2314260D
MOJE REPORT

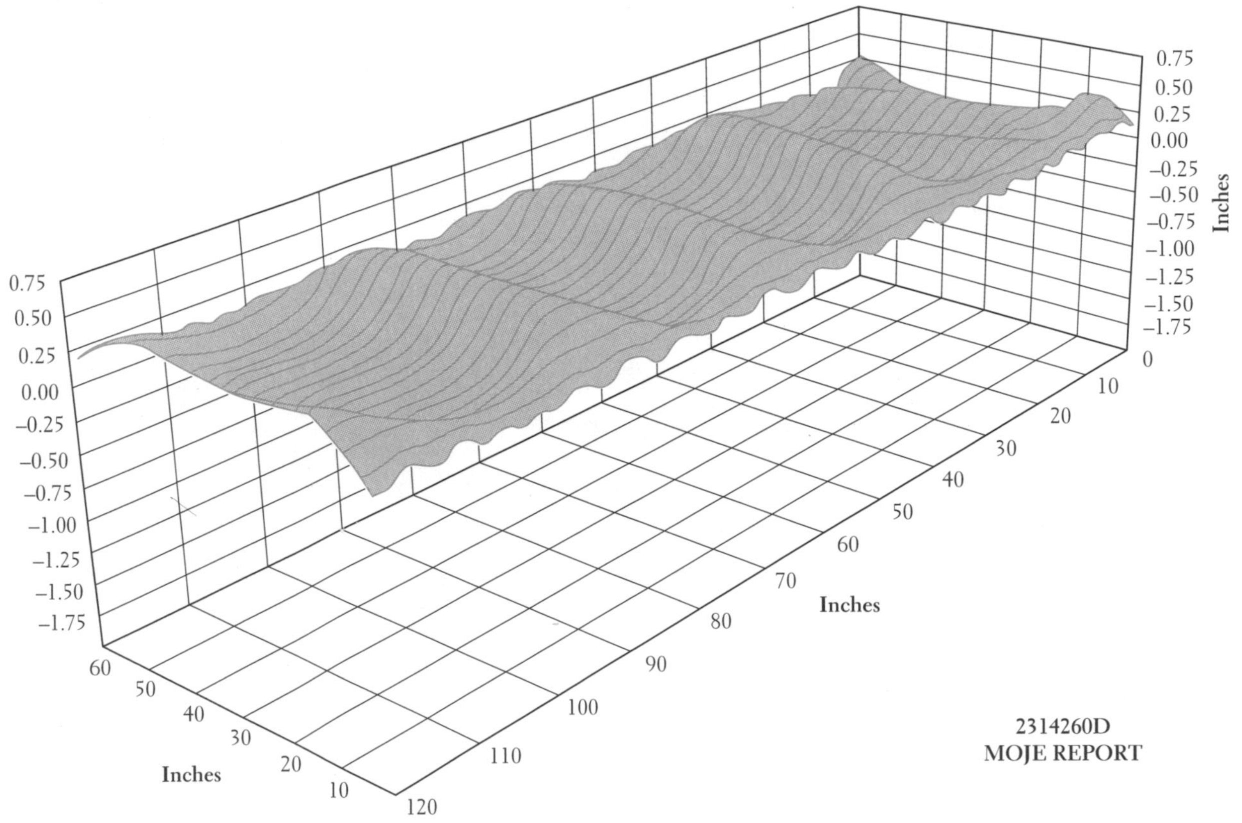

This is an exaggerated profile of a large aluminum sheet made from x-ray measurements. Quality engineers use this plot to monitor the flatness of each sheet, an essential characteristic to control for high quality. The idea of constantly improving quality by controlling variation is of vital importance and relies on a strong statistical foundation.

Instructor's Edition

UNDERSTANDING BUSINESS STATISTICS

Preface to the Instructor's Edition

We wrote this book in order to bridge the gap between the theoretical foundations of statistics and the need for business managers to extract useful decision-making information from data collections. The feedback we have received concerning the first edition of *Understanding Business Statistics* indicates that we accomplished this objective. In the second edition we retain the features that made the first edition successful while making some significant improvements. This Instructor's Preface will emphasize important features and offer teaching suggestions on how to get the most out of the book.

We understand that a study of statistics may, at first, not seem to be a very exciting endeavor. We also know that once the techniques become familiar, exciting results often follow, results that provide assistance and insight to the difficult task of making decisions.

Our teaching experience indicates that students often begin their first statistics course with feelings of apprehension and intimidation. For the course to be a successful learning experience, it is essential to overcome these feelings during the first two weeks. We have discovered that one way to build student rapport is to quickly provide students with the necessary mathematical and computer skills in a nonthreatening environment.

Instructor's Edition

In the Instructor's Edition only, we have added material in the margin to indicate:

Key figures or tables that are available as transparency masters (TM).

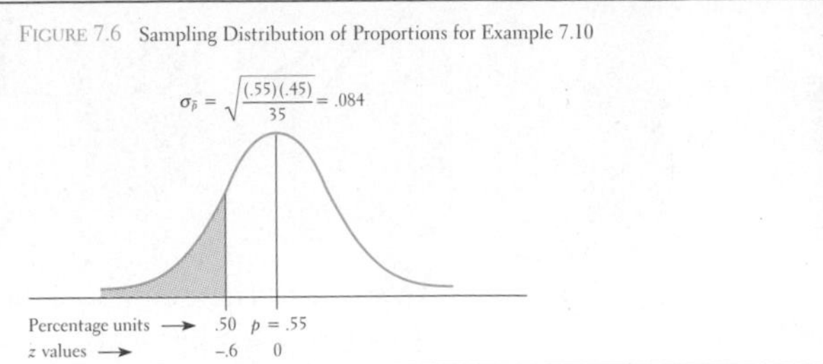

FIGURE 7.6 Sampling Distribution of Proportions for Example 7.10

Review lectures and actual on-site interviews with practitioners dealing with a key topic on videotape (V).

Coefficient of Variation

V

Another method sometimes used to measure the variability of a population or sample of data values is the **coefficient of variation.** This statistic specifies the size of the standard deviation as a percentage of the mean. It is calculated by dividing the standard deviation by the mean. The coefficient of variation indicates the *relative* amount of variability in a distribution.

V

SPOKANE TEACHERS CREDIT UNION

Steve Dahlstrom is president of Spokane Teachers Credit Union. The credit union regularly conducts a mail survey to determine members' attitudes toward its services. Among the demographic questions in each survey is whether a member is a teacher in the local area, since persons other than teachers can belong.

The credit union has been tracking the percentage of members who are teachers for several years. Each survey produces an estimate of this percentage, namely, the sample percentage. However, Steve recognizes that this point estimate can vary from survey to survey, even if the overall population percentage doesn't change. For this reason, an interval estimate is constructed around the point estimate each time a survey is taken. If this interval includes the historical percentage, the credit union assumes the population value hasn't shifted. Alternatively, when the interval estimate doesn't include this historical value, a shift is assumed to have occurred.

The credit union's marketing program assumes a high percentage of teachers in its membership, so a shift away from the historical percentage would affect the credit union's operations.

OTHER APPLICATIONS

The typical business estimates unknown population parameters daily. Speculation, guessing, and forecasting are common in modern business, whether done intuitively or

Check answers for most exercises.

Exercises containing data available on the data disk (DD).

39. .084 to .105

39. *The Wall Street Journal* (November 10, 1989) listed the leading mutual funds. A fund called Colonial Income Plus led the list with a 12-month return of 13.42%. Suppose an investor compared this figure with the average return of mutual funds currently available to investors.

A random sample of 30 mutual funds with assets of at least $100 million were selected and the mean and standard deviation of yield computed. The sample was selected from a population of 250 money market mutual funds with assets of at least $100 million. The mean was 9.43%, and the standard deviation was 2.79%. Construct a 90% interval estimate for the average yield of the 250 funds. What is the interval?

DD

40. This exercise refers to variable x_9, employee age, in Appendix C's company data base. It is known that the population is normally distributed. Select a simple random sample of 16 employees and construct a 95% interval estimate for the average employee age. Interpret the meaning of this interval.

PEDAGOGY

Most business statistics textbooks focus on the acquisition of sufficient knowledge to permit recall or recognition for examinations. It has been our earnest endeavor to move beyond this short-term objective and to give students the ability to truly comprehend what they are being asked to learn, and especially to gain the ability to apply these concepts in practical situations. We all know that knowledge acquired solely for the purpose of passing exams is soon forgotten. We believe that knowledge applied to simulated real situations is retained especially if positive practical results are observed.

This book attempts to make statistics relevant through the use of actual real-world situations and examples. The book also attempts to present the whole picture. Once a statistical concept is learned there are continuing references to situations where it could be of use. No technique is learned and then forgotten. Each procedure takes its place within the total statistical picture.

Chapter Objectives

Each chapter begins with behavioral objectives designed to explain what the student should be able to do after completing the chapter.

Chapter Introductions

The introduction includes the following features:

1. An article featuring an example that could be analyzed using the statistical techniques covered in the chapter.
2. An explanation of where the student has been and where the student is going.
3. A "Why Managers Need to Know" discussion of procedures covered in the chapter.

Chapter 5

BASIC PROBABILITY AND DISCRETE PROBABILITY DISTRIBUTIONS

And now sits Expectation in the air.
Shakespeare, *Henry V*

Objectives

When you have completed this chapter, you will be able to:

Explain the differences among the relative frequency, subjective, and classical approaches to probability.

Explain and use the basic rules of probability.

Construct discrete probability distributions—the binomial, hypergeometric, and Poisson distributions in particular.

Find the probabilities associated with particular outcomes for the binomial, hypergeometric, and Poisson distributions.

Compute the mean and standard deviation for discrete probability distributions.

SAMPLING DISTRIBUTIONS

In May 1989, *Business Month* featured an article entitled "Quest for Quality" describing quality-improvement efforts of Hewlett-Packard. The company had trimmed its defective rate on connections to 1,800 per million and was startled to find that a similar Japanese company had a rate of only 4 per million. Hewlett-Packard vowed to improve its defective rate.

The preceding chapter introduced the normal distribution and some of its applications. This chapter covers more important uses for this theoretical distribution and establishes the most important concept in statistics: the sampling distribution.

WHY MANAGERS NEED TO KNOW ABOUT SAMPLING DISTRIBUTIONS

Most statistical applications involve sampling items from the population being studied. Chapter 2 discussed ways to make the sample selection to ensure that a representative group of items is collected and measured. This selection process is important because the sample's characteristics are inferred to hold for the entire population, even though only a very small part of the population is actually sampled and measured.

This chapter deals with the accuracy of this inference process. Once the inference is made that the population possesses the same characteristics as the sample, the analyst must determine the extent of possible error involved in this process. Since sampling is commonplace in most organizations, knowing how to measure and understand this inherent error is vital to every manager. Assessing possible error involves a thorough understanding of statistics' most important concept: the sampling distribution.

Hewlett-Packard's attempts to reduce the defective rate must be closely monitored. A real quality improvement must be distinguished from a random fluctuation in the defective rate. The concept of sampling distributions is the key to understanding the difference.

Charts and Graphs

Charts and graphs are used wherever possible to help clarify and illustrate key concepts. They are also used to show the student how data are presented in a meaningful manner.

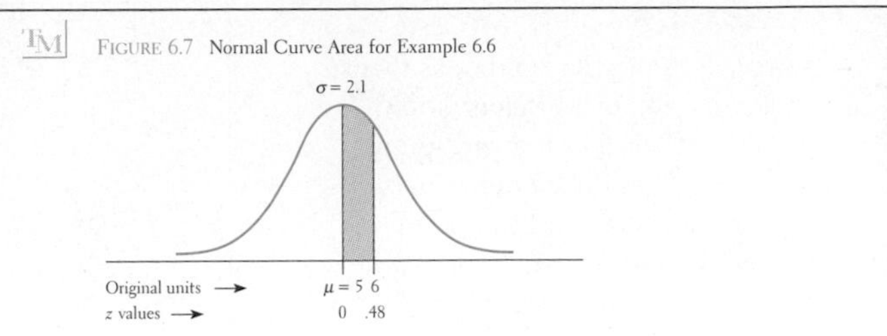

FIGURE 6.7 Normal Curve Area for Example 6.6

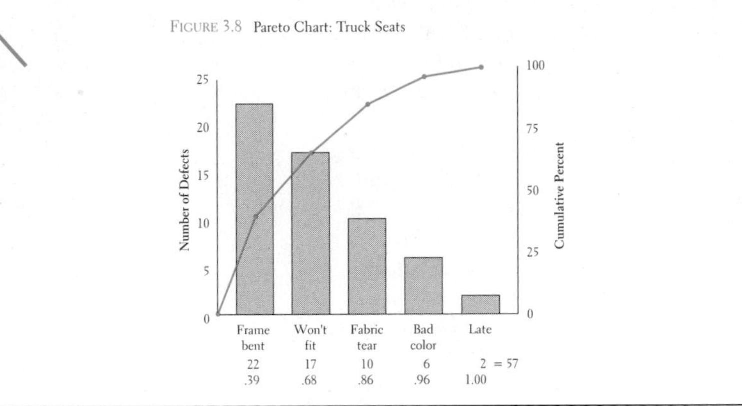

FIGURE 3.8 Pareto Chart: Truck Seats

Key Words, How-to Lists, and Boxed Definitions

The pedagogy makes use of boxes and color to define key works and concepts. We first introduced this concept 10 years ago in our *Business Forecasting* book. It must have been a good idea because most books have adopted it. Key words are bolded and pulled into the margin when first introduced.

Important characteristics and steps for key techniques are provided in screened boxes so that students will have further guidance in performing specific tasks such as constructing a frequency distribution.

Relative Frequencies

Relative frequencies, or percentages, are calculated for a frequency distribution by dividing the actual frequency for each class by the total number of objects classified. Table 3.6 does this for the Sunrunner Corporation executive incomes in Table 3.4. Note that in Table 3.6, each frequency is divided by 97, the total number of executives, to form the percentages in the last column. This column of percentages should total 1.000. (If calculation is done by hand, this sum may not precisely equal 1 due to rounding errors.)

Constructing a Frequency Distribution

Steps for constructing a frequency distribution

1. Determine the number of classes, usually 5 to 15 (see Table 3.3).
2. Determine the size of each class. Class size is determined by finding the difference between the largest value in the data set and the smallest value and dividing it by the number of classes desired.
3. Determine the starting point for the first class.
4. Tally the number of values that occur in each class.
5. Prepare a table of the distribution using actual counts and/or percentages (relative frequencies).

(*Note:* These steps should only be considered as rules of thumb and not as a rigorous process for constructing a frequency distribution.)

We have always tried to provide students with definitions that are easy to understand. Unfortunately, technically correct definitions of statistical terms are not always easy to understand. We have done our best to balance correctness with student abilities.

The **Poisson distribution** is used to model situations where there are random arrivals of events per unit of space or time, and where the probability of a specific number of successes is desired. It can be shown mathematically that a binomial distribution for which n becomes very large and p becomes very small approaches the Poisson distribution.

Notation

In order to make a difficult subject easier, we have used the easiest, most common statistical notation possible.

The formula for the Poisson distribution is

$$P(x) = \frac{\mu^x e^{-\mu}}{x!} \tag{5.8}$$

where μ = Mean number of arrivals per unit of time or space
x = Number of arrivals for which the probability is desired
e = Base of the natural logarithms, a mathematical constant approximately equal to 2.71828

Explanations and Examples

Our statistical explanations stress concepts rather than formulas. We want students to learn the "why" of statistics before working applications on their own. To do this, each explanation is followed by one or more pertinent examples.

Poisson Distribution

The **Poisson distribution** is used to model situations where the number of trials is very large and the number of successes is very small. The key issue to address before using the Poisson distribution involves the concept of randomness. That is, the arrival of the events in question mustn't follow any pattern. If the arrivals are truly random, the Poisson distribution can provide useful decision-making information.

EXAMPLE 5.22 *The American Statistician* (November 1992, pp. 246–53) reported on a study, "A Bayesian Analysis of a Poisson Random Effects Model for Home Run Hitters," that showed how the Poisson distribution could be used to estimate a hitter's ability to hit home runs. The statistic used for measuring a player's home run hitting ability is the observed rate, which divides the total number of home runs in a career by the total number of official at-bats. In baseball statistics books[1] this home run rate statistic is usually expressed as the number of at-bats for each home run hit. Babe Ruth was the greatest home run hitter with 714 career home runs in 8,389 career at-bats: a rate of .085. Using the Poisson distribution with an average rate of .085, what is the probability of Babe Ruth hitting no home runs in his next 10 at-bats? The rate is .085 for 1 at-bat or .85 for 10 at-bats. Hence $\mu = .85$ and $x = 0$. The probability is

$$P(x = 0) = \frac{.85^0(2.71828)^{-.85}}{0!} = \frac{1}{(2.71828)^{.85}} = .427$$

Situations

Situations are posed early in the discussion of Chapter 5 and 9 and are then resolved through the rest of those chapters as the appropriate techniques are presented. These situations are realistic descriptions of problems that can arise in an organization, and how they can be solved if the right statistical procedure is used. Our experience with the first edition, as well as comments from adopters and reviewers, indicated that this technique worked best in particular chapters, and so we confined them to those and eliminated the others.

■ SITUATION 5.2 Central Motors management is trying to decide whether to take out an insurance policy on its repair shop, which is separated from the main building complex. Central has evaluated the possible risks of fire loss on its building (Table 5.4). Although many dollar loss amounts are possible, Central has summarized possible losses in terms of the key values in Table 5.4. The possible losses and the corresponding probabilities estimated by management constitute a discrete probability distribution.

TABLE 5.4 Insurance Loss Probability Distribution (Situation 5.2)

x (loss)	P(x)	x · P(x)
$ 0	.925	0
5,000	.010	50
15,000	.010	150
30,000	.020	600
75,000	.020	1,500
100,000	.010	1,000
250,000	.005	1,250
	1.000	$4,550

Chapter Summaries, Glossaries, and Key Formulas

A summary paragraph helps to recap the important material in the chapter.

A glossary provides the student with easy access to the definitions of unfamiliar words.

A key formula section allows the student to quickly locate each formula without having to look through the chapter.

SUMMARY

This chapter has covered some basic ideas of probability and introduced the concepts of random variables and probability distributions. These concepts are necessary for the statistical procedures in the remainder of this book.

In addition, this chapter explained three important theoretical distributions and their applications to real-world business problems: the binomial, the hypergeometric, and the Poisson distributions. When a practical problem fits the specifications of one of these distributions, valuable decision-making information can be gained without doing expensive, time-consuming manipulations and real-world observations.

GLOSSARY

Probability A measure of the likelihood that a future event will occur; it can assume any value between 0 and 1, inclusive.

Sample space The collection of all possible outcomes for an experiment.

Multiplication rule A rule used when it's necessary to compute the probability that *both* event A and event B occur.

Random variable A variable defined by assigning one numerical value to each simple event of an experiment that yields random outcomes.

KEY FORMULAS

Expected value of a discrete random variable

$$E(x) = \Sigma[x \cdot P(x)] \quad (5.1)$$

Variance of a discrete random variable

$$\sigma^2 = \Sigma(x - \mu)^2 P(x) \quad (5.2)$$

Binomial probability distribution

$$P(x) = \binom{n}{x} p^x (1 - p)^{n-x} \quad (5.3)$$

Applications of Statistical Concepts in the Business World

An applications section is located after the summary section of each chapter. Its purpose is to give examples of how the chapter's concepts are applied in actual business situations.

APPLICATIONS OF STATISTICAL CONCEPTS IN THE BUSINESS WORLD

This chapter's procedures enjoy increasing practice in the business world. Their use in providing decision makers with reliable information is becoming more and more apparent as growing numbers of college students enter the business world armed with knowledge of these techniques. The concepts of probability, random variables, and probability distributions help decision makers assess the future with some degree of confidence. Indeed, an ability to deal with the uncertain future is vital for a modern business executive.

The concept of expected value is quite useful for establishing a baseline for assessing an opportunity's monetary aspects. Expected loss due to fire or theft can be used to determine the appropriate level of insurance payments, for example. The average number of defective units per shift can assist in a company's quality-control efforts. If a discrete probability distribution can be formed based on past history, then the expected value (or average value of this distribution) can provide management with valuable baseline performance information.

The binomial distribution is widely applicable in business because so many situations involve the concept of success versus failure. The key point, as this chapter stressed, is to make sure the trials are independent before using the binomial distribution as a model. Examples of situations that can be modeled with the binomial distribution, assuming this independence assumption is met, are:

1. Manufactured or purchased parts either meet quality-control specifications or don't.

Real-World Exercises

To quote one reviewer, "the book has the most extensive and well-thought-out problems of any book I have used." The examples and exercises have been drawn from our consulting work with statistics, relevant articles and professional research journals in business, and our own teaching notes and files. Each chapter has from 50 to 100 exercises. These appear at major divisions within each chapter and at chapter's end.

EXERCISES

31. What is the difference between a measure of central tendency and a measure of variability?
32. What is the difference between standard deviation and variance?
33. What is the difference between absolute variation and relative variation?

Discussion Questions

Discussion questions are presented at the beginning of each Exercise section. They can be used as homework assignments to encourage students to review and test their knowledge of the text material. This kind of question helps the student prepare for an essay or multiple-choice exam.

Answers or Solutions

Check answers are provided in the *Instructor's Edition* only. These provide a quick reference in class and help in choosing assignment problems.

A *Student's Solution Manual* containing detailed explanations of how to solve various exercises is available for student purchase. These problems are indicated in the student's text by the symbol below.

51. The following data collection shows the current number of enrollees, the number of companies or groups served, and the number of primary physicians for the top Spokane-area health care plans. Treat this data collection as a population.

Organization	Enrollees	Companies	Physicians
HMOs:			
HMO Washington	161	14	46
Foundation Health Plan	3,569	139	145
Group Health Northwest	30,000	350	26
HealthPlus	10,500	125	47
Maxicare Washington	173	11	12
PPOs:			
United Northwest Services	50,000	10	170
Inland Health Associates	29,000	9	86
Medical Services Corp.	17,373	580	541
First Choice Health Plan	3,836	291	43
Blue Cross Prudent Buyer	3,128	33	114

Source: "Hospitals Health Care & Insurance," *Journal of Business*, Nov. 25–Dec. 9, 1987.

a. Compute the mean and standard deviation of the number of enrollees in the 10 health plans.
b. Compute the mean and standard deviation of the number of companies or groups served by the 10 health plans.
c. Compute the mean and standard deviation of the number of primary physicians used by the 10 health plans.
d. Compute the median number of enrollees in the 10 health plans.
e. Compute the median number of companies or groups served by the 10 health plans.
f. Compute the median number of primary physicians used by the 10 health plans.
g. Is there any application for the weighted mean in this data collection?

51*a.* Mean = 14,774
SD = 16,692
b. Mean = 156
SD = 193
c. Mean = 123
SD = 156
d. Median = 7,168
e. Median = 79
f. Median = 66.5
g. No

Writing Integration

As with our first edition, this book contains numerous exercises that require the student to write a memo to management based on their statistical findings. We have included Appendix A on Effective Communication that shows students how to improve such memos and reports. Integrating writing into the statistics course is extremely important in our opinion and we hope this book will help you do so.

at least 380 acceptable cables. What is the probability that this shipment will fulfill the contract conditions?

54. You've worked part-time at Ranch Thrift, a large supermarket, for the past three years. Your boss knows that you're completing your business degree and asks you to study the average customer expenditure per visit. You sample 500 customer expenditures and determine that this variable is normally distributed with an average expenditure of \$31.28 and standard deviation of \$7.29. Write your boss a memo analyzing the average customer expenditure per visit.

Solved Exercises

One of the most popular innovations of the first edition was the use of solved exercises at the end of each chapter. Students indicated they found these extremely useful as a review on how to use key techniques before tackling homework assignments. They serve as an intermediate step between study of the chapter examples and solving the problems themselves.

4. COMPUTATION OF THE COEFFICIENT OF VARIATION

Refer to the data June Shapiro collected in Solved Exercise 2.

a. Compute the coefficient of variation for billings per agency.
b. Compute the coefficient of variation for number of employees per agency.

Solution:

a. $CV = \frac{s}{\bar{x}}(100) = \frac{2.276}{2.1455}(100) = 106\%$

b. $CV = \frac{s}{\bar{x}}(100) = \frac{10.52}{10.273}(100) = 102.4\%$

Extended Exercises

Our extended exercises are designed to be more challenging examples of the actual application of business statistics. We feel they might be considered mini-cases and provide the kinds of practical situations from which students need to learn.

56. RANCH LIFE INSURANCE COMPANY OF FLORIDA

Kim Carter, statistician for Ranch Life Insurance Company of Florida, notices that monthly premium receipts appear to follow a normal distribution. After plotting receipts for a typical month and observing their distribution, Kim decides that the normality assumption is reasonable.

Ranch wants to determine the percentage of monthly receipts that fall into the range \$125 to \$175, since such amounts are difficult to handle. They aren't large enough to warrant investment attention, unless there are many of them, nor are they small enough to ignore by putting them into the cash account.

To find the percentage of accounts in this range, Kim computes the mean and standard deviation of monthly premium receipts. She determines these values to be \$100 and \$38, respectively.

a. What percentage of monthly receipts can be expected to fall into the range \$125 to \$175?
b. Kim predicts that within two years the average monthly premium will rise to \$150. Assuming the standard deviation remains the same, how would this change the answer to Question *a*?
c. Describe how the assumption of normality might be verified in this case.

Use of the Computer

The use of microcomputers, along with powerful mainframes, has had tremendous impact on the application of statistics in business and economics. Our goal concerning student exposure to the computer is to keep is as simple as possible to use and understand. In order to acquaint students with the computer to learn statistics, Chapter 1 contains a section on Using Computers with This Text.

Examples of computer output appear throughout the text. Data analysis packages such as SAS, MINITAB, SPSS, and CBS (*Computerized Business Statistics*, 2/e by Hall/Adelman) have been chosen for these demonstrations, and they will be identified as they are used.

CBS consists of an instructional text and a microcomputer software package that can be purchased shrinkwrapped with the text. At the end of each chapter, instructions for solving one or two problems are given for statistical techniques available on the CBS package.

The MINITAB statistical package is explained in detail throughout most chapters so that students can use it with no prior preparation. At the end of each chapter, instructions for solving one or two problems are given using statistical techniques available on the MINITAB package.

The SAS statistical package is also explained. This package is more powerful than MINITAB and tends to be used more frequently in larger business applications and research. At the end of several chapters, instructions for solving a chapter problem are given for the SAS package.

In Example 8.4 an interval estimate was computed based on a sample size of 50. This interval estimate could also be constructed using the MINITAB software package. The MINITAB commands are:

```
MTB> RANDOM 50 C1;
SUBC> NORMAL 23.5 10.4.
MTB> DESCRIBE C1

C1    N    MEAN    MEDIAN    STDEV
     50   25.45    26.63     11.76

C1    MIN    MAX     Q1     Q3
     1.85  42.97  15.45  35.41

MTB> ZINTERVAL 95 PERCENT CONFIDENCE ASSUMED SIGMA 11.76 FOR C1
   N   MEAN     STDEV   SE MEAN   95.0 PERCENT C.I.
  50   25.45    11.76    1.66     (22.19, 28.72)

MTB> STOP
```

MINITAB Computer Package

The MINITAB commands to solve Extended Exercise 62 are:

```
MTB > RANDOM 30 C1;
SUBC> INTEGERS 1:200.
MTB > PRINT C1

C1
    173    138    180     76     69    141    130    140     84
     53    159     28    194    156     43    150     63    192
    173    171     83    109    158    106    189    160    104
     88     94     49

MTB > SET INTO C2
DATA> 2 4 3 7 2 1 1 4 1 2 3 2 1 5 2 2 2 2 3 2 2 2 3 7 5 4 4 2
MTB > END
MTB > DESCRIBE C2

                N      MEAN     MEDIAN     TRMEAN     STDEV     SEMEAN
C2             30     2.800      2.000      2.615     1.584      0.289


              MIN       MAX         Q1         Q3
C2          1.000     7.000      2.000      4.000

MTB > BOXPLOT C2

                      -----------------
             --------(+)               I-----------------------
                      -----------------

          ----+---------+---------+---------+---------+---------+--C1
             1.2       2.4       3.6       4.8       6.0       7.2

MTB > WRITE 'CH4EX62.DAT' C2
MTB > STOP
```

The **RANDOM** command and **INTEGERS** subcommand are used to generate 30 random numbers between 1 and 200. The **PRINT** command is used to list the random numbers stored in C1. The family sizes for each random number are included in the sample and entered into

SAS Computer Package

A data file called COURSE.DAT was created (see Table 2.8) to analyze data compiled from the class questionnaire (Table 1.1) for one of the authors' classes. SAS commands to provide descriptive statistics for the quantitative variables are:

```
TITLE ''STUDENT QUESTIONNAIRE RESULTS'';
DATA QUEST;
 INFILE 'COURSE.DAT';
 INPUT GPA 5–7 AGE 9–10;
PROC MEANS;
 VAR GPA AGE;
```

The **TITLE** statement names the SAS program.

The **DATA** statement provides a filename for the data.

The **INFILE** statement identifies an external file, COURSE.DAT, to be read with an **INPUT** statement.

The **INPUT** statement names the variable GPA and indicates that it is located in columns 5–7. The variable **AGE** is located in columns 9–10.

The **PROC MEANS** statement produces simple descriptive statistics for the variables listed on the VAR statement. In this example descriptive statistics will be printed for the variables GPA and AGE. Table 4.7 shows the SAS output.

Student Data Base

A questionnaire is provided in Chapter 1 for the student to complete. The data from this questionnaire can be compiled to create a data base for the whole class. This data can be used to illustrate key concepts such as data presentation, sampling distribution, hypothesis testing, and more. Examples are presented that use the results of this questionnaire from one of the author's classes.

There is also a larger version of the questionnaire in the *Instructor's Manual* for copying at your convenience.

TM

TABLE 1.1 Student Questionnaire for Class Data Base

1. My class standing is currently:
   ____ Freshman ____ Sophomore ____ Junior
   ____ Senior ____ Grad Student ____ Other
2. I am: ____ Female ____ Male
3. High school grade point average: __________
4. My age is: __________
5. I smoke cigarettes: ____ Regularly ____ Sometimes ____ Never

Please circle one of the following numbers to indicate your level of agreement with each of the statements below:

1—Strongly agree
2—Agree
3—Neutral or no opinion
4—Disagree
5—Strongly disagree

	SA	A	N	D	SD
6. A knowledge of statistics will be an important part of my working life after I leave college.	1	2	3	4	5
7. It would be a good idea to impose more stringent admission requirements for the business administration program.	1	2	3	4	5
8. Given the nature of statistics, I would prefer to have a quiz each week.	1	2	3	4	5
9. I usually do well in math classes.	1	2	3	4	5
10. In my business career, ethical considerations will be as important to me as making a profit.	1	2	3	4	5

Company Data Base

A data base of 200 company employees using nine variables is included in Appendix C. The data base is provided so that realistic assignments can be made that simulate real-world work with statistics. There are exercises at the end of most chapters that use and refer to this data base.

APPENDIX C COMPANY DATA BASE

The following data base contains nine variables measured on N = 200 fictitious company employees. Each row represents the values of the nine variables for a single employee. The number in the first column (1–200) is the employee number. Each subsequent column represents the values of one variable for all 200 employees.

The nine variables are defined as follows:

x_1 = Number of years with the company
x_2 = Number of overtime hours worked during the past six months
x_3 = Gender: 1 = Female, 2 = Male
x_4 = Number of continuing education courses completed
x_5 = Number of sick days taken during the past six months
x_6 = Score on company aptitude test
x_7 = Amount of education: 0 = High school diploma, 1 = Some college, 2 = College degree, 3 = Postgraduate education
x_8 = Annual base salary
x_9 = Employee age

n	x_1	x_2	x_3	x_4	x_5	x_6	x_7	x_8	x_9
1	11	125	1	4	9	121.89	2	23065	44
2	24	225	2	2	2	114.20	1	27180	50
3	17	115	2	3	5	134.11	1	34875	48
4	9	117	1	1	1	113.95	1	23685	53
5	15	26	1	2	0	151.41	2	33550	62
6	6	43	1	4	3	96.65	1	22635	45
7	4	124	2	2	4	98.43	2	19575	26
8	2	71	2	1	1	110.06	1	20430	28
9	17	166	2	2	5	101.98	1	18955	33
10	17	158	1	3	2	101.01	1	25595	40

New Quality-Control Chapter

The importance of producing high-quality products has increased dramatically in recent years. Many of the procedures designed to assure high-quality goods and operations rely on a statistical foundation that is based on a thorough knowledge of variability. Our new Chapter 13, "Quality Control Applications," presents some of the statistical concepts and techniques used to control and improve processes and thus deliver high-quality products. The chapter includes thorough discussions of all commonly used control charts, as well as other quality-control tools. At the end of the chapter we present a section on Kaiser Aluminum's award-winning efforts in quality improvement. This section includes a summary of their aluminum sheet process, output from their computerized monitoring and feedback process, and the control charts and graphs they utilize regularly in this quality effort. We have also integrated coverage of quality in appropriate places throughout the text.

Chapter 13

QUALITY-CONTROL APPLICATIONS

Come, give us a taste of your quality.
Shakespeare, "Hamlet"

Good things cost less than bad ones.
Italian proverb

Objectives
When you have completed this chapter, you will be able to:

Define the quality of a product or service.

Identify and differentiate between assignable and chance variation.

Explain the concept of statistical quality control.

Construct and interpret process control charts.

Describe the basic terms, procedures, and purposes of acceptance sampling.

THE EDUCATIONAL PACKAGE

The following materials can be obtained by adopters:

An *Instructor's Manual.*

A *Student Study Guide.*

A *Student Solutions Manual.*

A *Test Bank.*

CompuTest 3 Computerized Testing Service.

A *Transparency Masters* booklet.

A *Data Disk.*

A four–hour series of videos.

An optional shrinkwrapped disk and guide for the Computerized Business Statistics, 2/e (CBS) package.

The *Instructor's Manual* contains suggestions on how to teach the course and answers to all questions and exercises.

The *Study Guide,* written by Walt Hartman and Paul Van Ness, provides the student with additional explanations, exercises, and computer guidance.

The *Student Solutions Manual,* prepared by Paul Van Ness, contains completely worked out solutions to several key exercises for each chapter.

The *Test Bank,* prepared by Susan Simmons, provides over 1800 true/false, multiple-choice, and narrative problems. Along with the manual, a separate computerized testing package, *Computest* 3, is available from Irwin that includes a program disk, several data disks, and complete documentation. You will have access to the *TeleTest* service. You simply select the questions from the Test Bank and then call Educational Software Services and request as many as four versions of the test. The masters will be mailed first class within 24 hours.

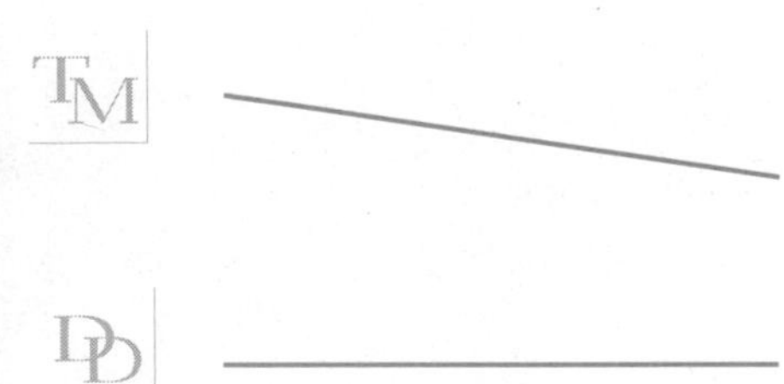

The *Transparency Masters* booklet contains important figures and tables from the text (indicated by the symbol TM) along with other material not found in the text that we have found useful in our classes.

A *Data Disk* is available to instructors upon request. The disk contains all large data sets from the text. Also, several large additional data sets are included. Exercises having data available on the disk are noted by the logo to the left.

Videotapes prepared by the authors allow students to obtain additional tutoring on key concepts. The first tape covers basic lecture material for Chapters 1 to 10. We have found these tapes to be very useful for students who need a basic review of key topics. The second tape contains interviews with several practitioners discussing the practical use of statistical procedures from several chapters. These interviews can be shown to the entire class in order to assist in the task of making statistics relevant. These are noted in the text margin by the logo to the left.

Supplementary Texts

There are a number of excellent supplementary texts we enthusiastically recommend. They include:

Campbell, S. K., *Flaws and Fallacies in Statistical Thinking*, Englewood Cliffs, N.J.: Prentice–Hall, Inc. 1974.

Huff, D. *How to Lie with Statistics*, NY: W.W. Norton & Company, 1954.

Reichman, W. J., *Use and Abuse of Statistics*, Baltimore: Penguin Books, 1971

Sachs, L. *Applied Statistics: A Handbook of Techniques*, 2nd ed. NY, NY: Springer-Verlag, 1984

Tanur, J.; F. Mosteller; W. Kruskal; E. Lehmann; R. Link; R. Pieters; and G. Rising. *Statistics: A Guide to the UnKnown*, 3rd ed., San Francisco: Holden-Day, 1989

Tufte, E. R., *The Visual Display of Quantitative Information*, Cheshire, CT: Graphics Press, 1983.

UNDERSTANDING BUSINESS STATISTICS

The Irwin Series in Production Operations Management

Aquilano and Chase
Fundamentals of Operations Management
First Edition

Chase and Aquilano
Production and Operations Management
Sixth Edition

Berry et al.
ITEK, Inc.
First Edition

Hill
Manufacturing Strategy: Text & Cases
Second Edition

Klein
Revitalizing Manufacturing: Text & Cases
First Edition

Lambert and Stock
Strategic Logistics Management
Third Edition

Leenders, Fearon, and England
Purchasing and Materials Management
Ninth Edition

Lotfi and Pegels
Decision Support Systems for Production & Operations Management for Use with IBM PC
Second Edition

Nahmias
Production and Operations Analysis
Second Edition

Niebel
Motion and Time Study
Eighth Edition

Sasser, Clark, Garvin, Graham, Jaikumar, and Maister
Cases in Operations Management: Analysis & Action
First Edition

Schonberger and Knod
Operations Management: Continuous Improvement
Fifth Edition

Stevenson
Production/Operations Management
Fourth Edition

Vollmann, Berry, and Whybark
Manufacturing Planning & Control Systems
Third Edition

Whybark
International Operations Management: A Selection of Imede Cases
First Edition

The Irwin Series in Statistics

Aczel
Complete Business Statistics
Second Edition

Duncan
Quality Control & Industrial Statistics
Fifth Edition

Emory and Cooper
Business Research Methods
Fourth Edition

Gitlow, Gitlow, Oppenheim, and Oppenheim
Tools and Methods for the Improvement of Quality
First Edition

Hall and Adelman
Computerized Business Statistics
Second Edition

Hanke and Reitsch
Understanding Business Statistics
Second Edition

Mason and Lind
Statistical Techniques in Business and Economics
Eighth Edition

Neter, Wasserman, and Kutner
Applied Linear Statistical Models
Third Edition

Neter, Wasserman, and Kutner
Applied Linear Regression Models
Second Edition

Siegel
Practical Business Statistics
Second Edition

Webster
Applied Statistics for Business and Economics
First Edition

Wilson and Keating
Business Forecasting
Second Edition

The Irwin Series in Quantitative Methods and Management Science

Bierman, Bonini, and Hausman
Quantitative Analysis for Business Decisions
Eighth Edition

Knowles
Management Science: Building and Using Models
First Edition

Lotfi and Pegels
Decision Support Systems for Management Science & Operations Research
Second Edition

Stevenson
Introduction to Management Science
Second Edition

Turban and Meredith
Fundamentals of Management Science
Sixth Edition

UNDERSTANDING BUSINESS STATISTICS

Second Edition

John E. Hanke
Arthur G. Reitsch

Both of Eastern Washington University

IRWIN

Burr Ridge, Illinois
Boston, Massachusetts
Sydney, Australia

This symbol indicates that the paper in this book is made of recycled paper. Its fiber content exceeds the recommended minimum of 50% waste paper fibers as specified by the EPA.

Senior sponsoring editor:	Richard T. Hercher, Jr.
Developmental editor:	Gail Korosa
Marketing manager:	Robb Linsky
Project editor:	Stephanie M. Britt
Production manager:	Ann Cassady
Art coordinator:	Mark Malloy
Compositor:	Weimer Graphics, Inc.
Typeface:	10/12 Electra
Printer:	R. R. Donnelley & Sons Company

Library of Congress Cataloging-in-Publication Data

Hanke, John E.,

Understanding business statistics / John E. Hanke, Arthur G. Reitsch.—2nd ed.

p. cm.

ISBN 0-256-11219-3 (acid-paper) 0-256-14505-9 (Instructor's Edition)

1. Industrial management—Statistical methods. I. Reitsch, Arthur G., II. Title.

HD30.215.H36 1994

650'.01'5195—dc20 93–16827

Printed in the United States of America

1 2 3 4 5 6 7 8 9 0 DOC 0 9 8 7 6 5 4 3

To produce a mighty book, you must choose a mighty theme.
No great and enduring volume can ever be written on the flea,
though many there be that have tried—Herman Melville, *Moby Dick*

Dedicated to Geri, Harry, Irene, and Jack (who don't need to read it);
Judy and Judy (who have and might, respectively);
Jill, Amy, Julie, Katrina, and Kevin (who should, but probably never will);
and especially all of our students (who had better).

PREFACE

But to go to school in a summer morn,
Oh, it drives all joy away!
Under a cruel eye outworn,
The little ones spend the day—
In sighing and dismay.
Blake, *The Schoolboy*

We have written this book in order to bridge the gap between the theoretical foundations of statistics and the need for business managers to extract useful decision-making information from data collections. We understand that a study of statistics may, at first, not seem to be a very exciting endeavor. We also know that once the techniques become familiar, exciting results often follow, results that provide assistance and insight to the difficult task of making decisions.

ACKNOWLEDGMENTS

We wish to thank several thousand previous students for their guidance in developing our writing style, and in particular to those students who helped us with the manuscript during class testing. We are particularly indebted to Judy Johnson, a rate analyst at Washington Water Power, who ran our SAS programs and provided data sets for both examples and exercises. A special thanks to Leonard Presby of William Paterson College for his help in problem checking. We also thank adopters and colleagues across the country (listed below) who reviewed the text and manuscript for this second edition and helped greatly in its refinement. We made an effort to respond to every suggestion. Nevertheless, we take responsibility for the final product and trust it will be pleasing to teach and learn from.

Michael Broida, *Miami University of Ohio*
Thomas MacFarland, *Nova University*
Anil Gulati, *Western New England College*
Elzbieta Trybus, *California State University, Northridge*
Walter Johnston, *Southwest Texas State University*
Mark Bomball, *Eastern Illinois University*

Nagraj Balakrishnan, *Tulane University*
Choonsan Kim, *Western Illinois University*
Robert Hull, *Western Illinois University*
Barbara McKinney, *Western Michigan University*
Steve Rigdon, *Southern Illinois University at Edwardsville*
Gayne Clifford, *North Idaho College*
Sandra Strasser, *Valparaiso University*

We would like to thank again the individuals who aided in developing the first edition of *Understanding Business Statistics*. We extend our sincere thanks to: Mary Jo Boehms, Jackson State Community College; John Briscoe, Indiana State University, Southeast; Alice Griswold, University of Dubuque; J. Morgan Jones, University of North Carolina, Chapel Hill; Someswar Kesh, University of Texas, Arlington; David D. Drueger, St. Cloud State University; Steven W. Lamb, Indiana State University; Frank Leroi, College of San Mateo; Mickey McCormick, Spokane Falls Community College; Peter Phung, El Paso Community College; John Shannon, Suffolk University; Lois Shufeldt, Southwest Missouri State; Scott Stevens, James Madison University; Paul A. Thompson, Ohio State University; Charles E. Tychsen, Northern Virginia Community College; George E. Vlahos, University of Dayton; Min-Chiang Wang, Washington State University; Ray Whitman, University of the District of Columbia; and Mark Wilson, University of Charleston.

Finally, we thank the makers of modern word processors, without whom we might have given up or settled for an inferior product. We also extend thanks to all the people at Irwin for their support. It was a pleasure to work with such a special group of professionals, especially, Dick Hercher, Gail Korosa, and Stephanie Britt. Portions of this text, particularly several data sets, are adapted from those that appeared in our *Business Forecasting* text published by Allyn & Bacon, whom we credit for this reuse.

To the students who attack the subject of business statistics with this book, we sincerely hope you gain an appreciation of the power of these techniques to assist business managers in their most important task: making decisions in the face of uncertainty.

John E. Hanke
Arthur G. Reitsch

Note to the Student

As you begin your study of business statistics you should know that this material is not here to weed out the faint of heart. Every quality business school requires a sound background in this subject because so many business decisions today are based on a proper analysis of collected data.

We have attempted to present the material, both the easy concepts and the more difficult ones, in an easy-to-understand way. There are numerous examples throughout the text, along with both solved and unsolved exercises. Be sure to check the back of the book for check figures on most of the odd-numbered exercises.

In order for you to master the subjects in this book it is necessary for you to read the material, work some of the exercises and attend class regularly. This is not a subject you can learn by cramming the night before an exam. You may find the video lectures that accompany this text to be useful in understanding the material. They cover the basic topics in Chapters 1 through 10 and are available through your instructor. There is also a Student Solutions Manual and a Study Guide available for additional help.

When you complete your study of statistics, you can be sure you are well prepared for the data analysis tasks that lie ahead in your business career. The topics in this book constitute a wide variety of ways to extract useful information from the data that exist, and that are constantly being collected, in every organization.

We hope your "bag of tricks" will serve you well during your career. Although you will forget some specific details of procedures that are not constantly used, our consulting experience has shown that business school graduates *do* retain the basic premise of statistics: If you know the right methods, almost any data collection can yield fruitful information.

We imagine a meeting sometime in the future attended by the leaders of your company and yourself. A thorny problem is being discussed when the company president turns to you and says, "You studied business in college; how do you see the situation?" We sincerely hope this book and your course have prepared you for this moment, as you begin: "My analysis of the data indicates that . . ."

Contents

Chapter 1 INTRODUCTION TO STATISTICS 1

- Why Statistics Is Important to Managers 2
- The Purpose of Statistics 2
- Student Data Base 3
- Using Computers with This Text 3
- MINITAB 4
- SAS 4
- Computerized Business Statistics 5
- Data Sets 5
- Study Guide 5
- Approach of This Book 5
- Summation Notation 6
- Summary 8
- Applications of Statistical Concepts in the Business World 8
- Glossary 9
- Key Formulas 9
- Exercises 9
- Introduction to the Microcomputer Package 10
- Introduction to the MINITAB Computer Package 10
- Introduction to the SAS Computer Package 12

Chapter 2 DATA COLLECTION 14

- Why Data Collection Procedures Are Important to Managers 15
- Types of Data 15
- Types of Data Sources 22
- Data-Gathering Techniques 24
- Populations and Samples 26
- Simple Random Sampling 28
- Other Sampling Techniques 32
- Data File Construction 37
- Summary 39
- Applications of Statistical Concepts in the Business World 39
- Glossary 41
- Solved Exercises 42
- Exercises 42
- Extended Exercises 44
- Microcomputer Package 46
- MINITAB Computer Package 47

Chapter 3 DATA PRESENTATION 48

- Why Data Presentation Methods Are Important to Managers 49
- Frequency Distributions 49
- Cumulative Frequency Distributions 57
- Charts and Graphs 60
- The Pareto Chart 63
- How to Lie with Statistics 69
- Summary 74
- Applications of Statistical Concepts in the Business World 74
- Glossary 76
- Solved Exercises 76
- Exercises 79
- Extended Exercises 83
- Microcomputer Package 85
- MINITAB Computer Package 86
- SAS Computer Package 87

Chapter 4 Descriptive Statistics 89

Why Descriptive Statistics Is Important to Managers 90
Measures of Central Tendency 90
Measures of Variability 104
Measures of Position 110
Summary 114
Applications of Statistical Concepts in the Business World 114
Glossary 115
Key Formulas 116
Solved Exercises 117
Exercises 119
Extended Exercises 123
Microcomputer Package 126
MINITAB Computer Package 127
SAS Computer Package 128

Chapter 5 Basic Probability and Discrete Probability Distributions 129

Why Discrete Probability Distributions Are Important to Managers 130
Basic Probability Definitions and Rules 130
Random Variables 138
Probability Distributions 140
Expected Value 143
The Binomial Distribution 146
The Binomial Table 152
Mean and Standard Deviation of the Binomial Distribution 156
The Hypergeometric Distribution 158
The Poisson Distribution 161
Poisson Distribution Table 164
Poisson Approximation to the Binomial 168
Summary 171
Applications of Statistical Concepts in the Business World 171
Glossary 172
Key Formulas 173
Solved Exercises 173
Exercises 178
Extended Exercises 180
Microcomputer Package 182
MINITAB Computer Package 183

Chapter 6 Continuous Probability Distribution 185

Why Managers Need to Know about Continuous Probability Distributions 186
Continuous Random Variables 186
The Uniform Distribution 187
Normal Distribution 192
Finding Normal Curve Areas 195
Normal Approximation to the Binomial 205
Summary 209
Applications of Statistical Concepts in the Business World 209
Glossary 210
Key Formulas 210
Solved Exercises 211
Exercises 213
Extended Exercises 215
Microcomputer Package 218
MINITAB Computer Package 218

Chapter 7 SAMPLING DISTRIBUTIONS 220

Why Managers Need to Know about Sampling Distributions 221
Sampling Error 221
Distribution of Sampling Means 222
Sampling Distribution of Sample Proportions 233
The Finite-Population Multiplier 239
Summary 243
Applications of Statistical Concepts in the Business World 243
Glossary 244
Key Formulas 244
Solved Exercises 245
Exercises 247
Extended Exercises 249
Microcomputer Package 252
MINITAB Computer Package 252

Chapter 8 ESTIMATION 254

Why Managers Need to Know about Estimation 255
Point and Interval Estimates of a Population Mean 255
Point and Interval Estimates of Population Proportions 263
Small-Sample Estimation 266
Sample Size and Estimation Error 271
Summary 277
Applications of Statistical Concepts in the Business World 278
Glossary 279
Key Formulas 279
Solved Exercices 280
Exercises 282
Extended Exercises 284
Microcomputer Package 287
MINITAB Computer Package 288

Chapter 9 HYPOTHESIS TESTING 289

Why Managers Need to Know about Hypothesis Testing 290
Introduction 290
Hypothesis-Testing Steps and Procedures 292
Errors in Hypothesis Testing 297
Developing Decision Rules 299
Hypothesis Tests about a Population Mean: Large Samples 302
p-Values and Hypothesis Testing 305
Hypothesis Tests about a Population Mean: Small Samples 310
Hypothesis Tests about a Population Proportion 314
Type II Errors, Operating Characteristic Curves, and Power Curves 320
Computing Sample Size for a Hypothesis Test 326
Choosing the Significance Level in Hypothesis Testing 328
Summary 329
Applications of Statistical Concepts in the Business World 329
Glossary 330
Key Formulas 331
Solved Exercises 331
Exercises 334
Extended Exercises 338
Microcomputer Package 341
MINITAB Computer package 342

Chapter 10 TWO-POPULATION HYPOTHESIS TESTS 343

Why Managers Need to Know about Hypothesis Testing for Two Populations 344
Hypothesis Tests about the Difference between Two Population Means: Large Samples 344
Hypothesis Testing about the Difference between Two Population Means: Small Samples 353
Hypothesis Testing for Means: Dependent Samples 358
Hypothesis Testing for Proportions from Two Populations 363
Summary 368
Applications of Statistical Concepts in the Business World 369
Glossary 370
Key Formulas 370
Solved Exercises 372
Exercises 376
Extended Exercises 378
Microcomputer Package 380
MINITAB Computer Package 381

Chapter 11 CHI-SQUARE TESTS 383

Why Managers Need to Know about Chi-Square Tests 384
Contingency Table Test 384
Goodness-of-Fit Test 394
Rule of Five 398
Final Notes on Chi-Square Tests 403
Summary 405
Applications of Statistical Concepts in the Business World 405
Glossary 406
Key Formulas 406
Solved Exercises 407
Exercises 410
Extended Exercises 413
Microcomputer Package 415
MINITAB Computer Package 417
SAS Computer Package 418

Chapter 12 VARIABILITY HYPOTHESIS TESTS AND ANALYSIS OF VARIANCE 420

Why Managers Need to Know about Analysis of Variance 421
Single-Population Variance Test 421
Two-Population Variance Test 424
ANOVA Basics 427
Within Method 428
Between Method 430
ANOVA *F* Test and Table 433
Two-Way Analysis of Variance 439
Other ANOVA Designs 448
Summary 449
Applications of Statistical Concepts in the Business World 450
Glossary 450
Key Formulas 451
Solved Exercises 452
Exercises 456
Extended Exercises 460
Microcomputer Package 462
MINITAB Computer Package 463
SAS Computer Package 465

Chapter 13 QUALITY-CONTROL APPLICATIONS 467

Why Managers Need to Know about Quality Control 468
Background 468
Quality—General Considerations 469
Statistical Process Control 473
Control Charts 481
Constructing a Chart to Monitor the Mean of a Process: The $\bar{x}$ Chart 485
Constructing a Chart to Monitor the Variation of a Process: The *R* Chart 501
Constructing a Chart to Monitor the Proportion of Defectives in a Process: The *p* Chart 508
Constructing a Chart to Monitor the Number of Defectives per Unit: the *c* Chart 514
Lot Acceptance 520
Power and Operating Characteristic (OC) Curves 523
Other Quality-Control Techniques 523
Summary 524
Applications of Statistical Concepts in the Business World 525
Glossary 530
Key Formulas 530
Solved Exercises 531
Exercises 539
Extended Exercises 544
MINITAB Computer Package 549

Chapter 14 CORRELATION AND SIMPLE REGRESSION 550

Why Managers Need to Know about Correlation and Regression Analysis 551
Scatter Diagrams 551
Correlation Coefficient 554
Hypothesis Testing in Correlation Analysis 556
Linear Equations 562
Functional and Statistical Models 563
Sample Regression Line 565
Residuals 571
Standard Error of Estimate 572
Prediction and Confidence Intervals 574
Coefficient of Simple Determination 579
Hypothesis Testing in Regression Analysis 586
Using the Regression Equation 592
Summary 595
Applications of Statistical Concepts in the Business World 596
Glossary 596
Key Formulas 597
Solved Exercises 599
Extended Exercises 607
Microcomputer Package 609
MINITAB Computer Package 611
SAS Computer Package 612

Chapter 15 MULTIPLE REGRESSION 613

Why Managers Need to Know about Multiple Regression Analysis 614
Selecting Predictor Variables 614
Notes on Multicollinearity 620
The Multiple Regression Equation 622
Standard Error of Estimate 626
Prediction and Confidence Intervals 627
Hypothesis Testing in Multiple Regression Analysis 630
Model Building 644
Curvilinear Models 644
Nonlinear Models 650
Qualitative Variables in Multiple Regression 652
Stepwise Regression 659
Final Notes on Stepwise Regression 664
Residual Analysis 665
Summary 672
Applications of Statistical Concepts in the Business World 673
Glossary 674
Key Formulas 674
Solved Exercises 675
Exercises 680
Extended Exercises 688
Microcomputer Package 696
MINITAB Computer Package 698
SAS Computer Package 701

Chapter 16 INDEX NUMBERS AND TIME SERIES ANALYSIS 703

Why Managers Need to Know about Index Numbers and Time Series Analysis 704
Purpose of Index Numbers 704
Constructing an Index 705
Types of Indexes 706
Consumer Price Index 710
Composite Index 713
Deflating a Time Series 714
Changing the Base Period 716
Decomposition of a Time Series 718
Trend 721
Cyclical 728
Seasonal Data 737
Summary 751
Applications of Statistical Concepts in the Business World 752
Glossary 754
Key Formulas 754
Solved Exercises 755
Exercises 761
Extended Exercises 767
Microcomputer Package 796
MINITAB Computer Package 771

Chapter 17 BUSINESS FORECASTING 773

Why Managers Need to Know about Business Forecasting 774
Choosing the Appropriate Forecasting Technique 774
Simple Forecasting Methods 777
Moving Averages 778
Exponential Smoothing 779
Forecasting Using Regression 787
Autocorrelation 792
The Problem of Autocorrelation in Regressing Time Series Data 808
Detection of Serial Correlation 811
Solutions to the Problem of Serial Correlation 814
Autoregressive Models 815
ARIMA Models 821
Summary 825
Applications of Statistical Concepts in the Business World 827
Glossary 828
Key Formulas 828
Solved Exercises 830
Exercises 839
Extended Exercises 846
Microcomputer Package 849
MINITAB Computer Package 850
SAS Computer Package 851

Chapter 18 DECISION MAKING UNDER UNCERTAINTY 854

Why Managers Need to Know about Decision Making 855
Decision Criteria and the Payoff Table 855
Expected Value of Perfect Information 860
Tree Diagram Analysis 862
Bayes' Theorem 866
Utility Considerations 870
Summary 873
Applications of Statistical Concepts in the Business World 874
Glossary 875
Key Formula 875
Solved Exercises 875
Exercises 879
Extended Exercises 884
Microcomputer Package 887

Chapter 19 NONPARAMETRIC STATISTICS 889

Why Managers Need to Know about Nonparametric Statistics 890
Nonparametric versus Parametric Tests 890
One-Sample Sign Test 891
One-Sample Runs Test 894
Mann-Whitney *U* Test 898
Spearman Rank Correlation 902
Summary 905
Applications of Statistical Concepts in the Business World 905
Glossary 906
Key Formulas 906
Solved Exercises 907
Exercises 911
Extended Exercises 916
Microcomputer Package 918
MINITAB Computer Package 919
SAS Computer Package 920

Appendix A Effective Communications 924

Appendix B Derivations 928

Appendix C Company Data Base 931

Appendix D Answers to Selected Odd-Numbered Exercises 936

Appendix E Statistical Tables 967

Index 999

Chapter 1

Introduction to Statistics

There are three kinds of lies: lies, damned lies, and statistics.
B. Disraeli

Objectives

When you have completed this chapter, you will be able to:

Explain the role of statistics in the decision-making process.

Explain the role of the computer in statistics.

Perform computations using summation notation.

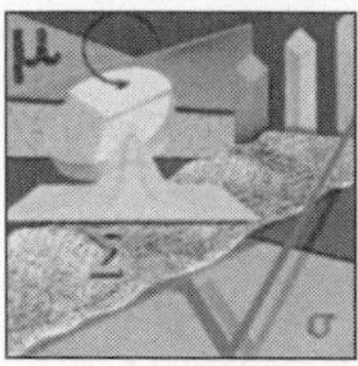

National spending on health care rose 11% between 1990 and 1991, the fifth consecutive year of double-digit increases. This trend, reported in *American Demographics* (April 1992, p. 19), is projected to continue through 1996. Health care accounted for 14% of the total output of goods and services in the United States in 1992, up from 12% in 1990. That's $817 billion a year spent on getting or staying well.

This chapter discusses topics essential to your study of business statistics. This book should aid your development as a business manager by improving your ability to make timely, efficient decisions. The authors sincerely hope that it will help you in your business career.

Why Statistics Is Important to Managers

Many entry-level business positions require a working knowledge of statistics. Many other beginning jobs require familiarity with data collection and analysis, or the analysis of reports and studies based on statistics. Knowledge of statistical principles is essential in such jobs. Midlevel and senior managers are also increasingly involved in statistical analysis, especially with personal computers and statistical software. One business leader recently told us, "The day of the seat-of-the-pants manager is almost gone."

The situation described at this chapter's beginning shows the need for a sound statistical background. It is a serious matter that health costs are increasing at a double-digit rate. But how was this information obtained? Was a sample of hospitals and/or doctors taken? If so, how many were sampled? Which hospitals and/or doctors were surveyed? Was the sample large enough to justify the reported increase? You'll deal with many such questions in this book.

The Purpose of Statistics

Every day people are bombarded by data. "Statistics" are associated with numbers generated in news reports, advertising claims, baseball earned run averages, opinion polls, and public debates. Modern organizations have millions of data items in their paper and computer records. Hundreds or thousands of data values are added to this total daily. Some of these additions come about through the normal course of business recordkeeping; others result from special studies and research efforts.

Without statistical procedures, an organization could never make sense of the mountain of data[1] that its business generates. The purpose of the statistical analyses you'll study in this text is to manipulate, summarize, and investigate data to obtain useful decision-making information.

[1]Throughout this book the term *data* is treated as a plural term. (The singular form of this word is *datum*.)

Purpose of Statistics

Statistical analysis is used to manipulate, summarize, and investigate data to obtain useful decision-making information.

Since the collection and study of data are important in many professions, a statistics background is valuable for a variety of careers. Government statistical offices release new numerical information on inflation and unemployment monthly. Forecasters, economists, financial advisors, and policymakers in business and government study these data to make informed decisions. To treat their patients effectively, dentists, doctors, and hospital personnel must understand statistics in research studies reported in medical journals. Elected officials use public opinion polls to gauge what legislation their constituents want. Businesses base decisions on market research studies of consumer buying patterns. Ranchers and farmers record data to study new feeds and crop varieties. Quality control engineers gather data on the reliability of manufactured parts and products. (Chapter 13 provides several examples.)

In the authors' experience, virtually every business manager needs a background in statistical analysis. Many jobs, especially in large companies, require extensive use of statistics. Such jobs often advertise for applicants with sound statistical or quantitative skills.

Although many other jobs don't require a statistical background, such a background may become increasingly important as a person achieves higher positions in management. In our consulting work we've helped managers in personnel, marketing, advertising, production, finance, computer applications, and public relations with their statistical problems. Just as the writing skills you began developing in grade school are vital in your college career, so will the statistical skills you develop through studying this book aid your business career.

STUDENT DATA BASE

Throughout this book are problems relating to the "student data base." These problems ask you to use the statistical techniques you've studied to analyze data generated in your own class. After each class member fills out the questionnaire in Table 1.1, the resulting data can be used in the end-of-chapter problems.

USING COMPUTERS WITH THIS TEXT

As you'll soon discover, statistical manipulation of data requires considerable arithmetic. For this reason, modern computers are essential for most statistical tasks.

This text will provide numerous examples of computer output. Typical data analysis packages have been chosen for these demonstrations. Keep in mind that literally hundreds of data analysis computer programs now available perform similar functions. During your career you may not use the packages in this text, but the ones you'll use will be similar in function and printed output.

TM

TABLE 1.1 Student Questionnaire for Class Data Base

1. My class standing is currently:
   ____ Freshman ____ Sophomore ____ Junior
   ____ Senior ____ Grad Student ____ Other
2. I am: ____ Female ____ Male
3. High school grade point average: ____________
4. My age is: ____________
5. I smoke cigarettes: ____ Regularly ____ Sometimes ____ Never

Please circle one of the following numbers to indicate your level of agreement with each of the statements below:

1—Strongly agree
2—Agree
3—Neutral or no opinion
4—Disagree
5—Strongly disagree

	SA	A	N	D	SD
6. A knowledge of statistics will be an important part of my working life after I leave college.	1	2	3	4	5
7. It would be a good idea to impose more stringent admission requirements for the business administration program.	1	2	3	4	5
8. Given the nature of statistics, I would prefer to have a quiz each week.	1	2	3	4	5
9. I usually do well in math classes.	1	2	3	4	5
10. In my business career, ethical considerations will be as important to me as making a profit.	1	2	3	4	5
11. Companies should have special programs and policies to help employees starting families.	1	2	3	4	5

Two of the best-known mainframe computer packages for statistical applications are MINITAB (MINITAB Project, University Park, Pennsylvania), and SAS (Statistical Analysis System, SAS Institute, Cary, North Carolina).

MINITAB

This book uses MINITAB since it's one of the easiest of the commonly available statistical packages and it can be employed on both mainframes and microcomputers. We aren't suggesting that you should use MINITAB during your career. Rather, we're showing how easily you can solve statistical applications using the computer. MINITAB instructions and examples are provided throughout the body and at the end of most chapters. Available in most university bookstores, *The Student Edition of MINITAB* is a helpful guide for using MINITAB.

SAS

More powerful than MINITAB, SAS is used more frequently in business applications. SAS instructions and examples appear at the end of selected chapters. The *SAS Guide for Use with Understanding Business Statistics* has been developed specifically for use with this textbook.

COMPUTERIZED BUSINESS STATISTICS

The microcomputer package *Computerized Business Statistics* (CBS), a statistical software package designed specifically for use with this textbook, runs on IBM and IBM-compatible microcomputers. It consists of an instructional text and either a 5.25-inch or 3.5-inch diskette. An overview of each statistical model plus illustrative examples appear at the end of most chapters in this text.

DATA SETS

Appendix C includes a data base of 200 company employees with nine variables so realistic assignments can be made that simulate real-world situations. A data disk with these data and over 50 data sets is also available.

STUDY GUIDE

The *Study Guide for Use with Understanding Business Statistics* available with this text contains input instructions for sample problems using MINITAB and CBS.

APPROACH OF THIS BOOK

This book begins by discussing ways to collect data in the business setting (Chapter 2) and presents easy-to-use graphical summaries of these values (Chapter 3). Numerical summary methods (Chapter 4) are then covered before the discussion moves on to certain important theoretical data distributions (Chapters 5, 6, and 7). The book's first part finishes with the important subjects of estimating unknown statistical values (Chapter 8) and testing the validity of statements made about these values (Chapters 9 and 10).

The second part of the book begins with a technique for determining the relationship between two qualitative variables (Chapter 11) and a variance ratio test (Chapter 12). The important topic of quality control, which uses most of the techniques learned in Chapters 1 through 12, appears in Chapter 13.

The final part of the book deals with sophisticated methods to examine relationships among two or more quantitative variables. All these methods are widely used in business today. Computer use is emphasized throughout these chapters since these procedures require complex arithmetic.

Each chapter contains numerous examples illustrating the concepts under discussion. In addition, Chapters 5 and 9 pose "situations" early in the discussion and resolve them after presenting the statistical technique. These situations realistically depict problems an organization can solve using the right statistical procedure.

A summary near the end of each chapter is followed by "Applications of Statistical Concepts in the Business World." A glossary of key terms, a list of key formulas, several solved exercises, and many unsolved exercises come next. By working through these brief problems, you should be able to master each chapter's topic before moving to the next. Three or four Extended Exercises (minicases) illustrating important chapter concepts follow the Exercises section. Some Extended Exercises are worked through or "solved"; others invite you to find the correct technique and apply it to a practical situation.

Finally, most chapters discuss using Computerized Business Statistics (CBS), MINITAB, or SAS to solve statistical problems. Detailed instructions will help computer novices use the computer to solve statistical problems.

SUMMATION NOTATION

Many statistical procedures call for the addition of several terms or factors. These addition procedures use a shorthand notation called *summation notation.* This method of indicating a sum will be used throughout this book, so you must understand this notation. If you already know summation notation, skip this section.

Summation Sign

The capital Greek letter sigma (Σ) is the **summation sign.** It instructs you to add all the terms that follow it. The key point is that all quantities covered by the summation sign must first be calculated, *then* added together. For example, the notation Σx means to identify all the values designated by x and add them together. The notation $\Sigma\ (x - y)$ means, first, to find the differences between each x and y pair and then add these differences. The following examples illustrate this concept.

EXAMPLE 1.1 Several data values have been collected and designated by the symbol x. Table 1.2 shows these values and their squared values. The table's columns are then added to form the totals shown.

TABLE 1.2 Data Values and Sums for Example 1.1

Value	x	x^2
x_1	3	9
x_2	5	25
x_3	−6	36
x_4	2	4
x_5	−9	81
Sums:	−5	155

Note that the summation notation presented in this section is a shorthand version. Complete summation notation uses an index of summation, often designated with the letter i. When several x values are to be added, the complete notation would designate the sum as

$$\sum_{i=1}^{n} x_i \tag{1.1}$$

This notation calls for the following sum. First, x_1 is identified, since the notation under the summation sign ($i = 1$) indicates that x_1 is the first term. In Example 1.1,

x_1 equals 3. Next, x_2 is identified (x_2 equals 5 in Example 1.1) and added to x_1. The index i is increased by one unit each time. This process is continued until x_n is added to the sum. In Example 1.1, n equals 5. Therefore, 5 will appear at the top of the summation sign, and x_5 will be the last term in the sum. Thus, the preceding notation calls for adding n values of x together, beginning with x_1 and continuing through x_n.

This book will employ the complete summation notation using a summation index when the computations are complex enough to require it for clarity. Otherwise, the simpler notation will be used.

EXAMPLE 1.2 Based on the sums in Table 1.2, the following summation notation is appropriate:

$$\Sigma x = -5 \qquad \Sigma x^2 = 155 \qquad (\Sigma x)^2 = -5^2 = 25$$

Note that for the sum of squared x values (Σx^2), each x must first be squared, *then* added; this sum is 155. Also note that the sum of x values squared, $(\Sigma x)^2$, produces a different sum, 25.

EXAMPLE 1.3 Two variables are measured for several objects. Table 1.3 shows these values, designated x and y, along with several values computed from them and their sums.

Based on the totals in Table 1.3, the following summation notation is used to summarize the calculations:

$$\Sigma x = 42 \qquad \Sigma y = 46 \qquad \Sigma(x - y) = -4$$
$$\Sigma(x - y)^2 = 62 \qquad \Sigma(x - 3)^2 = 243$$

TABLE 1.3 Data Values and Sums for Example 1.2

Value	x	y	$x - y$	$(x - y)^2$	$(x - 3)^2$
1	5	3	2	4	4
2	2	7	−5	25	1
3	12	8	4	16	81
4	9	10	−1	1	36
5	14	18	−4	16	121
Sums:	42	46	−4	62	243

EXAMPLE 1.4 In March 1992, U.S. industrial production rose to 107.2% of the 1987 average, according to a front-page graph in the April 16, 1992, *Wall Street Journal*. Suppose you wanted to investigate the relationship between industrial production and another economic variable such as the unemployment rate or personal disposable income.

Several data sums are needed to investigate the relationship between two such variables. Chapters 14 and 15 present techniques that require such sums. Table 1.4 presents the x–y data pairs that might result from a study of industrial production and a related variable, along with further necessary calculations and sums. Based on the values calculated in Table 1.4, the following statements can be made using summation notation:

$$\Sigma x = 66 \qquad \Sigma y = 48 \qquad \Sigma xy = -106$$
$$\Sigma x^2 = 3{,}390 \qquad \Sigma y^2 = 1{,}040$$

Based on Table 1.4, you should be able to verify the inequality

$$\Sigma x^2 \neq (\Sigma x)^2$$

TABLE 1.4 $x - y$ Data Values and Sums for Example 1.4

Value	x	y	xy	x^2	y^2
1	2	3	6	4	9
2	−4	10	−40	16	100
3	11	9	99	121	81
4	0	29	0	0	841
5	57	−3	−171	3,249	9
Sums:	66	48	−106	3,390	1,040

SUMMARY

This chapter has introduced some basic concepts of business statistics. Keep in mind as you study that the purpose of all statistical procedures, no matter how complex, is to extract useful information from available data. The purpose of this book, and of your business statistics course, is to improve your ability to perform this important function.

Summation notation was reviewed in this chapter. You should be familiar with this notation and its purpose. The exercises that follow will help you to master this simple concept.

Finally, this chapter covers some basic computer concepts used throughout the book. The section at the end of this chapter shows you how to use basic computer packages demonstrated at the end of most chapters.

APPLICATIONS OF STATISTICAL CONCEPTS IN THE BUSINESS WORLD

Following each chapter's Summary is a section called "Applications of Statistical Concepts in the Business World." Its purpose is to provide examples of how concepts discussed in the chapter are applied in the practical business world. There's not enough material in Chapter 1 to illustrate this approach, but you'll find this section useful in other chapters.

Any of the topics in this book could be used in a particular application, but the following chapter topics are quite widely used in the applications indicated.

Accounting: Data collection (Chapter 2), estimation (Chapter 8), hypothesis testing (Chapters 9 and 10).

Finance: Correlation and regression (Chapters 14 and 15), index numbers and time series analysis (Chapter 16).

General management: Data presentation (Chapter 3), business forecasting (Chapter 17), decision making (Chapter 18).

Management information systems: Data collection (Chapter 2), business forecasting (Chapter 17).

Marketing: Hypothesis testing (Chapters 9 and 10), chi-square tests (Chapter 11), analysis of variance (Chapter 12), nonparametric statistics (Chapter 19).

Operations management: Estimation (Chapter 8), hypothesis testing (Chapters 9 and 10), analysis of variance (Chapter 12), index numbers and time series analysis (Chapter 16).

Personnel: Hypothesis testing (Chapters 9 and 10), chi-square tests (Chapter 11), multiple regression (Chapter 15), nonparametric tests (Chapter 19).

Quality control: Data presentation (Chapter 3), descriptive statistics (Chapter 4), estimation (Chapter 8), quality control applications (Chapter 13).

GLOSSARY

Statistical analysis Used to manipulate, summarize, and investigate data to obtain useful decision-making information.

KEY FORMULAS

Summation notation

$$\sum_{i=1}^{n} x_i \qquad (1.1)$$

EXERCISES

1. Design a data collection of 10 values and use them to show that Σx^2 doesn't equal $(\Sigma x)^2$.
2. Consider the following x–y data values:

Value	x	y
1	5	4
2	7	9
3	3	8
4	0	5
5	10	3
6	2	9

a. Find the following sums: Σx, Σy, Σxy.

b. Show that Σx^2 isn't equal to $(\Sigma x)^2$.

2*a.* $\Sigma x = 27$
$\Sigma y = 38$
$\Sigma xy = 155$

b. $\Sigma x^2 = 187$
$(\Sigma x)^2 = 729$

3. Using the data collection

Value	x	y	z
1	−3	4	5
2	0	−12	14
3	15	7	−5
4	9	18	11
5	4	0	8

   a. Find the following sums: Σx, Σy, Σxy, $\Sigma(x - y + 2z)$.

   b. Show that Σy^2 isn't equal to $(\Sigma y)^2$.

3*a*. $\Sigma x = 25$
$\Sigma y = 17$
$\Sigma xy = 255$
$\Sigma(x - y + 2z) = 74$

b. $\Sigma y^2 = 533$
$(\Sigma y)^2 = 289$

4. For a certain data collection, the sum of the x's is 29, the sum of the y's is 48, the sum of their cross products is 357, and the sum of the x's after they're squared is 138. Summarize these results using summation notation.

4. $\Sigma x = 29$
$\Sigma y = 48$
$\Sigma xy = 357$
$\Sigma x^2 = 138$

INTRODUCTION TO THE MICROCOMPUTER PACKAGE

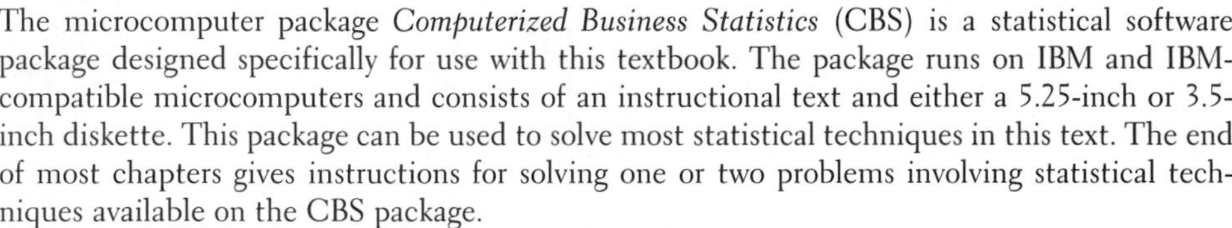

The microcomputer package *Computerized Business Statistics* (CBS) is a statistical software package designed specifically for use with this textbook. The package runs on IBM and IBM-compatible microcomputers and consists of an instructional text and either a 5.25-inch or 3.5-inch diskette. This package can be used to solve most statistical techniques in this text. The end of most chapters gives instructions for solving one or two problems involving statistical techniques available on the CBS package.

To access the package, type **CBS** after you receive the A> prompt on your screen. Your OPTIONS are C = configuration menu, M = main menu, and N = next page. You must choose the configuration menu the first time through to set up the package on your machine. Under the configuration (INPUT/OUTPUT SET UP MENU) your options are: Number of Disk Drives: ?, Program Disk Drive: ?, and Data Disk Drive: ?. After you make the appropriate choices for your machine, you can access the MAIN MENU. This menu lists all statistical techniques that you can run on CBS.

INTRODUCTION TO THE MINITAB COMPUTER PACKAGE

One popular software package used for statistical analysis is MINITAB. Available for both mainframes and microcomputers, MINITAB is one of the computer packages referred to throughout this book. For each MINITAB example in this text, assume that MINITAB has been executed. The MTB> prompt appears on the screen when the call up has been successful. The prompt at the left-most side of your screen tells you what kind of information MINITAB expects you to type.

MINITAB has long been recognized for its straightforward command structure, which will be presented throughout the text. But note that to further enhance ease of use, MINITAB has a new version called Release 8 for micros. It introduces menus and dialog boxes, with the command language retained for added flexibility and speed.

Understanding the MINITAB worksheet is the key to using this program. The worksheet contains columns (variables) and rows (observations). Columns are referred to by number, such as C1 and C2. Columns can also be assigned variable names, such as "Sales," "Price," or "Weight." The example commands discussed next refer to a typical worksheet shown below.

		Columns or variables					
		C1	C2	C3	C4	C5	C6
	1						
	2						
	3						
Rows or Observations	4						
	5						
	6						
	.						
	.						
	.						

As an example, MINITAB commands are presented to solve Exercise 2.

```
MTB > OUTFILE 'EXAMPLE.PRN'
MTB > SET C1
DATA> 5 7 3 0 10 2
DATA> END
MTB > SET C2
DATA> 4 9 8 5 3 9
DATA> END
MTB > LET C3 = C1*C2
MTB > PRINT C1-C3

 ROW   C1   C2   C3

   1    5    4   20
   2    7    9   63
   3    3    8   24
   4    0    5    0
   5   10    3   30
   6    2    9   18

MTB > LET K1 = SUM (C1)
MTB > LET K2 = SUM (C2)
MTB > LET K3 = SUM (C3)
MTB > PRINT K1-K3
K1       27.0000
K2       38.0000
K3       155.000

MTB > WRITE 'EXAMPLE.DAT' C1-C3
MTB > STOP
```

The **OUTFILE** command is used to save all the commands and output shown on the screen in the file specified "EXAMPLE.PRN" until the MINITAB session is ended with the command **STOP.**

The **SET** command is used to enter data into column 1 (C1) on the worksheet. The **DATA** subcommand is used to enter the data allowing at least one space between data values. The **END** subcommand is used to show that data entry is complete for column 1.

The **LET** command is used to do arithmetic using algebraic expressions such as multiplying C1 times C2 and storing the result in C3.

The **PRINT** command is used to print the contents of columns 1 through 3.

The **LET** command is used to sum the C1 column and store the result in row K1.

The **WRITE** command saves the data in a worksheet called EXAMPLE.DAT. For future use the worksheet can always be accessed by the command **READ 'EXAMPLE.DAT' C1–C3.**

INTRODUCTION TO THE SAS COMPUTER PACKAGE

The Statistical Analysis System (SAS) is one of the most versatile and popular software packages for statistical analysis in business and industry. Available for both mainframes and microcomputers, it's one of the packages referred to throughout this book.

To solve a statistical problem with SAS, we first define the data and then specify the statistical procedures (PROCS) to be used. Certain rules must be observed when running SAS programs:

1. SAS statements always end with a semicolon (;).
2. SAS names must start with a letter and must be eight characters or less.
3. SAS statements end in column 72. Longer statements are continued on the next line.
4. Data must be defined before a procedure can be run. Lines that contain data don't end with a semicolon. However, it's a good idea to include a semicolon at the end of the last line of data.
5. Several procedures can be performed by adding multiple procedure statements.
6. The decimal point must be included when entering data that contain a decimal (for example, 1.89).
7. Job Control Language (JCL) statements must be included with a SAS program. These statements are specific to a particular system and allow the SAS program to execute properly.

The SAS commands to solve Exercise 2 are:

```
$ SAS
OPTIONS PAGESIZE=60 LINESIZE=80;
TITLE "SAS SOLUTION TO EXERCISE 2";
DATA EXAMPLE;
 INPUT X Y;
    XY=X*Y;
CARDS;
5   4
7   9
3   8
0   5
10  3
2   9
PROC PRINT DATA=EXAMPLE;
 SUM X Y XY;
ENDSAS;
```

The OPTIONS statement indicates that the output page size will be 60 lines and that each line will contain 80 spaces.

The TITLE statement names the SAS program.

The DATA statement provides a filename for the data.

The INPUT statement names the variables and provides the correct order for the different fields on the data lines. Note that two variables will be read (X and Y) and a new variable will be created by multiplying ($XY = X^*Y$).

The CARDS statement indicates to SAS that the input data follow.

The next six lines contain the data values.

The PROC PRINT statement produces a listing of the data in the file EXAMPLE.

The SUM statement specifies variables to be totaled. The first line is a JCL statement. Table 1.5 shows the output for this SAS run.

TABLE 1.5 SAS Output for Exercise 2

SAS SOLUTION TO EXERCISE 2

OBS	X	Y	XY
1	5	4	20
2	7	9	63
3	3	8	24
4	0	5	0
5	10	3	30
6	2	9	18
	27	38	155

Chapter

2

Data Collection

Those who wish to succeed must ask the right preliminary questions.
Aristotle, *Metaphysics II*

Objectives

When you have completed this chapter, you will be able to:

Identify the various types of data that analysts collect.

Distinguish between nominal, ordinal, interval, and ratio levels of measurement.

Describe and know when to use various sampling techniques.

Describe the strengths and weaknesses of the more commonly used methods of data collection.

A cover story in the April 10, 1992, *Wall Street Journal* described the opening of Euro Disney, the new Disney theme park in France. The park and its adjoining resort complex cost $3.9 billion to construct.

Chapter 1 introduced the basic ideas of statistics to be presented in this book. In particular it stressed that the purpose of statistical analysis is to convert raw data into useful decision-making information.

WHY DATA COLLECTION PROCEDURES ARE IMPORTANT TO MANAGERS

Before data collections can be processed for decision-making purposes, the analyst must find relevant data. This chapter discusses data collection methods and illustrates the applications of the method. The collection of data that are relevant to the problem being studied is commonly the most difficult, expensive, and time-consuming part of the entire research project. Great care and skill must be exercised in the collection process; unfortunately, such care isn't always taken.

Euro Disney involved a multibillion-dollar gamble by Disney and the French government, which supplied a majority of the financing. This gamble was presumably based on sound research about the market potential for such a venture. Many data-gathering techniques discussed in this chapter were used to provide input into the decision-making process.

TYPES OF DATA

Variable

Statistical data are usually obtained by counting or measuring items. Examples of statistical data measures are the daily Dow Jones Average, unemployment rate, monthly sales of the Bay Point Corporation, and number of women executives at IBM. These data items are called **variables** because they can take on many different values.

Constant

Suppose a company wants to survey worker salaries in a particular industry. The company might also decide to compare salaries with other worker characteristics such as age, race, education level, and sex. In this instance the five characteristics—salary, age, race, education level, and sex—are variables in the survey. A variable has no fixed numerical value, whereas a **constant** does have a fixed value.

> A **variable** is an item of interest that can take on many different numerical values.
> A **constant** has a fixed numerical value.

Quantitative

Qualitative

Variables can be classified as quantitative or qualitative. A **quantitative variable** is one whose values are expressible as numerical quantities, such as measurements or counts. Weight (a measurement) and number of customers (a count) are examples of quantitative variables. A **qualitative variable** is not quantitative and can only be clas-

sified, but not measured. Qualitative variables can only be classified. A measurement taken on a qualitative variable conveys information regarding a characteristic (for example, classifying items on an assembly line as defective or not defective). As an example of a qualitative variable, Table 2.1 shows the number of firms classified by industry. It is important to recognize these two classifications when analyzing variables since different statistical techniques apply to different types of variables.

The type of data being analyzed is also important. Throughout this book, the type of data being treated will be identified using one of the data classification schemes discussed in the next section.

TABLE 2.1 Number of Firms by Industry, Spokane County, Washington, 1989

Services	3,059
Retail trade	2,058
Construction	874
Finance, insurance, and real estate	827
Wholesale trade	792
Unclassified	610
Manufacturing	505
Transportation and public utilities	327
Agriculture and mining	144
Total	9,196

Source: *County Business Patterns*, 1989.

> A **quantitative variable** is one whose values can be expressed as numerical quantities, such as measurements or counts. A **qualitative variable** is not quantitative and can only be classified, but not measured.

To prepare data for analysis, you must be familiar with a hierarchy of four numerical scales of measurement: *nominal, ordinal, interval,* and *ratio.* The higher the position of the data type in this hierarchy, the more information the data contain. Thus, data measured on a ratio scale contain more information than data measured on an interval scale, which contain more information than data on an ordinal scale, which in turn contain more information than data on a nominal scale.

Nominal Data

Data measured on a **nominal** scale represent the lowest level in the hierarchy and consist of categories in each of which the number of observations is recorded. Furthermore, the categories are in no logical order and have no particular relationship. The categories are said to be **mutually exclusive** since an individual, object, or measurement can be included in only one of them. The result is qualitative data usually measured by counting. The information in Table 2.1 is measured on a nominal scale: the number of firms has been counted for each industry. If a firm is counted as construction, for example, it cannot be counted as being in any other industry.

> Categories are **mutually exclusive** if an individual, object, or measurement can be included in only one of them.

People's favorite colors are another example of nominal data. If three colors are involved, the categories might be listed in order of preference as red, yellow, green or as green, yellow, red. Furthermore, if a color is red, it cannot be yellow or green. Since the order in which the categories are listed doesn't matter and the categories are mutually exclusive, the data are classified as nominal. Other examples of nominal data categories are male/female, Washington/Oregon/Idaho, urban/rural, train/bus/plane, and the college majors business/history/English/psychology/chemistry. In each of these situations, the categories could be arranged in any order.

> A **nominal** scale consists of mutually exclusive categories in which no logical order is implied.

Ordinal Data

Many data collections consist of qualitative categories where there is a progression or order. This type of data is referred to as **ordinal.** The information in Table 2.2 is measured on an ordinal scale. A rating of "excellent" is higher than a rating of "good," and so on; that is, order exists in the categories.

TABLE 2.2 Employee Ratings of Their Supervisor

Rating	Number of ratings
Excellent	4
Good	15
Fair	10
Poor	2
Total	31

> An **ordinal** scale consists of distinct categories in which order is implied.

Data measured on an ordinal scale contain more information than data measured on a nominal scale because the categories are ordered: values in one category are larger or smaller than values in other categories. Another example of data on an ordinal scale is the education categories on many questionnaires.

_______ Some high school
_______ High school graduate
_______ Some college
_______ College graduate
_______ Graduate school

This is an ordinal scale because each category indicates a higher level of education than the previous one. If the number of persons falling into each of these categories was recorded for a group being studied, ordinal data would result. The data are qualitative or categorical in nature, and the categories progress from little education to much education. Other examples of ordinal data categories are:

_______ Poor
_______ Average
_______ Good
_______ Superior

_______ Dislike
_______ Neutral
_______ Like

_______ Strongly agree
_______ Agree
_______ Neutral
_______ Disagree
_______ Strongly disagree

In each of these classification schemes, the occurrences in each category are counted, and the categories ascend or descend in some manner.

Interval Data

The next two types of scales involve quantitative data. The first type, the **interval** scale, results when numerical measurements are made on items and the intervals between measurements can be precisely determined. The Table 2.3 data are measured on an interval scale; the distance between any two temperature units is of a known, constant size.

TABLE 2.3 Temperature Desired by Factory Workers

65, 65, 65, 66, 66, 66
67, 67, 67, 67, 67, 67, 67, 67, 67, 68, 68, 68, 68, 68
69, 69, 69, 69, 69, 69, 69, 69, 69, 69, 69, 69, 70, 70, 70, 70, 70, 70, 70, 70, 70, 70, 70, 70, 70, 70, 70
71, 71, 71, 71, 71, 71, 71, 71, 71, 71, 71, 71, 72, 72, 72, 72, 72, 72, 72, 72, 72, 72
73, 73, 73, 73, 74, 74

Temperature	Number of respondents
65–66	6
67–68	14
69–70	27
71–72	22
73–74	6
Total	75

Note in Table 2.3 that the data collection has been summarized at the bottom of the table, where the number of occurrences in each category is shown. For this summary, the interval-scaled data have been converted to an ordinal scale (i.e., the categories are in ascending order). Such a data summary is called a *frequency distribution* and will be discussed in Chapter 3.

The interval scale is a stronger form of measurement than the ordinal or nominal scale because it allows you to discern not only which observed value is the largest, but also by how much. This is because there is a way of measuring the width of the interval between two values, rather than just ranking them. As an example, the interval cold/hot constitutes an ordinal scale while the interval 65°F/70°F is based on an interval scale. This is the key distinction between interval data and ordinal data: in ordinal data, distances between categories cannot be measured, whereas in interval data they can.

> The **interval** scale is a set of numerical values in which the distance between successive numbers is of measurable constant size.

By implication, data measured on an interval scale have an arbitrary zero point. That is, the person designing the scale arbitrarily decides where to locate the zero point. To qualify as an interval scale, the distance between numerical values needs only be definable. For example, in the consumer price index, if the base year is 1982, the price level during 1982 will be set at 100. Although this is an equal-interval measurement scale, the zero point is arbitrary.

A classic example of interval data is temperature measured in degrees Fahrenheit (Table 2.3). We can compute the amount of heat necessary to raise a room's temperature from 40°F to 60°F. The data values, 40 and 60, aren't arbitrary labels for categories. They are precisely defined numerical values, and the distance between them can also be precisely defined. Moreover, there's an arbitrary zero point for the Fahrenheit scale; the Celsius temperature scale uses a different zero point. Each of these scales constitutes an interval scale since the distance between any two numerical values can be precisely specified, and each scale has an arbitrary point defined to be zero.

Ratio Data

By contrast, data measured on a **ratio** scale have a fixed or nonarbitrary zero point. Such data are scaled using precisely defined intervals like interval-scaled data but have a fixed zero point as well. Data measured on a ratio scale constitute the highest level of measurement. The age data in Table 2.4 are measured on a ratio scale.

TABLE 2.4 Voter Opinion Survey: Age of Respondents

18, 19, 19, 19, 20, 20, 21, 21, 22, 25, 25, 28, 28, 29, 30, 32, 32,
33, 33, 35, 37, 37, 39, 41, 41, 42, 45, 45, 48, 48, 49, 49, 49, 50,
55, 55, 57, 60, 62, 65, 71, 72
Mean = 38.7

Note in Table 2.4 that the data values have been summarized by their average, or *mean*. This and similar ways to describe numerical collections using summary values are described in Chapter 4.

> The **ratio scale** consists of numerical measurements where the distances between numbers are of a known, constant size, and where the ratio of numbers has some meaning; in addition, there is a fixed, nonarbitrary zero point.

Most numerical measurements in practical situations result in data measured on a ratio scale. An example is the lifetime of a television picture tube. The difference between 500 days and 250 days is a measurable difference. Also, we could say that the 500-day tube lasted twice as long as the 250-day tube. By comparison, we wouldn't say that a 60° day is twice as warm as a 30° day. For interval data, the ratio of two numbers isn't appropriate. In addition, a true zero point exists for a ratio scale: zero lifetime means the tube didn't work at all; this zero value is clearly understood by everyone. Other examples of ratio-scaled data include automobile weights, annual salaries, elapsed times, shipping distances, and interest rates.

Before data are analyzed, it's important to first determine whether quantitative or qualitative data have been collected. In other words, it's vital whether (*a*) nominal- or ordinal-scaled data or (*b*) interval- or ratio-scaled data have been collected. Different statistical techniques are used for the two basic types of scales, and erroneous results can be expected if an inappropriate technique is applied.

Most statistical techniques in this book are for use with quantitative data. A few techniques discussed in later chapters are designed for nominal or ordinal data, and these will be clearly identified when they are presented. These techniques (sometimes referred to as *nonparametric techniques*) have entire books devoted to them. Chapters 11 and 19 of this book discuss several nonparametric data analysis procedures.

One final point should be made. It is possible, and sometimes desirable, to drop down the hierarchy scale. Suppose, for example, you've collected ratio-scaled data on people's ages. The numerical ages have been measured, and a fixed zero point is obvious; therefore, a ratio data scale exists. Converting these ratio-scaled ages to categories may be useful. For example, each age could be placed into one of the following categories:

________ Below 20
________ 20 to below 40
________ 40 to below 60
________ 60 to below 80
________ 80 to below 100

The result is data measured on an ordinal scale. However, suppose you had originally collected the age data in these categories. You couldn't convert these data into people's actual ages because the actual age of a person in the category "20 to below 40," for example, isn't known. In other words, it's possible to go down the hierarchy of data but not up.

One exception to this one-way rule is frequently employed in practical situations. The data collected to measure the performance of a department supervisor in Table 2.2 uses the following scale:

1. Excellent.
2. Good.
3. Fair.
4. Poor.

These are ordinal-scaled data since the frequencies in each category have been recorded and the categories are in order. Thus, the data would normally be analyzed using techniques designed for qualitative data (specifically, for ordinal-scaled data). But it's tempting to average the class responses by arbitrarily assigning numerical values to the categories as just shown. Averaging is a technique reserved for quantitative data, either interval or ratio, so it's not strictly appropriate for the ordinal data of Table 2.2.

However, it might be argued that the intervals between the categories are all equal. In other words, the same difference in performance exists between excellent and good as between good and fair as between fair and poor. If this argument is correct, the definition of interval-scaled data has been met; there are equal, measurable distances between successive data values. Therefore, numerical techniques such as averaging would be appropriate. These methods could only be used after numbers (1, 2, 3, . . .) have been assigned to the categories.

Analysts frequently use numerical techniques on ordinal data without addressing the issue of whether equal intervals exist between the categories. This can lead to serious error if unequal intervals actually exist and are ignored in the desire to use common numerical techniques. If the interval equality isn't addressed, the data analysis is suspect since qualitative data may have been converted to quantitative data without proper justification. Figure 2.1 summarizes the characteristics of the four measurement scales.

FIGURE 2.1 Characteristics of Levels of Measurement

Measurement scale	Characteristics	Appropriate statistics
Nominal	Unique classifications	Mode
Ordinal	Ranking or rating	Median, percentiles
Interval	Known difference between any two points	Mean, standard deviation
Ratio	Known difference between any two points Unique or true zero	Mean, standard deviation

EXERCISES

1. Explain the difference between a variable and a constant.

2. Explain the differences between qualitative and quantitative data.
3. State whether the following variables are qualitative or quantitative:
   a. The life of a light bulb.
   b. The brand of a light bulb.
   c. The rating of a particular stock.
   d. The expected return on investment for a particular stock.
   e. Number of accidents per week at a manufacturing plant.
   f. The types of accidents that occur at a manufacturing plant.
   g. Number of people who report to work per day at a manufacturing plant.

3*a.* Quantitative
b. Qualitative
c. Quantitative
d. Quantitative
e. Quantitative
f. Qualitative
g. Quantitative

4. Explain the difference between a nominal scale and an ordinal scale.
5. Explain the difference between an ordinal scale and an interval scale.
6. Explain the difference between an interval scale and a ratio scale.

7. Why are data measured on an interval or ratio scale preferred by statisticians?
8. The following information is included in John Johnson's personnel record:
   a. Sex: male.
   b. Marital status: single.
   c. Education completed: college.
   d. Height: six feet.
   e. Weight: 200 pounds.
   f. Amount of experience: seven years.
   g. Job: machine operator.
   h. Salary: $25,000 per year.

   Classify each of the personnel record items by type of data and method of measurement.

8*a.* Qualitative–nominal
b. Qualitative–nominal
c. Qualitative–ordinal
d. Quantitative–ratio
e. Quantitative–ratio
f. Quantitative–ratio
g. Qualitative–nominal
h. Quantitative–ratio

Types of Data Sources

Secondary Data

Primary Data

The data needed for a statistical analysis either are readily available or must be collected. Data that are already available are known as **secondary data,** and data that must be collected are known as **primary data.**

> **Primary data** are collected specifically for the analysis desired. **Secondary data** have already been compiled and are available for statistical analysis.

There are many sources of secondary data. Libraries are perhaps the most obvious example. Very powerful secondary data sources on the business scene include such computer networks as Compuserve, The Source, Dow Jones News Retrieval Service, Standard & Poor's Compustat, and Value Line. Subscribers to these services can access vast amounts of secondary data using the telephone and their own microcomputer.

The federal government generates large quantities of data each year. Published monthly, the *Survey of Current Business* covers many economic indicators. Published annually, the *Statistical Abstract of the United States* contains annual indicators of economic and other national activities. Anyone engaged in business or economic research should become familiar with these easily available sources of vast data on American life. Table 2.5 lists some other sources of data compiled by the federal government and other agencies.

TABLE 2.5 Selected Sources of Secondary Data

Data source	Subjects
American Statistics Index	Guide to sources of government data
Business Conditions Digest	Leading economic indicators
CIS/Index to Publications of the U.S. Government	Congressional publications
County and City Data Book	Data by city and county
Economic Report of the President	Various economic indicators of the United States
Federal Reserve Bulletin	Banks, financial markets, economic conditions
Handbook of Labor Statistics	Historical economic series
Statistics of Income Bulletin	Income and expense data

Data of interest to businesspeople can also be found in private publications and professional journals. The *Business Periodicals Index*, found in most libraries, lists published articles by subject area. People seeking sources of secondary data often consult it.

Secondary data are also available from commercial companies specializing in data services. Examples are the A. C. Nielsen Company, Market Facts, Inc., Market Research Corporation of America, and the J. Walter Thompson Company.

The advantage of using secondary data for a research or statistical investigation is that the data are already available and need not be collected for a specific project. Even purchasing the data from a commercial firm is usually less expensive than collecting primary data. The disadvantage of secondary data is that the specific needs of the analysis aren't always met by these sources. For this reason, many investigations require the collection of data directed specifically toward the matter being researched. The rest of this chapter concerns collecting such primary data.

EXERCISES

9. What are the advantages of primary data over secondary data?
10. Indicate a good secondary data source for each of the following types of information:
    a. Population information for the Pacific Northwest.
    b. A map of Lake County, Illinois.
    c. The birthrate in the United States.
    d. Annual sales of the top three airlines.
    e. Brands of diet cola recently introduced in the United States.

11. The Solomon Development Corporation asked a local research firm to conduct a market feasibility study to determine market factors that might affect the success of an athletic club in the Southwood Shopping Center in Lakeland, North Carolina. The research will require analysis of data on demographics, traffic flow, perceived image of competitors, area resident interest, and potential area growth.
    a. What secondary data sources could be used for this study?
    b. What primary data sources might be needed to complete this study?

DATA-GATHERING TECHNIQUES

The primary data-gathering techniques discussed in this section are widely used throughout business to collect information needed for analysis and decision making. It requires some practice and skill to determine which technique, or combination of techniques, best suits a specific task. The skilled researcher understands each data collection method and can use them to best advantage. The ability to perform good research is based largely on the analyst's skill in choosing among techniques.

Focus Groups

Focus groups are frequently used as a preliminary data-gathering method. These groups involve a small number of people in an informal discussion of items pertinent to the research. A skilled moderator conducts the sessions and leads the discussion into the areas of interest. Sessions last from one to two hours and are usually attended by 8 to 12 people. Since only a small number participate in a focus group, the results are used to direct further research.

It is important to select participants who match the larger group being studied. For example, if you wanted opinions on the adequacy of Medicare, it might be appropriate to choose for the focus group only participants over age 65. It might also be important to choose approximately equal numbers of men and women and to select participants from different areas of the region being studied. The key point is to try to get a fairly representative profile in the focus group so that their comments may be taken as reliable indicators of the opinions of the entire population being studied.

Usually it's wise to have at least three focus groups for each subject of interest. Each focus group will have its own character depending on its membership, and only after two or three sessions will the common themes begin to emerge. A single focus group could be misleading, especially if people with strong opinions dominate the session.

Telephone

Telephone interviewing is another popular technique for gathering information from residents. The advantages of this method are that it's fast, inexpensive, and relatively easy, and it provides a fairly high response rate. The disadvantages are that only simple questions can be asked, the survey must be short, and some people consider such telephone calls an invasion of their privacy and so won't answer.

Mail Questionnaires

Mailed questionnaires are frequently used to gather data when a mailing list exists or when respondents are scattered over a wide area. Detailed questions can be asked since people have time to reread questions and think about their answers. On the other hand, if the questionnaire is too long, people won't take the time to fill it out. The biggest problem with mail questionnaires is getting people to fill them out and return them. When a large group of people don't respond, the analyst faces the difficult problem of determining whether there's a difference between the respondents and nonrespondents. Working with a club or other tightly knit organization helps to minimize this problem. When the general population is surveyed, return rates are commonly very low, and this may lead to erroneous results.

Door-to-Door

The **door-to-door survey** is widely used because it is relatively easy to conduct and it generates high response rates. Care must be taken in selecting and training interviewers and ensuring that the questions are easy to understand. Also, the survey shouldn't be too lengthy. It is possible to cover a wide geographic area using this method and it's easy to obtain a good distribution of incomes of the respondents since people's incomes are usually reflected in their type of housing.

Mall Intercept

The **mall intercept** method is frequently used by market researchers interested in obtaining shoppers' opinions. Interviewers station themselves in heavily traveled shopping areas and invite selected people to answer a few questions. Visuals and other aids can be used in these interviews. People could be asked to taste a new product and comment on it, or people could be shown a new package and asked their opinions.

Registrations

Data are sometimes collected by **new product registrations.** Consumers are often asked to fill out survey forms when they "register" the product for warranty coverage. The obvious problem with the information is that not everyone returns the form. A bias may be introduced that could mislead the company collecting the data.

Observation

Sometimes data for business applications are collected by **observation.** Many such efforts involve the design of an *experiment* where conditions are carefully controlled so that the effects of introduced changes can be observed and analyzed. Experiments aren't as common in business as in science, but they're still used on occasion.

Interviews

The **personal interview** is used when the researcher needs to determine in-depth opinions and attitudes. Although this approach provides quality data, the cost and amount of time required to schedule and conduct personal interviews limit its usefulness.

The previous data-gathering methods all elicit the opinions or attitudes of people. However, many business problems concern the measurement of objects, such as television tubes, logs, or welded assemblies. Measuring objects avoids the problems of interacting and communicating with people, but involves questions of sample size and other considerations discussed in Chapter 8. Figure 2.2 summarizes advantages and disadvantages of each technique.

Experiments

Data sets of interest to the business community are often generated by experimental research. Experiments differ from other data-gathering techniques in terms of degree of control over the research situation. In an **experiment** one variable is manipulated and its effect on another variable is measured, while all other variables are controlled. Examples of business experiments include determining whether a customer prefers one of two brands of cola, whether presentation of unit price information changes average unit price paid, and whether a pay hike increases production. Experimental design is considered an integral part of quality-control operations.

EXERCISES

12. What are the advantages and disadvantages of the following data-gathering techniques?
    a. Focus groups.
    b. Telephone interviews.
    c. Mail questionnaires.

FIGURE 2.2 Advantages and Disadvantages of Data-Gathering Techniques

Data-gathering technique	Advantages	Disdvantages
Focus group	Good preliminary technique	Small sample Cannot project results
Telephone survey	Fast, inexpensive Easy to conduct, high response rate Interviewer flexibility	Simple questions must be asked Survey must be short
Mail survey	Can cover a wide geographical area Inexpensive, standardized questions	Low return rates Time-consuming
Door-to-door	Can cover a wide geographical area Easy to conduct, high return rates	Time-consuming Expensive
Mall intercept	Fast, inexpensive Easy to conduct, visual aids can be used Interviewer flexibility	Cannot project results Survey must be short
Personal interviews	Visual aids can be used Interviewer flexibility Answers can be probed	Expensive Time-consuming Small samples result

d. Mall intercept.

e. Door-to-door interviews.

f. Personal interviews.

13. The New York League of Credit Unions has decided to survey all credit unions in the state to determine how the league can improve service to its members. What type of data-gathering instrument should the league develop?

14. The Metro Association wants to determine voters' feelings about a county bond issue to be voted on next month. The issue involves replacing the present coliseum. Metro needs to determine who is most likely to vote for the proposal and who is most likely to vote against it. Once Metro has this information, it can create a target audience for its advertising. What type of data-gathering approach should Metro develop?

13. Mail survey

14. Telephone survey

POPULATIONS AND SAMPLES

Population

In statistical studies it's crucial to identify the **population** (the group of subjects or items being studied).

> A **population** is the entire set of individuals or items of interest.

There are times when you can measure or examine each item in the population. Each member of your statistics class, for example, might have filled out the questionnaire in Chapter 1 (Table 1.1). If 35 students are in your class, and if information is desired about only this class, the members constitute a population, and each member can be measured by his or her responses to the questionnaire. When an attempt to measure all members of a population of interest is made, a **census** results.

Census

> A **census** is an attempt to measure every item in the population of interest.

You can sometimes conduct a census when population items reside in a computer file. Even if the population is quite large, a computer can measure each item quickly and accurately. An example of this kind of census is the measurement of some variable for all employees in a firm. Records of 5,000 or more employees may be held in a computer file, so it could be easy and fast to obtain information on each if the files had data of interest such as time with the company, age, and performance rating.

In most statistical investigations, a census is difficult, costly, or even impossible. It would be difficult and very time-consuming to measure variables such as age and performance rating for a large company's employees, for instance, if these data were contained in file folders rather than on a computer. It would be impossible to survey each member of a large community since their telephone numbers aren't readily available and personal contact with such a large number couldn't be achieved even with several months' effort. Under such conditions, it's necessary to choose a **sample,** which is a population subset selected for analysis.

Sample

> A **sample** is a subset selected from the population.

Choosing *representative samples* is a key problem in statistical investigations. Unless it's easy and cost-effective to measure each population item through a census, the investigator faces the problem of how to select a representative sample from the larger population. A representative sample may provide useful insights into the nature of the population being studied, whereas an unrepresentative sample could suggest totally incorrect conclusions about the population.

EXAMPLE 2.1 A September 29, 1989, *Wall Street Journal* story indicated that the Gillette Company seeks to improve its share in the high-tech men's razor market. Suppose a market researcher is responsible for selecting a sample of men to interview about razors. Since it's not possible to contact all men in all selected cities, the researcher decides to sample men in several downtown areas and give them a short series of questions to answer. Interviewers query men during the busy afternoon hours Monday through Friday of a selected week.

The problem with this sample selection method is that many men don't shop during weekday afternoons. Those who work during the day away from downtown locations can't be selected during those hours. The researchers should have scheduled interviews weekends and evenings as well, along with interview areas away from downtown.

EXAMPLE 2.2 The Joe Dear Company, a manufacturer of farm tractors, receives component parts from several suppliers. To check incoming parts' quality, a few are selected for quality-control tests as they arrive in rail cars. For three days, boxcars are opened, and a few parts are removed for testing.

The time period for the test may be too short in this case. Perhaps only two suppliers had shipments due during the three-day test period. A longer sampling period could have ensured that all suppliers were being tested. Also, it might be misleading to select only parts that are easy to access when cars are opened. Suppliers might deliberately put parts known to be good at this location, disguising the real quality level of the entire boxcar load.

The key point in sampling is to be sure that the sampled items represent the population as closely as possible. This task is usually more difficult than it appears. Often we must devote much time and thought to this selection process since after the sample items are measured, it will be assumed that the sample is representative of the population. For example, analysts sampling 100 items from a population of 100,000 items must be sure they used a proper sampling plan before judging the condition of this large population. The rest of this chapter discusses methods of ensuring that a representative sample is drawn from the population of interest.

EXERCISES

15. What is the difference between a population and a sample?
16. What is the difference between a census and a sample?
17. When is a sample preferable to a complete census?
18. Is a census ever preferable to a sample? Give an example.

SIMPLE RANDOM SAMPLING

Random and Nonrandom Samples

There are two basic methods for selecting items from a population. If each item in the population has the same chance of being selected, this constitutes a **random sample.** In a random sample, each possible sample of n items has the same chance of being selected for analysis. If some population items have a greater chance of selection than others, this constitutes a **nonrandom sample.** These two sampling methods are sometimes referred to as *probability* samples (random) and *nonprobability* samples (nonrandom).

There are many different types of random samples. A simple random sample (the most frequently employed) results when n elements are selected from a population in such a way that every possible combination of n elements in the population has an equal probability of being selected.

Simple Random Sampling

> A **simple random sample** results when n elements are selected from a population in such a way that every possible combination of n elements in the population has an equal probability of being selected.

A simple random sample can be thought of as some variation of drawing names from a hat. A method is devised to reach into the population and randomly draw a single item. This procedure is repeated until the desired sample size is reached.

With and Without Replacement

In this sampling procedure, along with the others discussed in this chapter, it is assumed that the sampling is done **without replacement.** That is, an item selected for the sample isn't returned to the population for possible reselection. There are other circumstances when sampling is conducted **with replacement.** In these cases, each sampled item is returned to the population before the next selection takes place.

> When sampling is conducted **without replacement,** an item selected for the sample isn't returned to the population for possible reselection. When sampling is conducted **with replacement,** each sampled item is returned to the population before the next selection takes place.

EXAMPLE 2.3 A United Way committee of 10 people needs a three-person subcommittee to write its final report. Committee chair Jennifer Dahl decides to randomly select these people, so committee members write their names on pieces of paper and place them in a jar. Jennifer then selects three of them. The three names selected form the subcommittee. This procedure constitutes a simple random sample selected without replacement.

EXAMPLE 2.4 ACME TV just received an order for 150 TV sets. Fred Ward, owner of ACME, is concerned about the sets' quality. He decides to sample 10 sets and subject them to various tests. Each box containing a set is numbered, from 1 to 150. Then 150 pieces of paper are prepared, each with a number, covering the 1–150 number range. These pieces of paper are put into a jar, and 10 are randomly drawn. The 10 TV sets corresponding to these 10 numbers constitute a simple random sample selected without replacement.

The advantage of any random sample, including the simple random sample, is that it stands a better chance of providing a representative look at the population than does a nonrandom sample. This is because no population item is excluded from fair consideration for inclusion in the sample. In addition, a random sample is defensible. Critics of the sampling results can't fault the method of selection for bias in determining results. By contrast, nonrandom samples are subject to attack even if their results happen to be very representative of the population.

Random Number Table

Writing names or numbers on pieces of paper and randomly drawing them is a valid simple random sampling method. However, this method can prove time-consuming if the number of population items is large. The **random number table** provides a quick, easy method of randomly selecting population item numbers.

> The **random number table** provides lists of numbers that are randomly generated and can be used to select random samples.

Most computer software packages generate lists of random numbers for use in selecting random samples. One such package is MINITAB. The MINITAB commands to generate and print random numbers for selection of a sample of size 20 from a population of 200 observations are:

```
MTB> RANDOM 20 C1;
SUBC> INTEGER 1 200.
MTB> PRINT C1
C1

    32   135   165   140    73   198     8
   197   151    57    21    13   184    42
    77    99   108   114   128    37
MTB> STOP
```

These MINITAB commands are explained in the MINITAB Computer Package section at the end of this chapter.

Another example of a computerized random number generator (CBS) is presented at the end of this chapter. Appendix E.1 contains a table of random numbers generated with this program.

To use the table in Appendix E.1, choose an arbitrary starting point. Then choose a systematic way of picking numbers from the table. One way is to move from left to right along the arbitrarily chosen row. Another way is to go from top to bottom beginning in the arbitrarily chosen column. By preselecting the method of movement through the table, you remove any chance of bias and the randomness of the sampling procedure is ensured.

To use a random number table, follow these steps:

1. Obtain a list of the population, and consecutively number the items.
2. Identify the number of digits for the last item in the population. If the population contains 675 items, for example, you need three-digit random numbers.
3. Enter the random number table at some arbitrary point, and select numbers from the table in a predetermined way.
4. Determine whether sampling is to be done with or without replacement.
5. Omit any numbers that don't correspond to numbers on the list or that were previously selected from the table (if sampling is done without replacement). Continue until the desired number of items has been selected.
6. Include in the sample the items that correspond to the numbers selected.

EXAMPLE 2.5 Clipper Express Company's delivery fleet contains 80 trucks. Clipper's management is interested in their trucks' average miles per gallon. Clipper assigns the problem to analyst Jodi Lake, who decides to randomly select five trucks to undergo mileage tests during the next two weeks. Jodi would like to select a simple random sample. Rather than write 80 numbers on pieces of paper and randomly draw 5 of them, she decides to use a random number table.

Jodi obtains a list that identifies each truck by a number on the hood. Since there are fewer than 100 trucks in the fleet, two-digit random numbers are used to select the sample of trucks. Table 2.6 contains a portion of the random number table in Appendix E.1. Beginning at an arbitrarily chosen point, say, the upper left corner, and moving left to right, five random numbers are selected:

45, 72, 53, 84, 00

TM

TABLE 2.6 Partial Random Number Table

45725	38400	89452	31237	46598	31246	31002	32650	56421	89078
12457	32650	98740	56426	98451	02300	98450	59874	99544	56122
45112	00221	56446	23554	89710	56478	57410	00123	66658	45488
12450	56451	98451	98457	19457	32659	54201	00215	05579	65127
01245	61548	89700	23305	65704	65490	89567	32150	56401	66457
45618	23015	95781	65190	65734	56427	02455	54667	56102	65480
45611	23359	60058	67544	94567	88461	23346	56754	31216	64572
40015	50998	67723	33751	21334	56112	02240	97645	31278	56481
45002	21137	23199	89764	65722	34556	56420	12341	23498	88945
45500	65722	64977	65895	33348	56000	64559	56734	56779	56487

The first three numbers are valid, so Jodi includes their counterpart trucks in the sample. The next two numbers can't be used; no trucks are numbered 84 or 00. The next random numbers in the table are:

89, 45, 23, 12, 37

There's no truck number 89, and truck number 45 has already been selected (sampling is being done without replacement). Truck numbers 23 and 12 are valid numbers, and this completes the selection process. Jodi uses the trucks with the following numbers for mileage tests:

45, 72, 53, 23, 12

Jodi identifies the five trucks corresponding to the selected numbers and begins the mileage tests Monday morning. The selection process was completely random, and no charge of bias can be leveled at Jodi no matter what the mileage tests reveal. She has selected a simple random sample using a random number table.

EXAMPLE 2.6 From the general membership of the Postal Workers Union, 25 members are to be selected to constitute a committee to meet with management on labor issues. Since there are strong opinions throughout the union on these issues, it's important that union leadership use a completely random and defensible selection method. Union secretary Max Learner is to select the committee.

Max decides to use an existing list of union members, with the first person being number 1, the second number 2, and so on. Max produces a random number table and asks an objective witness to select a starting point on one page. Max has already explained to his witness that he intends to move left to right in picking numbers. Since there are 7,452 members in the union, four-digit numbers are used. After discarding duplicate numbers and those greater than 7,452, 25 valid numbers are selected. Persons corresponding to these numbers on the membership list constitute the committee.

Exercises

19. Explain the term *random sample.*
20. Describe some methods for selecting a random sample.
21. What is the difference between a random sample and a nonrandom sample?
22. Describe the steps necessary to use a table of random numbers.
23. A manufacturing association wants to develop a questionnaire to send all 8,250 members. The association decides to survey 30 members and requests assistance in finalizing the questionnaire. What type of sampling technique should be employed?
24. (This question refers to Exercise 23.) Describe the steps necessary to use a table of random numbers for selecting the sample of 30 members.

Other Sampling Techniques

If a simple random sample is possible and convenient, this is usually the best method. It is easy to perform, it's easy to understand, and no sampling bias can be charged after the selections are made. However, it's not always possible to take a simple random sample. For this method to be used, a list of the population must be available. If a store wanted to sample its credit card holders, for example, such a list would be available. But if it wanted to sample shoppers in its service area, there would be no list and it wouldn't be possible to match random numbers with shoppers.

Simple random sampling can be difficult if the population is quite large. It might be difficult, for example, to go through 50,000 personnel folders looking for those that correspond to 50 randomly selected numbers. Nevertheless, random samples are still desirable since they provide the best insurance against sample selection bias. This section discusses sampling methods other than simple random sampling.

Systematic Sample

Researchers have methods to ensure the randomness of sampled items that offer more convenience or lower cost than simple random sampling. In one such technique, **systematic sampling,** population items are arranged in a random sequence and every *n*th item is selected for the sample.

> A **systematic sample** is one in which every *n*th item in the population sequence is selected.

If systematic sampling is to be used, the population must be arranged in some random line or sequence. If N is the population size and n is the sample size, then N/n is the gap between successive sampled items. For example, if there are 1,000 items in a population and 100 items are to be sampled, then every 10th item (1,000/100) is selected. If 250 items are to be systematically selected from a population of 5,850 items, then every 23d item (5,850/250) is selected. In the latter example, as in most real-world situations, the calculation N/n doesn't produce a whole number for the sample interval. Since 5,850/250 = 23.4, the sample interval is rounded to 23. Note that if you round up, you'll run out of population items, so it's a good idea to always round down.

The starting point for sample selection is randomly determined from the first N/n items in the population. For example, if every 10th item is to be selected from a population, then a random starting point among the first 10 population items is selected using a random number table. If the random number 8 is selected, the items for the sample are numbers 8, 18, 28, 38, and so on.

EXAMPLE 2.7 A machine fills aluminum cans with soft drink, producing a line of cans that are then boxed and shipped. Zane Griffey, quality-control manager, wants to determine the line's average fill volume. This figure is an important measure of line quality since too much fill will cost the company money, while too little might create bad publicity if a consumer group detects the underfilling.

Zane decides to take a systematic sample of the can line since the can population is in a moving line and can be thought of as infinite in length. He decides to approach the line at an arbitrary time tomorrow and to take every 50th can as it passes the selection point. He'll repeat this procedure several times during various days and various shifts over the next two weeks. By measuring each sampled can's fill volume, Zane will have a good idea of how the machine is performing. He'll then use the lot acceptance procedures of Chapter 13 ("Quality-Control Applications") to decide if the line-filling volume is acceptable.

EXAMPLE 2.8 Ken Greenwood is personnel director for Waterworks Sprinkler Company, which produces commercial sprinkler systems. Ken wants to study his company's labor force. Specifically, he seeks information on overtime per week, on employees' age distribution, and on their education level. The personnel officer's employee file folders contain all these data. Since the company employs about 12,500 people and records aren't currently stored on a computer, some kind of sampling procedure must be employed. Ken wants to be sure that his sampling procedure will result in sample results that are representative of the entire labor force.

Ken decides to sample 350 personnel file folders from his company's total of 12,500 folders. Instead of taking a time-consuming simple random sample, Ken tells his staff to take a systematic sample since the file folders are arranged in alphabetical order. With population size of 12,500 and sample size of 350, the sample interval for a systematic sample is 12,500/350 = 35.7, rounded to 35.

Ken enters a random number table for a two-digit number and gets 18. He then computes all 350 of his random numbers as 18, 53 (18 + 35), 88 (18 + 35 + 35), and so on. Personnel files corresponding to these numbers are then pulled so Ken can record employee variables of overtime per week, age, and education level. He knows his sample will be representative of his company's total work force since he has a random sample.

Stratified Random Sample

Another method analysts frequently employ is the **stratified random sample.** Here, the population is broken into subgroups, or strata, and each group is individually sampled.

> In a **stratified random sample,** the population is broken into meaningful strata or subgroups and each group is randomly sampled.

Stratification is frequently performed on such demographic variables as gender, age, and income. For example, a city's residents might be stratified by income. Since residents' income level is reflected in housing type, separate samples could be taken for small houses, large houses, mobile homes, apartments, and so on. Age could also be used as a stratifying variable. Such a survey could include visits to a retirement community and a high school plus door-to-door interviews in a middle-income neighborhood.

It's important to stratify a population using variables that are relevant to the study. If the survey involves voting preference, stratifying based on age, income, and gender would make sense. Stratifying the population by height or eye color would not since these variables have no logical relationship with voting preference.

The advantage of stratifying a population prior to sampling is that the sample size—and hence the cost—can be reduced without sacrificing accuracy. If simple random sampling were used in a city study, you might have to sample 1,000 residents to ensure that the correct proportions of males and females, young and old, and wealthy and poor were included. If the population were first stratified according to age, income, and sex, the sample size might be reduced considerably, with attendant reductions in the time and cost needed for the study.

EXAMPLE 2.9 Cominco Electronics wants to sample electronic assemblies from its inventory as part of its continuing quality control efforts (Chapter 13 details quality control). Cominco supplies parts to the U.S. Navy. Management is concerned about a *U.S. Naval Institute Proceedings* article (May 1989, p. 205) outlining Congress's budgetary concerns and suggesting navy fleet size may be reduced. Such a cut would affect Cominco's business considerably, so management wants to carefully assess the quality of the assemblies it sends the Navy.

Cominco's president is also aware of Lockheed Corp.'s efforts to move more of its business from military to civilian work, as described in a February 10, 1992, *Wall Street Journal* front-page story. Cominco may have to consider a major effort to build its civilian business in the future. In the meantime, its electronic assemblies' quality is of primary concern.

Since three different companies supply parts to Cominco, the population of parts in inventory is first stratified by supplier. Past records indicate that 20% of the parts are supplied by supplier A, 70% by supplier B, and the other 10% by supplier C. Management has decided on a total sample size of 850 parts, which will reflect the proportions in the population. That is, 20% of the sample will be parts from supplier A, and so on. This results in the following sample sizes for the three strata:

Supplier A:	(.20)(850)	= 170
Supplier B:	(.70)(850)	= 595
Supplier C:	(.10)(850)	= 85
Total sample size		= 850

Now that the strata and their sample sizes have been determined, a simple random sample of parts is selected from each supplier. The sampling method used in this example is stratified sampling followed by simple random sampling within each stratum.

EXAMPLE 2.10 Michelle Sutcliffe, analyst for Professional Investment Group, is investigating earnings of large service companies. Once a year, *Fortune* magazine lists the largest service companies in the United States. This list (called the Fortune Service 500) is organized by six major industry groups (Table 2.7). Since collecting data for all 500 corporations would be extremely time-consuming, Michelle selects a random sample of 50 firms. She believes that firms in the same industry group share common earnings characteristics so she treats each group as a separate stratum. Table 2.7 shows how Michelle computed the appropriate number of companies to randomly select from each service group. For example, since 150 of the 500 companies, or 30%, are financial, she selects a simple random sample of 50 × .30 = 15 from this group.

TABLE 2.7 Fortune Service 500 Companies (Example 2.10)

Group	Number of companies	Percentage of population	Sample size
Financial	150	150/500 = .30	15*
Diversified	100	100/500 = .20	10
Commercial banking	100	100/500 = .20	10
Retailing	50	50/500 = .10	5
Transportation	50	50/500 = .10	5
Utilities	50	50/500 = .10	5
	500	1.00	50

*Thirty percent of 50 equals 15 financial service companies to be included in the final sample.

Cluster Sample 

The final random sampling technique discussed in this section is the **cluster sample.** In this method, instead of individual items, groups or clusters of items are selected to be in the sample.

> **Cluster sampling** involves randomly selecting groups or clusters of items for inclusion in the sample.

For this technique, the population must be grouped so that a random process can be used to select the sample groups. Once a group or cluster has been randomly picked, each item in the group is included in the sample. If the cluster groups are quite large, a simple random sample can be selected from each.

EXAMPLE 2.11 Forest Resources, a lumber company, wants to randomly sample logs to measure for moisture content and number of board-feet. Since the logs are in piles in the lumberyard, and since each pile contains similar logs, it's decided to regard the piles as clusters and randomly choose among them. There are 58 log piles, so two-digit random numbers are chosen. Log piles are prenumbered so piles corresponding to the random numbers can be identified. Each log in the chosen piles is then measured.

EXAMPLE 2.12 Panorex, Inc., uses a city map to randomly survey residents regarding their preferences for local TV news programs. Each city block is numbered for a total of 758 blocks. Twenty 3-digit random numbers are chosen, and blocks corresponding to these numbers are used in the sample. Interviewers are sent to interview each residence on the selected blocks. Several trips are needed to secure these interviews since many people aren't home on the first call. This interview process results in a cluster sample that's random.

V Three nonrandom sampling procedures are frequently used in practical situations. First, in a **judgment** sample, items selected for inclusion in the sample are chosen using the sampler's judgment. Second, the **convenience** sample is so named because the most convenient population items are selected. The third is a **quota** sample, selected on the basis of specific guidelines about which items and/or how many should be drawn.

EXAMPLE 2.13 Fidelity Associates' board of directors has decided to sample opinions of other companies around the country regarding the economic forecast for next year. Company president Sean Bradford chooses those persons to be interviewed by telephone. This is a judgment sample because the specific individuals to be called aren't selected randomly; rather, Bradford's judgment is used in the selection process. If the company president is experienced and personally selects a representative group to sample—a good sample should result. On the other hand, if Sean talks only to friends who aren't in a good position to assess economic conditions, a misleading picture of the company's operating environment could result. This is the danger of a judgment sample: the sampler must use good judgment in choosing items to be sampled. In addition, a judgment sample can be difficult to defend, especially when the results displease someone.

EXAMPLE 2.14 A market research class has decided to sample student opinion on several subjects for a class project. The team leader assigns each student a sample of 10 people and requests that interviews be completed in one week. This could be called a quota sample because each student's quota is a sample of 10, or it could be called a convenience sample because each student will presumably sample the 10 most convenient people in the absence of any other instructions. A poor sample will likely result. No thought has been given to the nature of the population or to whether the sampling team will be contacting students of various ages, majors, places of residence, and so on. If results of this sample are extended to the entire student population, inaccurate conclusions are quite possible.

EXAMPLE 2.15 A September 19, 1989, *Wall Street Journal* lead story stated, "In the Soviet Union, the newly elected are besieged by problems." Soviet politicians may discover the usefulness of a technique used for years by American politicians: the political poll. If such survey work were to be undertaken in the Soviet Union, identifying a representative sample would be crucial. Selecting such a sample would probably incorporate stratification and cluster sampling and would likely require a good bit of judgment as well.

Two conflicting objectives must be balanced in sampling from a population: accuracy and cost. If accuracy were the only objective, large, totally random samples would always be taken using methods that are fully defensible. If cost were the only objective, small samples would be selected using the fastest, most convenient method. Only when these two objectives are balanced through good judgment can a sampling procedure be determined that truly meets the researcher's needs.

In any sampling procedure, errors in estimating population characteristics are inevitable. Good sampling procedures keep these errors at an acceptably low level. Poor sampling procedures may generate misleading or erroneous results. Later this book will deal with recognition and measurement of these errors.

DATA FILE CONSTRUCTION

This chapter's emphasis is on recognizing the type of data to be collected in a research study, and on designing a plan to produce a representative sample of the population. Since data analysis is only as good as the data collected, this is a key concept and one sometimes overlooked in the haste to begin the analysis.

Of equal importance in ensuring that the final data analysis results are accurate is the careful coding of data and file construction after data have been collected. In our consulting work we sometimes see situations where careful collection of data is followed by careless, even sloppy keying of data into the computer and setting up of the data file. Subsequent analysis is then conducted on misleading or erroneous data, leading to improper conclusions.

The important point is to be sure that a carefully monitored process is involved in transferring data from the source documents to the computer file in a format that can be used by the data analysis software. It often helps to visualize the final data file as a rectangular block of numbers in the computer. There is a row for each respondent or entity measured, and a column for each variable recorded. Example 2.16 shows part of such a data block.

EXAMPLE 2.16 Table 1.1 in the previous chapter showed a student questionnaire used to generate a class data base. Table 2.8 shows a small portion of the data base we generated in a recent statistics class. Only 10 lines are shown, representing 10 student responses. Coding for the column variables was as follows (question numbers refer to the questions in Table 1.1):

1. 1 = Freshman, 2 = Sophomore, 3 = Junior, 4 = Senior, 5 = Grad, 6 = Other.
2. 1 = Female, 2 = Male.
3. GPA recorded with one decimal point (e.g., 3.1).
4. Age recorded with two digits.
5. Smoking recorded as 1 = Regularly, 2 = Sometimes, 3 = Never.

6 through 11. Responses recorded with response digit, 1 = Strongly agree, 2 = Agree, 3 = Neutral, 4 = Disagree, 5 = Strongly disagree.

Note: A nonresponse for any question is recorded as a zero.

TABLE 2.8 Student Questionnaire Data Block (Example 2.16)

2	1	3.1	22	3	1	3	2	4	5	2
2	1	2.9	21	3	1	4	2	3	5	4
3	2	3.0	25	3	5	2	3	4	2	3
2	2	2.2	29	1	3	3	3	2	2	3
3	2	3.5	23	3	2	4	3	3	4	5
2	1	2.7	35	3	2	1	1	2	1	2
2	1	3.8	21	3	2	4	2	4	3	5
3	2	2.5	20	2	2	1	3	3	3	3
3	1	2.4	24	3	4	4	5	5	3	4
3	1	3.3	23	3	3	2	2	2	2	2

EXERCISES

25. What are the advantages of each of the following sampling techniques?
    a. Simple random sample.
    b. Cluster sample.
    c. Convenience sample.
    d. Stratified random sample.
    e. Systematic sample.
    f. Judgment sample.

SM

26. Which of the sampling methods listed in Exercise 25 are random sampling techniques?
27. What is the danger of using a judgment sample?
28. The Illinois League of Credit Unions has decided to survey all credit unions in the state. The survey's purpose will be to determine how the league can improve service to its members. What type of sampling plan should the league use?

28. Mail survey

29. A large church wants to investigate its members' attitudes regarding level of financial support, desirability of building a new church, and popularity of the present pastor. A sum of

29. Focus group and then a mail survey

money has been allocated to research these matters, but the church leadership doesn't know how to proceed. What kind of research package would you recommend?

30. (This question refers to Exercise 29.) What variables should the research address so that the church's research objectives are reached?

SUMMARY

This chapter began by outlining the various kinds of data collected and analyzed in business studies. Sources of secondary data were then introduced along with methods used to collect primary data. Table 2.9 summarizes the sampling methods discussed.

TABLE 2.9 Sampling Methods

Method	Procedure
Random	
Simple	Items are randomly chosen one at a time.
Systematic	Every *n*th item is chosen from population sequence.
Stratified	The population is separated into meaningful subgroups prior to sampling.
Cluster	Groups or clusters of population items are selected for the sample.
Nonrandom	
Judgment	The researcher's judgment is used to decide which population items will be included in the sample.
Convenience	The most convenient items are selected for the sample.
Quota	Those choosing sampled items are given a quota.

The objective in any sampling method is to select sample items that are representative of the population. Each sampled item can represent hundreds or thousands of population items that weren't selected and won't be measured. For this reason, skilled researchers always strive to select a sound sampling plan. Random sampling provides the necessary assurance that the samples are representative.

APPLICATIONS OF STATISTICAL CONCEPTS IN THE BUSINESS WORLD

THE J & H RESEARCH SERVICE FEASIBILITY STUDY[1]

The applications of this chapter's data-gathering concepts are demonstrated in the activities of most successful organizations. Collecting data relevant to the problem being studied is often the most difficult, expensive, and time-consuming part of the entire research procedure. Let's look at J & H Research Service's approach to collecting reliable data for a feasibility study.

Metropolitan Mortgage donated land to a local university's College of Business. The land is located close to an interstate highway near the MeadowWood Industrial Park. The university decided to develop this property so as to encourage the community's

[1]"Physical Fitness Facility Market Analysis." *Decision Science Institute Proceedings*, San Francisco, 1992.

economic growth. The university contracted with J & H Research to determine whether a fitness facility was feasible. J & H agreed to accomplish the following objectives:

1. Determine whether MeadowWood Industrial Park employees are interested in a fitness facility. Determine potential use, reasonable costs, and what employees would pay to use a fitness facility.
2. Determine if the industrial park's employer's personnel office/management groups would be interested in a fitness facility.
3. Determine whether current residents of the surrounding area are interested in such facilities.
4. Define the primary market area and determine whether it would support a fitness facility.
5. Determine whether it's feasible to operate a fitness center at a profit.

J & H Research used the following data-gathering techniques to determine the fitness facility's feasibility:

Objective 1: Each of the seven firms in the industrial park administered a questionnaire to its employees (primary data). A 23% response rate was achieved.

Objective 2: Personal interviews were conducted with appropriate management personnel of each firm (primary data).

Objective 3: A door-to-door survey was conducted for residents of the surrounding area (primary data). A 63.4% response rate was achieved.

Objective 4: Census data were acquired for communities within a 10-mile radius of the proposed site (secondary data). A list of all fitness clubs in the area was compiled using both primary (telephone interviews) and secondary (*Journal of Business* articles) data sources. The list included size, staffing, type of programs offered, and physical facilities. A County Engineer's report was used to describe the site and determine access (secondary data). Articles in local business publications provided data on local business and residential development (secondary data). Observation and personal interviews were used to determine traffic flow (primary data).

Objective 5: An appraisal report was used to determine land and building costs for the area (secondary data). Telephone interviews were conducted to determine building and equipment costs (primary data).

Other Applications

Much information has already been collected and is available in libraries and computer data bases. Businesses of all types frequently use these sources rather than spend time and money to collect new data. *The Wall Street Journal,* read by many businesspeople daily, is a continuing source of secondary data.

Collecting primary data through sampling is common in the business world. Whenever information on a large population is desired, some kind of sampling is usually employed. Here are a few situations that call for sampling:

The accounting department wants to know the status of its accounts receivable.

A manufacturer of aluminum panels is interested in the quality level of its manufacturing process.

A car manufacturer needs to know a new model's average miles per gallon for advertising purposes.

The number of overtime hours per week in a large plant needs to be monitored on a monthly basis.

Company management needs to determine its large work force's opinion of a proposed union.

A large health care service must consider its clients' attitudes so that service may be improved.

Credit union customers need to be surveyed about their satisfaction with current service and interest in new services.

Supplier performance regarding the number of defective units shipped to a plant must be evaluated by a company's quality-control department.

A bank with over 10,000 customers wants to develop a profile of a highly profitable customer.

A restaurant is facing declining revenues each month and wants to know what customers think of their dining experience.

A university is interested in determining its graduates' attitudes toward a proposed fund-raising campaign.

GLOSSARY

Variable An item of interest that can take on many different numerical values.

Constant An item with a fixed numerical value.

Quantitative variable A variable whose values are expressible as numerical quantities, such as measurements or counts.

Qualitative variable A variable that isn't quantitative and can only be classified, but not measured.

Mutually exclusive Categories, only one of which can include a given individual, object, or measurement.

Nominal scale A scale consisting of mutually exclusive categories in which no logical order is implied.

Ordinal scale A scale consisting of distinct categories in which order is implied.

Interval scale A scale consisting of numerical values in which the distance between successive numbers is of measurable constant size.

Ratio scale A scale consisting of numerical measurements where the distances between numbers are of a known, constant size, and where the ratio of numbers has some meaning; in addition, there is a fixed, nonarbitrary zero point.

Primary data Data collected specifically for the analysis desired.

Secondary data Data already collected and available for statistical analysis.

Population The entire set of individuals or items of interest.

Census An attempt to measure every item in the population of interest.

Sample A subset selected from the population.

Simple random sample A sample that results when n elements are selected from a population in such a way that every possible combination of n elements in the population has an equal probability of being selected.

Sampling without replacement Sampling in which an item selected isn't returned to the population for possible reselection.

Sampling with replacement Sampling in which each selected item is returned to the population before the next selection takes place.

Random number table A table used to provide lists of numbers that are randomly generated and can be used to select random samples.

Systematic sample A sample in which every nth item in the population sequence is selected.

Stratified random sample A sample in which the population is broken into meaningful strata or subgroups, and each group is randomly sampled.

Cluster sample A sample in which groups or clusters of items are randomly selected for inclusion.

Solved Exercises

1. Levels of Measurement

Refer to the student questionnaire presented in Table 1.1. For each of the first six questions, identify the level of measurement.

Solution:

(1) ordinal, (2) nominal, (3) ratio, (4) ratio, (5) ordinal, (6) ordinal.

2. Secondary and Primary Data

Garfield Bay Marina, located on Lake Pend Oreille, was acquired by Westland Mortgage Service Company through repossession. The marina hasn't been producing revenue because it lacks a floating breakwater to protect it against high waves. To build the floating breakwater, Westland Mortgage must obtain permission from the Idaho Land Use Commission. Westland must convince the commission that the marina is needed. To do this, Westland must analyze competitive marinas on the lake, demonstrate that Garfield Bay can support the marina, and determine demand in the competitive market area for covered and uncovered boat slips.

a. What secondary data sources might be used to complete this study?

b. What primary data sources might be used to complete this study?

Solution:

a. Census data should be gathered to establish the market area's demographics. Boater registration data should be gathered from state government sources to help determine boat slip demand.

b. Marina operators and dealers should be interviewed. A physical survey of the number of occupied and vacant boat slips on Lake Pend Oreille should be completed.

3. Samples

(This question refers to Solved Exercise 2.) What kind of sampling plan should be used to determine the number of occupied and vacant boat slips on Lake Pend Oreille?

Solution:

A census of all the marinas located on Lake Pend Oreille should be completed.

Exercises

31. Specify whether each of the following variables is qualitative or quantitative. For each variable, identify its type of measurement scale.

    a. Gasoline mileage.

    b. Gasoline brand.

    c. A person's temperature.

31*a.* Quantity—Ratio
b. Quality—Nominal
c. Quantity—Interval

d. Quantity—Ratio
e. Quantity—Ratio
f. Quality—Nominal
g. Quality—Ordinal

d. A test score.

e. A worker's job performance rating.

f. A worker's job classification.

g. A football team's ranking.

32. Discuss the adequacy of each of the following sampling approaches:

    a. A radio disk jockey wishes to determine the most popular song in her city. She asks listeners to call and indicate their preference.

    b. A citizens' group interested in generating public and financial support for a waste-to-energy garbage-burning plant prints a questionnaire in a local newspaper. Readers are asked to return the questionnaires by mail.

    c. A drugstore wishes to examine whether it's losing or gaining customers. The manager chooses a sample from the store's list of credit card holders by selecting every 25th name.

    d. A research company obtains a sample for a focus group by randomly calling households and including every third respondent who's willing to participate.

    e. A research company obtains a sample for a focus group by selecting respondents through organized groups (church groups, clubs, and charitable organizations). The organizations are paid for securing a respondent, but no individual is directly compensated.

33. Uptown Radiology is developing a medical imaging center more complete and technologically advanced than any other currently located in the New England area. Uptown Radiology asked PMA Research to evaluate the market and project revenues for five years. The study's objectives are to:

    Identify market areas for each type of procedure the new facility will offer.

    Gather and analyze existing data on market area revenue for each such procedure.

    Identify health care industry trends that will positively or negatively affect revenue from these procedures.

    a. What secondary data sources might be used to complete this study?
    b. What primary data sources might be used to complete this study?

34. The Bay Area Rapid Transit (BART) wants to gather information from transit users and nonusers that it can use in developing marketing programs for maintaining present riders and attracting new riders. BART isn't sure what questions to ask, so it decides to do some preliminary research. Would focus groups be useful for this purpose? What method should be used to recruit participants?

35. Large = 240
Medium = 420
Small = 240
Compact = 300

35. A rental car company wants to estimate its fleet's average odometer mileage. Over 12,000 cars are in the fleet, so a sampling plan is needed. After analyzing the potential errors involved in sampling, the company decides on a sample size of 1,200 cars. A stratification on car size is also decided on, based on the following proportions of cars in the fleet.

Large cars	20%
Medium-sized cars	35
Small cars	20
Compact cars	25

    a. How many cars should be sampled from each size category?

b. Are there any other stratifications that should be made before the sample is taken?

c. How should the sample be taken from each stratum?

36. The Northtown Shopping Mall Association wants to develop a data base on kinds of people who shop at the mall. The association decides to conduct a study of people who shop there. What type of data-gathering approach should it use? What method should it use to recruit participants?

37. (This question refers to Exercise 36.) The interviewer asked each survey participant about the average amount spent per mall visit. The array of these amounts for the 100 people interviewed is

1. 10	21. 13	41. 15	61. 22	81. 62
2. 83	22. 10	42. 5	62. 7	82. 22
3. 71	23. 62	43. 59	63. 55	83. 9
4. 14	24. 10	44. 12	64. 92	84. 15
5. 82	25. 41	45. 52	65. 63	85. 95
6. 11	26. 22	46. 21	66. 55	86. 44
7. 47	27. 58	47. 13	67. 39	87. 15
8. 0	28. 45	48. 25	68. 89	88. 14
9. 25	29. 36	49. 54	69. 87	89. 25
10. 20	30. 65	50. 65	70. 25	90. 45
11. 95	31. 87	51. 74	71. 82	91. 35
12. 62	32. 41	52. 26	72. 29	92. 49
13. 36	33. 0	53. 32	73. 10	93. 4
14. 24	34. 48	54. 69	74. 75	94. 84
15. 42	35. 30	55. 80	75. 17	95. 15
16. 56	36. 50	56. 90	76. 96	96. 45
17. 55	37. 60	57. 84	77. 5	97. 66
18. 85	38. 70	58. 8	78. 36	98. 33
19. 99	39. 54	59. 24	79. 44	99. 18
20. 15	40. 82	60. 27	80. 22	100. 77

Use a table of random numbers to select a simple random sample of 30 dollar amounts, then compute the average of these values. Sampling should be done with replacement.

38. Identify whether each variable in the company data base found in Appendix C is qualitative or quantitative. For each variable, identify its type of measurement scale.

Extended Exercises

39. Deer Park Credit Union

The Deer Park Credit Union wants to improve its services to maintain its market share and possibly add members. It decides on a market research project consisting of two parts. First, names are randomly selected from its mailing list, and these people are invited to participate in a focus group. They're offered $25 to attend a one-hour session which is tape-recorded for review by management. A number of corrective-action ideas emerge from these meetings.

Next, a mail questionnaire is developed and mailed to a random sample of 350 persons selected from the credit union's membership list. This four-page questionnaire covers present usage of services, asks for a list of additional services desired, and contains a number of rating questions for evaluating the credit union's performance. About 75% of these questionnaires are returned within two weeks, and they're entered on the credit union's computer for analysis.

A final report is prepared that summarizes the focus group discussions and the tabulation of the questionnaires. A staff meeting is called to evaluate these results and to decide on actions to improve services, add new ones, and increase membership.

a. What is the advantage of holding the focus group meetings before the questionnaire is finalized?

b. Do you think the 75% return rate for the questionnaire is adequate? What might have been done to increase the return rate?

c. Do you think the credit union will learn what it wants to after reviewing this two-stage research?

40. THE SPOKANE INDIAN TRIBE FEASIBILITY STUDY[2]

The Spokane Indian Reservation in Eastern Washington is approximately 50 miles northwest of Spokane. The reservation's western and southern boundaries are comprised of 36 miles of Lake Roosevelt shoreline.

For the past two years, the tribe has investigated the potential for developing a recreational site at the confluence of the Spokane and Columbia Rivers on Lake Roosevelt. Plans include the possibility of building an RV park, motel (lodging and meeting rooms), marina (dock and rental slips), houseboat rental operation, grocery/fishing tackle store, picnic area, beach and swimming area, cultural center with gift shop, casino, and golf course. The Spokane Tribe has invited bids for a market analysis and feasibility study of these businesses. Before preparing your bid, do the following:

a. List primary sources of data that you would use to develop the market analysis. Explain how you would use each source.

b. List secondary sources of data that you would use. Explain how each would be used.

41. METROPOLITAN HOLDING COMPANY

The Metropolitan Holding Company has four subsidiaries, all in different cities. Top management, led by company president Wendy Watts, wants to determine company employees' attitudes toward the parent company and their subsidiary company. She decided to undertake this research after reading "The Champion of the Modern Corner Store," an article in *Working Woman* (September 1989). This article described the winning managerial formula of the woman who's president of her company, and Wendy wants to assess employees' attitudes in her own company as a first step in modifying her management style.

Wendy specifically wants to learn about employee loyalty to the holding company and to the employees' subsidiary company. If there's strong loyalty toward the subsidiary company and little loyalty toward the parent company, top management would hesitate to implement further plans for centralizing control of the firm.

Top management has developed a number of ideas to assess loyalty among the many employees. It is recognized that there are many different types of employees, including male and female, union and nonunion, short-term and long-term, and those from different subsidiary companies.

[2]"The Spokane Indian Tribe Feasibility Study." *Decision Science Institute Proceedings*, New Orleans, 1991.

A mail questionnaire has been suggested to measure employee attitudes, and a tentative set of questions has been developed.

a. Would you favor using a mail questionnaire in this case?

b. Would it be useful to stratify the population prior to the research? If so, how?

c. If you were to design this research, what methods would you employ?

MICROCOMPUTER PACKAGE

You can use the micro package *Computerized Business Statistics* to generate random numbers. In Exercise 37 you used a table of random numbers to select a simple random sample of 30 average dollar amounts from a population of 100 items.

Computer Solution

On the main menu of *Computerized Business Statistics*, a 7 is selected, which indicates Sampling and Estimation.

```
      Sampling and Estimation
      PROGRAM OPTIONS MENU
0. CBS Configuration
1. Generate Random Numbers
2. Central Limit Theorem Demonstration
3. Compute Sample Size
4. Interval Estimation
5. Quick Reviews
6. Exit to Main Menu
7. Exit to Operating System
Press ↵ to select option under hi-lite bar. Press number or up/down arrow keys to
move hi-lite bar.
```

This program generates random numbers, demonstrates the central limit theorem, determines sample sizes, and computes interval estimates.

Since the problem involves the generation of random numbers, 1 is selected.

```
Enter number of random numbers (10–1250) and press ↵ 30
```

The screen will now show a partial table of random numbers.

```
Send copy to the printer? Y/N press ↵ Y

Store random numbers in a data file? (Y/N, press ↵): Y
```

These features allow you to print out a copy of the random numbers and store them for future use.

MINITAB COMPUTER PACKAGE

The MINITAB commands to generate random numbers to solve Exercise 37 are:

```
MTB>  RANDOM 30 VALUES INTO C1;
SUBC> INTEGER 1 TO 100.
MTB>  PRINT C1

C1
40   20   90    8   67   47   65   12   85   26   28   80
27   56   61    1   12   81    1   43    7   58   14   84
61   78   33    8   22   85

MTB> STOP
```

The **RANDOM** command selects 30 values and stores them in column 1 of the worksheet (C1). The semicolon at the end of line 1 requests a subcommand prompt.

The **INTEGER** subcommand indicates that the 30 random numbers are to be integers from 1 to 100. A period must be placed at the end of the last subcommand line.

The **PRINT** command is used to print the 30 random numbers.

Chapter

3

Data Presentation

"The question is," said Alice, "whether you can make words mean so many different things."

"The question is," said Humpty Dumpty, "which is to be master— that's all."

Lewis Carroll, *Through the Looking-Glass*

Objectives

When you have completed this chapter, you will be able to:

Organize a data collection into a frequency distribution.

Determine the most effective method for presenting a data collection.

Construct various charts and graphs, such as pie charts, bar charts, histograms, frequency polygons, and ogives.

On Friday, April 17, 1992, *The Wall Street Journal* reported that the U.S. trade deficit had narrowed in February 1992 to a seasonally adjusted $3.38 billion from a revised $5.95 billion in January. These figures were obtained from the U.S. Department of Commerce.

Chapter 2 covered various ways of collecting data for decision making. It stressed the importance of carefully identifying needed data and ensuring that these data values are properly selected from the population under study.

WHY DATA PRESENTATION METHODS ARE IMPORTANT TO MANAGERS

Once data have been collected, they must be processed in some way so that any important patterns become apparent. The rest of this book discusses ways to convert raw data into the kinds of information decision makers need. Some of the most basic and most widely used techniques for summarizing important data collections appear in this chapter. These techniques are important for both qualitative data (nominal and ordinal) and quantitative data (interval and ratio). Additional methods for summarizing quantitative data collections are discussed in Chapter 4.

The U.S. trade deficit is an economic indicator business and government leaders watch closely. Charts and graphs are effective ways to track this important value over time. *The Wall Street Journal* uses graphs to show readers the history of important economic variables (Figure 3.1) and most issues have graphs on the front page to accompany lead stories. This chapter will show methods to construct effective charts and graphs.

FIGURE 3.1 U.S. Trade Deficit, 1989–92 (in billions of dollars)

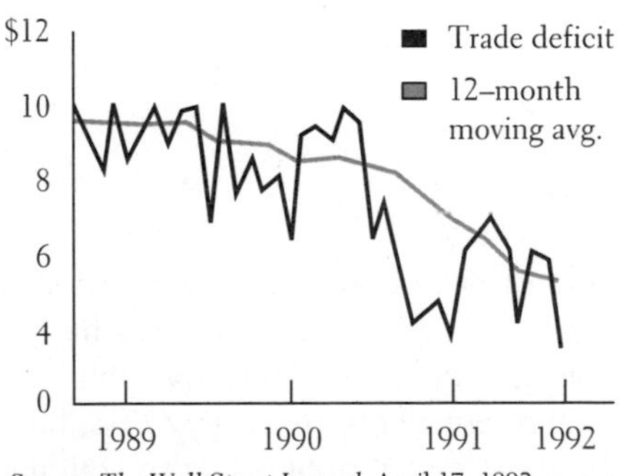

Source: *The Wall Street Journal*, April 17, 1992.

FREQUENCY DISTRIBUTIONS

The concept of a **distribution** is important in statistics. This is the term statisticians use to represent a collection, array, or group of numerical values.

> A **distribution** is a collection, array, or group of numerical values.

Frequency Distribution

A common, very helpful way to summarize data collections is through the **frequency distribution.** This data display method shows the frequency (number of occurrences) in each of several categories. Frequency distributions can summarize large volumes of data values so decision makers can extract useful information directly from the collection.

> A **frequency distribution** is a list of data classes or categories along with the number of values that fall into each.

EXAMPLE 3.1 The Brite Paint Company asked several people to indicate their favorite color. Tabulation of the results (Table 3.1) shows that 12 people indicated red as their favorite color, 8 chose green, 8 selected blue, and 4 picked yellow (nominal data). This tabulation represents a frequency distribution because various categories (colors) are listed along with the number of times (frequency) each was chosen. Unless some predetermined order exists, categories are listed in order of magnitude, the category with the largest frequency is listed first, and so forth.

TABLE 3.1 Favorite Colors (Example 3.1)

Color	Frequency
Red	12
Green	8
Blue	8
Yellow	4
	32

EXAMPLE 3.2 A sample of 86 shoppers was asked to what extent they agree with the statement, "Trudy's Apparel sells high-quality clothing." The frequency distribution in Table 3.2 summarizes the results (ordinal data). The table indicates fairly strong support for the statement. This frequency distribution concisely and clearly shows the reactions of the sample of shoppers to this statement.

Note that Tables 3.1 and 3.2 both summarize qualitative data.

When the raw data are measured on a quantitative scale, either interval or ratio, categories or classes must be designed for the data values before a frequency distribu-

TABLE 3.2 Reaction to the Statement, "Trudy's Apparel Sells High-Quality Clothing" (Example 3.2)

Reaction	Frequency
Strongly agree	12
Agree	35
Neutral or no opinion	27
Disagree	10
Strongly disagree	2
	86

tion can be formulated. No firm rule exists for determining the appropriate number of classes for a particular frequency distribution, but this number is usually between 5 and 15. If there are too few classes, the results may be too general to permit detection of underlying tendencies in the data. On the other hand, too many classes defeat the purpose of the frequency distribution, which is to summarize a large data collection so it can be easily understood and used in decision making.

The technical process of generating a frequency distribution is quite tedious and time-consuming. Therefore, a less rigorous approach will be suggested in the next section. Note that this approach uses several rules of thumb.

The first step in constructing a frequency distribution for quantitative data is to decide on the number of classes (usually 5 to 15). If there are a large number of items or observations (more than 1,000) in the data set, a relatively large number of classes (11 or more) is generally used. If the data set is small (say, fewer than 60 observations), a small number of classes (5 or 6) is used. Table 3.3 provides guidelines for selecting the number of classes.

The second step is to determine the size of each class. Frequency distributions are usually constructed using equal class widths. The exception occurs when it's necessary to leave the last class open-ended. Class width can be determined by finding the difference between the largest value in the data set and the smallest value and dividing

TABLE 3.3 Guidelines for Number of Classes in a Frequency Distribution

Number of observations	Number of classes
Fewer than 30	5
30 to fewer than 60	6
60 to fewer than 130	7
130 to fewer than 250	8
250 to fewer than 500	9
500 to fewer than 1,000	10
1,000 to fewer than 2,000	11
2,000 to fewer than 4,000	12
4,000 to fewer than 8,000	13
8,000 and over	14

it by the number of classes desired. Since people tend to be 5- and 10-oriented, class widths of these sizes are desirable and are used whenever possible.

The third step is to tally the number of values in each class. This involves listing the classes and then going through the data set, placing a tally mark by the appropriate class. Classes are organized so that their limits don't overlap (i.e., the classes are mutually exclusive).

The last step is to prepare a table of the distribution. It is common to show frequencies both as actual counts and as percentages, or relative frequencies. (The concept of relative frequencies will be explained in the next section.)

Constructing a Frequency Distribution

Steps for constructing a frequency distribution

1. Determine the number of classes, usually 5 to 15 (see Table 3.3).
2. Determine the size of each class. Class size is determined by finding the difference between the largest value in the data set and the smallest value and dividing it by the number of classes desired.
3. Determine the starting point for the first class.
4. Tally the number of values that occur in each class.
5. Prepare a table of the distribution using actual counts and/or percentages (relative frequencies).

(*Note:* These steps should only be considered as rules of thumb and not as a rigorous process for constructing a frequency distribution.)

EXAMPLE 3.3 The frequency distribution in Table 3.4 summarizes Sunrunner Corporation executives' incomes. Table 3.3 shows that with 97 observations, the frequency distribution should contain seven income classes. Notice that the choice of a convenient income class width, $10,000, makes the data summary easy to follow.

Table 3.4 illustrates the concept of mutually exclusive categories or classes. The class limits, such as "20,000 to less than 30,000," make it impossible for a person to

TABLE 3.4 Executive Incomes for the Sunrunner Corporation (Example 3.3)

Annual income ($)	Frequency
20,000 to less than 30,000	5
30,000 to less than 40,000	17
40,000 to less than 50,000	22
50,000 to less than 60,000	28
60,000 to less than 70,000	14
70,000 to less than 80,000	8
80,000 to less than 90,000	3
	97

belong to more than one income category since each begins where the previous one left off. This table is an example of a frequency distribution that neatly summarizes many raw data values.

EXAMPLE 3.4 Management of Atlas Contractors closely follows the number of trucks produced in the United States because demand for transmissions is closely related to this variable. The *New York Times* for September 10, 1989, indicated 66,427 trucks were produced for the most recent week.

While Atlas is excited about the recent truck volume, it is having trouble with its quality control. The company has had difficulty meeting demand this year because of the number of errors per shift (Table 3.5).

TABLE 3.5 Errors per Shift (Example 3.4)

Number of errors	Frequency (number of days)
0–4	11
5–9	22
10–14	13
15–19	8
20–24	3
25–29	2
	59

This table has six classes. It is easy to read, and it summarizes error occurrences in the manufacturing process. Note that the classes have an equal width, five units. Classes of unequal width (for example, 0–4, 5–10, 11–18, 19–25, and 26 or more) would make the underlying data more difficult to interpret. Also note that the variable, number of errors per shift, is measured in whole numbers. Thus, the classes (0–4, 5–9, etc.) are mutually exclusive.

When there are many observations or objects to classify in a frequency distribution, it may be more helpful to study the *percentage* of items falling into each class rather than the actual frequencies. It might be more meaningful, for example, to observe that 12% of a college's students are business majors than to know that there are 942 business majors.

Relative Frequencies

Relative frequencies, or percentages, are calculated for a frequency distribution by dividing the actual frequency for each class by the total number of objects classified. Table 3.6 does this for the Sunrunner Corporation executive incomes in Table 3.4. Note that in Table 3.6, each frequency is divided by 97, the total number of executives, to form the percentages in the last column. This column of percentages should total 1.000. (If calculation is done by hand, this sum may not precisely equal 1 due to rounding errors.)

TM

TABLE 3.6 Relative Frequencies for Executive Incomes (Example 3.3)

Annual income ($)	Frequency	Relative frequency
20,000 to less than 30,000	5	5/97 = .052
30,000 to less than 40,000	17	17/97 = .175
40,000 to less than 50,000	22	22/97 = .227
50,000 to less than 60,000	28	28/97 = .289
60,000 to less than 70,000	14	14/97 = .144
70,000 to less than 80,000	8	8/97 = .082
80,000 to less than 90,000	3	3/97 = .031
	97	1.000

Relative frequencies such as those in Table 3.6 can be very useful in summarizing large data collections.

> **Relative frequencies** are percentages calculated by dividing the actual frequency for each class by the total number of observations being classified.

EXAMPLE 3.5 Kyle Chang owns The Wash Tub, a dry cleaners. He wants to know the number of customer orders processed per day. A random sample of days is selected for study using sampling methods discussed in Chapter 2. Table 3.7 shows the resulting data. Kyle wants to use these data to understand the pattern of his customer load, but it's difficult to deal with so much raw data. Kyle knows a frequency distribution can summarize these values. He hopes the patterns that underlie the data will become more apparent and aid him in planning for future customer service.

TM

TABLE 3.7 Customers per Day for The Wash Tub (Example 3.5)

65	23	26	45	12	45	56	35	26	45	25
56	45	32	12	56	53	23	24	45	36	35
15	45	19	05	56	53	26	53	56	54	52
25	26	34	35	36	31	23	26	25	46	45
56	52	51	53	26	64	23	24	21	29	28
65	39	38	26	37	24	28	25	35	67	38
16	18	46	23	35	38	32	57	48	49	53
34	31	37	28	29	37	34	31	26	25	43

DD

Table 3.7 gives the raw data. Kyle follows the steps presented earlier in the chapter:

1. Table 3.3 shows that with 88 observations, Kyle should use about seven classes.
2. Class width is determined by finding the difference between the largest value in the data set (67) and the smallest value (5) and dividing it by the number of

classes desired [(67 − 5)/7 = 8.9]. A class width of 9 will provide approximately seven classes. However, people tend to think in terms of 5s and 10s, so Kyle decides that a class width of 10 will provide a frequency distribution that's easier to understand.

3. Next, Kyle organizes the classes so they don't overlap. He can now tally the number of values in each class (Table 3.8). Since the smallest value in the data is 5, he decides that a reasonable starting class is 0 to 9.

TABLE 3.8 Tally Sheet for Wash Tub Customers (Example 3.5)

Number of customers	Tallies	Count	Relative frequency
0–9	|	1	.011
10–19	𝍸 |	6	.068
20–29	𝍸 𝍸 𝍸 𝍸 𝍸 ||	27	.307
30–39	𝍸 𝍸 𝍸 𝍸 ||	22	.250
40–49	𝍸 𝍸 ||	12	.136
50–59	𝍸 𝍸 𝍸 |	16	.182
60–69	||||	4	.046
		88	1.000

4. Finally, Kyle constructs the distribution using actual counts and percentages (relative frequencies) (Table 3.8).

The basic frequency distribution of Table 3.8 helps Kyle evaluate his business's customer load. For instance, on 30.7% of the days studied, The Wash Tub had between 20 and 29 customers.

EXERCISES

1. Why are data collections organized into frequency distributions?
2. What is the difference between a frequency distribution and a relative frequency distribution?
3. Describe the steps necessary to convert a frequency distribution into a relative frequency distribution.

4. 7

4. If a data collection has 80 values, approximately how many classes should be included in its frequency distribution?

5. 10

5. If a data collection has 880 values, approximately how many classes should be included in its frequency distribution?

6. 20

6. A data collection contains 400 observations. The lowest value is 23, and the highest value is 60. What would be a good lower limit for the first class in a frequency distribution?
7. Jacob Palmer, the production manager of a food-processing plant, has recorded the number of batches rejected daily for the past 50 days. The lowest was 2 and the highest 36. Jacob wants to construct a frequency distribution for this series. How should he determine the following?

a. Approximate number of classes.

b. Class width.

c. Limits for the first class.

8. .2654
.1694
.1650
.1368
.1154
.0565
.0226
.0690

8. Football is still the most televised sport, but the summer Olympic Games are a quadrennial contender. Convert this frequency distribution into a relative frequency distribution.

Sport category	Hours aired, 1988
Football	423
Olympics	270
Basketball	263
Golf	218
Baseball	184
Tennis	90
Bowling	36
Other	110
Total	1,594

Source: Nielsen Media Research.

9. SAE Airlines has applied to the Civil Aeronautics Board (CAB) for a new route between Minneapolis and Billings. Carol Hart, company analyst, is estimating when the CAB is most likely to rule on the company's application. She assembles the waiting times for applications filed during the past year, acquiring observations for 120 filings. The data are stated in days from the date of application until a CAB ruling.

9. Class	f
40–49	18
50–59	18
60–69	22
70–79	22
80–89	20
90–99	20

52	63	72	95	99	77	65	43	58	67
64	54	78	98	82	84	75	77	69	49
58	57	69	71	80	90	85	96	87	44
42	73	82	65	79	67	85	73	88	77
84	44	98	58	82	64	95	67	99	69
98	47	79	41	90	50	45	56	47	54
54	67	78	95	94	75	69	41	52	65
65	54	79	98	86	85	78	71	63	44
56	58	67	71	81	95	85	92	84	42
48	70	84	65	70	66	87	74	86	75
89	42	90	58	87	67	96	63	90	68
97	49	77	40	98	54	46	59	48	59

a. Construct a frequency distribution for this data collection.

b. Construct a relative frequency distribution for this data collection.

10. Westland Investments is interested in purchasing Moreland Realty. As a part of the prepurchase negotiations, Jim Moreland, president of Moreland Realty, collects selling prices for 80 homes in the surrounding market area (prices are recorded in thousands of dollars):

35	110	37	58	72	102	39	125	31	48
64	54	108	98	82	84	75	77	69	49
42	73	32	65	109	67	85	73	88	77
98	47	79	41	90	30	45	56	47	114

54	67	78	95	94	75	69	41	122	65
89	42	90	58	87	27	96	63	90	68
36	58	27	71	81	95	85	92	84	42
48	70	104	65	70	66	87	34	86	75

a. Construct a frequency distribution for this data collection.

b. Construct a relative frequency distribution for this data collection.

CUMULATIVE FREQUENCY DISTRIBUTIONS

Cumulative Frequencies

The frequency distributions of Tables 3.1, 3.2, 3.4, 3.5, 3.6, and 3.8 show the number of items, or frequency, in each of several classes or categories. Sometimes it's useful to show the total number of occurrences above or below certain key values. The **cumulative frequency distribution** provides this kind of data summary.

> The **cumulative frequency distribution** shows the total number of occurrences that lie above or below certain key values.

Examples 3.6 and 3.7 show how to construct a cumulative frequency distribution.

EXAMPLE 3.6 The data of Table 3.4 are to be used to form a cumulative frequency distribution for Sunrunner Corporation executive incomes. As shown in Table 3.9, the cumulative frequency for each class is the sum of the frequencies for that class and all lower classes. For example, the cumulative frequency for the "$50,000 to less than $60,000" class is 72, which is the frequency of that class (28) plus the frequencies of all lower classes (5 + 17 + 22 + 28).

This type of cumulative frequency distribution is sometimes referred to as a *less-than* distribution because it enables one to readily see how many data values are less than some value. For instance, 72 of Sunrunner Corporation's executives earn less than

TM

TABLE 3.9 Less-than Cumulative Frequency Distribution of Executive Incomes (Example 3.6)

Annual income ($)	Frequency	Cumulative frequency	Relative frequency	Cumulative relative frequency
20,000 to less than 30,000	5	5	.052	.052
30,000 to less than 40,000	17	22	.175	.227
40,000 to less than 50,000	22	44	.227	.454
50,000 to less than 60,000	28	72	.289	.743
60,000 to less than 70,000	14	86	.144	.887
70,000 to less than 80,000	8	94	.082	.969
80,000 to less than 90,000	3	97	.031	1.000
	97		1.000	

$60,000. Note that the last value in the cumulative column (97) is equal to the total number of observations (the summation of the frequency column).

Similarly, the cumulative relative frequency (.743) for the $50,000–$60,000 class is computed by taking the relative frequency for the "$50,000 to less than $60,000" class (.289) and adding it to the relative frequencies of all the lower classes (.052 + .175 + .227 + .289 = .743). This means that 74.3% of Sunrunner's executives earn less than $60,000. Note that the last value in the cumulative relative frequency column is equal to 1.000, or 100%. This column will always sum to 1.000.

Sometimes a *more-than* cumulative frequency distribution is useful. Such a cumulative distribution shows the number and/or percentage of items in the data collection that are greater than certain key values as is shown in Example 3.7.

EXAMPLE 3.7 In Example 3.5, Kyle wanted to determine how frequently the customer load becomes unmanageable. A more-than cumulative frequency distribution will help identify the magnitude of this problem.

Table 3.10 is formed from the frequency distribution in Table 3.8. Kyle has determined that when 30 or more customers arrive in a single day, customers aren't helped in a timely manner and he loses business. Table 3.10 shows that there were 54 days when 30 or more customers arrived. In fact, the table shows that on 61.4% of the days 30 or more customers showed up. Kyle also knows that when 40 or more customers arrive in a single day, he must turn some of them away. Table 3.10 shows that this occurred on 32 days, or 36.4% of the time. These facts indicate to Kyle that he needs additional staff.

TABLE 3.10 The Wash Tub Customers per Day: More-than Cumulative Frequency Distribution (Example 3.7)

Customers per day	Frequency	More-than frequency	Relative frequency	More-than relative frequency
0–9	1	88	.011	1.000
10–19	6	87	.068	.989
20–29	27	81	.307	.921
30–39	22	54	.250	.614
40–49	12	32	.136	.364
50–59	16	20	.182	.228
60–69	4	4	.046	.046
	88		1.000	

EXERCISES

11. Why are data collections organized into cumulative frequency distributions?
12. What is the difference between a less-than cumulative frequency distribution and a more-than cumulative frequency distribution?
13. In a less-than cumulative frequency distribution, what percentage of the total frequencies fall below the upper limit of the highest class?

13. 100%

14. Alliance Pacific, Inc., conducted a voter opinion survey to provide input regarding a proposed waste-to-energy facility for the area. The following frequency distribution shows survey participants' family income levels.

Income level	Frequency
Under $15,000	296
$15,000 to less than $30,000	631
$30,000 to less than $50,000	404
$50,000 and over	130
Total	1,461

Source: "Waste-to-Energy Facility Voter Opinion Survey." Spokane: Alliance Pacific, Inc., August 1985.

14a. Eleven classes
b. .2026
.4319
.2765
.0890
c. .2026
.6345
.9110
1.000

a. How many classes should have been used to construct this frequency distribution?

b. Construct a relative frequency distribution for this data collection.

c. Construct a cumulative relative frequency distribution indicating the percentage of respondents with a family income less than $30,000.

15. An independent research firm surveyed households with residents age 55 or older. The following frequency distribution shows how respondents answered the question, "How many driving minutes from a hospital is the farthest that you would consider living during your retirement?"

Driving minutes	Frequency
5 minutes or less	47
6 to 10 minutes	150
11 to 15 minutes	128
16 to 20 minutes	67
21 minutes or more	94
Total	486

Source: "Surveys of Older Homeowners Concerning Retirement Attitudes." Spokane: Decision Science Associates, June 1986.

15a. Nine classes
b. .0967
.3086
.2643
.1379
.1934
c. .0967
.4053
.6687
.8066
1.0000

a. How could you improve this frequency distribution?

b. Construct a relative frequency distribution for this data collection.

c. Construct a cumulative relative frequency distribution.

16. Answerphone Service, Inc., wants to do a better job of billing customers for services rendered. Owner Sloan Spalding decides that he needs to know how long it takes to complete various incoming calls. The following data collection includes 150 random calls that were monitored and timed (calls are rounded to the nearest minute):

1	2	4	8	12	9	10	30	45	6
5	11	8	9	8	7	9	5	1	2
6	7	4	2	1	3	15	7	4	3
8	4	3	5	1	1	5	2	4	8
17	5	8	22	13	5	5	8	7	6
40	2	7	31	27	21	4	9	10	11

11	5	7	18	16	19	3	3	15	16
15	14	18	9	5	6	9	4	7	3
4	7	4	12	4	3	18	5	6	5
5	6	13	6	7	2	7	2	4	8
27	6	9	20	16	2	6	8	3	7
10	2	9	30	37	22	5	19	14	11
7	15	4	5	3	6	7	3	7	9
10	2	5	35	7	31	14	9	30	19
1	15	7	16	6	9	3	13	5	6

16*a*. Class	*f*
1–5	55
6–10	51
11–15	18
16–20	12
21–25	3
26–30	5
31–35	3
36–40	2
41–45	1

a. Construct a frequency distribution for this data collection.

b. Construct a relative frequency distribution for this data collection.

c. Construct a cumulative relative frequency distribution showing the likelihood that an incoming call will last less than 10 minutes.

d. What is the likelihood that an incoming call will last less than 25 minutes?

SM

17. Class	*f*	
100–199	9	.1250
200–299	22	.3056
300–399	24	.3373
400–499	13	.1806
500–599	4	.0556

17. Terry Anderson, analyst for Apple One Advertising, needs to develop a meaningful presentation for the following list of one-year advertising expenditures of a sample of 72 firms in the industry (expenditures are reported in thousands of dollars).

223	258	312	452	365	400	279	264	311
325	188	200	192	425	512	289	367	214
300	250	350	375	425	475	512	487	175
248	269	357	290	248	325	444	412	520
154	160	260	340	430	510	490	230	380
303	350	250	175	325	375	212	387	125
348	289	387	190	248	323	344	312	420
254	165	210	440	330	210	430	260	390

a. Construct a cumulative relative frequency distribution showing the likelihood that a firm will have expenditures less than \$300,000.

b. Construct a cumulative relative frequency distribution showing the likelihood that a firm will have expenditures more than \$400,000.

CHARTS AND GRAPHS

V

Frequency distributions are a good way to present the essential aspects of a data collections in concise, understandable terms. But pictures can be even more effective in displaying large data collections. This section presents various methods of using pictures to summarize a data collection.

The simplest charts and graphs to construct are for nominal and ordinal data. Because the data constitute categories, the classes are readily apparent and easily described graphically.

Pie Chart

The **pie chart** is an effective way of displaying the percentage breakdown of data by category. This type of chart is particularly useful if the relative sizes of the data components are to be emphasized. Budgets and other economic information are frequently depicted using pie charts. A complete circle, 360°, represents the total number of observations. Sizes of the slices are proportional to each category's relative frequency. For example, if a category's relative frequency is .25, that category's slice is 25% of 360°, or 90° (one fourth of the circle).

Table 3.1 showed 32 people's favorite colors. If the total number of people is divided into the number of people who selected each color, relative frequencies result: 12/32 = .375, 8/32 = .25, 8/32 = .25, and 4/32 = .125. Note that the relative frequencies sum to 1.000, or 100% (.375 + .25 + .25 + .125 = 1.000). Since 37.5 percent of the customers selected red, the slice assigned to this category is 37.5% of 360° [(.375)(360) = 135°]. Other arcs' lengths are calculated similarly (Figure 3.2—percentages are rounded).

Pie charts can also effectively present ratio- or interval-scaled data after they have been organized into categories.

EXAMPLE 3.8 The Washington Water Power Company's *1991 Annual Report* reveals total operating revenues were $566.8 million in 1991: $411.8 million from electric revenues, $73.3 million from natural gas revenues, and $81.7 million from nonutility revenues. One way to show where the company dollar came from is a pie chart. Total revenue is divided into each part: 411.8/566.8 = .727, 73.3/566.8 = .129, and 81.7/566.8 = .144 (Figure 3.3).

EXAMPLE 3.9 "Retailers' cash registers are ringing merrily," said *Barrons* magazine, August 28, 1989. Suppose the Itrex Company wants to expand its facilities to take advantage of these rising sales.

Itrex is to make a presentation to a group of bankers in preparation for a loan request. Itrex management wants to concisely indicate how company funds were expended during the past fiscal year. A pie chart is chosen for the purpose (Figure 3.4).

Figure 3.4 illustrates the advantage of the pie chart; it's easy to achieve a quick and fairly accurate picture of the numbers being represented. If greater details are needed, use some other method of summarizing raw data, such as a frequency distribution.

Bar Chart

The **bar chart** is another common method for graphically presenting nominal- and ordinal-scaled data. One bar represents the frequency for each category. The height of

FIGURE 3.2 Pie Chart: Favorite Colors of 32 People

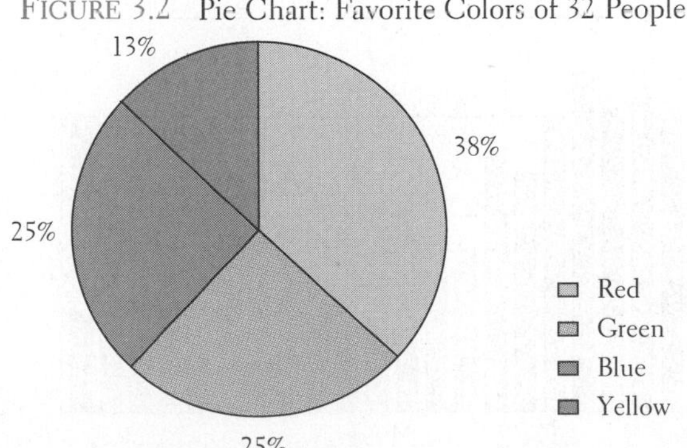

FIGURE 3.3 Pie Chart Showing Washington Water Power Operating Revenues

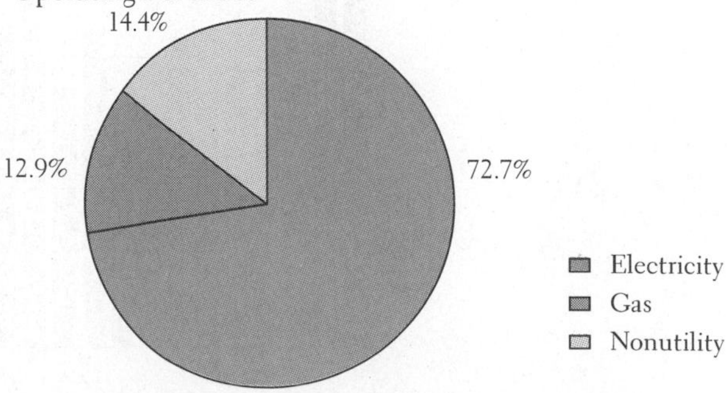

14.4%
12.9%
72.7%
Electricity
Gas
Nonutility

Source: Washington Water Power Co., 1991 Annual Report.

FIGURE 3.4 Pie Chart: Itrex Company Expenditures

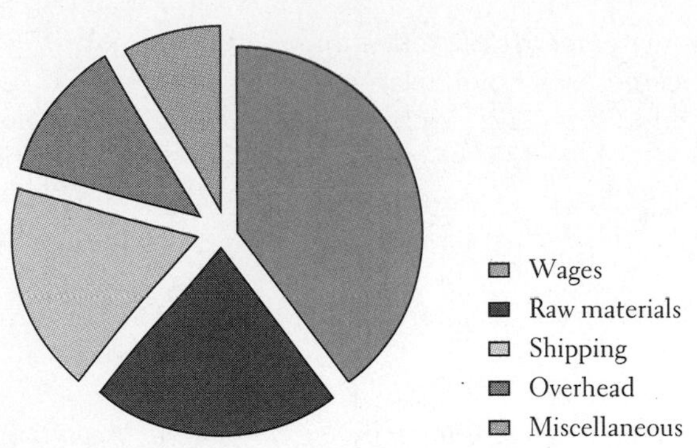

FIGURE 3.5 Bar Chart: Favorite Colors of 32 People

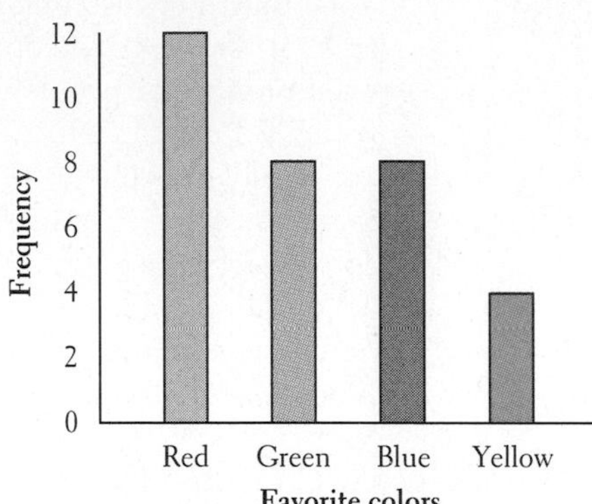

the bar is proportional to the number of items in its category. Bars are usually positioned vertically with their bases located on the horizontal axis of the graph. The bars are separated, and this is why such a graph is frequently used for nominal and ordinal data: the separations emphasize the plotting of frequencies for distinct categories.

Figure 3.2, a pie chart, showed 32 people's favorite colors. Figure 3.5 presents these data in a bar chart.

EXAMPLE 3.10 Bar charts are frequently used to compare a variable's values from one time period to another. Figure 3.6 shows U.S. raw steel production by month from 1989 until March 1992. It is easy to see the production trend by looking at this graph.

FIGURE 3.6 Bar Chart: Steel Production, 1989–92 (in millions of tons)

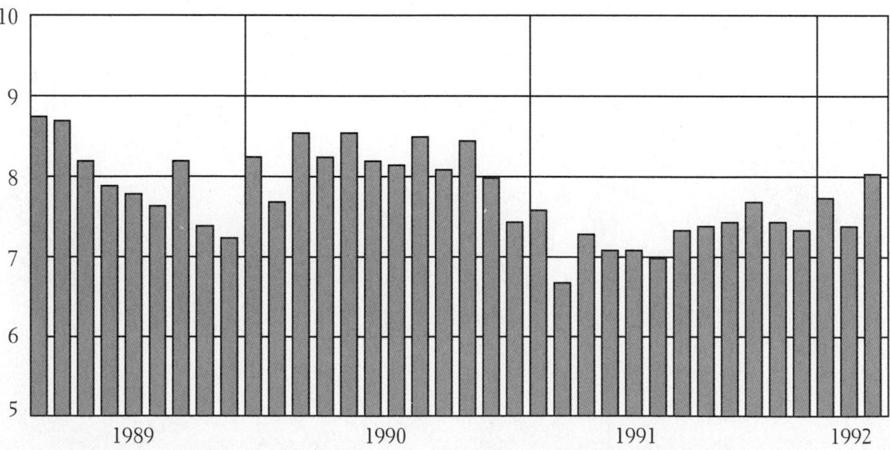

Source: *The Wall Street Journal*, April 27, 1992, p. 1.

Note from Figure 3.6 that the vertical scale begins at 5, not 0. This could possibly lead to problems of interpretation or a false picture of the original data. Watch for the possible distortion effects of such labeling in other graphs. This topic will be discussed further in a later section.

Bars are sometimes placed side by side to compare two different variables or a single variable for two different time periods (Figure 3.7). This bar chart reports how 1,997 adults responded to two questions concerning government regulation of airlines. Most bar charts are organized with the bars in a vertical position. Sometimes, however, for space reasons, the bars are in a horizontal position.

FIGURE 3.7 An Example of a Multiple Bar Chart

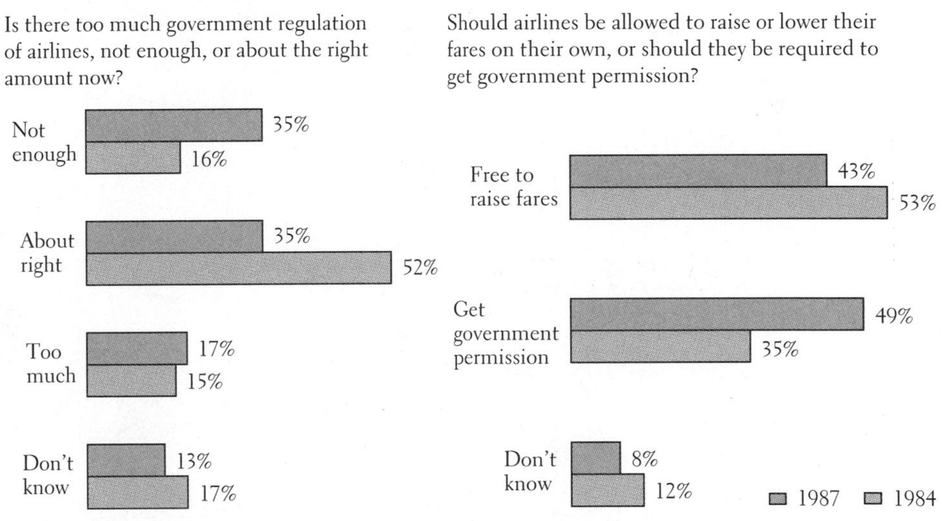

Source: *The Wall Street Journal,* November 9, 1987, p. 27.

THE PARETO CHART

Pareto Chart

The **Pareto chart** is a special case of the bar chart, which is frequently used in quality control. This type of chart consists of bars that describe components of a production or assembly line. Its purpose is to identify key causes of unacceptable quality. Each bar's height represents the number of occurrences of each problem, so the chart shows the degree of the quality problem for each variable measured. Figure 3.8 shows bar heights arranged in descending order of height.

> The **Pareto chart** is a bar chart used to identify and prioritize problems.

The Pareto chart may also include a second scale showing the cumulative percentages of the variables being measured across the bar chart's categories. The right vertical axis is scaled to accommodate percentages from 0 to 100. Figure 3.8 demonstrates both of these features.

EXAMPLE 3.11 Susan Delano is quality control manager for a small job shop making special truck seats to order. Her job includes tracking major quality problems in the shop, and she decides to construct a Pareto chart for the past month. Susan determines the major quality problems on the seat line and finds out how many of each type of problem occurred. Figure 3.8 shows these occurrences along with the cumulative percentages scaled on the right axis. Susan's chart will highlight the factory's quality problems during a meeting with top management.

FIGURE 3.8 Pareto Chart: Truck Seats

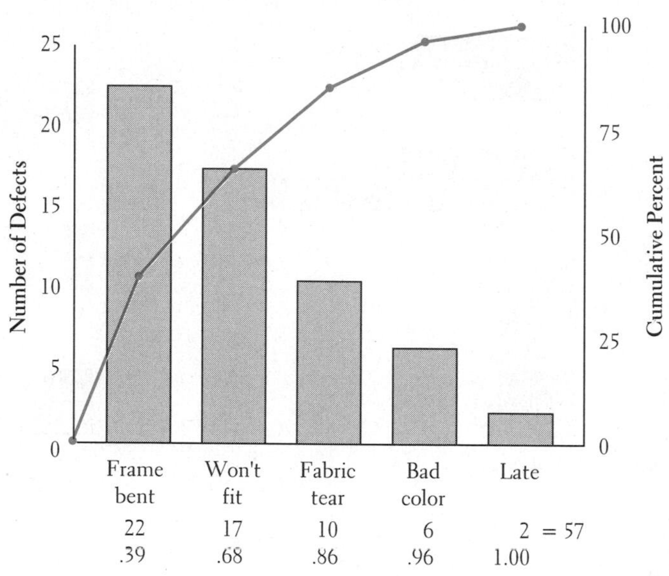

Histogram

The **histogram** is frequently used to graphically present interval and ratio data. In this graphing method, categories or classes are plotted along the horizontal axis of the graph, and numerical values of each class are represented by vertical bars. A histogram is like a bar chart except that there's no space between the bars. This is why the histogram is often used for interval and ratio data: the adjacent bars indicate that a numerical range is being summarized by indicating the frequencies in arbitrarily chosen classes.

EXAMPLE 3.12 The executive incomes in Table 3.4 are to be presented in a chart or graph. The histogram is chosen as an effective method (Figure 3.9). The seven income categories appear on the horizontal axis, and the frequencies appear as vertical bars.

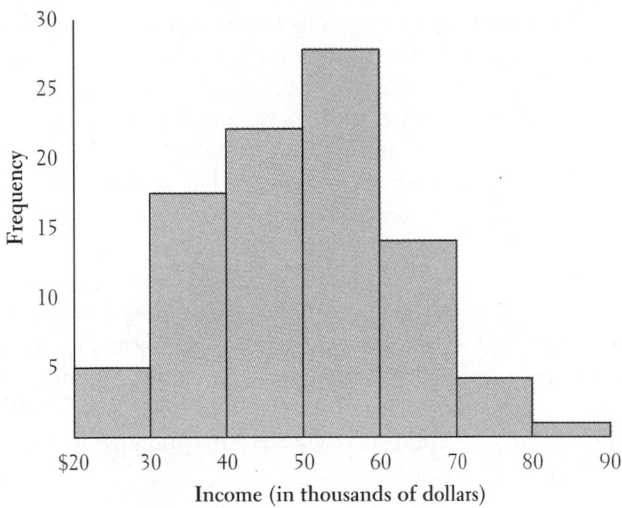

FIGURE 3.9 Histogram: Executive Incomes for the Sunrunner Corporation

Stem-and-Leaf Plot

A **stem-and-leaf plot** is an alternative way to show data. This approach is similar to the histogram except that the actual data are displayed instead of bars. Example 3.13 illustrates the stem-and-leaf plot.

EXAMPLE 3.13 Consider the data for number of customers per day for The Wash Tub (Table 3.7). To form a stem-and-leaf plot for these values, treat the first digit (the 10s place) as the stem. Next, treat the second digit (the 1s place) as the leaf. The first number in Table 3.7 is 65. Thus, the 5, which is in the 1s place, will be located in row 6 (the row corresponding to the stem, 6):

Stem	
0	
1	
2	
3	
4	
5	
6	5

When the values are placed in order, the stem-and-leaf plot looks like this:

Stem	Leaf
0	5
1	225689
2	1333334445555556666666688899
3	11122444555555667778889
4	355555556689
5	1223333346666667
6	4557

Note that the stem-and-leaf plot provides more information than a histogram because the actual digits are shown instead of bars.

Frequency Polygon

The **frequency polygon** is another common method for graphically presenting interval and ratio data. To construct a frequency polygon, mark the frequencies on the vertical axis and the values of the variable being measured on the horizontal axis, as with the histogram. Next, plot each class frequency by placing a dot above the class midpoint, and connect successive dots with straight lines to form a polygon. Two new classes with frequencies of zero are added at the ends of the horizontal scale. This allows the polygon to reach the horizontal axis at both ends of the distribution (Example 3.14).

EXAMPLE 3.14 A frequency polygon can be drawn for the executive incomes (Table 3.4) by plotting the income category on the horizontal axis, putting a dot above each midpoint to indicate frequency, and connecting the dots. Figure 3.10 shows that the polygon touches the horizontal axis at $15,000 and $95,000. These values represent the midpoints of the two new classes containing zero frequencies, which are added to the ends of the horizontal scale.

TM

FIGURE 3.10 Frequency Polygon: Executive Incomes

The frequency polygon of Table 3.10 outlines the data pattern clearly. If the purpose of presenting these executive incomes is to compare them with other distributions, the frequency polygon summarizes the data well.

Ogive

A graph of a cumulative frequency distribution is called an **ogive.** An ogive is used to determine how many observations lie above or below a certain value in a distribution. A *less-than* ogive tells how many items in the distribution have a value less than the upper limit of each class. First, a cumulative frequency distribution is constructed. Next, the cumulative frequencies are plotted at the upper class limit of each category. Finally, the points are connected with straight lines to form the ogive curve (Example 3.15).

A less-than ogive can also be constructed for a relative frequency distribution. The only difference involves the vertical scale. For a relative frequency distribution, this scale will range from 0 to 100%, indicating the fraction of the total number of observations that fall into or below each class. This approach is also demonstrated in Example 3.15.

EXAMPLE 3.15 Recall the less-than cumulative frequency distribution for Sunrunner Corporation executive incomes (Table 3.9). The cumulative frequency for each class is the sum of the frequencies for that class and for all lower classes. The less-than ogive curve is constructed by plotting these cumulative frequencies at the upper limit of each class. Figure 3.11 can be used to answer questions such as, "How many Sunrunner executives have incomes less than $60,000?" The answer is 72.

TM

FIGURE 3.11 Ogive: Executive Incomes (frequencies)

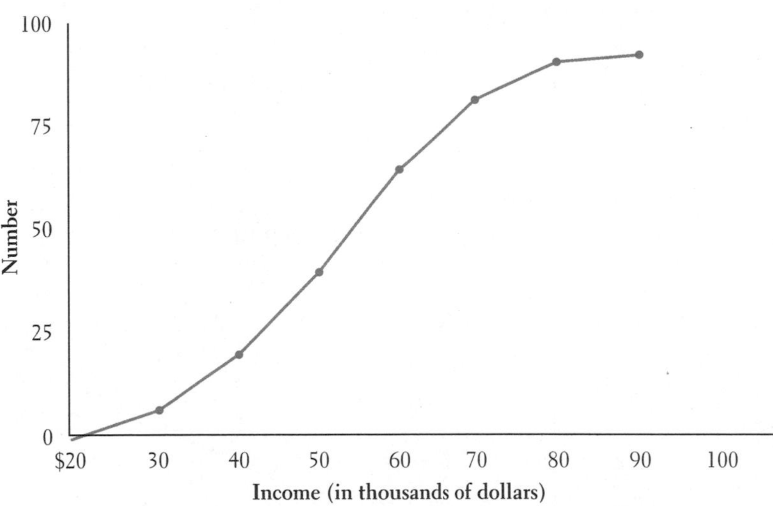

Similarly, Figure 3.12 shows the less-than ogive curve for *relative* frequencies. This curve can be used to answer questions such as, "What percentage of Sunrunner executives have incomes less than $60,000?" The answer is 74.3%.

A *more-than* ogive shows how many items in the distribution have a value greater than or equal to the lower limit of a particular class. This type of curve can also be developed for either a cumulative frequency distribution or a cumulative relative frequency distribution.

Time Series Graph V

The **time series graph** portrays data measured over time. The graph's horizontal axis represents time periods, and the vertical axis shows the numerical values corresponding to these time periods.

TM

FIGURE 3.12 Ogive: Executive Incomes (relative frequencies)

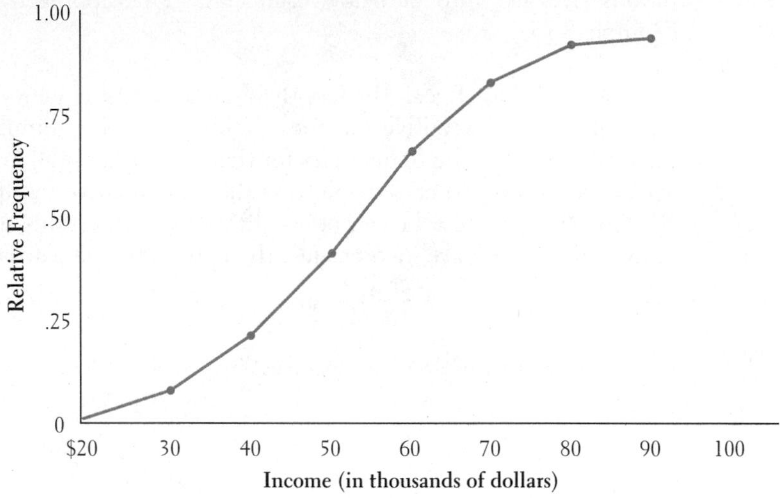

EXAMPLE 3.16 The Washington Water Power Company wants to show its average residential revenue per kilowatt-hour for the past six years in the *1991 Annual Report*. A time series graph is used for this purpose (Figure 3.13).

FIGURE 3.13 Time Series Graph: Average Residential Revenue per Kilowatt-Hour (WWP)

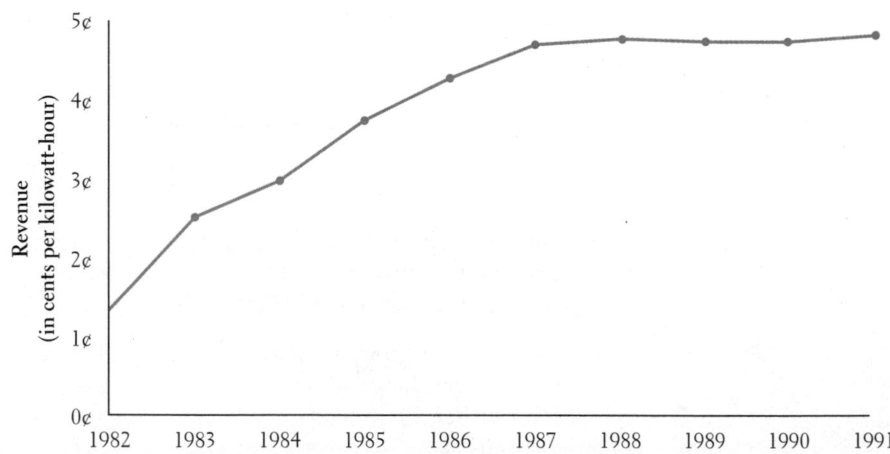

The advantage of the time series graph is that the rise or fall over time is usually obvious. It is apparent from Figure 3.13 that average residential revenue per kilowatt-hour for WWP has been increasing from 1982 to 1991. Time series data are important to almost all businesses, and will be covered thoroughly in Chapters 16 and 17.

It is important to note that many modern software packages for personal computers have graphing features. Small computers and the availability of data analysis programs have put sophisticated graphing capabilities within the reach of the smallest business and so choosing the most effective and accurate graphing method is increasingly important.

The MINITAB commands to generate a stem-and-leaf plot such as in Example 3.13 are:

```
MTB>  SET INTO C1
DATA> 65 23 26 . . . . . . . 26 25 43
DATA> END
MTB > STEM AND LEAF DISPLAY OF C1

Stem-and-leaf of C1       N = 88
Leaf Unit = 1.0

0              5
1              22
1              5689
2              133333444
2              555556666666688899
3              11122444
3              55555667778889
4              3
4              55555556689
5              122333334
5              6666667
6              4
6              557

MTB > STOP
```

Note that the MINITAB stem-and-leaf plot splits each 10s group into two groups to show more of the distribution of the number of customers per day. For example, the first 1 stem represents numbers from 10 to 14 and indicates that there were two days with 12 customers. The second 1 stem represents numbers from 15 to 19 and reveals that there was one day of 15 customers, one day of 16 customers, one day of 18 customers, and one day of 19 customers.

HOW TO LIE WITH STATISTICS

As a final note regarding creating and interpreting different kinds of graphs, be careful to avoid distortions. It is easy to deliberately distort a graph to give a misleading picture of the facts. A delightful little book, *How to Lie with Statistics*, exposes many graphing pitfalls that lead to distortions of original data.[1]

An example of such a distortion appears in Extended Exercise 44, " Kane's Chemicals." Can you see why the original data values were distorted as you look from the first barrel to the second?

[1]Darrell Huff, *How to Lie with Statistics* (New York: W. W. Norton, 1954).

As a second example of how two very different impressions can be developed from the same data, consider Figure 3.14 that appeared in *The Wall Street Journal* (July 29, 1992). This time series graph shows the Dow Jones Industrial Average's movement during one day's trading.

Note from Figure 3.14 that the Dow Jones was just under 3285 at the start of the day, and about 3335 at the end. With the vertical axis scaled as shown, this increase appears as a very significant growth. However, if the vertical axis is scaled over a wider range, the increase is difficult to detect (Figure 3.15). So which graph is correct? Both, or neither, depending on the graph's use. An investor that follows the market closely on a minute-to-minute basis would be interested in the market's sharp upturn shown in Figure 3.14. An investor looking at a portfolio's long-term growth probably wouldn't be interested in a daily graph at all, knowing in advance that it probably looks like Figure 3.15.

FIGURE 3.14 The Dow's Performance (DJIA at five-minute intervals yesterday)

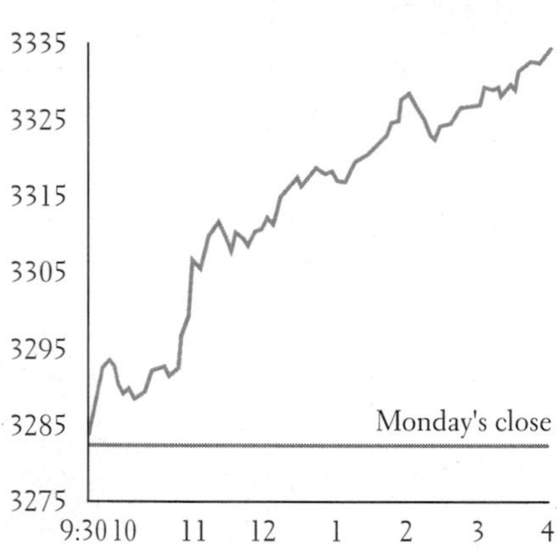

FIGURE 3.15 The Dow's Performance

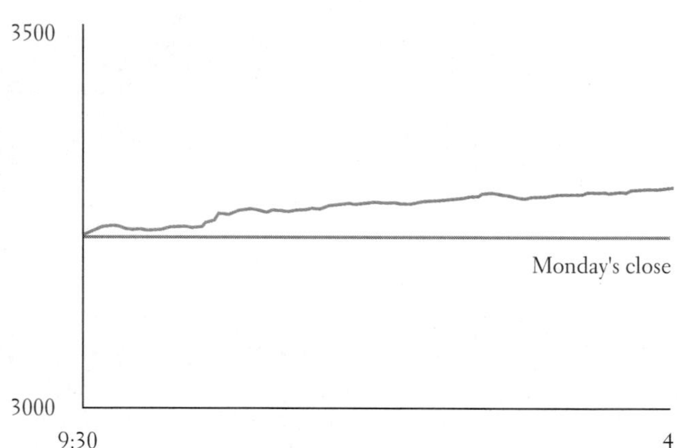

Figures 3.14 and 3.15 illustrate the point that great care must be taken in constructing a graph to ensure that it gives an accurate, appropriate impression of the original data.

As mentioned earlier, charts and graphs are widely used in almost all business publications because of the need to summarize important data collections. Figures 3.16 through 3.20 are examples of actual charts and graphs in national publications. Evaluate each figure, and indicate whether it does a fair job of displaying the data or whether it presents a distorted picture.

EXERCISES

18. What is the difference between a pie chart and a bar chart?
19. What is the difference between a histogram and a bar chart?
20. What is the difference between a histogram and a frequency polygon?
21. What are the advantages of a frequency polygon over a histogram?

FIGURE 3.16 Bar Chart: VCR Families

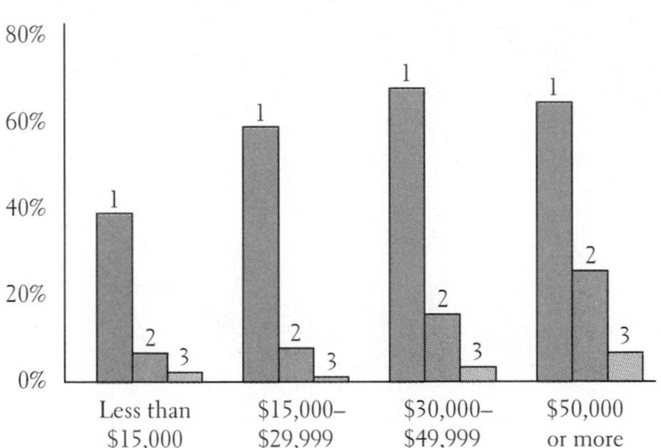

Source: The Roper Organization

FIGURE 3.17 Bar Chart: Class Standing for Questionnaire

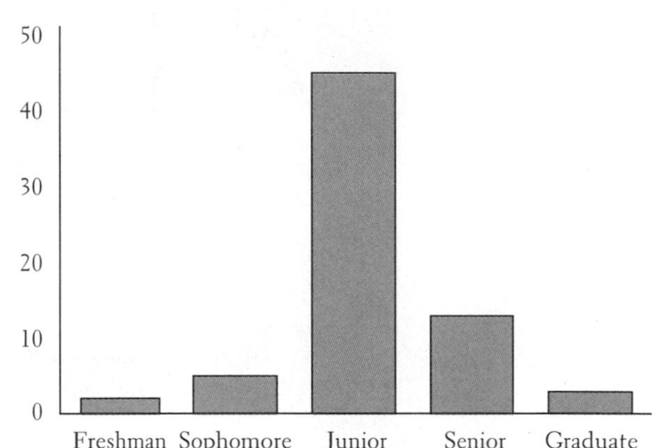

Source: Data was gathered from the questionnaire (Table 1.1) administered to one of the author's classes.

FIGURE 3.18 Pie Charts: Budget Breakdown

Fiscal Year 1993 Outlay Estimate: $1.52 trillion

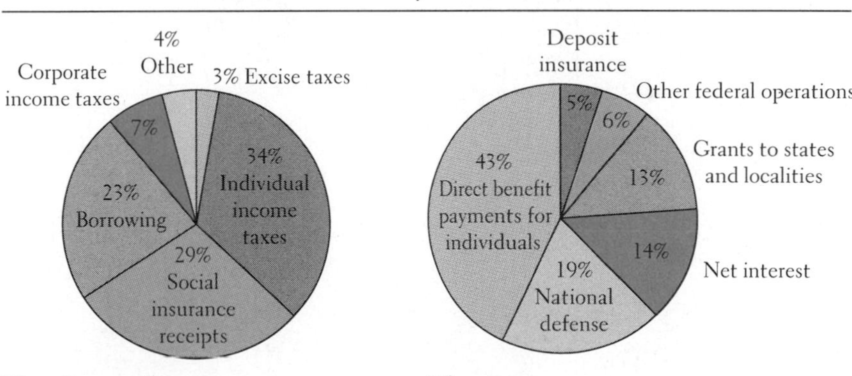

Source: *Spokesman-Review,* January 30, 1992, p. 1.

22. When should a less-than ogive be constructed?
23. How are time series graphs used?
24. A small-town PTA conducted a survey about drinking and driving via 166 telephone interviews. The following data reflect responses to the question, "Do you think the drinking driver problem has increased or decreased since 1988?"

Increased	96
Decreased	34
About the same	36
Total	166

FIGURE 3.19 Pictogram: Bungee Jumps, 1990–91

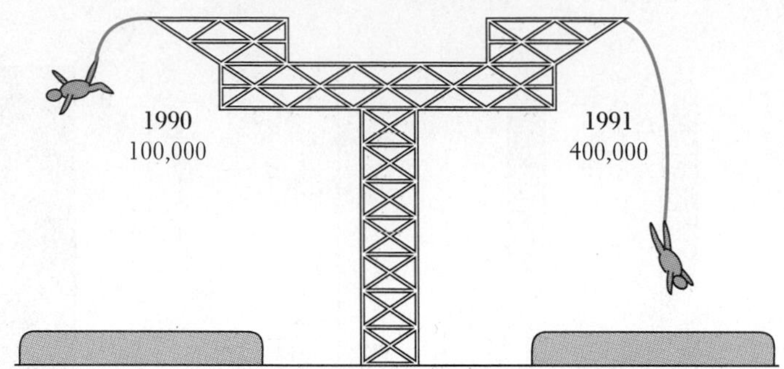

Source: North American Bungee Association

FIGURE 3.20 Time Series Graph: Shrinking Market, 1984–87

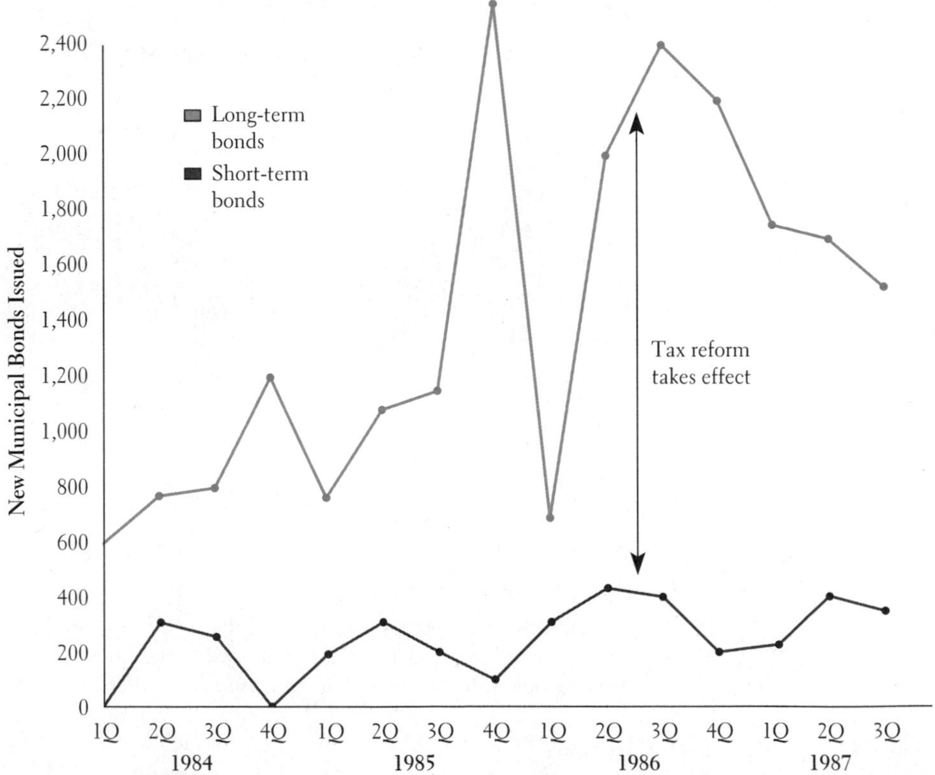

Source: *U.S. News & World Report,* October 26, 1987, p. 43.

a. Develop a pie chart.

b. Develop a bar chart.

c. Which chart is the better way to report these data?

25. During a pro football game's third quarter, a chart is to be presented to TV viewers to break down one team's scoring during the season. The data are:

Receivers	58%
Kickers	25
Running backs	11
Defense	6
Total	100%

a. What kind of chart should be used to present these data?

b. Construct this chart.

26. Finch Construction Company is negotiating with a local union and needs to present a chart of average hourly earnings in the construction industry from 1976 to 1985. What kind of chart would you recommend to Finch for the distribution that follows? Construct the appropriate chart.

Year	Hourly earnings
1976	$ 7.71
1977	8.10
1978	8.66
1979	9.27
1980	9.94
1981	10.82
1982	11.63
1983	11.92
1984	12.03
1985	12.20

Source: *U.S. Dept. of Labor Monthly Labor Review.*

27. An independent research firm surveyed households with residents 55 years of age or older. The following frequency distribution shows how respondents answered the question, "How many driving minutes from a hospital is the furthest that you would consider living during your retirement?"

Driving minutes	Frequency
5 minutes or less	47
6 to 10 minutes	150
11 to 15 minutes	128
16 to 20 minutes	67
21 minutes or more	94
Total	486

Source: "Surveys of Older Homeowners Concerning Retirement Attitudes." Spokane: Decision Science Associates, June 1986.

a. Construct a histogram.

b. Construct a frequency polygon.

c. Which type of graph would best show each separate class in the distribution?

d. Which type of graph shows the data pattern most clearly?

e. Construct a less-than ogive for the cumulative frequency distribution.

f. How many respondents would not consider living more than 20 minutes from a hospital?

28. Answerphone Service, Inc., wants to do a better job of billing customers for services rendered. Owner Sloan Spalding needs to know how long it takes to complete various incoming calls. For data collection, 150 random calls were monitored and timed, as shown in Exercise 16. Use the frequency distributions you constructed in Exercise 16 to:

    a. Construct a histogram.

    b. Construct a frequency polygon.

    c. Construct a more-than ogive for the cumulative relative frequency distribution.

    d. What percentage of the incoming calls will last more than 10 minutes?

SUMMARY

This chapter has presented important ways of summarizing data collections so that their important features can be quickly and easily understood and used in the decision-making process. These methods are especially important for qualitative data. Data measured on a nominal or ordinal scale are frequently summarized using the techniques of this chapter. Since such data often occur in practical situations, these techniques are prevalent in most business applications.

Frequency distributions were discussed as a way to present a data collection's essential features. Steps to be followed in preparing a frequency distribution were presented along with a discussion of relative frequencies and cumulative frequency distributions. Graphing methods to visually summarize collected data were shown. The purpose of charts and graphs is to briefly show the essential aspects of data arrays so the decision maker can understand and use their important information.

APPLICATIONS OF STATISTICAL CONCEPTS IN THE BUSINESS WORLD

KAISER ALUMINUM COMPANY'S USE OF CHARTS AND GRAPHS

Kaiser Aluminum Company's elaborate quality assurance system in the Trentwood plant has helped make it one of the world's leading aluminum suppliers. The applications section of Chapter 13 ("Quality-Control Applications") details this system.

Kaiser's computerized quality-control system generates huge amounts of raw data. These data values must somehow be displayed to those responsible for the operation of the aluminum production process. Charts and graphs are widely used for this purpose. Figures 3.21 through 3.23 (a pie chart, a bar chart, and a time series graph) were taken from quality-control reports Kaiser's system generated. These figures are rou-

FIGURE 3.21 Kaiser Aluminum Start Weight Breakdown

FIGURE 3.22 Kaiser Aluminum Recovery Distribution

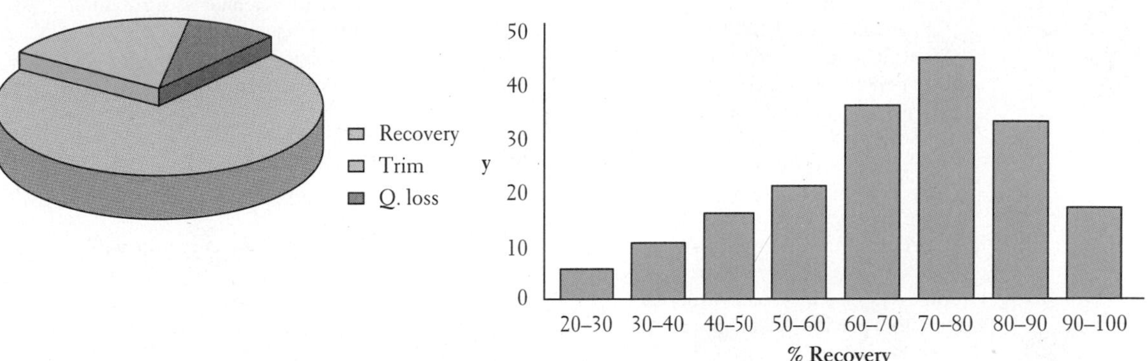

FIGURE 3.23 Kaiser Aluminum Recovery Defect Trends, Time Series Graph

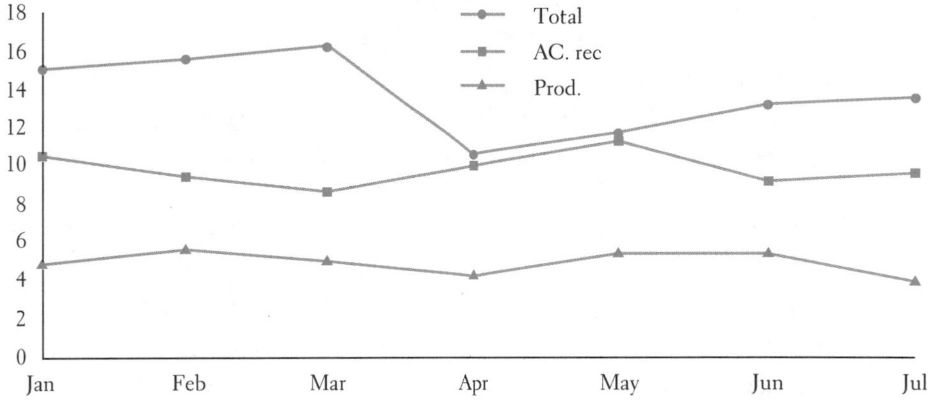

tinely reviewed by quality-control engineers and managers. As you see, Kaiser depends on graphical representations to ensure its products' quality.

OTHER APPLICATIONS

Here are additional areas where this chapter's techniques might prove useful. Data collection is described on the left; a possible summary technique is on the right.

Data collection	Possible summary technique
Ages of customers by category	Frequency distribution
Annual expenditures of company funds	Pie chart
Sales of wine by winery	Bar chart
Hourly wages of factory workers	Cumulative frequency distribution
Annual sales, 1979 to present	Time series graph
County government sources of revenue	Pie chart
Accounts receivable by store	Bar chart

Data collection	Possible summary technique
Credit card holders by state	Bar chart
Incomes of city residents	Cumulative frequency distribution
U.S. annual trade deficit	Time series graph
Monthly prime interest rate	Time series graph
U.S. population years of education	Frequency distribution
Annual sales of eight sales agents	Bar chart
Monthly sales by department	Bar chart
Average stock price per week	Time series graph
Dow Jones average, daily	Time series graph
State expenditures by department	Pie chart
VISA credit card purchase amounts	Cumulative frequency distribution
Company employee job rating scores	Histogram
Units shipped from factory monthly	Time series graph
Smokers per 100,000 by age category	Histogram
Annual sales of new cars	Time series graph
Scores on medical school exam	Cumulative frequency distribution
Graduating seniors' grade point averages	Frequency distribution
Percentage of defective parts by supplier	Pie chart
Quality control: bad units per week	Time series graph

Glossary

Distribution A collection, array, or group of numerical values.

Frequency distribution A list of several data classes or categories along with the number of values that fall into each.

Relative frequencies Percentages calculated by dividing the actual frequency for each class by the total number of observations being classified.

Cumulative frequency distribution A distribution showing the total number of occurrences that lie above or below certain key values.

Pie chart A method of presenting qualitative data summaries in which a circle is divided into sectors corresponding to the relative frequency for each class.

Bar chart A method of graphically presenting nominal and ordinal data in which one bar is used to represent the frequency for each category.

Pareto chart A bar chart used to identify and prioritize problems.

Histogram Used to graphically present interval and ratio data. The categories or classes are plotted along the graph's horizontal axis. Numerical values of each class are represented by vertical bars.

Stem and leaf Similar to histogram except that actual data are displayed instead of bars.

Frequency polygon Used to graphically present interval and ratio data. Formed by connecting the points corresponding to each class midpoint and frequency with straight lines.

Ogive A graph of a cumulative frequency distribution or cumulative relative frequency distribution.

Time series graph A graph of data values measured over time.

Solved Exercises

1. Frequency Distribution

Art Martinez, owner of a small jewelry store, has recorded the number of customers for each of the past 500 days. The smallest number was 7 and the largest 62. Art wants to construct a frequency distribution for this series. How should he set up the following?

a. Approximate number of classes.

b. Class width.

c. Limits for the first class.

Solution:

a. Table 3.3 shows that for 500 observations, about 10 classes should be used.

b. Class width is determined by subtracting the smallest value from the largest value and dividing the result by the appropriate number of classes: $(62 - 7)/10 = 5.5$. Thus, the class width should be 5 or 6. Since people are 5- and 10-oriented, a class width of 5 is chosen.

c. The first class must include the lowest value, 7. Since the variable (number of customers) is measured in whole numbers, the first class is 5–9.

2. RELATIVE AND CUMULATIVE FREQUENCY DISTRIBUTIONS

A voter opinion survey conducted by Alliance Pacific, Inc., provided voter input regarding a proposed waste-to-energy facility for the area. The following frequency distribution shows survey participants' age groups:

Age category	Frequency
18 to under 30	255
30 to under 45	510
45 to under 60	427
60 and over	405
Total	1,597

Source: *Waste-to-Energy Facility Voter Opinion Survey.* Spokane: Alliance Pacific, Inc., August 1985.

a. How could you improve this frequency distribution?

b. Construct a relative frequency distribution for this data collection.

c. Construct a cumulative relative frequency distribution indicating the percentage of respondents who are less than 45.

Solution:

a. Table 3.3 shows that around 11 classes should be used for n equal to 1,597.

b.

Age category	Frequency	Relative frequency	Cumulative frequency
18 to under 30	255	.160	.160
30 to under 45	510	.319	.479
45 to under 60	427	.267	.746
60 and over	405	.254	1.000
Total	1,597	1.000	

c. The cumulative relative frequency distribution shows that 47.9% of the respondents were less than 45 years old.

3. PIE AND BAR CHARTS

The December 14, 1987, edition of *U.S. News & World Report* reported the following values for the number of contact lenses worn by Americans:

Kind of contact lens	Number of Americans (millions)
Soft, daily wear	11.5
Rigid, gas-permeable	4.0
Soft, extended wear	3.5
Hard	1.5
Total	20.5

a. Construct a pie chart.

b. Construct a bar chart.

Solution:

a. The total number of Americans who have contact lenses is divided according to each different kind: 11.5/20.5 = .561, 4.0/20.5 = .195, 3.5/20.5 = .171, and 1.5/20.5 = .073. Figure 3.24 shows a pie chart for these data.

b. Figure 3.25 shows a bar chart for this distribution.

FIGURE 3.24 Pie Chart: Contact Lenses by Type in United States

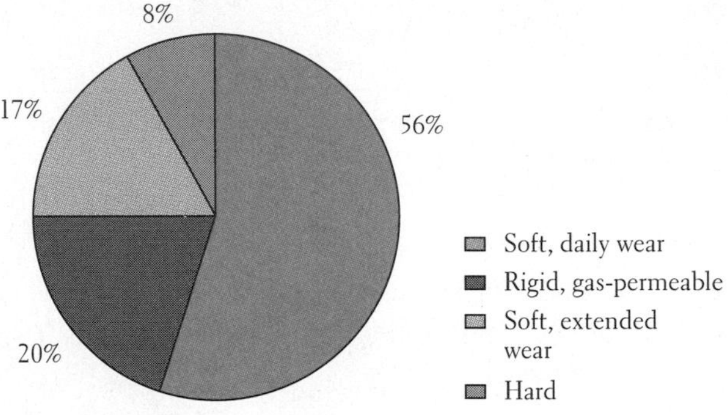

FIGURE 3.25 Bar Chart: Contact Lenses by Type in United States

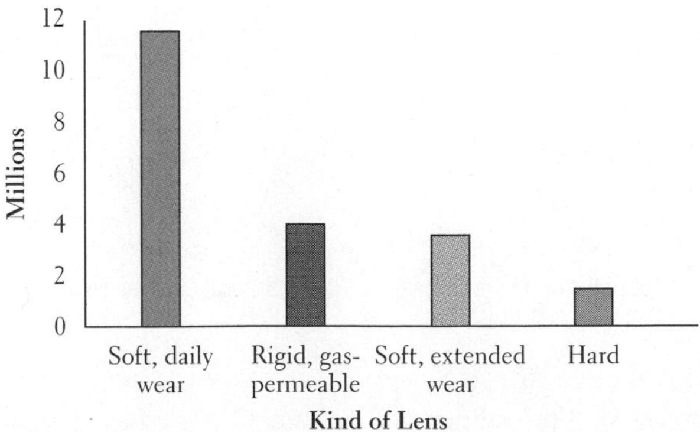

EXERCISES

29. Less-than cumulative frequency distribution

29. Bo Bosworth, statistician for the Omar Corporation, is preparing a frequency distribution that allows a person to determine the number of employees producing less than specified outputs. What kind of frequency distribution should Bo prepare?

30a. Eight classes
b. If 6 classes, width of 10
c. 40–49.99

30. April Marshall, manager of the university bookstore, has recorded the charge purchases made by students in one day. Of a total of 140 charges, the smallest was $40.58 and the largest $97.52. She wants to construct a frequency distribution for this series. How should she set up the following?

    a. Approximate number of classes.

    b. Class width.

    c. Limits for the first class.

31. Decision Science Associates conducted a survey of health care consumers to assess buying patterns and perceptions in the Missoula, Montana, market. The following frequency distribution shows who provided the respondents' health insurance coverage:

Coverage	Frequency
Employer	246
Spouse	150
Both	93
Total	489

Source: *Survey of Missoula Health Care Consumers with Employer-Paid Insurance.* Missoula: Decision Science Associates, February 1987.

    a. Construct a relative frequency distribution for this data collection.

    b. Construct a pie chart.

    c. Construct a bar chart.

32. The survey in Exercise 31 asked respondents, "How many people live in your household (including yourself)?" The following distribution classifies the responses:

Number of people	Frequency
1	52
2	147
3	102
4	116
5 to 7	66
8 or more	2
Total	485

Source: *Survey of Missoula Health Care Consumers with Employer-Paid Insurance.* Missoula: Decision Science Associates, February 1987.

    a. How could you improve this frequency distribution?

    b. Construct a relative frequency distribution for this data collection.

    c. Construct a less-than cumulative relative frequency distribution.

d. Construct a more-than cumulative relative frequency distribution.

e. What percentage of the households had five or more occupants?

33. Prior to putting a new tire on the market, Goodwheel Tire Company conducts tread life tests on a random sample of 150 tires. The following frequency distribution shows the results:

Number of miles (thousands)	Frequency
20 to under 25	7
25 to under 30	14
30 to under 35	28
35 to under 40	45
40 to under 45	30
45 to under 50	15
50 to under 55	11
Total	150

33*a.* .0467
.0933
.1867
.3000
.2000
.1000
.0733
b. 37.33%
e. 67.33%

a. Construct a relative frequency distribution for this data collection.

b. Construct a cumulative relative frequency distribution that will indicate the percentage of tires that lasted more than 40,000 miles.

c. Construct a frequency polygon.

d. Construct a less-than ogive for the cumulative relative frequency distribution.

e. What percentage of the tires lasted less than 40,000 miles?

34. In a feasibility study to determine whether to build a destination resort, Mark Craze analyzes the following data series on the number of visitors at the Coulee Dam Visitor Center.

Year	Visitors
1969	250,265
1970	250,929
1971	321,333
1972	342,269
1973	268,528
1974	468,136
1975	390,129
1976	300,140
1977	271,140
1978	282,752
1979	244,006
1980	161,524
1981	277,134
1982	382,343
1983	617,737
1984	453,881

Source: *Market Feasibility Study for a Proposed Resort Development at Crescent Bay on Lake Roosevelt.* Grand Coulee: Decision Science Associates, February 1985.

34*a*. Time series graph

a. What type of chart or graph should Mark construct?

b. Construct the appropriate graph for this data series.

35. For the market feasibility study in Exercise 34, Mark needs to present the following projected occupancy percentages:

Month	Percentage
January	10
February	15
March	30
April	45
May	70
June	90
July	100
August	100
September	80
October	60
November	25
December	15

Source: *Market Feasibility Study for a Proposed Resort Development at Crescent Bay on Lake Roosevelt*. Grand Coulee: Decision Science Associates, February 1985.

35*a*. Bar chart

a. What type of chart or graph should Mark construct?

b. Construct the appropriate chart for this data series.

36. Gene Madlock needs to display the following data of the top nine geographical distributions of 1983 capital commitments for independent private firms: California, $424.9 million; Connecticut, $4.3 million; Georgia, $43 million; Massachusetts, $322.5 million; Michigan, $18 million; New York, $215.1 million; Rhode Island, $30.4 million; Texas, $5 million; and Washington, $104 million (Source: *Venture Capital Journal*, July 1983).

36*a*. Bar or pie chart

a. What type of chart or graph should Gene construct?

b. Construct the appropriate chart or graph for this data series.

37.

Class	f
35<40	2
40<45	5
45<50	14
50<55	19
55<60	12
60<65	9
65<70	5
70<75	1
75<80	3
	70

37. The following data collection shows the normal daily mean temperatures of 70 selected cities:

67.5	40.0	71.2	61.9	62.6	60.6	56.6	50.3
49.8	54.0	57.5	68.0	75.6	61.2	77.0	51.1
49.2	50.4	52.1	49.7	56.4	56.2	68.2	45.0
55.1	51.5	48.6	39.7	38.2	44.7	64.6	54.1
55.4	44.7	51.1	49.4	45.3	53.1	56.2	47.3
47.6	54.5	60.0	59.0	41.3	54.5	49.6	51.7
59.9	53.0	54.3	50.3	50.3	63.3	45.3	61.8
59.2	66.0	63.4	66.3	51.7	44.1	59.5	57.7
51.4	47.2	54.8	46.1	45.7	79.7		

Source: 1987 *Statistical Abstract of the United States*.

a. Construct a frequency distribution.

b. Construct a histogram.

c. Construct a chart to show the number of cities that have a normal daily mean temperature less than 50°.

38.

Class	*f*
0–4	23
5–9	38
10–14	71
15–19	42
20–24	24
25–29	5
30–34	0
35–39	4
40–44	1
45–49	1
	209

38. The following data collection shows net income as a percentage of equity for a sample of 209 companies from the 1992 Fortune 500 survey:

17	17	3	23	19	21	16	39	11	16	27
23	15	22	6	21	35	13	4	17	18	11
22	25	11	21	18	20	14	3	11	12	19
18	18	18	9	9	18	8	10	22	11	12
8	12	2	23	14	28	12	7	16	0	22
7	20	18	7	2	17	6	15	11	10	3
12	7	14	14	20	15	15	16	12	9	14
2	5	11	25	17	9	10	12	11	12	14
49	11	36	12	11	12	22	13	9	22	7
14	0	16	12	16	5	19	12	11	18	18
14	22	7	8	13	10	16	11	13	44	11
36	14	14	11	12	14	4	18	0	4	1
16	10	12	5	22	1	20	10	12	3	3
7	14	14	18	16	17	18	13	3	17	17
3	19	10	13	7	14	2	7	9	12	8
8	8	8	14	6	14	3	13	9	8	7
10	12	20	9	14	14	20	12	13	16	5
11	13	13	16	10	6	7	14	27	7	19
20	21	8	2	1	22	15	8	1	16	22

a. Construct a frequency distribution.

b. Construct both a histogram and a frequency polygon.

c. Construct a chart to show the number of companies whose net income as a percentage of equity is greater than 20.

39. Referring to the company data base in Appendix C, select a random sample of 100 employees and:

a. Construct a frequency distribution for variable x_1, number of years with the company.

b. Construct a chart or graph to display this data series.

40. Referring to the company data base in Appendix C, select a random sample of 75 employees and:

a. Construct a frequency distribution for variable x_2, number of overtime hours worked during the past six months.

b. Construct a chart or graph to display this data series.

41. Referring to the company data base in Appendix C, use the population of employees and:

a. Construct a frequency distribution for variable x_8, annual base salary.

b. Construct a chart or graph to display this data series.

42. Referring to the company data base in Appendix C, select the first 150 employees and:

a. Construct a frequency distribution for variable x_9, employee age.

b. Construct a chart or graph to display this data series.

EXTENDED EXERCISES

43. AMSBURY GLASS SHOWERS

For five years, Amsbury Glass Company has been making and delivering fiberglass shower stalls, which have recently become its biggest revenue producer. Ron Murphy, president of Amsbury, has decided that this product's sales history justifies increasing plant manufacturing capacity, which will require additional financing. Ron is considering how best to state his case to the area banks.

The increase in unit sales of shower stalls has been particularly dramatic during the past fiscal year. Ron decides to focus on this increase in presenting his case. The numbers of units delivered during each of the past 12 months are 348, 412, 643, 658, 942, 789, 1,135, 1,247, 1,254, 1,562, 1,503, 1,829.

Ron confers with production manager Pete Roper. They agree that these sales levels justify additional plant capacity and that they want to display the current need in dramatic fashion. Ron decides to prepare a time series graph of these data (Figure 3.26) as a key component of management's presentation to the banks.

FIGURE 3.26 Time Series Graph: Sales of Amsbury Shower Stalls

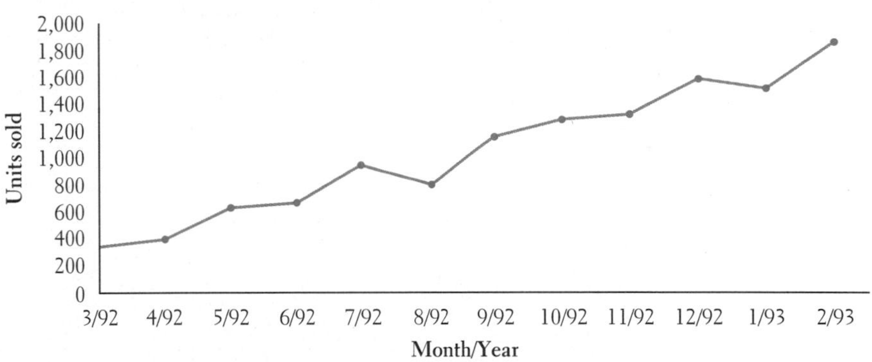

a. How effective do you think the graph will be in persuading the banks to grant additional loans?

b. What other graphing methods might have been used to show sales history?

44. KANE'S CHEMICALS

Kane's Chemicals makes film products, using crude oil in its manufacturing process. During last year's stockholders' meeting, management was severely criticized for using an excessive amount of foreign oil as opposed to domestic oil. Efforts to reduce foreign imports and increase domestic usage during the past year have resulted in a 50% reduction in the number of barrels of foreign oil used.

John Kane, company president, plans to continue reducing the company's imports of foreign oil. He's encouraged by a *Wall Street Journal* article (October 27, 1989) indicating that domestic oil activity is increasing. The journal stated that "fear is finally leaving the oil patch."

Mr. Kane decides to highlight the past year's reduction during his presentation to stockholders at the upcoming annual meeting. He wants to make sure stockholders understand the progress that has been made since the previous meeting. He decides to use a graph (Figure 3.27) to dramatize the reduction in foreign oil consumption.

FIGURE 3.27 An Example of a Pictogram

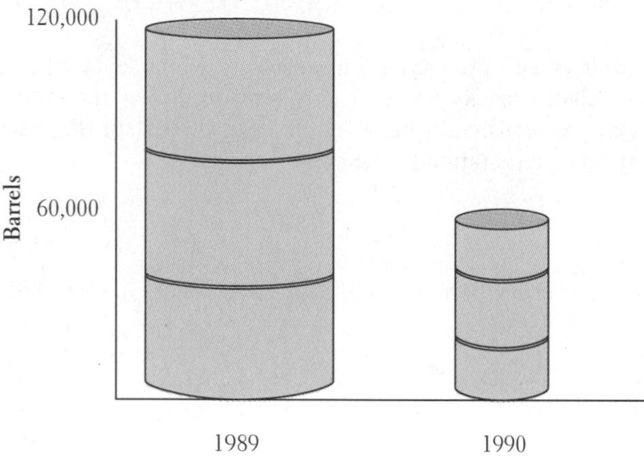

a. How effective do you think Figure 3.27's graph will be in convincing stockholders that dependence on foreign oil has been reduced?

b. Is the graph misleading in any way?

c. What do you think is the best way to visually depict the past year's import reduction?

45. WILCO VACUUM CENTER

Wilco Vacuum Center, a vacuum cleaner retailer, has recorded the number of units sold per day during the past several months. After assembling the raw data for the most recent month, store owner Mary Rose decides that the data represent a typical month and should be highlighted in an upcoming review with store employees. Unit sales per day for the past month are:

56, 89, 64, 23, 45, 65, 21, 78, 67, 59, 85, 63,
54, 21, 46, 49, 78, 86, 91, 65, 34, 64, 67, 56,
54, 23, 46, 34, 37, 38, 49

Mary wants to use both a tabular presentation and a graph for these values. It's important to show the data in an unbiased but effective manner. Mary assigns you the task of creating a frequency distribution for these data values and then determining what type of chart or graph will most effectively present them.

MICROCOMPUTER PACKAGE

You can use the micro package *Computerized Business Statistics* to construct a frequency distribution.

Kyle Chang wants to learn more about the number of customer orders processed per day in his retail operation. Table 3.7 showed a random sample of orders. Kyle wants to construct a frequency distribution for this data collection.

Computer Solution

On the main menu of *Computerized Business Statistics* a **3** is selected: Descriptive Statistics.

Since the data for this problem need to be entered on the keyboard a **1** is selected.

```
Descriptive Statistics - Define New Problem
 Raw or Group Data: Enter R/G, press ↵ R
```

Since the data are in raw form and not grouped, **R** is selected.

```
Population or Sample Data: Enter P/S, press ↵ P
```

The data will be treated as a population, so a **P** is selected.

```
Number of Data Points: Enter 1 – 125, press ↵ 88
```

Since the data collection consists of 88 customer counts, 88 is the correct entry.

```
Variable Name: Enter 0–5 char., press ↵ PRICE
```

The answer is **PRICE**.

```
Problem definition correct? Enter Y/N/Q, press ↵ Y
```

If the problem has been set up correctly, the answer is **Y**.

Next, the program provides spaces for the raw data to be entered. The data values are numbered from 1 to 88. The cursor allows you to replace the 0s on the screen with the actual data values.

```
Table Commands Enter Raw Data   File: None
               Price
1.              65
2.              23
3.              26
4.              45
5.              12
 .               .
 .               .
 .               .
88.             43
Press F when Finished
```

When the data have been entered and **F** pressed, the program asks:

```
Save data? Enter Y/N, press ↵ N
```

Now the program options menu reappears and you are instructed:

```
Enter number (1–9) for your selection from the menu & press ↵ 7
```

You are now ready to run the problem, so enter a 7. You will be asked:

```
Convert raw data to group data? Y/N & press ↵ Y
```

Since this problem involves the construction of a frequency distribution, the answer is **Y.** The lowest and highest values of the data collection appear on the screen, and you are asked to enter the number of groups.

```
Lowest Data Value:                  5
Highest Data Value:                67
Enter Number of Groups (2–10) & press ↵ 7
```

Since $n = 88$, seven groups are desired. Next, the program asks:

```
Enter Value for Lower Limit & press ↵ 0
```

Since the class width will be 10, the first class should start with 0. The program summarizes the situation:

```
Lowest Data Value:              5
Highest Data Value:            67
Number of Groups:               7
Lower Limit:                    0

Interval 10
```

The program computes the class width, or interval, and asks:

```
Is computed interval okay? Y/N & press ↵ Y
```

The program divides the data into seven groups of class width 10 (see Table 3.8) and calculates the mean, median, mode, range, variance, and standard deviation of the data (these concepts will be covered in Chapter 4). It then offers you the option of computing a relative frequency table (see Table 3.8). You may choose to save the solved problem on disk, print it, or merely view it on the screen.

```
S = Screen Output
P = Printer (hard copy)
D = Data Disk (text file)
R = Return to Descriptive Statistics Menu
Select Output Option: Enter letter and press ↵ P
```

Since a hard copy of the results is needed, **P,** or printer, is selected.

MINITAB Computer Package

The MINITAB commands to generate charts for Kyle Chang's data (Table 3.7) are:

```
MTB > READ 'CHANG.DAT' C1
      88 ROWS READ

C1
 65 23 26 45 · · ·

MTB > HISTOGRAM C1;
SUBC> INCREMENT = 10;
SUBC> START AT 0.

Histogram of C1 N = 88
```

```
Midpoint  Count
     0.0      0
    10.0      3  ***
    20.0     13  *************
    30.0     26  **************************
    40.0     15  ***************
    50.0     20  ********************
    60.0      8  ********
    70.0      3  ***
MTB > DOTPLOT C1

                                   .
                   :               :
                .  .:      .        :     .  :
                :.::.  . .: ..     :    .:  :
 .     :  : .. .:::::: :::::::.  . : .. ::. :.    .: .
-------+---------+---------+---------+---------+---------C1
      12        24        36        48        60        72
MTB > STOP
```

The **READ** command is used to read the customers per day data file called CHANG.DAT into column 1 (C1).

The **HISTOGRAM** command breaks the data range down into a reasonable set of intervals and assigns each datum to the midpoint of the interval within which it falls. The semicolon at the end of line 1 requests a subcommand prompt.

The **INCREMENT** subcommand allows you to choose the width of each interval, in this case 10.

The **START** subcommand specifies the midpoint for the first interval, in this case 0.

The **DOTPLOT** command generates a horizontal display similar to a histogram. The dotplot's bars are vertical, arrayed across what looks like a continuous range. However, the dotplot is broken down into intervals just like the histogram.

SAS Computer Package

The SAS commands to generate a histogram for Kyle Chang's data (Table 3.7) are:

```
TITLE ''SAS COMMANDS FOR THE WASH TUB DATA'';
DATA WASH;
 INFILE 'WASH.DAT';
 INPUT CUST 1–2;
PROC CHART;
 VBAR CUST;
```

The **TITLE** statement names the SAS program.

The **DATA** statement provides a filename for the data.

The **INFILE** statement identifies an external file that you want to read with an INPUT statement.

The **INPUT** statement names the variable CUST and indicates that it is located in columns 1–2.

The **PROC CHART** statement produces vertical and horizontal bar charts (also called histograms).

The **VBAR** statement lists the variables for which you want vertical bar charts. At the bottom of each bar, **CHART** prints a name or value. For qualitative variables, the category label is printed below each bar. For quantitative variables, the value is the midpoint of the interval represented by the bar.

The SAS output is shown in Table 3.11.

TABLE 3.11 SAS Histogram for The Washtub Data

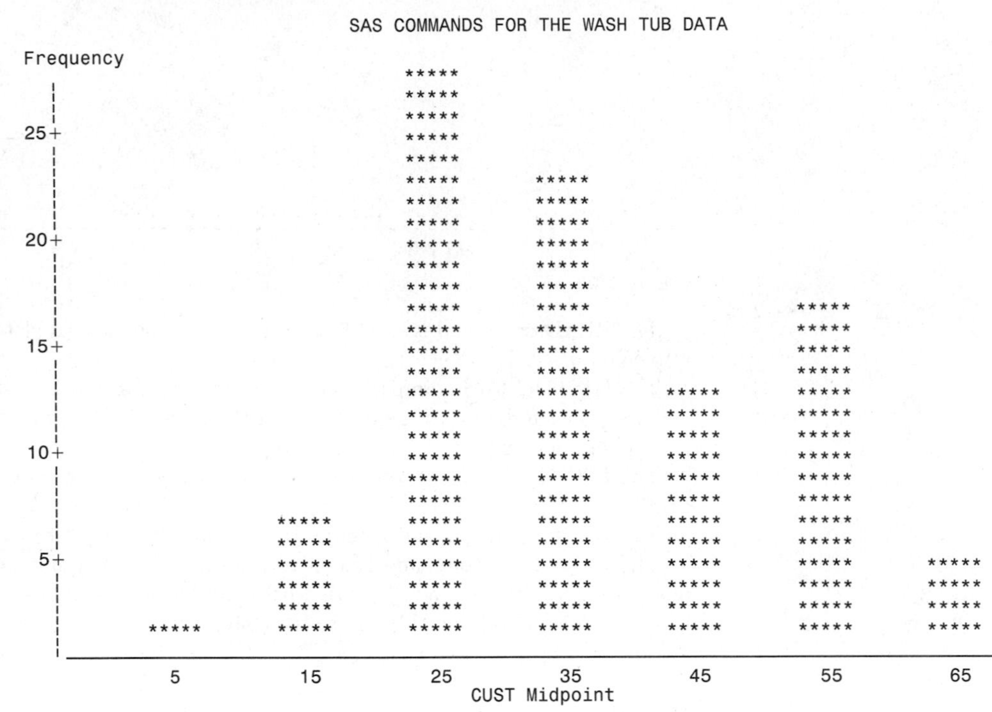

Chapter

4

Descriptive Statistics

Figures won't lie, but liars will figure.

Gen. C. H. Grosvenor

Objectives

When you have completed this chapter, you will be able to:

Compute the following measures of central tendency: mean, median, mode, and weighted mean.

Explain the advantages and disadvantages of each measure of central tendency.

Compute the following measures of variability: variance, standard deviation, and coefficient of variation.

Explain the advantages and disadvantages of using each measure of variability.

Financial Executive for May/June 1989 contained an article entitled, "Are Performance Fees Justified?" The *Yes* portion of this article argued that financial advisors should be paid based on the performance of their clients' portfolio accounts. The *No* position argued that advisors should be paid for their best efforts since portfolio performance depends on many factors other than the quality of advice.

The previous two chapters described various ways of collecting data and displaying them. Frequency distributions and graphs are important for showing the essential properties of data collections to assist in the decision-making process. These methods are especially important if the collected data are qualitative, that is, measured on either a nominal or an ordinal scale.

Why Descriptive Statistics Is Important to Managers

The methods for collecting and graphically presenting data discussed in Chapters 2 and 3 provide a starting point for data analysis. But managers also need to be acquainted with numerical descriptive measures that provide brief, easy-to-understand summaries of a data collection. These measures fall into two broad categories: measures of central tendency and measures of variability. Measures of central tendency describe the central location in a set of numerical observations. Measures of variability describe the spread or dispersion of the data values.

A possible way to resolve the issue posed by the *Financial Executive* article is to collect data on the performance of many different portfolio accounts, both those involving financial advisors and those not. These data values would need to be summarized in some way so that their essential characteristics become obvious. Important numerical methods of summarizing data collections are discussed in this chapter.

Measures of Central Tendency

In calculating summary values for a data collection, the first consideration is to find a central, or typical value for the data. This section presents four important measures of central tendency: mean, median, mode, and weighted mean.

Mean

The **arithmetic mean,** or simply the **mean,** is a summary value calculated by summing the numerical data values and dividing by the number of values.

> The **arithmetic mean** of a collection of numerical values is the sum of these values divided by the number of values. The symbol for the population mean is the Greek letter μ (mu), and the symbol for a sample mean is $\bar{x}$(*x*-bar).

Measurements of a data set are often denoted

$$x_1, x_2, x_3, \ldots, x_N$$

where x_1 is the first measurement in the data set, x_2 is the second measurement, and so on up to x_N, the last or Nth measurement in the data set. For four measurements, 3, 6, 4, and 9, the data set is

$$x_1 = 3, x_2 = 6, x_3 = 4, x_4 = 9$$

In any statistical study, there are usually two different data collections of interest: the population and the sample. Equation 4.1 is the formula for computing the mean of a population:

$$\mu = \frac{\Sigma x}{N} \tag{4.1}$$

where μ = Population mean
Σx = Sum of all population data values
N = Population size

To simplify the computations in this text, some shorthand notation is used. In the simplified notation for summing all x values, Σx, the summations are understood to extend from 1 to N. A more formal and complete notation system for this procedure is

$$\sum_{i=1}^{N} x_i$$

where the subscript i varies from its initial value of 1 to N in increments of 1. Since almost all sums run from 1 to N, the starting ($i = 1$) and ending (N) indices will be suppressed, and the simpler notation will be used except where the more complete notation is needed for clarity.

Any measurable characteristic of a population, for example, the population mean (μ) is called a **parameter.**

> A population **parameter** is any measurable characteristic of a population.

Equation 4.2 is used to compute the mean of a sample:

$$\bar{x} = \frac{\Sigma x}{n} \tag{4.2}$$

where $\bar{x}$ = Sample mean
Σx = Sum of all sample data values
n = sample size

Any measurable characteristic of a sample, for example, the sample mean ($\bar{x}$), is called a **statistic.** A sample statistic is frequently used to estimate a population parameter.

A sample **statistic** is any measurable characteristic of a sample.

TM

Characteristics of the arithmetic mean

1. Every data set measured on an interval or ratio level has a mean.
2. The mean has valuable mathematical properties that make it convenient to use in further computations.
3. The mean is sensitive to extreme values.
4. The sum of the deviations of the numbers in a data set from the mean is zero: $\Sigma(x - \mu) = 0$ and $\Sigma(x - \bar{x}) = 0$.
5. The sum of the squared deviations of the numbers in a data set from the mean is a minimum value: $\Sigma(x - \mu)^2$ is a minimum value, and $\Sigma(x - \bar{x})^2$ is a minimum value.

EXAMPLE 4.1 An instructor is interested in computing the mean age of the five people in a small class. Since the only people of interest are those in the class, this group constitutes a population, so Equation 4.1 is used to calculate the mean. Their ages are 21, 19, 25, 19, and 23. Their mean is calculated as

$$\mu = \frac{\Sigma x}{N} = \frac{21 + 19 + 25 + 19 + 23}{5} = 21.4$$

The mean or average age of the students in the class is 21.4 years. Note that the sum of deviations from the mean, $\Sigma(x - \mu)$, equals 0: $[(21 - 21.4) + (19 - 21.4) + (25 - 21.4) + (19 - 21.4) + (23 - 21.4)] = 0$.

EXAMPLE 4.2 The Atlas Welding & Sharpening Shop has 10 employees. Personnel records give the number of sick days each employee used during the past month. Equation 4.1 is used to calculate their mean. The data values and the mean calculation are

$$\mu = \frac{\Sigma x}{N} = \frac{3 + 0 + 5 + 6 + 1 + 0 + 11 + 8 + 0 + 4}{10} = 3.8$$

The computation reveals that an average of 3.8 sick days per hourly employee were taken during the past month.

Note that the sum of the squared deviations from the mean is equal to 127.6: $\Sigma(x - \mu)^2 = [(3 - 3.8)^2 + (0 - 3.8)^2 + (5 - 3.8)^2 + (6 - 3.8)^2 + (1 - 3.8)^2 + (0 - 3.8)^2 + (11 - 3.8)^2 + (8 - 3.8)^2 + (0 - 3.8)^2 + (4 - 3.8)^2] = 127.6$.

This is a minimum value because the population mean is the mathematical center of the distribution of 10 population values. If any value other than 3.8 is subtracted from the data values and the resulting deviations are squared and summed, the result will be a number larger than 127.6. Note that the results will be exactly the same if the data collection is treated as a sample.

The advantage of the arithmetic mean is that it's easy to compute, is understood by almost everyone, and is a good central value to use in summarizing a data collection, no matter how many values the collection contains. The disadvantage of the mean is that extreme values distort it. For this reason, the mean isn't the best summary statistic for all data collections.

EXAMPLE 4.3 Table 4.1 shows sales of the six largest restaurant chains. A mean sales amount of $5,280 million is computed using Equation 4.2:

$$\bar{x} = \frac{\Sigma x}{n} = \frac{14{,}110 + 5{,}590 + 3{,}700 + 3{,}030 + 2{,}800 + 2{,}450}{6} = 5{,}280$$

Note that this mean has been distorted upward by McDonald's sales of $14,110 million.

TABLE 4.1 Sales for the Six Largest Restaurant Chains, 1987 (Example 4.3)

Company	Sales ($ millions)
McDonald's	14,110
Burger King	5,590
Kentucky Fried Chicken	3,700
Hardee's	3,030
Wendy's	2,800
Pizza Hut	2,450

Source: C. Bovee and W. Arens, *Contemporary Advertising.* (Homewood, Ill.: Richard D. Irwin, 1989).

EXAMPLE 4.4 The journal *Accountancy* (July 1991, p. 78) reported on a study that computed the average (mean) monthly cost of leasing a car for employees of the major accounting firms in England. These costs ranged from a low of 284 pounds per month for the Volkswagen Golf, to a high of 1148 pounds per month for the Jaguar Sovereign. If the mean was also used to summarize the cost of all cars, it would be distorted upward by the high cost of the Jaguar.

Median V

In cases where you want a typical, central value that doesn't suffer the distorting effects of extreme values, use the **median** to summarize the data. Approximately half the data values in a set are less than the median, and approximately half are greater.

> The **median** of a data collection is the middle item in a set of observations that are arranged in order of magnitude.

Equation 4.3 is used to compute the *item number* of the median in a data set that is arranged in ascending or descending order:

$$\text{Median item number} = \frac{n + 1}{2} \tag{4.3}$$

> **Characteristics of the median**
> 1. Every ordinal-level, interval-level, and ratio-level data set has a median.
> 2. The median is not sensitive to extreme values.
> 3. The median does not have certain valuable mathematical properties for use in further computations.

EXAMPLE 4.5 Table 4.2 shows 1989 sales for a random sample of 11 of the top 50 retail chains. Clint Stone wants to compute a summary value to show the average sales for Table 4.2. The sample's mean, using Equation 4.2, is $8,383.5 million. This is considered a misleading summary statistic because it's distorted upward by two or three large values in the data collection.

TABLE 4.2 Sales for 11 of Top 50 Retail Chains, 1989 (Example 4.5)

Retail chain	Sales ($ millions)
Sears	$31,599
J.C. Penney	16,103
A & P	11,148
Albertsons	7,423
Walgreen	5,380
Toys "Я" Us	4,788
Tandy	4,181
Circle K	3,493
Costco	2,943
Nordstrom	2,671
Revco	2,490

Source: *Industry Surveys*, May 2, 1991, p. R80.

The median is the middle item in a set of observations. When data values are arrayed from highest to lowest as in Table 4.2, the median can be easily found. In this data collection, the median is $4,788 since half the values are greater than $4,788 and half are less. The median item can also be computed using Equation 4.3:

$$\text{Median item value} = \frac{n + 1}{2} = \frac{11 + 1}{2} = \text{6th item}$$

The median, $4,788, is the sixth item in the array. The value $4,788 is a central summary value that isn't distorted by Sears and J.C. Penney's comparatively high sales, which are now values that are only counted as ones in the analysis.

EXAMPLE 4.6 The median number of people treated daily at St. Luke's Hospital's emergency room must be determined from the following data for the past six days:

25, 26, 45, 52, 65, 78

Since the number of values is even, the two values in the center are used to compute the median; their average (mean) represents the median of the collection. The calculated average (mean) of the two central values, 45 and 52, is 48.5, so this is the median. Half of the values in the data array are less than 48.5, and half are greater. The median item can also be computed using Equation 4.3:

$$\text{Median item number} = \frac{n + 1}{2} = \frac{6 + 1}{2} = 3.5$$

Since the median is item 3.5 in the array, the third and fourth elements need to be averaged: $(45 + 52)/2 = 48.5$. Therefore, 48.5 is the median number of patients treated in St. Luke's emergency room during the six-day period.

The median separates a data array into two equal sections. If each section is subdivided by a new median, the result is four equal sections. Each of the three separating values is called a *quartile*; the middle quartile is the original median. An extension of this idea, which is often used on very large data arrays, is to separate the data into 100 sections, each with the same number of data elements. The separating values are then called *percentiles*.

Mode

It is sometimes important to know the most prevalent value in a data collection. The value that occurs most frequently is known as the **mode.**

V

The **mode** of a data collection is the value that occurs most frequently.

Characteristics of the mode

1. Some data sets do not have a mode.
2. Some data collections have more than one mode.
3. The mode does not have certain valuable mathematical properties for use in further computations.

EXAMPLE 4.7 A data collection consists of the values 2, 3, 3, 5, 6, 4, 3, 6, 7, 9, 3, 2, and 6. The mode of this collection is 3, since there are more 3s (four of them) than any other number.

EXAMPLE 4.8 The mode is to be determined for the following data values:

12, 14, 15, 16, 15, 18, 19, 20, 14

In this data array, two values (14 and 15) occur with a frequency of two. Therefore, the collection can be said to be bimodal, with modes 14 and 15. If no value appeared more than once, the data collection would have no mode.

Table 4.3 compares advantages and disadvantages of the mean, median, and mode.

TM

TABLE 4.3 A Comparison of the Mean, Median, and Mode

Average	Advantages	Disadvantages
Mean	Reflects the value of every data point Easy to compute and understand Has valuable mathematical properties; useful for further computations	Unduly influenced by extreme values
Median	Not distorted by extreme values	Lacking certain mathematical properties
Mode	Value that appears most frequently	Lacking certain mathematical properties Some data sets have no mode

In Chapter 3 frequency distributions were graphed as rectangles (histograms) or smooth curves (frequency polygons). A frequency polygon with many classes approaches a smooth curve (see Figure 4.1) with the frequency recorded on the *y*-axis and the class scale on the *x*-axis.

Analysts are frequently concerned about how data values are distributed, that is, how values in the data collection are spread out between the extremes. Differences among the mean, median, and mode can be easily seen from graphs of **symmetrical** and **skewed distributions.** Figure 4.1 shows three curves: one that is symmetrical (curve *a*) and two that are skewed (curves *b* and *c*). Curve *a* depicts a symmetrical distribution because a vertical line drawn from the peak of the curve to the horizontal axis will divide the area of the curve into two equal, symmetrical parts. Note that the mean, median, and mode are all located at the peak value of curve *a*.

TM FIGURE 4.1 Symmetrical and Skewed Distributions

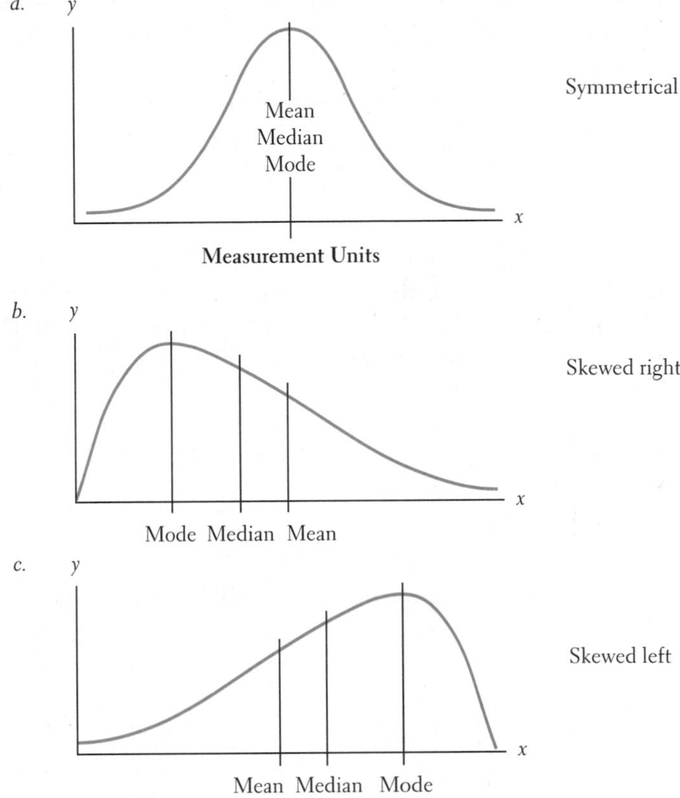

> A **symmetrical distribution** is represented by a curve that can be divided by a vertical line into two parts that are mirror images.

Curves *b* and *c* in Figure 4.1 are referred to as skewed curves because they lack symmetry. Values in such distributions are concentrated at either the low end or the high end of the scale along the horizontal axis. Curve *b* is skewed to the right, or the high end of the scale (such a distribution is sometimes referred to as *positively skewed*). The mean is drawn away from the highest point of the curve toward the skewed end. This is because the mean is sensitive to a few extreme values at that end of the curve. The mode (the value that occurs most frequently) is the *x* value corresponding to the highest point of the curve, and the median (the most typical value) is located between the mean and mode.

When the distribution is skewed to the left (curve *c* of Figure 4.1), the mean is pulled away from the highest point of the curve toward the low end of the scale. The median is pulled down, but not as much, and the mode remains at the highest point on the curve.

A **skewed distribution** is represented by a curve that lacks symmetry.

Figure 4.1 illustrates the effects of skewness on the three averages discussed in this section. In particular, this figure demonstrates the importance of determining the extent of skewness of a distribution before choosing among the averaging methods for a summary value. The median is generally the best measure of central tendency to use when a distribution is skewed.

Weighted Mean

The final measure of central tendency to be discussed in this chapter is the **weighted mean,** so named because in its calculation some data values are given more weight than others.

The **weighted mean** assigns more weight to some data values than to others.

In calculating the arithmetic mean of a data array using Equation 4.1 or 4.2, it's implicitly assumed that each data value carries the same weight. If, for some reason, certain data values are more important than others, different weights can be assigned to the values in calculating the mean.

Equation 4.4 is used to calculate the weighted mean for either a population or a sample:

$$\bar{x}_w = \frac{\sum_{i=1}^{n} w_i x_i}{\sum_{i=1}^{n} w_i} \tag{4.4}$$

where $\bar{x}_w$ = Weighted mean
x_i = Data values to be averaged
w_i = Weights applied to the x values

Note from Equation 4.4 that each selected weight is multiplied by the corresponding data value. Next these weighted values are summed. Finally, this summation of weighted values is divided by the summation of the weights. The result is the computation of a mean to which some data values contribute more than others.

EXAMPLE 4.9 Professor Chin gives three regular exams, a midterm, and a final exam in his statistics class each semester. These exam grades are averaged to determine each class member's final grade. The three regular exams each account for 15% of the grade, the midterm accounts for 25%, and the final accounts for 30%. Thus, the five exams' weights are .15, .15, .15, .25, .30. One class member achieves scores of 75, 82, 84, 79, and 91 during the quarter. Her final average score using the weighted mean is

$$\begin{aligned}\bar{x}_w &= \frac{w_1x_1 + w_2x_2 + w_3x_3 + w_4x_4 + w_5x_5}{w_1 + w_2 + w_3 + w_4 + w_5} \\ &= \frac{(.15)75 + (.15)82 + (.15)84 + (.25)79 + (.30)91}{.15 + .15 + .15 + .25 + .30} \\ &= \frac{83.2}{1} = 83.2\end{aligned}$$

EXAMPLE 4.10 Table 4.4 shows the percentage of the civilian labor force unemployed in three counties of Eastern Washington. Barbara McWilliams must make a presentation to the Spokane Economic Development Council showing the region's unemployment rate. Table 4.4 gives unemployment rates and labor force sizes for the three counties. She calculates the mean percentage unemployed for the three counties to be $(15.1 + 13.4 + 7.8)/3 = 12.1\%$. However, since Spokane County is much larger than the other two counties, Barbara feels that this figure doesn't truly reflect the region's unemployment rate. She decides that a weighted mean is more appropriate and calculates it using each county's civilian labor force as the weights:

$$\begin{aligned}\bar{x}_w &= \frac{(.151)(7{,}360) + (.134)(3{,}670) + (.078)(162{,}300)}{7{,}360 + 3{,}670 + 162{,}300} \\ &= \frac{14{,}263}{173{,}330} = .082\end{aligned}$$

The weighted average of the percentage of the labor force unemployed for the region is 8.2%. This value is much more representative of the region because it properly reflects the size of each county's labor force.

TABLE 4.4 Civilian Labor Force (Example 4.10)

County	Percentage unemployed	Civilian labor force
Adams	15.1	7,360
Pend Oreille	13.4	3,670
Spokane	7.8	162,300

Source: Washington State Employment Security Department, Labor Market and Economic Analysis Branch, July 1986.

The analyst must carefully choose which of the four methods of summarizing central tendency is most appropriate for a given data collection. The mean is commonly used but may not be appropriate if there are extreme values in the collection. In these cases, the median may provide a more accurate summary statistic. The mode is used when the value that occurs most frequently is desired. Its disadvantage is that this value may not accurately represent the entire collection. The weighted mean is used when certain data values are more important than others.

EXERCISES

1. Mean
2. Mode
3. Weighted mean
4. Median
5. Mean
6. Mean
7. Mean
8. Weighted mean

9. Median
11. Mean
12. Mode
13. Median
14. Mode

17*a*. Right
b. Symmetrical

1. Which measure of central tendency (mean, median, mode) is most sensitive to extreme values?
2. Which measure of central tendency is used to indicate the value with the greatest frequency?
3. Which measure of central tendency places differing amounts of importance on the values in a data collection?
4. When a data collection contains extreme values, which measure of central tendency should be used?
5. Which measure of central tendency takes into account the value of every item in a data collection in its computation?
6. Which measure of central tendency is useful for performing statistical procedures such as comparing central tendencies of several data sets?
7. Which measure of central tendency has mathematical properties that enable it to be easily used in further computations?
8. Which measure of central tendency allows different weights to be assigned to the values being averaged?
9. Which measure of central tendency would be a good choice for an average for a collection containing many small values and one very large value?
10. If one of the values slightly larger than the mean in a data collection is replaced by a very large value, does the mean go up, go down, or stay the same? How does this replacement affect the median?
11. If you wanted an average to be proportional to a community's total income, which measure of central tendency would you use?
12. If you wanted an average to represent income received by the most people in a community, which measure of central tendency would you use?
13. If you wanted an average to represent incomes of a community, in the sense that it would differ as little as possible from those incomes, which measure of central tendency would you use?
14. If you were to manufacture a new aluminum window screen and wished to produce only one size, which measure of central tendency would you use to assess market demand?
15. What is the difference between a sample statistic and a population parameter?
16. What is the difference between a symmetrical distribution and a skewed distribution?
17. Indicate whether the distribution for each of the following variables is symmetrical, skewed right, or skewed left:
    a. Annual household income.
    b. Lengths of rolls of wallpaper.

c. Left
d. Right
e. Symmetrical

c. Scores on a very easy statistics exam.

d. Family size.

e. Mileages of tires before wearout.

18. Indicate where the mean, median, and mode are located on each of the following types of distribution:

    a. Skewed right.

    b. Symmetrical.

    c. Skewed left.

    d. Values concentrated at the upper end of the scale.

    e. Symmetry lacking in the upper end.

19. Right

19. What is the shape of the distribution described by the following measures of central tendency: mean = 46, median = 42, mode = 39?

20. Symmetrical

20. What is the shape of the distribution described by the following measures of central tendency: mean = 3.1, median = 3.1, mode = 3.1?

21. Left

21. What is the shape of the distribution described by the following measures of central tendency: mean = 105, median = 110, mode = 115?

22. The following data show a population consisting of the number of Snickers candy bars purchased from a cafeteria vending machine on the first 10 days of operation: 7, 3, 0, 5, 8, b6, 7, 10, 1, 3.

22*a.* Mean = 5
Median = 5.5
Mode = 3 and 7
b. Median
c. Zero
d. 92, no

a. Calculate the mode, median, and mean for this data collection.

b. Which measure of central tendency would you use to estimate monthly sales of Snickers from this vending machine?

c. Compute the sum of the deviations from the mean: $\Sigma(x - \mu)$.

d. Compute the sum of the squared deviations from the mean: $\Sigma(x - \mu)^2$. Is it possible to obtain a smaller sum of squared deviations by using any number other than the mean?

23. Ten bear markets shown here have ravaged investors since the 1940s. In the rate of their descent, none of these declining markets rivaled what occurred in the fall of 1987. The most important question at that time was how long it would last.

Bear market	Months long
1948–1949	8
1953	8
1957	3
1960	10
1961–1962	7
1966	8
1968–1970	18
1973–1974	21
1976–1978	17
1981–1982	16

Source: "The Months Ahead," *Changing Times*, December 1987.

23a. 8
b. 9
c. 11.6
d. Median

a. What is the modal length of the bear market?
b. Which value divides the data collection into two equal parts?
c. Calculate the mean for this data collection.
d. Which of these measures of central tendency would you use to estimate the duration of the 1987 bear market?

24. Ted Mitchell, manager of Ted's Corner Grocery, investigates the average amount consumers spend on groceries during a one-week period. The following data represent the amounts spent last week by a randomly selected sample of 12 customers:

$ 65	$ 75	$ 85
153	250	99
80	191	55
131	93	182

24a. Mode = None
Median = 96
Mean = 121.58
b. Median

a. Calculate the mode, median, and mean for this data collection.
b. Which measure of central tendency would you use to indicate the typical amount of groceries purchased?

25. In 1989, franchise restaurant chains were expected to have U.S. sales of $70.4 billion, up 11.5% from the year before, according to an analysis prepared by *Restaurant Business* magazine and the consulting firm Technomic Inc. On a per-unit basis, 1989 sales for franchise chain outlets were expected to average $737,000. Here are data for the five leading chains based on total sales.

Restaurant chain	1989 sales (millions)	Number of units
McDonald's	$12,012	8,270
Burger King	5,110	5,361
Pizza Hut	3,100	6,050
Hardee's	3,040	3,327
Kentucky Fried Chicken	3,000	4,997

Source: *Industry Surveys*, March 15, 1990, p. L42.

25a. Median sales = $3,100 million
Median units = 5,361
Mean sales = $5,252.40 million
Mean units = 5,601
b. $937,761

a. Calculate the mode, median, and mean for both the 1989 sales and the number of franchises.
b. Compute the average per outlet for the five leading chains. Compare this value to what was expected from the consulting report.

26. Weighted mean, $7,920.67

26. Anderson Motors sold 53 Honda Civics in 1992 for the regular price of $8,250 (standard price, with options costing extra). In October, when the new models arrived, the 1993 standard price was reduced to $7,350. Anderson sold 15 Civics at this reduced price. In a December closeout sale Anderson sold 7 Civics for $6,650. What was the average price that Anderson received for Honda Civics in 1992 (not including cost of optional extras)?

27. Weighted mean, $2.11

27. Burt Distribution Corporation has a main office in Madison, Wisconsin, and a branch office in Cleveland. Branch manager Julie Pearson is concerned about the amount of money being spent on sending one- to two-pound packages to the main office. The following quantities indicate volumes of packages sent at different postal rates for the past year.

Type of mailing	Number of packages	Rate
Fourth class	2,023	$2.13
Third class	5,478	1.38
First class	8,457	2.40
Special delivery	1,023	2.95
Registered	423	3.60

What was the average cost of sending one- to two-pounds packages to the main office?

28. Perfection Tire Company wants to determine average mileage for a particular tire before wearout so it can establish a warranty policy. A sample is selected, and the following mileages are recorded to the nearest thousand miles:

33	41	55	47	38	45	47	46	48	39	40	40	41	42
38	48	50	49	36	44	44	45	42	35	46	43	47	47

28*a*. Mode = 47
Median = 44
Mean = 43.43
b. Left
c. Median

a. Calculate the mode, median, and mean for this data collection.
b. Is the data collection symmetrical or skewed?
c. Which measure of central tendency would you use to help determine the warranty policy?

29. Weighted mean, $37.86

29. Alton's Traction Headquarters sells four types of Goodyear tires, The following table lists the volume and price for each type of tire sold during a recent month:

Type of tire	Number sold	Price
F-32 radial	288	$49.95
Tiempo radial	940	29.95
Arriva radial	348	39.95
Vector radial	456	44.95

What was Alton's average revenue per Goodyear tire sold?

30. Jim Donaldson, marketing director of Clear Soft Drink Company, wants to determine the average selling price (in cents) for eight-ounce cans of soft drinks in Chicago supermarkets. He samples 44 brands and finds the following prices:

55	52	62	78	41	45	45	65	72	49	55
65	54	55	77	54	65	45	48	70	60	50
40	42	56	81	49	61	63	66	69	48	42
67	50	59	70	59	68	41	41	77	65	54

30*a*. Mode = 65
Median = 55.5
Mean = 57.5
b. Hard to tell
c. Median

a. Calculate the mode, median, and mean for this data collection.
b. Is the data collection symmetrical or skewed?
c. Which measure of central tendency should Jim Donaldson use if he's interested in determining the typical price of an eight-ounce can of pop?

MEASURES OF VARIABILITY

Computing a measure of central tendency for a data collection is a valuable way to summarize the numerical values, especially if there are a large number of them. There's another measurement of equal importance, however. We often need to know the extent of variability of the numbers in a data collection or distribution. The best descriptions of variability concern the deviations of the data values from some measure of central tendency, although other methods are also commonly used. This section presents three common measures of dispersion or variation: the range, variance, and standard deviation.

While measures of dispersion or variability are important in a variety of applications, there's probably no more important application area than quality control. It has been said that variability is the chief enemy of good quality. This is because consistency of output in a manufacturing operation is generally a sign of good quality, while extreme variability is generally a sign of poor quality. Chapter 13 ("Quality-Control Applications") explores variability and its relationship to the main job of business everywhere: achieving and maintaining good quality.

Range

The simplest measure of variability is the **range** (the difference between the highest and lowest values in a data set). Texaco's stock price varied from \$51 to \$54 in 1992, whereas Chevron's stock price varied from \$60 to \$78. Texaco's price range is \$54 − \$51 = \$3, while Chevron's is \$78 − \$60 = \$18. Comparison of ranges tells the analyst that Chevron's price was much more variable than Texaco's.

> The **range** is the difference between the highest and lowest values in a data set.

The range isn't always a good measure of variability. Whenever an extreme value is present in a distribution, the range will indicate excessive variation. For example, in Table 4.2 the range for retail chain sales is \$31,599 − \$2,490 = \$29,109. Sears' extremely large sales total has too much influence on the range.

The best descriptions of variability deal with deviations of the data values from some measure of central tendency. Since the mean has nice mathematical properties, it's a commonly used measure of central tendency. Next we'll look at two important measures of variability: variance and standard deviation.

Variance

The population **variance** is the average of the squared differences between the data values and the mean. It has certain mathematical properties that make it useful in other statistical applications; some of these uses will be presented in later chapters. However, interpreting the variance as the average of the squared differences isn't useful as a descriptive measure. Equation 4.5 shows how the variance for a population of data values is computed:

$$\sigma^2 = \frac{\Sigma(x - \mu)^2}{N} \tag{4.5}$$

where σ^2 = Population variance
x = Population values
μ = Population mean
N = Number of observations in the population

> The **variance** is the average of the squared differences between the data values and the mean.

V

EXAMPLE 4.11 Table 4.5 presents a population of five ages. The mean of this data array is found by summing the values and dividing by N, so $\mu = 200/5 = 40$. The mean age of 40 accurately describes the central tendency of the data collection. But what about variability? To what extent do the data values differ from their mean? Column 2 of Table 4.5 calculates and sums the deviations from the mean. However, taking the average of these deviations provides no indication of variability. The summation equals 0 since the mean is at the mathematical center of the array, and the negative values cancel out the positive values. Example 4.1 illustrated this concept.

TM

TABLE 4.5 Data Collection of Ages (Examples 4.11 and 4.12)

x	$x - \mu$	$(x - \mu)^2$
20	−20	400
30	−10	100
40	0	0
50	10	100
60	20	400
Sums: 200	0	1,000

$\Sigma x = 200$; $\Sigma(x - \mu) = 0$
$\Sigma(x - \mu)^2 = 1{,}000$
Mean $= \mu = 200/5 = 40$
Variance $= \sigma^2 = 1{,}000/5 = 200$
Standard deviation $= \sigma = \sqrt{200} = 14.1$

One mathematical approach to eliminating the minus signs is to square each deviation (column 3 of Table 4.5). After squaring the deviations, Equation 4.5 is applied and the variance of ages is computed:

$$\sigma^2 = \frac{\Sigma(x - \mu)^2}{N} = \frac{1{,}000}{5} = 200$$

Unfortunately, knowing that the average squared deviation in Example 4.11 equals 200 isn't very meaningful. One solution to this problem is to return to the original units of measure by taking the square root of the variance. Equation 4.6 shows how the square root of the variance, called the population **standard deviation,** is computed.

Standard Deviation

The standard deviation is the standard amount by which the values in a data collection differ from the mean:

$$\sigma = \sqrt{\frac{\Sigma(x - \mu)^2}{N}} \tag{4.6}$$

> The **standard deviation** measures the standard amount by which the values in a data collection differ from the mean.

EXAMPLE 4.12 The last column of Table 4.5 shows values for use in Equation 4.6 to compute the standard deviation of the population data. This column shows the squared difference between each data value and the mean of the distribution, 40. The sum of these squared deviations is 1,000, and their average is 200. The square root of 200 is 14.1, so this is the standard deviation of the data array. The data values have a mean of 40 and a standard deviation of 14.1. This means that the standard amount by which the values in the array differ from their mean (40) is about 14.1.

The standard deviation is commonly used to describe the extent to which a collection of data values is dispersed around its mean. A small standard deviation means that the values tend to be close to their mean. A large standard deviation means that the values are widely scattered about their mean.

V The data of Table 4.5 were defined to be a population and Equations 4.5 and 4.6 were used to calculate population variance and standard deviation. If the measured data constitute a sample, the calculation differs slightly and Equation 4.7 is used to calculate the sample variance. Also, the sample standard deviation is computed by taking the square root of the sample variance ($s = \sqrt{s^2}$). Note in Equation 4.7 that the denominator is 1 less than the sample size ($n - 1$) rather than the entire population size (N) used in Equations 4.5 and 4.6. Note also that while the Greek letter σ (sigma) was used to represent the population parameter, the letter s is used to represent the sample statistic:

Sample variance

$$s^2 = \frac{\Sigma(x - \bar{x})^2}{n - 1} \tag{4.7}$$

where s^2 = Sample variance
s = Sample standard deviation
x = The sample values
$\bar{x}$ = Sample mean
n = Number of observations in the sample

Degrees of Freedom V The denominator in Equation 4.7, ($n - 1$), represents **degrees of freedom.** This term appears frequently in statistical applications and refers to the number of data values in the sample that are free of each other in the sense that they carry unique information.

Degrees of freedom refers to the number of data elements that are free to vary.

The sample standard deviation calculation of Equation 4.7 uses the sample mean ($\bar{x}$) as an estimate of the population mean (μ). If the sum of the squared deviations in Equation 4.7's numerator were divided by the sample size, n, a biased variance would result. That is, the value of s^2, which is an estimate of the unknown population variance (σ^2), would tend, over many trials, to be slightly too small. This is because the $\Sigma(x - \bar{x})^2$ computation provides a minimum value, as Example 4.2 illustrated. Had the actual population mean been used in Equation 4.7, the numerator would probably have been slightly larger.

Mathematicians have discovered that the small-size bias of Equation 4.7's numerator is compensated for by reducing the denominator as well. By using $(n - 1)$ in the denominator of the sample variance calculation, the bias is removed and an unbiased estimate of the unknown population variance results.

In general, a piece of sample information is lost each time a sample statistic is used to estimate an unknown population parameter in an equation. In Equation 4.7, it would be preferable to measure the sampled items' variability around the true population mean, but since this value isn't known, an estimate—the sample mean—is used in its place.

A shortcut formula has been derived for calculating the sample variance and standard deviation. This is handy when the data being evaluated number more than a few items. Equation 4.8 is the shortcut formula to compute the sample variance. The sample standard deviation is computed by taking the square root of this variance:

$$s^2 = \frac{\Sigma x^2 - \dfrac{(\Sigma x)^2}{n}}{n - 1} \tag{4.8}$$

Both the sum of the sample x values and the sum of their squared values are needed for the calculation. Note that Σx^2 does not equal $(\Sigma x)^2$, as Chapter 1 pointed out.

It is easy to become confused by all the equations used to compute the variance and standard deviation. However, Equation 4.8 can be used in most cases since real-world situations usually involve samples.

EXAMPLE 4.13 Table 4.6 shows a data collection representing the number of units sold per day in a random sample of selling days for Jarms, an appliance dealer. As shown, the mean of the sample is 7.08 units. Since the data represent a sample,

TABLE 4.6 Jarms Appliances Sold (Example 4.13)

4	5	12	9	10	8
7	4	5	3	0	1
8	2	15	7	9	11
9	8	7	8	6	12

$n = 24$
$\Sigma x = 170$
$\bar{x} = 170/24 = 7.08$
$\Sigma x^2 = 1,512$

Equation 4.8 can be used to calculate the standard deviation. The x^2 values used to compute this sum are:

16	25	144	81	100	64
49	16	25	9	0	1
64	4	225	49	81	121
81	64	49	64	36	144

The variance can now be computed using Equation 4.8:

$$s^2 = \frac{\Sigma x^2 - \frac{(\Sigma x)^2}{n}}{n - 1} = \frac{1,512 - \frac{(170)^2}{24}}{24 - 1} = \frac{307.8}{23} = 13.38$$

The square root of the variance is the standard deviation:

$$s = \sqrt{13.38} = 3.66$$

Jarms Appliances sells an average (mean) of 7.08 units per day. Typical variation in these sales is 3.66 units from the mean of 7.08.

Many handheld calculators automatically figure the mean and standard deviation. In calculating standard deviation, we must know whether the data constitute a population or a sample so that the proper denominator can be used. Calculators commonly have two keys for this purpose: the N key for populations and the $(n - 1)$ key for samples.

In addition, most data analysis programs for either mainframe or personal computers include the mean and standard deviation as summary measures of data collections. The MINITAB commands for computing descriptive statistics for the Jarms Appliance Store example are:

```
MTB>   SET INTO C1
DATA> 4 5 12 9 10  8 7 4 5 3 0 1 8 2 15 7 9 11 9
DATA> 8 7 8 6 12
DATA> END
MTB>   DESCRIBE C1

             N      MEAN     MEDIAN     TRMEAN    STDEV    SEMEAN
C1          24     7.083      7.500      7.045    3.658     0.747

           MIN       MAX         Q1         Q3
C1       0.000    15.000      4.250      9.000

MTB > STOP
```

The "MINITAB Computer Package" section at the end of this chapter explains these MINITAB commands and the output.

Figure 4.2 shows the variability of the mean and standard deviation for different data distributions. In part *a,* three distributions appear. Since they all have the same shape, these three symmetrical distributions clearly have the same standard deviation. That is, data values in all three distributions are approximately the same distance from their respective means. However, their means are different; each is at a different point on the horizontal axis.

TM

FIGURE 4.2 Data Distributions

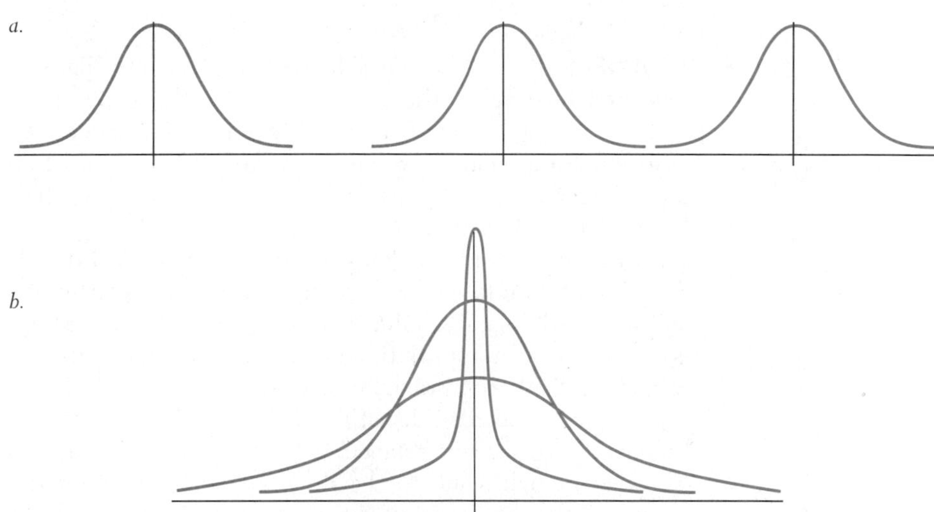

By contrast, the three symmetrical curves of part *b* all have the same mean. However, their standard deviations are different. The widest curves' data values are typically far from the mean compared with the middle curve's, and the inner-curve data values are even more tightly packed about the mean. Figure 4.2 illustrates the importance of knowing both the mean and standard deviation of a data distribution for an accurate summary of the distribution.

Coefficient of Variation

Another method sometimes used to measure the variability of a population or sample of data values is the **coefficient of variation.** This statistic specifies the size of the standard deviation as a percentage of the mean. It is calculated by dividing the standard deviation by the mean. The coefficient of variation indicates the *relative* amount of variability in a distribution.

V

> The **coefficient of variation** for a data collection expresses the standard deviation as a percentage of the mean.

Equation 4.9 is used to calculate the coefficient of variation for a sample. The abbreviation CV is used for this statistic:

$$\text{CV} = \frac{s}{\bar{x}}(100) \tag{4.9}$$

Note that for a population, s in the numerator would be replaced by σ, and $\bar{x}$ in the denominator would be replaced by μ.

Decision makers use the coefficient of variation to: (1) determine how reliable the mean is as a measure of central tendency, (2) assess whether the standard deviation is large, small, or somewhere in between, or (3) compare two or more distributions' variability.

EXAMPLE 4.14 The president of First Federal Bank was nervous about an attempted takeover of the bank, especially after reading a *Wall Street Journal* article (April 15, 1992) about Banc One's plans to buy Valley National Bank of Arizona, reportedly for around \$1.23 billion. Although there had been no specific threat against First Federal Bank, the president and bank board wanted certain facts and figures about the bank right away.

Kim Horns, a new analyst for the bank, was asked to collect a number of statistics for presentation to the bank board. She was to compare the average account balances at the downtown and suburban branches. A random sample of savings account balances was drawn from both locations. For the main office, the mean account balance was \$1,248.50 with standard deviation of \$537.93. At the branch, the mean was \$743.84 with standard deviation of \$325.10. Kim saw that the suburban branch had a lower average account balance, but she found it difficult to compare the variability of the two branches due to the difference in means. For this reason, Kim decided to compute the coefficient of variation for each branch:

Main office:

$$\text{CV} = \frac{s}{\bar{x}}(100) = \frac{537.93}{1{,}248.50}(100) = 43.1\%$$

Suburban office:

$$\text{CV} = \frac{s}{\bar{x}}(100) = \frac{325.10}{743.84}(100) = 43.7\%$$

Clearly, both the mean and standard deviation of account balances at the suburban branch are smaller than at the main office. However, as a percentage of their means, the two offices' standard deviations are about equal. In this sense, the variability of account balances at the two locations is relatively the same.

MEASURES OF POSITION

Suppose that a person feels he is drastically underpaid compared with other people with similar experience and background. One way to demonstrate this condition is to obtain these other employees' salaries and show the discrepancy. A measure of position

Percentile

or relative standing can be used to evaluate an individual salary compared with the entire group. One measure of the position of a particular observation is its **percentile ranking.** The pth percentile is the value of x such that p percent of the observations fall below the pth percentile and $(100 - p)$ percent lie above it.

> The pth **percentile** is the value of x such that p% of the observations fall below the pth percentile and $(100 - p)$% lie above it.

For example, the person who felt underpaid discovered that he was in the 20th percentile. This means that 20% of all employees with similar experience and background have salaries below his and 80% have higher salaries.

Percentiles divide observations into 100 parts of equal size. The procedure for obtaining a particular percentile is similar to the computation of the median. In fact, the median describes the 50th percentile. Deciles divide observations into 10 parts of equal size. Quartiles divide observations into four parts of equal size.

Another measure of position is a **standard score.** Like a percentile, a standard score determines the relative position of any particular data value, x. The standard score indicates the number of standard deviations by which a particular value lies above or below the mean. Standard scores are discussed in detail in Chapter 6.

Since the standard deviation is a measure of standard distance from the mean, knowing the mean and standard deviation provides the analyst with great insight about the data from which they were computed. Two important statistical concepts are often used in this process: Chebyshev's theorem and the empirical rule.

Chebyshev's Theorem

Chebyshev's theorem (sometimes referred to as *Tchebysheff's theorem*), credited to Russian mathematician P. L. Chebyshev, states that no matter what the shape of a distribution, at least 75% of the values will fall within ± 2 standard deviations of the mean of the distribution, and at least 89% of the values will lie within ± 3 standard deviations of the mean. Chebyshev's theorem will be discussed in detail in Chapter 6.

Empirical Rule

A popular rule of thumb in statistics, the **empirical rule,** involves a collection of data values that is symmetrical about its mean with most values close to the mean. Figure 4.3 shows a bell-shaped distribution with the following characteristics:

1. Approximately 68% of the values are within one standard deviation of the mean.
2. Approximately 95% of the values are within two standard deviations of the mean.
3. Approximately 99.7% of the values are within three standard deviations of the mean.

Note that Chebyshev's theorem is extremely conservative compared to the empirical rule (75% of the values instead of 95% lie within two standard deviations). The reason is that Chebyshev's theorem applies to any population or sample, without regard to the shape of the distribution. The empirical rule is also discussed in depth in Chapter 6.

Finally, it should be noted that the data used in this chapter to illustrate key concepts are **raw data,** that is, they consist of individual measurements. Table 4.6 is an

FIGURE 4.3 Bell-Shaped Distribution

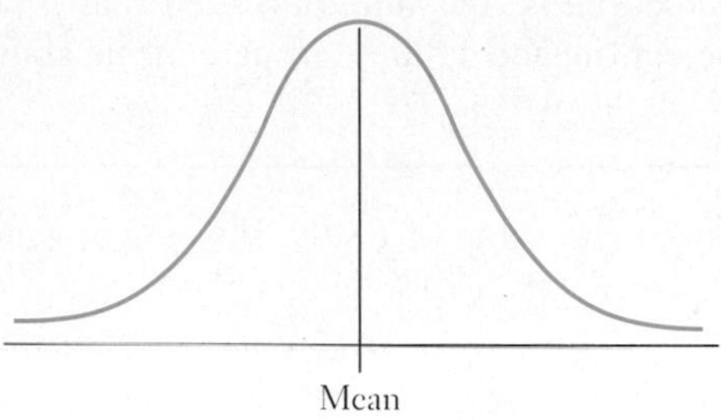

example of raw data. By contrast, many data sets are presented in **grouped data** form. The frequency distribution described in Chapter 3 is presenting grouped data (see Table 3.5).

Sometimes summary statistics must be calculated such as mean and standard deviation from grouped data. When this is necessary, each data value is assumed to have the value of the midpoint of its data category, since specific data values aren't given. After making this conversion, the formulas presented in this chapter can be used. Example 4.15 shows how the grouped data from a frequency distribution are converted to estimated raw data values so that formulas such as Equations 4.2 and 4.8 can be used.

EXAMPLE 4.15 The following frequency distribution has been constructed to show a data collection.

Class	Frequency
5–9	2
10–14	3
15–19	4

To calculate the estimated mean and standard deviation of the original data set, each value is assumed to take on the value of the middle or midpoint of its class. That is, each value in the 5–9 class is assumed to equal 7; values in the 10–14 class are all assumed to be 12; and values in the 15–19 range are assumed to be 17. This conversion results in the estimated original data set

7 7 12 12 12 17 17 17 17

We can now use the raw data formulas (Equations 4.2 and 4.8).

EXERCISES

SSM

31. What is the difference between a measure of central tendency and a measure of variability?
32. What is the difference between standard deviation and variance?
33. What is the difference between absolute variation and relative variation?

34. Why are deviations from the mean *squared* in computing standard deviation?

35. In the formula for sample standard deviation, why is the sum of squared deviations divided by $(n - 1)$ instead of by n?

36. Why is the concept of degrees of freedom important?

37. Suppose you live in an area where the standard deviation for the average weekly amount of rainfall is zero. Describe your climate.

SM

38. Jim Perez, customer service manager for National Tune-up Corporation, collected the following data representing the number of complaints his department received on each of eight randomly selected days:

    10, 12, 8, 5, 11, 10, 9, 14

    a. Compute the range.
    b. Compute the standard deviation.
    c. Compute the variance.
    d. Compute the coefficient of variation.
    e. Interpret each of these measures of variability.

38*a.* 9
b. 2.696
c. 7.268
d. 27.3%

39. Phoenix Body & Frame employs eight workers. The following data collection shows each worker's years of experience: 1, 7, 9, 15, 9, 1, 7, 15. Treat this data collection as a population.

    a. Compute the standard deviation.
    b. If a worker with 8 years of experience is added, how will this affect the standard deviation?
    c. If a worker with 15 years of experience replaces a worker with 7 years of experience, how will this affect the standard deviation?
    d. If a worker with no years of experience replaces a worker with 7 years of experience, how will this affect the standard deviation?

39*a.* 5
b. Reduce it
c. Increase
d. Increase

40. As a manufacturer of some product requiring great uniformity (interchangeability of parts), would you be interested in a product whose pertinent characteristics included a large or small standard deviation?

40. Small

41. The ages of some people in an office are 23, 25, 34, 35, 37, 41, 42, and 56. Treat this data collection as a sample.

    a. Compute the range.
    b. Compute the standard deviation.
    c. Compute the variance.
    d. Compute the coefficient of variation.

41*a.* 33
b. 10.38
c. 107.74
d. 28.3%

SM

42. Last year at this time, personal loan data at Farmers and Merchants Bank showed a mean of \$650 and a standard deviation of \$300. Recently the mean was calculated to be \$1,000 and the standard deviation \$350. Did loans last year show more or less relative variation than recent loans?

42. CV(1) = 46.2%
CV(2) = 35%

43. Michelle Wang wants to determine the variability of the amounts of checks she writes during a typical month. The following data collection represents 11 checks randomly selected from last month's personal checking account: \$8.63, \$102.36, \$45.00, \$50.12,

43. Mean = \$64.52
SD = \$62.18

$75.65, $9.87, $224.56, $78.95, $78.98, $15.62, $20.00. What is the average amount per check? What is the standard amount of variability per check?

44. $\bar{x}$ = $19,964.29
    s = 6,979.78
    CV = 34.96%
    CV = 14.29%

44. The annual salaries of Lake City Transmission's seven workers are $15,000, $22,000, $25,000, $17,500, $14,500, $32,500, and $13,250. A competitor, Transmission Exchange Company, pays workers a mean annual salary of $21,000 with standard deviation of $3,000. Compare the two companies' means and relative variability.

45*a*. 178.67
b. 13.37
c. 62.7%
d. Right
e. Increase
f. Decrease

45. Dick Hoover, owner of Modern Office Equipment, is concerned about freight costs and clerical costs incurred on small orders. To reduce expenditures in this area, he'll introduce a discount policy for orders over $40 to encourage customers to consolidate a number of small orders into large orders. The mean amounts per transaction for a sample of 28 customers are

    10, 15, 20, 25, 15, 17, 41, 50, 5, 9, 12, 14, 35, 18,
    19, 17, 28, 29, 11, 11, 43, 54, 7, 8, 16, 13, 37, 18

    a. Compute the variance.
    b. Compute the standard deviation.
    c. Compute the coefficient of variation.
    d. Is the distribution symmetrical, positively skewed, or negatively skewed?
    e. If the policy is successful, will the mean of the distribution increase, decrease, or remain the same?
    f. If the policy is successful, will the standard deviation of the distribution increase, decrease, or remain the same?

46. Describe what the standard deviation measures.

SUMMARY

This chapter has presented various quantitative measurements to summarize essential characteristics of data collections. It described methods to measure and summarize the two key elements of a data collection: central tendency and variability.

The mean, median, mode, and weighted mean were presented as methods of indicating a central summary value for a data collection. The range, variance, standard deviation, and coefficient of variation were presented as methods to indicate the degree of variability. The analyst must carefully choose among these methods in computing summary statistics so that they fairly and accurately summarize the underlying data collection.

APPLICATIONS OF STATISTICAL CONCEPTS IN THE BUSINESS WORLD

A HOSPITAL'S USE OF STANDARD DEVIATION

Bill Fisher is the chief financial officer at a hospital in Spokane, Washington. Several years ago he took two statistics classes from the authors while earning his bachelor's degree in business administration.

The federal government pays Bill's hospital in accordance with established dollar values for various procedures. The government recognizes that there is variability in the actual amount hospitals spend for various treatments, but makes a standard payment for each, with one exception. If the amount of the treatment exceeds three standard deviations above the mean, the government will make a special payment to the hospital to cover this procedure but only after careful review.

Bill keeps continuous track of the mean and standard deviation of each procedure covered by government reimbursement, and he compares the cost of each patient treatment with the three-standard-deviation upper limit. When the hospital's cost for a treatment exceeds the mean plus three standard deviations, he requests an additional payment.

During the previous year, one patient alone exceeded the three-standard-deviation upper limit by almost $300,000. By knowing the mean plus three-standard-deviation limit, Bill was able to claim this extra amount from Medicare for the hospital.

OTHER APPLICATIONS

The two essential components of any data collection, measures of central tendency and variability, are commonly used as summary values. Accountants, for example, constantly deal with numerical values and employ summary figures to describe various accounts' current condition and to make comparisons over time.

Financial data abound in the business world and are routinely summarized so their essential properties can be analyzed and used by decision makers. Production or manufacturing functions in businesses measure such things as output, temperature, and pressure. These data values must be briefly described using summary statistics if they are to be useful to managers.

Personnel records contain many quantitative variables (overtime hours per week, years of education, months with the company, and hourly rate of pay, for example) that must be summarized for use in intelligent decision making.

Although several measurements made in marketing result in categorical data, many quantitative measurements are used too. Examples are units sold per day, dollar volume per day for each department in a retail store, number of credit card uses per month by customers, and number of units sold for each type and style of product.

A key aspect of any business in this highly competitive age is quality control. Summary measures such as those discussed in this chapter are commonly used to measure such indications of quality as defective units per batch, variability of a manufacturing process, and sizes and weights of parts.

GLOSSARY

Arithmetic mean The sum of the numerical values in a collection divided by the number of values. The symbol for the population mean is the Greek letter μ (mu). The symbol for a sample mean is $\bar{x}$ (x-bar).

Parameter Any measurable characteristic of a population.

Statistic Any measurable characteristic of a sample.

Median The middle item in a set of observations that are arranged in order of magnitude.

Mode The value that occurs most frequently in a data collection.

Symmetrical distribution A curve that can be divided by a vertical line into two parts that are mirror images.

Skewed distribution A curve that lacks symmetry.

Weighted mean A mean computation in which some data values are assigned more weight than others.

Range The difference between the highest and lowest values in a data set.

Variance The average of the squared differences between the data values and the mean.

Standard deviation A measure of the standard amount by which the values in a data collection differ from the mean.

Degrees of freedom The number of data elements that are free to vary.

Coefficient of variation The standard deviation expressed as a percentage of the mean.

Percentile A value of x such that $p\%$ of the observations fall below the pth percentile and $(100 - p)\%$ lie above it.

Key Formulas

Arithmetic mean—population

$$\mu = \frac{\Sigma x}{N} \tag{4.1}$$

Arithmetic mean—sample

$$\bar{x} = \frac{\Sigma x}{n} \tag{4.2}$$

Median

$$\text{Median item number} = \frac{n + 1}{2} \tag{4.3}$$

Weighted mean

$$\bar{x}_w = \frac{\sum_{i=1}^{n} w_i x_i}{\sum_{i=1}^{n} w_i} \tag{4.4}$$

Variance—population

$$\sigma^2 = \frac{\Sigma(x - \mu)^2}{N} \tag{4.5}$$

Standard deviation—population

$$\sigma = \sqrt{\frac{\Sigma(x - \mu)^2}{N}} \tag{4.6}$$

Variance—sample

$$s^2 = \frac{\Sigma(x - \bar{x})^2}{n - 1} \tag{4.7}$$

Variance—sample

$$s^2 = \frac{\Sigma x^2 - \frac{(\Sigma x)^2}{n}}{n - 1} \quad (4.8)$$

Coefficient of variation

$$CV = \frac{s}{\bar{x}}(100) \quad (4.9)$$

SOLVED EXERCISES

1. CHOOSING AMONG THE MEAN, MEDIAN, MODE, AND WEIGHTED MEAN

Which measure of central tendency should be used in each of the following situations?

a. You want to determine the average annual percentage rate of net profit to sales for the General Electric Company for the past seven years.

b. You want to determine the average amount each worker receives per month to ensure a fair distribution in a profit-sharing plan.

c. You want to determine a representative wage value for use in arbitration for Precision Landscape Systems. The company employs 200 workers, including several highly paid specialists.

Solution:

a. The weighted mean should be used to weight the profit rates by the sales values for each year.

b. The mean should be used to divide the total profits to be shared by workers.

c. The median should be used so that the highly paid specialists' salaries don't distort the representative wage value.

2. COMPUTATION OF MEAN, MEDIAN, AND MODE

June Shapiro is thinking about starting an advertising agency and is interested in analyzing firms that operate in the Little Rock area. The following data collection shows a sample of the local agencies, 1992 total billings, and the number of full-time employees.

Agency	Billings ($ millions)	Employees
Wendt Advertising	7.4	29
Clark, White & Associates	5.0	31
Coons, Corker & Associates	3.5	10
Elgee Corporation	2.1	3
Pierce-Stuart & Associates	1.5	8
Robideaux & Associates	1.2	15
Pacific Advertising	1.0	4
Bright Ideas, Inc.	1.0	5
Creative Consultants	.4	1
Degerness & Associates	.3	3
Rasor & Associates	.2	4

a. Compare the mean, median, and mode for 1992 billings per agency.

b. Which measure of central tendency should June use if she wants the typical amount of 1992 billings?

c. Compute the mean, median, and mode for the number of employees per agency.

d. Which measure of central tendency should June use if she wants to measure variability as well?

Solution:

x	x^2	y	y^2
7.4	54.76	29	841
5.0	25.00	31	961
3.5	12.25	10	100
2.1	4.41	3	9
1.5	2.25	8	64
1.2	1.44	15	225
1.0	1.00	4	16
1.0	1.00	5	25
.4	.16	1	1
.3	.09	3	9
.2	.04	4	16
23.6	102.40	113	2,267

a. Mean $= \bar{x} = \dfrac{\Sigma x}{n} = \dfrac{23.6}{11} = 2.1455$

Median item number $= \dfrac{n+1}{2} = \dfrac{11+1}{2} = \dfrac{12}{2} = 6$

Median $= 1.2$
Mode $= 1.0$

b. June should use the median, 1.2, if she wants the typical amount. This value is not unduly influenced by the billings of $7.4 million for Wendt Advertising.

c. Mean $= \bar{x} = \dfrac{\Sigma x}{n} = \dfrac{113}{11} = 10.273$

Median item number $= \dfrac{n+1}{2} = \dfrac{11+1}{2} = \dfrac{12}{2} = 6$

Median $= 5$
Mode $= 3, 4$

d. Since June wants to perform further computations, such as finding the standard deviation, she should use the mean, 10.273.

3. COMPUTATION OF VARIANCE AND STANDARD DEVIATION
Refer to the data June Shapiro collected in Solved Exercise 2.

a. Compute the variance and standard deviation for billings per agency.

b. Compute the variance and standard deviation for number of employees per agency.

Solution:

a. Variance:

$$s^2 = \frac{\Sigma x^2 - \frac{(\Sigma x)^2}{n}}{n - 1} = \frac{102.4 - \frac{(23.6)^2}{11}}{11 - 1} = \frac{51.77}{10} = 5.18$$

Standard deviation:

$s = 2.276$

b. Variance:

$$s^2 = \frac{\Sigma x^2 - \frac{(\Sigma x)^2}{n}}{n - 1} = \frac{2{,}267 - \frac{(113)^2}{11}}{11 - 1} = \frac{1{,}106}{10} = 110.6$$

Standard deviation:

$s = 10.52$

4. COMPUTATION OF THE COEFFICIENT OF VARIATION

Refer to the data June Shapiro collected in Solved Exercise 2.

a. Compute the coefficient of variation for billings per agency.

b. Compute the coefficient of variation for number of employees per agency.

Solution:

a. $\text{CV} = \frac{s}{\bar{x}}(100) = \frac{2.276}{2.1455}(100) = 106\%$

b. $\text{CV} = \frac{s}{\bar{x}}(100) = \frac{10.52}{10.273}(100) = 102.4\%$

EXERCISES

47. Mean

48. Median

49*a*. Mean = 27
Median = 28
b. SD = 5.54
c. Decreases
d. Both decrease
e. Increases

47. Which measure of central tendency is a good choice for an average if further computations are needed?

48. For a certain operation, a factory supervisor is told to set a standard time that "differs as little as possible from the time now taken by all the employees in the shop." The supervisor should use which measure of central tendency?

49. Adams Tractor Company employs six workers aged 21, 27, 19, 35, 31, and 29. Treat this data collection as a population.

    a. Compute the mean and median.

    b. Compute the standard deviation.

    c. If a new worker of age 27 is added, how will this affect the standard deviation?

    d. (This question refers to the original six workers.) If a worker of age 20 replaces the worker who's 35, how will this affect the mean and standard deviation?

    e. (This question refers to the original six workers.) If a worker of age 38 replaces the worker who's 27, how will this affect the standard deviation?

50. Mean = 970,382
Median = 792,028

50. The largest 12 U.S. daily newspapers have daily circulations as listed below (as of March 31, 1988). Treat this data collection as a population. Compute the mean and median.

Newspaper	Circulation
The Wall Street Journal	2,025,176
USA Today	1,345,271
New York Daily News	1,283,302
Los Angeles Times	1,132,920
New York Times	1,078,443
Washington Post	810,011
Chicago Tribune	774,045
Detroit News	688,218
Newsday	665,218
Detroit Free Press	647,763
Chicago Sun Times	625,035
San Francisco Chronicle	569,185

Source: Audit Bureau of Circulation.

51. The following data collection shows the current number of enrollees, the number of companies or groups served, and the number of primary physicians for the top Spokane-area health care plans. Treat this data collection as a population.

Organization	Enrollees	Companies	Physicians
HMOs:			
HMO Washington	161	14	46
Foundation Health Plan	3,569	139	145
Group Health Northwest	30,000	350	26
HealthPlus	10,500	125	47
Maxicare Washington	173	11	12
PPOs:			
United Northwest Services	50,000	10	170
Inland Health Associates	29,000	9	86
Medical Services Corp.	17,373	580	541
First Choice Health Plan	3,836	291	43
Blue Cross Prudent Buyer	3,128	33	114

Source: "Hospitals Health Care & Insurance," *Journal of Business*, Nov. 25–Dec. 9, 1987.

51*a*. Mean = 14,774
SD = 16,692
b. Mean = 156
SD = 193
c. Mean = 123
SD = 156
d. Median = 7,168
e. Median = 79
f. Median = 66.5
g. No

a. Compute the mean and standard deviation of the number of enrollees in the 10 health plans.

b. Compute the mean and standard deviation of the number of companies or groups served by the 10 health plans.

c. Compute the mean and standard deviation of the number of primary physicians used by the 10 health plans.

d. Compute the median number of enrollees in the 10 health plans.

e. Compute the median number of companies or groups served by the 10 health plans.

f. Compute the median number of primary physicians used by the 10 health plans.

g. Is there any application for the weighted mean in this data collection?

51*h*. Median

h. Which average would you choose (mean or median) for each data collection if you wanted to describe the typical health care plan?

i. Compute the coefficient of variation for the five HMOs and the five preferred provider organizations (PPOs) for each of the three data collections. Compare the relative variability of the two types of health care plans.

52. The Hord Automobile Manufacturing Company is considering two brands of batteries for its latest model. The Telco battery has a mean lifetime of 55 months with a standard deviation of 5 months. The Long-Life battery has a mean lifetime of 45 months with a standard deviation of 3 months.

52*a*. Telco
b. Long-Life

a. If the decision criterion for selecting a brand of battery is maximum lifetime, which brand should be selected?

b. Which brand should be selected if consistency of service is the decision criterion?

53. Mean = 7.7
Median = 8
Mode = 8
SD = 2.01

53. The following data represent net income as a percentage of sales (rounded to the nearest full percentage during 1992 for a random sample of 70 of the 500 largest industrial corporations:

5	6	8	10	4	9	7
9	6	4	9	10	9	8
3	9	5	9	9	8	7
10	2	7	4	8	5	10
9	6	8	8	8	7	8
6	11	9	11	7	7	11
10	8	8	5	9	8	8
8	9	10	7	7	7	5
8	7	9	9	8	6	9
5	8	8	7	9	13	8

Compute summary measures for this distribution. Write a memo to management comparing your company's percentage, which is 9, to this distribution.

54. Before deciding on purchasing stock in the Electronic Research & Development Corporation, the management of Fidelity Investments, a mutual fund, wants data on price movements of the firm's stock during the past year. Thirty-five days of the past year were randomly selected, and the closing price (to the nearest dollar) was recorded for each day:

43	29	42	35	32	28	22
52	34	35	32	28	50	33
34	37	29	30	28	29	24
39	27	40	43	48	33	48
29	28	39	36	49	26	47

54*a*. Mean = 35.37
b. SD = 8.14
c. CV(ITS) = 19.7%
CV(ERDC) = 23%

a. Fidelity decides not to purchase the stock unless the mean closing price for last year is $34 or more. Is further analysis of these data necessary?

b. Fidelity is also interested in this stock's variability. They won't invest in it if the usual variation from the mean price is more than $10. Would they be interested?

c. Finally, Fidelity needs to compare Electronic Research & Development Corporation stock to that of Innovative Technology Systems. Fidelity is satisfied with both stocks and will purchase the one with less relative variability in price. If Innovative Technology Systems stock has a mean price of $61 and standard deviation of $12, which stock should Fidelity purchase?

55. Demand for both covered and open boat slips on Lake Pend Oreille in Idaho is:

	Covered		Open		
Marina	Occupied	Vacant	Occupied	Vacant	Total
The Captn's Table	0	0	22	3	25
Lee Peters Moorage	44	0	19	2	65
Sunset Resort	0	0	18	10	28
Bottle Bay Resort	0	0	20	2	22
Sandpoint Marina	26	0	109	0	135
Windbag Marina	0	0	60	0	60
Holiday Shores	0	0	33	2	35
Ellisport Marina	0	0	75	0	75
Pend Oreille Shores	0	0	33	32	65
Unknown name	0	0	63	7	70
Scenic Bay Marina	58	0	116	3	177
Vista Bay Resort	30	0	36	4	70
Bitter End Marina	0	0	103	2	105
Bayview Marina	65	0	13	2	80
Boileau's	119	1	20	4	144
McDonald's Hudson Bay Resort	90	0	90	0	180
Totals	432	1	830	73	1,336

Source: *Development Plan for Harbor View Marina in Garfield Bay on Lake Pend Oreille.* J & H Research Service, November 1987.

Metropolitan Mortgage & Securities Company has repossessed a vacant marina and is trying to decide how many slips to develop. Write a memo to Metropolitan summarizing the number of covered, open, and total boat slips presently on the lake, along with the percent vacant of each.

56. The *merchandise trade balance* is computed by finding the difference between merchandise exported and merchandise imported (exports minus imports). In 1980, the United States exported merchandise worth $221 billion and imported merchandise valued at $245 billion for a trade balance of negative $24 billion. In 1990, the United States exported merchandise worth $394 billion and imported merchandise valued at $495 billion for a trade balance of negative $101 billion. U.S. exports to and imports from a sample of nine countries in 1980 and 1990 (in millions of dollars) were:

	1980		1990	
Country	Exports	Imports	Exports	Imports
Austria	$ 447	$ 389	$ 873	$ 1,316
Bolivia	172	182	139	203
France	7,485	5,265	13,652	13,124
Japan	20,790	18,672	48,585	89,655
Mexico	15,145	12,580	28,378	30,172
Norway	843	2,632	1,281	1,848
Saudi Arabia	5,768	12,648	4,035	9,974
South Africa	2,463	3,321	1,732	1,701
Venezuela	4,573	5,321	3,107	9,447

Source: *Statistical Abstract of the United States* 1991, pp. 806–9.

a. Compute the merchandise trade balance in both 1980 and 1990 for the sample of nine countries.

b. Compute the 50th percentile for imports in 1990.

57. A wave of consolidation in 1986–88 changed the major airlines substantially. Several large mergers and acquisitions concentrated the industry. Market shares for the largest airlines in 1985 and 1988 were:

	1985	1988
American	13.2%	15.2%
United	12.5	15.1
Delta	9.0	13.2
Continental	4.9	9.9
Northwest	NA	9.1
TWA	9.6	8.4
Eastern	10.0	7.0
Pan Am	8.1	6.7
USAir	NA	4.2
Piedmont	NA	3.3
NWA	6.7	NA
People Express	3.3	NA
Republic	3.2	NA

Source: *Industry Surveys*, May 4, 1991, p. A17.

57*a.* Mean = 8.65
SD = 3.52
b. Mean = 9.21
SD = 4.2

a. Compute the mean and standard deviation for the 10 largest airlines in 1985 and 1988.

b. Write a paragraph discussing your findings.

58. This exercise refers to the company data base in Appendix C. Select a sample of 10 workers.

a. Compute the mean and standard deviation for each of the following variables.

x_1 = Number of years with the company
x_2 = Number of overtime hours worked during the past six months
x_4 = Number of continuing education courses completed
x_5 = Number of sick days taken during the past six months
x_6 = Score on company aptitude test
x_8 = Annual base salary
x_9 = Employee age

b. Indicate whether each variable is symmetrical, positively skewed, or negatively skewed.

EXTENDED EXERCISES

59. WORDAN WINE BOTTLING

Mike Wordan, a grape grower, is considering buying a wine-bottling plant and producing a line of quality table wines. Mike wants to know the bottling plant's capacity and works out an arrangement with Rick Roig, the current owner, to sample a number of production days. The number of bottles produced per day by the current process will be recorded. These data will help Mike decide if a purchase is feasible.

Test days are randomly selected during the busy bottling season. For each of the 25 days selected for the sample, the production line is observed, and the number of bottles produced is recorded. Since a backlog of wine awaits bottling, Mike believes that the output is a function of the capabilities of the process, not of raw material availability.

After sample values are recorded, the following statistics are calculated:

$$n = 25 \text{ days} \qquad \bar{x} = 584 \text{ bottles} \qquad s = 253 \text{ bottles}$$

Mike has not yet determined an appropriate price for the bottling facility and hasn't yet talked with bankers about financing. But Mike thinks the sample statistics will help him judge the purchase's feasibility.

a. What can Mike conclude after considering the statistics from the sampled days?

b. Was the sample size sufficiently large to make the statistics useful?

c. Are any problem areas revealed by the sample?

60. PIERONE'S CLOTHING COMPANY

Pierone's, a men's clothing company, sends salespeople to small retail establishments around the country. Every two years the company buys a large number of cars for salespeople to use in their travels. Bob Pierone, the owner, read an article in *Fortune* (September 25, 1989) indicating that automakers are trying to develop cars that run on methanol. Such a car would be much cleaner and would accelerate faster. Bob is interested in this concept, but meanwhile he must replace his current fleet.

The company has narrowed the choice of car to two models. Since the price and estimated upkeep costs for each are about the same, Bob must determine the miles per gallon of each car. If one car has substantially better mileage than the other, the choice will be made in its favor.

Pierone's arranges to test-drive a number of cars of each model for one week. Each car will be driven about 1,000 miles to produce a fair estimate of mileage. Sample statistics from this test are:

Model 1	Model 2
$\bar{x}$ = 19.4 mpg	$\bar{x}$ = 20.1 mpg
s = 1.7 mpg	s = 5.3 mpg
n = 12 cars	n = 15 cars

The company will use these data in deciding which model to buy. They'll be purchasing 500 to 600 cars.

a. What do you think about the sample sizes used for this test?

b. The standard deviation for model 2 is much larger than for model 1. In view of the number of cars to be purchased, is this a problem?

c. Overall, what direction do the sample results give Pierone's Clothing Company?

61. SECOND AVENUE CAR STEREOS

Second Avenue Radio produces car stereos. It is concerned about the number of units produced during the past several weeks. Owner Sally Dempsey decides to select a random sample of observation times. The number of units produced during each selected hour will be recorded.

Numbers recorded for the sample are:

5	6	8	4	5	9	7	5	8	4	9	8	7	6	8
4	6	5	7	5	7	6	8	9	3	4	8	2	9	5
5	1	5	6	8	6	6	9	5	9	0	5	7	8	6

a. What useful statistics can be calculated from the sample data?

b. Summarize the results of the sampling effort in a memo to Dempsey.

62. OUR LADY OF LOURDES HOSPITAL

One variable recorded for Our Lady of Lourdes Hospital employees is family size. Benefits director Curtis Huff asks you to quickly estimate the average family size per employee. Family sizes for the population of 200 employees are:

(1) 3	(35) 1	(69) 2	(102) 1	(135) 5	(168) 6
(2) 2	(36) 2	(70) 4	(103) 2	(136) 2	(169) 3
(3) 7	(37) 4	(71) 3	(104) 5	(137) 1	(170) 2
(4) 3	(38) 1	(72) 7	(105) 3	(138) 4	(171) 3
(5) 4	(39) 4	(73) 2	(106) 2	(139) 2	(172) 4
(6) 2	(40) 2	(74) 6	(107) 1	(140) 4	(173) 2
(7) 3	(41) 1	(75) 2	(108) 2	(141) 1	(174) 2
(8) 1	(42) 3	(76) 7	(109) 2	(142) 2	(175) 1
(9) 5	(43) 5	(77) 3	(110) 1	(143) 4	(176) 5
(10) 3	(44) 2	(78) 6	(111) 4	(144) 1	(177) 3
(11) 2	(45) 1	(79) 4	(112) 1	(145) 2	(178) 2
(12) 3	(46) 4	(80) 2	(113) 1	(146) 2	(179) 4
(13) 4	(47) 3	(81) 3	(114) 2	(147) 5	(180) 3
(14) 1	(48) 5	(82) 5	(115) 2	(148) 3	(181) 5
(15) 2	(49) 2	(83) 2	(116) 1	(149) 1	(182) 3
(16) 2	(50) 4	(84) 1	(117) 4	(150) 2	(183) 1
(17) 4	(51) 1	(85) 3	(118) 2	(151) 6	(184) 2
(18) 4	(52) 6	(86) 3	(119) 1	(152) 2	(185) 4
(19) 3	(53) 2	(87) 2	(120) 3	(153) 5	(186) 3
(20) 2	(54) 5	(88) 4	(121) 5	(154) 1	(187) 2
(21) 1	(55) 4	(89) 1	(122) 1	(155) 2	(188) 5
(22) 5	(56) 1	(90) 2	(123) 2	(156) 1	(189) 3
(23) 2	(57) 2	(91) 3	(124) 3	(157) 4	(190) 4
(24) 1	(58) 1	(92) 3	(125) 4	(158) 2	(191) 3
(25) 4	(59) 5	(93) 2	(126) 3	(159) 2	(192) 2
(26) 3	(60) 2	(94) 4	(127) 2	(160) 7	(193) 3
(27) 2	(61) 7	(95) 1	(128) 1	(161) 4	(194) 2
(28) 3	(62) 1	(96) 2	(129) 6	(162) 2	(195) 5
(29) 6	(63) 2	(97) 4	(130) 1	(163) 1	(196) 3
(30) 1	(64) 6	(98) 3	(131) 2	(164) 7	(197) 3
(31) 2	(65) 4	(99) 2	(132) 5	(165) 2	(198) 2
(32) 4	(66) 1	(100) 6	(133) 2	(166) 7	(199) 5
(33) 3	(67) 2	(101) 4	(134) 1	(167) 4	(200) 1
(34) 2	(68) 1				

a. Select a simple random sample of 30 family sizes and compute the mean. (See MINITAB section at the end of this chapter for instructions.)

b. You've decided to supply Curtis with additional information, so also compute the sample standard deviation. (Save these answers, since they'll be used in future exercises.)

Microcomputer Package

You can use the micro package *Computerized Business Statistics* to compute measures of central tendency and variability.

In Exercise 54, you analyzed price movements of Electronic Research & Development Corporation stock for 35 days. Computation of both mean and standard deviation of this data collection was necessary.

Computer Solution:

On the main menu of *Computerized Business Statistics*, a **3** is selected, indicating Descriptive Statistics.

Since the data for this problem need to be entered on the keyboard, **1** is selected.

```
Descriptive Statistics—Define New Problem
Raw or Group Data: Enter R/G, press ↵ R
```

Since the data are in raw form and haven't been grouped, **R** is selected.

```
Population or Sample Data: Enter P/S, press ↵ S
```

Since the data constitute a sample, choose **S.**

```
Number of Data Points: Enter 1 – 25, press ↵ 35
```

Since the data collection consists of 35 closing stock prices, **35** is the correct entry.

```
Variable Name Enter 0–5 Char. Press ↵ Price
```

The variable name used in this problem is **Price.**

```
Problem Definition Correct? Enter Y/N/Q, press ↵ Y
```

If the problem has been set up correctly, the answer is **Y.**

Next, the program provides spaces for the raw data to be entered. Data values are numbered from 1 to 35. The cursor allows you to replace the 0.0s on the screen with the actual data values.

```
Table Commands     Enter Raw Data     File: None
              Price
1.              43
2.              29
3.              42
4.              35
5.              32
 .               .
 .               .
 .               .
35.             47

Press F when Finished
```

After the data are entered and **F** pressed, you are asked:

```
Save data? Enter Y/N & press ↵ N
```

If you want to save these data in a disk file, answer **Y;** otherwise enter **N.**

The program options menu then reappears, and you are instructed to:

```
Enter number (1 - 9) for your selection from the menu & press ↵ 7
```

You are now ready to run the problem, so enter 7.

```
Convert raw data to group data? Y/N & press ↵ N
```

If you want to convert these raw data to group data, answer **Y**; otherwise answer **N.** Next, you are given output selections. Since a hard copy of the results is needed, **P**, or printer, is selected.

MINITAB COMPUTER PACKAGE

The MINITAB commands to solve Extended Exercise 62 are:

```
MTB > RANDOM 30 C1;
SUBC> INTEGERS 1:200.
MTB > PRINT C1

C1
     173    138    180     76     69    141    130    140     84
      53    159     28    194    156     43    150     63    192
     173    171     83    109    158    106    189    160    104
      88     94     49

MTB > SET INTO C2
DATA> 2 4 3 7 2 1 1 4 1 2 3 2 1 5 2 2 2 2 3 2 2 2 3 7 5 4 4 2
MTB > END
MTB > DESCRIBE C2

                 N     MEAN    MEDIAN    TRMEAN    STDEV    SEMEAN
C2              30    2.800     2.000     2.615    1.584     0.289


               MIN      MAX        Q1        Q3
C2           1.000    7.000     2.000     4.000

MTB > BOXPLOT C2

                      -----------------
            --------(+)                  I--------------------------
                      -----------------

          ----+---------+---------+---------+---------+---------+--C1
             1.2       2.4       3.6       4.8       6.0       7.2

MTB > WRITE 'CH4EX62.DAT' C2
MTB > STOP
```

The **RANDOM** command and **INTEGERS** subcommand are used to generate 30 random numbers between 1 and 200. The **PRINT** command is used to list the random numbers stored in C1. The family sizes for each random number are included in the sample and entered into C2 with the **SET** command. The **END** command is used when the data entry is complete.

Next, the **DESCRIBE** command is used to obtain descriptive statistics for C2. The output includes the sample size (N), the mean (**MEAN**), a mean for the remaining values after removing the smallest 5% and the largest 5% (**TRMEAN**), the median (**MEDIAN**), the standard deviation (**STDEV**), the standard error of the mean (**SEMEAN**) (which will be discussed in Chapter 7), the smallest number (**MIN**), the largest number (**MAX**), first quartile or 25th percentile (**Q1**), and third quartile or 75th percentile (**Q3**).

The **BOXPLOT** command generates a box plot (sometimes referred to as a box-and-whisker plot) that provides another way of looking at a data set in an effort to determine its central tendency, variability, and the existence of unusually large or small values. The box plot consists of five summary measures: median, lower quartile, upper quartile, smallest observation, and largest observation.

The rectangular box represents the middle half of the data, along with dashed lines extending to either side, indicating the data's variability. The median value, 2.0 in this case, is marked with a tick mark (+) inside the box. The box's left and right ends represent the data's first and third quartiles. In this example, the first quartile equals 2.0 and the third quartile equals 4.0.

Finally, the **WRITE** command is used to store the contents of column 2 in a file called CH4EX62.DAT for future use.

SAS Computer Package

A data file called COURSE.DAT was created (see Table 2.8) to analyze data compiled from the class questionnaire (Table 1.1) for one of the authors' classes. SAS commands to provide descriptive statistics for the quantitative variables are:

```
TITLE ''STUDENT QUESTIONNAIRE RESULTS'';
DATA QUEST;
 INFILE 'COURSE.DAT';
 INPUT GPA 5–7 AGE 9–10;
PROC MEANS;
 VAR GPA AGE;
```

The **TITLE** statement names the SAS program.

The **DATA** statement provides a filename for the data.

The **INFILE** statement identifies an external file, COURSE.DAT, to be read with an **INPUT** statement.

The **INPUT** statement names the variable GPA and indicates that it is located in columns 5–7. The variable **AGE** is located in columns 9–10.

The **PROC MEANS** statement produces simple descriptive statistics for the variables listed on the VAR statement. In this example descriptive statistics will be printed for the variables GPA and AGE. Table 4.7 shows the SAS output.

Table 4.7 Student Questionnaire Results

Variable	N	Mean	Std Dev	Minimum	Maximum
GPA	75	2.9733333	0.5176175	1.8000000	4.0000000
AGE	75	30.0533333	8.9335283	19.0000000	46.0000000

Chapter

5

Basic Probability and Discrete Probability Distributions

And now sits Expectation in the air.

Shakespeare, *Henry V*

Objectives

When you have completed this chapter, you will be able to:

Explain the differences among the relative frequency, subjective, and classical approaches to probability.

Explain and use the basic rules of probability.

Construct discrete probability distributions—the binomial, hypergeometric, and Poisson distributions in particular.

Find the probabilities associated with particular outcomes for the binomial, hypergeometric, and Poisson distributions.

Compute the mean and standard deviation for discrete probability distributions.

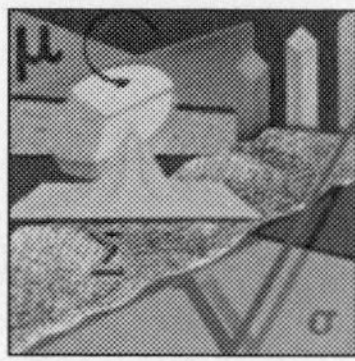

On January 12, 1992, the *New York Times* had a front-page article, "How to Sell More U.S. Cars: Japanese Drivers Offer Hints." With 33% of cars bought in the United States coming from Japan, U.S. automakers were very concerned about their companies' futures.

Previous chapters covered methods of collecting data and summarizing or presenting these numerical values. We saw how charts, graphs, averages, and measures of variability effectively summarize large data collections. Such summary methods bring out the key points of data collections for use in the decision-making process.

Why Discrete Probability Distributions Are Important to Managers

This chapter begins by introducing probability concepts. Entire textbooks have been written on this subject. You'll be studying simple probability principles needed to illustrate important concepts introduced later in this and the following chapters. If you've studied probability recently, you can skip this section. If you need some review on this subject, the material here will help you. If you're new to probability, study this section in depth.

Following the discussion of probability, important statistical background material will be introduced followed by three theoretical but very useful statistical distributions: the binomial, the hypergeometric, and the Poisson. Because these theoretical formulations are closely related to many real situations in the business world, they have great practical value.

Regarding the *New York Times* article just mentioned, one of the distributions discussed in this chapter might be of use in analyzing and forecasting U.S. auto sales patterns. Although these distributions are theoretical, one or more of them might model certain aspects of auto sales quite closely, and could therefore provide valuable information to an auto company's management.

Basic Probability Definitions and Rules

Probability

This section reviews basic probability definitions and rules. A **probability** indicates the likelihood that a future event will occur. Probability values vary between 0 and 1, reflecting the range of likelihood from impossible to totally certain.

> A **probability** is a measure of likelihood that a future event will occur; it can assume any value between 0 and 1, inclusive.

An easily understood probability is the likelihood of heads appearing on the flip of a fair coin. This probability is one half, or .50. This value means that there's a 50% chance of heads appearing on any flip.

Most business decisions have several possible outcomes. A **sample space** is the collection of all possible outcomes that can result from a business decision. Any process that generates well-defined outcomes is an **experiment.** Examples of experiments are the selection of a part for inspection, an investment decision, the choice of a plant location, and the completion of a sales call. The individual outcomes from an experiment are called **events.** Thus, an experiment's sample space consists of all the events that the experiment can produce. For example, the sample space for the selection and testing of a factory part might consist of the events *part okay,* and *part defective.*

> A **sample space** is the collection of all possible outcomes for an experiment. An **experiment** is any process that generates well-defined outcomes. An **event** is a possible outcome of an experiment.

There are three different ways to assign probabilities to events using relative frequencies, subjective probabilities, and classical probabilities. When probabilities are assigned to experimental outcomes, two basic requirements must be satisfied: (1) the probability values assigned to each event must be between 0 and 1, and (2) the probabilities of all events must add to 1.

Relative Frequency

The **relative frequency** method of assigning probabilities is based on experimentation or historical data. This type of probability is defined as the number of times an event occurs divided by the total number of times the experiment is performed. For example, if a consulting firm submits 100 proposals and 20 are accepted, the probability of a future successful proposal can be estimated as 20/100 or .20.

Subjective Probability

A **subjective probability** reflects feelings or opinions regarding the likelihood that an outcome will occur. If a management team think there's a .35 probability of a new product's success in the marketplace, this constitutes a subjective probability. The value .35 is an opinion rather than a value based on objective evidence.

Classical Probability

In the **classical probability** method, the assumption is the events of an experiment are equally likely. This method is most frequently used with games of chance. Since classical probability is not directly applicable to most business decision-making situations, it won't be discussed further.

> **Relative frequency** probabilities are defined as the number of times an event occurs divided by the total number of times the experiment is performed. **Subjective probabilities** reflect feelings or opinions concerning the likelihood that a particular outcome will occur.

Several terms are used in discussing probabilities and their applications. Some of the most important ones are defined in the following box and illustrated in Figure 5.1.

TM FIGURE 5.1 Probability Concepts: Venn Diagrams

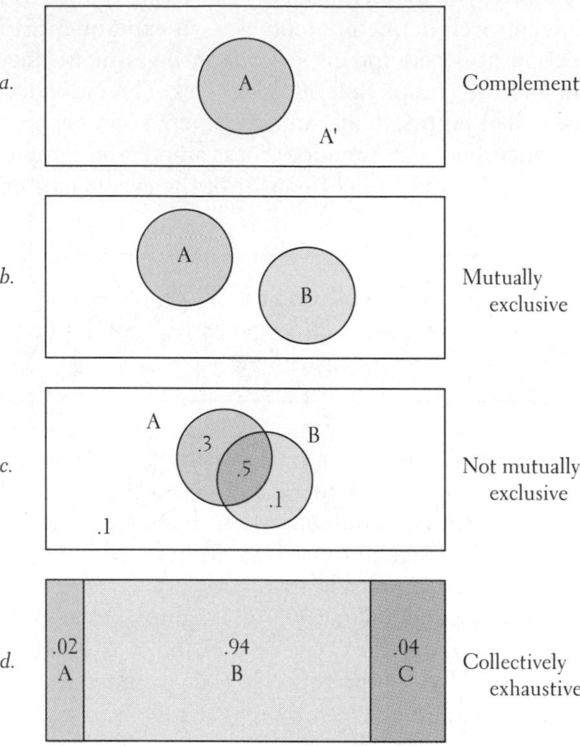

> The **complement** of any event is the collection of outcomes that are not contained in that event.
> A list of events is **collectively exhaustive** if it includes every possible event that can occur.
> Events are **mutually exclusive** if the occurrence of one precludes the occurrence of any other.

Figure 5.1*a* shows event A and its complement, event A′. The complement of event A is the collection of outcomes not contained in event A.

Figure 5.1*b* shows two events, A and B, that are mutually exclusive. If A occurs, for example, B has not occurred, by definition.

Parts *c* and *d* of Figure 5.1 are explained in Examples 5.1 and 5.2, respectively.

Various probability rules help us find the likelihood of future events. To use these rules, you must understand the two different types of event combinations that can occur in business applications. Suppose that two events, A and B, have been identified in a sample space. Some situations require determination of the probability *P*(A or B), which is the probability that *either* event A *or* event B occurs. Other problems require determination of the probability that *both* events will occur, $P(\text{A and B})$.

Addition Rule

For computing the probability that *either* event A or event B occurs, the **addition rule** is used. To use this rule, you must determine whether the events of interest are mutually exclusive.

Addition rule

For events that are *not* mutually exclusive,

$$P(\text{A or B}) = P(\text{A}) + P(\text{B}) - P(\text{A and B}).$$

For mutually exclusive events,

$$P(\text{A or B}) = P(\text{A}) + P(\text{B}) \qquad [\text{since } P(\text{A and B}) = 0]$$

In many probability situations, the outcome of interest can occur in more than one way. The addition rule requires that all such ways be identified and their probabilities computed. If these ways are mutually exclusive, their probabilities are added to determine the overall probability of the desired outcome.

EXAMPLE 5.1 Fairchild Credit Union records indicate that of a total of 1,000 customers, 800 have checking accounts, 600 have savings accounts, and 500 have both. What is the probability that a customer selected at random will have either a checking or a savings account?

Figure 5.1*c* illustrates this situation. The events *have a checking account* (denoted A) and *have a savings account* (denoted B) are *not* mutually exclusive because customers can have both types of accounts. Therefore, the computation is

$$\begin{aligned} P(\text{A or B}) &= P(\text{A}) + P(\text{B}) - P(\text{A and B}) \\ &= .8 + .6 - .5 \\ &= .9 \end{aligned}$$

Note in Figure 5.1*c* that 30% of the customers have a checking account only, 10% have a savings account only, 50% have both, and 10% have neither.

EXAMPLE 5.2 Diet Right Cola Company has an automatic machine that fills bottles with 16 ounces of the firm's beverage. Most bottles are filled properly; however, some are overfilled or underfilled. A random sample of 1,000 bottles tested showed:

Event	Ounces	Number of bottles	Probability
A	<16	20	.02
B	16	940	.94
C	>16	40	.04
		1,000	1.00

What is the probability that a particular bottle will be *either* underfilled or overfilled?

Figure 5.1*d* shows that the events are mutually exclusive and collectively exhaustive. Therefore, $P(\text{A or B or C}) = 1.00$. Applying the addition rule for mutually exclusive events,

$$\begin{aligned} P(\text{A or C}) &= P(\text{A}) + P(\text{C}) \\ &= .02 + .04 \\ &= .06 \end{aligned}$$

The probability that a particular bottle will be either underfilled or overfilled is .06.

Multiplication Rule

If you have to compute the probability that *both* event A and event B will occur, use the **multiplication rule.** To use this rule, you must determine whether the events are independent or dependent.

Independent

A formal mathematical definition of the terms that must be met for two events to be considered **independent** can be found in mathematical statistics textbooks. For practical purposes this formal definition states that two events are independent if one's occurrence in no way affects the likelihood that the second will occur. For example, when flipping a fair coin in a fair way, the event "heads appears on first flip" doesn't change the probability of observing heads on the second flip; this probability remains .50. In this case, the two events are independent.

> Events A and B are **independent** if the occurrence of one in no way affects the likelihood that the second will occur.

Dependent

Events A and B are **dependent** if one's occurrence alters the likelihood that the second will occur. For example, the event "person smokes" changes the probability of getting lung cancer since a medical connection between these two events has been established. In this case the two events (smoking and lung cancer) are considered dependent events with regard to probability assessment.

> Events A and B are **dependent** if the occurrence of one alters the likelihood that the second will occur.

For independent events, the probabilities of successive events are multiplied together to get the probability of that sequence. For dependent events, the idea is the same, but care must be taken to ascertain the events' exact probabilities since they may change depending on which events have previously occurred. The multiplication rules for independent and dependent events follow, along with several examples.

> **Multiplication rule**
> For events that are independent,
> $$P(\text{A and B}) = P(\text{A}) \times P(\text{B})$$
> For events that are dependent (the general multiplication rule),
> $$P(\text{A and } B) = P(\text{A}) \times P(B|\text{A})$$
> (Note: The vertical line means *given*.)

EXAMPLE 5.3 A company is considering introducing two new products to a local market. Management believes that the chance of success is about 50% for the first and 75% for the second. What is the probability that both products will be successful? Both probabilities are subjective because they're based on management opinion (expert though it might be) rather than on documented facts. If the assumption is that the two opinions are independent of each other, the multiplication rule for independent events calls for multiplying the two probabilities of success to find the desired probability:

$$\begin{aligned} P(\text{A and B}) &= P(\text{A}) \times P(\text{B}) \\ &= .50 \times .75 \\ &= .375 \end{aligned}$$

There's about a 37.5% chance that both products will be successful.

EXAMPLE 5.4 According to the Roper Organization, *American Demographics* (February 1993, p. 12), one in six customers who receive mail-ordered items indicate that delivery takes too long. The manager of a mail-order catalog distributor wants to determine the probability that all 10 of the orders sent out during a 12-hour period will be delivered in a timely fashion. The probability .167 is assigned to the event *delivery took too long*. Since this value is based on past experience, it's considered a relative frequency probability.

First the probability of the complement of *delivery took too long* needs to be calculated. Since the probability of delivery took too long is .167, the probability of a timely delivery is $(1 - .167) = .833$. If the status of each delivery is independent of every other delivery, the probability of all 10 deliveries being completed in a timely manner is computed using the multiplication rule for independent events:

$$.833^{10} = .161$$

There's about a 16% chance that all ten of the deliveries during the 12-hour period were delivered in a timely fashion.

EXAMPLE 5.5 A supervisor takes three feed bags from a filling machine and carefully weighs their contents. From past records she knows that the machine overfills the bags 10% of the time, so the probability .10 is assigned to the event *bag overfilled.* It is also known that such defective bags occur randomly, so one bag's status is independent of all others. What is the probability that no more than one bag in the sample of three is overfilled?

Both the addition rule and multiplication rule for independent events are used to answer this question. There's more than one way to properly fill two or three bags. Using C to represent a correctly filled bag and O to indicate an overfilled bag, the multiplication and addition rules can be employed to calculate the desired probability:

Qualifying events:
CCC, CCO, COC, OCC
Probability:

$$(.9)(.9)(.9) + (.9)(.9)(.1) + (.9)(.1)(.9) + (.1)(.9)(.9) = .972$$

It's quite likely (about a 97% chance) that no more than one overfilled bag will be found in the three bags sampled.

EXAMPLE 5.6 It is known that 25% of the persons taking the CPA exam in a certain city took a CPA review course from a local university. Of those who took the course, 60% passed the exam. What is the probability that a randomly selected person took the course and passed the exam?

The general multiplication rule for dependent events is used to calculate the answer. The probability of taking the course is $P(B) = .25\%$, followed by the probability of passing *given* the course was taken: $P(A|B) = 60\%$. So the correct probability is

$$P(A \text{ and } B) = P(B) \times P(A|B) = (.25)(.60) = .15$$

EXAMPLE 5.7 Past history shows that 15% of a laundromat's washers need a new motor during the first two years of operation. Of those needing new motors, 80% also need new drive belts during the same period. What is the probability that a machine will need both a new motor and new drive belts during its first two years?

The probability of needing a new motor, $P(B)$, is 15% and the probability of needing new belts is $P(A|B) = 80\%$ *given* a new motor is needed, so the probability is

$$P(A \text{ and } B) = P(B) \times P(A|B) = (.15)(.80) = .12$$

Chapter 18 provides additional material involving dependent events and their probabilities.

EXERCISES

1. Explain the concept of probability.
2. Why must a probability be a number between 0 and 1?
3. When is the multiplication rule of probability useful?
4. When is the addition rule of probability useful?

5. A local department store has collected data on TV sales for the past 50 days:

Number of TVs sold	Number of days
0	10
1	15
2	12
3	8
4 or more	5

5a. 5
b. P(0) = .20
P(1) = .30
P(2) = .24
P(3) = .16
P(4+) = .10
c. .20
d. .26
e. (.10) × (.10) = .01

a. Based on this history, how many outcomes are possible?

b. Assign probabilities to the various outcomes.

c. What is the probability that no TVs will be sold tomorrow?

d. What is the probability that more than two TVs will be sold tomorrow?

e. What is the probability that four or more TVs will be sold on each of the next two days?

6. Almost one in three Americans is a sports fan, according to a 1990 survey by Lieberman Research for *Sports Illustrated.* About 30% of American adults say they are very interested in sports. Around 43% are fairly interested, while 27% aren't interested in sports. Based on the study's results, what is the probability that:

6a. .73
b. .389
c. .16

a. An adult interviewed at random will be very or fairly interested in sports?

b. The next three adults interviewed will be sports fans?

c. Two of the next three adults interviewed will be nonfans?

7. Jill Sharp likes to play pool after school. She especially enjoys playing the Pigon brothers, Bob and Bill. Jill feels that she has a 90% chance of beating either brother on any given afternoon and that her second game isn't affected by an earlier win or loss. Find the probability that:

7a. .81
b. .18
c. .09
d. .01

a. Jill will beat both Pigon brothers this afternoon.

b. Jill will beat one brother and lose to the other this afternoon.

c. Jill will beat Bob and lose to Bill this afternoon.

d. Jill will lose to Bob Pigon two afternoons in a row.

8. .3

8. You own a small business and have contracted to supply your product at a fixed price of $20 per unit. You like the security provided by a guaranteed contract, but you're worried about either of two possible catastrophes: *(a)* the Federal Reserve will engineer a tight-money "credit crunch" that dries up the financing you need to buy raw materials and manufacture your product, or *(b)* the Fed will permit an easy-money inflation that increases your material and labor costs and prevents you from making a profit at a price of $20 per unit. You believe that the probability of tight money is .2 and the probability of easy money is .1. If tight money and easy money are mutually exclusive, what is the probability of one or the other?

9. S. Ward reported in "Children's Reactions to Commercials" (*Journal of Advertising Research,* April 1972) that children often have a very low understanding of commercials, even those designed to appeal to them. Ward's studies showed that only 45% of 5-to-7-

year-olds understand commercials. An advertising agent shows a TV commercial to three children randomly selected from this age group. Find the probability that:

9*a*. .091
b. .166
c. .408

a. The commercial's message is understood by all three children.

b. The commercial's message isn't understood by any of the three children.

c. The commercial's message is understood by one of the three children.

10. .18

10. Mike May, owner of Mike's Conoco, estimates that 90% of the motorists stopping at the station purchase gas. He also estimates that of those who buy gas, 20% also purchase oil. Find the probability that a customer entering the station will purchase both gas and oil.

11. .66

11. On Wall Street, tradition has it that if an NFC team or one of the old NFL teams now in the AFC (Indianapolis Colts, Cleveland Browns, and Pittsburgh Steelers) wins the Super Bowl, stock prices will be higher a year later. If an AFC team wins, the market will stumble ("An Examination of the Super Bowl Stock Market Predictor," *Decision Science Institute Proceedings*, November 21–23, 1988, p. 317). A *USA Today* article (January 23, 1992) indicates that it has worked 22 of 25 times. Suppose the probability in 1993 that the Dallas Cowboys of the NFC would win the game was .75. Find the probability that stock prices will increase in 1993.

Random Variables

Random Variable

An important concept in many statistical applications is the random variable. Experiments and their individual outcomes called *events* were discussed earlier in the chapter. Experiments result in simple events that correspond to values of some numerical variable. A **random variable** is defined by assigning one numerical value to each simple event of an experiment that yields random outcomes.

> A **random variable** is defined by assigning one numerical value to each simple event of an experiment that yields random outcomes.

An example of a random variable is the number of courses taken during a specific term by any of 100 college students. The number of courses varies from one to five from student to student. Other examples of random variables are the number of children per family, number of telephone calls to a mail order company per minute, and number of successful bids per month by a contractor.

Discrete Random Variable

In each of these situations, the random variable is measured by counting the number of *successes* that occur. Such variables are called **discrete random variables** because only certain values for the variable are possible. In each of the preceding examples, only integer values—0, 1, 2, 3, and so on—are possible.

> A **discrete random variable** is a variable that can assume only values from a predetermined set.

There are other random variables for which any value within some range is possible, such as a person's weight or a car's mileage. Known as *continuous random variables*, they will be discussed in the next chapter.

EXERCISES

SM

12. What is a random variable?
13. Four students have employment interviews scheduled at Keytronic, Inc. Each applicant will either get the job or be turned down.
    a. List the possible outcomes in terms of the results of the four interviews.
    b. Define a random variable that represents the number of offers made.
    c. Show what value the random variable will assume for each possible outcome.
14. Identify which of the following random variables can be classified as discrete.
    a. How long it took you to travel to school today.
    b. The number of students in this class.
    c. The number of questions you answered correctly on your first statistics test.
    d. The number of people in a sample of 50 who prefer a certain light beer over a competitor's brand.
    e. The length of time between tenants for a particular apartment.
    f. The number of finance majors in this class.
    g. The time of arrival of a bus.
    h. The amount of natural gas used per month to heat a hospital.
    i. The exact amount of diet pop in a can.
15. Which of the variables listed in the company data base from Appendix C are discrete variables?

14*a.* No
b. Yes
c. Yes
d. Yes
e. No
f. Yes
g. No
h. No
i. No

■ SITUATION 5.1 Central Motors sells new and used cars in a large city. Its owners are worried because their sales have been trending downward for the past three years. After one owner reads a March 12, 1992, *Wall Street Journal* front-page story about difficulties connected with sales and car salespeople, they do a serious study of their sales picture.

After some discussion, they focus on several key matters. One problem involves examining the number of cars sold per day in an effort to anticipate future stocking requirements. Management believes important decision-making information resides in data it collected on the number of cars sold over the past few months. The investigating team notices that sales per day seem to be random. That is, the number of sales one day doesn't seem to affect the number of sales the next day. In a recent team meeting, it was agreed that as much as possible needs to be learned from the collected data. (This situation will be solved at the end of this section.) ■

PROBABILITY DISTRIBUTIONS

V

Probability Distribution

Rather than consider the probability that a single, identified event will occur, it's often of interest to consider all the different values that a random variable can assume along with the probability of each. A listing of the possible values that a discrete random variable can assume along with their associated probabilities is called a **probability distribution.**

> A **probability distribution** is a listing of the possible values that a random variable can assume along with their probabilities.

Table 5.1 is an example of a probability distribution. Used in Example 5.8, it lists the values, x's, that the variable can assume along with the observed frequency of each. Figure 5.2 graphs this probability distribution.

TABLE 5.1 Probability Distribution of Absent Employees (Example 5.8)

Employees absent per day, x	Number of days, f	Probability, $P(x)$
1	18	.085
2	25	.118
3	39	.184
4	46	.217
5	27	.127
6	25	.118
7	22	.104
8	10	.047
	212	1.000

EXAMPLE 5.8 In Table 5.1, x represents the number of absent employees per day observed over the past 212 days, and f represents the number of times each x value was observed. For example, there were 18 days when only one employee was absent, and 25 days when two employees were absent. The first two columns constitute a frequency distribution of past employee absences.

Each frequency in Table 5.1 is divided by the total frequency, 212, to produce the relative frequencies in the third column (for example 18/212 = .085). The first and third columns constitute the probability distribution for future employees' absences. Inherent in these relative frequencies is the assumption that the future will reflect the conditions that prevailed in the past. In other words, a frequency distribution is a

FIGURE 5.2 Graph of Probability Distribution

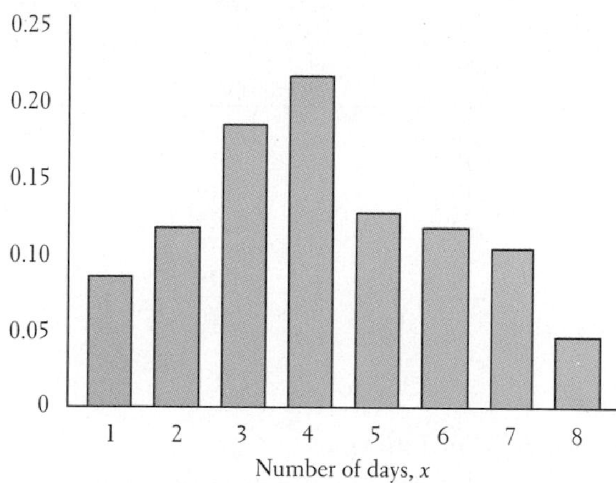

summary of what happened in the past, and a probability distribution is a summary of what might happen in the future.

Note in Table 5.1 that the sum of the relative frequencies is 1.00, or 100%. This is always the case for a probability distribution (disregarding rounding errors). The probability distribution must contain all possible values that the random variable can assume. Therefore, the sum of the probabilities must be 1.00.

■ SITUATION 5.1—RESOLVED The data in Table 5.2 were collected from company records and represent the cars Central Motors sold per day for the past 100 days. The company now has better information about unit sales per day, which will help in managing its business. The probability distribution in Table 5.2 is a good summary of the anticipated sales levels for the future. This table shows that the probability of selling 13 cars on any day is .23, for example.

TABLE 5.2 Probability Distribution of Cars Sold (Situation 5.1)

Cars sold per day, x	Number of days, f	Probability, $P(x)$
10	8	.08
11	12	.12
12	19	.19
13	23	.23
14	18	.18
15	20	.20
	100	1.00

Chapter 3 described how to construct a cumulative relative frequency distribution. Table 5.3 applies this technique to the Table 5.2 car sales data. Now management can see at a glance that the probability of selling 13 or fewer cars on a given day is .62.

TABLE 5.3 Cumulative Probability Distribution of Cars Sold (Situation 5.1)

Cars sold per day, x	Number of days, f	Probability, $P(x)$	Less than or equal cumulative probability	More than or equal cumulative probability
10	8	.08	.08	1.00
11	12	.12	.20	.92
12	19	.19	.39	.80
13	23	.23	.62	.61
14	18	.18	.80	.38
15	20	.20	1.00	.20
	100	1.00		

■

EXERCISES

16. What is a probability distribution?

17. What is the difference between a frequency distribution and a probability distribution?
18. Mr. Sands is considering making an offer to purchase a new home. He was inspired to find a home in the country after reading the article "Peaceable Kingdom for a Weekend Farmer" in the February 1989 issue of *Home Beautiful.*

    After looking at several homes for sale, he subjectively assessed this distribution for the purchase price:

Purchase price	$P(x)$
$80,000	.20
85,000	.50
90,000	.30

18*b*. .70

a. Is this a frequency distribution or a probability distribution?

b. What is the probability that the home will cost Mr. Sands no more than $85,000?

c. Why do the probabilities sum to 1?

19. Let x represent the number of days in which accidents occurred in the Kaypra plant during the past year.

Number of accidents	Number of days
0	185
1	102
2	55
3	12
4	11

19*a*. Frequency distribution
b. 0 .5068
1 .2795
2 .1507
3 .0329
4+ .0301
d. .151
e. .786

a. Is this a frequency distribution or a probability distribution?

b. Construct a probability distribution.

c. Graph the probability distribution.

d. What is the probability of two accidents tomorrow?

e. What is the probability of less than two accidents tomorrow?

20. Let x represent the number of defective units produced by an assembly line during a typical day.

Number of defectives	$P(x)$
0	.40
1	.30
2	.15
3	.10
4	.05

20*a*. Probability distribution
c. .40
d. .15
e. .16

a. Is this a frequency distribution or a probability distribution?
b. Graph the probability distribution.
c. What is the probability of no defectives tomorrow?
d. What is the probability of more than two defectives tomorrow?
e. What is the probability of no defectives in the next two days?

21. Construct a probability distribution for the variable for number of company courses completed in the company data base in Appendix C.

■ SITUATION 5.2 Central Motors management is trying to decide whether to take out an insurance policy on its repair shop, which is separated from the main building complex. Central has evaluated the possible risks of fire loss on its building (Table 5.4). Although many dollar loss amounts are possible, Central has summarized possible losses in terms of the key values in Table 5.4. The possible losses and the corresponding probabilities estimated by management constitute a discrete probability distribution.

TABLE 5.4 Insurance Loss Probability Distribution (Situation 5.2)

x (loss)	$P(x)$	$x \cdot P(x)$
$ 0	.925	0
5,000	.010	50
15,000	.010	150
30,000	.020	600
75,000	.020	1,500
100,000	.010	1,000
250,000	.005	1,250
	1.000	$4,550

■

EXPECTED VALUE

V

Expected Value

It is often helpful to summarize a probability distribution by specifying the average, or mean, value of the distribution. In statistics, this average or mean is known as the **expected value.**

The **expected value** of a discrete random variable is the average value that the random variable assumes over a large number of observations.

EXAMPLE 5.9 The expected value of a discrete probability distribution, such as the one in Table 5.1, is found by multiplying each value of x by its probability of occurrence and adding these products.

Table 5.5 repeats Table 5.1's probability distribution with the expected value calculated in the third column. The final column is the product of each x value in the distribution and its probability. The sum of these products is approximately 4.2. This is the average number of absent employees per day over the time of the collected data; it's the expected value of the probability distribution. (Of course, we wouldn't expect to find 4.2 employees absent during any particular day, because only integer values (0, 1, 2, 3, 4, etc.) can be assumed by the discrete variable *number of people*.)

TABLE 5.5 Expected Value for Absent Employees Distribution (Example 5.9)

x	$P(x)$	$x \cdot P(x)$
1	.085	.085
2	.118	.236
3	.184	.552
4	.217	.868
5	.127	.635
6	.118	.708
7	.104	.728
8	.047	.376
	1.000	$E(x) = 4.188$

The formula for computing the expected value from a discrete probability distribution is

$$E(x) = \Sigma[x \cdot P(x)] \tag{5.1}$$

where $E(x)$ = Expected value
x = Each value of the distribution
$P(x)$ = Probability of each x occurring

The computation of an expected value is actually an application of the weighted mean concept discussed in Chapter 4. The difference is that when the expected value is computed, the x's are weighted by probabilities that add to 1. Since the weights add to 1, the summation doesn't need to be divided by the total of the weights. Thus, the summation itself is the expected value.

Chapter 4 noted that an analyst should specify both the mean and standard deviation to adequately describe a population or sample. This is also true for probability distributions. The expected value is used to measure the central tendency of a probability distribution and the standard deviation is used to measure the variability.

The procedure for computing a probability distribution's standard deviation is similar to the one shown in Chapter 4. First, we compute the population variance:

$$\sigma^2 = \Sigma(x - \mu)^2 P(x) \tag{5.2}$$

The standard deviation of x is then computed by taking the square root of the variance. Example 5.10 demonstrates the computations.

EXAMPLE 5.10 The expected value for the absent employees probability distribution (see Table 5.1) computed in Example 5.9 was 4.2. We use Equation 5.2 to compute the variance for this distribution:

$$\begin{aligned}\sigma^2 &= \Sigma(x - \mu)^2 P(x) \\ &= (1 - 4.2)^2(.085) + (2 - 4.2)^2(.118) + \\ &\quad (3 - 4.2)^2(.184) + (4 - 4.2)^2(.217) + \\ &\quad (5 - 4.2)^2(.127) + (6 - 4.2)^2(.118) + \\ &\quad (7 - 4.2)^2(.104) + (8 - 4.2)^2(.047) \\ &= .870 + .571 + .265 + .009 + .081 + .382 + .815 + .679 \\ &= 3.67\end{aligned}$$

The standard deviation is

$$\sigma = \sqrt{\sigma^2} = \sqrt{3.67} = 1.92$$

The mean (4.2) and the standard deviation (1.92) can be used to describe the probability distribution in the same way that $\bar{x}$ and s were used to describe a relative frequency distribution in Chapter 4. The average number of absent employees per day over time is expected to be near 4.2. Similarly, $\sigma = 1.92$ measures the spread or variability of the probability distribution.

■ SITUATION 5.2—RESOLVED In forming the probability distribution of Table 5.4, Central Motors estimated key loss values along with their probabilities.

Central's analyst noticed that the sum of the probabilities of some type of loss equaled .075. This means that the probability of no loss must be .925 (1 − .075).

The third column of Table 5.4 shows the multiplication of each x times its probability. These products sum to $4,550, the expected value of the distribution. Central's management can now evaluate bids from insurance companies with the reasoning that this expected loss value should be covered by the face value of the insurance. Central's analyst realizes that in figuring its bid, an insurance company must add overhead and profit to this expected loss value. But $4,550, the expected annual loss due to fire, is a benchmark value that will help Central Motors decide which bid to accept. ■

EXERCISES

22. What is an expected value?

23. $E(x) = \$85,500$, $\sigma = \$3,482$

23. Mr. Sands is considering purchasing a new home. He subjectively determined a distribution for the purchase price:

Purchase price	$P(x)$
$80,000	.20
85,000	.50
90,000	.30

Compute the expected value and standard deviation for this probability distribution.

24. $E(x) = 1.1$
$\sigma = 1.18$

24. According to the March 1989 issue of *Electronics* magazine, the United States is attempting to develop a high-density television technology and reenter the consumer electronics market. A primary concern to Electo, a company hoping to enter this market, is the defective rate of its computer chip line.

Let x represent the number of defective units produced by this line during a typical day.

Number of defectives	$P(x)$
0	.40
1	.30
2	.15
3	.10
4 or more	.05

Compute the expected value and standard deviation for this probability distribution.

25. $E(x) = 48$

25. Demand for computer keyboards for the ISC Corporation varies greatly from month to month. The following probability distribution shows monthly demand for keyboards during the past two years. Find the expected value of demand for next month.

Monthly demand	$P(x)$
40	.15
45	.25
50	.45
55	.15

26. Compute the expected value and standard deviation for the variable *number of continuing education courses completed* (variable x_4) found in the company data base in Appendix C.

■ SITUATION 5.3 Central Motors is continuing to evaluate its daily sales volume. In particular, management wants to define a profitable day for the business. After talking with the dealership accountant, they decide that any day on which 13 or more cars are sold is profitable. Management now wishes to evaluate sales days based on this definition. ■

THE BINOMIAL DISTRIBUTION

Mathematicians have defined numerous theoretical distributions of numerical values. Some are of particular interest to businesspeople because they correspond closely to real-world events. One widely used probability distribution for a discrete random variable is the **binomial distribution.**

> The **binomial distribution** is a discrete probability distribution involving the likelihood of x successes in n trials of a binomial experiment.

The binomial distribution describes a situation that produces one of two possible outcomes on each trial. In addition, the probabilities of these outcomes must remain constant from trial to trial, and the trials must be independent. The binomial distribution is useful when the real situation being modeled meets the following criteria:

TM

Essential characteristics of the binomial distribution

1. There are n identical trials that lead to one of two outcomes: success or failure.
2. The probability of each outcome remains constant from trial to trial. The probability of one of these outcomes, called *success*, is designated p.
3. The trials are independent.

A good example of a binomial experiment is flipping a fair coin several times. There are only two possible outcomes for each trial, or flip (heads and tails); the probability of heads or tails remains constant from flip to flip (.50 each); and the flips are independent of each other.

EXAMPLE 5.11 A fair coin is to be flipped three times. What is the probability of obtaining exactly two heads?

One method of calculating probability in such a situation is to use a *tree diagram*, so called because it shows the various possible outcomes of an experiment in a drawing that looks like the branches of a tree. The tree diagram for the coin-flipping situation appears in Figure 5.3.

TM

FIGURE 5.3 Coin-Flip Tree Diagram

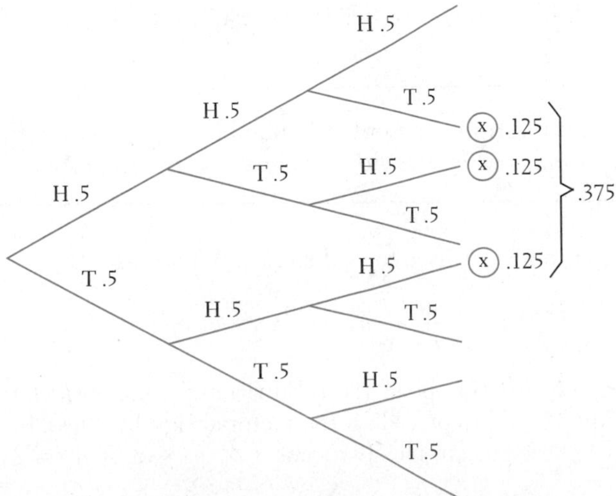

Each branch in Figure 5.3 represents a coin flip. The multiplication rule is used to compute the probability of every independent way in which two heads can result. Note that each way of getting two heads has the same probability, .125. The addition rule is then used to compute the final probability of getting two heads; this probability is .375.

To find the overall probability of two heads, first calculate the probability of achieving two heads in each of the several possible ways. Next, multiply this value by the number of possible ways of attaining this result. Thus, the final probability is

$$3 \times (.5 \times .5 \times .5) = .375$$

The first part of this calculation indicates the number of ways (3) in which the desired outcome (two heads) can occur. The second calculation $(.5 \times .5 \times .5 = .125)$ indicates the probability of achieving this result using one of the possible paths in the diagram. The final result (.375) is the probability of flipping a fair coin three times and obtaining exactly two heads.

Now Example 5.11 is modeled using the binomial distribution, already established as a good model of this situation. This calculation requires the binomial formula:

$$P(x) = \binom{n}{x} p^x (1 - p)^{n-x} \tag{5.3}$$

where $P(x)$ = Probability of x successes in n trials
n = Number of trials
$\binom{n}{x}$ = Number of ways of getting exactly x successes in n trials
p = Probability of success on any one trial
$(1 - p)$ = Probability of failure on any one trial.

Combination

The first term in Equation 5.3 is called "the combination of n things taken x at a time." A **combination** represents the number of ways we could reach into a collection of n items and choose x of them. For the coin-flipping example, it represents the number of different ways two heads can result from three coin flips.

> A **combination** represents the number of possible ways of choosing x things out of n things when the order of choosing isn't important.

Equation 5.4 is used to evaluate combinations:

$$\binom{n}{x} = \frac{n!}{x!(n - x)!} \tag{5.4}$$

The exclamation point (!) in Equation 5.4 means *factorial*. To calculate a factorial, multiply the value preceding the factorial sign by 1 less, by 1 less than that, and so on down to 1. For example, 4! means $4 \times 3 \times 2 \times 1 = 24$. To calculate 6!, find the product $6 \times 5 \times 4 \times 3 \times 2 \times 1$, which is 720. Mathematicians define 0! to be equal to 1 because there is only one way to choose 0 things. Some additional factorial expressions are solved in Example 5.12.

EXAMPLE 5.12

$$5! = (5)(4)(3)(2)(1) = 120$$
$$3! = (3)(2)(1) = 6$$
$$8! = (8)(7)(6)(5)(4)(3)(2)(1) = 40{,}320$$

Factorial expressions such as these are employed in computing combinations using Equation 5.4.

EXAMPLE 5.13 How many ways can we select a committee of three from a group of five people? This represents the combination $\binom{5}{3}$ and is evaluated

$$\binom{n}{x} = \frac{n!}{x!(n-x)!} = \frac{5!}{3!(5-3)!} = \frac{(5)(4)(3)(2)(1)}{(3)(2)(1)(2)(1)} = 10$$

There are 10 different ways to select a committee of three from a group of five.

In evaluating combinations, make sure that the order in which the items are selected doesn't matter. A committee consisting of Sue, Bill, and Joe is the same as a committee of Bill, Joe, and Sue; the order in which the names are listed isn't important.

EXAMPLE 5.14 Returning to the coin flip situation in Example 5.11, the problem can be solved using the binomial formula (Equation 5.3). There are three ways in which two heads can occur out of three flips of the fair coin:

$$\binom{n}{x} = \frac{n!}{x!(n-x)!} = \frac{3!}{2!(3-2)!} = \frac{(3)(2)(1)}{(2)(1)(1)} = 3$$

The probability of one of these three ways of obtaining two heads is

$$p^x(1-p)^{n-x} = (.5)^2(1-.5)^{3-2} = (.5)^2(.5)^1 = .125$$

Therefore, the probability of obtaining two heads on three flips of a fair coin is

$$P(x=2) = \binom{n}{x} p^x(1-p)^{n-x} = (3)(.5)^2(1-.5)^{3-2} = .375$$

This is the same probability calculated using the tree diagram of Figure 5.3.

Figure 5.4 charts the binomial distribution for the coin-flipping example just discussed. The horizontal axis indicates all possible numbers of heads that can occur, and the vertical axis lists the probability of each x occurring. The probability of two heads is highlighted in Figure 5.4 by the shaded bar for that event. As shown, this probability is .375. Note that the probabilities of the outcomes add to 1.0.

FIGURE 5.4 Binomial Distribution for Coin Flip ($n = 3, p = .5$)

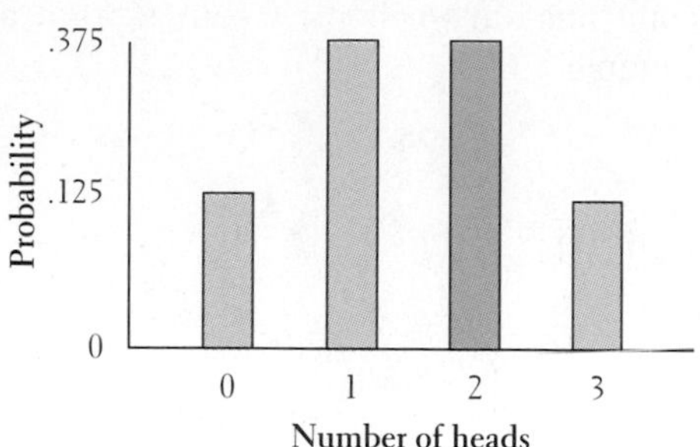

■ SITUATION 5.3—RESOLVED Central Motors' management team wants to use the binomial distribution to model the probabilities of profitable sales days and defines a profitable day as one in which 13 or more cars are sold. In conjunction with the established probability distribution for number of cars sold per day (Table 5.2), the probability of a profitable day can be computed using the addition rule. This is done by adding the probabilities of a 13-sale day (.23), 14-sale day (.18), and 15-sale day (.20). The total is .61. Central Motors concludes that there's about a 61% chance of profitable sales on any given day.

Deciding to use the binomial distribution in this situation was premature. All three criteria for this distribution need to be addressed for accurate results to be expected. Central's management considers these criteria with the following results:

1. The situation results in one of two possible outcomes each day: a profitable day or an unprofitable day.
2. Does the probability of a profitable day (.61) remain constant from day to day? This is management's critical question. If the probability changes due to the day of the week or as a result of changing economic conditions, the binomial distribution won't accurately model the situation. However, as suggested earlier, management believes that the number of cars sold is a random event, so the probability of a good day remains constant; one day's sales level doesn't seem to affect the next day's. Management decides that the criterion of constant probability is met.
3. Based on the preceding conclusion, management decides that the third criterion of the binomial distribution is also met: daily sales levels are indeed independent of each other. ■

EXERCISES

27. Describe a situation that would suggest use of the binomial distribution.
28. What are the essential properties of the binomial distribution?
29. Explain how combinations are useful.

30. Binomial *a, b, d, e*

30. Which of the following situations might be modeled by the binomial distribution assuming a large population?
    a. The number of trucks in a fleet that will need a major overhaul next year.
    b. The number of calls to a police dispatcher within an hour.

c. The length of time necessary to handle customer telephone inquiries.

d. The number of defective units per shipment.

e. The number of defective forks in a production run of 1,000.

31. 21

31. A TV picture tube may be purchased from one of seven suppliers. In how many ways can two suppliers be chosen from the seven?

Assume statistical independence for Exercises 32–34.

32. It is known that 30% of MasterCharge accounts in a local bank have balances over $2,000. Suppose four accounts are selected at random.

32*a.* .1029
b. .1029
c. 4
d. .4116

a. What is the probability that the first account selected is over $2,000 and the next three aren't?

b. What is the probability that the first three accounts selected are under $2,000 and the last account is over $2,000?

c. In how many different ways can a person select one account over $2,000 and three accounts under $2,000?

d. What is the probability of selecting one account over $2,000 and three accounts under $2,000?

33. Suppose it's determined that 30% of the people in Houston, Texas, read the evening paper. If three people are selected at random, what is the probability:

33*a.* .189
b. .343
c. .657

a. Of selecting exactly two people who read the evening paper?

b. That none reads the evening paper?

c. That at least one person reads the evening paper?

34. According to a declassified IRS audit manual, it's not just the items that appear on your tax return that can produce an audit. The absence of certain items can raise the DIF (Discriminate Function) number and cause your return to be targeted for examination. This DIF number indicates the likelihood that an audit of the return will result in an additional tax assessment. The DIF program is also highly effective in singling out incorrectly completed tax returns. Only about 17% of audits of taxpayers in the $25,000–$50,000 income category result in no change in the amount of tax due (*Tax Guide for College Teachers*, Academic Information Service, Inc., 1992).

34*a.* .17
b. .83
c. .1366

a. What is the probability that if the IRS audits a taxpayer with income of $45,000 it will produce no change in the tax due?

b. What is the probability that if the IRS audits a taxpayer with income of $30,000 it will produce some change in the tax due?

c. If the IRS randomly audits four taxpayers with income between $25,000 and $50,000, what is the probability that two or more audits will produce some change in the tax due?

■ SITUATION 5.4 Central Motors is examining the probabilities of different numbers of profitable days now that the binomial process has been deemed an appropriate model.

1. What is the probability that all six days in a work week will be profitable?
2. What is the probability of at least four profitable days in a work week?
3. What is the probability of no profitable days in a work week?
4. What is the probability of at least 10 profitable days in a 15-day period?

Answering these questions requires solving the binomial formula, Equation 5.3, several times. If Central's management wants answers to even more *what if* questions, the number of calculations will increase. Fortunately, statisticians have anticipated this situation and solved the binomial formula for hundreds of different problems. These computations appear in the binomial table in Appendix E.2, which is discussed in the next section. ■

THE BINOMIAL TABLE

Binomial Table

Before the binomial table can be used, the values of n, p, and x must be known. The number of trials in a binomial experiment is represented by n, the probability of success for each trial by p, and the number of successes for which the probability is desired by x. The following four examples illustrate the binomial table's use:

V

1. $n = 6,\quad p = .40,\quad x = 6$
2. $n = 8,\quad p = .50,\quad x \geq 4$
3. $n = 9,\quad p = .30,\quad x = 0$
4. $n = 15,\quad p = .20,\quad x \leq 3$

The binomial table is divided into blocks by n, the number of trials. The answer to the first problem is found in the block for $n = 6$. Find this section in the binomial table in Appendix E.2. The column headings represent values of p, so the desired column is the one headed .40. Now look at the left edge of the table. The row labels represent values of x. Reading probabilities using the appropriate x row and p column avoids the necessity of solving the binomial formula.

EXAMPLE 5.15 Find the probability that $x = 6$ if $n = 6$ and $p = .40$. The probability is .004, which is read directly from the intersection of the row $x = 6$ and the column $p = .40$ in the block for $n = 6$.

EXAMPLE 5.16 Find the probability that $x \geq 4$ if $n = 8$ and $p = .50$. This value is found by adding the individual probabilities for $x = 4$ through $x = 8$ in the $p = .50$ column of the $n = 8$ block; the sum is $.273 + .219 + .109 + .031 + .004 = .636$.

EXAMPLE 5.17 Find the probability that $x = 0$ if $n = 9$ and $p = .30$. The probability is .040, which is read directly from the intersection of the row $x = 0$ and the column $p = .30$ in the $n = 9$ block.

EXAMPLE 5.18 Find the probability that $x \leq 3$ if $n = 15$ and $p = .20$. The individual probabilities for $x = 0$ through $x = 3$ in the $n = 15$ block, $p = .20$ column, are added: $.035 + .132 + .231 + .250 = .648$.

Figure 5.5 plots the binomial distribution for Example 5.18. The number of possible successes is between 0 and 15 inclusive, and these values are shown on the horizontal

FIGURE 5.5 Binomial Distribution for Example 5.18 ($n = 15, p = .20$)

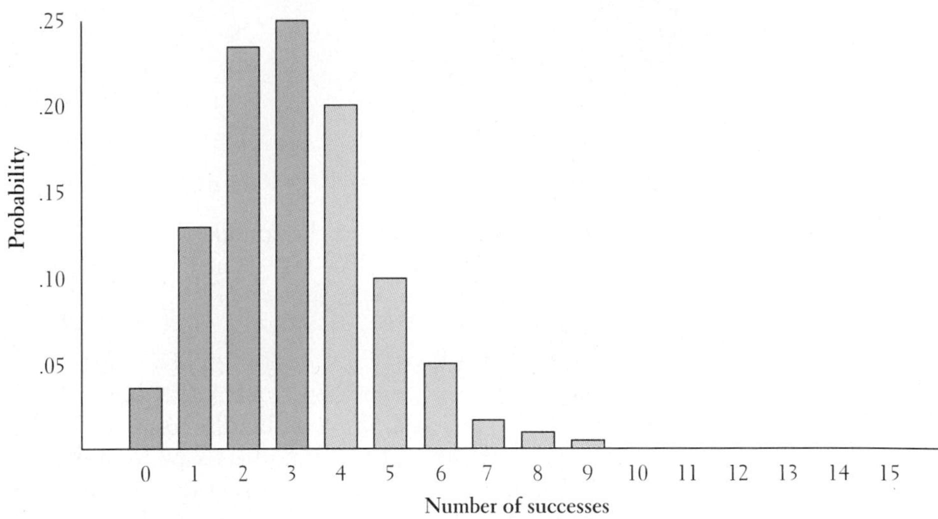

axis. Probabilities are scaled on the vertical axis. Figure 5.5 shades the appropriate probabilities, which add to .648.

In summary, the binomial table reflects the results of solving the binomial formula hundreds of times. It can be used to answer binomial problems if three values are known: the number of trials in the experiment (n), the probability of success on each trial (p), and the number of successes (x) for which the probability is to be computed. Remember that this process is only valid once it has been established that the binomial distribution is a good model of reality. That is, all three conditions that define the binomial distribution must be met.

The widespread use of microcomputers and software packages such as MINITAB may make tables like Appendix E.2's binomial table obsolete. Computer programs calculate binomial probabilities precisely. The MINITAB commands for computing the binomial probability for Example 5.17 are:

```
MTB> SET C1
DATA> 0
DATA> END
MTB> PDF C1;
SUBC> BINOMIAL 9 .3.
       K              P(X = K)
      0.00             0.0404
MTB> STOP
```

The PDF command calculates the probability for the specified value. In this case, the data value was set at $x = 0$ and the binomial subcommand was used to solve for $n = 9$ and $p = .3$.

The MINITAB commands for computing the binomial probability for Example 5.18 are:

```
MTB> SET C1
DATA> 0:3
DATA> END
MTB> CDF C1;
SUBC> BINOMIAL 15 .2.
      K          P(X LESS OR = K)
    0.00              0.0352
    1.00              0.1671
    2.00              0.3980
    3.00              0.6482
MTB> STOP
```

The CDF command computes the cumulative probability of a value less than or equal to x. In this case, the data value was set at $x = 0$ to $x = 3$ and the binomial subcommand used to solve for $n = 15$ and $p = .2$.

■ SITUATION 5.4—PARTIALLY RESOLVED Central Motors is now in a position to use the information from the binomial distribution in its decision-making process. The four desired probabilities must first be restated in appropriate terms. The probability of a profitable day (.61) is rounded to .60 for use in the binomial table. Table 5.6 shows the computations used to construct the binomial table for $n = 6$ and $p = .60$. Management's questions can easily be answered by referring to the binomial table in Appendix E.2.

1. $n = 6, p = .60, x = 6$: from the table, $P(x = 6) = .047$
2. $n = 6, p = .60, x \geq 4$: from the table,
   $P(x \geq 4) = .311 + .187 + .047 = .545$
3. $n = 6, p = .60, x = 0$; from the table, $P(x = 0) = .004$
4. $n = 15, p = .60, x \geq 10$; from the table,
   $P(x \geq 10) = .186 + .127 + .063 + .022 + .005 + .000 = .403$

TABLE 5.6 Probability Distribution for the Number of Profitable Days, Where $n = 6$ and $p = .60$ (Situation 5.4)

x		$P(x)$
0	$\frac{6!}{0!6!}(.60)^0\ (.40)^6 =$	.0041
1	$\frac{6!}{1!5!}(.60)^1\ (.40)^5 =$	.0369
2	$\frac{6!}{2!4!}(.60)^2\ (.40)^4 =$	.1382
3	$\frac{6!}{3!3!}(.60)^3\ (.40)^3 =$	.2765
4	$\frac{6!}{4!2!}(.60)^4\ (.40)^2 =$	.3110
5	$\frac{6!}{5!1!}(.60)^5\ (.40)^1 =$	.1866
6	$\frac{6!}{6!0!}(.60)^6\ (.40)^0 =$	.0467
		1.0000

From this analysis, management can see that it's almost impossible for each day of the week to be profitable (.047, from solution 1). Given the current probability of a good sales day, this level of weekly profit is extremely unlikely. The probability of four or more profitable days is slightly greater than 50% (.545, from solution 2).

On the other hand, Central is quite unlikely to have a bad week, that is, one with no profitable days (.004, from solution 3). Finally, there's less than an even chance (.403, from solution 4) of 10 or more profitable days out of 15.

Management must increase the probability of a profitable day to a larger value to obtain a more encouraging profit picture. It must emphasize salesperson training, increased advertising, and customer incentives if business is to improve. Modeling the sales volume situation with the binomial distribution helps management focus on its unsatisfactory profit picture. The end of the next section further analyzes Central's profit picture. ■

EXERCISES

For the following exercises, assume statistical independence.

35. For a binomial distribution with $n = 8$ and $p = .10$, find:
    a. $P(x = 4)$.
    b. $P(x \leq 3)$.
    c. $P(x \geq 7)$.
    d. $P(x \leq 2)$.

35*a*. .005 *b*. .995 *c*. .000 *d*. .962

36. For a binomial distribution with $n = 20$ and $p = .50$, find:
    a. $P(x = 14)$.
    b. $P(x \leq 13)$.
    c. $P(x \geq 7)$.
    d. $P(x \geq 2)$.

36*a*. .0370 *b*. .9423 *c*. .9423 *d*. 1.000

37. A lawyer who specializes in drug violations and litigation estimates that she wins 70% of her cases that go to court. She has just read "Drugs: The Case for Legalization" in the October 3, 1989, issue of *Financial World* and wants to use some of the article's arguments in her own trial work.

    Based on her estimated probability of success, if she presently represents five defendants in different cases, what is the probability that she'll win at least three cases?

37. .837

38. A film manufacturer advertises that 90 out of 100 prints will develop. Suppose you buy a roll of 20 prints but 5 don't develop. If the manufacturer's claim is true, what is the probability that 5 prints won't develop? Find the probability that 5 or more prints won't develop.

38. .0319 .0433

39. In the past, Phil Anderson has made mistakes on 5% of the tax returns he prepares. What is the probability that he'll make no mistakes on the first seven returns he prepares for the current tax year?

39. .6983

40. A project manager has determined that a subcontractor fails to deliver standard orders on schedule about 20% of the time. The project manager has six orders that this subcontractor has agreed to deliver. Calculate the probability that:

40*a*. .2621
b. .901
c. .3932

a. The subcontractor will deliver all of the orders.

b. The subcontractor will deliver at least four of the orders.

c. The subcontractor will deliver exactly five orders.

41. .0001

41. On Wall Street tradition says that if an NFC team or one of the old NFL teams now in the AFC (Indianapolis Colts, Cleveland Browns, and Pittsburgh Steelers) wins the Super Bowl, stock prices will be higher a year later. If an AFC team wins, the market will stumble ("An Examination of the Super Bowl Stock Market Predictor," *Decision Science Institute Proceedings*, November 21–23, 1988, p. 317). A *USA Today* article (January 23, 1992) indicates that it has worked 22 of 25 times. Suppose that the game outcome and stock price increases are unrelated. Find the probability of the game predicting increases in stock prices 22 times out of 25. Use a computer program.

42. If 40% of the employees in the company data base (see Appendix C) are females, and 10 employees are randomly chosen to serve on a committee, what is the probability that:

42*a*. .2508
b. .0060
c. .6331

a. Four women will be selected?

b. No women will be selected?

c. No more than four women will be selected?

Mean and Standard Deviation of the Binomial Distribution

Mean and Standard Deviation of Binomial

As demonstrated in Chapter 4, the mean and standard deviation are frequently used to summarize data collections. If possible outcomes of a binomial experiment are viewed as a data collection, the mean and standard deviation thus constitute good summary measures. The formulas for the mean (μ) and standard deviation (σ) of a binomial distribution are

$$\mu = np \tag{5.5}$$

$$\sigma = \sqrt{np(1 - p)} \tag{5.6}$$

■ Situation 5.4—Resolved Central Motors can use Equations 5.5 and 5.6 to find the mean and standard deviation of the number of profitable days per six-day work week. Since each day has a 61% chance of being profitable, $n = 6$ and $p = .61$. The mean and standard deviation are

$$\mu = np = (6)(.61) = 3.66$$
$$\sigma = \sqrt{np(1 - p)} = \sqrt{(6)(.61)(.39)} = 1.19$$

Central Motors now knows that if sales over a long period of time are studied, an average of 3.66 profitable days can be expected per week. The standard deviation of profitable days per week is 1.19. In other words, the number of profitable days per week typically varies from the mean by approximately 1.19 days. The low average number of profitable days isn't considered satisfactory, and management attention focuses on ways to improve profitability. Attention is directed specifically toward raising the probability of a profitable day, which now stands at only 61%. ■

EXERCISES

For the following exercises, assume statistical independence.

43. Yes

43. If four customers are asked whether they like a product, and the probability of any of them answering yes is .25, would you expect, on the average, about one yes from the four customers? If you keep asking samples of four customers if they like the product, what would you expect the variability in yes answers to be?

44. Mean = 1.8
SD = 1.2

44. For a binomial distribution with $n = 9$ and $p = .20$, find the mean and standard deviation.

45. Mean = 10
SD = 2.24

45. For a binomial distribution with $n = 20$ and $p = .50$, find the mean and standard deviation.

46. Fifty percent of the residents of Lake County are registered to vote. If 10 people are selected at random:

46*a*. 5
b. 1.58

a. Determine the average of this probability distribution.

b. Determine the variability of this probability distribution.

47. A project manager has determined that a subcontractor delivers standard orders on schedule about 90% of the time. The manager has placed 10 orders that this subcontractor has agreed to deliver.

47*a*. .349
b. 9
c. .95

a. What is the probability that the subcontractor will deliver all of the orders on schedule?

b. What is the mean of this probability distribution?

c. What is the standard deviation of this probability distribution?

48. A salesperson has a 20% chance of making a sale to any customer called upon. If five calls are made:

48*a*. .9421
b. .3277
c. 1
d. .89

a. What is the probability that fewer than three sales will be made?

b. What is the probability of no sales made?

c. What is the average number of sales?

d. What is the variability in the number of sales for each five calls made?

e. Is the binomial distribution a good model of this situation?

49. Mean = 20
SD = 3.46

49. Forty percent of the employees in the company data base (see Appendix C) are female. What are the mean and standard deviation of the number of females if random samples of 50 employees are taken?

■ SITUATION 5.5 On Monday morning, Central Motors management discovered that a batch containing bad parts may have been sent to a customer over the weekend. A bin containing 15 fuel pumps was used to select 5 pumps to be shipped to fill an order. It was discovered later that the 15 fuel pumps in the bin had been tested, and only 10 were in satisfactory condition. Management hopes that there were no defective pumps in the order. The Central analyst must determine the probability that all 5 of them are okay. ■

The Hypergeometric Distribution

The binomial distribution assumes that the population from which the sample is drawn is infinitely large. For this reason, the probability of success doesn't change with each trial. In the coin-flipping example, the number of "available" heads doesn't decrease as head flips occur. The "supply" of heads can be viewed as infinitely large so that the probability of flipping a head remains at .50 no matter how many are flipped.

When the population cannot be assumed to be infinitely large, or even very large, the binomial distribution isn't appropriate. This is because each time an item is selected from the population, the population size is reduced and the probability of success on the next trial changes. The *hypergeometric distribution* is used to model such situations.

An example of such a situation is the determination of the probability of forming a committee of all women if three persons are randomly chosen from a group of five women and four men. The binomial distribution doesn't model this situation because the probability of getting a female member changes each time a selection is made.

Another example is the determination of the probability of obtaining two good parts out of an inventory bin that contains four good parts and eight bad ones. Again, the probabilities keep changing with each draw so that the constant probability requirement of the binomial distribution is violated.

Hypergeometric Distribution

The **hypergeometric distribution** is used to model finite-population situations where samples are taken without replacement. The formula for this distribution is

$$P(x) = \frac{C_{n-x}^{N-r}\, C_x^r}{C_n^N} \tag{5.7}$$

where N = Population size
n = Sample size
r = Number of successes in population
x = Number of successes in sample for which a probability is desired
C = Combination

Note: C_x^n is an alternative way of expressing a combination.

> The **hypergeometric distribution** is used to model finite-population situations where sampling is done without replacement and where the probability of a certain number of successes is to be calculated.

Example 5.19 In a room containing eight people there are four members of a union. A random sample of three is selected for a committee. What is the probability that exactly one of them is a union member? Since the population is quite small ($N = 8$) and the sampling must be done without replacement, the binomial distribution isn't appropriate; the probability of selecting a union member changes each time a person is chosen. The hypergeometric distribution should be used with the following parameters:

$$N = 8 \qquad r = 4 \qquad n = 3 \qquad x = 1$$

The solution is

$$P(x = 1) = \frac{C_{3-1}^{8-4} C_1^4}{C_3^8} = \frac{\dfrac{4!}{2!2!}\,\dfrac{4!}{1!3!}}{\dfrac{8!}{3!5!}} = \frac{\dfrac{(4)(3)(2)(1)(4)(3)(2)(1)}{(2)(1)(2)(1)(1)(3)(2)(1)}}{\dfrac{(8)(7)(6)(5)(4)(3)(2)(1)}{(3)(2)(1)(5)(4)(3)(2)(1)}}$$

$$= \frac{24}{56} = .429$$

EXAMPLE 5.20 An auditor randomly selects 3 accounts from a group of 10 for careful examination. The company being audited knows that 4 of the tax accounts contain errors. What is the probability that all 3 of the accounts selected are error-free? Here $N = 10$, $n = 3$, $r = 6$ (the number of good accounts in the population), and $x = 3$ (the number of good accounts in the sample). The solution is

$$P(x = 3) = \frac{C_{3-3}^{10-6} C_3^6}{C_3^{10}} = \frac{\dfrac{4!}{0!4!}\,\dfrac{6!}{3!3!}}{\dfrac{10!}{3!7!}}$$

$$= \frac{\dfrac{(4)(3)(2)(1)(6)(5)(4)(3)(2)(1)}{(1)(4)(3)(2)(1)(3)(2)(1)(3)(2)(1)}}{\dfrac{(10)(9)(8)(7)(6)(5)(4)(3)(2)(1)}{(3)(2)(1)(7)(6)(5)(4)(3)(2)(1)}} = \frac{20}{120} = .167$$

■ SITUATION 5.5—RESOLVED The fuel pump problem can be modeled with the hypergeometric distribution but not the binomial. When the first pump is selected for shipment, the probability of getting a good one is 10 chances out of 15, or .67. But the chance of getting a good pump on the second try changes. Now there are only 14 pumps in the population and either 9 or 10 good ones, depending on whether the first one was good or bad. Although each pump drawn is either good or bad, this situation cannot be modeled with the binomial distribution because the small population size (15) results in a different probability of success each time a trial takes place.

The values required for the hypergeometric distribution formula are

$N = 15$ (the number of pumps in the population)
$n = 5$ (the number of pumps in the sample)
$r = 10$ (the number of good pumps in the population)
$x = 5$ (the number of good pumps in the sample for which the probability is to be determined)

Placing these values into Equation 5.7 produces the probability of a completely good shipment:

$$P(5) = \frac{C^{15-10}_{5-5}\,C^{10}_{5}}{C^{15}_{5}} = \frac{\dfrac{5!}{0!5!}\cdot\dfrac{10!}{5!5!}}{\dfrac{15!}{5!10!}} = \frac{(1)(252)}{3{,}003} = .0839$$

It is apparent that there's a very low probability (.0839) of a defect-free shipment. Management should contact the buyer and arrange to test the shipment and replace the defective pumps. ■

EXERCISES

50. Explain the similarities between the binomial distribution and the hypergeometric distribution.

51. Explain the differences between the binomial distribution and the hypergeometric distribution.

52. .238

52. Given $N = 10$, $n = 4$, $r = 5$, and $x = 3$, solve this hypergeometric problem.

53. A tire store has 20 identical grade A tires in stock. Five of these tires are slightly damaged. A customer purchases a set of four tires. Compute the probability distribution for the number of undamaged tires obtained by the customer.

54. .42

54. The Kingston Bank has 15 accounts receivable with open balances in its RV loan department. The bank president wants to modify the bank's business after reading a *Bankers Monthly* article entitled, "Banks that Make Money without Lending It" (February 1989, p. 58). He decides to sample some of the RV loans and study their profitability.

    Of the outstanding loans, six have balances above $1,000. The president selects at random five accounts receivable for study. Find the probability that exactly two of these audited accounts will have balances over $1,000.

55. .308

55. Local 429 has 25 members. Fifteen are in favor of a strike, and 10 are not. Find the probability that a random sample of 6 workers contains 3 who favor the strike and 3 who oppose it.

56. .138

56. A government agency is checking label specifications for a product. Suppose that in a particular crate, 6 out of 24 cans' contents don't meet their label specifications. The agency chooses 6 cans from a crate. What is the probability that the agency will find no mislabeled cans?

■ SITUATION 5.6 Another problem Central Motors management faces concerns the main office's telephone switchboard. The number of people answering the switchboard varies considerably during the day even though the number of incoming calls is steady over the entire working day. Management believes that analysis of this situation could provide useful information for deciding how many people to assign to the switchboard. ■

THE POISSON DISTRIBUTION

The Poisson distribution is another useful theoretical distribution for modeling certain real situations. Probabilities can be found without lengthy and costly observations of the real world.

Poisson Distribution

The **Poisson distribution** is used to model situations where the number of trials is very large and the number of successes is very small. The key issue to address before using the Poisson distribution involves the concept of randomness. That is, the arrival of the events in question mustn't follow any pattern. If the arrivals are truly random, the Poisson distribution can provide useful decision-making information.

V

> The **Poisson distribution** is used to model situations where there are random arrivals of events per unit of space or time, and where the probability of a specific number of successes is desired. It can be shown mathematically that a binomial distribution for which n becomes very large and p becomes very small approaches the Poisson distribution.

The formula for the Poisson distribution is

$$P(x) = \frac{\mu^x e^{-\mu}}{x!} \tag{5.8}$$

where μ = Mean number of arrivals per unit of time or space
x = Number of arrivals for which the probability is desired
e = Base of the natural logarithms, a mathematical constant approximately equal to 2.71828

Equation 5.8 shows that the Poisson distribution describes a discrete random variable that may assume any value in an infinite sequence ($x = 0, 1, 2, 3, \ldots$). Note that we need only one measure to compute the probability of a given x value: the mean number of arrivals per unit of time or space (μ). Examples 5.21 and 5.22 illustrate Equation 5.8's use.

EXAMPLE 5.21 A mail-order house switchboard receives an average of 3.5 orders per hour. These arrivals appear to be random; that is, there's no discernible pattern during the day or from day to day. What is the probability of exactly four calls arriving in a given hour? Since $\mu = 3.5$ and $x = 4$, the probability is

$$P(x = 4) = \frac{3.5^4(2.71828)^{-3.5}}{4!} = \frac{150.0625}{4 \cdot 3 \cdot 2 \cdot 1\,(2.71828)^{3.5}} = .189$$

EXAMPLE 5.22 *The American Statistician* (November 1992, pp. 246–53) reported on a study, "A Bayesian Analysis of a Poisson Random Effects Model for Home Run Hitters," that showed how the Poisson distribution could be used to estimate a hitter's ability to hit home runs. The statistic used for measuring a player's home run hitting ability is the observed rate, which divides the total number of home runs in a career by the total number of official at-bats. In baseball statistics books[1] this home run rate statistic is usually expressed as the number of at-bats for each home run hit. Babe Ruth was the greatest home run hitter with 714 career home runs in 8,389 career at-bats: a rate of .085. Using the Poisson distribution with an average rate of .085, what is the probability of Babe Ruth hitting no home runs in his next 10 at-bats? The rate is .085 for 1 at-bat or .85 for 10 at-bats. Hence $\mu = .85$ and $x = 0$. The probability is

$$P(x = 0) = \frac{.85^0(2.71828)^{-.85}}{0!} = \frac{1}{(2.71828)^{.85}} = .427$$

■ SITUATION 5.6—PARTIALLY RESOLVED After addressing the randomness issue, Central Motors management decides that phone calls are indeed random. There don't appear to be certain times of day when more calls arrive compared to others, and there doesn't seem to be any pattern. So they model the telephone situation using the Poisson process.

Management decides on a five-minute interval as the unit of time to evaluate. To use the Poisson distribution, Central's analyst must compute the mean, or average, number of arrivals per five-minute interval during the work day. Several five-minute intervals are selected at random during the next week. It is determined that the mean number of calls during these intervals is 4.8. This value is the mean of the Poisson distribution used to calculate probabilities.

Table 5.7 presents the probability distribution for the number of arrivals per five-minute interval. Figure 5.6 graphs this probability distribution. To find the probabilities to complete Table 5.7, we solve the Poisson formula (Equation 5.8) several times. Fortunately, statisticians have anticipated this situation and have solved the Poisson formula for hundreds of different problems. (Results of these computations, the Poisson Table in Appendix E.4, are discussed in the next section.) ■

EXERCISES

57. Explain the difference between the binomial distribution and the Poisson distribution.

58. .3679

58. Given $\mu = 1$, $x = 1$, solve this Poisson problem.

59. The Medical Lake fire station receives an average of two calls per day. Construct a probability distribution for the number of calls, assuming the Poisson distribution is an appropriate model.

60. .3679

60. In the past, trucks have randomly arrived at a loading dock at the rate of one per hour. What is the probability that no trucks will arrive in the next hour?

[1]S. Siwoff, S. Hirdt, T. Hirdt, and P. Hirdt, *The 1991 Elias Baseball Analyst* (New York: Fireside, 1991).

TABLE 5.7 Probability Distribution for the Arrival of Telephone Calls (Situation 5.6)

x	$P(x)$
0	$\frac{4.8^0\, 2.71828^{-4.8}}{0!} = .0082$
1	$\frac{4.8^1\, 2.71828^{-4.8}}{1!} = .0395$
2	$\frac{4.8^2\, 2.71828^{-4.8}}{2!} = .0948$
3	$\frac{4.8^3\, 2.71828^{-4.8}}{3!} = .1517$
4	$\frac{4.8^4\, 2.71828^{-4.8}}{4!} = .1820$
5	$\frac{4.8^5\, 2.71828^{-4.8}}{5!} = .1747$
6	$\frac{4.8^6\, 2.71828^{-4.8}}{6!} = .1398$
7	$\frac{4.8^7\, 2.71828^{-4.8}}{7!} = .0959$
8	$\frac{4.8^8\, 2.71828^{-4.8}}{8!} = .0575$
9	$\frac{4.8^9\, 2.71828^{-4.8}}{9!} = .0307$

FIGURE 5.6 Graphical Representation for the Probability Distribution of Telephone Call Arrivals

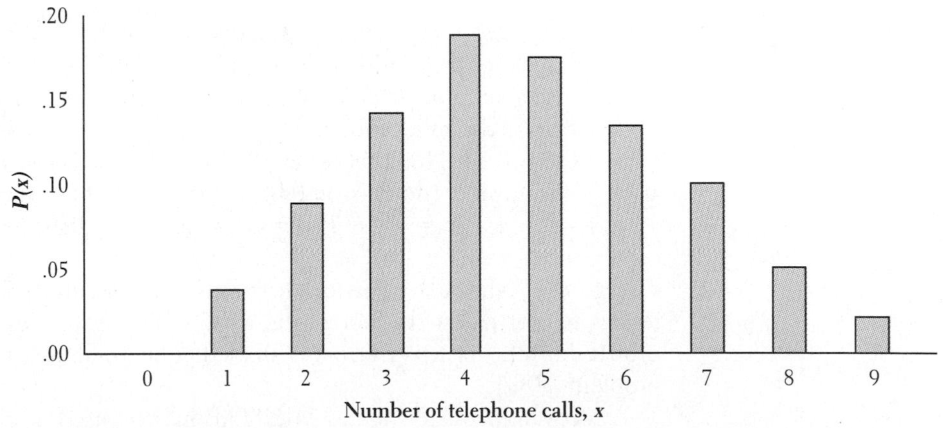

61. .2681

61. The Cheney Federal Credit Union receives, on the average, 2.2 applications for home improvement loans per week. What is the probability that it will receive two applications this week?

62. .1140

62. Inland Empire Telephone observes that 3.2 calls per minute come in on a certain line, on the average. What is the probability that five calls will come in on that line during the next minute?

63. .2231

63. The Pannell Corporation deposits cash reserves into its sick-leave fund on the assumption that its employees will require sick-leave pay for a total of 1.5 days, on the average, each month. What is the probability that no employees will call in sick this month?

POISSON DISTRIBUTION TABLE

Poisson Table

The Poisson distribution of Equation 5.8 has been solved for hundreds of values and compiled in a table (see Appendix E.4) for convenient use. The blocks of probabilities are headed by various values of μ, the mean or average number of occurrences per unit of time or space. Using the appropriate column, we can read the probabilities of the x values appearing on the left edge of the table.

EXAMPLE 5.23 From 1983 through 1987, the average number of fatal accidents for certificated route air carriers was 2.8 (*Statistical Abstract of the United States: 1989*, p. 611). Assume that the number of fatal accidents per year among certificated route air carriers can be adequately described by a Poisson probability distribution with mean 2.8. What is the probability of 3 or more fatal accidents in 1988? Look in the Poisson table in the column for $\mu = 2.8$. The probabilities of 0 through 2 accidents from this column are added: $P(x = 0) + P(x = 1) + P(x = 2) = .0608 + .1703 + .2384 = .4695$. The probability of 3 or more equals .5305 (1 − .4695).

EXAMPLE 5.24 If the mean value of a Poisson process is .90, what is the probability the x will be either 0 or 1? From the Poisson table for $\mu = .90$, the probabilities of 0 and 1 can be added: $P(x = 0) + P(x = 1) = .4066 + .3659 = .7725$.

EXAMPLE 5.25 According to *Fortune*, July 3, 1989, Westinghouse has been trying to make quality "the company religion," especially in the manufacturing processes.

Suppose a key process at Westinghouse generates errors at an average rate of 5.7 per hour. Errors arrive randomly, and the probability of 3 or fewer errors in a given hour is to be determined. This process can be modeled with the Poisson distribution. In the $\mu = 5.7$ column of the Poisson table, probabilities of 0 through 3 are added: $P(x = 0) + P(x = 1) + P(x = 2) + P(x = 3) = .0033 + .0191 + .0544 + .1033 = .1801$.

Figure 5.7 shows the Poisson distribution for Example 5.25. The number of occurrences is plotted on the horizontal axis, and probabilities are plotted vertically. The probability of 3 or fewer errors is shaded. This total area is the correct answer to the problem, .1801.

A software package such as MINITAB may be used in place of the Poisson table in Appendix E.4. MINITAB commands for computing Table 5.7's Poisson probability distribution are:

```
MTB> PDF;
SUBC> POISSON 4.8.
      K            P(X = K)
      0              0.0082
      SEE TABLE 5.7 FOR REST OF PROBABILITIES
MTB> STOP
```

FIGURE 5.7 Poisson Distribution for Example 5.25 ($\mu = 5.7$)

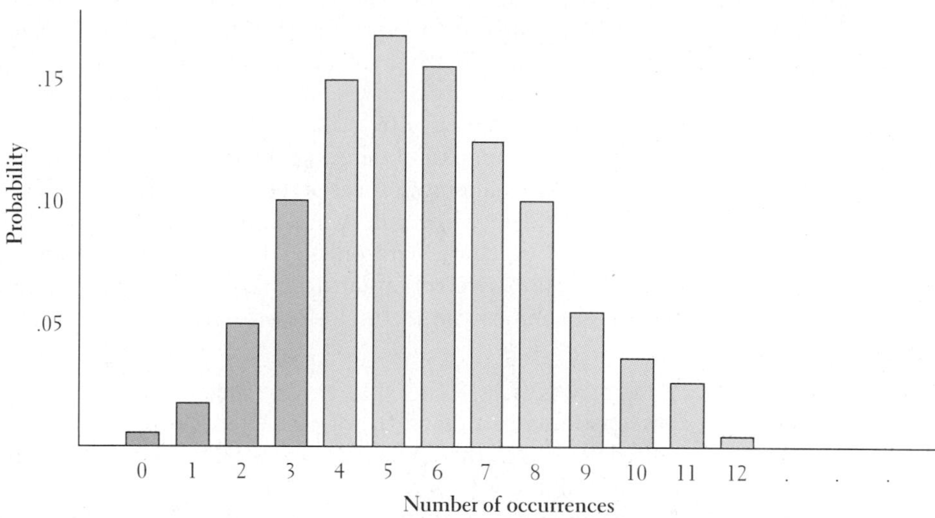

The PDF command calculates individual probabilities for the Poisson distribution with a mean of 4.8.

The MINITAB commands for computing the Poisson probability for Example 5.25 are:

```
MTB> SET C1
DATA> 0:3
DATA> END
MTB> CDF C1;
SUBC> POISSON 5.7.
          K        P(X LESS OR = K)
       0.00            0.0033
       1.00            0.0224
       2.00            0.0768
       3.00            0.1800
MTB> STOP
```

The CDF command computes the cumulative probability of a value less than or equal to x. In this case, the DATA command was used to specify the range $x = 0$ to $x = 3$, and the Poisson subcommand solved for a Poisson distribution with a mean of 5.7.

The definition of the Poisson distribution states that the mean number of arrivals per unit of time or space must be determined. The telephone example used a length of time as the measurement unit, namely, a five-minute period. The Poisson distribution can also be used to model the random arrivals of items per unit of space.

EXAMPLE 5.26 Suppose an aluminum sheet roll manufacturer wants to compute the probability of a defect-free roll. A roll of aluminum sheet is the unit of space to be modeled. To use the Poisson distribution, the mean number of defects that "arrive" on each roll must be known.

The aluminum sheet production process is watched over a period of several days, and it's decided that defects do occur on a random basis and the mean number of defects per roll is observed to be .30. The Poisson table can now be used to find the probability of a defect-free roll. Turn to this table and find the column headed by a μ of .30. The probability that x (number of defects on any given roll) equals 0 is the first number in the column: $P(x = 0) = .7408$.

If the mean number of defects per roll is .30 and these defects arrive randomly, the manager of the aluminum sheet process knows that there's a 74% chance of the process producing a defect-free roll. A decision can now be made as to whether this level of quality is satisfactory. With only a 74% chance of a defect-free roll, the manager decides that corrective action must be taken. A training process for operators is started, and the machine manufacturer is contacted about necessary improvements.

■ SITUATION 5.6—RESOLVED In Appendix E.4's Poisson table, locate the column corresponding to a mean (μ) of 4.8. This column indicates that the probability that x will be 0 is .0082, the probability that x will be 1 is .0395, and so on. These same values appear in Table 5.7.

Management can now determine the probabilities pertinent to the switchboard staffing problem. Remember that the time period being used is five minutes and that the mean number of phone calls during this interval is 4.8. Management seeks probabilities of the following events: no calls, three or fewer calls, and five or fewer calls.

The probabilities associated with these events are found in the Poisson table's $\mu = 4.8$ column. The first probability, for $x = 0$, is read directly from the table: .0082. The second probability is the sum of the probabilities for x values 0 through 3; the third is the sum of the probabilities for x values 0 through 5. The three desired probabilities are

$$P(x = 0) = .0082$$
$$P(x \leq 3) = .2942$$
$$P(x \leq 5) = .6509$$

Management is surprised at these low probabilities. It had hoped to use only one operator to staff the switchboard, but apparently many incoming calls can be expected.

The next key question is how long it takes an operator to service each call. If each call can be answered and processed in a few seconds, one operator might be enough. However, if each call averages one minute or more, additional operators will be needed. ■

EXERCISES

64. .1631

65. .7745

66. .1563

64. Given $\mu = 4.6$, $x = 3$, solve this Poisson problem.
65. Given $\mu = 5.3$, $x \geq 4$, solve this Poisson problem.
66. Customers arrive at the Country Counter supermarket at the rate of two every three minutes. What is the probability that five customers will arrive within the next six minutes?
67. The Bon Department Store has determined that demand for a certain model of camera is Poisson-distributed with a mean of two per week. The camera department manager wants

to study current camera demand to see if it justifies offering photography classes. She has just read "Into the Landscape" in *American Photographer* (August 1989, p. 34) and thinks such a class would be effective.

a. Determine the probability distribution of weekly demand for the camera.

b. If the store stocks four of these cameras in a particular week, what is the probability that demand will exceed supply?

67*b*. .0526

68. Cars arrive at the ZZ Car Wash at the average rate of 9 per hour. If arrivals per hour follow the Poisson distribution, find the probability of 15 or more arrivals during any given hour of operation.

68. .0415

69. Customer arrivals at the Federal Credit Union are Poisson-distributed and average 2.5 per minute.

a. What is the probability of exactly three arrivals in a one-minute period?

b. What is the probability of fewer than three arrivals in a one-minute period?

c. What is the probability of more than three arrivals in a one-minute period?

d. What is the probability of exactly three arrivals in a two-minute period?

69*a*. .2138
b. .5438
c. .2424
d. .1404

70. It is estimated that the number of taxis waiting to pick up customers in front of the JFK Terminal is Poisson-distributed with a mean of 5.5 cabs.

a. Find the probability that on random observation, exactly 6 cabs will be waiting.

b. Find the probability that on random observation, more than 10 cabs will be waiting.

c. Find the probability that on random observation, no cabs will be waiting.

70*a*. .1571
b. .0252
c. .0041

■ SITUATION 5.7 Central Motors' final problem involves inventory of a key part, engine spark plugs. Their large inventory has been supplied by a single manufacturer, which has recently informed them that some plugs may be defective. The supplier has found that about 2% of the plugs delivered during the past three years won't function properly. Since spark plugs will be randomly drawn from inventory, and since a plug either works properly or doesn't, Central decides that this situation can be modeled using the binomial distribution.

The problem would be simple if a tune-up for only one car were being considered. In that case, n, the number of plugs drawn from inventory, would be 4, 6, or 8, depending on the engine size. The binomial table could then be used to find, for example, the probability of no defective plugs used in a tune-up.

But Central is interested in the larger picture. Each week it draws approximately 100 plugs from inventory. They wish to model this situation with the binomial distribution; that is, management wants to know the probability of having no defective spark plugs drawn from inventory during a week. It also wants to know the probability of drawing five or fewer defective spark plugs. This problem can be characterized as follows:

$$n = 100 \qquad p = .02 \qquad P(x = 0) = ?$$
$$P(x \leq 5) = ?$$

The binomial formula can be used to find the probabilities for various numbers of defective plugs in each 100-plug batch. This would be very time-consuming, however, since the number of "trials" (100) is so large. Moreover, a binomial table rarely contains entries for n larger than 20. Thus, even though this situation is eligible for modeling with the binomial distribution, there doesn't seem to be a handy way to find the desired probabilities. ■

Poisson Approximation to the Binomial

Poisson Approximation to the Binomial

In binomial distribution problems where n is large and where the probability of success (p) is either quite small or quite large, probabilities can be approximated using the Poisson distribution. In this method, the "arrivals" of successes of the binomial are presumed to follow a Poisson process. Although probabilities computed using this approximation aren't precise, they're quite close to the true binomial probabilities.

> The Poisson distribution provides a close approximation to the binomial distribution when n is large and p is either quite small or quite large. As a rule of thumb, use of the approximation is appropriate when $n > 20$ and $np \leq 5$ or $n(1 - p) \leq 5$.

Figure 5.8 summarizes methods to find binomial probabilities. The vertical axis represents n, the number of independent trials in the binomial experiment. If n is small enough, the binomial table can be used to find the correct probability of the desired outcome. If n is larger than 20 (the maximum size of most binomial tables), the binomial probability must be approximated. If the rule of thumb holds ($np \leq 5$ or $n[1 - p] \leq 5$), this approximation can be made using the Poisson distribution. If this

TM

FIGURE 5.8 Methods of Solving Binomial Problems

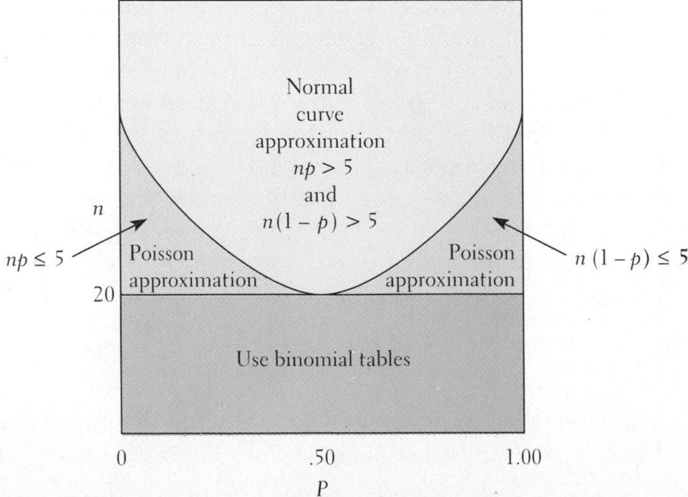

rule of thumb doesn't hold, the approximation is made using the normal distribution, which we will describe in Chapter 6.

EXAMPLE 5.27 One percent of the employees in a large factory are absent each day. If 70 employee names are randomly selected, what is the probability that no more than one is absent? Since n is quite large and $np \leq 5$ ($np = .7$), this binomial problem can be solved using the Poisson approximation. The mean number of absent employees calculated using Equation 5.5 is used to enter the Poisson table:

$$\mu = np = (70)(.01) = .7$$

The Poisson table column for $\mu = .7$ is used:

$$P(x = 0) + P(x = 1) = .4966 + .3476 = .8442$$

EXAMPLE 5.28 A sample of 116 parts is randomly drawn from inventory to be shipped to a customer. We know that the process that produced the parts generates 2.5% defective parts over time. What is the probability that the shipment contains exactly three defectives? Again, the large n and small p call for approximating the binomial probability using the Poisson distribution ($np = 2.9$):

$$\mu = np = (116)(.025) = 2.9$$

Referring to the Poisson table column for $\mu = 2.9$,

$$P(x = 3) = .2237$$

Note that software packages such as MINITAB make binomial approximations unnecessary. MINITAB commands for computing the binomial probability for Example 5.28 are:

```
MTB> SET C1
DATA> 3
DATA> END
MTB> PDF C1;
SUBC> BINOMIAL 116 .025.
       K            P(X = K)
    3.00             0.2266
MTB> STOP
```

Note how close the Poisson approximation .2237 is to the correct binomial probability, .2266.

■ SITUATION 5.7—RESOLVED In Central Motors' spark plug problem, n is large (100) and p is quite small (.02). Therefore, the Poisson distribution is used as an approximation of the true binomial distribution to find the probability that all the spark plugs used in a week are defect-free. The first step is to calculate the mean of this binomial situation:

$$\mu = np = (100)(.02) = 2 \qquad \text{(verifying that } np \leq 5\text{)}$$

The average number of faulty plugs in each week's supply of 100 is 2, so the Poisson table is entered using the column for a mean of 2. The reasoning is that defective plugs arrive at an average rate of 2 in each lot of 100.

Turn to the Poisson table in Appendix E.4 and find the column for a mean of 2. This column contains the probabilities of several occurrences of x, the number of defective plugs in each 100-plug batch. The first entry is for $x = 0$, the value desired by Central Motors. $P(x = 0) = .1353$, indicating a small probability that the plugs selected for the week will be defect-free. Central needs to work with its supplier to replace all the plugs in inventory or to establish a testing procedure for each plug prior to using it in a tune-up.

What is the probability that there will be 4 bad plugs in each week's 100-unit lot? The probability entry for $x = 4$ from the Poisson table is .0902.

The alternative would be to use the binomial formula:

$$P(x = 4) = \binom{100}{4}(.02)^4(.98)^{100-4} = .090208$$

Note how close the Poisson approximation is to the true binomial probability.

What is the probability of 5 or fewer bad plugs in each week's 100-unit lot? The answer is approximated by adding the probabilities for 0 through 5 in the $\mu = 2$ column in the Poisson table:

$$\begin{aligned} P(x \leq 5) &= .1353 + .2707 + .2707 + .1804 + .0902 + .0361 \\ &= .9834 \end{aligned}$$

There's about a 98% chance that the week's supply of 100 spark plugs will contain 5 or fewer defective units. ■

EXERCISES

71. When is the Poisson distribution a good approximation of the binomial distribution?
72. Why is the Poisson distribution used as an approximation of the binomial distribution?

73*a*. .3033
b. .0000

73. *a*. Given $n = 25$, $p = .02$, $x = 1$, solve this binomial problem.
    b. Given $n = 40$, $p = .97$, $x = 4$, solve this binomial problem.

74*a*. 3
b. .0498
c. .3528
d. .1991

74. Three percent of the hand calculators of a particular model fail within the first month of operation. F-Mart has just received a batch of 100.
    a. What is the expected number of calculators that will fail in the first month of operation?
    b. Find the probability that no calculators will fail.
    c. Find the probability that more than three calculators will fail.
    d. Find the probability that fewer than two calculators will fail.

75*a*. .1353
b. .0361
c. .0166

75. The Articulate Corporation has come to expect that 99% of its accounts receivable balances are error-free. A sample of 200 accounts has been selected for audit.
    a. What is the probability that none of the accounts will have errors?
    b. What is the probability that five of the accounts will have errors?
    c. What is the probability that more than five of the accounts will have errors?

76. .9972

76. TAB University has determined that 4% of newly accepted graduate students don't register for classes. Next fall's class list has 100 newly admitted graduate students. Find the probability that at least 90 will register for classes.

Summary

This chapter has covered some basic ideas of probability and introduced the concepts of random variables and probability distributions. These concepts are necessary for the statistical procedures in the remainder of this book.

In addition, this chapter explained three important theoretical distributions and their applications to real-world business problems: the binomial, the hypergeometric, and the Poisson distributions. When a practical problem fits the specifications of one of these distributions, valuable decision-making information can be gained without doing expensive, time-consuming manipulations and real-world observations.

Applications of Statistical Concepts in the Business World

This chapter's procedures enjoy increasing practice in the business world. Their use in providing decision makers with reliable information is becoming more and more apparent as growing numbers of college students enter the business world armed with knowledge of these techniques. The concepts of probability, random variables, and probability distributions help decision makers assess the future with some degree of confidence. Indeed, an ability to deal with the uncertain future is vital for a modern business executive.

The concept of expected value is quite useful for establishing a baseline for assessing an opportunity's monetary aspects. Expected loss due to fire or theft can be used to determine the appropriate level of insurance payments, for example. The average number of defective units per shift can assist in a company's quality-control efforts. If a discrete probability distribution can be formed based on past history, then the expected value (or average value of this distribution) can provide management with valuable baseline performance information.

The binomial distribution is widely applicable in business because so many situations involve the concept of success versus failure. The key point, as this chapter stressed, is to make sure the trials are independent before using the binomial distribution as a model. Examples of situations that can be modeled with the binomial distribution, assuming this independence assumption is met, are:

1. Manufactured or purchased parts either meet quality-control specifications or don't.
2. A customer buying a major appliance either returns for another purchase or goes elsewhere.
3. A bid for a contract job either is successful or results in failure.
4. An employee hired using the company's screening process either proves to be satisfactory or does not work out.
5. An account payable either results in the company being paid or becomes a bad-debt expense.
6. As a result of an intensive advertising campaign, a company's market share either increases or does not increase.

The Poisson distribution is widely applicable in business because many situations involve random arrivals. The key point, as stressed in this chapter, is to be sure the occurrences are random before using the Poisson distribution as a model. A few examples of situations that might be modeled with the Poisson, if this randomness assumption is met, are:

1. The arrivals of cars at a tollbooth, customers at a bank or checkout counter, or trucks at a weighing station.
2. The arrivals of telephone calls at a switchboard.
3. The number of defects per mile of underground cable.
4. The number of blemishes per panel.

Glossary

Probability A measure of the likelihood that a future event will occur; it can assume any value between 0 and 1, inclusive.

Sample space The collection of all possible outcomes for an experiment.

Experiment Any process that generates well-defined outcomes.

Event A possible outcome of an experiment.

Relative frequency A probability defined as the number of times an event occurs divided by the total number of times an experiment is performed.

Subjective probability A probability value that reflects the feelings or opinions concerning the likelihood that a particular outcome will occur.

Complement The collection of outcomes that aren't contained in a given event.

Collectively exhaustive Refers to a list containing every possible event that can occur.

Mutually exclusive Refers to events where the occurrence of one precludes the occurrence of any other.

Addition rule A rule used when it's necessary to compute the probability that *either* event A or event B occurs.

Independence A condition involving two events where one event's occurrence in no way influences the likelihood of the other's occurrence.

Dependence A condition involving two events where one event's occurrence alters the likelihood of the other's occurrence.

Multiplication rule A rule used when it's necessary to compute the probability that *both* event A and event B occur.

Random variable A variable defined by assigning one numerical value to each simple event of an experiment that yields random outcomes.

Discrete random variable A variable that can assume only values from a predetermined set.

Probability distribution A listing of the possible values that a random variable can assume along with their probabilities.

Expected value The average value assumed by a random variable over a large number of observations.

Binomial distribution A discrete probability distribution involving the likelihood of x successes in n trials of a binomial experiment.

Combination The number of ways in which x things can be chosen from a collection of n things when the order of choosing isn't important.

Hypergeometric distribution A distribution used to model finite-population situations where sampling is done without replacement and where the probability of a certain number of successes is to be calculated.

Poisson distribution A distribution used to model situations where the arrivals of events per unit of space or time are random and where the probability of a specific number of successes is to be determined.

KEY FORMULAS

Expected value of a discrete random variable

$$E(x) = \Sigma[x \cdot P(x)] \tag{5.1}$$

Variance of a discrete random variable

$$\sigma^2 = \Sigma(x - \mu)^2 P(x) \tag{5.2}$$

Binomial probability distribution

$$P(x) = \binom{n}{x} p^x(1 - p)^{n-x} \tag{5.3}$$

Combination formula

$$\binom{n}{x} = \frac{n!}{x!\,(n - x)!} \tag{5.4}$$

Expected value (mean) for a binomial probability distribution

$$\mu = np \tag{5.5}$$

Standard deviation for a binomial probability distribution

$$\sigma = \sqrt{np(1 - p)} \tag{5.6}$$

The hypergeometric probability distribution

$$P(x) = \frac{C^{N-r}_{n-x} C^r_x}{C^N_n} \tag{5.7}$$

The Poisson probability distribution

$$P(x) = \frac{\mu^x e^{-\mu}}{x!} \tag{5.8}$$

SOLVED EXERCISES

1. MULTIPLICATION AND ADDITION RULES

A motel keeps two vehicles ready for picking up patrons at the airport and railway station. Due to demand and chance of mechanical failure, the probability that a specific vehicle will be available when needed is .6. One vehicle's availability is independent of the other's.

a. In the event of two arrivals calling at the same time (one from the airport and one from the railway station) what is the probability that both vehicles will be available?

b. Find the probability that neither will be available.

c. If one call is placed from the airport, what is the probability that a vehicle is available?

Solution

a. The probability that one vehicle will be available is .6. The probability that both vehicles will be available is .6 × .6 = .36.

b. The probability that one vehicle won't be available is (1 − .6) = .4. The probability that both vehicles won't be available is .4 × .4 = .16.

c. There are three ways that at least one of the two vehicles will be available. Either only the first vehicle is available, only the second vehicle is available, or both vehicles are available. The probability that both are available is .36. The probability of just one vehicle being available is .6 × .4 = .24, and this can occur in two different ways. Therefore, the probability of at least one of the vehicles being available is .36 + .24 + .24 = .84. An alternative solution would be to compute the complement of neither vehicle being available: 1 − .16 = .84.

2. Random Variables

Identify which of the following random variables can be classified as discrete.

a. The number of people arriving at a checkout counter.

b. The number of ounces in a bottle of cola.

c. Tomorrow's temperature.

d. The number of sales made by a car salesperson today.

e. The weight of a roast bought at the supermarket.

f. The number of offers received on a house for sale.

Solution:

a. The number of people is a discrete variable.

b. The number of ounces is a continuous variable.

c. Temperature is a continuous variable.

d. The number of sales is a discrete variable.

e. Weight is a continuous variable.

f. The number of offers is a discrete variable.

3. Probability Distribution

Hanson Construction Company is having a problem with broken tools. A probability distribution of the number of broken tools each day for the past three months is:

Number of broken tools	$P(x)$
0	.30
1	.25
2	.15
3	.20
4 or more	.10

a. Find the probability of three broken tools tomorrow.

b. Find the probability of more than one broken tool tomorrow.

c. Find the probability of no broken tools in the next two days.

Solution:

a. $P(3) = .20.$

b. $P(2) + P(3) + P(4) = .15 + .20 + .10 = .45.$

c. $P(0) \times P(0) = .30 \times .30 = .09.$

4. EXPECTED VALUE

The Nutra Company has determined that if a new line of sweetener is marketed, the following probability distribution will describe its contribution to the firm's profits during the next three months:

Profit contribution	P(Profit contribution)
−$ 3,000	.2
$ 5,000	.5
$20,000	.3

Nutra has decided it should market the new sweetener if expected contribution to profit for the next three months is over $10,000. Based on the probability distribution, will it market the new sweetener?

Solution:

$$(.2 \times -3{,}000) + (.5 \times 5{,}000) + (.3 \times 20{,}000) = \$7{,}900$$

The company shouldn't market the new sweetener.

5. COMBINATIONS

Mary Livingston, president of the Maxell Corporation in Chicago, must prepare an itinerary for visiting three of the company's six plants. The trip's cost will depend on which plants she chooses to visit. How many different itineraries are possible?

Solution:

$$\binom{6}{3} = \frac{6!}{3!(6-3)!} = \frac{(6)\,(5)\,(4)\,(3)\,(2)\,(1)}{(3)\,(2)\,(1)\,(3)\,(2)\,(1)} = 20$$

6. BINOMIAL DISTRIBUTION

Large shipments of incoming parts at the Drummond Manufacturing plant are inspected for defective items using a random sampling scheme. Five items are to be examined; a lot is rejected if one or more defective items are observed. If the lot contains 5% defectives, what is the probability that it will be accepted? Rejected?

Solution:

The shipment will be accepted only when there are zero defectives. This can only happen one way:

$$\binom{5}{0} = \frac{5!}{0!(5-0)!} = \frac{(5)\,(4)\,(3)\,(2)\,(1)}{(1)\,(5)\,(4)\,(3)\,(2)\,(1)} = 1$$

Therefore, the probability of accepting the shipment is

$$P(0) = \binom{5}{0} p^0(1-p)^{5-0} = (1).05^0(1-.05)^5 = .7738$$

The probability of rejecting the shipment is

$$(1 - .7738) = .2262$$

7. BINOMIAL DISTRIBUTION

Sixty percent of the residents of King County are registered to vote. If 10 people who are old enough to vote are selected at random, find the probability of obtaining:

a. Ten registered voters.
b. Exactly five registered voters.
c. No registered voters.

Solution:

a. $n = 10, p = .60, x = 10$: from the table, $P(x = 10) = .006$.
b. $n = 10, p = .60, x = 5$: from the table, $P(x = 5) = .201$.
c. $n = 10, p = .60, x = 0$: from the table, $P(x = 0) = .000$.

8. BINOMIAL DISTRIBUTION

Colorado Power Company provides lower rates to customers who agree to use energy mainly at off-peak hours. Thirty percent of its customers take advantage of these savings. The consumer affairs department has randomly selected 12 customers to participate in a focus group discussing when people use the most energy. The department supervisor is concerned that the group will contain a large proportion of off-peak users.

a. What is the probability of obtaining fewer than three off-peak users in the focus group?
b. What is the probability of obtaining more than four off-peak users in the focus group?
c. What is the probability of obtaining fewer than eight regular customers in the focus group?
d. Compute the mean and the standard deviation of off-peak users in the focus group.

Solution:

a. $n = 12, p = .30, x < 3$: from the table, $P(x < 3) = .253$.
b. $n = 12, p = .30, x > 4$: from the table, $P(x > 4) = (1 - .724) = .276$.
c. $n = 12, p = .70, x < 8$: from the table, $P(x < 8) = .275$.
d. $\mu = np = 12(.30) = 3.6$
$\sigma = \sqrt{np(1-p)} = \sqrt{12(.30)(.70)} = 1.59$.

9. HYPERGEOMETRIC DISTRIBUTION

Mr. Heath is responsible for purchasing cases of wine for the Casa Blanca restaurant. Periodically, he selects a test case (12 bottles per case) to determine the adequacy of the sealing process.

For this test, he randomly selects and tests four bottles in the case. If a case contains two spoiled bottles of wine, find the probability that exactly one of them will appear in Mr. Heath's sample.

Solution

$$P(x = 1) = \frac{C_{n-x}^{N-r} C_x^r}{C_n^N} = \frac{\frac{10!}{3!7!} \frac{2!}{1!1!}}{\frac{12!}{4!8!}}$$

$$= \frac{\frac{(10)(9)(8)(7)(6)(5)(4)(3)(2)(1)(2)(1)}{(3)(2)(1)(7)(6)(5)(4)(3)(2)(1)(1)(1)}}{\frac{(12)(11)(10)(9)(8)(7)(6)(5)(4)(3)(2)(1)}{(4)(3)(2)(1)(8)(7)(6)(5)(4)(3)(2)(1)}} = \frac{240}{495} = .485$$

10. POISSON DISTRIBUTION

The Knoxville Economic Development Council has determined that the number of small businesses that declare bankruptcy per month has a Poisson distribution with a mean of 2.6. Find the probability of:

a. No bankruptcies occurring next month.

b. Three bankruptcies occurring next month.

c. Fewer than three bankruptcies occurring next month.

d. One or more bankruptcies occurring next month.

e. Two bankruptcies occurring within the next two months.

Solution:

a. $P(x = 0) = .0743$.

b. $P(x = 3) = .2176$.

c. $P(x < 3) = .5184$.

d. $P(x \geq 1) = 1 - P(x = 0) = 1 - .0743 = .9257$.

e. $\mu = 5.2$ for a two-month period.
$P(x = 2) = .0746$.

11. POISSON APPROXIMATION OF THE BINOMIAL DISTRIBUTION

The Citizen Company prides itself in meeting shipping deadlines. Jim Marshall, the president, boasts that out of every 100 orders, 98 are filled by the deadline. During a one-week period, 80 orders were processed. Assuming Marshall's claim is true, what is the probability that:

a. Exactly two orders weren't shipped on time?

b. Fewer than three orders weren't shipped on time?

c. Six or more orders weren't shipped on time?

Solution:

$$p = x/n = 2/100 = .02 \qquad np = 80(.02) = 1.6$$

a. $P(x = 2) = .2584$.

b. $P(x < 3) = .7833.$
c. $P(x \geq 6) = (1 - .9940) = .0060.$

Exercises

77a. Discrete
b. Continuous
c. Discrete
d. Continuous

77. State whether the following random variables are discrete or continuous.
    a. Number of errors found in an audit of a company's financial records.
    b. Length of time a customer waits for service at a supermarket checkout counter.
    c. Number of cars recalled by General Motors next year.
    d. Actual number of ounces of beer in a 12-ounce can.

78a. Poisson
b. Binomial
c. Binomial
d. Poisson
e. Poisson
f. Binomial
g. Neither
h. Neither

78. Which of the following situations should be modeled with the binomial distribution? Which should be modeled with the Poisson distribution?
    a. Telephone calls to a police department switchboard.
    b. Successive tosses of a coin weighted 70/30 in favor of heads.
    c. Items coming off a production line are classified as good or bad. The overall proportion of good items remains constant over time, and each successive item's quality is independent of the others'.
    d. Workers coming to a tool crib to check out an expensive tool.
    e. Orders lining up at a drill press for processing.
    f. Successive single births at a hospital, classified by gender.
    g. Each successive computer terminal entry made by an operator and classified as either correct or incorrect; the operator's accuracy is improving over time.
    h. Percent of parts produced on the night shift that are defective.

79. .9380

79. A major computer manufacturing company receives silicon chips in standard batches from a subcontractor. The plant manager has read an article on Intel's i486 processor in *Personal Computing* (July 1989, p. 25) and realizes that product quality is a primary ingredient of company success. He decides to examine recent batches of chips.

    Suppose there's an average of six defective chips per batch shipped by the subcontractor. What proportion of batches contains three or more defective chips?

80. .2969

80. A plan for reorganizing a corporation must be approved by 80% of the directors. If 15 directors are on the board, and if the probability that any of them will approve is .70, find the probability of the plan being approved by the board. Assume statistical independence.

81. .9810

81. The average number of customers per minute at a certain bank's window is 1. What is the probability that during a given minute three or fewer customers will appear?

82. 35

82. A shoe store has room for three pairs of boots in a window display and has seven styles from which to choose. How many different arrangements are possible, assuming the order of the shoe arrangement doesn't matter?

83. .8647

83. An automatic machine produces washers, 4% of which are defective. If a sample of 50 washers is drawn at random from the machine's production what is the probability of observing at least one defective?

84. .8319

84. A traveling salesperson makes a sale to 30% of potential customers. What is the probability that he gets at least one sale in the next five customer contacts?

85. .94

85. The two primary problems with a bottle-filling machine are overfilling and underfilling. If the machine overfills 3% of the time and underfills 3% of the time, find the probability that the next bottle will be filled properly.

86. .357

86. The Vis-a-Vis firm hires two new employees from a total of eight applicants (five men and three women). Both new employees are men. Find the probability that if the new employees were chosen randomly, neither would be a woman.

87. 6

87. For promotional consideration, Chet's Flower Shop provides fresh plants each day for Channel 3's "Noon Show." If six plants are on hand at the shop on a particular day, in how many ways can five be selected for delivery?

88. Dr. Moyer is considering investing a fixed sum of money in each of three business ventures. Assume that the probability distribution for the number of successful ventures out of the three is:

x	$P(x)$
0	.024
1	.178
2	.432
3	.366

Find the expected value of x. Find the probability that Dr. Moyer will enjoy:

88*a*. .798
b. .024
c. .202

a. At least two successful ventures.

b. No successful ventures.

c. Fewer than two successful ventures.

89. $480,000

89. J. & H. Research was asked to conduct a market feasibility study ("Market Analysis for Harbor Marina," J & H Research, August 1987) of the proposed redevelopment of the Harbor View Marina for Metropolitan Mortgage. Analysis of the three options Metropolitan faces was complicated by each option's range of possible selling prices. J. & H. Research decided that an accurate analysis would involve converting the range of selling prices and other costs under each option to a single dollar amount. The following price probabilities for the first option were estimated by commercial property brokers who knew the marina and the competitive market area:

Price	Probability
$400,000	.4
500,000	.4
600,000	.2

Compute a single dollar amount for this option.

90. Pam Stanley, personnel director for Portland Kleenex, has 10 people going through a communication skills training program. The company president has selected four of them to meet with him as a committee to discuss their current training. Pam is certain that two of the trainees are unhappy about the program. Find the probability that:

90*a*. .33
b. .53

a. No unhappy person will be on the committee.

b. One unhappy person will be on the committee.

91. Scott Ford has determined that a new car buyer will order factory-installed air conditioning about 30% of the time. Find the probability that:

91*a*. .0081
b. .3430
c. .2646

a. The next four buyers will all order factory air conditioning.

b. None of the next three buyers will order factory air conditioning.

c. Two out of the next four buyers will order factory air conditioning.

92. .0045

92. The Family Hospital emergency room is concerned about the increasing number of head injuries it treats. Emergency room chief physician Judy Sample has just received her October 27, 1989, issue of the *Journal of the American Medical Association* and reads an article on head injuries (p. 2251). She decides to study the problem of head injuries more closely.

Judy determines that the emergency room can handle a maximum of five head injuries per shift. She finds that the number of patients with head injuries averages 1.5 per shift. Find the probability that more than five head injuries will arrive during a given shift.

93. .9918

93. The probability of Allyn and Allyn Publishers binding a book upside-down is .008. If a run of 600 books is bound, what is the probability that at least one book will be bound upside-down?

94. .0498

94. An average of three misprints appear per issue in the *Denver Review* newspaper. If it's assumed that the number of misprints is Poisson-distributed and there are 60 pages in the average issue, find the probability that a randomly selected page has no misprints.

95. .4422

95. Anderson Manufacturing produces wallpaper. On the average, three rolls out of 1,000 have serious defects. If a retail store orders 500 rolls of wallpaper, what is the probability that two or more of them will have a serious defect?

96. $p = .10$

96. The La Junta city council has five members. Two are local contractors. If two members are selected at random to fill vacancies on the zoning committee, what is the probability that both contractors will be selected?

EXTENDED EXERCISES

97. ACE CUSTOM RACING TIRES

The Ace Corporation, a manufacturer of custom racing tires, is evaluating the market for a new line of tires. The proposed new tire will be test-marketed for one year only. If the tire is successful, it will be modified and incorporated into the company's regular line. For this reason, the company is considering costs and profits for the next year only.

After carefully analyzing the market, Ace estimates the following profits, along with the probability of obtaining each. Although the company recognizes that many other actual profits are possible, Ace considers these to be a good representation of the profit picture.

Profit	Probability
$ 5,000	.05
10,000	.20
20,000	.25
30,000	.25
40,000	.15
50,000	.10

Ace has determined that the fixed cost of producing the tire for a year is $20,000. Based on these figures, it decides to go ahead and manufacture the new tire. Ace's reasoning is that the expected value (expected profit) from the probability distribution is \$25,750, whereas the cost of achieving this expected profit is only \$20,000. This leaves an expected net profit of \$5,750.

a. Are the figures in the company's analysis correct?

b. What factors other than those considered by the company are relevant to this decision?

98. ALPHA MACHINE COMPANY

The Alpha Machine Company is developing a new device to fill small cardboard boxes with carefully measured quantities of material. The most interested client is a large breakfast cereal company and acquiring this account would mean considerable new business for Alpha.

The cereal company's quality-control standards are high—a matter receiving great attention at Alpha. Specifically, almost all boxes filled with cereal must be within a rather tight tolerance in terms of fill weight. The cereal company wants assurances that these standards will be met before it signs a contract.

Alpha decides to determine what percentage of the boxes filled in a trial run will fall outside the specified weight interval. Alpha estimates around 10%, based on tests of the filling machine, but it needs more definitive data on which to base the sales effort. Since the acceptable fill interval is specified, Alpha knows that this situation can be modeled by the binomial distribution: each box's fill weight either falls within this interval or doesn't, and repeated testing of the machine reveals no pattern to defective fills. In other words, misfilled boxes seem to appear randomly, and the trial independence requirement of the binomial definition is met.

In a trial run of 500 boxes, eight boxes are found to fall outside the acceptable fill interval. This represents a defective percentage of $8/500 = .016$. Alpha management now believes it can model the box-filling situation with the binomial distribution, where the probability of a defective unit is estimated to be .016.

Alpha's attention now turns to the basic unit of delivery used by the cereal company: a 250-box carton. Alpha decides that if it can show the cereal company the kind of quality performance the machine will provide on such cartons, Alpha might make a large sale. Alpha realizes that modeling this situation with the binomial distribution will require using the Poisson approximation to the binomial, because n is quite large ($n = 250$) and p is quite small ($p = .016$).

a. Is it a valid assumption that the binomial distribution is a good model for this situation?

b. Is the Poisson approximation appropriate here?

c. Construct a probability distribution for the number of defective boxes per 250-box carton. Does the quality level inherent in this distribution appear acceptable? Do you think the cereal company will be satisfied with the quality level reflected by this distribution?

99. INFRASTRUCTURE PROBLEMS

Suppose a major inner city problem in a large West coast city is an elevated roadway. Due to the heavy volume of truck traffic over this roadway, its bridge supports might fail. The city's Urban Commission considers restricting the number of trucks that may use the bridge during the day while it seeks funding for repairing the bridge. But local trucking firms exert pressure once this possibility becomes known. The commission wants to conduct an intense study of truck traffic but is uncertain about how to proceed.

Staff analysts suggest using the Poisson distribution to model truck traffic. They point out that trucks arrive randomly during the working day (a fact established in recent studies at the bridge) and that the Poisson distribution can provide probabilities of various numbers of truck arrivals. By looking at these probabilities, and by changing the mean arrival rate and examining other scenarios, the analysts think they can effectively model the situation and develop an approach that can counter local trucking firms' arguments. The current arrival rate of trucks is known to be four per minute.

a. Under the current conditions, what is the probability of more than three trucks arriving in any one minute?

b. Suppose the commission wants to reduce the probability of more than three trucks per minute to 20%. What would the mean arrival rate have to be reduced to in order to achieve this figure?

Microcomputer Package

You can use the micro package *Computerized Business Statistics* to solve binomial and Poisson problems.

In Situation 5.4, Central Motors needed to find the probability that a 15-day period will include at least 10 profitable days. Management determined that the probability of a profitable day was .61.

Computer Solution:

From the main menu of *Computerized Business Statistics*, a 5 is selected, which indicates Probability Distributions. The probability distributions menu appears on the screen:

```
Probability Distributions—PROGRAM OPTIONS MENU
          OPTIONS                      ----FUNCTIONS----
 1. Binomial                           P(x ≥ a)    P(x = a)            P(a ≤ x ≤ b)
 2. Poisson                            P(x ≥ a)    P(x = a)            P(a ≤ x ≤ b)
 3. Hypergeometric                     P(x ≥ a)    P(x = a)            P(a ≤ x ≤ b)
 4. Normal                             P(x ≥ a)    P(mean ≤ x ≤ a)     P(a ≤ x ≤ b)
 5. t                                  P(x ≥ a)    P(mean ≤ x ≤ a)     P(a ≤ x ≤ b)
 6. F                                  P(x ≥ a)
 7. Chi-Square                         P(x ≥ a)
 8. Quick Reviews
 9. Return to Main Menu
10. Exit to Operating System
Use arrow keys to move hi-lite to desired selection and press ↵
```

Central wants to know the probability of at least 10 profitable days, $P(x \geq 10)$, so the $P(x \geq a)$ function for the binomial is chosen. Instructions appear on the screen and the appropriate values are entered:

```
Enter Number of Trials (2 - 30000) and press ↵                 15
Enter Probability of an Occurrence (0-1) and press ↵           .61
Enter Number of Occurrences (0-15) and press ↵                 10
```

Next, the screen shows the probability distribution for $n = 15$, $p = .61$. The correct answer for $P(x \geq 10)$ is .4346.

In Situation 5.6, Central Motors needed to determine the probability that five or fewer calls will arrive at the telephone switchboard within a five-minute period. Central's analyst used a Poisson probability distribution with a mean of 4.8.

Computer Solution:

From the main menu of *Computerized Business Statistics*, a 5 is again selected. The probability distribution menu is then shown on the screen.

Central wants to know the probability of five or fewer calls $P(0 \leq x \leq 5)$, so Poisson–$P(a \leq x \leq b)$ is chosen.

```
Enter Average Number of Occurrences      (.1 - 25) and press ↵ 4.8
Enter Lower Limit                         (0 - 24) and press ↵   0
Enter Upper Limit                        (.1 - 24) and press ↵   5
```

The probability distribution for $\mu = 4.8$ is then shown on the screen. The correct answer for $P(0 \leq x \leq 5)$ is .6510.

MINITAB COMPUTER PACKAGE

Many common statistical distributions are available in MINITAB. All that's needed is an indication of the type of distribution (binomial or Poisson) and the value(s) of the parameter(s) that describe it (n and p for the binomial and μ for the Poisson). MINITAB also allows for the determination of both individual and cumulative probabilities. The **PDF** command calculates individual probabilities for discrete distributions. The **CDF** command calculates probabilities for the cumulative distribution function.

The MINITAB commands to solve Situation 5.4's Central Motors problem are shown next. First, find the probability that a 15-day period will include at least 10 profitable days if the probability of a profitable day is .61:

```
MTB > SET C1
DATA> 10:15
DATA> END
MTB > PDF C1;
SUBC> BINOMIAL 15 .61.
         K          P(X = K)
     10.00            0.1933
     11.00            0.1374
     12.00            0.0716
     13.00            0.0259
     14.00            0.0058
     15.00            0.0006
```

The **SET** command is used to indicate the required outcomes, 10 through 15.

The **PDF** command generates a probability density function. The **BINOMIAL** subcommand is used to generate the probability function for a binomial distribution with $n = 15$ and $p = .61$. This problem could also be solved using the commands:

```
MTB > SET C2
DATA> 5
DATA> END
MTB > CDF C2
SUBC> BINOMIAL 15 .39.
         K  P(X LESS OR = K)
      5.00            0.4346
```

Central Motors also wants to know the probability of five or fewer calls. The MINITAB commands are:

```
MTB > SET C3
DATA> 5
MTB > END
MTB > CDF C3;
SUBC> POISSON 4.8.
       K  P(X LESS OR = K)
     5.00            0.6510
MTB > STOP
```

Again the **SET** command is used to indicate the required outcome, 5.

The **CDF** command generates a cumulative probability density function. The **POISSON** subcommand is used to generate the probability function for a Poisson distribution with $\mu = 4.8$.

Chapter

6

Continuous Probability Distributions

This weighty business will not brook delay.
Shakespeare, *Henry VI*

Objectives

When you have completed this chapter, you will be able to:

Explain and apply the uniform distribution.

List the important properties of the normal probability distribution.

Determine the probability, using the standard normal distribution, that an observation will lie between two points or will be above or below some specified value.

Use the normal distribution as an approximation of the binomial.

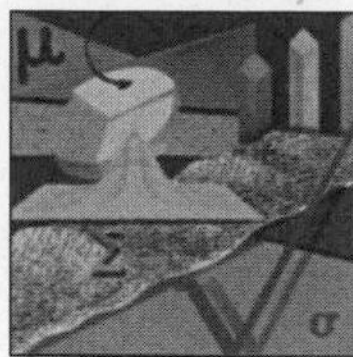

The second section of *The Wall Street Journal*, April 20, 1992, reported on the average length of leisure trips taken by upscale Americans. These travelers were classified as either "adventure enthusiasts" or members of the "country club set."

Chapter 5 discussed discrete probability distributions, where random variables assume only specific designated values. In contrast, continuous probability distributions involve random variables that can assume any value within a specified range. These variables are called *continuous random variables*. This chapter examines two special continuous variables of particular importance to managers.

Why Managers Need to Know about Continuous Probability

Many real-world observations can be modeled using the key distribution discussed in this chapter: the normal distribution. If the actual situation meets the conditions of this important model, valuable answers can be found without expensive, time-consuming observations. In addition, the normal distribution is the key to understanding the most important concept in statistics—the sampling distribution—the subject of Chapter 7.

In the just-mentioned article, the average length of leisure trips could be modeled by the most important distribution in statistics: the normal curve. If this theoretical distribution provided a good model, several important questions might be answered about the probabilities of the lengths of trips—valuable information to a leisure travel business.

Continuous Random Variables

Continuous Random Variable

Chapter 5 introduced the concept of a discrete random variable, one that can assume only certain predetermined values. A variable that can assume any value within some range is called a **continuous random variable.** Such a variable is measured on a numerical scale, that is, it constitutes either interval or ratio data.

> A **continuous random variable** is measured on a numerical scale. Each observation of the random variable can assume any value within some specified range.

There are numerous examples of continuous random variables, since most measurements made in business applications are of this type. The average number of miles per gallon of gas consumed by a car is one example. A small car might average between 25 and 30 miles per gallon, but its average mileage would be unlikely to *exactly* equal some specified value. A claimed mileage of 28 miles per gallon, for example, is commonly understood to mean *approximately* 28. In fact, it's almost impossible for this car to average *precisely* 28 miles per gallon, since that implies an average mileage of 28.0000 . . . , out to an infinite number of decimal places. Since there's only one value of interest, 28, out of an infinite number of possible values, the probability is equal to $1/\infty$, or approximately zero.

When dealing with a continuous random variable, the probability that the variable will fall within a specified range is sought, instead of the probability that the variable will assume a specific value. The following two questions illustrate the difference between discrete and continuous random variables:

1. What is the probability that the number of people arriving at the checkout counter in the next 30 seconds will be exactly two?
2. What is the probability that the lifetime of an electronic switch will be between four and six years?

The first question suggests the use of a discrete probability distribution. There can only be a discrete number of persons appearing at the checkout counter, such as zero, one, or two. In fact, if arrivals occur randomly and the average arrival rate is known, this answer can be computed using the Poisson distribution.

The second question suggests a continuous probability distribution. *Any* lifetime is possible within some reasonable range. A value between 4.385 and 4.587 years is possible, as is a value between 5 7/8 and 5 15/16 years. The probability that the observed lifetime will fall into a particular range is properly requested, since the probability of the lifetime precisely equaling some particular value is approximately zero.

THE UNIFORM DISTRIBUTION

Uniform Distribution

There are specific theoretical probability distributions for continuous random variables, just as there are for discrete random variables. The binomial and Poisson distributions, discussed in Chapter 5, are examples of the latter. The **uniform distribution** is sometimes appropriate when continuous random variables are being observed and where the outcome of an observation is equally likely to occur within any given segment of equal size in the specified range.

> The **uniform distribution** describes a random variable that is as likely to occur in one segment of a given size within a specified range as another.

Figure 6.1 shows a uniform distribution. The range within which the random variable can appear is specified by the values *a* and *b*. The probability "curve" is of uniform height at all points between *a* and *b*, which suggests equal probabilities of the random variable appearing within any segment of a given width in this range. Probability is equal to the area under the density curve. The area or probability of the rectangle equals 1.00, or 100%.

FIGURE 6.1 Uniform Distribution

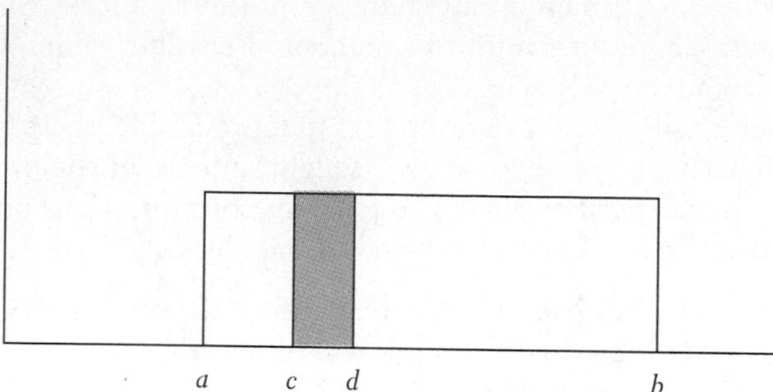

Furthermore, the probability of the variable falling between any two points c and d (see Figure 6.1) is equal to the percentage of the total range included between c and d.

$$P(c \leq x \leq d) = \frac{d - c}{b - a} \tag{6.1}$$

Note that since the probability of a value x being precisely equal to any specified value is approximately zero, the equality sign may or may not be included in the specification of a range. That is,

$$P(c < x < d) = P(c \leq x \leq d)$$

This applies to Equation 6.1 and to any other interval specification for a continuous variable.

EXAMPLE 6.1 Ernie Longnecker, foreman at Trentwood Aluminum, knows that weights of cast aluminum blocks are uniformly distributed within a range of 350 to 450 pounds. If Ernie selects a block at random, what is the probability that it weighs between 375 and 380 pounds? Since the random variable, block weight, is known to be uniformly distributed, a particular block weight has the same probability of appearing in any segment of specified width in the range 350 to 450. To answer the question, Ernie needs to compute the percentage of the desired range relative to the total possible range (see Figure 6.2):

$$P(c \leq x \leq d) = \frac{d - c}{b - a} = \frac{380 - 375}{450 - 350} = \frac{5}{100} = .05$$

So, five percent of the blocks fall in the interval or Ernie can say there's a 5% chance that any randomly selected block will have a weight in this interval.

EXAMPLE 6.2 Marilyn Horner knows that the years of company experience for Pacific Western Industries factory workers form a uniform distribution with a minimum of 0 and a maximum of 12.5 years. She wants to select an employee randomly and

FIGURE 6.2 Uniform Distribution

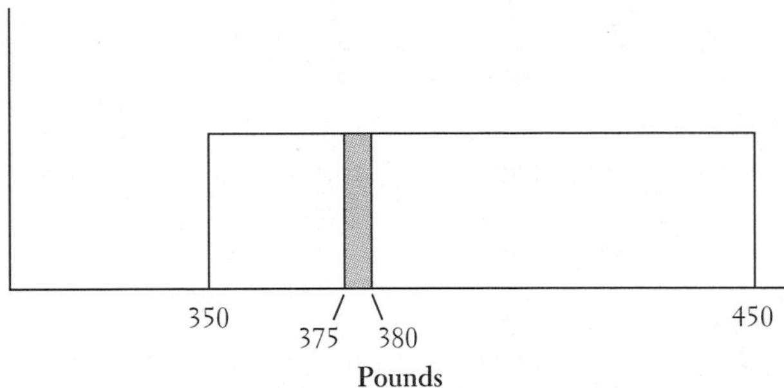

determine the probability that this person has between 2.5 and 7.4 years of experience with the company. This question can be reworded: What percentage of the total range, 0 to 12.5, is the interval 2.5 to 7.4? The answer is

$$P(c \leq x \leq d) = \frac{d - c}{b - a} = \frac{7.4 - 2.5}{12.5 - 0} = \frac{4.9}{12.5} = .392$$

There's about a 39% chance that an employee's time with Pacific Western Industries falls in the range 2.5 to 7.4 years.

Mean and Standard Deviation of Uniform

V

The mean and standard deviation of a uniform distribution are sometimes of interest. The average value of a random variable that follows a uniform distribution falls halfway between the range extremes. In other words, the mean is simply the average of the range boundaries (Equation 6.2). Equation 6.3 measures the standard deviation of a uniform distribution.

$$\text{Mean of uniform distribution} = \frac{a + b}{2} \tag{6.2}$$

$$\text{Standard deviation of uniform distribution} = \sqrt{\frac{(b - a)^2}{12}} \tag{6.3}$$

where a = Lower limit of range
b = Upper limit of range

EXAMPLE 6.3 Tamsen Stone, accountant for High-Performance Yard Care Tools Company, has determined that the ages of accounts receivable are uniformly distributed within a range of 4.7 weeks to 29.4 weeks. Tamsen needs to describe these account ages. The mean and standard deviation of these values provide easily understood summaries of the account age data. These values are calculated using Equations 6.2 and 6.3:

$$\text{Mean} = \frac{4.7 + 29.4}{2} = 17.05$$

$$\text{Standard deviation} = \sqrt{\frac{(29.4 - 4.7)^2}{12}} = 7.13$$

The distribution of account receivable ages has a mean of 17.05 weeks and a standard deviation of 7.13 weeks. Tamsen knows that the average account receivable is 17.05 weeks old and that the ages deviate from their mean by a standard amount of 7.13 weeks.

The MINITAB computer software package can be used to compute uniform probabilities. MINITAB commands for computing the probability for Example 6.2 are:

```
MTB> SET C1
DATA> 2.5
DATA> 7.4
DATA> END
MTB> CDF C1;
SUBC> UNIFORM  0  12.5.
     2.5            0.2000
     7.4            0.5920
MTB> STOP
```

The CDF command is used to compute the cumulative probability of a value less than or equal to x. In this case, the data values were set at $x = 2.5$ and $x = 7.4$. The UNIFORM subcommand is used to solve for the probability of an item falling below 2.5 (.2000) and the probability of an item falling below 7.4 (.5920). Therefore, the probability of an item falling between 2.5 and 7.4 is (.5920 − .2000) = .3920.

EXAMPLE 6.4 Joe Price, superintendent of the Justus Bag Company, wants to check the weight of grain bags filled by a machine that bags wheat. Joe knows that the correct weight for each bag is 125 pounds and that there's room for variability in this weight. A preliminary sample shows that bag weights are evenly distributed between 115 and 135 pounds. The range of tolerance for fill weight for shipping purposes has been determined as + or − five pounds. Mr. Price wants to know what percentage of the bags fall into this tolerance range.

Since he's observed that weights are equally distributed between 115 and 135 pounds, the uniform distribution can be used as a model. Joe needs to determine what percentage of the total range is constituted by the desired range using Equation 6.1:

$$P(c \le x \le d) = \frac{d - c}{b - a} = \frac{130 - 120}{135 - 115} = \frac{10}{20} = .50$$

Fifty percent of the bags will fall within five pounds of the desired weight of 125 pounds. Joe can now decide whether this is an acceptable quality level.

The mean and standard deviation of bag weight might also be relevant to Joe's decision. Using Equations 6.2 and 6.3, these summary values are

$$\text{Mean} = \frac{115 + 135}{2} = 125 \text{ pounds}$$

$$\text{Standard deviation} = \sqrt{\frac{(135 - 115)^2}{12}} = 5.77 \text{ pounds}$$

This is an example of a quality-control concern, a subject discussed at length in Chapter 13.

EXERCISES

1. Explain the difference between the uniform distribution and the Poisson distribution.
2. If you were to graph a uniform distribution, what would it look like?
3. What continuous random variables are of interest to a credit union studying daily customer transactions?

4. Which of the following random variables can be classified as continuous?
   a. The number of people arriving at a toll gate.
   b. The number of ounces in a bottle of milk.
   c. Tomorrow's temperature.
   d. The number of sales a real estate agent made this month.
   e. The weight of a steak bought at the supermarket.
   f. The number of offers received on a car for sale.
   g. Number of errors found in a company's accounts receivable records.
   h. Length of time a patient waits for a doctor.
   i. How long it took you to travel to school today.

4*a.* Discrete
b. Continuous
c. Continuous
d. Discrete
e. Continuous
f. Discrete
g. Discrete
h. Continuous
i. Continuous

5. Which of the variables listed in the company data base in Appendix C are continuous variables?

5. x_1, x_2, x_6, x_8, x_9

6. A West Coast commuter airline's manager of air operations has just read an article in *The Wall Street Journal* (November 6, 1989) indicating that air service between the United States and Japan is to be greatly expanded. She's concerned about flight time between San Diego and Los Angeles, as that route is a key link to the Orient flights. Flight time between Los Angeles and San Diego is known to be uniformly distributed between 80 and 100 minutes.
   a. What is the average flight time between the two cities?
   b. What is the standard variation in flight time between the two cities?
   c. What percentage of flights can be expected to take between 85 and 95 minutes?
   d. Find the probability that a flight will take more than 96 minutes.
   e. Determine the probability that a flight will take less than 80 minutes.

6*a.* 90
b. 5.77
c. 50%
d. 20%
e. 0%

7. General Equipment Manufacturing believes that one of its rolling machines is producing aluminum sheets of varying thickness. The machine typically produces sheets between 75 and 150 millimeters thick. It is known that this random variable is uniformly distributed. Sheets less than 100 millimeters thick are unacceptable to buyers and must be scrapped.
   a. Find the average thickness of the aluminum sheets produced by this machine.
   b. What is the standard variation in thickness of the aluminum sheets produced by this machine?
   c. Find the probability that a sheet produced by this machine will have to be scrapped.

7*a.* 112.5
b. 21.7
c. 33%

8. 30%

8. In a brick laying class the times students take to construct a standard two-by-three–foot test wall fall on a uniform distribution with a mean of 200 seconds. The difference between the longest and shortest time observed is 100 seconds. Find the probability that a student will take between 160 and 190 seconds to construct the wall.
9. A traffic light is set to switch from red to green according to a uniform distribution with a mean of 45 seconds. The difference between the smallest and largest number of seconds it takes the light to switch is eight seconds.

9*a*. 2.3
b. 75%
c. 25%

a. Compute the standard deviation of this distribution.
b. Find the probability that the light will take at least 43 seconds to switch.
c. What is the probability that the light will take less than 43 seconds to switch?

NORMAL DISTRIBUTION

In the 18th century, astronomers observed that repeated measurements of the same value (such as the mass of an object) tended to vary. When a large number of such observations were recorded, organized into a frequency distribution, and plotted on a graph, the recurring result was the shape in Figure 6.3. It was subsequently discovered that this distribution could be closely approximated with a continuous distribution sometimes referred to as the *normal distribution*. This distribution is also referred to as the *bell-shaped curve* or the *Gaussian curve*.

FIGURE 6.3 Normal Distribution

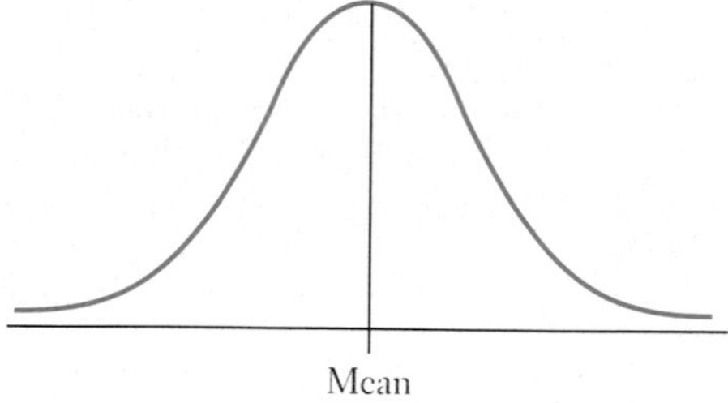

There are three reasons why the normal distribution is the most important theoretical distribution in business statistics:

1. The normal distribution approximates the observed frequency distributions of many natural and physical measurements, such as IQs, weights, heights, sales, product lifetimes, and variability of human and machine outputs.
2. The normal distribution can often be used to estimate binomial probabilities when n is greater than 20.
3. The normal distribution is a good approximation of distributions of both sample means and sample proportions of large samples ($n \geq 30$). Chapter 7 examines this concept in depth.

Many variables in nature and business have numerical observations that tend to cluster around their mean. In other words, it's more likely that an observation will be close to the mean of the data collection than far away. When this condition holds, the **normal distribution** will provide a good model of the data collection.

Normal Distribution

> The **normal distribution** is a continuous distribution that has a bell shape and is determined by its mean and standard deviation.

Figure 6.3 shows the shape of a typical normal curve. Note that the curve is symmetrical: half the area of the curve lies above the mean and half below it, and these halves are mirror images. Also note that away from the mean toward either of the tails, the height of the curve decreases. This corresponds to a decreasing probability of finding a value the further we move from the mean.

The theoretical normal distribution approaches infinity at the positive and negative ends of the curve. In practice this aspect is ignored since the probability of an observation occurring is very small as the distance from the mean increases. A discussion of the mathematical equation for the normal curve is beyond the scope of this text, but the formula is presented here to show its dependence on two key parameters: the mean and standard deviation of the distribution. The so-called probability density function for the normal distribution is

$$f(x) = \frac{1}{\sigma\sqrt{2\pi}}e^{-(1/2)\,[(x\,-\,\mu)/\sigma]^2} \tag{6.4}$$

where x = Any value of the continuous random variable
μ = Mean of the normal random variable
σ = Standard deviation of the normal random variable
e = 2.71828 . . . (natural log base)
π = 3.1416 . . . (used to find the circumference of a circle)

Note that there are two unspecified values in the equation: the mean of the distribution (μ) and the standard deviation (σ). Both e and π are constants with known values. If the mean and standard deviation are known, then a specific normal curve has been identified, and probabilities can be found.

Figure 6.4 shows three normal curves, each with a different mean. However, the three distributions have the same standard deviation. This can be seen by the identical shape or dispersion of each curve.

Figure 6.5 shows three normal curves, all with the same mean. However, the extent of their variability is different. Curve A has a larger standard deviation than curve B, and curve C has the smallest standard deviation of all.

Figures 6.4 and 6.5 show that both the mean and the standard deviation must be known before a specific normal curve can be identified out of the infinite number of curves available.

FIGURE 6.4 Normal Curves with Different Means but the Same Standard Deviation

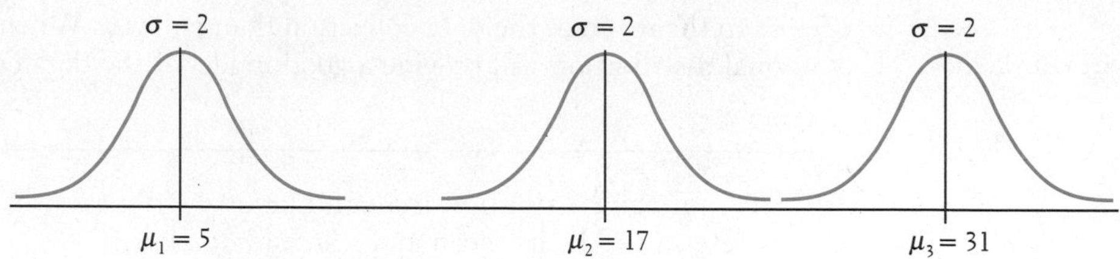

FIGURE 6.5 Normal Curves with the Same Mean but Different Standard Deviations

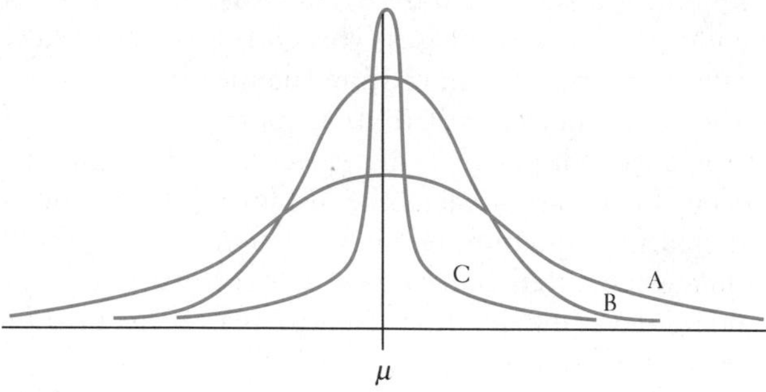

Characteristics of the normal distribution

1. The normal distribution has a bell shape and is symmetrical about its mean.
2. Knowledge of the mean and standard deviation is necessary to identify a specific normal distribution.
3. Each combination of mean and standard deviation specifies a unique normal distribution.
4. The normal distribution extends indefinitely in either direction from the mean.
5. The normal distribution is measured on a continuous scale, and the probability of obtaining a precise value is approximately zero.
6. The total area under the curve is equal to 1.0, or 100%. Fifty percent of the area is above the mean, and 50% is below the mean.
7. The probability that a random variable will have a value between any two points is equal to the area under the curve between those points. This area can be determined using either calculus or the standard normal table in Appendix E.6.

EXERCISES

10. Explain the difference between the uniform distribution and the normal distribution.
11. Explain the difference between the binomial distribution and the normal distribution.
12. If you were to graph a normal distribution, what would it look like?
13. Which of the following are characteristics of the normal distribution?
    a. The normal distribution is skewed.
    b. Knowledge of the median and standard deviation is necessary to construct a specific normal distribution.
    c. Each combination of mean and standard deviation defines a unique normal distribution.
    d. The normal distribution extends indefinitely in either direction from the mean.
    e. The normal distribution is measured on a discrete scale.
    f. The total area under the curve is equal to 1.0 or 100%.
    g. The probability that a random variable will have a value between any two points is equal to the area under the curve between those points.
14. Why is the normal distribution the most important theoretical distribution in business statistics?

13*a.* No
b. No
c. Yes
d. Yes
e. No
f. Yes
g. Yes

FINDING NORMAL CURVE AREAS

To find normal curve areas, we must use integral calculus along with Equation 6.4, and the computations are complex. For this reason, it would be convenient if a table for normal curve areas were available, as they are for the binomial and Poisson distributions. Unfortunately, more than one table would be necessary. Figures 6.4 and 6.5 show that the normal distribution is actually an infinitely large family of distributions, one for each possible combination of mean and standard deviation. The number of normal distributions is therefore unlimited, and providing a table of probabilities for each combination of mean and standard deviation wouldn't be practical.

Standard Normal Distribution

Fortunately, the problem of dealing with an infinite family of normal distributions can be solved by transforming all normal distributions to the **standard normal distribution,** which has a mean of 0 and a standard deviation of 1.

> The **standard normal distribution** has a mean of 0 and a standard deviation of 1.

z Value

Any normal distribution can be converted to the standard normal distribution by standardizing each of its observations in terms of ***z* values.** The z value measures the distance in standard deviations between the mean of the normal curve and the x value of interest.

> The **z value** is a measure of the number of standard deviations between the mean or center of a normal curve and the value of interest.

Equation 6.5 shows how the observations from any normal distribution can be standardized by forming a standard normal distribution of z values:

$$z = \frac{x - \mu}{\sigma} \tag{6.5}$$

where z = Number of standard deviations from mean
x = Value of interest
μ = Mean of distribution
σ = Standard deviation of distribution

Examples 6.5 and 6.6 illustrate applications of Equation 6.5.

Normal Curve Areas

EXAMPLE 6.5 A normal curve has a mean of 500 and standard deviation of 25. An analyst wants to find the normal curve areas both above and below the value 535.

What is the correct z value for 535? From Equation 6.5, the z value is

$$z = \frac{x - \mu}{\sigma} = \frac{535 - 500}{25} = 1.40$$

Figure 6.6 shows both the actual scale of this normal distribution and the standardized scale for the standard normal distribution. Note that the standard normal distribution is created by converting the actual values to z values.

TM

FIGURE 6.6 Normal Curve for Example 6.5

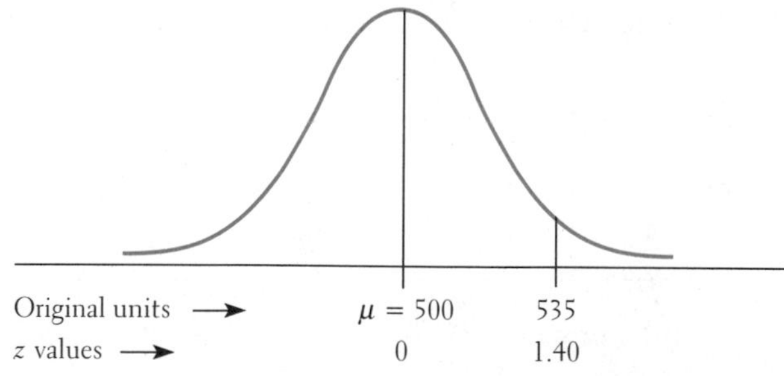

EXAMPLE 6.6 Coffee prices recently tumbled to a 14-year low of 76.5 cents a pound, according to *The Wall Street Journal* (October 4, 1989). Suppose a small importer in Florida watches these prices closely, as they're directly related to profits.

The importer averages 2,700 pounds per month with a standard deviation of 130 pounds. What is the z value for 2,200 pounds on this distribution?

$$z = \frac{2200 - 2700}{130} = -3.85$$

After the z value is calculated for the standard normal distribution, the next step is to use the standard normal table to look up the corresponding area under the curve. The standard normal table (Appendix E.6) is designed to be read in units of z, the number of standard deviations from the mean. The table shows the area under the curve between the mean and selected values of z. Remember that this table specifies the area between the *center* of the curve and the point specified by the z value.

Since the normal distribution is symmetrical about its mean, the left half of the curve is a mirror image of the right half. Because of this symmetry, the standard normal table provides only the right half (i.e., positive z values) of the distribution. If the z value of interest is negative, the minus sign is ignored, and the area is obtained in the same manner as if the z value were positive. For example, the area under the curve between the mean and $+2$ standard deviations is exactly equal to the area under the curve between the mean and -2 standard deviations.

Examples 6.7 through 6.14 illustrate applications of the standard normal table.

EXAMPLE 6.7 A normal distribution has a mean of 5 and standard deviation of 2.1. What is the probability that a numerical value randomly drawn from this distribution will lie between 5 and 6? In this example, the question is phrased properly because the normal distribution represents a continuous random variable, and probabilities must be stated for a range, not a specific value. Figure 6.7 shows the desired area. Using Equation 6.5, the z value is: $z = (6 - 5)/2.1 = 0.48$.

TM

FIGURE 6.7 Normal Curve Area for Example 6.6

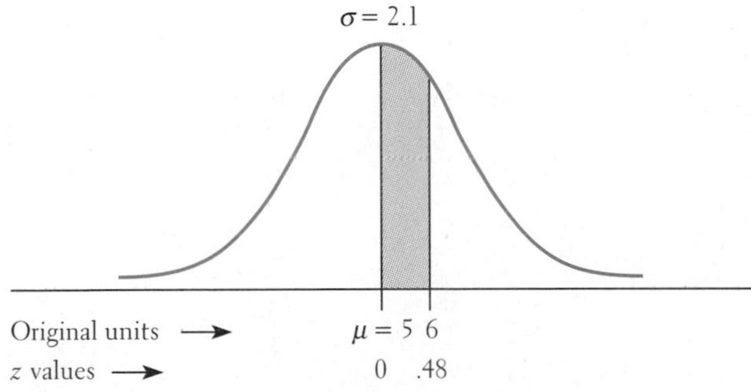

Since the area desired extends from the mean of the curve (5) to a point of interest, $x(6)$, the desired area can be read directly from the standard normal table using the calculated z value. Note the graph at the top of the table in Appendix E.6, which suggests that the areas under the curve are measured from the center of the curve to the point of interest.

The left column of the standard normal table lists the z value with only one digit on each side of the decimal point. Since the z value for this example is 0.48, the 0.4 row is used. The values across the top of the table give the second digit to the right of the decimal point. Since this digit is 8 in this example, the .08 column is used. At the intersection of the 0.4 row and the .08 column of the table is the value .1844. This is the percentage of the total area under the curve found between the center of the distribution and a point 0.48 standard deviations away. There's about an 18% chance of drawing a value from this normal distribution that lies between 5 and 6.

Now the reason for the empirical rule in Chapter 4 can be explained. Using the standard normal table, we can find the percentages of items on a standard normal distribution that will fall within 1, 2, and 3 standard deviations of the mean. Example 6.8 calculates these values.

EXAMPLE 6.8 What percentage of the values on a normal curve can be expected to fall within 1, 2, and 3 standard deviations of the mean? The standard normal table is entered with $z = 1$, $z = 2$, and $z = 3$, and the areas are determined using the process explained in Example 6.7. These areas are then doubled to account for values both above and below the mean:

$$z = 1: \quad (.3413)(2) = .6826$$
$$z = 2: \quad (.4772)(2) = .9544$$
$$z = 3: \quad (.4987)(2) = .9974$$

These values establish the empirical rule presented in Chapter 4: about 68% of the values are within one standard deviation of the mean, about 95.5% are within two standard deviations, and over 99.7% are within three standard deviations. Figure 6.8 shows these areas.

FIGURE 6.8 Normal Curve Areas for Example 6.7

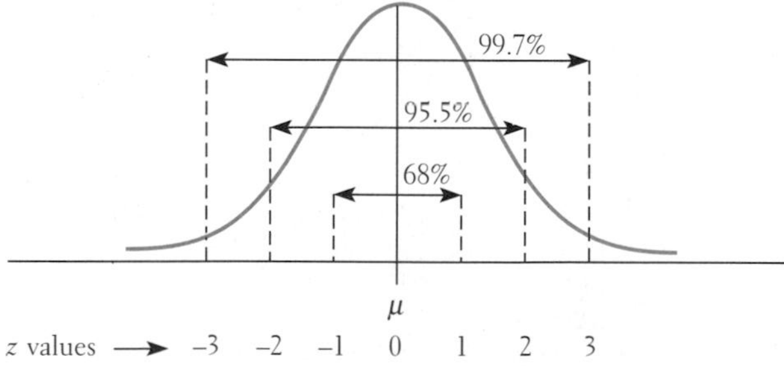

EXAMPLE 6.9 Fund managers noted that mutual fund sales nationally rose 4.2 billion in August 1989 to the highest value in two years (*The Wall Street Journal*, October 2, 1989). A study showed that the number of mutual fund shares traded on a local exchange was normally distributed with a mean of 250 and standard deviation of 12. Fund analyst Sherry Showalter needs to determine the probability that a share value

randomly selected from this distribution will fall between 225 and 250. The z value is $(225 - 250)/12 = -2.08$.

The negative sign of the z value indicates that the x value of interest (225) is less than the mean of the distribution (250); the negative sign is ignored when the z value is looked up in the standard normal table. As in Example 6.8, since this area is measured from the mean of the curve to some point, the desired area or probability can be read directly from the table. The 2.0 row of the table is used along with the .08 column, and the desired area is read from the table as .4812. Thus, there's about a 48% chance that a randomly selected item from this distribution will fall in the interval 225 to 250.

Examples 6.8 and 6.9 both involved areas measured from the mean or center of the normal curve to a point of interest. As a result, the normal curve area could be read directly from the table. Three other kinds of normal curve areas might also be of interest:

1. An area that lies at one end of the curve (see Example 6.10).
2. An area that spans the curve mean; that is, some of the area is above the mean, and some is below (see Example 6.11).
3. An area that is either above the mean or below it but does not include the mean (see Example 6.12).

EXAMPLE 6.10 A normal distribution has a mean of 4.9 and standard deviation of 1.2. What percentage of the area under this curve lies above 6? This question can be rephrased: What is the probability that an item randomly selected from this distribution will have a value above 6? Figure 6.9 shows the desired area.

FIGURE 6.9 Normal Curve Area for Example 6.10

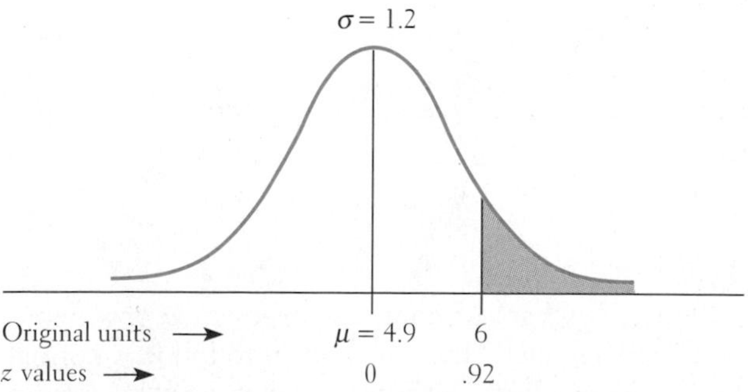

To solve this problem, we must first find the area from the mean of the curve (4.9) to the x value of interest (6). This area is found by calculating the z value and referring to the standard normal table. The z value is $(6 - 4.9)/1.2 = 0.92$.

The area from the standard normal table corresponding to a z value of 0.92 is .3212 (found at the intersection of the 0.9 row and the .02 column). To find the desired area, remember that exactly 50% of a normal curve lies above the mean and 50% lies below it. If half the normal curve area lies above the mean of 4.9, and if the area .3212 lies between 4.9 and 6, then the remaining portion of the half must lie above 6. Therefore, the desired area is .5000 − .3212 = .1788. There's about an 18% chance that a randomly selected item will have a value greater than 6 since about 18% of the curve area lies above this value.

EXAMPLE 6.11 What is the probability that an item drawn from an inventory of television tubes will have a shelf life between 2 and 10 weeks? The ages are known to follow a normal distribution with a mean of 5 weeks and standard deviation of 4 weeks. Figure 6.10 shows the desired area.

This problem actually involves two normal curve areas, each measured from the center of the curve, that must be determined separately. The two areas are added together to find the desired value. The two z values and their areas are

$$z = (2 - 5)/4 = -0.75 \rightarrow .2734 \quad \text{(area between 2 and 5)}$$
$$z = (10 - 5)/4 = 1.25 \rightarrow \underline{.3944} \quad \text{(area between 5 and 10)}$$
$$\text{Sum} = .6678 \quad \text{(area between 2 and 10)}$$

There's about a 67% chance that a randomly selected television tube will have a lifetime between 2 and 10 weeks.

FIGURE 6.10 Normal Curve Area for Example 6.11

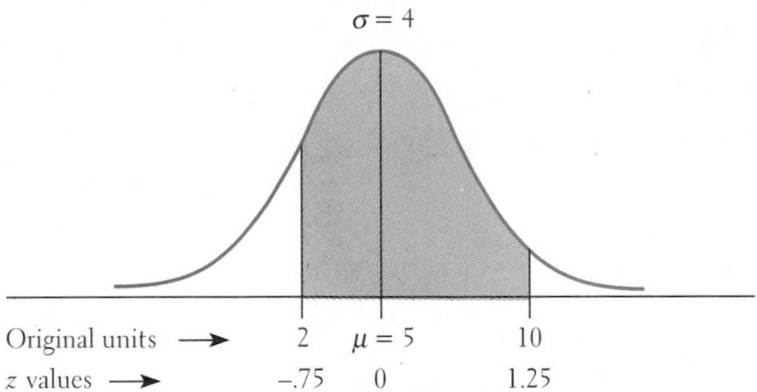

EXAMPLE 6.12 Years of company experience of a pool of first-line supervisors at Future Business Products, Inc., are known to follow a normal distribution with a mean of 7.8 years and standard deviation of 1.5 years. This information came to light when the company president investigated the firm's retention problem after reading an article (*Inc.* magazine, May 1989, p. 132) about the advantages of bonus and incentive systems for employees. Find the probability that a randomly selected supervisor has between 8 and 10 years of experience. Figure 6.11 shows the area to be determined.

To solve this problem, first find the area between the mean of the curve, 7.8, and 10, the upper value of interest. The area between 7.8 and 8 will then be subtracted

FIGURE 6.11 Normal Curve Area for Example 6.12

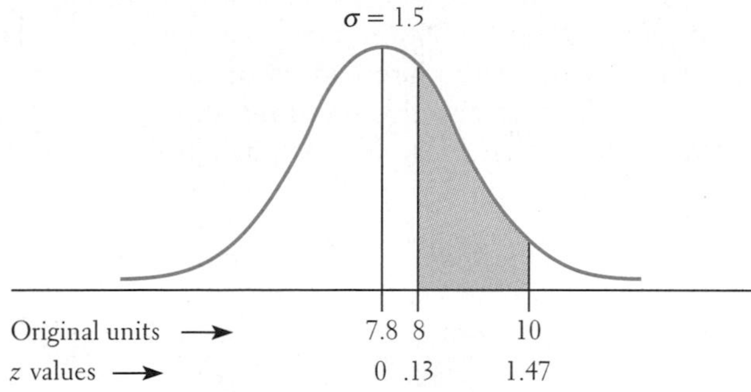

from it. The result is the area lying between 8 and 10. The two z values and their areas from the standard normal table are

$$\begin{aligned} z = (10 - 7.8)/1.5 = 1.47 &\rightarrow .4292 \quad \text{(area between 7.8 and 10)} \\ z = (8 - 7.8)/1.5 = 0.13 &\rightarrow \underline{.0517} \quad \text{(area between 7.8 and 8)} \\ \text{Difference} &= .3775 \quad \text{(area between 8 and 10)} \end{aligned}$$

There's about a 38% chance that a selected supervisor will have between 8 and 10 years of experience with Future Business Products, Inc.

Sometimes an analyst knows the area under the curve and must find an actual value or a z value. Example 6.13 illustrates this situation.

EXAMPLE 6.13 Alpine Tire Company has determined from road tests that the mean mileage of its main product is 50,000 miles with a standard deviation of 5,000 miles, and that the collected data are normally distributed. Alpine wishes to offer a warranty providing free replacement for any new tire that fails before the guaranteed mileage. If Alpine wishes to replace no more than 10% of the tires, what should the guaranteed mileage be?

Figure 6.12 shades the area of interest. To solve this problem, reverse the procedure for using the standard normal table. That is, instead of looking up the area for a par-

FIGURE 6.12 Normal Curve Area for Example 6.13

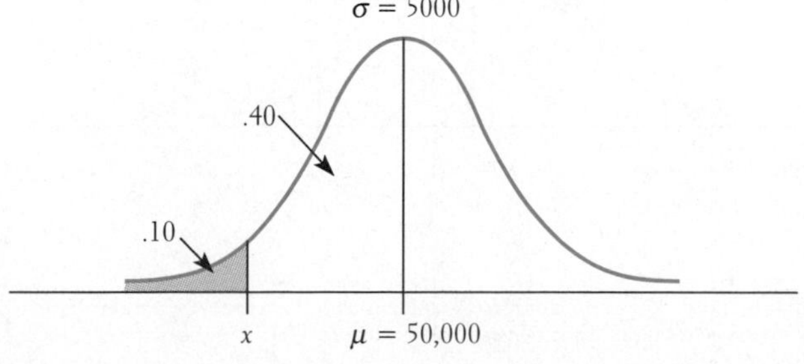

ticular z value, the analyst looks for the z value that coincides with the area of interest under the curve. This area equals 10%, but to find the appropriate z value in the table, the analyst must subtract 10% from 50% (see Figure 6.12). The area closest to .4000 is .3997, which is found at the intersection of the 1.2 row and the .08 column. The z value is thus -1.28 (the negative sign indicates that the z value is below the mean). To find the appropriate mileage for the guarantee, a z value of -1.28 is substituted into Equation 6.5:

$$\begin{aligned} z &= \frac{x - \mu}{\sigma} \\ -1.28 &= \frac{x - 50{,}000}{5{,}000} \\ x - 50{,}000 &= -1.28(5{,}000) \\ x - 50{,}000 &= -6{,}400 \\ x &= 43{,}600 \end{aligned}$$

Alpine should set its guarantee at about 43,600 miles since only 10% of failures will occur before that mileage has been reached.

As implied by the preceding example, Equation 6.5 can be manipulated so that x can be solved for directly: $x = \mu + z\sigma$.

EXAMPLE 6.14 A study reported in *Educational and Psychological Measurement*[1] used the Stanford-Binet Fourth Edition to measure a Composite Standard Age Score (CAS) for a sample of 5,013 subjects. Each of the four content areas had a mean SAS of 100 and a standard deviation of 16. If a person scores higher than 92% of the people who took the exam on the Quantitative Reasoning content area, what score did this person get if the scores are assumed to be normally distributed? With 92% of the scores below this x value, 42% of the scores must lie between the mean of 100 and x (see Figure 6.13). In the standard normal table, an area of .4207 is closest to the de-

FIGURE 6.13 Normal Curve Area for Example 6.14

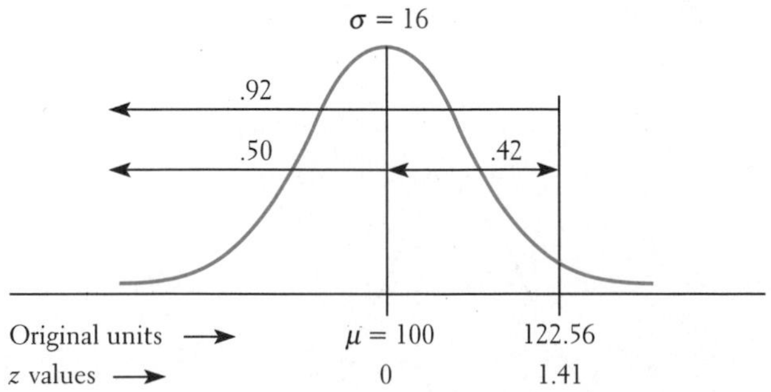

[1] V. E. Glaub and R. W. Kamphaus, "Construction of a nonverbal adaptation of the Stanford-Binet Fourth Edition," *Educational and Psychological Measurement*, Vol. 51, pp. 231–41.

sired value of .42. The z value for this area is 1.41, so x is 1.41 standard deviations above the mean:

$$x = \mu + z\sigma$$
$$x = 100 + (1.41)(16) = 122.56$$

Ninety-two percent of the people scored below 122.56 on Quantitative Reasoning.

The MINITAB computer software package can be used to compute normal curve probabilities. The MINITAB commands for computing the normal probability for Example 6.9 are:

```
MTB> SET C1
DATA> 225
DATA> 250
DATA> END
MTB> CDF C1;
SUBC> NORMAL 250 12.
 225     0.0186
 250     0.5000
MTB> STOP
```

The CDF command is used to compute the cumulative probability of a value less than or equal to x. In this case, the data values were set at $x = 225$ and $x = 250$. The NORMAL subcommand is used to solve for the probability of an item falling below 225 (.0186) and the probability of an item falling below 250 (.5000). Therefore, the probability of an item falling between 225 and 250 is $(.5000 - .0186) = .4814$.

Example 6.8 provided areas for the empirical rule, which applies only if the distribution in question follows a normal curve or can be closely approximated with one. For distributions that don't follow a normal curve, areas can be estimated through the use of **Chebyshev's theorem,** which was briefly mentioned in Chapter 4. This theorem states that regardless of how the data values are distributed, at least a certain percentage will lie within a specified range around the mean.

Chebyshev's Theorem

Chebyshev's theorem
Regardless of how the data values are distributed, at least $(1 - 1/k^2)$ of the values will lie within k standard deviations of the mean (for $k \geq 1$).

EXAMPLE 6.15 The distribution of ages in a factory do not follow a normal distribution but have a mean of 44.8 with a standard deviation of 9.7. Using Chebyshev's theorem, a lower bound for the percentage of ages within two standard deviations of the mean can be calculated:

$$(1 - 1/k^2) = 1 - 1/2^2 = 1 - 1/4 = .75$$

Thus, at least 75% of the ages in the factory are within two standard deviations of the mean. In other words, the ages of at least 75% of the employees range from $44.8 - (2)(9.7)$ to $44.8 + (2)(9.7)$, or from 25.4 to 64.2 years.

EXERCISES

15. Mean

15. In using the standard normal table to look up a z value, what point is used consistently as the reference point?
16. Why doesn't the standard normal table contain areas above .5000?

17. Why are x values converted to z values?
18. Draw a normal curve and shade the area under the curve for each of the following:
    - *a.* The area between the mean and $z = 0.75$.
    - *b.* The area between the mean and $z = -1.75$.
    - *c.* The area between $z = -1.25$ and $z = 0.25$.
    - *d.* The area between $z = 0.30$ and $z = 2.00$.
    - *e.* The area above $z = 1.00$.
    - *f.* The area below $z = -3.00$.

19*a.* .2734
b. .4599
c. .4931
d. .3593
e. .1587
f. .0013

19. Find the probability of an item falling into each of the shaded intervals drawn in Exercise 18.
20. Find the z value that corresponds to each of the areas described:
    - *a.* Seventy percent of the items lie above this z value.
    - *b.* Twenty percent of the items lie below this z value.
    - *c.* Ten percent of the items lie above this z value.
    - *d.* Sixty percent of the items lie above this z value.

20*a.* −.525
b. −.84
c. 1.28
d. −.25

21. $58,875 and below

21. Home loan applications are normally distributed with mean of $100,000 and standard deviation of $25,000 at the Rainier State Bank. Bank policy requires that applications involving loan amounts in the lowest 5% be submitted to a vice president in charge of authorizing low-income housing loans. What size home loan requests are submitted to this vice president?
22. Street lights in the residential areas served by Utah Power & Electric are constructed to have a mean lifetime of 500 days with standard deviation of 50 days. If it can be assumed that street light lifetimes are normally distributed, what percentage of the lamps:
    - *a.* Last longer than two years?
    - *b.* Last between 400 and 625 days?
    - *c.* Last longer than 600 days?
    - *d.* Last between 350 and 450 days?

22*a.* 0
b. 97.1%
c. 2.28%
d. 15.74%

23. Fuel consumption of a fleet of 1,000 trucks is normally distributed with a mean of 12 miles per gallon and standard deviation of 2 miles per gallon.
    - *a.* How many trucks will average 11 miles or more per gallon?
    - *b.* How many trucks will average less than 10 miles per gallon?
    - *c.* How many trucks will average between 9.5 and 14 miles per gallon?
    - *d.* How many trucks will average between 9 and 11 miles per gallon?
    - *e.* Find the probability that a truck selected at random will average over 13.5 miles per gallon.
    - *f.* Seventy percent of the trucks average more than what mileage?
    - *g.* Ten percent of the trucks average less than what mileage?

23*a.* 692
b. 159
c. 736
d. 242
e. .2266
f. 10.96
g. 9.44

24. 7.38

24. Horace Gainey, analyst for Splice Soft Drink Corporation, is setting the fill level for the company's new soft drink dispensers. If the ounces of fill are normally distributed with a mean of μ and standard deviation of 0.2 ounces, what should Horace set μ at so that eight-ounce cups will overflow only one time in a thousand?

25. 197,200

25. Brooks Publishing Company has discovered that the number of words contained in new manuscripts in excess of the number specified in the author's contract is normally distributed with a mean of 40,000 words and standard deviation of 10,000 words. If Brooks wants to be 90% certain that a new manuscript will be less than 250,000 words, how many words should be specified in the author's contract?

26. Workers' hourly wage at a state correctional institution is normally distributed with a mean of \$9.10 and a standard deviation of \$0.90.

26*a*. .1587
b. .9368
c. .2514
d. 9.10

a. Determine the probability that a worker's hourly wage exceeds \$10.00.

b. Find the probability that a worker's hourly rate is between \$7.70 and \$11.50.

c. What proportion of the workers earn less than \$8.50?

d. Half the workers earn more than what amount?

NORMAL APPROXIMATION TO THE BINOMIAL

Chapter 5 presented the binomial distribution and various methods of solving binomial problems. As Figure 5.8 shows, if the number of trials (n) is 20 or less, the correct binomial probabilities can be found in the binomial tables of Appendix E.2. If n is greater than 20 and the probability of success, p, is either very small or very large, the Poisson distribution can provide a good approximation using the method discussed in Chapter 5.

Suppose a binomial problem involves an n value larger than 20 (so that the binomial tables cannot be used) and a proportion that's neither very small nor very large. In such a case, the Poisson approximation isn't appropriate, and another method of solving the problem must be found.

As suggested by Figure 5.8, the normal curve provides a good approximation to the binomial distribution under these conditions. The approximation is made that the discrete binomial distribution follows the continuous normal distribution. This approximation introduces an error into the probability calculations, but this error has been found to be quite small.

When the normal approximation is used, the mean and standard deviation of the binomial distribution must be found so that they can be used to compute normal curve probabilities.

Normal Approximation to the Binomial

> The normal distribution provides a close approximation to the binomial distribution when n is large and p is close to .5. As a rule of thumb, this approximation is appropriate when $np > 5$ and $n(1 - p) > 5$.

Both the Poisson and binomial distributions are discrete, whereas the normal curve is continuous. Since discrete variables involve only specified values, intervals will have to be assigned to the continuous normal distribution to represent binomial values. For example, continuous values in the range 4.5 to 5.5 correspond to the discrete value 5. This addition and subtraction of .5 to the x value is commonly referred to as the **continuity correction factor.**

Continuity Correction Factor

To find the binomial probability of exactly 5 successes, the normal curve approximation is used based on the probability (i.e., the area under the normal curve) between 4.5 and 5.5. If the desired binomial probability is for 15 or more successes, the normal curve area from 14.5 to ∞ is found. If the binomial probability of interest involves 4 or fewer successes, the appropriate normal curve area is from 4.5 to $-\infty$.

Since the number of trials, or sample size, is usually large in practical situations where the normal distribution is used to approximate the binomial, the continuity correction factor typically has a negligible effect. However, this correction is made in the examples and exercises that follow.

Figure 6.14 shows how the normal curve can be used to give binomial probability approximations. The bars represent binomial probabilities for the distribution of x successes in 100 trials where the probability of success is .5. The normal curve superimposed over the binomial histogram has a mean and standard deviation equal to (from Equations 5.5 and 5.6):

$$\mu = np = (100)(.50) = 50$$
$$\sigma = \sqrt{np(1 - p)} = \sqrt{(100)(.50)(.50)} = 5$$

Figure 6.14 shows that the area in any set of bars (the binomial probability) approximately equals the corresponding area under the curve (the normal probability).

TM

FIGURE 6.14 Normal Approximation to the Binomial

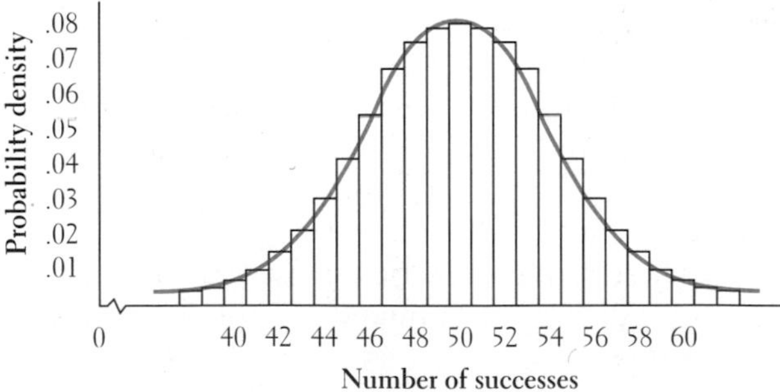

Figure 6.15 also shows how the binomial distribution can be approximated by the normal distribution. In Figure 6.15 three binomial probability distributions have been plotted for $p = .5$: $n = 5$, $n = 10$, and $n = 20$. Normal distributions with means of np and standard deviations of $\sqrt{np(1 - p)}$ have been superimposed on the binomial

FIGURE 6.15 Normal Approximation to the Binomial

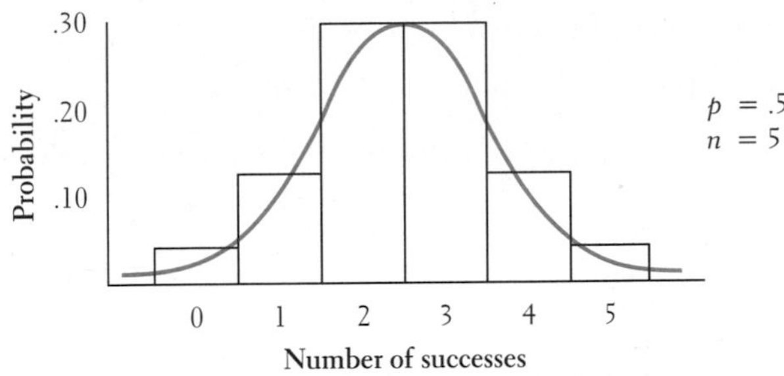

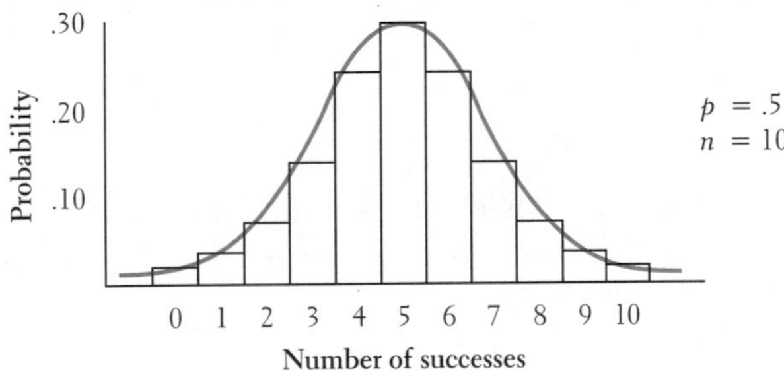

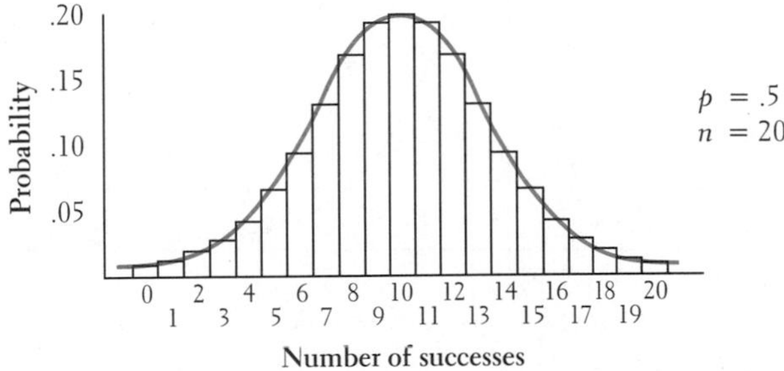

distributions. Figure 6.15 indicates that as n increases, the normal distribution more closely approximates the binomial distribution.

EXAMPLE 6.16 The librarian of the John Kennedy Library, Don Lake, randomly selects 100 books from the shelves and inspects their physical condition. In his last inspection, 40% of the books were in unsatisfactory condition. Assuming this percentage still holds, what is the probability that Don will find at least 50% of the sampled books unsatisfactory?

This is a binomial situation, since a book is either in good condition or not and since independence between selections is ensured due to random sampling. The binomial problem can be stated

$$n = 100 \qquad p = .40 \qquad P(x \geq 50) = ?$$

The normal curve can provide an approximation to the correct binomial answer, since n is too large for the binomial tables and the proportion (.40) precludes use of the Poisson approximation ($np = 40$). The mean and standard deviation of the binomial situation are found first:

$$\mu = np = (100)(.40) = 40$$
$$\sigma = \sqrt{np(1 - p)} = \sqrt{(100)(.40)(.60)} = 4.9$$

Figure 6.16 shows the area that needs to be computed from the standard normal table. Note that the continuity correction factor is used. The desired area to be found in the standard normal table is from 40 to 49.5. The z value for the desired area is

$$z = (49.5 - 40)/4.9 = 1.94$$

The standard normal table indicates an area of .4738 for a z value of 1.94. There is only a small chance (.5000 − .4738 = .0262) or 2.62%, that 50 or more of the sampled books will be unsatisfactory.

FIGURE 6.16 Normal Approximation to Binomial

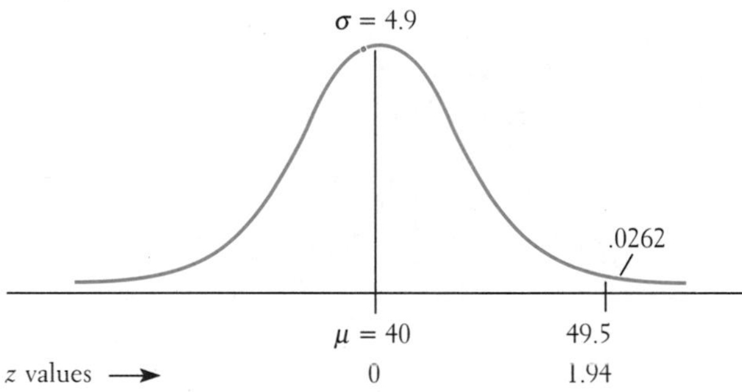

EXERCISES

27. When is the Poisson distribution a good approximation for the binomial distribution?
28. When is the normal distribution a good approximation for the binomial distribution?
29. What problem occurs when the normal distribution is used to approximate the binomial distribution? (*Hint:* This problem doesn't occur when the Poisson distribution is used.)
30. Explain the concept behind the continuity correction factor.
31. For a binomial distribution with $n = 50$ and $p = .40$, find:
    a. $P(x \geq 20)$.
    b. $P(x \leq 15)$.
    c. $P(x \geq 17)$.
    d. $P(x \leq 24)$.

31*a*. $\mu = 20$
$\sigma = 3.46$
.5557
b. .0968
c. .8438
d. .9032

32. $\mu = 7$
$\sigma = 2.51$
.1587

SSM

32. In the past, Sue Megard has made mistakes on 10% of the tax returns she's prepared. Find the probability that she'll make mistakes on 5 or fewer of the 70 returns she prepares for 1993. Assume statistical independence.

33*a*. $\mu = 33$
$\sigma = 4.8$
.7673
b. .9406

33. A salesperson has a 30% chance of making a sale to any customer called upon. If 110 calls are made during a particular month, determine the probability that:
    a. At least 30 sales are made.
    b. Forty or fewer sales are made.

34. $\mu = 12$
$\sigma = 3.39$
.7703

34. Four percent of the washers an automatic machine produces are defective. If a sample of 300 washers is drawn at random from the machine's production, what is the probability of observing at least 10 defectives?

35. $\mu = 202.5$
$\sigma = 13.2$
.2988

35. As of 1989, according to the *Statistical Abstract of the United States: 1991*, 13.5% of the country's 92.8 million households were classified as one-person households. If 1,500 households are randomly selected to participate in an Arbitron survey to determine TV ratings, find the probability that no more than 195 of these are one-person households.

36. $\mu = 54$
$\sigma = 4.65$
.8340

36. Boulevard Restaurant's management has been studying whether new customers return within a month. The collected data reveal that 60% of the new customers have returned. If 90 new customers dine at the Boulevard Restaurant this month, find the probability that at least 50 will return next month.

SUMMARY

This chapter has presented two continuous probability distributions that are useful models of many practical business situations: the uniform distribution and the normal distribution. The normal curve in particular is used frequently in business applications because so many business variables have values corresponding to the two key attributes of the normal curve: the values are symmetrically clustered around their mean, and there are more values close to the mean than far from it.

We must understand how to compute normal curve probabilities given the mean and standard deviation of the distribution because of the many situations that can be modeled with the normal curve. The next chapter gives an even more important reason for understanding normal curve areas. The normal curve underlies the inferential process that is the basis of all statistics: the process of reaching conclusions about populations based on sample evidence.

Finally, the normal approximation to the binomial distribution was presented. Along with the binomial procedures of Chapter 5, four methods of solving a binomial problem have been introduced: the binomial formula, the binomial tables, the Poisson approximation, and the normal approximation.

APPLICATIONS OF STATISTICAL CONCEPTS IN THE BUSINESS WORLD

Many numerical data arrays in the business world closely resemble a uniform distribution and can be modeled as discussed in this chapter. Also, at times the normal approximation is useful for computing binomial probabilities. But the greatest application of these concepts involves the many data collections found in the business world that approximate the shape of a normal curve.

When such a data array is found, percentages or probabilities can be easily determined using z values and the standard normal table. In fact, this method is so easy that it's frequently used even before the data distribution has been verified to resemble a normal curve. Obviously, it's important to verify the normality assumption if the results are to be accurate. Here are examples of variables that might follow a normal distribution and for which this chapter's techniques are useful.

Accounting: accounts receivable, accounts payable, cash balance, value of inventory, bad debt expense.

Manufacturing: dollar value of inventory, number of days to receive shipment, number of overtime hours per week, hours of labor per unit, weights of manufactured parts, lengths of parts.

Finance: interest rate paid as deviation from prime rate, company's stock price as percentage of Dow Jones, ratio of annual dividends to earnings, several companies' price/earnings ratios.

Marketing: ages of credit card holders, numerical ratings of store performance by customers, monthly market share, miles traveled by customers to store.

Personnel: time with company, years of education, score on company entrance test, job performance rating, number of dependents, annual salary, sick days taken per year.

Quality control: time between defects, defective items per shift, time until part failure, time until defective condition detected.

GLOSSARY

Continuous random variable A random variable that can assume any value within some specified range.

Uniform distribution A distribution describing a random variable that is as likely to occur in one segment of a given size within a specified range as another.

Normal distribution A continuous distribution that has a bell shape and is determined by its mean and standard deviation.

Standard normal distribution A normal distribution that has a mean of 0 and a standard deviation of 1.

***z* value** A measure of the number of standard deviations between the mean or center of a normal curve and the value of interest.

Chebyshev's theorem A rule stating that regardless of how the data values are distributed, at least $(1 - 1/k^2)$ of the values will lie within k standard deviations of the mean (for $k \geq 1$).

KEY FORMULAS

Uniform probabilities

$$P(c \leq x \leq d) = \frac{d - c}{b - a} \quad (6.1)$$

Mean of uniform distribution

$$\mu = \frac{a + b}{2} \quad (6.2)$$

Standard deviation of uniform distribution

$$\sigma = \sqrt{\frac{(b - a)^2}{12}} \tag{6.3}$$

Normal distribution probability density function

$$f(x) = \frac{1}{\sigma\sqrt{2\pi}} e^{-(1/2)\,[(x - \mu)/\sigma]^2} \tag{6.4}$$

***z* value or standardized value**

$$z = \frac{x - \mu}{\sigma} \tag{6.5}$$

SOLVED EXERCISES

1. UNIFORM DISTRIBUTION

The Latah Creek Winery produces between 200 and 300 gallons of wine each day. The uniform distribution best describes this process.

a. On average, how much wine is produced each day?

b. What is the amount of variability in the number of gallons of wine produced from day to day?

c. In what percentage of days can production be expected to fall between 220 and 270 gallons?

d. What is the probability that production will be more than 280 gallons tomorrow?

Solution:

a. $\text{Mean} = \frac{200 + 300}{2} = 250$

b. $\text{Standard deviation} = \sqrt{\frac{(300 - 200)^2}{12}} = 28.9$

c. $P(220 \le x \le 270) = \frac{270 - 220}{300 - 200} = \frac{50}{100} = .50$

d. $P(280 \le x \le 300) = \frac{300 - 280}{300 - 200} = \frac{20}{100} = .20$

2. NORMAL DISTRIBUTION

American Carpets has 2,000 accounts receivable. The mean and standard deviation are \$300 and \$50, respectively. Assume that the accounts are normally distributed.

a. How many accounts exceed \$400?

b. How many accounts are below \$250?

c. What is the probability that an account selected at random will be between \$200 and \$350?

d. What percentage of the accounts are between \$325 and \$375?

e. Forty percent of the accounts exceed what dollar amount? (*Hint:* Fifty percent of the accounts are for more than \$300.)

f. Twenty percent of the accounts are below what dollar amount?

Solution:

a. $z = (400 - 300)/50 = 2.0 \rightarrow .4772$ (area between 300 and 400)
$(.5000 - .4772) = .0228$ (area above 400)
$2{,}000 \times .0228 = 45.6$, or approximately 46 accounts

b. $z = (250 - 300)/50 = -1.0 \rightarrow .3413$ (area between 250 and 300)
$(.5000 - .3413) = .1587$ (area below 250)
$2{,}000 \times .1587 = 317.4$, or approximately 317 accounts

c. $z = (200 - 300)/50 = -2.0 \rightarrow .4772$ (area between 200 and 300)
$z = (350 - 300)/50 = 1.0 \rightarrow .3413$ (area between 300 and 350)
Sum $= .8185$ (area between 200 and 350)
The probability is approximately .82.

d. $z = (375 - 300)/50 = 1.5 \rightarrow .4332$ (area between 300 and 375)
$z = (325 - 300)/50 = 0.5 \rightarrow .1915$ (area between 300 and 325)
Difference $= .2417$ (area between 325 and 375)
The percentage is approximately 24%.

e. $(.5000 - .4000) = .1000 \rightarrow z = 0.25$
$x = \mu + z\sigma = 300 + 0.25(50) = 312.5$
Forty percent of the accounts are worth more than \$312.50.

f $(.5000 - .2000) = .3000 \rightarrow z = -0.84$
$x = \mu + z\sigma = 300 + (-0.84)(50) = 258$
Twenty percent of the accounts are worth less than \$258.

3. Normal Approximation to the Binomial Distribution

New Jersey Power Company provides lower rates to customers who agree to use energy mainly at off-peak hours. Thirty percent of their customers take advantage of these savings. The consumer affairs department has conducted a focus group and is preparing to conduct a random telephone survey of 500 customers. The department supervisor wants to make sure that the group will contain a sufficient proportion of off-peak users.

a. What is the probability of obtaining fewer than 150 off-peak users in the telephone survey?

b. What is the smallest number of off-peak users likely to be included in this sample? (*Hint:* Use three standard deviations below the mean, which will include .9987 of the area under the curve.)

Solution:

a. $\mu = np = 500(.30) = 150$
Since 50% of a normal curve lies below the mean, the probability of obtaining fewer than 150 customers is 50%.

b. $\sigma = \sqrt{np(1 - p)} = \sqrt{500(.30)(.70)} = 10.25$
$x = \mu + z\sigma = 150 + (-3.0)(10.25) = 119.25$
The probability of fewer than 119 off-peak users in the sample is .0013.

EXERCISES

37. Draw a normal curve and shade in the area under the curve for each of the following:
    a. The area between the mean and $z = 2.50$.
    b. The area between the mean and $z = -0.75$.
    c. The area between $z = -1.55$ and $z = 0.89$.
    d. The area between $z = -0.38$ and $z = -2.18$.
    e. The area above $z = 2.68$.
    f. The area below $z = -1.15$.

38a. .4946
b. .2734
c. .7527
d. .3374
e. .0037
f. .1251

38. Find the probability that an item would fall in each of the shaded intervals drawn in Exercise 37.

39. Find the z value that corresponds to each of the areas described:
    a. Fifty percent of the items lie above this z value.
    b. Thirty percent of the items lie below this z value.
    c. The chances are 1 in 10 that an item selected at random will deviate from the mean by more than this z value.
    d. Five percent of the items will lie more than this distance (measured in terms of a z value) from the mean.

39a. 0
b. $-.52$
c. ± 1.645
d. ± 1.96

40. The total time needed to process a mortgage loan application at Bancshares Mortgage Company is uniformly distributed between five and nine days.
    a. What is the average loan processing time?
    b. What is the variability in the loan processing time?
    c. What percentage of loans are processed within eight days?
    d. Find the probability that a loan will take more than six days to be processed.

40a. 7
b. 1.15
c. 75%
d. 75%

41. Mary Walsh is studying the records of the Valley Appliance Company to determine the adequacy of the present warranty policy for refrigerators. She finds that the length of time Valley Appliance refrigerators operate before requiring repairs is normally distributed with mean 5.7 years and standard deviation 2.1 years. The company presently repairs free any machine that fails to work properly within a two-year period after purchase. What percentage of Valley Appliance refrigerators require these free repairs?

41. 3.92%

42. The Barcellos' Tum Tum Resort staff tracks the number of days each guest stays. They've discovered that this variable is normally distributed with a mean of 9 and a standard deviation of 3. The forecast for next month indicates that 500 guests are expected.
    a. How many guests are expected to stay fewer than 5 days?
    b. How many guests are expected to stay more than 15 days?
    c. How many guests are expected to stay between 6 and 12 days?
    d. Fifteen percent of the guests leave after how many days?
    e. Seventy-five percent of the guests stay longer than how many days?

42a. 46
b. 11
c. 341
d. 6
e. 7

43. The label on Spic and Clean laundry detergent boxes indicates net weight of 27 ounces. A machine fills these boxes in a uniformly distributed manner, with the smallest box con-

taining 26 ounces and the largest 28 ounces. Quality control accepts boxes filled within 0.9 ounces of the amount stated on the box.

43*a*. .58
b. 35%
c. 10%

a. How much variability is there in the amount put in the boxes?

b. What is the probability that a box will be filled with between 26.8 and 27.5 ounces?

c. What is the probability that a box will fail to meet the quality-control standard?

44. 691

44. A large L-Mart discount store's maintenance department has been instructed to replace all light bulbs at the same time. Past experience indicates that light bulbs' life is normally distributed with a mean life of 750 hours and standard deviation of 40 hours. When should the lights be replaced so that no more than 7% burn out?

45. Forrest Paint Company accountant, Dan Joyner, has a history of making errors on 6% of the invoices he processes. Forrest Paint processed 400 invoices last month.

45*a*. $\mu = 24$
$\sigma = 4.75$
b. .1711
c. .0853

a. How many invoices would you expect to have errors?

b. Determine the probability that Don made fewer than 20 errors.

c. Determine the probability that Don made more than 30 errors.

46. 705

46. Jake runs the concession stand for a Chicago-area minor league baseball team. He knows that hot dog sales are normally distributed with an average of 600 hot dogs per day and standard deviation of 45. Jake reconsiders how much to stock in his business after reading an article in *Sport* magazine (March 1989) about Chicago-area baseball. This article predicted good crowds for Chicago teams, which Jake thinks will affect his business.

Jake wants to make sure that he doesn't run out of hot dogs. How many hot dogs should he order so that the probability of running out is less than 1% each day?

47. A swimming pool is filled at a rate between 32 and 39 gallons per minute. (Assume a uniform distribution.)

47*a*. 35.5
b. 42.9%

a. Find the average rate at which the pool is filled.

b. Find the probability that the rate at any one time is below 35 gallons per minute.

48. .0409

48. Automobile inspectors in New Mexico have determined that 11% of all cars coming in for annual inspection fail. What is the probability that 20 or more cars out of the next 130 cars tested will fail the inspection?

49. .0548

49. An automobile machine produces bearings, 2% of which are defective. If a sample of 600 bearings is drawn at random, what is the probability of observing six or fewer defectives?

50. 141

50. The personnel director of Kershaw's, Inc., Kelly Moreland, needs to administer an aptitude test to 30 job applicants. Kelly has just read an article about how managers cope with labor shortages (*Personnel Management*, May 1989). This article made Kelly think about how to improve the selection process for hirees, and she has bought an aptitude exam from a national company for use at Kershaw's.

The booklet for the test informs her that the average length of time required to complete the exam is 120 minutes with standard deviation of 25 minutes. When should she end the test if she wishes to allow sufficient time for 80% of the applicants to finish? (Assume that test times are normally distributed.)

51. Associated Investment Advisors sells annuities based on annual payout during the lifetimes of the participants in the plan. They've determined that participants' lifetimes are approximately normally distributed with a mean of 72 years and standard deviation of 4.7 years.

51*a*. .9319
.6664
.2611
.0446
b. 71

a. What is the probability that a plan participant will receive payments beyond age 65? Beyond age 70? Beyond age 75? Beyond age 80?

b. Sixty percent of the plan participants are beyond what age?

52. 19%

52. City planner Terry Novak knows that mean family income is $28,000 with a standard deviation of $9,000 in Bonners Ferry, Kentucky, a community of 20,000 households. He also knows that family income isn't a normally distributed variable. Terry is applying for a grant and must answer the following question: At least what percentage of incomes lie within $10,000 of the mean income?

53. .9936

53. Innovative Technology Systems manufactures electronic cables for computers. Innovative has found from past experience that 97% of the cables shipped are acceptable. It ships most of its cables to Compaq Computers. *The Wall Street Journal* (November 3, 1989) has just said that Compaq's stock plunged after it reported lower-than-expected fourth-quarter profits. This has Innovative concerned about the quality of its cables because Compaq has indicated it must cut production costs and may examine its commitment to Innovative.

A shipment of 400 cables has just been sent to Compaq. Innovative's contract calls for at least 380 acceptable cables. What is the probability that this shipment will fulfill the contract conditions?

54. You've worked part-time at Ranch Thrift, a large supermarket, for the past three years. Your boss knows that you're completing your business degree and asks you to study the average customer expenditure per visit. You sample 500 customer expenditures and determine that this variable is normally distributed with an average expenditure of $31.28 and standard deviation of $7.29. Write your boss a memo analyzing the average customer expenditure per visit.

EXTENDED EXERCISES

55. IRS REFUNDS

An IRS regional office plots a large sample of tax refund amounts, finding that they form a bell-shaped curve with refunds fairly close to this center value, suggesting a normal distribution. The average refund is $748 with standard deviation of $124. Since the data plot is so close to a normal curve, they decide that probability or percentage questions can be answered using the standard normal table.

A refund greater than $1,000 is considered "large" and the office manager wants to know what percentage of current refunds, based on the normal distribution, exceed this amount.

A second question involves new withholding guidelines for taxpayers. It is estimated that the average refund amount will rise by $150 after these guidelines go into effect. The office wonders how the percentage of large refunds will be affected.

The office wants to find the percentage of refunds over $1,000 that might be expected based on current guidelines. The z value is calculated, and the resulting area is subtracted from .50 to determine the area in the standard normal upper tail:

$$z = (1{,}000 - 748)/124 = 2.03 \rightarrow .4788 \quad \text{(area between 748 and 1,000)}$$
$$.5000 - .4788 = .0212 \quad \text{(area above 1,000)}$$

About 2% of the refunds under the current withholding guidelines can be expected to exceed $1,000.

With the new guidelines in effect, a $150 increase to $898, in the average refund can be expected. The office has assumed that the standard deviation of refund balances will remain the same, $124, even though the mean has shifted. Under this assumption, the percentage of the normal curve above $1,000 can be found using the z value and the standard normal table:

$$z = (1{,}000 - 898)/124 = 0.82 \rightarrow .2939 \quad \text{(area between 898 and 1,000)}$$
$$.5000 - .2939 = .2061 \quad \text{(area above 1,000)}$$

The increase in average refund raises the percentage of refunds of over $1,000 to about 21%. This increase from 2% to 21% is important to the IRS office for planning auditing time and clerical duties.

a. What would happen to the percentage of refunds over $1,000 if the average refund amount actually dropped $75?

b. After the 2% figure has been computed under the current withholding policy, how could the assumption of a normal distribution be checked?

56. Ranch Life Insurance Company of Florida

Kim Carter, statistician for Ranch Life Insurance Company of Florida, notices that monthly premium receipts appear to follow a normal distribution. After plotting receipts for a typical month and observing their distribution, Kim decides that the normality assumption is reasonable.

Ranch wants to determine the percentage of monthly receipts that fall into the range $125 to $175, since such amounts are difficult to handle. They aren't large enough to warrant investment attention, unless there are many of them, nor are they small enough to ignore by putting them into the cash account.

To find the percentage of accounts in this range, Kim computes the mean and standard deviation of monthly premium receipts. She determines these values to be $100 and $38, respectively.

a. What percentage of monthly receipts can be expected to fall into the range $125 to $175?

b. Kim predicts that within two years the average monthly premium will rise to $150. Assuming the standard deviation remains the same, how would this change the answer to Question *a*?

c. Describe how the assumption of normality might be verified in this case.

57. Specific Electric

Jess Franklin of Specific Electric Appliance Manufacturing Company's finance department has been studying interest rates on its short-term loans from the company's banks. For comparison purposes, he's been following the T-bill rate for several months. The most recent yield, as reported in *The Wall Street Journal* (February 23, 1990), is 7.80%. He has also been watching the rate Specific's bank charges.

Jess assumes that his bank rate, which varies from day to day, can be described by a normal curve and he uses normal curve procedures to compute various probabilities. These probabilities are used in preparing for market rate shifts under an acceptable level of risk.

In presenting his work to the firm's top management, Jess mentions the normality assumption and then shows the computations for market rate probabilities and the preparations based on these probabilities. Company president Mary Montana interrupts, saying, "I don't know about your assumption of a normal distribution for daily interest rates. It seems to me the assumption isn't valid, since rates often seem to be on a long-term increase or decrease. If that's true, the assumption of a normal distribution may be valid, but not the assumption of an unchanging average."

a. What are the strengths in Mary's statement?

b. What are the weaknesses in Mary's statement?

c. Is there any way Mary's concern about a shifting mean could be incorporated into Jess's calculations?

58. GMAT SCORES FOR CITY UNIVERSITY

Professors Williams, Ross, Stanley, and Richards are serving on the MBA Committee at City University. The committee is to set a cutoff level for admitting students into the MBA program using the GMAT (Graduate Management Admissions Test). Currently, the mean test score nationally is 475 with standard deviation of 75. Scores are thought to be approximately normally distributed.

Professor Ross suggests analyzing City's 100 most recent MBA applicants' scores to see if they resemble GMAT scores nationwide. If the sample is similar, Professor Ross proposes that a score be chosen that would permit 25% of the applicants to be admitted to the program. The 100 GMAT scores are:

568	395	489	288	396	442	672	492	465	523	494	513	486
606	486	514	497	399	562	507	457	449	553	492	330	375
365	415	575	432	378	403	518	476	355	470	512	527	366
422	506	542	452	579	400	429	383	569	381	514	465	439
505	429	564	438	350	595	476	469	462	446	565	450	
600	568	450	580	450	423	598	458	494	582	623	401	
461	564	519	375	553	543	480	322	490	436	446	465	
412	483	452	389	611	569	368	469	348	522	479	473	

a. Are City University applicants similar to the national average?

b. If Professor Ross's proposal is accepted, what cutoff score should be used for admittance?

c. Professor Richards feels that one third of the applicants should be admitted. What cutoff score would he propose?

59. EUREKA DAIRY

Jim Black is in charge of quality control at Eureka Dairy in Deer Park, Georgia. Jim is concerned about grade A milk's bacteria count per cubic centimeter. On July 15 the bacteria count was 31,000. Jim's problem is to determine whether something is wrong with the production process. Eureka Dairy over a long period of time has regulated its processing to achieve a mean bacteria count of 21,000 with standard deviation of 3,000. A distribution plotted from the bacteria counts over a long period of time is normal in form. Each day the count is plotted on a chart similar to Figure 6.17. Jim needs to determine whether this chart is useful.

a. What are the chances in 1,000 that the bacteria count will exceed 30,000 if the day-to-day variation in Figure 6.17 is purely random?

b. Determine the probability of a bacteria count of 31,000 or more.

c. Which is the more reasonable assumption: that a bacteria count of 31,000 might reasonably be expected, or that something is wrong? Explain your answer.

d. Is the charting device in Figure 6.17 helpful in maintaining high quality? Explain your answer.

e. Why would it be important for this dairy to find the mean value of these bacteria counts every month?

FIGURE 6.17 Bacteria Counts in Grade A Milk

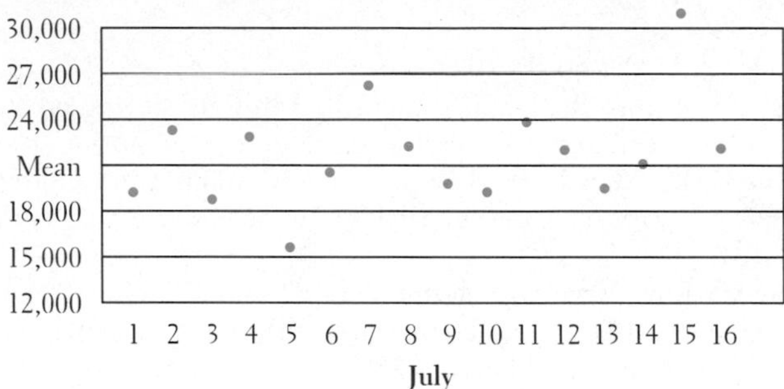

MICROCOMPUTER PACKAGE

The micro package *Computerized Business Statistics* can be used to solve normal curve problems. Suppose Applied Business Systems, Inc., needs to know what percentage of its orders exceeded 135 miles. Applied's analyst knows that shipping distances are normally distributed with a mean of 125 miles and standard deviation of 28 miles.

Computer Solution:

From the main menu of *Computerized Business Statistics*, a **5** is selected, indicating Probability Distributions. This menu appeared at the end of Chapter 5.

This problem involves the normal distribution. Since Applied needs to know what percentage of its orders exceeded 135 miles, the arrow is moved to normal $P(X \geq a)$.

```
Enter Mean and Press ↵ 125
Enter Standard Deviation and Press ↵ 28
Enter A and Press ↵ 135
```

The normal probability distribution for $\mu = 125$ and $\sigma = 28$ is shown on the screen. The correct answer for $P(x \geq 135)$ is .3601.

MINITAB COMPUTER PACKAGE

Two discrete statistical distributions (binomial and Poisson) were demonstrated at the end of Chapter 5. This section covers the MINITAB for two continuous statistical distributions: uniform and normal. All we need is to indicate the type of distribution and the value(s) of the parameter(s) that describe it (a to b for the uniform and μ and σ for the normal). The **CDF** command is used to calculate probabilities for the cumulative distribution function.

The **CDF** for any value *x* is the probability that a random variable with the specified distribution has a value less than or equal to *x*.

The MINITAB commands for Solved Exercise 1.*c* are shown to find the percentage of days that production can be expected to fall between 220 and 270 gallons for a uniform distribution with a range of 200 to 300.

```
MTB> SET C1
MTB> 220
MTB> 270
MTB> END
MTB> CDF C1;
SUBC> UNIFORM 200 300.
  220.0000     0.2000
  270.0000     0.7000
```

The **SET** command is used to identify the interval of interest. The **CDF** command is used to generate a cumulative probability density function. The **UNIFORM** subcommand is used to generate the probability function for a uniform distribution from 200 to 300. The percentage is (.7 − .2 = .5) or 50%.

The MINITAB commands for Solved Exercise 2.*a* to determine the probability that an account exceeds $400 if the accounts receivable are normally distributed with mean $300 and standard deviation $50 are:

```
MTB> SET C2
MTB> 400
MTB> END
MTB> CDF C2;
SUBC> NORMAL 300 50.
  400.0000     0.9772
```

The **SET** command is used to identify the interval of interest. The **CDF** command is used again to generate a cumulative probability density function. The **NORMAL** subcommand is used to generate the probability function for a normal distribution with a mean of $300 and standard deviation of $50. The probability is (1 − .9772) = .0228.

Chapter

7

Sampling Distributions

To see the world in a grain of sand.

Blake, *Auguries of Innocence*

Objectives

When you have completed this chapter, you will be able to:

Explain the concept of sampling distributions.

Construct a sampling distribution of sample means.

Construct a sampling distribution of sample proportions.

Explain why the central limit theorem is important to statistical decision making.

In May 1989, *Business Month* featured an article entitled "Quest for Quality" describing quality-improvement efforts of Hewlett-Packard. The company had trimmed its defective rate on connections to 1,800 per million and was startled to find that a similar Japanese company had a rate of only 4 per million. Hewlett-Packard vowed to improve its defective rate.

The preceding chapter introduced the normal distribution and some of its applications. This chapter covers more important uses for this theoretical distribution and establishes the most important concept in statistics: the sampling distribution.

WHY MANAGERS NEED TO KNOW ABOUT SAMPLING DISTRIBUTIONS

Most statistical applications involve sampling items from the population being studied. Chapter 2 discussed ways to make the sample selection to ensure that a representative group of items is collected and measured. This selection process is important because the sample's characteristics are inferred to hold for the entire population, even though only a very small part of the population is actually sampled and measured.

This chapter deals with the accuracy of this inference process. Once the inference is made that the population possesses the same characteristics as the sample, the analyst must determine the extent of possible error involved in this process. Since sampling is commonplace in most organizations, knowing how to measure and understand this inherent error is vital to every manager. Assessing possible error involves a thorough understanding of statistics' most important concept: the sampling distribution.

Hewlett-Packard's attempts to reduce the defective rate must be closely monitored. A real quality improvement must be distinguished from a random fluctuation in the defective rate. The concept of sampling distributions is the key to understanding the difference.

SAMPLING ERROR

A sample mean isn't likely to equal the mean of the population from which the sample was selected. Nor is a sample standard deviation or other sample measure likely to exactly equal its corresponding population value. Some difference between a sample statistic and its corresponding population parameter is to be expected. This difference, called the **sampling error,** is due purely to chance.

> **Sampling error** is the difference between a sample statistic and its corresponding population parameter.

EXAMPLE 7.1 Jarms Hardware's five workers have worked at the store for 2, 4, 5, 8, and 11 years, respectively, for an average (mean) of 6 years. If a sample of two workers with 5 and 11 years of experience is selected at random from this population, a sample mean of 8 results. The sampling error is 2, the difference between the sample statistic (8) and the corresponding population parameter (6) ($\bar{x} - \mu = 8 - 6 = 2$). If a second sample of two workers is selected at random from this population, and these workers have 2 and 8 years of experience, a sample mean of 5 results. In this case, the sampling error is -1, the difference between the sample statistic (5) and the corresponding population parameter (6) ($\bar{x} - \mu = 5 - 6 = -1$). Different combinations of two workers provide different sample means. How can analysts use sample means to estimate population means when there's almost always an error? To deal with the question of sample accuracy, we must understand the concept of sampling distributions.

Distribution of Sampling Means

Chapters 5 and 6 presented the binomial and normal distributions as models of certain realistic situations. This chapter's key concept involves a distribution of sample statistics. When a sample is taken from a population, a numerical sample statistic results. This statistic should be viewed *as if it were selected from the distribution of all possible values of that sample statistic.* This theoretical distribution of the sample statistic is called the **sampling distribution.**

Sampling Distribution

> A **sampling distribution** includes all possible values that a statistic, such as a sample mean, can assume for a given sample size.

V

Because population and sample sizes in practical situations are usually quite large, it's not feasible to actually formulate the array of possible sample results from which the statistic is drawn. There are countless ways to reach into a large population and select a sample and, hence, countless sample means from which to choose.

Even though in most real-life situations it's not possible to list all possible sample statistics, a limited-population example can be used to illustrate this concept.

Example 7.2 A population consists of ages 10, 20, 30, 40, and 50. A random sample of two is to be selected from this population and the sample mean computed. The sampling distribution consists of every possible sample mean. Since both N and n are quite small, we can find all possible samples and compute their means. Sampling for this example is done with replacement. That is, after the first population item is selected for the sample, it's returned to the population for possible selection again. In nearly all practical situations, the population size is sufficiently large that this replacement isn't necessary to ensure randomness.

Table 7.1 shows every possible sample pair that can be drawn from this population. Since $N = 5$ and $n = 2$, there are 25 possible sample pairs. The second column shows the mean value of each sample pair (the sample statistic); this column constitutes the sampling distribution for this example. Table 7.2 summarizes this sampling distribution, where duplicate sample means are combined to form a probability distribution. Figure 7.1 shows the probability distribution's shape.

TABLE 7.1 Sampling Distribution of Means (Example 7.2)

Sampled ages	Sample means	$(\bar{x} - \mu_{\bar{x}})$	$(\bar{x} - \mu_{\bar{x}})^2$
10, 10	10	−20	400
10, 20	15	−15	225
10, 30	20	−10	100
10, 40	25	−5	25
10, 50	30	0	0
20, 10	15	−15	225
20, 20	20	−10	100
20, 30	25	−5	25
20, 40	30	0	0
20, 50	35	5	25
30, 10	20	−10	100
30, 20	25	−5	25
30, 30	30	0	0
30, 40	35	5	25
30, 50	40	10	100
40, 10	25	−5	25
40, 20	30	0	0
40, 30	35	5	25
40, 40	40	10	100
40, 50	45	15	225
50, 10	30	0	0
50, 20	35	5	25
50, 30	40	10	100
50, 40	45	15	225
50, 50	50	20	400
	Sum = 750		2,500

TABLE 7.2 Probability Distribution of Means (Example 7.2)

Sample mean	Frequency	Probability
10	1	.04
15	2	.08
20	3	.12
25	4	.16
30	5	.20
35	4	.16
40	3	.12
45	2	.08
50	1	.04
		1.00

If a random sample of two ages is taken from the population (10, 20, 30, 40, 50) with replacement and the sample mean computed, it's *as if* this sample mean had been randomly selected from Table 7.1's sampling distribution. The sampling distribution underlies the inferential process in all statistical sampling situations, and you must have a mental image of this distribution. Chapters 8, 9, and 10, in particular, rely on

FIGURE 7.1 Distribution of Sample Means

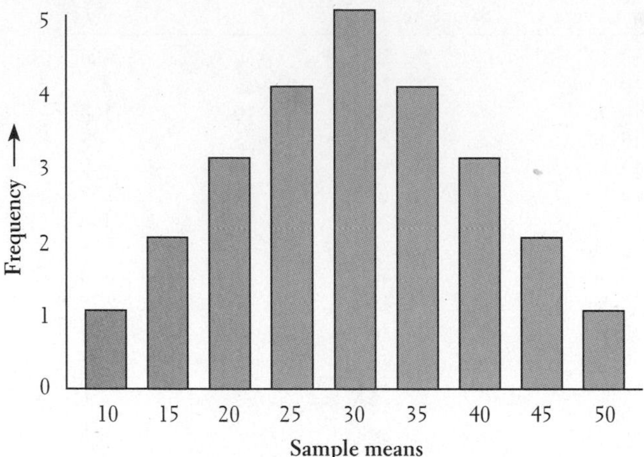

the concept of a sampling distribution in developing procedures for estimation and hypothesis testing.

Note the shape of Figure 7.1. The sample means seem to cluster about a central value, 30 (which happens to be the population mean). The distribution is also symmetrical, with as many values above 30 as below it. This description sounds like a normal distribution; in fact, this appearance isn't accidental, as will be discussed in the next section.

The population in Example 7.2 consists of ages 10, 20, 30, 40, and 50. From Equation 4.1, the population mean age is

$$\mu = \frac{\Sigma x}{N} = \frac{150}{5} = 30$$

The mean of the sampling distribution in Table 7.1 is also calculated using Equation 4.1:

$$\mu_{\bar{x}} = \frac{\Sigma \bar{x}}{n} = \frac{750}{25} = 30$$

The two means are the same. As specified by Equation 7.1, the mean of the population and mean of the sampling distribution are equal:

$$\mu_x = \mu_{\bar{x}} \tag{7.1}$$

where μ_x = Population mean

$\mu_{\bar{x}}$ = Mean of the sampling distribution

This is true for any sample or population size. This fact is intuitively appealing since we would expect sample means to cluster around the population mean. The frequency distribution of Table 7.2 shows this symmetrical clustering of sample means around the population mean value of 30.

From Equation 4.6, the standard deviation for the population ages 10, 20, 30, 40, and 50 can be computed.

$$\sigma = \sqrt{\frac{\Sigma(x - \mu)^2}{N}} = \sqrt{\frac{1{,}000}{5}} = \sqrt{200} = 14.1$$

The standard deviation of the sampling distribution is

$$\sigma_{\bar{x}} = \sqrt{\frac{\Sigma(\bar{x} - \mu_{\bar{x}})^2}{n}} = \sqrt{\frac{2{,}500}{25}} = \sqrt{100} = 10$$

Note that the standard deviation of the sampling distribution is less than the standard deviation of the population. This relationship is also intuitively appealing. It is reasonable to assume that the means of samples of two population values would tend to be closer to the population mean than would the individual population values themselves. Why the sampling distribution standard deviation happens to be 10 isn't intuitively obvious.

Equation 7.2 shows how to compute the standard deviation of the sampling distribution of means without requiring a listing of all the possible sample means:

$$\sigma_{\bar{x}} = \frac{\sigma}{\sqrt{n}} \tag{7.2}$$

where $\sigma_{\bar{x}}$ = Standard deviation of the sampling distribution (called the *standard error of the mean*)
σ = Population standard deviation
n = Sample size

Standard Error of the Mean

The term *standard error* is frequently used to identify the standard deviation of a sampling distribution. More precisely, the **standard error of the mean** is the standard deviation of the sampling distribution of sample means.

> The **standard error of the mean** is the standard deviation of the sampling distribution of sample means.

The standard error of the mean for Example 7.2 is

$$\sigma_{\bar{x}} = \frac{\sigma}{\sqrt{n}} = \frac{14.1}{\sqrt{2}} = \frac{14.1}{1.41} = 10$$

The value of the standard error of the mean depends on two factors:

1. The variability of the population as measured by its standard deviation (σ).
2. The sample size used (n).

EXAMPLE 7.3 A random sample of 50 Deaconess Medical Center employees is selected to determine the average amount of time since the last promotion. This action was prompted by an article on the increasing complexity of succession, reported in *Personnel Management* (January 1990). The president is concerned that time in rank, rather than competence, determines who'll be promoted.

The data values on time since promotion are collected from personnel files using a systematic sampling plan (covered in Chapter 2). Average (mean) time is computed to be 4.78 years. Analyst Pam Shore recognizes that if sampling were repeated and different people were selected by the random process, a different sample mean would result. It is as if 4.78 had been randomly drawn from the sampling distribution of means.

If the population standard deviation is known to be 1.2 years, the standard error of the mean for sample size 50 is

$$\sigma_{\bar{x}} = \frac{\sigma}{\sqrt{n}} = \frac{1.2}{\sqrt{50}} = \frac{1.2}{7.07} = 0.17$$

Note how the standard error of the mean is affected by both the variability of the population and the sample size selected. If the variability of the population is smaller, say, one year, then the standard error decreases:

$$\sigma_{\bar{x}} = \frac{\sigma}{\sqrt{n}} = \frac{1.0}{\sqrt{50}} = \frac{1.0}{7.07} = 0.14$$

If a larger sample size is used—say, 400—the standard error also decreases:

$$\sigma_{\bar{x}} = \frac{\sigma}{\sqrt{n}} = \frac{1.2}{\sqrt{400}} = \frac{1.2}{20} = 0.06$$

Having σ in the numerator makes sense, since we'd expect populations with high variability to have a more variable sampling distribution than populations with little variability. Placing the sample size, n, in the denominator seems reasonable also. This suggests that using a larger sample size decreases the variability (standard error) of the sampling distribution and results in sample means that are closer to the population mean than we'd get using a small sample size.

Central Limit Theorem

The population and sampling distributions in Example 7.2 illustrate the essential features of the **central limit theorem,** another important concept in statistics. This famous theorem states that the bell-shaped appearance of the sampling distribution of Table 7.2 and Figure 7.1 is no accident. The central limit theorem states that if a population is normally distributed, the distribution of sample means drawn from that population is also normally distributed. More important, if the population isn't normal, the distribution of sample means will be approximately normal if the sample is sufficiently large.

> The **central limit theorem** states that if a sufficiently large random sample of n observations is selected from any population, the sampling distribution of sample means will be approximately a normal distribution. The larger the sample size, n, the better will be the normal approximation to the sampling distribution of sample means.

The central limit theorem states that the distribution of sample means "approaches" a normal curve as the sample size increases. Table 7.1 shows the sampling distribution of means for a sample size of two. This distribution isn't perfectly normal since it is, in fact, a discrete distribution with only the specified values possible. In contrast, the normal distribution is a continuous distribution, as discussed in Chapter 6. However, had a sample size of 50 been used, the sampling distribution, although still not perfectly smooth, would be close to a smooth normal curve. And if a sample of 500 had been used, the resulting discrete distribution would be almost indistinguishable from the continuous normal curve. That's what is meant by the definition of the central limit theorem: the larger the sample size used, the closer the sampling distribution is to the normal curve.

The key feature of the central limit theorem is that the distribution of sample means approaches a normal curve *regardless of the population shape* if the sample is sufficiently large. This makes the central limit theorem valuable in statistical applications because analysts can use normal curve probability techniques for a sampling distribution even if there is no knowledge of the population's shape. Figure 7.2 illustrates this key feature of the central limit theorem.

Each population in Figure 7.2 has a different shape. Population *a* is skewed to the high side; population *b* is skewed to the lower end. Population *c*'s shape is even more nonnormal, while population *d* is the opposite of normal: data values are concentrated in the high and low regions with almost none in the middle. But when large enough samples are taken from each population and the mean is computed for each, these sample means approximate normal distributions, as the curves on the right side of Figure 7.2 show.

Probabilities can be computed for these normally distributed sampling distributions using the normal curve procedures of Chapter 6.

The central limit theorem provides the basic definition for the sampling distribution of sample means. If the sample size is reasonably large, these values form a normal curve with a mean equal to μ and standard error equal to $\sigma/\sqrt{n}$. As a rule of thumb, a sample size of 30 is the minimum needed to ensure the approximate normal shape of the sampling distribution. For smaller sample sizes, the shape of the population distribution must be known. If it's close to a normal distribution, the sampling distribution of means can still be assumed to be normal. If the population is nonnormal, and a small sample size is used, the sampling distribution may fail to follow a normal curve, and procedures discussed in Chapter 19 must be used.

FIGURE 7.2 Populations and Sampling Distributions

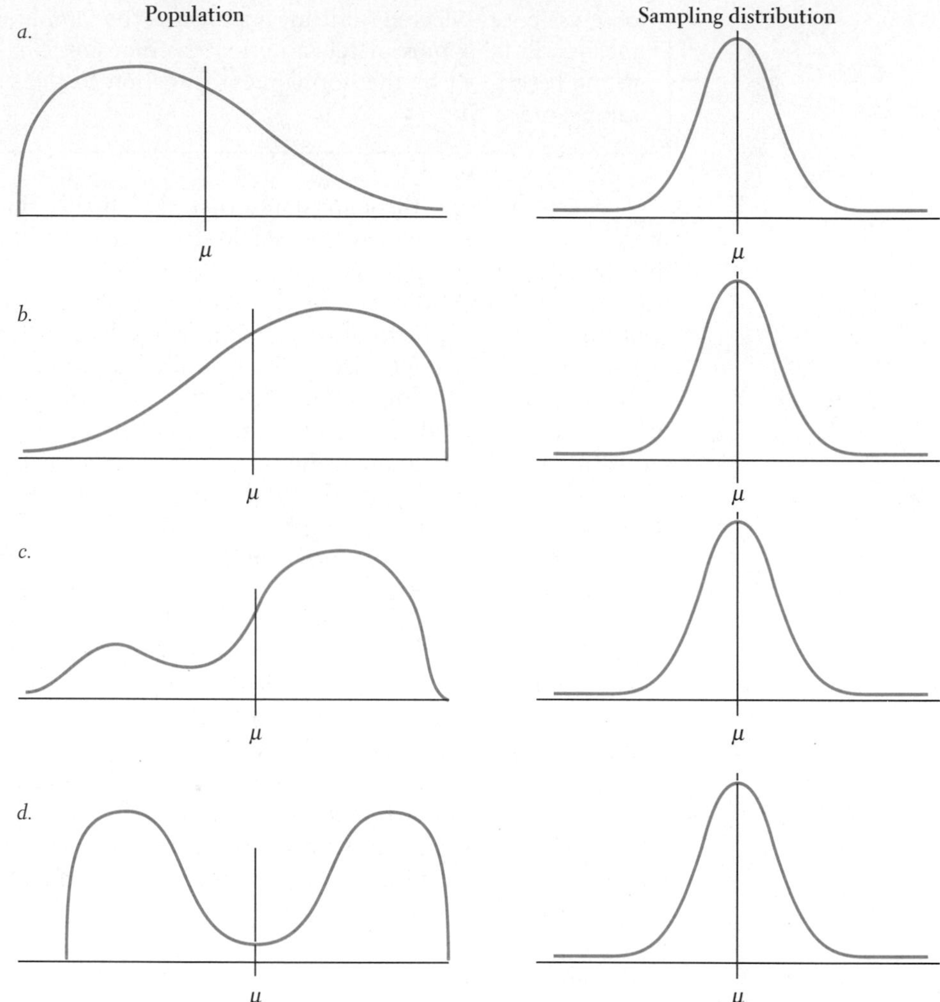

TM

Sampling Distribution of Means

Properties of the sampling distribution of means

1. The mean of the sampling distribution of means equals the population mean: $\mu_x = \mu_{\bar{x}}$.
2. The standard deviation of the sampling distribution of means (standard error) equals the population standard deviation divided by the square root of the sample size: $\sigma_{\bar{x}} = \sigma/\sqrt{n}$.
3. The sampling distribution of means is approximately normal for sufficiently large sample sizes ($n \geq 30$).

EXAMPLE 7.4 A population has a mean of 5.7 and standard deviation of 1.9. A sample of 50 items is randomly selected from this population. Find the probability that the sample mean lies between 5.5 and 5.8.

Two areas are found from the normal sampling distribution and added to determine the correct answer. Figure 7.3 shows the desired area.

FIGURE 7.3 Sampling Distribution of Means for Example 7.4

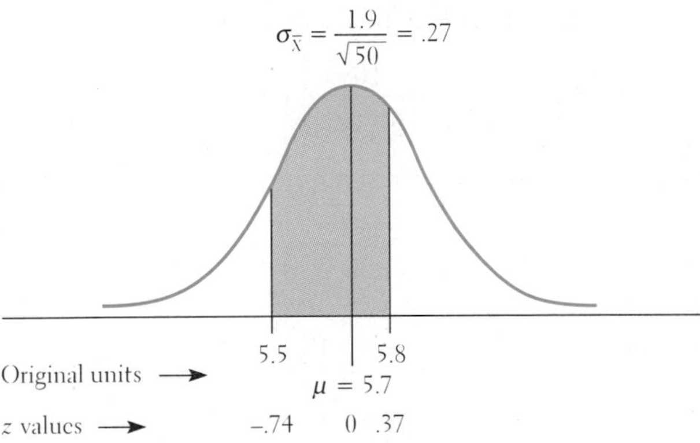

The calculations are

$$\sigma_{\bar{x}} = \frac{\sigma}{\sqrt{n}} = \frac{1.9}{\sqrt{50}} = \frac{1.9}{7.07} = 0.27$$

$$z = \frac{\bar{x} - \mu}{\sigma_{\bar{x}}} = \frac{5.5 - 5.7}{0.27} = -0.74 \rightarrow .2704 \text{ (area between 5.5 and 5.7)}$$

$$z = \frac{\bar{x} - \mu}{\sigma_{\bar{x}}} = \frac{5.8 - 5.7}{0.27} = 0.37 \rightarrow \underline{.1443} \text{ (area between 5.7 and 5.8)}$$

$$\text{Sum} = .4147 \text{ (area between 5.5 and 5.8)}$$

There's a 41.47% chance that the sample mean will fall between 5.5 and 5.8 if a sample size of 50 is used.

In real-life business situations, the population standard deviation is usually unknown. In such cases, the sample standard deviation, s, is used as an unbiased estimate of the population standard deviation, σ (i.e., s replaces σ in Equation 7.2). Whenever s is used, the t distribution, rather than the normal, is the theoretically correct distribution. (Chapter 8 discusses this concept.) However, whenever the sample size is sufficiently large (30 or greater) or the population is normally distributed, the central limit theorem indicates that the sampling distribution of means will be approximately normal.

EXAMPLE 7.5 A population is known to have a mean of 100. If a sample of 75 items is selected from this population, what is the probability that the sample mean will fall between 100 and 102 if the sample standard deviation is 10?

Since the sample size is greater than 30, a normal sampling distribution can be assumed. The mean of the sampling distribution, in accordance with Equation 7.1, is the population mean, 100. The standard error of the mean can't be calculated exactly because the standard deviation of the population isn't known. However, the sample standard deviation, $s = 10$, can be used as an estimate. In practical applications, this estimation process is typically used since only sample information is available.

The standard error of the mean, in accordance with Equation 7.2, is estimated as

$$s_{\bar{x}} = \frac{s}{\sqrt{n}} = \frac{10}{\sqrt{75}} = \frac{10}{8.66} = 1.15$$

These values are shown on the sampling distribution of Figure 7.4.

FIGURE 7.4 Sampling Distribution of Means for Example 7.5

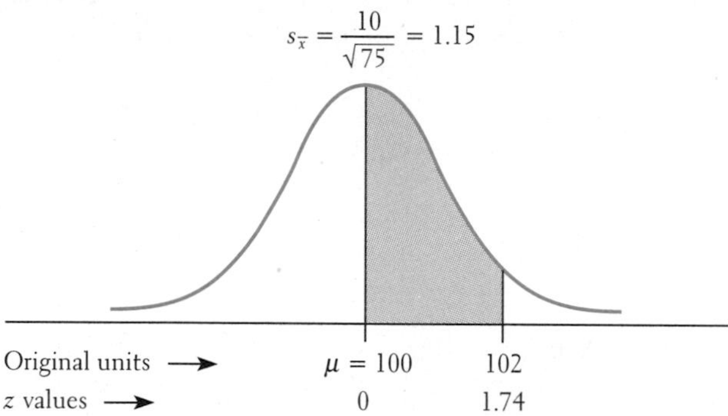

The desired area can be found by computing the z value as demonstrated in Figure 7.3. This calculation and the resulting area in the right side of the curve are

$$z = \frac{102 - 100}{1.15} = 1.74 \rightarrow .4591 \text{ (area between 100 and 102)}$$

There's about a 46% chance that the sample mean will lie between 100 and 102 when a sample size of 75 is used.

A good way to understand the concept of the sampling distribution of a statistic is to use MINITAB for simulating the sampling process. The MINITAB Computer Package section at this chapter's end gives an example.

EXERCISES

1. What is sampling error?
2. What is meant by the statement "Sampling error is due to chance"?

3. What is a sampling distribution?

4. Why are sampling distributions important?
5. What thought should the term *standard error* bring to mind?

6. Why is the central limit theorem important?
7. Why is it important for a statistician to assume that a sampling distribution is normally distributed?
8. What effect does each of the following changes have on the variability of a sampling distribution of means?

8*a*. Increases
b. Decreases
c. No effect

   a. The population standard deviation is increased.
   b. The sample size is increased.
   c. The population mean is decreased.
9. Describe the shape of the sampling distribution of means when:

9*a*. Normal
b. Not normal
c. Normal

   a. The population is normally distributed.
   b. The population is not normally distributed, but the sample size is small (less than 30).
   c. The population is not normally distributed, but the sample size is large (30 or greater).

10. Distinguish the following measures: population mean (μ), sample mean (x), and sampling distribution mean ($\mu_{\bar{x}}$). How do these means compare in size for a specific case?
11. Distinguish the following measures: population standard deviation (σ), sample standard deviation (s), and standard error of the mean ($\sigma_{\bar{x}}$). How do these standard deviations compare in size for a specific case?
12. A normally distributed variable has a mean of 100 and standard deviation of 15. What is the probability that:

12*a*. .7486
b. .2120
c. .0681
d. 0
e. 0

   a. A value selected at random will be less than 110?
   b. A value selected at random will be between 85 and 95?
   c. A sample of 20 items will have a mean less than 95?
   d. A sample of 200 items will have a mean less than 95?
   e. A sample of 500 items will have a mean less than 95?

13. .33

13. A sample of 36 employees has a mean education level of 14 years with a standard deviation of 2 years. What is the standard deviation of the sampling distribution of sample means?

14. Smaller
.5

14. A sample of 100 batteries has been selected from a production line that yields batteries with a mean lifetime of 40 months and standard deviation of 10 months. If a different sample of 400 is taken from the same population, will the standard error of the mean be larger, the same, or smaller? Calculate the new standard error of the mean.
15. Suppose an analyst wants to use the information on commodity prices introduced in an article "Commodity-Indexed Debt" (*Columbia Journal of World Business*, Winter, 1988, p. 57). Under the assumption that these prices are normally distributed with a mean of 75 cents and a standard deviation of 9 cents, a random sample of 81 commodity prices is selected. What is the probability that:

15*a*. .1587
b. 0
c. .6826
d. .0668

   a. The first price selected at random from the population will be larger than 84 cents?
   b. The mean of the sample will be larger than 84 cents?
   c. The mean of the sample will be between 74 and 76 cents?
   d. The mean of the sample will be smaller than 73.5 cents?

16a. .0808
b. .5160

16. An automatic machine used to fill cans of soup has mean filling weight of 16 ounces and $\sigma = 0.5$.
    a. What is the probability of obtaining a sample of 49 cans with a mean larger than 16.1 ounces?
    b. Find the probability that the sample mean will be within 0.05 ounces of the population mean, 16 ounces.

17. 96.8 to 103.2

17. If all possible samples of size 64 are selected from a population whose mean is 100 and whose standard deviation is 20, between what limits would the middle 80% of the sample means be expected to fall?

18. .2802

18. Family income distribution in St. Paul, Minnesota, is skewed to the right. The latest census reveals mean family income of $24,000 with standard deviation of $4,000. In a simple random sample of 75 families, find the probability that the sample mean family income will differ from St. Paul's mean income by more than $500.

19. A random sample of 40 computer chips is drawn from a population and the weight of each recorded. A previous study showed that the population mean weight was 0.8 ounces with a standard deviation of 0.1 ounces.

    This action is being taken in response to an article on a new PC, the Compaq Systempro (*PC Magazine*, February 27, 1990). The subject of this article has direct application to a chip supplier that now wants to investigate chip weight, a key aspect of a new system involving computer graphics.

19a. .9992
b. 0
c. Variability would decrease

    a. What is the probability that the sample has a mean weight between 0.75 and 0.90 ounces?
    b. Determine the probability that the sample has a mean weight less than 0.5 ounces.
    c. How would the sampling distribution of sample means change if the sample size were increased from 40 to 400?

20. A population consists of the following units produced today by four workers:

Worker	Units produced
A	5
B	3
C	7
D	8

20a. $\mu = 5.75$
$\sigma = 1.92$
d. 5.75, yes
e. 1.362
f. 1.362, yes
g. Sampling distribution

    a. Compute the population mean and standard deviation.
    b. Develop a table showing every possible sample of size two (sample with replacement).
    c. Compute the mean of each of the samples of size two.
    d. Compute the mean of this sampling distribution. Does this mean equal the population mean?
    e. Compute the standard error of the mean for this sampling distribution using Equation 7.2.
    f. Compute the standard deviation of the sampling distribution of means. Does this standard deviation equal the standard error of the mean?
    g. Which distribution has less variability: the population distribution or the sampling distribution of sample means?

SAMPLING DISTRIBUTION OF SAMPLE PROPORTIONS

The binomial distribution (Chapter 5) involves finding the probabilities of different numbers of "successes" in a binomial experiment. The binomial distribution is a discrete probability distribution showing the probability of x successes in n trials of a binomial experiment, where each trial results in either success or failure. It is frequently relevant to inquire about the proportion of successes rather than the actual number. Equation 7.3 shows that for a sample of n trials of a binomial experiment, the proportion of successes, the statistic $\bar{p}$, is computed by dividing the number of successes, x, by the number of trials, n:

$$\bar{p} = \frac{x}{n} \tag{7.3}$$

EXAMPLE 7.6 Table 7.3 shows a population of five employees that includes two college graduates. Using Equation 7.3, the proportion of college graduates is

$$p = \frac{2}{5} = .40$$

Forty percent of the workers are college graduates.

TABLE 7.3 Population of Workers (Example 7.6)

Worker	College graduate
A	Yes
B	No
C	No
D	Yes
E	No

EXAMPLE 7.7 Example 7.6 involved a population of five employees including two college graduates. A random sample of two employees is to be selected from this population and the sample proportion of college graduates computed. Several different samples could be selected.

Table 7.4 shows every possible sample pair that can be drawn from the population when sampling is done with replacement. Since N = 5 and n = 2, there are 25 possible sample pairs. The third column of Table 7.4 shows the proportion of college graduates for each sample pair (the sample statistic). This column constitutes the sampling distribution of proportions for this example. The probability distribution of Table 7.5 summarizes the sampling distribution's values.

Now the mean proportion of the sampling distribution for a sample size of two is calculated:

$$\mu_{\bar{p}} = \frac{10.0}{25} = .40$$

TABLE 7.4 Sampling Distribution of Proportions (Example 7.6)

Sampled workers	Sample characteristics	Sample proportion of college graduates	$(\bar{p} - \mu_{\bar{p}})$	$(\bar{p} - \mu_{\bar{p}})^2$
A, A	Y, Y	1.00	.60	.36
A, B	Y, N	.50	.10	.01
A, C	Y, N	.50	.10	.01
A, D	Y, Y	1.00	.60	.36
A, E	Y, N	.50	.10	.01
B, A	N, Y	.50	.10	.01
B, B	N, N	.00	−.40	.16
B, C	N, N	.00	−.40	.16
B, D	N, Y	.50	.10	.01
B, E	N, N	.00	−.40	.16
C, A	N, Y	.50	.10	.01
C, B	N, N	.00	−.40	.16
C, C	N, N	.00	−.40	.16
C, D	N, Y	.50	.10	.01
C, E	N, N	.00	−.40	.16
D, A	Y, Y	1.00	.60	.36
D, B	Y, N	.50	.10	.01
D, C	Y, N	.50	.10	.01
D, D	Y, Y	1.00	.60	.36
D, E	Y, N	.50	.10	.01
E, A	N, Y	.50	.10	.01
E, B	N, N	.00	−.40	.16
E, C	N, N	.00	−.40	.16
E, D	N, Y	.50	.10	.01
E, E	N, N	.00	−.40	.16
		$\Sigma\bar{p} = 10.00$		3.00

TABLE 7.5 Probability Distribution of Proportions

$\bar{p}$	Frequency	Probability
.00	9	.36
.50	12	.48
1.00	4	.16

Note in the preceding example that the two mean proportions are the same. Equation 7.4 shows that the true population proportion and the mean of the sampling distribution of proportions are equal:

$$p = \mu_{\bar{p}} \tag{7.4}$$

where p = Population proportion
$\mu_{\bar{p}}$ = Mean of the sampling distribution of proportions

When the population is infinite or very large, or when sampling is conducted with replacement, the standard deviation of the sampling distribution of proportions is computed as

$$\sigma_{\bar{p}} = \sqrt{\frac{p(1-p)}{n}} \tag{7.5}$$

where $\sigma_{\bar{p}}$ = Standard deviation of the sampling distribution (the standard error of the proportion)
p = Population proportion
n = Sample size

Standard Error of the Proportion

Remember that the term *standard error* is frequently used to identify the standard deviation of a sampling distribution. In the same way, the standard deviation of the sampling distribution of sample proportions is referred to as the **standard error of the proportion.**

> The **standard error of the proportion** is the standard deviation of the sampling distribution of sample proportions.

EXAMPLE 7.8 The standard error of the proportion for Example 7.7 is

$$\sigma_{\bar{p}} = \sqrt{\frac{p(1-p)}{n}} = \sqrt{\frac{.40(1-.40)}{2}} = \sqrt{.12} = .3464$$

Computation of the standard deviation for Table 7.4's sampling distribution confirms that the standard error of the proportion is the standard deviation of the sampling distribution of proportions:

$$\sigma_{\bar{p}} = \sqrt{\frac{\Sigma(\bar{p} - \mu_{\bar{p}})^2}{n}} = \sqrt{\frac{3.00}{25}} = \sqrt{.12} = .3464$$

We can show that the proportion of successes in a binomial experiment approaches a normal distribution as the number of trials, n, increases. Chapter 6 emphasized that the normal distribution provides a close approximation to the binomial distribution when n is large and p is neither small nor large. Specifically, to use the normal curve for proportion problems, both np and $n(1-p)$ should be 5 or greater. Since most real-life business situations that involve the binomial distribution require fairly large sample sizes, the normal approximation to the binomial distribution is frequently used.

EXAMPLE 7.9 Five percent of the cathode ray tubes the Jaypro Company makes for PC monitors are returned by the monitor manufacturer as defective. This is of great concern to Jaypro, especially after a March 1992 article in *PC World*, "Buyer's Guide: Super VGA Monitors" (page 178). Jaypro considers it essential to improve its quality performance if it's to continue supplying tubes to the industry.

After a quality-improvement program, Jaypro will sample its cathode ray tubes to see if quality has risen. A random sample of 125 tubes will be pulled from inventory during the next few days. What is the probability that more than 8% of them will be defective, assuming that the overall defective rate is still 5 percent? Figure 7.5 shows the desired area.

FIGURE 7.5 Sampling Distribution of Proportions for Example 7.9

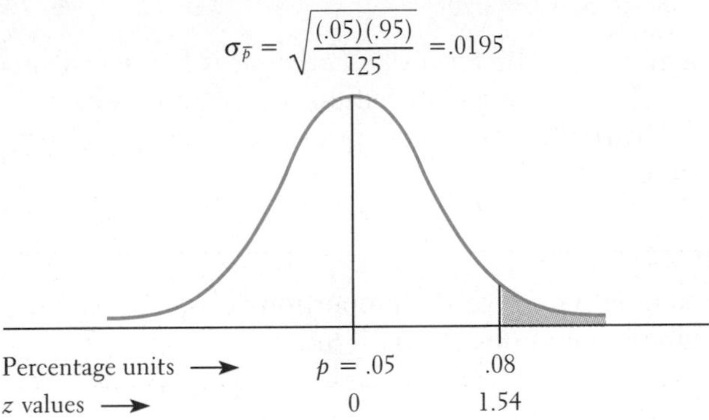

The calculations for the desired area are

$$\sigma_{\bar{p}} = \sqrt{\frac{p(1-p)}{n}} = \sqrt{\frac{.05(1-.05)}{125}} = \sqrt{.00038} = .0195$$

$$z = \frac{\bar{p} - p}{\sigma_{\bar{p}}} = \frac{.08 - .05}{.0195} = 1.54 \rightarrow .4382 \text{ (area between .05 and .08)}$$

$$.5000 - .4382 = .0618 \text{ (area above .08)}$$

There's approximately a .0618 chance that 8% or more of the tubes will be defective, assuming a population defective rate of 5%.

EXAMPLE 7.10 The following quote appeared in *The Spokesman-Review* on October 30, 1989:

> City Councilwoman Sheri Bernard appears to be riding a wave of anti-incinerator sentiment into the Spokane mayor's office. A survey, conducted Oct. 19–25 for *The Spokesman-Review* and *Spokane Chronicle*, shows Bernard far ahead of her campaign rival and fellow councilman, Rob Higgins. Of the 200 city voters selected at random and surveyed by Market Trends Inc. of Spokane, 46% said they would vote for Bernard if the election were held tomorrow. . . . Another 19% were undecided when the survey was taken, some two weeks before the election.

Sheri's campaign manager, counting on about half of the undecided voters, feels confident that 55% of the population of voters will choose Sheri Bernard.

On November 6, one day before the election, a random sample of 35 voters is taken to assess voting preference. What is the probability that this sample will indicate that Sheri will lose (i.e., that fewer than 50% of the sampled voters prefer her) if in fact, she has a population preference of 55%? Figure 7.6 shows the area to be found.

TM

FIGURE 7.6 Sampling Distribution of Proportions for Example 7.10

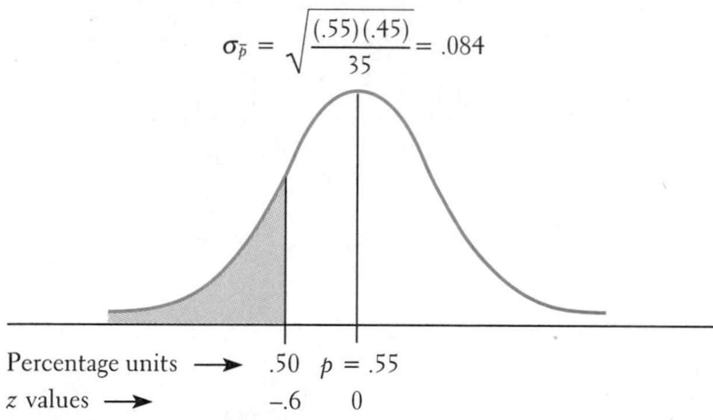

The calculations for the desired area are

$$\sigma_{\bar{p}} = \sqrt{\frac{p(1-p)}{n}} = \sqrt{\frac{.55(1-.55)}{35}} = \sqrt{.007} = .084$$

$$z = \frac{\bar{p} - p}{\sigma_{\bar{p}}} = \frac{.50 - .55}{.084} = -0.60 \rightarrow \text{ .2257 (area between .50 and .55)}$$

$$.5000 - .2257 = .2743 \text{ (area below .50)}$$

There's about a 27% chance that the sample of 35 will mislead Sheri's campaign manager into thinking she'll lose when, in fact, she has a 55% population voter preference. A larger sample size would reduce this probability of error.

EXAMPLE 7.11 How would a sample size of 150 alter the risk of error in Example 7.10 if Sheri is still assumed to have a population voter preference of 55%? Figure 7.7 shows the area to be found.

FIGURE 7.7 Sampling Distribution of Proportions for Example 7.11

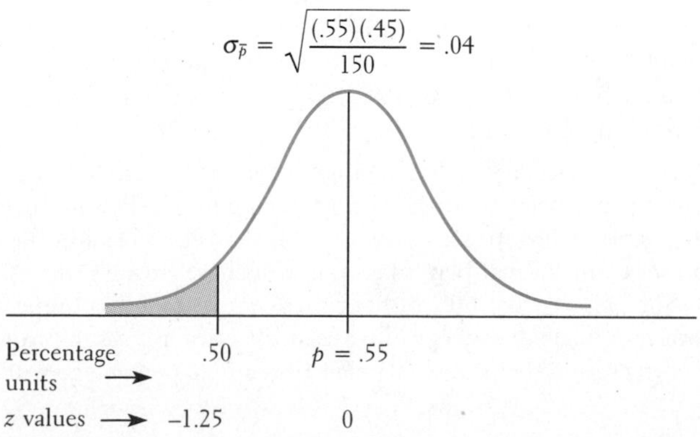

The calculations for the desired area are

$$\sigma_{\bar{p}} = \sqrt{\frac{p(1-p)}{n}} = \sqrt{\frac{.55(1-.55)}{150}} = \sqrt{.00165} = .04$$

$$z = \frac{\bar{p} - p}{\sigma_{\bar{p}}} = \frac{.50 - .55}{.04} = -1.25 \rightarrow .3944 \text{ (area between .50 and .55)}$$

$$.5000 - .3944 = .1056 \text{ (area below .50)}$$

The increased sample size reduces the probability of misleading results from 27.43% to 10.56%.

Exercises

21. Explain the difference between the number of successes in a binomial experiment and the percentage of successes.

22. If you took a statistics quiz and answered 16 out of the 20 questions correctly, what percentage of the questions did you get right?

22. 80%

23. What effect does increasing the sample size have on the variability of a sampling distribution of proportions?

23. Decreases

24. When is it appropriate to use the normal approximation for the sampling distribution of proportions?

25. Seventy percent of a population of employees are male. In a sample of 10 employees, what are the mean and standard deviation of the sampling distribution for the proportion of males selected?

25. Mean = .70, SD = .145

26. (This question refers to Exercise 25.) How will increasing the sample size to 100 affect the mean and standard deviation of the sampling distribution? Calculate the new standard error of the proportion.

26. Mean = .70, SD = .046

27. Approximately 20% of the independent grocery stores in Bonner County offer trading stamps. If a sample of 50 stores is selected, find the probability that:
    a. The first store selected at random from the population will offer trading stamps.
    b. The proportion of stores offering trading stamps will be greater than 25%.
    c. The proportion of stores offering trading stamps will be less than 22%.
    d. The proportion of stores offering trading stamps will be between 17% and 23%.

27a. .20; b. .1894; c. .6368; d. .4038

28. Seventeen percent of the people who file tax returns in the state of Georgia have gross taxable incomes of more than $50,000. If a sample of 400 Georgia returns is randomly selected, what is the probability that more than 20% of these people have gross taxable incomes in excess of $50,000?

28. .0559

29. Doyle's Wholesale Toys' marketing manager is interested in computer-assisted toys after reading an article about them in *PC Computing* ("PCs in Toyland," August 1989, p. 90). She wants to investigate entry into this market and thinks the extent of repeat customers for her company will play a key role in such a venture's success.

    She believes that 60% of her firm's orders come from repeat customers. A simple random sample of 80 orders will be used to verify this assumption. Assuming that her belief is correct, find the probability that the sample percentage will be less than 50%.

29. .0336

30. Last year 75% of Hart Department Store's credit card purchases were for less than $150. In a random sample of 200 credit card purchases, what is the probability that purchases less than $150 amount to:

30*a*. .8968
b. .0516
c. 1.0

a. Between 70% and 80%?

b. More than 80%?

c. More than 20%?

31. A population consists of the following six units produced today. One unit is defective.

Item	Condition
A	OK
B	Defective
C	OK
D	OK
E	OK
F	OK

31*a*. .17
d. .17, yes
e. .266
f. .266, yes

a. Compute the population proportion for defective units.

b. Develop a table showing every possible sample of size two (sample with replacement).

c. Compute the proportion defective of each of the samples of size two shown in part *b*.

d. Compute the mean of this sampling distribution of sample proportions. Does this mean proportion equal the population proportion?

e. Compute the standard error of the proportion for this sampling distribution.

f. Compute the standard deviation of the sampling distribution of proportions. Does this standard deviation equal the standard error of the proportion?

THE FINITE-POPULATION MULTIPLIER

Many populations that decision makers examine are limited in size (finite). However, Equation 7.2 is based on a population that's infinite or very large. This is why analysts frequently sample from finite populations with replacement (each item selected for inclusion in a sample is immediately put back into the population so that it might be chosen again). But sometimes we can't sample with replacement, as when items are destroyed in the sampling process. For example, if TV picture tube lifetimes are tested to determine the time until failure, sampling without replacement is mandatory.

For reasons of cost and convenience, sampling is frequently done without replacement. As long as the sample size is small relative to the population, sampling without replacement yields essentially the same results as sampling with replacement. However, as a rule of thumb, if the sample size is more than 5% of the population, the results of sampling with and without replacement will differ. This occurs because the probabilities change significantly from selection to selection when sampling without replacement from a small population. Chapter 5 stated that the hypergeometric distribution is appropriate for determining sample probabilities in this situation. Fortunately, the

Finite-Population Multiplier

hypergeometric modification can be reduced to the simple form known as the **finite-population multiplier:**

$$\text{Finite-population multiplier} = \sqrt{\frac{N - n}{N - 1}} \tag{7.6}$$

where N = Population size
n = Sample size

Equation 7.6 is used to modify the standard error formula to reflect changing probabilities when the sample size exceeds 5% of the population ($n/N > .05$). The standard error is simply multiplied by the finite-population multiplier.

> The **finite-population multiplier** is used to modify a standard error formula to reflect changing probabilities, when sampling is done without replacement from a finite population and the sample size exceeds 5% of the population ($n/N > .05$).

EXAMPLE 7.12 In Example 7.6, Table 7.3 showed a population of five employees including two college graduates. Table 7.4 showed the 25 possible samples of two that could be selected using sampling with replacement. Table 7.6 shows the 10 possible samples of two that can be selected using sampling without replacement.

TABLE 7.6 Sampling Distribution of Proportions for Example 7.6 without Replacement (Example 7.12)

Sampled workers	Sample characteristics	Sample proportion of college graduates
A, B	Y, N	.50
A, C	Y, N	.50
A, D	Y, Y	1.00
A, E	Y, N	.50
B, C	N, N	.00
B, D	N, Y	.50
B, E	N, N	.00
C, D	N, Y	.50
C, E	N, N	.00
D, E	Y, N	.50
		$\Sigma \bar{p} = 4.00$

Since the sample represents over 5% of the population ($n/N = 2/5$, or 40%, of the population), the standard error of the proportion should be modified using the finite-population multiplier:

$$\sigma_{\bar{p}} = \sqrt{\frac{p(1-p)}{n}}\sqrt{\frac{N-n}{N-1}} = \sqrt{\frac{.40(1-.40)}{2}}\sqrt{\frac{5-2}{5-1}} = \sqrt{.12}\sqrt{.75} = .30$$

You can compute the standard deviation for the sampling distribution in Table 7.6 and confirm that the standard error of the proportion modified by the finite-population multiplier is the standard deviation of the sampling distribution of proportions.

EXAMPLE 7.13 In Example 7.2 all possible samples of two ages were selected with replacement from the population of five ages: 10, 20, 30, 40, and 50. Table 7.1 gave the resulting sampling distribution of 25 sample means. The mean of this sampling distribution was 30 and the standard deviation was

$$\sigma_{\bar{x}} = \sigma/\sqrt{n} = 14.1/\sqrt{2} = 10$$

What if the samples of two ages were selected without replacement? Table 7.7 shows the resulting sampling distribution of 10 sample means. The mean of this sampling distribution is still 30. However, the standard deviation must be calculated using the finite-population multiplier because the sample size exceeds 5% of the population $[(n/N = 2/5 = .4)$. The standard deviation of this sampling distribution is

$$\sigma_{\bar{x}} = \frac{\sigma}{\sqrt{n}}\sqrt{\frac{N-n}{N-1}} = \frac{14.1}{\sqrt{2}}\sqrt{\frac{5-2}{5-1}} = 10\sqrt{.75} = 8.66$$

You can compute the standard deviation for the sampling distribution of Table 7.7 and confirm that the standard error of the mean modified by the finite-population multiplier is the standard deviation of the sampling distribution of means.

TABLE 7.7 Sampling Distribution of Sample Means for Example 7.2 without Replacement (Example 7.13)

Sampled ages	Sample means
10, 20	15
10, 30	20
10, 40	25
10, 50	30
20, 30	25
20, 40	30
20, 50	35
30, 40	35
30, 50	40
40, 50	45
	$\Sigma\bar{x} = 300$

EXERCISES

32. Explain the difference between sampling with replacement and sampling without replacement.

33. Why is it necessary to use the finite-population multiplier?

34. When is it necessary to use the finite-population multiplier?

35. For a normally distributed population of $N = 750$ with a mean of 20 and standard deviation of 2, find the standard error of the mean for sampling distributions based on the following sample sizes (sampling is done without replacement):

35*a*. .40
b. .248
c. .186

a. 25.

b. 60.

c. 100.

36. The mean of a normally distributed population of 500 items is 175, and the standard deviation is 19. A sample of 81 items is selected without replacement from this population. What is the probability that:

36*a*. .3192
b. .0048
c. .7016
d. .0606

a. The first item selected at random from the population will be greater than 184?

b. The mean of the sample will be greater than 180?

c. The mean of the sample will be between 173 and 177?

d. The mean of the sample will be smaller than 172?

37. Approximately 20% of the 200 independent grocery stores in Alameda offer trading stamps. In a sample of 50 stores selected without replacement, what is the probability that:

37*a*. .0764
b. .1112
c. .2668

a. The percentage of stores offering trading stamps will be greater than 27%?

b. The percentage of stores offering trading stamps will be less than 14%?

c. The percentage of stores offering trading stamps will be between 15% and 19%?

38. .1446

38. After reading that "premature deaths cost American industry more than $25 billion and 132 million workdays of lost production each year" (*World Traveler,* May 1992, p. 30), Mary Upton, president of SCI Corporation, is considering implementing a physical fitness program for her 800 employees. A simple random sample of 100 employees selected without replacement is taken to estimate what percentage would participate. Mary will implement the program if at least 50% of her employees would participate. If 400 out of 800 is the true population proportion, what is the probability that fewer than 45 out of the 100 people surveyed will show a desire to participate in the program?

39. This question refers to the population in Exercise 20:

Worker	Units produced
A	5
B	3
C	7
D	8

39*a*. Mean = 5.75
SD = 1.92
c. 5.75, yes
d. 1.111
e. 1.111, yes

a. Develop a table showing every possible sample of size two (sample without replacement).

b. Compute the mean of each of the samples in part *a*.

c. Compute the mean of this sampling distribution. Does this mean equal the population mean?

d. Compute the standard error of the mean for this sampling distribution (remember the correction factor).

e. Compute the standard deviation of the sampling distribution of means. Does this standard deviation equal the standard error of the mean?

40. This question refers to the population in Exercise 31:

Item	Condition
A	OK
B	Defective
C	OK
D	OK
E	OK
F	OK

40*b.* .17
c. .17, yes
d. .238
e. .238, yes

a. Develop a table showing every possible sample of size two (sample without replacement).

b. Compute the proportion of each of the samples in part *a*.

c. Compute the mean proportion of this sampling distribution of sample proportions. Does this mean proportion equal the population proportion?

d. Compute the standard error of the proportion for this sampling distribution.

e. Compute the standard deviation of the sampling distribution of proportions. Is this standard deviation equal to the standard error of the proportion?

SUMMARY

This chapter presented the most important concept in statistics, the sampling distribution. Whenever a sample is taken from the population being studied, a statistic computed from this sample should be viewed as being drawn from the distribution of all possible sample statistics. This key concept of statistical inference will be used throughout the rest of this book.

This chapter discussed two sampling distributions: the sampling distribution of means and the sampling distribution of proportions. More sampling distributions appear in later chapters. Both distributions discussed here are used in the next two chapters when procedures for estimation and hypothesis testing are developed.

It is vital that you understand the basic concept of the sampling distribution. Spend as much time as necessary with this chapter to gain this understanding. If you have a firm grasp of the idea of a sampling distribution, you'll find the rest of the text much easier to understand.

APPLICATIONS OF STATISTICAL CONCEPTS IN THE BUSINESS WORLD

Whenever the variability of sample results is called into question, the concept of the sampling distribution is applicable. Here are some sample statistics that may or may not signal an important shift, depending on the position in the sampling distribution.

1. A new manager in a branch bank reports an increase of $125 in the average savings account balance after one month on the job.

2. Accounts receivable has a new average balance "significantly" below the previous level due to a new campaign to reduce receivables.
3. The percentage of customers returning merchandise, based on a random sample of buyers, falls after a new "be a friend" campaign is started at the returns desk.
4. A small loan office manager notices that the average amount requested by loan customers has increased a bit during the past two weeks.
5. The personnel department of a large company is proud of its "pride in excellence" program, which, it claims, has reduced the absenteeism rate during the past six months. The claim is based on a sample of workers over a two-week period.
6. The average number of times a store's credit card is used per customer has dropped below the average of a year ago.
7. A quality-control manager points with pride to a reduction in nonfunctioning units from 5.8% to 4.3%. The latter figure is based on a random sample of 35.

GLOSSARY

Sampling error The difference between a sample statistic and its corresponding population parameter.

Sampling distribution A distribution that includes all possible values a statistic, such as a sample mean, can assume for a given sample size.

Standard error of the mean The standard deviation of the sampling distribution of sample means.

Central limit theorem A theorem stating that if a sufficiently large random sample of n observations is selected from any population, the sampling distribution of sample means will be approximately a normal distribution.

Standard error of the proportion The standard deviation of the sampling distribution of sample proportions.

Finite-population multiplier A factor used to modify standard error formulas to reflect changing probabilities if sampling is done without replacement from a finite population and the sample constitutes more than 5% of the population ($n/N > .05$).

KEY FORMULAS

Mean of the sampling distribution of means

$$\mu_x = \mu_{\bar{x}} \tag{7.1}$$

Standard error of the mean

$$\sigma_{\bar{x}} = \frac{\sigma}{\sqrt{n}} \tag{7.2}$$

Percentage or proportion of successes

$$\bar{p} = \frac{x}{n} \tag{7.3}$$

Mean of the sampling distribution of proportions

$$p = \mu_{\bar{p}}$$

Standard error of the proportion

$$\sigma_{\bar{p}} = \sqrt{\frac{p(1-p)}{n}} \tag{7.5}$$

Finite-population multiplier

$$\sqrt{\frac{N-n}{N-1}} \tag{7.6}$$

SOLVED EXERCISES

1. SAMPLING DISTRIBUTION OF MEANS

The Timeless Battery Company claims that its batteries have a mean life of 60 months and standard deviation of 9 months. A consumer group testing this claim purchases 36 batteries and determines the mean lifetime.

a. Compute the standard error of the mean.

b. Assuming that Timeless's claim is true, what is the probability that the sample's mean life is less than 58?

c. Determine the probability that the mean life of the sample is between 57 and 63.

d. Assume that the actual population mean lifetime for Timeless batteries is 55 months. Find the probability that the mean life of the sample is at least 60.

e. If the consumer group's sample mean is 55, what would you conclude if you were its analyst?

Solution:

a. $\sigma_{\bar{x}} = \dfrac{\sigma}{\sqrt{n}} = \dfrac{9}{\sqrt{36}} = \dfrac{9}{6} = 1.5$

b. $z = \dfrac{\bar{x} - \mu}{\sigma_{\bar{x}}} = \dfrac{58 - 60}{1.5} = -1.33 \rightarrow$ .4082 (area between 58 and 60)

$.5000 - .4082 = .0918$ (area below 58)

The probability is about 9%.

c. $z = \dfrac{\bar{x} - \mu}{\sigma_{\bar{x}}} = \dfrac{63 - 60}{1.5} = 2.00 \rightarrow$ .4772 (area between 60 and 63)

$.4772 + .4772 = .9544$ (area betwen 57 and 63)

The probability is about 95%.

d. $z = \dfrac{\bar{x} - \mu}{\sigma_{\bar{x}}} = \dfrac{60 - 55}{1.5} = 3.33 \rightarrow$ almost .5000 (area between 55 and 60)

$.5000 - .5000 = .0000$ (area above 60)

The probability is approximately zero.

e. You should conclude that Timeless's claim is false. It is almost impossible to get a sample mean of 55 from a population with a mean of 60 using a sample size of 36.

2. Sampling Distribution of Proportions

Laser Dynamics Corporation is considering advertising on the TV show, "Roseanne." The A.C. Nielsen ratings in *U.S.A. Today* (July 1, 1992) showed that "Roseanne" had a rating share (shares are the percentage of sets in use) of 25 on June 23, 1992. Vicki Laser, public relations director, suspects that the actual percentage is less than 25%. Vicki hires an independent research agency to take a random sample of 750 viewers watching TV at 9 P.M. Tuesday, June 30, 1992. The agency finds that 175 were watching "Roseanne." Do these data present sufficient evidence to contradict the A.C. Nielsen ratings?

Solution:

$$\bar{p} = \frac{x}{n} = \frac{175}{750} = .233$$

$$\sigma_{\bar{p}} = \sqrt{\frac{p(1-p)}{n}} = \sqrt{\frac{.25(1-.25)}{750}} = \sqrt{.00025} = .0158$$

$$z = \frac{\bar{p} - p}{\sigma_{\bar{p}}} = \frac{.233 - .25}{.0158} = -1.08 \rightarrow .3599 \text{ (area between .25 and .233)}$$

$$.5000 - .3599 = .1401 \text{ (area below .233)}$$

The probability of finding 175 or fewer viewers watching "Roseanne" out of a sample of 750 is approximately .14 (14%) if the true population percentage is 25%.

3. Finite-Population Multiplier

The hourly wages for the Hem Iron Works plant's 500 workers average (mean) \$8.50 with standard deviation of \$2.20. What is the probability that the mean wage of a sample of 100 workers will be:

a. More than \$9?

b. Between \$8.15 and \$8.40?

Solution:

a. $$\sigma_{\bar{x}} = \frac{\sigma}{\sqrt{n}}\sqrt{\frac{N-n}{N-1}} = \frac{2.20}{\sqrt{100}}\sqrt{\frac{500-100}{500-1}} = 0.22(.8953) = 0.197$$

$$z = \frac{\bar{x} - \mu}{\sigma_{\bar{x}}} = \frac{9 - 8.5}{0.197} = 2.54 \rightarrow .4945 \quad \text{(area between 8.50 and 9.00)}$$

$$.5000 - .4945 = .0055 \quad \text{(area above 9)}$$

The probability is about .55%.

b. $$z = \frac{\bar{x} - \mu}{\sigma_{\bar{x}}} = \frac{8.4 - 8.5}{0.197} = -0.51 \rightarrow .1950 \text{ (area between 8.40 and 8.50)}$$

$$.5000 - .1950 = .3050 \text{ (area below 8.4)}$$

$$z = \frac{\bar{x} - \mu}{\sigma_{\bar{x}}} = \frac{8.15 - 8.5}{0.197} = -1.78 \rightarrow .4625 \text{ (area between 8.15 and 8.50)}$$

$$.5000 - .4625 = .0375 \text{ (area below 8.15)}$$

$$.3050 - .0375 = .2675 \text{ (area between 8.15 and 8.40)}$$

The probability is almost 27%.

EXERCISES

41. "College Mergers: An Emerging Alternative," *Community, Technical and Junior College Journal,* (August/September 1988, p. 37) interests Niagara Falls and Niagara Central Community College officials, who are considering a merger. One question critical to a merger is the number of credit hours students have completed at each institution. If total credit hours per student at Niagara Falls Community College are normally distributed with a mean of 50 and a standard deviation of 5, what is the probability that:

41*a.* .3085
b. .2684
c. .2148
d. .0062
e. About 0

a. A student at random will have more than 55 credit hours?
b. A student at random will have between 55 and 60 credit hours?
c. A sample of 10 students will have a mean less than 49 hours?
d. A sample of 100 students will have a mean less than 49 hours?
e. A sample of 400 students will have a mean less than 49 hours?

42. A variable representing the probability that a person entering a shop will buy something follows a binomial distribution and has a population proportion equal to .25. What is the probability that:

42*a.* .25
b. .7627
c. .1230
d. .0104

a. A person entering the shop will buy something?
b. At least 1 person out of a sample of 5 people entering the shop will buy something?
c. More than 30 people out of a sample of 100 entering the shop will buy something?
d. More than 120 people out of a sample of 400 entering the shop will buy something?

43. For a normally distributed population of $N = 250$ with a mean of 60 and standard deviation of 5, find the standard error of the mean for sampling distributions based on the following sample sizes, if sampling is done without replacement:

43*a.* 1.58
b. .63
c. .39

a. 10.
b. 50.
c. 100.

44. .3372

44. California had 9.5% unemployment in June 1992 (*The Spokane-Review,* July 3, 1992). Find the probability that the percentage of unemployed in a random sample of 600 people is over 10%.

45. Bill Barkley believes that 25% of all persons with incomes above $75,000 will be audited by the IRS on a random basis at least once in a 10-year period.

45*a.* .0778
b. .9544

a. What is the probability that of a sample of 150 people with incomes over $75,000, at least 45 will have been audited at least once in the past 10 years?
b. If a random sample of 300 is selected, what is the probability that the proportion of the sample who were audited at least once is between 20% and 30%?

46. The number of column inches of classified advertisements appearing on Fridays in the *Tampa Bay Chronicle* is roughly normally distributed with mean 427 and standard deviation 44 inches. Assume that results for the past 20 consecutive Fridays can be regarded as a random sample ($n = 20$).

46*a.* .3015
b. Mean = 427
SD = 9.84
c. .9969

a. What is the probability that the number of column inches appearing last Friday was more than 450?
b. Find the mean and standard error of the total number of column inches of classified advertisements for a sampling distribution of 20 Fridays.

c. Find the probability that the average number of column inches per Friday will be between 400 and 500.

47. .9641

47. There are about 1,400 automobile dealers in the Chicago area with average (mean) dollar sales per dealer around $750,000. A random sample of 250 dealers is selected, and the mean and standard deviation are computed. If the standard deviation is $95,000, what is the probability that the sample mean is between $740,000 and $765,000?

48. .7888

48. Linda Rice, Western Life Insurance Company analyst, is concerned with whether insurance applications provide complete information. From past experience, Linda has found that 80% of the applications provide complete information. If the next 100 applications are considered a random sample, what is the probability that the proportion of completed applications will fall within 5 percentage points of the population percentage?

49. .9836

49. A tax analyst wishes to sample a population of 5,000 tax returns after reading an article in *Accountancy* (June 1989, p. 27) on tax planning for the year 1992. In this population of returns, the proportion of people who authorized $1 for support of political parties is 60%. If the analyst randomly selects a sample of 500 returns, find the probability that the sample percentage authorizing $1 of support will be between 55% and 65%.

50. There is significant difference

50. A consumer magazine reported that families in the Southwest spend an average of $23.54 for eating out each week. An economist checks this value for the Midwest. He selects a random sample of 121 families and calculates a mean weekly expenditure for eating out of $25.34 with standard deviation of $4.62. Would you say that families in the Midwest spend more eating out, or is the difference in mean expenditures due to chance sampling error?

51. .2776

51. A mortgage company knows that 8% of its home loan recipients default within the first five years. What is the probability that out of 350 loan recipients, fewer than 25 will default within the next five years?

52. A population of high school students has a mean grade point average (GPA) of 2.98 with standard deviation of 0.39. Suppose federal education auditors conduct a random sample of students to determine whether their mean GPA meets certain federal guidelines. They take a random sample of 75 students and calculate the sample GPA.

52*a.* .5000
b. .3300
c. .9578

a. Find the probability that the sample GPA is less than 2.98.

b. Find the probability that the sample GPA is greater than 3.00.

c. Find the probability that the sample GPA is between 2.9 and 3.1.

53. Touch, a well-known cold remedy, is advertised to relieve cold symptoms for an average (mean) of 12 hours with standard deviation of 3 hours. Assuming this claim is true, if a sample of 50 patients with colds are given this medicine, what is the probability that the average relief will last:

53*a.* .7620
b. .0091
c. 0

a. Between 11.5 and 12.5 hours?

b. More than 13 hours?

c. Less than 10 hours?

54. .1286

54. In a population of 900 business majors at a large midwestern university, mean GPA is 3.0 with standard deviation of 0.3. If a random sample of 75 students is selected, find the probability that the sample mean GPA will differ from the population mean GPA by more than 0.05.

55. The following data show how many computers each of four Computer Korner salespeople sold last week and whether each salesperson had previous computer sales experience before working at Computer Korner.

Salesperson	Sales	Experience
A	5	Y
B	4	Y
C	2	Y
D	1	N

55*a*. Mean = 3
SD = 1.58
d. 3, yes
e. .9129
f. .9129, yes

a. Compute the population mean and standard deviation for the number of sales last week.

b. Develop a table showing every possible sample of two (sample without replacement).

c. Compute the mean of each of the samples in part *b*.

d. Compute the mean of this sampling distribution. Does this mean equal the population mean?

e. Compute the standard error of the mean for this sampling distribution.

f. Compute the standard deviation of the sampling distribution of means. Does this standard deviation equal the standard error of the mean?

56. This question refers to Exercise 55.

56*a*. .75
d. .75, yes
e. .25
f. .25, yes

a. Compute the population proportion for the percentage of salespeople who have previous experience.

b. Develop a table showing every possible sample of two (sample without replacement).

c. Compute the proportion of each of the samples in part *b*.

d. Compute the mean proportion of this sampling distribution of sample proportions. Does this mean proportion equal the population proportion?

e. Compute the standard error of the proportion for this sampling distribution.

f. Compute the standard deviation of the sampling distribution of proportions. Does this standard deviation equal the standard error of the proportion?

EXTENDED EXERCISES

57. THE WICKLAND CORPORATION

This exercise is a class project. The Wickland Corporation has examined the number of sales for the past 200 days, which are listed below. Past experience has shown the variable to be normally distributed with a mean of 100 and standard deviation of 10. Select a random sample of 30 sales values (sample with replacement). Each class member should select his or her own individual random sample. For each sample, calculate the sample mean and standard deviation. These values should then be assembled for the class.

100	89	95	103	82	77	97	109	99	100
99	105	99	109	108	96	104	111	90	99

96	100	88	103	99	112	88	101	102	99
100	91	112	96	107	106	82	90	96	84
105	85	99	91	109	85	107	99	80	94
99	92	83	111	104	110	80	127	118	110
117	85	114	105	96	89	105	87	98	96
109	80	98	94	102	98	93	103	102	97
107	98	96	107	101	104	88	109	87	93
92	104	111	91	106	94	80	102	104	81
121	90	87	95	85	111	98	110	121	90
118	120	99	115	105	117	99	101	84	103
112	107	92	87	109	110	105	98	99	104
101	115	97	120	113	110	96	100	126	95
107	114	114	93	86	100	93	105	121	112
93	120	84	95	77	89	96	105	115	109
111	89	84	94	104	105	86	92	98	109
102	103	99	114	99	101	104	110	97	96
90	100	105	107	95	100	97	85	96	105
104	98	104	101	111	107	95	98	87	90

a. How do your sample mean and standard deviation compare with the population parameters?

b. The class as a whole should construct a sampling distribution of sample means and compute the mean and standard deviation.

c. Does the sampling distribution of sample means appear to approximate a normal distribution?

d. Are the mean and standard error of the class sampling distribution close to the values expected from the population data?

58. Gady Electronics

Gady Electronics, Inc., makes keyboards for use in personal computers. One small chip whose operation is critical in the keyboard is made by a supplier in California. The supplier has had quality-control problems, but Gady is reluctant to switch to another supplier because of the chip's unique capabilities.

The problem is acute since Al Gady, the company's quality-control officer, read an article about Microsoft bringing stereo sound and synchronized audio/video to some of its software. These changes underline the importance of properly operating keyboards in the future.

In a meeting with the supplier two weeks ago, Al pointed out that about 10% of the chips arriving at the Gady plant were defective. This caused Gady many problems such as the expense of inspection and replacement of defective units. The supplier assured Al that measures would be taken to improve the quality.

Al decided to inspect a random sample of the chips that arrived at the plant a week after this meeting. A random sampling plan was designed for selecting chips from various shipments over a week's time. A total of 50 chips were selected and subjected to tests. Of the 50 chips in the sample, 4, or 8%, were found to be defective.

Al complained to the supplier about the lack of significant progress in reducing the defective percentage of the chips. The manager of the chip operation replied, "A defective rate of

8% shows significant progress in improving the quality level of the chips; after all, 8% is less than 10%."

a. By using correct statistical procedures, determine who is right.

b. Specifically, what is the probability of getting a sample percentage of 8% or less if the true population defective percentage is 10%?

c. Based on the answers to the preceding questions, what should Al tell the supplier?

59. BOARDSTROM DEPARTMENT STORE

Julie Elway (manager of Boardstrom Department Store in Tulsa, Oklahoma) and her management team are considering allowing the store to issue its own credit card to customers. First, Julie wants to know whether Boardstrom customers' average dollar purchase is the same as the national average for such stores, $73. The standard deviation for this population of stores is $8. The team formulates a plan to take a random sample of customer purchase amounts. Each department in the store is to be sampled during a three-week period, and various days of the week and times of day will be used in collecting the data.

The management team isn't sure how to use the data once it's collected. They recognize that even if the population average purchase amount for the store is $73, a sample average might differ from this amount. The team has discussed the variability of sample means from sample to sample and wonders how the results should be interpreted after the sampling process is completed.

A random sampling plan of purchase amounts is developed, but management is concerned about the variability of sample means. Store manager Elway decides to sample 100 purchase amounts taken from various departments of the store at various times of the day and days of the week. After the sample is taken, a mean of $70 is computed.

Next, it is assumed that the store's average purchase amount is $73, the national average. Figure 7.8 shows the sampling distribution that applies when the population standard deviation of $8 is used to calculate the standard error of the mean:

$$\sigma_{\bar{x}} = \frac{\sigma}{\sqrt{n}} = \frac{8}{\sqrt{100}} = \frac{8}{10} = 0.8$$

FIGURE 7.8 Sampling Distribution of Means for Exercise 59

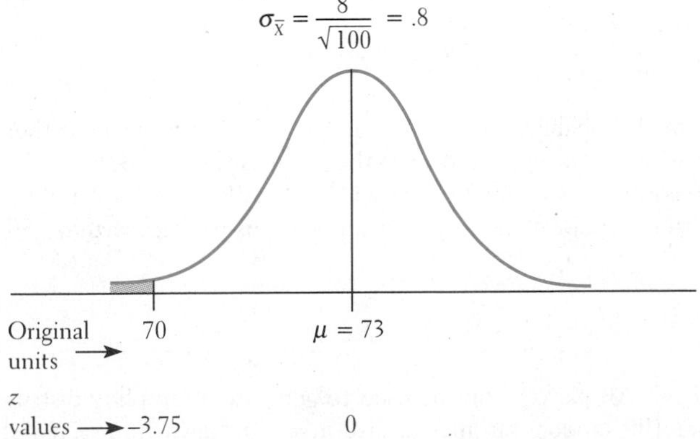

If the population standard deviation were unknown, the sample standard deviation could have been used to estimate it.

Store management can now evaluate the $70 sample mean. How likely is it that this value was drawn from Figure 7.8's sampling distribution? The answer to this question will help Julie's team decide how likely it is that the population mean for the store equals the national average. Write a memo to management on this subject.

60. OUR LADY OF LOURDES HOSPITAL

Chapter 4 presented family sizes for a population of 200 Our Lady of Lourdes Hospital employees. You were asked to select a random sample of size 30 and compute the mean and standard deviation. Assume that the population mean is 2.9.

a. By how much does your sample mean differ from the population mean? Explain this difference.

b. The class as a whole should construct a sampling distribution of sample means and compute its mean and standard deviation.

c. Does the sampling distribution of sample means appear to approximate a normal distribution?

MICROCOMPUTER PACKAGE

The micro package *Computerized Business Statistics* may be used to solve sampling distribution problems based on the normal curve.

In Exercise 59, Julie Elway, Boardstrom Department Store manager, wanted to know whether Boardstrom customers' average dollar purchase matched the national average for such stores, $73.

Computer Solution

From the main menu of *Computerized Business Statistics* a **5** is selected, indicating Probability Distributions.

This problem involves the normal distribution. Since Julie wanted to know whether the Boardstrom average dollar purchase, $70, differed significantly from the national average for such stores, $73, the arrow is moved to normal $P(\text{Mean} \leq x \leq a)$.

```
Enter Mean and Press ↵ 73
Enter Standard Deviation and Press ↵ .8
Enter A and Press ↵ 76
```

The normal probability distribution for $\mu = 73$ and $\sigma = 0.8$ is then shown on the screen. Note that the area between 76 and 73 is the same as the area between 70 and 73.

The correct answer for $P(70 \leq x \leq 73)$ is .4987. The probability of obtaining a sample mean of $70 from a population with a mean of $73 is practically zero (.5000 − .4987 = .0013).

MINITAB COMPUTER PACKAGE

The MINITAB package can be used to generate a sampling distribution. Suppose you want to simulate 100 random samples of size $n = 40$ drawn from a population including the integer numbers 1 to 100. The MINITAB commands necessary to accomplish this task are:

```
MTB> RANDOM 100 C1-C40;
SUBC> INTEGER 1 100.
MTB> ADD C1-C40, PUT SUM IN C41
MTB> DIVIDE C41 BY 40, PUT SAMPLE AVERAGES IN C42
MTB> DESCRIBE C42
C42  N       MEAN    MEDIAN   STDEV
    100     50.498   50.288   3.860

C42    MIN      MAX       Q1       Q3
    41.525   60.250   47.806   53.225
MRB> STOP
```

The RANDOM and INTEGER commands generate 40 samples of size 100. Each sample consists of numbers in the range 1 to 100. The ADD command adds the values in each row across the 40 columns and places the sums in column C41. The DIVIDE command divides each sum by 40, thus calculating the sample mean. At this point, the columns C1, . . . , C40, C41, and C42 look like:

```
ROW     C1    . . .    C40      C41        C42
  1     52             48     2145.542    53.639
  2     40             62     1934.678    48.367
  .      .              .        .          .
  .      .              .        .          .
  .      .              .        .          .
100     72             31     2047.112    51.178
```

Column C42 contains the 100 sample means. The DESCRIBE command calculates the mean, standard deviation, minimum, and maximum for these 100 sample means. The mean of the sampling distribution is 50.5 (the population mean is also 50.5), and the standard deviation of the sampling distribution is 3.86 (the standard deviation of *all* possible sample means of sample size 40 is $\sigma/\sqrt{n} = 29/\sqrt{40} = 4.59$).

The HISTOGRAM command produces:

```
MTB> HISTOGRAM C42

Histogram of C42   N = 100

Midpoint  Count
      42      1  /
      44      5  /////
      46     13  /////////////
      48     14  //////////////
      50     23  ///////////////////////
      52     17  /////////////////
      54     14  //////////////
      56      8  ////////
      58      3  ///
      60      2  //

MTB>STOP
```

The central limit theorem indicates that the sampling distribution should be a normal distribution (with a mean of 50.5 and a standard deviation of 4.59). The histogram does look very much like a normal distribution.

Chapter

8

ESTIMATION

Errors, like straws, upon the surface flow; he who would search for pearls must dive below. Dryden, "All for Love"

Objectives

When you have completed this chapter, you will be able to:

Describe the mean and proportion of a population using point and interval estimates.

Construct interval estimates for a population mean and a population proportion.

Determine the impact of sample size on an interval estimate.

Compute the required sample size for an estimation problem involving a population mean and a population proportion.

Compute the maximum tolerable error for a specific sample size.

A front-page April 30, 1992, *Wall Street Journal* story covered Ross Perot's independent bid for the U.S. presidency. His bid was based on the belief that many voters preferred his brand of leadership.

Chapter 7 covered sampling distributions. It mentioned that sampling distributions provide the foundation for two important statistical concepts: estimation and hypothesis testing. This chapter concerns estimation. Chapters 9 and 10 examine hypothesis testing.

WHY MANAGERS NEED TO KNOW ABOUT ESTIMATION

Decision makers frequently investigate certain characteristics of populations of data values. As you've already learned, usually it is necessary to sample such populations and infer that the characteristics of the sample apply to the population as well. This chapter examines the inferential process with emphasis on the amount of error that is inherent. Understanding the concepts of this chapter is vital to any sampling procedure.

Regarding *The Wall Street Journal*'s article on Ross Perot, any candidate must estimate the voters' inclinations on a constant basis. The estimation procedures in this chapter are commonly used in political polls and many other places.

POINT AND INTERVAL ESTIMATES OF A POPULATION MEAN

Point Estimate

A **point estimate** is a single value measured from a sample and used as an estimate of the corresponding population value (parameter). Although there are many population parameters of potential interest to a decision maker, the two most important are the population mean and population proportion.

> A **point estimate** is a single value that is measured from a sample and used as an estimate of the corresponding population parameter.

When a point estimate of the population mean is desired, the sample mean is used. When the population proportion is of interest, the sample proportion is used as a point estimate.

EXAMPLE 8.1 Espinoza Construction, a building contractor, needs to estimate the average (mean) weight of a certain structural steel beam used in large buildings. A sampling plan is devised to select such beams over the next two months from the three firms that make them. This process produces a sample of 150 beams, that are weighed at the manufacturers' sites. Their average weight is calculated to be 125.7 tons; this is the point estimate of the mean weight of all such beams.

EXAMPLE 8.2 A study designed to answer these questions was reported in *The Accounting Review*: Are government contractors more profitable than other firms, and do such contractors shift some of the overhead and pension costs of their commercial operations to the government?[1] The results of the study were based on a large sample of government contractors who also have commercial business. The author, Lichtenberg, concluded these contractors have a profit rate (return on assets) that is 68 to 82 percent higher than other companies. This conclusion required the inference that the sample contractor profit rate (a percentage) could be inferred or projected to all such firms.

The problem with a point estimate is that it conveys no sense of accuracy. For example, the statement, "The sample mean, an estimate of the population mean, is 150 pounds," doesn't reflect the sample size or the extent of the population's variability. This point estimate might be very accurate or very misleading depending on these two factors.

Interval Estimate

Confidence Level

An **interval estimate** indicates the sample estimate accuracy. The interval estimate specifies an interval within which the true population parameter is quite likely to lie and a **confidence coefficient** is used to indicate the likelihood that the population parameter lies within that interval. The confidence coefficient can be expressed as a percentage and called a **confidence level.**

> An **interval estimate** establishes an interval within which it's quite likely that the population parameter lies. A **confidence coefficient** is used to indicate the likelihood that an interval estimate contains the population parameter. A **confidence level** is the confidence coefficient expressed as a percentage.

Interval estimates are based on the theory developed in Chapter 7. The normal sampling distribution, as established by the central limit theorem, is used to construct interval estimates. Figure 8.1 illustrates this process.

Suppose that the mean, μ, of a population is known, and the sampling distribution, consisting of all possible sample means for a certain sample size, has been constructed. Such a distribution appears in Figure 8.1. The interval a–b is constructed such that a and b are equally distant from the mean of the curve, μ, and include 95% of the sample means.

Next, suppose a person takes a random sample and computes the mean as if this mean were selected from the sampling distribution of means in Figure 8.1. Suppose the value obtained is the sample mean $\bar{x}_1$. The person is now instructed to calculate an interval of width a–b and place the chosen sample mean in the middle of this interval. The resulting interval is shown below the curve in Figure 8.1. This sampler

[1]Frank P. Lichtenberg, "A Perspective on Accounting for Defense Contracts," *The Accounting Review* (October 1992), pp. 741–52.

FIGURE 8.1 Sampling Distribution of Means

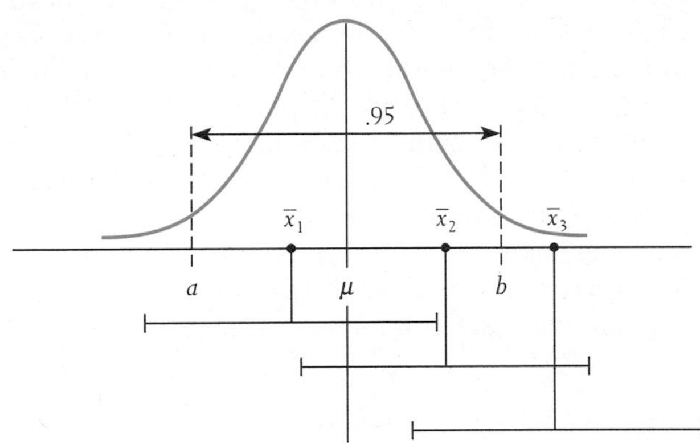

would be pleased to be told that this interval contains the true population mean, μ, even though he or she wouldn't know where in the interval μ is.

Now a second sampler approaches the sampling distribution, selects sample mean $\bar{x}_2$, and constructs an interval of the same width *a–b*, centering it on the sample mean. This interval is shown in Figure 8.1 and also contains the population mean, μ.

Finally, a third person randomly selects a sample mean from Figure 8.1's sampling distribution, calculates the mean $\bar{x}_3$, and constructs the *a–b* interval around it. Unfortunately, this interval does not contain the population mean. This happened to sampler 3, not because of errors in the sampling process, but because of the randomness of sample results. Actually, sampler 3 had only a 5% chance of having such bad luck since only 5% of the sample means in Figure 8.1 lead to intervals that don't contain the population mean.

An analyst cannot see the sampling distribution from which the sample mean is drawn. However, the process of constructing an interval around the point estimate $\bar{x}$ is undertaken with the understanding that there's a high probability, but not a certainty, that the resulting interval will contain the population mean. The formula used to construct an interval estimate for the population mean is

Interval Estimate for Means

$$\bar{x} \pm z\frac{\sigma}{\sqrt{n}} \tag{8.1}$$

where $\bar{x}$ = Sample mean
z = Value from standard normal table reflecting confidence level
σ = Population standard deviation
n = Sample size

This equation is used whenever the population standard deviation is known.

Note that four values must be known before an interval estimate for the population mean can be constructed. First, the sample mean, $\bar{x}$, must be known. This value is computed from the sample values.

Next, the degree of confidence in the interval estimate must be established. This leads to the selection of a z value. In Figure 8.1, 95% of the curve is included in the width of the a–b interval. This translates to 95% confidence that the resulting interval contains the population mean. To find the correct z value, this percentage is divided in half since one half of the 95% lies on either side of the normal curve mean. Half of .95 is .4750, and in the standard normal table in Appendix E.6, this area is found in the 1.9 row and the .06 column. Thus, the correct z value is 1.96. In other words, a distance of 1.96 standard deviations on either side of the mean of any normal curve defines an area that includes 95% of the curve's values. You can use the standard normal table to verify the confidence levels and corresponding z values in Table 8.1. These are values commonly used for interval estimates.

TM

TABLE 8.1 Interval Estimate z Values

Confidence level	z value
.90	1.645
.95	1.96
.98	2.33
.99	2.575

Equation 8.1 indicates that the population standard deviation, σ, must also be known. In practice, this usually isn't possible; the only way to identify σ without error is to conduct a census. Instead, an estimate of σ is used to construct the interval estimate. The sample standard deviation, s, provides an unbiased estimate of the unknown σ and is substituted in Equation 8.1 to construct the interval. This introduces a certain amount of error, but this error is usually quite small, especially if large samples are used.

When the sample value s is used, the t distribution rather than the z distribution is theoretically correct; this distribution will be discussed in depth later in this chapter. The t value replaces the z value in Equation 8.1. If the sample size is 30 or greater, however, the z value is quite close to t, and its use introduces only minor error. Equation 8.2 is used to compute the interval estimate for means when both of the following conditions apply: the population standard deviation (σ) is estimated using the sample standard deviation (s), and the sample size is 30 or greater:

$$\bar{x} \pm z\frac{s}{\sqrt{n}} \tag{8.2}$$

where $\bar{x}$ = Sample mean
z = Value from standard normal table reflecting confidence level
s = Sample standard deviation
n = Sample size

Remember that if the sample size constitutes more than 5% of a finite population, the standard error of the mean must be modified by the finite-population multiplier.

Finally, Equation 8.1 or 8.2 requires that the sample size, n, be known. Note that the equation for an interval estimate specifies an area z standard errors around the sample mean. In Equation 8.1, the standard error is the standard deviation of the sampling distribution of means, $\sigma/\sqrt{n}$. An estimate of this standard error, $s/\sqrt{n}$, is used in Equation 8.2.

As Equations 8.1 and 8.2 show and as common sense suggests, three factors determine the interval estimate's width and, hence, its accuracy. First, the z value is multiplied by the standard error of the mean to create the interval estimate. This suggests that a higher confidence level (going from a 95% level to a 99% level, for example) requires the use of a larger z value, which leads to a wider interval.

Second, note that σ (or its estimator, s) is in the numerator of the standard error of the mean. As discussed in Chapter 7, populations with high variability have a larger standard error of the mean. Therefore, the more variable the population, as measured by σ, the wider the interval. Remember that wider intervals mean less accurate interval estimates.

Third, the sample size, n, is in the denominator of the standard error of the mean. As discussed in Chapter 7, larger sample sizes produce smaller standard errors and, thus, narrower or more accurate interval estimates. This is intuitively appealing since we would expect larger samples to yield better estimates of population values than smaller samples. The larger the sample, the more information from the population is contained in the sample.

> The normal curve is the appropriate distribution for constructing an interval estimate when:
>
> 1. The population standard deviation is known, or
> 2. The population standard deviation is unknown and the sample size is 30 or greater.

EXAMPLE 8.3 A random sample of 500 shoppers is selected from Northgate Shopping Center to determine the average distance customers travel to the mall. An analysis of the sample results reveal $\bar{x} = 23.5$ miles and $s = 10.4$ miles.

The point estimate for the unknown population mean of all shoppers at the mall is 23.5 miles, the sample mean. The interval estimate for μ, using 95% confidence and Equation 8.2, is

$$\begin{aligned} \bar{x} \pm z\frac{s}{\sqrt{n}} &= 23.5 \pm 1.96\frac{10.4}{\sqrt{500}} \\ &= 23.5 \pm 1.96(0.465) \\ &= 23.5 \pm 0.91 \\ &= 22.6 \text{ to } 24.4 \end{aligned}$$

It can be stated with 95% confidence that the average distance traveled to the mall by the population of shoppers is somewhere between 22.6 and 24.4 miles. More precisely, a statistician would state that if 100 samples of size 500 were selected, their means and standard deviations computed, and interval estimates constructed, 95 out of the 100 intervals would be expected to contain the population mean.

EXAMPLE 8.4 Suppose the sample results in Example 8.3 had been misstated. The sample measurements were correct, but the sample size was actually 50, not 500. What would happen to the interval estimate? The new calculations are

$$\begin{aligned} 23.5 \pm 1.96\frac{10.4}{\sqrt{50}} &= 23.5 \pm 1.96(1.47) \\ &= 23.5 \pm 2.88 \\ &= 20.6 \text{ to } 26.4 \end{aligned}$$

The population standard deviation is still estimated at 10.4 miles, and the confidence level for the interval is still 95%. But because the sample size is smaller, the interval is wider and hence less accurate. For this case, it can be said with 95% confidence that the unknown population mean is somewhere in the interval 20.6–26.4 miles.

In Example 8.4 an interval estimate was computed based on a sample size of 50. This interval estimate could also be constructed using the MINITAB software package. The MINITAB commands are:

```
MTB> RANDOM 50 C1;
SUBC> NORMAL 23.5 10.4.
MTB> DESCRIBE C1

C1    N    MEAN    MEDIAN    STDEV
     50   25.45    26.63     11.76

C1    MIN     MAX      Q1      Q3
     1.85   42.97   15.45   35.41

MTB> ZINTERVAL 95 PERCENT CONFIDENCE ASSUMED SIGMA 11.76 FOR C1
    N   MEAN     STDEV   SE MEAN   95.0 PERCENT C.I.
   50  25.45     11.76    1.66      (22.19, 28.72)

MTB> STOP
```

The RANDOM command is used to generate a sample of 50 observations and the NORMAL subcommand generates these 50 observations from a normal population with a mean of 23.5 and standard deviation of 10.4. The ZINTERVAL command is used to compute a 95% interval estimate for the data stored in C1 using the sample standard deviation, 11.76, as an estimate of the population standard deviation. Note that the ZINTERVAL command consists of the confidence level, assumed sigma, and column where the data are located.

EXAMPLE 8.5 A large automobile retailer, Avanti Southwest, studies the 1,300 customers who've taken delivery on new cars during the past year. Brad Peterson, sales manager, is attempting to measure customer satisfaction. He designs a systematic sampling plan for use with company records on the past year's customers. The selected individuals are called and asked to rate satisfaction with their car on a 1–10 scale, with 1 being the worst and 10 the best rating. Brad recognizes that this scale constitutes ordinal data, as discussed in Chapter 2, but because he believes equal intervals exist between successive rating numbers, he decides to treat the data as interval-scaled. He samples 375 customers, computes the sample mean and standard deviation, and develops an interval estimate of the population average customer rating. He recognizes that he should use the finite-population multiplier because he is sampling without replacement and the sample size exceeds 5% of the population ($n/N = 375/1{,}300 = .288$). The sample measures are $\bar{x} = 7.81$, $s = 2.3$.

Brad chooses the 95% confidence level and calculates the interval estimate:

$$
\begin{aligned}
7.81 \pm 1.96\frac{2.3}{\sqrt{375}}\sqrt{\frac{1{,}300 - 375}{1{,}300 - 1}} &= 7.81 \pm 1.96(0.119)\sqrt{0.712} \\
&= 7.81 \pm 1.96(0.119)(0.844) \\
&= 7.81 \pm 0.197 \\
&= 7.61 \text{ to } 8.01
\end{aligned}
$$

Brad can say with 95% confidence that if a census were taken of all the firm's customers from the past year, the average satisfaction rating would be somewhere between 7.61 and 8.01 on a 1–10 scale.

EXERCISES

SM

1. Explain the difference between a point estimate and an interval estimate.
2. What advantage does an interval estimate provide an analyst compared with a point estimate?
3. How does a reduced sample size affect an interval estimate?
4. How does decreasing the level of confidence affect an interval estimate?
5. How does decreased population variability affect an interval estimate?
6. What is the appropriate z value for the following confidence levels?
   a. 80%.
   b. 88%.
   c. 94%.
   d. 98%.

6*a.* 1.28
b. 1.555
c. 1.88
d. 2.33

7. The Fresh-Juice Company packages frozen lemonade in cans claimed to have a mean weight of 16 ounces. The population standard deviation is known to be 0.1. Determine a point estimate for the population mean if a random sample of 12 cans have the following weights, in ounces:

15.94	16.04	16.26	15.87	16.03	16.01
16.14	15.95	15.98	16.07	15.83	15.90

7. $\bar{x} = 16$

8. Determine interval estimates for each of the following:

8*a*. 96.61 to 103.39
b. 23.07 to 26.53
c. 7.37 to 7.63
d. .753 to .847

	Sample mean	σ	Sample size	Confidence level
a.	100	15	75	95%
b.	24.8	4.5	45	99
c.	7.5	1.4	300	90
d.	0.8	0.2	100	98

9. 11.17 to 12.83

9. The average amount of gas purchased is recorded for a sample of 50 customers at Gary's Union Service Station. If the sample mean is 12 gallons and standard deviation is 3 gallons, compute the 95% interval estimate of the mean number of gallons purchased per customer.

10. (This question refers to Exercise 9.) Compute the 95% interval estimate of the mean number of gallons purchased per customer.

10*a*. 11.41 to 12.59
b. 11.02 to 12.98
c. Increasing size reduces width

a. If the sample of customers was actually 100.

b. If the sample size was actually 36.

c. Explain what effect sample size has on the width of the interval estimate.

11. (This question refers to Exercise 9.) Compute the interval estimate of the mean number of gallons purchased by the 50 customers using:

11*a*. 10.91 to 13.09
b. 11.3 to 12.7
c. Higher confidence yields a wider interval

a. A 99% confidence level.

b. A 90% confidence level.

c. Explain what effect the confidence level has on the width of the interval estimate.

12. (This question refers to Exercise 9.) Compute the 95% interval estimate of the mean number of gallons purchased by the 50 customers using:

12*a*. 10.89 to 13.11
b. 11.45 to 12.55

a. A sample standard deviation of 4.

b. A sample standard deviation of 2.

c. Explain what effect population variability has on the width of the interval estimate.

13. 1,891.75 to 2,008.25
98% likely

13. The First Federal Credit Union wants to estimate the mean amount of outstanding automobile loans. Past experience reveals that the standard deviation is $250. Determine a 98% interval estimate for the population mean if a random sample of size 100 has a sample mean of $1,950. Interpret the meaning of this interval.

SM

14. 27.1 to 32.1

14. The length of time between billing and receipt of payment was recorded for a random sample of 50 clients (of a total of 950) of the legal firm of Schwan, Schwan, and Waldo. The sample mean and standard deviation for the 50 accounts were 29.6 days and 11.8 days, respectively. Calculate an 88% confidence interval estimate for the mean time between billing and receipt of payment for all of the firm's accounts. Describe the meaning of the interval.

15. 7.54 to 8.66

15. New Horizons Airlines wants to estimate the mean number of unoccupied seats per flight to Germany over the past year. New Horizons is looking for increased business with the two Germanies after the liberalizing political events of November 1989 in East Germany, and after studying the technical progress in East Germany as described in the *GDR Review* (April 1989 issue).

To accomplish this investigation, records of 400 flights are randomly selected from the files, and the number of unoccupied seats is noted for each flight. The sample mean and standard deviation are 8.1 seats and 5.7 seats, respectively. Estimate the mean number of unoccupied seats per flight during the past year using a 95% interval estimate. Interpret this interval's meaning.

16. This exercise refers to variable x_1, number of years with the company, in Appendix C's company data base. Assume that the population standard deviation is 5. Select a simple random sample of 36 employees and construct a 95% interval estimate for the average number of years with the company. Write a memo summarizing the results.

POINT AND INTERVAL ESTIMATES OF POPULATION PROPORTIONS

Chapter 6 demonstrated that the normal distribution provides a good approximation for the binomial distribution when $np > 5$ and $n(1 - p) > 5$. Since most proportion situations meet these criteria, the normal distribution is usually used to create interval estimates for population proportions.

Once the sample proportion has been computed as a point estimate of the population proportion, an interval is formed around this sample value, and this becomes the interval estimate for the unknown population parameter. Equation 8.3 uses the formula for the standard error of the proportion established in Chapter 7 to compute the interval estimate for a population proportion:

Interval Estimate for Proportions

$$\bar{p} \pm z\sqrt{\frac{p(1 - p)}{n}} \tag{8.3}$$

where $\bar{p}$ = Sample proportion
z = Value from standard normal table reflecting confidence level
n = Sample size
p = Population proportion

Equation 8.3 presents the same difficulty as Equation 8.2 for the population mean interval estimate. A population parameter, in this case p, must be known before the interval can be computed. The solution to this problem is the same as for means: a sample estimate is used in place of the population value to form the interval. The sample proportion, $\bar{p}$, is used as an estimate of the unknown population proportion, p. This substitution leads to a small amount of error in the estimation process.

Remember that if the sample makes up more than 5% of a finite population, the standard error of the proportion must be modified by the finite-population multiplier.

EXAMPLE 8.6 Example 7.10 referred to a newspaper article in *The Spokesman-Review* (October 30, 1989) with the quote:

> A survey, conducted Oct. 19–25 for *The Spokesman-Review* and *Spokane Chronicle*, shows Bernard far ahead of her campaign rival and fellow councilman, Rob Higgins. Of the 200 city voters selected at random and surveyed by Market Trends Inc. of Spokane, 46% said they would vote for Bernard if the election were held tomorrow; 26.5% said they would vote for Higgins. Another 19% were undecided when the survey was taken, some two weeks before the election. Market Trends vice president William Robinson, project manager for the survey, said that he believes a turnaround is extremely unlikely at this point in the campaign. Even

> giving Higgins the most favorable break under the sample's 7% margin of error—in which he would gain 7% and Bernard would lose 7%—and allowing him an even split of the undecided voters, Bernard is still leading, Robinson explained.

The point estimate of the population preference for Sheri Bernard is .46, the sample proportion. A 95% interval estimate is computed by substituting $\bar{p}$ for p in Equation 8.3:

$$\begin{aligned}\bar{p} \pm z\sqrt{\frac{p(1-p)}{n}} &= .46 \pm 1.96\sqrt{\frac{(.46)(.54)}{200}}\\ &= .46 \pm 1.96\sqrt{.0012}\\ &= .46 \pm 1.96(.035)\\ &= .46 \pm .069\\ &= .391 \text{ to } .529\end{aligned}$$

Note that, as the article stated, the margin of error is 7% (.069). It can be said with 95% confidence that if the vote were held at this time, between 39.1% and 52.9% of the voting public would vote for Sheri Bernard. This is the procedure pollsters and the news media use prior to an election. These results might have been reported as, "Forty-six percent of the registered voters prefer Sheri Bernard, with a margin of error of 7%."

EXAMPLE 8.7 The Kenless Corporation has been getting complaints about the toaster it markets in the eastern part of the country. To deal with this problem, the company first wants to know the percentage of the toasters sold that have problems. A rebate program has been in effect for six months, so the company decides to use the names on the rebate list as a population from which to sample. A random sample of 1,800 names is chosen from this list, and a brief questionnaire is mailed to these people along with an additional $5 gift certificate. A total of 1,675 questionnaires came back, which represents a good return rate, 93% [(1,675/1,800)100]. The company is satisfied that a representative sample has been obtained.

Twelve percent of the respondents said they experienced problems. The interval estimate is computed at the 99% confidence level. To find the correct z value for 99% confidence, this percentage is divided in half, producing a standard normal table area of .4950. In Appendix E.6, the z value is found in the 2.5 row halfway between the .07 and .08 columns. Thus, the z value is approximately 2.575. The interval estimate is

$$\begin{aligned}.12 \pm 2.575\sqrt{\frac{(.12)(.88)}{1{,}675}} &= .12 \pm 2.575\sqrt{.000063}\\ &= .12 \pm 2.575(.0079)\\ &= .12 \pm .02\\ &= .10 \text{ to } .14\end{aligned}$$

Kenless can state with 99% confidence that the percentage of buyers who have had problems with the toaster is between 10% and 14%. This quality level is considered unsatisfactory by company management, and a quality improvement program is initiated. (Chapter 13 discusses relevant procedures for ensuring good quality.)

EXERCISES

17. Why is the normal curve used in most problems requiring an interval estimate for a proportion?

18. Determine confidence intervals for each of the following:

	Sample proportion	Sample size	Confidence level
a.	.30	55	95%
b.	.50	35	99
c.	.75	200	90
d.	.10	400	98

18*a.* .18 to .42
b. .28 to .72
c. .70 to .80
d. .0655 to .1345

19. The Target Corporation personnel director wants to estimate the number of employees within one year of retirement. A simple random sample of 80 employee records is selected, and four people are found to be within one year of retirement. Formulate a 98% interval estimate for the true proportion of employees within one year of retirement in the entire corporation.

19. 0 to .106

20. (This question refers to Exercise 19.) Compute the 98% interval estimate of the proportion of employees within one year of retirement (with $\bar{p}$ still .05):
    a. For a sample of 200 employees.
    b. For a sample size of 40.
    c. Explain what effect sample size has on the width of the interval estimate.

20*a.* .014 to .086
b. 0 to .13

21. (This question refers to Exercise 19.) Compute the interval estimate of the proportion of employees within one year of retirement for a sample of 80 using:
    a. A 99% confidence level.
    b. A 90% confidence level.
    c. Explain what effect the confidence level has on the width of the interval estimate.

21*a.* 0 to .113
b. .01 to .09

22. (This question refers to Exercise 19.) Compute the 98% interval estimate of the proportion of employees within one year of retirement for a sample of 80 using:
    a. A population proportion of .10.
    b. A population proportion of .01.

22*a.* .022 to .178
b. 0 to .036

23. The IRS is estimating the total number of tax accountants who had their own tax returns audited last year. If a random sample of 100 returns showed that 16 were audited, develop a 90% interval estimate for the true proportion of tax accountants whose returns were audited last year. Interpret the meaning of this interval.

23. .10 to .22

24. Taco Now is studying its market penetration in Tampa. Taco Now's analyst asks 900 randomly selected residents whether they've been to Taco Now in the past month. Of those surveyed, 300 responded yes. Compute a 99% interval estimate for the true percentage of city residents who've been to Taco Now in the past month. Describe the meaning of this interval.

24. .29 to .37

25. Radio Castle tests a sample of 200 transistors and finds that 8 are defective. Calculate a 98% interval estimate for p, the true proportion of defectives. Interpret the meaning of this interval.

25. .0077 to .0723

SM

26. The *Spokane Chronicle* randomly sampled 500 registered voters to determine if they would vote for the annexation of Spokane Valley, a small adjoining community. Find a 90% inter-

26. .364 to .436

27. .508 to .617

val estimate for the proportion of the population favoring annexation if 200 of the sampled voters said they would vote favorably. Interpret the meaning of this interval.

27. In a market research study, a sample of 320 individuals are asked if they're aware of a soft drink product. If 180 of the respondents indicate awareness, develop a 95% interval estimate for the proportion of individuals in the population who are aware of the product. What does this interval suggest?

28. This exercise refers to variable x_3, gender, in Appendix C's company data base. Select a simple random sample of 50 employees and construct a 95% interval estimate for the proportion of females with the company. Interpret this interval's meaning.

SMALL-SAMPLE ESTIMATION

So far in this chapter the examples have involved rather large sample sizes. As a rule of thumb, large samples are considered to be those with 30 or more observations. In most practical situations, you can acquire a large sample, in which case these procedures will apply.

Small-Sample Estimation for Means

There are times, however, when it is practical to use a small sample. For example, some sampled items must be destroyed to be measured, and if these items are expensive, a small sample size is almost mandatory. Other samples consist of historical evidence, and if only a few measurements are available, you can't go back and collect more.

Small samples are rarely used to estimate population proportions because this causes very wide (i.e., inaccurate) intervals. For example, if 5 out of 25 people prefer a particular product, the 95% interval estimate for the population proportion, using Equation 8.3, is

$$
\begin{aligned}
.20 \pm 1.96\sqrt{\frac{(.20)(.80)}{25}} &= .20 \pm 1.96\sqrt{.0064} \\
&= .20 \pm 1.96(.08) \\
&= .20 \pm .1568 \\
&= .043 \text{ to } .357
\end{aligned}
$$

This interval is too wide to be useful. Management judgment alone could probably produce a much tighter interval estimate.

Using small samples to estimate the population mean can produce useful intervals if the population standard deviation isn't too large, and if it can be assumed that the population is approximately normally distributed. In these cases, the t distribution is used to form the interval estimate. Again, as a rule of thumb, a sample size less than 30 suggests use of the t distribution. Also, as stated earlier in this chapter, the t distribution is appropriate whenever the sample statistic s is used to estimate the population parameter σ.

t Distribution

The t distribution is a theoretical distribution that has many applications in statistics. It was first developed by W. S. Gosset, a scientist in the Guiness brewery in Ireland, who published his discovery in 1908 under the pen name Student. Gosset discovered that when sampling from a normal distribution, the t statistic has a sampling distribution much like the z statistic. The primary difference between the t and z sampling distributions is that the t statistic is more variable than the z. This is because the t statistic contains two random quantities ($\bar{x}$ and s) while the z statistic contains only one ($\bar{x}$).

The t distribution is a family of distributions similar to the standard normal distribution. There's a specific t distribution for each number of degrees of freedom, $n - 1$. There's a unique t distribution for 2 degrees of freedom, for 7 degrees of freedom, for 15 degrees of freedom, and so forth. Figure 8.2 shows the standard normal distribution (z distribution) and its relationship to t distributions with 12 and 25 degrees of freedom.

TM

FIGURE 8.2 Normal Distribution and t Distributions

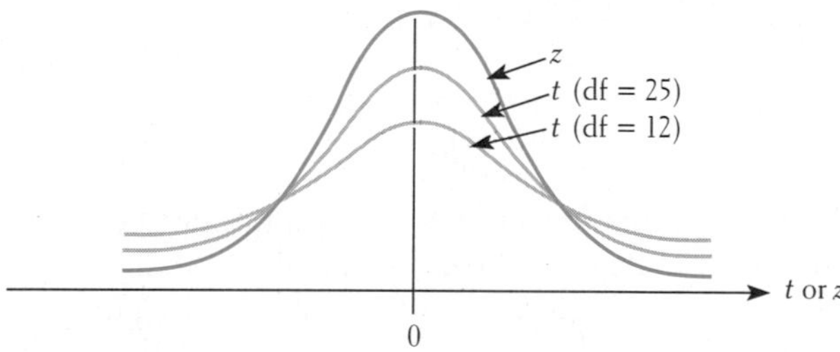

Note that the increased variability in the sampling distribution of t depends on the sample size, n. If n is small, the sampling distribution of t is more variable. You can see in Figure 8.2 that the increased variability of the t statistic means that the t value that locates the area in the lower or upper tail will be larger than the corresponding value of z, especially for small sample sizes.

Equation 8.4 forms an interval estimate for the population mean when the sample size is small and σ is unknown. This equation also requires that the population values be approximately normally distributed. The small-sample interval estimate is

$$\bar{x} \pm t\frac{s}{\sqrt{n}} \tag{8.4}$$

where $\bar{x}$ = Sample mean
t = Value from t distribution reflecting confidence level
s = Sample standard deviation
n = Sample size

Note the similarity between Equations 8.2 and 8.4. The only difference is that the t distribution, instead of the normal curve, is used to reflect the confidence level. The flowchart of Figure 8.3 summarizes the steps for determining when the t distribution is appropriate.

Use of the t table in Appendix E.7 requires that the area in the curve's lower and upper tails be known, as suggested by the shaded graph at the top of the table. Sup-

FIGURE 8.3 Sampling Distribution for Test of Population Mean

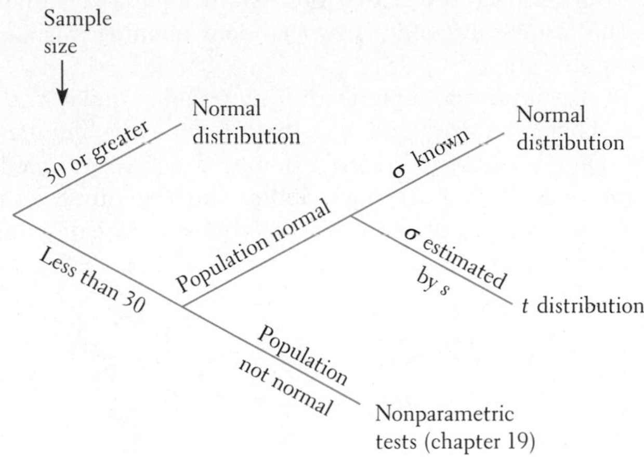

pose a 95% confidence level is desired for an interval estimate. With 95% of the curve inside the interval, there must be 5% outside it, or 2.5% in each tail.

The second value required for the t table is the number of degrees of freedom (a concept discussed in Chapter 4). We stated there that a piece of sample information is lost each time a sample statistic is used to estimate an unknown population parameter in an equation. Thus, when the sample standard deviation (s) is used as an estimate of the population standard deviation (σ) for computing the standard error of the mean, the degrees of freedom equal $n - 1$. If a sample of 10 has been selected, the degrees of freedom total $n - 1 = 9$.

> The ***t* distribution** is the appropriate distribution for constructing an interval estimate when the population is approximately normally distributed, the population standard deviation is unknown, and the sample size is less than 30.

Once again, remember that if the sample constitutes more than 5% of a finite population, the standard error of the mean must be modified by the finite-population multiplier.

EXAMPLE 8.8 An interval estimate is to be formed around a sample mean. A sample of eight has been selected, and a 98% confidence level is chosen. What is the correct t value?

A 98% confidence level implies an area of .01 in each tail of the t distribution, and the number of degrees of freedom is 7 (8 − 1). Therefore, the t table is entered using row 7 and column .02 for a two-tailed area. The correct t value from the table is 2.998.

EXAMPLE 8.9 Jean Simmons, a health store owner in Dallas, Texas, has just read an article entitled "The Cholesterol Myth" in *The Atlantic Monthly*, September 1989. It prompted Jean to estimate the average fat content per pound of hamburger sold in Dallas stores. For her sample, she purchased one pound of hamburger from each of nine randomly selected stores. She cooked the hamburger, poured off the fat, and weighed it. The results for each of the stores, in ounces of fat, are

3.3 4.8 5.1 4.5 4.0 3.9 4.7 5.0 3.6

Jean now wants to compute a 90% interval estimate for the average fat content per pound of hamburger. The mean and standard deviation for the sample are $\bar{x} = 4.322$, $s = 0.644$. The interval estimate is

$$\begin{aligned} 4.322 \pm 1.86\frac{0.644}{\sqrt{9}} &= 4.322 \pm 1.86(0.2147) \\ &= 4.322 \pm 0.3993 \\ &= 3.923 \text{ to } 4.721 \end{aligned}$$

Using a very small sample size (nine), it can be stated with 90% confidence that the average fat content per pound of hamburger is between 3.923 and 4.721 ounces.

An interval estimate using the t distribution can also be computed using the MINITAB software package. The MINITAB commands for estimating the interval in Example 8.9 are:

```
MTB> SET INTO C1
DATA> 3.3 4.8 5.1 4.5 4.0 3.9 4.7 5.0 3.6
DATA> END
MTB> DESCRIBE C1

C1          N          MEAN          MEDIAN          STDEV
            9          4.322         4.500           0.644

C1         MIN          MAX          Q1          Q3
           3.30         5.100        3.750       4.9400

MTB> TINTERVAL 90 PERCENT CONFIDENCE FOR C1
    N        MEAN            STDEV           SE MEAN          90.0 PERCENT C.I.
    9        4.322           0.644            0.215           (3.923, 4.721)

MTB> STOP
```

The TINTERVAL command is used to compute a 90% interval estimate for the data stored in C1 using the sample standard deviation as an estimate of the population standard deviation. Note that the TINTERVAL command consists of the confidence level and column where the data are located. The population standard deviation is estimated from the sample data located in the column indicated.

EXERCISES

For exercises 32 through 40, assume you're sampling from a normal population.

SM 29. When is it appropriate to use the t distribution?

30. Explain the differences between the normal curve and the t distribution.

31. Why is $n - 1$ the number of degrees of freedom used to construct an interval estimate using the t distribution?

32. Find the appropriate t value for each of the following situations:

32*a*. 2.306
b. 2.977
c. 1.796
d. 1.706

a. 95% interval estimate for 8 degrees of freedom.
b. 99% interval estimate for 14 degrees of freedom.
c. 90% interval estimate for a sample size of 12.
d. 90% interval estimate for a sample size of 27.

33. In each of the following cases, should the normal distribution or the t distribution be used to form an interval estimate?

33*a*. *t*
b. Normal
c. *t*
d. Normal

	Sample mean	s	Sample size	Interval estimate
a.	10	2	25	95%
b.	30	5.5	55	99
c.	50	9.4	10	90
d.	1	0.2	100	98

34*a*. 9.17 to 10.83
b. 28.09 to 31.91
c. 44.55 to 55.45
d. .95 to 1.05

35. 2.75 to 3.16

34. Determine an interval estimate for each of the cases in Exercise 33.

35. Quality Foods' regional manager wants to determine the average fat content per pound of steak sold in Portland, Maine. She's considering quitting her job and starting a cattle ranch after reading the article "Queen of the Range" in the January 1989 issue of *Successful Farming*. Her ranch would produce low-fat beef for sale to upscale consumers. Her interest is increased by an article in *Successful Farming* (February 1990), in which columnist Bill Helming discussed the critical factor of beef demand in the market of the 1990s.

She purchases one steak from each of the 20 stores in the area and determines average fat content per pound:

2.1	3.2	2.8	3.0	2.5	3.2	2.7	2.6	4.1	2.9
2.4	3.7	3.8	2.9	3.3	3.5	2.8	2.2	2.7	2.7

Construct a 90% interval estimate for the average fat content of steaks in the region. Interpret this interval's meaning.

36. 30.87 to 39.13

36. A dentist wishes to improve appointment scheduling. He tracks the average (mean) time he spends with each patient over a one-week period. The sample of 25 patients results in a mean time of 35 minutes with standard deviation of 10 minutes. Construct a 95% interval estimate for the mean time spent per patient. Interpret this interval's meaning.

37. 2,443 to 2,531

37. The Microspace Corporation produces an electronic component used in microcomputers. To fulfill government regulations, Microspace must estimate this component's average lifetime, in hours, before failure. A random sample of 22 components are found to last an average (mean) of 2,487 hours with standard deviation of 73 hours. Construct a 99% interval estimate for this component's mean lifetime before failure. Write a brief statement describing the interval.

38. 189.41 to 204.59

38. The United Paint Company tests a new brand of paint for square feet of coverage per gallon, a measure to be specified on the can label. A sample of 15 different gallons are tested, with average (mean) coverage of 197 square feet and standard deviation of 11.2

square feet. Construct a 98% interval estimate for the mean square feet of coverage per gallon. Interpret this interval's meaning.

39. .084 to .105

39. *The Wall Street Journal* (November 10, 1989) listed the leading mutual funds. A fund called Colonial Income Plus led the list with a 12-month return of 13.42%. Suppose an investor compared this figure with the average return of mutual funds currently available to investors.

A random sample of 30 mutual funds with assets of at least $100 million were selected and the mean and standard deviation of yield computed. The sample was selected from a population of 250 money market mutual funds with assets of at least $100 million. The mean was 9.43%, and the standard deviation was 2.79%. Construct a 90% interval estimate for the average yield of the 250 funds. What is the interval?

DB

40. This exercise refers to variable x_9, employee age, in Appendix C's company data base. It is known that the population is normally distributed. Select a simple random sample of 16 employees and construct a 95% interval estimate for the average employee age. Interpret the meaning of this interval.

SAMPLE SIZE AND ESTIMATION ERROR

One frequently asked question in statistics is: How large a sample should be taken? It is a difficult question, and a clear understanding of the concept of sampling distributions is necessary to answer it.

Three factors affect the determination of sample size for estimating a population mean: (1) the confidence level, (2) the maximum tolerable error, and (3) the population variation. Note that none of these factors has any direct relationship to the population's size.

Maximum Tolerable Error

V

The **maximum tolerable error** is a concept that refers to the maximum amount by which the sample statistic (the estimate) differs from the population parameter, for a specified confidence level.

> The **maximum tolerable error** is the maximum amount by which the sample statistic (the estimate) differs from the population parameter for a specified confidence level.

If the sample statistic is normally distributed in accordance with the central limit theorem, sample size can be estimated by using the following four steps.

Sample Size for Means

Step 1 Determine the confidence level, usually .90, .95, or .99. A higher confidence level requires a larger sample size. The appropriate z value is then found, just as in the procedure for interval estimates.

Step 2 Determine how much error, E, is tolerable. The magnitude of error will depend on how critical an accurate estimate is. A smaller tolerable error requires a larger sample size. The value of E calls for a subjective decision by the analyst.

Step 3 Determine the population standard deviation, or, if it's unknown, estimate it. This can be done by using a standard deviation based on past experience with similar analyses. Another possibility is to conduct a pilot study, taking a small sample and using the sample standard deviation, *s*, to estimate the population standard deviation, σ.

Step 4 Use the information gathered in Steps 1 through 3 in Equation 8.5,

$$n = \frac{z^2\sigma^2}{E^2} \tag{8.5}$$

where n = Sample size
z = Value from standard normal table reflecting confidence level
σ = Population standard deviation
E = Maximum tolerable error

EXAMPLE 8.10 What if the Northgate Shopping Center manager (see Example 8.4) decides that the interval estimate is too wide? Instead of accepting an error of 2.9 on either side of the mean (23.5 − 20.6 = 2.9), he states, "I want a 95% chance that the mean obtained from the random sample is no more than one mile from the true population mean. I'd like it to be even closer, but one mile is the maximum error I can tolerate."

The manager is essentially saying, "Based on a sample size of *n*, if the estimate of the population mean is computed to be 23.5 miles, I want to be confident that the population mean falls in the interval 22.5 to 24.5 miles."

Figure 8.4 shows the sampling distribution for this example and indicates that the maximum tolerable error, *E*, is $z(\sigma/\sqrt{n})$:

$$E = z\frac{\sigma}{\sqrt{n}} \tag{8.6}$$

Equation 8.6 can be rearranged so that *n*, the sample size, is the value to be solved for. This is how Equation 8.5 was derived.

TM

FIGURE 8.4 Sampling Distribution of Means

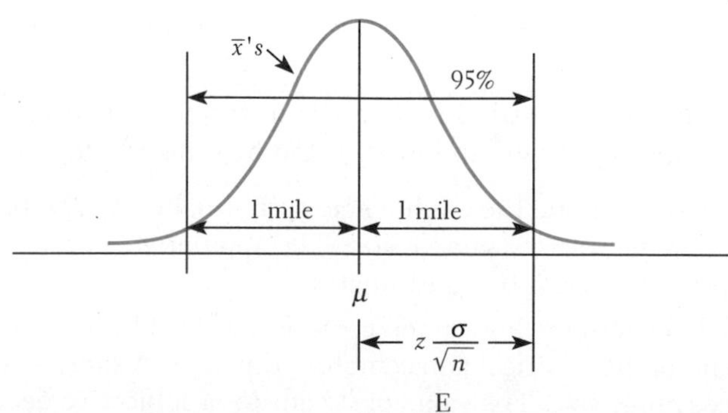

In general, if an analyst requires more precision, the sample size must be increased. The maximum tolerable error is proportional to $1/\sqrt{n}$, so to decrease the maximum tolerable error by half, four times as many observations are needed in the sample ($1/\sqrt{n} = 1/\sqrt{4} = 1/2$). To reduce the error to one-fourth its original value, 16 times as many observations are needed in the sample.

EXAMPLE 8.11 As stated in Example 8.10, the manager wants a sample large enough that the maximum tolerable error is one mile. The sample size, from Equation 8.6, is

$$\begin{aligned} 1 &= 1.96\frac{10.4}{\sqrt{n}} \\ \sqrt{n} &= 1.96(10.4) \\ \sqrt{n} &= 20.384 \\ n &= 20.384^2 \\ n &= 415.5\text{, rounded to }416 \end{aligned}$$

The manager needs a sample of at least 416 shoppers. (*Note:* The sample size figure is always rounded upward. This ensures that the criteria for maximum tolerable error are met.) Equation 8.5 produces the same result:

$$n = \frac{z^2\,\sigma^2}{E^2} = \frac{1.96^2(10.4)^2}{1^2} = 415.5$$

EXAMPLE 8.12 Herb Kau wants to estimate the mean weight of cartons shipped from a plant. The sample mean is to be no more than 2 pounds from the population mean with 95% confidence. The population standard deviation is estimated to be 10 pounds. How large a sample is needed? Using Equation 8.5, the calculations are

$$n = \frac{z^2\,\sigma^2}{E^2} = \frac{1.96^2(10)^2}{2^2} = 96.04\text{, rounded to }97$$

A sample size of 97 cartons will give 95% assurance that the sample mean is no more than 2 pounds from the population mean.

EXAMPLE 8.13 (Refer to Example 8.12.) Herb Kau decides that his budget will permit a sample size of 200 cartons. Using this sample size, what is the maximum tolerable error? Equation 8.6 is used to solve for E:

$$\begin{aligned} E &= z\frac{\sigma}{\sqrt{n}} \\ &= 1.96\frac{10}{\sqrt{200}} \\ &= 1.4 \end{aligned}$$

With the larger sample size of 200, there's a 95% chance that the sample mean will be no more than 1.4 pounds from the population mean.

The procedure for determining the appropriate sample size for estimating a proportion is similar to the one used for sample means. Steps 1 and 2 are essentially the same. Steps 3 and 4 are revised as follows:

Sample Size for Proportions

Step 3 Determine the population proportion or, if it's unknown, estimate it. If information is available on the population proportion (p), possibly from a previous study, use this value. Another method is to take a small preliminary sample and use the sample proportion, $\bar{p}$, as an estimate of p.

Step 4 Use the information gathered in steps 1 through 3 in Equation 8.7:

$$n = \frac{z^2 p(1 - p)}{E^2} \tag{8.7}$$

where n = Sample size
z = Value from standard normal table reflecting confidence level
p = Population proportion
E = Maximum tolerable error

The maximum tolerable error is computed using Equation 8.8:

$$E = z\sqrt{\frac{p(1 - p)}{n}} \tag{8.8}$$

Equation 8.8 can be rearranged so that n, the sample size, is the value to be solved for. This is how Equation 8.7 was derived.

The z value for Equation 8.7 is found in the standard normal table after the confidence level has been chosen. For a confidence level of 95%, a z value of 1.96 is used. If n is to be solved for, the decision maker must specify the maximum tolerable error, E. If E is to be solved for, the sample size, n, and the value p must be estimated and inserted in Equation 8.8.

EXAMPLE 8.14 A study published (July 31, 1992) in the *Annals of Surgery* says the use of positron emission tomography could help women detect breast tumors earlier. The study, funded by the U.S. Energy Department and the Revlon Group, looked at 14 women and correctly determined the status of the women's tumors in 12 cases. John Glaspy, an assistant professor of medicine at the University of California, Los Angeles, cautioned in *The Wall Street Journal* (July 31, 1992) that such a small study cannot be deemed statistically significant. A much larger sample of cases would be needed to show what promise, if any, the technology holds for breast cancer patients. If the percentage of successful determinations is around 85% and it is convenient for a sample of 196 women to be tested, what is the maximum tolerable error at the 95% confidence level? The value E is computed using Equation 8.8:

$$E = z\sqrt{\frac{p(1 - p)}{n}}$$

$$= 1.96\sqrt{\frac{(.85)(.15)}{196}}$$

$$= 1.96\ (.0255)$$
$$= .05$$

There is a 95% chance that the sample percentage of successful determinations, based on a sample size of 196, is within 5% of the true population percentage.

The estimated population proportion affects the width of the interval estimate. The width is greatest when p is .5, and it decreases as p gets larger or smaller. This can be seen by multiplying p by $(1 - p)$ in the numerator of the standard error of the proportion in Equation 8.8. If p equals .5, $p(1 - p)$ equals .25. If p is larger or smaller, $p(1 - p)$ is smaller than .25. Because of this, when p is not known or cannot be estimated, it is assumed to be .5. This is a conservative approach since using .5 results in the largest sample size possible.

Steps for computing sample size

1. Determine the confidence level.
2. Determine how much error, E, is tolerable.
3. Determine the population standard deviation or proportion. If it is unknown, estimate it.
4. Compute the sample size using either Equation 8.5 or Equation 8.7.

EXAMPLE 8.15 Suppose Dr. John Glaspy is unhappy with the 5.0% value for E (see Example 8.14); it is too large. When asked about the maximum error that would be acceptable, he decides on 2.5%. If this value of E is used, what sample size is necessary? Equation 8.7 is solved:

$$n = \frac{z^2\, p(1 - p)}{E^2} = \frac{1.96^2\ (.85)(.15)}{.025^2} = 783.7, \text{ rounded to } 784$$

The sample size must be increased from 196 to 784 to reduce the maximum tolerable error from 5% to 2.5%. Note that to cut the maximum tolerable error in half, the sample size had to be multiplied by 4.

EXAMPLE 8.16 Jenna Webster is manager of Easy-Quit, a program that has helped thousands of people stop smoking. She wants a rough idea of the proportion of previous clients who still are not smoking. She has just read an article in *Health* (March 1989) about the effects of air pollutants, including tobacco smoke. Because of the increased emphasis on quality air, Jenna believes her program could expand considerably if it's truly effective.

How large a sample of previous clients should she take to test the program's effectiveness? Jenna wants to be quite sure (99% confident) that the sample estimate is no more than .03 from the true population proportion. Easy-Quit has no idea what proportion of its past clients still aren't smoking. Equation 8.7 is used to solve for sample size, using .5 as the estimate of the population proportion:

$$n = \frac{z^2 p(1-p)}{E^2} = \frac{2.575^2(.5)(.5)}{.03^2} = 1{,}841.8, \text{ rounded to } 1{,}842$$

A sample size of 1,842 will provide 99% confidence that the sample proportion of those still not smoking will be within 3 percentage points of the true population value.

EXAMPLE 8.17 (Refer to Example 8.16.) Jenna decides Easy-Quit cannot afford to take a sample of 1,842. What would happen to E if the sample size were reduced to 1,000? Equation 8.8 is used to answer this question:

$$\begin{aligned} E &= 2.575\sqrt{\frac{(.5)(.5)}{1{,}000}} \\ &= 2.575(.0158) \\ &= .0407 \end{aligned}$$

Reducing the sample size to 1,000 increases the maximum tolerable error slightly. Easy-Quit now has a maximum error of about .04, which is considered acceptable.

EXERCISES

SSM

41. What is maximum tolerable error?
42. Explain the relationship between maximum tolerable error and the width of an interval estimate.
43. Joey August, a local beer distributor, is aware that weather conditions influence the volume of beer sold. Joey would like to know with 98% certainty the true mean daily precipitation in his region within 0.08 inch. Past experience indicates that the standard deviation can be assumed to be 0.20 inch.

43*a*. 34
b. 87
c. .047

a. How many observations of daily precipitation are required?

b. What sample size is required to reduce the maximum tolerable error to 0.05 inch?

c. Compute the maximum tolerable error for a sample of 100 observations.

44. Chet Lemon is interested in opening a health spa for smokers. His interest was intensified after reading the cover story on health spas in the April 1989 issue of *Health*. He thinks there might be a market for such a service, since many people want to improve their health but are having difficulty quitting smoking.

    To accurately forecast the demand for such a service, Chet needs to estimate the percentage of smokers in the neighborhood he's considering for his spa. Chet has decided to select a sample of 400 people and construct a 95% interval estimate for the proportion of smokers. Chet estimates that 25% of the target population smokes.

44*a*. .042
b. .027
c. 201

a. Compute the maximum tolerable error.

b. Compute the maximum tolerable error for a sample size of 1,000.

c. How many people need to be interviewed for the sample percentage to be no more than 6% from the population percentage?

45. 1,068

45. A national research firm wants to estimate the proportion of TV households that will watch a "Cheers" rerun next week. The research director decides to select a random sample and ask viewers whether they'll watch the show. The A.C. Nielsen ratings reported in *USA Today*, July 1, 1992, showed "Cheers" with a market share of 23% on June 25, 1992. (Market share comprises the percentage of sets in use that watched "Cheers.") How many viewers should be randomly selected to produce a 98% interval estimate for the true proportion of viewers if a maximum tolerable error of 3 percentage points is desired?

46. The Davis Real Estate Appraisers Agency has a client who wishes to know the average value of one-acre lots in Bend County. The client requires Davis to be 99% confident that its estimate is within $2,000 of the correct value. From past data, the standard deviation is believed to be $8,000.

46*a*. 107
b. 425
c. $2,913.28

a. How many estimates are required?

b. What sample size is needed to reduce the maximum tolerable error to $1,000?

c. Compute the maximum tolerable error for a sample of 50 estimates.

SM

47. 189

47. The Mountain View Treatment Center would like to estimate the mean time a counselor spends with each patient. If the population standard deviation is estimated to be 35 minutes, how large should the sample be for a maximum tolerable error of 5 minutes? Use a confidence level of 95%.

48. 423

48. The Cameron Advertising Agency wants to measure the proportion of the population that responds favorably to a new commercial for Safe Band-Aids. The agency seeks to estimate the proportion of favorable responses within .04 at the 90% confidence level. What sample size should be used if the agency has no idea what the population proportion is?

49. 19

49. This exercise refers to variable x_8, annual base salary, found in Appendix C's company data base. Assume that the population standard deviation is $6,500 and that a maximum tolerable error of $3,000 is desired. How large should the sample be for a 95% interval estimate of average annual base salary?

50. 11.76

50. This exercise refers to variable x_2, number of overtime hours worked during the past six months, found in Appendix C's company data base. Assume that the population standard deviation is 30. If a sample of 25 is selected, compute the maximum tolerable error for a 95% interval estimate for average number of overtime hours worked during the past six months.

SUMMARY

This chapter developed one of the primary uses of the sampling distribution. The estimation process for the population mean and the population proportion was covered, with emphasis on formulating interval estimates. An interval estimate provides the decision maker with a sense of the estimate's accuracy, which a point estimate does not.

An adjunct of the interval estimation process is using the sampling distribution to determine the needed sample size or the maximum tolerable error in estimating a population mean or proportion. This process is extremely useful, since almost every sampling situation requires decisions on how many items or persons to sample and how much accuracy attends the estimation process.

Applications of Statistical Concepts in the Business World

Spokane Teachers Credit Union

Steve Dahlstrom is president of Spokane Teachers Credit Union. The credit union regularly conducts a mail survey to determine members' attitudes toward its services. Among the demographic questions in each survey is whether a member is a teacher in the local area, since persons other than teachers can belong.

The credit union has been tracking the percentage of members who are teachers for several years. Each survey produces an estimate of this percentage, namely, the sample percentage. However, Steve recognizes that this point estimate can vary from survey to survey, even if the overall population percentage doesn't change. For this reason, an interval estimate is constructed around the point estimate each time a survey is taken. If this interval includes the historical percentage, the credit union assumes the population value hasn't shifted. Alternatively, when the interval estimate doesn't include this historical value, a shift is assumed to have occurred.

The credit union's marketing program assumes a high percentage of teachers in its membership, so a shift away from the historical percentage would affect the credit union's operations.

Other Applications

The typical business estimates unknown population parameters daily. Speculation, guessing, and forecasting are common in modern business, whether done intuitively or more formally. Because of the need to continually assess the condition of a population of interest, estimating key population parameters is an ongoing management concern.

For this reason, the formal estimating procedures in this chapter are important. This is especially true for the procedures for risk assessment, since risk is often difficult to determine intuitively. Determining sample size is also a constant problem in any business where samples are used to estimate population parameters. Examples of population parameters whose values might be of great interest to a business include:

Average savings account balance in a branch bank
Average number of sick days taken per year
Percentage of the market that will be captured by a new product
Average lifetime of TV sets (quality control department)
Percentage of population that recognizes an advertising theme
Mean number of products returned for service each week
Average shipping distance for mail-order customers
Average delay, in days, between ordering and receiving parts
Percentage of the work force absent any given day
Average inventory turnover, in days, for a company's products
Percentage of cartons incorrectly filled in a packing plant (for quality-control records)
Average income per household
Average days per stay in a hospital

GLOSSARY

Point estimate A single value that is measured from a sample and used as an estimate of the corresponding population parameter.

Interval estimate An interval within which the population parameter quite likely lies.

Confidence coefficient A coefficient used to indicate the likelihood that an interval estimate contains the population parameter.

Confidence level A confidence coefficient expressed as a percentage.

***t* distribution** A distribution used to construct an interval estimate when the population is approximately normally distributed, the population standard deviation is unknown, and the sample size is less than 30.

Maximum tolerable error The maximum amount by which the sample statistic (the estimate) differs from the population parameter for a specified confidence level.

KEY FORMULAS

Interval estimate for sample mean—population standard deviation known

$$\bar{x} \pm z \frac{\sigma}{\sqrt{n}} \tag{8.1}$$

Interval estimate for sample mean—population standard deviation unknown

$$\bar{x} \pm z \frac{s}{\sqrt{n}} \tag{8.2}$$

Interval estimate for population proportion

$$\bar{p} \pm z \sqrt{\frac{p(1 - p)}{n}} \tag{8.3}$$

Interval estimate for sample means—small samples

$$\bar{x} \pm t \frac{s}{\sqrt{n}} \tag{8.4}$$

Sample size determination—mean

$$n = \frac{z^2 \sigma^2}{E^2} \tag{8.5}$$

Maximum tolerable error—mean

$$E = z \frac{\sigma}{\sqrt{n}} \tag{8.6}$$

Sample size determination—proportion

$$n = \frac{z^2 p(1 - p)}{E^2} \tag{8.7}$$

Maximum tolerable error—proportion

$$E = z\sqrt{\frac{p(1-p)}{n}} \tag{8.8}$$

SOLVED EXERCISES

1. INTERVAL ESTIMATION OF A POPULATION MEAN—LARGE SAMPLE

Gattos Pizza specializes in home delivery and is considering a special two-for-one deal designed to increase the size of customer orders. To determine if the deal works, Gattos estimates the average size of customer orders at this time. A sample of 36 orders is selected, and the mean amount is \$14.37 with standard deviation of \$4.02.

a. Construct a 95% interval estimate. Interpret the meaning of this interval.

b. If the population standard deviation is known to be \$3.50, construct a 90% interval estimate. Interpret the meaning of this interval.

Solution:

a.
$$\begin{aligned} \bar{x} \pm z\frac{s}{\sqrt{n}} &= 14.37 \pm 1.96\frac{4.02}{\sqrt{36}} \\ &= 14.37 \pm 1.96(0.67) \\ &= 14.37 \pm 1.31 \\ &= \$13.06 \text{ to } \$15.68 \end{aligned}$$

Gattos can say with 95% confidence that the average amount of a customer order is between \$13.06 and \$15.68.

b.
$$\begin{aligned} \bar{x} \pm z\frac{\sigma}{\sqrt{n}} &= 14.37 \pm 1.645\frac{3.50}{\sqrt{36}} \\ &= 14.37 \pm 1.645(0.58) \\ &= 14.37 \pm 0.96 \\ &= \$13.41 \text{ to } \$15.33 \end{aligned}$$

Gattos can say with 90% confidence that the average amount of a customer order is between \$13.41 and \$15.33.

2. INTERVAL ESTIMATION OF A POPULATION PROPORTION

A new cheese spread is tested in five local supermarkets. A sample of 600 shoppers try the product, and 348 indicate that they like it. Construct a 98% interval estimate for the percentage of shoppers who like the new cheese spread, and interpret this interval's meaning.

Solution:

$$\begin{aligned} \bar{p} \pm z\sqrt{\frac{p(1-p)}{n}} &= .58 \pm 2.33\sqrt{\frac{(.58)(.42)}{600}} \\ &= .58 \pm 2.33\sqrt{.0004} \\ &= .58 \pm 2.33(.02) \\ &= .58 \pm .047 \\ &= .533 \text{ to } .627 \end{aligned}$$

It can be said with 98% confidence that the percentage of the population of shoppers who like the new cheese spread is between 53.3% and 62.7%.

3. INTERVAL ESTIMATION OF A POPULATION MEAN—SMALL SAMPLE, σ UNKNOWN

The Mass Bay Transit Authority (MBTA) must estimate the average number of passenger miles traveled per person per route for a federal agency. MBTA employee Trudy Monk rides the streetcar each day and calculates the number of passenger miles per person per route. Trudy has ridden the Beacon Street route 22 times this year and computed an average number of passenger miles of 3.2 with a standard deviation of 0.6. Construct a 99% interval estimate for average passenger miles traveled per person on the Beacon Street route, and interpret this interval's meaning. It is known that passenger miles closely follow a normal distribution.

Solution:

$$\begin{aligned} \bar{x} \pm t\frac{s}{\sqrt{n}} &= 3.2 \pm 2.831\frac{0.6}{\sqrt{22}} \\ &= 3.2 \pm 2.831(0.128) \\ &= 3.2 \pm 0.36 \\ &= 2.84 \text{ to } 3.56 \end{aligned}$$

The MBTA can now report to the federal agency, with 99% confidence, that the average number of passenger miles traveled per person on the Beacon Street route last year was between 2.84 and 3.56.

4. SAMPLE SIZE FOR INTERVAL ESTIMATE OF A POPULATION MEAN

A gift shop is interested in the charges made by credit card customers. The owner wants an estimate of the mean purchase amount for credit card customers that's within $1.00 of the actual population mean. For a 90% confidence level, how large a sample is necessary if the population standard deviation is estimated at $4.75?

Solution:

$$n = \frac{z^2\sigma^2}{E^2} = \frac{1.645^2(4.75^2)}{1.00^2} = 61$$

5. MAXIMUM TOLERABLE ERROR FOR INTERVAL ESTIMATE OF A POPULATION MEAN

If the gift shop owner in Solved Exercise 4 uses a sample of 100 credit card customers, what is the maximum tolerable error?

Solution:

$$\begin{aligned} E &= z\frac{\sigma}{\sqrt{n}} \\ &= 1.645\frac{4.75}{\sqrt{100}} \\ &= \$0.78 \end{aligned}$$

6. SAMPLE SIZE FOR INTERVAL ESTIMATE OF A POPULATION PROPORTION

The California Institute for Tourism plans to survey out-of-state visitors to determine if they plan to stay in the state more than one week. It would like to be 95% confident of its estimate.

How many tourists should be sampled if the institute wants the sample proportion of visitors staying longer than one week to be within .03 of the true proportion?

Solution:

$$n = \frac{z^2 p(1-p)}{E^2} = \frac{1.96^2(.5)(.5)}{.03^2} = 1{,}067.1, \text{ rounded to } 1{,}068$$

7. Maximum Tolerable Error for Interval Estimate of a Population Proportion

If the California Institute for Tourism (see Solved Exercise 6) uses a sample of 400 credit card customers, what is the maximum tolerable error?

Solution:

$$\begin{aligned} E &= z\sqrt{\frac{p(1-p)}{n}} \\ &= 1.96\sqrt{\frac{(.5)(.5)}{400}} \\ &= 1.96(.025) \\ &= .049 \end{aligned}$$

Exercises

51*a*. 13.32 to 14.68
b. 122.74 to 133.26
c. .508 to .732
d. 1.795 to 1.805

51. Construct an interval estimate for each of the following situations:
    a. $\bar{x} = 14, \sigma = 2, n = 25$, 90% confidence level.
    b. $\bar{x} = 128, s = 24, n = 80$, 95% confidence level.
    c. $\bar{p} = .62, n = 125$, 99% confidence level.
    d. $\bar{x} = 1.8, s = 0.02, n = 25$, 80% confidence level.

52*a*. 117
b. 198
c. 277

52. Find the appropriate sample size for each of the following situations:
    a. $\bar{x} = 147, \sigma = 11, E = 2$, 95% confidence level.
    b. $\bar{p} = .24, E = .05$ (5%), 90% confidence level.
    c. $E = .07$ (7%), 98% confidence level.

53. 15.0 to 18.6

53. Decision Science Associates, an independent research firm, employs people to call households weekday evenings, 5 to 9 P.M., to conduct telephone interviews. President Paul Dawson needs to estimate how many people to hire to complete a job requiring 2,000 interviews. His preliminary test of 36 calls reveals that they require an average of 16.8 minutes with standard deviation of 4.2 minutes. Calculate a 99% interval estimate for the true mean length of all 2,000 interviews.

54. .008 to .112

54. A random sample of 50 workers on a shopping mall construction project indicated that 3 weren't wearing hard hats. The project's population is 500 workers. Construct a 90% interval estimate for the proportion of workers not wearing hard hats.

55. 89.85 to 100.15

55. A quality-control engineer conducted a test of the tensile strength of 15 aluminum wires and found a mean tensile strength of 95 with a standard deviation of 7.6. Construct a 98% interval estimate for the average tensile strength of aluminum wires.

56. 736.18 to 747.82

56. The Mutual Insurance Company needs to study the annual health insurance claims for men between the ages of 40 and 50 to determine the necessity of a rate increase. A random sample of 450 claims produced a sample mean of \$742 and sample standard deviation of \$53. Find the 98% interval estimate for the population mean claim.

57. \$29,070 to \$34,490

57. The Klassic Design Corporation would like to compare its employees' annual salaries with those of similar companies in the industry. Klassic hasn't been using an employment agency for its staffing needs but is considering doing so after reading the article "Employing a Private Employment Firm" in the *Personnel Journal* (September 1989 issue).

In a random sample of 18 companies, average salary is found to be \$31,780 with standard deviation of \$5,450. Find the 95% interval estimate for the mean salary of companies in the industry.

58. .845 to .955

58. The auditors of Litho-Art Printers want to know the proportion of accurate accounts receivable based on an audit verification letter sent to customers. On the basis of the letter, 180 out of 200 responses were verified as accurate. Find the 99% interval estimate for the true proportion of accurate accounts receivable.

59. 62
151

59. The Specific Tire Corporation wants to be sure that its estimate of a new brand's average mileage is no more than 525 miles off the true average. It is known that the standard deviation for this type of tire is about 2,500 miles. If Specific wants to be 90% certain that the sample mean is within the desired interval, how many tires should be tested? If Specific wants to be 99% certain, how many tires should be tested?

60. 277

60. Inland Market Research conducts telephone interviews to test advertising recall. Swanson's has just developed a new advertising campaign and has asked Inland to bid on a contract to test people's recall. Swanson's wants to be 98% confident that the sample percentage is within 7% of the actual population percentage of individuals who recall the new advertising slogan. How many telephone interviews should Inland plan?

61. .2595 to .3905

61. Using the sample size determined for the 98% interval estimate in Exercise 60, Inland Market Research completed the telephone interviews and found that 90 respondents recalled the new advertising slogan. Find the 98% interval estimate.

62. 35.35 to 37.05

62. A 1989 study by Jones at the Massachusetts Institute of Technology compared world auto manufacturers, finding that the average European large-volume car plant took 36.2 hours to build a car (*Business Week*, January 15, 1992). Compute a 90% interval estimate for this study if the standard deviation was 2.6 and sample size was 27 plants.

63. 423

63. In his book, *Customers for Life*, Dallas Cadillac dealer Carl Sewell figures a lifetime customer will spend a total of \$332,000 at one of his 10 dealerships. Nissan Motors luxury Infiniti brand was founded with the idea that superior customer service by its dealers would distinguish it from other brands. General Manager William R. Bruce decides to determine the proportion of Infiniti owners who rate Nissan's customer service as superior. If he can tolerate a maximum error of 4%, how large a sample should he select for a 90% interval estimate?

64. This exercise refers to variable x_6, score on company aptitude test, found in Appendix C's company data base. Select a simple random sample of 40 employees (sample with replacement) and construct a 90% interval estimate for the average score on the company aptitude test. Interpret the meaning of this interval.

65. The following data consist of the prime interest rates for 100 randomly chosen weeks. Select a random sample of 20 weeks (sample without replacement), and construct a 95% inter-

val estimate. Assume this population is normally distributed, and remember the finite-population correction factor.

10.9	11.6	14.0	7.7	10.0	11.3	8.7	13.1
10.3	11.9	12.0	11.7	6.7	9.3	8.8	10.7
11.8	9.5	13.0	11.6	7.1	10.6	8.0	9.8
11.6	8.6	9.5	8.2	10.8	11.6	8.6	10.8
12.7	12.8	6.9	9.0	11.9	11.7	10.5	8.9
7.6	7.3	9.9	8.5	14.0	10.2	10.3	6.5
11.5	12.2	7.8	10.5	12.9	10.5	8.0	9.7
7.3	13.5	11.1	9.8	13.3	11.5	6.3	11.4
7.1	12.1	8.0	10.6	12.1	8.6	11.6	6.8
8.3	12.6	8.9	9.9	9.1	9.8	12.9	8.3
10.1	11.9	9.9	10.2	7.5	9.1	12.0	10.1
11.5	10.6	5.9	11.8	8.7	12.1	6.1	8.9
9.4	11.0	7.8	8.3				

Extended Exercises

66. Tenth Key Mail Orders

Tenth Key, a mail-order company with a small retail store, does most of its business through the mail. Customer satisfaction is important in the company's philosophy, and questionnaires are frequently used to assess customers' satisfaction with the firm's products.

A major aspect of customer satisfaction has just come to light as a result of an open-ended question on a recent mail survey. When asked what single thing would most improve the company's service, many people indicated faster service. Company president Grace Slick would like to know the average time between a customer's mailing or calling in an order and the company's filling the order.

Grace decides to conduct a telephone survey of current customers since there's only one key question to be asked. A random sample of customers can easily be selected from recent customer orders using a systematic sampling plan. The remaining issue is how many customers to call.

Equation 8.5 is used to compute sample size. Grace decides the margin of error for time between ordering and receipt of goods should be 1.5 days. A 95% confidence level will be used. The standard deviation of times is unknown, and there are many guesses about this value.

Grace takes a preliminary sample to estimate the variability in receipt times. Fifty names are randomly selected from the current customer list and called. Each person is asked how long it took for their most recent order to arrive, from the time of order placement. The average time for the sample of 50 wasn't of interest, but the standard deviation of 2.7 days was used as an estimate of the population standard deviation.

Once the values needed for Equation 8.5 were determined, the necessary sample size was computed:

$$n = \frac{z^2 \sigma^2}{E^2} = \frac{1.96^2(2.7^2)}{1.5^2} = 12.45$$

Rounded to $n = 13$, this seemed a very small sample size. It was apparent that the degree of accuracy Grace requested had already been exceeded by the preliminary sample of 50. Based on the time needed to call the 50 people, she estimated that a sample of 500 would be quickly and easily accomplished. The maximum tolerable error for a sample of this size was computed using Equation 8.6:

$$E = 1.96\frac{2.7}{\sqrt{500}}$$
$$= 1.96(0.12)$$
$$= 0.24$$

a. Summarize the accuracy for a sample size of 500 in one statement.

b. Suppose the maximum tolerable error of 0.24 day is considered more accurate than necessary. What should the sample size be if this error were changed to one day?

c. The assumption that the population standard deviation is 2.7 days was based on a sample of 50. How could this be checked as the sample continues to be taken?

67. CEA PENSION FUND

The CEA (a state teachers association) has invested a considerable portion of its pension fund in the stock market. The total portfolio value is constantly monitored by CEA officials and by their investment advisors. The holdings' yield or dividend payout hasn't been followed in the past, and the association would like to know its approximate average value.

CEA's portfolio contains several hundred stocks, each with a different yield. The yield is calculated as the annual dividend divided by the current stock price. As each stock's price fluctuates on a day-to-day basis, the yield changes also. To sample yields, we must not only sample different stocks in the portfolio, but also check them at different points in time. A sampling plan is needed to select the stock yields, which will be averaged and used to estimate the total portfolio yield over time.

It will take time to select the stocks and the points in time to use in the sample, which argues for a small sample size. On the other hand, CEA would like a fairly accurate average yield figure to report to its membership. More accuracy suggests a larger sample. Therefore, a sample size that balances cost against accuracy must be determined.

Key association officials differ in their opinions of a tolerable margin of error. The maximum tolerable error ranges from .5% to 2% among these officials. It is assumed that the yield of the total holdings is around 5%.

a. Construct a table that shows several maximum tolerable errors and their associated sample sizes.

b. How long a period should be used to define the population of yields from which the sample will be taken?

c. Based on the table constructed for question *a*, what sample size would you choose if you were the association president, considering both accuracy and the implied cost of sampling?

68. WHITFIELD UNIVERSITY BASKETBALL

Bobby Day, basketball coach for Whitfield University, is curious about male high school seniors' heights, especially after reading an article in *Coach* (August 1989) that described a new zone defense. Bobby thinks player height is the key to its success. It seems to him that senior males' average height has been increasing sharply over the past five years. Bobby wants to know the average height of graduating high school males in the five-state area that supplies most of Whitfield's basketball players.

Bobby has two things to consider in selecting a sample of high school graduating seniors. First, how will the sample be taken? There are hundreds of high schools in the five-state area and hundreds of students in each school. Some method of randomly sampling these students will have to be devised.

Second, how many students should be sampled? Bobby wants a certain amount of accuracy, but understands that accuracy must be paid for with increased sample size.

a. How should students be sampled from the high schools in the five-state area?

b. Write a statement that the coach can understand and that, complete with information supplied by the coach, will provide the information necessary to compute sample size.

c. Suppose that after questions *a* and *b* are answered and a survey is designed, the cost of estimating high school males' average height is found to be $1,500. Do you think the coach will ask the university administration for the money to conduct this study?

69. PARK AND FLY CAR RENTAL

Park and Fly Car Rental has a 150-car fleet. Manager Shawn Birch is concerned about his cars' average miles per gallon of gas since he needs to determine how much to charge customers per mile for usage of the automobiles. Shawn selects and tests a sample of 20 cars.

You work for Park and Fly and are assigned to estimate the average mileage per auto. Actual mileages for the entire fleet of 150 cars (rounded to the nearest whole number) are:

27	24	22	23	25	30	26	24	23	23	26
22	21	27	28	27	27	27	24	21	26	18
27	20	23	30	25	25	21	24	25	27	24
26	24	26	23	31	25	22	23	31	25	26
21	28	27	23	23	23	29	25	24	24	20
26	25	29	18	20	17	28	22	26	22	21
25	25	25	25	21	21	28	29	24	23	26
22	20	30	24	22	23	22	22	23	23	20
26	21	28	28	27	24	22	23	33	20	21
24	24	21	29	29	26	24	28	26	21	22
25	23	25	25	24	23	25	23	27	23	20
20	28	20	22	20	24	25	23	24	25	25
26	23	28	22	23	23	24	21	25	25	25
24	23	23	18	16	24	22				

a. Select a random sample of 20 mileages (sample with replacement) and construct a 95% interval estimate.

b. If you're told that the maximum tolerable error is one mile per gallon, what sample size would you recommend?

c. What is the maximum tolerable error if a sample size of 40 is used?

70. OUR LADY OF LOURDES HOSPITAL

Chapter 4 presented family sizes for a population of 200 Our Lady of Lourdes Hospital employees. Customer benefits director Curtis Huff has asked you to quickly estimate average family size per employee. You've computed the mean and presented it to the director as a point estimate of the population mean. Mr. Huff isn't satisfied with your work. He wants to know how accurate your estimate is.

a. Develop 90%, 95%, and 99% interval estimates for the mean.

b. Discuss whether the finite-population multiplier should be used in this situation.

c. If the sample size were increased to 50, what effect would this have on your interval?

d. Write a memo to Mr. Huff summarizing your results.

MICROCOMPUTER PACKAGE

The micro package *Computerized Business Statistics* can be used to compute sample size.

Suppose you wanted to find the sample size needed to estimate the average annual billing amount for your clients. The population standard deviation of annual billing amounts is estimated to be about \$2,500. A confidence level of 95% is chosen, and sample sizes are to be computed for maximum tolerable errors of \$200, \$300, and \$500.

Computer Solution:

From the main menu of *Computerized Business Statistics*, a 7 is selected, indicating Sampling and Estimation. The sampling and estimation menu is then shown on the screen. This menu was presented at the end of Chapter 2.

Since the problem involves the determination of sample size, **Compute Sample Size** is selected.

```
SAMPLE SIZE ANALYSIS

1. Sample Size from Alpha/Beta Error
2. Sample Size from Sampling Error

    Enter Option (1-2) and press ↵ 2
```

Alpha/beta error has not been discussed, so the correct response is **2,** "sample size from sampling error."

```
Enter Standard Deviation and press ↵ 2500
```

The estimated population standard deviation for this exercise is \$2,500.

```
Enter Alpha error: 1 = .1, 2 = .05, 3 = .025, 4 = .01, 5 = .005, 6 = Other
Select Alpha: Enter 1–6 and press ↵ 3
```

The concept of alpha error hasn't been covered yet. Alpha error refers to the area in one tail. For a confidence level of 95%, the alpha error is $(1 - .95)/2 = .025$, and a **3** is entered.

```
Critical Z for Alpha = .025 and press ↵ 1.96
```

The correct z value for a 95% confidence level is 1.96.

```
Enter the Sampling Error and press ↵ 200
```

Sampling error is the same as maximum tolerable error. The maximum tolerable error for this exercise is \$200.

Finally, the program provides the answer:

```
Sample Size = 600
```

This process can be repeated for maximum tolerable errors of \$300 and \$500.

MINITAB Computer Package

The following commands show how the MINITAB package is used to solve the Our Lady of Lourdes Hospital exercise (Extended Exercise 70).

First, the program is used to generate 30 random numbers.

```
MTB> RANDOM 30 C1;
SUBC> INTEGER 1 200.
MTB> PRINT C1
C1

   78  106   75   68  104   41    2   73
   53   53   24  101   42  189   57   42
  155   19   15   88  161   93  111   35
   57  193  106   94   23  182
```

Next, the family sizes that correspond to the random numbers are entered as data, and the mean and standard deviation are computed:

```
MTB> SET INTO C2
DATA> 6 2 2 1 5 1 2 2 2 2 1 4 3 3 2 3 2 3 2 4 4 2
DATA> 4 1 2 3 2 4 2 3
DATA> END
MTB> DESCRIBE C2

   C2          N      MEAN    MEDIAN    STDEV
              30     2.633    2.0000    1.217
   C2        MIN       MAX        Q1       Q3
           1.000     6.000     2.000    3.250
```

Finally, a 95% interval estimate is computed using the sample standard deviation, 1.217, as an estimate of the population standard deviation.

```
MTB> ZINTERVAL 95 1.217 C2

   N      MEAN    STDEV    SE MEAN    95.0 PERCENT C.I.
   30    2.633    1.217       .222       (2.197, 3.069)

MTB> STOP
```

The ZINTERVAL command is used to compute a 95% interval estimate for the data stored in C2 using the sample standard deviation, 1.217, as an estimate of the population standard deviation. Note that the ZINTERVAL command consists of the confidence level, assumed σ, and column where the data are located. If 100 students develop interval estimates using the population in Extended Exercise 62 in Chapter 4, 95 of the intervals will contain the actual population mean. The interval estimate developed in this example, 2.197 to 3.069, does include the actual population mean, which is 2.9.

Chapter

9

Hypothesis Testing

Say not, "This is the truth," but "So it seems to me to be as I now see the things I think I see."

Inscription above a doorway at the German Naval Officers School in Kiel

Objectives

When you have completed this chapter, you will be able to:

Describe the difference between estimation and hypothesis testing.

Use the four-step hypothesis-testing procedure to solve practical business problems.

Identify the two forms of potential error in the hypothesis-testing procedure and understand their consequences.

Develop decision rules.

Conduct tests of hypotheses about population means and population proportions.

Develop the operating characteristic curve and power curve for each decision rule.

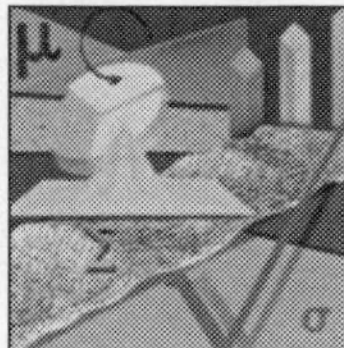

According to *The Wall Street Journal,* February 27, 1990, Waldenbooks is launching a new membership program. Frequent book buyers will receive benefits including discounts on future purchases.

The preceding chapters have set the stage for one of the most important statistical applications: hypothesis testing. Most real-world statistical analyses to assist the decision-making process involve this important concept. This chapter and the next cover this topic, that is based on the sampling distribution ideas of Chapter 7. If you can't fully understand this chapter's concepts, a review of Chapter 7 may prove helpful.

Why Managers Need to Know about Hypothesis Testing

Managers receive data signals each day from various aspects of their businesses. Some of these might be called false signals because they simply reflect chance or random fluctuations in daily operations. Other changes signal significant shifts in important measures of company health. This chapter concerns understanding the difference between random and significant changes.

For the Waldenbooks program management of the chain must carefully monitor sales to detect the effect. They must distinguish between a significant sales upturn and a temporary increase due to random effects. This chapter deals with how to do this.

Introduction

It is important at the outset to understand the difference between hypothesis testing (the subject of this chapter) and estimation (the subject of Chapter 8). Both procedures involve the use of sampling distributions. The major difference is whether a predetermined notion of the state of the population being sampled has been established. If nothing is known about the population, estimation is used to provide point and interval estimates about population parameters of interest. If information about the population is claimed or suspected, **hypothesis testing** is used to determine the feasibility of this information.

Estimation versus Hypothesis Testing

> **Estimation** involves using sample evidence to estimate the unknown characteristics of a population. **Hypothesis testing** involves using sample evidence to assess the likelihood that an assumption about some characteristic of a population is true.

The difference between estimation and hypothesis testing may be easier to understand by determining which of these two questions is relevant to a particular statistical study:

1. What is the state of the population? Since no information about it exists, a random sample will be selected, appropriate statistics computed, and inferences about population parameters made. The likelihood of error in this estimation process is recognized and measured.
2. Does the population possess the characteristics that are claimed, suggested, or hypothesized? The claim being made about the population is in doubt, so a random sample from this population is selected, appropriate statistics computed, and, once these sample results are examined, the decision of whether to reject the claim about the population is made. The likelihood of error in this hypothesis-testing process is then assessed.

■ SITUATION 9.1 Five months ago Sue and Bill Johnson took over a chemical manufacturing company started by Bill's parents. The company supplies a variety of basic chemicals to many firms, including the Anderson Corporation. One of the Johnson's big accounts with Anderson involves a chemical that Anderson uses in making a medication that helps control high cholesterol.

In their early contacts, Anderson's purchasing manager suggested that Bill and Sue read a study that appeared in *The Journal of the American Medical Association.*[1] Among other things, it indicated that of those persons seeing a doctor about high cholesterol, 19.2% were given a prescription for medication. Anderson's product is often prescribed for these people.

Anderson has developed a test for incoming shipments of Johnson's chemical that combines measures of acidity and potency. According to the contract between them, this measure is supposed to be at least 425 units. In checking their own records from the factory floor, Bill and Sue find the following information:

1. A total of 55 batches have been tested using the Anderson acidity/potency measure during the past three years. This sample of 55 batches was randomly selected from the several hundred batches produced.
2. The average measurement for the sample batches was 415 acidity/potency units with a standard deviation of 30.

When first confronted with this sample evidence, Sue and Bill conclude that their process is not meeting specification. On second thought, however, they are not so sure. Perhaps the process is performing as specified and the 415 figure is due to random variability inherent in sampling. Also, they note that Anderson has never indicated

[1]W. H. Giles, R. F. Anda, D. H. Jones, M. K. Serdula, R. K. Merritt, and F. DeStefano, "Recent Trends in the Identification and Treatment of High Blood Cholesterol by Physicians," *The Journal of the American Medical Association* (March 3, 1993), pp. 1133–38.

displeasure with the quality of their product. Sue realizes from her experience in a college statistics course that the 10-unit deficit (425–415) could be due to randomness, but she and Bill decide the matter must be investigated. ■

Hypothesis-Testing Steps and Procedures

The following steps constitute the procedure for testing a hypothesis about the state of a population. The specific calculations vary from test to test.

Hypothesis-Testing Steps

Step 1 State the null and alternative hypotheses (these terms will be explained in depth later in this section).

V

The first step in the hypothesis-testing procedure is to state the null, or no-change, hypothesis. The null hypothesis states that the difference between a sample statistic and the corresponding claimed population parameter is due to the chance variation involved in sampling. The alternative hypothesis is the opposite statement about the population, which must be true if the null hypothesis is false.

Step 2 Assume the null hypothesis is true, and determine the appropriate sampling distribution for this assumption.

The null hypothesis stands on trial much as a person charged with a crime: innocence is assumed unless sufficient evidence is produced to indicate guilt. That is, the null hypothesis is assumed to be true unless sample evidence can be produced to indicate that this assumption is extremely unlikely, in which case the null hypothesis will be judged "guilty" or false.

Under the assumption that the null hypothesis is true, a sampling distribution is developed from which the calculated test statistic will be drawn. The specific sampling distribution will vary from test to test.

Step 3 Take a random sample from the population under investigation and compute the appropriate test statistic from the collected data.

Random samples are required to ensure that the sample is representative of the population. After the sample has been selected, the appropriate statistic, a single numerical value, is calculated from the data. This statistic is commonly the sample mean or sample proportion.

Step 4 Assess the likelihood of selecting the test statistic from the assumed sampling distribution.

If it seems quite unlikely that the computed test statistic could be drawn from the sampling distribution, the null hypothesis is rejected. The testing process assumes that the null hypothesis is true, and if an extremely unlikely occurrence accompanies this assumption, the assumption must be abandoned.

On the other hand, if the test statistic seems likely to have come from the assumed sampling distribution, the null hypothesis isn't rejected. In this case the sample hasn't produced evidence strong enough to suggest that the null hypothesis is false.

Example 9.1 A sales brochure for a new light bulb claims that such bulbs' average lifetime is 1,000 hours. A random sample of 250 bulbs is taken from inventory, and each is tested until failure. These test bulbs' average lifetime is computed and used to test the null hypothesis that all such bulbs' average lifetime is 1,000 hours. Suppose one of the following test results occurs:

1. The sample average (mean) lifetime is 999 hours. This sample average is less than the claimed 1,000-hour average for the population of light bulbs; however, it seems quite reasonable that if the population averages 1,000 hours, the sample could average 999 hours. The sample evidence doesn't seem to contradict the null hypothesis, so the null hypothesis isn't rejected.
2. The sample average (mean) lifetime is 700 hours. This sample evidence seems incompatible with the claimed population average of 1,000 hours. Observing such a low sample average seems extremely unlikely if the null hypothesis is true, especially since such a large sample was used (250). The null hypothesis is rejected.

The two hypothesis-testing outcomes in the preceding example are intuitively obvious. It isn't necessary to understand hypothesis-testing procedures to arrive at the correct conclusion if the sample evidence is this clear. Most situations, however, are not intuitively obvious. One must usually follow the four hypothesis-testing steps to correctly assess the probability that the null hypothesis is true.

The hypothesis to be tested about a population can come about in any of several ways. Someone may claim that the population of interest has certain characteristics. A salesperson, for example, might claim that a new machine averages nine months between breakdowns. A sales brochure might claim that no more than 5% of the electronic components ordered from a company will prove defective when installed in larger assemblies.

Other hypothesis-testing applications involve hypotheses or claims that aren't as apparent. The following four situations relevant to a business setting illustrate this point.

EXAMPLE 9.2 A study conducted to determine the annual salaries of company trainers around the United States found that the average (mean) salary was $63,627 ("Honey, They Shrunk My Paycheck," *Training*, November 1992, p. 21). The study pointed out that salaries differed by several demographic characteristics including location, number of company employees, gross sales/assets of company, industry, sex, education level, age, and years of experience. An analyst wants to determine whether the average salary of company trainers in New York state is similar to the national average. The appropriate hypothesis is that the average salary is $63,627. A random sample of salaries will be acquired, and if the sample mean is different enough, it will be concluded that company trainers are paid differently in the state of New York.

EXAMPLE 9.3 The management team at a bank wonders whether the average savings account balances for two of its branches are the same or different. One branch has just had its interior remodeled, an action that management took based on an article in *The Banker*, "Putting on the Ritz" (February 1989 issue). This article pointed out the profit advantages of making a bank's interior appealing to customers.

The appropriate hypothesis is that the average balances are equal. Sample accounts will be selected from each branch and, if there's a large enough difference between them, it will be concluded that the population of account balances at the two branches have different averages.

EXAMPLE 9.4 A state government agency is concerned about unemployment rates in the state's two major cities. Random samples are selected from each city and the sample unemployment rates determined. The appropriate hypothesis is that the two population unemployment rates are equal. If the sample rates are very close, it will be concluded that the cities have the same unemployment rate. If the sample rates are quite different, it will be concluded that they have different unemployment rates.

EXAMPLE 9.5 A new machine purchased by the Sun Company to fill containers with orange juice is supposed to have an average fill volume of 16 ounces. Before using the machine in the production process, the company decides to sample its output volumes to see if the claim is true. The appropriate hypothesis is that the machine does indeed average 16 ounces of fill. Several containers are filled under production conditions, and the sample mean volume is computed. If this sample average is close to 16 ounces, it will be concluded that the claimed machine average is correct. If the sample average volume isn't close to 16 ounces, the company that sold the machine will be called to adjust or replace it.

Each of the previous examples involves the testing of a single hypothesis or claim about the state of the population of interest. In statistics, these claims are tested in the form of null hypotheses.

Null Hypothesis

Step 1 in the hypothesis-testing procedure calls for stating the null and alternative hypotheses. The **null hypothesis** states that the difference between a sample statistic and its assumed population parameter is due to the chance variation inherent in sampling.

> The **null hypothesis** is the assumption about the population that is tested using sample evidence. It states that the difference between a sample statistic and the assumed population parameter is due to chance variation in sampling. The symbol for the null hypothesis is H_0.

Analysts usually design their tests based on the assumption that there has been no change in the population of interest. Why not state the hypothesis in a positive form? Why not claim that a difference exists between the sample statistic and the population parameter, due to some cause? Unfortunately, this type of hypothesis cannot be tested definitively. Evidence that's consistent with a hypothesis stated in a positive form can almost never be taken as conclusive grounds for accepting the hypothesis. A finding that is consistent with such a hypothesis might be consistent with other hypotheses too and, thus, doesn't establish the truth of the given hypothesis. Example 9.6 illustrates this point.

EXAMPLE 9.6 Suppose a coin is suspected of being biased in favor of tails. The coin is flipped 100 times, and the outcome is 53 tails. It would *not* be correct to jump to the conclusion that the coin is biased simply because more than the expected number of tails (50) resulted. In fact, a total of 53 tails is consistent with the hypothesis that the coin is fair. It wouldn't be surprising to flip a fair coin 100 times and observe 53 tails. On the other hand, 85 or 90 tails in 100 flips would seen to contradict the hypothesis of a fair coin. In this event, there would be a strong case for a biased coin.

Alternative Hypothesis

Suppose the null hypothesis being tested is false. In hypothesis testing, an **alternative hypothesis** is stated that holds true if the null hypothesis is false. The objective of a hypothesis test is to use sample evidence to choose between these two statements about the state of the population of interest.

> The **alternative hypothesis** in a hypothesis test is the statement about the population that must be true if the null hypothesis is false. The symbol for the alternative hypothesis is H_1.

An alternative hypothesis may indicate a change from the null hypothesis in a particular direction, or it may indicate a change without specifying direction. In Example 9.5, the machine was claimed to fill containers with 16 ounces each; thus, the null hypothesis is H_0: $\mu = 16$. This hypothesis would be rejected if the sample mean was found to be either too large or too small; so the alternative hypothesis is H_1: $\mu \neq 16$. Because no direction is specified in the alternative hypothesis (the sample mean could be greater than or less than 16 ounces), this is called a **two-tailed test.**

Frequently, the analyst is concerned with only one alternative. In Example 9.2, the manager wonders if a quality improvement program has reduced the percentage of defective units produced below the previous rate of 15%; thus, the null hypothesis is H_0: $p \geq .15$. This hypothesis would be rejected if the sample defective rate was found to be reduced; so the alternative hypothesis is H_1: $p < .15$. If the analyst is concerned only with an alternative in a single direction, this is called a **one-tailed test.**

One- and Two-Tailed Tests

> A **one-tailed test** is one in which the alternative hypothesis indicates a direction (either greater or less than); a **two-tailed test** is one in which the alternative hypothesis does not specify direction.

■ SITUATION 9.1—PARTIALLY RESOLVED Sue and Bill Johnson have records from a sample of 55 chemical batches showing an average acidity/potency measurement of 415 units. Since their contract with Anderson specifies a mean of 425 units, they are concerned about maintaining a good relationship with Anderson. Since a mean below 425 is of concern, their hypothesis test will be one-tailed. The null and alternative hypotheses are:

$$H_0: \mu \geq 425$$
$$H_1: \mu < 425$$

An alternative hypothesis uses one of three signs: the unequal sign ($\neq$), the less-than sign ($<$), or the greater-than sign ($>$). The Johnsons have chosen among three possible situations and specified the alternative hypothesis accordingly:

1. If the population mean isn't 425, it would be either less than or greater than 425. The alternative hypothesis is two-tailed and uses the unequal sign (H_1: $\mu \neq 425$).
2. If the population mean isn't greater than or equal to 425, it's less than 425. The less-than sign is used in the alternative hypothesis (H_1: $\mu < 425$); this is a one-tailed test.
3. If the population mean isn't less than or equal to 425, it's greater than 425. The alternative hypothesis utilizes the greater-than sign (H_1: $\mu > 425$); this is also a one-tailed test.

Because their sole concern is deterioration in the chemical process, the Johnsons chose alternative 2. They'll examine the sample evidence to decide between the null hypothesis (population mean greater than or equal to 425) and the alternative hypothesis (population mean less than 425).

For any hypothesis test, one of the three alternative hypothesis types must be chosen. The choice depends on the state of the population that's believed to exist if the null hypothesis is false. ■

EXERCISES

1. Explain the similarities and differences between hypothesis testing and estimation.

2. Why do analysts test the null hypothesis?
3. What are the steps used in hypothesis testing?
4. Why is it necessary to assume that the null hypothesis is true?
5. Jim Young is considering running for mayor. He would like to have some idea of the possibility of winning. He wants you as a consultant to tell him how to get information to help him make a decision. In the context of hypothesis testing, what would you recommend to Jim?
6. Explain the difference between the null hypothesis and the alternative hypothesis.
7. Explain the difference between a one-tailed test and a two-tailed test.
8. What are the two possible conclusions in a test of a hypothesis?
9. State the appropriate null hypothesis and alternative hypothesis to test the following statements:
   a. A supplier of plastic strips has agreed to send a manufacturing firm shipments containing no more than 2% defectives.

9a. $p \leq .02, p > .02$
b. $\mu = 7, \mu \neq 7$
c. $\mu \geq 600, \mu < 600$
d. $\mu = 21, \mu \neq 21$
e. $\mu \leq 5, \mu > 5$
f. $p = .10, p \neq .10$

b. The average time for delivery of Leading Edge Computers is seven days.

c. A manufacturer claims that the average life of a transistor battery is at least 600 hours.

d. The average age of Tech University students is 21 years.

e. The Headache Pharmaceutical Company claims that the average time for a pain reliever to take effect is five minutes.

f. A random sample of accounts receivable were checked to determine whether the proportion that were delinquent has changed from 10%.

ERRORS IN HYPOTHESIS TESTING

As discussed in Chapter 8, an important aspect of estimation is determining the possibility of error. Error assessment is an integral part of estimating population characteristics using sample evidence. Likewise, in testing a hypothesis the analyst must assess the likelihood that the conclusion reached is wrong.

EXAMPLE 9.7 A company is testing the claim that the average weight of parts produced by a new machine is 2 pounds. The null hypothesis is H_0: $\mu = 2$, and the alternative hypothesis is H_1: $\mu \neq 2$. A random sample of parts is selected from the output of the new machine and their average weight determined. Now the company must decide whether to reject the null hypothesis that the population average weight is 2 pounds.

Two types of errors might occur in this situation:

1. If the company decides to reject the 2-pound claim, it could be making a mistake. Perhaps the machine actually produces parts with an average weight of exactly 2 pounds. An erroneous conclusion might be reached because the sample average was misleading.
2. If the company fails to reject the 2-pound claim, it could also be making a mistake. The machine might actually be producing parts that average 1 or 3 pounds, and if the sample average is close to 2 pounds, the company might erroneously fail to reject the null hypothesis.

In hypothesis testing, one of the two types of error just described is always a possibility. The sample, although selected randomly, could lead to an incorrect rejection of the null hypothesis or an incorrect acceptance of the null hypothesis. These two types of hypothesis-testing errors are known as **type I** and **type II errors,** respectively.

Type I and Type II Errors

In hypothesis testing, rejecting a true null hypothesis is known as a **type I error;** the probability of committing such an error is denoted alpha (α). Failing to reject a false null hypothesis is known as a **type II error;** the probability of committing this error is denoted beta (β).

Table 9.1 summarizes the risks inherent in testing any null hypothesis. Note that the table's rows represent the world's true state, or the actual condition (true versus false) of the null hypothesis being tested. Unfortunately, we can't determine which state of the world is true without some risk of error if sample evidence is used to make the decision. In terms of time and money we can rarely conduct a complete census of the population and thus arrive at an error-free conclusion regarding the null hypothesis. Instead, a sample is selected from the population and, based on this sample's characteristics, the null hypothesis is either rejected or not rejected. Since this decision is based on examination of a sample that forms only part of the population, an erroneous conclusion is always possible.

TABLE 9.1 Type I and Type II Errors

	Conclusion based on sample evidence	
True state of the world	Fail to reject null hypothesis	Reject null hypothesis
Null hypothesis true	Correct decision	Type I error
Null hypothesis false	Type II error	Correct decision

As Table 9.1 shows, there are four possible outcomes to a hypothesis test. This is because there are two possible states of the world (null hypothesis true, null hypothesis false) and two possible conclusions based on the sample evidence (fail to reject null hypothesis, reject null hypothesis). Two of the four possible outcomes represent correct conclusions: failing to reject a true null hypothesis and rejecting a false null hypothesis. Note that if a decision maker reaches the correct conclusion, this will probably not be known until some future time.

Table 9.1 also indicates the two possible ways to commit an error in reaching a conclusion about a population on the basis of sample information. A null hypothesis that turns out to be correct might be rejected on the basis of the sample evidence; this is a type I error. On the other hand, a null hypothesis that turns out to be false might not be rejected based on the sample evidence; this is a type II error. Again, note that, at the moment of decision, there's no way of knowing whether the decision is correct. This will become evident later and, if the conclusion is incorrect, there's usually a price or penalty to be paid.

> A **type I error** is only possible if the null hypothesis is rejected, while a **type II error** is only possible if the null hypothesis is not rejected.

The penalties associated with committing type I and type II errors concern decision makers. If there's no penalty for an incorrect decision, there's no need to spend time and money collecting sample information in an attempt to make the correct decision.

Businesspeople, however, strive to make correct decisions, usually based on sample, or incomplete, information about the true state of the world. It is particularly important in hypothesis testing to balance the penalties of type I and type II errors against each other before reaching a conclusion. This important subject is discussed later in this chapter.

EXERCISES

10. Explain the difference between a type I error and a type II error.
11. Which type of error is it more important to control: type I or type II?
12. When does an analyst risk making a type II error?
13. When does an analyst risk making a type I error?

14. Type I

14. If the null hypothesis is true, what type of error might be made?

15. Type II

15. If the null hypothesis is false, what type of error might be made?

16. Type I

16. Coffee Delight claims on their labels that each can contains 2 pounds of coffee. If an experiment is conducted and the null hypothesis rejected, what kind of error could be made? Explain the implications of such an error. If the null hypothesis is not rejected, what kind of error could be made? Explain the implications of such an error.

17. $\mu = \$34,000$
$\mu \neq \$34,000$

17. State the null and alternative hypotheses for testing the claim that the average salary of the employees listed in the Appendix C company data base is $34,000. If a study is conducted and the null hypothesis rejected, what kind of error could be made? Explain the implications of such an error. If the null hypothesis is not rejected, what kind of error could be made? Explain the implications of such an error.

18*a*. Type I—calling a truth-teller a liar
Type II—calling a liar a truth-teller
b. 185/500 = .37

18. The American Management Association surveyed 1,005 firms in December 1988, discovering that polygraph testing is declining in U.S. firms (*Personnel*, May 1989, p. 39). The article "Lie Detectors Can Make a Liar of You" (*Discover*, June 1986, p. 7) may explain this decline. The article indicates that if 1,000 people took a polygraph test and 500 told the truth and 500 lied, the polygraph would indicate that approximately 185 of the people who told the truth were liars and 120 of the liars told the truth.
    a. The null hypothesis is that a person is telling the truth and the alternative hypothesis is that a person is lying. In this context, describe type I and type II errors.
    b. Based on the survey results, what is the approximate probability that a polygraph test will result in a type I error?

DEVELOPING DECISION RULES

Step 2 in the hypothesis-testing procedure calls for determining the appropriate sampling distribution, assuming the null hypothesis is true. The central limit theorem (Chapter 7) indicates that the sampling distribution of means is a normal distribution for sample sizes that are sufficiently large (30 or greater).

Step 3 of the hypothesis-testing procedure involves computing a statistic from the sample. For testing a hypothesis about a population mean, this statistic will be the sample mean. However, to complete Step 4 (determining the probability of getting the sample statistic from the assumed sampling distribution), a significance level must be chosen.

We hope that the correct decision concerning the null hypothesis will be reached based on sample evidence, but there's always a possibility of rejecting a true H_0 or failing to reject a false H_0. The probabilities of these events are known as alpha (α) and beta (β), respectively. The probability of rejecting a null hypothesis that's true is called the **level of significance** of a hypothesis test. It is fairly common to designate a particular significance level—usually .01, .02, .05, or .10—without any thought as to why this value is chosen. In real decision-making situations, the analyst must choose the significance level by asking: What probability of rejecting a true null hypothesis am I willing to accept? We must understand that a low probability of committing a type I or alpha error generates a higher probability of committing a type II or beta error, and vice versa, for any given sample size.

Level of Significance

> The **level of significance** of a hypothesis test is the probability of rejecting a null hypothesis that is true. It is designated by the symbol α (alpha).

How does an analyst choose an appropriate value for alpha? The answer depends on the relative penalties associated with type I and type II errors. If rejecting a true H_0 is more costly than failing to reject a false H_0, a small alpha should be chosen. If failing to reject a false H_0 is more costly than rejecting a true H_0, a larger alpha should be chosen.

Decision Rule

A **decision rule** indicates the conditions under which the null hypothesis will be rejected. This rule specifies the action to be taken for each possible sample outcome.

V

> A hypothesis-testing **decision rule** specifies the action to be taken for each possible sample outcome.

Figure 9.1 illustrates the development of the decision rule in a hypothesis test for a population mean. If the null hypothesis is assumed true, the sampling distribution in Figure 9.1 is the appropriate distribution from which to draw the sample mean.

Note that two numerical values, a and b, appear on the ends of the curve. These are the decision rule critical values. They represent the points beyond which a sample mean drawn from this distribution may be viewed as unlikely. In general terms, using Figure 9.1, the decision rule for this example might be stated:

> If the mean computed from the sample data is between a and b, fail to reject the null hypothesis, since such a result is compatible with the assumed sampling distribution. If the sample mean is less than a or greater than b, reject the null hypothesis, since such extreme values are unlikely to have been drawn from this sampling distribution.

Rather than state the decision rule and test statistic in units of measurement (such as hours, dollars, or seconds), the usual method is to specify these two important val-

TM

FIGURE 9.1 Sampling Distribution of Means

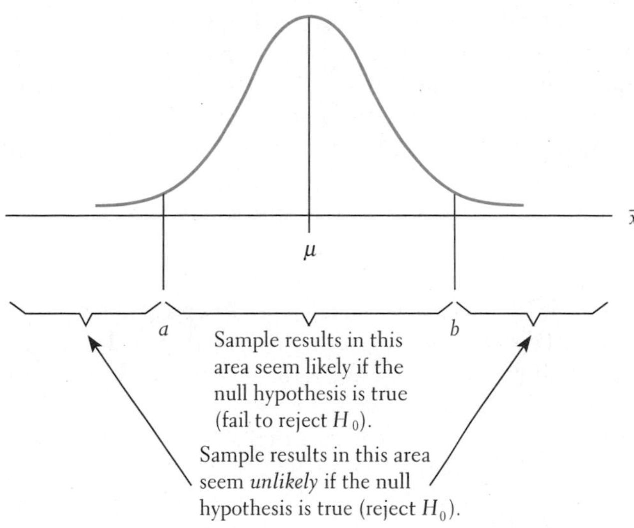

ues in terms of standardized z scores. In this approach (discussed in Chapter 6), the sample statistic is expressed in terms of the number of standard deviations between it and its mean; that value is then compared with a table value of z. In Equation 9.1, z is computed as the difference between the observed sample value and the hypothesized or assumed population value, divided by the standard error of the appropriate sampling distribution:

$$z = \frac{\text{Observed value} - \text{Assumed value}}{\text{Standard error of sampling distribution}} \tag{9.1}$$

Equation 9.1 is used throughout this chapter to compute the sample test statistic. The standardized method is the common way of using sample data to determine the likelihood that the null hypothesis is true.

EXERCISES

19. No

19. In a hypothesis test, is it necessary to assume that the population is approximately normally distributed? Why or why not?

SM

20. What is meant by a significance level of .05?
21. What is the difference between a significance level and an alpha level?
22. An analyst decides to change the significance level from .05 to .10. What happens to beta when this change is made?

23. No

23. Alpha has been set at .01 in a hypothesis test. It is determined that the cost of a type I error is relatively low compared with the cost of a type II error. Is the significance level appropriate for this test?
24. Comment on the statement: The risks in a hypothesis test can be minimized by using a very low significance level.

Hypothesis Tests about a Population Mean: Large Samples

This chapter has provided the background material necessary to test a hypothesis about a population mean. Recall the hypothesis-testing steps established early in the chapter. First, the null and alternative hypotheses are stated. Second, the null hypothesis is assumed true and the appropriate sampling distribution under this assumption identified. Third, a random sample is taken and the appropriate test statistic computed. Finally, the likelihood that the test statistic came from the assumed sampling distribution is computed, and this leads to acceptance or rejection of the null hypothesis.

Example 9.8 The American work force's average age is decreasing according to an article in *Personnel Management* (August 1989). Honeycutt, Inc., wants to determine if its shareholders' average age is also dropping. In 1985 a study showed that its shareholders' mean age was 55.

Since the question involves a downward change only, a one-tailed test is in order. The null and alternative hypotheses are

$$H_0: \mu \geq 55$$
$$H_1: \mu < 55$$

If the null hypothesis is assumed true, the sampling distribution from which the sample mean will be drawn is normal with a mean of 55 years. A random sample of 250 stockholders is drawn from the company's stockholder list and contacted about their ages. The standard deviation of ages in the population of stockholders is assumed to be 12 years, the value established in the 1985 study. Based on these values, the assumed sampling distribution is developed as shown in Figure 9.2.

TM

Figure 9.2 Sampling Distribution of Means for Example 9.8

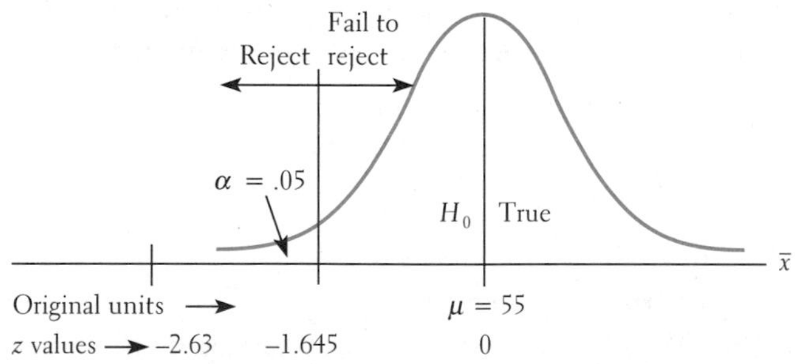

The sampling distribution in Figure 9.2 is based on the assumption that H_0 is true. The sampling distribution has a mean of 55 and standard error of 0.76, based on the known standard deviation of the population and the chosen sample size. A significance level of .05 is chosen, as shown in the figure. With 5% of the curve on the lower end, 45% must lie between the curve mean and the critical value. From the standard normal table, this area corresponds to a z value of 1.645, which is negative since the area lies below the mean.

The decision rule for this hypothesis test is

If the sample mean lies more than 1.645 standard errors below the mean of 55 years, reject the null hypothesis; otherwise fail to reject it (if $z < -1.645$ reject H_0).

We must now compute the sample mean and find how many standard errors below the curve mean it lies. Suppose the sample reveals a mean of 53 years. The sample z value is computed using Equation 9.1. This equation states the necessary calculations in general terms, whereas Equation 9.2 is used specifically to test a hypothesis about a population mean:

$$z = \frac{\bar{x} - \mu}{\sigma_{\bar{x}}} \tag{9.2}$$

where $\bar{x}$ = Sample mean
μ = Hypothesized population mean
$\sigma_{\bar{x}}$ = Standard error of mean

The standard deviation of the sampling distribution (the standard error of the mean) is

$$\sigma_{\bar{x}} = \frac{\sigma}{\sqrt{n}} = \frac{12}{\sqrt{250}} = 0.76$$

$$z = \frac{\bar{x} - \mu}{\sigma_{\bar{x}}} = \frac{53 - 55}{0.76} = -2.63$$

The computed z value (-2.63) is below the critical z value from the standard normal table (-1.645). The decision rule calls for rejection of the null hypothesis. The reasoning is that such a low sample mean is quite unlikely to have come from a sampling distribution with a mean of 55. There is a small chance of error in rejecting the null hypothesis.

EXAMPLE 9.9 Has the average time between telephone orders changed from 3.8 minutes, the mean of two years ago? This is the question facing a telephone mailorder company that has just started selling items based on special promotional materials. Company management is familiar with an article discussing the reasons for reduced business after such an action ("An Alternative Explanation for Lower Repeat Rates after Promotion Purchases," *Journal of Marketing Research*, May 1989, p. 205) and wants to follow repeat business carefully.

A random sample of 100 telephone orders reveals a sample mean of 4 minutes with a standard deviation of 0.5 minutes. A significance level of .02 is chosen for this hypothesis test. Since the question involves a change in either direction from the previous average, the alternative hypothesis will be stated as a two-tailed test. The null and alternative hypotheses are

H_0: $\mu = 3.8$
H_1: $\mu \neq 3.8$

The population standard deviation is unknown but will be estimated using the sample standard deviation, $s = 0.5$. Figure 9.3 shows the appropriate sampling distribution, assuming the null hypothesis is true.

FIGURE 9.3 Sampling Distribution of Means for Example 9.9

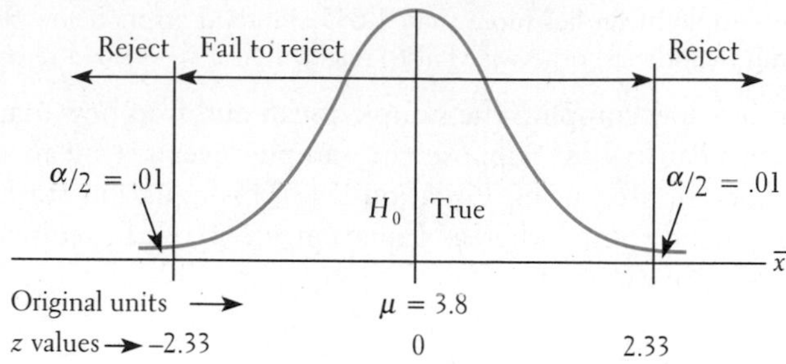

Note in Figure 9.3 that alpha (.02) has been split between the two ends of the curve. Since the alternative hypothesis is nondirectional, a sample mean that's either too large or too small will result in rejection of the null hypothesis. The two critical z values are 2.33 and -2.33, as shown.

The decision rule for this hypothesis test is

> If the sample mean lies more than 2.33 standard errors below or above the mean of 3.8 minutes, reject the null hypothesis; otherwise, fail to reject it (if $z < -2.33$ or $z > 2.33$ reject H_0).

The test z value is calculated from the sample and used to make the decision:

$$s_{\bar{x}} = \frac{s}{\sqrt{n}} = \frac{0.5}{\sqrt{100}} = 0.05$$

$$z = \frac{\bar{x} - \mu}{s_{\bar{x}}} = \frac{4 - 3.8}{0.05} = 4.00$$

Since the test value for z (4.00) is greater than the upper limit ($z = 2.33$), the null hypothesis is rejected. There is, as always, a possibility that a type I error has been committed (the rejected null hypothesis might actually be true).

EXAMPLE 9.10 Human Affairs, a company that markets a motivational training program, claims that the performance ratings of factory workers will rise after completion of the course. To test this claim, the Eastland Corporation, which is considering buying the program, randomly samples 75 employees from the Prentice Hill Corporation, which recently used the program. The average worker rating for Prentice Hill was 75 before the training program; no follow-up study was conducted after completion of the program. The sample evidence is

$$\bar{x} = 77 \qquad s = 13 \qquad n = 75$$

The null and alternative hypotheses for this test are

H_0: $\mu \leq 75$
H_1: $\mu > 75$

If the null hypothesis is assumed true, the sample mean will be drawn from the sampling distribution of Figure 9.4.

FIGURE 9.4 Sampling Distribution of Means for Example 9.10

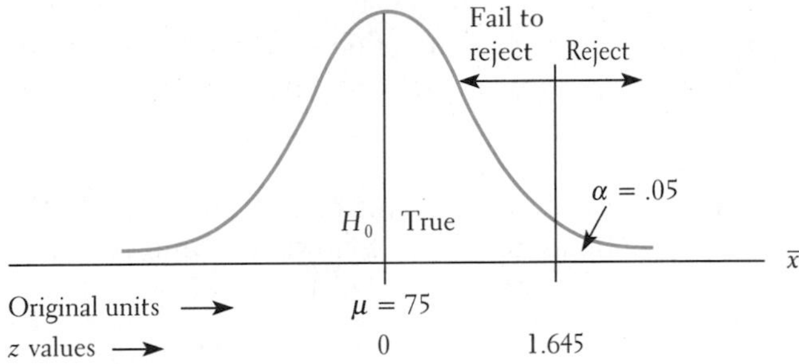

A significance level of .05 is chosen for the test, resulting in the decision rule:

If the sample mean is more than 1.645 standard errors above the assumed population mean of 75, reject the null hypothesis. Otherwise, fail to reject it (if $z > 1.645$ reject H_0).

The z value from the sample data is then calculated:

$$s_{\bar{x}} = \frac{s}{\sqrt{n}} = \frac{13}{\sqrt{75}} = 1.5$$

$$z = \frac{\bar{x} - \mu}{s_{\bar{x}}} = \frac{77 - 75}{1.5} = 1.33$$

Since the calculated z value (1.33) is less than the critical z value (1.645), the null hypothesis is not rejected. There's not enough sample evidence to reject the hypothesis that the population mean is still 75 following completion of the training program. Of course, there's some chance of a type II error, since the null hypothesis might actually be false.

p-VALUES AND HYPOTHESIS TESTING

According to the statistical test procedure illustrated in Examples 9.8 through 9.10, the conclusion is stated in terms of rejecting or not rejecting the null hypothesis based on a reject region (alpha) selected prior to conducting the test. A second method of presenting the results of a statistical test reports the extent to which the test statistic disagrees with the null hypothesis. This method has become popular because analysts want to know what percentage of the sampling distribution lies beyond the sample statistic on the curve, and most statistical computer programs report this result in terms of a *p*-value (probability value). The *p*-value is the probability of observing a sample value as extreme as, or more extreme than, the value observed, given that H_0 is true. This area represents the probability of a type I error if the null hypothesis is rejected. The *p*-value is compared to the alpha value, and, on this basis, the null hypothesis is either rejected or not rejected. If p is less than alpha, the null hypothesis is rejected (if $p < \alpha$, reject H_0). If p is greater than or equal to alpha, the null hypothesis is not rejected (if $p \geq \alpha$, don't reject H_0).

p-Value

The ***p*-value** is the probability of observing a sample value as extreme as, or more extreme than, the value actually observed, given that H_0 is true.

Statistical data analysis programs commonly compute the p-value during the execution of a hypothesis test. The following examples illustrate the way to interpret p-values.

EXAMPLE 9.11 Gene Rice, an assistant coach in the NFL, is preparing for the college draft and wants to test the hypothesis that NFL linemen's mean weight is at least 270 pounds, as reported in a 1992 *Sporting News* article. Gene feels that the mean weight is more than 270 pounds and decides to use the .05 significance level to test the null and alternative hypotheses:

$$H_0: \mu \leq 270$$
$$H_1: \mu > 270$$

Figure 9.5 shows the sampling distribution based on the assumption that the population mean is really 270. The decision rule for this hypothesis test is

If the sample mean is more than 1.645 standard errors above the assumed population mean of 270 pounds, reject the null hypothesis. Otherwise, fail to reject it (if $z > 1.645$ reject H_0).

A random sample of 50 players yields

$$\bar{x} = 281 \qquad s = 35$$

FIGURE 9.5 p-Value Computation for Example 9.11

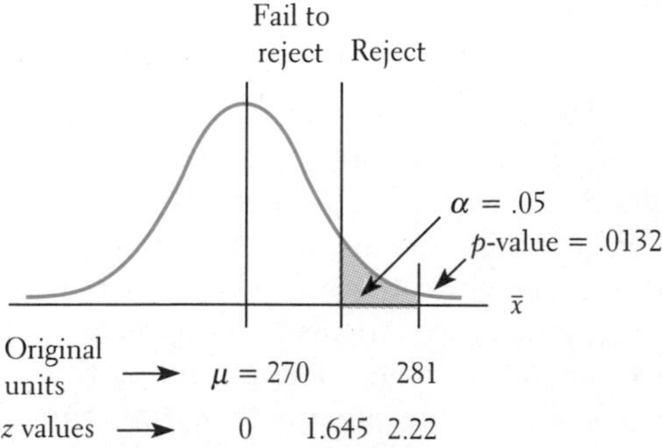

The estimated standard deviation of this sampling distribution is

$$s_{\bar{x}} = \frac{s}{\sqrt{n}} = \frac{35}{\sqrt{50}} = 4.95$$

The z value is

$$z = \frac{281 - 270}{4.95} = 2.22$$

The p-value is determined using the standard normal table. The area between the mean and a z value of 2.22 is .4868. The p-value is the area above the z value (.5000 − .4868 = .0132). The probability of observing a z value at least as large as 2.22 is only .0132 if the null hypothesis is true.

This small p-value represents the risk of rejecting a true null hypothesis. The decision rule is

If p-value $< \alpha$, reject H_0.
If p-value $\geq \alpha$, fail to reject H_0.

Since the p-value is less than the significance level ($.0132 < .05$), the null hypothesis is rejected. Gene has concluded that the mean weight for linemen is more than 270 pounds. The probability that this conclusion is wrong is .0132. Note that if Gene had chosen a .01 significance level, his conclusion would have been to fail to reject. The significance level choice clearly plays a critical part in the hypothesis-testing procedure.

The MINITAB commands to perform the hypothesis test for Example 9.11 are:

```
MTB> ZTEST OF MU=270, ASSUMING SIGMA=35, ON C1;
SUBC> ALTERNATIVE +1.
```

The output for this test is:

```
TEST OF MU = 270 VS MU G.T. 270
THE ASSUMED SIGMA = 35

      N   MEAN  STDEV  SE MEAN     Z   P VALUE
C1   50    281     35     4.95  2.22     .0132

MTB> STOP
```

The ZTEST command is used to test the null hypothesis that $\mu = 270$. The standard deviation of 35 is assumed based on the sample data stored in C1. The ALTERNATIVE +1 subcommand tests the null against the alternative hypothesis that $\mu >$ 270. Note that the ALTERNATIVE +1 subcommand tells the program to do a one-tailed test above the mean. ALTERNATIVE −1 means to test one-tailed below the mean. If there is no ALTERNATIVE subcommand, a two-tailed test is performed.

The p-values for Examples 9.8 through 9.10 are now computed. When Example 9.8 is run on a computer program, a p-value of .0043 results. Since this p-value is less than the significance level ($.0043 < .05$), the null hypothesis is rejected.

A z value of -2.63, from the standard normal table, represents an area of .4957 below the mean. Since the area on the lower end of the curve below the z value is wanted, .4957 is subtracted from .5000. Thus, the p-value is

$$p\text{-value} = .5000 - .4957 = .0043 \text{ (area below a } z \text{ value of } -2.63)$$

When Example 9.9 is run on a computer program, the result is a p-value of .00006. Since the p-value is less than the significance level ($.00006 < .02$), the null hypothesis is rejected. Note that for a two-tailed test the p-value is determined by doubling the area above the z value.

A z value of 4.00, from the standard normal table, includes an area of .49997 above the mean. Since the area on the upper end of the curve above the z value is wanted, .49997 is subtracted from .5000. The p-value is

$$p\text{-value} = 2(.5000 - .49997) = 2(.00003) = .00006$$

When Example 9.10 is run on a computer program, the result is a p-value of .0918. Since the p-value is greater than the significance level ($.0918 > .05$), the null hypothesis is not rejected.

A z value of 1.33, from the standard normal table, includes an area of .4082 above the mean. Since the area above the z value of 1.33 is wanted, .4082 is subtracted from .5000:

$$p\text{-value} = .5000 - .4082 = .0918 \text{ (area above a } z \text{ value of } 1.33)$$

Steps for computing p-values:

1. Determine the value of the test statistic (z or t) computed using the sample data.

2a. If the test is one-tailed, the p-value is equal to the area beyond the z or t.

2b. If the test is two-tailed, the p-value equals twice the area beyond the observed z or t.

■ SITUATION 9.1—RESOLVED The hypothesis test formulated by the Johnsons can now be executed. The sample data are

$$\bar{x} = 415 \qquad s = 30 \qquad n = 55$$

The null and alternative hypotheses are

$$H_0\colon \mu \geq 425$$
$$H_1\colon \mu < 425$$

Since the sample size is greater than 30, the sampling distribution of means can be assumed normal without knowledge of the shape of the population distribution. The sampling distribution has a mean of 425, assuming the null hypothesis is true.

Figure 9.6 shows the sampling distribution and the decision rule z value based on a significance level of .05. The decision rule is

> If the sample mean is more than 1.645 standard errors below the assumed population mean of 425 hours, reject the null hypothesis; otherwise, fail to reject it (if $z < -1.645$ reject H_0).

FIGURE 9.6 Sampling Distribution of Means for Situation 9.1

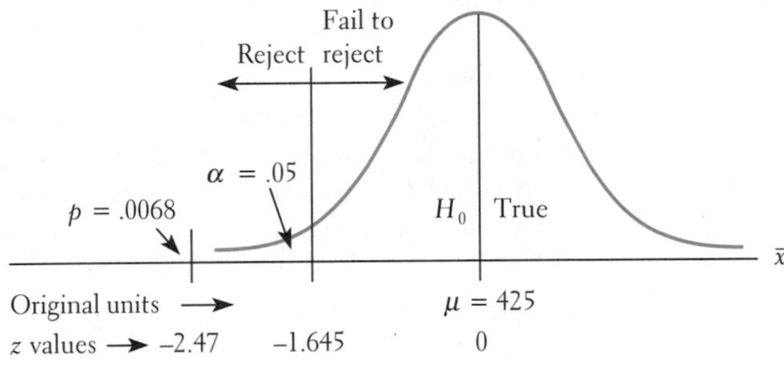

The sample z value is now calculated and compared with the table z value of -1.645. The calculation is

$$s_{\bar{x}} = \frac{s}{\sqrt{n}} = \frac{30}{\sqrt{55}} = 4.05$$

$$z = \frac{\bar{x} - \mu}{s_{\bar{x}}} = \frac{415 - 425}{4.05} = -2.47$$

Since the calculated z value (-2.47) is less than the critical value of z (-1.645), the null hypothesis is rejected. The possibility of a type I error must be considered; however, the chance of this error is quite low. In fact, there is only a 5% chance that the Johnsons could reject a true null hypothesis since 5% was the significance level, or alpha, chosen at the start of the test.

When Situation 9.1 is run on a computer program, the result is a p-value of .0068. Since the p-value is less than the significance level ($.0068 < .05$), the null hypothesis is rejected.

A z value of -2.47, from the standard normal table, includes an area of .4932 below the mean, as shown in Figure 9.6. Since the area on the lower end of the curve beyond the z value is wanted, .4932 is subtracted from .5000:

$$p\text{-value} = .5000 - .4932 = .0068 \text{ (area below a } z \text{ value of } -2.47)$$

The probability of observing a sample mean as extreme as 415, given that the population mean is actually 425, is .0068. ■

EXERCISES

25. Under what conditions is it necessary to assume that the population being sampled is approximately normal?

26. Reject H_0 if $z < -1.04$
$z = -2.92$, reject type I
p-value = .0018

26. Bill Ford, manager of the Bon Resort Hotel, believes that the average guest bill is at least \$400. The population is normally distributed with a standard deviation of \$60. State the decision rule for a significance level of .15 if a sample of 49 guest bills are surveyed. If the sample mean is \$375, what should Bill's conclusion be? Explain what type of error might have been made. Compute the p-value.

27. $z = 10$, reject
p-value = .0000

27. A manufacturing assembly line operation has a scheduled mean completion time of 30 minutes. The population has a standard deviation of 4 minutes. State the decision rule for a sample of 64 observations tested at the .01 significance level. State the appropriate conclusion if the sample mean is 35 minutes. Explain what type of error might have been made. Compute the p-value.

28. $z = -7.3$, reject
p-value = .0000

28. The Howell Manufacturing Company produces bearings. Past experience shows that the production process is normally distributed and produces bearings with an average diameter of 2.1 inches and standard deviation of 0.12 inch. Nineteen bearings are randomly selected from the production process and have a mean diameter of 1.9 inches. What would you conclude if you tested at the .05 significance level? Compute the p-value.

29. $z = 7.5$, reject
p-value = .0000

29. A university statistics professor has been asked to develop a way of determining profitable bank customers. The bank hired the professor after management read "Teaching Old Bankers New Tricks," in *Bankers Monthly* (February 1990, p. 58). This article discusses ways of improving bankers' performance and generating higher profits. Management wants a good description of a profitable customer, and the professor begins studying profitability.

Five years ago a study was conducted that showed an average service charge for checking accounts of \$3.20 with standard deviation of \$0.40. The professor is interested in detecting a situation for which the average service charge is either greater than or less than \$3.20. What should she conclude at the .01 significance level if a sample of 100 accounts has a mean service charge of \$3.50?

Hypothesis Tests about a Population Mean: Small Samples

Small-Sample Mean Test

When the sample size is small (less than 30), the distribution of the population from which the sample was selected must be assumed to be approximately normal. If this assumption can be made and the population standard deviation is known, the sampling distribution of sample means can be assumed to be normally distributed. If the population standard deviation is unknown, the sampling distribution of sample means is described by the t distribution. The test statistic is computed using Equation 9.3:

$$t = \frac{\bar{x} - \mu}{s_{\bar{x}}} \qquad (9.3)$$

where $\bar{x}$ = Sample mean
μ = Hypothesized population mean
$s_{\bar{x}}$ = Estimated standard error of the mean $\left(\frac{s}{\sqrt{n}}\right)$

When the sample size is small and the population is nonnormal, nonparametric tests such as those discussed in Chapter 19 are used. Figure 8.3 summarized the procedure for determining the appropriate sampling distribution of sample means for hypothesis tests about a population mean.

EXAMPLE 9.12 The Tapico Corporation is concerned about the breaking strength of the steel cables made in its plant. A major buyer is interested in purchasing a large number of cables and has stated that the average breaking point must not be less than one ton. Tapico thinks that one ton is the approximate breaking point of the cables, but decides to test the hypothesis that the average (mean) breaking strength is one ton against the alternative that it is less.

This situation suggests a very small sample size. The cables to be tested will each be broken and the weight at breakage recorded. The average of these breaking points will then be used to test the null hypothesis. A small sample size is appropriate because each sampled item is destroyed in the process. A large sample would be too costly.

The null and alternative hypotheses are

$$H_0: \mu \geq 1$$
$$H_1: \mu < 1$$

Tapico decides it can afford to break 10 cables and designs a process to do so. A significance level of .05 is chosen for the test. The sample results are

$$\bar{x} = 0.96 \text{ tons} \qquad s = 0.15 \text{ tons} \qquad n = 10$$

This hypothesis test involves a different sampling distribution. When there's a small sample size (usually considered less than 30) and the population standard deviation is unknown (and estimated by the sample standard deviation, s), the t distribution is the correct sampling distribution if the population is assumed to be normal. After reviewing its cables' breaking points, the company decides that these weights are probably distributed in a bell-shaped manner about their mean, and that a normal distribution is an appropriate assumption. Figure 9.7 summarizes the test.

TM

FIGURE 9.7 t Distribution Hypothesis Test for Example 9.12

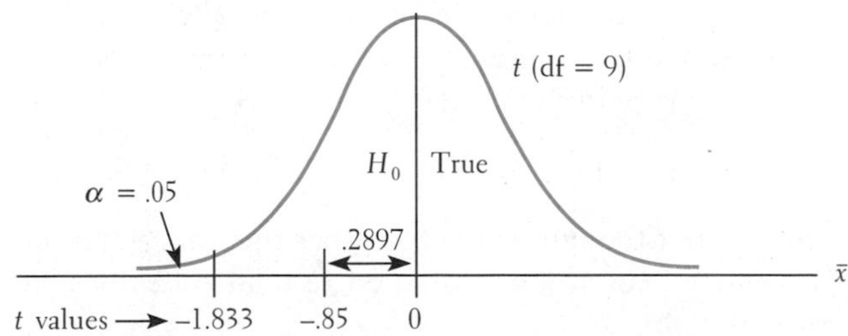

The critical value for the test is found in the t table in Appendix E.7. As demonstrated in Chapter 8, to use this table, you must know the area on one end of the curve. Since this is a one-tailed test and alpha is .05, this area is .05. Thus, the .05 column at the bottom of the t table is used to find the critical value.

You must also know the degrees of freedom ($n - 1$) for the test. For a sample size of 10, the number of degrees of freedom is 9 ($10 - 1$). The critical value observed from the t table is 1.833. Since this value is below the curve mean, it's negative (−1.833), as Figure 9.7 shows.

The decision rule is

> If the sample mean is more than 1.833 standard errors below the assumed population mean of one ton, reject the null hypothesis; otherwise, fail to reject it (if $t < -1.833$ reject H_0).

For this test, using Equation 9.3

$$s_{\bar{x}} = \frac{s}{\sqrt{n}} = \frac{0.15}{\sqrt{10}} = 0.047$$

$$t = \frac{\bar{x} - \mu}{s_{\bar{x}}} = \frac{0.96 - 1}{0.047} = -0.85$$

Since the test t value (−0.85) isn't below the critical value (−1.833), the null hypothesis is not rejected. According to this hypothesis test, the company is justified in advertising an average breaking weight of one ton. However, a type II error is possible. If the average breaking weight is less than one ton, a type II error could be very costly. Perhaps the expense of a larger sample should be incurred to ensure that customer problems don't arise later.

When Example 9.12 is run on a computer program, the result is a p-value of approximately .2087. Since the p-value is greater than the significance level (.2087 > .05), the null hypothesis is not rejected.

The MINITAB commands to find the p-value for Example 9.12 are

```
MTB> CDE -.85;
SUBC> +.9.
-.85   .2087
```

EXAMPLE 9.13 In Example 8.9, Jean Simmons, a Dallas health store owner, decided to test the average fat content per pound of hamburger sold in Dallas stores. To do so, she purchased one pound of hamburger from each of nine randomly selected stores. She cooked the hamburger, poured off the fat, and weighed it. The results for each of the stores, in ounces of fat, were

3.3 4.8 5.1 4.5 4.0 3.9 4.7 5.0 3.6

Jean wants to test the null hypothesis that the average fat level is 4.0 ounces using the .05 significance level and a two-tailed test. She assumes that the population is normally distributed.

Since the sample size is only 9 and the population standard deviation isn't known, the t test based on 8 degrees of freedom is appropriate. The decision rule is

> If the sample mean is more than 2.306 standard errors below or above the assumed population mean of 4.0 ounces, reject the null hypothesis; otherwise, fail to reject it (if $t < -2.306$ or $t > 2.306$ reject H_0).

For this test, using Equation 9.3

$$s_{\bar{x}} = \frac{s}{\sqrt{n}} = \frac{0.644}{\sqrt{9}} = 0.215$$

$$t = \frac{\bar{x} - \mu}{s_{\bar{x}}} = \frac{(4.322 - 4.0)}{0.215} = 1.5$$

Since the test t value (1.5) is not greater than the critical value (2.306), the null hypothesis is not rejected. According to this hypothesis test, Jean can't reject the premise that the average fat content of the hamburger is 4.0 ounces. The p-value, .17, shown in the MINITAB output, gives the probability of observing a sample mean as extreme as 4.322, if the population mean is actually 4.0.

The MINITAB software package can be used for hypothesis testing. The MINITAB commands to solve Example 9.13 are:

```
MTB> SET INTO C1
DATA> 3.3 4.8 5.1 4.5 4.0 3.9 4.7 5.0 3.6
DATA> END
MTB> DESCRIBE C1

C1    N    MEAN    MEDIAN    STDEV
      9   4.322    4.500     0.644

C1    MIN     MAX      Q1       Q3
      3.30    5.100    3.750    4.9400

MTB> TTEST OF MU = 4.0 ON C1

TEST OF MU = 4.0 VS MU N.E. 4.0

  N     MEAN    STDEV    SE MEAN          T    P VALUE
  9    4.322    0.644      0.215        1.5    .17

MTB> STOP
```

The TTEST command is used to test the null hypothesis that $\mu = 4$. Since there's no ALTERNATIVE subcommand, the alternative hypothesis is two-tailed, H_1: $\mu \neq 4$. This t test will use the standard deviation of the sample data stored in C1.

EXERCISES

30. When should the t distribution be used?

31. Steel Wheel Tires claims that its tires have a mean tread life of at least 45,000 miles. Suppose a test yielded results of $n = 22$, $\bar{x} = 43{,}000$, $s = 3{,}000$.
    a. State the null and alternative hypotheses.
    b. State the decision rule if the hypothesis is tested at the 1% significance level.
    c. State the appropriate conclusion.
    d. What type of error might be made?
    e. Estimate the p-value.

31*a.* $\mu \geq 45{,}000$
$\mu < 45{,}000$
b. Reject H_0 if $t < -2.518$
c. Reject
d. Type I
e. .007

32. $z = -3.5$, reject

32. The employees' union claims that average seniority is at least 12 years for the TCA Corporation. In a random sample of 49 employees, average seniority is found to be 11.5 years with standard deviation of 1 year. Test the union's claim at the .02 significance level.

33. $s = .9$, $t = -.74$, fail to reject

33. The Canon Toy Company buys batteries for its electric toys. The supplier guarantees that the batteries will last an average of 19 hours. After receiving customer complaints, Canon randomly selects 10 batteries from its stock and measures their duration. The results are

1	18.0
2	18.4
3	19.0
4	20.2
5	19.6
6	18.6
7	19.4
8	19.2
9	17.0
10	18.5

Assuming that these batteries' lifetimes are normally distributed, test the supplier's guarantee at the .10 significance level.

Hypothesis Tests about a Population Proportion

So far, this chapter has presented situations where the average (mean) value of a population is tested (e.g., the average time between machine breakdowns, the average age of stockholders, and the average breaking strength of steel cables).

Analysts are also interested in the percentage of items in a population that meet certain specifications. Politicians are concerned with the percentage of voters who favor a particular issue, government agencies want to know about the percentage of people unemployed, and business managers are interested in the percentage of parts produced or purchased that are defective.

As with the population mean, if the population percentage is unknown and information about its value is desired, a random sample is drawn from the population, the sample percentage computed, and this value used as an estimate of the unknown population value. (Chapter 8 discussed this estimation process.) On the other hand, if a claim about the population percentage has been made sample evidence can be used to reject or fail to reject this claim. This hypothesis-testing procedure for proportions is discussed next.

The testing methodology depends on whether a small sample or a large sample is used. For small samples ($n \leq 20$) the binomial distribution is used. For large samples ($n > 20$) the normal distribution is acceptable if $np > 5$ and $n(1 - p) > 5$. Since most proportion analyses involve large samples, only the large-sample test is discussed here.

Test for a Population Proportion

Large-sample tests of means and proportions are very similar, since the sampling distribution for each is the normal distribution. As Equation 9.4 shows, the difference between the sample proportion and the hypothesized or claimed population proportion is divided by the standard error of the sampling distribution of proportions to produce the test statistic:

$$z = \frac{x/n - p}{\sigma_{\bar{p}}} \tag{9.4}$$

where x = Number of sample successes
n = Sample size
p = Hypothesized population proportion
$\sigma_{\bar{p}}$ = Standard error of the proportion

Remember from Equation 7.3 that x/n is equal to the sample proportion, $\bar{p}$.

■ SITUATION 9.2 Sue and Bill Johnson turn their attention to the quality of another product their company makes: an acidic compound used in making an over-the-counter pain relief product. According to their own quality-control standards, no more than 3% of the 200-pound batches produced in the factory can fail a very thorough and time-consuming series of chemical analysis tests. A failure means that the product is not acceptable to Johnson's customers.

The null hypothesis to be tested is that the percentage of failed batches over a long period of time is 3% or less, against the alternative that it is more than 3%. Thus, the one-tailed test involves the following two hypotheses:

H_0: $p \leq .03$
H_1: $p > .03$

As discussed in Chapter 8, the appropriate sampling distribution for large-sample proportions is the normal distribution. The mean of this distribution is the population proportion, and the standard error of the distribution is $\sigma_{\bar{p}} = \sqrt{p(1 - p)/n}$. ■

EXAMPLE 9.14 Kawneer Architectural Products is checking the production of steel cable conduits in its main plant. Since these components are usually enclosed in walls and other structures, the quality level must be quite high. A quality improvement program has been underway on the conduit line for the past six months, and the foreman claims that the previous defective rate of 2% has been reduced. Kawneer's management decides to test this claim.

Since the foreman claims a difference on the down side, a one-tailed test is appropriate. Thus, the hypotheses are

H_0: $p \geq .02$
H_1: $p < .02$

A random sample of conduits is selected over the next two weeks. A total of 358 are chosen, and, of these, 4 are found to be defective. The sample evidence is

$$n = 358 \qquad \bar{p} = 4/358 = .0112$$

Kawneer Architectural Products decides to take a 10% chance of rejecting the null hypothesis if it's true. Since the test is one-tailed, an area of .4000 (.5000 − .1000) is looked up in the standard normal table. This results in a critical z value of -1.28 (negative because it's below the curve mean). Figure 9.8 summarizes the hypothesis test.

FIGURE 9.8 Sampling Distribution of $\bar{p}$ for Example 9.14

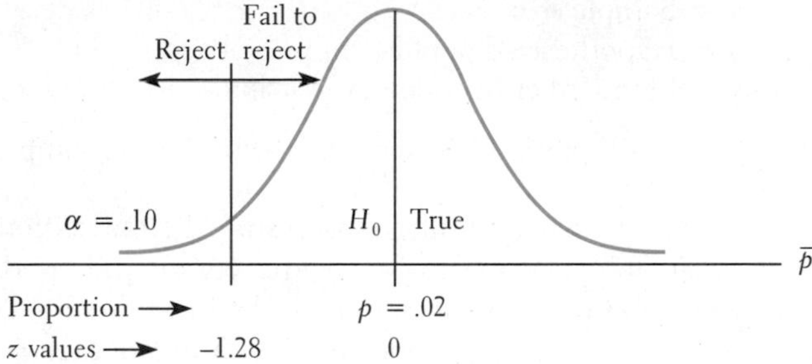

The decision rule for this hypothesis test is

If the sample proportion lies more than 1.28 standard errors below the proportion of .02 defectives, reject the null hypothesis; otherwise, fail to reject it (if $z < -1.28$ reject H_0).

The test value of z is computed:

$$\sigma_{\bar{p}} = \sqrt{\frac{p(1-p)}{n}} = \sqrt{\frac{.02(1-.02)}{358}} = .0074$$

$$z = \frac{\bar{p}-p}{\sigma_{\bar{p}}} = \frac{.0112-.02}{.0074} = \frac{-.0088}{.0074} = -1.19$$

Since the test value of z (-1.19) isn't below the critical value of z (-1.28), the null hypothesis is not rejected. At the .10 significance level, the conduit foreman is *not* justified in claiming improved quality. Based on the sample evidence, Kawneer can't conclude that their conduit production line's quality improvement program has been successful.

When Example 9.14 is run on a computer program, the result is a p-value of .1170. Since the p-value is greater than the significance level $(.1170 > .10)$, the null hypothesis is not rejected.

A z value of -1.19, from the standard normal table, includes an area of .3830 below the mean. Since the area on the lower end of the curve beyond the z value is wanted, .3830 is subtracted from .5000. The p-value is

$$p\text{-value} = .5000 - .3830 = .1170 \text{ (area below a } z \text{ value of } -1.19)$$

EXAMPLE 9.15 An article in the *Free China Review* (May 1992, page 26) discusses the severe competition from newly opened banks, forcing existing financial institutions to improve their products and services. Stockton International, such an institution, is trying to improve its accounts receivable levels in Taiwan.

For several years, the percentage of accounts receivable that are past due each month has been around 6%. The accounting department thinks it has evidence that economic conditions have caused this percentage to increase. A hypothesis test seems in order.

During the past month, Stockton issued invoices to 478 suppliers. Of these, 42 are past due. The sample evidence is

$$n = 478 \qquad \bar{p} = 42/478 = .0879$$

The accounting department points to the past-due rate of nearly 9% as an indication that measures need to be taken to ensure prompt payment on the part of all suppliers. Stockton management isn't sure the sample size justifies this action. The null and alternative hypotheses are formulated:

$$H_0\colon p \le .06$$
$$H_1\colon p > .06$$

Stockton chooses a significance level of 5%, resulting in the hypothesis test diagram in Figure 9.9.

FIGURE 9.9 Sampling Distribution of $\bar{p}$ for Example 9.15

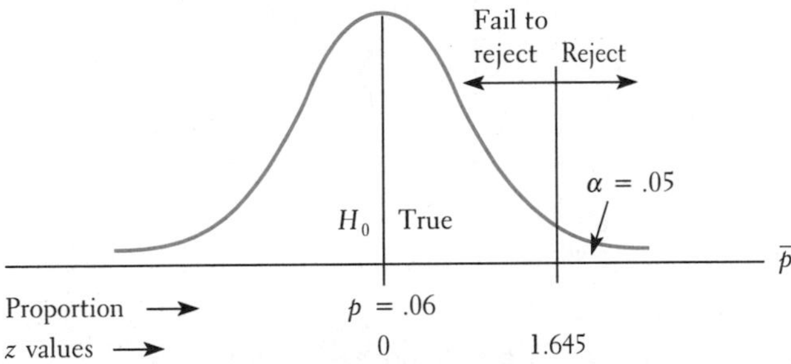

The decision rule for this hypothesis test is

If the sample proportion lies more than 1.645 standard errors above the proportion .06, reject the null hypothesis; otherwise, fail to reject it (if $z > 1.645$ reject H_0).

The test z value is computed:

$$\sigma_{\bar{p}} = \sqrt{\frac{p(1-p)}{n}} = \sqrt{\frac{.06(1-.06)}{478}} = .011$$

$$z = \frac{\bar{p} - p}{\sigma_{\bar{p}}} = \frac{.0879 - .06}{.011} = \frac{.0279}{.011} = 2.54$$

The large test z value results in rejection of the null hypothesis (since $2.54 > 1.645$). It appears that the accounting department is right: there seems to have been an increase in the percentage of past-due accounts receivable, and corrective action is required.

When Example 9.15 is run on a computer program, the result is a p-value of .0055. Since the p-value is less than the significance level ($.0055 < .05$), the null hypothesis is rejected. The probability of observing a sample proportion as extreme as .0879, given that the population proportion is actually .06, is .0055.

The p-value was computed by looking up a z value of 2.54, from the standard normal table, which includes an area of .4945 above the mean. Since the area on the upper end of the curve beyond the z value is wanted, .4945 is subtracted from .5000:

$$p\text{-value} = .5000 - .4945 = .0055 \text{ (area above a } z \text{ value of 2.54)}$$

■ SITUATION 9.2—RESOLVED The Johnsons wish to test the hypothesis that substandard batches still amount to 3% of total production against the alternative that this percentage has increased. A significance level of .02 is chosen for this one-tailed test, resulting in the sampling distribution in Figure 9.10.

FIGURE 9.10 Sampling Distribution of $\bar{p}$ for Situation 9.2

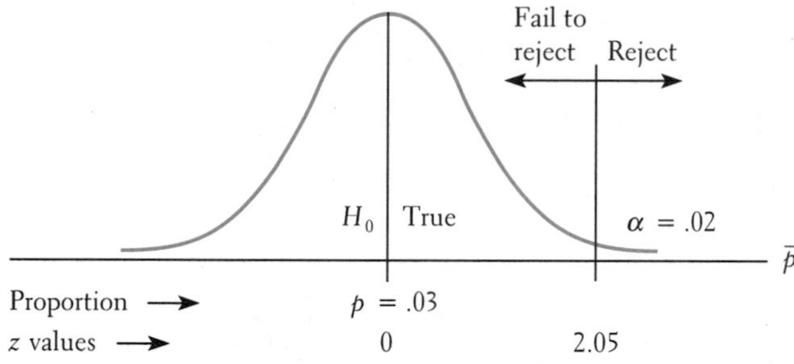

The decision rule for this hypothesis test is

If the sample proportion lies more than 2.05 standard errors above the proportion of .03 defectives, reject the null hypothesis; otherwise, fail to reject it (if $z > 2.05$ reject H_0).

A random sample of batches is drawn from various shifts over the next month. Each batch is closely inspected to determine whether it is substandard. At the end of the month, it's found that of the 180 batches inspected, 8 are substandard. The sample evidence can be stated as

$$n = 180 \qquad \bar{p} = 8/180 = .0444$$

The sample proportion (.0444) is above the acceptable population proportion specified in the null hypothesis (.03). Does the sample size of 180 provide enough sample evidence to reject the null hypothesis?

The test value for z is computed based on the sample proportion of .0444 and the sample size of 180:

$$\sigma_{\bar{p}} = \sqrt{\frac{p(1-p)}{n}} = \sqrt{\frac{.03(1-.03)}{180}} = .0127$$

$$z = \frac{\bar{p} - p}{\sigma_{\bar{p}}} = \frac{.0444 - .03}{.0127} = 1.13$$

The computed z value (1.13) is less than the critical z value from the standard normal table (2.05). The null hypothesis that the substandard rate for the batches is still 3% is not rejected. Since the null hypothesis has not been rejected, there's some chance that a type II error has occurred.

Running Situation 9.2 on a computer program results in a p-value of .1292. Since the p-value is greater than the significance level ($.1292 > .02$), the null hypothesis is not rejected.

A z value of 1.13, from the standard normal table, represents an area of .3708 above the mean. Since the area on the upper end of the curve beyond the z value is wanted, .3708 is subtracted from .5000:

$$p\text{-value} = .5000 - .3708 = .1292 \text{ (area above a } z \text{ value of } 1.13) \quad ■$$

EXERCISES

34. What are the similarities and differences between the test procedure for means and the test procedure for proportions?

35. What sampling distribution is appropriate for tests of proportions when the sample size is small? When the sample size is large?

36. Steve Peel is considering purchasing a business. The business has stated that no more than 25% of its accounts receivable are more than 30 days past due. In a sample of 50 accounts, the sample proportion is tested at the .05 significance level. State the null and alternative hypotheses and the appropriate decision rule. State the conclusion if the sample proportion, $\bar{p}$, is .29. Explain what type of error might have been made.

36. $p \leq .25$; $p > .25$; Reject H_0 if $z > 1.645$; $z = .653$; fail to reject

37. Jack Knive knows from past experience that 12% of the recipients of auto loans from the Community Credit Union default within the first year. Jack feels that the default rate is increasing. If he obtains evidence that the percentage of customers who default is now greater than 12%, the credit union will revise its guidelines for granting auto loans. A random sample of 150 customers who received loans a year ago indicates that 23 have since defaulted. State the null and alternative hypotheses and the appropriate decision rule. State your conclusion and explain what type of error might have been made.

37. $p \leq .12$; $p > .12$

38. The Neptune Automobile Company advertises that 90% of the owners of new Neptunes are satisfied with their purchase. Center Neptune in Green Bay, Wisconsin, wants to determine if this is true for its own customers. Of 40 customers contacted, 35 indicate they're satisfied. Is the percentage of all Center Neptune customers that are satisfied as high as the advertisement indicates? Test at the .01 significance level.

38. $p \geq .90$; $p < .90$; Reject H_0 if $z < -2.575$; $z = -.527$, fail to reject

39. According to *The Wall Street Journal* (May 25, 1988), the percentage of 10-to-19 year-olds who drink coffee was 8.9% in 1984. In 1988, a sample of 742 young people showed that 5.3% drank coffee. Is the conclusion that a lower percentage of young people were drinking coffee in 1988 justified using a .01 significance level?

39. $z = -3.44$, reject

40. Four years ago the proportion of college graduates in Appendix C's company data base was .25. You feel that this proportion has increased. State the null and alternative hypotheses. Select a simple random sample of 25 observations from the data base and test your hypothesis at the .15 significance level.

Type II Errors, Operating Characteristic Curves, and Power Curves

So far in this chapter, attention has been directed toward assessing the probability of a type I error. Each figure summarizing a hypothesis test reflects the necessary assumption that the null hypothesis is true. But what if it's false? A type II error occurs when a false null hypothesis is not rejected.

Under the assumption that the null hypothesis is true, a single value for the population parameter under test is specified. For example, in Situation 9.1 the Johnsons tested the hypothesis that the mean acidity/potency measurement of batches sent to Anderson was 425 units. If this hypothesis is assumed true, the correct sampling distribution is the one with a population mean of 425 (see Figure 9.11*a*). Figure 9.11*a* also shows the probability of the sample results leading to an incorrect decision. This error is the incorrect rejection of a true null hypothesis—a type I error—and the probability of it occurring is alpha.

However, suppose the null hypothesis is false. If the true population mean isn't 425, what is it? There are many—in fact, an infinite number of—values that the population mean could be if it's not 425. For this reason, asking for the probability of a type II error in a hypothesis test isn't a fair question. The probability of a type II error can be determined only if the population mean is specified.

Referring to the Johnson's batch problem (Situation 9.1), the Johnsons decide to assess the probability of a type II error. They're satisfied with the type I error probability chosen ($\alpha = .05$), but are now concerned about the chances of failing to reject the null hypothesis if it is false. The situation summarized is

$$H_0: \mu \geq 425$$
$$H_1: \mu < 425$$
$$n = 55 \qquad s = 30 \qquad \alpha = .05$$

Note that these specifications don't include the sample mean. The present concern is with assessing the probabilities of error, not with failing to reject or rejecting the null hypothesis, so the sample mean isn't needed.

In the selection of alpha (the probability of a type I error), the Johnsons must think about the penalty associated with such an error and decide on the acceptable probability of incurring this penalty. They have decided that a 5% chance of rejecting a true null hypothesis is acceptable.

Determining the chance of a type II error is more difficult. Since there are many values that the population mean could be, if it's not as specified in the null hypothesis, several representative values of the mean must be chosen. For each of these, the probability of a type II error (beta) is computed. The Johnsons pick three possible values for the population mean, other than the null hypothesis value of 425, and then compute the probability of a type II error for each. The chosen values are 421, 418, and

FIGURE 9.11 Type II Error

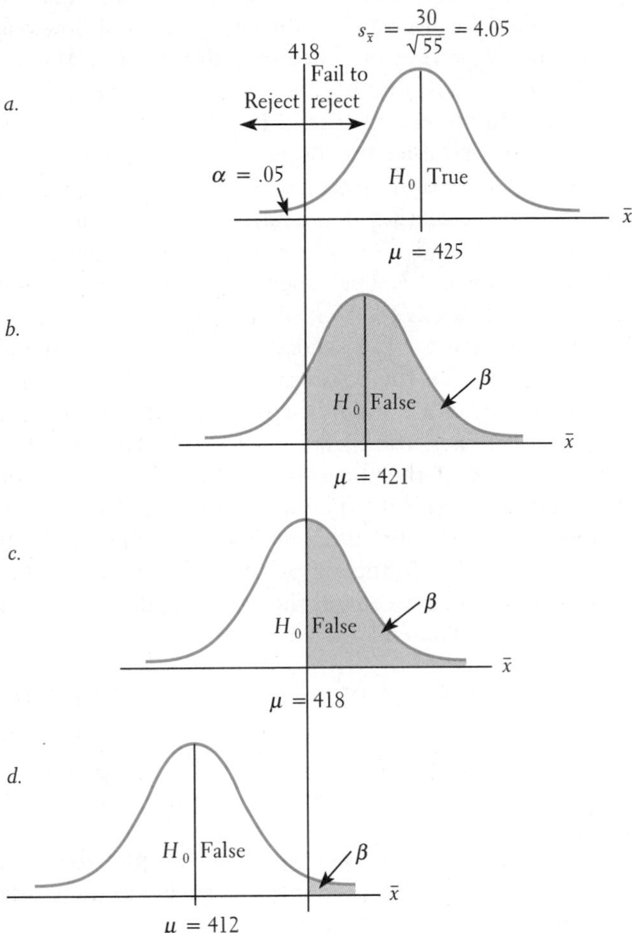

412 units. The Johnsons believe that knowing the probabilities of accepting the false null hypothesis for each of these three values will enable them to assess the level of accuracy for their chosen sample size. In other words, they wish to complete the entries in Table 9.2.

TABLE 9.2 Type II Errors

Population mean (μ)	Probability of accepting a false null hypothesis (β)
421	?
418	?
412	?

By choosing several representative values for the unknown population mean, they can assess the risks associated with failing to reject a false null hypothesis. The three values in Table 9.2 will give the Johnsons an idea of how risky their hypothesis test is with regard to a type II error. Since they already know the probability of a type I error, this will put them in a good position to decide if the risk level is acceptable.

The probability of committing a type II error must be computed for each of the three representative values for the population mean in Table 9.2. Figure 9.11*a* shows the sampling distribution associated with the null hypothesis being true, along with the probability of rejecting it (alpha). Figure 9.11 also shows three other sampling distributions—*b*, *c*, and *d*—each reflecting one of the chosen alternative population mean values of Table 9.2. The probability that the false null hypothesis won't be rejected (beta) is shown as the shaded area in each diagram.

After each of Figure 9.11's shaded areas is determined and the values for Table 9.2 computed, a picture of the potential for a type II error emerges. Each shaded area in Figure 9.11 is part of a normal distribution. To use a normal curve to find areas, we must know two things: the mean and the standard deviation (standard error). Table 9.2 lists the means of the three distributions in Figure 9.11. The standard error for each is assumed to be 4.05. This assumption is based on the idea that even if the population mean is slightly different from 425, the standard deviation of the population will still be about 30, the sample standard deviation. If this is true, then the same standard error should exist for all the sampling distributions being considered, since $n = 55$ for each. The shaded areas for each of the alternative hypothesis curves in Figure 9.11 are now found.

The critical value for rejection of the null hypothesis is the point on the curve that is z standard errors below the assumed population mean of 425, or

$$425 - 1.645(4.05) = 418.34 \text{ (rounded to 418)}$$

Figure 9.11*a* shows this value.

If the population mean is actually 421, the probability of failing to reject a false null hypothesis (making a type II error) is shown as the shaded region in Figure 9.11*b*. The computations for this area are

$$z = \frac{418 - 421}{4.05} = -0.74 \rightarrow .2704 \text{ (area between 418 and 421 in Figure 9.11}b\text{)}$$

$$\beta = .5000 + .2704 = .7704 \quad \text{(area above 418 in Figure 9.11}b\text{)}$$

If the population mean is actually 418, the probability of making a type II error is shown in Figure 9.11*c*. In this case, $\beta = .5000$, since half of the curve is above 418.

If the population mean is actually 412, the probability of making a type II error is shown in Figure 9.11*d*. The computations are

$$z = \frac{418 - 412}{4.05} = 1.48 \rightarrow .4306 \text{ (area between 412 and 418 in Figure 9.11}d\text{)}$$

$$\beta = .5000 - .4306 = .0694 \quad \text{(area above 418 in Figure 9.11}d\text{)}$$

OC Curve

The three beta values are entered beside their respective population mean values in Table 9.3. When these values are plotted, the result is called the **operating characteristic curve** (OC curve) for the hypothesis test (see Figure 9.12). Note that the curve has been hand-fitted to the three calculated values.

TABLE 9.3 Operating Characteristic Curve Values

Population mean (μ)	β (error)
421	.77
418	.50
412	.07

FIGURE 9.12 Operating Characteristic Curve

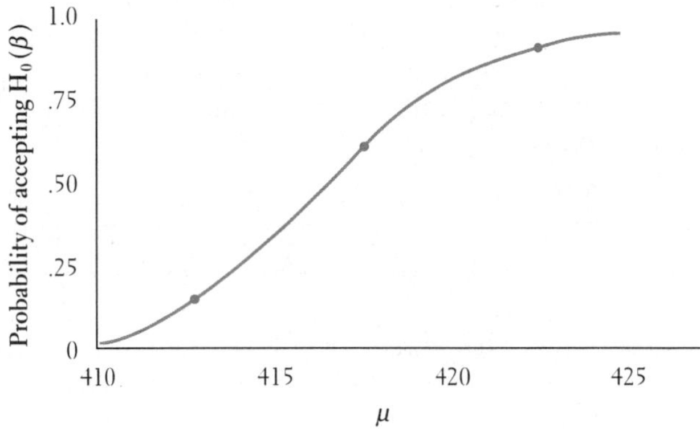

Power Curve

We can also designate the probability of correctly rejecting a false null hypothesis $(1 - \beta)$. Table 9.4 gives these values for the selected population means. A curve plotted through these values is called the **power curve** of the test and appears in Figure 9.13.

TABLE 9.4 Power Curve Values

Population mean (μ)	$1 - \beta$ (correct decision)
421	.23
418	.50
412	.93

Table 9.3 and Figure 9.12 show the probabilities of committing a type II error under three different population mean alternatives. Table 9.4 and Figure 9.13 show the likelihood of reaching the correct conclusion under these same conditions. The operating characteristic curve shows the probability of making a type II error, and the power

FIGURE 9.13 Power Curve

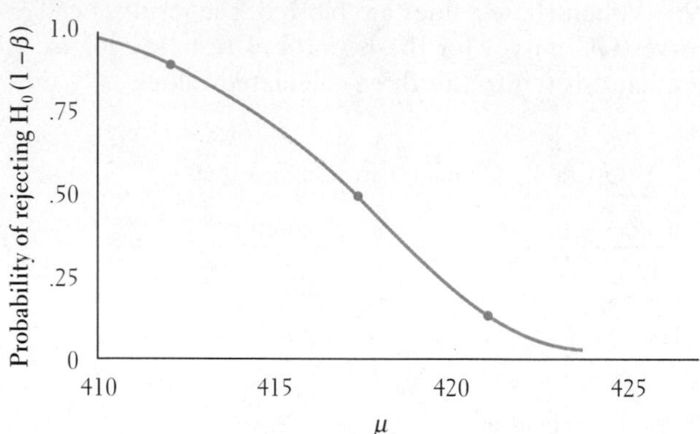

curve shows the probability of correctly rejecting a false null hypothesis. The power curve is used more frequently because it indicates the power of the test to correctly detect a false null hypothesis.

> The **operating characteristic curve** for a hypothesis test shows the probability of failing to reject a false null hypothesis for each possible value of the true population parameter. The **power curve** shows the probability of rejecting a false null hypothesis for each possible value of the true population parameter.

This "power" to detect a false null hypothesis is often the key to maintaining high quality, among other applications. The maintenance and improvement of quality are examined in Chapter 13—hypothesis testing is a vital part of this process.

The Johnsons can now assess the risks associated with their hypothesis test. The probability of incorrectly rejecting a true null hypothesis is 5% (alpha). The probabilities of incorrectly failing to reject a false null hypothesis, or of correctly rejecting a false null hypothesis, are summarized by the operating characteristic curve and the power curve, respectively. The Johnsons can now use their management judgment to decide if their chosen sample size ($n = 55$) has produced acceptable levels of risk.

EXERCISES

41. When we fail to reject H_0

42. No

41. When can a type II error occur?
42. If a population mean is unspecified, can the probability of a type II error be determined?
43. If the probability of making a type I error is decreased, how does this affect the probability of making a type II error?

44. If the probability of making a type II error is decreased, how does this affect the probability of making a type I error?

46. When H_0 is rejected

45. Which is more important to control: type I error or type II error?

46. When does an analyst risk making a type I error?

47. Explain the difference between an operating characteristic curve and a power curve.

48. A French auto manufacturer claims that a new company model will average at least 50 miles per gallon of gas. The population has a standard deviation of 5 miles per gallon. State the decision rule for a sample of 50 cars tested at the .02 significance level.

48*a*. 0
b. .0143
c. .2177
d. $z = -2.83$, reject

a. What is the probability of committing a type II error if actual mileage is 50 miles per gallon?

b. What is the probability of committing a type II error if actual mileage is 47 miles per gallon?

c. What is the probability of committing a type II error if actual mileage is 48 miles per gallon?

d. State the appropriate conclusion if the sample mean, $\bar{x}$, is 48 miles per gallon.

49. Draw the operating characteristic curve for Exercise 48.

50. Draw the power curve for Exercise 48.

51. $z = 1.2$, fail to reject $\beta = .7703$

51. Each week the Florida State Patrol intercepts an average of $56 million worth of drugs being transported north on Interstate 95. Over 36 randomly chosen weeks in 1992, the patrol intercepted an average of $60 million in drugs per week with a standard deviation of $20 million. Does this sample evidence indicate increasing movement of drugs through Florida? Test at the .05 significance level. Compute the probability of a type II error if the population mean is actually $59 million.

52. Draw the operating characteristic curve for Exercise 51.

53. Draw the power curve for Exercise 51.

54. Reject $\bar{x} < 391.1$ $\beta = .0301$

54. Bill Ford, Bon Resort Hotel manager, believes that the average guest bill is at least $400. The population is normally distributed with standard deviation of $60. In Exercise 26 you were asked to state the decision rule for a significance level of .15 using a sample of 49 guest bills. You were also asked "if the sample mean is $375, what should Bill's conclusion be?" What is the probability of a type II error if the population average guest bill is actually $375?

55. $z = .51$ $\beta = .6950$

55. Jack Knive knows from past experience that 12% of Community Credit Union's auto loan recipients default within the first year. Jack feels that the default rate is increasing. If he obtains evidence that the percentage of customers who default is now greater than 12%, the credit union will revise its guidelines for granting auto loans. In a random sample of 150 customers who received loans one year ago, 23 have since defaulted. Find the probability of a type II error if the population percentage is actually 15%.

56. Reject $\bar{p} > .34$ $\beta = .6772$

56. Four years ago the percentage of college graduates in Appendix C's company data base was 25%. You feel that this percentage has increased. In Exercise 40 you were asked to select a simple random sample of 25 observations from the data base and test a hypothesis at the .15 significance level. Find the probability of a type II error if the population percentage of college graduates is actually 30%.

Computing Sample Size for a Hypothesis Test

Finding Sample Size in H_0 Test

Chapter 8 discussed how sample size decisions are made for interval estimation problems once the analyst has specified the desired degree of precision. This section shows how sample size decisions are made for hypothesis-testing problems once the analyst has specified allowable probabilities for type I and type II errors.

After considering the situation for their hypothesis test, the Johnsons decide the risk level is too high. They're comfortable with the type I error probability, since they set it at 5%, but they find too much risk associated with the power curve in Figure 9.13. The power of the test to detect a drop in mean chemical batch to 421 units is rather low (23%). A drop to this level would signal a significant deterioration in acidity/potency performance, and they decide to increase the power of the test to detect such a drop. To do this, they need to increase the sample size.

To determine sample size in a hypothesis-testing situation, three things must be known or estimated. First, the population standard deviation, or an estimate of it, must be specified. The Johnsons' initial sample of 55 revealed a sample standard deviation of 30 units; this will be used as the estimate of the population standard deviation.

Next, the risks of both type I and type II errors must be specified. The alpha level has already been established: $\alpha = .05$. Specifying the beta risk requires that a value for the population mean also be specified. In other words, the Johnsons must complete the following statement:

> Beta equals ________ when the population mean equals ________.

Completing this statement indicates not only the tolerable probability of failing to reject a false null hypothesis but also the population mean value for which this risk is appropriate. Suppose the value .02 is chosen for beta. The statement for acceptable type II error can then be reworded:

> If the population mean has dropped from 425 to ________, we want only a 2% chance of failing to reject the false claim that the population mean is still 425.

By filling in the blank in this statement, the Johnsons will have all the information they need to solve for the appropriate sample size. This sample size will guarantee that the desired risk levels for both type I and type II errors are met.

The Johnsons decide the population mean value for the beta specification should be 415. They reason that if the population mean has dropped as low as 415, they want to be almost certain that the hypothesis test will detect this fact and that the false null hypothesis will be rejected. They want to take only a 2% chance that the test will fail to detect this shift, leading to acceptance of the false null hypothesis.

The sample size needed in this hypothesis test can now be found. Figure 9.14 summarizes this situation. The top curve is the sampling distribution that applies if the null hypothesis is true. The mean of the curve is 425, and the probability of rejecting the true null hypothesis (alpha) is shown on the left end of the curve. The lower curve indicates that the population mean is in fact 415. The probability of failing to reject the false null hypothesis is shown on the upper end of this curve (beta). Note that the critical z value for the upper curve is -1.645 (since 5% of the curve is excluded on

TM FIGURE 9.14 Hypothesis Test

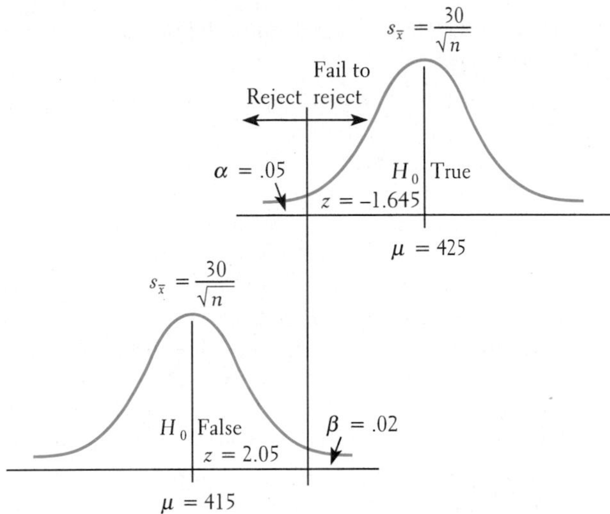

the lower end), and for the lower curve it is $z = 2.05$ (since 2% of the curve is excluded on the upper end).

The vertical line extending through both the curves of Figure 9.14 is the decision rule critical value. A sample mean above this value will lead to a failure to reject the null hypothesis, and a sample mean below this value will lead to rejection. This value can be specified using both curves. The following calculation states the decision rule value on the left using the upper curve and on the right using the lower curve. These two specifications are for the same value, as reflected by the equal sign between them. The result is one equation with one unknown: the sample size, n. The equation can thus be solved for the appropriate sample size:

$$\begin{aligned} 425 - 1.645(30/\sqrt{n}) &= 415 + 2.05(30/\sqrt{n}) \\ 10 &= 49.35/\sqrt{n} + 61.5/\sqrt{n} \\ \sqrt{n} &= 110.85/10 \\ \sqrt{n} &= 11.085 \\ n &= 122.9, \text{ rounded to } 123 \end{aligned}$$

The Johnsons should increase their sample size from the original value of 55 to 123 batches. This larger sample size, although costing more time and money, will yield the desired risk levels they specified.

EXERCISES

57. Yes

57. Is it possible to control the probabilities of both a type I and a type II error in a particular hypothesis test? If so, how is this accomplished?
58. If the sample size is increased in a hypothesis test after the acceptable type I and type II errors have been specified, increasing accuracy will result. Would this accuracy be

reflected in a lower alpha, would beta be decreased, or could both alpha and beta be decreased?

59. Increase sample size

59. How could an analyst decrease the probabilities of both a type I error and a type II error in a hypothesis test?

60. σ, along with probabilities of type I and II errors

60. What three things must an analyst know to determine the appropriate sample size for a hypothesis test?

61. $n = 54$

61. Swingline Products produces bags of charcoal with a mean weight of 5 pounds and standard deviation of 1 pound. Quality Control samples the production process to determine whether standards are being met. A hypothesis test is conducted at the 5% significance level. The firm wants to guard against failing to reject the null hypothesis if the true mean is 5.4 pounds at a level of .10. What sample size should be selected for a one-tailed test?

62. $n = 9$

62. The Genesis Company produces bearings. Past experience shows that the process produces bearings with an average diameter of 4 inches and standard deviation of 0.2 inch. An alpha level of .10 is desired. If the population mean isn't 4 inches but has dropped to 3.8 inches, Genesis wants only a 5% chance of accepting the false notion that the population mean is still 4 inches. What sample size should Genesis select?

63. Approximately 500

63. The Neptune Automobile Company advertised in *Business Week* that 90% of the owners of new Neptunes are satisfied with their purchase. It wants to check whether this percentage has dropped. An alpha level of .01 is desired for the hypothesis test. If the population percentage has dropped to 85%, Neptune wants only a 10% chance of accepting the false notion that the population percentage is actually 90%. What sample size should Neptune select?

Choosing the Significance Level in Hypothesis Testing

Choosing Alpha

Some final thoughts are in order regarding the selection of a significance level in a hypothesis test. Throughout this chapter the significance level has been set arbitrarily or has been based on "consideration of the costs of a type I error." In practice, too often, little thought is given to the choice of alpha. The most common significance level in use is 5% and in fact, the authors have encountered situations where the choice of a significance level other than 5% was deemed "incorrect." Not considering the significance level might be expensive.

Some business leaders indicate that students are incorrectly taught to always select low significance levels in their business classes. The automatic selection of a low significance level, or a low chance of committing a type I error, might reflect the point of view: I'll continue to believe that the conditions of the past are unchanged; unless I see overwhelming evidence to the contrary, I'll continue to accept the status quo.

Such a statement can be regarded as extremely conservative. Most businesspeople need to take more risk in their decisions if they're to discover new opportunities and remain competitive. In addition, analysts must recognize that for a given amount of evidence (a given sample size), reducing the probability of a type I error increases the probability of a type II error. In other words, having too much faith in the status quo can lead to failure to detect a change in conditions.

The key point is that the costs associated with type I and type II errors need to be weighed in the choice of alpha. If the cost of a type I error is low compared with the cost of a type II error, then alpha should be relatively high. If committing a type I error is quite costly and a type II error is inexpensive, then a very low value of alpha should be chosen. By considering the costs of an error in a hypothesis test, the decision maker is in a better position to set the proper level of risk exposure.

SUMMARY

This chapter has covered one of statistics' most important topics: hypothesis testing. It may seem, at first glance, that estimation (Chapter 8) is more widely used, but, in fact, hypothesis testing is very common in business applications of all kinds.

Hypothesis tests of both a population mean and a population proportion were discussed. These two population parameters are involved in many practical applications; numerous examples follow.

This chapter also discussed the risk of a type II error. These risks are summarized by the operating characteristic curve or the power curve and, along with the chosen alpha value, show the analyst to what extent the chosen sample size creates exposure to risk. As always in statistical applications, the analyst must choose between a large expensive sample size with low risk, and a small inexpensive sample size with much risk.

Finally, the chapter addressed how to answer the most popular question in statistics: How large a sample should be used? As shown, the answer basically depends on how much risk of error the analyst is willing to take.

APPLICATIONS OF STATISTICAL CONCEPTS IN THE BUSINESS WORLD

THE KAISER ALUMINUM COMPANY'S USE OF HYPOTHESIS TESTING

Kaiser Aluminum is a supplier of aluminum stock to many industries around the world. Its award-winning quality improvement program is detailed in Chapter 13, "Quality-Control Applications." One of Kaiser's quality practices is to take a sample from each batch of aluminum stock and subject it to a number of tests.

Lori Anderson (a recent business graduate) is an accountant at Kaiser. Part of her job is to help design sampling plans for the aluminum-producing factory. She recently explained one of the tests to us: the "ultimate" test. Several dog-bone–shaped segments are cut from samples of aluminum stock and subjected to a pull test. The number of pounds required to break the dog bone is recorded for each test, and the average of these values becomes the sample statistic, measured in pounds.

The sample mean breaking point is used in a hypothesis test to see if the specification breaking point hypothesis can be rejected. If not, the batch is judged to be of high quality on the strength factor. If the null hypothesis is rejected because of a low average breaking point, the batch is suspect and an investigation is launched. Lori uses her business statistics courses regularly in her involvement in Kaiser's sampling process.

Other Applications

Hypothesis testing is widely used in accounting, finance, production, marketing, personnel, quality control, and all other areas involving measuring items of interest. Questions that suggest that the test of a population mean is in order include:

1. Has the average value of a company's accounts receivable balance changed during the past year?
2. Has the average lifetime of an electronics part decreased since a new supplier of components began deliveries?
3. Has the average age of employees changed since the company began hiring significant numbers of women three years ago?
4. Has the average interest rate a company paid on its many loans changed over the past six months?
5. The average number of defectives per truckload, as measured by a company's quality-control department, has been 4.5 for several months. Has it decreased as a result of the QC department's improvement efforts?

Hypothesis tests involving a population percentage are also common. Again, all functional areas of business are candidates for this kind of hypothesis test since the percentage of items in the total population that are in a particular condition is frequently of interest. Questions that might arise regarding a population percentage include:

1. Has the percentage of minorities in a large company work force, previously known to be 12%, increased as a result of affirmative action efforts?
2. Has the percentage of accounts receivable that result in bad-debt expense increased as a result of depressed economic conditions?
3. Has the percentage of manufactured components that are defective responded to a recent quality-control effort?
4. Has the percentage of loan applications accepted by all branches of the bank changed during the past year?
5. In a taste test a year ago, only 35% of a consumer panel rated our soft drink superior to that of our competitor. A new-formula drink has been developed, and the taste test will again be tried. Will there be an improvement?

Glossary

Hypothesis testing Using sample evidence to assess the likelihood that an assumption about some characteristic of a population is true.

Null hypothesis (H_0) The assumption about the population that is tested using sample evidence. It states that any difference between a sample statistic and its assumed population parameter is due to chance variation in sampling.

Alternative hypothesis (H_1) The statement about the population that must be true if the null hypothesis is false.

One-tailed test A hypothesis test in which the alternative hypothesis indicates direction (either greater or less than).

Two-tailed test A hypothesis test in which the alternative hypothesis does not specify direction.

Type I error Rejection of a true null hypothesis.

Type II error Failure to reject a false null hypothesis.

Level of significance The probability of rejecting a null hypothesis that is true. It is designated by the symbol α (alpha).

Decision rule A hypothesis test rule that specifies the action to be taken for each possible sample outcome.

***p*-value** The probability of observing a sample value as extreme as, or more extreme than, the value actually observed, given that H_0 is true.

Operating characteristic curve A curve that shows the probability of failing to reject a false null hypothesis for each possible value of the true population parameter.

Power curve A curve that shows the probability of rejecting a false null hypothesis for each possible value of the true population parameter.

KEY FORMULAS

Standardized test statistic

$$z = \frac{\text{Observed value} - \text{Assumed value}}{\text{Standard error of sampling distribution}} \tag{9.1}$$

Standardized test statistic—population mean (large-sample case)

$$z = \frac{\bar{x} - \mu}{\sigma_{\bar{x}}} \tag{9.2}$$

Standardized test statistic—population mean (small-sample case)

$$t = \frac{\bar{x} - \mu}{s_{\bar{x}}} \tag{9.3}$$

Standardized test statistic—population proportion

$$z = \frac{x/n - p}{\sigma_{\bar{p}}} \tag{9.4}$$

SOLVED EXERCISES

1. ONE-SAMPLE HYPOTHESIS TEST FOR MEANS—LARGE SAMPLE

A company claims that the rubber belts it manufactures have a mean service life of at least 800 hours. A simple random sample of 36 belts from a large shipment reveals a mean life of 780 hours and standard deviation of 90 hours.

a. What is the appropriate conclusion of a hypothesis test done at the .05 significance level?

b. If a computer program is used for this problem, what *p*-value would it compute?

Solution:

a. The null and alternative hypotheses are

$$H_0: \mu \geq 800$$
$$H_1: \mu < 800$$

The decision rule is:

If the sample mean lies more than 1.645 standard errors below the assumed population mean of 800 hours, reject the null hypothesis; otherwise, fail to reject it (reject H_0 if $z < -1.645$).

$$s_{\bar{x}} = \frac{s}{\sqrt{n}} = \frac{90}{\sqrt{36}} = 15$$

$$z = \frac{\bar{x} - \mu}{s_{\bar{x}}} = \frac{780 - 800}{15} = -1.33$$

Since the test value for z (-1.33) is larger than the critical value ($z = -1.645$), the null hypothesis is not rejected. There's insufficient evidence to dispute the company's claim. There's a possibility that a type II error has been committed, since the accepted null hypothesis might actually be false.

b. Look up the z value of -1.33 in the standard normal table. The area between the mean and a z value of -1.33 is .4082. Therefore, the p-value is (.5000 − .4082), or .0918.

2. ONE-SAMPLE HYPOTHESIS TEST FOR MEANS—SMALL SAMPLE

The maker of a certain car model claims that the car averages 31 miles per gallon of unleaded gas. A random sample of nine cars is selected, and each car is driven on a supply of one gallon of unleaded gas.

a. State the decision rule in terms of mileage if an alpha of .01 is used and the sample standard deviation equals three miles per gallon.

b. What is the appropriate conclusion if the nine cars average 29.5 miles per gallon?

Solution:

a. The null and alternative hypotheses are

$$H_0: \mu \geq 31$$
$$H_1: \mu < 31$$

Degrees of freedom equal $(n - 1) = (9 - 1) = 8$. The decision rule is to reject the null hypothesis if the test value for t is less than -2.896 (reject H_0 if $t < -2.896$).

b.

$$s_{\bar{x}} = \frac{s}{\sqrt{n}} = \frac{3}{\sqrt{9}} = 1$$

$$t = \frac{\bar{x} - \mu}{s_{\bar{x}}} = \frac{29.5 - 31}{1} = -1.50$$

Since the test value for t (-1.50) is larger than the critical value ($t = -2.896$), the null hypothesis is not rejected. The car maker's claim appears to be true. Of course, a type II error may have been committed.

3. ONE-SAMPLE HYPOTHESIS TEST FOR PROPORTIONS

A certain manufacturing process turns out 20% defective items. The manufacturer will continue the process as long as the percentage of defective items isn't significantly larger than the norm of 20%. A random sample of 100 items is selected and tested. If 30 items are defective, what is the correct decision at the .02 significance level?

Solution:

The null and alternative hypotheses are

$$H_0: p \leq .20$$
$$H_1: p > .20$$

The decision rule is:

If the sample proportion of defectives lies more than 2.05 standard errors above the assumed population percentage of 20%, reject the null hypothesis; otherwise, fail to reject it (reject H_0 if $z > 2.05$).

$$\sigma_{\bar{p}} = \sqrt{\frac{p(1-p)}{n}} = \sqrt{\frac{.20(1-.20)}{100}} = .04$$

$$z = \frac{(x/n - p)}{\sigma_{\bar{p}}} = \frac{(30/100 - .20)}{.04} = \frac{.10}{.04} = 2.5$$

Since the test value of z (2.5) is greater than z's critical value (2.05), the null hypothesis is rejected. The percentage of defective items is significantly larger than the normal 20%. There's a possibility that a type I error has been committed.

4. TYPE II ERROR

The hypothesis-testing procedure in Solved Exercise 1 led to the conclusion that the null hypothesis should not be rejected. The possibility of a type II error was mentioned. Calculate the probability of a type II error if it's assumed that the rubber belts have a mean service life of 780 hours.

Solution:

Figure 9.15 illustrates the solution. The decision rule was to reject the null hypothesis if the computed z value is less than -1.645. If this z value is converted to hours, the null hypothesis will be rejected if the sample has an average service life less than 775.3 hours:

$$-1.645 = \frac{\bar{x} - 800}{15}$$
$$-24.7 = \bar{x} - 800$$
$$\bar{x} = 775.3$$

If the population mean is actually 780, the probability of obtaining a sample mean greater than 775.3 by chance is $(.5000 + .1217) = .6217$. This is the probability of a type II error.

$$z = \frac{\bar{x} - \mu}{s_{\bar{x}}} = \frac{775.3 - 780}{15} = -0.31 \rightarrow .1217 \text{ (area between 775.3 and 780)}$$

5. SAMPLE SIZE FOR A HYPOTHESIS TEST

Manufacturers' advertising claims are sometimes tested by the Federal Trade Commission (FTC) to verify their accuracy. The makers of Venetian Spaghetti Sauce have advertised that their 32-ounce jar is always filled to the top. Management is concerned that the FTC will test this claim and find it untrue. Venetian wants to determine the appropriate sample size for a test of its own. The population standard deviation is 0.5 ounce. A significance level of .05 is desired. If the population mean isn't 32 ounces, but has dropped to 31.8 ounces, Venetian wants only a

FIGURE 9.15 Type II Error Calculation

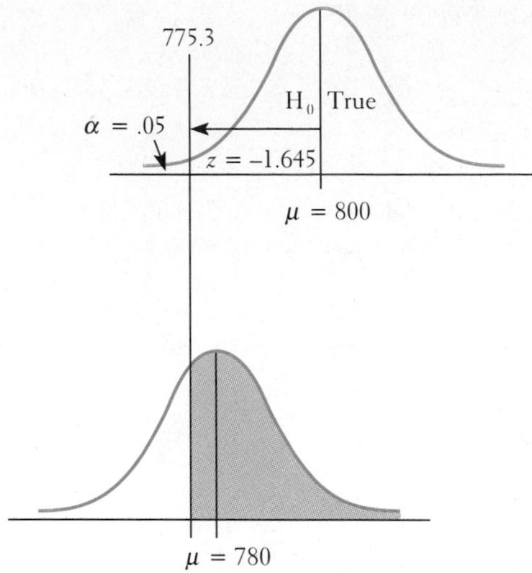

10% chance of accepting the false notion that the population mean is still 32 ounces. What sample size should Venetian select?

Solution:

A significance level, or alpha, of .05 is equivalent to the value

$$32 - 1.645(0.5/\sqrt{n})$$

If the population mean has dropped to 31.8 ounces, Venetian wants only a 10% chance of failing to reject the false notion that the population mean is still 32 ounces. This corresponds to a value of

$$31.8 + 1.28(0.5/\sqrt{n})$$

The appropriate sample size is computed by equating these two expressions and solving for n:

$$\begin{aligned} 32 - 1.645(0.5/\sqrt{n}) &= 31.8 + 1.28(0.5/\sqrt{n}) \\ 0.2 &= 0.8225/\sqrt{n} + 0.64/\sqrt{n} \\ \sqrt{n} &= 1.4625/0.2 \\ \sqrt{n} &= 7.3125 \\ n &= 53.5 \end{aligned}$$

Venetian should use a sample size of 54.

EXERCISES

64. How do hypothesis-testing procedures differ when the population standard deviation is unknown?
65. Does rejecting a null hypothesis disprove it? Why or why not?

66. Does a sample result that is inconsistent with the null hypothesis lead to its rejection? Why or why not?

67. What is meant when a null hypothesis is rejected on the basis of sample information?

68. Explain why no single level of probability is used to reject or accept a hypothesis.

69. .0228

69. If a hypothesized value is rejected because it differs from a sample statistic by two or more standard deviation units, what is the likelihood that a true hypothesis has been rejected?

70. $\mu \geq 20$
$\mu < 20$

70. If minimum load-bearing capacity of New Mexico's bridges is 20 tons, state the null and alternative hypotheses to test a sample of bridges.

71*a*. Normal
b. t
c. t
d. Binomial
e. Binomial

71. State the appropriate sampling distribution for each of the following hypothesis tests. Also state the necessary assumptions.

a. H_0: $\mu = 40$; $\sigma = 3$; $n = 25$.

b. H_0: $\mu = 70$; $s = 8$; $n = 25$.

c. H_0: $\mu = 20$, $s = 4$; $n = 25$.

d. H_0: $p = .10$; $n = 58$.

e. H_0: $p = .05$; $n = 39$.

72. The null hypothesis is that the old tire manufacturing process is as good as the new one. What kind of cost would a type I error create in this situation?

73. The null hypothesis is that a television tube manufacturing process is producing no more than the maximum allowable rate of defective tubes. What kind of cost would a type II error create in this situation?

74*a*. True
b. True
c. True
d. True
e. False

74. Which of the following statements about the probabilities of type I and type II errors are *not* correct?

a. A type I error can never occur if H_0 is false.

b. A type II error can never occur if H_0 is true.

c. If H_0 is true, it is possible to make a type I error or make a correct decision.

d. If H_0 is false, it is possible to make a type II error or make a correct decision.

e. It's not possible to specify the probabilities of both type I and type II errors in the same hypothesis test because only one or the other can occur.

75. $z = -7.89$, reject

75. For a sample of 35, the sample mean is 96 and the standard deviation is 3. Using the .02 level of significance, test the hypothesis that the population mean is 100.

76. $t = 8.49$, reject

76. For a sample of 18, the sample mean is 6 and the standard deviation is 0.5. Using the .05 level of significance, test that the sample mean is greater than the hypothesized population mean of 5.

77. $z = .883$, fail to reject

77. For a sample of 50, the sample proportion is .85. Using the .01 level of significance, test the hypothesis that the population proportion is .80.

78. $z = -1.23$,
fail to reject

78. A company has purchased a large quantity of steel wire. The supplier claims that the wire has a mean tensile strength of 80 pounds or more. The company tests a sample of 13 pieces of the wire and finds a mean of 78.64 and standard deviation of 4 pounds. Should the company dispute the claimed mean tensile strength on the basis of this evidence at the .05 significance level?

79. $z = 1.52$, reject

79. The May 5, 1988, *Wall Street Journal* reported an increase in the percentage of taxpayers who used professional preparers from 45% in 1986 to 47% in 1987. In a 1988 study to see

if a significant increase in the usage of professional preparers had occurred, of a random sample of 1,000 taxpayers, 494 indicated they used a professional preparer. Using the 10% significance level, can it be concluded that there has been an increase since 1987?

80. $z = 2.7$, reject

80. A package-filling device is set to fill cereal boxes with a mean weight of 20 ounces of cereal per box. The standard deviation of the amount actually put into the boxes is 0.5 ounces. A random sample of 25 filled boxes is weighed, yielding a mean weight of 20.27 ounces. Test at the .05 significance level to determinc whether the device is working properly.

81. $z = -1.6$, fail to reject

81. Under a standard manufacturing process, the breaking strength of nylon thread is normally distributed, with mean of 100 and standard deviation of 5. A new, cheaper process is tested, and a sample of 25 threads is drawn, with the results $\bar{x} = 98.4$, $s = 5.5$. Your assistant has noted, "Since the sample mean isn't significantly less than 100 at alpha .05, we have strong justification for installing the new process." Do you agree?

82. $z = 3.125$, reject

82. A manufacturer claims that a customer will find no more than 8% defective knee braces in a large shipment. A customer decides to test this claim after reading an article in the *American Journal of Sports Medicine* (July/August 1989, p. 535). This article discusses the forces exerted on a knee brace used for injured athletes and convinces the customer that high quality is essential.

A random sample of 200 braces is selected from the shipment, and 28 defectives are found. Should the manufacturer's claim be disputed at the .01 significance level?

83. $z = -.6$, fail to reject

83. Investigators for the National Transportation Safety Board (NTSB) stopped 1,500 heavy trucks by surprise in five states and ordered 46.1% off the road because their brakes were out of adjustment, the *Detroit News* reported (*The Spokesman-Review*, July 20, 1992). About 10% of the trucks inspected had other serious brake problems, the newspaper said. The state patrol in another state decides to stop a random sample of 200 trucks to determine whether the problem is as widespread as reported and finds 88 of the trucks with brakes out of adjustment. Does this provide evidence that the actual percentage of 46.1% reported by the NTSB is too high? (Test using the .01 significance level.)

84. $\mu = 12$
$\mu \neq 12$
Reject if $z > 1.96$ or $z < -1.96$
$z = 15$, reject
Type I

84. The manufacturer of Cola Pop is in the process of producing 12-ounce cans. The automated pouring device needs frequent checking to verify that it's actually putting 12 ounces in each can. Cans' weights are known to be normally distributed with a standard deviation of 0.2 ounce. State the null and alternative hypotheses. State the decision rule if the hypothesis is to be tested at the 5% significance level for a sample of 36 cans. State the appropriate conclusion if the sample mean is 12.5 ounces. Explain what type of error might be made.

85. $z = -1.35$, fail to reject

85. According to a survey of family travel plans conducted by the U.S. Travel Data Center for *Better Homes and Gardens*, 49% of the family vacationers intending to travel with children in 1992 planned to visit a theme park (*The Wall Street Journal*, April 15, 1992). Brandon Kim, president of Wild Kingdom, is interested in building a theme park in Madison, Wisconsin. He decides to survey 700 families in the surrounding area and determine whether at least 49% intend to visit a theme park on their vacation. If 325 respondents indicate they intend to do so, what should Brandon conclude? (Use the .01 significance level.)

86. $z = .75$, fail to reject

86. In a certain year, the mean interest rate on loans to all large retailers was 6%, and the standard deviation was 0.2 percentage points. Two years later, a simple random sample of 100 loans to large retailers yielded a mean interest rate of 6.015%. Assume you're willing to run a 1% risk of concluding a change has occurred when in fact there has been no change. Would you conclude that there has been a change in the average level of interest

rates for large retailers? If, in fact, the average interest rate for all large retailers was 6.015%, would the conclusion that a change has occurred in the average interest rate for large retailers result in a correct decision, a type I error, or a type II error?

87. $z = 1.41$, fail to reject

87. The Slick Corporation manufactures razor blades and wishes to test if men appreciate its new extra-sharp blade. The company hires a research firm to recruit people to test the new blade. The research firm randomly selects 50 men to use the blade for a one-week trial period. At the end of the experiment, participants are asked if they would purchase the new blade. When this experiment was done last year, 50% of the respondents indicated that they would buy the blade. Slick wants to charge more for the new blade, so it hopes that the percentage will increase. Of the 50 men, 30 say they would buy the new blade. Testing at the .01 significance level, is there a significant increase in the proportion of men who say they'll purchase the new blade?

88. $t = 5$, reject

88. A photographic processing stage is supposed to last an average of 30 seconds. If the process takes more or less than 30 seconds, the picture's quality will suffer. This is especially true for certain high-quality film used for professional purposes. The Sanders Company is expecting a rush of such film after reading a notice in *American Photographer* about Ilford's new XPI film. Sanders knows that professional photographers expect perfection and is concerned about its processing times.

Sanders decides to select 25 pieces of film and run them through the process. If the sample mean is 33 seconds and sample standard deviation is 3 seconds, what should Sanders conclude if it tests at the .05 significance level? Assume that the process is normally distributed.

89. $z = 2.12$, reject

89. The California Power Company wants to determine whether mean residential electricity usage per household increased during January. Past experience indicates that usage is normally distributed with a mean of 700 kwh and standard deviation of 50 kwh. A simple random sample of 50 households was selected for January, and mean usage was found to be 715 kwh. Test at the .02 significance level whether mean residential electricity usage per household has increased for the month of January.

90. $z = -.73$, fail to reject

90. Western, Inc., manufactures men's sports shirts carried in 24% of the men's clothing stores on the West Coast. Western recently sampled 60 men's clothing stores on the East Coast and found that 12 stores carried its brand. At the .10 significance level, is there evidence that Western has poorer distribution on the East Coast?

91*a*. $\beta = .48$, power $= .52$
b. $\beta = .61$, power $= .39$

91. A coin-operated coffee machine was designed to discharge at least 8 ounces of beverage per cup, with standard deviation .9 ounce. An analyst selects a random sample of 36 cupfuls for a consumer-testing service and is willing to have an alpha risk of 10%. Compute the test's power and the probability of a type II error if the population average amount dispensed is:

a. 7.8 ounces.

b. 7.85 ounces.

92. $n = 899$

92. (This question refers to Exercise 91.) If the analyst wants 98% power to detect a shift in the population mean from 8 ounces to 7.9 ounces, what sample size must be selected?

93*a*. $\beta = .6293$
b. $\beta = .7486$

93. (This question refers to Exercise 91.) If the analyst wishes an alpha risk of 5%, compute the test's power and the probability of a type II error if the population average amount dispensed is:

a. 7.8 ounces.

b. 7.85 ounces.

94. Using Appendix C's company data base, test the null hypothesis that the mean number of years with the company for the 200 employees is 12.6. Use the .02 significance level for a simple random sample of 40 employees selected with replacement.

95. Using Appendix C's company data base, test the null hypothesis that the proportions of males and females employed by the company are equal. Use the .01 significance level for a simple random sample of 35 employees selected with replacement.

EXTENDED EXERCISES

96. RICH HEALTH PRODUCTS

The Rich Health Products Company wants to know if its six-month effort to reduce absenteeism has produced results. The campaign resulted from a study that revealed an average of 2.9 sick days taken per employee in the company's main manufacturing plant. Concern over this matter increased after the personnel manager read an article about absenteeism in the nursing profession ("Absenteeism among Hospital Nurses: An Idiographic-Longitudinal Analysis," *Academy of Management Journal*, June 1989).

A random sample of 50 employee records will be used to determine any improvement. The company decides to test the null hypothesis that the average number of sick days taken per month is still 2.9 against the alternative that the average has decreased. Rich management considers the penalty associated with a type I error, which would mean concluding that the absentee rate has declined when in fact it hasn't. This would divert management attention away from a continuing absentee problem. In view of this undesirable situation, management decides on a significance level of 2%: they will accept only a 2% chance of thinking there has been an improvement when there really hasn't.

The hypothesis test is summarized as follows:

$$H_0: \mu \geq 2.9 \qquad n = 50$$
$$H_1: \mu < 2.9 \qquad \alpha = .02$$

The sample mean and sample standard deviation are computed to be 2.75 and 0.83 days per month, respectively. The personnel director is anxious to conclude that the absentee reduction campaign has been a success, but other members of management aren't sure the sample results are significant. They decide to continue with the hypothesis test.

The critical z value is the one that yields an area of .48 on a normal curve, since this is a one-tailed test and $\alpha = .02$. This z value is -2.05, which leads to the decision rule:

> If the sample mean is more than 2.05 standard errors below the assumed population mean of 2.9, reject the null hypothesis; otherwise, fail to reject it (reject if $z < -2.05$).

The test value for z is computed next. The unknown population standard deviation is estimated using the sample standard deviation, $s = 0.83$:

$$z = \frac{2.75 - 2.9}{0.83/\sqrt{50}} = \frac{-0.15}{0.117} = -1.28$$

The test value of z, -1.28, isn't low enough to fall into the rejection range ($z < -2.05$), so the null hypothesis cannot be rejected. The personnel director insists that the absentee reduction program has been successful and can't understand why a reduced sample average doesn't bear this out. A colleague points out that the combination of sample mean, the variability of absent days (as measured by s) and, most important, the sample size ($n = 50$) don't constitute enough evidence to claim that a reduction has taken place among all of Rich's employees. The personnel director is determined to establish the reduction campaign's validity and asks what it would take to do so. It is agreed that if the 2.75 average is shown to hold up over a larger sample size, the null hypothesis of no change can be rejected. The personnel director decides to sample more worker records to build the sample size.

a. What considerations are important in selecting persons to be in the sample from all of Rich's employees?

b. What is the minimum sample size that would result in rejection of the null hypothesis, under the assumption that the sample mean again turned out to be 2.75?

c. What does a type II error mean in this situation?

97. CHERRY LANE APPLE ORCHARD

Cherry Lane Orchards grows and processes apples. Its share of the applesauce market has been around 30% for several years. Recently its other apple products have been losing ground, and management has decided to try to increase the applesauce market share in an attempt to maintain plant capacity.

A marketing firm was retained to develop a campaign for the firm's applesauce. When the campaign was first presented to management, it was rejected as offbeat and possibly even offensive. The marketing firm, pointing out the success of similar approaches in other markets, finally convinced Cherry Lane to try the campaign. After the deal was signed, management stated they would watch the results closely to determine whether the company's market share was still around 30%. Since the new campaign was so different, it was agreed that the market share could change in either direction. That is, the new campaign might either increase or decrease the present share.

A method of randomly sampling consumers across many geographical markets was designed, with sampling to begin shortly after initiation of the new advertising campaign. A sample size of 1,000 consumers was planned, and the sample distribution convinced management that the sample was random and representative. The percentage of applesauce buyers in this sample who chose the Cherry Lane brand would be used to determine the new campaign's effectiveness.

a. What are the null and alternative hypotheses?

b. In view of the risks involved, what is an appropriate significance level for the test?

c. What is the decision rule for this test?

d. How far from 30% can the sample percentage be before the null hypothesis is rejected?

98. MILGARD ALUMINUM

Milgard Manufacturing, an aluminum processing company, decides to check the weights of the large rolls of aluminum foil one of its processing plants produces. Rolls are supposed to average 950 pounds, but increased raw material costs have led management to suspect that this average has increased. If so, valuable aluminum is being lost. Corrective action could save the company many dollars over a year's time.

Milgard wants to test the hypothesis that the rolls' average weight is 950 pounds against the alternative that it is actually greater. A total of 250 rolls are to be randomly sampled and weighed to test the null hypothesis. A preliminary sample indicates a sample standard deviation of 5.8 pounds. Since this is similar to standard deviation figures of past studies, it's used as an estimate of the population standard deviation.

Milgard's management is familiar with hypothesis testing and the risks that must be assumed. After considering the consequences of rejecting a true null hypothesis (believing that the average has increased beyond 950 pounds when it hasn't), they decide on a significance level of 5%.

a. What are the null and alternative hypotheses?

b. What is the decision rule?

c. What does a type II error mean in this situation?

d. Choose three values for the average weight of the aluminum rolls, other than 950 pounds, and compute the probabilities of failing to reject and of rejecting the null hypothesis for each. Summarize these calculations by forming the operating characteristic curve and the power curve.

After reviewing the risk situation, as indicated by the significance level and the power curve, along with the cost of individually weighing 250 aluminum rolls, management decides that they've allowed for more test accuracy than they're willing to pay for. After thinking carefully about the risks they're willing to take, they formulate the following risk specifications:

$$\alpha = .05$$
$$\beta = .05 \text{ if } \mu = 952$$

e. What sample size will meet these risk specifications, assuming that the population standard deviation is 5.8 pounds?

99. WHITFIELD UNIVERSITY BASKETBALL

Bobby Day, basketball coach for Whitfield University, has just been fired, and the administration is attempting to hire a new coach. President Fredrickson must determine the new coach's salary. He feels that a coach's average salary for a school the size of Whitfield is $100,000. The president orders his assistant, Ken Dolan, to study this issue. Ken decides to sample 54 schools and test the president's hypothesis. The 54 salaries are:

99,541	88,946	95,292	102,677	82,200	77,331
96,805	108,830	98,584	100,358	99,326	105,207
98,957	108,827	108,239	95,867	104,182	111,255
90,446	99,483	96,166	99,956	88,452	103,121
98,897	111,854	88,209	100,381	102,281	99,076
99,892	91,353	111,597	96,003	106,994	105,967
82,139	89,856	96,377	84,055	104,997	85,154
99,206	90,775	109,276	85,210	106,501	98,986
80,008	93,535	99,388	92,242	82,518	111,352

a. What significance level should Ken use?

b. What is Ken's conclusion concerning the president's hypothesis?

c. What kind of error might Ken be making?

100. OUR LADY OF LOURDES HOSPITAL

Chapter 4 gave family sizes for a population of 200 Our Lady of Lourdes Hospital employees. Customer benefits director Curtis Huff believes that the average family size has decreased since the last time this variable was studied, five years ago. At that time, family size averaged 2.9.

a. Develop the null and alternative hypotheses to test Mr. Huff's belief.

b. Use the .02 significance level to test the null hypothesis. Use the sample results you computed in Chapter 4.

c. In Chapter 8, a new random sample was generated. The new sample's descriptive statistics using MINITAB are:

```
MTB> DESCRIBE C2

C2      N      MEAN     MEDIAN     STDEV
       30     2.633     2.0000     1.217

C2    MIN       MAX         Q1        Q3
    1.000     6.000      2.000     3.250
```

Test the hypothesis developed in part *a* using the results presented on the MINITAB output. What is your conclusion using the .05 significance level? The MINITAB commands to perform this hypothesis test appear in the "MINITAB Computer Package" section.

MICROCOMPUTER PACKAGE

The micro package *Computerized Business Statistics* may be used to solve hypothesis-testing problems.

Sue and Bill Johnson (Situation 9.1) have records from the past three years showing that the acidity/potency measure is 415 units. The Johnsons are worried that the process is not meeting specification. Sue and Bill decide that a hypothesis test is in order.

Computer Solution:

From the main menu of *Computerized Business Statistics* an 8 is selected, which indicates Hypothesis Testing. Since the problem involves entering data from the keyboard, a 1 is selected. The following choices appear on the screen:

```
Data Type: (R) Raw (S) Summary                                   S

Data Form: (M) Means (P) Proportion                              M
Proportion data consists of values from 0 to 1

Population: (1) One Population (2) Two Populations               1

Variance: (P) Population (S) Sample                              S

Testing: (1) One Sided (2) Two Sided                             1
         (L) Lower Limit (U) Upper Limit                         L

Hypothesis Value:                                              425

Enter F when finished  Instructions for each option are provided here.
```

The choices are

S = Summary
M = Means
1 = One Population
S = Sample
1 = One Sided
L = Lower Limit
425 = Hypothesized population mean (μ)

F is entered to indicate that you are finished with this menu.

```
Sample Size:                                                          55
Sample Mean:                                                         415
Standard Deviation (S):                                               30
Enter F when finished  Instructions for each option
                       are provided here.
```

The choices are

$$n = 55$$
$$\bar{x} = 415$$
$$s = 30$$

Next, the screen shows:

```
Alpha Error 1 = 0.1, 2 = 0.05, 3 = 0.025, 4 = 0.01, 5 = 0.005,
            6 = Other
Select Alpha: enter 1–6 and press ↵ 2
```

A 2 is entered for the .05 significance level and the screen shows:

```
Degrees of Freedom: 54
Critical Z (Test Statistic)................... 1.645
```

Next, the hypothesis-testing program options menu reappears. A 7 is entered so that the problem can be run. The hypothesis-testing output menu then appears. The choice in this case is **P** for printer.

MINITAB Computer Package

The MINITAB commands to perform the hypothesis test for Extended Exercise 100 are

```
MTB> ZTEST OF MU=2.9, ASSUMING SIGMA=1.217, ON C2;
SUBC> ALTERNATIVE -1.
```

The output of this test is

```
TEST OF MU = 2.9 VS MU L.T. 2.9
THE ASSUMED SIGMA = 1.22

     N      MEAN     STDEV   SE MEAN      Z      P VALUE
C2  30     2.633     1.217       .22    -1.20     .1200

MTB> STOP
```

The ZTEST command is used to test the null hypothesis that $\mu \geq 2.9$. The standard deviation of 1.217 is assumed based on the sample data stored in C2. The ALTERNATIVE -1 subcommand tests the null against the alternative hypothesis that $\mu < 2.9$. Note that the ALTERNATIVE $+1$ subcommand tells the program to do a one-tailed test above the mean. If there is no ALTERNATIVE subcommand, a two-tailed test is performed.

Chapter 10

Two-Population Hypothesis Tests

Some circumstantial evidence is very strong, as when you find a trout in the milk.
Thoreau, *Journal*

Objectives

When you have completed this chapter, you will be able to:

Conduct two-population hypothesis tests for population means.

Conduct two-population hypothesis tests for population proportions.

Recognize business applications in which two-population hypothesis testing can be applied.

In its February 1989 issue, *Personnel Management* featured an article comparing on-the-job training and training through off-site courses and seminars. On-the-job training was recognized as more expensive, but the relative effectiveness of the two methods was in question.

Chapter 9 developed two very useful hypothesis-testing procedures: the test of a single population mean and the test of a single population proportion. Comparison of two populations of interest frequently occurs in practice. This chapter covers these important hypothesis tests.

WHY MANAGERS NEED TO KNOW ABOUT HYPOTHESIS TESTING FOR TWO POPULATIONS

We sometimes want to compare two populations to see whether they can be regarded as the same or different. Two-sample tests are used to evaluate claims about the equality of the means or proportions of two populations. Occasionally, the analyst's objective is to evaluate a claim about a specific difference between the means or proportions of two populations. For example, a claim may be that the means of two populations are equal, or a claim may be that the mean of one population is greater (or less) than the mean of another population.

At the completion of this chapter, you'll have examined one-sample tests for both means and proportions, discussed in Chapter 9, and the two-sample tests introduced in this chapter. All these hypothesis tests use the four basic steps presented early in Chapter 9. These steps apply to all other hypothesis tests as well.

Regarding the *Personnel Management* article, specific measures of worker productivity need to be developed and recorded for two samples of trainees, one for each training method. The two methods can then be compared and observed differences tested.

HYPOTHESIS TESTS ABOUT THE DIFFERENCE BETWEEN TWO POPULATION MEANS: LARGE SAMPLES

When testing two populations for equality of means, the null hypothesis under test is that the two population means are equal. This hypothesis won't be rejected unless sufficient evidence is gathered to reject it with small chance of error. The alternative hypothesis can use the unequal sign, the greater-than sign, or the less-than sign. This choice depends on the claim being made about the populations of interest. For a two-tailed test, the null and alternative hypotheses are

$$H_0: \mu_1 - \mu_2 = 0$$
$$H_1: \mu_1 - \mu_2 \neq 0$$

For a one-tailed test the null and alternative hypotheses are either

$$H_0: \mu_1 - \mu_2 \leq 0 \qquad \text{or} \qquad H_0: \mu_1 - \mu_2 \geq 0$$
$$H_1: \mu_1 - \mu_2 > 0 \qquad \qquad H_1: \mu_1 - \mu_2 < 0$$

Note that 0 could be replaced in these hypotheses with any value of interest. For example, the null and alternative hypotheses might be

$$H_0: \mu_1 - \mu_2 = 5$$
$$H_1: \mu_1 - \mu_2 \neq 5$$

Independent samples are selected from two populations, and the observations making up one sample are chosen independently of the observations making up the other sample. After random samples are taken from each of the two populations, the sample means are computed and the difference between them calculated. This difference is the test statistic used to reject or fail to reject the null hypothesis. If this difference is large, the null hypothesis is rejected. If this difference is small, the null hypothesis isn't rejected. To determine whether the sample mean difference is large or small, the sampling distribution for this statistic is consulted. The specifications for this distribution depend on the two sample sizes and their population variances. Since the population variances are usually unknown, sample variances are generally used to approximate them.

The sampling distribution for sample mean differences for large samples (each 30 or larger) is the normal distribution. This distribution has a mean of 0, which is intuitively obvious based on this reasoning. If the null hypothesis is true (no difference between the population means), we would expect sample mean differences to cluster around the difference between the population means, which is 0. There would be as many sample mean differences above 0 as below, and they would tend to be close to 0 rather than far away.

The sampling distribution for sample mean differences appears in Figure 10.1. Note that the sample mean differences are clustered around 0. If the difference between the sample means is close to 0, which is likely if the two populations have the same mean, the null hypothesis is not rejected. If a large difference is found, the null hypothesis is rejected.

TM

FIGURE 10.1 Sampling Distribution of Sample Mean Differences

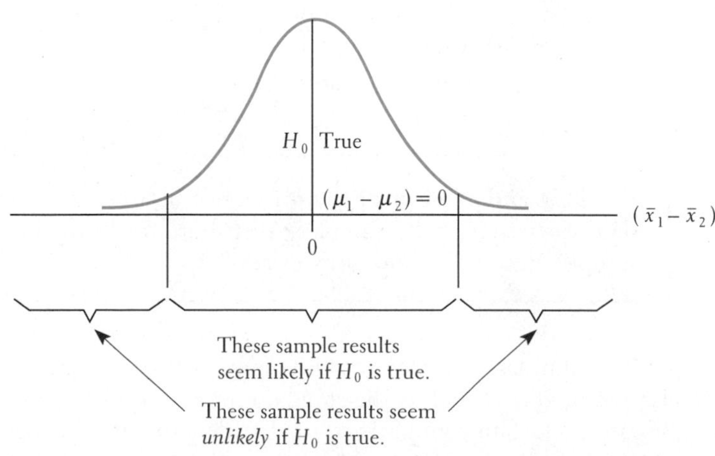

The test statistic for the two-population mean test is a z value since the sampling distribution is normally distributed. The z value measures the number of standard errors between 0, the mean of the curve, and the difference between the two sample means. The use of the normal distribution is based on the assumptions:

1. The observations in the two samples are independent.
2. The sample sizes are each 30 or larger.

If sample sizes less than 30 are used, we must assume that the populations are normally distributed.

Standard Error of the Difference between Population Means

Equation 10.1 shows the calculation for the **standard error of the difference between population means,** $\sigma_{\bar{x}_1 - \bar{x}_2}$:

$$\sigma_{\bar{x}_1 - \bar{x}_2} = \sqrt{\frac{\sigma_1^2}{n_1} + \frac{\sigma_2^2}{n_2}} \tag{10.1}$$

where $\sigma_{\bar{x}_1 - \bar{x}_2}$ = Standard error of the difference between population means
σ_1^2 = Variance of population 1
σ_2^2 = Variance of population 2
n_1 = Size of sample 1
n_2 = Size of sample 2

Note that to solve Equation 10.1 the variances of the populations under test must be known. In practice, the sample variances are usually used to estimate the unknown population parameters:

$$s_{\bar{x}_1 - \bar{x}_2} = \sqrt{\frac{s_1^2}{n_1} + \frac{s_2^2}{n_2}} \tag{10.2}$$

where $s_{\bar{x}_1 - \bar{x}_2}$ = Estimated standard error of the difference between population means
s_1^2 = Variance of sample 1
s_2^2 = Variance of sample 2
n_1 = Size of sample 1
n_2 = Size of sample 2

> The **standard error of the difference between population means** is the standard deviation of the sampling distribution of differences between all possible sample means of given sample sizes.

The standard error of the difference between population means calculated using Equation 10.1 or 10.2 is the standard deviation of the sampling distribution shown in Figure 10.1. This standard error is the denominator in the equation used to calculate the standardized difference between the sample means and the hypothesized population means:

$$z = \frac{(\bar{x}_1 - \bar{x}_2) - (\mu_1 - \mu_2)}{\sigma_{\bar{x}_1 - \bar{x}_2}}$$

Since we hypothesized that the difference between the population means is 0, Equation 10.3 omits the $(\mu_1 - \mu_2)$ term:

$$z = \frac{(\bar{x}_1 - \bar{x}_2)}{\sigma_{\bar{x}_1 - \bar{x}_2}} \qquad (10.3)$$

where $\sigma_{\bar{x}_1 - \bar{x}_2}$ = Standard error of the difference between population means
$\bar{x}_1$ = Mean from sample 1
$\bar{x}_2$ = Mean from sample 2

The following three examples illustrate the hypothesis test for two population means.

EXAMPLE 10.1 In preparing for upcoming union negotiations, Debbie Rush, chief labor negotiator for the Belmont Company, wants to know if there is more absenteeism among the company's unionized employees than among its nonunion employees. She has just read an article in *The Wall Street Journal* (May 19, 1992) describing a problem with disability claims in Ohio. Such claims accounted for almost 12% of employment discrimination cases in that state between 1985 and 1990. This article convinces Debbie that she must learn all she can about health problems in her company's work force, and she decides to start with absenteeism based on claimed health problems.

The null hypothesis she wants to test is that the average number of absent days per year is the same for both union and nonunion groups. Since Debbie is interested only in knowing if union absenteeism is higher, a one-tailed test is appropriate.

A random sample of workers is taken from each of the two groups: union and nonunion. The mean and standard deviation of absent days are calculated for each group:

$\bar{x}_1$ = 9.3 days $\quad s_1$ = 3.1 days $\quad n_1$ = 50 (Union)
$\bar{x}_2$ = 8.7 days $\quad s_2$ = 2.3 days $\quad n_2$ = 45 (Nonunion)

Debbie is tempted to cite the sample means as evidence in upcoming discussions with the union, but she realizes that the difference in sample means could be due to chance sampling error. The null and alternative hypotheses she decides to test are

$$H_0: (\mu_1 - \mu_2) \leq 0$$
$$H_1: (\mu_1 - \mu_2) > 0$$

If the null hypothesis is assumed true, the difference between the two sample means will be drawn from the sampling distribution in Figure 10.2.

Debbie decides to use a significance level of .05 for the test, which results in the following decision rule:

TM

FIGURE 10.2 Sampling Distribution of Sample Mean Differences for Example 10.1

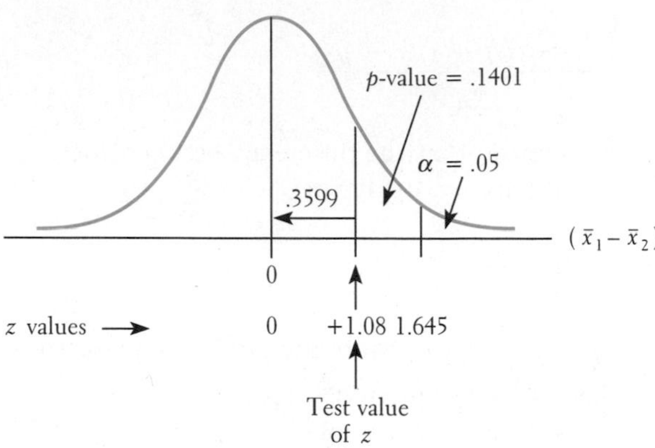

If the difference between the two sample means is more than 1.645 standard errors above the assumed mean (0) of the sampling distribution, reject the null hypothesis; otherwise, fail to reject it (reject H_0 if $z > 1.645$).

The estimate of the standard error of the difference between population means is calculated using Equation 10.2. Note that the sample standard deviations have been squared to produce the sample variances used as estimates of the unknown population variances:

$$s_{\bar{x}_1-\bar{x}_2} = \sqrt{\frac{s_1^2}{n_1} + \frac{s_2^2}{n_2}}$$

$$= \sqrt{\frac{3.1^2}{50} + \frac{2.3^2}{45}} = \sqrt{0.1922 + 0.1176} = \sqrt{0.3098}$$

$$= 0.557$$

Since n_1 and n_2 are each 30 or greater, the samples are considered large and the z test can be used for the test of significance. The selection process must also meet another criterion underlying the use of the z test: sample independence. This means that the selection of one employee doesn't affect the selection of any other employee. The z value is calculated using the standard error of 0.557 as the denominator.

$$z = \frac{\bar{x}_1 - \bar{x}_2}{s_{\bar{x}_1-\bar{x}_2}} = \frac{9.3 - 8.7}{0.557} = 1.08$$

The calculated z value is 1.08, indicating that the difference between the two sample means is 1.08 standard errors above 0, the mean of the assumed sampling distribution. Since the test value of z (1.08) isn't larger than the critical value of z from the standard normal table (1.645), the null hypothesis cannot be rejected. Debbie's evidence isn't strong enough for her to say that union employees have more absent days per year than nonunion employees. Although this is probably the correct conclusion, a type II error is possible.

When this example is run on a computer program, the result is a p-value of .1401. Since the p-value is greater than the significance level (.1401 > .05), the null hypothesis is not rejected.

A z value of 1.08, from the standard normal table, includes an area of .3599 above the mean as shown in Figure 10.2. Since the area on the upper end of the curve beyond the z value is wanted, .3599 is subtracted from .5000. The p-value is:

$$p\text{-value} = .5000 - .3599 = .1401 \text{ (area above a } z \text{ value of 1.08)}$$

EXAMPLE 10.2 Gene Marsh, the manager of a large mall, is very interested in the results of a study published in *The Journal of Social Psychology*.[1] The study tested whether fat customers experience longer response times from salespersons than their thinner counterparts. Observations were collected during 15-minute intervals on four consecutive Saturday afternoons in an urban shopping mall at two separate shoe stores. A total of 181 customers were classified as either fat or nonfat and the average time it took the salesperson to wait on them recorded. The mean response time to the nonfat group was 16.6 seconds while the mean response time to the fat group was 29.7 seconds. The null and alternative hypotheses are

$$H_0: \mu_1 - \mu_2 \geq 0$$
$$H_1: \mu_1 - \mu_2 < 0$$

A .10 significance level is chosen for this one-tailed test. The decision rule is

If the difference between the two sample means is more than 1.28 standard errors below the assumed mean (0) of the sampling distribution, reject the null hypothesis; otherwise, fail to reject it (reject H_0 if $z < -1.28$).

Suppose the sample results are:

$$\bar{x}_1 = 16.6 \text{ seconds} \qquad s_1 = 11.6 \text{ seconds} \qquad n_1 = 106$$
$$\bar{x}_2 = 29.7 \text{ seconds} \qquad s_2 = 18.6 \text{ seconds} \qquad n_2 = 75$$

The estimate of the standard error of the difference between population means is calculated using Equation 10.2:

$$s_{\bar{x}_1 - \bar{x}_2} = \sqrt{\frac{11.6^2}{106} + \frac{18.6^2}{75}} = \sqrt{1.269 + 4.613} = \sqrt{5.882}$$
$$s_{\bar{x}_1 - \bar{x}_2} = 2.425$$

The z value is then calculated using the standard error of 2.425 as the denominator:

$$z = \frac{16.6 - 29.7}{2.425} = \frac{-13.1}{2.425} = -5.4$$

[1] L. L. Pauley, "Customer Weight as a Variable in Salespersons' Response Time." *The Journal of Social Psychology* (1989), pp. 713–14.

Since the calculated value for z (-5.4) is lower than the critical value (-1.28), the hypothesis is rejected. Fat customers experienced longer response times from salespersons than nonfat customers. While this is probably the correct conclusion, a type I error is possible.

When Example 10.2 is run on a computer program, the result is a p-value of .0000. Since the p-value is less than the significance level (.0000 $<$ .10), the null hypothesis is rejected.

A z value of -5.4, from the standard normal table, includes an area of approximately .5000 below the mean. Since the area on the lower end of the curve beyond the z value is wanted, .5000 is subtracted from .5000: p-value $= .5000 - .5000 = .0000$ (area below a z value of -5.4).

The probability of observing a difference in sample means as extreme as 13.1, given that the population mean difference is actually 0, is approximately .0000.

EXAMPLE 10.3 Colleen Heaton, a college grants writer, wants to know if the average age of students at her university is greater than the average for other universities in Alabama. If it is, this would strengthen the chances of a favorable response to her application for funds for adult education programs. At a conference, Colleen participates in a panel discussion involving on-the-job training's importance as an extension of college study. Each panel member is required to read an article about the value of learning in developing competitive improvements in a company (*Training and Development*, February 7, 1992, p. 33). Colleen takes a random sample of student records from her own university (population 1) and devises a method to randomly select student ages from the other three universities in the state (population 2). She chooses a significance level of .02 for this one-tailed test.

The hypotheses under test are

$$H_0: (\mu_1 - \mu_2) \leq 0$$
$$H_1: (\mu_1 - \mu_2) > 0$$

The decision rule is

> If the difference between the two sample means is more than 2.05 standard errors above the assumed mean (0) of the sampling distribution, reject the null hypothesis (reject H_0 if $z > 2.05$).

The samples are selected and provide the following results:

$$\bar{x}_1 = 28.7 \text{ years} \qquad s_1 = 5.1 \text{ years} \qquad n_1 = 125$$
$$\bar{x}_2 = 24.9 \text{ years} \qquad s_2 = 3.5 \text{ years} \qquad n_2 = 250$$

The estimate of the standard error of the difference between population means is calculated using Equation 10.2:

$$s_{\bar{x}_1 - \bar{x}_2} = \sqrt{\frac{5.1^2}{125} + \frac{3.5^2}{250}} = \sqrt{0.208 + 0.049} = \sqrt{0.257}$$
$$= 0.507$$

The z value is calculated using the standard error of 0.507 as the denominator in Equation 10.3:

$$z = \frac{28.7 - 24.9}{0.507} = \frac{3.8}{0.507} = 7.50$$

Since the calculated z value is greater than the critical z value ($7.50 > 2.05$), the null hypothesis is rejected with small chance of error. Colleen is justified in claiming that the average age of students at her university is greater than the average for the other universities in the state.

When a computer program is used to test the three null hypotheses in this section, p-values appear in the printout. Recall from Chapter 9 that a p-value represents the area under the sampling distribution curve that lies beyond the z value calculated from the sample data. It thus constitutes the risk of a type I error that must be assumed if the null hypothesis is rejected. Table 10.1 shows the p-values for this chapter's hypothesis tests.

TABLE 10.1 Hypothesis Test p-Values

Example	Test z or t value	p-value (alpha for rejection)	Test conclusion
Example 10.1	1.08	.1401	Don't reject H_0
Example 10.2	−5.4	.0000	Reject H_0
Example 10.3	7.50	.0000	Reject H_0
Example 10.4	2.49	.0128*	Reject H_0
Example 10.5	2.19	.0561*	Reject H_0
Example 10.6	−1.11	.1335	Don't reject H_0
Example 10.7	−2.40	.0082	Reject H_0

*Computed using the CBS computer package.

EXERCISES

1. What is the difference between a one-sample test and a two-sample test?
2. When a two-sample test for the difference in population means is performed, what is the null hypothesis?
3. What is the test statistic for Exercise 2?
4. What does the sampling distribution for the difference between two population means depend on?

5. What do we call the standard deviation for the sampling distribution of the difference between two population means?
6. What is the mean of the sampling distribution of differences in population means?
7. What is the appropriate sampling distribution for a two-sample test when each of the sample sizes is 30 or greater?
8. What assumptions are made when the sampling distribution for Exercise 7 is used?

For the rest of the exercises in this section, assume that the observations in the two samples are independent.

9. Ted Gibbons, analyst for the National Painter's Union, is evaluating the mean drying times of two types of paint. The results of his experiment are

$$\bar{x}_1 = 320 \text{ minutes} \qquad s_1 = 25 \text{ minutes} \qquad n_1 = 32$$
$$\bar{x}_2 = 350 \text{ minutes} \qquad s_2 = 29 \text{ minutes} \qquad n_2 = 37$$

9*a.* No
b. Yes
c. No
d. Yes
e. 6.5
f. Reject if $z > 1.96$ or $z < -1.96$
g. $z = -4.62$
h. Reject

a. Does Ted have to assume equal variances?

b. Does Ted have to assume independent samples?

c. Does Ted have to assume normal populations?

d. Is the appropriate sampling distribution the normal curve?

e. Compute the standard error of the difference.

f. State the decision rule.

g. Using the .05 significance level, test to determine whether there is a difference between the mean drying times of the two types of paints.

h. What is Ted's conclusion?

10. For the past 10 years, Payless Rental Agency has been purchasing tires from the Union Tire Company to mount on its fleet of rental cars. A representative of the Goodwheel Tire Corporation claims that its brand gets better mileage. Payless decides to test the Goodwheel claim. Each company is asked to submit a random sample of 36 tires for a simulated road-wear test to determine the average time until wearout. The results are

$$\bar{x}_1 = 44{,}000 \text{ miles} \qquad s_1 = 3{,}500 \text{ miles} \qquad n_1 = 36 \text{ (Goodwheel)}$$
$$\bar{x}_2 = 41{,}000 \text{ miles} \qquad s_2 = 4{,}000 \text{ miles} \qquad n_2 = 36 \text{ (Union)}$$

Payless decides to test the Goodwheel claim at the .02 significance level.

10*a.* $\mu_1 - \mu_2 = 0$
b. Normal
c. Reject H_0 if $z > 2.05$
d. $z = 3.39$
e. Reject

a. State the null and alternative hypothesis.

b. Is the appropriate sampling distribution the normal curve or the *t* distribution?

c. State the decision rule.

d. Test to determine whether the Goodwheel claim is valid.

e. What should Payless conclude?

11. $z = -4.76$, reject

11. Chris Todd, personnel director of the Macro Corporation, has been instructed to determine if wage discrimination exists between the company's male and female employees. Chris decides to test a random sample of hourly wages for company employees. The results are

$$\bar{x}_1 = \$8.10 \qquad s_1 = \$0.95 \qquad n_1 = 75 \text{ (females)}$$
$$\bar{x}_2 = \$8.90 \qquad s_2 = \$1.10 \qquad n_2 = 75 \text{ (males)}$$

Chris tests at the .10 significance level to determine whether females have lower hourly wages than males. What is Chris's conclusion?

12. $z = 2.42$, fail to reject

12. The Hewlet-Desoto Corporation is planning on locating a new plant in either Waukegan, Illinois, or Madison, Wisconsin. If the cost of new homes is significantly lower in either city relative to the other, the plant will be located there. A study is conducted to deter-

mine whether the average cost of new homes is significantly lower in Waukegan or Madison. The random sample results are

$$\bar{x}_1 = \$82{,}000 \qquad s_1 = \$10{,}525 \qquad n_1 = 60 \text{ (Waukegan)}$$
$$\bar{x}_2 = \$77{,}500 \qquad s_2 = \$9{,}830 \qquad n_2 = 60 \text{ (Madison)}$$

If the Hewlet-Desoto Corporation tests at the .01 significance level, will it find a difference in the cost of new homes between the two cities?

13. $z = .992$, fail to reject

13. The Environmental Protection Agency (EPA) conducts studies designed to estimate cars' gas mileages. The EPA has been asked to compare highway mileages for cars using supreme unleaded versus regular unleaded gasoline. The EPA selects 80 cars and tests the number of miles per gallon obtained for each of 40 cars using supreme unleaded gasoline and each of 40 cars using regular unleaded gasoline. The results are

$$\bar{x}_1 = 29.3 \text{ mpg} \qquad s_1 = 1.9 \text{ mpg} \qquad n_1 = 40 \text{ (supreme unleaded)}$$
$$\bar{x}_2 = 28.9 \text{ mpg} \qquad s_2 = 1.7 \text{ mpg} \qquad n_2 = 40 \text{ (regular unleaded)}$$

What should the EPA conclude if the test is conducted using the .01 significance level?

14. $z = -25.5$, reject

14. According to *The Wall Street Journal* (May 16, 1988), the average annual hours per worker in the United States total 1,898; in Japan, this figure is 2,152. Suppose these values are based on random samples of 800 U.S. workers and 500 Japanese workers. The standard deviations of annual hours are 153 for the U.S. workers and 187 for the Japanese. Do Japanese workers spend more hours on the job than American workers? Use a significance level of .05.

HYPOTHESIS TESTING ABOUT THE DIFFERENCE BETWEEN TWO POPULATION MEANS: SMALL SAMPLES

Analysts must sometimes test for a difference between two population means using small samples. This test is used when sampling items means destroying them, when sampling is very expensive, or when only a few historical values can be obtained.

The test is the same as the two-population mean test for large samples, except that the *t* distribution is used instead of the normal curve. The *t* test is considered appropriate when either sample size is less than 30. Use of the *t* distribution assumes:

1. The observations in the two samples are independent.
2. The two populations are approximately normal.
3. The two populations have equal variances.

Equation 10.1 showed that the standard error of the difference between two population means equals the square root of the sum of the two population variances, which are adjusted for sample size. Since it's assumed that the two populations have equal variances ($\sigma_1^2 = \sigma_2^2$), Equation 10.1 can be rewritten as

$$\sigma_{\bar{x}_1-\bar{x}_2} = \sigma\sqrt{\frac{1}{n_1} + \frac{1}{n_2}} \qquad (10.4)$$

Pooled Estimate of the Variance

If the variance, σ^2, is unknown, the two sample variances can be used to compute a **pooled estimate of the variance.** Equation 10.5 is used to solve for the square root of this pooled estimate of the variance:

$$s_{\text{pooled}} = \sqrt{\frac{s_1^2(n_1 - 1) + s_2^2(n_2 - 1)}{n_1 + n_2 - 2}} \tag{10.5}$$

A **pooled estimate of the variance** of a population is based on the combination of two or more sample variances and is appropriate whenever the variances of two or more populations are assumed equal.

If the square root of the pooled estimate of the variance (s) is substituted for σ in Equation 10.4, the result is the estimate of the standard deviation of the sampling distribution (called the standard error of the difference):

$$s_{\bar{x}_1 - \bar{x}_2} = s\sqrt{\frac{1}{n_1} + \frac{1}{n_2}} \tag{10.6}$$

The standard error of the difference between population means forms the denominator in Equation 10.7, which is used to calculate the test t value.

$$t = \frac{\bar{x}_1 - \bar{x}_2}{s_{\bar{x}_1 - \bar{x}_2}} \tag{10.7}$$

where $s_{\bar{x}_1 - \bar{x}_2}$ = Standard error of the difference between population means
$\bar{x}_1$ = Mean from sample 1
$\bar{x}_2$ = Mean from sample 2

The null hypothesis to be tested is that the two populations from which the samples were taken have the same mean. Under the assumption that this hypothesis is true, the sample statistic is computed using Equation 10.7. A significance level is then chosen, and the t table is consulted for the critical test value, where the correct number of degrees of freedom is $(n_1 - 1) + (n_2 - 1)$, or $(n_1 + n_2 - 2)$. Two degrees of freedom are lost because two sample statistics (the sample variances) are used as estimates of population parameters in the computation of the pooled variance. If the test statistic is less than this critical value, the null hypothesis is not rejected. If it is greater than the critical value, the null hypothesis is rejected at the chosen significance level.

EXAMPLE 10.4 The Bates Company has come up with a new manufacturing process for making the tubing used in high-quality bicycle frames. Because strength is such an important element in the design of a bicycle frame, a few of the frames made with the new tubing are to be stress-tested and the failure points compared with those of the conventional frames made by the company. Because the frames are quite expensive in terms of both materials and labor, it's decided to stress-test eight new frames and seven old ones; each frame will be subjected to an increasing load force until failure. The company will use a machine that gives a combined stress reading as it increases the stress load.

The null and alternative hypotheses are

$$H_0: (\mu_1 - \mu_2) \leq 0$$
$$H_1: (\mu_1 - \mu_2) > 0$$

If the null hypothesis is assumed true, the difference between the two sample means will be drawn from the sampling distribution in Figure 10.3. A significance level of .05 is chosen for the test. The t table is consulted using df $= (8 + 7 - 2) = 13$. The critical t value for a one-tailed test, found in the .05 column of the t table, is 1.771. The decision rule is

> If the difference between the two sample means is more than 1.771 standard errors above the assumed mean (0) of the sampling distributions, reject the null hypothesis (reject H_0 if $t > 1.771$).

The samples are selected and provide the following results:

New frames	Old frames
$\bar{x}_1 = 27.8$ units	$\bar{x}_2 = 23.7$ units
$n_1 = 8$	$n_2 = 7$
$s_1 = 3.4$ units	$s_2 = 2.9$ units

The square root of the pooled estimate of the variance is computed using Equation 10.5:

$$s_{\text{pooled}} = \sqrt{\frac{s_1^2(n_1 - 1) + s_2^2(n_2 - 1)}{n_1 + n_2 - 2}}$$

FIGURE 10.3 Sampling Distribution of Sample Mean Differences for Example 10.4

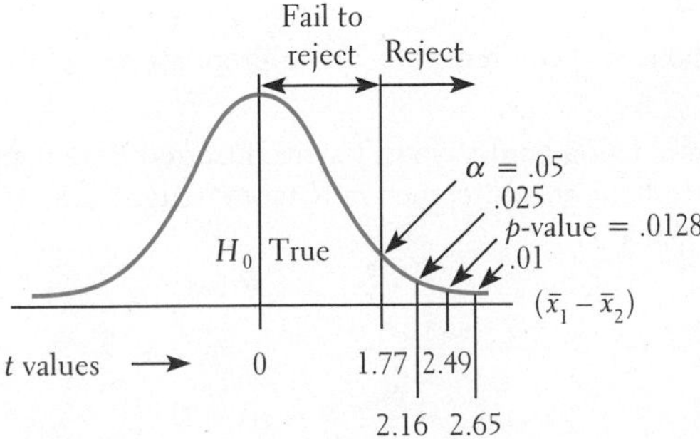

$$= \sqrt{\frac{3.4^2(8 - 1) + 2.9^2(7 - 1)}{8 + 7 - 2}}$$
$$= \sqrt{10.106}$$
$$= 3.18$$

This value, 3.18, is substituted into Equation 10.6 to compute the standard error of the difference.

$$s_{\bar{x}_1 - \bar{x}_2} = 3.18\sqrt{\frac{1}{8} + \frac{1}{7}} = 3.18(0.518) = 1.647$$

The standard error of the difference between population means, calculated using Equation 10.6, forms the denominator of Equation 10.7, which is used to calculate the t value:

$$t = \frac{\bar{x}_1 - \bar{x}_2}{s_{\bar{x}_1 - \bar{x}_2}} = \frac{27.8 - 23.7}{1.647} = \frac{4.1}{1.647} = 2.49$$

Since the test value for t (2.49) is larger than the critical t value (1.771), the null hypothesis is rejected at the .05 significance level. Bates concludes, based on its small sample, that the new frames do exceed the old frames in terms of strength. Bates believes it may have made a breakthrough in bicycle frame construction. However, the company would feel much better about this conclusion if a larger sample had been used.

When this example is run on a computer program, the result is a p-value of .0128. Since the p-value is less than the significance level ($.0128 < .05$), the null hypothesis is rejected.

A t value of 2.49 lies between 2.160 and 2.650 in the t table for 13 degrees of freedom. Figure 10.3 shows that .025 represents the area above the t value of 2.16, and .01 represents the area above the t value of 2.65. The CBS computer program provides a p-value of .0128 shown as the area above 2.49 in Figure 10.3.

Exercises

15. *t*

15. What is the appropriate sampling distribution for a two-sample test when sample sizes are smaller than 30?

16. What assumptions are required when the appropriate sampling distribution for Exercise 15 is used?
17. Two shipments of nylon cord have just arrived from different suppliers. The company analyst decides to test for any difference in tensile strength. The results of the test, in pounds per square inch, are:

Supplier A	Supplier B
37	41
39	42
41	38

Supplier A	Supplier B
35	45
36	40
34	39
38	

17*a*. Yes
b. Yes
c. Yes
d. t
e. −2.43
f. 11
g. 1.35
h. Reject H_0 if $t > 2.101$ or $t < -2.101$
i. Reject

a. Does the analyst have to assume equal variances?

b. Does the analyst have to assume independence?

c. Does the analyst have to assume normal populations?

d. Is the appropriate sampling distribution the normal curve or the t distribution?

e. Compute the square root of the pooled estimate of the variance for the two samples.

f. Compute the appropriate number of degrees of freedom.

g. Compute the standard error of the difference.

h. State the decision rule.

i. Using the .05 significance level, test to determine whether the two suppliers' nylon cords have the same mean tensile strength.

For the rest of the exercises in this section, assume that the observations in the two samples are independent, the two populations are approximately normal, and the populations have equal variances.

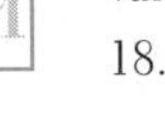

18. The Eastern Publishing Company hires college students to sell books during the summer. The company wants to evaluate the effectiveness of the new training program. To measure its efficiency, a company representative randomly selects a group of salespeople, records for each person the number of sales consummated during the past summer, and indicates whether the salesperson participated in the new training program. The results are

$\bar{x}_1 = 482$ books $\quad s_1 = 43$ books $\quad n_1 = 22$ (training)
$\bar{x}_2 = 465$ books $\quad s_2 = 39$ books $\quad n_2 = 27$ (no training)

18*a*. $\mu_1 - \mu_2 \leq 0$
$\mu_1 - \mu_2 > 0$
b. t
c. Reject H_0 if $t > 1.684$
d. $t = 1.45$, no difference

a. State the null and alternative hypotheses.

b. Is the appropriate sampling distribution the normal curve or the t distribution?

c. State the decision rule.

d. Do these data present sufficient evidence to indicate a difference in the average number of books sold at the .05 significance level?

19. Exercise 13 discussed EPA studies designed to estimate auto gas mileage. Suppose the EPA is comparing city mileages for station wagons versus four-door sedans. The EPA selects 24 station wagons and 22 sedans and determines the miles per gallon rating (mpg) for each. The results are

$\bar{x}_1 = 28.2$ mpg $\quad s_1 = 1.9$ mpg $\quad n_1 = 24$ (wagons)
$\bar{x}_2 = 31.5$ mpg $\quad s_2 = 2.1$ mpg $\quad n_2 = 22$ (sedans)

19*a*. $\mu_1 - \mu_2 = 0$
$\mu_1 - \mu_2 \neq 0$
b. t
c. Reject H_0 if $t > 2.02$ or $t < -2.02$
d. $t = -5.59$, reject

a. State the null and alternative hypotheses.

b. Is the appropriate sampling distribution the normal curve or the t distribution?

c. State the decision rule.

d. What should the EPA conclude if the test is conducted at the .05 significance level?

20. The Tendy Corporation wants to determine if productivity will be increased by instituting a bonus plan. The corporation decides to use the bonus plan in 13 randomly selected plants and compare the results with 15 plants that operate on the usual salary basis. The number of units produced per day is

$$\bar{x}_1 = 45 \text{ units} \quad s_1 = 7 \text{ units} \quad n_1 = 13 \text{ (bonus)}$$
$$\bar{x}_2 = 43 \text{ units} \quad s_2 = 6 \text{ units} \quad n_2 = 15 \text{ (salary)}$$

a. State the null and alternative hypotheses.

b. What should the Tendy Corporation conclude if the test is conducted at the .01 significance level?

20*a*. $\mu_1 - \mu_2 \leq 0$
$\mu_1 - \mu_2 > 0$
b. $t = .81$, fail to reject

21. The General Automobile Company is considering the purchase of batteries in bulk from two suppliers. A sample of 15 batteries is randomly selected from each supplier and tested. The mean lifetimes are

$$\bar{x}_1 = 1{,}345 \text{ hours} \quad s_1 = 31 \text{ hours} \quad n_1 = 15 \text{ (A)}$$
$$\bar{x}_2 = 1{,}310 \text{ hours} \quad s_2 = 28 \text{ hours} \quad n_2 = 15 \text{ (B)}$$

a. State the null and alternative hypotheses.

b. What should General Automobile conclude if the test is conducted at the .05 significance level?

21*a*. $\mu_1 - \mu_2 = 0$
$\mu_1 - \mu_2 \neq 0$
b. $s_{pooled} = 29.54$
$s_{\bar{x}_1 - \bar{x}_2} = 10.79$
$t = 3.24$, reject

Hypothesis Testing for Means: Dependent Samples

In Exercise 13 of this chapter, the Environmental Protection Agency compared highway mileages for automobiles using supreme unleaded versus regular unleaded gasoline. A total of 80 cars were tested: 40 used supreme unleaded gas, and the other 40 used regular unleaded gas. Different samples were used because one of the underlying assumptions of the two-sample mean test is independence of samples.

What if the EPA had tested the same 40 cars using supreme unleaded gas in one trial and regular unleaded gas in another? This would eliminate the possibility of one sample containing a large number of cars that normally get excellent gas mileage. Unlike the test in Exercise 13, which involved independent samples, the EPA could have used **matched pairs,** so called because two sets of measurements are taken for each automobile: one for supreme unleaded gas and a second for regular unleaded gas. The same number of cars with excellent gas mileage would be contained in both the supreme unleaded and the regular unleaded groups. In the matched-pairs test, there's no need to assume that the two underlying populations have equal variances. The only assumption necessary is that the population of differences is normal.

Matched Pairs

Note that it is difficult to design a matched-pairs experiment. One criterion for this type of test is that the treatment doesn't change the subjects or objects being examined.

Matched pairs result when each data value in one sample is matched with a corresponding data value in the other sample.

The matched-pair t test focuses on the differences in paired observations. It involves computing the mean and standard deviation of the differences. Equation 10.8 simply substitutes the difference (d) for x in Equation 4.1 to compute the mean:

$$\bar{d} = \frac{\Sigma d}{n} \tag{10.8}$$

where $\bar{d}$ = Average difference between the paired observations
d = Difference
n = Number of differences

Equation 10.9 substitutes the difference (d) for x in Equation 4.8 and takes the square root to compute the standard deviation of the differences:

$$s_d = \sqrt{\frac{\Sigma d^2 - \frac{(\Sigma d)^2}{n}}{n - 1}} \tag{10.9}$$

The standard deviation of the sampling distribution is the sample standard deviation, computed using Equation 10.9, divided by the square root of the sample size. Equation 10.10 shows this standard deviation as the denominator of the formula for the matched-pairs t test for dependent samples:

$$t = \frac{\bar{d}}{s_d/\sqrt{n}} \tag{10.10}$$

where s_d = Standard deviation of the differences
$\bar{d}$ = Average difference between the paired observations
n = Number of differences

EXAMPLE 10.5 The EPA selects a sample of 10 cars to determine if there's a significant difference in mileage between supreme unleaded gas and regular unleaded gas. The null and alternative hypotheses are

H_0: $(\mu_1 - \mu_2) = 0$
H_1: $(\mu_1 - \mu_2) \neq 0$

A significance level of .10 is chosen for the test. The number of degrees of freedom for the matched-pairs t test is $n - 1$, so the t table is consulted for df $= (10 - 1) = 9$. The critical t value for a two-tailed test is found in the .10 column of the t table, indicating a critical value of 1.833. The decision rule is

If the average difference between the paired observations is more than 1.833 standard errors above or below the assumed mean (0) of the sampling distribution, reject the null hypothesis (reject H_0 if $t < -1.833$ or $t > 1.833$).

The results of the EPA test are:

Automobile	Supreme unleaded	Regular unleaded	Difference (d)	Squared difference (d^2)
1	28.2	27.4	0.8	0.64
2	30.1	29.0	1.1	1.21
3	32.8	29.4	3.4	11.56
4	30.0	28.0	2.0	4.00
5	28.9	31.0	−2.1	4.41
6	31.0	29.6	1.4	1.96
7	32.3	28.3	4.0	16.00
8	30.4	29.6	0.8	0.64
9	27.0	27.0	0.0	0.00
10	28.5	28.0	0.5	0.25
			11.9	40.67

From Equation 10.8, the average difference between the paired observations is

$$\bar{d} = \frac{\Sigma d}{n} = \frac{11.9}{10} = 1.19$$

From Equation 10.9, the standard deviation of the differences is

$$s_d = \sqrt{\frac{\Sigma d^2 - \frac{(\Sigma d)^2}{n}}{n - 1}} = \sqrt{\frac{40.67 - \frac{(11.9)^2}{10}}{10 - 1}}$$

$$= \sqrt{\frac{40.67 - 14.16}{9}} = \sqrt{\frac{26.51}{9}} = \sqrt{2.95} = 1.72$$

The matched-pairs t statistic is

$$t = \frac{\bar{d}}{s_d/\sqrt{n}} = \frac{1.19}{1.72/\sqrt{10}} = \frac{1.19}{0.544} = 2.19$$

Since the test value for t (2.19) is larger than the critical t value of 1.833, the null hypothesis is rejected at the .10 significance level. The EPA concludes, based on its small sample, that the supreme unleaded gas gave significantly better mileage than the regular unleaded gas. Although this is probably the correct conclusion, a type I error, which would occur if the mileage is the same for the two types of gasoline, is possible.

Exercises

22. Explain the difference between dependent and independent samples.
23. Burgans Furniture has asked the Create America Advertising Agency to develop a new advertising campaign. Burgans' marketing manager, Megan Hubble, decides to evaluate the

campaign's effectiveness. Megan collects data on monthly sales before and during the campaign for eight regional stores. The results are:

Store	Average sales before	Average sales during
1	$63,458	$65,496
2	48,510	52,462
3	51,203	50,864
4	75,241	79,520
5	60,123	71,145
6	55,555	55,600
7	45,456	48,654
8	57,438	60,897

a. State the null and alternative hypotheses.

b. Is the appropriate sampling distribution the normal curve or the t distribution?

c. State the decision rule.

d. Using the .05 significance level, test to determine if the advertising campaign was effective.

e. What should Megan conclude?

24. Pam Soltaro teaches typing and word processing at City Community College. Pam feels that students type faster on computer-based word processors than on electronic typewriters. She decides to test this hypothesis on nine advanced students. The results, in words per minute, are:

Student	Word processor	Electronic typewriter
1	55	51
2	69	65
3	70	70
4	75	76
5	82	80
6	65	62
7	60	57
8	73	71
9	77	72

a. State the null and alternative hypotheses.

b. Is the appropriate sampling distribution the normal curve or the t distribution?

c. State the decision rule.

d. Using the .025 significance level, test to determine if students type faster on word processors.

e. What should Pam conclude?

25. The Gilbert Research Company is testing two commercials for the Detroit Edison Electric Company. Both commercials were shown to 12 customers, who were asked to rate the commercials on a dial with a scale from 1 to 100. The results are:

Customer	Value received commercial	Electric card commercial
1	95	87
2	59	65
3	73	80
4	65	73
5	32	45
6	45	39
7	60	57
8	83	81
9	27	33
10	50	40
11	63	66
12	95	93

25*a*. $\mu_1 - \mu_2 = 0$
$\mu_1 - \mu_2 \neq 0$
b. t
c. Reject H_0 if $t > 1.796$ or $t < -1.796$
d. $t = -.48$
e. Fail to reject

a. State the null and alternative hypotheses.

b. Is the appropriate sampling distribution the normal curve or the t distribution?

c. State the decision rule.

d. Using the .10 significance level, test to determine whether customers liked one campaign better than the other.

e. What should Gilbert Research conclude?

26. Jim Dyke, owner of the Westside Bowling Alley, wants to offer a special promotion. Jim would like to advertise bowling lessons that are guaranteed to improve a person's score. Before offering a money-back guarantee, Jim decides to test the claim on a sample of 15 people. Jim records participant scores for three games bowled before the lessons and compares them with scores from three games bowled after the lessons are completed. The results are:

Participant	Before lessons	After lessons
1	270	300
2	300	325
3	175	280
4	243	298
5	305	291
6	330	356
7	350	382
8	274	273
9	297	361
10	306	326
11	385	412
12	411	458
13	241	287
14	258	264
15	308	342

26*a*. $\mu_1 - \mu_2 \geq 0$
$\mu_1 - \mu_2 < 0$
c. $t = 4.53$
d. Reject

a. State the null and alternative hypotheses.

b. State the decision rule using the .05 significance level.

c. Test to determine whether participants improved after the bowling lessons.

d. What should Jim conclude?

HYPOTHESIS TESTING FOR PROPORTIONS FROM TWO POPULATIONS

An analyst may wish to compare two populations on the basis of the proportion or percentage of their members that meet certain conditions. The four hypothesis-testing steps from Chapter 9 are used for this test.

To test for the difference between two population proportions, a random sample from each population is taken and the sample proportion calculated for each. The difference between the sample proportions is the test statistic, and its sampling distribution is the normal distribution. The null hypothesis under test is that the two populations have the same proportion. This hypothesis will not be rejected unless sufficient evidence is gathered to reject it with small chance of error. For a two-tailed test, the null and alternative hypotheses are

$$H_0: p_1 - p_2 = 0$$
$$H_1: p_1 - p_2 \neq 0$$

For a one-tailed test, the null and alternative hypotheses are either

$$H_0: p_1 - p_2 \leq 0 \qquad \text{or} \qquad H_0: p_1 - p_2 \geq 0$$
$$H_1: p_1 - p_2 > 0 \qquad\qquad\quad H_1: p_1 - p_2 < 0$$

Note that 0 could be replaced in these hypotheses with any value of interest. For example, the null and alternative hypotheses might be

$$H_0: p_1 - p_2 = .20$$
$$H_1: p_1 - p_2 \neq .20$$

If the null hypothesis is assumed true, the sampling distribution will have a mean of 0, the difference between the population proportions. Sample proportion differences are thus arrayed about the mean of 0 on a normal curve, as shown in Figure 10.4.

As suggested by Figure 10.4, if the difference between the sample proportions is close to 0, this supports the null hypothesis that the populations have the same

FIGURE 10.4 Sampling Distribution of Sample Proportion Differences

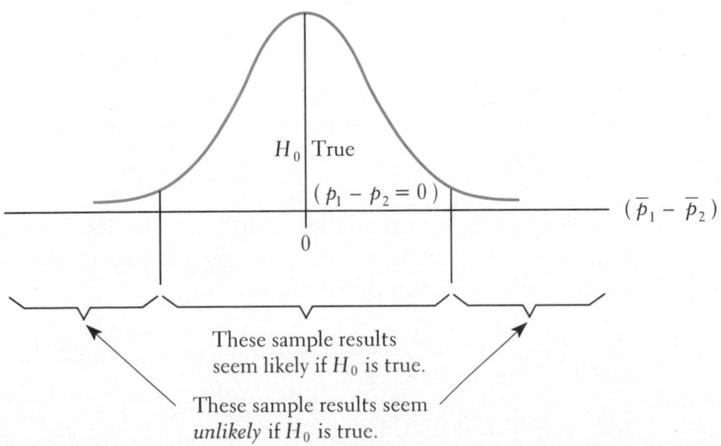

proportion. In this case, the null hypothesis will not be rejected. If the samples have very different proportions, the null hypothesis will be rejected.

In the two-sample test for proportions, the pooled estimate of the population proportion ($\hat{p}$) is computed by averaging the two sample proportions:

$$\hat{p} = \frac{x_1 + x_2}{n_1 + n_2} \tag{10.11}$$

where x_1 = Number of successes in sample 1
x_2 = Number of successes in sample 2
n_1 = Size of sample 1
n_2 = Size of sample 2

Note that if the population proportions are equal ($p_1 = p_2$), then the two samples came from the same population. If each sample proportion is viewed as an estimate of the same population proportion, combining the two samples, as is done in Equation 10.11, should provide an improved estimate of the true value of the population proportion.

The pooled estimate of the population proportion ($\hat{p}$) is used in Equation 10.12 to compute the standard deviation of the sampling distribution of the differences (called the **standard error of the difference between population proportions**):

$$\sigma_{\bar{p}_1 - \bar{p}_2} = \sqrt{\hat{p}(1 - \hat{p})\left(\frac{1}{n_1} + \frac{1}{n_2}\right)} \tag{10.12}$$

where $\sigma_{\bar{p}_1 - \bar{p}_2}$ = Estimate of the standard error of the difference between population proportions
$\hat{p}$ = Pooled estimate of the population proportion
n_1 = Size of sample 1
n_2 = Size of sample 2

> The **standard error of the difference between population proportions** is the standard deviation of the sampling distribution of differences between all possible sample proportions for given sample sizes.

The standard error calculated using Equation 10.12 constitutes the denominator in the equation that analyzes the difference between the sample proportions and the hypothesized population proportions:

$$z = \frac{(\bar{p}_1 - \bar{p}_2) - (p_1 - p_2)}{\sigma_{\bar{p}_1 - \bar{p}_2}}$$

Since it's hypothesized that the difference between the population proportions is 0, Equation 10.13 is developed without the $(p_1 - p_2)$ term:

$$z = \frac{\bar{p}_1 - \bar{p}_2}{\sigma_{\bar{p}_1 - \bar{p}_2}} \tag{10.13}$$

where $\sigma_{\bar{p}_1 - \bar{p}_2}$ = Standard error of the difference between population proportions
$\bar{p}_1$ = Proportion of successes for sample 1
$\bar{p}_2$ = Proportion of successes for sample 2

The null hypothesis being tested is that the two populations from which the samples were taken have the same proportion. Under the assumption that this hypothesis is true, the sample statistic is computed using Equation 10.13. A significance level is then chosen, and the z table is consulted for the critical test value. If the test statistic is less than this critical value, the null hypothesis is not rejected. If it's greater than the critical value, the null hypothesis is rejected at the chosen significance level.

It is usually not helpful to compare two population proportions using small samples. This test is not sensitive enough to detect a difference when small samples are used; therefore, the normal distribution will be used along with large sample sizes in the following examples.

EXAMPLE 10.6 Joseph Conrad, an economic analyst for the state of West Virginia, wants to determine whether the unemployment rate is the same or different for two towns in the state's coal mining region. The null and alternative hypotheses are

$$H_0: (p_1 - p_2) = 0$$
$$H_1: (p_1 - p_2) \neq 0$$

Joseph decides to use a significance level of .05 for the test, resulting in the following decision rule:

> If the difference between the two sample proportions is more than 1.96 standard errors below or above the assumed mean (0) of the sampling distribution, reject the null hypothesis (reject H_0 if $z < -1.96$ or $z > 1.96$).

Joseph selects random samples of people from each town and computes these results:

$x_1 = 55$ people unemployed $\quad n_1 = 550$ people
$x_2 = 90$ people unemployed $\quad n_2 = 750$ people

The pooled estimate of the population proportion ($\hat{p}$) is computed by averaging the two sample proportions using Equation 10.11:

$$\hat{p} = \frac{x_1 + x_2}{n_1 + n_2} = \frac{55 + 90}{550 + 750} = \frac{145}{1{,}300} = .1115$$

The standard deviation of the sampling distribution of the differences between proportions (the standard error of the difference) is computed by inserting the pooled estimate of the population proportion (.1115) into Equation 10.12:

$$\sigma_{\bar{p}_1-\bar{p}_2} = \sqrt{\hat{p}(1-\hat{p})\left(\frac{1}{n_1}+\frac{1}{n_2}\right)} = \sqrt{.1115(.8885)\left(\frac{1}{550}+\frac{1}{750}\right)}$$
$$= \sqrt{(.099)(.0032)} = \sqrt{.000317} = .018$$

The z value is calculated using the standard error of .018 as the denominator in Equation 10.13:

$$z = \frac{\bar{p}_1 - \bar{p}_2}{\sigma_{\bar{p}_1-\bar{p}_2}} = \frac{.10 - .12}{.018} = -1.11$$

The calculated z value is -1.11, indicating that the difference between the two sample proportions is 1.11 standard errors below 0, the mean of the assumed sampling distribution. Since the test value of z (-1.11) isn't lower than the critical value of z from the standard normal table (-1.96), the null hypothesis cannot be rejected. The sample evidence isn't strong enough to reject the hypothesis that the two towns have the same unemployment rate. Although this is probably the correct conclusion, a type II error is possible.

EXAMPLE 10.7 A union suspects that more men than women work over 40 hours per week in a large plant. The union complains to management about discrimination toward women in assigning overtime. The union and the company agree to use a random sample of worker records from the past year to decide this issue. Since the suspicion is that the population of women working overtime is less than that of men, a one-tailed test is suggested. The null and alternative hypotheses, along with the sample evidence resulting from a large random sample of employee records, are

$$H_0: (p_1 - p_2) \geq 0$$
$$H_1: (p_1 - p_2) < 0$$

where p_1 = Population proportion of women
p_2 = Population proportion of men
x_1 = 114 women worked overtime $\quad n_1$ = 875 women
x_2 = 162 men worked overtime $\quad n_2$ = 950 men

The union and management analysts agree to use a significance level of .05 for the test, leading to the following decision rule:

> If the difference between the two sample proportions is more than 1.645 standard errors below the assumed mean (0) of the sampling distribution, reject the null hypothesis (reject H_0 if $z < -1.645$).

The pooled estimate of the population proportion ($\hat{p}$) is computed by averaging the two sample proportions using Equation 10.11:

$$\hat{p} = \frac{114 + 162}{875 + 950} = \frac{276}{1{,}825} = .15$$

The standard error of the difference is computed by using the pooled estimate of the population proportion (.15) in Equation 10.12:

$$\sigma_{\bar{p}_1-\bar{p}_2} = \sqrt{(.15)(.85)\left(\frac{1}{875} + \frac{1}{950}\right)} = .0167$$

The z value is calculated using the standard error of .0167 as the denominator in Equation 10.13:

$$z = \frac{\bar{p}_1 - \bar{p}_2}{\sigma_{\bar{p}_1-\bar{p}_2}} = \frac{.13 - .17}{.0167} = -2.40$$

Since the z value from the sample exceeds the critical z value from the standard normal table ($-2.40 < -1.645$), the null hypothesis is rejected. It is concluded that women workers are putting in less overtime than men. Company management can argue that the sample results are misleading, that discrimination in overtime doesn't really exist. In effect, they would be arguing that a type I error has been committed. However, since there's only a 5% chance of such an error, the company would be wise to modify its overtime policy rather than fight the sample findings.

Table 10.1 lists the calculated z values for the tests of this section along with the computed p-values.

EXERCISES

27. For a two-sample test for the difference in population proportions, what is the null hypothesis?
28. What is the test statistic for Exercise 27?
29. What assumptions does the sampling distribution for the difference between two population proportions depend on?
30. What is the standard deviation of the sampling distribution for the difference between two population proportions called?
31. What is the mean of the sampling distribution of differences in population proportions?

31. 0

32. According to a *USA Today*/CNN Gallup poll of 755 registered voters conducted on July 17–18, 1992 (*USA Today*), 56% supported Bill Clinton. *Newsweek* (July 27, 1992) reported a survey that indicated 59% favored Clinton. Suppose the *Newsweek* survey was based on a sample of 1,032 voters. If the two samples were randomly selected from the same population, what is the pooled estimate of the variance for the percentage of voters who favor Clinton? If tested at the .05 significance level, do the data provide sufficient evidence to indicate that the two samples were selected from different populations?

32. $S_{\bar{p}} = .5775$
$z = -1.27$, fail to reject

33. The Latah Creek Winery presently markets in the state of Oregon. The winery is considering expansion to Idaho and must determine if a new marketing strategy is needed for this market. One of its best white wines is taste-tested in both regions, and the proportions of wine drinkers who liked the wine are recorded:

$x_1 = 372$ liked the wine $\quad n_1 = 600$ (Idaho)
$x_2 = 544$ liked the wine $\quad n_2 = 800$ (Oregon)

33*a*. $p_1 - p_2 = 0$
$p_1 - p_2 \neq 0$
b. Normal
c. .0257
d. Reject H_0 if $z > 2.575$ or $z < -2.575$
e. $z = -2.335$
f. Fail to reject

a. State the null and alternative hypotheses.

b. Is the appropriate sampling distribution the normal curve or the *t* distribution?

c. Compute the standard error of the difference.

d. State the decision rule.

e. Using the .01 significance level, test to determine whether there's a difference between the proportions of wine drinkers who liked the wine.

f. What should the Latah Creek Winery conclude?

34. In Exercise 25, the Gilbert Research Company agreed to test two advertising campaigns for the Detroit Edison Electric Company. Two TV commercials were developed and shown in the company's market area on the three local channels over a three-day period. The following week Gilbert Research conducted a telephone survey to identify people who had seen the commercials. People who had seen only one commercial were asked to state its primary message. The results are

$x_1 = 72$ recalled primary message $\quad n_1 = 152$ (value received commercial)
$x_2 = 74$ recalled primary message $\quad n_2 = 171$ (electric card commercial)

34*a*. $p_1 - p_2 = 0$
$p_1 - p_2 \neq 0$
b. Normal
c. .0555
d. Reject H_0 if $z > 1.645$ or $z < -1.645$
e. $z = .738$
f. Fail to reject

a. State the null and alternative hypotheses.

b. Is the appropriate sampling distribution the normal curve or the *t* distribution?

c. Compute the standard error of the difference.

d. State the decision rule.

e. Using the .10 significance level, test to determine whether there's a difference between the proportions of people who recalled the primary message of each commercial.

f. What should Gilbert Research conclude?

35. $z = 1.02$, fail to reject

35. *The Wall Street Journal*, May 23, 1988, reported the percentage of fatal accidents involving car rollovers to be different for small cars and large cars. For the former, the percentage was 26%; for the latter, it was 21%. If these results were based on samples of 150 from each group, would you conclude that large cars are safer?

SUMMARY

You have now been exposed to several kinds of hypothesis tests widely used in the business world. Each of these tests follows the same four steps discussed early in Chapter 9:

1. The null and alternative hypotheses are stated.
2. The null hypothesis is assumed true, and the sampling distribution for the test is identified based on this assumption.
3. A random sample is taken from the population(s) under study and the appropriate sample statistic computed.
4. The likelihood that the sample statistic could have been drawn from the assumed sampling distribution is assessed. If this probability is high, the null hypothesis is not rejected. If this probability is low, the null hypothesis is rejected.

Table 10.2 summarizes the hypothesis tests that have been presented. The null hypothesis to be tested appears in the first column. The second column provides the appropriate sample statistic to be computed from the sample data. The third column shows the sampling distribution for the test, and the fourth column shows the parameters of that distribution under the assumption that the null hypothesis is true.

TABLE 10.2 Hypothesis Test Summary

H_0	Test statistic	Sampling distribution	Parameters of sampling distribution
$\mu = 150$*	$\bar{x}$	Normal or t	μ and $\sigma/\sqrt{n}$
$p = .75$*	$\bar{p}$	Normal	p and $\sqrt{\frac{p(1-p)}{n}}$
$(\mu_1 - \mu_2) = 0$	$\bar{x}_1 - \bar{x}_2$	Normal or t	0 and $\sqrt{\frac{\sigma_1^2}{n_1} + \frac{\sigma_2^2}{n_2}}$
$(p_1 - p_2) = 0$	$\bar{p}_1 - \bar{p}_2$	Normal	0 and $\sqrt{p(1-p)\left(\frac{1}{n_1} + \frac{1}{n_2}\right)}$

*Example value

By referring to Table 10.2, you should be able to conduct any of the hypothesis tests discussed so far. Also, additional hypothesis tests that you'll encounter in this text and in the business world should be easy for you to conduct. The same four steps are followed in every hypothesis test; you need only know the correct sample statistic to compute, the correct sampling distribution to consult, and the parameters of that distribution.

APPLICATIONS OF STATISTICAL CONCEPTS IN THE BUSINESS WORLD

THE SPOKANE TRANSIT AUTHORITY'S USE OF HYPOTHESIS TESTING

Christine Fueston is planning manager for the Spokane Transit Authority (STA). One of her responsibilities is ensuring that the data reported to the Urban Mass Transit Authority (UMTA) are collected in accordance with the Uniform System of Accounts and Records and Reporting System requirements. She must report fixed-route motorbus passenger mile data along with van pool ridership and mileage data.

Christine has developed a sampling plan that's in compliance with the sampling procedures for obtaining fixed-route bus operating data. Using this plan, she sends surveyors out to ride the buses and collect the appropriate information. Statistical issues that concern her are sample size, precision, and confidence levels. Christine frequently must test hypotheses about population parameters using sample statistics. Since bus routes change from year to year, she must sometimes perform a two-population hypothesis test to determine whether the statistical base has shifted from year to year. If so, funding relationships with the federal government could change.

After Christine has completed her analysis each year, she is required to hire an independent statistician to verify and validate her work.

Other Applications

As mentioned in Chapter 9, hypothesis tests are widely employed in practical situations to test claims or suspicions about populations using sample data. The hypothesis tests covered in this chapter are two-population tests for means and proportions. Here are examples of questions that might be answered by one of the hypothesis tests presented in this chapter.

How do two alcoholic treatment centers compare on the percentage of clients who are alcohol-free one year after treatment?

Is the average price of a basket of food the same or different between Safeway and Dominick's food stores?

Are the percentages of defective parts from two suppliers the same or different?

Is the percentage of clients over age 65 the same or different for Blue Cross compared with Group Health?

Glossary

Standard error of the difference between population means The standard deviation of the sampling distribution of differences between all possible sample means for given sample sizes.

Pooled estimate of the variance The combination of two or more sample variances, which is appropriate whenever the variances of two or more populations are assumed equal.

Matched pairs The matching of each data value in one sample with a corresponding data value in the other sample.

Standard error of the difference between population proportions The standard deviation of the sampling distribution of differences between all possible sample proportions for given sample sizes.

Key Formulas

Standard error of the difference between two population means

$$\sigma_{\bar{x}_1 - \bar{x}_2} = \sqrt{\frac{\sigma_1^2}{n_1} + \frac{\sigma_2^2}{n_2}} \qquad (10.1)$$

Estimated standard error of the difference between two population means

$$s_{\bar{x}_1 - \bar{x}_2} = \sqrt{\frac{s_1^2}{n_1} + \frac{s_2^2}{n_2}} \qquad (10.2)$$

Two-sample mean z test statistic

$$z = \frac{\bar{x}_1 - \bar{x}_2}{\sigma_{\bar{x}_1 - \bar{x}_2}} \qquad (10.3)$$

Standard error of the difference between two population means when the variances are equal

$$\sigma_{\bar{x}_1-\bar{x}_2} = \sigma\sqrt{\frac{1}{n_1} + \frac{1}{n_2}} \tag{10.4}$$

Pooled variance estimate

$$s_{\text{pooled}} = \sqrt{\frac{s_1^2(n_1 - 1) + s_2^2(n_2 - 1)}{n_1 + n_2 - 2}} \tag{10.5}$$

Estimated standard error of the difference between two population means when the variances are equal

$$s_{\bar{x}_1-\bar{x}_2} = s\sqrt{\frac{1}{n_1} + \frac{1}{n_2}} \tag{10.6}$$

Two-sample mean *t* test statistic

$$t = \frac{\bar{x}_1 - \bar{x}_2}{s_{\bar{x}_1-\bar{x}_2}} \tag{10.7}$$

Sample mean—matched samples

$$\bar{d} = \frac{\Sigma d}{n} \tag{10.8}$$

Sample standard deviation—matched samples

$$s_d = \sqrt{\frac{\Sigma d^2 - \dfrac{(\Sigma d)^2}{n}}{n - 1}} \tag{10.9}$$

Matched-pairs *t* test statistic

$$t = \frac{\bar{d}}{s_d/\sqrt{n}} \tag{10.10}$$

Pooled estimator of the population proportion

$$\hat{p} = \frac{x_1 + x_2}{n_1 + n_2} \tag{10.11}$$

Estimated standard error of the difference between two population proportions

$$\sigma_{\bar{p}_1-\bar{p}_2} = \sqrt{\hat{p}(1 - \hat{p})\left(\frac{1}{n_1} + \frac{1}{n_2}\right)} \tag{10.12}$$

Two-sample z test statistic for proportions

$$z = \frac{\bar{p}_1 - \bar{p}_2}{\sigma_{\bar{p}_1 - \bar{p}_2}} \tag{10.13}$$

SOLVED EXERCISES

1. TWO POPULATION MEANS—LARGE SAMPLES

"Greater Reliance on Foreign Oil Feared as U.S. Output Tumbles," reported the *New York Times* on its front page, January 18, 1990. The Puget Power Company wonders if higher oil prices might result, which, in turn, could cause higher electrical usage for home heating. To measure changes over the past year, a simple random sample of 40 households was selected for January 1989 and compared with a sample of 50 households for January 1990. The sample results are

$$\bar{x}_1 = 1{,}645 \text{ kwh} \qquad s_1 = 298 \text{ kwh} \qquad n_1 = 40 \ (1989)$$
$$\bar{x}_2 = 1{,}803 \text{ kwh} \qquad s_2 = 305 \text{ kwh} \qquad n_2 = 50 \ (1990)$$

Test at the .10 significance level if the average residential electricity usage per household has changed for the month of January.

a. State the null and alternative hypotheses.

b. Is the appropriate sampling distribution the normal curve or the t distribution?

c. State the decision rule.

d. What should Puget Power conclude?

Solution:

a. The null and alternative hypotheses are

$$H_0\!: (\mu_1 - \mu_2) = 0$$
$$H_1\!: (\mu_1 - \mu_2) \neq 0$$

b. The sampling distribution for sample mean differences in the two-sample mean test for large samples (30 or larger) is the normal distribution.

c. This is a two-tailed test at the .10 significance level using the z value. Divide the significance level in half: .10/2 = .05. Look up (.5000 − .0500) = .4500 in the body of the standard normal table. The appropriate z value is 1.645. Therefore, the decision rule is

> If the difference between the two sample means is more than 1.645 standard errors above or below the assumed mean (0) of the sampling distribution, reject the null hypothesis (reject H_0 if $z < -1.645$ or $z > 1.645$).

d. $$s_{\bar{x}_1 - \bar{x}_2} = \sqrt{\frac{s_1^2}{n_1} + \frac{s_2^2}{n_2}} = \sqrt{\frac{298^2}{40} + \frac{305^2}{50}} = 63.88$$

$$z = \frac{\bar{x}_1 - \bar{x}_2}{s_{\bar{x}_1 - \bar{x}_2}} = \frac{1{,}645 - 1{,}803}{63.88} = -2.47$$

Since the computed z value (−2.47) is below the critical z value (−1.645), reject the null hypothesis and conclude that the average residential electricity usage per household has changed for the month of January.

2. TWO POPULATION MEANS—SMALL SAMPLES

Gale Marrs, personnel manager of the Baxter Richfield Company, suspects that older workers miss more days per year due to illness than younger workers. Gale decides to test this hypothesis and randomly samples the records of 10 older (40 years or over) and 10 younger (under 40 years old) employees. Gale feels that the populations are normally distributed. The results are:

Older	Younger
37	24
19	42
21	18
35	15
16	0
4	9
0	10
12	20
63	22
25	13

a. State the null and alternative hypotheses.

b. Is the appropriate sampling distribution the normal curve or the t distribution?

c. State the decision rule if Gale tests at the .05 significance level.

d. What should Gale Marrs conclude?

Solution:

a. The null and alternative hypotheses are

$$H_0: (\mu_1 - \mu_2) \leq 0$$
$$H_1: (\mu_1 - \mu_2) > 0$$

b. The t test is considered appropriate when either sample size is less than 30 and the populations from which they are selected are normally distributed.

c. This is a one-tailed test at the .05 significance level using the t value. The number of degrees of freedom for this t test is df $= (n_1 + n_2 - 2) = (10 + 10 - 2) = 18$. Look up the value in the t table for 18 degrees of freedom in the .05 significance column. The appropriate t value is 1.734. Therefore, the decision rule is

If the difference between the two sample means is more than 1.734 standard errors above the assumed mean (0) of the sampling distribution, reject the null hypothesis (reject H_0 if $t > 1.734$).

d. $\bar{x}_1 = 23.2 \quad s_1 = 18.3 \quad n_1 = 10$
$\bar{x}_2 = 17.3 \quad s_2 = 11.2 \quad n_2 = 10$

$$s_{\text{pooled}} = \sqrt{\frac{s_1^2(n_1 - 1) + s_2^2(n_2 - 1)}{n_1 + n_2 - 2}}$$

$$= \sqrt{\frac{18.3^2(10 - 1) + 11.2^2(10 - 1)}{10 + 10 - 2}} = 15.17$$

$$s_{\bar{x}_1 - \bar{x}_2} = 15.17\sqrt{\frac{1}{10} + \frac{1}{10}} = 6.78$$

$$t = \frac{\bar{x}_1 - \bar{x}_2}{s_{\bar{x}_1 - \bar{x}_2}} = \frac{23.2 - 17.3}{6.78} = 0.87$$

Since 0.87 does not exceed the critical t value (1.734), fail to reject the null hypothesis. Based on the sample evidence, Gale cannot conclude that older workers miss more days due to illness per year than younger workers.

3. TWO POPULATION MEANS—DEPENDENT SAMPLES

Katrina Bell, analyst for the Hexaco Oil Company, has been assigned to investigate the claim that Hexaco dealers charge more for unleaded gas than independent dealers. Katrina is afraid that if she chooses two independent random samples of stations for each type of dealer, the variability in price due to geographic location might be a factor. To eliminate this source of variability, she chooses a pair of stations—one independent and one Hexaco—in close geographic proximity. The results of Katrina's sampling are:

Region	Hexaco	Independent	Difference (d)	Squared difference (d^2)
1	90.5	89.9	0.6	0.36
2	91.9	90.9	1.0	1.00
3	92.7	90.9	1.8	3.24
4	91.9	90.9	1.0	1.00
5	93.6	91.8	1.8	3.24
6	89.9	90.9	−1.0	1.00
7	90.9	90.9	0.0	0.00
8	89.8	88.9	0.9	0.81
9	88.7	88.9	−0.2	0.04
10	87.9	88.6	−0.7	0.49
11	92.7	91.9	0.8	0.64
			6.0	11.82

a. State the null and alternative hypotheses.

b. State the decision rule if Katrina tests at the .01 significance level.

c. What should Katrina conclude?

Solution:

a. The null and alternative hypotheses are

$$H_0: (\mu_1 - \mu_2) \leq 0$$
$$H_1: (\mu_1 - \mu_2) > 0$$

b. This is a one-tailed test at the .01 significance level using the t value. The degrees of freedom for this t test total $(n - 1) = (11 - 1) = 10$. Look up the value in the t table for 10 degrees of freedom in the .01 significance column. The appropriate t value is 2.764. Therefore, the decision rule is

> If the difference between the two sample means is more than 2.764 standard errors above the assumed mean (0) of the sampling distribution, reject the null hypothesis (reject H_0 if $t > 2.764$).

c. $\bar{d} = \frac{\Sigma d}{n} = \frac{6}{11} = 0.545$

$$s_d = \sqrt{\frac{\Sigma d^2 - \frac{(\Sigma d)^2}{n}}{n - 1}} = \sqrt{\frac{11.82 - \frac{(6.0)^2}{11}}{11 - 1}}$$

$$= \sqrt{\frac{11.82 - 3.27}{10}} = \sqrt{\frac{8.55}{10}} = \sqrt{0.855} = 0.925$$

$$t = \frac{\bar{d}}{s_d / \sqrt{n}} = \frac{0.545}{0.925 / \sqrt{11}} = \frac{0.545}{0.279} = 1.95$$

Since the test value for t (1.95) is smaller than the critical t value (2.764), the null hypothesis is not rejected. Katrina concludes that she does not have sufficient evidence to support the claim that Hexaco dealers charge more than independent dealers.

4. TWO POPULATION PROPORTIONS

Pacific Northwest Electric, a major gas and electric company, is attempting to take over a smaller concern, Idaho Light and Power. Pacific's securities consultant reports that a larger proportion of male Idaho shareholders support the takeover bid than female shareholders. Kim Gamble, Pacific's president, has asked Eddie Kennedy, Pacific's statistician, to conduct a telephone survey of a random sample of shareholders to confirm this report. Eddie samples 1,000 shareholders (400 male and 600 female) and finds that 220 males and 320 females support the takeover bid.

a. State the null and alternative hypotheses.

b. State the decision rule if Eddie tests at the .05 significance level.

c. What should Eddie conclude?

Solution:

a. The null and alternative hypotheses are

$$H_0: (p_1 - p_2) \leq 0$$
$$H_1: (p_1 - p_2) > 0$$

b. This is a one-tailed test at the .05 significance level using the z value. Look up (.5000 − .0500) = .4500 in the body of the standard normal table. The appropriate z value is 1.645. Therefore, the decision rule is

If the difference between the two sample means is more than 1.645 standard errors above the assumed mean (0) of the sampling distribution, reject the null hypothesis (reject H_0 if $z > 1.645$).

c. $\hat{p} = \frac{x_1 + x_2}{n_1 + n_2} = \frac{220 + 320}{400 + 600} = \frac{540}{1,000} = .54$

$$\sigma_{\bar{p}_1 - \bar{p}_2} = \sqrt{\hat{p}(1 - \hat{p})\left(\frac{1}{n_1} + \frac{1}{n_2}\right)} = \sqrt{.54(.46)\left(\frac{1}{400} + \frac{1}{600}\right)}$$

$$\sigma_{\bar{p}_1 - \bar{p}_2} = \sqrt{(.2484)(.0042)} = \sqrt{.001} = .032$$

$$z = \frac{\bar{p}_1 - \bar{p}_2}{\sigma_{\bar{p}_1 - \bar{p}_2}} = \frac{.55 - .533}{.032} = 0.53$$

Since the test value for z (0.53) is smaller than the critical z value of 1.645, the null hypothesis is not rejected. Eddie concludes that he doesn't have sufficient evidence to support the securities consultant's report.

EXERCISES

36. Why are two-sample tests performed?

37. State the three types of claims that can be made about means or proportions in a two-sample test.

38. Explain when the t distribution instead of the normal curve is used to test a hypothesis.

39. $\mu_1 - \mu_2 = 0$
$\mu_1 - \mu_2 \neq 0$
$z = -2.89$
Yes

39. Cary Richey, a history student, wants to compare the average height of ancient Romans and Greeks. After considerable reading, she can find only a few references to height, and those for men only. Based on the following data, where heights are recorded in inches, can she conclude that the Greek and Roman populations had different average heights if she tests at the .10 significance level?

$\bar{x}_1 = 61.4$ inches $\quad s_1 = 3.7$ inches $\quad n_1 = 32$ (Greeks)
$\bar{x}_2 = 63.8$ inches $\quad s_2 = 2.9$ inches $\quad n_2 = 32$ (Romans)

40. $\sigma_{\bar{x}_1-\bar{x}_2} = .8$, $z = 8.75$, reject

40. On May 5, 1988, *The Wall Street Journal* reported that the average age of the industrial base in Japan was 10 years and that in the United States was 17 years. The implication is that Japan has a more modern industrial base than the United States. Suppose the stated averages were based on a survey of 75 Japanese firms and 80 U.S. firms, and the standard deviations of equipment age were 4.9 years for Japanese firms and 5.1 years for U.S. firms. At the .05 significance level, what conclusion can be reached?

41. $s_{\bar{x}_1-\bar{x}_2} = 2.75$, $t = 5.78$, reject

41. A car company wants to test the collision characteristics of two of its car designs. Dummies are to be the "drivers" for these cars and are designed to record impact forces on the head and chest. Cars equipped with these dummies are then crashed into a solid wall at a speed of 30 miles per hour. The company hopes that its new L car will show a lower impact force than its conventional car. Since each car is destroyed by the test, only a few cars are tested. Based on the following sample evidence, can the company conclude that the new L car is safer if the test is done at the .05 significance level? (The variable recorded is a combined measurement of the head and chest forces on impact.)

$n_1 = 5 \quad \bar{x}_1 = 129.7 \quad s_1 = 5.3$ (old car)
$n_2 = 7 \quad \bar{x}_2 = 113.8 \quad s_2 = 4.3$ (L car)

42. $z = -2.33$, reject

42. *The Miami Herald* surveyed a number of subscribers to determine who was reading its Sunday edition. Of 400 men surveyed, 78% read it, and 85% of the 300 surveyed women read it. Is there a significant difference at the .10 significance level?

43. $z = -5.7$, reject

43. After a fire, a company can find only a few of its records. The accounting department was about to test the difference between the average sales per customer for two of the company's stores. The recovered records, consisting of only a few customer accounts, produced the following results. Based on this small sample, and using a .05 significance level, is one store selling more per customer than the other?

$n_1 = 38 \quad \bar{x}_1 = \$53.87 \quad s_1 = \$10.43$ (store 1)
$n_2 = 42 \quad \bar{x}_2 = \$68.13 \quad s_2 = \$11.94$ (store 2)

44. $z = 23.7$, reject

44. A Harris poll reported in *Newsweek* (March 28, 1988) revealed a decrease in Americans' average number of leisure hours per week. In 1980 there were 19 hours per week, but in

1987 only 17. This conclusion was based on a sample of 1,500 adults in each poll. If the standard deviation was 2.5 in 1980 and 2.1 in 1987, can we conclude at the .01 significance level that there has been a decrease in Americans' average number of weekly leisure hours?

45a. $t = 5.04$
b. $t = 9.72$
c. $t = 3.33$

45. In each of the following situations, test to see whether one group has a larger average (mean) value than the other. For each test, use a significance level of .05.

a. $n_1 = 5$ $\bar{x}_1 = 12{,}569$ $s_1 = 2{,}439$
$n_2 = 7$ $\bar{x}_2 = 22{,}736$ $s_2 = 3{,}981$

b. $n_1 = 26$ $\bar{x}_1 = 34.7$ $s_1 = 3.9$
$n_2 = 19$ $\bar{x}_2 = 24.1$ $s_2 = 3.2$

c. $n_1 = 18$ $\bar{x}_1 = 235.8$ $s_1 = 34.9$
$n_2 = 13$ $\bar{x}_2 = 199.3$ $s_2 = 21.5$

46. $z = 27.9$, reject

46. *Playboy* magazine (July 1988) reported that the distance of an average commute in Southern California is 10.7 miles each way. Assume this conclusion is based on a random sample of 350 commuters. Suppose the average commute in Illinois is 5 miles, based on the same sample size. Use the .02 significance level to determine if the evidence supports the conclusion that commuters in California drive farther than those in Illinois, if both standard deviations are 2.7 miles.

47. $z = -.5$, fail to reject

47. According to the *Statistical Bulletin* (October–December 1982), the average number of deaths per 1,000 troops was 1.20 for the Army and 1.57 for the Marine Corps. Is this difference significant at the .10 level? Assume that the figures are based on random samples of 5,000 from each service. (*Note:* Since each sampled person either did or did not die, this should be treated as a proportion problem.)

48. $z = -4.91$, reject

48. On May 25, 1988, *The Wall Street Journal* reported a difference in the prison return rate between inmates who had a furlough and those who didn't. The former had a return rate of 12%, and the latter had a return rate of 31%. Assuming that this conclusion is based on random samples of 225 inmates from each of the two populations, can you conclude that furloughs reduce the return rate at the .05 significance level?

49. $z = .69$, fail to reject

49. In 1992, the National League of Cities conducted a survey of 620 cities and towns. It found that 54% have negative balance sheets, up from 52% in 1991 (*USA Today*, July 9, 1992). The 1991 sample consisted of 580 cities and towns. Test at the .10 significance level to determine whether the percentage of cities and towns with negative balance sheets has changed significantly since 1991.

50. $\bar{x}_1 = 173.125$, $\bar{x}_2 = 172.125$, $s_1 = .791$, $s_2 = .835$, $t = 2.46$, reject

50. A study reported in *Industrial Quality Control* provided two analysts' 16 independent determinations of hydroquinone's melting point.

Analyst I	Analyst II
174.0	173.0
173.5	173.0
173.0	172.0
173.5	173.0
171.5	171.0
172.5	172.0
173.5	171.0
173.5	172.0

Source: *Quality Control and Industrial Statistics* (Homewood, IL: Irwin, 1986).

Is there enough evidence to conclude at the .05 significance level that there's a tendency for one analyst to get higher results than the other?

51. Baseball fans like to argue about which league is better: the National or the American. American League fans claim that because of the designated hitter, there's more offense in American League games. To test this claim, data were gathered on the number of runs scored by each team in the 1991 season (*The Sporting News 1992 Yearbook*). The results are:

51. $\bar{x}_1 = 726.6, \bar{x}_2 = 662.9$, $s_1 = 69.8, s_2 = 55$, Pooled SD = 63.5, $t = 2.55$, reject

American	Runs	National	Runs
Boston	731	New York	640
Milwaukee	799	Cincinnati	689
Seattle	702	Montreal	579
Detroit	817	Pittsburgh	768
Toronto	684	Chicago	695
Texas	829	St. Louis	651
Cleveland	576	San Diego	636
Kansas City	727	San Francisco	649
New York	674	Atlanta	749
Minnesota	776	Philadelphia	629
Oakland	760	Houston	605
Baltimore	686	Los Angeles	665
Chicago	758		
California	653		

Test at the .025 significance level the claim that there are typically more runs scored per team in the American League.

EXTENDED EXERCISES

52. BRICE COMPANY

The Brice Company needs to replace a machine that produces bolts of various sizes from steel stock. Two machines are being considered for purchase, and research to date has revealed that they cost about the same, have about the same lifetime, and have comparable warranties. Tom Brice, the owner's son and a recent college graduate, has just joined the company. His first job is to make a recommendation to his father about which machine to buy.

Tom calls several other companies around the country, locating five that are using one of the machines and four that are using the other. He discusses his problem with their manufacturing managers, and two of them agree to let him visit their facilities to sample the bolt production line. Tom conducts the visits and, over the course of several days, obtains what he thinks are good random samples of each machine's output. Measurements are made to determine the number of bolts in each sample that fall outside specifications, as well as the variability in diameter, the key factor in a precision bolt. Here are the data Tony collects:

Machine 1: n = 25 bolts, percentage outside specifications = 4%
Standard deviation of diameter = 0.02 inch

Machine 2: n = 31 bolts, percentage outside specifications = 3.2%
Standard deviation of diameter = 0.08 inch

Tom thinks he has enough data to decide which machine to buy. He tests the hypothesis that the two machines produce the same percentage of bolts outside specifications:

$$H_0: \ (p_1 - p_2) = 0$$
$$H_1: \ (p_1 - p_2) \neq 0$$

Tom computes a test value of 1.14, that is smaller than the critical values of z found in the standard normal table for small values of alpha. Tom thus fails to reject the null hypothesis of equal rates for the two machines with small chance of error.

a Has Tom conducted the hypothesis test correctly?

b. Has the test statistic of 1.14 been computed correctly?

c. Are there any factors that should be considered in the machine purchase decision that Tom has not addressed?

d. How would you react to the statement: "Machine 2 has a lower percentage of out-of-tolerance parts than Machine 1 (3.2% compared to 4.0%) and is therefore superior"?

e. If machine 1 costs less, what should Tom recommend to his father?

53. SUBURBAN REGIONAL UNIVERSITY

Suburban Regional University is competing with Downtown University for funding from the state legislature and has been accused of lowering its admission standards to attract more students. Tom Douglas, an outside consultant, is hired to see if this is true. He decides to randomly select student files to collect high school grade point averages and SAT scores.

Both universities agree to the process, and the results are to be made available to both. Mr. Douglas is familiar with the situation described in *The Wall Street Journal* (September 12, 1989) regarding a general decline in college entrance test scores during the past school year. He knows his analysis must take this decline into account.

Mr. Douglas conducts his test with 250 student files randomly selected from each university. The results are:

	Suburban	Downtown
High school GPA:		
Mean	2.63	2.94
Standard deviation	0.38	0.41
SAT score:		
Mean	985	935
Standard deviation	21	105

a. Test the hypothesis that the two universities have the same quality of student as measured by high school grade point average.

b. Test for quality of student by using the two universities' SAT scores.

c. What are your conclusions about student quality based on these two hypothesis tests?

d. What does the large difference between the SAT score standard deviations suggest?

54. OLYMPIC MANUFACTURING

The Olympic Manufacturing Company uses both ABC and XYZ placement companies to recruit management talent. The two companies' service levels appear to be about equal, but ABC has just raised its rates. ABC claims that more of the people it places are still on the job after one year, and that this is due to its superior screening procedures.

As personnel director for Olympic, it's your job to decide if ABC is worth the higher rate. You're aware of the many other placement agencies available, having just seen several of their ads in *The Wall Street Journal* section "The Mart" (June 17, 1992, pp. B13–B15). The performance of the two agencies currently being used is thus of great importance.

A sample of employees placed by each agency is easily obtained, so getting a reasonable sample size is no problem. Files on all employees are available in the personnel office.

a. How would you take a random sample in this case?

b. Suppose 85% of XYZ's placements are still on the job after one year, a value obtained from a sample of 300 employees from this placement agency. At the .05 significance level, how high would ABC's retention rate have to be for the null hypothesis of equal population retention rates to be rejected?

c. What other factors besides retention rate might you consider in evaluating ABC's new, higher cost?

MICROCOMPUTER PACKAGE

The micro package *Computerized Business Statistics* can be used to solve two-population hypothesis-testing problems.

The Puget Power Company (see Solved Exercise 1) wants to determine whether the average electricity usage per household has changed for the month of January. A simple random sample of 40 households was selected for January 1989 and compared with a sample of 50 households for January 1990. A two-population hypothesis test was conducted to determine whether the average has changed.

Computer Solution:

From the main menu of *Computerized Business Statistics* an 8 is selected, which indicates hypothesis testing. The hypothesis-testing menu appears on the screen.

Since the problem involves entering data from the keyboard, a 1 is selected.

```
Data Type:      (R) Row      (S) Summary                              S
Data Form:      (M) Means    (P) Proportion                           M
Proportion data consists of values from 0 to 1
Population:       (1) One Population (2) Two Populations              2
                  (U) Unmatched Samples  (M) Matched Samples          U
Variance:   (P) Population     (S) Sample                             S
Testing:      (1) One Sided    (2) Two Sided                          2
Hypothesis Value:                                                     0
Enter F when finished          Instructions for each option
                               are provided here
```

The choices are

S = Summary
M = Means
2 = Two populations
U = Unmatched

S = Sample
2 = Two-sided
0 = Hypothesized population mean $(\mu_1 - \mu_2) = 0$

F is entered to indicate that you are finished with this menu.

```
Sample Size for Group 1:                                  40
Sample Size for Group 2                                   50
Sample Mean for Group 1:                                1645
Sample Mean for Group 2:                                1803
Standard Deviation for Group 1:                          298
Standard Deviation for Group 2:                          305
```

The choices are

$n_1 = 40$
$n_2 = 50$
$\bar{x}_1 = 1{,}645$
$\bar{x}_2 = 1{,}803$
$s_1 = 298$
$s_2 = 305$

```
Alpha Error:    1 = 0.2, 2 = 0.1, 3 = 0.05, 4 = 0.02,
                5 = 0.01, 6 = Other
Select Alpha:   enter 1-6 and press ↵ 2
```

A **2** is entered for the .10 significance level and the screen shows:

```
Degrees of Freedom:   88
Critical Z (Test Statistic)  ................................1.645
```

Next, the hypothesis-testing program options menu reappears. A **7** is entered so that the problem can be run. The hypothesis-testing output menu then appears. The choice in this case is **P** for printer.

MINITAB COMPUTER PACKAGE

The MINITAB commands to perform the hypothesis test for Solved Exercise 2 are

```
MTB> SET OLDER INTO C1
DATA> 37 19 21 35 16 4 0 12 63 25
DATA> END
MTB> SET YOUNGER INTO C2
DATA> 24 42 18 15 0 9 10 20 22 13
DATA> END
MTB> TWOSAMPLE T .95 FOR C1 VS C2;
SUBC> ALTERNATIVE +1;
SUBC> POOLED.

TWOSAMPLE T FOR C1 VS C2
      N       MEAN      STDEV      SE MEAN
C1   10       23.2      18.3        5.80
C2   10       17.3      11.2        3.54
```

```
95 PCT CI FOR MU C1 - MU C2: (-8.4, 20.2)
TTEST MU C1 - MU C2 (VS GT): T = .87 P = .20 DF = 18
POOLED STDEV = 15.2
MTB> STOP
```

The TWOSAMPLE T command is used to test the null hypothesis that $\mu_1 - \mu_2 \leq 0$. The command calculates a $K\%$ confidence interval for $\mu_1 - \mu_2$. The ALTERNATIVE +1 subcommand tests the null against the alternative hypothesis that $\mu_1 - \mu_2 > 0$. If there is no ALTERNATIVE subcommand, a two-tailed test is performed. The POOLED subcommand assumes the two populations have equal variances and that the common variance is estimated by the pooled variance.

Chapter

11

CHI-SQUARE TESTS

Ye shall know the truth, and the truth shall make you free.
St. John 8:32

Objectives

When you have completed this chapter, you will be able to:

Explain the difference between the test of independence and the goodness-of-fit test.

Compute expected frequencies and the chi-square statistic.

Apply the contingency table in a decision-making application.

Apply the goodness-of-fit test in a decision-making application.

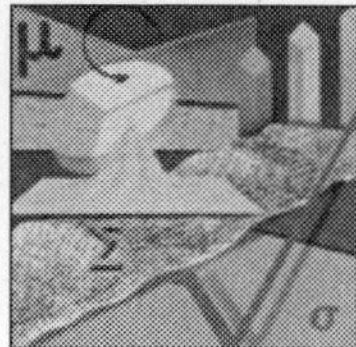

Men are losing their grip on the labor force, according to an *American Demographics* article, "Workers in 2000" (March 1990, p. 36). The increasing impact of American women on the labor force is predicted for the 1990s.

Chapters 8 through 10 introduced estimation and hypothesis testing. Hypothesis tests about a population mean or proportion were constructed for one and two samples. For these tests it was assumed that the populations being sampled were normally distributed. These tests dealt with data that were at least interval-scaled, such as heights, ages, and incomes. There are some situations where the data aren't interval or ratio, but are nominal or ordinal. In these situations, no assumptions can be made about the population's shape. This chapter will introduce chi-square tests, which cover some of these situations.

Why Managers Need to Know about Chi-Square Tests

This chapter discusses two hypothesis tests for which the chi-square distribution is the appropriate sampling distribution. Because of the frequency with which nominal and ordinal data are collected in practical situations, these techniques are particularly useful in business. Additional hypothesis tests of this type for qualitative data are covered in Chapter 19.

Regarding the *American Demographics* article, the changing nature of the work force could be monitored year by year by recording the numbers of men and women in such job categories as executive, professional, sales, service, and laborer. The techniques in this chapter could be used to detect significant changes.

Contingency Table Test

Contingency Table Test

The **contingency table test** is designed to determine whether two categorical variables are related. It is sometimes called the *test of independence* since the null hypothesis being tested states that the two categorical variables are *independent*. This test is quite useful because the analyst is often interested in finding whether one categorical variable is related to another.

> The **contingency table test** determines whether two categorical variables are related to each other.

The data necessary for the contingency table test consist of sample measurements on two categorical variables (nominal- or ordinal-scaled). These data values are arrayed in tabular form, which enables the analyst to see a *display* of the collected data. This type of table is sometimes referred to as a *cross-classification table* (*crosstabs* for short).

The null and alternative hypotheses that the analyst must choose between after examining the sample data are

H_0: The row and column variables are independent.

H_1: The row and column variables are dependent.

The contingency table test is often used to analyze important aspects of survey data. Surveys typically contain questions designed to measure certain demographic characteristics of the sample (for instance, age category, sex, income level, marital status, and educational level). Another type of question frequently found in a survey instrument elicits respondents' attitudes and opinions. Many contingency table tests contrast a demographic variable with an attitude variable. For example, the male/female variable might be cross-tabulated with a rating on store prices, or age categories might be cross-tabulated with the response to a statement about a presidential candidate. The purpose of such tests is to determine if different population types, as distinguished by the demographic questions, have different attitudes regarding the subjects investigated by the survey. "Applications of Statistical Concepts in the Business World" at this chapter's end gives additional examples of contingency table applications.

EXAMPLE 11.1 Jim Moore, marketing director for Bell Manufacturing Corporation, wants to know if there's a difference in brand awareness between men and women concerning the company's environmental control system. Jim randomly surveyed 100 people. Table 11.1 gives the results. The column totals show that 60 men and 40 women were surveyed. The row totals show that of the 100 respondents, 70 were aware of the company's environmental control system and 30 were unaware. These row and column totals are the result of random sampling.

TABLE 11.1 Contingency Table for Gender and Brand Awareness (Example 11.1)

	Gender		
Brand awareness	Male	Female	Totals
Aware	36	34	70
Unaware	24	6	30
Totals	60	40	100

As stated in Chapter 9, the first step in the hypothesis-testing procedure is to state the null and alternative hypotheses. The null hypothesis for this contingency table test is that the two categorical variables are independent of each other. This hypothesis states that a person's gender in no way indicates whether the person is aware of Bell's environmental control system. In other words, knowledge of which column a person is in, is of no value in trying to guess in which row that person falls. In the case of Table 11.1, if all females were aware of the control system and all males were unaware, it would be obvious that males and females differed in their awareness level. The null hypothesis would obviously be false under these conditions.

Table 11.1 is typical of most contingency tables in that it is not immediately obvious from the table whether the null hypothesis is true or false. A statistical test is needed to determine whether there's a relationship between the row and column variables.

The null and alternative hypotheses for this situation are

H_0: Gender and brand awareness are independent.

H_1: Gender and brand awareness are dependent.

The second step in the hypothesis-testing procedure is to assume that the null hypothesis is true. For Example 11.1, if gender and brand awareness are assumed to be independent, how many observations would be expected to fall in each cell of Table 11.1? Example 11.2 demonstrates the computation of the expected number of observations in each cell.

EXAMPLE 11.2 The probability that a person is aware of the Bell environmental control system in Example 11.1 is found by noting that there are 70 aware persons out of the 100 people sampled:

$$\bar{p} = x/n = 70/100 = .70$$

If gender and brand awareness are independent, as stated in the null hypothesis, Jim would expect 70% of the 60 males to be aware of the Bell system. In other words, he expects that 42 males (.70 × 60 = 42) would be aware of the company's product. Likewise, Jim would expect 70% of the 40 females, or 28, to be aware of the Bell system. Note that the expected frequencies for the "aware" row must sum to the total observed frequencies: 42 + 28 = 70. The upper right corner of each cell in Table 11.2 shows the expected frequencies.

TABLE 11.2 Expected Frequencies for Example 11.2

	Gender		
Brand awareness	Male	Female	Totals
Aware	36 (expected 42)	34 (expected 28)	70
Unaware	24 (expected 18)	6 (expected 12)	30
Totals	60	40	100

Equation 11.1 provides an easy method for computing expected frequencies. Chapter 5 showed that independence of events A and B implies that $P(\text{A and B}) = P(\text{A}) \times P(\text{B})$. Similarly, in the contingency table analysis, if the categories are independent, the probability that an item is classified in any particular cell of the table is the product of the corresponding marginal probabilities. To calculate the expected frequency for a particular cell, multiply the row total by the column total and then divide this product by the total sample size:

$$f_e = \frac{\text{(Row total)(Column total)}}{\text{Sample size}} \tag{11.1}$$

The expected frequency for the male-unaware cell of Table 11.2 is

$$f_e = \frac{\text{(Row total)(Column total)}}{\text{Sample size}} = \frac{(30)(60)}{100} = 18$$

A widely used rule of thumb for this test states that each expected frequency in a contingency table must be five or greater ($f_e \geq 5$) for the test to be accurate.

A test statistic is now needed that compares the observed and expected frequencies for each cell of Table 11.2. If the observed frequencies are quite close to the expected frequencies, the statistic should indicate a failure to reject the null hypothesis of independence. This is the appropriate conclusion because the expected frequencies are computed under the assumption that the two categorical variables are independent. If the observed and expected frequencies are quite different, the test statistic should lead to rejection of the null hypothesis.

Equation 11.2 is used for the cell-by-cell comparisons. The computed value is called a *chi-square* (χ^2) *statistic.* If the null hypothesis is true, the distribution of this computed value is approximately a chi-square distribution. Actually, the chi-square is a family of probability distributions. As with the t distribution, the χ^2 probability distribution is characterized by a single parameter, the degrees of freedom. Figure 11.1 shows the chi-square distribution for selected df values. The distribution is skewed positively, but as df increases, it approaches the shape of the normal distribution:

$$\chi^2 = \sum \frac{(f_o - f_e)^2}{f_e} \tag{11.2}$$

where: f_o = Observed frequency
f_e = Expected frequency

TM

FIGURE 11.1 Chi-Square Distributions for Various df

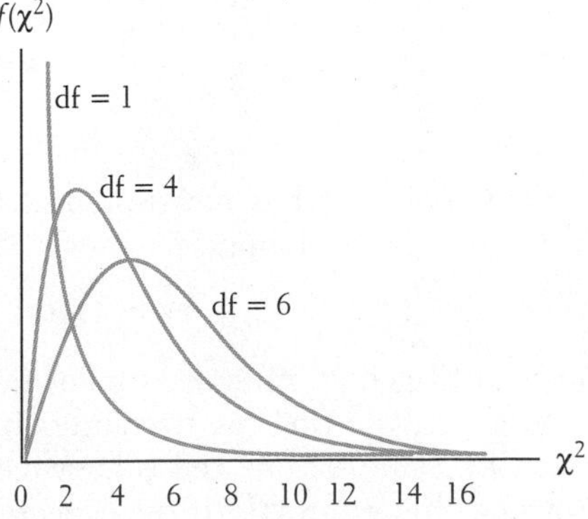

Note that the comparison between the observed and expected frequencies for each cell is being made in the numerator. If large differences exist from cell to cell, a large statistic results; small differences produce a small statistic. The contingency table hypothesis test is therefore a one-tailed test to the right. As Figure 11.2 shows, a large test statistic leads to a rejection of the null hypothesis while a small statistic leads to a failure to reject.

If the null hypothesis is true, the test value is drawn from the chi-square distribution. To determine the specific distribution from which it is drawn, we must calculate the degrees of freedom using Equation 11.3:

$$\text{df} = (r - 1)(c - 1) \tag{11.3}$$

where: r = Number of rows
c = Number of columns

Examples 11.3 and 11.4 illustrate these concepts.

EXAMPLE 11.3 Table 11.3 shows chi-square calculations from the cell values in Table 11.2. Note in Equation 11.2 that each value of the fraction following the summation sign is calculated; then these are added together. Since there are two rows and two columns in Table 11.2, there are four terms to calculate and sum using Equation 11.2.

Table 11.3 shows that the test statistic computed from the sample data is 7.143. If this calculated value is judged to be small, it's because the observed values in the cells are close to those that would be expected if the null hypothesis is true. If the test statistic turns out to be large, it's because the observed and expected frequencies are not close.

TM

TABLE 11.3 Chi-Square Computations for Example 11.3

f_o	f_e	$(f_o - f_e)$	$(f_o - f_e)^2$	$(f_o - f_e)^2/f_e$
36	42	−6	36	36/42 = 0.857
34	28	6	36	36/28 = 1.286
24	18	6	36	36/18 = 2.000
6	12	−6	36	36/12 = 3.000
				χ^2 = 7.143

The null hypothesis for Example 11.1 is now tested at the 5% significance level. From Equation 11.3, the degrees of freedom are

$$\text{df} = (r - 1)(c - 1) = (2 - 1)(2 - 1) = (1)(1) = 1$$

The rationale for this degree of freedom value is as follows: Of the four cells in Table 11.2, how many are free to vary, given that the row and column totals must be maintained? The answer is one. If a value for one cell is known, the rest of the cell values are determined by the row and column totals. If the expected frequency for the male-aware cell is known to be 42, then the expected frequency for the female-aware cell must be 28 because the expected frequencies for the awareness row must add to 70. Likewise, if the expected frequency for the male-aware cell is 42, the expected frequency for the male-unaware cell must be 18 because the expected frequencies for the male column must add to 60.

Use Appendix E.8's chi-square table to find the critical chi-square value. As this table shows, the critical value for a chi-square distribution with one degree of freedom at the .05 significance level is 3.841. The decision rule is

> If the calculated chi-square statistic is larger than 3.841, reject the null hypothesis; otherwise, fail to reject it (reject H_0 if $\chi^2 > 3.841$).

The chi-square statistic of 7.143 exceeds the critical value. This statistic's large value is due to the large differences between the observed and expected frequencies in the four cells of the contingency table. The null hypothesis is rejected with small chance of error (5%). These sample data reveal a dependence between gender and brand awareness.

Table 11.2 illuminates the dependency between gender and brand awareness now that it has been supported statistically. The table shows that although 28 females were expected to be aware of Bell's environmental control system, 34 females were actually aware. Evidently, females are more likely to be aware of this system than males.

Figure 11.2 summarizes this situation. If the null hypothesis is true, the test statistic is drawn from this distribution. However, since the test value is larger than the critical value, this seems quite unlikely, so the null hypothesis is rejected.

FIGURE 11.2 Chi-Square Distribution (Example 11.3)

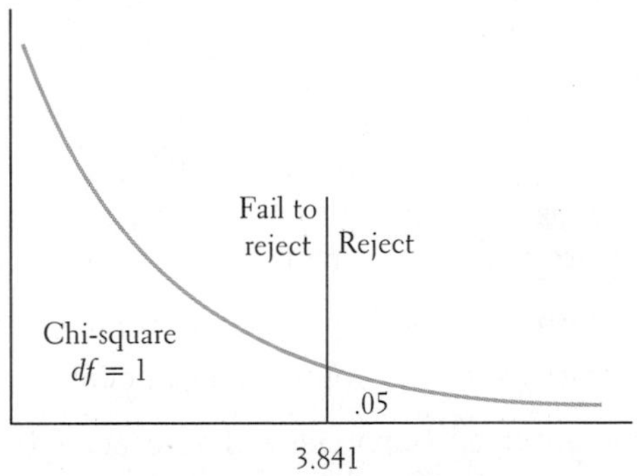

The chi-square contingency table test can be performed using MINITAB. The appropriate commands to solve Example 11.3 are:

```
MTB > READ C1 C2
DATA> 36 34
DATA> 24 6
DATA> END
      2 ROWS READ
MTB > NAME C1 'MALE' C2 'FEMALE'
MTB > CHISQUARE C1 C2
```

```
Expected counts are printed below observed counts

              MALE    FEMALE    Total
      1         36        34       70
             42.00     28.00

      2         24         6       30
             18.00     12.00

  Total         60        40      100

ChiSq =  0.857 + 1.286 +
         2.000 + 3.000 = 7.143
df = 1

MTB > CDF 7.143;
SUBC> CHISQUARE WITH DF = 1.
    7.1430    0.9925
MTB > STOP
```

Note that the READ command is used to input the data instead of the SET command. The READ command puts 36 and 24 into C1 and 34 and 6 into C2. The NAME command is used to name the columns of the table. The CHISQUARE command performs the analysis. The output produces a table that contains both the observed frequencies and the expected frequencies.

The CDF command is used to generate a cumulative probability density function. The CHISQUARE subcommand is used to generate the probability function for a chi-square distribution with one degree of freedom. Note that the p-value (.0075) is computed by subtracting .9925 from 1 ($1.0000 - .9925 = .0075$).

EXAMPLE 11.4 Are baby boomers (25- to 44-year-olds) more likely to be employed than other age groups? A custom telephone survey of 4,000 respondents completed by Bruskin/Goldring Research indicates that of Americans 18 years of age or older: 63% are currently employed full-time, or are part-time employees not looking for full-time employment; 10% are unemployed or employed looking for full-time work, and 27% are unemployed and not looking.[1]

Table 11.4 shows the data classified by employment status and age. Do the data present sufficient evidence to indicate that employment status varies according to age group? The null and alternative hypotheses are

H_0: Employment status and age group are independent.

H_1: Employment status and age group are dependent.

Table 11.4 shows the observed frequencies. The expected frequencies, under the assumption that the null hypothesis is true, are calculated using Equation 11.1. For example, the expected frequency for the new workers-employed cell in the contingency table is

$$f_e = \frac{(2{,}520)(560)}{4{,}000} = 352.8$$

[1]"Where Workers Live," *American Demographics Desk Reference Series: American Workers*, Dow-Jones, Inc. December 1992, pp. 2–3.

TABLE 11.4 Contingency Table for Employment Status and Age Group (Example 11.4)

	Employment status			
Age group	Employed	Looking	Not looking	Totals
New Workers (18–24)	360	120	80	560
Boomers (25–44)	1440	160	200	1800
Peak Earners (45–54)	440	40	80	560
Seniors (55–64)	200	40	200	440
Retires (65+)	80	40	520	640
Totals	2520	400	1080	4000

Source: Adapted from American Workers, a supplement to *American Demographics*, December 1992,
pp. 2–3.

The expected frequencies, along with the calculation of the chi-square statistic, appear in Table 11.5. The calculations begin in the upper left corner of the table and move from left to right.

TABLE 11.5 Chi-Square Computations for Example 11.4

f_o	f_e	$\frac{(f_o - f_e)^2}{f_e}$
360	352.8	.147
120	56.0	73.143
80	151.2	33.528
1440	1134.0	82.571
160	180.0	2.222
200	486.0	168.305
440	352.8	21.553
40	56.0	4.571
80	151.2	33.528
200	277.2	21.500
40	44.0	0.364
200	118.8	55.500
80	403.2	259.073
40	64.0	9.000
520	172.8	697.615
	Sum:	1462.620

The test statistic, as shown in Table 11.5, is 1462.62. This value reflects the large differences between the observed frequencies and the expected frequencies if the null hypothesis of independence is true. The number of degrees of freedom for the test is

$$\text{df} = (5 - 1)(3 - 1) = (4)(2) = 8$$

Table 11.6 shows the rationale for computing the degrees of freedom for the contingency table (Table 11.4). Of the 15 cells, how many are free to vary when the expected frequencies are computed? The answer is eight. If eight expected frequencies are specified, the rest are determined by the row and column totals. For instance, if the eight

TABLE 11.6 Illustration of Degrees of Freedom for Table 11.4

	Employment status			
Age group	Employed	Looking	Not looking	Totals
New Workers (18–24)	f_e	f_e		560
Boomers (25–44)	f_e	f_e		1800
Peak Earners (45–54)	f_e	f_e		560
Seniors (55–64)	f_e	f_e		440
Retires (65+)				640
Totals	2520	400	1080	4000

values represented by f_e in Table 11.6 are known, the remaining values can be computed. Thus, there are $(r - 1)(c - 1)$ degrees of freedom in this table and in all contingency tables.

The critical chi-square value (from the table) for 8 degrees of freedom is 20.09 for a significance level of .01. The decision rule is

> If the calculated chi-square statistic is larger than 20.09, reject the null hypothesis (reject H_0 if $\chi^2 > 20.09$).

The null hypothesis is rejected since the test value (1462.62) is larger than the critical value (20.09). The sample data lead to the conclusion that employment status and age group are dependent. Tables 11.4 and 11.5 show that baby boomers are more likely to be employed than other age groups.

EXERCISES

1. What kind of data are used for the chi-square contingency table test?
2. Why is the chi-square contingency table test useful in business applications?
3. What is the goal of the contingency table test?
4. State the null and alternative hypotheses for a contingency table test.
5. How are the expected frequencies computed for a contingency table test?
6. If a contingency table has four columns and three rows, how many degrees of freedom are there for the chi-square contingency table test?
7. Core-Mark Distributors classifies its accounts receivable as either paid on time or overdue. Core-Mark also classifies the accounts as local or national. The data from the past few weeks are:

	Payment status	
Proximity	Paid	Overdue
Local	75	95
National	60	110

   a. State the null and alternative hypotheses.
   b. Compute the degrees of freedom.
   c. State the decision rule using the .02 significance level.
   d. Test whether the proximity of the debtor has any bearing on payment status.

1. Qualitative

6. 6

7*a*. Independent, dependent
b. 1
c. Reject H_0 if $\chi^2 > 5.412$
d. $\chi^2 = 2.76$, fail to reject

8. Pacific Advertising researches the relationship between favorite type of advertising message and income level for a sample of customers. The data are:

	Favorite advertisement		
Income	A	B	C
Low	25	40	70
Medium	30	30	30
High	45	20	10

8*b*. 4
c. Reject H_0 if $\chi^2 > 9.488$
d. $\chi^2 = 45.4$, reject

a. State the null and alternative hypotheses.
b. Compute the degrees of freedom.
c. State the decision rule using the .05 significance level.
d. Test whether income level is related to advertising preference.

9. The Computervision Corporation researches whether part quality is independent of production shift. The data on numbers of good versus defective parts are:

	Part quality	
Shift	Defective	Good
Day	67	726
Swing	33	575
Night	61	363

9*b*. 2
c. Reject H_0 if $\chi^2 > 5.99$
d. $\chi^2 = 25.17$, reject

a. State the null and alternative hypotheses.
b. Compute the degrees of freedom.
c. State the decision rule using the .05 significance level.
d. Test whether part quality is independent of production shift.

10. The A. D. Nickel Department Store sells gift certificates during the Christmas season. Sales manager Leo Henneman wants to determine if the value of a certificate has anything to do with what a customer purchases with it. The data collected from a sample of customers are:

	Certificate value		
Department	\$10	\$50	\$100+
Appliances	22	26	54
Clothing	33	31	22
Hardware	41	43	19

10*b*. 4
c. Reject H_0 if $\chi^2 > 13.277$
d. $\chi^2 = 30.83$, reject

a. State the null and alternative hypotheses.
b. Compute the degrees of freedom.
c. State the decision rule using the .01 significance level.
d. Test whether certificate value has anything to do with what a customer purchases.

11. The Metropolitan Improvement Association is planning to build a new coliseum in Pueblo, Colorado. The group undertook a market research study for Southern Colorado to

determine sports preferences of males in various age groups. A random sample of 680 males provided these results:

	Age group			
Sport	18–30	31–45	46–60	61 +
Hockey	25	50	75	100
Basketball	100	80	30	10
Football	5	25	25	30
Soccer	20	30	40	35

a. State the null and alternative hypotheses.

b. Compute the degrees of freedom.

c. State the decision rule using the .10 significance level.

d. Is age related to sport preference?

11*b.* 9
 c. Reject H_0 if $\chi^2 > 14.684$
 d. $\chi^2 = 173.8$, reject

GOODNESS-OF-FIT TEST

Goodness-of-Fit Test

The contingency table measures the "fit" of observed category frequencies to those frequencies expected under the assumption that the null hypothesis is true. A more general application of this procedure is the **goodness-of-fit test,** which determines whether frequencies observed for some categorical variable could have been drawn from a hypothesized population distribution.

The null and alternative hypotheses that the analyst must choose between after examining the sample data are

H_0: The sample is from the specified population.
H_1: The sample is not from the specified population.

> The **goodness-of-fit test** determines the likelihood that the frequencies observed for a categorical variable could have been drawn from a hypothesized population.

As stated in the definition of this test, only one categorical variable is involved. In contrast, the contingency table test covered earlier in this chapter involved the comparison of *two* categorical variables. The exercises at the end of this chapter will help distinguish between these two chi-square tests.

Equation 11.2 is used to calculate the chi-square test value for the goodness-of-fit test just as for the contingency table test. If the numbers of observed and expected frequencies among the categories are quite close, the resulting statistic will be small and the null hypothesis not rejected. If large differences exist among categories, a large statistic results and the null hypothesis will be rejected. Thus, like the contingency table test, the goodness-of-fit test is a one-tailed test to the right.

In using the chi-square table to find the critical value, we must determine the degrees of freedom. For the goodness-of-fit test, this number is calculated using Equation 11.4. Note that one degree of freedom is always lost because the expected frequencies must sum to the total number of observed frequencies. Additional degrees of freedom are lost whenever sample statistics are used to estimate population parameters in the computations for the expected frequencies:

$$\text{df} = k - 1 - c \tag{11.4}$$

where k = Number of categories
c = Number of unknown population parameters estimated by sample statistics

EXAMPLE 11.5 Equinox Food Exchange, an international food distributor, wants to know if there has been a shift in the size of shipments exported to Poland since that country began moving away from a state-controlled economy. An article in *Financial World* (March 3, 1992, p. 38) intensified Equinox's interest. If the export pattern has shifted, Equinox must adjust its purchasing pattern.

A random sample of shipments exported within the past five months, one from each month, was selected and the size (measured in 1,000 pounds) recorded:

Type:	A	B	C	D	E	Total
Number of shipments:	12	15	21	9	11	68

These numbers constitute the observed frequencies for the five shipments. The null and alternative hypotheses are

H_0: The populations of sizes of shipments are equal ($p = .20$).
H_1: At least one p_i is not equal to .20.

Under the assumption that the null hypothesis of equal type preference is true, how many shipments are expected to fall into each of the five categories? The answer is one fifth (20%) of the total sample size. Since $n = 68$, the null hypothesis implies that $(68 \times .20) = 13.6$ shipments would, on the average, be sent for each month. The value 13.6 is the expected frequency for each category. The observed and expected frequencies are displayed together:

Brand:	A	B	C	D	E	Total
Observed frequency:	12	15	21	9	11	68
Expected frequency:	13.6	13.6	13.6	13.6	13.6	68

The chi-square statistic calculated from Equation 11.2 is 6.411, as Table 11.7 shows.

In this example, there are five categories ($k = 5$), and there are no unknown population parameters to be estimated with sample statistics ($c = 0$). Thus, degrees of freedom is $5 - 1 - 0 = 4$. Figure 11.3 shows several significance levels and critical

TABLE 11.7 Chi-Square Computations for Example 11.5

f_o	f_e	$(f_o - f_e)^2/f_e$
12	13.6	0.188
15	13.6	0.144
21	13.6	4.026
9	13.6	1.556
11	13.6	0.497
		χ^2 = 6.411

FIGURE 11.3 Chi-Square Distribution for Four df (Example 11.5)

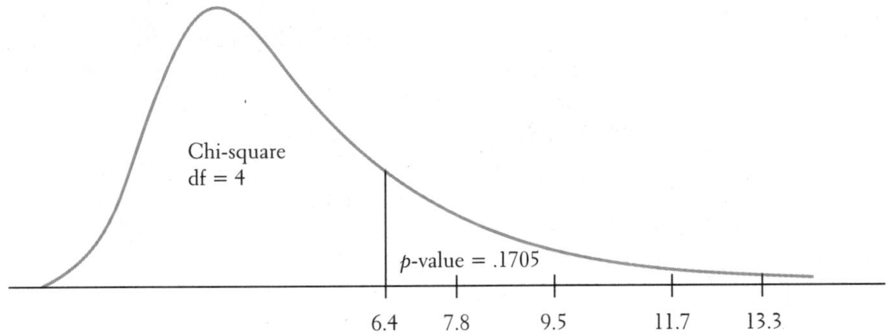

values selected from Appendix E.8's chi-square table for the distribution based on four degrees of freedom:

Alpha	.10	.05	.02	.01
Chi-square:	7.779	9.488	11.668	13.277

The computed test value (χ^2 = 6.411) is smaller than any of the critical values shown in Figure 11.3. The exact probability of rejecting a true null hypothesis is the *p*-value, .1705. The null hypothesis should not be rejected. There doesn't appear to be any difference among the five sizes of shipments Equinox Food Exchange exported to Poland.

EXAMPLE 11.6 *Shopping Journal* reported a recent study indicating that the breakdown of mall shoppers by age in a large city was:

Age category:	<21	21–35	36–50	51–65	66+
Percentage:	10%	32%	31%	16%	11%

In a random sample of shoppers in the Marshall Department Store's main branch, shoppers were asked to indicate their age categories. The following observed frequencies resulted:

Age category:	< 21	21–35	36–50	51–65	66+
Observed frequency:	18	51	42	89	50

Do the ages found in the Marshall study correspond to the age distribution reported by *Shopping Journal*?

The null and alternative hypotheses are

H_0: $p_1 = .10, p_2 = .32, p_3 = .31, p_4 = .16, p_5 = .11.$
H_1: The population proportions are not $p_1 = .10, p_2 = .32, p_3 = .31, p_4 = .16, p_5 = .11.$

The expected frequencies were calculated by taking the percentages from the *Shopping Journal* study and multiplying them by the sample size, 250. For example, the expected frequency for shoppers under age 21 is 25 ($.10 \times 250$). The expected and observed frequencies are:

Age category:	< 21	21–35	36–50	51–65	66+
Observed frequency:	18	51	42	89	50
Expected frequency:	25.0	80.0	77.5	40.0	27.5

Equation 11.2 is used to compute the chi-square test statistic and determine how well the age distribution obtained in the department store fits the age statistics of the large city. Table 11.8 shows the chi-square value for the test.

TABLE 11.8 Chi-Square Computations for Example 11.6

f_o	f_e	$(f_o - f_e)^2/f_e$
18	25.0	2.0
51	80.0	10.5
42	77.5	16.3
89	40.0	60.0
50	27.5	18.4
		$\chi^2 = 107.2$

The test value of 107.2 is compared with the table value of chi-square, again using the distribution for four degrees of freedom ($k = 5$, $c = 0$). At the .01 significance level, the decision rule is

If the calculated chi-square statistic is larger than 13.277, reject the null hypothesis (reject H_0 if $\chi^2 > 13.277$).

Since the sample chi-square statistic (107.2) is larger than the critical value (13.277), the null hypothesis is rejected. Marshall Department Store shoppers don't appear to conform to the large city's age distribution reported by *Shopping Journal*.

RULE OF FIVE

The test statistic used to compare the relative sizes of expected and observed frequencies has an approximate chi-square distribution. The distribution of this test statistic is actually discrete, but it can be approximated by using a continuous chi-square distribution when sample size n is large. This is the approach used in Chapter 6 to approximate the discrete binomial distribution using the normal distribution. The discrete distribution of the test statistic χ^2 is approximated using the continuous chi-square distribution. To assure that n is large enough, the conservative rule is to require that the expected frequency for each cell be at least 5. If a cell's expected frequency is less than 5, cells should be combined in such a way that meaningful categories result. Example 11.7 illustrates the use of the rule of five.

EXAMPLE 11.7 Lilah Novak, factory manager for a transmissions manufacturer, wants to use a simulation computer program to model the movement of goods on the factory floor. She's interested in improving the factory's efficiency, especially after reading an editorial in *Management Accounting* (August 1989), which described the increasing pressure on U.S. manufacturing from overseas competition. She also read a front-page *Wall Street Journal* (March 2, 1990) article describing the rapid expansion of Korean car companies.

A key assumption of the program is that the arrival of finished goods off the assembly line follow a Poisson distribution. Since Lilah has no idea whether this assumption is valid, she selects a random sample of factory hours and records the arrivals per hour (Table 11.9).

TABLE 11.9 Shipment Arrivals per Hour (Example 11.7)

Arrivals/hour	Frequency
0	3
1	15
2	23
3	20
4	12
5	10
6	7
7 or more	5
	$n = 95$

The null hypothesis under test is that the sample data were drawn from a population that follows a Poisson distribution:

H_0: The population is Poisson-distributed.

H_1: The population is not Poisson-distributed.

Under the assumption that the null hypothesis is true, Table 11.9's observed frequencies are compared with the expected frequencies based on the appropriate Poisson distribution. The chi-square statistic for the test is then calculated using Equation 11.2.

To find the expected frequencies, Lilah must know the mean number of population arrivals so that the correct column of the Poisson table can be consulted. However, the population mean is not known, so the sample mean from Table 11.9 must be calculated and used as an estimate. This is the same as the process for computing a weighted mean, which was introduced in Chapter 4. Each value in the first column of Table 11.9 is multiplied by the frequency (second column), and these products are added. This sum is divided by the total number of sample hours (95) to produce the sample mean:

$$\bar{x}_w = \frac{\Sigma wx}{\Sigma w}$$

$$= \frac{(0\times3) + (1\times15) + (2\times23) + (3\times20) + (4\times12) + (5\times10) + (6\times7) + (7\times5)}{3 + 15 + 23 + 20 + 12 + 10 + 7 + 5}$$

$$= \frac{296}{95} = 3.1$$

The average number of arrivals per hour for the sample, 3.1, is used as an estimate of the unknown population mean.

We now consult the Poisson table in Appendix E.4 to find the expected frequencies, under the assumption that the population is Poisson-distributed. The probabilities from the $\mu = 3.1$ column of the Poisson table are shown in Table 11.10. These probabilities are multiplied by 95, the number of sampled hours, to form the expected frequencies. Table 11.10 shows these values as well.

TABLE 11.10 Expected Frequencies for Example 11.7

Frequency	Poisson probability ($\mu = 3.1$)	f_e (probability × 95)
0	.0450	4.275*
1	.1397	13.272
2	.2165	20.568
3	.2237	21.252
4	.1734	16.473
5	.1075	10.213
6	.0555	5.273
7 or more	.0387	3.677

*95 × .0450 = 4.275

Based on the rule of five, none of the expected frequencies in Table 11.10's f_e column should be less than five. However, the first category, the one for 0 arrivals per hour, has an expected frequency of 4.275. Also, the last category, the one for 7 or more arrivals per hour, has an expected frequency of 3.677. These values violate the rule of five. Lilah must combine the "0" and "1" categories and also the "6" and "7 or more" categories so that none of the expected frequencies is less than 5. This reduces the number of categories, and the degrees of freedom, but results in a valid test. Once these categories have been combined in Table 11.11, the expected frequency of the "0 and 1" category is 17.547, and its observed frequency equals 18. The expected frequency of the "6 or more" category is 8.949, and the observed frequency now equals 12.

TM

TABLE 11.11 Goodness-of-Fit Test for Example 11.7

Frequency	Poisson prob. for $\mu = 3.1$	f_e (prob. $\times$ 95)	f_o	$\frac{(f_o - f_e)^2}{f_e}$
0 or 1	.1847	17.547*	18	.012
2	.2165	20.568	23	.288
3	.2237	21.252	20	.074
4	.1734	16.473	12	1.215
5	.1075	10.213	10	.004
6 or more	.0942	8.949	12	1.040
			Sum: 95	2.633

*95 × .1847 = 17.547

After the expected frequencies are computed, they're compared with the observed frequencies, and the chi-square statistic is calculated. As shown in Table 11.11, this test value is 2.633. For this equation, there are six categories ($k = 6$). One population parameter, the mean, wasn't known and was estimated using a sample statistic, so $c = 1$. Finally, the expected frequencies must sum to 95, so one more degree of freedom is lost. Thus, the degrees of freedom is

$$\text{df} = k - 1 - c = 6 - 1 - 1 = 4$$

In the chi-square table for four degrees of freedom, the critical value for $\alpha = .10$ is 7.779. Smaller significance levels have even larger critical values. At the .10 significance level, the decision rule is

> If the calculated chi-square statistic is larger than 7.779, reject the null hypothesis (reject H_0 if $\chi^2 > 7.779$).

Since the test statistic (2.633) is smaller than the critical value (7.779), the null hypothesis is not rejected. The sample data support the assumption that the population is Poisson-distributed, and Lilah can use the computer simulation program based on this assumption.

Figure 11.4 shows the test statistic compared to the critical or table chi-square value. Note that the p-value is .6220. This means that Lilah must assume a .6220 risk of making a type I error if she rejects the null hypothesis.

FIGURE 11.4 Chi-Square Distribution for Four df (Example 11.7)

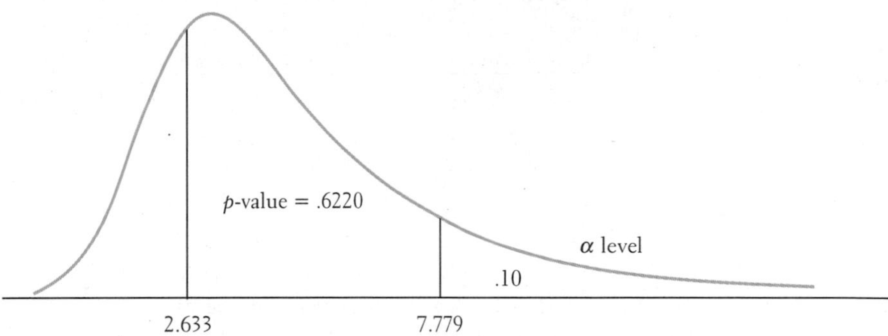

EXERCISES

12. What kind of data are used in the chi-square goodness-of-fit test?
13. Why is the chi-square goodness-of-fit test useful in business applications?
14. What is the goal of the goodness-of-fit test?
15. State the null and alternative hypotheses for a goodness-of-fit test.
16. How are the expected frequencies computed for a goodness-of-fit test?

17. 3

17. If a goodness-of-fit test to investigate equal brand preference has four categories, how many degrees of freedom are involved in the test?

18. 5

18. If a goodness-of-fit test to investigate whether a variable is normally distributed has eight categories, how many degrees of freedom are involved in the test?
19. How do the contingency table test and the goodness-of-fit test differ?

20. The Shaga Soft Drink Company is about to enter the diet cola market and wants to know if consumers prefer a certain brand in a blind taste test. Two hundred diet cola drinkers are offered four different beverages in identical containers and asked to indicate their favorite. The results are:

Favorite diet cola			
A	B	C	D
60	43	46	51

a. State the null and alternative hypotheses.
b. Compute the degrees of freedom.
c. State the decision rule using the .01 significance level.
d. Test if people prefer one brand over another.

20*b.* 3
c. Reject H_0 if $\chi^2 > 11.345$
d. $\chi^2 = 3.32$, fail to reject

21. Kay Bright, accounting supervisor for Westman Corporation, wants to know if the company's accounting process can be simulated using the Poisson distribution to describe the

incidence of error. Kay takes a random sample of 400 accounts from the firm's accounting records and summarizes the number of errors found in each account. The results are:

Number of errors	Number of accounts
0	102
1	140
2	75
3	52
4 or more	31
	400

21*b*. 3
c. Reject H_0 if $\chi^2 > 7.815$
d. $\chi^2 = 10.28$, reject

a. State the null and alternative hypotheses.
b. Compute the degrees of freedom.
c. State the decision rule using the .05 significance level.
d. Test whether the Poisson distribution describes the incidence of error in the firm's accounting records.

22. The First Intercounty Bank surveyed the number of business failures in those counties where it has branches. Vice President Cal Worship is trying to obtain data to help him decide how to distribute the bank's staff of commercial loan officers specially trained to handle bankruptcies. The results of the sampling are:

County:	A	B	C	D	E	Sum
Observed failures:	17	23	25	12	23	100

22*b*. 4
c. Reject H_0 if $\chi^2 > 7.779$
d. $\chi^2 = 5.8$, fail to reject

a. State the null and alternative hypotheses.
b. Compute the degrees of freedom.
c. State the decision rule using the .10 significance level.
d. Determine whether or not it's reasonable for Cal to make loan officer assignments under the assumption that all five counties have the same number of problem businesses.

23. df = 3, reject H_0 if $\chi^2 > 7.815$
$\chi^2 = 17.34$, reject

23. Past records indicate that the average number of service calls received at the Magna service facility is four per one-hour interval. A random sample of 200 hour intervals is taken and the frequencies of service calls recorded. The results are:

Number of calls	Number of 200 hour intervals
0	45
1	99
2	32
3	19
4 or more	5
	Sum = 200

Use the .05 significance level to test whether the Poisson distribution describes the number of service calls received at the Magna service facility.

FINAL NOTES ON CHI-SQUARE TESTS

Several important things should be noted about the use of the chi-square tests discussed in this chapter. First, the expected frequencies should, as a rule of thumb, all be 5 or greater. If expected frequencies are lower, the test may be invalidated since the chi-square distribution may not represent the true sampling distribution.

Most data analysis computer programs can conduct the contingency table test, and some are capable of the goodness-of-fit test. These analyses' results usually include a display of the data along with the computed chi-square value and the p-value. The analyst can make a rational decision to reject or fail to reject the null hypothesis based on knowledge of the p-value.

When the null hypothesis is rejected for the contingency table test, the conclusion is that there is a dependence between the row and column variables. The analyst's next task is to determine the nature of this dependence. That is, after the hypothesis of independence is rejected, the analyst's interest shifts to finding which rows tend to influence which columns. This task is most easily accomplished by an inspection of the contingency table.

Likewise, a rejection in a goodness-of-fit test leads to an investigation of the ways in which the sample data fail to conform to the hypothesized population distribution. Those categories with more than the expected number of items are contrasted with categories that have less than the expected number. Insights into the nature of the population are thus gained.

Quantitative data, either interval or ratio, are frequently collected in statistical analyses. Since the chi-square tests discussed in this chapter are used only with categorical data, it's often desirable to convert quantitative data to categorical data so that these tests may be employed. For example, ages of sampled people from a night college program might be collected along with a variable measuring graduate/undergraduate status. If the analyst wants to investigate the relationship between age and status using a contingency table, it's necessary to first convert the ratio-scaled age data to ordinal data. Several age categories can be established and each person placed into one of them; this type of problem is illustrated in Exercise 34. Each person is also classified as a graduate or undergraduate.

EXERCISES

24. What is the rule of thumb regarding the number of expected frequencies necessary to conduct a valid chi-square test?
25. How is the p-value helpful to an analyst conducting a chi-square test?
26. After rejecting a null hypothesis in a contingency table test, what should the analyst do?
27. Alliance Pacific, Inc., conducted a voter opinion survey to elicit input from area voters regarding a proposed aquifer protection area. People were asked how they would vote on the ballot, and this variable was tested against income level, in thousands. The results are:

Income level ($000)	*Voter preference* Yes	No	Undecided
Under 15	155	55	35
15 to under 30	409	110	30
30 to under 50	269	45	26
50 and over	84	11	9

Source: "Spokane Aquifer Protection Area Voter Opinion Survey," Spokane: Alliance Pacific, Inc., August 1985.

27*b*. 6
c. Reject H_0 if $\chi^2 > 12.592$
d. $\chi^2 = 33.64$, reject

a. State the null and alternative hypotheses.
b. Compute the degrees of freedom.
c. State the decision rule using the .05 significance level.
d. Test whether income level is related to a person's vote on the aquifer protection area.

28. In the survey in Exercise 27, the variable *educational level* was also tested against how people plan to vote on the ballot measure. The results are:

Educational level	*Voter preference* Yes	No	Undecided
High school	303	65	30
Some college	282	70	40
College graduate	332	86	30

Source: "Spokane Aquifer Protection Area Voter Opinion Survey," Spokane: Alliance Pacific, Inc., August 1985.

28*b*. 4
c. Reject H_0 if $\chi^2 > 13.277$
d. $\chi^2 = 4.83$, fail to reject

a. State the null and alternative hypotheses.
b. Compute the degrees of freedom.
c. State the decision rule using the .01 significance level.
d. Test whether educational level is related to whether a person voted yes for the aquifer protection area.

29. The Dayton Corporation is trying to decide how to allot its advertising budget. Harold Ellis, company analyst, suggests that the company study how effective other firms have been with different types of advertising. He obtains the following data:

Type of advertisement	*Number of stores* Increased sales	Stable sales	Decreased sales
Newspaper	18	12	4
Radio	12	16	3
TV	14	16	2

29*b*. 2
c. Reject H_0 if $\chi^2 > 4.605$
d. $\chi^2 = 1.375$, fail to reject

a. State the null and alternative hypotheses.
b. Compute the degrees of freedom.
c. State the decision rule using the .10 significance level.
d. Test whether type of advertising affects sales.

Summary

This chapter presented two important statistical tests designed for qualitative or categorical data. These tests are widely used in business because many business applications involve measurements on people rather than things. Surveying people's attitudes usually results in categorical data, and investigating the relationships involved in such data requires the use of qualitative data techniques such as the tests discussed in this chapter. Additional methods of analyzing qualitative data appear in Chapter 19.

The contingency table test is designed to examine the relationship between two categorical variables. One of the variables is arrayed in the rows of the contingency table, and the other appears in the columns. The chi-square statistic is then computed. This statistic measures the degree of conformity between the observed frequencies in each cell of the table and the frequencies that are expected under the assumption of independence between the two variables.

The goodness-of-fit test measures the extent to which the frequencies observed in each category of a single variable conform to the frequencies that are expected for a hypothesized population. The nature of the population under test must be specified before the test is conducted. Under the assumption that the sample conforms to this hypothesized population, the expected frequencies are determined and compared with the observed frequencies using the chi-square statistic. The population condition specified in the null hypothesis is then either rejected or not rejected.

Applications of Statistical Concepts in the Business World

Alliance Pacific's Use of Chi-Square Tests

Jack Geraghty is president of Alliance Pacific, Inc. (API), a public relations and public affairs firm that specializes in crisis management and community awareness campaigns. API has determined public opinion on such issues as recycling, the police and fire departments staffing, electrical magnetic fields, sewers, whether to build a coliseum, and whether to build a waste-to-energy plant. The firm also specializes in helping local school districts obtain voter approval of bond levies.

Jack frequently conducts public opinion surveys. In each survey, one section asks respondents for demographic data to be used for statistical analysis. Jack uses the chi-square test of independence (crosstabs) to determine the relationship between each demographic variable and respondents' attitudes on various issues. For example, Jack uses crosstabs to determine the demographics (gender, education, age, income, etc.) of the type of person who will vote yes on a particular bond issue.

Other Applications

The contingency table test is widely used in business because market research often involves collecting categorical data. Here are examples of cross-tabulations that might appear in a business setting. The demographic variables in the left column would be compared with any one of the opinion variables in the right column through the use of a contingency table test.

Demographic variables	Opinion variables
Age category	Automobile preference
Sex	Favorite department store
Marital status	Health care provider
Educational level	Opinion on social security
Area of residence	Preferred presidential candidate
Occupation	Rating on 1-to-5 scale of:
Type of residence	Prices
Number in household	Service
Income level	Value
Years in community	Safety of funds invested
Employment status	Quality of management
Own home versus rent	Career satisfaction

The goodness-of-fit test is not as widely used as the contingency table test but still has many business applications. Following are several variables that might be examined and compared with the indicated population distribution.

Variable	Hypothetical population
Age	Age distribution from different state
Local candidate preference	National candidate preference
Telephone call arrivals	Poisson distribution
Time of completion	Normal distribution
Weight of parts	Normal distribution
Time of delivery	Normal distribution
Product preference	Equal preference
TV show preference	Equal preference
Defectives by plant	Equal defective rates

Glossary

Contingency table test A test to determine whether two categorical variables are related to each other.

Goodness-of-fit test A test to determine the likelihood that the frequencies observed for a categorical variable could have been drawn from a hypothesized population.

Key Formulas

Expected frequencies

$$f_e = \frac{(\text{Row total})(\text{Column total})}{\text{Sample size}} \tag{11.1}$$

Chi-square statistic

$$\chi^2 = \sum \frac{(f_o - f_e)^2}{f_e} \tag{11.2}$$

Contingency table test degrees of freedom

$$\text{df} = (r - 1)(c - 1) \tag{11.3}$$

Goodness-of-fit test degrees of freedom

$$\text{df} = k - 1 - c \tag{11.4}$$

SOLVED EXERCISES

1. CONTINGENCY TABLE TEST

Decision Science Associates conducted a telephone survey to assess older homeowners' attitudes toward retirement. People 55 years of age or older were asked, "How important to you is 24-hour community security in deciding where to live during your retirement?" Respondents indicated this factor was either "important" or "not important." This variable was tested against gender to determine if males and females answered the question differently. The results are:

Gender	*Important*	*Not important*
Male	140	60
Female	180	20

Source: "Survey of Older Homeowners Concerning Retirement Attitudes," Spokane: Decision Science Associates, June 1986.

a. State the null and alternative hypotheses.

b. Compute the degrees of freedom.

c. State the decision rule using the .05 significance level.

d. Test if gender is related to whether a person feels 24-hour security is important in determining where to live during retirement.

Solution:

a. H_0: Gender and the importance of 24-hour security are independent.

H_1: Gender and the importance of 24-hour security are dependent.

b. $\text{df} = (r - 1)(c - 1) = (2 - 1)(2 - 1) = 1.$

c. If the calculated chi-square statistic is larger than 3.841, reject the null hypothesis (reject H_0 if $\chi^2 > 3.841$).

d. The computations for the expected frequencies are

$$(200)(320)/400 = 160$$
$$(200)(80)/400 = 40$$
$$(200)(320)/400 = 160$$
$$(200)(80)/400 = 40$$

The observed and expected frequencies are shown in Table 11.12.

The chi-square computations are shown in Table 11.13. Since the calculated chi-square statistic (25) is larger than the critical value at the .05 significance level (3.841), reject the null hypothesis and conclude that gender and the importance of 24-hour security are dependent. Inspection of the table shows that females are more likely than males to want 24-hour security.

TABLE 11.12 Expected Frequencies for Solved Exercise 11.1

Gender	*Important*	*Not important*	
Male	160 140	40 60	200
Female	160 180	40 20	200
Totals	320	80	400

TABLE 11.13 Chi-Square Computations for Solved Exercise 11.1

f_o	f_e	$(f_o - f_e)^2/f_e$
140	160	2.5
60	40	10.0
180	160	2.5
20	40	10.0
		$\chi^2 = 25.0$

2. GOODNESS-OF-FIT TEST—NORMAL DISTRIBUTION

The Hewlet-Desoto Corporation has several thousand hourly workers. Company analyst Peggy Flaherty wants to determine if a normal distribution can be used to describe the firm's hourly wage scale. She selects a random sample of hourly workers and records their wage rates. Peggy finds that the sample mean and standard deviation are \$8.00 and \$0.78, respectively. She develops a frequency distribution of hourly workers (Table 11.14) and tests at the .05 significance level to see whether the hourly wage scale for the company is normally distributed.

TABLE 11.14 Data for Solved Exercise 11.2

Hourly wage (\$)	Number of workers
6.00 to under 6.50	12
6.50 to under 7.00	38
7.00 to under 7.50	104
7.50 to under 8.00	131
8.00 to under 8.50	117
8.50 to under 9.00	98
9.00 to under 9.50	47
9.50 to under 10.00	13
	560

a. State the null and alternative hypotheses.

b. Compute the degrees of freedom.

c. State the decision rule using the .05 significance level.

d. Test whether the company's hourly wage scale is normally distributed.

Solution:

a. H_0: The population of hourly wages is normally distributed.
   H_1: The population of hourly wages is not normally distributed.

b. df $= k - 1 - c = 8 - 1 - 2 = 5$. $c = 2$ because two sample statistics (the sample mean and standard deviation) are used to estimate population parameters (the population mean and standard deviation).

c. If the calculated chi-square statistic is larger than 11.07, reject the null hypothesis at the .05 significance level (reject H_0 if $\chi^2 > 11.07$).

d. The null hypothesis is assumed to be true, so the sample mean and standard deviation are used to develop a theoretical distribution that is assumed to be normal. The computations for the expected frequencies are presented in Table 11.15.

TABLE 11.15 Expected Frequencies for Solved Exercise 11.2

Hourly wage ($)	$\bar{x}$	z	Area	f_e
6.00 to under 6.50	6.50	−1.92	.0274	15*
6.50 to under 7.00	7.00	−1.28	.0729	41
7.00 to under 7.50	7.50	−0.64	.1608	90
7.50 to under 8.00	8.00	0.00	.2389	134
8.00 to under 8.50	8.50	0.64	.2389	134
8.50 to under 9.00	9.00	1.28	.1608	90
9.00 to under 9.50	9.50	1.92	.0729	41
9.50 to under 10.00	10.00	2.56	.0274	15
			1.0000	560

*560 × .0274 = 15

Since a normally distributed variable theoretically ranges from $-\infty$ to $+\infty$, the area between the mean of the distribution (8.00) and the lower limit of the first class (6.00) is .5000 (the area from $-\infty$ to the mean).

The next step is to compute z values for the upper boundaries of each class. The upper boundary for the first class is 6.50. The z value for 6.50 is

$$z = \frac{x - \bar{x}}{s} = \frac{6.50 - 8.00}{0.78} = -1.92$$

From Appendix E.6's standard normal table, the area between a z value of -1.92 and the mean is .4726. If this area is subtracted from the area between the mean and $-\infty$ (.5000), the area of the class "6.00 to under 6.50" is .0274 (.5000 − .4726).

The z value for the upper boundary of the second class is

$$z = \frac{x - \bar{x}}{s} = \frac{7.00 - 8.00}{0.78} = -1.28$$

The standard normal table shows that the area between a z value of -1.28 and the mean is .3997. If this area is subtracted from the area between the mean and -1.92, the area of the class "6.50 to under 7.00" is .0729 (.4726 − .3997). Table 11.15 shows similar computations for the other class intervals.

Finally, Table 11.16 shows the differences between the observed and expected frequencies along with the chi-square computation.

TABLE 11.16 Chi-Square Computations for Solved Exercise 11.2

Hourly wage ($)	f_o	f_e	$(f_o - f_e)^2/f_e$
6.00 to under 6.50	12	15	0.60
6.50 to under 7.00	38	41	0.22
7.00 to under 7.50	104	90	2.18
7.50 to under 8.00	131	134	0.07
8.00 to under 8.50	117	134	2.16
8.50 to under 9.00	98	90	0.71
9.00 to under 9.50	47	41	0.88
9.50 to under 10.00	13	15	0.27
		560	$\chi^2 = 7.09$

Since the calculated chi-square statistic (7.09) is smaller than the critical value (11.07), Peggy fails to reject the null hypothesis and concludes that the hourly wage scale is normally distributed.

EXERCISES

30. When the chi-square test is used, is it necessary to assume that the population is normally distributed?
31. What are the similarities between the chi-square distribution and the t distribution? What are the differences?
32. Why is the alternative hypothesis one-tailed for chi-square tests?
33. Janis Yee, Financial Fleet Corporation director of marketing, conducts an experiment to determine if the type of postage used on the envelope containing a questionnaire affects whether a respondent returns it. Janis mails out 4,000 questionnaires, half using a postage meter and half using a regular stamp. The results are:

	Type of postage	
	Meter	Stamp
Response	750	775
No response	1,250	1,225

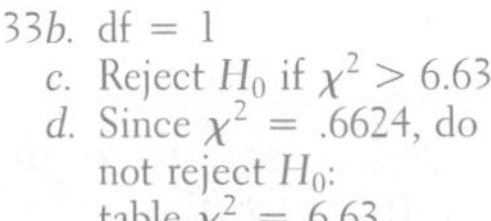
33*b*. df = 1
c. Reject H_0 if $\chi^2 > 6.63$
d. Since $\chi^2 = .6624$, do not reject H_0: table $\chi^2 = 6.63$

a. State the null and alternative hypotheses.
b. Compute the degrees of freedom.
c. State the decision rule using the .01 significance level.
d. Test if the response rate varies with the type of postage used.

34. Tony Greenwell, Wise Insurance Company analyst, believes younger drivers have more auto accidents and should be charged more for car insurance. To test this hypothesis, Tony gathers statistical evidence on claim rates for various age groups over a five-year period:

Age group	*Claim*	*No claim*
16 to under 21	50	175
21 to under 35	45	225
35 to under 50	38	375
50 and over	34	225

a. State the null and alternative hypotheses.

b. Compute the degrees of freedom.

c. State the decision rule using the .05 significance level.

d. Test if the number of claims is dependent on age.

34*b.* df = 3
c. Reject H_0 if $\chi^2 > 7.81$
d. Since $\chi^2 = 21.7965$, reject H_0

35. Holly Largent, vice president of computing at Northern University, has collected data on the number of times service to users was interrupted per day over the past year. Holly wants to determine the appropriate probability distribution for this variable so that she can create a simulation process. The data are:

Interruptions per day	Number of days
0	117
1	128
2	63
3	30
4	13
5 or more	14
	365

What should Holly conclude?

35. Test against Poisson, df = 4. Reject H_0 since $\chi^2 = 17.64$ (not a Poisson)

36. Bif Peanut Butter Company is worried that consumers prefer other brands to Bif. It hires an independent research firm to conduct a telephone survey in a market test area. The research firm calls 400 households and obtains the following brand preferences:

Brand A	Bif	Brand C	Brand D	Brand E
75	65	90	82	88

Write a brief memo for the research firm summarizing the results.

36. Test against uniform, df = 4. Since $\chi^2 = 5.22$, do not reject H_0

37. Diane Morton, marketing director of the Spokane Transit Authority, has hired Decision Science Associates to conduct a marketing research study. Diane wants to determine if riders live closer to a bus stop than nonriders. DSA surveys 1,201 Spokane County residents. The results are:

Proximity to bus stop	*Riders*	*Nonriders*	
Less than 1 block	200	234	434
1 or 2 blocks	170	221	391
3 or 4 blocks	55	112	167
5 or more blocks	52	117	169
Don't know	12	28	40
Totals	489	712	1,201

Source: "1984 Market Survey for Spokane Transit Authority," Spokane: Decision Science Associates, April 1984.

Write a memo to Diane explaining the results of this study.

37. df = 4. Since $\chi^2 = 19.4346$, reject H_0

38. Test against uniform, df = 9. $\chi^2 = 12.02$, table $\chi^2 = 16.92$, so do not reject H_0

38. Berry Wise has written a computer program to generate single-digit random numbers and wants to make sure it works properly. His friend, Michelle Conrath, is taking a statistics course and agrees to test the program. Michelle uses the program to generate 1,000 numbers.

Numbers	Frequency
0	90
1	85
2	115
3	101
4	92
5	107
6	85
7	112
8	113
9	100
	$n =$ 1,000

What should Michelle tell Berry about the program?

39. Test against normal df = 2. $\chi^2 = 3.38$ and table $\chi^2 = 5.99$ so do not reject H_0

39. Carla Parrish believes demand for jelly doughnuts on weekends at the Strick's Doughnut Company is normally distributed. If she's correct, the inventory problem of how many doughnuts to produce on Friday can be solved. Carla gathers data for the past 100 weekends:

40	45	34	35	40	37	36	44	42	39	39	42
45	39	38	37	42	37	35	42	40	41	40	36
42	42	33	33	34	39	38	37	36	39	36	31
41	39	45	43	30	40	38	39	42	38	38	37
34	36	40	42	45	31	47	35	37	39	43	45
35	43	40	40	33	39	44	37	49	45	45	39
47	40	38	44	38	39	31	37	36	41	36	44
37	37	48	50	45	43	42	35	37	40	37	42
31	42	40	41								

If Carla uses the .05 significance level, what should she conclude?

40. df = 3. Using $\alpha = .05$, critical $\chi^2 = 7.81$, $\chi^2 = 102.45$ so reject H_0

40. "Videophiles," an *American Demographics* (July 1992) article, reports demographics of media users. Once a year, Simmons Market Research Bureau asks nearly 20,000 Americans to give a detailed picture of their buying behavior, media use, demographics, and attitudes. The survey asks about most forms of media use, including magazine and newspaper reading, movie going, radio listening, TV viewing, videotape renting, and the buying of books, video games, and compact discs. Simmons identified seven types of media users, each with distinct demographic characteristics. A total of 2,800 respondents were identified as either videophiles or CD buyers; the accompanying table breaks down the results by household income categories.

Household income	Videophiles	CD buyers	Total
Less than \$15,000	208	84	292
\$15,000 to under \$35,000	512	300	812
\$35,000 to under \$60,000	560	384	944
\$60,000 or more	320	432	752
	1,600	1,200	2,800

Todd Corlett is interested in opening a store for videophiles (heavy users of videotapes, video games, and cable TV) and wants to know whether CD buyers are prevalent in the same household income categories as videophiles. This information will help him determine where to locate his new store.

Should Todd conclude that people's classification as either videophiles or CD buyers is independent of household income categories?

41. If α = .05, critical χ^2 = 12.59, df = 6, χ^2 = 27.82 so reject H_0

41. Robinson Research conducts a market segmentation study for the Atlanta area. Company president Bill Robinson identified seven types of media users, each with distinct demographic characteristics. To determine whether these findings are consistent with the entire U.S. population, Robinson compared his results with those reported by Simmons Market Research Bureau (*American Demographics*, July 1992). Simmons' percentages for each segmentation group were: TV fans (22%), radio listeners (22%), newspaper readers (20%), movie goers (12%), book buyers (10%), videophiles (8%), and CD buyers (6%). When Robinson classified its 500 sampled people, the results were: TV fans (100), radio listeners (120), newspaper readers (80), movie goers (80), book buyers (35), videophiles (60), and CD buyers (25). Are Bill Robinson's findings distributed the same as those reported by Simmons Market Research Bureau?

42. This question refers to Appendix C's company data base. Test the null hypothesis that the proportion of males and females (variable x_3) employed by the company is independent of amount of education (variable x_7). Use the .05 significance level and a sample size of 50.

43. This question refers to Appendix C's company data base. Test to determine whether the number of sick days taken during the past six months (variable x_5) is a Poisson-distributed variable. Use the .10 significance level and a sample size of 35.

44. This question refers to Appendix C's company data base. Test to determine whether employee age (variable x_9) is a normally distributed variable. Use the .05 significance level and a sample of 100.

EXTENDED EXERCISES

45. BABBET ELECTRONICS

Joe Burt is quality-control manager for the Babbet Electronics Company factory that produces compact discs (CDs). His boss, the plant manager, recently told a meeting of company executives that he'd read an article in *Gramophone* magazine (August 1989) about CD sales in the Japanese market. The manager stated that the quality of units produced by Babbet had slipped during the past year, making the company ineffective in this market.

Joe replied that quality had not gone down, but he had no data to back him up. He decided to seek sound evidence that would either confirm or contradict the plant manager's statement.

Company records prior to a year ago were obtained to get an idea of the quality level at that time. Then a random sample of quality reports for 224 CDs was taken from records for the past six months. Five categories were established for the CDs' condition (Table 11.17). The historical

TABLE 11.17 Data for Extended Exercise 45

	Product quality				
	OK	Slight rework	Major rework	Sell at discount	Discard
Then	163	37	10	8	6
Now	125	56	12	15	16

percentages were multiplied by 224, the sample size, to produce the expected frequencies. These were then compared with the observed frequencies in each category so a goodness-of-fit test could be conducted. The null hypothesis under test is that quality had not changed during the past few months.

Using Table 11.17's data, Joe calculates a test value of 41.82 for the goodness-of-fit test. He considers this a very large test value and realizes that his boss is right: the CD line's quality has deteriorated during the past year, and something must be done about it.

a. Did Joe calculate the test statistic correctly?

b. What are the critical table values for chi-square for several significance levels?

c. Is Joe's final conclusion correct?

46. SHELTY OIL COMPANY

For many years, Shelty Oil Company (a national retailer of gasoline and other car products) has offered its own credit card. Maintaining this service is expensive, and Shelty management wonders if the card should be dropped. There's a feeling that general credit cards, so popular in recent years, are preferred by customers over cards that can be used only with one company.

A consultant hired by the company designs a survey to be sent to a random sample of 1,383 holders. One of the demographic questions asks respondents whether they're heavy, medium, or light users of the Shelty card. Another question uses a 1-to-7 point scale to determine the respondent's opinion about the desirability of continuing the Shelty card. Table 11.18 shows the resulting data.

a. What is the null hypothesis in this situation?

b. What is the test statistic, the number of degrees of freedom for the test, and the critical value for a significance level of .05?

c. Using the .05 significance level, state the result of this test in simple terms.

TABLE 11.18 Data for Extended Exercise 46

	Not desirable					*Quite desirable*	
Card use	1	2	3	4	5	6	7
Heavy	56	79	87	93	128	59	21
Medium	67	89	94	132	32	21	16
Light	87	128	90	64	21	10	9

47. VALLEY HOSPITAL[2]

Lane Samson, chief administrator for a small hospital in western Washington, has hired a consultant to conduct a research study in his hospital's service area. A series of focus groups is conducted, along with a door-to-door survey. Among the matters of interest to Lane is the survey response to the following statement:

For most health problems, I would be comfortable being treated at Valley Hospital.

[2]This exercise is based on a study completed in May 1988 for a small hospital located in western Washington.

Survey respondents were asked to react to this statement with one of the following responses:

Strongly disagree, Disagree, Neutral or no opinion, Agree, Strongly agree.

Lane has seen the tabulation of responses for the entire sample, but he wants to compare responses by two key geographic areas. The first (area 1) is the area in the immediate vicinity of the hospital (within four miles). The second area (area 2) consists of the county the hospital is in, outside the four-mile area.

The data have been run on the SPSS computer program, version x. Here are the SPSS commands to generate a cross-tabulation of area by statement response:

```
CROSSTABS TABLES=VAR5 BY VAR14
STATISTICS 1
```

When the data were being keyed into the computer, the area number (1 or 2) was the fifth variable, so this variable received the name VAR5. Responses to the statement of interest to Lane were keyed in as variable 14, so that variable received the name VAR14. The second command line shown asks the program to compute the chi-square value and the p-value for the data.

After the computer run was completed, the following output was produced and printed:

```
            VAR 14
             SD    D     N     A     SA
VAR5    1     9   30    53    65    17
        2    21   45    42    15    11
        Chi-Square = 36.97     P = .0000
```

Lane interprets the output as follows. The cross-tabulation shows the number of responses in each of the 10 possible response categories. The total number of responses is 308, the door-to-door sample size.

The chi-square statistic, 36.97, was computed using Equation 11.2. Lane computes the degrees of freedom to be 4, leading to a table value of 13.277 at the .01 significance level. He thus rejects the null hypothesis of independence between rows and columns and concludes that the two areas react differently to being treated at Valley Hospital. In analyzing the cross-tabulation, Lane finds that people in area 1 (near the hospital) are more comfortable with being treated at Valley Hospital than those living farther away. Lane decides that an advertising campaign might improve this situation.

a. Did Lane reach the correct conclusion based on the computer output?

b. Did he use the correct degrees of freedom value and the correct value from the chi-square table?

c. Lane didn't know how to interpret the p-value printed on the computer output. Write a brief paragraph that explains this value to him.

MICROCOMPUTER PACKAGE

The micro package *Computerized Business Statistics* can be used to solve chi-square problems.

In Solved Exercise 11.1, Decision Science Associates attempted to determine if there was dependence between gender and whether people 55 years of age or older felt 24-hour security was important in deciding where they live during retirement.

Computer Solution:

From the main menu of *Computerized Business Statistics* a **12** is selected, indicating chi-square analysis. Since the problem involves entering data from the keyboard, a **1** is selected.

```
Chi-Square Analysis—Define New Problem
OPTIONS          1 = Goodness of Fit
                 2 = Test for Independence
Select Test: Enter 1/2, Press ↵ 2
```

Since a contingency table test, or test for independence, is needed, a **2** is selected.

```
Number of Columns: Enter 2–10, Press ↵ 2
Number of Rows: Enter 2–10, Press ↵ 2
```

Solved Exercise 11.1 involves a contingency table with 2 columns and 2 rows.

```
Alpha Error 1 = 0.1, 2 = 0.05, 3 = 0.025, 4 = 0.01, 5 = Other
Select Alpha: Enter 1–5, Press ↵ 2
```

The significance level selected for this exercise is .05.

```
Degrees of Freedom:  ............................... 1
Critical Chi-Square: ............................ 3.84

Chi-Square Analysis—Enter Column Labels
            Column 1    X1
            Column 2    X2
Press end when Finished
```

Variable 1 is entered as **IMP** and variable 2 as **SEX,** and end is pressed.

```
Problem definition correct? Enter Y/N/Q, Press ↵ Y
```

Following the **Y** response, the program is ready for the data to be entered.

```
Enter Observations
         IMP  SEX
      1  0    0
      2  0    0
```

After the data have been entered, the screen shows:

```
   IMP  SEX
1  140   60
2  180   20
```

F is entered to indicate that you are finished with this menu.

```
Save Data? Enter Y/N, Press ↵ N
```

Next, the chi-square analysis program options menu reappears.

A 7 is entered so that the problem can be run, and the chi-square analysis output menu appears. The choice in this case was **P** for printer.

Now, the program asks:

```
Want Graphic?
Enter Y/N and press enter: Y
```

The choice in this case was **Y** for yes. The resulting graph is shown in Figure 11.5.

FIGURE 11.5 Computer Output

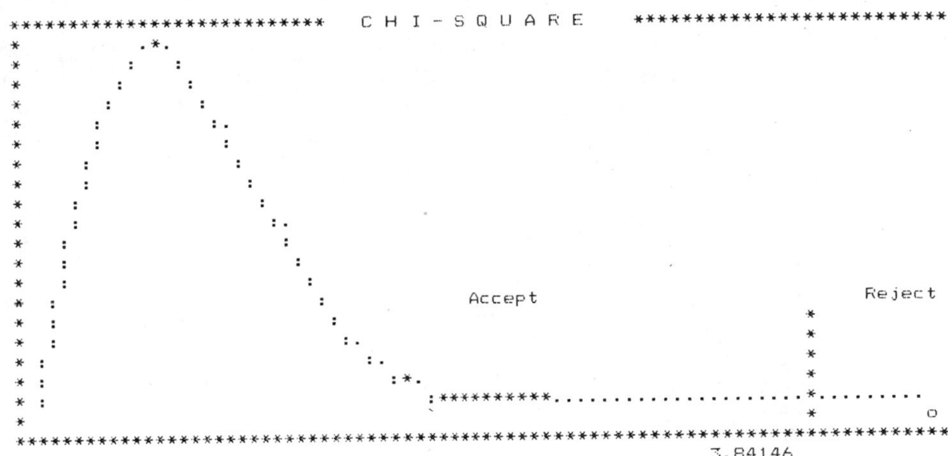

MINITAB COMPUTER PACKAGE

The MINITAB commands to perform the chi-square test of independence for Exercise 28 are:

```
MTB > READ C1–C3
DATA> 303 65 30
DATA> 282 70 40
DATA> 332 86 30
DATA> END
      3 ROWS READ

MTB > NAME C1 'YES' C2 'NO' C3 'UNDECID'
MTB > CHISQUARE FOR TABLE IN C1-C3
```

Expected counts are printed below observed counts

```
          YES       NO    UNDECID    Total
   1      303       65         30      398
       294.80    71.05      32.15

   2      282       70         40      392
       290.36    69.98      31.66

   3      332       86         30      448
       331.84    79.97      36.19

Total     917      221        100     1238


ChiSq  = 0.228 + 0.515 + 0.144 +
         0.241 + 0.000 + 2.195 +
         0.000 + 0.454 + 1.058 = 4.834
df = 4

MTB > CDF 4.834;
SUBC> CHISQUARE FOR DF = 4.
    4.8340     0.6952
MTB > STOP
```

The READ command is used to input the data instead of the SET command. The READ command puts 303, 282, and 332 into C1; 65, 70, and 86 into C2; and 30, 40, and 30 into C3. The NAME command is used to name the columns of the table. The CHISQUARE command performs the analysis. The output produces a table that contains both the observed frequencies and the expected frequencies.

The CDF command is used to generate a cumulative probability density function. The CHISQUARE subcommand is used to generate the probability function for a chi-square distribution with four degrees of freedom. Note that the p-value (.3048) is computed by subtracting .6952 from 1 (1.0000 − .6952 = .3048). Since the p-value is greater than the significance level, .3048 > .01, the null hypothesis is not rejected.

SAS Computer Package

```
TITLE ''CHI-SQUARE TEST FOR EXAMPLE 11-4'';
DATA DEFECTS;
INPUT COMPANY $ DEFECT $ COUNT@@;
CARDS;
A MINOR 14 A MAJOR 25 A REPLACE 18
B MINOR 5 B MAJOR 16 B REPLACE 10
PROC PRINT;
PROC FREQ;
 WEIGHT COUNT;
 TABLES COMPANY*DEFECT/CHISQ;
```

The TITLE command names the SAS run. The DATA command gives the data a name. The INPUT command names and orders the different fields on the data lines. The $ indicates that both COMPANY and DEFECT are character data. The @@ indicates that each card image contains two additional sets of data, and the CARDS command is a message that the input data will follow. The next line specifies that 14 defects from supplier A were minor, 25 were major, and 18 required replacement. The next line summarizes the defects for supplier B. The PROC PRINT command directs SAS to list the data. The PROC FREQ command and WEIGHT COUNT subcommand specify that the values of the variable COUNT are relative weights for the observations. The TABLES subcommand directs SAS to produce a contingency table of the variables COMPANY and DEFECT. Finally, the CHISQ command produces the chi-square statistic. The results are presented in Table 11.19.

TABLE 11.19 SAS Output for Example 11.4

```
                CHI-SQUARE TEST FOR EXAMPLE 11-4

                  TABLE OF COMPANY BY DEFECT

COMPANY       DEFECT
         |
Frequency|
Percent  |
Row Pct  |        |        |        |
Col Pct  |MAJOR   |MINOR   |REPLACE |  Total
---------+--------+--------+--------+
A        |     25 |     14 |     18 |     57
         |  28.41 |  15.91 |  20.45 |  64.77
         |  43.86 |  24.56 |  31.58 |
         |  60.98 |  73.68 |  64.29 |
---------+--------+--------+--------+
B        |     16 |      5 |     10 |     31
         |  18.18 |   5.68 |  11.36 |  35.23
         |  51.61 |  16.13 |  32.26 |
         |  39.02 |  26.32 |  35.71 |
---------+--------+--------+--------+
Total          41       19       28       88
            46.59    21.59    31.82   100.00

          STATISTICS FOR TABLE OF COMPANY BY DEFECT

Statistic                     DF     Value      Prob
------------------------------------------------------
Chi-Square                     2     0.923     0.630
Likelihood Ratio Chi-Square    2     0.951     0.622
Mantel-Haenszel Chi-Square     1     0.130     0.718
Phi Coefficient                      0.102
Contingency Coefficient              0.102
Cramer's V                           0.102

Sample Size = 88
```

Chapter 12

Variability Hypothesis Tests and Analysis of Variance

Strange! All this difference should be 'twixt Tweedledum and Tweedledee.

John Byron

Objectives

When you have completed this chapter, you will be able to:

Apply the single-population variance test to a business situation.

Apply the hypothesis test for the difference between two population variances to a business situation.

Estimate variance using both the *within* method and the *between* method.

Describe the *F* distribution and apply it to an analysis of variance.

Perform an analysis of variance for a one-way design.

Perform an analysis of variance for a two-way design.

List the assumptions behind the analysis of variance.

An April 1992 *Personnel Journal* article, "An Incentive Pay Success Story," described how a new incentive pay system at Viking Freight Company raised worker productivity.

Chapter 9 showed how to evaluate claims about the means and proportions of a population. Chapter 10 discussed how to evaluate claims about the equality of the means and proportions of two populations. This chapter will explain how to evaluate claims about the variance of a population and claims about the equality of the variances of two populations. Most important, you'll learn how to test the null hypothesis that the means of several populations are equal.

WHY MANAGERS NEED TO KNOW ABOUT ANALYSIS OF VARIANCE

One hypothesis test covered in Chapter 10 was the two-population mean test. In this test, the equality of two population means was tested using sample evidence taken from each population. An important subject of Chapter 12 is the hypothesis test for three or more population means. Even though population *means* are being compared, this test is conducted by focusing on the variances of these populations. For this reason, the test is called *analysis of variance,* usually abbreviated ANOVA.

Judging by the *Personnel Journal* article, a freight company might be very interested in investigating several incentive pay systems involving hourly employees. A method of measuring worker productivity would be determined and various freight firms sampled that use a variety of incentive plans. The sample results would be analyzed using the ANOVA procedures described in this chapter to determine if the plans were the same or different with regard to raising productivity.

SINGLE-POPULATION VARIANCE TEST

One-Population Variance Test

Analysts are sometimes interested in investigating the variability of a population rather than its mean or proportion. This is because uniformity of output is often critical in industrial applications. In fact, excessive variability is considered the number one enemy of high quality, as discussed at length in Chapter 13. The hypothesis test discussed in this section is designed to determine whether a population's variance equals some predetermined value.

The standard deviation of a data collection is used to describe the variability in that collection. As discussed in Chapter 4, the standard deviation can be thought of as the standard difference between the items in a data collection and their mean. Chapter 4 also defined the variance of a data set as the square of its standard deviation. The sample variance, although not particularly useful as a descriptive measure, is used to test the null hypothesis involving variability and is useful in understanding the procedure for analysis of variance.

The null hypothesis for the variance test is that the population variance is equal to some prespecified value. Since the usual issue of interest is whether the population variance is greater than this value, a one-tailed test is generally performed.

To test the null hypothesis, a random sample of items is taken from the population under investigation and a test statistic computed from these data. Equation 12.1 is used to compute the test statistic:

$$\chi^2 = \frac{(n-1)s^2}{\sigma^2} \tag{12.1}$$

where $n - 1$ = Degrees of freedom for the test where n is the sample size
s^2 = Sample variance
σ^2 = Population variance, assuming the null hypothesis is true

Note that the appropriate sampling distribution for this test is the chi-square distribution. In other words, if the null hypothesis is true, the test statistic computed using Equation 12.1 is taken from the chi-square distribution. In Chapter 11 you learned that a particular chi-square distribution is specified by a single parameter, its degrees of freedom. For this test, the degrees of freedom is one less than the sample size $(n - 1)$.

EXAMPLE 12.1 Ellie Gordan, an analyst with the Economic Development Council, wants to know if the variability of ages in a local community is the same or greater than that of the entire state. The standard deviation of state ages, known from a recent study, is 12 years. Ellie plans to take a random sample of 25 people from the community and determine their ages. She'll then calculate the sample variance and use Equation 12.1 to produce the sample statistic. The null and alternative hypotheses are

H_0: $\sigma^2 \leq 144$
H_1: $\sigma^2 > 144$

The sample is taken and results in a sample standard deviation of 15 years. The sample variance is thus 225, and the sample chi-square statistic is

$$\chi^2 = \frac{(n-1)s^2}{\sigma^2} = \frac{(25-1)(15)^2}{12^2} = 37.5$$

If the null hypothesis is true, the sample statistic of 37.5 is drawn from the theoretical chi-square distribution—specifically, the distribution with 24 degrees of freedom $(25 - 1 = 24)$. Note from Equation 12.1 that the larger the sample variance is compared to the hypothesized population variance, the larger the test statistic produced. Thus, a large sample statistic leads to rejection of the null hypothesis, and a small statistic results in failure to reject. The chi-square table (Appendix E.8) is used to determine whether it's likely or unlikely for the value 37.5 to be drawn from the assumed chi-square sampling distribution.

Suppose this test is to be conducted at the .02 significance level. From the .02 column of the chi-square table and the 24 row, the critical value is found to be 40.27. The decision rule is

If $\chi^2 > 40.27$, reject the null hypothesis that the population variance is 144 (reject H_0 if $\chi^2 > 40.27$).

Since the calculated test statistic is 37.5, the null hypothesis is not rejected (at the risk of a type II error). Note from the chi-square table that if an alpha of .05 had been chosen, the critical table value would be 36.415, and the null hypothesis would have been rejected (37.5 > 36.415). This example illustrates the importance of thinking carefully about the appropriate risk of a type I error in a hypothesis test.

Figure 12.1 summarizes Example 12.1. The null hypothesis is assumed true, leading to the drawing of a sample statistic from a chi-square distribution with 24 degrees of freedom. The test statistic along with three critical values are shown in Figure 12.1.

FIGURE 12.1 Chi-Square Test

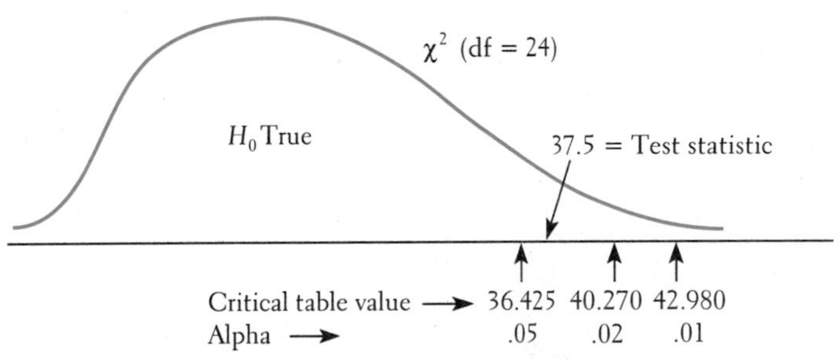

EXERCISES

1. Why is the variance test useful in business applications?
2. State the null and alternative hypotheses for a single-population variance test of your choice.
3. Alan Roberts, production manager of the Mountain Tire Company, believes there is too much variability in the life of tires produced by the night shift. If the process is working properly, Mountain Tires should last an average of 45,000 miles with a standard deviation of 4,000 miles. Alan decides to test to determine if the variability of tire mileages produced by the night shift is greater than 4,000 miles. He selects a sample of 12 tires and computes a sample standard deviation of 4,112 miles.
   a. State the null and alternative hypotheses.
   b. Compute the degrees of freedom.
   c. State the decision rule using the .02 significance level.
   d. Test whether the standard deviation of tires produced by the night shift is greater than 4,000 miles.

3a. $\sigma^2 \leq 16{,}000{,}000$
$\sigma^2 > 16{,}000{,}000$
b. 11
c. Reject H_0 if $\chi^2 >$ 22.618
d. $\chi^2 = 11.62$, fail to reject

4. Chris Karst, owner of a large chain of pet kennels, would like to determine the feasibility of providing a dental insurance plan for her employees. She's concerned about both the average cost and whether the standard deviation exceeds $200. A random sample of eight employees reveals the following dental expenses, in dollars, for the previous year:

342 425 625 975 141 52 342 459

4a. $\bar{x}$ = \$420.13
s = 287.11
180.03 to 660.23
b. $\sigma^2 \leq 10{,}000$
$\sigma^2 > 10{,}000$
df = 7
$\chi^2 = 14.42$, reject.

a. Using a 95% confidence interval, estimate the average cost of providing dental insurance.

b. If Chris uses the .05 significance level, is there evidence that the population standard deviation of dental expenses is above \$200?

TWO-POPULATION VARIANCE TEST

Two-Population Variance Test

Sometimes it's of interest to compare two populations to see if one is more variable in some important measurement than the other. The null hypothesis is that the two populations have the same variance, and the alternative hypothesis is that one has a greater variance than the other. Random samples are taken from each population and the sample variances computed. These values are then used in Equation 12.2 to compute the sample statistic:

F-ratio

$$F = \frac{s_1^2}{s_2^2} \tag{12.2}$$

where s_1^2 = Variance of sample 1
s_2^2 = Variance of sample 2

Note: for convenience in finding F values, the largest sample variance is usually placed in the numerator.

The test statistic for Equation 12.2 is called the *F ratio.* If the null hypothesis of equal population variances is true, the ratio of sample variances is drawn from the theoretical F distribution. By consulting the F table in Appendix E.9, we can assess the likelihood of this event. If it seems likely that the F ratio could have come from the assumed sampling distribution, the null hypothesis is not rejected. If it's quite unlikely the F ratio could be drawn from the assumed distribution, the null hypothesis is rejected.

The particular F distribution that applies to a specific test is determined by two parameters: the degrees of freedom for the numerator and the degrees of freedom for the denominator. Each of these values is $n - 1$. If these values are known and a value for alpha chosen, the critical F value can be found from the F table.

EXAMPLE 12.2 Wanda Flikke, president of Fidelity Mutual, wants to know if the hourly wage variability is the same at two of her branches, or if the variability of the Highland Branch (branch 1) is greater than that of the Oakwood Branch (branch 2). Her interest in salaries at Fidelity increased after she read an article in *Dollars & Sense* (May 1989) on significant income inequality in the United States. Comparing the income variability of the two branches is the first step of a complete income study.

Random samples are taken of hourly wages from each branch to determine the sample variances. Wanda chooses the .05 significance level. The null and alternative hypotheses are

$$H_0: \sigma_1^2 - \sigma_2^2 \leq 0$$
$$H_1: \sigma_1^2 - \sigma_2^2 > 0$$

The sample results are

$$s_1 = \$3.79 \qquad s_1^2 = 14.3641 \qquad n_1 = 21 \text{ (branch 1)}$$
$$s_2 = \$2.48 \qquad s_2^2 = 6.1504 \qquad n_2 = 25 \text{ (branch 2)}$$

The F statistic is calculated using Equation 12.2:

$$F = \frac{s_1^2}{s_2^2} = \frac{14.3641}{6.1504} = 2.34$$

The F ratio indicates that the sample variance from population 1 is 2.34 times the sample variance from population 2. However, given the sample sizes, is this enough evidence to reject the hypothesis that the two populations have the same variance? The critical F value is needed to answer this question. First, the degrees of freedom for the numerator and denominator are calculated:

$$\text{df (numerator)} = (n_1 - 1) = (21 - 1) = 20$$
$$\text{df (denominator)} = (n_2 - 1) = (25 - 1) = 24$$

The F table in Appendix E.9 is used to find the critical value. There are two F values in the table: one for the .05 significance level and one for the .01 level. Since this is a one-tailed test, as suggested by the alternative hypothesis, the entire .05 or .01 area will lie on the upper end of the curve.

The columns of the F table represent the numerator degrees of freedom, so column 20 is selected. The row labels correspond to denominator degrees of freedom, so row 24 is selected. The critical F value at the .05 significance level for 20 degrees of freedom in the numerator and 24 degrees of freedom in the denominator is 2.02.

The F ratio calculated from the sample data is 2.34. Based on this test value, the null hypothesis is rejected ($2.34 > 2.02$). If a 5% risk of a type I error is acceptable, Wanda can conclude that the populations don't have the same variance.

EXAMPLE 12.3 Are the variances of two populations of inventory part ages the same or does population 2 have a greater variance? To answer this question, random samples of 53 parts are taken from each of these inventory populations and the sample variances calculated. The test is to be conducted at the .01 significance level. The null and alternative hypotheses are

$$H_0: \sigma_2^2 - \sigma_1^2 \leq 0$$
$$H_1: \sigma_2^2 - \sigma_1^2 > 0$$

The numerator and denominator degrees of freedom are each 52 (53 − 1). In the abbreviated F table in Appendix E.9, the 50 row and the 50 column are used as approximations of the degrees of freedom. The decision rule is

If the calculated F ratio is larger than 1.94, reject the null hypothesis (reject H_0 if $F > 1.94$).

The sample results are

$$s_1^2 = 489 \qquad n_1 = 53 \text{ (inventory 1)}$$
$$s_2^2 = 1{,}370 \qquad n_2 = 53 \text{ (inventory 2)}$$

The F statistic is calculated using Equation 12.2:

$$F = \frac{s_2^2}{s_1^2} = \frac{1{,}370}{489} = 2.8$$

One of the sample variances is 2.8 times as large as the other. The null hypothesis is rejected since the test statistic (2.8) exceeds the critical value (1.94) from the F table. It is safe to conclude that inventory 2 has more variability in age than inventory 1.

Exercises

5. Why is the larger sample variance placed in the numerator in the equation for the F statistic?

6. Explain how the F test helps to determine whether two sample variances are equal or different.

7. State the null and alternative hypotheses for a two-population variance test of your choice.

8. How many parameters determine the particular F distribution that applies to a specific test?

8. 2

9. The Vantage Company uses two machines to produce ball bearings used in wheel assemblies. It is essential that the diameter of these bearings not vary significantly from the specification of 0.3 inch. Production Manager Pedro Hernandez is afraid that one of the machines is producing bearings that vary from specifications by an excessive amount, and he decides to compare the two machines. He selects a random sample of 20 bearings from each machine's production lot and computes the standard deviation of the diameters:

$$s_1 = 0.002 \qquad n_1 = 20 \text{ (machine 1)}$$
$$s_2 = 0.0015 \qquad n_2 = 20 \text{ (machine 2)}$$

a. State the null and alternative hypotheses.

b. Compute the degrees of freedom.

c. State the decision rule using the .05 significance level.

d. Test if the variability of ball bearing diameters differs for the two machines.

9*a.* $\sigma_1^2 - \sigma_2^2 \leq 0$
$\sigma_1^2 - \sigma_2^2 > 0$
b. 19, 19
c. Reject H_0 if $F > 2.21$
d. $F = 1.78$

10. The American Car Association is conducting an experiment to refute the claim that foreign automobiles get better gas mileage than American-made cars. Sue Wainwright, president of the association, feels that the variance in gas mileage obtained by foreign-made models is greater than for American-made models. A mileage test is conducted on 16 vehicles. The results, in miles per gallon, are:

American	35.3	32.6	37.1	34.1	31.9	36.4	35.7	33.3
Foreign	41.3	36.8	37.8	37.1	35.0	37.9	34.8	31.3

a. Write a memo to Sue reporting the results of the test that foreign cars get better mileage.

b. Write a memo to Sue reporting the results of the test of her belief that the variance in gas mileage obtained by foreign models is greater than for American models.

10*a.* df = 14
$\bar{x}_F = 36.5$ $\bar{x}_A = 34.6$
$s_F = 2.91$ $s_A = 1.87$
$t = 1.59$
fail to reject
b. Reject H_0 if $F < 3.79$, $F = 2.43$ fail to reject

ANOVA BASICS

Analysis of Variance

The **analysis of variance,** or **ANOVA,** procedure uses a single numerical variable measured on the sample items to test the null hypothesis of equal population means. This variable can be either interval- or ratio-scaled. It must be, in other words, a quantitative rather than a qualitative variable. This variable is sometimes called the *dependent variable,* especially in computer programs that perform ANOVA.

The null hypothesis under test in ANOVA is that all the populations being studied (at least three) have the same mean value for the dependent variable. The null and alternative hypotheses in ANOVA are

H_0: $\mu_1 = \mu_2 = \mu_3 = \cdots = \mu_c$.
H_1: Not all populations have the same mean.

> **Analysis of variance (ANOVA)** is a statistical procedure for determining whether the means of three or more populations are equal.

In the ANOVA test, sample evidence is gathered from each of the populations under study, and these data are used to compute a sample statistic. The appropriate sampling distribution is then consulted to see if the sample statistic contradicts the assumption that the null hypothesis is true. If so, it's rejected; otherwise, it's not rejected. This hypothesis test uses the same steps outlined at the beginning of Chapter 9.

Recall for the two-population variance test that the ratio of the sample variances is computed and checked against the F distribution. This procedure is also used in ANOVA to test the null hypothesis.

In analysis of variance we assume that all the populations being studied have the same variance, regardless of whether their means are equal. That is, whether the populations have equal or unequal means, the variability of items around their respective means is the same. If this assumption is sound, the null hypothesis of equal population means can be tested using the F distribution.

Under this key assumption, it becomes important to be able to estimate what the variance is and we will describe two methods here. The first method produces a valid estimate of the unknown common variance of the populations *regardless* of whether the populations have equal means. This method is known as the ***within* method** of variance estimation. The second method produces a valid estimate of the variance of the populations *only if* the null hypothesis of equal population means is true. This method is known as the ***between* method.**

Within *Method*

Between *Method*

> The ***within* method** of estimating the variance of the populations produces a valid estimate whether or not the null hypothesis is true. The ***between* method** produces a valid estimate only if the null hypothesis is true.

The final step in ANOVA involves calculating a ratio with the *between* method estimate in the numerator and the *within* method estimate in the denominator. If the null hypothesis that the populations have the same mean is true, this ratio consists of two separate estimates of the same population variance and is thus drawn from the F distribution. However, if the population means are not equal, the estimate in the numerator will be inflated, resulting in a very large ratio. It will be obvious upon consulting the F distribution that such a large ratio isn't likely to have been drawn from this distribution, and the null hypothesis will be rejected. The hypothesis test in ANOVA is one-tailed: a large F statistic will lead to rejection of the null hypothesis, and a small value will lead to failure to reject.

EXERCISES

11. What is the purpose of analysis of variance?
12. What kinds of data are used with analysis of variance?
13. State the null and alternative hypotheses for an analysis of variance.
14. What is the difference between the *within* method estimate and the *between* method estimate of the variance?

WITHIN METHOD

The *within* method of variance estimation will produce a valid estimate regardless of whether the null hypothesis of equal population means is true. This is because the variability of sample values is determined by comparing each data item with its own sample mean. Each sample value drawn from population A is compared with sample mean A, each item drawn from population B is compared with sample mean B, and so on. Equation 12.3 is used to compute the variance estimate using the *within* method:

$$s_w^2 = \frac{\sum_j \sum_i (x_{ij} - \bar{x}_j)^2}{c(n - 1)} \tag{12.3}$$

where s_w^2 = Estimate of the sample variance using *within* method
x_{ij} = ith data item in group j
$\bar{x}_j$ = Mean of group j
c = Number of groups
n = Number of sample items in each group

The double summation signs in Equation 12.3 call for first summing the values indicated by the right summation sign, and then summing the values indicated by the left one. First, the differences between each x value and its group mean are found, squared, and summed. Then, these sums for each group are added. The result is the sum of the squared deviations between each sample measurement and its group mean. This value is frequently called the *sum of squares within* (SS_w). This sum is then divided by the appropriate degrees of freedom to produce an estimate of the unknown population variance.

The appropriate number of degrees of freedom for the *within* method is computed as $c(n - 1)$ if the number of observations in each group is equal. Since the mean of each group is subtracted from each item in that group, only $(n - 1)$ items within each group are free to vary. And since there are c groups, c is multiplied by $(n - 1)$ to obtain the *within* method degrees of freedom.

Equation 12.3's key point is that each sample measurement is compared to the mean of its *own* group. Example 12.4 illustrates this concept.

EXAMPLE 12.4 The fill weights of four packages of frozen spinach are sampled from each of three crates. The question is whether the average weights of the packages are the same or different among the three crates. Here are the sampled weights (in ounces), group means, grand mean, and estimate of the *within* method variance using Equation 12.3:

	Group 1	Group 2	Group 3	
	12.4	11.9	10.3	
	13.7	9.3	12.4	
	11.5	12.1	11.9	
	10.3	10.6	10.2	
Mean:	12.0	11.0	11.2	Grand mean: 11.4

$$\Sigma(x_i - \bar{x}_1)^2 = (12.4 - 12)^2 + (13.7 - 12)^2 + (11.5 - 12)^2 + (10.3 - 12)^2 = 6.19$$

$$\Sigma(x_i - \bar{x}_2)^2 = (11.9 - 11)^2 + (9.3 - 11)^2 + (12.1 - 11)^2 + (10.6 - 11)^2 = 5.07$$

$$\Sigma(x_i - \bar{x}_3)^2 = (10.3 - 11.2)^2 + (12.4 - 11.2)^2 + (11.9 - 11.2)^2 + (10.2 - 11.2)^2 = 3.74$$

$$s_w^2 = \frac{\sum(x_{ij} - \bar{x}_j)^2}{c(n - 1)} = \frac{6.19 + 5.07 + 3.74}{3(4 - 1)} = \frac{15}{9} = 1.67$$

Note that each x value in the sample is compared with the mean of its own group. These differences are then squared and summed in accordance with Equation 12.3. The resulting values are added and divided by the degrees of freedom. The result, 1.67, is an estimate of the common variance of the three populations. The s_w^2 term is frequently referred to as the *mean square error (MSE)*.

The reason the *within* method produces a valid estimate of the unknown population variance, regardless of the status of H_0, appears in Figure 12.2. Figure 12.2*a* shows a situation for which the null hypothesis is true: the sample values drawn from each of the three populations, although not precisely equal, are nearly equal, so the three sample means are very close.

By contrast, Figure 12.2*b* reflects a situation where the null hypothesis is obviously false. The sampled items from each population have very different values, resulting in very different sample means. However, using the *within* method, the *same* variance

FIGURE 12.2 Variance Estimation

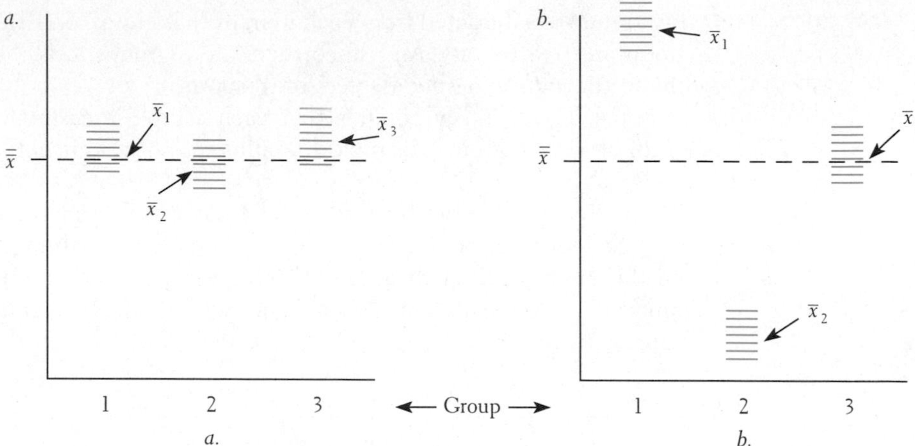

estimate will result for part *b* as for part *a*. This is because each item in each sample is compared with its own group mean. The fact that the group means are all quite different is not reflected in the calculation of Equation 12.3. Note that the assumption of equal population variances appears to be true for both plots: the scatter of data values around their means is the same for each group.

EXERCISES

15. What assumption must be valid for the *within* method to be used to estimate the variance?
16. Explain why the number of degrees of freedom for the *within* method is $c(n - 1)$.
17. How is the sum of squares within (SS_w) computed?

18. $s_w^2 = 5.25$

18. Four persons who drink a particular brand of coffee were asked to record the number of cups consumed during a day. The same was done for drinkers of three other brands. The results are shown below. Estimate the common population variance using the *within* method.

	Brand A	Brand B	Brand C	Brand D	
	3	5	2	3	
	2	1	10	6	
	5	4	5	4	
	6	6	7	5	
Mean	4	4	6	4.5	$\bar{\bar{x}} = 4.625$

BETWEEN METHOD

The second method of estimating the common variance of the populations produces a valid estimate only if the null hypothesis is true. To understand the *between* method, recall the central limit theorem presented in Chapter 7. This key theorem in statistics states that the distribution of sample means tends toward a normal distribution as the sample size increases, with a mean of μ and a standard error of $\sigma/\sqrt{n}$. If the standard error of the mean is $\sigma/\sqrt{n}$, then the variance of the distribution equals the standard error squared, σ^2/n.

This variance is a measure of the differences between all sample means that could be drawn from the distribution and the mean of the population. The square root of this variance is the standard error of the mean, the standard difference between a sample mean and the population mean. The standard error was described in Chapter 7.

In ANOVA, to estimate the variance of the sampling distribution of means, we must first estimate the population mean. The mean of all sample values provides such an estimate. Next, the difference between each group mean and this estimated population mean is determined, and these differences are squared and summed. This value is frequently called the *sum of squares between* (SS_b). This sum is then divided by the appropriate number of degrees of freedom to produce the estimate of the sampling distribution variance. Equation 12.4 shows the computation of the estimate of the variance of the sampling distribution of means:

$$s_{\bar{x}}^2 = \frac{\sum_j (\bar{x}_j - \bar{\bar{x}})^2}{c - 1} \tag{12.4}$$

where $s_{\bar{x}}^2$ = Estimate of the variance of the sampling distribution of means
$\bar{x}_j$ = Mean of group j
$\bar{\bar{x}}$ = Grand mean (mean of all data values), used as an estimate of μ
c = Number of groups

Remember from the sampling distribution of sample means that $\sigma_{\bar{x}}^2 = \sigma^2/n$, where n is the sample size, or number of items in each group. Evaluating this equation for an estimate of the variance (σ^2) produces

$$\sigma_{\bar{x}}^2 = \frac{\sigma^2}{n}$$
$$n\sigma_{\bar{x}}^2 = \sigma^2$$
$$\sigma^2 = n\sigma_{\bar{x}}^2$$

Therefore, an estimate of σ^2 can be computed by multiplying n by the estimate of $\sigma_{\bar{x}}^2$, or

$$s^2 = ns_{\bar{x}}^2$$

Thus, the *between* method estimate of the variance can be computed by substituting Equation 12.4 for $s_{\bar{x}}^2$:

$$s_b^2 = \frac{n\sum_j (\bar{x}_j - \bar{\bar{x}})^2}{c - 1} \tag{12.5}$$

where s_b^2 = *Between* method estimate of the common population variance
$\bar{x}_j$ = Mean of group j
$\bar{\bar{x}}$ = Grand mean (mean of all data values), used as estimate of μ

c = Number of groups

n = Number of sample items in each group if the number of observations in each group is equal

The appropriate degrees of freedom value for the *between* method is $c - 1$. Since the grand mean is subtracted from the mean of each group, only $(c - 1)$ means are free to vary. Note that Equation 12.5 assumes that the number of observations in each group, n, is equal.

EXAMPLE 12.5 In Example 12.4 the fill weights of four packages of frozen spinach were sampled from each of three crates and an estimate of the unknown population variance was calculated using the *within* method. In this example the unknown population variance will be estimated using the *between* method:

$$(12.0 - 11.4)^2 + (11.0 - 11.4)^2 + (11.2 - 11.4)^2 = 0.56$$

$$s_b^2 = \frac{n\sum_j(\bar{x}_j - \bar{\bar{x}})^2}{c - 1} = \frac{4(0.56)}{3 - 1} = \frac{2.24}{2} = 1.12$$

The estimate of the population variance computed using the *between* method is 1.12.

Figure 12.2 illustrates why this "estimate" is valid only if the null hypothesis is true. In part *a* of Figure 12.2, the null hypothesis appears to be true, and the variability of the three sample means around the grand mean ($\bar{\bar{x}}$) can be measured and used as a reliable estimate. In part *b* the situation is different. Because the null hypothesis is obviously false (that is, the populations have different means), the squared differences between the three sample means and the grand mean are quite large. The result is an inflated estimate of the population variance, not a true estimate. Figure 12.2 shows why the *between* method works only if the null hypothesis is true. In the next section we will introduce a statistical test to determine whether the *between* method has produced an inflated estimate.

EXERCISES

19. When is the *between* method of estimating the variance a valid approach?
20. Explain why df for the *between* method equals $c - 1$.
21. How is the sum of squares between (SS_b) computed?

22. Four persons who drink a particular brand of coffee were asked to record the number of cups consumed during a day. The same was done for drinkers of three other brands. The results are shown below. Estimate the population variance using the *between* method.

22. $s_b^2 = 3.583$.

Brand A	Brand B	Brand C	Brand D
3	5	2	3
2	1	10	6
5	4	5	4
6	6	7	5

ANOVA *F* TEST AND TABLE

After the *within* and *between* methods have been used to estimate the unknown variance of the populations, a ratio is formed from these two estimates:

$$F = \frac{s_b^2 \text{ (\textit{Between} method estimate of } \sigma^2)}{s_w^2 \text{ (\textit{Within} method estimate of } \sigma^2)} \tag{12.6}$$

If the null hypothesis is true, both the numerator and denominator of Equation 12.6 are valid estimates of the common variance of the populations being studied. This ratio will thus conform to the *F* distribution. However, if the null hypothesis is false, Equation 12.6's numerator is actually an inflated estimate of σ^2; the denominator will remain a valid estimate. Under this condition, the *F* value will be very large, and we conclude that the null hypothesis is false. Figure 12.3 shows the sampling distribution for the ANOVA test along with the acceptance and rejection regions.

Figure 12.3 illustrates the final step in the ANOVA hypothesis test. If the null hypothesis of equal population means is true, the calculated *F* statistic was drawn from this distribution. As the figure indicates, this appears reasonable as long as the *F* value is not too large. If a large *F* value results from the sample data, we conclude that unequal population means have caused the numerator in the *F* calculation to become inflated, and the null hypothesis is rejected. Note in Figure 12.3 that alpha (α), the probability of a type I error, is indicated in the upper (right-hand) tail. If the null hypothesis is actually true, there's some chance that it will be erroneously declared false. The chance of this occurring is equal to alpha, or the significance level of the test.

TM

FIGURE 12.3 *F* Distribution

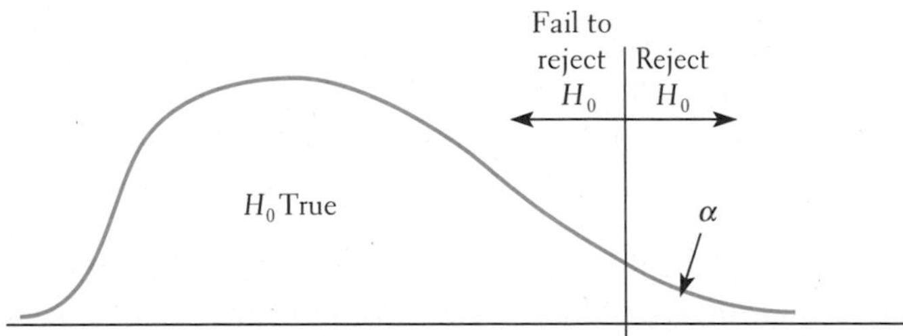

The results of an analysis of variance are usually displayed in an ANOVA table that summarizes the key values for the test. This table has a standard format that is used in most textbooks and computer programs that perform ANOVA. Table 12.1 shows the general form of the ANOVA table.

Table 12.1 summarizes the calculations needed to test the equality of several population means using analysis of variance. First, the *within* method is used to estimate σ^2. Each data value is compared with its own group mean, and the sum of squared differences is divided by the degrees of freedom, $c(n - 1)$.

TM

ANOVA *Table*

TABLE 12.1 ANOVA Table

Source of variation	SS	df	Estimate of σ^2	F ratio
Between groups	$n\sum_{j} (\bar{x}_j - \bar{\bar{x}})^2$	$c - 1$	SS_b/df_b	s_b^2/s_w^2
Within groups	$\sum_{j}\sum_{i} (x_{ij} - \bar{x}_j)^2$	$c(n - 1)$	SS_w/df_w	
Total	$\sum_{j}\sum_{i} (x_{ij} - \bar{\bar{x}})^2$	$nc - 1$		

j = Column number

i = Row number

c = Number of columns (groups)

n = Number of items in each group (sample size)

Next, the *between* method is used to estimate the common but unknown variance of the populations. As shown in the sum of squares (SS) column of Table 12.1, the sample mean for each group is compared with $\bar{\bar{x}}$, the estimate of the common population mean. This sum is multiplied by n, the number of items in each group. The sum of squares is then divided by the appropriate degrees of freedom, $(c - 1)$. This "estimate" of σ^2 is used in the numerator of the F ratio calculation. Finally, the *between* method estimate is divided by the *within* method estimate. The result is the computed F ratio for the test.

Note that Table 12.1 also shows the total sum of squares and the total degrees of freedom. These values, typically included in a computer printout for ANOVA, are simply the sum of the *between* and *within* values for SS and df.

> The **ANOVA table** contains columns showing the sources of variation, the sums of squares, the degrees of freedom, the estimates of the variance, and the F value for the analysis of variance procedure.

An example will illustrate the test calculations needed to complete an ANOVA table. If you understand the calculations in this example, you'll understand the numerous calculations performed by computer programs that compute analysis of variance and produce an ANOVA table in the final printout.

EXAMPLE 12.6 Joanne Herr, an analyst for the Best Foods grocery chain, wants to know if three stores have the same average dollar amount per purchase. A random sample of six purchases is chosen from each store. Table 12.2 presents the data collected from this sample along with the sample mean for each store and the grand mean of all the sample data. Joanne will test at the .01 significance level.

The null hypothesis under test is that all three populations from which the sample data were drawn have the same mean. The alternative hypothesis is that the popula-

TABLE 12.2 ANOVA Sample Data (in Dollars) for Example 12.6

	Store 1	Store 2	Store 3
	12.05	15.17	9.48
	23.94	18.52	6.92
	14.63	19.57	10.47
	25.78	21.40	7.63
	17.52	13.59	11.90
	18.45	20.57	5.92
Mean:	18.73	18.14	8.72

Grand mean $= \bar{\bar{x}} = 15.20$, $c = 3$, $n = 6$

tions don't have the same mean. The first two sample means in Table 12.2 suggest that the null hypothesis is true, since they're very close. However, the third sample mean, 8.72, is considerably smaller than the other two. But is this difference due to chance sampling or to the fact that the populations have different means? This is the question addressed in the ANOVA procedure.

Both the *within* and *between* methods are used to estimate the variance of the three populations. Remember the key assumption behind ANOVA: all populations have the same variance regardless of whether they have the same mean. Table 12.3 shows the calculations for the *within* method, and Table 12.4 shows calculations for the *between* method.

TABLE 12.3 *Within* Method Calculation for Example 12.6

Store 1:

$$(12.05 - 18.73)^2 + (23.94 - 18.73)^2 + (14.63 - 18.73)^2 + (25.78 - 18.73)^2 + (17.52 - 18.73)^2 + (18.45 - 18.73)^2 = 139.82$$

Store 2:

$$(15.17 - 18.14)^2 + (18.52 - 18.14)^2 + (19.57 - 18.14)^2 + (21.40 - 18.14)^2 + (13.59 - 18.14)^2 + (20.57 - 18.14)^2 = 48.25$$

Store 3:

$$(9.48 - 8.72)^2 + (6.92 - 8.72)^2 + (10.47 - 8.72)^2 + (7.63 - 8.72)^2 + (11.90 - 8.72)^2 + (5.92 - 8.72)^2 = 26.02$$

Sum of squares within $(SS_w) = 139.82 + 48.25 + 26.02 = 214.09$

TABLE 12.4 *Between* Method Calculation for Example 12.6

$$(18.73 - 15.20)^2 + (18.14 - 15.20)^2 + (8.72 - 15.20)^2 = 63.09$$

Sum of squares between $(SS_b) = 6(63.09) = 378.54$

The values calculated in Tables 12.3 and 12.4 are used to complete the ANOVA table. Since there are three populations being tested, $c = 3$. A sample of six values was drawn from each population, so $n = 6$. Table 12.5 shows the ANOVA table for this example.

TABLE 12.5 ANOVA Table for Example 12.6

Source of variation	SS	df	Estimate of σ^2	F ratio
Between groups	378.54	2	189.27	13.26
Within groups	214.09	15	14.27	
Total	592.63	17		

Note: The degrees of freedom were calculated as follows:

$$c - 1 = 3 - 1 = 2 \text{ (between groups)}$$
$$c(n - 1) = 3(6 - 1) = 15 \text{ (within groups)}$$

As shown in Table 12.5, the *between* method of estimating σ^2 produces a value of 189.27, whereas the *within* method estimate is 14.27. The F ratio indicates that the *between* method estimate is 13.26 times the *within* method value. Is this difference due to chance sampling error, or is it due to the fact that the null hypothesis is false? To answer this question, the F table is consulted and a critical value determined.

Two degrees of freedom are associated with the numerator of the F ratio, and 15 degrees of freedom are associated with the denominator. From the F table in Appendix E.9, the critical value is 6.36 for these degrees of freedom at the .01 level. The calculated F value of 13.26 is larger than the critical value, which means there is enough sample evidence to reject the null hypothesis of equal population means.

When a computer program is used to solve this example, as will be discussed next, a p-value of .0005 results. The p-value indicates that the probability of obtaining an F value greater than 13.26 by chance alone is .0005, if H_0 is true.

Since one of the group means is smaller than the others, Joanne concludes that although stores 1 and 2 might have equal average purchase amounts, store 3 appears to be below the average of the other two. This conclusion is not based on an intuitive inspection of the data shown in Table 12.2, but on a statistical rejection of the null hypothesis of equal means. Joanne has used the ANOVA procedure to conclude that corrective action is needed to bring store 3 up to the average of the other two stores.

The MINITAB commands to perform analysis of variance for Example 12.6 are:

```
MTB > SET C1
DATA> 12.05 23.94 14.63 25.78 17.52 18.45
DATA> 15.17 18.52 19.57 21.40 13.59 20.57
DATA>  9.48  6.92 10.47  7.63 11.90  5.92
MTB > END
MTB > SET C2
DATA> 1 1 1 1 1 1 2 2 2 2 2 2 3 3 3 3 3 3
MTB > END
MTB > NAME C1 'AMOUNT' C2 'STORES'
MTB > ONEWAY C1 C2

ANALYSIS OF VARIANCE ON AMOUNT
SOURCE     DF        SS        MS        F        P
STORES      2     378.4     189.2    13.26   0.0005
ERROR      15     214.1      14.3
TOTAL      17     592.5
```

```
                                    INDIVIDUAL 95 PCT CI'S FOR MEAN
                                    BASED ON POOLED STDEV
LEVEL      N      MEAN      STDEV   ---------+---------+---------+-------
    1      6    18.728      5.288                       (-----*------)
    2      6    18.137      3.106                       (-----*------)
    3      6     8.720      2.281    (-----*------)
                                    ---------+---------+---------+-------
POOLED STDEV =   3.778                    10.0      15.0      20.0
```

The SET command is used to enter the average dollar amount per purchase into C1, and to identify in which store the purchase was made in C2. The ONEWAY command performs the one-way analysis of variance. The output produces an ANOVA table and also analyzes the differences between the group means.

Note that $3.778^2 = 14.3$, the value listed in the sum of squares column for the ERROR row. Thus, the mean square error is equivalent to the pooled estimate of σ^2.

Note also that the MINITAB output includes a 95% confidence interval for the population mean corresponding to each group. Each of these confidence intervals is calculated using the POOLED STDEV = 3.778 and the t distribution based on the degrees of freedom for the error mean square. The confidence interval for the mean of store (level) 1 is

$$\begin{aligned}\bar{x}_1 \pm t\frac{s_p}{\sqrt{n}} &= 18.728 \pm 2.131\,\frac{3.778}{\sqrt{6}}\\ &= 18.728 \pm 2.131(1.542)\\ &= 18.728 \pm 3.286\\ &= 15.442 \text{ to } 22.014\end{aligned}$$

A few comments are in order regarding the analysis of variance procedure discussed in this chapter. First, the examples have implicitly assumed that the same sample size is used for each of the populations under test. In the ANOVA table, this sample size is denoted n, the number of items in each group. More complex versions of the ANOVA procedure can accommodate different sample sizes for the different groups. The simple procedure presented here, which assumes equal sample sizes, is the preferable method if equal samples are possible and convenient.

As mentioned in earlier chapters for other hypothesis tests, computer programs often print the p-value for the test along with the test statistic. In ANOVA, the p-value represents the area of the F distribution that lies above the calculated F value. As with other tests, this p-value is the risk of a type I error that must be assumed if the null hypothesis is rejected.

The key assumption in ANOVA is that the populations have the same variance regardless of whether they have the same means. This assumption can be checked after the sample data have been collected. The sample variances can be examined to see if they are about the same. Pairwise comparisons between sample variances can also be made using the two-population variance test discussed earlier in this chapter. If the null hypotheses of equal population variances are not rejected for all possible pairs, the assumption of equal variances necessary for ANOVA can be made with confidence.

Finally, if the populations don't have the same mean, then which populations have unequal means? The quickest and easiest way to answer this question is to inspect the sample means to see if any are either much higher or much lower than the others. In Example 12.6, it was concluded that store 3, with a mean of 8.72, had a lower average purchase amount than the other two stores. More formal procedures exist for finding the significant sample mean differences once the null hypothesis has been rejected. More advanced texts on analysis of variance describe these procedures.

EXERCISES

SM

23. What is an *F* ratio?

SM

24. What is an ANOVA table?

25. Four persons who drink a particular brand of coffee were asked to record the number of cups consumed during a day. The same was done for drinkers of three other brands. The results are shown below. (Exercises 18 and 22 asked you to estimate the variance using the *within* and *between* methods for these data.) Construct an ANOVA table to test if there's a difference in the average number of cups consumed for each brand.

25.	SS	df	σ^2
Between	10.75	3	3.58
Within	63.00	12	5.25
	73.75	15	

$F = .683$

Brand A	Brand B	Brand C	Brand D
3	5	2	3
2	1	10	6
5	4	5	4
6	6	7	5

26. The Economy Fuel Company delivers home-heating oil in a four-city area. Owner Jill Grover is interested in determining the speed with which bills are paid in the four cities. Random samples of six accounts are selected in each area, and the numbers of days between delivery and payment of the bill are recorded. The results are partially summarized below:

Source of variation	SS	df	Estimate of σ^2	*F* ratio
Between groups	128.14	3		
Within groups	864.35	20		
Total				

26*a*. H_0: $\mu_1 = \mu_2 = \mu_3 = \mu_4$
b. Reject H_0 if $F > 3.10$
c. $F = .99$
d. Fail to reject

a. State the null and alternative hypotheses.

b. State the decision rule if the null hypothesis is tested at the .05 significance level.

c. Complete the ANOVA table.

d. What should Jill conclude?

27. The Harrington Corporation manufactures VCRs. Tom Roberts, production manager, has a choice of three subcontractors from which to buy parts. Tom purchases five batches from each subcontractor, with the same number of items in each batch. The number of defectives per batch is determined, and an analysis of variance is run on the computer.

The results are partially summarized below:

Source of variation	SS	df	Estimate of σ^2	F ratio
Between groups	496.54			
Within groups	333.20			
Total		14		

27*a*. H_0: $\mu_1 = \mu_2 = \mu_3$
b. 2, 12
c. Reject H_0 if $F > 6.93$
d. $F = 8.94$
e. Reject
f. No

a. State the null and alternative hypotheses.

b. Compute the appropriate degrees of freedom values.

c. State the decision rule if the null hypothesis is tested at the .01 significance level.

d. Complete the ANOVA table.

e. What should Tom conclude?

f. Can Tom determine which subcontractor is best by examining the ANOVA table?

28. The Bandy Corporation, an electronics firm, has sent a number of employees to four educational institutions for technical training. This action was initiated by an article on assessing training needs in the *Training and Development Journal* (April 1989, p. 61). The company hoped that the training would improve employee productivity and product quality.

At the end of the program, Bandy tested the 40 graduates. The scores are:

	Program A	Program B	Program C	Program D	
	95	92	85	98	
	88	88	81	65	
	90	80	86	74	
	99	75	91	82	
	89	67	78	90	
	93	78	81	62	
	95	92	86	75	
	97	80	90	85	
	85	77	75	70	
	90	69	83	82	
Mean	92.1	79.8	83.6	78.3	$\bar{\bar{x}} = 83.45$

28*a*. H_0: $\mu_1 = \mu_2 = \mu_3$
b. 3, 36
c. Reject H_0 if $F > 2.86$
d. $F = 6.197$, reject
e. Yes

a. State the null and alternative hypotheses.

b. Compute the degrees of freedom.

c. State the decision rule if the null hypothesis is tested at the .05 significance level.

d. What should Bandy conclude?

e. Can Bandy determine which program is best by examining the data presented?

TWO-WAY ANALYSIS OF VARIANCE

The ANOVA discussion and examples to this point have taken into account only one source for the variability in the dependent variable: the groups identified in the populations under test. In Example 12.6, only the different stores could explain differences in average purchase amount. This situation is an example of a *one-way* ANOVA because there is only one factor identified to explain the sample mean differences.

Two-Way ANOVA

It is sometimes desirable to identify *two* possible causes for differences in the dependent variable. In such a case, a *two-way* ANOVA is conducted. In this procedure, two possible causes for the variability in the dependent variable are identified. Random samples are taken from the populations of interest, and the sample results are used to test the relevant null hypotheses.

To conduct a two-way ANOVA, we must measure the dependent variable for every combination of the two factors being considered. Examples 12.7 and 12.8 illustrate a two-way design.

EXAMPLE 12.7 In Example 12.6, Joanne Herr sought to determine if there was a difference in the average dollar amount per purchase among three stores. What if she also wishes to determine if there's a difference in the average dollar amount per purchase due to the effects of two different advertising campaigns?

The data in Table 12.2 are rearranged so that they can be examined using two-way analysis of variance. As Table 12.6 shows, there are three groups in factor 1 (store) and two groups in factor 2 (advertising campaign). A sample of three items ($n = 3$) were taken and measured for each of the six cells of the table ($3 \times 2 = 6$).

TM

TABLE 12.6 ANOVA Sample Data (Dollars) for Example 12.7

Advertising campaign	Store 1	Store 2	Store 3	Means
	12.05	15.17	9.48	
A	(16.87) 23.94	(17.75) 18.52	(8.96) 6.92	14.53
	14.63	19.57	10.47	
	25.78	21.40	7.63	
B	(20.58) 17.52	(18.52) 13.59	(8.48) 11.90	15.86
	18.45	20.57	5.92	
Mean:	18.73	18.14	8.72	15.20

Grand mean = 15.20, $r = 2$, $c = 3$, $n = 3$
Store 1 mean = 18.73
Store 2 mean = 18.14
Store 3 mean = 8.72
Advertising campaign A mean = 14.53
Advertising campaign B mean = 15.86
Store 1 and advertising campaign A mean = 16.87
Store 2 and advertising campaign A mean = 17.75
Store 3 and advertising campaign A mean = 8.96
Store 1 and advertising campaign B mean = 20.58
Store 2 and advertising campaign B mean = 18.52
Store 3 and advertising campaign B mean = 8.48

EXAMPLE 12.8 Ginny Nash, a professor at Midwestern University, has received a grant to study effects of different types of fertilizers and different types of soils. In her grant application, she quoted extensively from an article in *The Futurist* (July–August 1989) discussing drought-reduced harvests around the world and the need for increased efficiency in farming.

Ginny decides to investigate four different fertilizers (classified A, B, C, and D) on several acres planted in soybeans. Ginny plants the soybeans in five different soil types labeled 1, 2, 3, 4, and 5. At the end of the growing season, certain acres will be sampled and carefully measured for soybean yield. She hopes that this experiment will reveal fertilizer and soil combinations that produce heavy yields. The data will be collected by measuring the yield for every possible combination of fertilizer and soil type. A sample of n plots of land will be used for each of these 20 combinations, and a two-way ANOVA will be performed.

The two-way analysis of variance procedure will be used to test for differences in the dependent variable that are produced by the column variable. The null hypothesis being tested is that the various levels of the column variable all have the same population mean; this is the same test that was performed for the one-way analysis of variance. Likewise, another null hypothesis will state that the various levels of the row variable have the same average value in the population. These two null hypotheses could be tested separately, which would involve two one-way ANOVAs utilizing the procedure described earlier in this chapter. However, it's more convenient and time-efficient to test the row and column variables at the same time. This results in two null hypotheses under test: one for the rows and one for the columns.

A more important reason for using two-way ANOVA is that it enables a third hypothesis to be tested. Since every combination of the row and column variables will be sampled, we can examine the **interaction** effect of these variables. In Example 12.8, some unexpected result might occur when a particular fertilizer is used with a particular soil type. If so, interaction is present. The following two situations illustrate the concept of interaction for Example 12.8.

Interaction

1. The average yield of fertilizer A is 100 units per acre. The average yield of soil type 1 is 98 units per acre. When fertilizer A is used with soil type 1, an average of 99 units per acre is produced. Since nothing unexpected has happened when fertilizer A is used with soil type 1, no interaction is present.
2. Fertilizer B averages 110 units per acre, and soil type 1 averages 98. When the two are used together, the average yield is 150 units per acre. Apparently, something unusual is occurring when fertilizer B is used on soil type 1. Interaction is present.

> **Interaction** occurs when the levels of one factor interrelate significantly with the levels of the second factor in influencing the dependent variable.

In a two-way ANOVA, the first null hypothesis under test concerns the presence of interaction:

H_0: There is no interaction between the row and column factors in the populations under test.

If interaction is found, the analyst usually turns next to determining why certain levels of one factor interact with certain levels of the second factor. This is done by examining the various cell means. Interaction is found infrequently; however, when it is found, the analyst may not be interested in testing other hypotheses.

If no interaction is found, the row and column variables are examined for differences in the dependent variable. The null hypotheses under test are

H_0: There is no difference in the average value of the dependent variable for the row populations.

H_0: There is no difference in the average value of the dependent variable for the column populations.

EXAMPLE 12.9 William McGonigle, a personnel analyst, wants to conduct a two-way analysis of variance to see if the variable *time with company* is affected by either of two factors: the employee's location in the company's work areas and the employee's pay status. Each employee is assigned to one of four company work areas in various parts of the city. There are three types of employee in terms of method of payment: hourly, monthly, and annual. The data collection consists of samples from every possible combination of company location and payment method. This will result in a data table with 12 cells (four locations times three payment types). The null hypotheses to be tested are:

H_0: There is no interaction between work location and payment method.

H_0: There is no difference in time with company by work location.

H_0: There is no difference in time with company by payment method.

EXAMPLE 12.10 A study reported in the *Journal of Marketing Research* investigated the effects of price, brand, and store information on buyers' product evaluations.[1] Suppose the dependent variable was the buyer's perception of product quality as measured by a numerical value. Two of the factors studied were price and brand. There were five prices for handheld calculators ($17, $28, $39, $50, and the absence of a price) and three brands (Hewlett Packard, Royal, and Sony). The data collection consisted of samples from every possible combination of price and brand. This resulted in a data table with 15 cells. The null hypotheses to be tested are:

H_0: There is no interaction between price and brand.

H_0: There is no difference in perception of product quality for the different price levels.

H_0: There is no difference in perception of product quality for the different brands.

[1]Dodds, W. B., K. B. Monroe, and D. Grewal, "Effects of Price, Brand, and Store Information on Buyers' Product Evaluations," *Journal of Marketing Research*, August 1991, pp. 307–19.

The calculations involved in a two-way analysis of variance are considerable. The wide availability of computer programs that perform ANOVA has virtually eliminated hand calculations for this technique. As with all computer data analysis programs, however, knowing what's being done with the data is important for proper interpretation and understanding. The specific calculations for two-way ANOVA won't be presented here, but we will describe the general nature of the analysis and interpret the computer output.

The key assumption behind two-way ANOVA is the same as for one-way ANOVA: all populations under test are assumed to have the same variance. If there are three rows in the data table and five columns, there are 15 cells and 15 separate populations from which to sample. Regardless of whether the means of these 15 populations are the same, it must be assumed that they vary to the same extent. They must all have the same variance if the ANOVA procedure is to work properly.

There are four ways of estimating the unknown common variance of the populations in the two-way ANOVA procedure. One of these ways, the *within* method, produces a reliable estimate of this variance regardless of whether any of the three null hypotheses are true. As with one-way ANOVA, the *within* method measures the variability of each sample value around its *own cell mean.* Even if several of the cells in the data table have very different means, this won't influence the calculation of the variance estimate using the *within* method. Computing the sum of squares using the *within* method calls for comparing the first data value to the mean of the cell it's in. This difference is squared and added to the squared differences between all the other sample data measurements and their own cell means. The resulting value is divided by the appropriate number of degrees of freedom, $rc(n-1)$. Since the cell mean is subtracted from each of the n items in the cell, one of these items is not free to vary. Each cell thus has $(n-1)$ degrees of freedom, and there are r (the number of rows) times c (the number of columns) cells. This *within* estimate of the variance is the denominator of each of the F ratios.

The second method of estimating the variance is valid only if there is no interaction among the populations. If there is interaction, this method produces an inflated estimate. The df value is computed in the same manner as for the contingency table test: $(r-1)(c-1)$.

The third method of estimating the variance produces a valid estimate only if the null hypothesis about column mean equality is true. If this hypothesis is false, an inflated estimate will result. This is the same as using the *between* method to estimate the variance in one-way ANOVA. The degrees of freedom equal the number of columns minus 1 $(c-1)$.

Likewise, the final method of estimating the variance is valid only if the null hypothesis about row mean equality is true. If it is not, an inflated estimate results. Again, the procedure is similar to the *between* method estimate of the variance in one-way ANOVA. The degrees of freedom equal the number of rows minus 1 $(r-1)$. Table 12.7 shows the formulas for two-way ANOVA.

The final result of a two-way ANOVA is the calculation of three F ratios. As just mentioned, the denominator for each of these ratios is the *within* method estimate of the unknown variance of the populations. The numerators of the ratios are the

TABLE 12.7 Two-Way Analysis of Variance Table

Source of variation	SS	df	Estimate of σ^2	F ratio
Rows	$cn\sum_i (\bar{x}_{ri} - \bar{\bar{x}})^2$	$r - 1$	SS_r/df_r	s_r^2/s_w^2
Columns	$rn\sum_j (\bar{x}_{cj} - \bar{\bar{x}})^2$	$c - 1$	SS_c/df_c	s_c^2/s_w^2
Interactions	$n[\sum_i\sum_j (\bar{x}_{ij} - \bar{x}_{ri} - \bar{x}_{cj} + \bar{\bar{x}})^2]$	$(r - 1)(c - 1)$	SS_i/df_i	s_i^2/s_w^2
Within groups	$\sum_i\sum_j\sum_k (x_{ijk} - \bar{x}_{ij})^2$	$rc(n - 1)$	SS_w/df_w	
Total	$\sum_i\sum_j\sum_k (x_{ijk} - \bar{\bar{x}})^2$	$nrc - 1$		

j = Column number

i = Row number

k = Observation number within a cell

r = Number of rows

c = Number of columns

n = Number of observations in each cell

"estimates" produced under the assumption that each of the three null hypotheses is true. Each F ratio is examined to see if it's unusually large. Any F ratio that's larger than the table value for F results in rejection of the corresponding null hypothesis. The general form of each of the three final F ratios is

$$F = \frac{s_i^2 \text{ (}\textit{Interaction}\text{ estimate of } \sigma^2)}{s_w^2 \text{ (}\textit{Within}\text{ method estimate of } \sigma^2)} \quad \text{(Interaction)}$$

$$F = \frac{s_c^2 \text{ (}\textit{Between column}\text{ method estimate of } \sigma^2)}{s_w^2 \text{ (}\textit{Within}\text{ method estimate of } \sigma^2)} \quad \text{(Columns)}$$

$$F = \frac{s_r^2 \text{ (}\textit{Between row}\text{ method estimate of } \sigma^2)}{s_w^2 \text{ (}\textit{Within}\text{ method estimate of } \sigma^2)} \quad \text{(Rows)}$$

If all three null hypotheses are true, the numerators and denominators of these F ratio calculations will all be valid estimates of the same unknown population variance. As you have seen, such a ratio is drawn from the F distribution. However, if any of the three null hypotheses are false, the numerator in the corresponding ratio will be inflated and a large F value will result leading to a rejection of the null hypothesis.

EXAMPLE 12.11 Table 12.8 presents the two-way ANOVA table for Example 12.7. Four "estimates" of the common variance of all populations have been calculated. However, only the *within* method produces a valid estimate regardless of the status of any null hypothesis. The sample evidence has produced the value 16.019 as the *within* method estimate of σ^2.

TABLE 12.8 ANOVA Table for Example 12.11

Source of variation	SS	df	Estimate of σ^2	*F* ratio
Rows	8.013	1	8.013	0.50
Columns	378.381	2	189.190	11.81
Interaction	13.851	2	6.925	0.43
Within	192.223	12	16.019	
Total	592.468	17		

The three null hypotheses under test in Table 12.8 are:

H_0: There is no interaction between store and advertising campaign in the population.

H_0: The row populations (advertising campaigns) both have the same mean.

H_0: The column populations (stores) all have the same mean.

Note that in Example 12.6 Joanne Herr has already tested the null hypothesis that the column populations, or stores, all have the same mean.

The *F* ratios of Table 12.8 are calculated by dividing each of the three "estimates" of σ^2 corresponding to the three null hypotheses by 16.019, the valid estimate of σ^2. These calculations are:

F ratio	Degrees of freedom	Critical *F* (.05)
8.013/16.019 = 0.500	1, 12	4.75
189.190/16.019 = 11.810	2, 12	3.88
6.925/16.019 = 0.432	2, 12	3.88

Note that the *within* estimate of σ^2 ($s_w^2 = 16.019$) is used in each of the denominators. Also shown are the degrees of freedom for the numerator and denominator for each hypothesis test. These values appear in Table 12.8 for each row of the table. Note that the sum of squares (378.381) and the degrees of freedom (2) for the columns from Table 12.8 match (subject to rounding errors) the *between groups* row of Table 12.5. In both cases, the difference between store means is being tested.

The critical ratios from the *F* table are found for the .05 significance level and compared to the calculated *F* ratios. The calculated *F* value for interaction (0.432) is less than the critical value (3.88), so the null hypothesis is not rejected. The calculated *F* value for rows (0.500) is less than the critical value (4.75), so the null hypothesis for rows is not rejected. The calculated *F* value for columns (11.810) is larger than the critical value (3.88), so the null hypothesis for columns is rejected.

The conclusions for the two-way analysis of variance are:

1. There is no interaction between the stores and advertising campaigns in the population.
2. The advertising campaigns both have the same mean.
3. The stores have different means.

For the first two conclusions, the possibility of a type II error exists. In either case, the null hypothesis might actually be false. For the last conclusion, there's a chance that the rejected null hypothesis might actually be true. An assessment of the risks of error and the associated penalties is an important final step in any hypothesis test.

The third conclusion states that the different stores do not have the same mean in the population. This is the same conclusion reached following the analysis in Example 12.6.

Some final comments are in order regarding both one-way and two-way analysis of variance procedures. As has been mentioned several times in this chapter, the key assumption of ANOVA is that all populations have the same variance. Actually, there are three assumptions that must hold for the ANOVA procedure to work properly:

1. All populations under test must have the same variance for the dependent variable.
2. All populations under test must be normally distributed for the dependent variable.
3. The samples taken from the populations under test must be drawn randomly.

These three assumptions should be verified to ensure a valid analysis of variance. These assumptions are sometimes ignored, especially since computer programs that perform ANOVA don't ask the analyst if the assumptions have been addressed. The analyst should at least have some intuitive assurance that the first two assumptions are met and that random samples are being used.

Exercises

29. What is the difference between a one-way and a two-way analysis of variance test?
30. What causes interaction in a two-way analysis of variance test?
31. What are the three hypotheses tested in a two-way analysis of variance test?
32. Empire Television Repair Service decided to study the effect of television brand and service center type on set repair time, measured in minutes. Four television brands (A, B, C, D) and four service centers were selected for analysis. Each service center was assigned three television sets of each brand for repair. The results are partially summarized below. The columns refer to television brands, and the rows refer to service centers. Test at the .01 significance level.

Source of variation	SS	df	Estimate of σ^2	F ratio
Rows	3,200	3		
Columns	300	3		
Interaction	800	9		
Within	300	32		
Total	4,600	47		

a. State the null and alternative hypotheses.

b. Is there interaction between service center and television brand?

c. Is there a difference in brands?

d. Is there a difference in service centers?

32*b.* $F_r = 113.8$
$F_c = 10.67$
$F_i = 9.48$
Yes, there is interaction
c. Yes
d. Yes

33. The accompanying table shows a partially completed ANOVA table for a two-way analysis of variance test.

Source of variation	SS	df	Estimate of σ^2	*F* ratio
Rows	5.1	3		
Columns	18.1	2		
Interaction			2.9	
Within	37.6			
Total		47		

33*a*. $F_r = 1.63$
$F_c = 8.72$
$F_i = 2.78$
b. 4
c. 3
d. 4
e. There is no interaction

a. Complete the ANOVA table.

b. How many rows were in the original data table?

c. How many columns were in the original data table?

d. How many items were found in each cell in the original data table?

e. If you test at the .01 significance level, what are your conclusions concerning the three hypotheses tested?

34. Jeff Norton, manager of Coldpoint Appliances (a large appliance retailer), feels that the number of units sold depends both on a salesperson's ability and on the brand being sold. For the six most recent monthly periods, he recorded the number of units sold in the downtown store:

Brand sold	Salesperson A			B			C			D		
1	4	5	6	3	5	7	8	9	10	2	0	1
	8	3	5	3	4	2	12	9	13	5	1	3
2	5	7	7	9	9	9	8	7	9	3	2	5
	8	6	4	7	5	8	10	8	6	4	1	6

34*b*. $F_r = 4.458$
$F_c = 27.53$
$F_i = 6.265$
c. There is interaction

a. State the null and alternative hypotheses.

b. Use a computer program to produce an ANOVA table.

c. Test all of the relevant hypotheses at the .05 significance level.

d. Write Jeff a short memo summarizing your conclusions.

35*b*. $F_r = .368$
$F_c = 27.444$
$F_i = .752$
c. No interaction
d. No difference between machines; difference between operators

35. Tim Russell, production manager of the Tetronic Corporation, feels that the variation in the number of units produced per hour might be related to both the operator and the machine used to produce the units. This matter is of particular concern to Tim after he read a *Wall Street Journal* article (November 27, 1989) on the Fed's attempt to reverse a manufacturing slump by driving down interest rates. He thinks that this is a good time to study the production issue.

Three Tetronic operators (A, B, C) are observed using each of three different machines (1, 2, 3) for two separate hours:

Machine	Operator A		B		C	
1	12	15	17	23	10	14
2	9	12	20	25	12	12
3	8	11	19	22	13	11

a. State the null and alternative hypotheses.

b. Use a computer program to produce an ANOVA table.

c. Test all of the relevant hypotheses at the .01 significance level.

d. Write Tim a short memo summarizing your conclusions.

Other ANOVA Designs

The one-way and two-way designs described in this chapter are the basic ANOVA procedures used in most applications. Modifications to these procedures are sometimes employed in examining the effects of different factors on a variable of interest. Four of the more common variations are described in this section.

1. As mentioned earlier, the basic ANOVA designs assume that sample sizes are equal. For one-way ANOVA, the same sample size is used for each of the treatments. For the two-way design, the same sample size is used in each cell of the data table. More complex designs can accommodate unequal sample sizes. This might be desirable if there were different proportions of items in the populations and the analyst wanted to reflect these differences in the sample. For a two-way ANOVA involving machines and operators, for example, if a particular machine group accounted for 75% of the output, the analyst might want to oversample that group and undersample the others.

   Sometimes it's not possible to obtain the same sample size per treatment or cell. If historical records are being used to generate the sample measurements, for instance, the unavailability of data may lead to unequal sample sizes.
2. In the designs described in this chapter, all populations of interest were sampled. Suppose, for the machine and operator example, there were 3 operators and 5 machines. Since all operators use all machines, there are 15 different populations, one for every combination of machine and operator. In a basic two-way ANOVA, all 15 of these combinations are sampled. Now suppose there are 10 machine groups and 50 operators. A basic design would involve a huge sample size if all 500 populations were sampled. An alternative ANOVA design randomly chooses those populations to be sampled and extends the results to all populations.
3. The basic ANOVA procedure can be broadened to cover three or more factors. In the machine/operator example, a third factor that might affect hourly output is the factory shift during which production took place. If there are 3 shifts, 3 operators, and 5 machine groups, a total of 45 different combinations or populations are involved. In a basic ANOVA design, all 45 combinations would be sampled. An alternative is to randomly choose the operators, machines, and shifts to be sampled and extend the ANOVA results to all of the populations.

   The two-way factorial ANOVA study mentioned in Example 12.10, "Effects of Price, Brand, and Store Information on Buyers' Product Evaluations," (*Journal of Marketing Research*, August 1991) investigated the effects of price, brand, and store information on buyers' perception of product quality. This three-way factorial design actually sampled five price levels, three brand names, and three store names.

4. In the basic one-way ANOVA design, subjects are randomly assigned to treatments. This random assignment provides some assurance that the subjects in each treatment are more or less the same, eliminating the effects of differing subjects. If the subjects are people subjected to differing TV ads, for example, the analyst hopes, through random assignment, that not all the young people end up watching one ad and all the older people end up watching another.

   The *randomized block design* removes the effect of differences among treatment subjects by subjecting each subject to all treatments. For example, suppose there are 12 supermarkets in the experiment along with three different display methods for a new product. A simple random ANOVA design would randomly assign display methods to stores, but each store would only use one display type. In a randomized block design, each store uses all three display methods over a period of time, thus eliminating the possible effect of different store types. The order of assigning display methods to stores is done randomly; assignments might appear as follows:

	Store (blocks)											
	1	2	3	4	5	6	7	8	9	10	11	12
	1	2	3	1	2	3	1	2	3	1	2	3
Method	2	3	1	2	3	1	2	3	1	2	3	1
	3	1	2	3	1	2	3	1	2	3	1	2

The different methods of conducting the analysis of variance procedure are sometimes referred to as *experimental designs*. The term *experiment* suggests a scientific application more than a business application, and this is generally true. Business applications often involve observation rather than the manipulation of variables, so the advanced experimental design procedures are not widely used. However, there are certainly times when business situations can be controlled so that the effect of different factors on the variable of interest can be examined. In these cases, the more advanced procedures of experimental design can be quite useful and in fact quality control and research into the design of products are two such important areas.

SUMMARY

In addition to means and proportions, the variabilities of populations are frequently of interest. This chapter has presented methods to test the variability of a single population and to compare the variabilities of two populations.

This chapter has also presented ways to examine the effects of different factors on a variable of interest (the dependent variable). In the one-way analysis of variance, measurements on the dependent variable are made for each level of the single factor believed to affect this variable. Two relevant factors can be examined simultaneously in the two-way ANOVA procedure, and the effects of three or more factors on the dependent variable can be examined through the use of more advanced procedures.

Analysis of variance is a good example of a statistical technique that has become practical due to widespread use of computers. The volume of calculations is such that a design of any useful size is very difficult to perform using hand calculations. Computer programs that perform ANOVA are widely available for personal computers as well as mainframe computers. These programs typically perform both one-way and two-way analyses, and more advanced techniques are sometimes available. An example of the use of a microcomputer program is demonstrated at the end of this chapter.

Applications of Statistical Concepts in the Business World

There are many business applications of the ANOVA techniques discussed in this chapter. When the average value of some variable is compared across three or more populations, the conclusions that result from an ANOVA study can be very useful to management. Often production variables are varied to see which combination yields the optimum manufacturing process. Here are examples of dependent variables whose means for different population groups might be of interest.

Dependent variable	Populations under study
Overtime hours per month	Employees: union hourly, nonunion hourly, salaried
Shipping time	Size of container: small, medium, large
Time to repay loan	Age of customer: under 30, 31–45, 46–65, over 65
Units produced per hour	Shift: 1, 2, 3 Plant: A, B, C, D
Savings account balance	Account holders' age: under 35, 36–50, 51 + Age of account: under 5 years, 5–10 years, over 10 years
Defective units produced	Shift, material supplier, foreman
College GPA	Class: freshman, sophomore, junior, senior Major: business, liberal arts, health sciences Age: under 22, 22–30, 31 +
Annual cost of repair for ordered parts	Supplier: A, B, C, D Part cost: under \$25, \$25–\$100, over \$100
Points scored by NFL team	Day played: Sunday, Monday, other Opponent: same division, same conference, other
Employee time with company	Plant: 1, 2, 3 Education: high school, some college, college graduate
Age of account receivable	Public corporation, private corporation, partnership
Monthly cash balance	Busy season, moderate season, slow season
Interest rate paid on short-term loan	Bank: A, B, C Season: summer, fall, winter, spring Bull market, bear market, neutral market
Sales per customer	Catalog sale, store sale, discount store sale
Customer rating of store employees	Downtown store, valley store, north store
Time in hospital	Age: under 45, 45–65, 66 + Medical insurance, no medical insurance, Medicare
Complaints per 1,000 customers	Store: 1, 2, 3 Value of item: under \$25, \$25–\$250, over \$250
Monthly sales per salesperson	Company car, lease car, own car

Glossary

Analysis of variance (ANOVA) A statistical procedure for determining whether the means of three or more populations are equal.

***Within* method** A method of estimating the variance of populations that produces a valid estimate whether or not the null hypothesis is true.

***Between* method** A method of estimating the variance of populations that produces a valid estimate only if the null hypothesis is true.

ANOVA table A table that contains columns showing the sources of variation, the sums of squares, the degrees of freedom, the estimates of the variance, and the F value for the analysis of variance procedure.

Interaction A significant interrelationship between the levels of one factor and the levels of a second factor in influencing the dependent variable.

KEY FORMULAS

Chi-square variance test

$$\chi^2 = \frac{(n-1)s^2}{\sigma^2} \tag{12.1}$$

***F* ratio for two-population variance test**

$$F = \frac{s_1^2}{s_2^2} \tag{12.2}$$

***Within* method estimate of σ^2**

$$s_w^2 = \frac{\sum_j \sum_i (x_{ij} - \bar{x}_j)^2}{c(n-1)} \tag{12.3}$$

Estimate of the sampling distribution variance

$$s_{\bar{x}}^2 = \frac{\sum_j (\bar{x}_j - \bar{\bar{x}})^2}{c-1} \tag{12.4}$$

***Between* method estimate of σ^2**

$$s_b^2 = \frac{n\sum_j (\bar{x}_j - \bar{\bar{x}})^2}{c-1} \tag{12.5}$$

***F* ratio for ANOVA**

$$F = \frac{s_b^2 \text{ (\textit{Between} method estimate of } \sigma^2)}{s_w^2 \text{ (\textit{Within} method estimate of } \sigma^2)} \tag{12.6}$$

Two-way ANOVA formulas

Estimate of the variance between columns

$$s_c^2 = \frac{rn\sum_j (\bar{x}_{cj} - \bar{\bar{x}})^2}{c-1}$$

Estimate of the variance between rows

$$s_r^2 = \frac{cn\sum_i (\bar{x}_{ri} - \bar{\bar{x}})^2}{r-1}$$

Estimate of the variance for interaction

$$s_i^2 = \frac{n\left[\sum_i \sum_j (\bar{x}_{ij} - \bar{x}_{ri} - \bar{x}_{cj} + \bar{\bar{x}})^2\right]}{(r - 1)(c - 1)}$$

Estimate of the variance for *within*

$$s_w^2 = \frac{\sum_i \sum_j \sum_k (x_{ijk} - \bar{x}_{ij})}{rc(n - 1)}$$

SOLVED EXERCISES

1. ONE-POPULATION VARIANCE TEST

Scientific measuring instruments such as an aircraft altimeter must provide unbiased readings with a small measurement error. The production manager for Hulk Aircraft, Fred Sterling, is concerned about the amount of variation in the readings produced by his company's altimeters. The altimeters are designed to have a standard deviation of 200 feet. Fred decides to test whether the variability of altimeters is greater than 200 feet. He selects a sample of seven altimeters and computes a sample standard deviation of 250 feet.

a. State the null and alternative hypotheses.

b. Compute the degrees of freedom.

c. State the decision rule using the .05 significance level.

d. Test if the variability of the company's altimeters is greater than 200 feet.

Solution:

a. The null and alternative hypotheses are

$$H_0: \sigma^2 \leq 40{,}000$$
$$H_1: \sigma^2 > 40{,}000$$

b. $\text{df} = (n - 1) = (7 - 1) = 6$

c. The decision rule is

If $\chi^2 > 12.59$, reject the null hypothesis that the population variance is 40,000 (reject H_0 if $\chi^2 > 12.59$).

d. $\chi^2 = \frac{(n - 1)s^2}{\sigma^2} = \frac{(7 - 1)(250)^2}{200^2} = 9.375$

Since the calculated test statistic (9.375) is lower than the critical table value (12.59), the null hypothesis can't be rejected at the .05 significance level. There isn't sufficient sample evidence to conclude that the population standard deviation is more than 200 feet.

2. TWO-POPULATION VARIANCE TEST

Carla Mitchell, analyst for Abbott Laboratories, a national drug manufacturer, is concerned about the quality of one of its products. Abbott purchases a particular material used to manufacture the product of concern from two different suppliers. The level of defects in the raw material is approximately the same between the two suppliers, but Carla is concerned about the variability from shipment to shipment. If the level of defects tends to vary excessively for either supplier, the quality of the drug product could be affected. To compare the relative variation of the two suppliers, Carla selects 11 shipments from each supplier and measures the percentage of defects in the raw material for each shipment, along with the standard deviations. The results are

$$s_1 = 0.61 \qquad n_1 = 11 \text{ (supplier 1)}$$
$$s_2 = 0.29 \qquad n_2 = 11 \text{ (supplier 2)}$$

a. State the null and alternative hypotheses.

b. Compute the degrees of freedom.

c. State the decision rule using the .05 significance level.

d. Test whether the variability of the shipment defect levels for supplier 1 is greater than for supplier 2.

Solution:

a. The null and alternative hypotheses are

$$H_0: \sigma_1^2 - \sigma_2^2 \leq 0$$
$$H_1: \sigma_1^2 - \sigma_2^2 > 0$$

b. $\text{df}_1 = (n_1 - 1) = (11 - 1) = 10$
$\text{df}_2 = (n_2 - 1) = (11 - 1) = 10$

c. The critical F value is 2.97. The decision rule is

If the calculated F ratio is larger than 2.97, reject H_0 (reject H_0 if $F > 2.97$).

d. $F = \dfrac{s_1^2}{s_2^2} = \dfrac{(0.61)^2}{(0.29)^2} = 4.42$

One of the sample variances is 4.42 times the other. The null hypothesis is rejected since the test statistic (4.42) exceeds the critical value (2.97). Carla should conclude that the variability of shipment defect levels for supplier 1 is greater than for supplier 2.

3. ONE-WAY ANALYSIS OF VARIANCE

Color Paint Corporation owner Marlene Perez decides to replace several paint sprayers. After researching the situation, she concludes that four brands appear to be comparable in terms of cost and projected lifetime. Marlene determines that the deciding factor among the four brands is the amount of paint used in normal operation. She measures paint thickness, in millimeters, for several paint tests, with the following results:

	Sprayer A	Sprayer B	Sprayer C	Sprayer D
	5.4	6.1	8.2	7.2
	5.9	5.9	8.5	6.5
	6.2	6.3	6.9	6.8
	7.0	6.5	9.4	7.1
	5.1	7.2	7.9	7.4
	5.5	6.9	8.6	6.7
Mean =	5.85	6.48	8.25	6.95

Grand mean = $\bar{\bar{x}}$ = 6.88

a. State the null and alternative hypotheses.
b. Compute the degrees of freedom.
c. State the decision rule if the null hypothesis is tested at the .01 significance level.
d. What should Marlene conclude?

Solution:

a. The null and alternative hypotheses are

H_0: $\mu_1 = \mu_2 = \mu_3 = \mu_4$.
H_1: Not all populations have the same mean.

b. $df_w = c(n - 1) = 4(6 - 1) = 20$
$df_b = (c - 1) = (4 - 1) = 3$

c. Find the F table entry for column 3 and row 20. At the .01 significance level, this critical value is 4.94. The decision rule is

If the calculated F ratio is larger than 4.94, reject the null hypothesis (reject H_0 if $F > 4.94$).

d. Table 12.9 shows the ANOVA table for this problem.

TABLE 12.9 ANOVA Table for Solved Exercise 3

Source of variation	SS	df	Estimate of σ^2	F ratio
Between groups	18.61	3	6.203	16.37
Within groups	7.57	20	0.379	
Total	26.18	23		

The sums of squares in this table are:

$$(5.4 - 5.85)^2 + (5.9 - 5.85)^2 + (6.2 - 5.85)^2 +$$
$$(7.0 - 5.85)^2 + (5.1 - 5.85)^2 + (5.5 - 5.85)^2 +$$
$$(6.1 - 6.48)^2 + (5.9 - 6.48)^2 + (6.3 - 6.48)^2 +$$
$$(6.5 - 6.48)^2 + (7.2 - 6.48)^2 + (6.9 - 6.48)^2 +$$
$$(8.2 - 8.25)^2 + (8.5 - 8.25)^2 + (6.9 - 8.25)^2 +$$
$$(9.4 - 8.25)^2 + (7.9 - 8.25)^2 + (8.6 - 8.25)^2 +$$
$$(7.2 - 6.95)^2 + (6.5 - 6.95)^2 + (6.8 - 6.95)^2 +$$
$$(7.1 - 6.95)^2 + (7.4 - 6.95)^2 + (6.7 - 6.95)^2 =$$
$$SS_w = 7.57$$

$$(5.85 - 6.88)^2 + (6.48 - 6.88)^2 + (8.25 - 6.88)^2 +$$
$$(6.95 - 6.88)^2 = 3.1$$

$$SS_b = 6(3.1) = 18.6$$

$$F = \frac{s_b^2/df_b}{s_w^2/df_w} = \frac{(18.6/3)}{(7.57/20)} = \frac{6.2}{0.379} = 16.36$$

The null hypothesis is rejected since the test statistic (16.36) is larger than the critical value (4.94). Marlene should conclude that paint thickness differs among these four brands of sprayers.

4. TWO-WAY ANALYSIS OF VARIANCE

Julie Barnes, analyst for the marketing research firm Professional Marketing Associates, is conducting research for a client to determine if age and level of education affect income. Table 12.10 shows the results of Julie's data collection. What should Julie conclude if she tests the hypotheses at the .05 significance level?

TABLE 12.10 Income Data for Solved Exercise 4

Age group	High school	Some college	College graduate
18 to <30	$25,000	$36,250	$42,500
	31,450	39,400	46,000
	27,500	35,450	47,250
30 to <50	28,000	46,250	52,600
	30,950	44,400	56,700
	26,250	48,450	57,750
50 +	35,000	46,250	62,800
	38,250	49,400	66,700
	37,700	55,450	70,250

Solution:

The data are run on a microcomputer program demonstrated at the end of this chapter. Table 12.11 shows the results.

TABLE 12.11 Computer Output for Solved Exercise 4

```
                              Information Entered
Number of Variables:                      2
Number of Rows:                           3
Number of Columns:                        3
Alpha Error:                              .05
GP 1      A        B        C         GP 3      G        H        I
 1 =  25,000   36,250   42,500         1 =  35,000   46,250   62,800
 2 =  31,450   39,400   46,000         2 =  38,250   49,400   66,700
 3 =  27,500   35,450   47,250         3 =  37,700   55,450   70,250
GP 2      D        E        F
 1 =  28,000   46,250   52,600
 2 =  30,950   44,400   56,700
 3 =  26,250   48,450   57,750
```

Results

Source of variation	SS	df	Estimate of σ^2	F ratio
Rows	955,230.9	2	477,601.9	55.87
Columns	2,756,481.8	2	1,378,240.9	161.24
Interaction	163,307.8	4	40,826.9	4.78
Error	153,861.7	18	8,547.9	
Total	4,028,855	26		

```
Critical F-Value (Row):3.55                          Reject Null Hypothesis
Critical F-Value (Int):2.93                          Reject Null Hypothesis
Critical F-Value (Col):3.55                          Reject Null Hypothesis
```

The calculated F ratios are compared with the critical F values:

df	Critical F ($\alpha = .05$)	Calculated F test statistic
2, 18	3.55	55.87
2, 18	3.55	161.24
4, 18	2.93	4.78

Based on the appropriate critical values and the calculated F ratios in Table 12.11, all three null hypotheses are rejected. On this basis, Julie concludes:

1. There is interaction between age and education level. There seem to be unexpected differences when certain age groups are compared to certain education levels. A rejection of the null hypothesis of no interaction sends Julie back to the sample data to search for the age/education level combinations that produced unexpected results.
2. The age groups have different income levels.
3. The educational groups have different income levels.

EXERCISES

36. What is the key assumption that must hold for the analysis of variance procedure to work properly?
37. How is the F distribution similar to the t distribution? How do the distributions differ?
38. What does the term *sum of squares* refer to?

39. Fail to reject

39. Suppose there are 4 degrees of freedom for a chi-square test at the .05 significance level. How would you interpret a chi-square test statistic of 8.4?

40. Reject

40. Suppose the degrees of freedom for an F test are 2 for the numerator and 6 for the denominator. At the .05 significance level, how would you interpret a test statistic of 8.4?
41. Here is a partially completed ANOVA table.

Source of variation	SS	df	Estimate of σ^2	F ratio
Between groups	14,398	3		
Within groups				
Total	19,654	23		

41*a*. $F = 18.3$
b. 4
c. Table $F = 3.10$
d. $F = 18.3$
e. Reject

a. Complete the ANOVA table.

b. How many groups are being compared?

c. What is the appropriate critical value if the null hypothesis is tested at the .05 significance level?

d. Compute the test statistic (F ratio).

e. Would you reject or fail to reject the null hypothesis?

42. The Hullpak Manufacturing Company produces a part for the aluminum industry that has a critical outside diameter of 2.2 inches. Production manager Albert Moore knows that the standard deviation should not exceed 0.032 inch. Albert knows that cutting is on a

42. $\sigma^2 \leq .001$
$\sigma^2 > .001$
df = 19.
Reject H_0 if
$\chi^2 > 30.14$,
$\chi^2 = 40.99$, reject

43. $\sigma_1^2 - \sigma_2^2 \leq 0$
$\sigma_1^2 - \sigma_2^2 > 0$
df = 29, 29.
Reject H_0 if F > 1.90,
F = 1.87,
fail to reject

44. F = 12.05,
reject

45a. F = 64.4
b. 3
c. F = 5.61
d. F = 64.4
e. Reject

timed basis, which means that the longer the same cutting tool is used, the greater the amount of play. As a result, the average diameter remains relatively constant, but the variability can increase. Albert has inspected a recent sample of 20 parts and determined a sample standard deviation of 0.047 inch. Can Albert conclude at the .05 significance level that the cutting tool should be changed?

43. Stock analyst Robin Booth wants to compare the risks associated with two different stocks. She decides to measure the risk of a given stock on the basis of the variation in daily price changes. Robin selects a random sample of 30 daily price changes for each stock. The results are

$$s_1 = 0.93 \quad n_1 = 30 \text{ (stock A)}$$
$$s_2 = 0.68 \quad n_2 = 30 \text{ (stock B)}$$

Robin compares the risks associated with the two stocks in a test at the .05 significance level. What is her conclusion?

44. *Consumer Digest* wants to determine if any differences in average (mean) life exist among five different brands of TV picture tubes. Random samples of three picture tubes of each brand were tested. The results (in hours) are:

Brand A	Brand B	Brand C	Brand D	Brand E
3,520	4,025	4,520	3,987	3,620
3,631	3,901	4,325	4,123	3,358
3,954	3,756	4,189	3,852	3,428

At the .05 significance level, is there evidence of a difference in average life among these five brands of tubes?

45. Here is a partially completed ANOVA table.

Source of variation	SS	df	Estimate of σ^2	*F* ratio
Between groups		2		
Within groups	129.6	_	5.4	
Total	825.4			

a. Complete the ANOVA table.

b. How many groups are being compared?

c. What is the appropriate critical value if the null hypothesis is tested at the .01 significance level?

d. Compute the test statistic (*F* ratio).

e. Would you reject the null hypothesis?

46. Here is a partially completed ANOVA table.

Source of variation	SS	df	Estimate of σ^2	*F* ratio
Rows	1,488	2		
Columns	48	2		
Interaction	32	4		
Within	520	9		
Total	2,088	17		

46a. $F_r = 12.88$,
$F_c = .42$,
$F_i = .14$
b. 3
c. 3
d. 6.42
e. 8.02

a. Complete the ANOVA table.

b. How many rows are being compared?

c. How many columns are being compared?

d. What is the appropriate critical value to test for interaction if the null hypothesis is tested at the .01 significance level?

e. What is the appropriate critical value to test for the difference between columns if the null hypothesis is tested at the .01 significance level?

f. Compute the test statistic (*F* ratio) for each hypothesis.

g. Would you reject each of the null hypotheses?

h. State your conclusions for this exercise.

47. $F = 2.12$,
fail to reject

47. Fred Burks, manager of the Monty Card Department Store, wonders if his customers are charging more on their Monty Card credit cards than on MasterCharge or VISA. Fred decides to examine nine randomly chosen charges from sales using each of the three cards. The results are:

Monty Card	MasterCharge	VISA
$103	$ 71	$ 98
91	102	111
62	83	72
47	21	9
85	15	24
175	49	39
23	36	64
80	58	71
121	68	40

Can Fred conclude there is a difference in the mean amount charged among the three credit cards? Test at the .05 significance level.

48. $F = 9.06$
Reject H_0 if
$F > 5.78$, reject

48. Trudy Runge, a government analyst, has conducted a study to determine corporation executives' attitudes toward government economic policy. Trudy wants to find out if attitudes differ for different corporation sizes. Executives of 24 corporations are interviewed, and their scores on several rating scales are averaged. The results (where highest average score represents most favorable attitude) are:

Small	Medium	Large
45	61	68
51	58	70
62	73	72
47	81	59
35	45	74
55	49	69
23	46	64
50	59	71

Can Trudy conclude there is a difference in the average executive attitude toward government economic policy based on corporation size? Test at the .01 significance level.

49. $F = 13.06$
Reject H_0 if
$F > 6.36$, reject

49. Charles Tortorelli, manager of an assembly line at a vacuum cleaner manufacturing plant, believes that the rate of defective units produced in an eight-hour shift on one of the conveyor belts is affected by which shift is operating the belt. He decides to test this hypothesis by sampling the belt six times for each eight-hour shift and counting the defective units. The results are:

Day	Swing	Night
14	11	28
12	15	27
12	17	17
17	18	25
15	25	24
10	13	26

At the .01 significance level, do the three shifts produce the same mean rate of defective units?

50. Following is a partially completed ANOVA table.

Source of variation	SS	df	Estimate of σ^2	F ratio
Rows	15.4	3		
Columns			6.40	
Interaction	17.1	6		
Within		24		
Total	192.8	35		

50*a*. $F_r = .84$
$F_c = 1.05$
$F_i = .48$
b. $F = 3.67$
c. $F = 5.61$
d. Fail to reject all three

a. Complete the ANOVA table.

b. What is the appropriate critical value to test for interaction if the null hypothesis is tested at the .01 significance level?

c. What is the appropriate critical value to test for a difference between columns if the null hypothesis is tested at the .01 significance level?

d. State your conclusions for this exercise.

51. $F_r = 24.12$
$F_c = 22.32$
$F_i = 1.98$
Fail to reject interaction; reject row and column differences

51. The Sweet Treat Ice Cream Company is planning a test of three new flavors: brandy, peach, and apricot. Cathy Gant, company analyst, also wishes to measure the effects of four different retail price levels: \$1.09, \$1.19, \$1.29, and \$1.39 per pint. For test sites Cathy selected 12 geographically separated stores with similar levels of ice cream sales. Cathy arranged to have the new flavors delivered to the stores each week and to see to the proper displaying and pricing of the ice cream in all stores throughout a three-week period. At the end of each week, pints sold of each flavor were recorded for each price level.

	Flavors								
Price	Brandy			Peach			Apricot		
1.09	17	18	15	17	15	14	10	12	13
1.19	16	16	13	17	14	12	9	10	11
1.29	14	11	10	14	14	14	8	9	7
1.39	8	9	6	10	9	11	5	7	10

Run the data on a computer program, and write a memo to Cathy summarizing the results.

52. $\bar{x}_1 = 200.2$
$\bar{x}_2 = 188.5$
$s_1^2 = 687.7$
$s_2^2 = 87$
$s_{pooled} = 20.7$
$s_{\bar{x}1-\bar{x}2} = 13.89$
$t = .84$
sales are same
$F = 7.9$
variabilities are same

52. Darlene Spooner (manager of a large discount chain) must choose where to place a popular battery display. Darlene is concerned with both the level and the variability of sales. She's considering placing the display either in the hardware department or next to the checkout counter. Darlene locates the display at the checkout counter in five stores and in the hardware section in four other stores. The results, in number of batteries sold per week, are:

Checkout counter	Hardware department
205	185
185	191
170	178
240	200
201	

Based on the appropriate statistical test, does one location produce better average sales than the other? Based on the appropriate statistical test, does one location show less variability than the other? Use the .01 significance level to reach your decisions.

53. $F_r = .018$
$F_c = .031$
$F_i = .535$
Fail to reject
all null hypotheses

53. Debbie Majors (Stoneway Corporation training director) is experimenting with three different training methods to determine if there's a difference in their effectiveness. Debbie has a group of 12 new trainees, and is concerned that trainees with previous experience may react to the training methods differently. Therefore, she divides the trainees into two groups: *no experience* and *experienced.* She then exposes two trainees from each group to one of three training methods. Once the training is completed, each trainee is given a test designed to measure the effectiveness of the training. The resulting test scores are:

	Training method		
	A	B	C
No experience	72 78	75 79	81 74
Experienced	82 76	73 78	80 72

Run the data on a computer program, and write a memo to Debbie summarizing the results.

EXTENDED EXERCISES

54. BEST BUY STORES

Stu Owens, president of the Best Buy retail bookstore chain, is planning a major study to find reasons for the variability in sales per customer throughout its store system. Stu has just read a *Wall Street Journal* article (November 21, 1989) describing how book publishers face a painful future austerity. He's concerned about how this might affect his stores' sales and profits.

There are a number of factors that Stu considers relevant to purchase amount. After discussing these matters at several management meetings, he focuses on the following factors of interest:

Male/female customers

Downtown store, valley store, northside store, southside store

Active credit card user, light card user, no card

His attention now turns to designing a study to investigate the effects of these three factors on the key variable of interest to the store: sales amount per customer transaction.

a. How would you design a study to investigate the areas of interest to Best Buy?

b. Design the data table to be used to collect data for the study.

c. Describe how a representative sample could be taken to ensure that Best Buy's objectives are met.

55. CURTIS MYERS COMPANY

The Curtis Myers Company makes TV sets and has recently begun using production teams in an attempt to build morale and improve quality. After a six-month trial period, this effort appears to be successful, based on the company's usual means of measuring the quality of its products. Now the company's attention turns to ways of assessing differences from team to team and from shift to shift. This information is needed so that the company can follow through on its pledge to award bonus payments to teams with superior quality records.

At first glance, the four teams involved seem to have different quality levels as measured by the number of units returned under warranty per week. However, the differences may be due to random error, especially given the limited period of measurement. Curtis Myers' management decides that an analysis of variance would be useful, in which the dependent variable is the weekly number of units returned under warranty. A two-way ANOVA is planned: one factor will be the production team, and the other will be the shift. The three shifts will be used as the row factor, and the four production teams will be used as the column factor.

A random sample of five weeks is used for each of the 12 combinations of team and shift. The resulting data are keyed into the company's small computer, which performs analysis of variance. The ANOVA table in Table 12.12 is produced by this program.

TABLE 12.12 ANOVA Table for Extended Exercise 55

Source of variation	SS	df	Estimate of σ^2	F ratio
Rows	205	2	102.5	6.83
Columns	51	3	17.0	1.13
Interaction	98	6	16.3	1.09
Within	720	48	15.0	
Total	1,074	59		

a. State the null and alternative hypotheses being tested.

b. State, in the simplest language possible, the conclusions of interest to Curtis Myers' management.

56. CONSUMERS AUTOMOBILE INSURANCE

The Consumer Automobile Insurance Company examines its policy of hiring mostly college graduates for its sales force. Some of its salespeople have a high school education, some have limited college education, and some have a college diploma. It would be fairly easy to randomly select a sample from each group and measure the key variable of interest to the company: annual sales of auto insurance. A one-way analysis of variance is planned.

The company decides to randomly sample four persons from each of the three categories of education and measure annual sales, in thousands of dollars. If education doesn't seem to make a difference in annual sales, the company will abandon its policy of seeking college graduates for its sales force and use lower-cost high school graduates. On the other hand, if a college degree makes a significant difference in sales level, Consumer's current policy will be continued.

Here are annual sales levels, in thousands of dollars, for the sample:

High school	Some college	College graduate
125	98	137
110	115	122
101	103	118
114	112	132

After looking at the sample data, personnel manager Linda Bell states, "College graduates are obviously outperforming those with less education. The policy of seeking college grads should continue."

a. What is your immediate response to Linda Bell's statement?

b. Perform a one-way analysis of variance and produce the appropriate ANOVA table.

c. Now what is your reaction to the personnel manager's statement?

Microcomputer Package

The micro package *Computerized Business Statistics* can be used to solve two-way ANOVA problems.

In Solved Exercise 4, Julie Barnes, analyst for the marketing research firm Professional Marketing Associates, conducted research for a client to determine whether age and level of education have an effect on income.

Computer Solution:

From the main menu of *Computerized Business Statistics* a **13** is selected, indicating analysis of variance. The analysis of variance menu is shown on the screen.

Since the problem involves entering data from the keyboard, a **1** is selected.

```
Analysis of Variance—Define New Problem
 Number of Variables: Enter 1–2, Press ↵ 2
```

Since two variables (age and level of education) are to be analyzed, a **2** is selected.

```
Variable #1 (Rows)
Number of Groups: Enter 2–5, Press ↵ 3
Variable #2 (Columns)
Number of Groups: Enter 2–5, Press ↵ 3
Alpha Error: Enter 0–1, Press ↵ .05
```

There are three age categories (rows) and three education levels (columns). The significance level for this exercise is .05.

```
Analysis of Variance—Enter Number of Data Points
             Column 1       Column 2       Column 3
Row 1         – 3 –          – 3 –          – 3 –
Row 2         – 3 –          – 3 –          – 3 –
Row 3         – 3 –          – 3 –          – 3 –
Press F when Finished
```

There are three data points in each cell. **F** is entered once the blanks have been completed.

```
Analysis of Variance—Enter Variable Labels
           Column 1      Column 2      Column 3
Row 1         X1            X2            X3
Row 2         X4            X5            X6
Row 3         X7            X8            X9
Press end when Finished
```

The cells are named A, B, C, D, E, F, G, H, and I. **END** is pressed once the X's have been replaced.

Next, the program asks:

```
Problem definition correct Y/N/Q, Press ↵ Y
```

After a **Y** response, the program is ready for the data to be entered:

```
Enter Data Values Group 1
     A       B       C
1 = 0       0       0
2 = 0       0       0
3 = 0       0       0
```

After the data have been entered, the screen shows:

```
       A       B      C
1 = 25000  36250  42500
2 = 31450  39400  46000
3 = 27500  35450  47250
```

Next, the screen asks you to enter data values for Group 2. After you've finished, the screen shows:

```
       D      E      F
1 = 28000  46250  52600
2 = 30950  44400  56700
3 = 26250  48450  57750
```

This process is repeated for the third group. **F** is pressed when you're finished. Next, you're asked:

```
Save data? Y/N, Press ↵ N
```

The analysis of variance menu reappears.

A 7 is entered so that the problem can be run.

The computer responds with the output menu. The choice in this case is **P** for printer. The results are shown in Table 12.11.

MINITAB COMPUTER PACKAGE

The two-way analysis of variance can be performed using MINITAB. The appropriate commands to solve Example 12.11 are:

```
MTB> SET C1
DATA> 12.05 23.94 14.63 25.78 17.52 18.45
```

```
DATA> 15.17 18.52 19.57 21.4 13.59 20.57
DATA> 9.48 6.92 10.47 7.63 11.9 5.92
DATA> END
MTB> SET C2
DATA> 1 1 1 1 1 1 2 2 2 2 2 2 3 3 3 3 3 3
DATA> END
MTB> SET C3
DATA> 1 1 1 2 2 2 1 1 1 2 2 2 1 1 1 2 2 2
DATA> END
MTB> NAME C1 'AMOUNT' C2 'COLUMNS' C3 'ROWS'
MTB> TWOWAY C1 C2 C3

ANALYSIS OF VARIANCE AMOUNT

SOURCE          DF       SS        MS
COLUMNS          2    378.4     189.2
ROWS             1      8.0       8.0
INTERACTION      2     13.9       6.9
ERROR           12    192.2      16.0
TOTAL           17    592.5

MTB > LET C4=6.9/16
MTB > LET C5=8/16
MTB > LET C6=189.2/16
MTB > PRINT C4-C6

 ROW        C4      C5         C6

   1   0.43125     0.5     11.825

MTB > CDF .43125;
SUBC> F DF NUMERATOR = 2, DF DENOMINATOR = 12.
    0.4313     0.3406
MTB > CDF .5;
SUBC> F DF = 1, DF = 12.
    0.5000     0.5070
MTB > CDF 11.825;
SUBC> F DF = 2, DF = 12.
   11.8250     0.9985
MTB > STOP
```

Note that the amounts are entered in a single column, C1, using the SET command. A code is developed (1 = store 1, 2 = store 2, and 3 = store 3) to identify each column or store in C2. A code is also developed (1 = campaign A and 2 = campaign B) to identify each row or advertising campaign in C3. The NAME command is used to name the rows of the table. The TWOWAY command performs the analysis. The computer output produces a table similar to Table 12.8.

The LET command is used to divide the estimate of the variance for the interaction term (6.9) by the estimate of the variance for the *within* (labeled ERROR on the output) term (16). The result is stored in C4. The PRINT command shows the resulting F ratios.

The CDF command is used to generate a cumulative probability density function. The F subcommand is used to generate the probability function for an F distribution with 2 degrees of freedom in the numerator and 12 degrees of freedom in the denominator for the interaction F ratio of .4313. Note that the p-value (.6594) is computed by subtracting .3406 from 1 (1.0000 − .3406 = .6594). Since the p-value is greater than the significance level (.6594 > .01), the null hypothesis is not rejected.

SAS COMPUTER PACKAGE

The SAS computer package can be used to solve ANOVA problems. The SAS commands to solve Example 12.6 are as follows.

```
TITLE ''ANOVA ANALYSIS FOR EXAMPLE 12-6'':
DATA STORES;
INPUT STORE DOLLARS;
CARDS;
1  12.05
1  23.94
1  14.63
1  25.78
1  17.52
1  18.45
2  15.17
2  18.52
2  19.57
2  21.40
2  13.59
2  20.57
3  9.48
3  6.92
3  10.47
3  7.63
3  11.90
3  5.92
PROC PRINT;
PROC ANOVA;
 CLASS STORE;
 MODEL DOLLARS=STORE;
 MEANS STORE;
```

The title command names the SAS run. The data command gives the data a name. The next 18 lines are card images that represent the stores and average purchase amounts. The PROC PRINT command directs SAS to list the data. The PROC ANOVA command performs analysis of variance. The CLASS subcommand identifies STORE as the variable to be classified. The MODEL subcommand indicates that the average purchase amount is the dependent variable and the type of store is the independent variable. The MEANS subcommand indicates that means are printed for each level of the variable STORE. Table 12.13, on the next page, shows the computer output for this SAS run. This output provides a p-value equal to .0005 (represented as PR > F on the output).

Table 12.13 SAS Output for Example 12–6

```
                         ANOVA ANALYSIS FOR EXAMPLE 12-6
                          Analysis of Variance Procedure

Dependent Variable: DOLLARS
                                    Sum of             Mean
Source                  DF         Squares           Square     F Value      Pr > F
Model                    2    378.38083333     189.19041667       13.26      0.0005
Error                   15    214.08721667      14.27248111
Corrected Total         17    592.46805000
              R-Square                C.V.         Root MSE            DOLLARS MEAN

              0.638652            24.86274        3.7778937               15.195000

Source                  DF         Anova SS     Mean Square     F Value      Pr > F

STORE                    2    378.38083333     189.19041667       13.26      0.0005

       Analysis of Variance Procedure

Level of          -----------DOLLARS-----------
STORE       N        Mean                SD

1           6     18.7283333         5.28812790
2           6     18.1366667         3.10628825
3           6      8.7200000         2.28125404
```

Chapter 13

Quality-Control Applications

Come, give us a taste of your quality.
Shakespeare, "Hamlet"

Good things cost less than bad ones.
Italian proverb

Objectives

When you have completed this chapter, you will be able to:

Define the quality of a product or service.

Identify and differentiate between assignable and chance variation.

Explain the concept of statistical quality control.

Construct and interpret process control charts.

Describe the basic terms, procedures, and purposes of acceptance sampling.

On February 26, 1992, Kaiser Aluminum Company received Miller Brewing Company's Aluminum Supplier of the Year Award for the second year in a row. This award is based on the quality of material shipped to Miller.

Why Managers Need to Know about Quality Control

The importance of producing high-quality products has increased dramatically in recent years. A primary reason for this increase has been foreign competition, particularly from Japan.

Consider what a special edition of *Business Week* said about quality:

> In 40 years, a focus on quality has turned Japan from a maker of knick-knacks into an economic powerhouse—and U.S. and European companies are being forced to respond. The result: a global revolution affecting every facet of business. As it becomes clear that higher quality means lower costs, products will improve, and so will services. For the 1990s and far beyond, quality must remain the priority for business.[1]

Many procedures designed to ensure high-quality production operations rely on a strong statistical foundation with particular attention to understanding variability. This chapter presents statistical concepts and techniques to provide good process control and, thus, high-quality products.

The just-mentioned award to Kaiser Aluminum was due, in the opinion of Kaiser management, to its intensive Total Quality Improvement program. Aspects of this impressive program are discussed at the end of this chapter in the "Applications" section.

Background

The concepts of statistical quality control were first developed during the 1920s, primarily through the work of Dr. Walter A. Shewhart of Bell Telephone Laboratories. Dr. Shewhart introduced the idea of controlling production quality rather than inspecting it into each part.

At the end of World War II, the United States enjoyed a tremendous competitive advantage as the only major power with its industrial base left intact. Demand for consumer products kept increasing. Management's number one priority was to make production more efficient. Little attention was paid to controlling product quality.

After the war, Japan faced the difficult task of rebuilding its economy. The country was devoid of abundant natural resources, so redevelopment of industry was based on a management approach that took advantage of its only real resource, the labor force. With the assistance of managerial expertise exported to Japan from the United States

---

[1] *Business Week*, bonus issue, January 15, 1992.

(individuals like W. Edwards Deming, Joseph Juran, and A. V. Feigenbaum), a new managerial approach was developed that emphasized continuous improvement of product quality. This management style, called *management by process*, has helped Japan become the major threat to U.S. industrial superiority. In management by process, the industrial effort's goal is to constantly work on methods for improving the product or service. This approach utilizes new technology, focuses on the customer, and reacts to change quickly.

QUALITY—GENERAL CONSIDERATIONS

Quality

Before various tools and methods for measuring quality can be developed, the term must be defined. The **quality** of a product or service is determined by the extent to which it satisfies all the needs and preferences of its users.

> The **quality** of a product or service is the extent to which it satisfies its users' needs and preferences.

It is important, of course, to have good product designs. But in the production process itself, the key concern is often centered around process variability. It might be said that quality is the absence of variation and that variation is the firm's constant threat. If the variability of parts and assemblies is controlled, higher quality will result in almost any process.

The basic notion of monitoring product quality involves distinguishing between random and caused variability. In fact, it could be said that variability is the key concern in quality-control efforts. All processes produce results that vary from unit to unit. If this variability is slight and of consistent magnitude, good quality is generally indicated. If units are highly variable from one to another, or if the variability pattern is suddenly altered, poor quality is usually indicated.

EXAMPLE 13.1 Suppose the key quality factor for steel ingots is their weight. Each ingot has a different weight than the one produced before or after it. If the process is "in control," this weight variability is said to be randomly determined. That is, the observed variability of weights is presumed to be satisfactory for a process that's producing ingots of acceptable weight quality. By contrast, if the process shifts out of control, one or more ingot weights are judged to be outside the established range of acceptability. In this case, the observed variability is caused by something, namely, a process that's out of control and requires corrective action.

Figure 13.1 graphically demonstrates variability. Imagine a gun shot several times at a target. Plot *a* of Figure 13.1 shows excessive variability, even though the shots are centered on the target. In plot *b*, the variability is acceptable (a tight pattern), but it's centered off the target. In plot *c*, both the variability (scatter) and the center point are acceptable; in this case, the quality, in terms of variability, is acceptable.

FIGURE 13.1 Variability

a.

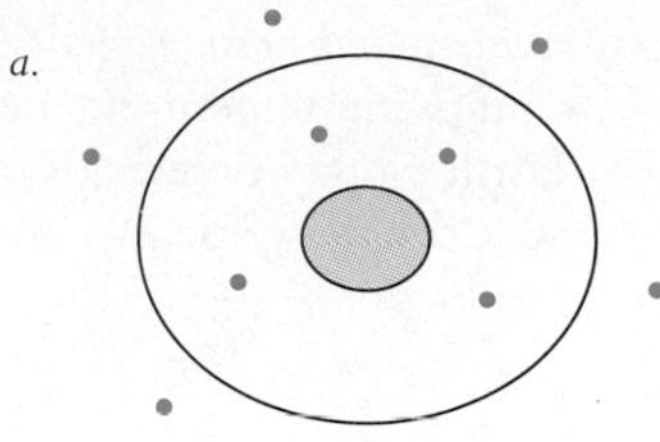

b.

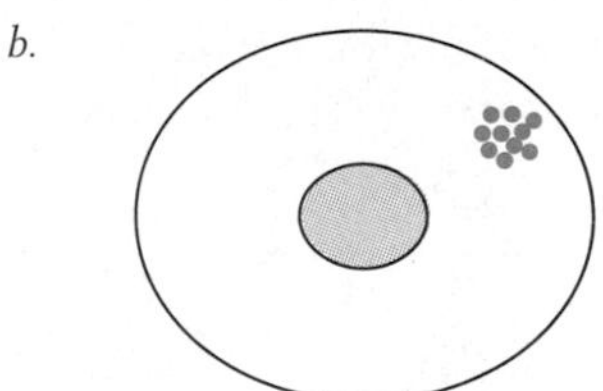

c.

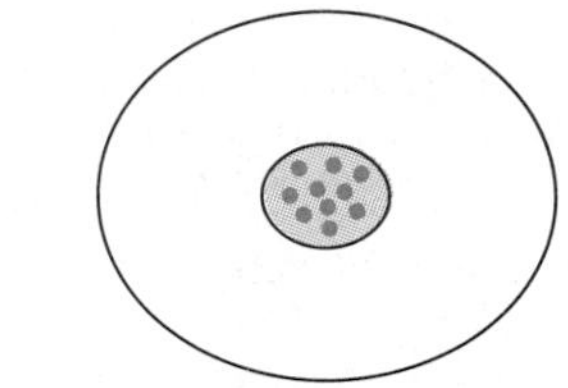

Deming

Before looking at specific quality-control procedures, a few additional comments on the general quality picture are appropriate. W. Edwards Deming, an American statistician, helped to establish effective quality-control methods in Japan in the 1950s, and subsequently helped firms around the world with their quality-improvement efforts. Among his accomplishments was the establishment of 14 key points for managing a quality-improvement and -maintenance program. Deming indicated that following the 14 guidelines creates an organizational climate in which process-management efforts can flourish. For a more complete discussion of these points, see Deming (1986)[2] or Gitlow, Gitlow, Oppenheim, and Oppenheim (1989).[3] The 14 points are:

1. Create constancy of purpose toward improving product and service.
2. Adopt a new philosophy based on the new economic age of high quality, not delays, mistakes, and defective products.

[2]W. E. Deming. *Out of the Crisis.* Cambridge, Mass.: M.I.T. Center for Advanced Engineering Study, 1986.

[3]H. Gitlow, S. Gitlow, A. Oppenheim, and R. Oppenheim. . . . *Tools and Methods for the Improvement of Quality.* Homewood, Ill.: Irwin, 1989.

3. Cease dependence on inspection to achieve quality. Instead, build quality into the product in the first place.
4. End the practice of awarding business on the basis of price alone. Instead, minimize total cost by recognizing the hidden cost of buying poor quality.
5. Improve constantly and forever the system of production and service to improve quality and productivity.
6. Institute training on the job.
7. Institute supervision designed to help people and machines produce a better product.
8. Drive out fear so that everyone can concentrate on quality work.
9. Break down barriers between departments so that the entire production team, from design to final delivery, pulls together in the quality effort.
10. Eliminate slogans, exhortations, and targets for the work force that ask for zero defects and new levels of productivity. Such exhortations only create adversarial relationships.
11. Eliminate work standards that prescribe numerical quotas for the day.
12. Remove the barriers that rob the hourly worker of the right to pride of workmanship.
13. Institute a vigorous program of education and training.
14. Put everybody in the company to work to accomplish the transformation.

These 14 points lay the groundwork for a fundamental change in old-style American business methods that involved production and cost objectives without proper attention to quality goals. As such, the 14 points represent the new philosophy business firms need if they're to maintain and improve their sales, profits, and reputations, and remain in business into the next century.

Juran and Deming are two names familiar to all those who've studied quality control. These two pioneers have increased their followings as the importance of improving the quality of U.S. products has become critical. Japan's 40-year-old Deming Prize for quality is Japanese industry's most coveted award.

Deming Prize

Baldrige Award

A more recent development is the Malcolm Baldrige National Quality Award started in 1987. A 1991 *Harvard Business Review* article describes its progress:

> In just four years, the Malcolm Baldrige National Quality Award has become the most important catalyst for transforming American business. More than any other initiative, public or private, it has reshaped managers' thinking and behavior. The Baldrige Award provides companies with a comprehensive framework for assessing their progress toward the new paradigm of management and such commonly acknowledged goals as customer satisfaction and increased employee involvement.[4]

The Baldrige examiners look for the following, to be outlined in no more than 75 pages by the applying firm:

[4]David A. Garvin, "How the Baldrige Award Really Works," *Harvard Business Review*, November 1991, pp. 80–93.

Top executives incorporate quality values into day-to-day management.

Its products are as good as or better than those of its competitors.

It is working with suppliers to improve the quality of their products or services.

Customer needs and wants are being met—and customer satisfaction ratings are as good as or better than competitors'.

The company trains workers in quality techniques and has systems in place to ensure that products are high quality.

The quality system yields concrete results, such as gains in market share and reduction in product-cycle time.

Consider these additional points regarding efforts to improve U.S. quality:

Eastman Kodak has all managers attend a four-month course in quality control.

Total Quality Management(TQM) is the new watchword for many firms. This slogan reflects efforts at every level of the organization to make improvements.

The move toward better quality is considered by enthusiastic companies to be a culture-transforming approach.

Many firms have reached the conclusion that most quality problems are the fault of management, not workers.

It is increasingly recognized that workers themselves are in the best position to find and correct quality problems.

The "perfect factory" is being designed. Under this concept, a part is measured, then the part that it must fit is designed around that measurement. In this way, each final product becomes a made-to-order assembly.

The term *fourth-generation management* is being used to describe the new emphasis on total quality.

Quality efforts are increasing in the service sector as well as the manufacturing sector. Examples are mail and product carriers, airlines, the finance industry, insurance companies, and retailing.

The quest for quality has focused attention on research and development efforts. Specific contributions to product quality are demanded of R&D expenditures.

Quality is designed into the product, instead of inspected in. This is accomplished through design and analysis of appropriate experiments.

Once a company adopts the new quality philosophy, many changes in operations and management approaches may be needed. One slogan of the new quality effort is "Design quality into the product, don't inspect it in." Even so, traditional statistical quality-control methods are still needed to assess the process. This chapter addresses these statistical procedures.

Exercises

1. What is quality?
2. Why is quality important?

3. Explain why the management style called management by process has become a major challenge to U.S. industrial competitiveness.
4. Who is Dr. Walter A. Shewhart? What is his contribution to the concept of quality control?
5. Who is W. Edwards Deming? What is his contribution to the concept of quality control?
6. What is the Malcolm Baldrige National Quality Award?

STATISTICAL PROCESS CONTROL

Statistical Process Control

Among managers concerned with quality control, one fundamental goal is to identify out-of-control processes and to bring and keep them in statistical control. The series of activities used to attain this goal is referred to as **statistical process control** (SPC).

> **Statistical process control** (SPC) is the series of actions used to monitor and eliminate variation in order to keep a process in a state of statistical control.

One key to statistical process control is use of a control chart (a time series graph with the *x*-axis scaled in hours, days, weeks, months, years, and so on). The purpose of the chart is to track process variability—the key component in quality control. The time series graph was discussed in Chapter 3.

The control chart's vertical axis is scaled to accommodate the variable being tracked. This variable is the key indicator of quality in the process being monitored. For each time period, this key variable is measured and plotted on the control chart, forming a time series graph as time passes.

In addition to providing a visual display of a process, the control chart separates assignable causes of variation from chance causes of variation.

Assignable Causes

Assignable causes of variation are fluctuations in variation due to events or actions that aren't part of the process design. Examples of assignable causes of variation include dust getting into the air and interfering with microchip production, a worker accidentally setting a machine's controls improperly, or a supplier shipping a batch of defective raw materials to the process. Assignable variation is usually nonrandom in nature and can be eliminated or reduced without modifying the process.

Chance Causes

Chance causes of variation are attributable to design of the process. Examples include the small amount of variation in liquid from one soft drink can to another and the variability in the miles per gallon of a fleet of autos. Chance variation is usually random in nature and can be eliminated or reduced only by changing the process.

> **Assignable causes** of variation are fluctuations in variation due to events or actions that aren't part of the process design. **Chance causes** of variation are attributable to the design of the process.

The most typical format for a control chart will set control limits within ±3 standard deviations of the statistical measure of interest (average, proportion, or range). These limits are called the upper control limit (UCL) and lower control limit (LCL). Recall that in Chapter 6, you learned that for a normal distribution, the mean ±3 standard deviations included almost all (99.74%) of the observations. The 3 standard deviation limits also reduce the likelihood of tampering with the process. Once these control limits are set, the control chart is evaluated from the perspective of (1) discerning any pattern that might exist in the values over time and (2) determining whether any points fall outside the control limits.

Figure 13.2 illustrates several different control charts. The process in plot A is said to be stable because no points fall outside the 3 standard deviation control limits and there doesn't appear to be any pattern in the ordering of values over time.

FIGURE 13.2 Control Chart Patterns of Variation

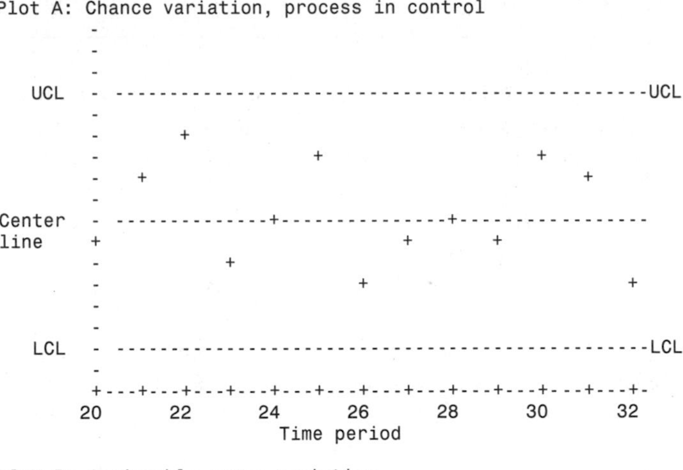

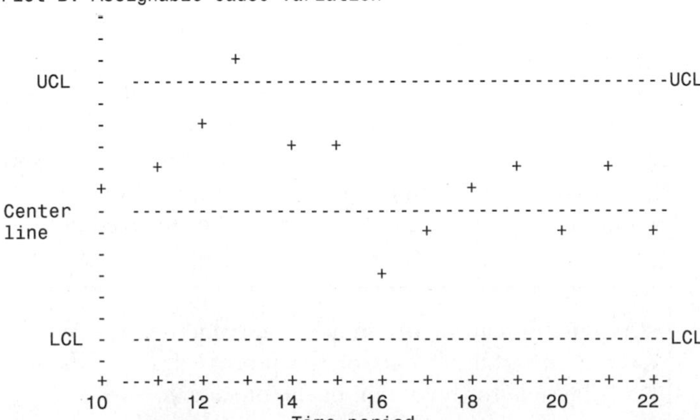

FIGURE 13.2 *continued*

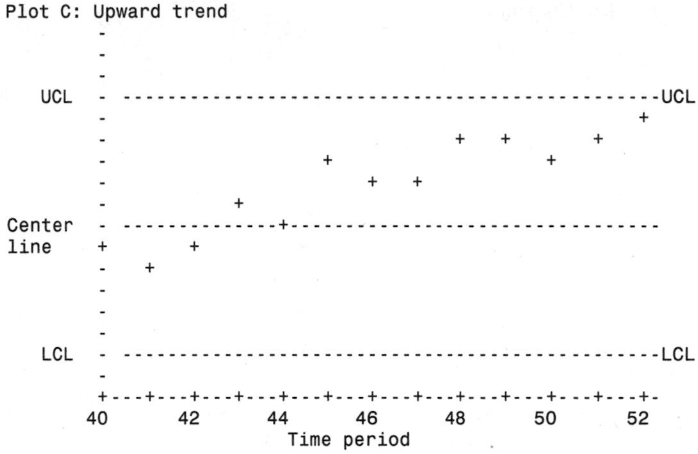

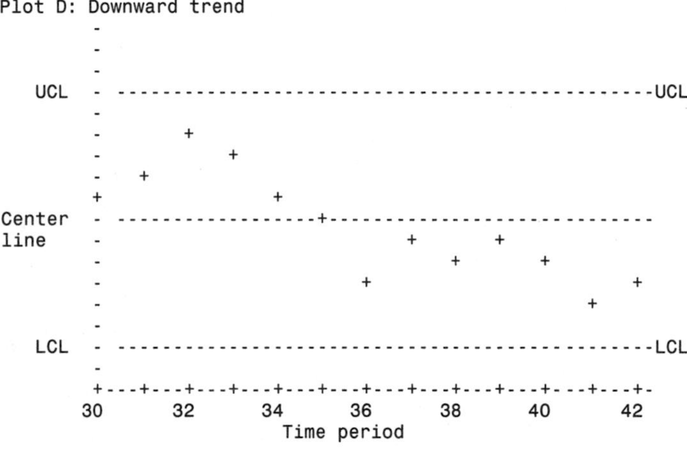

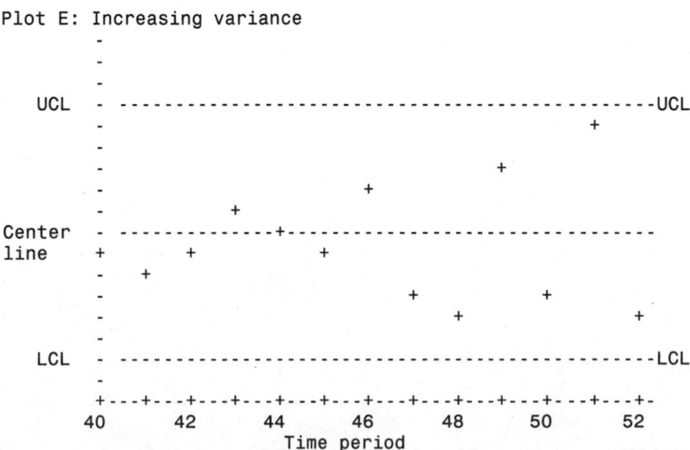

FIGURE 13.2 *continued*

Plot F: Hugging

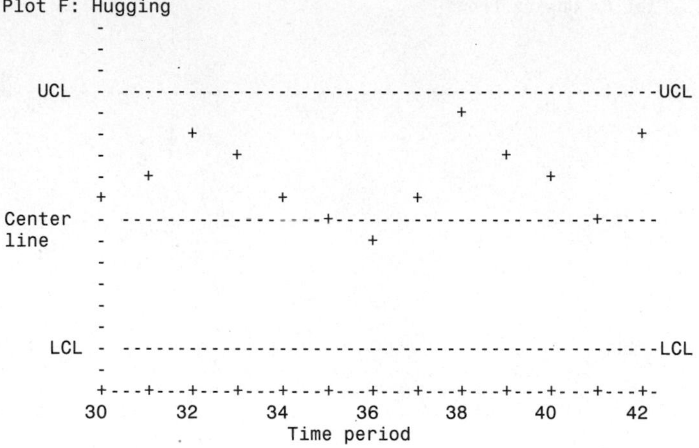

Plot G: Run

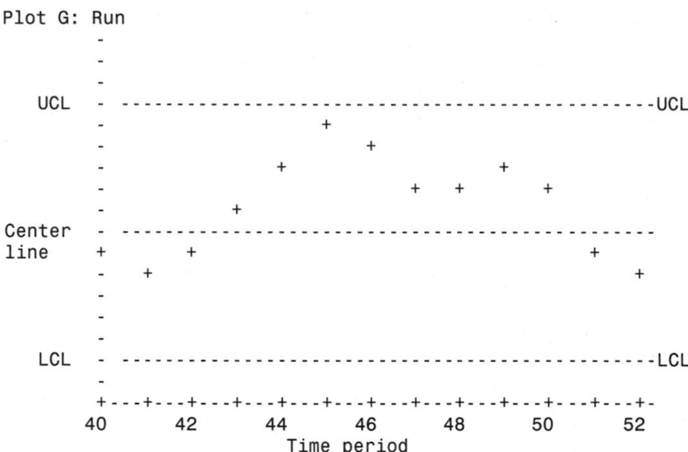

Plot H: Cycling

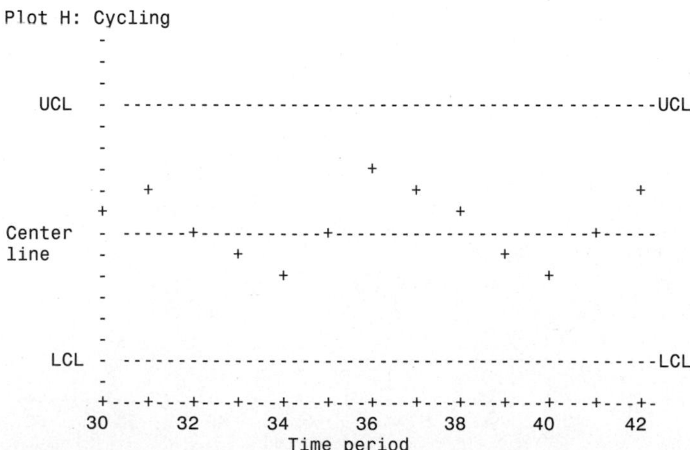

FIGURE 13.2 *concluded*

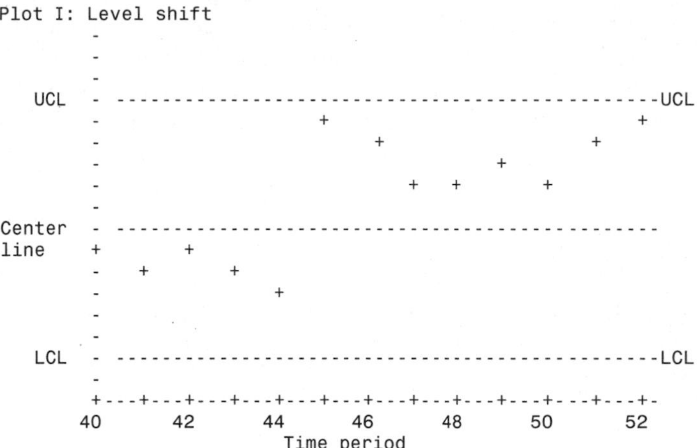

The process in plot B may or may not be in control since an unusually high measurement appears. One point falls above the 3 standard deviation control limit. The process for this unusually high observation may be in control with a randomly high measurement, or it may be out of control. Management attention is directed toward the process in this time period. This point will have to be further investigated to determine any assignable causes that could have influenced the result.

Plot C shows an upward-trending plot. Plot D shows a downward-trending plot. These processes seem to be in control since each measurement is within the control limits. However, they are obviously drifting out of control. The upward-trending plot can be characterized as resulting from a process whose mean is gradually shifting upward over time. Gradual shifts like these are common in manufacturing processes as machines wear out over time. The downward-trending plot can be characterized as resulting from a process whose mean is gradually shifting downward over time.

Plot E shows a process that's in control but for which the amount of variability is increasing. This results from a process whose mean remains constant but whose variance increases over time. This type of deterioration in a process sometimes results from worker fatigue. Workers pay close attention to every item that they process at the beginning of a shift. However, toward the end of a shift, concentration wanes and workers become careless and/or easily distracted. As a result, some items receive more attention than other items, causing the variance of workers' output to gradually increase.

Plot F shows a process that's in control but with most or all measurements above (or below) the desired process mean. Such a process could be costing money or reflect a quality level that, while satisfactory, could be improved. Also, only a slight shift in process quality could drive the process outside the control limits. Management attention is called for to discover the reasons for the condition and make improvements.

Plot G shows a run of several plots either above or below the desired process average. While all data values are within the control limits, management attention might uncover an undesirable element in the process. Perhaps a particular machine is drifting in and out of tolerance causing the plot pattern.

Plot H illustrates a cycling process. Again, each data plot is within the control limits, but something other than randomness is obviously affecting the output. Management attention might determine the problem and improve the process.

Plot I shows a process with a sudden shift in the level of measurements. This results from a process whose mean suddenly increases but whose variance remains constant. Introducing a new operator, new machine, or different-quality raw materials into the process can cause such a shift.

The rest of this chapter introduces you to statistical methods used in statistical process control. The next section describes how to use control charts to determine whether a particular process is in control.

EXERCISES

7. SPC

7. What term is used to describe a series of actions used to monitor and eliminate variation in order to keep a process in control?
8. What is a control chart? For what purpose is it used?
9. Describe the difference between assignable causes of variation and chance causes of variation. Give examples.
10. Figure 13.3 shows several quality-control plots. Which are in control? If a plot isn't in control, what type of problem exists?

FIGURE 13.3 Control Chart Patterns of Variation (Exercise 10)

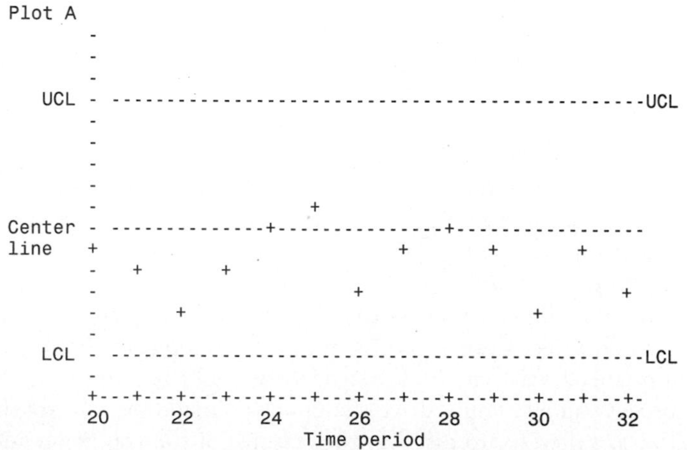

FIGURE 13.3 *continued*

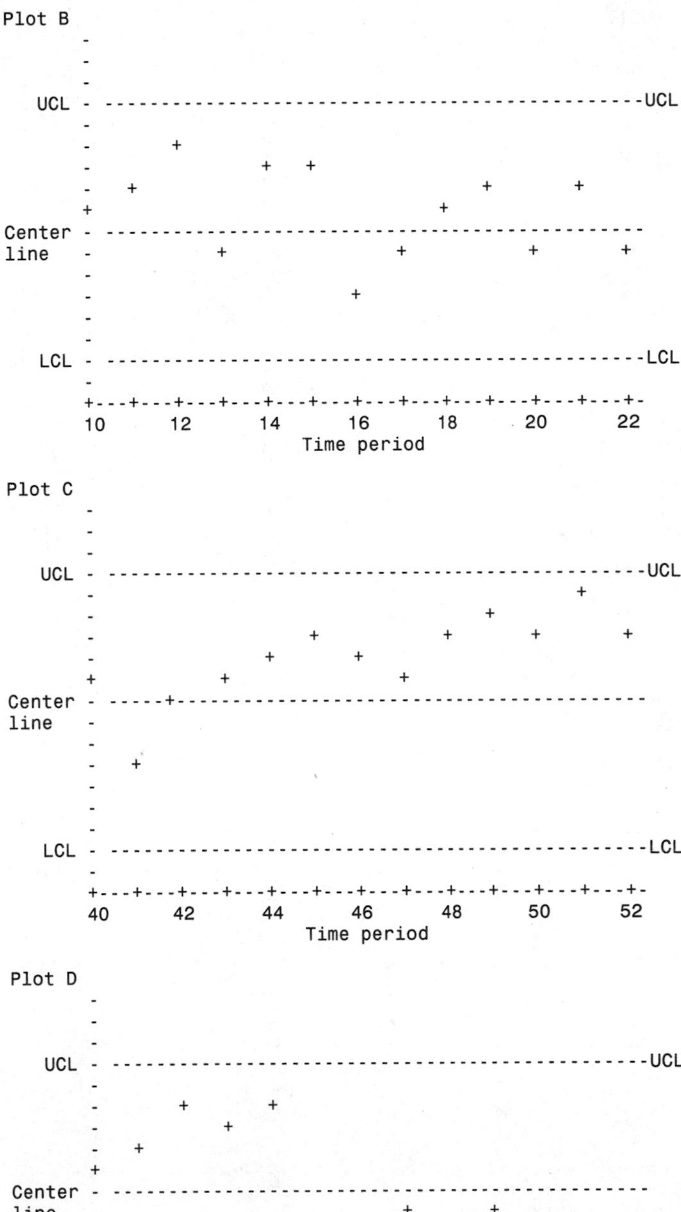

FIGURE 13.3 *continued*

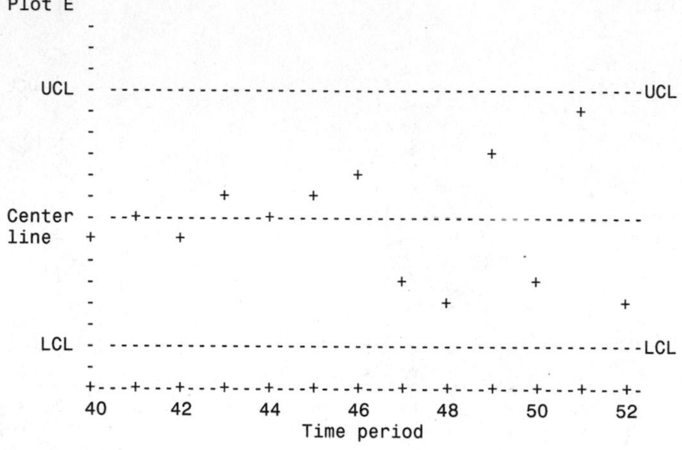

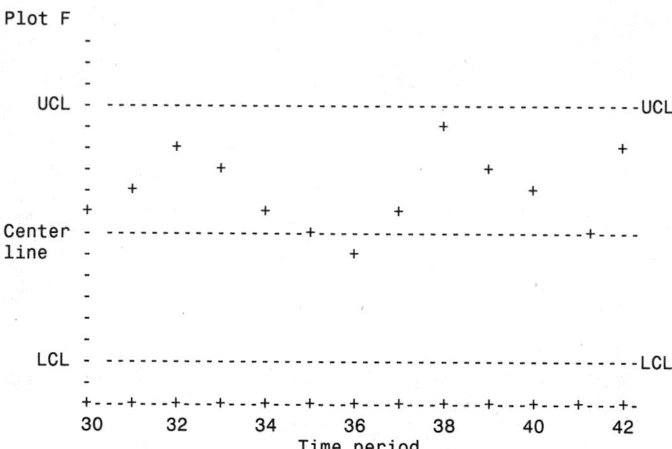

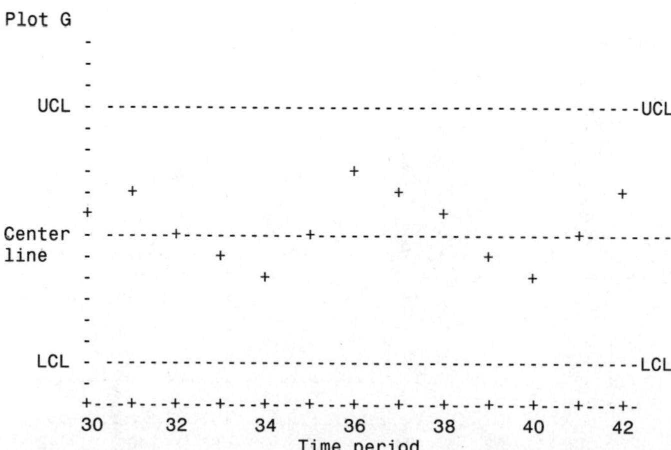

FIGURE 13.3 *concluded*

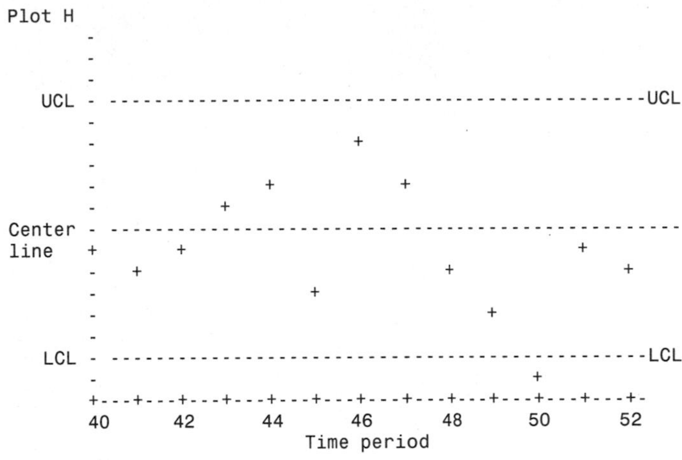

CONTROL CHARTS

Control Charts

The **control chart** is a time series graph that tracks a key variable of interest in the quality effort. Control charts are useful for evaluating a process's past performance as well as for monitoring its current performance. As the previous section indicated, in addition to providing a visual display of a process, the major function of the control chart is to separate assignable causes of variation from chance causes of variation.

> The **control chart** is a time series graph that tracks a key variable of interest in the quality effort.

Figure 13.4 presents an example of an individual measurement control chart. Note that the upper control and lower control limits are positioned (3 standard deviations above and below the mean) so that when the process is in control, the probability of an individual value of the variable of interest falling outside the control limits is small (.0026 = 1 − .9974). Note also the assumption that the variable of interest is normally distributed. This assumption is made after examining a plot of this variable and determining that the values approximate a normal distribution. Better yet, a goodness-of-fit test that assumes that the population from which the sample was taken is normally distributed can be conducted. Solved Exercise 11.2 showed this procedure.

The basic idea behind this normality assumption is that when the process is in control, or acceptable, the measured variable is likely to be close to the process mean rather than far away: it's assumed, in fact, that a normal distribution generates the value in each time period. An acceptable region is defined within which each value of

FIGURE 13.4 Individual Measurement Control Chart Showing the Normality Assumption

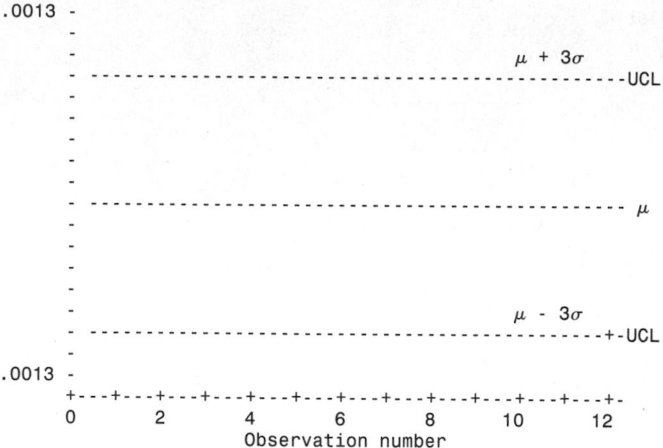

the variable is considered to be acceptable, and outside of which a problem in the process is being signaled.

Under the normality assumption, the acceptable interval can be established by knowing the process mean, the process standard deviation, and the confidence level for the interval. This notion is similar to the range established for the acceptance of a null hypothesis (Chapter 9). Attention is focused on making an inference about a process rather than a specific population of items, so the null and alternative hypotheses are

H_0: The process is in control.
H_1: The process is not in control.

A two-tailed hypothesis test is conducted with the control limits operating as the critical values. Each time a new point is plotted, a decision is made to fail to reject the null hypothesis (the point is within the control limits) or reject it (the point is outside the control limits). Anytime we reject the null hypothesis and conclude that the process isn't in control, we run the risk of making a type I error. Anytime the null hypothesis is not rejected and it's concluded that the process is in control, we run the risk of making a type II error. Example 13.2 illustrates the acceptance or rejection problem in statistical process control.

EXAMPLE 13.2 A large assembly line produces over 10,000 fuel pumps each week. Most of the line is automated, including high technology equipment that measures the volume of output for each pump as assembly is completed. This volume is the key indicator of part quality and is of vital concern to the car manufacturer using the pumps.

Management decides to plot each pump's output volume since the automated machinery is making this measurement. Past experience with the data has shown that pump volume will average .10 gallons per minute with standard deviation of .01 gallons per minute. For control chart purposes, these values are multiplied by 100 for a mean of 10 and standard deviation of 1.

Three standard deviations are used around the mean to form the control chart upper and lower limits. While a lower limit is needed to signal an inadequate pump, the upper limit is also established; while a pump that has "excessive" pump volume isn't a quality problem at first glance, management wants to know why such a measurement happens. The upper and lower control limits, with 99.74% confidence, are

$$\mu \pm 3\sigma = 10 \pm (3)(1) = 7 \text{ to } 13$$

Large rolls of paper with these limits printed on them are loaded into a printer electronically attached to the pump measurement machine. Each pump's volume is plotted on this paper as the completed pump is measured. Each hour, an assembly line worker scans several feet of this paper to observe the volume pattern of completed pumps. Since control limits are printed on the paper, it's very easy to spot out-of-control measurements and look for patterns. Figure 13.5 shows five minutes of this control chart. Most pumps produced during these five minutes are in control, that is, acceptable for shipment to the car manufacturer. However, pump number 25 has a low volume. Since this is the only such pump, the floor supervisor decides that there's no problem with the process; the pump is removed from the line and scrapped.

FIGURE 13.5 Individual Chart for Volume Developed Using MINITAB (Example 13.2)

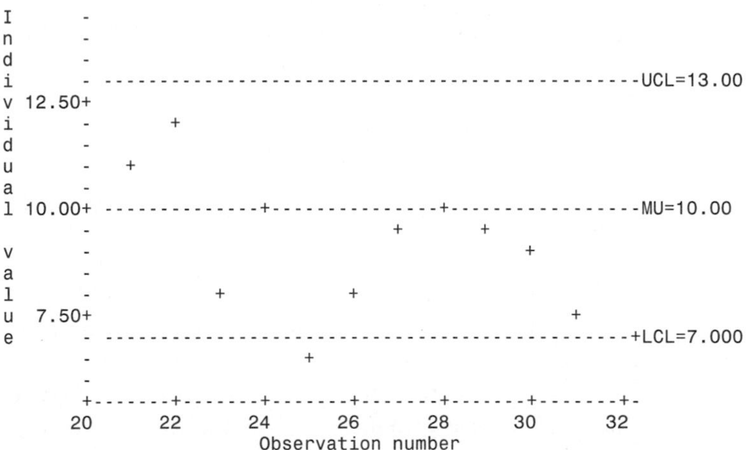

A second problem is revealed by pumps 28 through 32. While all these pumps are within the established control limits, the process seems to drift downward. The automatic machinery may be slipping or deteriorating, resulting in pumps that will soon be below standard. The floor supervisor immediately visits the production line and is prepared to stop the line and determine the reason for the apparent deterioration in quality.

The MINITAB Computer Package section at the end of this chapter gives the MINITAB commands to develop Figure 13.5.

In Example 13.2, the key quality variable being tracked is the volume of output for each pump used by a car manufacturer. In other applications, other variables are deemed to be of key importance in the quality-control effort. Here's a brief description of some quality variables typically tracked on a control chart.

Individual measurements: For very large or expensive assemblies, careful measurement of each unit is sometimes appropriate. These measurements are plotted individually over time, not averaged and plotted. An example is the measured electrical output of large industrial generators. Example 13.2 illustrated a situation where individual pump measurements were monitored. Figure 13.5 showed an individual control chart.

Process mean: This is the average value of the process for each time period. If a small number of items is produced, the entire batch is measured and this population mean is recorded on the chart. More often, a random sample of items is taken and their sample mean is used to estimate the mean of the entire time period's output; then this sample value is plotted on the control chart. Examples 13.3 and 13.4 illustrate situations where process quality is monitored using sample means. Figure 13.6 presents a mean control chart.

Range of measured values: This variable tracks the process variability. In almost all processes, the less variability, the better, as noted earlier. Tracking the difference between the largest and smallest value (the range) is a way of monitoring variability. If the range becomes too great, corrective action is called for as illustrated in Example 13.5. A range control chart appears in Figure 13.11.

Standard deviation: This would seem to be a better way of tracking variability than using the range. The range can be distorted by even a single very large or small value. The standard deviation tends to be less affected by extreme values; however, practitioners use the range much more widely, primarily because it's easier to calculate and interpret than the standard deviation.

Proportion defective: The number of defective units in each time period is calculated (a census) or estimated (a sample) and divided by the total number of items measured. The result is the proportion defective and this value is recorded on the control chart for each time period. This measurement is used when attention is focused on the correct functioning of units as a whole: either one works or it doesn't. Example 13.6 illustrates a situation where the proportion of defective units is monitored. Figure 13.14 shows a proportion control chart.

Number of defects per unit: In large assemblies, the number of nonconforming items per unit is often the focus. For each time period, this value is averaged for the units tested and plotted on the control chart. Examples 13.7 and 13.8 illustrate situations where the number of defects per unit are monitored. The appropriate control charts appear in Figures 13.15 and 13.17.

Number of nonconforming units: Instead of tracking the proportion defective, the total number of nonconforming units is measured for each time period. This variable is appropriate when the batch size remains relatively constant.

EXERCISES

11. Describe how a control chart is used.

12. Three standard deviations around mean

12. Where are the upper and lower control limits set for a control chart?

13. .0026

13. When a process is in control, what is the probability of an individual value of the variable of interest falling outside the control limits? Explain how you computed this value.

14. Explain the basic idea behind the normality assumption.

SM

15. Albert Hughes (quality-control engineer for Dillon Aircraft) understands that viscosity of an aircraft primer paint is an important quality characteristic. Since the product is produced in batches and each batch takes several hours to produce, the production rate is slow and an individual control chart is necessary for quality monitoring. Past experience indicates that the average paint viscosity will be 30 units with a standard deviation of 1.2.

15*a*. LCL = 26.4, UCL = 33.6, in control
b. Potentially out of control

a. Viscosity readings for 18 observations are shown below (sample 1). Albert instructs you to construct a control chart for individual measures and test to determine whether the process is in control. You're to write Albert a report indicating whether the process is in control and, if not, what type of pattern you've observed.

b. One week later, Albert asks you to take another sample (sample 2) and develop a new control chart. Write Albert a second report.

	Viscosity	
Batch number	Sample 1	Sample 2
1	30.11	30.02
2	30.03	29.79
3	29.89	32.11
4	31.11	29.03
5	29.00	29.59
6	29.54	31.04
7	30.04	29.95
8	29.95	30.26
9	30.26	30.74
10	30.74	32.24
11	31.24	32.02
12	31.02	26.87
13	30.87	27.99
14	29.99	28.57
15	29.57	28.55
16	30.55	29.00
17	30.25	27.81
18	29.81	28.43

CONSTRUCTING A CHART TO MONITOR THE MEAN OF A PROCESS: THE $\bar{x}$ CHART

$\bar{x}$ Chart

Example 13.2 focused on using a control chart to measure the variation in individual observations of a process to determine whether the process was in control. In this section the **$\bar{x}$ chart** is used to detect changes in the process mean by monitoring the variation in the means of samples drawn from the process. Instead of plotting individual observations on the control chart, the analyst plots sample means. (Each sample mean is computed from a sample of n individual observations.) As a rule of thumb, many analysts obtain at least 20 samples of n observations each (where $n > 2$). Since sample means involve more observations, the $\bar{x}$ chart is more sensitive than the individual measurement chart for detecting shifts in the process mean.

> The $\bar{x}$ **chart (mean chart)** is used to detect changes in a process mean by monitoring the variation in the means of samples drawn from the process.

To determine the centerline and control limits for the $\bar{x}$ chart, the analyst must understand the sampling distribution of $\bar{x}$'s. A quick review of the properties of this sampling distribution of means will be helpful.

> Properties of the **sampling distribution of means:**
>
> 1. The mean of the sampling distribution of means equals the population mean:
>
> $$\mu_{\bar{x}} = \mu_x$$
>
> 2. The standard deviation of the sampling distribution of means (standard error) equals the population standard deviation divided by the square root of the sample size:
>
> $$\sigma_{\bar{x}} = \sigma/\sqrt{n}$$
>
> 3. The sampling distribution of means is approximately normal for sufficiently large sample sizes ($n \geq 30$).

The process mean (μ) may either be known from past experience with the process or be estimated on the basis of sample data. The usual case in industry is to estimate the process mean using the available sample means. The $\bar{x}$ chart centerline, which represents the mean of the process, is computed by averaging the sample means. This mean of the sample means is denoted by $\bar{\bar{x}}$:

$$\bar{\bar{x}} = \frac{\bar{x}_1 + \bar{x}_2 + \bar{x}_3 + \cdots + \bar{x}_k}{k} \tag{13.1}$$

where $\bar{\bar{x}}$ = Estimate of the process mean (chart centerline)
$\bar{x}_i$ = Mean of each sample
k = Number of samples of size n

The process standard deviation (σ) may also either be known from past experience with the process or be estimated using sample data. If the process standard deviation is known, the relevant standard deviation is the standard error of the mean, $\sigma/\sqrt{n}$. This is because the chart is tracking sample means rather than individual observations.

The $\bar{x}$ chart's control limits are determined from the sampling distribution of the means, not the distribution of individual x's. Since the control limits are usually set at three standard deviations, the standard deviation of the sampling distribution is multiplied by 3:

$$\begin{aligned} \text{LCL} &= \bar{\bar{x}} - 3(\sigma/\sqrt{n}) \\ \text{UCL} &= \bar{\bar{x}} + 3(\sigma/\sqrt{n}) \end{aligned} \tag{13.2}$$

where $\bar{\bar{x}}$ = Estimate of the process mean (centerline)
σ = Process standard deviation
n = Size of each sample

The resulting control limits are referred to as the 3-sigma control limits. Note that the value 3 can be changed to reflect the quality requirements of the process. Using the value 3 produces control limits that will be exceeded approximately 26 times in 10,000 (.0026) by chance if the process mean and variation remain stable. A value of 2 would produce control limits exceeded approximately 4.6 times in 1,000 (.0456).

Example 13.3 shows how lower and upper control limits are constructed when the population standard deviation is known.

EXAMPLE 13.3 A machine produces cylinders used as the center for 3½-inch computer disks. A total of 25 samples have been selected. Each sample contains nine cylinders ($n = 9$). The average of the sample means is a diameter of $\bar{\bar{x}} = 2.5$ centimeters. Based on past experience, the process standard deviation is known to be $\sigma = 0.003$ centimeters. Quality-control analyst Evelyn Black must develop upper and lower control limits for determining whether the process is in control. She uses Equation 13.2 to compute them:

$$\begin{aligned} \text{LCL} &= \bar{\bar{x}} - 3(\sigma/\sqrt{n}) \\ &= 2.5 - 3\ (.003/\sqrt{9}) = 2.5 - 3(.001) = 2.497 \\ \text{UCL} &= \bar{\bar{x}} + 3(\sigma/\sqrt{n}) \\ &= 2.5 + 3(.003/\sqrt{9}) = 2.5 + 3(.001) = 2.503 \end{aligned}$$

Whenever a sample of nine cylinders produces a mean between 2.497 and 2.503, Evelyn concludes that the process is in control. Whenever a sample mean falls outside these limits, she concludes that the process is not in control. If the process is in control, the probability of obtaining a sample mean outside the control limits (making a type I error) is $2(.5000 - .4987) = .0026$.

The process standard deviation is usually unknown and must be estimated from sample data. The most effective approach (and the one used most frequently in industry, especially when small samples are used) is to utilize the ranges of the k samples as an estimate of the process variability. Recall from Chapter 4 that the range, R, of a sample is the difference between the maximum and minimum observations in a data set. The process standard deviation is estimated using Equation 13.3:

$$\hat{\sigma} = \frac{\bar{R}}{d_2} \tag{13.3}$$

where $\hat{\sigma}$ = Estimate of the process standard deviation
$\overline{R}$ = Average of the sample ranges
d_2 = Value selected from the control chart constants table (Table 13.1)

The estimate of the process standard deviation is substituted into Equation 13.2 forming Equation 13.4:

$$\text{LCL} = \bar{\bar{x}} - 3(\hat{\sigma}/\sqrt{n})$$
$$\text{UCL} = \bar{\bar{x}} + 3(\hat{\sigma}/\sqrt{n}) \tag{13.4}$$

The steps for construction of an $\bar{x}$ chart are:

Steps for constructing an $\bar{x}$ chart:

1. Select k samples of data, each of size n.
2. Compute the mean of each sample.
3. Estimate the process mean ($\bar{\bar{x}}$) by averaging the sample means. Use this process mean as the centerline of the chart.
4. Estimate the population standard deviation using $\hat{\sigma} = \overline{R}/d_2$. ($d_2$ is found in Table 13.1.)
5. Compute the 3-sigma control limits:

$$\text{LCL} = \bar{\bar{x}} - 3(\hat{\sigma}/\sqrt{n})$$
$$\text{UCL} = \bar{\bar{x}} + 3(\hat{\sigma}/\sqrt{n})$$

Example 13.4 illustrates the procedure for constructing lower and upper control limits when the population standard deviation is unknown.

EXAMPLE 13.4 Management of the Mead Corporation is considering entering the European market. However, the company controller has recently read an article in *Management Accounting* (July 1992) that points out that even if the company makes good products, if its quality system does not conform to ISO 9000 standards Europeans will not buy.[5] Jeff Frost, Quality Engineer, has been informed that the company's quality system must conform to ISO 9000 standards in order for the company to sell products or services in Europe. Jeff has been told that the quality system described in the ISO 9000 series is the only one that meets European Economic Area (EEA) directives requiring sellers to have quality systems.

Jeff decides to improve the quality of the tensile strength of a textile fiber produced by the company. He selects 16 samples from the first eight hours of a production run.

[5] A. F. Borthick and H. P. Roth, "Will Europeans Buy Your Company's Products" *Management Accounting*, July 1992, p. 28.

TABLE 13.1 Control Chart Constants

Number of observations in subgroup, n	A_2	A_3	d_2	d_3	D_3	D_4
2	1.880	2.659	1.128	0.853	0.000	3.267
3	1.023	1.954	1.693	0.888	0.000	2.574
4	0.729	1.628	2.059	0.880	0.000	2.282
5	0.577	1.427	2.326	0.864	0.000	2.114
6	0.483	1.287	2.534	0.848	0.000	2.004
7	0.419	1.182	2.704	0.833	0.076	1.924
8	0.373	1.099	2.847	0.820	0.136	1.864
9	0.337	1.032	2.970	0.808	0.184	1.816
10	0.308	0.975	3.078	0.797	0.223	1.777
11	0.285	0.927	3.173	0.787	0.256	1.744
12	0.266	0.886	3.258	0.778	0.283	1.717
13	0.249	0.850	3.336	0.770	0.307	1.693
14	0.235	0.817	3.407	0.762	0.328	1.672
15	0.223	0.789	3.472	0.755	0.347	1.653
16	0.212	0.763	3.532	0.749	0.363	1.637
17	0.203	0.739	3.588	0.743	0.378	1.622
18	0.194	0.718	3.640	0.738	0.391	1.608
19	0.187	0.698	3.689	0.733	0.403	1.597
20	0.180	0.680	3.735	0.729	0.415	1.585
21	0.173	0.663	3.778	0.724	0.425	1.575
22	0.167	0.647	3.819	0.720	0.434	1.566
23	0.162	0.633	3.858	0.716	0.443	1.557
24	0.157	0.619	3.895	0.712	0.451	1.548
25	0.153	0.606	3.931	0.709	0.459	1.541
Over 25	$3/\sqrt{n}$					

Source: Adapted from *Tools and Methods for the Improvement of Quality*, H. Gitlow, S. Gitlow, A. Oppenheim, and R. Oppenheim (Homewood, IL: Richard D. Irwin, 1989).

Samples are taken at 30-minute intervals. Each sample consists of $n = 4$ fiber specimens.

Table 13.2 summarizes the results. As it shows, the mean of the 16 sample means is $\bar{\bar{x}} = 120$. Since the process standard deviation isn't known, it's estimated using Equation 13.3. The average range and the appropriate d_2 value from Table 13.1 are used to estimate the standard deviation. Each sample's range is computed in the R column in Table 13.2. For example, the range or difference between the largest and smallest fiber strengths for sample number 1 is $(120.85 - 119.50) = 1.35$. At the bottom of Table 13.2, the average range for these samples is computed: $\bar{R} = .92375$. Referring to Table 13.1 for a sample of $n = 4$ fibers, the appropriate d_2 value is 2.059. Using Equation 13.3, the estimate of σ is:

$$\hat{\sigma} = \frac{\bar{R}}{d_2} = \frac{.92375}{2.059} = .449$$

TM

TABLE 13.2 Sixteen Samples of Size 4 from the Tensile Strength Process of Example 13.4

Sample number	Strength of fiber 1	2	3	4	$\bar{x}$	Range R
1	120.15	119.50	120.85	119.95	120.11	1.35
2	119.89	119.40	120.45	119.87	119.90	1.05
3	119.62	120.03	120.74	120.13	120.13	1.12
4	120.47	119.89	120.24	120.15	120.19	0.58
5	120.00	119.21	119.68	120.24	119.78	1.03
6	119.99	119.87	119.85	119.84	119.89	0.15
7	120.11	120.01	120.42	119.93	120.12	0.49
8	119.75	120.25	120.14	119.86	120.00	0.50
9	120.18	119.87	119.81	119.77	119.91	0.41
10	120.87	120.57	119.24	120.09	120.19	1.63
11	119.86	119.20	120.30	119.72	119.70	1.10
12	118.86	120.41	119.87	120.53	119.92	1.67
13	119.90	121.12	119.54	120.07	120.16	1.58
14	119.99	120.18	120.06	119.88	120.03	0.30
15	120.03	120.05	120.14	119.33	119.89	0.81
16	119.55	120.56	120.17	119.64	119.98	1.01
					1,919.99	14.78

$$\bar{\bar{x}} = \frac{1{,}919.99}{16} = 120$$

$$\bar{R} = \frac{14.78}{16} = .92375$$

Equation 13.4 is used to calculate the control limits:

$$\begin{aligned}
\text{LCL} &= \bar{\bar{x}} - 3(\hat{\sigma}/\sqrt{n}) \\
&= 120 - 3(.449/\sqrt{4}) = 119.327 \\
\text{UCL} &= \bar{\bar{x}} + 3(\hat{\sigma}/\sqrt{n}) \\
&= 120 + 3(.449/\sqrt{4}) = 120.674
\end{aligned}$$

Figure 13.6 shows these lower and upper control limits along with the centerline and 16 sample means plotted in sequence. The sample means are all within the control limits so Jeff concludes that the process is in control.

The MINITAB computer package can be used to develop Figure 13.6. The MINITAB commands are:

```
MTB> SET C1
DATA> 120.15   119.50   120.85   119.95
DATA> 119.89   119.40   120.45   119.87
DATA> 119.62   120.03   120.74   120.13
DATA> 120.47   119.89   120.24   120.15
DATA> 120.00   119.21   119.68   120.24
DATA> 119.99   119.87   119.85   119.84
DATA> 120.11   120.01   120.42   119.93
DATA> 119.75   120.25   120.14   119.86
DATA> 120.18   119.87   119.81   119.77
DATA> 120.87   120.57   119.24   120.09
DATA> 119.86   119.20   120.30   119.72
```

Figure 13.6 $\bar{x}$ Chart for Strength Developed Using MINITAB (Example 13.4)

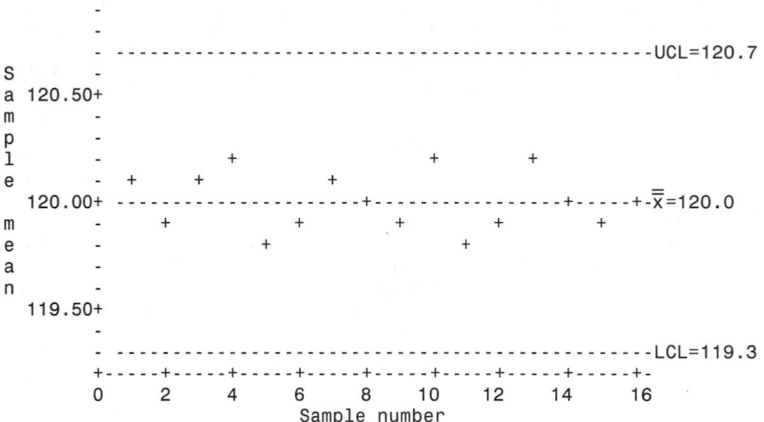


```
DATA> 118.86   120.41   119.87   120.53
DATA> 119.90   121.12   119.54   120.07
DATA> 119.99   120.18   120.06   119.88
DATA> 120.03   120.05   120.14   119.33
DATA> 119.55   120.56   120.17   119.64
DATA> END
MTB> NAME C1 'STRENGTH'
MTB> XBARCHART FOR DATA IN C1, SAMPLE SIZE 4
     OUTPUT SHOWN AS FIGURE 13.6

MTB> WRITE 'FIBER.DAT' C1
MTB> STOP
```

The data are entered in sequence into C1. The XBARCHART command plots sample means of size $n = 4$ on an $\bar{x}$ chart (Figure 13.6). The WRITE command is used to save the data located in C1 in a file called FIBER.DAT.

Up to this point, the discussion has focused on determining that a process is not in control by identifying values beyond the control limits on the $\bar{x}$ chart. A closer look at the pattern of all control chart values may also reveal a process that's not in control. This is true even though all of the values may be within the control limits. For example, six points in a row, all increasing or decreasing, indicate that a process is not in control, possibly due to operator fatigue. The process can probably be improved by identifying and eliminating this source of variation. Assorted plot patterns appeared in Figure 13.2.

Analysts use pattern analysis to recognize systematic patterns in an $\bar{x}$ control chart and to identify the source of such process variation. To help detect systematic patterns in $\bar{x}$ charts, each chart is divided into three zones (Figure 13.7). Zone A is defined as the area between 2 and 3 standard deviation units above and below the centerline. Zone B is defined as the area between 1 and 2 standard deviation units above and below the centerline. Zone C is defined as the area between the centerline and $\pm$ 1 standard deviation unit.

FIGURE 13.7 $\bar{x}$ Chart Using Zones A, B, and C

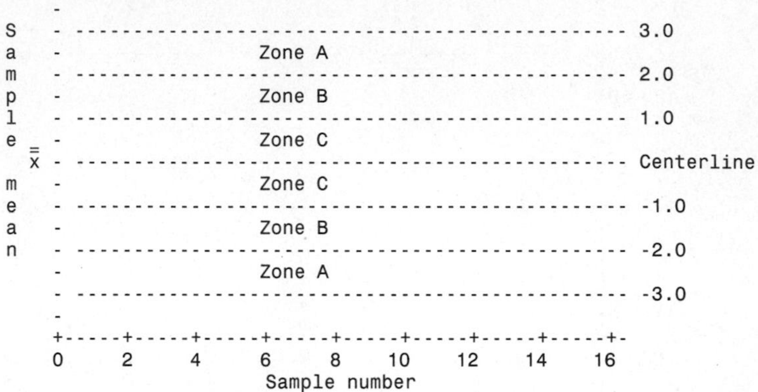

Analysts don't agree about the specific systematic patterns that indicate nonrandom variation. The following specific patterns are used by the MINITAB computer program.[6] Each pattern is illustrated in Figure 13.8.

PATTERN	DESCRIPTION
1	One point beyond zone A (the out-of-control pattern discussed previously).
2	Nine points in a row in zone C or beyond, all on one side of centerline.
3	Six points in a row, all increasing or all decreasing.
4	Fourteen points in a row, alternating up and down.
5	Two out of three points in a row in zone A or beyond.
6	Four out of five points in a row in zone B or beyond (on one side of centerline).
7	Fifteen points in a row in zone C (above or below centerline).
8	Eight points in a row beyond zone C (above or below centerline).

FIGURE 13.8 Eight Patterns Tested for by MINITAB

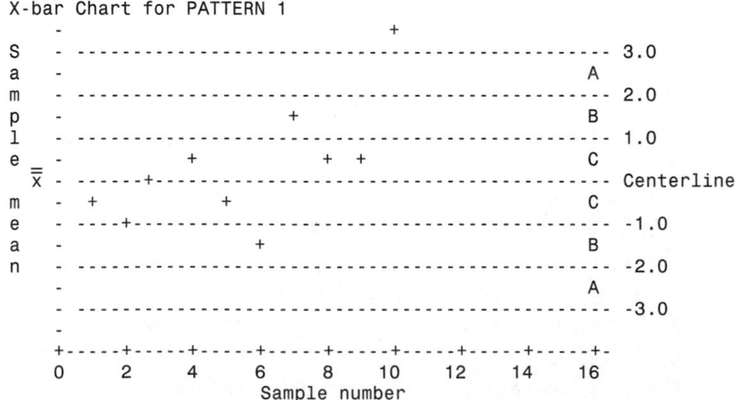

[6]*MINITAB Reference Manual Release 8 PC Version,* State College, PA: MINITAB Statistical Software, 1991.

FIGURE 13.8 *continued*

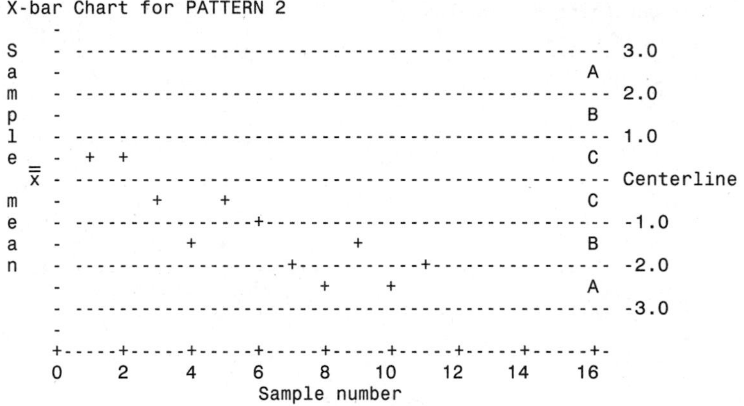

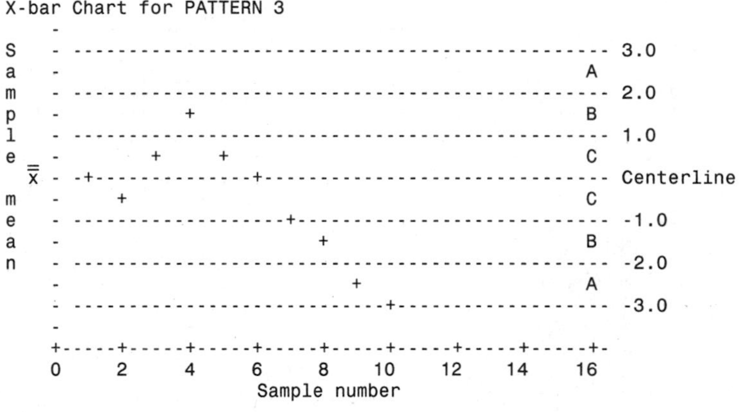

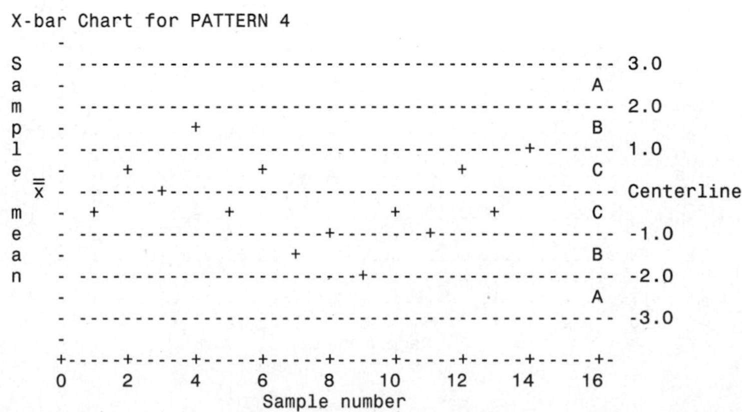

FIGURE 13.8 *continued*

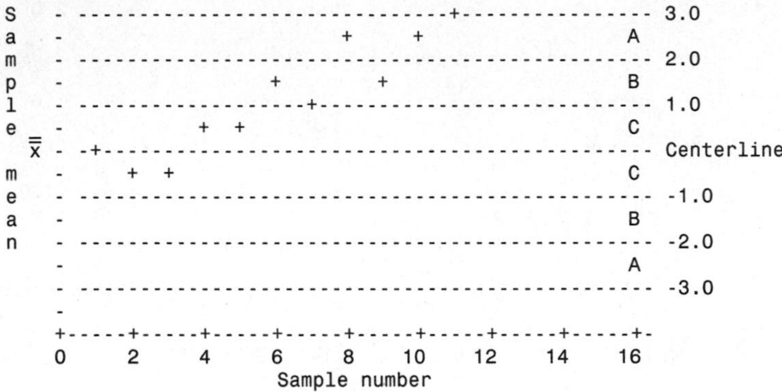

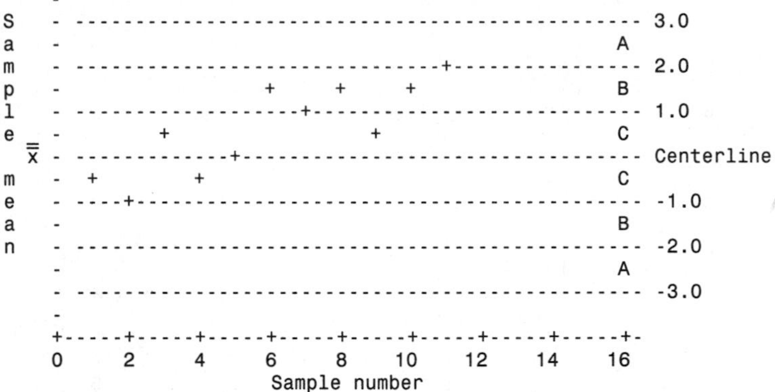

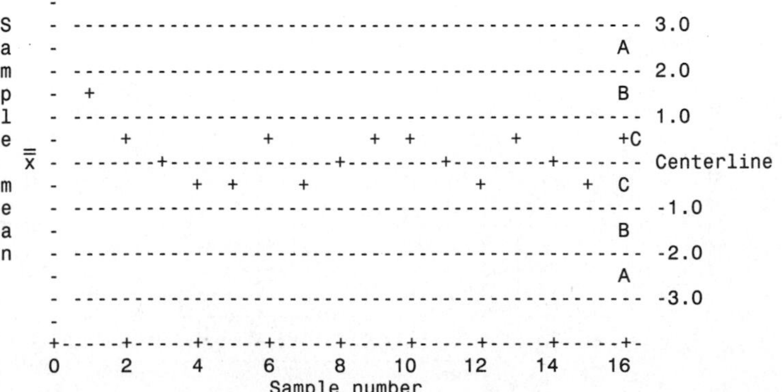

FIGURE 13.8 *concluded*

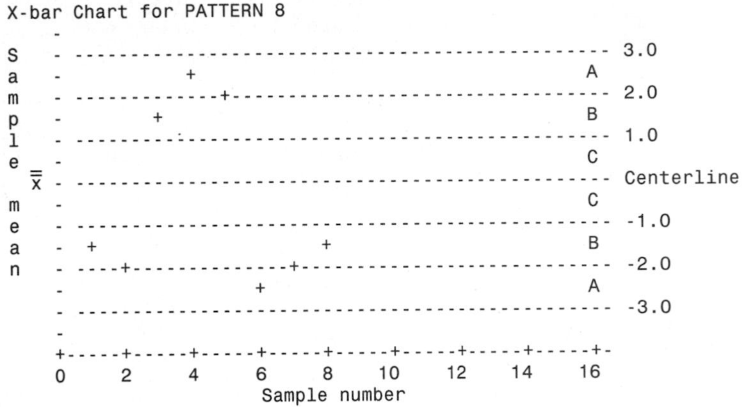

After examining Figure 13.8, it should be obvious that there's more to control chart inspection than looking for values outside the control limits. In actual practice, analysts need a great deal of knowledge and experience to interpret the particular pattern or assignable causes. Several good textbooks are available if more information on pattern interpretation is needed.

The MINITAB computer package can be used to develop zones A, B, and C for Example 13.4. The MINITAB commands are:

```
MTB >  READ 'FIBER.DAT' C1
     64 ROWS READ

C1
  120.15   119.50   120.85   119.95 . . .

MTB > NAME C1 'STRENGTH'
MTB > XBARCHART FOR DATA IN C1, SAMPLE SIZE 4;
SUBC> SIGMA = .449;
SUBC> SLIMITS 1 2 3;
SUBC> TEST 1:8.
      OUTPUT SHOWN AS FIGURE 13.9
MTB > STOP
```

The READ command is used to read the data from the file FIBER.DAT into C1. The XBARCHART command plots sample means of size $n = 4$ on an $\bar{x}$ chart. Equation 13.3 is used to estimate the process standard deviation. The subcommand SIGMA = .449 is used to provide this information. Zones A, B, and C are included using subcommand SLIMITS 1 2 3, and MINITAB is instructed to search for patterns 1 through 8 using subcommand TEST 1:8. Figure 13.9 shows that no patterns were identified. If MINITAB does detect a pattern, the sample at which the pattern is completed is flagged by placing a value (1 for pattern 1, 2 for pattern 2, and so forth) above or below the plotted value.

FIGURE 13.9 $\bar{x}$ Chart for Strength with Zones A, B, and C (Example 13.4)

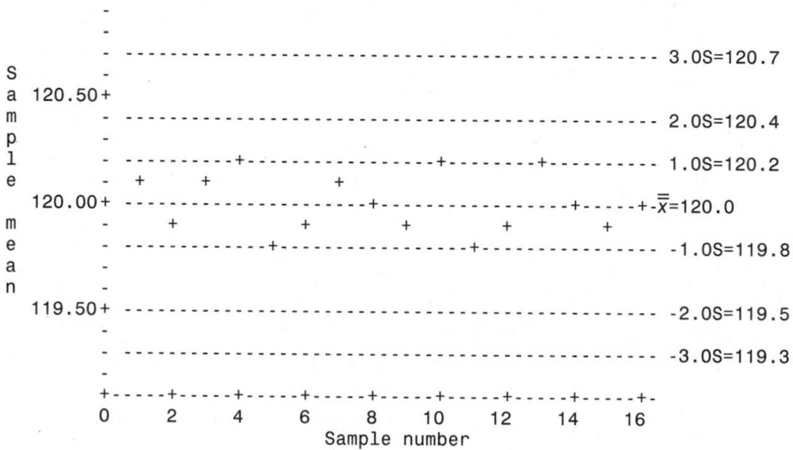

In practice, the $\bar{x}$ chart is typically used in conjunction with a range chart (R chart) that monitors the variation of the process. Used together, these two charts make it possible to determine whether a process is in control.

You've just learned how to determine when a process is not in control because of a shift in the mean. In the next section, you'll learn how to determine whether a variation change indicates an out-of-control process.

EXERCISES

16. The individual measurement chart's control limits are determined from the sampling distribution of individual x's. How are the control limits of an $\bar{x}$ chart determined?
17. Explain how the properties of the sampling distribution of sample means are used to construct an $\bar{x}$ chart.
18. Even if all the values on an $\bar{x}$ chart fall between the control limits, the process may not be in control. Explain.
19. Use pattern analysis to determine which of the processes plotted in the six $\bar{x}$ charts in Figure 13.10 are in control.

FIGURE 13.10 Plots to Be Analyzed Using Pattern Analysis (Exercise 19)

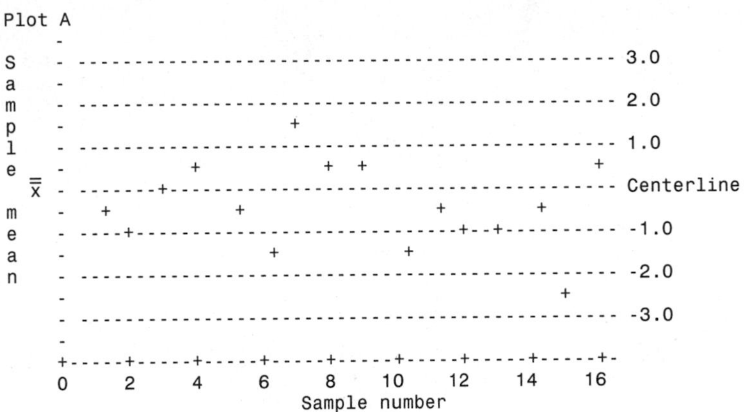

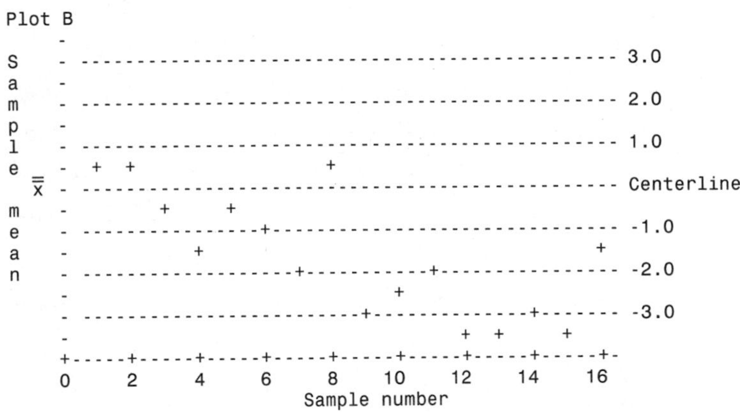

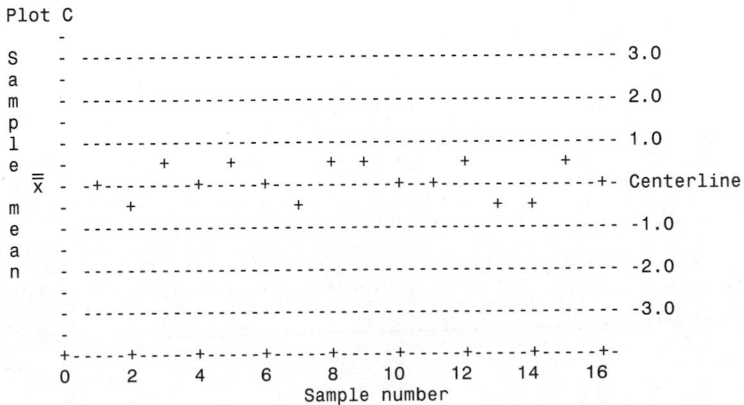

FIGURE 13.10 *concluded*

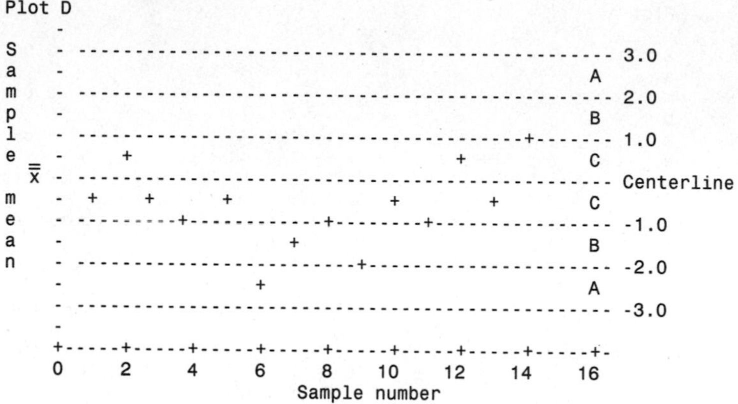

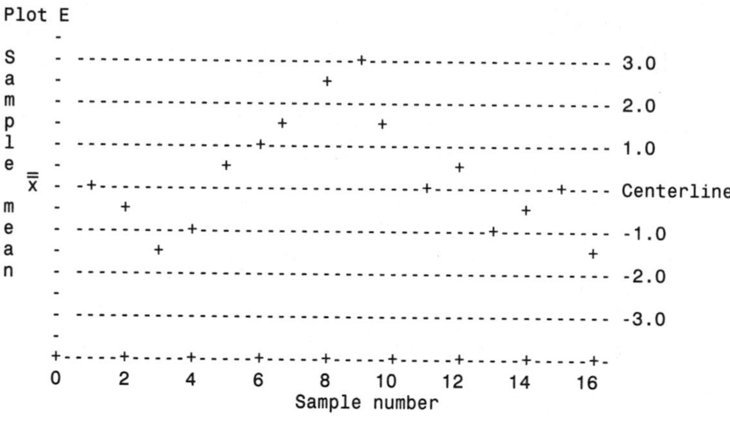

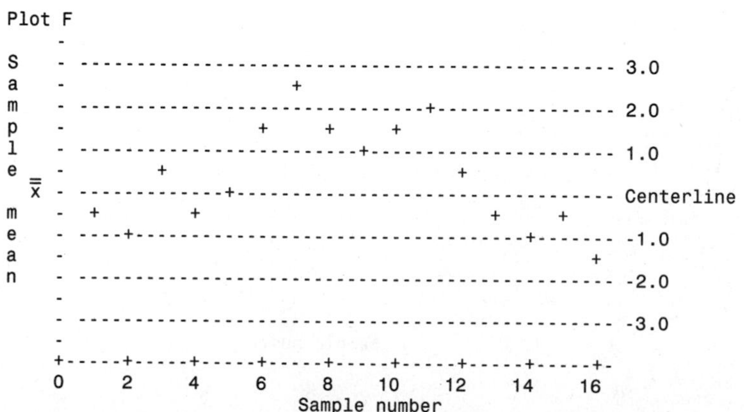

20. LCL = 3,839, UCL = 4,161

20. Natural gas cylinders are produced by a robot welder to have an average burst strength of 4,000 psi, with standard deviation of 120 psi. Determine upper and lower control limits for a 3-sigma mean control chart in which each sample consists of five cylinders.

21. In control

21. (Refer to Exercise 20.) Determine whether the process is in control given the following nine sample means:

Mean Burst Strengths								
4005	4058	3995	3854	4001	3897	4112	4067	4012

22. LCL = 11.955, UCL = 12.045

22. Taft Manufacturing produces softballs that historically have a circumference averaging 12 inches with standard deviation of .04 inches. Determine upper and lower control limits for a 3-sigma mean control chart in which each sample consists of seven softballs.

23. Potentially out of control

23. (Refer to Exercise 22.) Determine whether the process is in control given the following eight sample mean circumferences: 12.051, 11.966, 11.981, 11.945, 12.072, 11.998, 12.008, 12.033.

24. Chuck Jackson, manager of the Chariot Inn, monitors the swimming pool's pH level by taking readings every two hours from 9 A.M. to 9 P.M. daily. The past two weeks' results are:

Day 1	Average pH	Range
1	8.21	.17
2	8.26	.15
3	8.08	.19
4	8.26	.22
5	8.19	.18
6	8.14	.13
7	8.09	.10
8	8.21	.16
9	8.20	.21
10	8.09	.12
11	8.16	.21
12	8.09	.08
13	8.24	.16
14	8.19	.19

24*a*. LCL = 8.104, UCL = 8.240
b. $\bar{\bar{x}}$ = 8.172 Zone C: LCL 8.150, UCL 8.195 Zone B: 8.150 to 8.127, 8.195 to 8.217. Zone A: 8.127 to 8.140, 8.217 to 8.240
c. Potentially out of control

a. Develop the centerline and upper and lower control limits for a 3-sigma $\bar{x}$ chart.

b. Compute the limits of the six zones (A, B, C).

c. Plot the means and test to determine whether the process is in control.

25. The Wearing Corporation manufactures precision parts such as bolts used in helicopters. Charlene Richards is in charge of quality control. She samples six bolts each hour and measures them using a computerized precision measuring instrument. The data for the past 22 hours are:

Hour	Bolt lengths (centimeters)					
1	21.02	23.41	22.01	24.12	23.88	22.87
2	22.01	22.45	21.21	23.82	24.08	22.37
3	21.54	21.99	23.56	22.35	23.12	23.93
4	24.12	23.83	22.76	24.54	23.21	22.34
5	22.32	22.44	24.31	22.22	23.23	21.89

Hour	Bolt lengths (centimeters)					
6	22.35	23.56	22.87	23.35	25.11	22.27
7	21.92	23.51	24.31	22.52	23.56	21.74
8	21.32	21.41	22.41	21.92	21.86	23.81
9	22.21	22.45	21.31	22.82	22.06	22.35
10	21.44	23.99	23.16	23.75	23.16	22.94
11	22.12	24.83	22.26	24.55	24.26	21.34
12	22.34	21.44	24.41	21.23	24.23	23.85
13	21.35	23.43	22.57	24.36	23.18	24.47
14	23.92	21.51	23.31	22.57	22.56	24.44
15	21.32	22.41	22.31	24.15	21.89	23.87
16	22.31	23.45	23.41	23.82	21.98	21.38
17	21.67	20.99	23.54	22.35	22.12	22.96
18	24.09	22.83	21.76	24.54	23.21	23.34
19	22.34	21.44	24.31	23.62	24.83	24.59
20	21.35	24.56	23.84	23.65	23.18	24.27
21	22.96	22.51	21.31	22.55	22.56	23.44
22	23.95	21.51	24.33	21.32	21.26	22.34

25*a*. $\bar{x}$ chart
b. $\bar{\bar{x}}$ = 22.88, LCL = 21.57, UCL = 24.20, in control

a. Construct the appropriate control chart to monitor this process.

b. Is the process in control?

c. Give an example of an assignable cause that could potentially affect this process.

26. The Circuit Corporation manufactures circuit boards for new personal computers. Board length is very important since they're eventually slipped into slots in a chassis. Company quality analyst Phil Conrath is in charge of stabilizing the length dimension. Boards are cut from large sheets of material by a single rotary cutter continuously fed from a hopper. Phil develops a control chart for the length of the circuit boards produced by the process. The circuit boards' mean length is supposed to be 6 inches with a standard deviation of .08 inch. Phil decides to select five units every hour from the production process. The accompanying table shows the resulting lengths for a two-day period.

Sample number	Cut circuit board lengths 1	2	3	4	5
Day 1					
7 A.M.	5.83	6.09	5.91	6.18	5.91
8	6.13	5.99	5.76	6.12	6.19
9	5.94	5.81	6.11	6.28	6.00
10	6.03	5.89	6.01	6.08	6.10
11	5.93	5.99	6.01	6.19	6.11
12 P.M.	6.11	6.01	5.96	5.92	6.09
1	5.84	5.91	6.13	6.28	5.99
2	6.13	6.10	6.01	6.00	6.10
3	6.03	6.19	5.93	5.89	5.91
4	6.14	6.19	5.86	6.17	6.04
5	5.94	5.91	6.01	6.07	6.04
6	6.13	5.88	6.14	6.18	6.14
Day 2					
7 A.M.	6.15	5.95	5.78	6.18	6.10
8	5.94	5.91	6.01	6.20	6.13

Sample number	Cut circuit board lengths 1	2	3	4	5
9	5.83	5.88	6.08	6.12	6.11
10	5.97	6.19	5.81	6.08	5.91
11	6.13	5.87	5.77	6.16	6.29
12 P.M.	5.94	5.91	6.21	6.08	6.03
1	6.04	5.93	6.04	6.18	6.13
2	6.13	6.09	5.92	6.08	5.95
3	6.03	5.89	5.97	6.14	6.13
4	5.94	5.83	6.13	6.11	5.90
5	6.01	5.81	6.02	6.03	6.14
6	5.85	6.06	5.97	6.19	5.81

26*a*. $\bar{x}$ chart
b. Potentially out of control. Test 5 indicates two out of three points in a row in Zone A failed at point 12
c. Yes
d. Yes

a. Construct the appropriate control chart to monitor this process.

b. Is the process in control?

c. Assume that the population standard deviation is known to be .1 inch. Now is the process in control?

d. Assume that the population standard deviation is unknown and must be estimated. Now is the process in control?

CONSTRUCTING A CHART TO MONITOR THE VARIATION OF A PROCESS: THE *R* CHART

R Chart

Figure 13.2 demonstrated that a process may be out of statistical control because the mean or variance or both are changing over time. The last section focused on using the $\bar{x}$ chart to detect changes in the process mean by monitoring the variation in the means of samples drawn from the process. In this section, the **range chart (*R* chart)** is used to detect changes in the process variation by monitoring sample ranges. As a rule of thumb, many analysts obtain at least 20 samples of n observations each (where $n > 2$).

> The ***R* chart (range chart)** is used to detect changes in the process variation by monitoring sample ranges drawn from the process.

To determine the centerline and control limits for the R chart, we need to understand the sampling distribution for R. The centerline of the $\bar{x}$ chart represented the process mean and was computed by averaging the sample means. Similarly, the centerline of the R chart is the average of the sample ranges (denoted by $\bar{R}$):

$$\bar{R} = \frac{R_1 + R_2 + R_3 + \cdots + R_k}{k} \qquad (13.5)$$

where $\bar{R}$ = Average range for the samples (centerline)
R_i = Range of each sample
k = Number of samples of size n

To construct the control limits, a measure of the variability of the sampling distribution of R is needed. The estimated standard deviation is denoted s_R. Values d_2 and d_3 are taken from the control chart constants table (Table 13.1) and used to estimate s_R:

$$s_R = \overline{R}\,\frac{d_3}{d_2} \tag{13.6}$$

The control limits for the R chart are constructed in the same way as for the $\bar{x}$ chart. $\overline{R}$ and s_R are substituted for $\bar{x}$ and $\sigma_{\bar{x}}$ in Equation 13.4, forming

$$\text{Control limits} = \overline{R} \pm 3s_R$$

After substituting $\overline{R}(d_3/d_2)$ for s_R, the equation becomes

$$\overline{R} \pm 3\overline{R}\frac{d_3}{d_2} = \overline{R}\left(1 \pm 3\frac{d_3}{d_2}\right)$$

To simplify the computations, the values D_3 and D_4 are defined as

$$D_3 = 1 - 3\frac{d_3}{d_2}$$

$$D_4 = 1 + 3\frac{d_3}{d_2}$$

and found using Table 13.1. The R chart control limits are constructed using Equation 13.7:

$$\begin{aligned} \text{LCL} &= D_3\overline{R} \\ \text{UCL} &= D_4\overline{R} \end{aligned} \tag{13.7}$$

Steps for constructing an *R* chart:

1. Select *k* samples of data, each of size *n*.
2. Compute the range for each sample.
3. Compute the average range ($\overline{R}$). Use the average range as the centerline of the chart.
4. Compute the 3-sigma control limits:

$$\text{LCL} = D_3\overline{R} \quad (D_3 \text{ and } D_4 \text{ are found in Table 13.1})$$
$$\text{UCL} = D_4\overline{R}$$

Example 13.5 shows how an *R* chart is developed.

EXAMPLE 13.5 In Example 13.4, Jeff Frost was monitoring the process mean for textile fibers and discovered that the mean of the process is in control. Now he needs to find out about the process variation.

Each sample's ranges are computed (Table 13.2). So is the average range for these samples ($\bar{R}$ = .92375), which will be the centerline for the control chart. Referring to Table 13.1 for a sample of n = 4 fibers, the appropriate D_3 value is 0 and the appropriate D_4 value is 2.282. Equation 13.7 is used to calculate the control limits:

$$\text{LCL} = D_3\bar{R} = 0(.924) = 0$$
$$\text{UCL} = D_4\bar{R} = 2.282(.92375) = 2.108$$

Figure 13.11 shows these lower and upper control limits along with the centerline and the 16 average sample ranges plotted in sequence. The average sample ranges are all within the control limits so the process is deemed to be in control.

Figure 13.11 *R* Chart for Strength Developed Using MINITAB (Example 13.5)

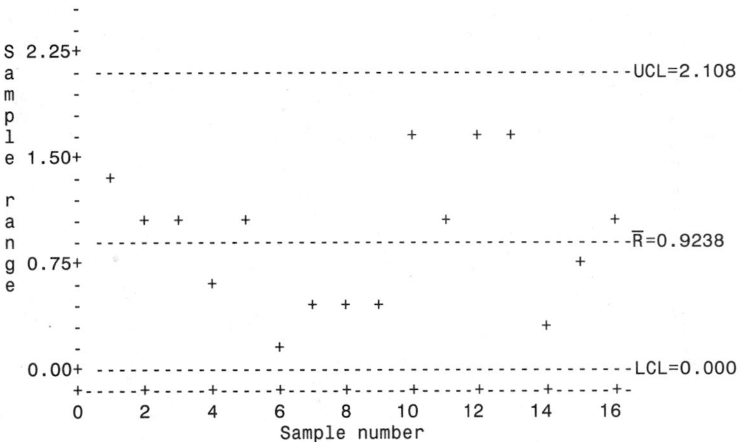

The MINITAB computer package can be used to develop Figure 13.11, The MINITAB commands are:

```
MTB > READ 'FIBER.DAT' C1
     64 ROWS READ

C1
  120.15    119.50    120.85 119.95 . . .

MTB > NAME C1 'STRENGTH'
MTB > RCHART FOR DATA IN C1, SAMPLE SIZE 4
    OUTPUT IS SHOWN IN FIGURE 13.11

MTB > STOP
```

The READ command is used to read the data from the file FIBER.DAT into C1. The RCHART command plots the average sample ranges of samples of size n = 4 on an R chart as shown in Figure 13.11

As mentioned earlier, the $\bar{x}$ chart and R charts are usually used together to monitor the mean and variation of a process. Actually, the appropriate procedure is to first construct the R chart. If we conclude that the process variation is in control, then it makes sense to construct an $\bar{x}$ chart. Remember, the $\bar{x}$ chart's control limits are dependent on the variation of the process. Thus, if the process variation is out of control, the $\bar{x}$ control limits are not correct either. In other words, if the process variation is changing, any single estimate of the variation won't be representative of the process.

In Figure 13.12, the sample ranges are within their control limits, but the means have drifted downward and the process is no longer in control. In Figure 13.13, the sample means remain within the control limits while the variability of the process has shifted upward and out of control.

A process that's not in control can also be identified by a lone sample value that falls outside the control limits. When this happens, an investigation is usually conducted to determine whether there's an assignable cause.

FIGURE 13.12 $\bar{x}$ and R Charts Showing the Mean Out of Control

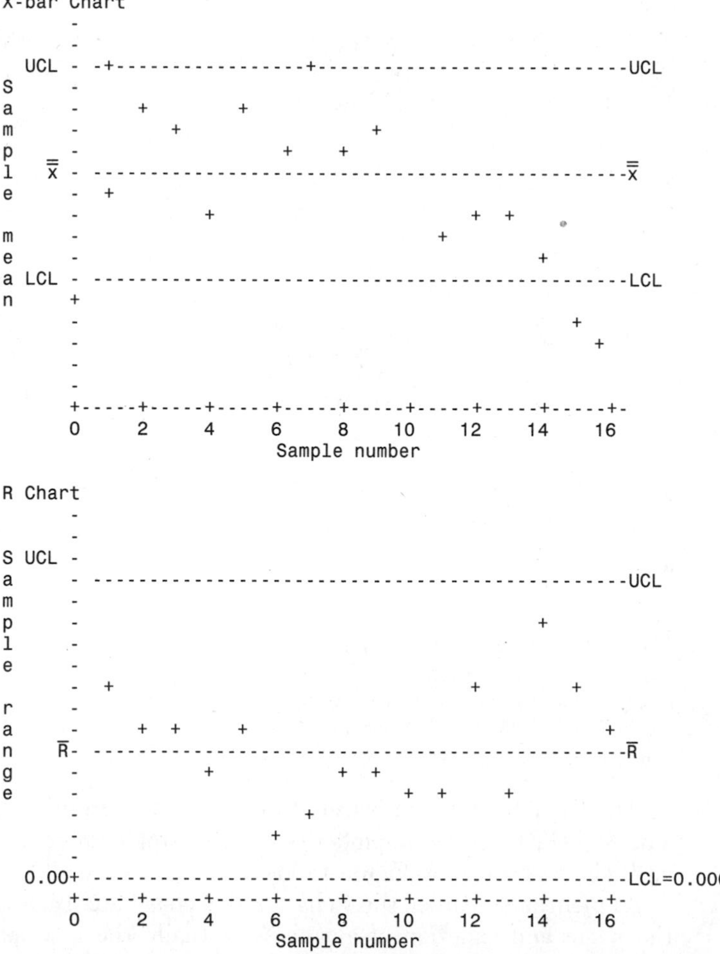

FIGURE 13.13 $\bar{x}$ and R Charts Showing the Variation Out of Control

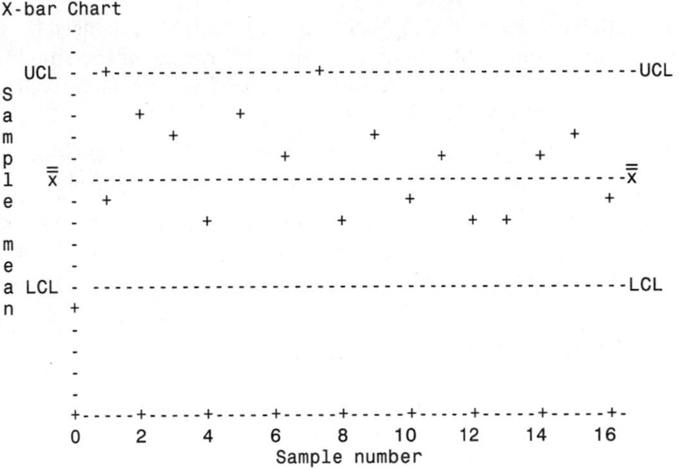

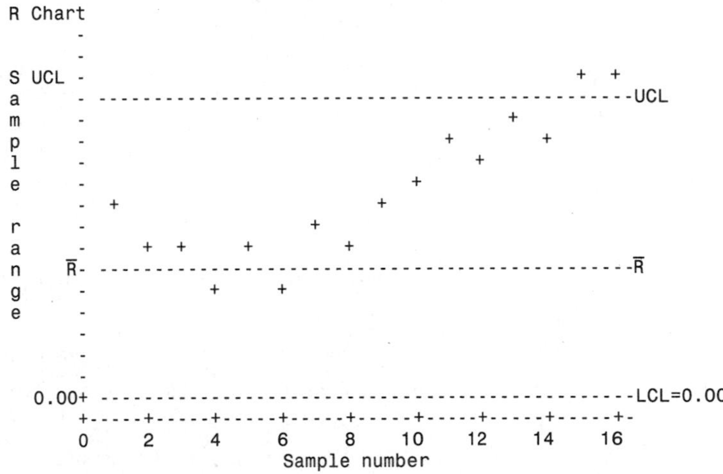

EXERCISES

27. How are the control limits of an R chart determined?

28. What characteristic of a process is an R chart used to monitor?

28. Variation

29. Why is an R chart used in conjunction with an $\bar{x}$ chart? Which chart should be analyzed first? Why?

30. (Refer to Exercise 22.) Taft Manufacturing produces softballs that historically have a circumference averaging 12 inches. Estimate s_R if the average of the sample ranges is .13 inches. Determine upper and lower control limits for a 3-sigma mean control chart in which each sample consists of seven softballs.

30. LCL = .0099, UCL = .2501

31. In control

31. (Refer to Exercise 30.) Determine whether the process is in control given the following eight sample ranges: .141, .102, .163, .215, .047, .111, .138, .211.

32. LCL = 0, UCL = 634.2

32. (Refer to Exercise 20.) Natural gas cylinders are produced by a robot welder to have an average burst strength of 4,000 psi. The average of the sample ranges is 300 psi. Determine upper and lower control limits for a 3-sigma range control chart in which each sample consists of five cylinders.

33. Potentially out of control

33. (Refer to Exercise 32.) Determine whether the process is in control given the following nine sample ranges: 300, 245, 741, 100, 458, 641, 406, 401, 258.

34. (Refer to Exercise 24.) The Chariot Inn manager monitors the swimming pool's pH level by taking readings every two hours from 9 A.M. to 9 P.M. daily. The past two weeks' results are:

Day 1	Average pH	Range
1	8.21	.17
2	8.26	.15
3	8.08	.19
4	8.26	.22
5	8.19	.18
6	8.14	.13
7	8.09	.10
8	8.21	.16
9	8.20	.21
10	8.09	.12
11	8.16	.21
12	8.09	.08
13	8.24	.16
14	8.19	.19

34*a*. $\overline{R}$ = .1621, s_R = .0499, LCL = .0124, MCL = .3118
b. Zone C: .1122 to .2120. Zone B: .0623 to .1122, .2120 to .2619. Zone A: .0124 to .0623, .2619 to .3118

a. Develop the centerline and upper and lower control limits for a 3-sigma *R* chart.

b. Compute the limits of the six zones.

c. Plot the ranges and test to determine whether the process is in control.

d. In exercise 24, the manager computed an $\bar{x}$ chart. Now that he has both an *R* chart and an $\bar{x}$ chart, what is his conclusion?

SM DD

35. (Refer to Exercise 25.) The Wearing Corporation manufactures precision parts such as bolts used in helicopters. Six bolts are sampled each hour and measured using a computerized precision measuring instrument. The data for the past 22 hours are:

Hour	Bolt lengths (centimeters)					
1	21.02	23.41	22.01	24.12	23.88	22.87
2	22.01	22.45	21.21	23.82	24.08	22.37
3	21.54	21.99	23.56	22.35	23.12	23.93
4	24.12	23.83	22.76	24.54	23.21	22.34
5	22.32	22.44	24.31	22.22	23.23	21.89
6	22.35	23.56	22.87	23.35	25.11	22.27
7	21.92	23.51	24.31	22.52	23.56	21.74
8	21.32	21.41	22.41	21.92	21.86	23.81
9	22.21	22.45	21.31	22.82	22.06	22.35
10	21.44	23.99	23.16	23.75	23.16	22.94

Hour	Bolt lengths (centimeters)					
11	22.12	24.83	22.26	24.55	24.26	21.34
12	22.34	21.44	24.41	21.23	24.23	23.85
13	21.35	23.43	22.57	24.36	23.18	24.47
14	23.92	21.51	23.31	22.57	22.56	24.44
15	21.32	22.41	22.31	24.15	21.89	23.87
16	22.31	23.45	23.41	23.82	21.98	21.38
17	21.67	20.99	23.54	22.35	22.12	22.96
18	24.09	22.83	21.76	24.54	23.21	23.34
19	22.34	21.44	24.31	23.62	24.83	24.59
20	21.35	24.56	23.84	23.65	23.18	24.27
21	22.96	22.51	21.31	22.55	22.56	23.44
22	23.95	21.51	24.33	21.32	21.26	22.34

35*a*. R chart, $\overline{R} = 2.722$, LCL = 0, UCL = 5.456
b. Yes

a. Construct the appropriate control chart to monitor the variation of this process.

b. Is the process variation in control?

c. Give an example of an assignable cause that could potentially affect this process variation.

d. In Exercise 25, an $\bar{x}$ chart was constructed. Now that you've examined both an *R* chart and an $\bar{x}$ chart, what is your conclusion?

36. The Slim-rite Company produces several diet cola drinks. Lynn Stephens, quality-control inspector, monitors the amount of cola injected into 12-ounce cans by one of the filling heads on the automated process. She decides to sample five cans of diet cola each half hour beginning at 6 A.M.. The data for 25 consecutive half-hour periods are:

Hour	Ounces per can				
1	12.0000	12.0225	11.9858	12.0075	12.0180
2	12.0225	12.0150	11.9775	11.9963	11.9850
3	11.9850	12.0045	12.0225	12.0300	11.9955
4	12.0000	12.0225	12.0173	11.9850	11.9850
5	11.9782	11.9925	12.0225	12.0075	12.0367
6	12.0075	12.0225	12.0300	11.9797	11.9955
7	12.0300	12.0420	11.9775	11.9700	12.0000
8	12.0210	12.0375	12.0225	11.9775	11.9850
9	11.9775	11.9992	12.0150	12.0225	11.9625
10	12.0000	12.0120	11.9625	12.0300	12.0488
11	11.9625	12.0338	12.0525	11.9528	12.0225
12	11.9910	12.0525	11.9618	12.0600	12.0150
13	11.9700	12.0000	12.0120	12.0000	11.9850
14	11.9850	12.0075	12.0173	11.9925	11.9925
15	11.9932	12.0225	12.0000	11.9880	12.0075
16	12.0188	12.0150	12.0120	11.9835	12.0000
17	12.0075	12.0443	11.9925	11.9978	12.0225
18	11.9880	12.0225	12.0300	11.9850	12.0075
19	11.9797	11.9700	11.9925	11.9955	12.0075
20	12.0233	12.0075	12.0300	11.9700	11.9925
21	11.9932	12.0225	11.9805	12.0413	12.0225
22	11.9850	11.9677	12.0525	12.0075	12.0300
23	11.9925	12.0450	11.9663	12.0225	12.0525
24	12.0000	12.0075	12.0600	11.9565	11.9475
25	12.0525	12.0150	12.0225	11.9400	11.9580

36*a*. *R* chart, $\bar{R}$ = .06433, LCL = 0, UCL = .136
b. Yes

a. Construct the appropriate control chart to monitor the variation of this process.

b. Is the process variation in control?

c. Give an example of an assignable cause that could potentially affect this process variation.

d. Should an $\bar{x}$ chart be constructed to monitor the process mean?

CONSTRUCTING A CHART TO MONITOR THE PROPORTION OF DEFECTIVES IN A PROCESS: THE *p* Chart

p Chart

The $\bar{x}$ and *R* charts are used most often to monitor quantitative variables (height, weight, length, etc.). The chart used to monitor qualitative or categorical variables (successful or unsuccessful, defective or nondefective, conforming or nonconforming) is called the ***p* chart.** This chart is used to monitor the proportion of defective or nonconforming units produced by a process.

> The ***p* chart** is used to monitor the proportion of defective or nonconforming units produced by a process.

A p chart is constructed in the same way as the $\bar{x}$ chart. A collection of samples (usually 20 to 30) is obtained while the process is believed to be in control. The p chart is based on the assumption that the number of defectives observed in each sample is a binomial random variable. The process proportion is actually the binomial probability, p (discussed in Chapter 5). When the process is in a state of statistical control, p remains constant over time.

To determine the p chart centerline and control limits, the analyst needs to know the sampling distribution of $\bar{p}$. A quick review of the properties of this sampling distribution of proportions will be helpful.

> Properties of the **sampling distribution of proportions:**
>
> 1. The mean of the sampling distribution of proportions equals the population proportion: $\mu_{\bar{p}} = p$.
> 2. The standard deviation of the sampling distribution of proportions (standard error) equals $\sigma_{\bar{p}} = \sqrt{p(1-p)/n}$.
> 3. The proportion of successes in a binomial experiment approaches a normal distribution as the number of trials, n, increases.

The process proportion (p) may either be known from past experience with the process or be estimated on the basis of sample data. Using sample data, the p chart centerline is computed by averaging the sample proportions. This is done by letting x_i be the number of defective units in each sample, and n be the sample size. This results in Equation 13.8, which is used to compute the proportion of defective units in each sample:

$$\bar{p}_i = \frac{x_i}{n} \tag{13.8}$$

where $\bar{p}_i$ = Proportion of defective units in sample i
x_i = Number of defective units in sample i
n = Sample size

The appropriate estimator $\hat{p}$ is computed by dividing the total number of defective units in all of the samples by the total number of units sampled:

$$\hat{p} = \frac{\text{Total number of defective units in all } k \text{ samples}}{\text{Total number of units sampled}} \tag{13.9}$$

where $\hat{p}$ = Estimate of the process proportion.

Equation 13.10 is used to compute the 3-sigma control limits. Note that $\hat{p}$ is substituted for p when the process proportion is unknown.

$$\text{LCL} = \hat{p} - 3\sqrt{\frac{\hat{p}(1-\hat{p})}{n}}$$
$$\text{UCL} = \hat{p} + 3\sqrt{\frac{\hat{p}(1-\hat{p})}{n}} \tag{13.10}$$

When constructing a p chart, the sample size must be much larger than for $\bar{x}$ and R charts. A large sample size is needed because most processes monitored in industry have relatively small process proportions (often lower than 5%). Samples drawn using small sample sizes would likely not contain any defective items. As a result, most sample proportions would equal 0. Montgomery (1991) provides a formula that computes a sample size large enough to give an analyst a 50% chance of detecting a process shift of some specified proportion.[7]

[7]D. C. Montgomery, *Introduction to Statistical Quality Control*, 2nd ed. New York: Wiley, 1991.

Steps for constructing a p chart:

1. Select some number of samples of data, each of size n. Select a large sample size (n), especially if the process proportion is small.
2. Compute the proportion of defective units in each sample: $p_i = x_i/n$.
3. If the process proportion isn't known, estimate it:

$$\hat{p} = \frac{\text{Total number of defective units in all samples}}{\text{Total number of units sampled}}$$

4. Compute the 3-sigma control limits:

$$\text{LCL} = \hat{p} - 3\sqrt{\hat{p}(1 - \hat{p})/n}$$
$$\text{UCL} = \hat{p} + 3\sqrt{\hat{p}(1 - \hat{p})/n}$$

Example 13.6 shows how a p chart is developed.

EXAMPLE 13.6 The Goodlight Headlight Company wants to monitor the filament integrity of headlights coming off the manufacturing line. Quality Vice President Ruth Chang is responsible for determining when assignable causes are affecting the process. Headlights coming off the manufacturing line are sampled and subjected to a voltage 25% higher than that for which they're rated. Each sample consists of 100 bulbs. A bulb is categorized as defective if it burns out during a three-second exposure to this higher voltage. Table 13.3 covers 20 samples from last week's production run.

The proportion of defective units in each sample is computed using Equation 13.8. For sample 1, the proportion of defectives is

$$\hat{p}_1 = \frac{x_1}{n} = \frac{18}{100} = .18$$

The process proportion is estimated using Equation 13.9:

$$\hat{p} = \frac{408}{20(100)} = .204$$

Note that this estimate can also be computed by adding up the sample proportions and dividing by the number of samples (4.08/20 = .204).

Equation 13.10 is used to compute the 3-sigma control limits:

$$\begin{aligned}\text{LCL} &= \hat{p} - 3\sqrt{\frac{\hat{p}(1 - \hat{p})}{n}}\\ &= .204 - 3\sqrt{\frac{.204(1 - .204)}{100}}\\ &= .204 - 3(.04025) = .08325\end{aligned}$$

TABLE 13.3 Twenty Samples of Size 100 from a Headlight Production Run (Example 13.6)

Sample number	Number of defectives	Proportion defective
1	18	.18
2	15	.15
3	26	.26
4	15	.15
5	28	.28
6	12	.12
7	24	.24
8	15	.15
9	23	.23
10	41	.41
11	16	.16
12	18	.18
13	24	.24
14	14	.14
15	16	.16
16	18	.18
17	25	.25
18	19	.19
19	15	.15
20	26	.26
	408	4.08

$$\begin{aligned}\text{UCL} &= \hat{p} + 3\sqrt{\frac{\hat{p}(1-\hat{p})}{n}}\\ &= .204 + 3\sqrt{\frac{.204(1-.204)}{100}}\\ &= .204 + 3(.04025) = .32475\end{aligned}$$

Figure 13.14 shows these lower and upper control limits along with the centerline and the 20 sample proportions plotted in sequence. The high proportion of defectives in sample 10 places this sample outside the control limits. Ruth decides to conduct an investigation to determine why so many defectives occurred in sample 10.

The MINITAB computer package can be used to develop Figure 13.14. The MINITAB commands are:

```
MTB > SET C1
DATA> 18 15 26 15 28 12 24 15 23 41
DATA> 16 18 24 14 16 18 25 19 15 26
DATA> END
MTB > NAME C1 'DEFECTS'
MTB > PCHART USING DATA IN C1, SAMPLE SIZE 100
     OUTPUT SHOWN AS FIGURE 13.14
MTB > STOP
```

The data are entered in sequence into C1. The PCHART command plots sample proportions for samples of size 100.

FIGURE 13.14 p Chart for Defects Developed Using MINITAB (Example 13.6)

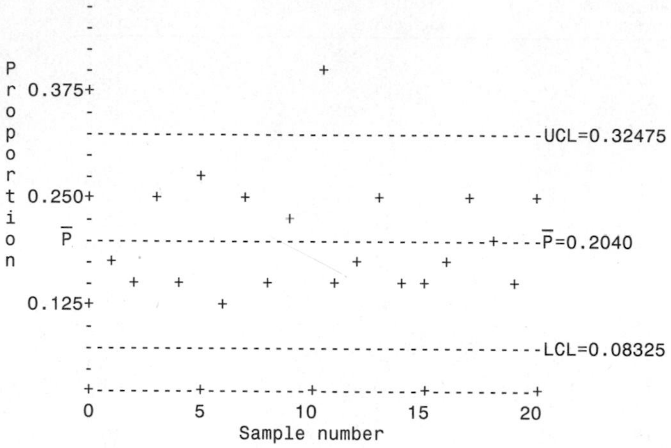

EXERCISES

37. Explain how the properties of the sampling distribution of proportions are used to construct a p chart.

38. How are the control limits of a p chart determined?

39. What characteristic of a process is a p chart used to monitor?

40. LCL = 0, UCL = .0497

40. When a production process is operating properly, the proportion of defectives is .02. Compute lower and upper control limits for a p chart if each sample consists of 200 observations.

41*a*. LCL = 0, UCL = .102
b. LCL = 0, UCL = .072
c. LCL = .001, UCL = .059

41. The Willow Springs Hotel chain is studying the percentage of guest rooms that weren't ready when guests attempted to check in. Assume that from previous research, the population percentage is estimated to be 3%.

    a. What are the control limits if samples of 50 are selected?

    b. What are the control limits if samples of 150 are selected?

    c. What are the control limits if samples of 300 are selected?

    d. How does sample size affect p chart control limits?

42. The Bing Corporation uses an injection molding process to provide a bracket used on aircraft passenger seats. Sue Darling, who's in charge of quality, is especially concerned with examining each bracket for cracks, splits, or other imperfections. Daily samples of 100 have been examined for 20 days.

Date	Sample size	Number defective
March 1	100	2
2	100	3
3	100	4
4	100	8

Date	Sample size	Number defective
5	100	4
6	100	3
7	100	6
8	100	1
9	100	3
10	100	4
11	100	1
12	100	8
13	100	4
14	100	2
15	100	5
16	100	4
17	100	6
18	100	4
19	100	3
20	100	5

a. Calculate the proportion defective in each sample.

b. Develop the centerline and upper and lower control limits for a 3-sigma p chart.

c. Compute the limits of the six zones (A, B, C).

d. Plot the proportions and determine whether the process is in control.

42*b.* CL = .04, LCL = 0, UCL = .099
c. Zone C: .02 to .06. Zone B: 0 to .02, .06 to .079. Zone A: .079 to .099
d. In control

43. The Empire Company produces floppy disks for microcomputers. President Larry Williams has recently received several complaints concerning quality. Retailers have indicated that customers keep returning disks containing bad sectors. Larry implements a quality-control program to correct this problem. He instructs his production manager to select a sample of 300 disks from each production run. Here are the proportion of disks with bad sectors taken from 12 production runs:

Sample	Proportion defective
1	.06
2	.08
3	.05
4	.10
5	.03
6	.04
7	.09
8	.12
9	.07
10	.06
11	.09
12	.05

a. Develop a centerline and upper and lower control limits for a 3-sigma p chart.

b. Compute the limits of the six zones.

c. Plot the proportions and test to determine whether the process is in control.

43*a.* CL = .07, LCL = .026, UCL = .114
b. Zone C: .055 to .085. Zone B: .041 to .055, .085 to .099. Zone A: .026 to .041, .099 to .114
c. Potentially out of control

Constructing a Chart to Monitor the Number of Defectives per Unit: The c Chart

c Chart

The p chart was used to monitor the proportion of defective units in a sample of n units. The c chart is used to monitor the number of defects per unit. The c chart is used to control a single type of defect or to control all types of defects without distinguishing between types. c charts are used to monitor such variables as the number of blemishes on aluminum panels, number of scratches on a CRT screen, or number of defects in a length of wire.

> The **c chart** is used to monitor the number of defects per unit.

A c chart is constructed in the same way as the p chart. A collection of samples (usually 20 to 30) is selected where each sample is obtained by observing a single unit. The c chart is appropriate when the sample size per unit is very large and the probability of a defect in any part of the unit is very small. Recall that the situation just described fits the assumption behind the Poisson process discussed in Chapter 5.

The average number of defects ($\bar{c}$) may either be known from past experience with the process or be estimated on the basis of sample data. If the system is stable, an estimate may be available for the average number of defects per unit. If no prior estimate is available, the average number of defects is estimated from the sample data:

$$\bar{c} = \frac{\sum c_i}{n} \tag{13.11}$$

where $\bar{c}$ = Estimate of the average number of defects per unit
c_i = Number of defects in unit i
n = Number of units sampled

An important property of the Poisson random variable is that the mean and variance are equal. Therefore, the standard deviation equals the square root of the mean. Using this information, Equation 13.12 is developed to compute the 3-sigma control limits:

$$\begin{aligned} \text{LCL} &= \bar{c} - 3\sqrt{\bar{c}} \\ \text{UCL} &= \bar{c} + 3\sqrt{\bar{c}} \end{aligned} \tag{13.12}$$

Steps for constructing a *c* chart:

1. Select some number of samples of data (20 to 30 units), where each sample is obtained by observing a single unit.
2. Determine the number of defects for each unit (c_i).
3. Estimate the average number of defects per unit, $\bar{c} = \dfrac{\Sigma c_i}{n}$.
4. Compute the 3-sigma control limits.

$$\text{LCL} = \bar{c} - 3\sqrt{\bar{c}}$$
$$\text{UCL} = \bar{c} + 3\sqrt{\bar{c}}$$

Example 13.7 shows how a *c* chart is developed.

EXAMPLE 13.7 According to an American Management Association Human Resource publication, *HR Focus* (May 1992), Handy HRM Corporation, a New York management consulting firm, surveyed 78 of the largest U.S. corporations and found that 92 percent said they are beginning to measure and base employee remuneration on quality satisfaction from a customer's perspective.[8] Customers of the Mars Automobile Company have recently complained about dirt specks and poor alignment of door panels. Quality engineer Faye Sandberg has been assigned the task of implementing a program to base employee pay on whether the assembly process for these door panels can be kept in control. Cars are randomly selected for a close examination for fit-and-finish defects. Each week, 20 cars are inspected. Table 13.4 shows the results from last week's inspection.

The average number of defects for the sample of 20 vehicles is computed using Equation 13.11:

$$\bar{c} = \frac{\sum c_i}{n} = \frac{36}{20} = 1.8$$

Equation 13.12 is used to compute the 3-sigma control limits:

$$\begin{aligned}\text{LCL} &= \bar{c} - 3\sqrt{\bar{c}} \\ &= 1.8 - 3\sqrt{1.8} = 1.8 - 4.02 = -2.22 \\ \text{UCL} &= \bar{c} + 3\sqrt{\bar{c}} \\ &= 1.8 + 3\sqrt{1.8} = 1.8 + 4.02 = 5.82\end{aligned}$$

[8] "Quality Movement Grows, Influences More Paychecks." *HR Focus: American Management Association Human Resources Publication.* May 1992, 69:18.

TABLE 13.4 Number of Defects from the Inspection of Twenty Automobiles (Example 13.7)

Vehicle number	Number of defects
1	0
2	1
3	2
4	3
5	0
6	5
7	2
8	0
9	1
10	2
11	1
12	7
13	1
14	0
15	2
16	4
17	1
18	0
19	1
20	3
	36

Since it's impossible to have a negative number of defects, the lower control limit, −2.22, is replaced by 0. Figure 13.15 shows these lower and upper control limits along with the centerline and the 20 c values plotted in sequence. The control chart shows vehicle 12's c value falling outside the control limits so Faye investigates why vehicle 12 had so many defects.

FIGURE 13.15 c Chart for Defects Developed Using MINITAB (Example 13.7)

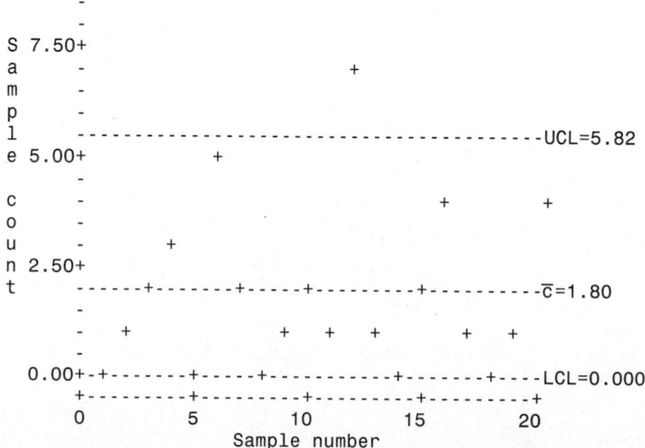

The MINITAB computer package can be used to develop Figure 13.15. The MINITAB commands are:

```
MTB > SET C1
DATA> 0 1 2 3 0 5 2 0 1 2 1 7 1 0 2 4 1 0 1 3
DATA> END
MTB > NAME C1 'DEFECTS'
MTB > CCHART USING DATA IN C1
    OUTPUT SHOWN AS FIGURE 13.15
MTB > STOP
```

The data are entered in sequence into C1. The CCHART command plots the c values for the 20 vehicles.

EXAMPLE 13.8 Sam Gangee has just been appointed quality-control manager for Clinton Lawnmowers, which manufactures power mowers. Quality-control manager is a new position for the company, reflecting management's growing concern about quality's importance in the competitive marketplace. Sam decides to take a look at the factory quality records as a first step.

Talking with factory supervisors, he finds two major problems. First, the number of defects for each component in lawnmowers varies from one part to the next. It seems that chassis problems are most severe, while painting quality problems are least severe.

Second, the key variable sometimes monitored on the factory floor is total number of defects per lawnmower. Sam agrees that this is the key variable of interest, but he's distressed to find that this variable hasn't always been recorded. In fact, historical records are spotty. Sam decides that his first job is to begin a systematic program of sampling the lawnmower line to measure defects per machine. He then wonders about how to display this variable over time.

After carefully examining the quality of mowers over several weeks, he constructs a Pareto chart (Figure 13.16). (The Pareto chart was discussed in Chapter 3.) It shows that the chassis line is causing the most serious quality problem, that is, it's responsible for the highest number of defects per mower. The next most serious component is the engine; the least serious is painting. Sam plots the cumulative percentage of defects against the right axis of the Pareto chart.

Next, Sam tackles the lawnmower line's key quality-control problem, number of defects per machine. For each lawnmower he has his new inspection team determine the number of defects as the machine nears the end of the final assembly line. Sam records the defect measurements on a c chart for the first 18 lawnmowers inspected, (Figure 13.17). It shows the average number of defects for the sample of 18 lawnmowers is 1.667. The control limits are computed using Equation 13.11:

$$\begin{aligned}
\text{LCL} &= \bar{c} - 3\sqrt{\bar{c}} \\
&= 1.667 - 3\sqrt{1.667} = 1.667 - 3.87 = -2.2 \\
\text{UCL} &= \bar{c} + 3\sqrt{\bar{c}} \\
&= 1.667 + 3\sqrt{1.667} = 1.667 + 3.87 = 5.537
\end{aligned}$$

Sam reached several conclusions after studying his control chart. First, he didn't see a trend in the defect numbers, either up or down. Next, he noted an out-of-control

FIGURE 13.16 Pareto Chart: Defectives per Mower (Example 13.8)

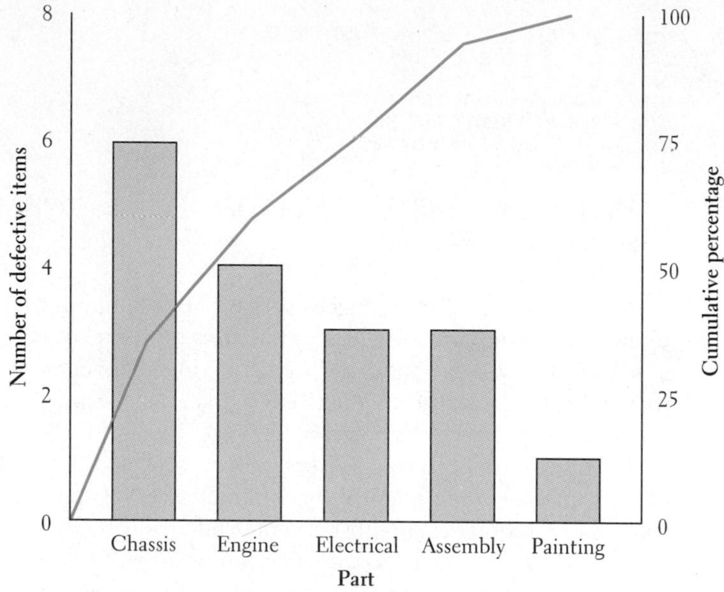

FIGURE 13.17 *c* Chart for Defects Developed Using MINITAB (Example 13.8)

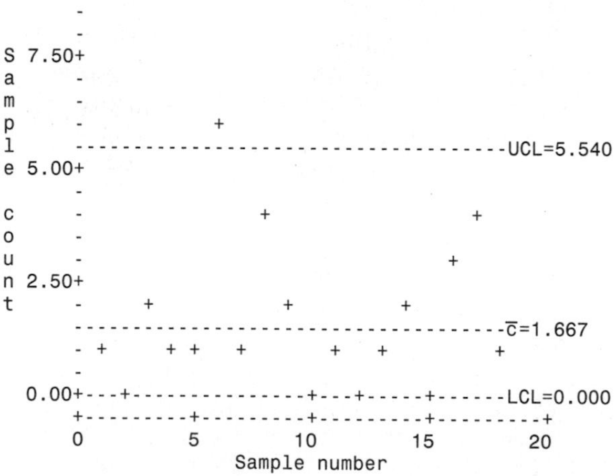

value of six defects for machine 6. At the time, he and his floor supervisors visited the line and determined that there wasn't a problem. He was pleased to see that this high defect rate didn't continue during subsequent lawnmowers.

Finally, Sam noted the estimated mean number of defects per machine (1.667) and decided to take some corrective action regarding this value. Although the control chart indicates that the production process is stabilized around this value, he considers it too high. Sam thinks his first big challenge will be to reduce the average number of defects per lawnmower to a more acceptable figure.

EXERCISES

44. What is the difference between the c chart and the p chart? Indicate the circumstances in which each would be the most appropriate chart.

45. For the following list of variables, indicate whether a c chart or p chart would be most appropriate.

45.*a.* p Chart
b. c Chart
c. p Chart
d. c Chart
e. c Chart

a. The number of late arrivals out of 325 trains that are scheduled to arrive at a particular station each week.

b. Periodic samples consisting of 25-foot lengths examined during the production of continuous sheet steel to determine the number of surface scratches, blemishes, or other flaws.

c. The number of defective switches in samples of 400.

d. The number of cracks in an engine block.

e. The number of defects per unit on the final assembly line of a personal computer manufacturer.

46. Jane Lot is vice president of quality for Outdoor Paper Company. The paper is produced so that it appears at the end of a web and is rolled onto a reel. Every reel is examined for imperfections. Results for the past 24 reels are:

Reel	Blemishes	Reel	Blemishes
1	6	13	12
2	9	14	8
3	7	15	7
4	4	16	6
5	8	17	2
6	4	18	5
7	2	19	6
8	11	20	4
9	6	21	6
10	1	22	9
11	2	23	5
12	10	24	4

46*a.* CL = 6, LCL = 0, UCL = 13.35
b. Zone C: 3.55 to 8.45. Zone B: 1.1 to 3.55, 8.45 to 10.9. Zone A: 0 to 1.1, 10.9 to 13.35
c. In control

a. Develop the centerline and upper and lower control limits for a 3-sigma c chart.

b. Compute the limits of the six zones.

c. Plot the number of blemishes and test to determine whether the process is in control.

47. The Richard Irving Publishing Company counts the number of errors that make their way into 18 finished books of approximately equal pages.

Book	Errors	Book	Errors
1	31	4	42
2	25	5	55
3	73	6	88

Book	Errors	Book	Errors
7	41	13	18
8	49	14	92
9	60	15	39
10	65	16	71
11	50	17	51
12	78	18	68

47*a*. CL = 55.33, LCL = 33.02, UCL = 77.65
b. Zone C: 47.89 to 62.77. Zone B: 40.46 to 47.89, 62.77 to 70.21. Zone A: 33.02 to 40.46, 70.21 to 77.65
c. Potentially out of control

a. Develop the centerline and upper and lower control limits for a 3-sigma *c* chart.
b. Compute the limits of the six zones.
c. Plot the number of errors and test to determine whether the process is in control.

LOT ACCEPTANCE

Lot acceptance and process control are the two primary settings for the application of effective quality-control techniques. In lot acceptance, a sample from a batch or lot of items is inspected to determine the quality level of the entire batch. This batch might be produced by our factory and bound for customers, might be our own lot to be sent forward to another segment of our company, or might be an incoming lot from a supplier. In all these cases, statistical procedures are used to select a sample of items, measure their quality, and reach a decision about the whole lot.

Acceptance Sampling

Acceptance sampling involves risks for both the manufacturer and the consumer of a particular shipment. These risks are comparable to the type I and type II errors discussed in hypotheses testing (Chapter 9). The acceptance procedure is of great importance due to the possibility of these errors and their attendant costs. Only rarely is it possible and cost effective to conduct a census of the entire lot. This is done only when there are few items which are high-priced or of vital importance in later assemblies. For the most part, sampling is the basis for the decision regarding the lot of items, but, as always, when conclusions are reached about all the items after examining only some of them, errors are possible.

The null hypothesis tested in lot acceptance sampling is that the lot has the acceptable level of quality. If the sample quality results seem reasonable against this hypothesis, the hypothesis is not rejected and the entire lot is deemed to have sufficient quality. The danger here is that a false null hypothesis may not be rejected (i.e., a type II error could be committed). The type II error represents the failure to reject a lot that should have been rejected. This is referred to as the **consumer's risk,** since the consumer is incurring the risk of the manufacturer failing to reject a lot that should have been rejected. The penalty for such an error is the acceptance into the next production phase of parts that don't meet specified quality standards, or the delivery of substandard parts to customers.

Consumer's Risk

Alternatively, if the sample results seem unlikely when compared with the null hypothesis, it's rejected. This means that the entire lot will be returned to the manufacturer (either our own company's manufacturing process or a supplier's). The danger here is that a type I error may be committed (i.e., a lot with acceptable quality is

Producer's Risk

erroneously rejected). This is referred to as the **producer's risk,** since the producer is incurring the risk that an acceptable lot will be returned. The cost of such an error is the discarding or "fixing" of a lot that was acceptable in the first place.

> **Consumer's risk** (β) is the probability of failing to reject a product of unacceptable quality. **Producer's risk** (α) is the probability of rejecting a product of acceptable quality.

The basic steps in lot acceptance sampling are covered in Chapter 9. Specifically, the steps are:

1. The null and alternative hypotheses are developed:

   H_0: The lot is of acceptable quality.
   H_1: The lot is not of acceptable quality.
2. The null hypothesis regarding the quality of the population (the entire lot) is assumed true and the appropriate sampling distribution for this assumption is identified.
3. A sample of items is selected from the lot. (See Chapter 2 for sampling methods.) The key quality variable is measured for the sample of items and the sample statistic is computed. This statistic is usually a mean or proportion.
4. If it's likely that the sample statistic could have come from the sampling distribution, the null hypothesis is not rejected (lot acceptance). If it's unlikely that the sample statistic could have come from the sampling distribution, the null hypothesis is rejected (lot rejection).

Example 13.9 illustrates this procedure.

EXAMPLE 13.9 Jenny Fife is responsible for lot acceptance sampling in the receiving area of a company that makes motorized hydraulic pumps. Engines for this product are received in lots of 1,000 every two or three weeks from the engine supplier.

Each time a lot arrives, Jenny randomly selects 50 engines for extensive testing by numbering the engines as they're removed from the packing crate. Next, 50 random numbers are drawn from a random number table and the engines corresponding to these numbers make up the sample. The statistic determined from the sample of engines is the proportion that do not meet specified quality standards for her company, that is, are deemed defective. If this sample proportion is too high, the entire lot of engines is repacked and returned to the supplier for corrective action.

The contract with the supplier specifies that no more than 4% of the engines it ships will be defective. For the most recent shipment, Jenny finds four of the engines in her sample to be defective. Her sample proportion, 4/50 = .08, is in excess of the permitted defective rate for the entire lot. But this high proportion could be due to random variation in sampling, or the lot could be unacceptable. Jenny's task is to determine which.

The null and alternative hypotheses and the sample results are

$$H_0: p \leq .04 \qquad n = 50$$
$$H_1: p > .04 \qquad \bar{p} = .08$$

Jenny chooses the .01 significance level due to the importance of minimizing the probability of a type I error and its associated cost. At this significance level, for a one-tailed test (see the standard normal table), the critical z value is 2.33. The decision rule is

If $z > 2.33$, reject that the process proportion is .04.

The computed z value (see Equation 9.4) is

$$z = \frac{x/n - p}{\sigma_{\bar{p}}} = \frac{.08 - .04}{.0277} = 1.444$$

Since $z = 1.444$, the null hypothesis isn't rejected and the entire lot of 1,000 engines is deemed to have sufficient quality ($1.444 < 2.33$). Jenny allows the engines to enter the factory floor for assembly in hydraulic pumps.

Since Jenny conducts this test several times a month, she develops the following chart to use in summarizing the actions to be taken under several sample outcomes for a sampling plan for $n = 50$:

Number defective	z	Conclusion
4	1.44	Accept lot
5	2.16	Accept lot
6	2.88	Reject lot

Based on these calculations, Jenny issues sampling instructions to her quality-control staff:

Each time a lot of 1,000 engines comes in, take a random sample of 50 engines using the random number table. If five or fewer are defective, accept the lot of engines and enter them into the production process. If six or more are defective, the lot is deemed unacceptable so call me at once.

Jenny reasons that with this set of instructions, she need not be present when each batch arrives. Her staff will inform her if an unacceptable batch is discovered.

Note that most companies are moving away from acceptance sampling. Since acceptance sampling looks at units that have already been produced, the effect on improving quality is minimal. Most companies now rely on using fewer suppliers and making sure that the suppliers they do use demonstrate a capable process that remains in control.

POWER AND OPERATING CHARACTERISTIC (OC) CURVES

A key aspect of any acceptance sampling plan is that it should offer protection, both to the consumer (who doesn't want to accept a bad lot) and to the producer (who doesn't want a good lot rejected).

Power of a Hypothesis Test

The power of any hypothesis test is its ability to detect a false null hypothesis. Chapter 9 defined the power of a test as

$$\text{Power} = 1 - \beta$$

where β is the probability of a type II error. The power of a test is increased by using a larger sample size. In the case of lot acceptance or process control, the higher the power of the test, the better one can detect a quality level below specification. In other words, the larger the sample size, the lower is the probability of a type II error, holding the significance level (probability of a type I error) constant.

As is usually the case in statistical applications, the analyst is torn between little power (at low cost) and high power (at high cost). These factors must be balanced against each other in choosing the desired sample size with its attendant cost and risk.

The alpha or significance level indicates the probability of making a type I error (producer's risk). In considering the type II error, an analyst can choose between using either a power curve showing the probability of rejecting a false null hypothesis or an operating characteristic curve showing the probability of accepting a false null hypothesis (consumer's risk). The power curve plots the probability of rejecting a lot versus a range of possible values that could reflect the shipment's actual quality. The operating characteristic curve plots the probability of accepting a lot versus a range of possible values that could reflect the shipment's actual quality. Procedures for computing these curves were covered late in Chapter 9.

Power Curve

OC Curve

OTHER QUALITY-CONTROL TECHNIQUES

Although the control chart and the lot and process control hypothesis tests are most commonly used in quality control, other statistical techniques can be used as well. As discussed in Chapter 12, analysis of variance tests the hypothesis that several populations have the same mean. In quality control, these populations might represent five different suppliers where the average number of defectives per lot might be compared. For a production line, the three shifts producing parts might be the populations being compared. In general, whenever three or more populations have means that are to be compared, analysis of variance should come to mind.

The contingency table test (Chapter 11) can be used to compare one variable with another, if both variables are measured on a categorical scale (nominal or ordinal data). An example is the comparison of males and females against their quality-control rating (good, average, poor). Or, the different shifts (day, evening, graveyard) might be compared with the quality of output (high, OK, poor). As long as the two variables being compared are both categorical variables, the contingency table test can determine if they're dependent or independent.

Chapter 11 also describes the goodness-of-fit test. This statistical test determines the goodness of fit between the number of observations in each category and the number expected under a specified population. An example is comparing the number of monthly defects per supplier against the same distribution from a year ago. If there has been no change, a good fit will result. If the fit is poor, changes in the defect pattern have occurred among the suppliers. The goodness-of-fit procedure can also be used to check the shape of a distribution against a hypothesized population distribution such as the normal.

In more general terms, many statistical techniques are candidates for inclusion in quality-control efforts. Experimental design has become an especially important aspect of designing quality into products. Imaginative use of any technique in this text might result in an effective quality-control effort. It is even possible that two or more techniques might be combined in certain circumstances to allow management to measure the quality of a firm's efforts.

EXERCISES

48. What is the difference between lot acceptance and process control?
49. What is meant by the term *producer's risk?*
50. What is meant by the term *consumer's risk?*
51. Briefly summarize the basic steps in lot acceptance sampling.
52. How does the power of a test affect a lot acceptance situation?
53. What function does an operating characteristic curve serve in a lot acceptance situation?
54. Clark Equipment, a wholesaler, has received a shipment of 6,000 can openers. Royce Clayton, vice president of quality, considers a 1% defective rate to be an acceptable quality level. He selects a random sample of 200 can openers and tests to determine whether they work properly. What should Royce conclude if seven of the sampled can openers are defective?
55. (Refer to Exercise 54.) Royce wishes to avoid shipments whose percentage of defectives is as high as 3%. He implements a sampling plan that will select 200 can openers from each shipment. Royce accepts the shipment if the number of defectives in the sample is no more than six. Construct the operating characteristic curve for this acceptance sampling plan.

54. $z = 3.57$. Unacceptable quality level

SUMMARY

This chapter began with an overview of the quality-control and improvement process. No greater challenge faces corporate America today than the continual improvement of its products and services. The former chairman of Ford Motor Company, Donald Peterson, has stated that firms unable or unwilling to adopt this attitude won't be around in the next century.

Next we presented the concept of control charts, detailing construction and use of four widely used charts: the $\bar{x}$ chart, range chart (R chart), p chart, and c chart.

Statistical quality-control procedures were discussed next. They are generally applicable in two areas: process control and lot acceptance. In both areas, the focus is on the amount of variability in the key measurements being made.

In process control, a continuous production process is checked on a regular basis. The objective is to assure that the quality level meets or exceeds specifications. An example of such a process is an assembly line that produces small engines. This line runs continuously during working hours, and will continue to do so for the foreseeable future. To assure adequate quality, this process needs to be sampled and measured on a routine basis. Many quality-control procedures are directed toward this end.

By contrast, lot acceptance procedures are designed for batches of products. These batches, or lots, might be purchased from an outside supplier. In this case, sampling procedures are designed either to accept the lot as having sufficient quality, or to reject the entire lot on the basis of the sample quality. Other lots might be produced by a company's own factory, but constitute a batch or lot rather than a continuous stream of products. An example is a batch of small engines to be shipped to a customer. Or, the batch of engines just produced might be sent to another branch of the same company for inclusion in a larger product such as garden tractors. After the lot is manufactured, the production process will shift to another product. In all such cases, the question becomes whether the lot is of sufficient quality to be sent on. This decision is made on the basis of examining the quality of a sample of items taken from the lot.

APPLICATIONS OF STATISTICAL CONCEPTS IN THE BUSINESS WORLD

KAISER ALUMINUM COMPANY'S USE OF QUALITY CONTROL

Successful implementation of quality principles is illustrated by the Total Quality Improvement program at Kaiser Aluminum Company's Trentwood plant in Spokane, Washington. As mentioned at the start of this chapter, Kaiser received the Aluminum Supplier of the Year Award from Miller Brewing Company for the second year in a row in early 1992. Kaiser also received the Ball Corporation Packaging Product Group's first Aluminum Supplier of the Year Award in 1992. These awards reflect Kaiser's commitment to the constant improvement of quality since 1981.

Kaiser's Trentwood plant makes aluminum sheeting and plate with thickness between .008 and 3 inches. In the smaller sizes, enormous rolling mills successively reduce the aluminum stock's thickness. This rolling process is constantly monitored by X-ray and beta-ray sensors in the rolling mills that measure, among other things, thickness of the sheets moving at speeds of up to a mile a minute. These sensors are accurate enough to enable control of the aluminum sheet thickness to within .0002 inch (1/20 the diameter of a human hair)—the tolerance currently deemed necessary for acceptable quality. However, as one of the quality-control engineers told us, Kaiser's efforts are devoted to constantly reducing this figure, resulting in even tighter standards. Many other measurements are constantly made on the aluminum sheet stock, such as speed of the sheet, sheet flatness, and process temperature.

Measurements made on the moving aluminum sheet are fed into a series of computers that analyze the data. If problems are detected or if a trend is apparent that will lead to problems later, the computer makes adjustments in the ongoing process. If these adjustments still don't correct the problem or trend, the operator's control console is signaled so that corrective action can be taken. Such action sometimes involves shutting the line down to avoid producing unacceptable product.

The basic concepts discussed throughout this chapter are utilized in this monitoring process. At Kaiser, however, measurements and analyses are made by sophisticated measuring devices and high-speed computers, not by hand.

Figure 13.18 shows a flow diagram of the Kaiser computer control process.

FIGURE 13.18 Kaiser's Computer Control Process

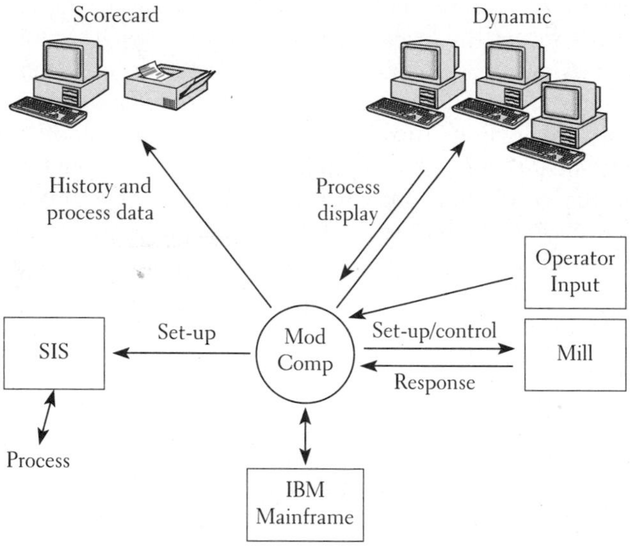

The minicomputer that controls the data collection and analysis is called "ModComp," while "SIS" stands for surface inspection system. The mainframe computer stores vast amounts of historical data and performs some of the more sophisticated data analyses. The system is designed to provide almost instant adjustments to the process and to provide control information to the line operator. A vast data base for analysis by Kaiser's engineers is also generated.

Figure 13.19 shows one of the key reports produced by Kaiser's computerized quality system. This "scorecard" report includes summary information at the top of the page along with several key measurements for each roll of stock: sheet gauge thickness measured by the beta gage and X-ray sensors, the speed of the sheet through the rolling mill, and flatness.

Note that these plots, with the exception of the speed plot, have horizontal lines around the actual measurements. These lines are the tolerance limits. Should a measurement exceed these limits at any time, the green light at the operator's console turns either yellow or red, depending on the problem's severity. This procedure is fol-

FIGURE 13.19 A Report from Kaiser's Computerized Quality System

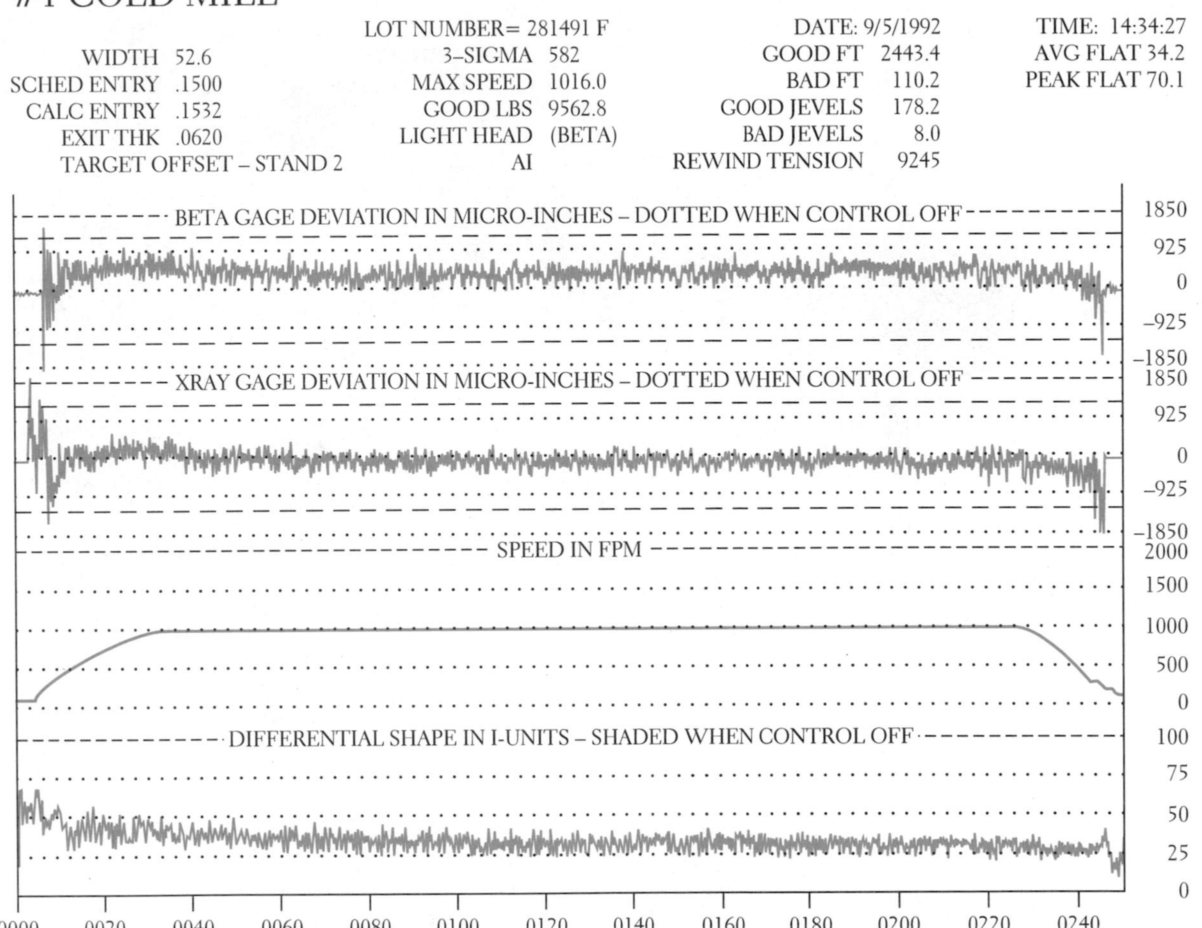

lowed so that the operator can easily and quickly detect a problem and take corrective action, rather than wait until the damage is done and the problem is found through inspection. As a Kaiser engineer told us, "The operators and first-line supervisors have neither the time nor the inclination to wade through columns and rows of numbers."

Figure 13.20 shows an exaggerated profile of a large aluminum sheet made from the X-ray measurements. Quality engineers use this plot to monitor the flatness of each sheet of stock, an essential feature for controlling high quality.

Figures 13.21 through 13.23 show additional charts and graphs generated by Kaiser's computerized data collection and analysis system (chart types discussed in Chapter 3, "Data Presentation"). Among them you'll find the bar chart, pie chart, and time series graph. These charts, along with supporting data, appear in reports generated in various

FIGURE 13.20 Aluminum Sheet Profile at Kaiser

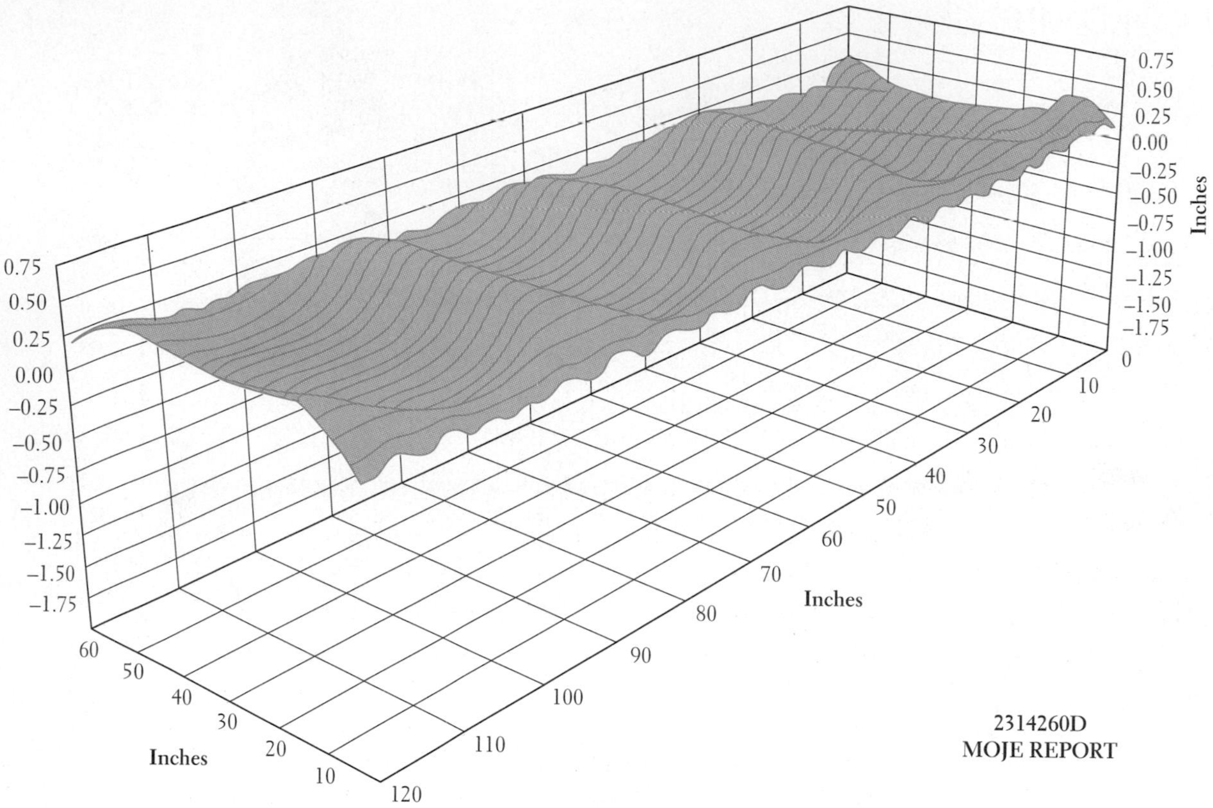

Inches

Inches

Inches

2314260D
MOJE REPORT

FIGURE 13.21 Kaiser Aluminum Recovery Defect Trends, Time Series Graph

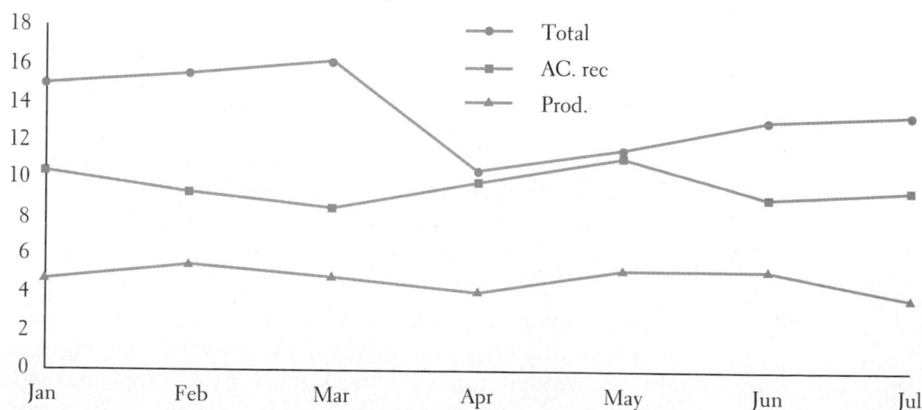

FIGURE 13.22 Recovery Trend

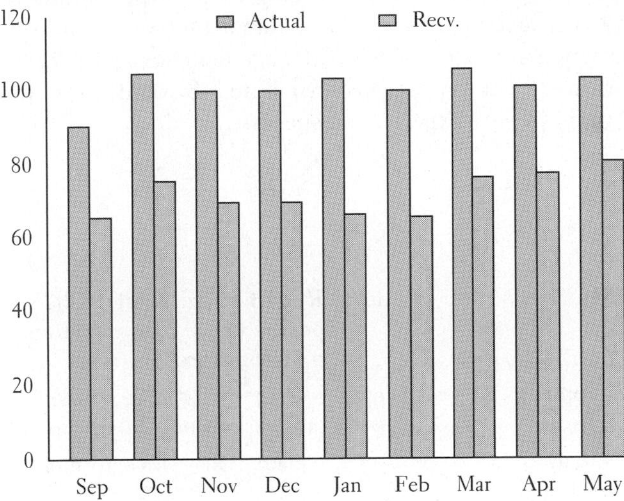

FIGURE 13.23 Start Weight Breakdown

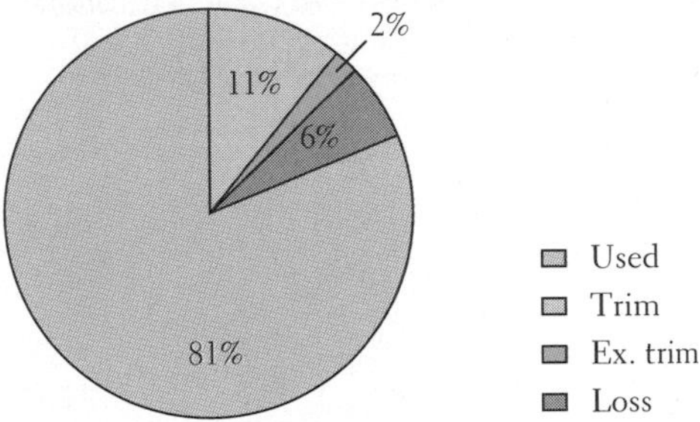

combinations for first-line supervisors, midlevel managers, quality-control engineers, and top management.

Kaiser Aluminum's Total Quality Improvement system is a good example of what is going right in American industry today. The idea of constantly improving quality by controlling variation is a pervasive theme at Kaiser, and all employees from the production line to top management are aware of its vital importance. No more important lesson can be learned by today's business students than the necessity of constantly improving the quality of American goods and services.

OTHER APPLICATIONS

Applications of quality concepts are everywhere in business. As mentioned before, many observers have argued that constant improvement of quality is the most important task facing business in this country. But improving quality isn't easy. According to

Newsweek (September 7, 1992), numerous firms are dropping their Total Quality Management (TQM) programs. In many cases, expectations exceeded results, especially when firms faced layoffs and other labor problems. The key concepts, said *Newsweek*, are patience and labor peace. "Managements expect it to be instant gratification, and that is one of the key reasons for failure." By contrast, companies that use TQM over the long haul have experienced success.

Glossary

Quality The extent to which a product or service satisfies its users' needs and preferences.

Statistical process control (SPC) A series of actions used to monitor and eliminate variation in order to keep a process in a state of statistical control.

Assignable causes Fluctuations in variation due to events or actions that aren't part of the process design.

Chance causes Causes of variation that are attributable to the design of the process.

Control chart A time series graph that tracks a key variable of interest in the quality effort.

$\bar{x}$ chart (mean chart) Chart used to detect changes in the process mean by monitoring the variation in the means of samples drawn from the process.

***R* chart (range chart)** Chart used to detect changes in the process variation by monitoring the ranges of samples drawn from the process.

***p* chart** Chart used to monitor the proportion of defective or nonconforming units produced by a process.

***c* chart** Chart used to monitor the number of defects per unit.

Consumer's risk (β) The probability of failing to reject a product of unacceptable quality.

Producer's risk (α) The probability of rejecting a product of acceptable quality.

Key Formulas

$\bar{x}$ chart centerline

$$\bar{\bar{x}} = \frac{\bar{x}_1 + \bar{x}_2 + \bar{x}_3 + \cdots + \bar{x}_k}{k} \tag{13.1}$$

$\bar{x}$ chart upper and lower control limits (population standard deviation known)

$$\begin{aligned} LCL &= \bar{\bar{x}} - 3(\sigma/\sqrt{n}) \\ UCL &= \bar{\bar{x}} + 3(\sigma/\sqrt{n}) \end{aligned} \tag{13.2}$$

Estimate of the process standard deviation

$$\hat{\sigma} = \frac{\bar{R}}{d_2} \tag{13.3}$$

$\bar{x}$ chart upper and lower control limits (population standard deviation unknown)

$$\begin{aligned} LCL &= \bar{\bar{x}} - 3(\hat{\sigma}/\sqrt{n}) \\ UCL &= \bar{\bar{x}} + 3(\hat{\sigma}/\sqrt{n}) \end{aligned} \tag{13.4}$$

Average range

$$\bar{R} = \frac{R_1 + R_2 + R_3 + \cdots + R_k}{k} \tag{13.5}$$

Estimate of standard error of the average ranges

$$s_R = \bar{R}\frac{d_3}{d_2} \tag{13.6}$$

***R* chart upper and lower control limits**

$$\begin{aligned} LCL &= D_3\bar{R} \\ UCL &= D_4\bar{R} \end{aligned} \tag{13.7}$$

Proportion of defective units for each sample

$$p_i = \frac{x_i}{n} \tag{13.8}$$

Estimate of the process proportion

$$\hat{p} = \frac{\text{Total number of defective units in all } k \text{ samples}}{\text{Total number of units sampled}} \tag{13.9}$$

***p* chart upper and lower control limits**

$$\begin{aligned} LCL &= \hat{p} - 3\sqrt{\frac{\hat{p}(1-\hat{p})}{n}} \\ UCL &= \hat{p} + 3\sqrt{\frac{\hat{p}(1-\hat{p})}{n}} \end{aligned} \tag{13.10}$$

Estimate of the average number of defects per unit

$$\bar{c} = \frac{\sum c_i}{n} \tag{13.11}$$

***c* chart upper and lower control limits**

$$\begin{aligned} LCL &= \bar{c} - 3\sqrt{\bar{c}} \\ UCL &= \bar{c} + 3\sqrt{\bar{c}} \end{aligned} \tag{13.12}$$

SOLVED EXERCISES

1. $\bar{X}$ CHART

The Circuit Corporation manufactures circuit boards for personal computers. The overall length of boards is important since boards are eventually slipped into slots in a chassis. Company quality analyst Phil Sheppard is in charge of stabilizing the length dimension. Boards are cut from large sheets of material by a single rotary cutter continuously fed from a hopper. Phil decides to develop a control chart for the length of the circuit boards produced by the process. The control chart is to be based on five units selected each hour. The accompanying table shows the resulting lengths for a two-day period.

Sample number	Cut circuit board lengths						
	1	2	3	4	5	$\bar{x}$	Range R
Day 1							
7 A.M.	5.83	6.09	5.91	6.18	5.91	5.984	0.35
8	6.13	5.99	5.76	6.12	6.19	6.038	0.43
9	5.94	5.81	6.11	6.28	6.00	6.028	0.47
10	6.03	5.89	6.01	6.08	6.10	6.022	0.21
11	5.93	5.99	6.01	6.19	6.11	6.046	0.26
12 P.M.	6.11	6.01	5.96	5.92	6.09	6.018	0.19
1	5.84	5.91	6.13	6.28	5.99	6.030	0.44
2	6.13	6.10	6.01	6.00	6.10	6.068	0.13
3	6.03	6.19	5.93	5.89	5.91	5.990	0.30
4	6.14	6.19	5.86	6.17	6.04	6.080	0.33
5	5.94	5.91	6.01	6.07	6.04	5.994	0.16
6	6.13	5.88	6.14	6.18	6.14	6.094	0.30
Day 2							
7 A.M.	6.15	5.95	5.78	6.18	6.10	6.032	0.40
8	5.94	5.91	6.01	6.20	6.13	6.038	0.29
9	5.83	5.88	6.08	6.12	6.11	6.004	0.29
10	5.97	6.19	5.81	6.08	5.91	5.992	0.38
11	6.13	5.87	5.77	6.16	6.29	6.044	0.52
12 P.M.	5.94	5.91	6.21	6.08	6.03	6.034	0.30
1	6.04	5.93	6.04	6.18	6.13	6.064	0.25
2	6.13	6.09	5.92	6.08	5.95	6.034	0.21
3	6.03	5.89	5.97	6.14	6.13	6.032	0.25
4	5.94	5.83	6.13	6.11	5.90	5.982	0.30
5	6.01	5.81	6.02	6.03	6.14	6.002	0.33
6	5.85	6.06	5.97	6.19	5.81	5.976	0.38
						144.626	7.47

a. Construct an $\bar{x}$ chart to monitor this process.

b. Is the process in control?

Solution:

a. The mean for the first sample is

$$\bar{x} = \frac{5.83 + 6.09 + 5.91 + 6.18 + 5.91}{5} = 5.984$$

The process mean is estimated

$$\bar{\bar{x}} = \frac{\bar{x}_1 + \bar{x}_2 + \cdots + \bar{x}_k}{k} = \frac{5.984 + 6.038 + \cdots + 5.976}{24}$$

$$= \frac{144.626}{24} = 6.026$$

The range for the first sample is

$$R = 6.18 - 5.83 = 0.35$$

The average of the ranges is

$$\overline{R} = \frac{R_1 + R_2 + \cdots + R_k}{k} = \frac{0.35 + 0.43 + \cdots + 0.38}{24} = \frac{7.47}{24}$$
$$= .3113$$

The process standard deviation is estimated

$$\hat{\sigma} = \frac{\overline{R}}{d_2} = \frac{.3113}{2.326} = 0.1338$$

The control limits are

$$\begin{aligned} LCL &= \bar{\bar{x}} - 3(\hat{\sigma}/\sqrt{n}) \\ &= 6.026 - 3(.1338/\sqrt{5}) = 5.846 \\ UCL &= \bar{\bar{x}} + 3(\hat{\sigma}/\sqrt{n}) \\ &= 6.026 + 3(.1338/\sqrt{5}) = 6.205 \end{aligned}$$

b. Figure 13.24 shows these lower and upper control limits along with the centerline and the 24 sample means plotted in sequence. The sample means are all within the control limits so Phil concludes that the process is in control.

FIGURE 13.24 $\bar{x}$ Chart for Lengths (Solved Exercise 1)

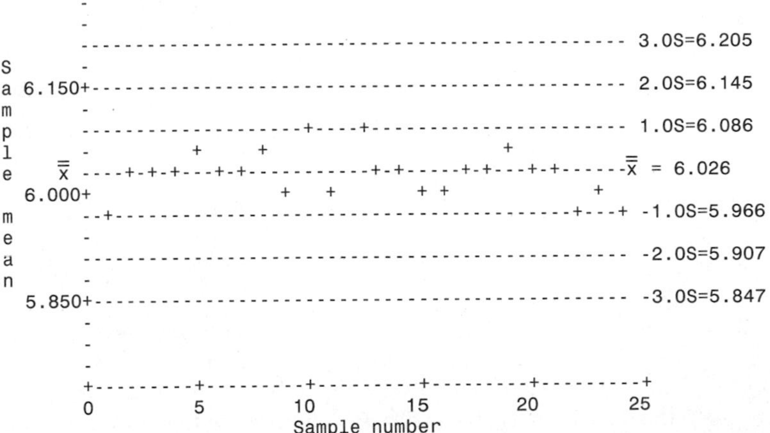

2. RANGE CHART

Refer to Solved Exercise 1.

a. Construct the appropriate control chart to monitor the variation of this process.

b. Is the process variation in control?

c. In Solved Exercise 1, Phil constructed an $\bar{x}$ chart. Now that he has both an R chart and an $\bar{x}$ chart, what is his conclusion?

Solution:

a. The appropriate control chart is the *R* chart.

b. The average of the ranges is computed in Solved Exercise 1, $\overline{R}$ = .3113. This will be the centerline for the control chart.

Referring to Table 13.1 for a sample of n = 5 lengths, the appropriate D_3 and D_4 values are 0 and 2.114. Equation 13.7 is used to calculate the control limits:

$$LCL = D_3\overline{R} = 0(.3113) = 0$$
$$UCL = D_4\overline{R} = 2.114(.3113) = .658$$

c. Figure 13.25 shows these lower and upper control limits along with the centerline and the 24 average sample ranges plotted in sequence. The average sample ranges are all within the control limits so the process is concluded to be in control.

FIGURE 13.25 *R* Chart for Lengths (Solved Exercise 1)

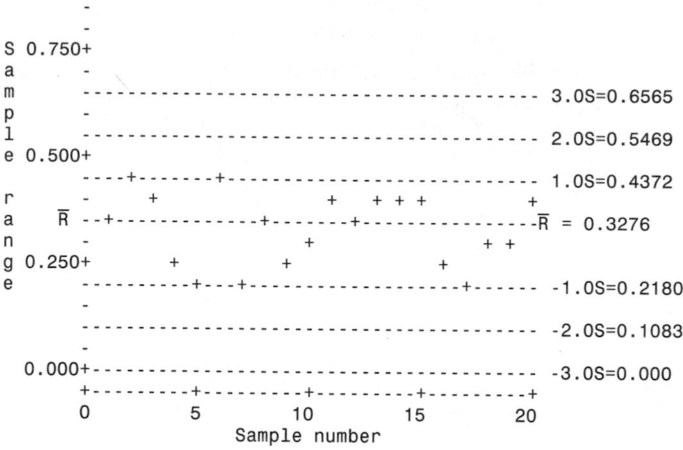

3. *p* CHART

The Sunshine Fruit Juice Company produces frozen juice concentrate packed in 12-ounce cardboard cans. These cans are formed on a machine by spinning them from cardboard stock and attaching metal top and bottom panels. A plastic strip is attached around the can's top. When this strip is pulled, the cardboard tears and the top of the can comes open. Unfortunately, quality-control inspector Clare King has been informed that a large percentage of strips don't open the can when pulled. She must implement an inspection procedure to monitor this process. Clare selects samples of 200 for 22 days and determines the number of defective cans:

Date	Sample size	Number defective	Proportion defective
April 1	200	4	.020
2	200	6	.030
3	200	10	.050
4	200	21	.105
5	200	5	.025

Date	Sample size	Number defective	Proportion defective
6	200	15	.075
7	200	19	.095
8	200	16	.080
9	200	11	.055
10	200	14	.070
11	200	13	.065
12	200	15	.075
13	200	7	.035
14	200	12	.060
15	200	9	.045
16	200	13	.065
17	200	12	.060
18	200	15	.075
19	200	3	.015
20	200	11	.055
21	200	6	.030
22	200	8	.040

a. Show how the proportion defective for sample 1 was computed.

b. Develop the centerline and upper and lower control limits for a 3-sigma p chart.

c. Compute the limits of the six zones.

d. Plot the proportions and test to determine whether the process is in control.

Solution:

a. For sample 1, the proportion of defectives is

$$p_1 = \frac{x_1}{n} = \frac{4}{200} = .02$$

The proportion for each sample is shown above.

b. The process proportion estimate is

$$\hat{p} = \frac{245}{22(200)} = .0557$$

The 3-sigma control limits are

$$\begin{aligned}
\text{LCL} &= \hat{p} - 3\sqrt{\frac{\hat{p}(1-\hat{p})}{n}} \\
&= .0557 - 3\sqrt{\frac{.0557(1-.0557)}{200}} \\
&= .0557 - 3(.0162) = .0071 \\
\text{UCL} &= \hat{p} + 3\sqrt{\frac{\hat{p}(1-\hat{p})}{n}} \\
&= .0557 + 3\sqrt{\frac{.0557(1-.0557)}{200}} \\
&= .0557 + 3(.0162) = .1043
\end{aligned}$$

c. Zone C: .0557 − .0162 = .0395
.0557 + .0162 = .0719
(.0395 to .0719)
Zone B: (.0233 to .0395) and (.0719 to .0881)
Zone A: (.0071 to .0233) and (.0881 to .1043)

d. Figure 13.26 shows these lower and upper control limits along with the centerline and the 22 sample proportions plotted in sequence. The high proportion of defectives in day 4 places this sample outside the control limits. Clare investigates why so many defectives occurred during day 4.

FIGURE 13.26 *p* Chart for Defects (Solved Exercise 3)

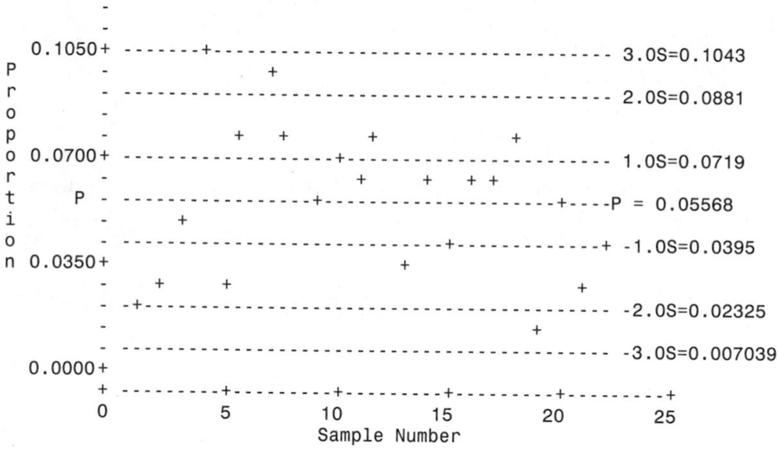

4. *c* CHART

The Neptune Motors Company builds compact cars. Frank Nelson inspects dashboard assemblies and records the number of total assembly defects. Here are the results for 20 dashboards:

Dashboard	Defects	Dashboard	Defects
1	5	11	2
2	4	12	7
3	7	13	4
4	3	14	6
5	8	15	8
6	6	16	3
7	5	17	10
8	6	18	7
9	10	19	4
10	9	20	5

a. Develop the centerline and upper and lower control limits for a 3-sigma *c* chart.

b. Compute the limits of the six zones.

c. Plot the number of defects and test to determine whether the process is in control.

Solution:

a. The average number of defects is

$$\bar{c} = \frac{\sum c_i}{n} = \frac{119}{20} = 5.95$$

The 3-sigma control limits are

$$\begin{aligned}\text{LCL} &= \bar{c} - 3\sqrt{\bar{c}} \\ &= 5.95 - 3\sqrt{5.95} = 5.95 - 3(2.44) = -1.37 \\ \text{UCL} &= \bar{c} + 3\sqrt{\bar{c}} \\ &= 5.95 + 3\sqrt{5.95} = 5.95 + 3(2.44) = 13.27\end{aligned}$$

b. Zone C: 5.95 − 2.44 = 3.51
5.95 + 2.44 = 8.39
(3.51 to 8.39)
Zone B: (1.07 to 3.51) and (8.39 to 10.83)
Zone A: (0 to 1.07) and (10.83 to 13.27)

c. Figure 13.27 shows these lower and upper control limits along with the centerline and the number of defects plotted in sequence. The number of defects is all within the control limits so Frank concludes that the process is in control.

FIGURE 13.27 *c* Chart for Defects (Solved Exercise 4)

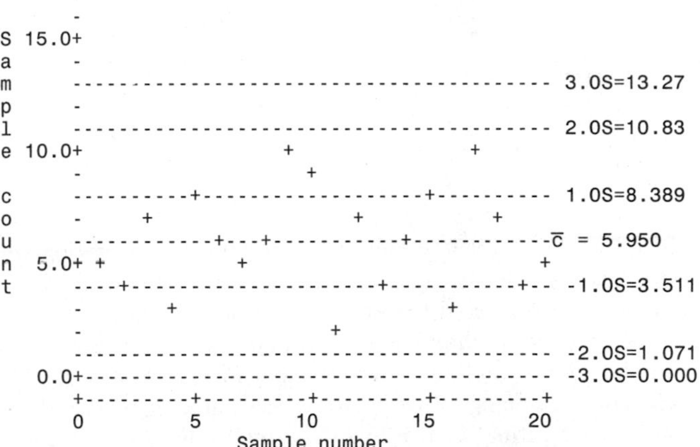

5. LOT ACCEPTANCE

Carlene Foss is in charge of final buyoff for lots of 10,000 transistors manufactured by her company. She judges each lot's quality and either passes it on to the shipping department or junks the entire lot due to poor quality. Management has decided that a lot with 2% or fewer defective transistors is acceptable.

Determine a sampling plan for Carlene to use in accepting or rejecting a lot, given management's definition of a good lot.

Solution:

Carlene decides to sample 100 transistors from each lot and use the sample results to determine the lot's fate. She calculates the probabilities of various sample outcomes, assuming the lot has 2% defectives, as follows:

$$H_0: p \leq .02, \qquad n = 100$$
$$H_1: p > .02$$
$$\sigma_{\bar{p}} = \sqrt{\frac{.02(.98)}{100}} = .014$$

Sample results, number of defectives	Sample results, % defective	Probability if H_0 is true
3	.03	.2389
4	.04	.0764
5	.05	.0162
6	.06	.0021

The values in the last column were calculated using normal curve procedures (Chapter 6). For example, the first z value is $(.03 - .02)/.014 = .71$. The normal curve table indicates an area of .2611 for this z value, leaving $.5 - .2611 = .2389$ on the end of the curve. This latter value is the probability of getting a value as large, or larger, than .03 from the sampling distribution, assuming H_0 is true ($p = .02$). Carlene's worksheet for calculating the values in the final column is:

Assuming H_0 is true:			
Sample value	z	Area	.5 − Area
.03	.71	.2611	.2389
.04	1.43	.4236	.0764
.05	2.14	.4838	.0162
.06	2.86	.4979	.0021

Based on the preceding table, Carlene tells her inspection staff, "When each lot is completed, take a random sample of 100 transistors and have the lab people test them thoroughly. From this sample, record the number that don't work properly. If this number is four or less, send the entire lot to shipping. If the number of defectives is five or more, call me at once—the lot will be rejected and we need to find out what went wrong."

Carlene's reasoning is that if a lot is acceptable ($p = .02$), there's only a .0162 probability of erroneously rejecting it since that's the probability of getting five or more defectives from a sample taken from a good lot.

6. Operating Characteristic Curve

In Solved Exercise 5, Carlene Foss developed a sampling plan for accepting or rejecting lots of 10,000 transistors. She's satisfied with her type I error since there's only a .0162 probability of erroneously rejecting a good lot ($\alpha = .0162$). She considers this an acceptably low probability for the producer's risk. She now wonders about the consumer's risk, that is, whether her sampling plan offers sufficient protection for her company's transistor customers.

Develop the operating characteristic (OC) curve for Carlene's sampling plan and evaluate the risks of the plan.

Solution:

Carlene's predetermined decison rule point, from Solved Exercise 5, is five defectives or 5% defective. She decides to calculate the probabilities of failing to reject the false null hypothesis that $p = .02$ for each of three population defective percentages. These values and their corresponding beta values are:

p	Beta
.03	.9236
.05	.5000
.07	.0764

Carlene calculated these beta values using normal curve procedures. If $p = .05$, then exactly half the curve lies below the decision rule point (which is .05). A value in this region would lead to erroneous acceptance of the null hypothesis.

If $p = .03$, the calculated z value is $(.03 - .05)/.014 = -1.43$, and the standard normal area for this z value is .4236. Half the standard normal area must be added to this value since most of the sampling distribution lies below the decision rule point of .05 if $p = .03$. So $\beta = .5000 + .4236 = .9236$.

If $p = .07$, the calculated z value is $(.07 - .05)/.014 = 1.43$ and the standard normal area is .4236. This value must be subtracted from .5000 since only a small part of the sampling distribution lies below .05 if $p = .07$. So $\beta = .5000 - .4236 = .0764$.

Carlene plots her three values on graph paper and draws a smooth line through these points to produce her OC curve (Figure 13.28).

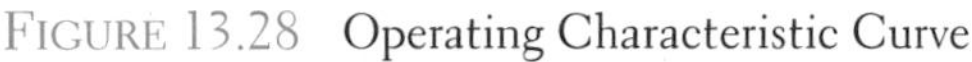

FIGURE 13.28 Operating Characteristic Curve

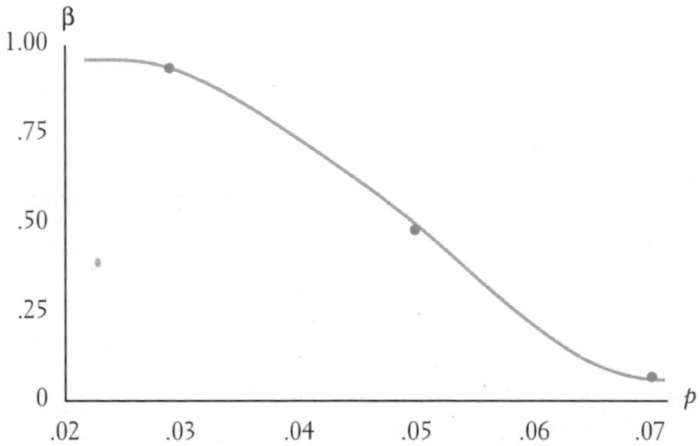

EXERCISES

56. Improving quality is often cited as the most important challenge facing American business today. Define what is meant by *quality* in this regard.
57. Your boss has just read about using control charts to improve quality in a manufacturing operation and asks how to do this. Write a brief memo explaining how the correct use of control charts can help in the quality improvement effort.

58. How are the upper and lower control limits on a control chart established?
59. There are two possible explanations for a measurement on a control chart exceeding the control limits. Explain.
60. Sketch a control chart with several observations for each of the following situations:
    a. Process in control, a single out-of-control observation.
    b. Process in control but drifting upward.
    c. Process in control but drifting downward.
    d. Process in control with strings of measurements above centerline.
    e. Process in control but cycling.
61. Consider a manufacturing operation such as Kaiser Aluminum's Trentwood aluminum factory. (See the "Applications" section for a description of this operation.) Describe an application for each of the following types of control chart for this operation: individual measurements, $\bar{x}$, R, p, and c.
62. Consider a service operation such as a credit union. Describe an application for each of the following types of control chart for this business: individual measurements, $\bar{x}$, R, p, and c.
63. Theory X and Theory Y are discussed in management classes as two different ways of viewing workers and dealing with them in the workplace. Discuss W. Edwards Deming's teachings with regard to these two opposing theories.
64. The Beamer Company makes ball bearings for high-quality bicycle components that demand very close tolerances. Beamer randomly selects 10 ball bearings every hour. Past experience shows the average (mean) diameter to be .37 with an average range of .04 ($\bar{R}$ = .04).
    a. Set up the $\bar{x}$ control chart.
    b. Set up an R chart.

64*a.* $\hat{\sigma}$ = .013, LCL = .3577, UCL = .3823
b. LCL = .0089, UCL = .0710

65. (Refer to Exercise 64.) The results of the past five samples are:

Mean	Range
.3691	.020
.3705	.063
.3722	.040
.3699	.057
.3702	.088

    a. Plot the means on the $\bar{x}$ chart.
    b. Plot the ranges on the R chart.
    c. Write a memo to Beamer management indicating the results of your study.
66. A light truck factory has 128 key indicators of quality for completed trucks. During final inspection, each indicator is inspected and either performs properly or does not. Costly rework is necessary for items that don't perform properly, so management wants to track the percentage of nonconforming items per truck. During a trial period, the following percentages were recorded; the period was considered by management to be "normal."

Truck number	% nonconforming
1	3
2	6
3	0
4	7
5	2
6	4
7	0
8	0
9	1
10	4

66*a*. CL = 2.7, LCL = 0, UCL = 7.63

a. Set up a *c* chart using the preceding data and plot these values.

b. Write a brief memo to management indicating the purpose of the *c* chart, how data are to be recorded on it for each completed truck, and how to interpret the results.

67. Boxes of apples received at a processing plant are supposed to have an average weight of 20 pounds. The standard deviation of weights is believed to be 2 pounds. Each boxcar load of boxes is sampled randomly, with 30 boxes being selected and weighed. The receiving inspection plan calls for a one-tailed test (down) and a significance level of .05.

   a. State the null and alternative hypotheses.

   b. State the decision rule for the test.

   c. Pick three key values below 20 pounds and indicate both β and $1 - \beta$ for these values.

   d. Plot the values found in part *c* to form the OC and power curves.

   e. What should be done with a boxcar load of apples whose sampled boxes' mean weight is 19 pounds?

   f. Based on your decision in part *e*, what type of error might have been committed? If this error has been made, what is the nature of the penalty and who will pay it?

68. Johnson and Dumas's article "How to Improve Quality If You're NOT in Manufacturing" (*Training*, November 1992) listed several steps to follow in improving a service firm's quality and hence its market share and profits. Steps range from establishing customer needs to implementing the plan. Suppose you own a formal wear rental shop and you face increased competition. Describe some steps you would take to improve your quality image with your market.

69. "America's Best Plants" (*Industry Week*, October 19, 1992) identified one of the best companies as Air Products and Chemicals, Inc. This company makes polymer emulsion products such as paint and paper coatings. "Foot soldiers run the show" at this company where employees are involved in every aspect of the plant's activities.

   A highlight of the article on Air Products and Chemicals was the 97.9% first-pass yield on its production line. This figure strongly suggests the use of a percentage control chart (*p* chart). Such a chart is also used by Kaiser Aluminum. (See this chapter's "Applications" section.)

   Construct a *p* chart for Air Products and Chemicals using fictitious values. Indicate the time values you choose for the *x*-axis.

70. A manager begins a control chart for the mean weight of steel ingots. She measures the average weights of the 24 ingots produced this week and then forms a control chart. Upon posting it, she says, "It makes no sense to measure quality against the standard established last week. Maybe the process was way out of control then." Evaluate this statement, and either refute it or indicate how to meet the objection it raises.

71. A company intends to use an acceptance sampling plan to monitor the average time between power-up and proper current readings for an electronic component it makes for electronic camera controls. Components are made in batches of 500. Among other things, the company wants to know how many components it must sample and test from each batch. A preliminary sample indicates a sample standard deviation of 1.5 seconds.

When asked about how accurate the sampling plan should be, the plant manager finally subscribes to the following statements:

1. If the actual time in the entire batch meets specification (5 seconds), I want only a 2% chance of concluding that this time is more than 5 seconds.
2. If the actual time in the entire batch is really 6 seconds, I want only a 5% chance of thinking it's 5 seconds.

a. How big a sample should be taken from each batch?

b. Select three key values for the key time variable and compute both β and $1 - \beta$ for each.

c. Plot the values found in part *b* to form the OC and power curves for this test.

72. The Concave Computer Company is enjoying a considerable increase in business volume. As a result, the accounting department now needs more than the normal 30-day period to process check requests. Unfortunately, the company is no longer getting the discounts its suppliers give for timely payment. Chip Weeks analyzes the amount of time it takes for a check request to flow through the accounting department. Six completed check requests are selected each day, and $\bar{x}$ and R charts are developed for the flow time variable. Flow time data for the past 20 days are:

Day	Days required to process a check request					
1	31	34	25	28	29	31
2	29	32	28	34	30	33
3	24	27	29	31	35	31
4	30	27	29	34	32	38
5	39	37	34	29	30	31
6	32	34	35	38	29	34
7	25	29	32	35	31	32
8	24	33	39	31	34	32
9	26	29	33	35	33	32
10	26	35	33	28	32	30
11	27	34	25	38	39	35
12	29	31	28	32	27	34
13	28	27	26	27	35	31
14	33	27	28	34	32	38
15	31	31	32	29	33	31
16	31	34	35	38	29	34

Day	Days required to process a check request					
17	29	29	32	35	31	32
18	28	33	35	31	34	32
19	36	29	28	35	33	32
20	34	35	32	28	32	30

72*a*. $\bar{x}$ chart: CL = 31.5, LCL = 27.29, UCL = 35.71
R chart: CL = 8.707, LCL = 0, UCL = 17.45
b. Yes

a. Construct the appropriate control charts to monitor the mean and variation of this process.

b. Is the process in control?

c. Write a report to Chip Weeks that explains the current flow time situation.

73. The Precision Manufacturing Company (which makes needlelike operating instruments for hospital operating rooms) implements statistical process control procedures in its production operation. The company collects one sample of 150 randomly selected manufactured instruments each day for 15 days.

Day	Sample size	Defectives
1	150	5
2	150	7
3	150	3
4	150	2
5	150	4
6	150	5
7	150	8
8	150	6
9	150	3
10	150	1
11	150	2
12	150	6
13	150	7
14	150	14
15	150	5

73*a*. *p* chart: CL = .03467, LCL = 0, UCL = .07948
b. Potentially out of control

a. Construct the appropriate control chart to monitor this process.

b. Is the process in control?

c. Write a memo to management that explains the defective instrument situation.

74. In a large chain that sells washers and dryers, the service department decides to improve the effectiveness of its repair work. Maintenance requests that require a second call to complete the repair are monitored for 16 months. Eighty requests are randomly selected for each month.

Month	Total requests	Second visits
1	80	1
2	80	0
3	80	2
4	80	5

Month	Total requests	Second visits
5	80	4
6	80	2
7	80	3
8	80	3
9	80	0
10	80	1
11	80	2
12	80	4
13	80	1
14	80	0
15	80	3
16	80	2

74*a*. *p* chart: CL = .02578, LCL = 0, UCL = .07894
b. In control

a. Construct the appropriate control chart to monitor this process.

b. Is the process in control? Is the service department's objective of improving the effectiveness of its repair work accomplished?

c. Write a memo to management that explains the repair work's present status. Propose a plan for determining whether the effectiveness of repair work has improved.

75. A production line assembles electric clocks. Clocks are periodically examined for imperfections. Results for the past 20 clocks examined are:

Clock	Defects	Clock	Defects
1	0	11	2
2	1	12	0
3	2	13	0
4	0	14	1
5	1	15	2
6	3	16	2
7	0	17	0
8	1	18	4
9	2	19	1
10	7	20	2

75*a*. *c* chart: CL = 1.55, LCL = 0, UCL = 5.285
b. Out of control

a. Construct the appropriate control chart to monitor this process.

b. Is the process in control?

c. Write a memo to management that summarizes the stability of the process.

Extended Exercises

76. Valley Electronics

Valley Electronics makes components for commercial electronics assemblies such as oscilloscopes and circuit testers. A large manufacturer of these items has contracted with Valley to make thousands of chassis assemblies, one of Valley's specialties. Each chassis requires certain dimensions and must have two holes drilled in precise locations; a complex electronic component is then attached in these holes.

At Valley's weekly management council meeting, Susan Boyer, who recently joined the company because of her expertise in quality control, suggested tracking the key dimension (distance between holes) and recording values for a sample of chassis components. She planned to construct $\bar{x}$ and R charts whose purposes she then explained to the council.

According to contract specifications, the chassis measurement between mounting holes is 7.6 inches, measured from the edges nearest to each other.

Susan began taking samples of 25 chassis components from the line until she had 10 such samples. After calculating the mean between-hole measurement for each of the 10 samples, she averaged them and found a mean for all sampled chassis of 7.61 inches. The 10 samples' average range was .05 inches. Using a d_2 value from Table 13.1 of 3.931, she estimated the standard deviation for the between-hole measurement to be .0127 inches. Susan called the buyer of the chassis assemblies and, after reporting these values, was assured that they were satisfactory, that is, met the terms of the contract.

a. Check Susan's estimate of the process standard deviation using Table 13.1.

b. Construct $\bar{x}$ and R charts for Susan.

c. Susan wants to show the management council example plots to watch out for as the chassis line continues operations. Use both charts, along with fictitious plot values, to illustrate key future dangers for the chassis line.

77. VALLEY ELECTRONICS #2

(See Extended Exercise 76.) Susan Boyer of Valley Electronics is concerned about the defective rate for Valley's best profit producer, a programmable control for home electronics products. A few customer complaints have raised concerns about the possibility of deteriorating quality.

Susan designs a sampling plan for these components and pulls them from the assembly line over a period of three weeks. She samples them from all shifts, various days of the week, and various times of the day for a total of 20 samplings. Her sample size for each is 25 controllers. Although it takes a lot of time to individually test all aspects of each unit, she's convinced that this is very important for the company's reputation and long-term profitability.

For each sample of 500 controllers, Susan computes the percentage that don't perform properly. After averaging these defective rates, she has an estimate of the defective rate for the entire process, 3.7%. Since the company produces thousands of these units each year, this defective rate means that hundreds of defective units are being sold by the company. Valley's management council agrees with her that this rate is too high so steps are begun to lower it.

At Susan's urging, these attempts are designed around Deming's 14 points for quality improvement discussed earlier in this chapter. The management council agrees that this effort constitutes a change of corporate culture at Valley, but they recognize that the electronic controller isn't the only component facing quality problems and competitive challenges. They agree to hire an outside consultant to help Susan create the necessary changes.

In the meantime, Susan decides to construct a p chart to track the defective rate. She hopes that she'll be able to spot the hoped-for improving trend, as well as watch for any deterioration in the process that may need direct corrective action. Her sampling plan involves sampling from each shift every other day; samples of 500 controllers will be used.

a. Construct the p chart for Susan.

b. Prepare several plots on this chart for Susan to use in her next management council meeting. She wants to show the management team how various plots that might result can help them take appropriate corrective action.

78. CLINTON LAWNMOWERS

Sam Gangee of Example 13.8 has turned to a key quality-control problem in his lawnmower factory, the quality of incoming carburetors received from a supplier. The volume of gasoline that carburetors hold at rest is an important factor in how long it takes to start a lawnmower when cold.

After discussions with design engineers, it's agreed that an average of two cubic inches of gas per carburetor (or less) will constitute the definition of an acceptable lot. A volume greater than two cubic inches can create problems on a cold start. Carburetors arrive in lots of 500 units.

Sam uses a systematic sample (Chapter 2) to randomly select those carburetors that will constitute the sample and be subjected to several quality tests. In each arriving truckload, the sequence of carburetors for sampling purposes is determined by the order in which they're unloaded.

He chooses a sample size of 25, so every 20th item will be sampled (500/25 = 20). For each batch, a random number is chosen between 1 and 20, which is the item number for the first sampled carburetor as it's unloaded. Each 20th item thereafter is also chosen. In his most recent sampling effort, the random number 11 was chosen, so carburetors 11, 31, 51, 71, and so on were marked with special paint as they were unloaded from the truck. These 25 items were then taken to the test lab and measured for gas volume. If the entire lot passed inspection on the basis of sample results, it would be sent to final assembly. If the lot failed due to poor quality in the sample, each of the 500 carburetors would be returned to the supplier. On Wednesday, Sam received the following information from his quality-control staff:

Lot number 275: $n = 25$
$\bar{x}$ (average gas volume per carburetor) = 4.7
s (standard deviation of carburetor volume) = 1.4

Sam decided to use the normal curve in his hypothesis test since he judged the sample size (25) to be sufficiently large. He made this decision after looking at both the t and normal curve tables and noting how close the values are for samples of 25. The hypotheses under test are:

$$H_0: \mu \leq 2$$
$$H_1: \mu > 2$$

He computed the test z value from the sample data contained in his report. (See Chapter 9.)

$$z = \frac{4.7 - 2}{1.4/\sqrt{25}} = 9.64$$

From the standard normal table, Sam found the table critical value to be 2.05, using a significance level of .02 for a one-tail test. Since 9.64 > 2.05, the null hypothesis was rejected. The sample results ($\bar{x} = 4.7$) don't seem reasonable when compared with the null hypothesis ($\mu \leq 2$).

Sam decided that it's necessary to return the entire lot to the carburetor supplier. In addition, he'll visit the supplier's plant to try to learn what has gone wrong, and to impress on the supplier's management the importance of correct gas volume. He hopes he isn't wasting his time with this effort. (He hopes that he hasn't made a type I error.) Such an error would be embarrassing and might create future problems with the supplier. In addition, lawnmower assembly time would be lost without justification.

Sam next wants to determine the power of this test for $n = 25$ and decide whether he has chosen an adequate sample size. Here are the facts Sam needs to accomplish this task:

H_0: $\mu \leq 2$ $\quad n = 25$
H_1: $\mu > 2$ $\quad s = 1.4$
$s_{\bar{x}} = s/\sqrt{n} \quad = 1.4/\sqrt{25} = .28$

Sam previously established a critical z value of 2.05 for a one-tailed hypothesis test using a significance level of .02. In units of gasoline volume, this number of standard errors is 2.574 cubic inches $(2 + 2.05[.28] = 2.574)$. Figure 13.29 shows three areas Sam chooses to calculate beta (probability of type II error) for three different possible values of the population mean.

FIGURE 13.29 Normal Curve Areas

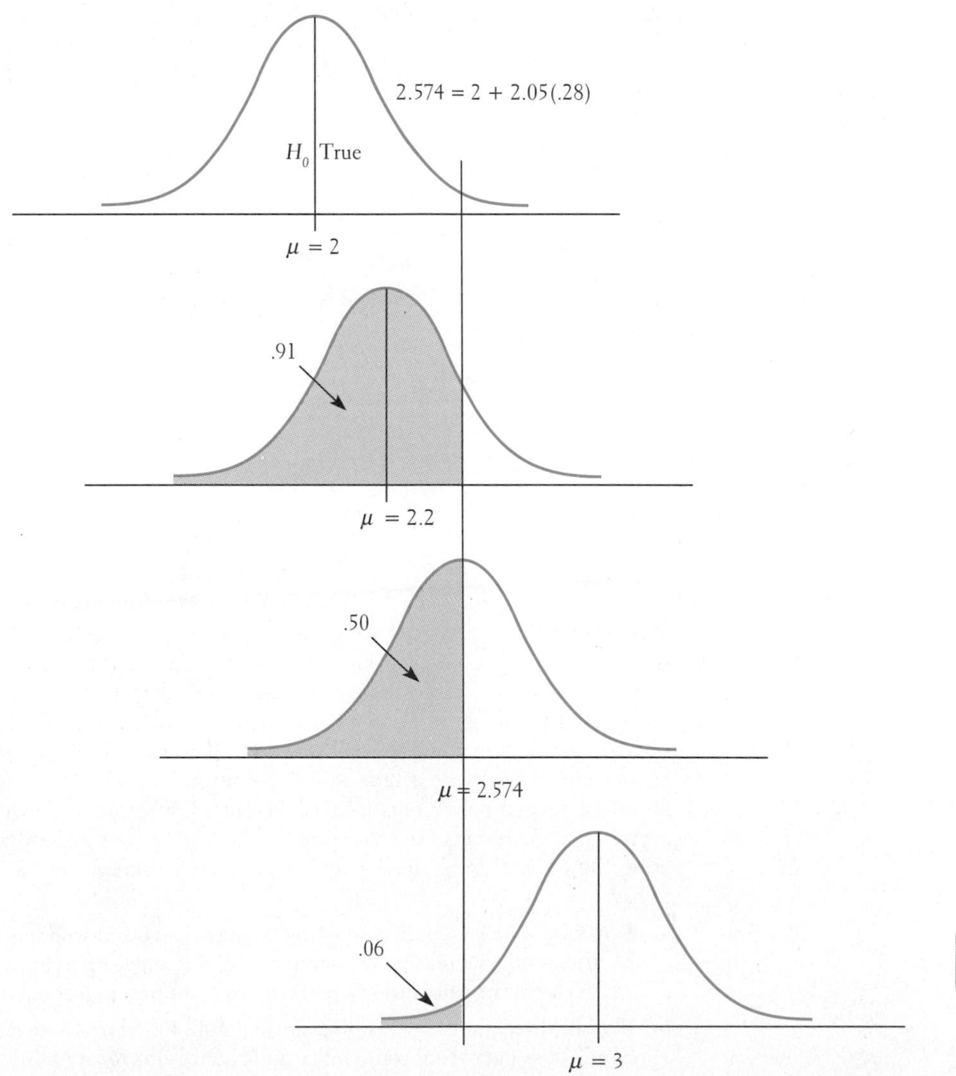

By subtracting the beta values in Figure 13.29 from 1, he computes the power of the test for the three designated population mean values. He summarizes these as follows and plots them on a power curve (Figure 13.30).

Population mean	Power $(1 - \beta)$
2.200	.09
2.574	.50
3.000	.94

FIGURE 13.30 Power Curve

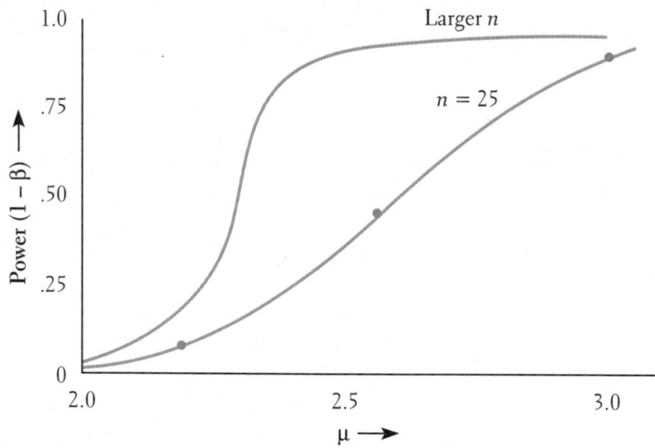

Using Figure 13.30, Sam can find the power of his statistical test to correctly reject the null hypothesis that $\mu \leq 2$. He has connected the three points on his graph with a curved line to obtain this power curve. After studying this curve, Sam decides that perhaps his chosen sample size ($n = 25$) isn't powerful enough. He can increase the test power by increasing the sample size. Although this will be more costly, Sam considers it a good investment.

Notice that in Figure 13.30, another power curve has been plotted, one for a larger n. Increasing the sample size above 25 will move the power curve to the left in Figure 13.30, providing greater power to detect a false null hypothesis. After thinking about this matter, Sam plots a family of several power curves using Figure 13.30's format; each curve represents a different sample size. Sam thinks that by studying the test's power for several sample sizes and by considering the cost of using these sample sizes, he can choose the sample size that best meets his needs.

a. Sam's boss indicates that sampling is inexpensive and wonders how the test's power would be affected by increasing the sample size. She suggests trying a sample of 50 and another of 75. Perform the calculations necessary to form new power curves for each.

b. Plot all three power curves on a single graph. Based on these curves, write a brief memo to Sam's boss indicating your choice and the reasons for it.

MINITAB COMPUTER PACKAGE

MINITAB was used to generate the individual chart for average pump volume in Figure 13.5.

```
MTB> SET C1
DATA> 12.1 11 9.7 8.4 10.2 10.4 11 12.6 13 8.8
DATA> 9 7.7 10 11.2 12.2 13 12.1 10.2 10.3 9.7
DATA> 11 12 8 10.2 6.8 8 9.5 10.2 9.4 8.9 7.3 7.2
DATA> END
MTB > NAME C1 'VOLUME'
MTB > ICHART C1;
SUBC> MU=10;
SUBC> SIGMA= 1;
SUBC> XSTART at 21 END 32.
     OUTPUT SHOWN AS FIGURE 13.5
MTB> STOP
```

The data are entered in sequence into C1. The ICHART command plots the pump volumes on an individual chart. The MU and SIGMA subcommands indicate that the mean and standard deviation for this chart should be 10 and 1, respectively. The XSTART subcommand indicates that the chart should begin with pump 21 and end with pump 32.

MINITAB can produce the following statistical process control charts:

XBARCHART produces a chart of sample means.

RCHART produces a chart of sample ranges.

SCHART produces a chart of sample standard deviations.

ICHART produces a chart of individual observations.

MACHART produces a chart of moving averages.

EWMACHART produces a chart of exponentially weighted moving averages.

MRCHART produces a chart of moving ranges.

PCHART produces a chart for proportion of nonconformities.

NCHART produces a chart for number of nonconformities.

CCHART produces a chart for Poisson counts.

UCHART produces a chart for Poisson counts per unit.

Chapter

14

Correlation and Simple Regression

There's some difference between Peter and Peter.
Cervantes,
Don Quixote

Objectives

When you have completed this chapter, you will be able to:

Construct and interpret scatter diagrams.

Calculate the correlation coefficient between two variables.

Develop a regression equation using the least squares procedure.

Interpret the slope (regression coefficient) and y-intercept.

Compute and interpret the standard error of estimate and develop prediction interval estimates.

Explain the underlying assumptions of regression analysis.

Compute and interpret the simple coefficient of determination.

Test a hypothesis to determine if two variables are linearly related.

An extensive article in *Financial World* (July 7, 1992) discussed the financial health of professional baseball, football, basketball, and hockey franchises. It included a two-page summary of major financial statistics for all teams (pp. 50–51).

Chapter 11 discussed methods of determining the relationship between two categorical variables. Either nominal or ordinal data were needed for these techniques. This chapter explores the relationship between two continuous or quantitative variables. Since so many variables in the business setting are measured on an interval or ratio scale, correlation and regression techniques are widely used to assist the decision-making process.

WHY MANAGERS NEED TO KNOW ABOUT CORRELATION AND REGRESSION ANALYSIS

The basic notions of regression and correlation are examined in this chapter. Extensions of these techniques to situations involving more than two variables appear in Chapter 15. Since regression analysis requires a great many calculations, computer applications for the techniques discussed are emphasized.

This chapter and the next cover regression, one of the most popular techniques in data analysis. Every manager encounters the procedures of correlation and regression in his or her career, and understanding them is essential. Since numerical data abound in the business world, there's a frequent need to examine the relationships among different variables.

Regarding the *Financial World* article just mentioned, it might be of interest to focus on one financial statistic such as "value of franchise" and attempt to find other variables that are highly related. Candidates in the article's financial data were total revenue, player costs, operating income, and media revenue. The procedures this chapter describes can be used to search for important relationships.

SCATTER DIAGRAMS

In both correlation and regression analysis, the linear relationship between two continuous variables, designated x and y, is investigated. A sample of items is measured for both x and y, with the focus on the extent to which these two variables are related or correlated.

One useful way of examining the x-y relationship is to view the data using a graph. An x-y plotting system is used for this purpose. The x axis is scaled to accommodate the range of values needed for the x variable, and the y axis is scaled to accommodate the y values. The data pairs are then plotted in two-dimensional space. This x-y plot is called a **scatter diagram.**

Scatter Diagram

> A **scatter diagram** plots a series of x-y data pairs in two-dimensional space.

EXAMPLE 14.1 Five cars are randomly selected from a rental fleet. Each car is weighed and then driven 100 miles to determine its mileage per gallon. The results are:

Car	Weight (pounds)	Miles per gallon
1	2,743	21.4
2	3,518	15.2
3	1,855	38.9
4	5,214	12.7
5	4,341	17.8

The five x-y data points can be plotted in two-dimensional space to form a scatter diagram of the data. Weight is chosen to be the x variable, so the x axis is scaled from 0 to 6,000 pounds. Miles per gallon is the y variable, so the y axis is scaled from 0 to 40. Each of the five data points is plotted using this x-y system (Figure 14.1).

FIGURE 14.1 Weight-Mileage Scatter Diagram

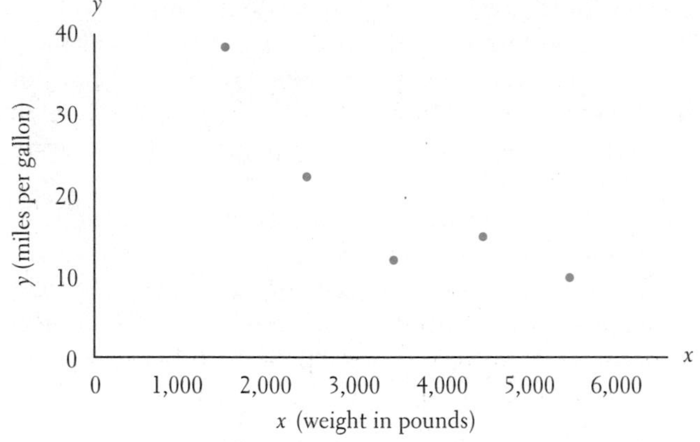

The advantage of the scatter diagram is that it enables one to visualize the relationship between x and y. Figure 14.1 shows that as a car's weight increases, its mileage tends to decrease. Based on the small sample of five cars, a relationship between weight and mileage seems to exist. It would be preferable to select a much larger sample before drawing any conclusions, of course, and also to measure the extent of the x-y relationship.

MINITAB can be used to develop a scatter diagram. The appropriate commands to plot the data from Example 14.1 are:

```
MTB> SET C1
DATA> 21.4 15.2 38.9 12.7 17.8
DATA> END
MTB> SET C2
DATA> 2743 3518 1855 5214 4341
```

```
DATA> END
MTB> NAME C1 'MPG' C2 'WEIGHT'
MTB> PLOT C1 VS C2
   OUTPUT WILL BE SHOWN HERE
MTB> STOP
```

The output for this MINITAB run is similar to the scatter diagram in Figure 14.1.

Figure 14.2 shows some important scatter diagram patterns that should be looked for when examining a particular *x*-*y* relationship. (The number of data points has been deliberately kept small in these examples. Plots of real data usually involve many more data points.)

FIGURE 14.2 Scatter Diagrams

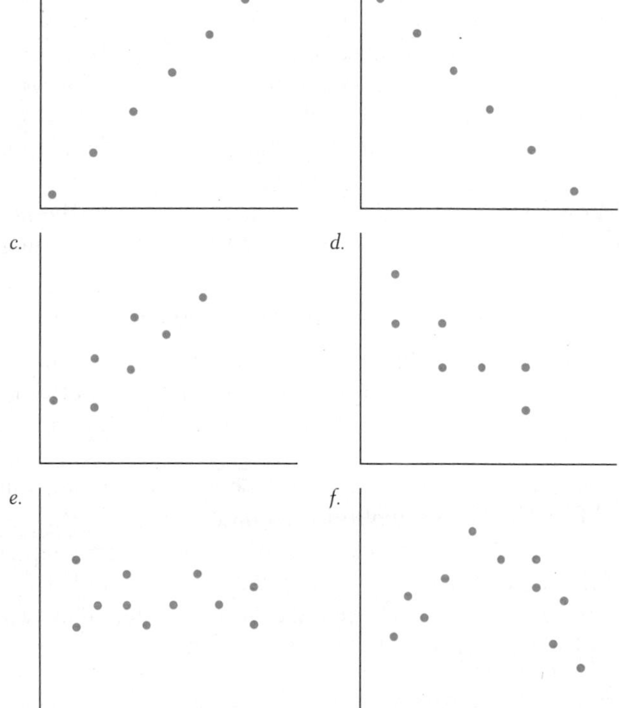

Plot *a* in Figure 14.2 illustrates a perfect positive linear relationship. It is linear because the plotted points lie on a straight line. It is positive because as *x* increases, *y* increases also. And it's perfect because the plotted *x*-*y* points all lie on this line. Plot *b* shows a perfect negative linear relationship. The relationship is negative because as *x* increases, *y* decreases. Plots such as *a* and *b* are rarely seen in practical situations; they're included here to illustrate the extreme cases of linear *x*-*y* relationships.

Plots *c* and *d* in Figure 14.2 illustrate relationships typically seen in real-life scatter diagrams. The points in plot *c* represent a positive linear relationship, but not a perfect relationship, since the points don't all lie precisely on a straight line. Plot *d* is similar, except that an imperfect negative relationship is shown. Most scatter diagrams encountered in practical situations are variations of plots *c* and *d*.

Plot *e* illustrates a complete lack of relationship between *x* and *y*. Knowledge of the *x* variable provides no useful information about the *y* variable. This lack of linear relationship is an important concept in hypothesis testing, which is discussed later in this chapter.

Finally, plot *f* illustrates a curved relationship between *x* and *y*. Note that although plot *f* shows a relationship between *x* and *y*, it's not a linear relationship.

Correlation Coefficient

The advantage of the scatter diagram is that it enables the analyst to *see* the relationship between the two variables of interest. It is particularly valuable for revealing the presence of curved relationships, which can be missed when numerical measurements of linear correlation are computed.

Correlation Coefficient

It is usually desirable to measure the extent of the relationship between *x* and *y* as well as observe it in a scatter diagram. The measurement used for this purpose is the **correlation coefficient,** which is a numerical value in the range -1 to $+1$ that measures the strength of the linear relationship between two quantitative variables.

> The **correlation coefficient** is a value between -1 and $+1$ that indicates the strength of the linear relationship between two quantitative variables.

Correlation coefficients exist for a population of data values and for each sample selected from it. The symbol for the population correlation coefficient is ρ, the Greek letter rho. For the sample, the correlation coefficient is represented by the letter *r*. As Table 14.1 shows, both ρ and r range between -1 and $+1$. As usual, the sample statistic is used to estimate the population parameter. This process will be examined in depth in the next section.

TABLE 14.1 Correlation Coefficients

Data collection	Correlation coefficient	Range of values
Population	ρ	$-1 \leq \rho \leq +1$
Sample	r	$-1 \leq r \leq +1$

For both ρ and r:

-1: Perfect negative linear relationship
0: No linear relationship
$+1$: Perfect positive linear relationship

As Table 14.1 states, a correlation coefficient of $+1$ indicates a perfect positive linear relationship, a value of 0 indicates no relationship, and a value of -1 indicates a perfect negative linear relationship. These values are rarely encountered in real situations, but they're good benchmarks for evaluating the correlation coefficient of any data collection.

Equation 14.1 is used to calculate the sample correlation coefficient. For the population correlation coefficient, the same equation is used, except the population size, N, is substituted for the sample size, n:

$$r = \frac{n\Sigma xy - (\Sigma x)\,(\Sigma y)}{\sqrt{n\Sigma x^2 - (\Sigma x)^2}\,\sqrt{n\Sigma y^2 - (\Sigma y)^2}} \tag{14.1}$$

where
Σx = Sum of the x values
Σy = Sum of the y values
Σx^2 = Sum of the squared x values
Σy^2 = Sum of the squared y values
$(\Sigma x)^2$ = Sum of the x values squared
$(\Sigma y)^2$ = Sum of the y values squared
Σxy = Sum of the product of x and y for each paired observation
n = Number of x-y observations

Equation 14.1 is used only for quantitative data and is known as the *Pearson product-moment correlation coefficient.*

EXAMPLE 14.2 A calculator should be used to form a data table of the various sums required for computing r using Equation 14.1. The data in Example 14.1 will be used to form such a table so that the correlation coefficient between car weight and mileage for the sample of five cars can be found. The data, along with the calculations of the necessary sums, appear in Table 14.2.

The values calculated in Table 14.2 are used in Equation 14.1 to calculate the sample correlation coefficient for the sample of five cars:

$$\begin{aligned} r &= \frac{n\Sigma xy - (\Sigma x)(\Sigma y)}{\sqrt{n\Sigma x^2 - (\Sigma x)^2}\,\sqrt{n\Sigma y^2 - (\Sigma y)^2}} \\ &= \frac{5(327{,}820.9) - (17{,}671)(106)}{\sqrt{5(69{,}371{,}475) - (17{,}671)^2}\,\sqrt{5(2{,}680.34) - (106)^2}} \\ &= \frac{-234{,}021.5}{273{,}494.4} = -.855 \text{ rounded to } -.86 \end{aligned}$$

The correlation coefficient for the sample of five data points is $r = -.86$. This indicates a rather strong negative linear relationship between car weight and miles per gallon in the sample. The correlation coefficient verifies what was apparent in Figure 14.1's scatter diagram.

While both the scatter diagram and the sample correlation coefficient suggest a strong relationship between weight and mileage: (on a scale of 0 to -1, $r = -.86$) the sample size is extremely small and may not provide the analyst with enough

TABLE 14.2 Correlation Coefficient Calculations for Example 14.2

	x	y	xy	x^2	y^2
	2,743	21.4	58,700.2	7,524,049	457.96
	3,518	15.2	53,473.6	12,376,324	231.04
	1,855	38.9	72,159.5	3,441,025	1,513.21
	5,214	12.7	66,217.8	27,185,796	161.29
	4,341	17.8	77,269.8	18,844,281	316.84
Sums:	17,671	106.0	327,820.9	69,371,475	2,680.34

information to infer a significant relationship in the population. A statistical hypothesis test will be developed in the next section to allow us to determine whether a sample relationship can be extended to the population.

MINITAB can be used to compute a correlation coefficient. The appropriate command to compute the correlation coefficient for Example 14.2 is:

```
MTB> CORR C1 C2
Correlation of MPG AND WEIGHT = -0.855
MTB> STOP
```

EXAMPLE 14.3 Queen Hardware Store manager Robin Nash conducts exit interviews of 150 shoppers. She requests several statistics, including number of miles driven to the store (x) and dollar amount of purchase in the store (y). Wanting to know the relationship between these two variables, she keys the x-y pairs into a computer using a program that calculates the correlation coefficient. This program computes r to be .09. Robin concludes that the extremely weak linear relationship between miles driven and purchase amount does not warrant further examination.

The correlation coefficients for the scatter diagrams in Figure 14.2 can be estimated based on the apparent relationships between x and y. In Figure 14.2*a*, the correlation coefficient is $+1$, since a perfect positive linear relationship is apparent. In plot *b*, the correlation coefficient is -1. Figure 14.2 *c* and *d* show relationships that are not perfect; values for r might be estimated at about $+.75$ for plot *c* and about $-.75$ for plot *d*. In plot *e*, $r = 0$ since there appears to be no x-y relationship. In plot *f*, r also is approximately 0. This means that there's no *linear* relationship, although the scatter diagram of plot *f* clearly shows that a nonlinear relationship exists.

HYPOTHESIS TESTING IN CORRELATION ANALYSIS

A statistical question should always be asked when a sample is taken and measurements are made on the sample items: Can the sample results be assumed to hold for the entire population of interest?

The specific concern in correlation analysis is whether it can be concluded, based on sample evidence, that a linear relationship exists between the two continuous variables in the population. The null hypothesis under test states that no correlation exists in the population, that is, $\rho = 0$. The null and two-tailed alternative hypotheses for a correlation analysis are

$$H_0\colon \rho = 0$$
$$H_1\colon \rho \neq 0$$

A two-tailed alternative is used when the analyst is testing to determine if any linear relationship exists in the population. A one-tailed alternative is used when the analyst's goal is to determine if either a positive (H_1: $\rho > 0$) or a negative (H_1: $\rho < 0$) relationship exists.

After a sample of *x-y* pairs has been randomly drawn from the population, the sample correlation coefficient is computed using Equation 14.1. The value of r along with the sample size n are then used to compute the sample statistic for the test. If this statistic is close to 0, the null hypothesis is not rejected. If the statistic is far from 0, the null hypothesis is rejected.

If samples of the same size (n) are selected from a population, and if the r values computed from each sample are distributed normally around $\rho = 0$, only the standard error of r need be known for the usual test involving the normal distribution to be performed, as introduced in Chapter 9:

$$z = \frac{\text{Observed value} - \text{Assumed or hypothesized value}}{\text{Standard error of sampling distribution}}$$

Unfortunately, r values aren't normally distributed, so the normal curve can't be used. However, if the null hypothesis is true, then the appropriate sampling distribution for this test is the t distribution with $n - 2$ degrees of freedom. Two degrees of freedom are lost because two population parameters (μ_x and μ_y) are estimated using sample statistics ($\bar{x}$ and $\bar{y}$). The value for the estimated standard error of r is computed using Equation 14.2:

$$s_r = \sqrt{\frac{1 - r^2}{n - 2}} \tag{14.2}$$

where s_r = Standard error of the correlation coefficient
r = Sample correlation coefficient
n = Number of paired observations

Equation 14.3 shows the appropriate test statistic:

$$t = \frac{(r - \rho)}{s_r} \tag{14.3}$$

where r = Sample correlation coefficient
ρ = Hypothesized population correlation coefficient
s_r = Standard error of the correlation coefficient (computed using Equation 14.2)

EXAMPLE 14.4 An article in *The Academy of Management Review* reports the results of a study examining the roles organization design and culture play in the varying levels of success experienced by advanced manufacturing technologies in organizations.[1] The study conducted by Zammuto and Krakower (1991) examined the relationship between organizations' competing values profiles and a number of organizational characteristics. The study surveyed 332 colleges and universities. One of several hypotheses tested was that a hierarchical value system, reflecting the values and norms associated with bureaucracy, is correlated with the organizational characteristic of formalization.[2] The correlation between the hierarchical value score and the formalization score for the sampled organization was $r = .42$.

The null and a two-tailed alternative hypothesis for this correlation analysis are

$$H_0: \rho = 0$$
$$H_1: \rho \neq 0$$

If the null hypothesis is assumed true, the sampling distribution from which the ratio r/s_r will be drawn is the t distribution with a mean of 0. There are 330 degrees of freedom associated with this test ($n - 2 = 332 - 2 = 330$). If the .05 significance level is chosen, the t table in Appendix E.7 is used to find the critical t value. A choice must be made between the 120 or infinity row. The conservative approach is to select the row providing the highest critical t value. At the intersection of the 120 row and the .05 column (read from the top of the table) is the value 1.98. Since this is a two-tailed test, ± 1.98 are the critical values for the test. The decision rule is:

> If the sample t statistic lies more than 1.98 standard errors below or above the assumed mean (0) of the sampling distribution, reject the null hypothesis (reject H_0 if $t < -1.98$ or $t > 1.98$).

The test statistic is calculated using Equations 14.2 and 14.3. The standard error of r is

$$s_r = \sqrt{\frac{1 - r^2}{n - 2}} = \sqrt{\frac{1 - (.42)^2}{330}} = .05$$

The t statistic is

$$t = \frac{r - \rho}{s_r} = \frac{.42 - 0}{.05} = 8.4$$

The appropriate sampling distribution, assuming the null hypothesis is true, appears in Figure 14.3. The calculated t statistic (8.4) is in the rejection area specified by the decision rule ($t < 1.98$), so the null hypothesis is rejected. Zammuto and Krakower conclude that there is a correlation between a hierarchical value system and the organizational characteristic of formalization.

---

[1] R. F. Zammuto and J. Y. Krakower, "Quantitative and Qualitative Studies in Organizational Culture," *Research in Organizational Change and Development* 5 (1991), p. 95.

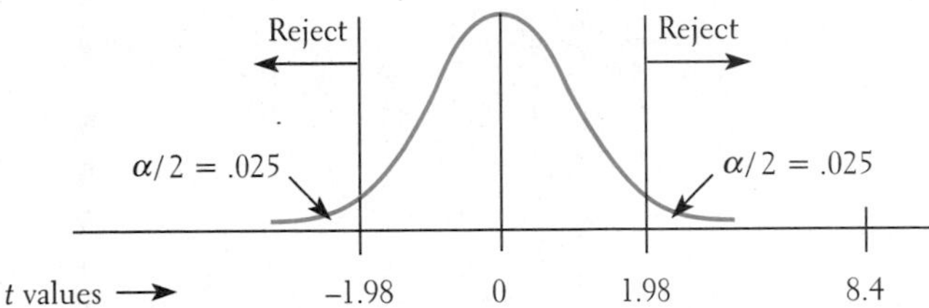

FIGURE 14.3 Sampling Distribution of $\frac{r}{s_r}$ for Example 14.4

A couple of words of caution about correlation should be mentioned. A correlation between two variables doesn't necessarily mean that one variable causes the other one. Correlation analysis can't be used to directly determine causality. Furthermore, two variables being correlated in a statistical sense doesn't necessarily mean that they're correlated in any direct, meaningful way. For example, we might determine statistically that church attendance and alcohol consumption are highly correlated in a certain large city. However, it might not be possible to determine which is the dependent and which is the independent variable. Whenever population-related variables increase together, it is often a reflection of a general increase in population rather than any direct connection between the two variables.

The next section will consider the problem of finding the best-fitting line for a given set of data. This line will provide a regression equation, a term first used by English scientist Francis Galton (1822–1911) in describing certain relationships in the theory of heredity.[2]

EXERCISES

1. What is a scatter diagram?
2. Why are scatter diagrams important?
3. Why are the magnitude and sign of a correlation coefficient important?
4. What does $r = 0$ imply?
5. What does it mean when r is shown not to be significant?
6. Interpret each of the following correlation coefficients.
   a. $r = -1.00$
   b. $r = 0$
   c. $r = .85$
   d. $r = -.20$
7. Using five data points, show what each relationship in Exercise 6 would look like if plotted on a scatter diagram.

[2]W. H. Kruskal, J. M. Tanur, eds., *International Encyclopedia of Statistics* (New York: The Free Press, 1968), Vol. 1, p. 524.

8. Director of Research and Development Donna Pico must defend her budget request for increased funding. Sampling eight pharmaceutical companies, she collects the following data:

Company	Annual profit ($ millions), y	Research and development ($ millions), x
1	$25	$ 5
2	30	7
3	20	4
4	50	10
5	40	8
6	60	12
7	50	6
8	35	11

a. Plot a scatter diagram.

b. What kind of relationship exists between these two variables?

c. Estimate the correlation coefficient.

d. Compute the correlation coefficient.

e. Test the correlation coefficient at the .05 significance level.

f. Write a short memo summarizing the results of this analysis for Donna.

8d. $r = .708$
e. $t = 2.458$, reject H_0 since $2.458 > 2.447$

9. Suppose that $n = 400$ and $r = .38$ in a correlation analysis. What is your conclusion concerning the population correlation at the .05 significance level?

9. $t = 8.17$, reject H_0 since $8.17 > 1.98$

10. Ralph Ludwigson, Danielson Tool & Die Corporation personnel director, feels that there's a relationship between the ages of the firm's computer operators and the number of days they were absent from work last month. After reading "Will the New Software Deliver What It Promises?" in *Today's Office* (June 1989, p. 27), he's thinking about the absenteeism problem since his company's computer operators are using the kind of software the article describes. Ralph selects a random sample of 10 workers and collects the following data:

Worker	Days absent, y	Age, x
1	5	25
2	0	30
3	1	62
4	7	33
5	8	45
6	12	27
7	6	55
8	11	41
9	2	22
10	3	58

a. Plot a scatter diagram.

b. What kind of relationship exists between these two variables?

c. Estimate the correlation coefficient.

d. Compute the correlation coefficient.

10*d.* $r = -.1635$
e. Fail to reject H_0 since $.469 < 3.355$

e. Test the correlation coefficient at the .01 significance level.

f. What should Ralph conclude?

11. Keith Mikelson, president of the Northeast Siding Company, feels that the amount of time a salesperson spends with a client should be positively related to the size of that client's account. To see if this relationship exists, Keith gathers the following sample data:

Client	Account size, y	Minutes spent, x
1	$1,056	108
2	825	132
3	651	62
4	748	95
5	894	58
6	1,242	134
7	1,058	87
8	1,112	78
9	1,259	120

a. Plot a scatter diagram.

b. What kind of relationship exists between these two variables?

11*c.* $r = .483$
d. Fail to reject H_0 since $1.455 < 2.365$

c. Compute the correlation coefficient.

d. Test the correlation coefficient at the .05 significance level.

e. What should Keith conclude?

12. Consider the 200 observations in the accompanying table. The dependent variable, y, is the population of the number of shares of Golden Mining stock traded on the Denver exchange each day. The independent variable, x, is the high temperature of Denver, Colorado, for each day. Randomly select observations for 15 days.

12*a.* $\rho = 0$ for this population

a. Compute the coefficient of correlation for your sample.

b. Test the hypothesis that there is no relationship between high temperature and shares of stock traded at the .05 significance level.

Observation	y	x	Observation	y	x	Observation	y	x	Observation	y	x
(1)	50	37	(14)	97	46	(27)	42	64	(40)	84	53
(2)	90	77	(15)	69	88	(28)	60	24	(41)	56	61
(3)	46	55	(16)	87	87	(29)	22	29	(42)	48	18
(4)	47	27	(17)	52	82	(30)	91	40	(43)	0	45
(5)	12	49	(18)	52	56	(31)	68	35	(44)	58	4
(6)	23	23	(19)	15	22	(32)	36	37	(45)	27	23
(7)	65	18	(20)	85	49	(33)	22	28	(46)	78	68
(8)	37	1	(21)	41	44	(34)	92	56	(47)	78	79
(9)	87	41	(22)	82	33	(35)	34	33	(48)	72	66
(10)	83	73	(23)	98	77	(36)	34	82	(49)	21	80
(11)	87	61	(24)	99	87	(37)	63	89	(50)	73	99
(12)	39	85	(25)	23	54	(38)	30	78	(51)	54	86
(13)	28	16	(26)	77	8	(39)	31	24	(52)	76	48

Observation	y	x	Observation	y	x	Observation	y	x	Observation	y	x
(53)	55	48	(90)	55	71	(127)	73	44	(164)	69	78
(54)	12	15	(91)	13	53	(128)	13	63	(165)	62	93
(55)	5	70	(92)	50	13	(129)	18	74	(166)	0	51
(56)	2	9	(93)	60	12	(130)	70	40	(167)	8	68
(57)	77	52	(94)	61	30	(131)	9	53	(168)	47	30
(58)	6	71	(95)	73	57	(132)	93	79	(169)	7	81
(59)	67	38	(96)	20	66	(133)	41	9	(170)	48	30
(60)	30	69	(97)	36	27	(134)	17	52	(171)	59	46
(61)	3	13	(98)	85	41	(135)	10	82	(172)	76	99
(62)	6	63	(99)	49	20	(136)	69	37	(173)	54	98
(63)	70	65	(100)	83	66	(137)	5	57	(174)	95	11
(64)	33	87	(101)	22	43	(138)	18	62	(175)	7	6
(65)	13	18	(102)	32	5	(139)	88	21	(176)	24	83
(66)	10	4	(103)	24	13	(140)	99	94	(177)	55	49
(67)	21	29	(104)	63	3	(141)	86	99	(178)	41	39
(68)	56	21	(105)	16	58	(142)	95	45	(179)	14	16
(69)	74	9	(106)	4	13	(143)	78	19	(180)	24	13
(70)	47	8	(107)	79	18	(144)	3	76	(181)	36	31
(71)	34	18	(108)	5	5	(145)	38	81	(182)	62	44
(72)	38	84	(109)	59	26	(146)	57	95	(183)	77	11
(73)	75	64	(110)	99	9	(147)	77	30	(184)	32	60
(74)	0	81	(111)	76	96	(148)	25	59	(185)	12	82
(75)	51	98	(112)	15	94	(149)	99	93	(186)	85	7
(76)	47	55	(113)	10	30	(150)	9	28	(187)	90	68
(77)	63	40	(114)	20	41	(151)	79	85	(188)	78	10
(78)	7	14	(115)	37	1	(152)	79	27	(189)	60	27
(79)	6	11	(116)	56	27	(153)	48	61	(190)	96	90
(80)	68	42	(117)	6	73	(154)	5	7	(191)	51	6
(81)	72	43	(118)	86	19	(155)	24	79	(192)	9	62
(82)	95	73	(119)	27	94	(156)	47	49	(193)	93	78
(83)	82	45	(120)	67	5	(157)	65	71	(194)	61	22
(84)	91	16	(121)	22	31	(158)	56	27	(195)	5	99
(85)	83	21	(122)	32	13	(159)	52	15	(196)	88	51
(86)	27	85	(123)	90	11	(160)	17	88	(197)	45	44
(87)	13	37	(124)	88	50	(161)	45	38	(198)	34	86
(88)	6	89	(125)	35	40	(162)	45	31	(199)	28	47
(89)	76	76	(126)	57	80	(163)	90	35	(200)	44	49

LINEAR EQUATIONS

Dependent and Predictor Variables

When two variables are examined for their correlation, it's usually for the purpose of using one to predict the other. Most correlation and regression studies are initiated based on the desire to examine and explain the changing value of this variable, which, in regression analysis, is called the *dependent variable.* The symbol chosen for the dependent variable is y. A second variable is identified that is believed to be associated with y and is called the *independent* or *predictor variable;* its symbol is x.

When only one predictor variable is identified, the analysis is called *simple regression.* When there are two or more predictor variables, a *multiple regression* analysis is being conducted (as Chapter 15 discusses).

The scatter diagram displays the *x-y* relationship in graphic terms. After the strength of this relationship has been measured with the correlation coefficient, the next step is to draw a straight line through the data points of the scatter diagram so that knowledge of the *x* variable can be used to predict the *y* variable.

Equation 14.4 is used to construct the straight line. The symbols β_0 (beta zero) and β_1 (beta one) represent the line's parameters; once they're specified, the line is fixed. The first parameter, β_0, is the *y*-intercept, or the point where the line crosses the *y* axis, the value of *y* when *x* is 0. The second parameter, β_1, is the slope of the line, or the amount by which *y* changes when *x* increases by one unit:

$$y = \beta_0 + \beta_1 x \tag{14.4}$$

where β_0 = *y*-intercept
β_1 = Slope of the line

EXAMPLE 14.5 Suppose that $\beta_0 = 8$ and $\beta_1 = 3$. Using Equation 14.4, the linear equation is

$$\begin{aligned} y &= \beta_0 + \beta_1 x \\ &= 8 + 3x \end{aligned}$$

If $x = 0$, then $y = 8$, which is the *y*-intercept (β_0):

$$y = 8 + 3(0) = 8$$

Note that as the value of *x* is increased by 1, the value of *y* increases by 3, which is the slope of the line (β_1):

$$\begin{aligned} y &= 8 + 3(1) = 11 \qquad x = 1 \\ y &= 8 + 3(2) = 14 \qquad x = 2 \\ y &= 8 + 3(3) = 17 \qquad x = 3 \end{aligned}$$

FUNCTIONAL AND STATISTICAL MODELS

The *x-y* points determined by Equation 14.4 all lie on a straight line. This is considered a *functional* relationship. In plots *c* and *d* in Figure 14.2, the points don't all lie on a straight line. Such relationships are considered *statistical* relationships.

An important question in regression analysis is: Does a perfect relationship exist between the independent (*x*) and dependent (*y*) variables? For example, can the exact value of sales revenue (*y*) be predicted if price per unit (*x*) is specified? This is probably not possible, for several reasons. Sales depend on many variables other than price per unit—such as advertising expense, time of year, state of the economy, etc. In most cases, there's also some variation due strictly to chance or random error, which can't be modeled or explained.

Functional Model

If a model is constructed that hypothesizes an exact relationship between variables, it's called a **functional** or **deterministic model.** Consider the relation between dollar sales (y) of a particular book and number of units sold (x). If the selling price is $8 per book, the relationship is

$$y = 0 + 8x$$

This equation represents a functional relationship between the variables *dollar sales* (y) and *units sold* (x). A perfect relationship exists. If 10 books are sold, sales revenue equals exactly $80.

Statistical Model

Based on the recognition that most real-world variables can't be predicted exactly, a model is constructed that hypothesizes a relationship between variables allowing for random error. Equation 14.5 is called a **statistical** or **probabilistic model:**

$$y = \beta_0 + \beta_1 x + \varepsilon \tag{14.5}$$

where β_0 = y-intercept
β_1 = Slope of the line
ε = Error

In Equation 14.5, ε (the Greek letter epsilon) represents the error involved when an independent variable is used to predict the dependent variable. This error term accounts for independent variables that affect y but are not included in the model. It also accounts for chance, or random, variability. Thus, ε encompasses two kinds of error: model error (which means that all relevant independent variables aren't included) and chance or random error.

> A **functional model** hypothesizes an exact relationship between variables. A **statistical model** hypothesizes a functional relationship plus some random error.

The probability distribution of ε determines how well the regression model describes the relationship between the independent and dependent variables. Four key assumptions about the general form of the probability distribution of ε underlie the regression analysis procedures discussed in this chapter:

1. The probability distribution of ε is normal.
2. The variance of the probability distribution of ε is constant for all values of x.
3. The mean of the probability distribution of ε is 0. This assumption implies that the mean value of y for a given value of x is $E(y) = \beta_0 + \beta_1 x$.
4. The values of ε are independent of each other. This assumption implies that a random sample of objects has been selected from the population for measurement.

Figure 14.4 shows distributions of errors for three specific values of x. Note that the relative frequency distributions of the errors are normal, with a mean of 0 and a constant variance. The straight line in Figure 14.4 shows the means. It indicates the mean value $E(y)$ for a given value of x and is given by the equation $E(y) = \beta_0 + \beta_1 x$.

TM

FIGURE 14.4 The Probability Distribution of ε

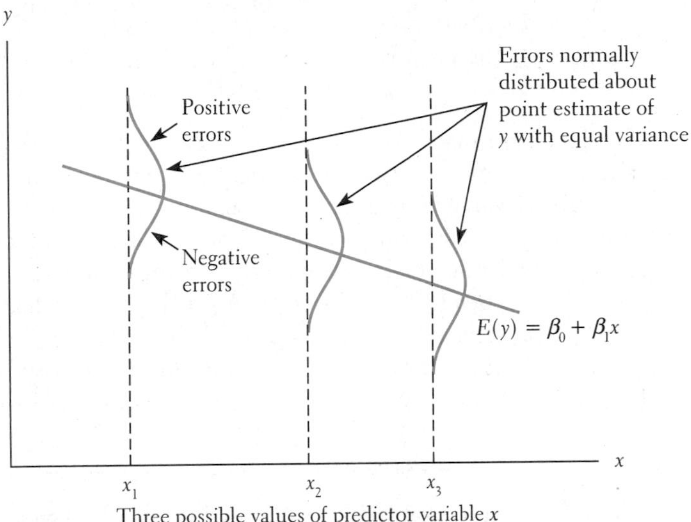

The four assumptions make it possible for analysts to develop measures of reliability for the least squares estimators. Chapter 15 discusses techniques for checking the validity of these assumptions along with remedies to be applied when they appear to be invalid.

EXAMPLE 14.6 Suppose a bookstore conducts a 12-week experiment to determine the effect of advertising on sales revenue. The relationship between sales revenue (y) and advertising expenditure (x) is expressed as a statistical model:

$$\begin{aligned} y &= \beta_0 + \beta_1(x) + \varepsilon \\ &= 0 + 20(x) + \varepsilon \end{aligned}$$

Note that the functional component ($20x$) of the model indicates that if \$10 is spent on advertising, sales revenue will equal \$200. However, the statistical model indicates that sales revenue isn't exactly related to advertising expenditure. That is, the random error component (ε) indicates that sales revenue may depend on variables other than advertising expenditure.

SAMPLE REGRESSION LINE

Sample Regression Line

Normally, the exact values of the regression parameters β_0, β_1, and ε are never actually known. From the sample data, estimates of these parameters are found, and the straight line that best fits the set of data points, called the **sample regression line,** is determined. Equation 14.6 uses b_0 and b_1 to estimate β_0 and β_1:

$$\hat{y} = b_0 + b_1x \tag{14.6}$$

where $\hat{y}$ = Predicted value of the dependent variable
x = Independent variable
b_0 = Estimate of the population y-intercept
b_1 = Estimate of the population line slope

The line determined by Equation 14.6 should pass through the data points so that the y value for a given value of x can be predicted. Note that $\hat{y}$, the predicted value of the dependent variable, is actually the mean y value for the given x value. Also note that for any specified x value in the sample, there are two corresponding y values: the actual, observed value of y corresponding to the observed x, and the predicted mean of y for this x. Therefore, (x,y) is a point on the scatter diagram, and $(x,\hat{y})$ is a point on the regression line $\hat{y} = b_0 + b_1x$. The difference $(y - \hat{y})$ measures the error involved in predicting the dependent variable, and is discussed in the next section. Note that the line will always pass through a point determined by the means, $(\bar{x},\bar{y})$.

> The **sample regression line** is a straight line that best fits a set of sample *x-y* data points.

The definition of the regression line isn't really adequate. The term *best fits* could be interpreted in different ways. Specifically, the method used to fit a straight line to the collected *x-y* data values needs to be defined.

Method of Least Squares

The method commonly used to determine the sample regression line for a collection of *x-y* pairs is called the **method of least squares.** This is a mathematical procedure to find the equation for the straight line that minimizes the sum of the squared distances between the line and the data points, as measured in the vertical (y) direction.

> The **method of least squares** determines the equation for the straight line that minimizes the sum of the squared vertical distances between the data points and the line.

The derivation of the equations needed to find the y-intercept and slope of a regression line using the method of least squares requires the use of calculus. This derivation is found in Appendix B; only the results are presented here. Equations 14.7 and 14.8 are used in regression analysis to find the slope and y-intercept of the sample regression line:

$$b_1 = \frac{n\Sigma xy - (\Sigma x)(\Sigma y)}{n\Sigma x^2 - (\Sigma x)^2} \tag{14.7}$$

where Σx = Sum of the x values
Σy = Sum of the y values
Σx^2 = Sum of the squared x values
$(\Sigma x)^2$ = Sum of the x values squared
Σxy = Sum of the product of x and y for each paired observation
n = Number of x-y observations

$$b_0 = \frac{\Sigma y}{n} - \frac{b_1 \Sigma x}{n} \tag{14.8}$$

where Σx = Sum of the x values
Σy = Sum of the y values
b_1 = Slope of the line computed using Equation 14.7
n = Number of x-y observations

It should be noted that Equation 14.8 is frequently written as $b_0 = \bar{y} - b_1\bar{x}$.

Equations 14.7 and 14.8 call for several familiar sums. If you've already calculated the correlation coefficient, these sums are available. Almost all data analysis computer packages calculate both the correlation coefficient and the regression equation. Many handheld calculators can calculate the slope and intercept of the regression equation along with the correlation coefficient. (Note that the term *regression coefficient* is synonymous with slope and will be used throughout the rest of the text.)

EXAMPLE 14.7 Amy Green, Green Garden Company president, wants to see if her company's weekly sales volume is related to some other variable. Her company sells garden supplies through its store in a city's suburbs. "1990 Buyers Guide" in *Organic Gardening* (March 1990) got her thinking about how to increase sales.

Amy randomly selects eight weeks from the past two years and records weekly sales volume in thousands of dollars. After reviewing the situation, she decides that the number of TV ads for the store run per week might be correlated with sales; so she also records this variable for each selected week. Table 14.3 presents the collected sample data along with the sums necessary for further calculations.

TABLE 14.3 Regression Analysis Calculations for Example 14.7

	y	x	xy	x^2	y^2
	125	3	375	9	15,625
	152	5	760	25	23,104
	131	4	524	16	17,161
	133	4	532	16	17,689
	142	5	710	25	20,164
	116	3	348	9	13,456
	127	3	381	9	16,129
	163	6	978	36	26,569
Sums:	1,089	33	4,608	145	149,897

$n = 8$
$\bar{y} = 1{,}089/8 = 136.125$
$\bar{x} = 33/8 = 4.125$

The sums in Table 14.3 are used in Equations 14.1, 14.2, 14.3, 14.7, and 14.8 to examine the correlation between x and y and to calculate the sample regression line. First, the correlation coefficient and t value are calculated:

$$r = \frac{8(4{,}608) - (33)(1{,}089)}{\sqrt{8(145) - (33)^2}\sqrt{8(149{,}897) - (1{,}089)^2}} = .956$$

There appears to be a strong positive correlation between x and y since $r = .956$. However, a sample of only eight data points has been examined. Can it be said that the correlation in the population differs from 0 based on such a small sample? To answer this question, a hypothesis test is conducted at the .01 significance level.

The standard error of r is

$$s_r = \sqrt{\frac{1 - (.956)^2}{8 - 2}} = .12$$

The t value is

$$t = \frac{r - \rho}{s_r} = \frac{.956 - 0}{.12} = 7.97$$

The critical t value from the t table for 6 ($n - 2 = 8 - 2 = 6$) degrees of freedom in the .01 column is 3.707. Since the calculated t value (7.97) exceeds this value, the null hypothesis of no population correlation is rejected at the .01 significance level.

Next, the sample regression line is calculated using the method of least squares:

$$b_1 = \frac{n\Sigma xy - (\Sigma x)(\Sigma y)}{n\Sigma x^2 - (\Sigma x)^2} = \frac{8(4{,}608) - (33)(1{,}089)}{8(145) - (33)^2} = 13.056$$

$$b_0 = \frac{\Sigma y}{n} - \frac{b_1\Sigma x}{n} = \frac{1{,}089}{8} - \frac{13.056\,(33)}{8} = 82.268$$

$$\hat{y} = 82.268 + 13.056x$$

Amy can now interpret the values in the sample regression equation. The y-intercept, 82.268, is the expected value of y if $x = 0$. Since Green Garden runs TV ads each week, this is a case where the interpretation of the y-intercept isn't useful. Most situations are like this, but there are some where useful information can be gained from knowing the expected y value if x is 0.

The interpretation of the slope of the regression line usually produces useful information. From the regression equation, Amy can see that for each increase of one unit in x, the y value is expected to increase by an average of 13.056. In practical terms, the regression equation suggests that for each additional TV ad run by Green Garden, an average of 13.056 additional sales dollars (in thousands) can be expected. This information may be useful to Amy Green in planning next year's advertising budget.

MINITAB can be used to run regression analysis problems. The MINITAB commands to solve Example 14.7 are:

```
MTB > READ C1-C2
DATA> 125 3
```

```
DATA> 152 5
DATA> 131 4
DATA> 133 4
DATA> 142 5
DATA> 116 3
DATA> 127 3
DATA> 163 6
DATA> END
      8 ROWS READ

MTB > NAME C1 'SALES' C2 'ADS'
MTB > CORR C1 C2

Correlation of SALES and ADS = 0.956

MTB > REGRESS C1 ON 1 PREDICTOR C2

The regression equation is
SALES = 82.3 + 13.1 ADS

Predictor        Coef       Stdev      t ratio          p
Constant       82.268       7.000        11.75      0.000
ADS            13.056       1.644         7.94      0.000

s = 4.899    R-sq = 91.3%    R-sq(adj) = 89.9%

Analysis of Variance

SOURCE          DF        SS          MS        F          P
Regression       1     1512.9      1512.9    63.05      0.000
Error            6      144.0        24.0
Total            7     1656.9

MTB > WRITE 'CH14EX8.DAT' C1-C2
MTB > STOP
```

Note that the READ command is used to input the data instead of the SET command. The READ command puts the sales variable into C1 and the TV ads variable into C2. The NAME command is used to name the columns. The CORR command provides the correlation coefficient for these two variables. The REGRESS command is used to develop a regression analysis with sales as the dependent (y) variable (C1) and TV ads as the independent (x) variable (C2). Finally, the WRITE command is used to store the contents of columns C1 and C2 in a file called CH14EX8.DAT.

EXERCISES

13. What is the difference between an independent variable and a dependent variable?
14. What is the difference between a functional model and a statistical model?
15. If $r = 0$, what is the slope for the regression equation?
16. Which of the following situations is inconsistent?

    16*b.* is inconsistent

    a. $\hat{y} = 500 + 0.01x$ and $r = .75$
    b. $\hat{y} = 200 + 0.8x$ and $r = -.80$
    c. $\hat{y} = -10 + 2x$ and $r = .50$
    d. $\hat{y} = -8 - 3x$ and $r = -.95$

17. (This question refers to Exercise 8.) Would it be appropriate for Donna to develop a regression equation to predict annual profits based on the amount she has requested for her department? If so, compute the regression equation.

    17. Yes $\hat{y} = 12.1656 + 3.3758x$

18. (This question refers to Exercise 10.) Would it be appropriate for Ralph to develop a regression equation to predict the number of absent days based on an employee's age? If so, compute the regression equation.

19. AT&T (American Telephone and Telegraph) earnings per share are estimated using GNP (gross national product). The regression equation is $\hat{y} = 0.058 + 0.05x$, where GNP is measured in billions of dollars.

    a. Interpret the slope.

    b. Interpret the y-intercept.

SSM

20. James Dobbins, Atlanta Transit Authority maintenance supervisor, must determine whether there's a positive relationship between a bus's annual maintenance cost and its age. If such a relationship exists, James feels that he can do a better job of predicting the annual bus maintenance budget. He collects the following data:

Bus	Maintenance cost (\$), y	Age (years), x
1	859	8
2	682	5
3	471	3
4	708	9
5	1,094	11
6	224	2
7	320	1
8	651	8
9	1,049	12

a. Plot a scatter diagram.

b. What kind of relationship exists between these two variables?

c. Compute the correlation coefficient.

d. Test the correlation coefficient at the .05 significance level.

e. Should James use regression analysis to predict the annual bus maintenance budget?

f. Determine the sample regression analysis equation.

g. Estimate the annual maintenance cost for a five-year-old bus.

20c. $r = .938$
d. Reject H_0 since $7.21 > 2.365$
f. $\hat{y} = 208.2033 + 70.9181x$
g. $\hat{y} = \$562.80$

21. Anna Sheehan (manager of the Spendwise supermarket chain) would like to be able to predict paperback book sales per week based on the amount of shelf display space (in feet) provided. Anna gathers a sample of 11 weeks:

Week	Number of books sold, y	Feet of shelf space, x
1	275	6.8
2	142	3.3
3	168	4.1
4	197	4.2
5	215	4.8
6	188	3.9
7	241	4.9
8	295	7.7

Week	Number of books sold, y	Feet of shelf space, x
9	125	3.1
10	266	5.9
11	200	5.0

a. Plot a scatter diagram.

b. What kind of relationship exists between these two variables?

c. Compute the correlation coefficient.

d. Test the correlation coefficient at the .10 significance level.

e. Should Anna use regression analysis to predict paperback book sales?

f. Determine the sample regression equation.

g. Estimate paperback book sales for a week in which four feet of shelf space are provided.

21*c.* $r = .95$
d. Reject H_0 since $9.13 > 1.833$
f. $\hat{y} = 32.5 + 36.4x$
g. 178.08

RESIDUALS

Residuals

The difference between an observed y and the mean of y predicted from the sample regression equation, $\hat{y}$, is called a **residual.** Equation 14.9 is used to compute a residual:

$$e = y - \hat{y} \tag{14.9}$$

where e = Residual
y = Actual value of y
$\hat{y}$ = Estimated value of the dependent variable using the sample regression equation

It should be emphasized that the residual is the vertical deviation of the observed y from the sample regression line, which is known. The residual is different from the model error term, ε, which is the vertical deviation of y from the *unknown* population regression line and, hence, is unknown.

> A **residual** is the difference between an actual y and the value, $\hat{y}$, predicted using the sample regression equation.

EXAMPLE 14.8 Figure 14.5 presents a scatter diagram for the data used in this example (introduced in Example 14.7). The regression equation that best fits these data points is

$$\hat{y} = 82.268 + 13.056x$$

The first two columns in Table 14.4 show the original x-y data points. The $\hat{y}$ value predicted using the x value for each data pair and the regression equation are shown

FIGURE 14.5 Residuals for Example 14.8

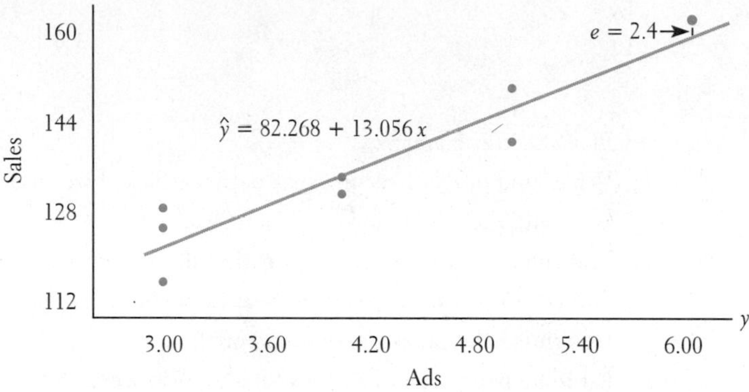

TABLE 14.4 Standard Error of Estimate Calculation for Example 14.9

y	x	$\hat{y}$	$(y - \hat{y})$	$(y - \hat{y})^2$
125	3	121.4	3.6	12.96
152	5	147.6	4.4	19.36
131	4	134.5	−3.5	12.25
133	4	134.5	−1.5	2.25
142	5	147.6	−5.6	31.36
116	3	121.4	−5.4	29.16
127	3	121.4	5.6	31.36
163	6	160.6	2.4	5.30
				Sum: 144.0

$$\hat{y} = 82.268 + 13.056x$$

$$s_{y \cdot x} = \sqrt{\frac{\Sigma(y - \hat{y})^2}{n - 2}} = \sqrt{\frac{144.0}{6}} = 4.9$$

in column 3. For example, the last $\hat{y}$ value is calculated from the regression equation using the sample x value 6:

$$\hat{y} = 82.268 + 13.056(6) = 160.604$$

The residual for each pair of observations is in Table 14.4's fourth column. The residual for the last pair of observations (163,6) is

$$\begin{aligned} e &= y - \hat{y} \\ &= 163.0 - 160.6 = 2.4 \text{ (see Figure 14.5)} \end{aligned}$$

STANDARD ERROR OF ESTIMATE

Standard Error of Estimate

The standard deviation of a simple data collection is used to measure the variability, or scatter of data values, about their mean. The **standard error of estimate** is used to measure the variability, or scatter, of the observed sample y values around the sample regression line. It measures the standard or typical difference between the values predicted by the regression equation and the actual y values. This can be seen by the formula for the standard error of estimate:

$$s_{y \cdot x} = \sqrt{\frac{\Sigma(y - \hat{y})^2}{n - 2}} \tag{14.10}$$

where $s_{y \cdot x}$ = Standard error of estimate
y = Sample y values
$\hat{y}$ = Values of y calculated from the regression equation
n = Sample size

> The **standard error of estimate** is a measure of the variability, or scatter, of the observed sample y values around the regression line.

The $\hat{y}$ values are calculated by substituting the x value of each data pair into the regression equation. The differences between these regression equation estimates and the actual y values (i.e., the residuals) are squared, added, and divided by the degrees of freedom $(n - 2)$. The square root of this value is the standard error of estimate. The value $(n - 2)$ represents the number of degrees of freedom around the fitted regression line. Two degrees of freedom are lost because b_0 and b_1 are used as estimates of β_0 and β_1 in the sample regression equation.

EXAMPLE 14.9 The data used in this example were introduced in Example 14.7. The fourth column of Table 14.4 shows the residuals for each pair of observations. The last column shows the sum of squared residuals (sum of squares error) between the $\hat{y}$ values calculated from the regression equation and the actual y values. Incidentally, this is the value that is minimized by the least squares procedure. If any y-intercept and slope values other than 82.268 and 13.056 were used, the resulting sum of squared residuals would be larger than 144.

When the sum of squared residuals (sum of squares error) is divided by the degrees of freedom and the square root taken, the result is the standard error of estimate. As Table 14.4 shows, for this example the standard error is 4.9. It can be said that the typical or standard difference between the sample y values and their regression line estimates is 4.9 (in thousands of dollars).

EXAMPLE 14.10 According to an article by Adel Novin (1992) in *Management Accounting*, regression analysis is one of the few quantitative techniques available for determining and analyzing the extent of the relationship between overhead costs and various cost drivers.[3] Adel collected data from 12 consecutive months on overhead

[3]A. M. Novin, "Applying Overhead: How to Find the Right Bases and Rates," *Management Accounting*, March 1992, pp. 40–43.

costs and machine hours. He used a Lotus 1-2-3 worksheet to develop a regression equation that used machine hours to estimate monthly overhead costs.

$$\hat{y} = 72{,}794 + 74.72x$$
$$s_{y \cdot x} = 9{,}799$$
$$n = 12$$
$$r = .877$$

The y-intercept ($72,794) is an estimate of total monthly fixed overhead costs. The slope of the regression equation ($74.72) is the rate for the application of variable overhead costs (i.e., $74.72 per machine hour). For each additional machine hour (x), monthly overhead costs (y) can be expected to increase by an average of $74.72.

Adel plans to use the regression equation to forecast monthly overhead costs using machine hours. First, however, he notes the size of the standard error of estimate: $9,799. He interprets this to mean since the sample y values (overhead costs) typically differ from this regression estimate by this amount, he can expect his future forecast values of y to have a similar error. The size of this standard error of estimate troubles him since accurate overhead cost forecasts are needed.

Prediction and Confidence Intervals

The sample regression equation is frequently used to make forecasts for y. If a given value of x is substituted in the regression equation, the expected value of y can be found. This y value is similar to the point estimate of the mean discussed in Chapter 8. That is, a single numerical estimate of y is produced without any indication of its accuracy.

A point estimate provides no sense of how far off it may be from the population parameter. To determine that information, a prediction or confidence interval is developed. In fact, analysts can choose between two types of intervals: the **prediction interval** (for a particular value of y) or the **confidence interval** estimate (for the expected value of y). Prediction intervals are used to predict a particular y value for a given value of x. Confidence intervals are used to estimate the mean value of y for a specific value of x.

Prediction Interval

Confidence Interval

Whenever we want to predict one particular value of the dependent variable, given a specific value of the independent variable, we calculate a prediction interval:

$$\hat{y} \pm t\, s_{\hat{y} \cdot x} \tag{14.11}$$

where $\hat{y}$ = Sample regression estimate of y
t = Value from t distribution based on $n - 2$ degrees of freedom for a given prediction level
$s_{\hat{y} \cdot x}$ = Estimated standard error of the prediction

The estimated standard error of the prediction $s_{\hat{y} \cdot x}$ is an estimate of the standard deviation of the sampling distribution for the estimator y:

$$s_{\hat{y} \cdot x} = s_{y \cdot x} \sqrt{1 + \frac{1}{n} + \frac{(x_p - \bar{x})^2}{\Sigma(x_i - \bar{x})^2}} \tag{14.12}$$

where $s_{\hat{y}\cdot x}$ = Estimated standard error of the prediction
$s_{y\cdot x}$ = Standard error of estimate
x_p = The given value of x
$\bar{x}$ = The mean of x
$\Sigma(x_i - \bar{x})^2$ = The sum of squares total for the x variable

The sum of squares total for the x variable is computed using

$$\Sigma(x_i - \bar{x})^2 = \Sigma x_i^2 - \frac{(\Sigma x_i)^2}{n}$$

The standard error of estimate ($s_{y\cdot x}$) in Equation 14.12 measures the dispersion of sample data points around the sample regression line. The two terms after the 1 under the square-root sign [$1/n$ and $(x_p - \bar{x})^2/\Sigma(x_i - \bar{x})^2$] measure the dispersion of many sample regression lines around the true population regression line. Example 14.11 illustrates the use of a prediction interval.

EXAMPLE 14.11 Amy Green, Green Garden Company president, wants to estimate sales for next week if she were to run six TV ads. Using the data and the regression equation computed in Example 14.7, she develops a point estimate for next week's sales: $\hat{y} = 82.268 + 13.056(6) = 160.604$. But Amy isn't satisfied with her prediction. She doesn't know anything about this estimate's accuracy so she uses Equations 14.11 and 14.12 to develop a 95% prediction interval to predict next week's sales if six TV ads are run.

The standard error of the prediction is

$$\begin{aligned} s_{\hat{y}\cdot x} &= s_{y\cdot x}\sqrt{1 + \frac{1}{n} + \frac{(x_p - \bar{x})^2}{\Sigma(x_i - \bar{x})^2}} \\ &= (4.9)\sqrt{1 + \frac{1}{8} + \frac{(6 - 4.125)^2}{8.875}} \\ &= (4.9)\sqrt{1 + .125 + .396} \\ &= (4.9)\,(1.233) \\ &= 6.042 \end{aligned}$$

The computation for the sum of squares total for the x variable is

$$\Sigma(x_i - \bar{x})^2 = \Sigma x_i^2 - \frac{(\Sigma x_i)^2}{n} = 145 - \frac{33^2}{8} = 8.875$$

The prediction interval is

$$\hat{y} \pm t\, s_{\hat{y}\cdot x}$$
$$160.604 \pm 2.447\,(6.042)$$
$$160.604 \pm 14.788$$
$$145.816 \text{ to } 175.392$$

Amy predicts with 95% confidence that weekly sales next week will fall in the interval \$145,816 to \$175,392 if six TV ads are run.

Instead of trying to predict the outcome of a single experiment at the given x value, an analyst may want to attempt to estimate the mean result of a very large number of experiments at the given x value. The same value is used to predict the y value for a given x value. Equation 14.13 is used to develop a confidence interval:

$$\hat{y} \pm t\, s_{\hat{\mu}\cdot x} \tag{14.13}$$

For the confidence interval, the estimated standard error of estimate, $s_{\hat{\mu}\cdot x}$, is used as the estimate of the standard deviation of the sampling distribution for the estimator y. Amy computes the standard deviation of estimate as

$$s_{\hat{\mu}\cdot x} = s_{y\cdot x}\sqrt{\frac{1}{n} + \frac{(x_p - \bar{x})^2}{\Sigma(x_i - \bar{x})^2}} \tag{14.14}$$

Unlike Equation 14.12, Equation 14.14 doesn't include the 1 under the square root sign. As a result, it produces an interval that's narrower than the prediction interval. This is reasonable, given that predicting a single value is more difficult than estimating the average of a population of values. Figure 14.6 illustrates the difference between prediction intervals and confidence intervals.

Example 14.12 shows the use of a confidence interval.

FIGURE 14.6 Prediction Intervals for Individual Values and Confidence Intervals for Mean Values

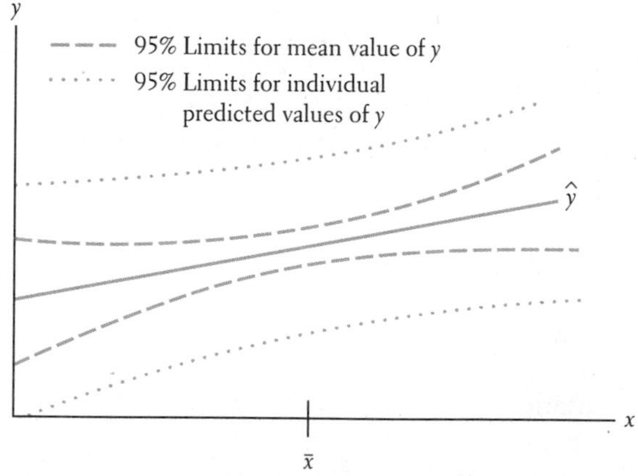

Prediction intervals are used to predict a particular y value for a given value of x. **Confidence intervals** are used to estimate the mean value of y for a specific value of x.

EXAMPLE 14.12 This example is a continuation of Example 14.12. Amy Green decides that it might be more informative to develop a 95% confidence interval for mean weekly sales when six TV ads are run.

The estimated standard error of estimate is

$$\begin{aligned} s_{\hat{\mu}\cdot x} &= s_{y\cdot x}\sqrt{\frac{1}{n} + \frac{(x_p - \bar{x})^2}{\Sigma(x_i - \bar{x})^2}} \\ &= (4.9)\sqrt{\frac{1}{8} + \frac{(6 - 4.125)^2}{8.875}} \\ &= (4.9)\sqrt{.125 + .396} \\ &= (4.9)\ (0.722) \\ &= 3.538 \end{aligned}$$

The confidence interval is

$$\begin{gathered} \hat{y} \pm t\, s_{\hat{\mu}\cdot x} \\ 160.604 \pm 2.447\ (3.538) \\ 160.604 \pm 8.654 \\ 151.950 \text{ to } 169.258 \end{gathered}$$

Amy is 95% confident that the interval from \$151,950 to \$169,258 contains the mean sales revenue for a week when six TV ads are run. One reason why the intervals are so large is the small number of data points used to fit the least squares line. The width of the prediction interval could be reduced by using a larger number of data points.

Note that the prediction interval for an individual value of y will always be wider than the confidence interval for a mean value of y. The error in estimating the mean value of y, for a given value of x, is the distance between the least squares line and the true line of means. In contrast, the error in predicting some future value of y is the sum of two errors: the error of estimating the mean value of y plus the random error that's a component of the value of y to be predicted. Note that in Equations 14.12 and 14.14, both the error of prediction and error of estimation take their smallest values when $x_p = \bar{x}$. The further x_p lies from $\bar{x}$, the larger will be the errors of prediction and estimation. This concept is seen in Figure 14.6, which shows prediction intervals for individual values and confidence intervals for mean values.

Also note that the standard normal z value can be used in place of t in Equations 14.11 and 14.13 for sample sizes of 30 or more.

The MINITAB commands to solve Examples 14.8, 14.9, 14.11, and 14.12 are shown in the MINITAB Computer package section. Note that the data were stored in a file called CH14EX8.DAT at the end of Example 14.7.

EXERCISES

22. What does a residual measure?

23. What is the difference between a residual and the model error term?

24. What does the standard error of estimate measure?

25. If two variables have a correlation coefficient (r) of 1, what is the standard error of estimate ($s_{y \cdot x}$)?

26. Can the standard error of estimate ($s_{y \cdot x}$) ever exceed the standard deviation of the dependent variable (s_y)? Can the standard error of estimate ($s_{y \cdot x}$) ever equal the standard deviation of the dependent variable (s_y)? Explain your answers.

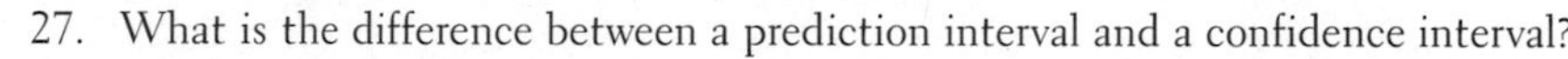

27. What is the difference between a prediction interval and a confidence interval?

28. $s_{y \cdot x} = 111.61$

28. This question refers to Exercise 20. Compute the residual for each bus. Compute the standard error of the estimate. Interpret $s_{y \cdot x}$ in terms of the variables used in this exercise.

29. PI: 627.6 to 1,207.2.
 CI: 797.8 to 1,036.9.

29. This question refers to Exercise 20. Develop both a 95% prediction interval and a 95% confidence interval for a 10-year-old bus.

30. Mario Padilla (an accountant for Palmer Furniture Corporation) must determine whether overhead can be estimated based on the number of chairs produced. Mario collects the following monthly data on overhead expenses and chairs produced at seven different plants:

Plant	Overhead expenses y	Number of chairs x
1	\$576	112
2	497	122
3	789	147
4	862	173
5	361	94
6	688	151
7	532	109

30*b*. $\hat{y} = -147.4 + 5.88x$
c. \$5.88
d. 65.118
e. 64.772
g. 734.2
h. 549.5 to 919.0
i. 654.3 to 814.2

a. Plot the data on a scatter diagram.

b. Determine the sample regression equation.

c. When an extra chair is produced, what is the average increase in overhead expense?

d. Compute the residual for plant 1.

e. Compute the standard error of estimate.

f. Interpret $s_{y \cdot x}$ in terms of the variables used in this exercise.

g. Compute a point estimate of the overhead expense if 150 chairs are produced.

h. Compute a 95% prediction interval for your prediction for part *g*.

i. Compute a 95% confidence interval for your prediction for part *g*.

j. What should Mario conclude?

31. Anna Sheehan, manager of the Spendwise supermarket chain, would like to determine whether a relationship exists between the time it takes to check out a customer and the amount the person purchases. Anna wants to study current purchase amounts before trying such new techniques in future advertising. She collects data for a sample of 12 customers:

Customer	Checkout time (minutes) y	Purchases (rounded to nearest dollar) x
1	3.1	$ 35
2	1.1	14
3	.4	4
4	6.4	78
5	5.8	81
6	8.4	106
7	4.9	61
8	7.9	66
9	2.1	22
10	5.9	54
11	.8	12
12	1.3	19

a. Plot the data on a scatter diagram.

b. Determine the sample regression equation.

c. Compute the residual for customer 12.

d. Compute the standard error of estimate.

e. Interpret $s_{y \cdot x}$ in terms of the variables used in this exercise.

f. Compute a point estimate of the checkout time for a $75 purchase.

g. Compute a 90% prediction interval for your prediction for part *f.*

h. Compute a 90% confidence interval for your prediction for part *f.*

i. What should Anna conclude?

31*b.* $\hat{y} = .1774 + .0833x$
c. $-.46$
d. .9338
f. 6.423
g. 5.607 to 7.240
h. 4.596 to 8.250

COEFFICIENT OF SIMPLE DETERMINATION

Coefficient of Determination

A statistic consulted frequently in regression analysis is the **coefficient of simple determination** (r^2). It is useful because it measures the percentage of the variability in the dependent variable, y, that can be explained by the predictor variable, x.

> The **coefficient of simple determination,** r^2, measures the percentage of the variability in y that can be explained by the predictor variable, x.

It is not a coincidence that the same symbol is used for the coefficient of simple determination (r^2) and the correlation coefficient (r). In fact, the correlation coefficient squared equals the coefficient of simple determination. If the correlation coefficient between two variables is .80, for example, then $r^2 = .64$ or 64% ($.80^2 = .64$).

To calculate r^2, simply square the correlation coefficient, r. However, to understand why r^2 measures the percentage of the variability in y explained by x, we must understand the formula defining r^2. First, a few terms need to be explained.

Sum of Squares Total

The amount of total deviation in the dependent variable is called the *sum of squares total* (SST). This value measures the variability of y *without* taking into consideration the predictor variable, x. The SST is the sum of the squared differences between the sample y values and their mean, as shown by Equation 14.15. If this sum is divided by the appropriate number of degrees of freedom $(n - 1)$, the variance of y results. If the square root of this variance is computed, the standard deviation of y results. These computations are defined by the equations for the standard deviation of a single variable in Chapter 4.

$$\text{SST} = \sum_{i=1}^{n} (y_i - \bar{y})^2 \qquad (14.15)$$

where SST = Sum of squares total
y_i = ith value of the dependent variable
$\bar{y}$ = Mean of the dependent variable

EXAMPLE 14.13 The data used in this example were introduced in Example 14.7. The sum of squares total (SST) is computed in Table 14.5, where the mean of y, 136.125, is subtracted from each y value, and the difference is squared. These squared differences are then summed. The sum of squares total (SST) is 1,656.877. Therefore, the standard deviation of the y variable (s_y) is

$$s_y = \sqrt{\frac{\Sigma(y - \bar{y})^2}{n - 1}} = \sqrt{\frac{1{,}656.877}{8 - 1}} = 15.4$$

TABLE 14.5 Sum of Squares Total Calculation for Example 14.14

y	$\bar{y}$	$(y - \bar{y})$	$(y - \bar{y})^2$
125	136.125	−11.125	123.765
152	136.125	15.875	252.016
131	136.125	−5.125	26.266
133	136.125	−3.125	9.766
142	136.125	5.875	34.516
116	136.125	−20.125	405.016
127	136.125	−9.125	83.266
163	136.125	26.875	722.266
	Sums:	0.000	1,656.877

Figure 14.7*a* plots the data in Table 14.4 on a scatter diagram. Figure 14.7*b* shows the case where x contributes no information and the mean of y is used to predict y $(\bar{y} = \hat{y})$. Figure 14.7*c* shows the case where knowledge of x is used to predict y using the regression equation $\hat{y} = b_0 + b_1x$.

Sum of Squares Error

The least squares regression line minimizes the *sum of squares error* (SSE). The SSE measures the variability of the sample y values around $\hat{y}$. It represents the amount of deviation in the dependent variable that is *not* explained by the regression equation. If

FIGURE 14.7 Measuring the Sum of Squares Error for Two Cases

a. Scatter diagram of data presented in Table 14.4

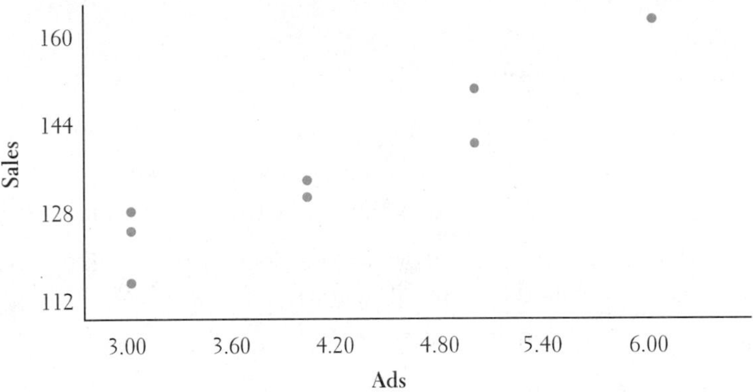

b. Case when x contributes no information for predicting y, $\bar{y} = \hat{y}$.

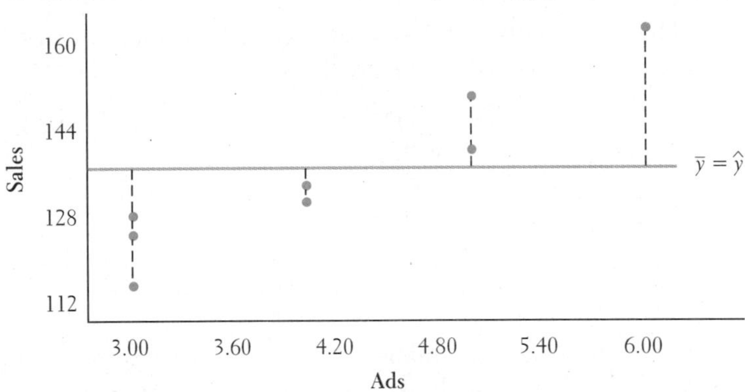

c. Case when knowledge of x contributes to predicting y, $\hat{y} = b_0 + b_1x$.

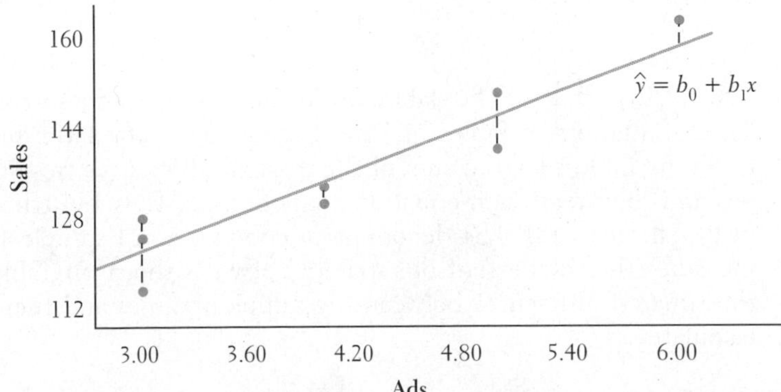

this sum is divided by the appropriate number of degrees of freedom $(n - 2)$, the unexplained variance of y results. The square root of this unexplained variance is the standard error of estimate:

$$SSE = \sum_{i=1}^{n} (y_i - \hat{y})^2 \qquad (14.16)$$

where SSE = Sum of squares error
y_i = ith value of the dependent variable
$\hat{y}$ = Estimated y value for each given x value

The amount of deviation in the dependent variable explained by the regression equation is called the *sum of squares regression* (SSR).

$$SSR = SST - SSE \qquad (14.17)$$

where SSR = Sum of squares regression
SST = Sum of squares total
SSE = Sum of squares error

The equation for r^2, the percentage of the variability in the dependent variable, y, that can be explained by the predictor variable, x, can now be defined.

$$r^2 = 1 - \frac{\Sigma(y - \hat{y})^2}{\Sigma(y - \bar{y})^2} \qquad (14.18)$$

or

$$r^2 = 1 - \frac{SSE}{SST}$$

The ratio following the minus sign represents the percentage of the variability of y that is still unexplained by the regression equation. Since this ratio is the percentage that is *unexplained* by x and the regression equation, 1 minus this value is the percentage that is *explained*. The coefficient of simple determination, r^2, thus measures the percentage of variability in y that is explained when x is used to predict y.

EXAMPLE 14.14 The data used in this example were introduced in Example 14.7. The summations in Tables 14.4 and 14.5 can be inserted in Equation 14.18 to calculate r^2. From Table 14.4, the sum of the squared differences (residuals) between the y values and their regression equation predictions, SSE, is 144 (the numerator of the ratio in Equation 14.18). The denominator computed in Example 14.14, SST = 1,656.88, measures the total extent of variability of y. As shown in Table 14.5, it is the sum of the squared differences between the sample y values and their own mean. Amy then calculates r^2:

$$r^2 = 1 - \frac{SSE}{SST} = 1 - \frac{144}{1{,}656.88} = 1 - .09 = .91$$

When y is predicted using only knowledge of its mean (Figure 14.7*b*), the total sum of squares or unexplained deviation is 1,656.88. When y is predicted using knowledge of the linear relationship between x and y ($r = .956$) (Figure 14.7*c*), the sum of squares error or unexplained deviation is reduced to 144. If the ratio of these two values is expressed as a percentage, we can say that only 9% (144/1,656.88) of the variability of y remains unexplained after information on the linear relationship between x and y has been introduced. Therefore, the other 91% ($1 - .09 = .91$) is explained by knowledge of the linear relationship between x and y ($r = .956$). These calculations illustrate the previous definition of r^2.

Since r^2 is the correlation coefficient squared, that is, a number between -1 and $+1$ squared, it must be a number between 0 and $+1$. This is true for all percentages expressed in decimal form and is why r^2 is interpreted as the *percentage* of the variability of y that is explained by x; r^2 is one of the most frequently consulted statistics in regression analysis because it so briefly and accurately reflects the ability of the chosen predictor variable, x, to explain the variability of y.

Figure 14.8 illustrates the coefficient of simple determination, r^2. This figure shows a particular x value along with the average value of y ($\bar{y}$), the regression prediction value for y ($\hat{y}$), and the actual value of y (y). Without knowledge of x, we predict an unknown y value to equal the mean of y. That is, $\bar{y}$ is the best estimate of any unknown value of y. However, if a linear relationship between x and y has been specified, the sample regression equation can be used to predict y. Thus, for any specific value of x, we use $\hat{y}$ rather than $\bar{y}$. Knowledge of the linear relationship between x and y generally produces more accurate predictions of y.

Figure 14.8 also shows how the deviation is explained for a specific x, y data point that lies above the mean. If the linear relationship between x and y is unknown, the mean of y is used to predict y. The total deviation to be explained is the difference

TM

FIGURE 14.8 Explained and Unexplained Variation of y

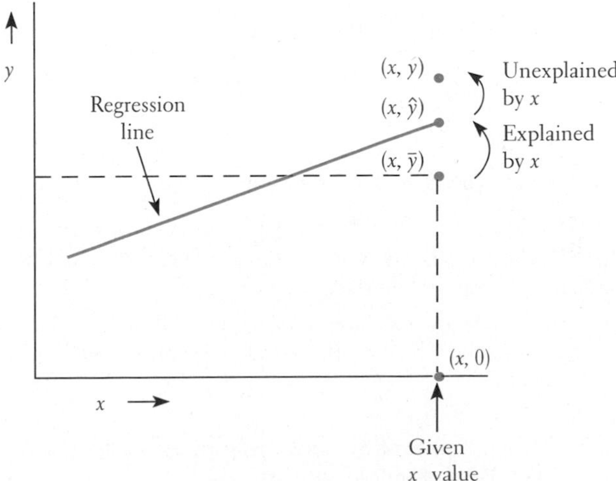

between the actual value of y and its mean $(y - \bar{y})$. Some of this difference is explained by the fact that x is a fairly large value. Since the regression line has a positive slope, a large value of x is associated with a large value of y. The difference, $\hat{y} - \bar{y}$ is explained by the linear relationship between the given x value and y $(r = .956)$.

However, y isn't equal to $\hat{y}$; it lies above this value. The distance $y - \hat{y}$ is *not* explained by the linear relationship between x and y. If it were, the x-y value would lie on the regression equation line. This difference is explained by independent variables that affect y, but aren't included in the model, and also by chance, or random, variability, which can't be explained. Of course, the analyst isn't interested in a single data point, but in all the sample data. Equation 14.16 sums the differences for all the data points.

EXAMPLE 14.15 Consider the last data point listed, $(x = 6, y = 163)$. If the linear relationship between x and y was not known, the best estimate of y would be its mean (136.1). The distance between the actual value of y and its mean is

$$(y - \bar{y}) = (163.0 - 136.1) = 26.9$$

In Example 14.7, a high positive linear relationship $(r = .956)$ was found between the number of television ads run per week (x) and weekly sales (y). This correlation implies that if a large number of ads are run next week, sales will be higher than the weekly average $(\bar{y} = 136.1)$.

Table 14.4 used the sample regression line to estimate y for each week based on knowledge of the number of TV ads run that week. Six ads were run during the last week, so sales were predicted to be \$160,604 (see Example 14.9). The high positive linear relationship between x and y has allowed the analyst to explain a large amount of the variation in the prediction of y (i.e., it has reduced the unexplained deviation from 26.9 to 2.4):

$$(y - \hat{y}) = 163.0 - 160.6 = 2.4$$

The r^2 value of .914 $(.956^2)$ indicates that 91.4% of the variance in the weekly sales variable can be explained by the strong linear relationship with the number of TV ads run during the week.

EXERCISES

32. What does the coefficient of simple determination measure?
33. Why is it useful to know both r and r^2?
34. What correlation between x and y is required for the assertion that 85% of the variance of y can be explained by knowledge of x?

34. $r = .92$

35. Mary Union owns a gas station in Cleveland, Ohio. Mary has developed the following regression equation based on the weekly sales of unleaded gas:

$$\hat{y} = 100 - 5x, \qquad n = 64$$

where $\hat{y}$ = Estimate of volume of unleaded gas sold (thousands of gallons)
x = Price of unleaded gas

a. Interpret the regression coefficient.

35*b.* 95.25

b. Compute a point estimate of the weekly sales volume of unleaded gas if the price is 95 cents.

36. Ed Bogdanski, owner of the American Precast Company, has hired you as a part-time analyst. Ed was extremely pleased when you uncovered a positive relationship between the number of building permits issued and the amount of work available to his company. Now he wonders if it's possible to use knowledge of interest rates on first mortgages to predict the number of building permits that will be issued each month. You collect a random sample of data covering nine months:

Month	Building permits, y	Interest rate, x
1	786	10.2%
2	494	12.6
3	289	13.5
4	892	9.7
5	343	10.8
6	888	9.5
7	509	10.9
8	987	9.2
9	187	14.2

36*b.* $r = -.8907$
c. Reject H_0 since $5.1842 > 2.365$
d. $\hat{y} = 2{,}217.4 - 144.95x$
e. 144.95
f. $r^2 = .7934$

a. Plot the data on a scatter diagram.

b. Compute the correlation coefficient.

c. Test the correlation coefficient at the .05 significance level.

d. Determine the sample regression equation.

e. When the interest rate increases by 1%, what is the average decrease in the number of building permits issued?

f. Compute the coefficient of simple determination.

g. Write a sentence to Ed, in simple language, interpreting the r^2 value computed in part *f.*

h. Write Ed a memo explaining the results of your analysis.

37. Ginny Peters has the following data on a mail order business for 10 cities:

City	Number of mail orders received (thousands), y	Number of catalogs distributed (thousands), x
1	23	7
2	17	3
3	23	5
4	14	2
5	31	10
6	24	8
7	37	14
8	19	4
9	15	1
10	33	12

37*b.* $r = .9846$
c. Reject H_0 since $15.94 > 2.306$
d. $\hat{y} = 11.95 + 1.77x$
e. Up by 1,770
f. $r^2 = .9695$

a. Plot the data on a scatter diagram.
b. Compute the correlation coefficient.
c. Test the correlation coefficient at the .05 significance level.
d. Determine the sample regression equation.
e. When the number of catalogs issued increases by one, what is the effect on the number of mail orders received?
f. Compute the coefficient of simple determination.
g. Write a sentence that Ginny can understand interpreting the r^2 value computed in part *f.*
h. Write Ginny a memo explaining the results of your analysis.

Hypothesis Testing in Regression Analysis

Hypothesis Test for Slope

Another key statistic is the *t* value, which is used to test the null hypothesis that the slope of the regression equation in the population is 0. If a regression equation has 0 slope, a change in *x* doesn't affect *y*. In other words, *x* and *y* have no correlation in the population. The symbol for the slope in the population regression equation is β_1. The null hypothesis and two-tailed alternative hypothesis for testing the slope are

$$H_0: \beta_1 = 0$$
$$H_1: \beta_1 \neq 0$$

A two-tailed alternative is used when the goal is to determine whether the slope of the regression equation in the population is not 0. A one-tailed alternative is used when testing to determine whether the slope is positive (H_1: $\beta_1 > 0$) or negative (H_1: $\beta_1 < 0$).

As with the correlation coefficient hypothesis test, we can show that if the null hypothesis (the population slope is 0) is true, then the appropriate sampling distribution for this test is the *t* distribution with $(n - 2)$ degrees of freedom. Two degrees of freedom are lost because two population parameters (β_0 and β_1) are estimated using sample statistics (b_0 and b_1). The value for the estimated standard error of b_1 (s_b) is computed using Equation 14.19:

$$s_b = \frac{s_{y \cdot x}}{\sqrt{\Sigma(x - \bar{x})^2}} \tag{14.19}$$

where s_b = Standard error of the regression coefficient
$s_{y \cdot x}$ = Standard error of estimate
$\Sigma(x - \bar{x})^2$ = Sum of the squared differences between each observed *x* and the mean of *x*

Equation 14.20 shows the appropriate test statistic:

$$t = \frac{b_1 - \beta_1}{s_b} \tag{14.20}$$

where b_1 = Sample regression coefficient
β_1 = Hypothesized population regression coefficient
s_b = Standard error of the regression coefficient

EXAMPLE 14.16 The data in Table 14.4 are used to calculate the t statistic to test the null hypothesis that $\beta_1 = 0$. The null and two-tailed alternative hypotheses for testing the slope are

$$H_0: \beta_1 = 0$$
$$H_1: \beta_1 \neq 0$$

There are 6 degrees of freedom associated with this test: $(n - 2) = (8 - 2) = 6$. The .01 significance level is chosen. The t table in Appendix E.7 is used to find the critical t value. In the 6 row and the .01 column is the value 3.707. Since this is a two-tailed test, 3.707 and -3.707 are the critical values. The decision rule is

> If the sample t statistic lies more than 3.707 standard errors below or above the assumed mean (0) of the sampling distribution, reject the null hypothesis (reject H_0 if $t < -3.707$ or $t > 3.707$).

Table 14.4 shows the $s_{y \cdot x}$ computation (4.9). This is one of the values needed to calculate the standard error of the regression coefficient using Equation 14.19. We also need the sum of the squared differences between x and its mean. This sum is calculated in Example 14.11: 8.875.

The values necessary to calculate the t statistic using Equation 14.20 are now available. Computation of the standard error of b using Equation 14.19 produces

$$s_b = \frac{s_{y \cdot x}}{\sqrt{\Sigma(x - \bar{x})^2}} = \frac{4.9}{\sqrt{8.875}} = 1.645$$

The sample regression line slope of 13.056 from Example 14.7 is used in Equation 14.20 to compute the test statistic:

$$t = \frac{b_1 - \beta_1}{s_b} = \frac{13.056 - 0}{1.645} = 7.94$$

The computed t (7.94) is larger than the critical t (3.707). Therefore, the null hypothesis is rejected. We conclude that the population regression line does *not* have a slope of 0. There is some linear relationship between x and y in the population.

Incidentally, the hypothesis test just discussed is the same as the test of the hypothesis that the population correlation coefficient is 0. That is, the following two null hypotheses describe the same situation:

$$H_0: \rho = 0 \qquad\qquad H_0: \beta_1 = 0$$

The first hypothesis states that there's no correlation between x and y. The second states that if a regression line is fitted to the population data, this line will be horizontal; that is, it will have a slope of 0. If one of these hypotheses is true, the other is also.

In fact, if these two null hypotheses are tested separately, the same t statistic and test conclusion will result. The reason for learning both tests is that each has its own real-world applications. You can conduct a hypothesis test for the correlation coefficient of Example 14.7 and confirm that the test statistic is also approximately 7.94.

F *Test*

Another key statistic in regression analysis, the F statistic, is used to test the null hypothesis that the sample regression equation does not explain a significant percentage of the y variable's variance. The null and alternative hypotheses are

$$H_0: \rho^2 = 0$$
$$H_1: \rho^2 > 0$$

At first glance, it appears that this null hypothesis and the null hypothesis tested by the t statistic are the same: they both claim that the sample results can't be assumed to hold for the population. These two null hypotheses are indeed similar for a simple regression analysis, but for multiple regression, to be discussed in the next chapter, they serve two different purposes. For this reason, both approaches are presented.

The test statistic for the null hypothesis just stated is drawn from the theoretical F distribution if the null hypothesis is true. This is a one-tailed test since ρ^2 can only be 0 or greater. A large F statistic will result in rejection of the null hypothesis; a small statistic won't. The F statistic is calculated by most regression computer programs and found in the "analysis of variance for the regression" section of the computer output.

Table 14.6 shows a typical ANOVA table for the regression. First, the portion concerning degrees of freedom is explained. You've already learned that the total degrees of freedom equal $n - 1$: one degree of freedom is lost when the mean of y is used to predict y. You've also learned that when a sample regression equation is used to predict y, the degrees of freedom equal $n - 2$ because β_0 and β_1 are estimated using b_0 and b_1 in the equation. This leaves one degree of freedom for the regression. Thus, in simple regression, the number of degrees of freedom for regression will always be 1.

TABLE 14.6 Analysis of Variance for the Regression

Source of variation	df	Sum of squares	Estimate of σ^2	F ratio
Regression	$k - 1$	SSR	SSR/$(k - 1)$	Eq. 14.21
Error or residual	$n - k$	SSE	SSE/$(n - k)$	
Total	$n - 1$	SST		

There are three sources of variation in regression analysis: the total variation, the explained variation (due to regression), and the unexplained variation (error or residual). Note in Table 14.6 that the sum of squares for the total variation is SST. The sum of squares for the unexplained variation is SSE. The estimate of the unexplained variance is computed by dividing this sum of squares by the appropriate degrees of freedom: SSE/$(n - k)$. The sum of squares for the explained variation is SSR. The estimate of the explained variance is also computed by dividing this sum of squares by the appropriate degrees of freedom: SSR/$(k - 1)$. The ratio of these two estimates, the estimate of the variance that is explained divided by the estimate of the variance that is unexplained, provides the F ratio:

$$F = \frac{\text{SSR}/(k - 1)}{\text{SSE}/(n - k)} \tag{14.21}$$

where SSR = Sum of squares regression
SSE = Sum of squares error
k = Number of linearly independent parameters to be estimated (the number of bs in the equation, unless the predictor variables are linearly dependent)
n = Sample size

Thus, the F test can be used to determine the existence of a linear relationship between x and y. In simple linear regression, this test is equivalent to the t test. In the next chapter, on multiple regression, the F test is used to determine whether a particular equation explains a significant percentage of the variance in the dependent variable; separate t tests are then used to evaluate the significance of each predictor variable. For simple linear regression, you may conduct either an F test or a t test. The results lead to the same conclusion.

EXAMPLE 14.17 Table 14.7 is the regression ANOVA table for the data of Table 14.4. An explanation of the values in this table follows.

TABLE 14.7 ANOVA Regression Table for Example 14.18

Source of variation	df	Sum of squares	Estimate of σ^2*	F ratio
Regression	1	1,512.88	1,512.898	63.0
Error or residual	6	144.00	24.0	
Total	7	1,656.88		

*The estimate of σ^2 is frequently referred to as *mean square.*

The value 1,656.88, which represents SST, is the sum of the squared differences between the y values and their mean. It is a measure of the variability of y before the x-y linear relationship is introduced:

$$\text{SST} = \Sigma(y - \bar{y})^2 = 1{,}656.88$$

The value 144 in Table 14.7 is the sum of the squared differences between the y values and their estimates based on x and the regression equation:

$$\text{SSE} = \Sigma(y - \hat{y})^2 = 144$$

The SSR value, 1,512.88, is the sum of squared differences "explained" with the introduction of x. It is the difference between the measure of the total of y variability (1,656.88) and the sum of squares error using x as a predictor (144):

$$SSR = SST - SSE = 1{,}656.88 - 144 = 1{,}512.88$$

The appropriate number of degrees of freedom associated with the regression sum of squares equals the number of independent variables. In simple linear regression, the degrees of freedom always equal 1. Table 14.7 shows one degree of freedom for the "regression" source of variation.

The degrees of freedom for the sum of squares error equal $(n - k)$, the sample size n, minus the number of regression coefficients estimated in the regression equation. In simple regression, β_0 and β_1 are the only regression coefficients estimated, so the degrees of freedom always equal $(n - 2)$. Table 14.7 shows six degrees of freedom $(n - k = 8 - 2 = 6)$ for the "residual" source of variation.

The loss of one degree of freedom for the total is due to the estimate of the population mean of y using the sample mean. Table 14.7 indicates a total of seven degrees of freedom $(n - 1 = 8 - 1 = 7)$.

The two sums of squares are divided by their degrees of freedom to produce the estimates of the unknown population variance listed in the fourth column of Table 14.7. The value 24.0 is a valid estimate of this variance regardless of the state of the null hypothesis. However, the estimate in the first row (1,512.88) is valid only if the null hypothesis is true. As shown in Chapter 12 (ANOVA), the ratio of these two "estimates" is drawn from the F distribution if the null hypothesis is true. This ratio (63.0) is computed using Equation 14.21 and is shown in the last column:

$$F = \frac{SSR/(k - 1)}{SSE/(n - k)} = \frac{1{,}512.88/(2 - 1)}{144/(8 - 2)} = 63.0$$

To determine whether an F value of 63.0 is "large," consult the F table in Appendix E.9. The df reference values for the table are 1 for the numerator and 6 for the denominator. For these degrees of freedom and a significance level of .05, the F table indicates a critical value of 5.99. The decision rule is

> If the calculated F value is greater than 5.99, reject the null hypothesis (reject H_0 if $F > 5.99$).

Therefore, reject the null hypothesis with small chance of error. We conclude that the sample regression equation explains a significant percentage of the y variance.

EXAMPLE 14.18 In Table 14.2, the variable of interest is car mileage per gallon, so this is the dependent variable, y. A variable that may be associated with y is car weight; this is the predictor variable, x. These data values were keyed into a computer program that performs regression analysis, SPSS-PC (Statistical Package for the Social Sciences, PC version). Table 14.8 displays the key regression values produced by this program.

The regression constant (b_0) and the regression coefficient (b_1) for the predictor variable are combined to form the regression equation,

$$\hat{y} = 45.109 - .00676x$$

TABLE 14.8 SPSS-PC Computer Output for Example 14.18

```
r-Squared: .73101                      Standard Error: 6.23192

                 Variables in the Equation
Variable                B                 t                Sig t
Weight             -.00676            -2.855               .0648
Constant            45.109             5.111               .0145

                   Analysis of Variance
                 df       Sum of Squares          Mean Square
Regression        1            316.62967            316.62967
Residual          3            116.51033             38.83678
            F = 8.15283        Sig F = .0648
```

The following symbols may help you read this computer output.

$r^2 = .73101$
$s_{y \cdot x} = 6.23192$
$b_1 = -.00676$
$b_0 = 45.109$
SSR = 316.62967
SSE = 116.51033

The regression slope means that for each increase in car weight of one pound, the mileage may be expected to decrease by an average of 0.00676 miles per gallon.

The t value for the equation slope is -2.855. The p-value for this statistic (.0648) indicates the probability of a type I error. To reject the hypothesis that $\beta_1 = 0$ and conclude that there's a nonzero slope in the population, we must risk about a 6% chance of being wrong.

The regression equation has caused a reduction in the sum of squares error. The null hypothesis stating that the sample regression equation doesn't explain a significant percentage of the y variance is tested by the F statistic. The null hypothesis may be rejected if a .0648 risk is acceptable (Sig F = .0648). Note that this is the same p-value computed for the t statistic. This is always true for a simple regression analysis.

Overall, we can conclude that this regression equation is rather weak, even though the r^2 value (73%) might appear promising. The small sample size (5) has produced a regression equation that can be used to predict in the population only if a somewhat high degree of risk is assumed (6.48%). If this were a real-world situation, a much larger sample size would be needed.

EXAMPLE 14.19 Washington Water Power rate analyst Tony Perez wants to study the relationship between temperature and the amount of electricity used by small commercial customers. He needs to determine how sensitive usage is to temperature. Tony uses "cooling degree days" to measure how cold a day is (the higher this value, the colder the day). He has taken a random sample of 22 months and computed the average value of this index, along with the average kilowatt-hours per small commercial customer. Tony runs his data using the SAS computer package. The SAS commands are shown at the end of this chapter. (*Note:* The actual data on usage and cooling degree days were collected for Washington Water Power for a sample of months selected from 1988 through 1989.)

Table 14.9 presents the SAS output. The analyst concludes that temperature is a fairly good predictor of the number of kilowatt-hours consumed by small commercial customers. With large t and F values, the regression equation is significant and can be used in the future to forecast power needs ($t = 7.62$, $F = 58.13$). He's somewhat disappointed, however, that only about 74% of the power consumption variance is explained by temperature. Tony had hoped for a larger r^2 value and wonders if additional predictor variables would explain a higher percentage of the variance.

TABLE 14.9 SAS Computer Output for Example 14.19

```
PEARSON CORRELATION COEFFICIENTS/PROB > :R: UNDER HO = RHO = 0/N = 22
            X            Y
X      1.00000       .86256
Y       .86256      1.00000

DEPENDENT VARIABLE: Y
SOURCE     DF     SUM OF SQUARES     MEAN SQUARE     F VALUE     PR > F     R-SQUARE
MODEL       1         1029495.82      1029495.82       58.13      .0001         .744
ERROR      20          354219.50        17710.97              ROOT MSE            Y-MEAN
TOTAL      21         1383715.32                               133.0826           1399.6
SOURCE     DF    TYPE I SS    F VALUE   PR > F   DF   TYPE III SS   F VALUE   PR > F
X           1   1029495.82      58.13    .0001    1    1029495.82     58.13    .0001
                                  T FOR HO =                        STD ERROR OF  ESTIMATE
PARAMETER          ESTIMATE     PARAMETER = 0       PR > [T]
INTERCEPT       1135.613175
X                  0.491662          7.62              .0001                       0.06449
                SUM OF RESIDUALS                                                      0.00
                SUM OF SQUARED RESIDUALS                                         354219.50
```

The following symbols may help you read this computer output:

$SSR = 1{,}029{,}495.82$ $\bar{y} = 1{,}399.6$
$SSE = 354{,}219.50$ $b_0 = 1{,}135.613175$
$SST = 1{,}383{,}715.32$ $b_1 = .491662$
$r^2 = .744$

USING THE REGRESSION EQUATION

The first step in evaluating a sample regression equation is to check the key values in the computer output. The r^2 value must be sufficiently high to encourage the analysis to continue. The t value must be high enough to reject the null hypotheses of zero population slope. Once a regression equation passes these tests, the analyst can use the equation for the intended purposes.

There are generally two purposes for a regression equation once it has been formed from the sample data and deemed significant. The first purpose is to gain insights into the effect of the predictor variable on the dependent variable. In Example 14.19, Tony found that electricity use by small commercial customers is significantly related to temperature. This relationship may prove quite valuable to both the power company and the customer in projecting power needs for the near future. In multiple regression (discussed in Chapter 15), there will be many more opportunities to explore the relationships between predictor variables and the dependent variable, since there are many potential predictor variables to examine.

The second important use of the sample regression equation is to make predictions for y given specified values for x.

EXAMPLE 14.20 Shop owner Carol Hartman is interested in examining the most important variable identified with shop success: number of customers who enter the shop per week. Carol believes that one variable that might be correlated with weekly visits is the county unemployment rate. She selects a random sample of 60 weeks from shop records for the past two years and records the relevant information for the two variables of interest. The data are keyed into the shop's small computer, that has a regression analysis package. Table 14.10 presents the key elements of the computer output.

TABLE 14.10 Computer Output for Example 14.20

r-Squared: .893 Standard Error: 2.1

Variables in the Equation

Variable	B	t	Sig t
V1	−53.8	10.4	.000
Constant	1147.9	9.7	.000

Analysis of Variance

	df	Sum of Squares	Mean Square
Regression	1	112,842	112,842
Residual	58	101,628	1,752.2

F = 64.4 Sig F = .000

Note the significant t statistic in Table 14.10. There's a very small risk (less than .001) of committing a type I error if the null hypothesis is rejected. It can be safely concluded that the slope of the population regression equation is not 0 (based on the large t value). The sample regression equation can be used in conjunction with the population of shop weeks. This regression equation is

$$\hat{y} = 1{,}147.9 - 53.8x$$

where x is the unemployment rate for the county and $\hat{y}$ is the expected value of y given the value of x. The slope of this equation can be interpreted to mean that for each increase of 1 percentage point in the unemployment rate, an average loss of 53.8 customers per week is expected. The r^2 of 89% means that most of the variability in shop visits can be explained by the linear relationship between visits and the unemployment rate.

Carol has judged the regression equation significant and can use it to estimate the number of visits per week given various values for x, the county unemployment rate. The county has issued its unemployment forecast for the next three months, predicting rates of 5.2%, 5.8%, and 7.0%. Based on these forecasts, the regression equation can be used to predict the expected number of shop visits per week for the next three months.

$$\hat{y} = 1147.9 - 53.8(5.2) = 868$$
$$\hat{y} = 1147.9 - 53.8(5.8) = 836$$
$$\hat{y} = 1147.9 - 53.8(7.0) = 771$$

Carol can use these predictions to plan shop operations, especially if she has information on profit per shop visit.

EXERCISES

38. What does it mean when b_1 is shown not to be significant?

SM

39. What is the F statistic used for in regression analysis? What is the t statistic used for in regression analysis?

40. What is the meaning of the statement, "A percentage of the y variance can be explained by x?"

41. Can the number of games a major league baseball team wins be explained by the number of home runs the team hits? The following data come from the *Sporting News 1992 Baseball Yearbook:*

Team	Wins y	Home runs x
Pittsburgh	98	126
Atlanta	94	141
Los Angeles	93	108
San Diego	84	121
St. Louis	84	68
Philadelphia	78	111
Chicago Cubs	77	159
New York Mets	77	117
San Francisco	75	141
Cincinnati	74	164
Montreal	71	95
Houston	65	79

a. Plot the data on a scatter diagram.

b. Develop a regression equation.

c. Compute the residuals.

d. Compute the sum of squares error (SSE).

e. Compute the total sum of squares (SST).

f. What percentage of the variance in games won can be explained by the number of home runs the team hit?

g. Test to determine whether the regression equation explains a significant percentage of the variance in the dependent variable.

41*b.* $\hat{y} = 75.49 + .0449x$
d. SSE = 1082.31
e. SST = 1101.67
f. $r^2 = .0176$
g. It doesn't, p-value = .6812. Fail to reject H_0

42. Jane Davis, manager of Quantum Realty, Inc., wants to determine if a home's selling price can be explained by its size. She's familiar with a 1980 study by Cho and Reichert that

used regression analysis to predict house price using a number of predictor variables.[4] They found that size of living space was the most significant factor, and Jane wants to use this finding in her own area. Jane has collected the following data:

Home	Selling price ($000), y	Number of rooms, x
1	90.4	8
2	127.3	9
3	109.6	8
4	131.2	12
5	81.3	6
6	107.9	10
7	135.8	11
8	97.8	7
9	116.7	10
10	164.8	14
11	88.8	7
12	120.5	11
13	109.8	10

a. Plot the data on a scatter diagram.

b. Develop a regression equation.

c. Compute the residuals.

d. Compute the sum of squares error (SSE).

e. Compute the total sum of squares (SST).

f. What percentage of the selling price variance can be explained by the number of rooms?

g. Test to determine whether the regression equation explains a significant percentage of the variance in selling price.

h. Write Jane a memo explaining the results of your analysis.

42*b.* $\hat{y} = 26.85 + 9.2x$
d. SSE = 989.59
e. SST = 6182.64
f. $r^2 = .84$
g. Yes. Reject H_0 since $F = 57.73 > 4.96$

SUMMARY

This chapter has presented the basic concepts of correlation and simple regression analysis. Correlation is used to measure the extent of the linear relationship between two continuous variables. In regression analysis, a dependent variable is identified along with a predictor or explanatory variable. Using the method of least squares, a regression equation is calculated along with other summary statistics, such as r^2, the t statistic, and the F statistic.

It is important in regression analysis to test the relevant hypotheses before using the regression equation for prediction. Either the t statistic or the F value should be examined and used to determine if the sample regression results can be extended to the

[4]C. C. Cho and A. Reichert, "An Application of Multiple Regression Analysis for Appraising Single-family Housing Values," *Business Economics* 15 (January 1980), pp. 47–52.

population from which the sample came. Analysts often make the mistake of looking only at r^2 when evaluating the results of a regression, and this can lead to erroneous conclusions, especially if a small sample size is involved.

The concepts presented in this chapter provide the background necessary for consideration of the more common case in regression analysis: the use of multiple predictor variables—the subject of the next chapter.

Applications of Statistical Concepts in the Business World

As mentioned early in this chapter, regression and correlation analysis are common methods of analyzing data to produce useful decision-making information. There are many numerical variables to consider in the business setting, and often managers want to understand the relationships among them. Correlation analysis is used when knowledge of the relationship between two variables is desired. Regression analysis is used when one variable (y) is to be predicted based on knowledge of another variable (x). Here are several examples of variables that might be of interest in a correlation and regression analysis. The manager would probably want to first see the correlation coefficient between the two variables, and then study the regression equation and determine its ability to produce accurate estimates.

Dependent variable	Predictor variable
Defectives per shift	Temperature of factory
Cost of goods sold/month	Number of employees/month
Number of overtime hours	Average temperature
Employee hourly wage	Employee age
Years with company	High school GPA
Number of defectives per factory branch	Wage rate per branch
Company dividends per share	Earnings per share
Number of shares outstanding	Annual sales
Seconds per computer transaction	Size of computer memory
Student GPA	Age of student
Student rating of professor	Student's class grade
Company cost of capital	Prime interest rate
Time until machine breakdown	Cost of monthly machine maintenance
Cost of rental car per day	Size of rental car company
Salesperson's monthly gross	Number of miles driven
Lifetime of TV picture tube	Temperature of operating space
Pounds of oats per bag	Time since filling machine adjustment
Viscosity of truck oil	Temperature of engine

Glossary

Scatter diagram A plot of x-y data pairs in two-dimensional space.

Correlation coefficient A value between -1 and $+1$ that indicates the strength of the linear relationship between two quantitative variables.

Functional model A model that hypothesizes an exact relationship between variables.

Statistical model A model that hypothesizes a functional relationship plus some random error.

Sample regression line The straight line that best fits a set of sample x-y data points.

Method of least squares A method that determines the equation of the straight line that minimizes the sum of the squared vertical distances between the line and the data points.

Residual The difference between an actual y and the value, $\hat{y}$, predicted using the sample regression equation.

Standard error of estimate A measure of the variability, or scatter, of the observed sample y values around the regression line.

Prediction interval An interval used to predict a particular y value for a given value of x.

Confidence interval An interval used to estimate the mean value of y for a specific value of x.

Coefficient of simple determination A measure of the percentage of the variability in y that can be explained by the predictor variable, x.

KEY FORMULAS

Pearson product-moment correlation coefficient

$$r = \frac{n\Sigma xy - (\Sigma x)(\Sigma y)}{\sqrt{n\Sigma x^2 - (\Sigma x)^2}\sqrt{n\Sigma y^2 - (\Sigma y)^2}} \tag{14.1}$$

Standard error of r

$$s_r = \sqrt{\frac{1 - r^2}{n - 2}} \tag{14.2}$$

t statistic for testing if the correlation coefficient differs from 0

$$t = \frac{(r - \rho)}{s_r} \tag{14.3}$$

Functional model for a straight line

$$y = \beta_0 + \beta_1 x \tag{14.4}$$

Statistical model for a straight line

$$y = \beta_0 + \beta_1 x + \varepsilon \tag{14.5}$$

Sample regression equation

$$\hat{y} = b_0 + b_1 x \tag{14.6}$$

Slope or regression coefficient formula

$$b_1 = \frac{n\Sigma xy - (\Sigma x)(\Sigma y)}{n\Sigma x^2 - (\Sigma x)^2} \tag{14.7}$$

y-intercept formula

$$b_0 = \frac{\Sigma y}{n} - \frac{b_1 \Sigma x}{n} \tag{14.8}$$

Residual

$$e = y - \hat{y} \tag{14.9}$$

Standard error of estimate

$$s_{y \cdot x} = \sqrt{\frac{\Sigma(y - \hat{y})^2}{n - 2}} \tag{14.10}$$

Prediction interval

$$\hat{y} \pm t\, s_{\hat{y} \cdot x} \tag{14.11}$$

Standard error of the prediction

$$s_{\hat{y} \cdot x} = s_{y \cdot x}\sqrt{1 + \frac{1}{n} + \frac{(x_p - \bar{x})^2}{\Sigma(x_i - \bar{x})^2}} \tag{14.12}$$

Confidence interval

$$\hat{y} \pm t\, s_{\hat{\mu} \cdot x} \tag{14.13}$$

Estimated standard error of estimate

$$s_{\hat{\mu} \cdot x} = s_{y \cdot x}\sqrt{\frac{1}{n} + \frac{(x_p - \bar{x})^2}{\Sigma(x_i - \bar{x})^2}} \tag{14.14}$$

Sum of squares total

$$\text{SST} = \sum_{i=1}^{n} (y_i - \bar{y})^2 \tag{14.15}$$

Sum of squares error

$$\text{SSE} = \sum_{i=1}^{n} (y_i - \hat{y})^2 \tag{14.16}$$

Sum of squares regression

$$\text{SSR} = \text{SST} - \text{SSE} \tag{14.17}$$

Coefficient of simple determination

$$r^2 = 1 - \frac{\Sigma(y - \hat{y})^2}{\Sigma(y - \bar{y})^2} \tag{14.18}$$

or

$$r^2 = 1 - \frac{\text{SSE}}{\text{SST}}$$

Standard error of the regression coefficient, b_1

$$s_b = \frac{s_{y \cdot x}}{\sqrt{\Sigma(x - \bar{x})^2}} \tag{14.19}$$

***t* statistic for testing if a regression coefficient differs from 0**

$$t = \frac{b_1 - \beta_1}{s_b} \tag{14.20}$$

***F* statistic**

$$F = \frac{\text{SSR}/(k - 1)}{\text{SSE}/(n - k)} \tag{14.21}$$

SOLVED EXERCISES

1. CORRELATION ANALYSIS

Carlene Larsen owns several ice cream stands in San Pedro, Texas. She's trying to find some variable that's positively related to daily sales and decides to investigate average temperature. She collects the following data for a random sample of 10 days:

Day	Daily sales (gallons), y	Average temperature (°F), x
1	110	72
2	127	79
3	140	85
4	151	90
5	89	66
6	187	95
7	205	100
8	190	98
9	136	82
10	165	91

a. Compute the correlation coefficient.

b. Test the correlation coefficient at the .025 significance level to determine if there's a positive relationship.

Solution:

a.

Day	y	x	y^2	x^2	xy
1	110	72	12,100	5,184	7,920
2	127	79	16,129	6,241	10,033
3	140	85	19,600	7,225	11,900
4	151	90	22,801	8,100	13,590

Day	y	x	y^2	x^2	xy
5	89	66	7,921	4,356	5,874
6	187	95	34,969	9,025	17,765
7	205	100	42,025	10,000	20,500
8	190	98	36,100	9,604	18,620
9	136	82	18,496	6,724	11,152
10	165	91	27,225	8,281	15,015
Sums:	1,500	858	237,366	74,740	132,369

$$r = \frac{n\Sigma xy - (\Sigma x)(\Sigma y)}{\sqrt{n\Sigma x^2 - (\Sigma x)^2}\sqrt{n\Sigma y^2 - (\Sigma y)^2}}$$
$$= \frac{10(132{,}369) - (858)(1{,}500)}{\sqrt{10(74{,}740) - (858)^2}\sqrt{10(237{,}366) - (1{,}500)^2}}$$
$$= \frac{36{,}690}{\sqrt{11{,}236}\sqrt{123{,}660}} = \frac{36{,}690}{37{,}275} = .984$$

b. The null and alternative hypotheses are

H_0: $\rho \leq 0$
H_1: $\rho > 0$
$\text{df} = (n - 2) = (10 - 2) = 8$

The decision rule is

If the sample t statistic is greater than 2.306, reject the null hypothesis (reject H_0 if $t > 2.306$).

The standard error of r is

$$s_r = \sqrt{\frac{1 - r^2}{n - 2}} = \sqrt{\frac{1 - (.984)^2}{8}} = .063$$

The t statistic is

$$t = \frac{r - \rho}{s_r} = \frac{.984 - 0}{.063} = 15.6$$

The calculated t statistic (15.6) is greater than the t value (2.306), so the null hypothesis is rejected. Carlene concludes that there is a positive linear relationship between average temperature and daily ice cream sales.

2. Regression Analysis

Since Carlene found a positive relationship between the two variables, she would like to use knowledge of average temperature to predict daily ice cream sales.

a. Compute the sample regression equation.

b. Interpret the slope or regression coefficient.

c. Compute the residual for the first day.

d. Compute the standard error of estimate.

e. Test the regression coefficient at the .025 significance level. Use a one-tailed test.

f. Compute the coefficient of simple determination.

g. Compute a 95% prediction interval for a day when the temperature is 90°.

h. Compute a 95% confidence interval for a day when the temperature is 90°.

Solution:

a.

$$b_1 = \frac{n\Sigma xy - (\Sigma x)(\Sigma y)}{n\Sigma x^2 - (\Sigma x)^2}$$

$$= \frac{10(132{,}369) - (858)(1{,}500)}{10(74{,}740) - (858)^2} = \frac{36{,}690}{11{,}236} = 3.265$$

$$b_0 = \frac{\Sigma y}{n} - \frac{b_1 \Sigma x}{n} = \frac{1{,}500}{10} - \frac{3.265(858)}{10} = -130.14$$

$$\hat{y} = -130.14 + 3.265x$$

b. If the average temperature increases 1°, daily ice cream sales will increase, on the average, 3.265 gallons.

c. $\hat{y} = -130.14 + 3.265(72) = 104.94$
$e = y - \hat{y} = 110 - 104.94 = 5.06$

d.

Day	y	$\hat{y}$	$y - \hat{y}$	$(y - \hat{y})^2$
1	110	104.94	5.06	25.60
2	127	127.79	−0.80	0.64
3	140	147.39	−7.39	54.61
4	151	163.71	−12.71	161.54
5	89	85.35	3.65	13.32
6	187	180.04	6.96	48.44
7	205	196.37	8.63	74.48
8	190	189.84	0.16	0.03
9	136	137.59	−1.59	2.53
10	165	166.98	−1.98	3.92
			0.00	385.26

$$s_{y \cdot x} = \sqrt{\frac{\Sigma(y - \hat{y})^2}{n - 2}} = \sqrt{\frac{385.26}{8}} = 6.94$$

e. The null and alternative hypotheses are

H_0: $\beta_1 \leq 0$
H_1: $\beta_1 > 0$
df $= (n - 2) = (10 - 2) = 8$

The decision rule is

If the sample t statistic is greater than 2.306, reject the null hypothesis.

The standard error of b_1 is

$$s_b = \frac{s_{y \cdot x}}{\sqrt{\Sigma(x - \bar{x})^2}} = \frac{6.94}{\sqrt{1{,}123.6}} = .207$$

where

$$\Sigma(x-\bar{x})^2 = \Sigma x^2 - \frac{(\Sigma x)^2}{n} = 74{,}740 - \frac{(858)^2}{10} = 1{,}123.6$$

The t statistic is

$$t = \frac{b_1 - \beta_1}{s_b} = \frac{3.265 - 0}{.207} = 15.8$$

This is the same result obtained when the correlation coefficient was tested. Carlene concludes that there's a positive linear relationship between average temperature and daily ice cream sales. The slope of the regression line is significantly different from 0.

f. $\Sigma(y-\hat{y})^2 = 385.26, \qquad \Sigma(y-\bar{y})^2 = 12{,}366$

$$r^2 = 1 - \frac{\Sigma(y-\hat{y})^2}{\Sigma(y-\bar{y})^2} = 1 - \frac{385.26}{12{,}366} = 1 - .031 = .969$$

g. $\hat{y} = -130.14 + 3.265(90) = 163.71$

$$\hat{y} \pm t\, s_{y \cdot x}\sqrt{1 + \frac{1}{n} + \frac{(x_p-\bar{x})^2}{\Sigma(x_i-\bar{x})^2}}$$

$$163.71 \pm 2.306(6.94)\sqrt{1 + \frac{1}{10} + \frac{(90-85.8)^2}{1{,}123.6}}$$

$$163.71 \pm 2.306(6.94)\sqrt{1.1157}$$

$$163.71 \pm 2.306(6.94)\ (1.056)$$

$$163.71 \pm 16.9$$

$$146.81 \text{ to } 180.61$$

h. $\hat{y} \pm t\, s_{y \cdot x}\sqrt{\frac{1}{n} + \frac{(x_p-\bar{x})^2}{\Sigma(x_1-\bar{x})^2}}$

$$163.71 \pm 2.306(6.94)\sqrt{\frac{1}{10} + \frac{(90-85.8)^2}{1{,}123.6}}$$

$$163.71 \pm 2.306(6.94)\sqrt{.1157}$$

$$163.71 \pm 2.306(6.94)(.34)$$

$$163.71 \pm 5.44$$

$$158.27 \text{ to } 169.15$$

Note that since the sample size is less than 30, the t distribution is consulted for 6 degrees of freedom $(10 - 2 = 8)$. Carlene is 95% confident that gas sales in gallons will fall in the interval from 146.81 to 180.61 for a day of 90° temperature. She's also 95% confident that the interval from 158.27 to 169.15 encloses the mean sales of gas in gallons when a prediction is made for a day of 90° temperature.

EXERCISES

43. What is a sample regression? How is it used?
44. What is the difference between correlation analysis and regression analysis?
45. If two variables have a correlation coefficient (r) equal to 0, what is the value of the standard error of estimate ($s_{y \cdot x}$)?

46. What are two ways in which the slope or regression coefficient can be tested for significance?
47. What is the difference between testing that the population correlation coefficient is 0 and testing that the population regression coefficient is 0?
48. What null hypothesis is tested using the F statistic in simple regression analysis?

49*b*. $r = 1$

49. For the following set of data:

y:	10	15	20	25	30	35	40
x:	6	8	10	12	14	16	18

a. Plot the data on a scatter diagram.
b. Compute the correlation coefficient.

50. For the following set of data:

y:	90	80	70	60	50	40	30
x:	20	24	28	32	36	40	44

a. Plot the data on a scatter diagram.

50*b*. $\hat{y} = 140 - 2.5x$

b. Compute the sample regression equation.

51. For the following set of data:

y:	12	17	18	22	16	11	21	26
x:	5	8	8	9	6	6	10	12

a. Plot the data on a scatter diagram.

51*b*. $\hat{y} = 1.45 + 2.05x$
c. 21.98

b. Compute the sample regression equation.
c. Compute a point estimate for an x value of 10.

52. Reject H_0 since $4.62 > 2.75$

52. A sample correlation coefficient of $r = .60$ was calculated based on a sample of size $n = 40$. Test at the .01 significance level the hypothesis H_0: $\rho = 0$ versus the alternative H_1: $\rho \neq 0$.

53. Fail to reject H_0 since $-.26 > -1.711$

53. Test at the .05 significance level the hypothesis H_0: $\beta_1 \geq 0$ versus the alternative H_1: $\beta_1 < 0$, given that a simple linear regression based on a sample of size $n = 26$ produced the sample regression equation $\hat{y} = -2.5 - .6x$, with $s_b = 2.3$.
54. Given the following summary measures:

$$n = 20, \quad \Sigma x = 154.2, \quad \Sigma x^2 = 2{,}281.3,$$
$$\Sigma xy = 4{,}002.8, \quad \Sigma y = 613.4, \quad \Sigma y^2 = 19{,}418.9$$

54*a*. $r = -.893$
b. Reject H_0 since $-8.51 < -1.734$
c. $\hat{y} = 35.827 - .665x$

a. Compute the correlation coefficient.
b. Test the correlation coefficient at the .10 significance level. Use a two-tailed test.
c. Compute the sample regression equation.

55. City Parcel Delivery Service accountant Jean Foster has been asked to compute a new rate schedule for local deliveries. Jean already has data on the average cost per mile of delivery

truck operation, but she needs to determine the average amount of time needed per mile to make a delivery. She collects data on the next 13 runs:

Delivery	Minutes, y	Miles, x
1	28	11
2	27	10
3	35	15
4	15	7
5	8	2
6	14	5
7	20	8
8	29	9
9	13	4
10	16	3
11	40	14
12	9	3
13	31	12

a. Plot the data on a scatter diagram.

b. Compute the correlation coefficient.

c. Test the correlation coefficient at the .05 significance level. Use a two-tailed test.

d. Determine the sample regression equation.

e. What is the average amount of time needed per mile to make a delivery?

f. Compute the coefficient of simple determination.

g. Write a sentence that Jean can understand interpreting the r^2 value computed in part *f.*

h. Compute the residuals.

i. Compute the sum of squares error (SSE).

j. Compute the sum of squares total (SST).

k. Test to determine whether the regression equation explains a significant percentage of the dependent variable variance. Use the .05 significance level.

l. Predict how long it will take to deliver a package to a business 10 miles away.

m. Develop a 90% prediction interval for part *l.*

n. Construct a regression ANOVA table.

55*b.* $r = .9562$
c. Reject H_0 since 10.87 > 2.2
d. $\hat{y} = 3.91 + 2.27x$
e. 2.27 minutes
f. $r^2 = .9143$
i. SSE = 109.94
j. SST = 1282.9231
k. Reject H_0 since F = 117.42 > 4.84
l. 26.2 minutes
m. 20.28 to 32.12

56. Jim Larkin owns a service station in an area where a large construction project is planned. Jim feels that his gasoline sales are dependent on traffic flow along the street where his station is located. *The Wall Street Journal,* March 2, 1990, predicted that world crude oil prices would rise because of cutbacks in North Sea production. Jim is concerned that this may lead to higher gas prices, which could hurt his business.

As well, Jim fears that sales will decrease significantly once the construction project begins. Jeff Brunner, a part-time employee and full-time business student, disagrees with Jim. Jeff feels that the station's success is based on customer loyalty and not on traffic flow. Jeff and another student are assigned to do a project in their statistics course. Jeff obtains permission from Jim to study the relationship between gas sales and traffic count and collects a sample of eight days of data:

56. $\hat{y} = 67.47 + 22.52x$
$r^2 = .9495$
$t = 10.62$

Day	Total gallons sold (thousands), y	Traffic count (hundreds), x
1	284	9
2	381	13
3	271	11
4	287	9
5	452	17
6	192	5
7	204	7
8	158	4

Write a report for Jeff and his classmate to turn in to their professor. Write a second report for Jeff to give to Jim Larkin.

57. $\hat{y} = 3.24 + .39x$
$r^2 = .6189$
$t = 4.03$

57. Brian Bosley, a rate analyst for Northeast Power, was asked to determine if there's a linear relationship between electricity consumption and the number of rooms in a single-family dwelling. Because electricity consumption varies from month to month, Brian decided to study usage during January. He collected the following data:

House	Kilowatt-hours (thousands), y	Number of rooms, x
1	8	13
2	6	10
3	9	15
4	5	7
5	8	9
6	5	5
7	7	8
8	9	9
9	3	4
10	6	6
11	8	14
12	6	5

Write a report for Brian's supervisor that analyzes the relationship between these variables.

58. The Dillon Investment Company bids on investments offered by various firms that desire additional financing. Martin Hughes, manager of Dillon, wonders if there's a relationship between Dillon's bid and the bid of Dillon's major competitor, Amfco Securities. He feels that Dillon might be using the same rationale in preparing bids as Amfco. In other words, could Dillon's bid be used to predict Amfco's bid? Martin has tabulated data on the past 12 issues bid on, in terms of the bid's percentage of par value, for both firms:

Issue	Amfco, y	Dillon, x
1	101.5	101.9
2	98.9	99.1
3	100.3	101.1
4	105.9	106.8
5	102.0	102.1
6	97.4	97.1
7	99.3	99.5
8	98.8	99.4

Issue	Amfco, y	Dillon, x
9	103.6	104.1
10	100.1	99.7
11	98.5	99.0
12	100.1	100.3

58*a*. $y = .9913$
b. $\hat{y} = 8.88 + .91x$
c. $\hat{y} = 101.6$
d. .1131
e. 101.6, 101.38

a. To what extent are the two firms using the same rationale in preparing bids?

b. Develop a regression equation for Mr. Hughes.

c. Predict Amfco's bid if Dillon bids 102% of par value.

d. For the prediction made in part *c*, what is the probability of Dillon winning this particular bid (if lowest bid wins)?

e. What should Martin bid if he wants a 50% probability of winning the bid? A 75% probability of winning the bid?

59. An investor is considering putting funds into a mutual fund managed by Fidelity—specifically, its Blue Chip fund. She collects a small sample of issues in *The Wall Street Journal* and records the fund's selling price per share (y) along with that day's Dow Jones Industrial Average (x):

Date	y	x
Nov. 8	13.61	2597.13
Dec. 1	14.14	2706.27
Oct. 19	14.02	2643.65
Oct. 11	14.55	2785.33
Oct. 3	14.18	2713.72
Oct. 6	14.50	2773.56
Oct. 24	14.21	2662.91

Values are from *The Wall Street Journal* of the dates shown, all 1989.

59*a*. $r = .92$
b. Yes, $t = 5.276$
d. $\hat{y} = 2.753 + .0042x$

a. What is the correlation between x and y?

b. Is the correlation found in part *a* significant?

c. How would you interpret your findings?

d. What is the sample regression equation?

e. What would you recommend to this investor?

60. This exercise refers to the company data base in Appendix C. Select a random sample of 10 workers. Determine if there's a significant relationship between the number of years with the company (x_1) and the number of overtime hours worked during the past six months (x_2).

61. This exercise refers to the company data base in Appendix C. Select a random sample of 15 workers. Develop a regression equation using employee age (x_9) to predict annual base salary (x_8). Use the .05 significance level to determine if this equation explains a significant percentage of the variance in the dependent variable.

62. This exercise refers to the company data base in Appendix C. Select a random sample of 12 workers. Develop a regression equation using employee age (x_9) to predict the number of sick days taken during the past six months (x_5). Use the .10 significance level to determine if the regression coefficient is significantly different from 0.

EXTENDED EXERCISES

63. MURFORD ELECTRONICS

Susan and Charles Murford own a company that retails various kinds of electronic equipment such as TV sets, VCRs, stereo equipment, and video cameras. A variable of great concern to them is their monthly gross sales. Since they have records for this variable over the past five years, it's easy to take a random sample of months to use in a regression analysis.

After thinking about variables that might be related to their extreme variability in monthly sales, the Murfords decide that occupancy rate of the largest hotel in town might correlate well. They base this conclusion on a recent newspaper article that noted the unusually high correlation between this variable and other indicators of local economic activity.

The Murfords randomly select the 10 months for their sample and record their gross sales, in dollars, for each month. They then obtain hotel occupancy rates for these same months from the local chamber of commerce. Table 14.11 shows the data they collected along with the summary statistics generated by a computer program that performs simple regression analysis.

TABLE 14.11 Data and Regression Computer Results for Extended Exercise 63

x (hotel occupancy rate, %)	y (monthly sales, $000)
63	85.2
79	88.4
55	79.7
88	91.3
85	89.9
42	74.3
54	79.8
60	81.4
78	85.6
62	82.7

```
r-Squared: .94780                 Standard Error: 1.27683
                  Variables in the Equation

Variable            B                t              Sig t
Rate V1           .33934          12.052            .0000
Constant        61.22992          31.920            .0000

                        Analysis of Variance

                df      Sum of Squares        Mean Square
Regression       1         236.79865          236.79865
Residual         8          13.04235            1.63029
             F = 145.24912    Sig F = .0000
```

a. Can these results be extended to the population of all months? Explain.

b. What is the regression equation? If the current occupancy rate is 75%, what is the expected sales level for Murford Electronics?

c. About how far off would you expect the prediction made in part *b* to be?

64. THE SHIVES INVESTMENT SEMINAR

Cindy Shives has been conducting investment seminars for about three years in a large city. She has heard favorable comments from a number of former attendees and would like to gather some evidence regarding personal attributes that affect success in the investment world. She thinks this knowledge would contribute greatly to her seminars. A *Financial Executive* article, "Corporate Investments—Do You Play the Loser's Game?" (May/June 1989), makes her think carefully about the approach she's using in her seminars.

She randomly chooses 28 former attendees from her files, and they agree to fill out a brief, anonymous questionnaire. She asks them to estimate the percentage increase in their net asset worth during the 12-month period following their attending her seminar. She'll use this variable as the dependent variable in a regression analysis.

Cindy then considers variables that might be related to investment success as measured by the dependent variable. Her files contain the questionnaires that participants filled out at the beginning of her seminar. After looking over these forms, she decides to test two variables (age and number of years of investment experience) against the dependent variable. She matches these data values for each person in the sample with the dependent variable and keys the resulting data into a regression analysis computer program. After the program has run, she tries to interpret the results but can't.

a. Provide some general advice to Cindy Shives about what to look for on the regression output.

b. Describe how Cindy can tell which of her two predictor variables is better.

c. Give some specific benchmark values that Cindy can use in studying the statistics on her computer printout.

65. PLATEN PRINTING

Consider the population of 140 observations in the table below. The Platen Printing Company wishes to determine the relationship between the number of copies produced by an offset printing technique (x) and the associated direct labor cost (y). Select a random sample of 25 observations.

a. Use the .05 significance level to determine if there is a significant relationship.

b. If there is a significant relationship, develop a sample regression equation and use it to predict the direct labor cost for a job involving 275 copies.

c. Develop a 95% prediction interval for your prediction in part *b.*

d. Develop a 95% confidence interval for your prediction in part *b.*

e. How accurate is your regression equation?

Observation	y	x	Observation	y	x	Observation	y	x
(1)	1.0	10	(10)	1.4	40	(19)	1.5	70
(2)	0.9	10	(11)	1.2	40	(20)	2.0	70
(3)	0.8	10	(12)	1.7	50	(21)	0.8	80
(4)	1.3	20	(13)	0.9	50	(22)	0.6	80
(5)	0.9	20	(14)	1.2	50	(23)	1.8	80
(6)	0.6	30	(15)	1.3	50	(24)	1.0	90
(7)	1.1	30	(16)	0.7	60	(25)	2.0	100
(8)	1.0	30	(17)	1.0	60	(26)	0.5	100
(9)	1.4	40	(18)	1.3	70	(27)	1.5	100

Observation	y	x	Observation	y	x	Observation	y	x
(28)	1.3	110	(66)	1.4	240	(104)	3.1	360
(29)	1.7	110	(67)	1.6	240	(105)	2.5	370
(30)	1.2	110	(68)	1.7	240	(106)	2.9	370
(31)	0.8	110	(69)	1.5	250	(107)	2.6	370
(32)	1.0	120	(70)	2.2	250	(108)	3.0	380
(33)	1.8	120	(71)	2.5	250	(109)	3.2	380
(34)	2.1	120	(72)	2.4	260	(110)	2.9	390
(35)	1.5	130	(73)	2.0	260	(111)	2.6	390
(36)	1.9	130	(74)	2.7	260	(112)	2.5	390
(37)	1.7	140	(75)	2.0	270	(113)	2.7	400
(38)	1.2	150	(76)	2.2	270	(114)	3.1	400
(39)	1.4	150	(77)	2.4	270	(115)	2.4	400
(40)	2.1	150	(78)	1.8	280	(116)	3.0	400
(41)	0.9	160	(79)	2.8	290	(117)	3.4	420
(42)	1.1	160	(80)	2.2	290	(118)	3.5	420
(43)	1.7	160	(81)	2.4	290	(119)	3.1	420
(44)	2.0	160	(82)	2.1	290	(120)	2.9	420
(45)	1.6	170	(83)	1.9	290	(121)	2.8	430
(46)	1.9	170	(84)	2.4	300	(122)	3.3	430
(47)	1.7	170	(85)	2.5	300	(123)	2.5	440
(48)	2.2	180	(86)	2.9	300	(124)	2.8	440
(49)	2.4	180	(87)	2.0	300	(125)	2.4	450
(50)	1.6	180	(88)	1.9	310	(126)	2.6	450
(51)	1.8	190	(89)	2.5	310	(127)	3.0	450
(52)	4.1	190	(90)	2.6	310	(128)	3.4	460
(53)	2.0	190	(91)	3.2	320	(129)	3.0	460
(54)	1.5	200	(92)	2.8	320	(130)	3.3	470
(55)	2.1	200	(93)	2.4	320	(131)	3.4	470
(56)	2.5	200	(94)	2.5	320	(132)	3.1	470
(57)	1.7	220	(95)	2.0	330	(133)	3.6	480
(58)	2.0	220	(96)	2.4	340	(134)	3.0	480
(59)	2.3	220	(97)	2.2	340	(135)	2.9	480
(60)	1.8	220	(98)	2.0	340	(136)	3.2	480
(61)	1.3	230	(99)	2.5	350	(137)	2.6	490
(62)	1.6	230	(100)	2.8	350	(138)	3.8	490
(63)	2.8	230	(101)	2.3	350	(139)	3.3	490
(64)	2.2	230	(102)	2.7	350	(140)	2.9	500
(65)	2.6	230	(103)	2.8	360			

MICROCOMPUTER PACKAGE

The micro package *Computerized Business Statistics* can be used to solve correlation and regression analysis problems.

In Solved Exercises 1 and 2, Carlene Larsen is trying to find some variable that's positively related to daily sales. She investigates average temperature, which she'd like to use to predict daily ice cream sales.

Computer Solution:

From the main menu of *Computerized Business Statistics* a 9 is selected, which indicates Simple Correlation and Regression. The simple correlation and regression menu appears on the screen.

Since the problem involves entering data from the keyboard, a 1 is selected.

```
Simple Correlation and Regression-Define New Problem
Number of Data Points: Enter 4–125, Press ↵ 10
```

Since 10 days were sampled, **10** is selected.

```
Alpha Error 1 = 0.2, 2 = 0.1, 3 = 0.05, 4 = 0.02, 5 = 0.01, 6 = Other
Select Alpha: Enter 1–6, Press ↵ 3
Degrees of Freedom ......................................... 8
Critical t (Alpha/2) .................................... 2.306
Simple Correlation and Regression-Enter Variable Labels
                     Independent Variable X1
                     Dependent Variable    Y
Press END when Finished
```

The variable names are *x* for average temperature and *y* for ice cream sales. **END** is pressed once the blanks have been completed.

Next, the program asks:

```
Problem definition correct Y/N/Q, Press ↵ Y
```

After a **Y** response, the program is ready for the data to be entered:

```
Enter Data Values
      x   y
 1 =  0   0
 2 =  0   0
 3 =  0   0
 4 =  0   0
 5 =  0   0
 6 =  0   0
 7 =  0   0
 8 =  0   0
 9 =  0   0
10 =  0   0
Press F when Finished
```

There are 10 pairs of data points. An **F** is entered once the blanks have been filled.

After the data have been entered, the screen shows:

```
        x    y
 1 =   72  110
 2 =   79  127
 3 =   85  140
 4 =   90  151
 5 =   66   89
 6 =   95  187
 7 =  100  205
 8 =   98  190
 9 =   82  136
10 =   91  165
```

You are asked:

```
Save Data? Y/N, Press ↵ N
```

The simple correlation and regression menu then reappears.

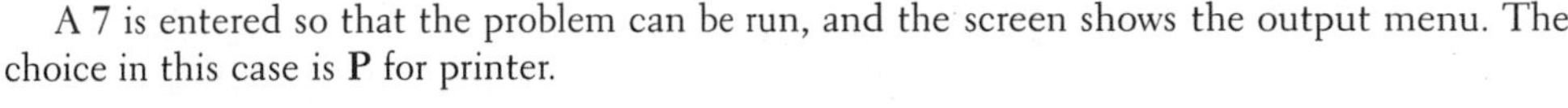

A 7 is entered so that the problem can be run, and the screen shows the output menu. The choice in this case is **P** for printer.

```
Residual analysis?
Enter Y/N, Press ↵ Y

Forecast, Interval analysis?
Enter Y/N, Press ↵ Y
```

Finally, the program asks:

```
Graphics?
Enter Y/N, Press ↵ Y
```

MINITAB COMPUTER PACKAGE

The MINITAB commands to solve Examples 14.9, 14.10, 14.12, and 14.13 are:

```
MTB > READ 'CH14EX8.DAT' C1-C2
MTB > BRIEF 3
MTB > REGRESS C1 ON 1 PREDICTOR C2;
SUBC> PREDICT 6.

The regression equation is
SALES = 82.3 + 13.1 ADS

Predictor       Coef      Stdev      t ratio        P
Constant      82.268      7.000        11.75    0.000
ADS           13.056      1.644         7.94    0.000

s = 4.899        R-sq = 91.3%        R-sq(adj) = 89.9%

Analysis of Variance

SOURCE          DF         SS         MS         F        P
Regression       1     1512.9     1512.9     63.05    0.000
Error            6      144.0       24.0
Total            7     1656.9

   Fit  Stdev.Fit        95% C.I.            95% P.I.
160.61       3.54  (151.95,  169.26)   (145.82, 175.39)

Obs.      ADS      SALES       Fit    Stdev.Fit    Residual    St.Resid
   1     3.00     125.00    121.44         2.53        3.56        0.85
   2     5.00     152.00    147.55         2.25        4.45        1.02
   3     4.00     131.00    134.49         1.74       -3.49       -0.76
   4     4.00     133.00    134.49         1.74       -1.49       -0.33
   5     5.00     142.00    147.55         2.25       -5.55       -1.28
   6     3.00     116.00    121.44         2.53       -5.44       -1.30
   7     3.00     127.00    121.44         2.53        5.56        1.33
   8     6.00     163.00    160.61         3.54        2.39        0.71

MTB > STOP
```

The BRIEF 3 command is used to provide an output that includes a table of residuals. The REGRESS command is used again to develop a regression analysis with sales as the dependent (y) variable and TV ads as the independent (x) variable. The PREDICT subcommand is used to compute a point estimate, a confidence interval estimate, and a prediction interval for a week when six ads are planned.

SAS Computer Package

The SAS computer package can be used to run regression analysis problems. The SAS commands to solve Example 14.19 are:

```
TITLE ''REGRESSION ANALYSIS FOR EXAMPLE 14.19'';
DATA USAGE;
INPUT Y X;
CARDS;
1174  246
1202  124
1283   26
1220   61
1182  253
1177  370
1150  634
1812 1069
1887 1225
1762 1212
1641 1066
1292  547
1213  242
1231   67
1443   20
1296  109
1205  272
1201  414
1308  631
1573  774
1684 1066
1855 1384
PROC PRINT;
PROC CORR;
PROC REG;
 MODEL Y=X;
```

Table 14.9 shows the SAS output for this run.

The TITLE command names the SAS run. The DATA command gives the data a name. The INPUT command names and specifies the order for the two data fields. The next 22 lines are card images that represent the y variable (average kilowatt-hours used per small commercial customer for the month) and the x variable (average cooling degree days for the month). The PROC PRINT command directs SAS to list the data. The PROC CORR command indicates that a correlation matrix is desired. The PROC REG command and MODEL subcommand indicate that y and x are the regression variables, with y being the dependent variable and x the independent variable.

Chapter

15

MULTIPLE REGRESSION

Once upon a midnight dreary, while I pondered, weak and weary, . . .
Poe, "The Raven"

Objectives

When you have completed this chapter, you will be able to:

Select good predictor variables.

Interpret a correlation matrix.

Test hypotheses to determine the significance of a multiple regression model and the independent variables in the model.

Recognize potential problems in using multiple regression analysis, especially the problem of multicollinearity.

Develop curvilinear models.

Incorporate qualitative variables into the multiple regression model.

Apply the stepwise regression approach.

Analyze computer output for a multiple regression model.

The June 16, 1992, *PC Magazine* compared the 486–50 PC chips' increased speed to its predecessors. It reported that machines with this chip are the most powerful on the market.

Chapter 14 covered simple regression analysis, where one independent variable is used to predict a dependent variable. When there are two or more predictor variables, the analysis is called *multiple regression*, the subject of this chapter.

Why Managers Need to Know about Multiple Regression Analysis

The same logic applies in multiple regression as in simple regression. A single dependent variable is identified whose movements or variance the analyst wishes to explain. The analyst then identifies two or more potential predictor variables that may be correlated with the dependent variable. A random sample of items is selected from the population being studied, and an attempt is made to find a combination of predictor variables that produces a good prediction or regression equation for y.

Since there are many instances in business where movement of a quantitative variable is of great interest, multiple regression is one of the most widely used techniques in practical applications.

Regarding the 486–50 chip in the *PC Magazine* article, it might be interesting to study the effect of various factors on PC chip speed over the past few years. A number of variables that might possibly be related to chip speed could be identified, measured, and analyzed to observe their correlations with chip speed. The ultimate objective might be to find a good prediction equation for chip speed, and possibly extend the equation past current data to predict future speeds.

Selecting Predictor Variables

In a multiple regression analysis, the first step is to identify the dependent and predictor variables to be included in the prediction model. Next, a random sample is taken, and all the variables are recorded for each sampled item. The third step is to identify the relationships between the dependent and the predictor variables, and also among the predictor variables. This is done by analyzing the data using a computer program that produces a **correlation matrix** for the variables. This matrix is sized in accordance with the number of variables being investigated. If three variables are being analyzed, the correlation matrix will be 3 × 3 (three rows by three columns). If there are 10 variables, the correlation matrix will be 10 × 10.

Correlation Matrix

A correlation coefficient for each combination of two variables appears at the intersection of every row and column of the correlation matrix. The two variables being measured are designated by the row number and the column number. Table 15.1 is an example of a correlation matrix for four variables (4 × 4). The correlation coefficient that indicates the linear relationship between variables 2 and 3 is represented as $r_{2,3}$. Note that the first subscript refers to the row and the second subscript refers to the column. Also note that the relationship between variables 2 and 3 ($r_{2,3}$) is exactly the

TABLE 15.1 Correlation Matrix

Variables	1	2	3	4
1	$r_{1,1}$	$r_{1,2}$	$r_{1,3}$	$r_{1,4}$
2	$r_{2,1}$	$r_{2,2}$	$r_{2,3}$	$r_{2,4}$
3	$r_{3,1}$	$r_{3,2}$	$r_{3,3}$	$r_{3,4}$
4	$r_{4,1}$	$r_{4,2}$	$r_{4,3}$	$r_{4,4}$

same as that between variables 3 and 2 ($r_{3,2}$). Finally, the coefficients along the primary diagonal ($r_{1,1}$, $r_{2,2}$, $r_{3,3}$, $r_{4,4}$) will always be 1 since a variable is always related to itself in a perfect positive way.

> A **correlation matrix** displays the correlation coefficients for every possible pair of variables in the analysis.

For the sake of consistency, and to make it easy to read a typical computer output in this text, the y variable will be entered first and represented as variable 1, or x_1. This means that the first predictor variable will be represented as variable 2, or x_2.

EXAMPLE 15.1 An analyst has identified the dependent variable *job evaluation rating* for hourly employees of a large factory. He also identifies four possible predictor variables: age, entry test score, number of dependents, and years with the company. A random sample of 200 workers is selected from company files, and these four variables are recorded. A correlation matrix is calculated so that the strength of the association between the dependent variable and each predictor variable can be examined (Table 15.2).

The program numbers the variables keyed into the computer from left to right, beginning with number 1. Since the analyst chose to enter y first, the dependent variable in Table 15.2 is variable 1. Row 1 (or column 1) in the correlation matrix should be examined first to determine the correlations between y and the various predictor variables.

TABLE 15.2 Correlation Matrix for Example 15.1

	1	2	3	4	5
1	1	−.27	.78	−.83	.65
2	−.27	1	−.63	.47	−.46
3	.78	−.63	1	−.89	.17
4	−.83	.47	−.89	1	−.21
5	.65	−.46	.17	−.21	1

Inspection of Table 15.2 indicates that variable 2 isn't highly related to variable 1 ($r_{1,2} = -.27$), so it won't be a good predictor of y. Variables 3 and 4 have good potential as predictor variables since their correlations are fairly high: $r_{1,3} = .78$ and $r_{1,4} = -.83$. Variable 5 has only fair potential: $r_{1,5} = .65$. The purpose of this analysis is to find the strength of the associations between the dependent variable and the variables chosen as potential predictor variables. In this case, two good potential predictor variables have been found (entry test score and number of dependents), along with a predictor with fair potential (years with company).

There are two guidelines for selecting predictor variables for a multiple regression equation. The first of these is illustrated in Example 15.1. A predictor variable should be strongly correlated with the dependent variable. This is the same logic used in Chapter 14 for identifying a single predictor variable in a simple regression. In multiple regression, however, there's a second guideline that should be followed in selecting predictor variables.

If any two predictor variables in a multiple regression are too highly correlated, they interfere with each other by explaining the same variance in the dependent variable. This condition of high correlation between predictor variables is called **multicollinearity.** Multicollinearity is undesirable because it suggests that the predictor variables are not independent, and, as a consequence, it's difficult to say how much of the observed effect is due to an individual predictor variable. In other words, if two variables are highly correlated, they supply almost the same predictive information.

Multicollinearity

When two predictor variables are highly correlated, the sample regression coefficient estimators, $b_0, b_2, b_3, \ldots, b_k$ of the population regression coefficient parameters, $\beta_0, \beta_2, \beta_3, \ldots, \beta_k$ are undependable. The estimate b_2 of β_2 may not even be close to the true value of β_2 due to the high variability in the sampling distribution of β_2. In extreme cases, b_2 might even be negative when it should be positive. This phenomenon will be illustrated in Example 15.15. Since two variables that are highly correlated add little to the explanation of the dependent variable variance and create undependable regression coefficients, one of them should be dropped from the model.

> **Multicollinearity** results when predictor variables are too highly correlated among themselves.

The ideal in multiple regression analysis is to have uncorrelated predictor variables so that each explains a separate portion of the variation in the dependent variable. Figure 15.1 illustrates this concept. The pie chart represents the total variation of the dependent variable, y. The xs are separate pieces of the pie labeled A and B, and each explains a separate portion of the variability of y. Area C indicates the overlap (that portion of the y variance being explained by both predictor variables). Area D represents the unexplained portion of y's variability.

FIGURE 15.1 Multicollinearity

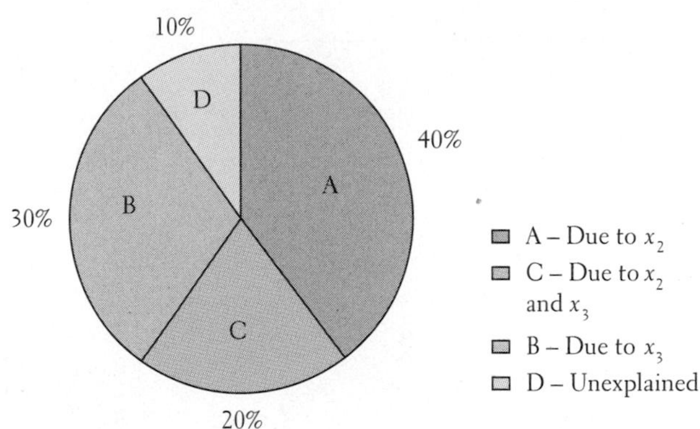

Predictor Variable Selection

The following two rules summarize the considerations that should prevail in selecting predictor variables in a multiple regression.

> Rules for selecting predictor variables in a multiple regression:
> 1. A predictor variable should have a strong correlation with the dependent variable.
> 2. A predictor variable should not be too highly correlated with any other predictor variable.

EXAMPLE 15.2 In Example 14.7, Amy Green, Green Garden Company president, developed a simple regression model that used the number of TV ads run per week to predict weekly sales of garden supplies. She was able to explain 91.3% of the variance in sales through her knowledge of the linear relationship (r = .956) between the number of TV ads and sales. Amy wants to find another predictor variable to explain the remaining 8.7%.

Amy decides that the average temperature during a week should be related to weekly sales of garden supplies. Table 15.3 shows the data and the correlation matrix that result from running the analysis on a multiple regression program.

Both x variables are highly related to the dependent variable ($r_{1,2}$ = .956 and $r_{1,3}$ = .921) and thus have potential for being good predictor variables. However, the two predictor variables are highly related to each other ($r_{2,3}$ = .805), so multicollinearity might be a problem.

EXAMPLE 15.3 The analyst in Example 15.1 can study Table 15.2 further to conduct a multiple regression analysis. The dependent variable (job evaluation rating) is

TABLE 15.3 Data and Correlation Matrix for Example 15.2

y	x_2	x_3
125	3	41
152	5	86
131	4	33
133	4	47
142	5	64
116	3	22
127	3	55
163	6	84

	Variables 1	2	3
1	1	.956	.921
2	.956	1	.805
3	.921	.805	1

variable one! Based on the correlation matrix and the two selection rules, the following predictor variable combinations are considered:

1. $y(x_1)$ should be predicted by x_4. *Reason:* x_4 has the highest correlation with the dependent variable of all the predictor variables collected ($r_{1,4} = -.83$) and will explain 69% ($-.83^2$) of the y variance. It is often of interest to run a simple regression analysis using the best single predictor.
2. y shouldn't be predicted by x_3 and x_4 together. *Reason:* Although both x_3 and x_4 have good correlations with the dependent variable ($r_{1,3} = .78$ and $r_{1,4} = -.83$), they are too highly correlated with each other ($r_{3,4} = -.89$). Multicollinearity is quite likely, as these two variables will be explaining the same y variance. When analysts examine correlations for multicollinearity, they use the following rule of thumb: The correlation between the two predictor variables should be well below the lower of the two correlations between the predictor variables and the dependent variable. This rule applies only to the magnitude of the correlation coefficients and ignores their signs. In this case, the correlation between predictor variables ($r_{3,4} = -.89$) *exceeds* the smaller of the dependent-predictor variable correlations ($r_{1,3} = .78$), ignoring the sign, so multicollinearity is likely.
3. y should be predicted by x_4 and x_5 together. *Reason:* x_4 has a good correlation with the dependent variable ($r_{1,4} = -.83$), and x_5 has a fair correlation ($r_{1,5} = .65$). However, the correlation between x_4 and x_5 is low ($r_{4,5} = -.21$), so multicollinearity won't be a problem. This combination should be examined since each predictor variable will explain a separate portion of the y variable variance, and a good prediction equation is likely to result.
4. y should be predicted by x_3 and x_5 together. *Reason:* x_3 and x_5 both have reasonable correlations with y ($r_{1,3} = .78$ and $r_{1,5} = .65$) and a low correlation with each other ($r_{3,5} = .17$). This combination should also produce a good prediction equation with no multicollinearity.

Note that none of these predictor variable combinations involves x_2. This variable has a low correlation with y ($r_{1,2} = -.27$) and so would not be used alone or in any combination.

The three promising predictor variable combinations identified should be run using a computer program that performs multiple regression. The resulting regressions can then be analyzed to find the best sample prediction equation. Finally, the best sample equation can be evaluated to see if its predictive power for y is strong enough to use in the population.

EXAMPLE 15.4 Example 14.10 developed a regression equation to predict monthly overhead costs using machine hours. However, in a complex manufacturing environment, variable overhead costs may be driven by several equally important factors. Under such circumstances, using more than one base for applying variable overhead costs to products and jobs results in a more accurate cost estimate.[1]

As reported in *Management Accounting*, Nevin (1992) developed a multiple regression equation to forecast monthly overhead costs using direct labor hours, machine hours, and number of setups, as predictor variables. The data and a correlation matrix are presented in Table 15.4. Row 1 of the correlation matrix indicates variable x_3, machine hours, has the best potential ($r_{13} = .878$) as a predictor variable. Variables x_2 and x_4, direct labor hours and number of setups, both have only fair potential ($r_{12} = .535$)

TABLE 15.4 Data and Correlation Matrix (Example 15.4)

FOH costs	Direct labor hours	Machine hours	Number of setups
155,000	985	1,060	200
160,000	1,068	1,080	225
170,000	1,095	1,100	250
165,000	1,105	1,200	202
185,000	1,200	1,600	210
135,000	1,160	1,100	150
145,000	1,145	1,080	165
150,000	1,025	1,090	180
180,000	1,115	1,300	204
175,000	1,136	1,400	206
190,000	1,185	1,500	208
200,000	1,220	1,700	212

	1 Costs	2 Labor	3 Machine	4 Setups
Costs	1	.535	.878	.627
Labor	.535	1	.768	−.047
Machine	.878	.768	1	.251
Setups	.627	−.047	.251	1

[1]A. M. Novin, "Applying Overhead: How to Find the Right Bases and Rates," *Management Accounting*, March 1992, pp. 40–43.

and (r_{14} = .627). The first rule for selecting predictor variables has indicated all three predictor variables have some potential since they are correlated with the dependent variable. Using both rules for selecting predictor variables, the following combinations are considered:

1. A simple regression using machine hours, x_3, as the predictor variable for y should be run. Reason: x_3 has the highest correlation with the dependent variable of all the predictor variables collected (r_{13} = .878) and will explain 77.1 percent $(.878)^2$ of the monthly overhead cost variance.
2. The combination of x_2 and x_3 should not be run. Reason: Although x_2 and x_3 are good potential predictor variables (correlations of .535 and .878 with y), they are also highly correlated with each other (r_{23} = .768). The correlation of .768 exceeds the smaller of the dependent-predictor variable correlations (r_{12} = .535), so multicollinearity is likely. The detection of multicollinearity in a multiple regression will be discussed later in this chapter.
3. The combination of x_3 and x_4 should be used together. Reason: x_3 is the best single predictor and x_4 is a fair predictor (correlation with y is .627). Their correlation with each other (r_{34} = .251) is lower than the two correlations with y. The run should be made so the outcome can be assessed.
4. There is no combination of three predictor variables that should be tried. Reason: The correlation matrix does not reveal any combination of three predictor variables that have good correlations with y and low correlations with each other.

Adel can now instruct a computer program to run the desired regressions. The result is presented in Example 15.7.

NOTES ON MULTICOLLINEARITY

When multicollinearity is present, how severe is the problem? Actually, if the analyst only wishes to use the regression model for prediction purposes, multicollinearity may not cause any serious difficulties. The adverse consequences of multicollinearity are:

1. Estimates of the regression coefficients fluctuate markedly from sample to sample.
2. An independent variable that's positively related to the dependent variable can produce a negative regression coefficient if it's highly correlated to another independent variable.
3. Multiple regression is often used as an interpretative tool to evaluate the relative importance of various independent variables. When predictor variables are intercorrelated, they explain the same variance in the prediction of the dependent variable. For this reason, it's difficult to separate the individual influences of each of the independent variables when multicollinearity is present.

It was mentioned earlier that the presence of multicollinearity may not be serious for applications where the analyst only wants to use the regression model for prediction purposes. In this case, the effects of unstable regression coefficients may cancel each other out, resulting in an accurate prediction of y. One example might be a site location study, such as where to locate a new McDonalds or Taco Time. Several highly related independent variables such as traffic count, traffic flow, population density, number of households, and number of registered drivers may be used to predict potential sales volume. Since the model is only being used to predict the best location (potential sales volume), the presence of multicollinearity may not be a severe problem.

EXERCISES

1. Explain the difference between a simple regression model and a multiple regression model.
2. Why does a correlation matrix contain 1s down the primary diagonal?
3. What is multicollinearity? How can it be prevented?
4. What are the characteristics of a good predictor variable?
5. In the following correlation matrix, variable 1 is the dependent variable.

	1	2	3	4
1	1	−.87	.78	.23
2	−.87	1	−.43	−.07
3	.78	−.43	1	.09
4	.23	−.07	.09	1

5a. 2 and 3 are
b. No, $r_{23} = -.43$
c. 2 and 3

a. Are variables 2, 3, and 4 good potential predictor variables?
b. Will multicollinearity be a problem for any combination? Explain your answer.
c. Which variable(s) will be included in the final model?

6. This exercise refers to the following correlation matrix where variable 1 is the dependent variable.

	1	2	3	4
1	1	.77	.84	.92
2	.77	1	.75	.81
3	.84	.75	1	.21
4	.92	.81	.21	1

6a. Yes
b. Yes, 2 and 3, 2 and 4
c. 3 and 4

a. Are variables 2, 3, and 4 good potential predictor variables?
b. Will multicollinearity be a problem for any combination? Explain your answer.
c. Which variable(s) will be included in the final model?

7. In the following correlation matrix, variable 1 is the dependent variable.

	1	2	3	4	5	6
1	1	.571	.098	−.539	.810	.764
2		1	.258	−.112	.387	.418
3			1	−.007	.245	.187
4				1	−.419	−.158
5					1	.755
6						1

7*b.* 5 and 6, maybe 2 and 4
c. Negative
d. 5, $r^2 = .66$
e. 5 and 6
f. 2–4–5, 2–4–6

a. Why is half of the matrix below the primary diagonal blank?
b. Which predictor variables are related to the dependent variable?
c. What kind of relationship exists between variables 1 and 4?
d. Which predictor variable will explain the largest portion of the dependent variable's variance? What percentage will it explain?
e. Is there any evidence of multicollinearity?
f. Which combination or combinations of variables should be investigated further?

The Multiple Regression Equation

Equation 15.1 shows how the population multiple regression model is written:

$$y = \beta_0 + \beta_2 x_2 + \beta_3 x_3 + \cdots + \beta_k x_k + \varepsilon \qquad (15.1)$$

where
y = Dependent variable
$x_2, x_3, \ldots, x_k$ = Predictor variables
$\beta_0, \beta_2, \beta_3, \ldots, \beta_k$ = Parameters in the population model
ε = Random error component

Regression Assumptions

The assumptions of the multiple regression model are similar to those for the simple linear regression model:

1. The probability distribution of ε is normal.
2. The variance of the probability distribution of ε is constant for all values of x.
3. The mean of the probability distribution of ε is 0. This assumption implies that the mean value of y for a given value of x is $E(y) = \beta_0 + \beta_2 x_2 + \beta_3 x_3 + \cdots + \beta_k x_k$.
4. The values of ε are independent of each other. This assumption implies that a random sample of objects has been selected from the population for measurement.

The least squares method produced the best-fitting straight line for two variables in Chapter 14. When three variables are analyzed, the least squares method produces a plane (Figure 15.2). When more than three variables are analyzed, the multiple regression model forms a hyperplane (or response surface) through multidimensional space. Note that whenever the term *plane* is used throughout the rest of the text, it will refer to a plane in three-dimensional space or a hyperplane in multidimensional space.

The multiple regression equation minimizes the sum of the squared vertical distances between the actual y values and their estimates based on the regression plane. In other words, in developing the multiple regression equation, $\Sigma(y - \hat{y})^2$ is minimized by the least squares procedure. This is the same quantity minimized in simple regression, as explained in Chapter 14. The difference in multiple regression is that the $\hat{y}$ values are calculated using more than one predictor variable. In other words, two or more predictor variable values are used in the prediction equation to calculate each $\hat{y}$.

Normally, the exact values of the regression parameters $\beta_0, \beta_2, \beta_3, \ldots, \beta_k$, and ε of Equation 15.1 aren't actually known but must be estimated from sample data. From

FIGURE 15.2 Multiple Regression Plane

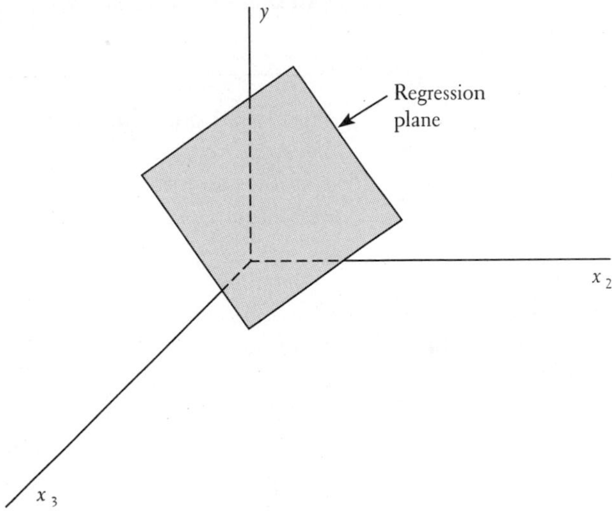

the sample data, estimates of the parameters are found, and the hyperplane that best fits the set of data points, called the *sample regression hyperplane*, is determined. Equation 15.2 uses $b_0, b_2, b_3, \ldots,$ and b_k to estimate $\beta_0, \beta_2, \beta_3, \ldots,$ and β_k:

Sample Regression Equation

$$\hat{y} = b_0 + b_2x_2 + b_3x_3 + \cdots + b_kx_k \tag{15.2}$$

where $\hat{y}$ = Estimated value of the dependent variable
$x_2, x_3, \ldots, x_k$ = Predictor variables
$b_0, b_2, b_3, \ldots, b_k$ = Sample estimates of $\beta_0, \beta_2, \beta_3, \ldots, \beta_k$

As in the case of the simple regression model, the sample estimates $b_0, b_2, b_3, \ldots,$ b_k are obtained as solutions to a set of simultaneous linear equations. These are difficult to solve without the use of a computer program. For this reason, computer programs will be used to solve multiple regression exercises throughout the rest of this text.

If two predictor variables are used in multiple regression, the equation will have a y-intercept and two regression coefficients, one for each predictor (x). As in simple regression, the value b_0 is the y-intercept. If both x_2 and x_3 are 0, the regression equation value for $\hat{y}$ is b_0, the y-intercept. If it's possible for both x_2 and x_3 to approach 0, this interpretation might prove useful. In most cases, however, the two predictor variables are such that they can't be near 0. As in simple regression, the y-intercept rarely has a useful interpretation.

Estimated Regression Coefficient

The $b_2, b_3, \ldots, b_k$ values are referred to as **estimated regression coefficients.** Each coefficient measures the average change in y per unit change in the relevant predictor variable. However, since the simultaneous influence of all predictor variables on y is being measured, the net effect of x_2 (or any other x) must be measured apart from any influence of other predictor variables. Therefore, we say that b_2 measures the average change in y per unit increase in x_2, *holding the other predictor variables constant.*

A particular **estimated regression coefficient** measures the average change in the dependent variable for a one-unit increase in the relevant predictor variable, holding the other predictor variables constant.

EXAMPLE 15.5 In Example 15.2, Amy Green used the number of TV ads and average temperature to predict weekly sales. She used MINITAB to produce the following multiple regression equation:

$$\hat{y} = 86.255 + 8.324x_2 + 0.2877x_3$$

The regression coefficients in the equation are interpreted as follows:

1. If the number of ads run per week increases by one, and average daily high temperature during the week is held constant, weekly sales are expected to increase by an average of 8.324 (thousand dollars).
2. If average daily temperature during the week increases by 1°, and the number of ads run per week is held constant, weekly sales are expected to increase by an average of 0.2877 (thousand dollars).

After interpreting the regression coefficients, the analyst can develop point estimates or predictions for y using the regression equation. Values for the predictor variables are substituted into the regression equation, and the $\hat{y}$ value is computed. This is the most common application for multiple regression analysis in the business world, since forecasts of important dependent variables are often desired.

EXAMPLE 15.6 Amy can now use the multiple regression equation in Example 15.5 to predict weekly sales if the number of ads and the average temperature are specified. Suppose these values are known to be

$$x_2 = 4 \text{ (Number of ads)}$$
$$x_3 = 70 \text{ (Average weekly temperature)}$$

The prediction of weekly sales is

$$\begin{aligned}\hat{y} &= 86.255 + 8.324(4) + 0.2877(70)\\ &= 86.255 + 33.296 + 20.160\\ &= 139.688 \text{ (thousand dollars)}\end{aligned}$$

The predicted weekly sales based on the sample multiple regression equation and the specified values of the predictor variables is \$139,688. Now Amy wants to interpret the values in the equation.

How would an increase of one ad per week affect sales if average temperature is held constant?

$$\hat{y} = 86.255 + 8.324(5) + 0.2877(70)$$
$$= 148.012$$

Note that sales have increased by $8,324 (148,012 − 139,688).

What is the effect on sales of an increase of 1° in the average temperature if the number of ads is held constant?

$$\hat{y} = 86.255 + 8.324(4) + 0.2877(71)$$
$$= 139.976$$

Note that sales have increased by $288 (139,976 − 139,688).

MINITAB can be used to run multiple regression problems. The MINITAB commands to solve Examples 15.5 and 15.6 are:

```
MTB > READ C1-C3
DATA> 125 3 41
DATA> 152 5 86
DATA> 131 4 33
DATA> 133 4 47
DATA> 142 5 64
DATA> 116 3 22
DATA> 127 3 55
DATA> 163 6 84
DATA> END
      8 ROWS READ

MTB > NAME C1 'SALES' C2 'ADS' C3 'TEMP'
MTB > CORR C1-C3

          SALES       ADS
ADS       0.956
TEMP      0.921      0.805

MTB > REGRESS C1 ON 2 PREDICTORS C2 C3;
SUBC> PREDICT 4 70;
SUBC> PREDICT 5 70;
SUBC> PREDICT 4 71.
```

The regression equation is

```
SALES = 86.3 + 8.32 ADS + 0.288 TEMP
    Fit     Stdev.Fit         95% C.I.                95% P.I.
139.688         1.643    (135.463, 143.912)    (131.608, 147.767)
148.011         1.237    (144.831, 151.191)    (140.426, 155.597)
139.975         1.704    (135.594, 144.357)    (131.813, 148.138)
```

The rest of the regression output is shown in Table 15.6.

```
MTB > STOP
```

Note that the READ command is used to input the data instead of the SET command. The READ command puts the sales variable into C1, the TV ads variable into C2, and the average temperature variable in C3. The NAME command is used to name the table's columns. The CORR command provides the correlation matrix for these three variables. The REGRESS command is used to develop a regression analysis with sales as the dependent (y) variable and TV ads and average temperature as the independent (x) variables. The first PREDICT subcommand is used to compute both a point and 95% interval estimate for a week when four TV ads are planned and average temperature will be 70°. Note that the output is only partially shown here. Table 15.6 shows complete output.

EXAMPLE 15.7 In Example 15.4, Adel Nevin developed a multiple regression equation to forecast monthly overhead costs. He was able to explain 94.7 percent of the dependent variable variance using machine hours and number of setups as predictor variables.[2] He found:

$$y = 19{,}796.43 + 65.44(MH) + 322.21(NS)$$

where y = Estimated monthly overhead costs
MH = Machine hours
NS = Number of setups

Adel can use this equation to predict monthly overhead costs if he specifies the values of the predictor variables. Suppose he wants to predict the monthly overhead costs for next month. He plans on 1,400 machine hours and 205 setups. The predicted value y is

$$y = 19{,}796.43 + 65.44(MH) + 322.21(NS)$$
$$y = 19{,}796.43 + 65.44(1400) + 322.21(205) = 177{,}465.48$$

The multiple regression equation predicts that monthly overhead costs will be $177,465.48 next month. Adel wonders about this prediction's accuracy.

STANDARD ERROR OF ESTIMATE

Standard Error of Estimate

In simple regression, as discussed in Chapter 14, the standard error of estimate is used to measure the variability, or scatter, of the observed sample y values around the sample regression line. In multiple regression, the **standard error of estimate** measures the variability, or scatter, of the observed sample y values around the regression plane. Equation 15.3 shows how the standard error of estimate is computed in multiple regression. This equation is identical to Equation 14.10 except for the computation of the degrees of freedom in the denominator:

$$s_{y \cdot x's} = \sqrt{\frac{\Sigma(y - \hat{y})^2}{n - k}} \tag{15.3}$$

where $s_{y \cdot x's}$ = Standard error of estimate
y = Sample y values
$\hat{y}$ = Values of y calculated from the regression plane or hyperplane
k = Number of linearly independent parameters to be estimated (the

---

[2] A. M. Novin, "Applying Overhead: How to Find the Right Bases and Rates," *Management Accounting*, March 1992, pp. 40–43.

number of *b*s in the equation assuming the predictor variables are linearly independent)

n = Sample size

> The **standard error of estimate** measures the variability, or scatter, of the observed sample y values around the regression plane.

EXAMPLE 15.8 Joyce Miller, financial analyst for Edwall Chemical Corporation (a fertilizer company), wants to predict the weekly interest rate Edwall pays for short-term funds. The company president has ordered an intensive study of Edwall's financial and sales position after reading a *Wall Street Journal* article (November 2, 1989, p. C16) indicating that U.S. farmers set an income record in 1988. The president can't understand why Edwall's 1988 profits were so low.

Joyce randomly selects 100 weeks from the company files and records the interest paid for each week (the dependent variable), along with several other variables that she thinks will correlate well. After examining the correlation matrix produced by her regression computer program, she finds a good predictor combination:

$$\hat{y} = -0.05 + 0.55x_4 - 0.42x_6$$

Joyce analyzes the following summary values

t value for x_4 = 4.79
t value for x_6 = −5.83
$R^2 = .91 \quad F = 89.44$
$s_{y \cdot x\text{'s}} = 0.004$

She decides that the t values, F value, and R^2 all indicate that the regression equation will do a good job of predicting the weekly interest Edwall paid. But how close will the predictions based on this regression equation be? The standard error of estimate indicates that for the sample of 100 weeks, $\hat{y}$ typically differs from the actual value of y by 0.004. Joyce considers this typical error to be quite acceptable and is pleased with the accuracy of the equation. It is easy to measure the two predictor variables, x_4 and x_6, at the beginning of each week, so she can now make accurate predictions.

PREDICTION AND CONFIDENCE INTERVALS

The sample multiple regression equation is frequently used to make forecasts for y. If a given set of x values are substituted in the regression equation, the expected value of y can be found. This y value is called a *point estimate*. However, as stated in Chapter 14, this point estimate doesn't provide any knowledge about the degree of accuracy of the forecast.

Chapter 14's prediction interval and confidence interval concepts can also be applied to multiple regression analysis. Equation 15.4 is used to compute a prediction interval for y:

$$\hat{y} \pm t\, s_{\hat{y} \cdot x\text{'s}}$$

where $\hat{y}$ = Regression equation prediction of y
t = Value from t distribution based on $n - k$ degrees of freedom for a given prediction level
$s_{\hat{y}\cdot x\text{'s}}$ = Estimated standard error of the prediction

Equation 15.5 is used to compute a confidence interval for y:

$$\hat{y} \pm t\, s_{\hat{\mu}\cdot x\text{'s}} \tag{15.5}$$

where $s_{\hat{\mu}\cdot x\text{'s}}$ = Estimated standard error of the estimate

The assumptions made when we use Equations 15.4 and 15.5 to compute prediction and confidence intervals for y were introduced in Chapter 14 and restated earlier in this chapter. For multiple regression models, the formulas for the standard deviation of the sampling distributions for the estimator y, $s_{\hat{y}\cdot x\text{'s}}$ and $s_{\hat{\mu}\cdot x\text{'s}}$, are rather complex and won't be discussed in this text. Those who use regression computer packages will usually be provided both prediction and confidence intervals.

EXAMPLE 15.9 In Example 15.6, Amy Green wants to determine the accuracy of her prediction of $139,688. She decides to develop 95% prediction and confidence intervals. First, she checks the MINITAB computer output and finds the prediction interval is 131.608 to 147.767. Using Equation 15.4 to compute this prediction interval, she gets

$$\hat{y} \pm t\, s_{\hat{y}\cdot x\text{'s}}$$
$$139.688 \pm 2.571(3.143)$$
$$139.688 \pm 8.080$$
$$131.608 \text{ to } 147.767$$

The t value for five degrees of freedom ($\text{df} = n - k = 8 - 3 = 5$) is used. If Amy runs four TV ads and average temperature is 70° next week, she's 95% confident that sales will be between $131,608 and $147,767.

Next, Amy checks the MINITAB computer output and finds the confidence interval is 135.463 to 143.912. Using Equation 15.5 to compute this confidence interval, she gets

$$\hat{y} \pm t\, s_{\hat{\mu}\cdot x\text{'s}}$$
$$139.688 \pm 2.571(1.643)$$
$$139.688 \pm 4.225$$
$$135.463 \text{ to } 143.912$$

Amy is 95% confident that the mean of the subpopulation of y for a week when she runs four TV ads and average temperature is 70° is between $135,463 and $143,912.

EXAMPLE 15.10 In Example 15.7, Adel Nevin wondered about the accuracy of his prediction of $177,465.48 for the monthly overhead costs for next month. He notices on his computer output that the standard error of fit is 1,670. Adel decides to develop a 90% confidence interval. He substitutes the appropriate values into Equation 15.5:

$$\hat{y} \pm t\, s_{\hat{\mu}\cdot x\text{'s}}$$
$$177{,}465.48 \pm 1.833(1670)$$
$$177{,}465.48 \pm 3061.11$$
$$174{,}404.37 \text{ to } \$180{,}526.59$$

Note that since the sample size is 12, the t value for 9 degrees of freedom is used.

Adel is 90% confident that the interval from \$174,404.37 to \$180,526.59 contains the mean variable overhead costs for next month if 1,400 machine hours and 205 set-ups are used.

EXERCISES

SM

8. What assumptions underlie the multiple regression model?
9. What is minimized when the least squares method is used to develop a multiple regression equation?

SM

10. What does the estimated regression coefficient measure in multiple regression?
11. What does a residual measure?
12. What does the standard error of estimate measure in multiple regression?

SM

13. Your multiple regression equation is $\hat{y} = 4.72 + 13x_2 - 4.2x_3$. Make a point estimate given $x_2 = 40$ and $x_3 = 20$.

13. 440.72

14. Develop a 90% prediction interval for Exercise 13 if $s_{\hat{y}\cdot x\text{'s}} = 2.8$. Compute this interval for a sample size of 25. Develop a 90% confidence interval for Exercise 13 if $s_{\hat{\mu}\cdot x\text{'s}} = 1.5$ and the sample size is 43.

14. 435.91 to 445.53; 438.25 to 443.19

15. Mario Padilla (an accountant for the Palmer Furniture Corporation) wants to determine if overhead can be estimated based on the number of chairs and tables produced. Mario collects the following data on overhead expenses for chairs and tables produced at seven different plants:

Plant	Overhead expenses, y	Number of chairs, x_2	Number of tables, x_3
1	\$576	112	95
2	497	122	84
3	789	147	102
4	862	173	108
5	361	94	75
6	688	151	99
7	532	109	91

a. Determine the sample multiple regression equation.

b. When an extra chair is produced, what is the average increase in overhead expense?

c. Compute the residual for plant 1.

d. Compute the standard error of estimate.

e. Interpret $s_{y\cdot x\text{'s}}$ in terms of the variables used in this exercise.

f. Compute a point estimate of the overhead expense if 150 chairs and 100 tables are produced.

g. Calculate a 95% prediction interval for part *f*.

15*a.* $\hat{y} = -622.3 + 2.398x_2 + 9.914x_3$
b. \$2.40
c. -12.1050
d. 31.0086
f. 728.8
g. 633.25 to 824.35
h. 687.33 to 770.27

h. Calculate a 95% confidence interval for part *f*.

i. What should Mario conclude?

16. Spendwise supermarket chain manager Anna Sheehan wants to know if a relationship exists between the time it takes to check out a customer and the amount the person purchases. She chooses two predictor variables: the amount a person purchases and the number of purchased items. Anna collects data for a sample of 12 customers:

Customer	Checkout time (minutes), y	Purchase amount (dollars), x_2	Number of items, x_3
1	3.1	35	8
2	1.1	14	6
3	0.4	4	2
4	6.4	78	13
5	5.8	81	12
6	8.4	106	18
7	4.9	61	11
8	7.9	66	12
9	2.1	22	6
10	5.9	54	12
11	0.8	12	3
12	1.3	19	9

16*a*. $\hat{y} = -.242 + .06655x_2 + .1274x_3$
b. .127 minutes
c. $-.874$
d. .9609
f. 6.66
g. 4.66 to 8.66
h. 5.71 to 7.61

a. Determine the sample multiple regression equation.

b. When an extra item is purchased, what is the average increase in the checkout time?

c. Compute the residual for customer 12.

d. Compute the standard error of estimate.

e. Interpret $s_{y \cdot x\text{'s}}$ in terms of the variables used in this exercise.

f. Compute a point estimate of the checkout time if a customer purchases 15 items that amount to $75.

g. Calculate a 90% prediction interval for part *f*.

h. Calculate a 90% confidence interval for part *f*.

i. Write a memo to Anna summarizing the results.

Hypothesis Testing in Multiple Regression Analysis

After the random sample has been collected, the variables measured, and the correlation matrix examined to find those predictor variable combinations that are of interest, the models with the best potential are analyzed. The objective is to find the best equation for predicting y and to then determine whether this equation meets the analyst's accuracy needs.

The criteria in Chapter 14 for evaluating a simple regression equation are used for multiple regression as well. Specifically, three key statistics should be examined in considering the quality of any regression equation, whether it has one predictor variable or many.

Coefficient of Multiple Determination (R^2)

One statistic consulted frequently in multiple regression analysis is the **coefficient of multiple determination,** represented by the symbol R^2. It is useful for measuring the percentage of the variability in the dependent variable, y, that can be explained by the predictor variables.

> The **coefficient of multiple determination,** R^2, measures the percentage of the variability in y that can be explained by the predictor variables.

An R^2 value close to 1 means that the equation is very accurate because a large portion of the variability of y is being explained. Equation 15.6 is used to calculate R^2 in a multiple regression. Note that this equation is similar to Equation 14.18 except that the calculations for $\hat{y}$ involve two or more predictor variables; this is denoted by capitalizing the symbol R^2:

$$R^2 = 1 - \frac{\Sigma(y - \hat{y})^2}{\Sigma(y - \bar{y})^2} \qquad (15.6)$$

Note that the numerator of the ratio is the sum of squares error (SSE), which is used to measure how well the regression plane fits a set of sample data points. As SSE is reduced by adding new predictor variables to the model, R^2 increases. If a regression plane fits a set of sample data points perfectly, SSE equals 0 and R^2 equals 1.

EXAMPLE 15.11 Amy Green's data were introduced in Example 15.2. When the mean of y was used to predict weekly sales in Example 14.13, the sum of squares total (SST) was 1,656.88 and r^2 was 0:

$$r^2 = 1 - \frac{\text{SSE}}{\text{SST}} = 1 - \frac{1{,}656.88}{1{,}656.88} = 1 - 1 = 0$$

In Example 14.14, when knowledge of the relationship between the number of TV ads and weekly sales ($r = .956$) was used to predict the dependent variable, the sum of squares error (SSE) was reduced to 144, and r^2 increased to .913:

$$r^2 = 1 - \frac{\text{SSE}}{\text{SST}} = 1 - \frac{144}{1{,}656.88} = 1 - .087 = .913$$

Table 15.5 shows the residuals for the data in Example 15.2. The computation of the residual for week 1 (three TV ads were run, and average high temperature for the week was 41°) is

$$\hat{y} = 86.255 + 8.324(3) + 0.2877(41) = 123.021$$
$$e = y - \hat{y} = 125 - 123.021 = 1.979$$

TABLE 15.5 Sum of Squares Error Calculation for Example 15.11

y	x_2	x_3	$\hat{y}$	$(y - \hat{y})$	$(y - \hat{y})^2$
125	3	41	123.021	1.979	3.916
152	5	86	152.614	−0.614	0.377
131	4	33	129.043	1.957	3.830
133	4	47	133.071	−0.071	0.005
142	5	64	146.285	−4.285	18.361
116	3	22	117.555	−1.555	2.418
127	3	55	127.049	−0.049	0.002
163	6	84	160.363	2.638	6.959
			Sums:	0.00	35.868

$$\hat{y} = 86.255 + 8.324x_2 + 0.2877x_3$$

When the residual column is squared and summed, SSE falls to 35.868. R^2 increases to .978:

$$R^2 = 1 - \frac{\text{SSE}}{\text{SST}} = 1 - \frac{35.868}{1{,}656.88} = 1 - .022 = .978$$

The information collected up to this point is summarized:

Variables used to explain variance of y	R^2	SSE
None	0	1,656.88
Number of TV ads	.913	144.00
Number of TV ads and average high temperature	.978	35.87

Analysts often make the mistake of looking only at R^2 in evaluating a regression equation. This can lead to problems since R^2 reflects only the reduction in the sum of squares error, as shown in Equation 15.6. The contributions of individual predictor variables should be analyzed and hypotheses tested to see if the sample results can be extrapolated to the population. For these reasons, the t and F statistics in the regression output should also be examined.

The t values in the regression analysis test the hypotheses that the population regression coefficients equal 0. Suppose the following regression equation has been calculated:

$$\hat{y} = 14 - 7x_2 + 5x_3$$

The sample regression coefficient for predictor variable 2 is −7. This can be interpreted to mean that for each increase of one unit in x_2, holding x_3 constant, y can be expected to decrease by an average of seven units. But can this statement be made about the population? This question is answered by examining the t value for the regression coefficient for x_2.

The null hypothesis being tested is

$$H_0\colon \beta_2 = 0$$

This null hypothesis states that in the population, regardless of the sample results, when x_2 increases by one, y is unaffected by this increase and assumes a random value. In other words, x_2 is contributing nothing to the predictive ability of the regression equation. If this null hypothesis is true, the test value for t is drawn from the t distribution with $(n - k)$ degrees of freedom (where n is the sample size and k is the number of linearly independent parameters, or βs, estimated in the analysis). A large t value ($t > 3$ or $t < -3$) will usually lead to rejection of the null hypothesis, and a t value close to 0 won't. The analyst therefore hopes for a large t value, either positive or negative, so that the sample regression coefficient can be generalized to the population.

Regression t Test

We must also test the null hypothesis that $\beta_3 = 0$. The sample regression coefficient for x_3, which is 5, can't be generalized to the population until this null hypothesis is rejected. Before using the regression equation, we must be sure that all t values in the computer printout are larger than the critical values from the t table for the appropriate degrees of freedom at the significance level being tested.

The computed t values are of particular importance in a multiple regression because they constitute the primary way to detect multicollinearity. If the analyst is unsure about including two variables in the same regression because of their high relationship to each other, the regression is run and the t values are checked. If they are sufficiently large, the correlation between the two predictor variables isn't a problem. If one or both t values fall below the table value for t, multicollinearity is present, rendering the regression coefficients unreliable. The following examples show the use of the t test.

EXAMPLE 15.12 In Example 15.2, Amy Green, Green Garden Company president, developed a multiple regression model that used the number of TV ads run per week and the average temperature for the week to predict weekly sales of garden supplies. When she examined the correlation matrix in Table 15.3, she became concerned about the problem of multicollinearity. Amy decides to test the regression coefficients to make sure that each predictor variable is contributing to the prediction of the dependent variable. First, she tests the number of TV ads run per week (x_2) at the .05 significance level:

$$H_0: \beta_2 = 0$$
$$H_1: \beta_2 \neq 0$$

The decision rule based on 5 degrees of freedom $(n - k) = (8 - 3) = 5$ is

> If the calculated t value is less than -2.571 or greater than 2.571, reject the null hypothesis (reject H_0 if $t < -2.571$ or $t > 2.571$).

Table 15.6 presents the results of a multiple regression computer analysis. The computed t value for the number of ads is 5.5. Since the computed t value is greater than the critical t value (2.571), the null hypothesis is rejected. The regression coefficient for the number of ads variable is significantly different from 0.

The same hypothesis test is performed for the regression coefficient for the variable representing average temperature. Table 15.6 shows that the computed t value for this variable is 3.88. Therefore, the regression coefficient for average high temperature is

TABLE 15.6 Computer Output for Examples 15.5, 15.6, and 15.12

```
The regression equation is
SALES = 86.3 + 8.32 ADS + 0.288 TEMP

Predictor        Coef       Stdev      t ratio       p
Constant       86.255       3.963        21.77   0.000
ADS             8.324       1.515         5.50   0.003
TEMP          0.28769     0.07411         3.88   0.012

s = 2.678       R-sq = 97.8%      R-sq (adj) = 97.0%

Analysis of Variance

SOURCE          DF          SS          MS          F          P
Regression       2     1621.01      810.50     112.99      0.000
Error            5       35.87        7.17
Total            7     1656.88

SOURCE          DF      SEQ SS
ADS              1     1512.90
TEMP             1      108.11

Obs.   ADS     SALES       Fit  Stdev.Fit  Residual  St.Resid
1     3.00   125.000   123.021      1.444     1.979      0.88
2     5.00   152.000   152.614      1.794    -0.614     -0.31
3     4.00   131.000   129.043      1.697     1.957      0.94
4     4.00   133.000   133.071      1.022    -0.071     -0.03
5     5.00   142.000   146.285      1.273    -4.285     -1.82
6     3.00   116.000   117.555      1.709    -1.555     -0.75
7     3.00   127.000   127.049      2.002    -0.049     -0.03
8     6.00   163.000   160.363      1.934     2.637      1.42
```

The following symbols may help you read this computer output.

$b_0 = 86.255$	$R^2 = 97.8\%$
$b_2 = 8.324$	$SSR = 1621.01$
$b_3 = .28769$	$SSE = 35.87$
$s_{y \cdot x} = 2.678$	$SST = 1656.88$

also significantly different from 0. Evidently, both variables explain some of the sales variance, so multicollinearity isn't a problem.

The F value is another statistic checked before the regression equation is used to explain the variability in y or to predict y. Just as in a simple regression, the F value tests the null hypothesis that the sample regression equation doesn't explain a significant percent of the y variance. This null hypothesis is

H_0: $\rho^2 = 0$ (The sample regression equation does not explain a significant percent of the variance in y.)

Regression F Test

This hypothesis is rejected if the F statistic computed from the sample data is larger than the value from the F table.

Proper consideration of the three key factors in evaluating a regression analysis requires some practice and judgment. The following examples illustrate the process that the analyst follows in identifying the best prediction equation for y once those predictor combinations of interest have been determined from the correlation matrix and run on a computer program.

EXAMPLE 15.13 Continuing from Example 15.12, Amy Green tests the F value for her multiple regression equation at the .05 significance level. The null and alternative hypotheses are

$$H_0: \rho^2 = 0$$
$$H_1: \rho^2 > 0$$

Correct values for the degrees of freedom are 2 for the numerator and 5 for the denominator (see Table 15.6). The appropriate number of degrees of freedom associated with the regression sum of squares is the number of independent variables. Since the multiple regression equation in this example has two independent (x) variables, there are 2 degrees of freedom, as Table 15.6 shows for the "regression" source of variation.

Similarly, the degrees of freedom for the "residual" source of variation equal $(n - k)$, the sample size, n, minus the number of coefficients estimated in the regression equation (β_0, β_2, and β_3). Therefore, Table 15.6 shows 5 degrees of freedom $(n - k) = (8 - 3) = 5$ for this source of variation.

Finally, the loss of the degree of freedom for the total is due to the estimate of the population mean of y using the sample mean. Thus, Table 15.6 shows 7 degrees of freedom $(n - 1) = (8 - 1) = 7$ for the "total" row in the ANOVA table.

For 2 and 5 degrees of freedom, Appendix E.9's F table indicates a critical F value of 5.79 for the .05 significance level. The decision rule is

If the calculated F value is greater than 5.79, reject the null hypothesis.

The following sums of squares are found in Table 15.6: SSR = 1,621.01, SSE = 35.87, and SST = 1,656.88. The sums of squares are divided by the appropriate degrees of freedom to produce the estimates of the unknown population variance, referred to as the mean square values (MS) on the computer output. The mean square for the "regression" row is 1,621.01/2 = 810.5. The mean square for the "residual" row is 35.87/5 = 7.17. The F value is the ratio of these two estimates of the variance and is computed using Equation 14.21:

$$F = \frac{\text{SSR}/(k - 1)}{\text{SSE}/(n - k)} = \frac{1{,}621.01/(3 - 1)}{35.87/(8 - 3)} = \frac{810.5}{7.17} = 113$$

Since the computed F value (113) is larger than the critical F value (5.79), the null hypothesis is rejected. The sample regression equation is explaining a significant percentage of the y variance.

EXAMPLE 15.14 Bank of San Francisco analyst Shane Bahoney seeks a way to accurately predict a customer's profitability. He discovers a measure called the *profitability index* in "Case Study: Old Regional Bank" in *Statistical Decision Models for Management* by Hanke and Reitsch (Allyn & Bacon, 1985). This index is based on the activities of customers, including provisions for loans, savings accounts, and checking accounts.

Shane identifies two potential variables that might correlate well with the profitability index (y): monthly checking account charge and number of checks written per month. He hopes that these two variables will enable the bank to explain the index's variability and to predict customer profitability.

A random sample of 10 customers is selected, and the three numerical measurements are made on each. Table 15.7 shows the resulting data along with the correlation matrix computed from them.

TABLE 15.7 Data and Correlation Matrix for Example 15.14

Profitability index (y)	Monthly checking charge (x_2)	Checks per month (x_3)
31	2.65	35
18	4.08	29
16	3.59	22
37	3.03	55
30	3.41	61
44	2.51	52
15	3.18	25
35	2.75	38
51	2.10	58
59	2.14	83

	Variables		
	1	2	3
1	1	−.867	.885
2	−.867	1	−.630
3	.885	−.630	1

Examination of the correlation matrix in Table 15.7 indicates two potentially good predictor variables. Both x_2 and x_3 have good correlations with the dependent variable ($r_{1,2} = -.867$ and $r_{1,3} = .885$). The best single predictor variable is x_3 because it has the highest correlation with y ($r_{1,3} = .885$) and would explain 78.3% of its variance ($.885^2 = .783$) if used in a simple regression equation.

The F test is used to determine whether the multiple regression equation explains a significant percent of the y variance. The null and alternative hypotheses are

$$H_0: \rho^2 = 0$$
$$H_1: \rho^2 > 0$$

The instructions to run these data on the SAS program are shown at the end of this chapter. Table 15.8 gives the results for this multiple regression run.

There are 2 degrees of freedom for the numerator and 7 for the denominator, as Table 15.8 shows. For the regression row, referred to as "model" on the SAS computer output, df $= (k - 1) = (3 - 1) = 2$. For the residual row, referred to as "error" on the SAS computer output, df $= (n - k) = (10 - 3) = 7$. Finally, for the "total" row, df $= (n - 1) = (10 - 1) = 9$.

For 2 and 7 degrees of freedom, the F table in Appendix E.9 indicates a critical value of 4.74 for the .05 significance level. The decision rule is

If the calculated F value is greater than 4.74, reject the null hypothesis.

The following sums of squares are found in Table 15.8: SSR = 1,874.57, SSE = 113.82, and SST = 1,988.40. The mean square for the "model" row is 1,874.57/2 = 937.29. The mean square for the "error" row is 113.82/7 = 16.26. The F value is

$$F = \frac{\text{SSR}/(k-1)}{\text{SSE}/(n-k)} = \frac{1{,}874.57/(3-1)}{113.82/(10-3)} = \frac{937.29}{16.26} = 57.6$$

Since the calculated F value (57.6) is considerably larger than the critical value (4.74), the null hypothesis is rejected with small chance of error. Shane concludes that the sample regression equation explains a significant percentage of the y variance ($\rho^2 > 0$).

The p value provided by the SAS program in Table 15.8 leads to the same conclusion. The p-value for the F statistic is .0001, meaning that the probability of obtaining an R^2 value as large as .943 by chance alone is very small (.0001). The analyst should

TABLE 15.8 SAS Computer Output for Example 15.14

```
DEPENDENT VARIABLE: INDEX
SOURCE    DF   SUM OF SQUARES   MEAN SQUARE   F VALUE     PR > F    R-SQUARE
MODEL      2        1874.57         937.29      57.6       .0001      .943
ERROR      7         113.82          16.26               ROOT MSE                Y-MEAN
TOTAL      9        1988.40                               4.0325                  33.6
SOURCE    DF   TYPE I SS   F VALUE   PR > F   DF   TYPE III SS   F VALUE   PR > F
X2         1    1496.24     92.01     .0001    1     316.41       19.46     .0031
X3         1     378.33     23.27     .0019    1     378.33       23.27     .0019
                                  T FOR HO =                          STD ERROR OF
PARAMETER        ESTIMATE         PARAMETER = 0       PR > [T]        ESTIMATE
INTERCEPT          49.02
X2                -11.97              -4.41            .0031             2.71
X3                  0.43               4.82            .0019             0.09
                    OBSERVED          PREDICTED
OBSERVATION         VALUE             VALUE                RESIDUAL
      1               31                32.44                 -1.44
      2               18                12.72                  5.28
      3               16                15.56                  0.44
      4               37                36.55                  0.45
      5               30                34.60                 -4.60
      6               44                41.48                  2.52
      7               15                21.77                 -6.77
      8               35                32.55                  2.45
      9               51                48.99                  2.01
     10               59                59.33                 -0.33

               SUM OF RESIDUALS                                0.00
               SUM OF SQUARED RESIDUALS                      113.82
```

The following symbols may help you read this computer output. Some items have been left out of the output to make it easier to read.

SSR = 1,874.57	b_0	= 49.02
SSE = 113.82	b_2	= −11.97
SST = 1,988.40	b_3	= 0.43
R^2 = .943	$(y - \hat{y})$	= −1.44 (Obs. 1)
$\bar{y}$ = 33.6		

conclude that R^2 is significantly different from 0. The multiple regression equation explains a significant percentage of the dependent variable variance.

Attention now turns to the question of whether using x_2 and x_3 together in a multiple regression equation is a good idea. Since both have strong correlations with y, they pass the first test for good predictor variables. But what about the correlation between them? The correlation matrix in Table 15.7 indicates this correlation ($r_{2,3}$) to be $-.63$. Although this value is below both correlations with y ($-.867$ and $.855$), it's still high enough to cause concern about multicollinearity.

The regression should be run and the t values tested to see if multicollinearity is a problem. There are 7 degrees of freedom for the t test, as shown in the "df" column and "error" row. This value is calculated as $(n - k)$, where k is the number of βs, or linearly independent parameters to be estimated in the analysis. Since three parameters are involved (β_0, β_2, and β_3), the degrees of freedom is $(10 - 3) = 7$. For 7 degrees of freedom, the t table indicates a critical value of 2.365 for a two-tailed test at an alpha level of .05. The decision rule is

If the calculated t value is less than -2.365 or greater than 2.365, reject the null hypothesis.

Since both t values (-4.41 and 4.82) are significant, both null hypotheses are rejected. Both regression coefficients are significant, and the regression equation is used to estimate values in the population. The correlation between x_2 and x_3 ($r_{2,3} = -.63$) has not led to multicollinearity.

The p-values provided by the SAS program lead to the same conclusion. The p-values for the t statistics are .0031 and .0019, indicating that probabilities of obtaining regression coefficients as large as -11.97 and .43 by chance alone are very small. The analyst should therefore conclude that the regression coefficients are significantly different from 0. Both predictor variables explain a significant portion of the variance.

Table 15.8's multiple regression equation

$$\hat{y} = 49.02 - 11.97x_2 + 0.43x_3$$

can be interpreted for the population of bank customers as follows: Holding x_3 constant, a \$1 increase in monthly checking charge (x_2) will decrease the profitability index by an average of about 12 units (-11.97). With x_2 held constant, an increase of one check per month (x_3) will increase the profitability index by an average of 0.43 units. Bank management can use these values to evaluate the effects of these two key variables on the important profitability index.

In addition, the multiple regression equation can be used to predict the profitability index for a customer if both x_2 and x_3 are known. For example, a customer who incurs a monthly checking charge of \$1.25 and writes 62 checks is predicted to have a profitability index of 60.72:

$$\begin{aligned}\hat{y} &= 49.02 - 11.97x_2 + 0.43x_3\\ &= 49.02 - 11.97(1.25) + 0.43(62) = 60.72\end{aligned}$$

EXAMPLE 15.15 Rashid Al-Qamra, vice president of a manufacturing firm, wants to promote physical fitness for his company's employees. He first became interested in this idea after reading an article on the rewards of having fit employees, "Let's Get Physical" (*Business Monthly*, March 1990).

While flying to a board of directors meeting, Rashid read in Northwest Airlines' *World Traveler* that "premature deaths cost American industry more than $25 billion and 132 million workdays of lost production each year." Rashid asks statistician Sue Ableson to analyze the effectiveness of the company's fitness center. Sue collects data on several employees for y, the score on a fitness rating scale; x_2, the perceived level of exertion during exercise at the fitness center; and x_3, the average number of visits to the fitness center per week.

Table 15.9 displays the variables along with the correlation matrix generated by a computer program.

TABLE 15.9 Data and Correlation Matrix for Example 15.15

y	x_2	x_3
36	9.6	5.5
12	2.6	1.8
24	3.5	0.9
27	6.1	2.8
36	7.8	4.6
34	6.9	3.7
17	4.4	1.9
23	6.1	1.8
31	7.0	2.7
30	6.8	2.0

	Variables		
	1	2	3
1	1	.896	.748
2	.896	1	.842
3	.748	.842	

After studying the correlation matrix, Sue is pleased to find that both x variables correlate well with y: $r_{1,2} = .896$ and $r_{1,3} = .748$. She decides to run two regressions. First, y will be explained by x_2 alone; she observes that x_2 is the single best predictor, since it has the higher correlation with y. Second, y will be predicted by x_2 and x_3 together; Sue reasons that these two potentially good predictor variables should produce a strong prediction equation when used together. Tables 15.10 and 15.11 show the MINITAB computer results from these two regressions.

Sue notes that R^2 for the multiple regression equation is the same as r^2 using x_2 alone (80.3%), and she decides to use both variables to predict y. The equation, from Table 15.11, is

$$\hat{y} = 5.79 + 3.54x_2 - 0.115x_3$$

She gives this equation to her boss and indicates that it will produce fairly accurate predictions for y, based on the R^2 of about 80%.

TABLE 15.10 MINITAB Computer Output for Example 15.15

```
The regression equation is
Y = 5.88 + 3.48X2
Predictor        Coef        Stdev       t ratio
Constant        5.880
X2              3.480        1.206         5.70
s = 3.802       R-sq = 80.3%
Analysis of Variance
SOURCE           DF          SS           MS
Regression        1        470.37       470.37
Error             8        115.63        14.45
Total             9        586.00
```

TABLE 15.11 MINITAB Computer Output for Example 15.15

```
The regression equation is
Y = 5.79 + 3.54 X2 - 0.11 X3
Predictor        Coef       Stdev      t ratio
Constant        5.793
X2              3.540       1.206        2.94
X3             -0.115       1.755       -0.07
s = 4.063          R-sq = 80.3%
Analysis of Variance
SOURCE             DF        SS          MS
Regression          2      470.44      235.22
Error               7      115.56
Total               9      586.00
SOURCE             DF      SEQ SS
X2                  1      470.37
X3                  1        0.07
```

The following symbols may help you read this computer output:

$b_0 = 5.793$	$R^2 = 80.3\%$
$b_2 = 3.540$	$SSR = 470.44$
$b_3 = -0.115$	$SSE = 115.56$
$s_{y \cdot x's} = 4.063$	$SST = 586.00$

Unfortunately, Sue hasn't guarded against multicollinearity. Table 15.9's correlation matrix indicates that x_2 and x_3 should *not* be used in the same regression equation since the correlation between them is too high ($r_{2,3} = .842$). This correlation is nearly as high as the correlation between x_2 and y (.896) and higher than the correlation between x_3 and y (.748). For this reason, multicollinearity is sure to result.

Table 15.11 shows symptoms of multicollinearity. The t value for x_2 has dropped from what it was when x_2 was used alone (2.94 compared with 5.70). Worse, the t value for x_3 (-0.07) is not significant. Based on this t value, x_3 shouldn't be used in conjunction with x_2. This conclusion renders the regression equation useless in the population for which it's intended.

There's an even more serious problem caused by multicollinearity: the sign on the regression coefficient for x_3 is the opposite of what it should be. There's a *positive* correlation between x_3 and y ($r_{1,3} = .748$) but a *negative* regression coefficient

($b_3 = -0.115$). The latter value is interpreted to mean that when x_3 increases, holding x_2 constant, y *decreases* by an average of 0.115 units. This regression coefficient doesn't make sense since x_3 and y are positively correlated.

The basic problem caused by multicollinearity is that the sample regression coefficients vary excessively from sample to sample. One sample may produce a small positive value, another may produce a large negative value, the next may produce a large positive value, and so on. As Table 15.11 shows, this particular sample has produced a regression coefficient for x_3 that has varied so much that it's negative instead of positive. If this equation is used, the results are sure to be erroneous. Sue would be much better off using the simple regression equation in Table 15.10, which has an r^2 of 80% along with a valid t value.

EXERCISES

17. What does the coefficient of multiple determination measure?

18. Gary Texaco owns a gas station in Cleveland, Ohio. Gary has developed the following multiple regression equation based on weekly sales of unleaded gas:

$$\hat{y} = 100 - 50x_2 + 4x_3 \qquad s_y = 20 \qquad s_{\hat{\mu}\cdot x's} = 6 \qquad n = 36$$

where $\hat{y}$ = Estimated sales of unleaded gasoline (gallons)
x_2 = Price of unleaded gasoline (cents)
x_3 = Traffic count

18*b*. 17,876.50
c. 17.864.7 to 17,888.3

a. Interpret the estimated regression coefficients.

b. Compute a point estimate of weekly sales of unleaded gas if price is .95 and traffic count is 4,456 cars.

c. Compute a 95% confidence interval for your prediction for part *b*.

19. Rob Higgens, a real estate broker, wants to develop a regression equation to predict the sale price of homes (in thousands of dollars) in Flint, Michigan. Rob read "An Application of Multiple Regression Analysis for Appraising Single-Family Housing Values" in *Business Economics* (January 1980, pp. 47–52), indicating predictor variables that could be utilized in predicting price (including total living area, number of rooms, number of baths, and age of property). Rob decided to use age of house (x_2), square feet of living space (x_3), measured in hundreds, and number of rooms (x_4) as predictor variables. He collected data for 22 houses and gives it to you to perform an analysis on a microcomputer. A portion of the analysis of variance table follows:

ANALYSIS OF VARIANCE

SOURCE OF VARIATION	DEGREES OF FREEDOM	SUM OF SQUARES
ATTRIBUTABLE TO REGRESSION	3	2448.65
DEVIATION FROM REGRESSION	18	424.81
TOTAL	21	2873.46

19*a*. $R^2 = .852$
b. df $= n - k = 22 - 4 = 18$

a. Calculate R^2.

b. Show how the degrees of freedom for the "deviation from regression" was computed.

c. Should Rob use this multiple regression equation? Why or why not?

20. In Exercise 19, the computer output for housing value appraisal also contained the following information:

VARIABLE NO.	REGRESSION COEFFICIENT	STD. ERROR OF REG COEF.	COMPUTED T VALUE
2	3.15241	0.92010	3.426
3	1.52483	0.39568	3.854
4	2.52752	2.68925	0.940

20*a*. Reject H_0 if $t > 2.552$ so 2 and 3 are significant

a. Which variables are contributing significantly to the prediction of sales price at the .01 significance level (one-tailed test)?

b. Interpret the estimated regression coefficients.

c. Is multicollinearity a problem in this analysis?

d. Write a short memo to Rob summarizing your conclusions.

21. Fast Service Food Mart owner Sue McGinty wants to predict the number of quart bottles of pop (y) sold each day. She decides to investigate using the number of people on the street (x_2) and the predicted high temperature (x_3) as predictor variables. A random sample of 30 (nonconsecutive) days is selected. A partial computer output shows the following results:

CORRELATION MATRIX: 3 BY 3

	1	2	3
1	1	.792	.826
2	.792	1	.653
3	.826	.653	1

VARIABLE NO.	MEAN	STANDARD DEVIATION	REGRESSION COEFFICIENT	STD. ERROR OF REG COEF.	COMPUTED T VALUE
2	985.28	240.850	0.13589	0.04855	______
3	65.87	21.48	0.81245	0.19568	______
DEPENDENT					
1	62.20	25.90			

INTERCEPT −31.85

STD. ERROR OF ESTIMATE ______ R-Squared ______

ANALYSIS OF VARIANCE

SOURCE OF VARIATION	DEGREES OF FREEDOM	SUM OF SQUARES	MEAN SQUARES	F VALUE
ATTRIBUTABLE TO REGRESSION	2	12145.54	______	______
DEVIATION FROM REGRESSION	______	3125.61	______	
TOTAL		15271.15		

a. Analyze the correlation matrix.

b. Test the significance of the estimated regression coefficients at the .05 significance level (one-tailed).

c. Explain how pop sales are affected by an increase of 1° in predicted high temperature.

d. Estimate the number of quart bottles that will be sold tomorrow if the traffic count is 900 people and the high temperature is predicted to be 70°.

e. Calculate the standard error of estimate.

f. Calculate R^2 and interpret its meaning.

g. Calculate the F value and test to determine if the multiple regression equation has increased R^2 significantly. Use the .01 significance level.

h. Is multicollinearity a problem?

i. What should Sue McGinty conclude?

21*b*. t table = 1.703, $t_2 = 2.8$, $t_3 = 4.15$ Both are significant
c. Plus .81
d. 147.3
e. 10.76
f. $R^2 = .795$
g. $F = 52.46$ Table $F = 5.57$ so significant
h. No

22. A large manufacturing firm's personnel department interviewed and tested a random sample of 21 workers. On the basis of the test results, the following variables were investigated:

x_2 = Dexterity score
x_3 = Aptitude score
x_4 = Anxiety score

Subsequently, the workers were observed to determine the average number of units of work completed (y) in a given time period for each worker. Regression analysis yielded

$$\hat{y} = -212 + 2.12x_2 + 1.80x_3 - 0.45x_4$$
$$(.070) \quad (.050) \quad (0.30)$$

The quantities in parentheses are the standard errors of the regression coefficients. Also, $s_{y \cdot x\text{'s}} = 4.2$ and $s_y = 15.4$.

a. Which variables are making significant contributions to the prediction of work units completed at the .05 significance level (two-tailed test)?

b. Interpret the estimated regression coefficient for the aptitude score variable.

c. Estimate the number of work units completed for a worker with a dexterity score of 100, an aptitude score of 80, and an anxiety score of 10.

d. Calculate the sum of squares error (SSE).

e. Calculate the sum of squares total (SST).

f. Calculate R^2 and interpret its meaning.

22*a.* $t_2 = 30.3$
$t_3 = 36$
$t_4 = 1.5$
2 and 3 are significant
c. 139.5
d. SSE = 299.9
e. SST = 4743.2
f. $R^2 = .937$

23. Stan Birch, owner of Komputer Korner, needs to predict the number of Leading Edge computers he'll sell next month. He collects data on the selling price and amount spent on advertising for 10 randomly selected months:

Month	Sales, y	Selling price, x_2	Advertising expenditures, x_3
1	10	1,300	900
2	6	2,000	700
3	5	1,700	500
4	12	1,500	1,400
5	10	1,600	1,500
6	15	1,200	1,200
7	5	1,600	600
8	12	1,400	1,000
9	17	1,000	1,500
10	20	1,100	2,100

Run the data on a multiple regression program.

a. Analyze the correlation matrix.

b. Which variables are making significant contributions to the prediction of sales at the .05 significance level (two-tailed test)?

c. What is the prediction equation?

d. Interpret the estimated regression coefficients.

e. What percentage of the sales variance can be explained with this equation?

23*b.* $t_2 = -3.756$,
$t_3 = 4.377$
Both are significant
c. $\hat{y} = 16.406 - .0082x_2 + .0059x_3$
e. $R^2 = .932$
f. No
g. 10.006

f. Is multicollinearity a problem in this analysis?

g. Predict sales for next month if the selling price is \$1,500 and \$1,000 is spent on advertising.

Model Building

The major function of regression analysis is to test several possible models, each based on a sound economic and scientific foundation. When this approach is followed, the regression tests simply serve to determine which model is best.

Model building is the key to the success or failure of regression analysis. If the regression model doesn't represent the true nature of the relationship between the dependent variable and independent variables, the modeling effort will usually be unproductive. Model building involves developing a model that will provide a good fit to a set of data not only mathematically but also intuitively. The process should lead to adopting a model that gives good estimates of the mean value of y and good predictions of future values of y for given values of x.

> **Model building** is the development of a regression equation that will provide a good fit to a particular set of data.

In regression analysis, the two primary activities in model building are determining the form of the model and selecting the variables to be included in the model. The form of the model may be linear, curvilinear, or nonlinear.

So far you've learned that a linear model is a model that's linear in the regression coefficients and the error term. Sometimes the data of interest don't exhibit a linear relationship. When this is the case, some way must be found to deal with a relationship that can't be approximated with a linear model. There are two basic approaches for dealing with curvilinear and nonlinear relationships. The first approach is to fit the data with a curved model. The second approach is to convert one or more variables to another form so that the resulting relationship with y is linear. Once the data are plotted, it's often evident that a transformation of the data (such as taking logarithms, square roots, or reciprocals) will produce relatively linear patterns, so that a straight line may be adequate.

A model that's linear in the regression coefficients and the error term may be nonlinear with respect to the independent variables. Such a model is referred to as a *curvilinear model.*

Curvilinear Models

One important type of curvilinear response model is the polynomial regression model:

$$y = \beta_0 + \beta_1 x + \beta_2 x^2 + \cdots + \beta_k x^k + \varepsilon \tag{15.7}$$

In this model, k is the order of the equation. The value of the highest power of an independent variable in a model is referred to as *order of the model.* For example, the simple linear regression model presented in Equation 14.5

$$y = \beta_0 + \beta_1 x + \varepsilon$$

is a first-order model.

The second-order model is

$$y = \beta_0 + \beta_1 x + \beta_2 x^2 + \varepsilon \tag{15.8}$$

where y = Dependent variable
x = Independent variable
β_0 = y-intercept
β_1 = Parabola shifter
β_2 = Curvature coefficient
ε = Random error component

This equation provides a curve shaped like a parabola. The β_0 coefficient still represents the intercept where the curve intersects the y axis. The value of β_1 shifts the parabola to the right or left. If $\beta_1 = 0$, for example, the parabola is symmetrical and centered at $y = 0$. Increasing the value of β_1 causes the parabola to shift to the left. The β_2 coefficient describes the curvature. If $\beta_2 = 0$, there's no curvature. If $\beta_2 > 0$, the equation opens upward or is convex (Figure 15.3a). If $\beta_2 < 0$, the equation opens downward or is concave (Figure 15.3b).

The third-order model is

$$y = \beta_0 + \beta_1 x + \beta_2 x^2 + \beta_3 x^3 + \varepsilon \tag{15.9}$$

where β_3 = Controls the rate of reversal of curvature for the curve

This equation provides a model that contains one reversal in curvature and one peak and one trough (Figure 15.4). Reversals in curvature aren't common, but such relationships can be modeled by third- and higher-order polynomials. Example 15.16 illustrates a second-order model.

EXAMPLE 15.16 Gilbert Garcia owns a chain of hardware stores in Chicago. He wants to predict monthly sales using knowledge of the corresponding monthly advertising expenditures. Gil suspects that sales will increase as the amount spent on advertising increases. However, he also believes that at a certain point, sales will begin to increase at a slower rate. Gil feels that he'll reach a point where there will be little to gain in sales by spending a larger amount on advertising.

Gil selected a random sample of 14 weeks of data from company records (Table 15.12). Figure 15.5 shows a scatter diagram of the data. He notes that sales do appear to level off after a certain amount is spent on advertising. A curvilinear relationship seems to exist between sales and advertising expense.

FIGURE 15.3 Second-Order Models

a. Model with $\beta_2 > 0$ (convex)

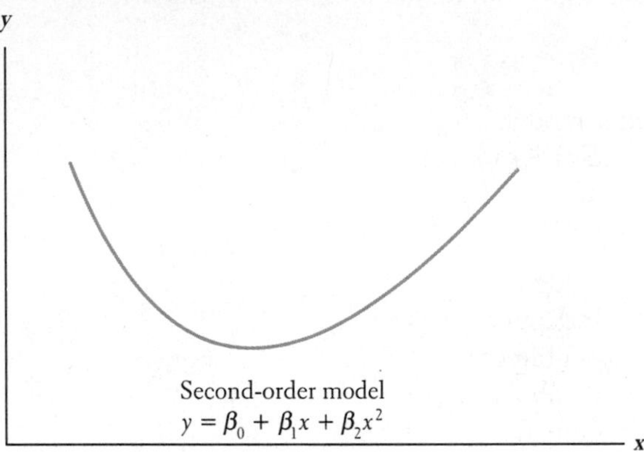

b. Model with $\beta_2 < 0$ (concave)

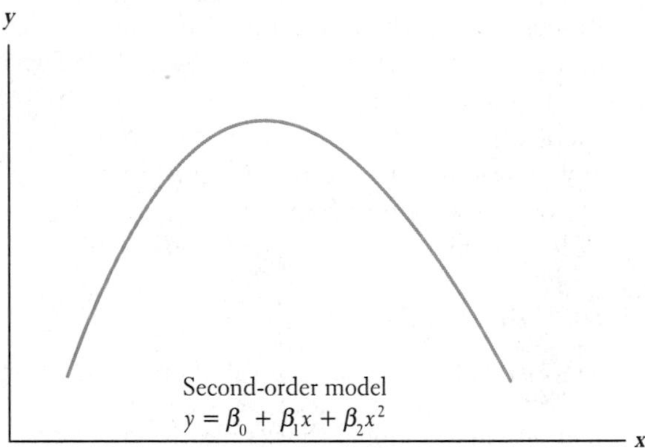

Gil uses the following MINITAB commands to run a curvilinear model:

```
MTB> SET C1
DATA> 1.1 1.7 2.6 2.4 2.3 2.9 .4 3.2 3.3 3.1 3.2
DATA> 3.0 3.7 3.3
DATA> END
MTB> SET C2
DATA> 3.9 4.9 7.6 6.8 5.9 9.1 3.4 11.6 14.1 14.9
DATA> 10.5 9.9 17.1 12.4
DATA> END
MTB> MULT C2 BY C2 PUT INTO C3
MTB> NAME C1 'SALES' C2 'EXP' C3 'EXPSQR'
MTB> REGRESS C1 ON 1 PREDICTOR C2
     OUTPUT IS SHOWN IN TABLE 15.13
MTB> REGRESS C1 ON 2 PREDICTORS C2 C3
     OUTPUT IS SHOWN IN TABLE 15.14
MTB> STOP
```

FIGURE 15.4 Third-Order Models

a. Model with $\beta_3 > 0$

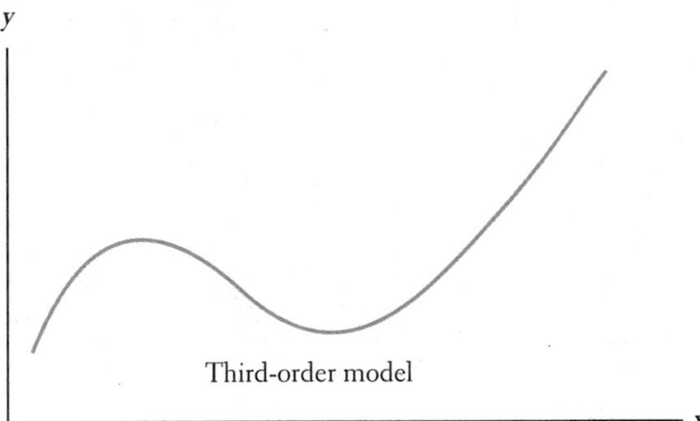

b. Model with $\beta_3 < 0$

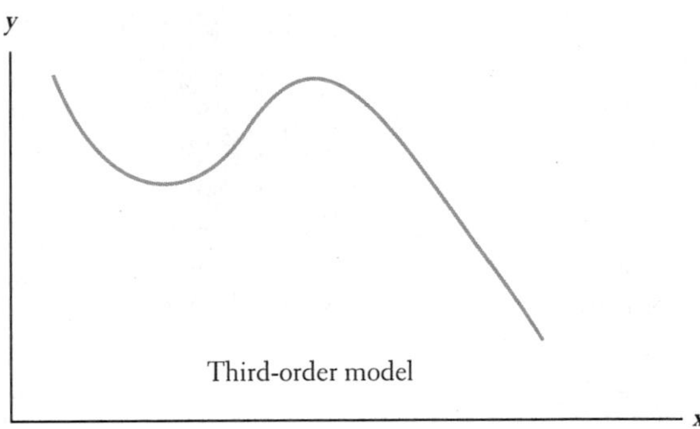

TABLE 15.12 Data for Example 15.16

Week	Sales ($000)	Advertising expenditures ($00)
1	1.1	3.9
2	1.7	4.9
3	2.6	7.6
4	2.4	6.8
5	2.3	5.9
6	2.9	9.1
7	0.4	3.4
8	3.2	11.6
9	3.3	14.1
10	3.1	14.9
11	3.2	10.5
12	3.0	9.9
13	3.7	17.1
14	3.3	12.4

FIGURE 15.5 Data Plot for Example 15.16

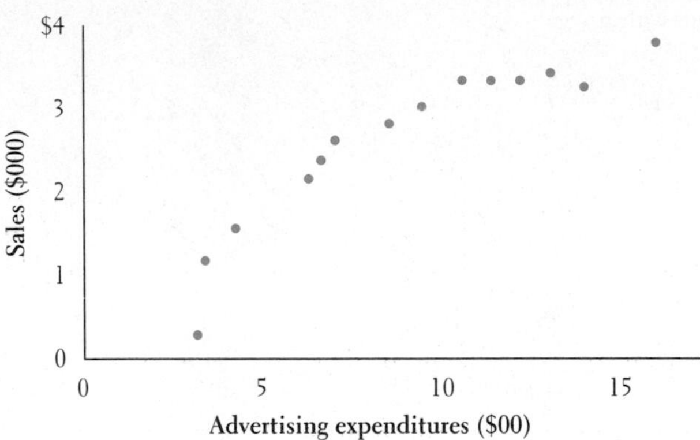

Table 15.13 presents the output for a simple linear regression equation. The linear regression equation, $\hat{y} = 0.754 + 0.194x$, explains 77.7% of the variance in the dependent variable.

Next, Gil instructs the program to square the x_2 variable, thus generating a new variable, x_3 ($x_2^2 = x_3$), which will model the curvilinear effect. Table 15.14 shows the MINITAB output. The multiple regression equation $\hat{y} = -1.01 + 0.627x_2 - 0.022x_3$, explains 93.2% of the variance in y. This equation explains an additional 15.5% of the variance; therefore, if the regression coefficients are both significant, Gil should use it.

The appropriate hypotheses to test the β_1 coefficient are

$$H_0: \beta_1 = 0$$
$$H_1: \beta_1 \neq 0$$

The appropriate degrees of freedom to test this hypothesis is df $= (n - k) = (14 - 3) = 11$. The decision rule if the hypothesis is tested at the .05 significance level is

If the calculated t statistic is less than -2.201 or greater than 2.201, reject the null hypothesis (reject H_0 if $t < -2.201$ or $t > 2.201$).

TABLE 15.13 MINITAB Computer Output for Example 15.16

```
The regression equation is
SALES = 0.754 + 0.194 EXP

Predictor      Coef    Stdev    t ratio
Constant      0.754
EXP           0.194    0.030       6.44

s = 0.461      R-sq = 77.7%

Analysis of Variance

SOURCE         DF        SS          MS
Regression      1      8.89        8.89
Error          12      2.55        0.21
Total          13     11.44
```

TABLE 15.14 MINITAB Computer Output for Example 15.16

```
The regression equation is
SALES = -1.01 + 0.627 EXP - 0.022 EXPSQR

Predictor        Coef        Stdev       t ratio
Constant       -1.009
EXP             0.627        0.088          7.14
EXPSQR         -0.022        0.004         -5.03

s = 0.265     R-sq = 93.2%

Analysis of Variance
SOURCE             DF           SS            MS
Regression          2        10.66          5.33
Error              11         0.77          0.07
Total              13        11.43

SOURCE             DF       SEQ SS
X2                  1         8.89
X3                  1         1.78
```

The null hypothesis is rejected (7.14 > 2.201) and Gil should conclude that the β_1 coefficient is significantly different from 0. The appropriate hypotheses to test the β_2 coefficient are

$$H_0\colon \beta_2 = 0$$
$$H_1\colon \beta_2 \neq 0$$

The decision rule is the same as when β_1 was tested.

Table 15.14 shows that the computed t value is -5.03. The null hypothesis is rejected ($-5.03 < -2.201$) and Gil should conclude that the β_2 coefficient is also significantly different from 0. Gil should use the second-order model to predict monthly sales.

If the β_2 coefficient had been significant but the β_1 coefficient not significant, Gil could have tried a model that included only the rate of curvature coefficient (β_2). Equation 15.10 presents this type of quadratic model:

$$y = \beta_0 + \beta_2 x^2 + \varepsilon \tag{15.10}$$

One of the assumptions of regression analysis is that a linear relationship exists between y and each predictor variable. However, the multiple regression model can be generalized to handle curvilinear relationships involving some or all of the predictor variables. A linear model is a model that's linear in the unknown βs. As long as a model is linear in the βs (β^x is not present), the linear statistical model can be used to model curvilinear relationships between the dependent and predictor variables.

Here are examples of curvilinear models. Equation 15.11 shows a reciprocal model:

$$y = \beta_0 + \beta_1(1/x) + \varepsilon \tag{15.11}$$

This is a simple linear regression model because it's linear in the unknown parameters (βs). Equation 15.11, unlike Equations 15.9 and 15.10, involves a transformation of the predictor variable, x. By substituting a transformed x ($1/x$), the analyst can simplify the relationship to one that's linear in its transformation. Unfortunately, the choice of an appropriate transformation is not easy. Analysts often need to study data plots to gain insight into which transformation will be successful. Equations 15.12 and 15.13 show two of the more common transformations. Equation 15.12 shows a square-root transformation:

$$y = \beta_0 + \beta_1\sqrt{x} + \varepsilon \tag{15.12}$$

Equation 15.13 shows an exponential model:

$$y = \beta_0\,[e(\beta_1 x)]\varepsilon \tag{15.13}$$

that is nonlinear in the parameters β_0 and β_1. This model can be transformed into the linear form by using the logarithmic transformation:

$$\mathrm{Log}_e y = \mathrm{Log}_e\beta_0 + \beta_1\mathrm{Log}_e x + \log_e\varepsilon \tag{15.14}$$

Figure 15.6 shows the shape of the exponential model. The MINITAB program can be used to perform transformations. The MINITAB Computer Package section at the end of this chapter demonstrates the commands to accomplish this task.

FIGURE 15.6 Exponential Models

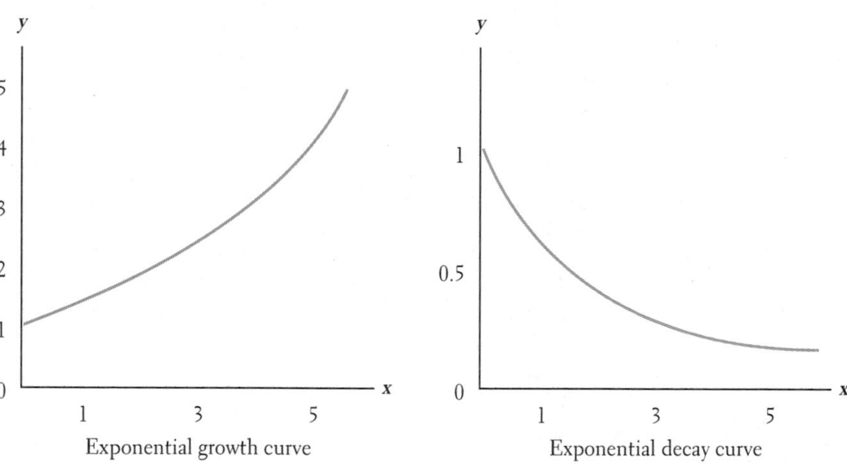

NONLINEAR MODELS

The term *nonlinear regression model* is used to designate any regression model that's not linear in the parameters (β^x is present) and can't be made so by transformation. For example, the exponential model of Equation 15.13 with an additive error term is nonlinear.

Here are examples of nonlinear models:

A logistic growth curve:

$$y = \beta_0/(1 + \beta_1\rho^x) + \varepsilon \tag{15.15}$$

An asymptotic regression curve:

$$y = \beta_0 - \beta_1 \rho^x + \varepsilon \tag{15.16}$$

Figure 15.7 shows the shapes of these nonlinear curves.

FIGURE 15.7 Nonlinear Models

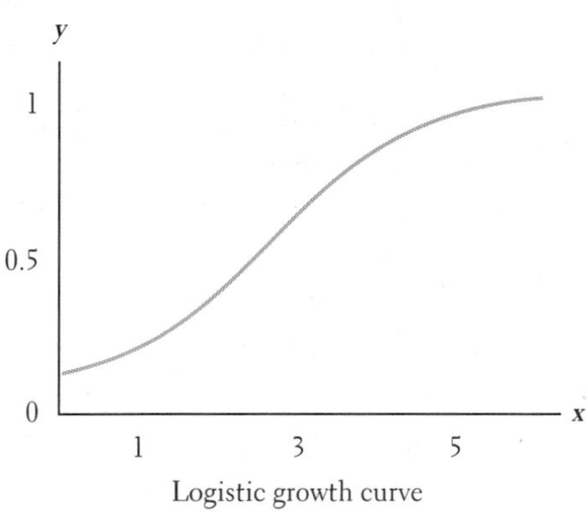

Logistic growth curve

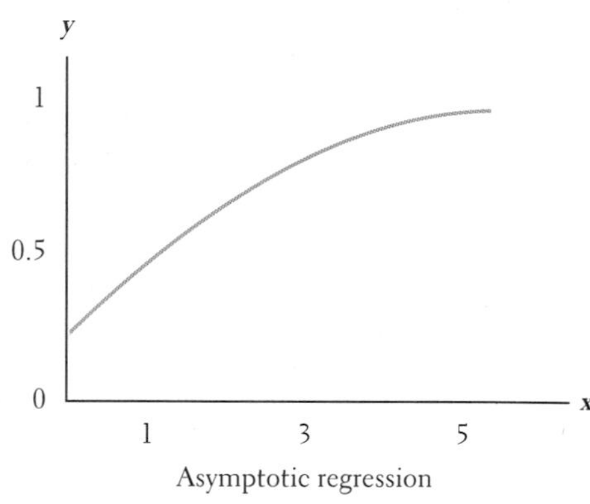

Asymptotic regression

EXERCISES

24. Explain the concept of model building.
25. Explain the differences between linear, curvilinear, and nonlinear models.
26. Briefly sketch the following models:
    a. Parabola.
    b. Third-order.
    c. Second-order.
    d. Exponential model.
    e. Logistic growth curve.

SSM

27. Jeff Paco, an analyst at Inland Power & Electric, has been assigned the task of predicting the maximum amount of power that must be generated each day to meet demand during summer. Jeff decides to investigate the relationship between average temperature and demand, measured in megawatts. He knows that demand will increase as the average temperature increases. However, Jeff suspects that as the average temperature rises, demand for electricity will grow at an increasing rate. He's interested in investigating a curvilinear model, so he obtains a random sample of 30 summer days and runs the data on a computer program. The results of running the $\hat{y} = b_0 + b_1x + b_2x^2$ model are:

VARIABLE NO.	REGRESSION COEFFICIENT	STD. ERROR OF REG COEF.	COMPUTED T VALUE
X	−10.35489	1.52145	−6.806
X2	0.07012	0.00854	8.211

```
INTERCEPT    403.68501
R SQUARED      0.962
```

a. Test the curvilinear model using the .01 significance level.

27*b.* 43.97

b. Predict the demand in megawatts for a day with average temperature of 92°.

c. Write a very brief memo summarizing the results.

28. Shelly Daniels is a quality-control engineer for Specific Electric Corporation, which manufactures electric motors. In one step of the manufacturing process, an automatic milling machine produces slots in the motors' shafts. Each batch of shafts is tested, and all shafts that don't meet dimensional tolerances are discarded. The milling machine must be readjusted at the beginning of each new batch because its cutter head wears slightly during production. Shelly must determine how a batch's size affects the number of defective shafts in the batch so that she can select the best batch size. She collects the following data for the average batch size of 13 batches and asks you to analyze it.

Batch	Number of defectives, y	Batch size, x
1	4	25
2	8	50
3	6	75
4	16	100
5	22	125
6	27	150
7	36	175
8	49	200
9	53	225
10	70	250
11	82	275
12	95	300
13	109	325

28*b.* $\hat{y} = -17.7 + .355x_2$
c. $\hat{y} = 1.9 + .0408x_2 + .0009x_3$
d. Quadratic model $\hat{y} = 4.6973 + .001008x_2$
e. 95.4

a. Plot the data on a scatter diagram.

b. Develop a first-order model.

c. Develop a second-order model.

d. Find the best model.

e. Predict the number of defectives for a batch size of 300 using the better model.

f. Write Harry a memo summarizing your results.

Qualitative Variables in Multiple Regression

Throughout the discussion of regression analysis in this chapter and Chapter 14, we've assumed that all variables in the analysis are quantitative, that is, measured on either an interval or a ratio scale. However, many real-world variables are qualitative, measured on an ordinal or nominal scale. For this reason, a technique has been developed for using qualitative variables in multiple regression equations.

Sometimes a variable of interest in a regression can't possibly be considered quantitative. An example is the variable *gender* (female/male). Although it may be important in predicting a quantitative dependent variable, it's obviously a nominally scaled variable. The best course of action in such a case is to take separate samples of males and females and conduct two separate regression analyses. The result for males can be compared with the results for females to see if the same predictor variables and the same regression coefficients result. Valuable insights can be gained from such a process.

Dummy Variable

If a large sample size isn't possible or is cost-prohibitive, a **dummy variable** can be employed to introduce a qualitative variable into the analysis. For example, a male could be designated with the code 0 and a female could be coded as 1. Each person sampled could then be measured as either a 0 or a 1 for the variable *gender*, and this variable, along with the quantitative variables for these persons, could be entered into a multiple regression program and analyzed.

A **dummy variable** in a regression analysis is a qualitative or categorical variable that is used as a predictor.

EXAMPLE 15.17 A sample of 15 hourly workers in a factory is selected for analysis. The dependent variable is the company's annual job performance rating. Management believes that the company's aptitude test score might be well correlated with the dependent variable, so they record this test score for each person in the sample. Management also thinks that a person's union affiliation might affect job performance rating. All hourly workers belong to either union A or union B. Members of union A are coded as 0s and members of union B as 1s. This is an arbitrary choice—the coding could have been reversed (union A as 1s and union B as 0s). Data for the regression analysis appear in Table 15.15.

TABLE 15.15 Data for Example 15.17

Worker	Job performance rating	Aptitude test score	Union membership
1	5	60	0
2	4	55	0
3	3	35	0
4	10	96	0
5	2	35	0
6	7	81	0
7	6	65	0
8	9	85	0
9	9	99	1
10	2	43	1
11	8	98	1
12	6	91	1
13	7	95	1
14	3	70	1
15	6	85	1

The data in Table 15.15 are keyed into a computer program that performs regression analysis. The dependent variable is numbered 1; the predictor variables are variables 2 and 3. Table 15.16 shows the results.

TABLE 15.16 Computer Output for Example 15.17

VARIABLE NO.	MEAN	STANDARD DEVIATION	CORRELATION X VS Y	REGRESSION COEFFICIENT	STD. ERROR OF REG COEF.	COMPUTED T VALUE
2	76.87	22.90	0.876	0.12041	0.01015	11.86
3	0.47	0.52	0.021	−2.18072	0.45035	−4.84
DEPENDENT						
1	5.80	2.60				

INTERCEPT	−1.95646	MULTIPLE CORRELATION	0.96
STD. ERROR OF ESTIMATE	0.78627	R SQUARED	0.92

ANALYSIS OF VARIANCE

SOURCE OF VARIATION	DEGREES OF FREEDOM	SUM OF SQUARES	MEAN SQUARES	F VALUE
ATTRIBUTABLE TO REGRESSION	2	86.981	43.491	70.349
DEVIATION FROM REGRESSION	12	7.419	0.618	
TOTAL	14	94.400		

The following symbols may help you read this computer output:

$s_{x2} = 22.9$	$b_3 = -2.18072$	$s_{y \cdot x} = 0.78627$
$s_{x3} = 0.52$	$s_{b2} = 0.01015$	$R^2 = .92$
$r_{1,2} = .876$	$s_{b3} = 0.45035$	SSR = 86.981
$r_{1,3} = .021$	$s_y = 2.6$	SSE = 7.419
$b_2 = 0.12041$	$b_0 = -1.95646$	SST = 94.400

The multiple regression equation is

$$\hat{y} = -1.96 + 0.12x_2 - 2.18x_3$$

The two t values, the F value, and R^2 all indicate that the regression equation will do a good job of predicting the job performance ratings of all hourly workers in the factory. Now we can interpret the values in the regression equation. The regression coefficient for x_3 is particularly interesting.

Union membership (variable 3) is coded as either a 0 or a 1. If a worker is a member of union A (code 0), the last term in the regression equation drops out (since $x_3 = 0$). If a worker belongs to union B, x_3 equals 1, so the third term in the equation is -2.18. This leads to two separate regression equations: one for members of union A and another for members of union B:

$$\hat{y} = -1.96 + 0.12x_2 \qquad \text{(union A)}$$
$$\hat{y} = -1.96 + 0.12x_2 - 2.18(1)$$
$$= -4.14 + 0.12x_2 \qquad \text{(union B)}$$

In effect, membership in union B reduces a worker's job performance rating by an average of 2.18 points on the average. For both unions' workers, each increase of 1 point in the company's aptitude test score increases the job performance rating by an average of 0.12 points. However, union membership has a definite effect on job performance rating. If two workers, one from each union, each scored 87 on the aptitude test, the regression equation would predict the following job performance ratings for these two employees:

$$\hat{y} = -1.96 + 0.12(87) = 8.48 \qquad \text{(union A)}$$
$$\hat{y} = -4.14 + 0.12(87) = 6.30 \qquad \text{(union B)}$$

Company management may be able to use this information to advantage, although a larger sample size would greatly strengthen the conclusions' validity.

Remember that the choice of coding for this example could have been reversed. If this had been the case, the sign for the regression coefficient for the union membership variable would have been reversed (b_3 would have been 2.18 instead of -2.18).

Example 15.18 illustrates the use of dummy variables in a multiple regression equation as an alternative approach to solving analysis of variance problems.

EXAMPLE 15.18 In Example 12.6, Joanne Herr, analyst for the Best Foods grocery chain, wanted to know whether three stores have the same average dollar amount per purchase. Stores can be thought of as a single qualitative variable set at three levels: A, B, and C. Note that with a qualitative or dummy predictor variable, Joanne cannot attach a quantitative meaning to a given level; all she can do is describe it.

A model can be set up to predict the mean dollar amount per purchase:

$$\hat{y} = \beta_0 + \beta_2 x_2 + \beta_3 x_3$$

where $\hat{y}$ = Expected dollar amount per purchase

$$x_2 = \begin{cases} 1 \text{ if the purchase is made in store A} \\ 0 \text{ if the purchase is not made in store A} \end{cases}$$

$$x_3 = \begin{cases} 1 \text{ if the purchase is made in store B} \\ 0 \text{ if the purchase is not made in store B} \end{cases}$$

Table 15.17 presents the data.

x_2 and x_3 are dummy variables representing purchases in store A or store B, respectively. Note that the three levels of the qualitative variable have been described with only two dummy variables. This is because the mean of store C is accounted for by the intercept β_0. If both x_2 and x_3 equal 0, the purchase must have been made in store C and is represented by the mean purchase for that store. The mean value of y when the purchase is made in store C is

$$\begin{aligned} \mu_c &= \beta_0 + \beta_2(0) + \beta_3(0) \\ &= \beta_0 \end{aligned}$$

In Chapter 12, on analysis of variance, the null hypothesis under test was that all three populations from which the sample data were drawn have the same mean. If the three stores have the same average dollar amount per purchase, this hypothesis won't be rejected. However, if a multiple regression model can be developed that allows the

TABLE 15.17 Sample Data for Example 15.18

Purchase (dollars), y	Store A, x_2	Store B, x_3
12.05	1	0
23.94	1	0
14.63	1	0
25.78	1	0
17.52	1	0
18.45	1	0
15.17	0	1
18.52	0	1
19.57	0	1
21.40	0	1
13.59	0	1
20.57	0	1
9.48	0	0
6.92	0	0
10.47	0	0
7.63	0	0
11.90	0	0
5.92	0	0

analyst to predict the average dollar amount per purchase based on knowledge of which store the purchase was made in, this hypothesis can be rejected.

Table 15.18 shows the results of running the data in Table 15.17 on a multiple regression computer program. The regression equation $\hat{y} = 8.72 + 10.01x_2 + 9.42x_3$ explains 64% of the variance in average dollar amount per purchase. Note that the mean purchase for store C, \$8.72, equals β_0. The table shows that 8.72 is the predicted value for each person who purchased in store C. Also note that the regression coefficient for x_2, 10.01, equals β_0 subtracted from the mean purchase for store A (18.73 − 8.72). The table of residuals shows that the mean for store A (18.73) is the predicted value for each person who purchased in store A. Finally, the regression coefficient for x_3, 9.42, equals β_0 subtracted from the mean purchase for store B (18.14 − 8.72). The table shows that the mean for store B (18.14) is the predicted value for each person who purchased in store B. Obviously, the multiple regression uses the store means to predict the average dollar amount of purchase for each person.

Note that the "analysis of variance" section of the output is identical to Table 12.5. Using multiple regression, Joanne comes to the same conclusion as she did using analysis of variance.

EXERCISES

29. What is a dummy variable?
30. Why are dummy variables used in multiple regression analysis?
31. The values 0 and 1 are frequently used to create dummy variables. Could 1 and 2 be used instead?

TABLE 15.18 Computer Output for Example 15.18

VARIABLE NO.	MEAN	STANDARD DEVIATION	REGRESSION COEFFICIENT	STD. ERROR OF REG COEF.	COMPUTED T VALUE
2	0.33	0.485	10.008	0.822	4.59
3	0.33	0.485	9.417	0.774	4.32
DEPENDENT					
1	15.20	5.90			

INTERCEPT	8.72	MULTIPLE CORRELATION	0.80
STD. ERROR OF ESTIMATE	3.7779	R SQUARED	0.64

ANALYSIS OF VARIANCE

SOURCE OF VARIATION	DEGREES OF FREEDOM	SUM OF SQUARES	MEAN SQUARES	F VALUE
ATTRIBUTABLE TO REGRESSION	2	378.54	189.27	13.26
DEVIATION FROM REGRESSION	15	214.06	14.27	
TOTAL	17	592.60		

OBSERVATION	OBSERVED VALUE	PREDICTED VALUE	RESIDUAL
1	12.05	18.73	−6.68
2	23.94	18.73	5.21
3	14.63	18.73	−4.10
4	25.78	18.73	7.05
5	17.52	18.73	−1.21
6	18.45	18.73	−0.28
7	15.17	18.14	−2.97
8	18.52	18.14	0.38
9	19.57	18.14	1.43
10	21.40	18.14	3.26
11	13.59	18.14	−4.55
12	20.57	18.14	2.43
13	9.48	8.72	0.76
14	6.92	8.72	−1.80
15	10.47	8.72	1.75
16	7.63	8.72	−1.09
17	11.90	8.72	3.18
18	5.92	8.72	−2.80

32. Ellie Burks is personnel director for the JVC Corporation. Presently, JVC hires prospective salespeople and trains them using an expensive program. Ellie has decided to administer an aptitude test to predict which applicants will be most successful on the job. Ellie also wonders if college graduates become better salespeople than do nongraduates. She decides to test the next 15 applicants. She determines whether they're college graduates and codes each person 1 if he or she graduated from college and 0 if not. The 15 prospective salespeople are trained in the program and placed on the job. After one month, their total sales are recorded, and the following data result:

Applicant	Sales, y	Test score, x_2	College graduate, x_3
1	345	52	1
2	405	46	1
3	475	60	1
4	205	20	1
5	355	38	1

Applicant	Sales, y	Test score, x_2	College graduate, x_3
6	300	44	1
7	133	14	0
8	280	28	0
9	165	30	0
10	145	18	0
11	165	32	0
12	340	50	0
13	140	22	0
14	215	30	0
15	145	20	0

a. Plot the data on a scatter diagram. Use 1s for college graduates and 0s for nongraduates.

b. Is test score a good predictor variable?

c. Is knowledge of whether a person is a college graduate a good predictor variable?

d. Indicate the regression equation Ellie should use to predict successful salespeople.

e. Interpret the estimated regression coefficients.

f. Estimate the first month's sales for a college graduate who scored 50 on the test.

g. Estimate the first month's sales for an applicant who didn't graduate from college and who scored 50 on the test.

h. Write a memo to Ellie summarizing your conclusions concerning this situation.

32*b.* Yes, r = .9034
c. t_2 = 5.723, t_3 = 2.172, both OK
d. $\hat{y} = 34.478 + 5.81x_2 + 61.245x_3$
f. 386.223
g. 324.978

33. Color Paint Corporation owner Marlene Perez is replacing several paint sprayers. After researching the situation, she concludes that four brands appear to be comparable in terms of cost and projected lifetime. Marlene determines that the deciding factor among the four brands will be the amount of paint used in normal operation. She measures the paints' thickness in millimeters, for several tests, with the following results:

	Sprayer A	Sprayer B	Sprayer C	Sprayer D
	5.4	6.1	8.2	7.2
	5.9	5.9	8.5	6.5
	6.2	6.3	6.9	6.8
	7.0	6.5	9.4	7.1
	5.1	7.2	7.9	7.4
	5.5	6.9	8.6	6.7
Means:	5.85	6.48	8.25	6.95

Solve this ANOVA problem using multiple regression. Compare your results to those obtained in Solved Exercise 3 in Chapter 12.

33. $\hat{y} = 6.95 - 1.1x_2 - .467x_3 + 1.3x_4$
R^2 = .7106

34. *Consumer Digest* wants to determine if any differences in average life exist for five brands of TV picture tubes. Random samples of three tubes of each brand were tested. The results (in hours) are:

Brand A	Brand B	Brand C	Brand D	Brand E
3,520	4,025	4,520	3,987	3,620
3,631	3,901	4,325	4,123	3,358
3,954	3,756	4,189	3,852	3,428

34. $\hat{y} = 3468.7 + 233x_2 + 425.3x_3 + 876x_4 + 518.7x_5$
R^2 = .8282
F = 12.05

At the .05 significance level, is there evidence of a difference in average life among these five brands of tubes? Solve this analysis of variance problem using multiple regression. Compare your answer to that for Exercise 44 in Chapter 12.

35. Rosanna Staben is studying bus drivers' average hourly wages in three northeastern states to determine if there are significant differences. She collects the following hourly wage data:

	State		
Observation	New York	New Hampshire	New Jersey
1	10	7	8
2	11	6	11
3	9	9	9
4	12	10	9
5	8	8	10
6	13	8	11

35*a*. $\hat{y} = 9.7 + .833x_2 - 1.67x_3$
b. 10.5
c. 8.0
d. 9.7
e. It's significant since $F = 4.19 > 3.68$

a. Develop the appropriate regression model, $\hat{y} = \beta_0 + \beta_2 x_2 + \beta_3 x_3$, to determine whether there are differences in average wages.

b. Predict the average wage for New York bus drivers.

c. Predict the average wage for New Hampshire bus drivers.

d. Predict the average wage for New Jersey bus drivers.

e. Test for significant differences at the .05 significance level.

STEPWISE REGRESSION

Stepwise Regression

A popular multiple regression technique called **stepwise regression analysis** introduces predictor variables into the regression equation one at a time until all potential predictor variables have been analyzed.

> The **stepwise regression analysis** technique enters variables into the regression equation one at a time until all have been analyzed.

Almost all computer programs for stepwise analysis begin by running a simple regression equation using the predictor variable that has the highest correlation with y. This variable is entered first because it explains the largest percentage of y's variance. Next, the stepwise program adds a new variable that's related to the dependent variable but not too highly correlated to the predictor variable already entered into the model. At each subsequent step, a new variable is entered that explains the largest percentage of the variance in y left unexplained by the variables already in the equation.

The stepwise process works as follows. The analyst provides the stepwise computer package with a dependent variable (y) and several potentially important independent variables (x's).

Step 1 The computer fits all possible simple regression models of the form

$$y = \beta_0 + \beta_1 x_1 + \varepsilon$$

The independent variable that produces the largest (absolute) t value is used as the best predictor of y and identified as x_1. Note that at Step 1 the computer will always choose the independent variable with the highest (absolute) correlation with the dependent variable.

Step 2 The computer fits all possible two-variable models that contain x_1. Each of the other independent variables is run in combination with x_1 to form

$$y = \beta_0 + \beta_1 x_1 + \beta_2 x_2 + \varepsilon$$

The new independent variable that produces the largest (absolute) t value is retained and used to predict y in conjunction with x_1. This new predictor is identified as x_2. Note that while x_2 will be correlated to y, it won't be too highly correlated to x_1.

Note that x_1 and x_2 will probably be correlated to some degree and the inclusion of x_2 changes the value of β_1 and its t statistic. Some of the better computer programs recheck β_1 to ensure that it remains sufficiently useful to remain in the model. If it doesn't, the computer searches for the best replacement variable.

Step 3 The computer fits all possible three-variable models that contain x_1 and x_2. Each other independent variable is run in combination with x_1 and x_2 to form

$$y = \beta_0 + \beta_1 x_1 + \beta_2 x_2 + \beta_3 x_3 + \varepsilon$$

The independent variable that produces the largest (absolute) t value is retained and used to predict y in conjunction with x_1 and x_2. This new predictor is identified as x_3. Note that while x_3 will be correlated to y, it won't be too highly correlated to x_1 or x_2.

The stepwise process continues until the step is reached where none of the remaining variables has a β coefficient significantly different from 0 at some specified alpha level. At this point, the computer can't add a new variable that will contribute to the prediction of y. Hence, the result of the stepwise procedure is a model that contains only independent variables with t values that are significant at the specified significance level. Example 15.19 illustrates the stepwise procedure.

EXAMPLE 15.19 Betty Butler, personnel director for Executive Choice, wants to predict whether a particular applicant will become a good secretary. Her interest in this matter increased after she read "Employee Training: Hands On Pays Off" in *The Office* (October 1989, p. 32), which gave Betty some new ideas about training in the workplace.

After her applicants successfully complete a six-month training program, they're placed on a new job, and their performance is rated at the end of the first month. Betty decides to use this performance rating as the dependent variable. Next, she chooses to investigate the following predictor variables:

x_2 = Motivation test score
x_3 = Aptitude test score

x_4 = Anxiety test score
x_5 = Keyboarding speed and accuracy score
x_6 = Computer test score

Betty gathers data on 30 applicants and inputs their scores and first-month performance rating into a data file called BUTLER.DAT.

The MINITAB commands to enter the data and run a correlation matrix for Example 15.19 are:

```
MTB > READ 'BUTLER.DAT' C1-C6
     30 ROWS READ

 ROW   C1    C2     C3    C4    C5    C6
   1   44   22.1    10   4.9    0    2.4
   2   47   22.5    19   3.0    1    2.6
   3   60   23.1    27   1.5    0    2.8
   4   71   24.0    31   0.6    3    2.7
  .  .  .

MTB > NAME C1 'RATING' C2 'APTITUDE' C3 'MOTIVATE' C4 'ANXIETY'
MTB > NAME C5 'KEYBOARD' C6 'COMPUTER'
MTB > CORR C1-C6

                  C1        C2          C3         C4         C5
                RATING  APTITUDE   MOTIVATE   ANXIETY   KEYBOARD
C2 APTITUDE     0.798
C3 MOTIVATE     0.676     0.228
C4 ANXIETY     -0.296    -0.287     -0.222
C5 KEYBOARD     0.550     0.540      0.350    -0.279
C6 COMPUTER     0.622     0.695      0.318    -0.244      0.312
```

The READ command is used to read a file called BUTLER.DAT into the MINITAB worksheet. The NAME command is used to identify each variable. The CORR command provides a correlation matrix for the six variables.

Betty examines the correlation matrix and decides that when she runs the stepwise analysis, the aptitude test score will enter the model first because it has the largest correlation with performance rating ($r_{1,2} = .798$) and will explain 63.68% ($.798^2$) of the performance rating variable variance.

She notes that the motivation test score will enter the model second because it's strongly related to performance rating ($r_{1,3} = .676$) but not highly related to the aptitude test score ($r_{2,3} = .228$) already in the model.

Betty also notices that the other variables don't qualify as good predictor variables. The anxiety test score won't be a good predictor because it's not well related to performance rating ($r_{1,4} = -.296$). The keyboarding speed and computer test score variables have potential as good predictor variables ($r_{1,5} = .550$, $r_{1,6} = .622$). However, both of these predictor variables have a multicollinearity problem with the aptitude test score ($r_{2,5} = .540$, $r_{2,6} = .695$).

The MINITAB commands to run a stepwise regression analysis for Example 15.19 are:

```
MTB > STEP C1-C6;
SUBC> FENTER 4.2.

STEPWISE REGRESSION OF RATING ON 5 PREDICTORS, WITH N = 30
```

```
     STEP              1          2
CONSTANT         -100.85     -86.79

APTITUDE            6.97       5.93
T RATIO             7.01      10.60

MOTIVATE                      0.200
T RATIO                        8.13

S                   6.85       3.75
R-SQ               63.70      89.48
 MORE? (YES, NO, SUBCOMMAND, OR HELP)
SUBC> NO
MTB > STOP
```

The STEP command runs a stepwise analysis using C1 as the dependent variable and C2 through C6 as the independent variables. The FENTER subcommand indicates that the criterion for allowing a new variable to enter the model is $F = 4.2$. If no FENTER subcommand is used, the default is $F = 4$.

Although the printout for MINITAB's stepwise procedure contains t statistics, MINITAB actually uses the F statistic to decide whether a variable should be added to the model. But note that there's a mathematical relationship between the t and F statistics ($t^2 = F$). At each step, the MINITAB program calculates an F statistic for each of the variables not in the model. The variable with the largest F statistic is added, provided its F statistic is larger than the specified cutoff value; FENTER = 4.2 in this example ($F = 4$ is used unless some other value is specified). MINITAB's stepwise procedure does check to make sure that variables entered into the model on an earlier step are still valid.

The stepwise analysis proceeds in the following manner:

Step 1 The model after step one is

$$\text{RATING} = -100.85 + 6.97(\text{APTITUDE})$$

This model explains 63.70% of the performance rating variable variance. This model had the largest F statistic, $F = 49.14$. Since 49.14 is greater than 4.2, APTITUDE is added to the model.

If the analysis is performed using the t statistic from the printout, the null and alternative hypotheses to determine whether the aptitude test score's regression coefficient is significantly different from 0 are

$$H_0: \beta_2 = 0$$
$$H_1: \beta_2 \neq 0$$

If the test is conducted at the .05 significance level, the critical t statistic based on 28 ($n - k = 30 - 2$) degrees of freedom is 2.048. The decision rule is

> If the calculated t statistic is greater than 2.048 or less than -2.048, reject the null hypothesis (reject H_0 if $t > 2.048$ or $t < -2.048$).

Since the computed t ratio found on the MINITAB output, 7.01 ($t^2 = F = 49.13$), is greater than the critical value ($7.01 > 2.048$), the null hypothesis is rejected. The APTITUDE variable's regression coefficient is significantly different from 0. This result means that the aptitude test score is a good variable and the procedure now moves on to Step 2.

Step 2 The model after Step 2 is

$$\text{RATING} = -86.79 + 5.93(\text{APTITUDE}) + 0.200(\text{MOTIVATE})$$

This model explains 89.48% of the performance rating variable variance. The null and alternative hypotheses to determine whether the motivation test score's regression coefficient is significantly different from 0 are

$$H_0\colon \beta_3 = 0$$
$$H_1\colon \beta_3 \neq 0$$

If the test is conducted at the .05 significance level, the critical t statistic based on 27 ($n - k = 30 - 3$) degrees of freedom is 2.052. The decision rule is

If the calculated t statistic is greater than 2.052 or less than -2.052, reject the null hypothesis (reject H_0 if $t > 2.052$ or $t < -2.052$).

Since the computed t ratio found on the MINITAB output is 8.13, the null hypothesis is rejected. The MOTIVATE variable's regression coefficient is significantly different from 0. This result means that motivation test score is a good variable when used in conjunction with aptitude test score. Note that the t ratio for the APTITUDE variable's regression coefficient, 10.6, is still significant. The procedure now moves on to Step 3.

Step 3 The computer fits all possible three-variable models that contain x_1 and x_2. None of the other independent variables is significant when run in combination with x_1 and x_2 so the stepwise procedure is completed.

Actually, the best three-variable model is developed and discarded because all of the t ratios aren't significant. The best three-variable model is

$$\text{RATING} = -89.42 + 6.12(\text{APTITUDE}) + 0.202(\text{MOTIVATE}) - .592(\text{COMPUTER})$$

This model explains 89.50% of the performance rating variable variance. The null and alternative hypotheses to determine whether the computer test score's regression coefficient is significantly different from 0 are

$$H_0\colon \beta_6 = 0$$
$$H_1\colon \beta_6 \neq 0$$

If the test is conducted at the .05 significance level, the critical t statistic based on 26 ($n - k = 30 - 4$) degrees of freedom is 2.056. The decision rule is

If the calculated t statistic is greater than 2.056 or less than -2.056, reject the null hypothesis (reject H_0 if $t > 2.056$ or $t < -2.056$).

If this run is made, the computed t ratio on the MINITAB output is $-.36$. The null hypothesis isn't rejected. The COMPUTER variable's regression coefficient isn't significantly different from 0. This result means that the computer test score isn't a good variable when used in conjunction with the aptitude and motivation test scores.

Final Notes on Stepwise Regression

The stepwise regression technique is extremely easy to use. Unfortunately, it's also extremely easy to misuse. Analysts developing a regression model often produce a large set of potential independent variables and then let the stepwise procedure determine which are significant. The problem is that when a large set of independent variables are analyzed, many t tests are performed, and a type I error will likely result. For this reason, the final model might contain some variable that's not linearly related to the dependent variable but entered the model just by chance.

A second problem involves initial selection of potential independent variables. When these variables are selected, high-order terms (curvilinear, nonlinear, and interaction) are often omitted to keep the number of variables manageable. Consequently, several important variables may be initially omitted from the model. Obviously, an analyst's intuitive choice of the initial independent variables is critical to the development of a successful regression model.

Exercises

36. Why is stepwise regression used? When should stepwise regression be used?
37. Examine the following correlation matrix, where variable 1 is the dependent variable.

	1	2	3	4
1	1	−.87	.78	.23
2	−.87	1	−.43	−.07
3	.78	−.43	1	.09
4	.23	−.07	.09	1

37*a*. 2, $r = -.87$
b. 3
c. 2 and 3

a. Which variable would enter the model first? Why?
b. Which variable would enter the model second? Why?
c. Which variable or variables would be included in the best prediction equation?

38. Examine the following correlation matrix, where variable 1 is the dependent variable.

	1	2	3	4	5	6
1	1	.571	.098	−.539	.810	.764
2		1	.258	−.112	.387	.418
3			1	−.007	.245	.187
4				1	−.419	−.158
5					1	.755
6						1

38*a*. 5, $r = .81$
b. 2
c. 2 and 5 or 4 and 6

a. Which variable would enter the model first? Why?
b. Which variable would enter the model second? Why?
c. Which variable or variables would be included in the best prediction equation?

39. Real estate broker Marilyn Roig wishes to estimate the importance of four factors in determining the price of lots. She runs data for 60 lots on a multiple regression program. Examine the following correlation matrix, where price is the dependent variable.

	Price	View	Slope	Elevation	Area
Price	1	.86	.66	.62	.57
View	.86	1	.65	.73	.38
Slope	.66	.65	1	.09	.61
Elevation	.62	.73	.09	1	.11
Area	.57	.38	.61	.11	1

39*a*. View, $r = .86$
b. Area
c. View and area

a. Which variable would enter the model first? Why?

b. Which variable would enter the model second? Why?

c. Which variable or variables would be included in the best prediction equation?

40. Stepwise enters runs, era.
$t = 10.9$ and -9.5
$F = 82.1$
$\hat{y} = 71.2 + .1148$ Runs $- 18.0$ ERA
$R^2 = .877$

40. Cindy Lawson just bought a major league baseball team. She has been receiving a lot of advice on how to create a winning ballclub. Cindy asks you to study this problem. You decide to use multiple regression analysis to determine which statistics are important in developing a winning team (measured by number of games won during the 1991 season). You gather the following statistics from *The Sporting News 1992 Baseball Yearbook* and run them on a stepwise regression program. Write Cindy a report. Make sure you discuss any multicollinearity problems and provide her with a final regression equation.

Team	Wins	ERA	SO	BA	Runs	HR	SB
Giants	75	4.03	905	.246	649	141	95
Mets	77	3.56	1028	.244	640	117	153
Cubs	77	4.03	927	.253	695	159	123
Reds	74	3.83	997	.258	689	164	124
Pirates	98	3.44	919	.263	768	126	124
Cardinals	84	3.69	822	.255	651	68	202
Phillies	78	3.86	988	.241	629	111	92
Astros	65	4.00	1033	.244	605	79	125
Dodgers	93	3.06	1028	.253	665	108	126
Expos	71	3.64	909	.246	579	95	221
Braves	94	3.49	969	.258	749	141	165
Padres	84	3.57	921	.244	636	121	101
Red Sox	84	4.01	999	.269	731	126	59
White Sox	87	3.79	923	.262	758	139	134
Yankees	71	4.42	936	.256	674	147	109
Tigers	84	4.51	739	.247	817	209	109
Orioles	67	4.59	868	.254	686	170	50
Brewers	83	4.14	859	.271	799	116	106
Indians	57	4.23	862	.254	576	79	84
Blue Jays	91	3.50	971	.257	684	133	148
Mariners	83	3.79	1003	.255	702	126	97
Rangers	85	4.47	1022	.270	829	177	102
Athletics	84	4.57	892	.248	760	159	151
Royals	82	3.92	1004	.264	727	117	119
Angels	81	3.69	990	.255	653	115	94
Twins	95	3.69	876	.280	776	140	107

RESIDUAL ANALYSIS

Model building has been defined as the general process of finding a regression equation that fits the sample data well. A valid model will provide good predictions of y for given values of x. Choosing the appropriate model is the key to successfully implementing regression analysis.

In Chapter 14, we used Equation 14.9 to compute the residual, or the difference between an actual observed y value and the predicted value, $\hat{y}$:

$$e = y - \hat{y}$$

Residual Analysis

Note that the mean of the residuals equals 0: $\Sigma(y - \hat{y}) = 0$. Also, the standard deviation of the residuals equals the standard error of estimate: $s_{y \cdot x\text{'s}} = \sqrt{\Sigma(y - \hat{y})^2/(n - k)}$.

Examination of a table of residuals or a residual plot can help determine whether a particular regression equation fits the sample data properly. The MINITAB commands to develop a residual plot for Example 15.15 are:

```
MTB> SET C1
DATA> 36 12 24 27 36 34 17 23 31 30
DATA> END
MTB> SET C2
DATA> 9.6 2.6 3.5 6.1 7.8 6.9 4.4 6.1 7.0 6.8
DATA> END
MTB> SET C3
DATA> 5.5 1.8 0.9 2.8 4.6 3.7 1.9 1.8 2.7 2.0
DATA> END

MTB> NAME C1 'Y' C2 'X2' C3 'X3'
MTB> REGRESS C1 ON 2 PREDICTORS C2 C3;
SUBC> RESIDS C4.
    THE REGRESSION OUTPUT IS SHOWN IN TABLE 15.11

MTB> NAME C4 'RESIDUAL' C5 'STAND'

MTB> PLOT C4 VS C1
    THE RESIDUAL PLOT IS SHOWN IN FIGURE 15.8
MTB> STOP
```

Note that the residuals were computed and stored in column C4 by the RESIDS subcommand. The PLOT command shows the residuals (C4) scaled on the y axis and plotted against the y values (C1) scaled on the x axis.

TM

FIGURE 15.8 The Residuals Plotted against y for Example 15.15

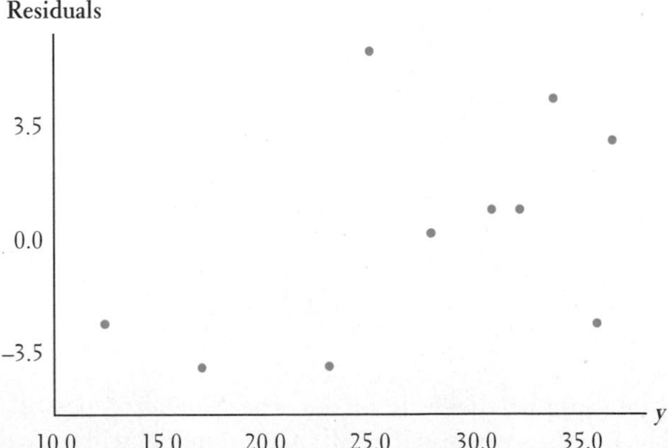

Residuals can also be standardized and plotted for examination. There are several ways to do this. However, the computations are complex, and computer analysis is essential. A description of the computational procedures is left to more advanced texts. The MINITAB commands to generate and plot standardized residuals for Example 15.15 are:

```
MTB> REGRESS C1 ON 2 PREDICTORS C2 C3;
SUBC> TRESIDS C5.
    THE REGRESSION OUTPUT IS SHOWN IN TABLE 15.11
MTB> PRINT C1-C5

ROW    Y     X2     X3      RESID        STAND
  1   36    9.6    5.5   -3.14846     -1.12525
  2   12    2.6    1.8   -2.79083     -1.12587
  3   24    3.5    0.9    5.91932      2.13424
  4   27    6.1    2.8   -0.06736     -0.01618
  5   36    7.8    4.6    3.12084      0.91071
  6   34    6.9    3.7    4.20376      1.15225
  7   17    4.4    1.9   -4.15210     -1.15032
  8   23    6.1    1.8   -4.18232     -1.26348
  9   31    7.0    2.7    0.73476      0.18649
 10   30    6.8    2.0    0.36238      0.10461

MTB> PLOT C5 VS C1
    THE RESIDUAL PLOT IS SHOWN IN FIGURE 15.9
MTB> STOP
```

FIGURE 15.9 The Standardized Residuals Plotted against y for Example 15.15

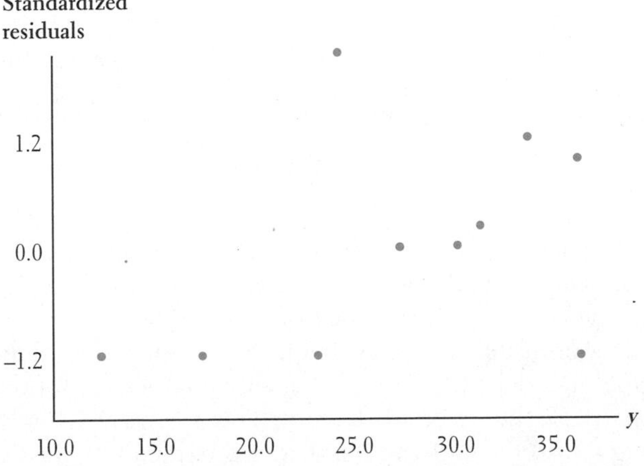

The standardized residuals were computed and stored in column C5 by the TRESIDS subcommand. The PRINT command shows what has been stored in columns C1 through C5. The PLOT command shows the standardized residuals (C5) scaled on the y axis and plotted against the y values (C1) scaled on the x axis.

FIGURE 15.10 Valid Model

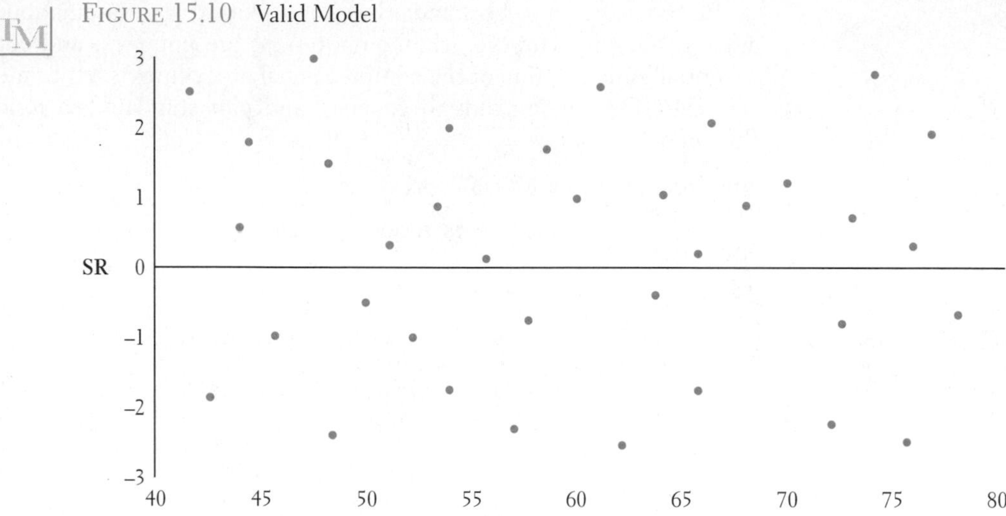

The residuals should satisfy the regression model assumption: they should be normally distributed, uncorrelated, and have the same variance. Figure 15.10 shows a residual plot that appears to meet these assumptions. Characteristics of a good residual plot include:

1. The numbers of positive and negative residuals are approximately equal.
2. When the residuals are standardized, about 68% of them should lie within 1 standard deviation ($s_{y \cdot x\text{'s}}$) of the regression line or plane, about 95% of them should lie within 2 standard deviations, and about 99% of them should lie within 3 standard deviations.
3. The variability of the residuals should be approximately constant for all values of $\hat{y}$.

When analysts examine a residual plot, they look for obvious indications that the assumptions have been violated. The next section addresses residual plots that clearly indicate violation of at least one assumption.

One assumption for regression analysis is that the population distribution of ε is normal. Small departures from normality don't create serious problems. However, major departures should be of concern. This assumption can be checked by visually inspecting a histogram of the standardized residuals. As just stated, approximately 68% of these residuals should lie within 1 standard deviation, and about 95% of them should lie within 2 standard deviations. Also, if the residuals are normally distributed, the positive and negative residuals should be approximately equal in number. Figure 15.11 shows a distribution that's seriously skewed toward the positive residuals. Since the normal distribution is symmetric, Figure 15.11 suggests that the residuals aren't normally distributed.

FIGURE 15.11 Nonnormality

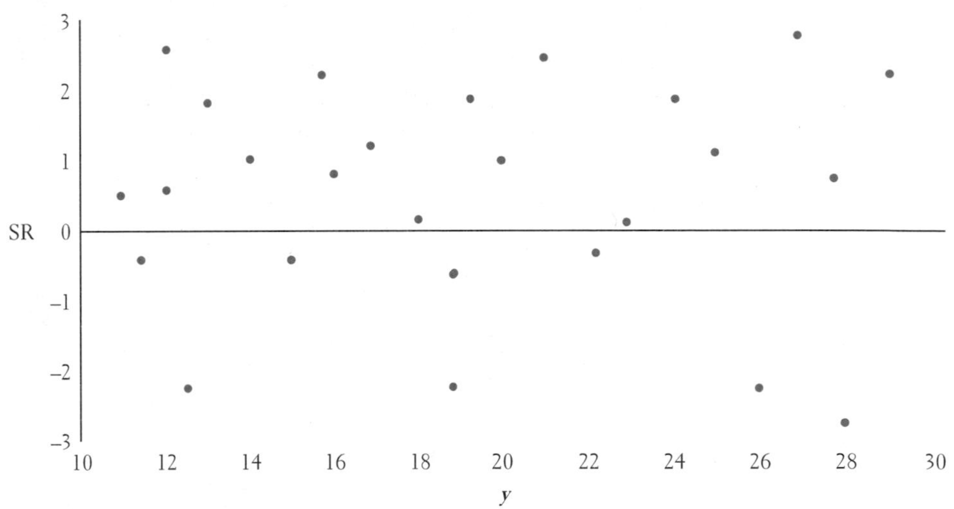

The MINITAB HISTOGRAM command, introduced in Chapter 3, can be used to check the assumption of normality for Example 15.15.

```
MTB> HISTOGRAM C5

Histogram of C5    N = 10

Midpoint   Count
   -1.5        1   *
   -1.0        3 ***
   -0.5        0
    0.0        3 ***
    0.5        0
    1.0        2  **
    1.5        0
    2.0        1   *
MTB> STOP
```

A second assumption of regression analysis is that the dispersion of errors around the regression line or plane is constant. Figure 15.10 showed how the residuals should be dispersed. Figure 15.12 illustrates a residual plot where the error variance increases with x. We may also encounter plots where the error variance decreases as x increases.

A third assumption of regression analysis is that the mean of the probability distribution of the residuals is 0. This assumption implies that the mean value of y for a given value of x is $E(y) = \beta_0 + \beta_2 x_2 + \beta_3 x_3 + \cdots + \beta_k x_k$. Examining a scatter diagram of the relationship between each predictor variable and the dependent variable can help determine whether this assumption has been violated. Figure 15.13 illustrates a parabolic relationship.

A fourth assumption of regression analysis is that the values of the residuals are independent of each other, implying a random sample. Such residuals should

FIGURE 15.12 Unequal Variance

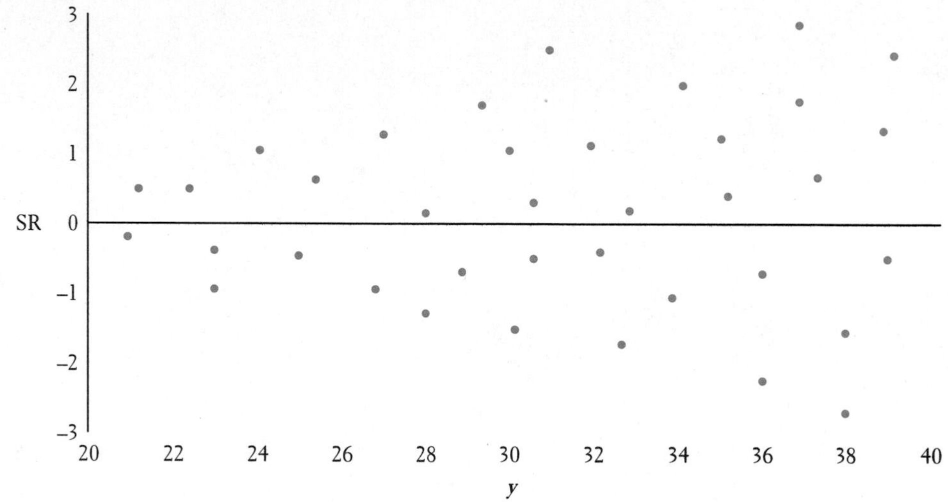

FIGURE 15.13 Nonlinearity

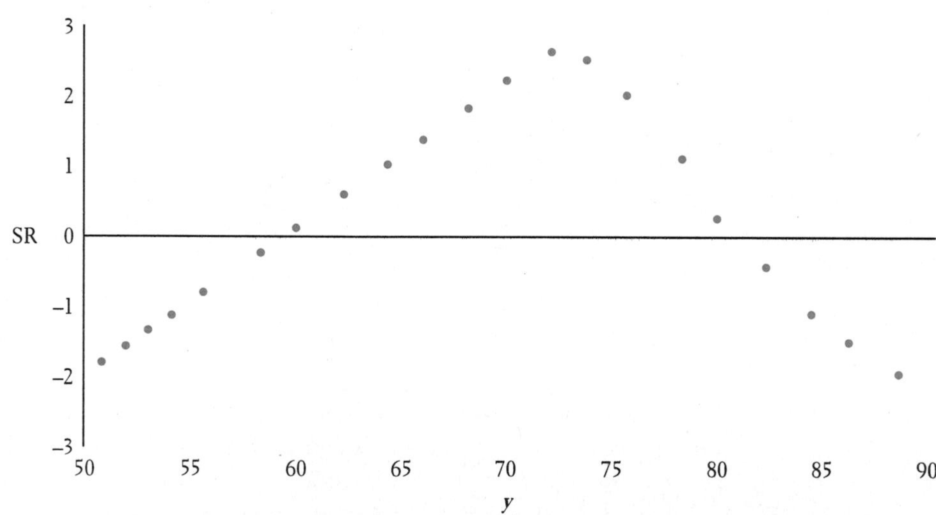

fluctuate in a random pattern around the baseline, 0. If the residuals are uncorrelated, then there should be no patterns in the residual plot. Figure 15.14 illustrates a residual plot with correlated error terms. Whenever data are obtained in a time sequence, there's the potential that the residuals are correlated over time, as discussed in Chapter 17.

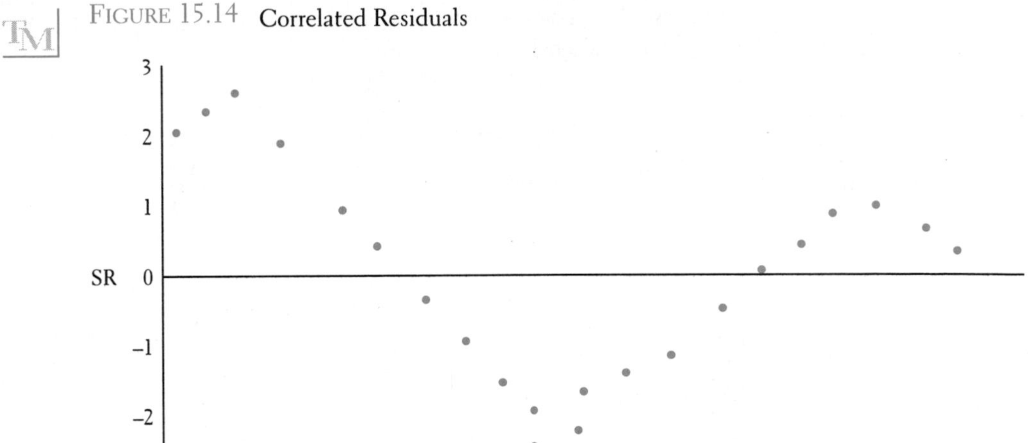

FIGURE 15.14 Correlated Residuals

Figure 15.15 shows the presence of an *outlier* (a point that lies far beyond the scatter of the remaining residuals). Outliers can lead to violation of one or both assumptions of equal variance and normality. They can create many problems for the analyst. The reason that an outlier occurred in the first place frequently dictates how it should

FIGURE 15.15 Outlier Plot

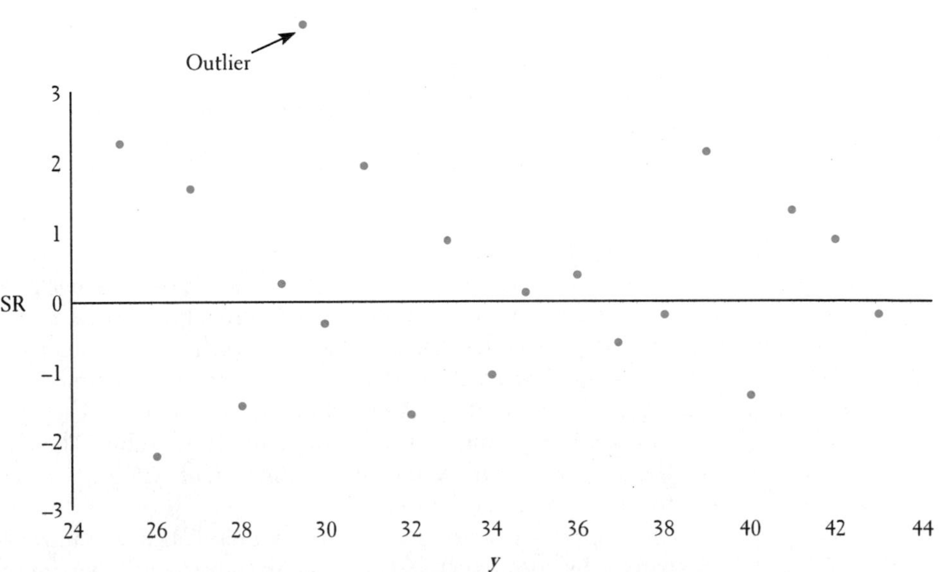

be treated. Alternatives include discarding the point, using mean values in its place, or leaving it in the analysis.

An **outlier** is a point that lies far beyond the scatter of the remaining residuals.

Refer to Extended Exercise 65 for an additional example of how the regression assumptions are checked.

EXERCISES

41. What is the difference between residuals and standardized residuals?
42. List the characteristics of a good residual plot.
43. Whenever data are obtained in a time sequence, there is the potential that the error terms are correlated over time. In this case, which assumption of regression has been violated? How can an analyst determine whether this assumption has been violated?
44. If the numbers of positive and negative residuals aren't approximately equal, which assumption of regression has been violated? How can an analyst determine whether this assumption has been violated?
45. If a residual plot shows that the error variance is increasing as x increases, which assumption of regression has been violated?
46. What is meant when a point is referred to as an outlier?

47. This exercise uses Appendix C's Company Data Base. Select a random sample of 30 employees and develop a multiple regression equation to predict annual base salary (x_8). Examine a residual plot to determine whether your regression equation fits the sample data properly. Write a memo to the company president summarizing results of this analysis.

SUMMARY

This chapter has extended the basic regression and correlation concepts of Chapter 14 to situations involving two or more predictor variables. The objective in a regression analysis is to identify as many variables as possible that might be correlated with the dependent variable of interest. The correlation matrix is then examined to find those predictor variables that correlate well with the dependent variable but not with each other. Next, predictor variable combinations are formed and tested using a multiple regression computer program. Finally, the quality of each regression equation is determined by checking R^2, the t values, and the F value. The best prediction equation can then be used, if it's found to be of sufficient quality, to explain the variability of y and to make predictions for y.

In multiple regression, we must guard against multicollinearity. This condition, caused by correlations between predictor variables that are too high, leads to unreliable regression coefficients.

The basic assumptions for simple regression analysis, stated near the end of Chapter 14, hold for multiple regression as well:

1. The probability distribution of ε is normal.
2. The variance of the probability distribution of ε is constant for all values of x.
3. The mean of the probability distribution of ε is 0. This assumption implies that the mean value of y for a given value of x is $E(y) = \beta_0 + \beta_1 x_1 + \beta_2 x_2 + \cdots + \beta_k x_k$.
4. The values of ε are independent of each other. This assumption implies that a random sample of objects has been selected from the population for measurement.

Assumption 4 is of particular importance in business applications. Many business situations involve data measured over months, quarters, or years. When the dependent and predictor variables are measured for these time periods, assumption 4 is often violated because the sampled time periods are in sequence, not randomly selected. Ways to solve this problem are covered in Chapter 17.

APPLICATIONS OF STATISTICAL CONCEPTS IN THE BUSINESS WORLD

Regression analysis is a popular technique in most areas of science and social science, including business. The problem isn't that this powerful technique is underutilized, but that it's used on inappropriate data and that analysts aren't skilled in interpreting the results. This danger has become increasingly acute since the advent of powerful personal computers, which enable almost anyone to perform sophisticated regression analyses.

Here are some areas for which the application of regression analysis might prove fruitful. The dependent variable is listed along with some potential predictor variables. Note that all variables are quantitative.

Dependent variable	Predictor variables
Employee job rating	Age, years with company, number of dependents, years of education
Annual cost of goods sold	Annual measurements of unemployment rate, GNP, total sales dollars, wholesale price index
Product's market share	Advertising budget, number of company employees, length of time product has been on market, time since last product "improvement"
Defects per shift	Number of workers on shift, average age of workers, number of floor supervisors
Employee turnover rate	Percentage of company wages compared with competitor average, average employee age
Local TV news rating	Station power in watts, percentage of newscast commercial time, time since last change of on-camera personnel
Hardness of steel batch	Temperature of process, humidity, time of process
Quality-control index	Hours of overtime, employees per shift

Glossary

Correlation matrix A display of the correlation coefficients for every possible pair of variables in the analysis.

Multicollinearity A condition that results when predictor variables are too highly correlated among themselves.

Estimated regression coefficient A measure of the average change in the dependent variable for a one-unit increase in the relevant predictor variable, holding the other predictor variables constant.

Standard error of estimate A measure of the variability, or scatter, of the observed sample y values around the regression plane.

Coefficient of multiple determination A measure of the percentage of the variability in y that can be explained by the predictor variables.

Model building The development of a regression equation that will provide a good fit to a particular set of data.

Dummy variable A qualitative or categorical variable used as a predictor.

Stepwise regression analysis A technique that enters variables into the regression equation one at a time until all have been analyzed.

Outlier A point that lies far beyond the scatter of the remaining residuals.

Key Formulas

Population multiple regression model

$$y = \beta_0 + \beta_2 x_2 + \beta_3 x_3 + \cdots + \beta_k x_k + \varepsilon \qquad (15.1)$$

Sample multiple regression model

$$\hat{y} = b_0 + b_2 x_2 + b_3 x_3 + \cdots + b_k x_k \qquad (15.2)$$

Standard error of estimate for multiple regression

$$s_{y \cdot x\text{'s}} = \sqrt{\frac{\Sigma(y - \hat{y})^2}{n - k}} \qquad (15.3)$$

Prediction interval

$$\hat{y} \pm t\, s_{\hat{y} \cdot x\text{'s}} \qquad (15.4)$$

Confidence interval

$$\hat{y} \pm t\, s_{\hat{\mu} \cdot x\text{'s}} \qquad (15.5)$$

Coefficient of multiple determination

$$R^2 = 1 - \frac{\Sigma(y - \hat{y})^2}{\Sigma(y - \bar{y})^2} \qquad (15.6)$$

Polynomial model

$$y = \beta_0 + \beta_1 x + \beta_2 x^2 + \cdots + \beta_k x^k + \varepsilon \qquad (15.7)$$

Second-order model

$$y = \beta_0 + \beta_1 x + \beta_2 x^2 + \varepsilon \qquad (15.8)$$

Third-order model

$$y = \beta_0 + \beta_1 x + \beta_2 x^2 + \beta_3 x^3 + \varepsilon \tag{15.9}$$

Quadratic model

$$y = \beta_0 + \beta_2 x^2 + \varepsilon \tag{15.10}$$

Reciprocal model

$$y = \beta_0 + \beta_1(1/x) + \varepsilon \tag{15.11}$$

Square-root transformation

$$y = \beta_0 + \beta_1\sqrt{x} + \varepsilon \tag{15.12}$$

Exponential model

$$y = \beta_0[e(\beta_1 x)]\varepsilon \tag{15.13}$$

Logarithmic transformation

$$\text{Log}_e\, y = \text{Log}_e\, \beta_0 + \beta_1 \text{Log}_e\, x + \text{Log}_e\, \varepsilon \tag{15.14}$$

Logistic growth curve

$$y = \beta_0/(1 + \beta_1 \rho^x) + \varepsilon \tag{15.15}$$

Asymptotic regression curve

$$y = \beta_0 - \beta_1 \rho^x + \varepsilon \tag{15.16}$$

SOLVED EXERCISE

1. MULTICOLLINEARITY

Herb Hancock, sales manager of the NAPE Company (a large automotive parts distributor), wants to develop a model to predict total annual sales for a region as early as April. If regional sales can be predicted, then total company sales can be estimated. The number of retail outlets in the region that stock the company's parts and the number of cars registered for each region as of April 1 are the two predictor variables Herb wants to investigate. Herb collects the following data:

Region	Sales (millions), y	Number of retail outlets, x_2	Number of cars registered (millions), x_3
1	52.3	2,011	24.6
2	26.0	2,850	22.1
3	20.2	650	7.9
4	16.0	480	12.5
5	30.0	1,694	9.0
6	46.2	2,302	11.5
7	35.0	2,214	20.5
8	3.5	125	4.1
9	33.1	1,840	8.9
10	25.2	1,233	6.1
11	38.2	1,699	9.5

a. Analyze the correlation matrix.

b. Are the regression coefficients valid?

c. How much error is involved in the prediction for region 1?

d. Show how the standard error of estimate was computed.

e. How can this regression equation be improved?

The data are run on a multiple regression program. Table 15.19 shows the computer output.

TABLE 15.19 Computer Output for Solved Exercise 1

CORRELATION MATRIX: 3 BY 3

VAR.	1	2	3
1	1.000	0.739	0.548
2	0.739	1.000	0.670
3	0.548	0.670	1.000

VARIABLE NO.	MEAN	STANDARD DEVIATION	REGRESSION COEFFICIENT	STD. ERROR OF REG COEF.	COMPUTED T VALUE
2	1554.36	843.91	0.01099	0.00520	2.11
3	12.43	6.86	0.19466	0.63984	0.30
DEPENDENT					
1	29.61	13.76			

INTERCEPT	10.109	MULTIPLE CORRELATION	0.74
STD. ERROR OF ESTIMATE	10.305	R SQUARED	0.55

ANALYSIS OF VARIANCE

SOURCE OF VARIATION	DEGREES OF FREEDOM	SUM OF SQUARES	MEAN SQUARES	F VALUE
ATTRIBUTABLE TO REGRESSION	2	1043.66	521.83	4.91
DEVIATION FROM REGRESSION	8	849.56	106.20	
TOTAL	10	1893.23		

TABLE OF RESIDUALS

OBSERVATION	OBSERVED VALUE	PREDICTED VALUE	RESIDUAL
1	52.30	36.99657	15.30343
2	26.00	45.72960	−19.72960
3	20.20	18.78986	1.41014
4	16.00	17.81718	−1.81718
5	30.00	30.47639	−0.47639
6	46.20	37.64429	8.55571
7	35.00	38.42921	−3.42921
8	3.50	12.28098	−8.78098
9	33.10	32.06130	1.03870
10	25.20	24.84600	0.35400
11	38.20	30.62867	7.57133

Solution:

a. The number of retail outlets is related to annual sales ($r_{1,2}$ = .739) and is potentially a good predictor variable. Number of cars registered is moderately related to annual sales ($r_{1,3}$ = .548) and, because of multicollinearity ($r_{2,3}$ = .670), won't be a good predictor variable in conjunction with number of retail outlets.

b. No. Multicollinearity is present, causing the regression coefficients to be undependable.

c. $\hat{y} = 10.109 + 0.01099(2{,}011) + 0.19466(24.6)$
$= 36.997$ million
$e = (y - \hat{y}) = 52.300 - 36.997 = 15.303$

d. $$s_{y \cdot x} = \sqrt{\frac{\Sigma(y - \hat{y})^2}{n - k}} = \sqrt{\frac{849.56}{11 - 3}} = \sqrt{106.195} = 10.3$$

e. New predictor variables should be tried.

Herb decides to investigate a new predictor variable, personal income by region. The data for this new variable are:

Region	Personal income (billions)
1	98.5
2	31.1
3	34.8
4	32.7
5	68.8
6	94.7
7	67.6
8	19.7
9	67.9
10	61.4
11	85.6

The data are run on a multiple regression program. Table 15.20 presents the computer output.

TABLE 15.20 Computer Output for Solved Exercise 1

```
                 CORRELATION MATRIX: 4 BY 4
                 VAR.      1        2         3        4
                 1       1.000    0.739     0.548    0.936
                 2       0.739    1.000     0.670    0.556
                 3       0.548    0.670     1.000    0.281
                 4       0.936    0.556     0.281    1.000

RUN NUMBER 1

VARIABLE                STANDARD   REGRESSION   STD. ERROR     COMPUTED
NO.          MEAN       DEVIATION  COEFFICIENT  OF REG. COEF.  T VALUE

   2       1554.36     843.91       0.00238        0.00157        1.52
   3         12.43       6.86       0.45743        0.16750        2.73
   4         60.25      27.17       0.40058        0.03779       10.60

DEPENDENT

   1         29.61      13.76

INTERCEPT                       -3.91771    MULTIPLE CORRELATION     0.987

STD. ERROR OF ESTIMATE            2.668     R SQUARED                0.974

                                  ANALYSIS OF VARIANCE

                               DEGREES     SUM OF     MEAN
SOURCE OF VARIATION           OF FREEDOM   SQUARES    SQUARES    F VALUE

ATTRIBUTABLE TO REGRESSION        3        1843.40    614.47      86.33
DEVIATION FROM REGRESSION         7          49.83      7.12
     TOTAL                       10        1893.23

END RUN NO. 1
```

TABLE 15.20 *concluded*

RUN NUMBER 2

VARIABLE NO.	MEAN	STANDARD DEVIATION	REGRESSION COEFFICIENT	STD. ERROR OF REG COEF.	COMPUTED T VALUE
3	12.43	6.86	0.62092	0.13821	4.49
4	60.25	27.17	0.43017	0.03489	12.33
DEPENDENT					
1	29.61	13.76			

INTERCEPT −4.02690 MULTIPLE CORRELATION 0.982

STD. ERROR OF ESTIMATE 2.877 R SQUARED 0.965

ANALYSIS OF VARIANCE

SOURCE OF VARIATION	DEGREES OF FREEDOM	SUM OF SQUARES	MEAN SQUARES	F VALUE
ATTRIBUTABLE TO REGRESSION	2	1827.03	913.52	110.41
DEVIATION FROM REGRESSION	8	66.20	8.27	
TOTAL	10	1893.23		

END RUN NO. 2

RUN NUMBER 3

VARIABLE NO.	MEAN	STANDARD DEVIATION	REGRESSION COEFFICIENT	STD. ERROR OF REG COEF.	COMPUTED T VALUE
2	1554.36	843.91	0.00515	0.00162	3.18
4	60.25	27.17	0.38530	0.05024	7.67
DEPENDENT					
1	29.61	13.76			

INTERCEPT −1.60819 MULTIPLE CORRELATION 0.972

STD. ERROR OF ESTIMATE 3.587 R SQUARED 0.946

ANALYSIS OF VARIANCE

SOURCE OF VARIATION	DEGREES OF FREEDOM	SUM OF SQUARES	MEAN SQUARES	F VALUE
ATTRIBUTABLE TO REGRESSION	2	1790.32	895.16	69.59
DEVIATION FROM REGRESSION	8	102.91	12.86	
TOTAL	10	1893.23		

END RUN NO. 3

f. Is personal income by region a good potential predictor variable?

g. What percentage of the variance in sales will be explained by using only personal income as a predictor variable?

h. What percentage of the variance in sales will be explained by using all three predictor variables?

i. Is the prediction equation in run 1 explaining a significant percentage of the sales variance? Test at the .05 significance level.

j. Test at the .05 significance level to determine if each of the three predictor variables should be used to predict sales.

k. Test at the .05 significance level to determine if personal income and number of retail outlets (x_2 and x_4) should be used to predict sales.

l. Test at the .05 significance level to determine if personal income and number of registered automobiles (x_3 and x_4) should be used to predict sales.

m. Which model should Herb use?

n. Interpret the estimated regression coefficients for the equation in part *j*.

o. Are these regression coefficients valid?

p. Discuss the accuracy of this model.

Solution:

f. Yes. Personal income is highly related to annual sales ($r_{1,4} = .936$).

g. $(.936)^2 = .876$

h. $R^2 = .974$

i. The null and alternative hypotheses are

$$H_0: \rho^2 = 0$$
$$H_1: \rho^2 > 0$$

The decision rule is

Reject the null hypothesis if the computed F statistic is greater than 4.35.

The following sums of squares are found in Table 15.20: SSR = 1,843.40, SSE = 49.83, and SST = 1,893.23. The sums of squares are divided by the appropriate degrees of freedom to produce the estimates of the unknown population variance, referred to as the mean square values on the computer output. The mean square for the "attributable to regression" row is 1,843.40/3 = 614.47. The mean square for the "error" row is 49.83/7 = 7.12. The F value is the ratio of these two estimates of the variance:

$$F = \frac{SSR/(k-1)}{SSE/(n-k)} = \frac{1{,}843.40/(4-1)}{49.83/(11-4)} = \frac{614.47}{7.12} = 86.33$$

Since the calculated F value (86.33) is considerably larger than the critical value (4.35), the null hypothesis is rejected. Herb concludes that the sample regression equation is explaining a significant percentage of the sales variance.

j. The appropriate hypotheses are

$$H_0: \beta_2 = 0, \quad \beta_3 = 0, \quad \beta_4 = 0$$
$$H_1: \beta_2 \neq 0, \quad \beta_3 \neq 0, \quad \beta_4 \neq 0$$

The decision rule is based on $(n - k) = (11 - 4) = 7$ degrees of freedom:

Reject the null hypothesis if the computed t statistic is smaller than -2.365 or greater than 2.365.

Personal income is a significant variable (10.6 > 2.365), as is number of registrations (2.73 > 2.365). However, sales isn't a significant variable (1.52 < 2.365).

k. The variables to be tested are in run 3. The appropriate hypotheses are

$$H_0: \beta_2 = 0, \quad \beta_4 = 0$$
$$H_1: \beta_2 \neq 0, \quad \beta_4 \neq 0$$

The decision rule is based on $(n - k) = (11 - 3) = 8$ degrees of freedom:

> Reject the null hypothesis if the computed t statistic is smaller than -2.306 or greater than 2.306.

Since the computed t statistics for both number of retail outlets, 3.18, and personal income, 7.67, are greater than 2.306, the null hypotheses are rejected. Herb concludes that the variables both explain a significant portion of the sales variance.

l. The variables to be tested are in run 2. The appropriate hypotheses are

$$H_0: \beta_3 = 0, \quad \beta_4 = 0$$
$$H_1: \beta_3 \neq 0, \quad \beta_4 \neq 0$$

The decision rule is based on $(n - k) = (11 - 3) = 8$ degrees of freedom:

> Reject the null hypothesis if the computed t statistic is smaller than -2.306 or greater than 2.306.

Since the computed t statistics for both number of registered automobiles, 4.49, and personal income, 12.33, are greater than 2.306, the null hypotheses are rejected. Herb concludes that the variables both explain a significant portion of the sales variance.

m. Herb should choose the model containing registered autos and personal income (x_3 and x_4) because it explains a higher percentage of the variance ($R^2 = .965$).

n. The equation is $\hat{y} = -4.0269 + 0.62092x_3 + 0.43017x_4$. If the number of registered cars in the region increases by 1 million while personal income remains constant, sales will increase by an average of 620,920. If personal income increases by $1 billion while the number of cars registered remains constant, sales will increase by an average of 430,170.

o. The regression coefficients should be valid since variables 3 and 4 aren't too highly related to each other ($r_{3,4} = .281$) so multicollinearity isn't a problem.

p. The model explains 96.5% of the sales variance and should be fairly accurate. Each prediction is typically off by about 2.877 million (the value of the standard error of estimate).

EXERCISES

48. Explain each of the following concepts:
    a. Correlation matrix.
    b. Estimated regression coefficient.
    c. R^2.
    d. Coefficient of multiple determination.
    e. Multicollinearity.
    f. Residual.
    g. Dummy variable.
    h. Stepwise regression.

49. 36.35

49. Your multiple regression equation is $\hat{y} = 7.81 + 1.5x_2 - 8.46x_3 + 10.68x_4$. Make a point estimate given $x_2 = 2, x_3 = 1.4, x_4 = 3.5$.

50. 30.99 to 41.71

51. $F = 49.88$, significant since $49.88 > 3.71$

52. Adding x_3 increases R^2 to only 73.5%: collinear, low t values: −1.84 and −.516

50. Make a 98% confidence interval for Exercise 49 if $s_{\hat{\mu} \cdot x\text{'s}} = 2.3$. Compute this interval for a sample size of 45.

51. Jack Raines works for a government regulatory agency that wants to determine what miles per gallon (mpg) rating new cars should achieve. Jack builds a multiple regression model using engine size (x_2), car weight (x_3), and rear axle ratio (x_4) to predict miles per gallon (y). He takes a random sample of 14 new cars, records the data for the three potential predictor variables, and determines mpg. The computer output containing the analysis of variance is:

ANALYSIS OF VARIANCE

SOURCE OF VARIATION	DEGREES OF FREEDOM	SUM OF SQUARES	MEAN SQUARES	F-VALUE
ATTRIBUTABLE TO REGRESSION	3	567.12	189.04	
DEVIATION FROM REGRESSION	10	37.89	3.79	
TOTAL	13	605.01		

Test the regression equation at the .05 significance level. State the appropriate hypotheses, decision rule, and conclusion.

52. Government economist Tracy Wilder is trying to predict the demand function for passenger car fuel in the United States. Tracy developed a model that used the actual price of a gallon of regular gas to predict fuel consumption per year. She could only explain 72.8% of the variance with this model. Tracy has decided to add a variable representing the population of the United States to the model. The data are:

Year	Fuel consumed by cars (billions of gallons), y	Price of gasoline, x_2	U.S. population (millions), x_3
1973	78.8	0.39	211.9
1974	75.1	0.53	213.9
1975	76.4	0.57	216.0
1976	79.7	0.59	218.0
1977	80.4	0.62	220.2
1978	81.7	0.63	222.6
1979	77.1	0.86	225.1
1980	71.9	1.19	227.7
1981	71.0	1.31	230.1
1982	70.1	1.22	232.5
1983	69.9	1.16	234.8
1984	68.7	1.13	237.0
1985	69.3	1.12	239.3

Source: *Statistical Abstract of the United States,* various years.

Run the data on a multiple regression program. Write a memo to Tracy summarizing the results of adding the population variable to the model. Recommend to Tracy what she should do next.

53. Ralph Ludwigson, personnel director for Danielson Tool & Die Corporation, feels that there's a relationship between ages of the firm's employees and number of days they were

absent from work last month. He selects a random sample of 10 workers and collects the following data:

Worker	Days absent, y	Age, x
1	5	25
2	0	30
3	1	62
4	7	33
5	8	45
6	12	27
7	6	55
8	11	41
9	2	22
10	3	58

a. Plot the data on a scatter diagram.

b. Develop a linear model.

c. Test this model at the .05 significance level.

d. Develop a curvilinear model.

e. Test this model using the .05 significance level.

f. If you've found a valid model, predict the number of absent days for a 30-year-old employee.

53*b.* $\hat{y} = 7.319 - 0.0457x$
c. Not significant, $t = -.47$
d. $\hat{y} = -18.6 + 1.347x - .017x^2$
e. Low t values: 1.86 and -1.94
f. No significant model

54. This exercise refers to the following correlation matrix, where variable 1 is the dependent variable.

	1	2	3	4
1	1	.77	.84	.92
2	.77	1	.75	.81
3	.84	.75	1	.21
4	.92	.81	.21	1

a. Which variable would enter the model first? Why?

b. Which variable would enter the model second? Why?

c. Which variable or variables would be included in the best prediction equation?

54*a.* 4, $r = .92$
b. 3
c. 3 and 4

55. Monty Card Department Store manager Fred Burks wonders if his customers are charging more on their Monty Card credit cards than on MasterCharge and VISA. Fred examines nine randomly chosen charges from sales using each of the three cards:

Monty Card	MasterCharge	VISA
$103	$ 71	$ 98
91	102	111
62	83	72
47	21	9
85	15	24
175	49	39
23	36	64
80	58	71
121	68	40

55. $F = 2.12$, $t = 1.69$ and $-.16$; not significant

Construct the ANOVA table using multiple regression. Compare your results to the ANOVA table for Exercise 47 in Chapter 12.

56. Decision Science Associates has been asked to do a feasibility study for a proposed destination resort one half mile from the Grand Coulee Dam. Mark Craze isn't happy with the regression model that used the price of a gallon of regular gas to predict the number of visitors to the Grand Coulee Dam Visitors Center. After plotting the data on a scatter diagram, Mark decides to use a dummy variable to represent significant celebrations in the general area. Mark uses a 1 to represent a celebration and a 0 to represent no celebration. In the following table, note that the 1 for 1974 represents the Expo '74 World's Fair in Spokane, Washington, and the 1 for 1983 represents the celebration of the 50th anniversary of the Grand Coulee Dam's construction. Mark also decides to use time as a predictor variable.

Year	Number of visitors, y	Time, x_2	Price of gasoline, x_3	Celebration, x_4
1973	268,528	1	0.39	0
1974	468,136	2	0.53	1
1975	390,129	3	0.57	0
1976	300,140	4	0.59	0
1977	271,140	5	0.62	0
1978	282,752	6	0.63	0
1979	244,006	7	0.86	0
1980	161,524	8	1.19	0
1981	277,134	9	1.31	0
1982	382,343	10	1.22	0
1983	617,737	11	1.16	1
1984	453,881	12	1.13	0

Source: Grand Coulee Dam Visitors Center and *Statistical Abstract of the United States, 1988.*

56*a*. t values: 2.2, −1.7, 4.1
b. Full model: $\hat{y}$ = 325,399 + 33,570(Time) − 282,546(Price) + 238,084(Cel.)
c. R^2 = .74, low t values, not a good model

a. Run a model that utilizes all three predictor variables. Test the t values to determine which predictor variables are significance at the .20 significance level. Use a two-tailed test.

b. Determine the best model and predict the number of visitors for 1986 if the price of gasoline is estimated to be 86 cents and the World's Fair is to be celebrated in Vancouver, Canada, within a day's drive of Grand Coulee Dam.

c. How accurate is the model that you used in part *b*?

d. Write a report for Mark to present to his boss. Indicate what additional information would be important in deciding whether to recommend that the destination resort be built.

57. Washington Water Power Company rate analyst Judy Johnson is preparing for a rate case and needs to estimate electric residential revenue for 1992. Judy investigates three potential predictor variables: residential use per kilowatt-hour (kwh), residential charge per kwh (cents/kwh), and number of residential electric customers. She collects data from 1968 to 1991:

Year	Revenue (millions of \$) y	Use per kwh x_2	Charge (cents/kwh) x_3	Number of customers x_4
1968	19.3	10,413	1.33	139,881
1969	20.4	11,129	1.29	142,806

Year	Revenue (millions of $) y	Use per kwh x_2	Charge (cents/kwh) x_3	Number of customers x_4
1970	20.9	11,361	1.25	146,616
1971	21.9	11,960	1.21	151,640
1972	23.4	12,498	1.19	157,205
1973	24.5	12,667	1.19	162,328
1974	25.8	12,857	1.21	166,558
1975	30.5	13,843	1.29	170,317
1976	33.3	14,223	1.33	175,536
1977	37.2	14,427	1.42	181,553
1978	42.5	14,878	1.52	188,325
1979	48.8	15,763	1.59	194,237
1980	55.4	15,130	1.84	198,847
1981	64.3	14,697	2.17	201,465
1982	78.9	15,221	2.55	203,444
1983	86.5	14,166	2.97	205,533
1984	114.6	14,854	3.70	208,574
1985	129.7	14,997	4.10	210,811
1986	126.1	13,674	4.34	212,865
1987	132.0	13,062	4.71	214,479
1988	138.1	13,284	4.82	215,610
1989	141.2	13,531	4.81	217,164
1990	143.7	13,589	4.81	219,968
1991	149.2	13,800	4.84	223,364

Source: "Financial and Operating Supplement," *Washington Water Power Annual Report*, 1978, 1986, 1991.

57*a*. Stepwise: $\hat{y} = -69.1 + 31.7x_3 + .0044x_2$
$t = 102.6, 13.1$
b. 135.15
c. $R^2 = .984$

a. Develop a good model for Judy to use.

b. Use the model selected in part *a* to predict 1992 revenue given the following estimates: residential use per kwh, 14,000; residential charge per kwh, 4.50; and number of residential electric customers, 215,000.

c. How accurate is the model selected in part *a*?

d. Write documentation supporting your choice so that Judy can testify before the rate commission.

58. Jeff Hawkins, an economist, is studying how important an area's economics are in influencing people's choices of where to live. He feels that people will change jobs and even careers if the money is right. Based on these beliefs, Jeff feels that economics play an important role in determining which cities are rated as the best places to live. He gathers data from Rand McNally & Company, *Places Rated Almanac*, 1981; Moody's Investors Service, *Bond Rating Guide*, 1981; the Bureau of Economic Analysis, "County and Metropolitan Area Personal Income," *Survey of Current Business*, 1981; Commerce Clearing House, *State Tax Handbook*, 1981; and Bureau of Labor Statistics, "State and Metropolitan Area Unemployment," *News*, March 1981. Jeff selects a systematic sample of 31 cities and records data on five variables: overall rank (y), Moody's bond rating (x_2), average household income (x_3), average household taxes (x_4), and local unemployment rate (x_5). Jeff coded the Moody's bond rating as a dummy variable, with 1 representing a rating of AAA, AA, A1 or A. Zero was used to represent any other bond rating, such as BAA1.

Metro area	Ranking, y	Moody's rating, x_2	Average income (\$), x_3	Average taxes (\$), x_4	Unemployment rate (%), x_5
Amarillo, TX	84	1	28,388	214	4.4
Atlanta, GA	1	1	27,051	1,721	5.5
Billings, MT	125	1	26,943	1,954	4.1
Bridgeport, CT	92	1	33,518	420	6.0
Charleston, WV	52	1	26,738	1,306	7.4
Cleveland, OH	14	0	28,677	716	8.1
Detroit, MI	43	0	30,243	1,541	13.0
Erie, PA	55	0	24,125	740	9.3
Gadsden, AL	244	0	20,928	991	8.7
Greeley, CO	270	1	23,325	1,535	6.4
Jackson, MS	68	1	24,929	1,046	5.0
Kenosha, WI	190	1	26,568	2,593	8.4
Las Vegas, NV	172	0	30,526	194	7.4
Lincoln, NE	79	1	26,922	997	3.5
Los Angeles, CA	47	1	29,792	2,716	8.1
Memphis, TN	66	1	23,614	299	5.9
Miami, FL	20	1	28,042	222	5.2
Modesto, CA	258	1	26,819	2,372	11.8
Monroe, LA	206	0	20,920	567	8.5
Nashua, NH	197	1	25,456	000	4.5
New York, NY	26	0	26,938	2,773	7.6
Peoria, IL	206	1	30,563	1,051	8.4
Phoenix, AZ	45	1	27,975	2,089	6.0
Portland, ME	108	1	23,906	1,572	6.3
Richmond, VA	29	1	28,671	1,605	3.6
St. Louis, MO	24	0	26,136	1,631	7.9
Salem, OR	97	1	23,231	1,943	7.4
Seattle, WA	5	1	30,802	324	6.3
Topeka, KA	140	1	25,620	1,880	5.8
Waterbury, CT	266	0	25,393	341	6.8
Wilmington, DE	109	1	27,232	2,411	6.9

58*a*. $\hat{y} = 404.5 - .011x_3$
e. 74.5

a. Develop a model to predict a city's overall ranking.

b. Test Jeff's theory that economics play an important role in determining which cities are rated as the best places to live.

c. What variables would you add to improve the prediction model? Look in the *Places Rated Almanac* if you need help.

d. Could the Moody's rating variable be coded differently?

e. Use the best model to predict a city's rating if the following information is available: Moody's rating is 1, average income is \$30,000, average taxes are \$1,000, and unemployment rate is 8%.

59. Professional Investment Group analyst Michelle Sutcliffe is investigating earnings per share for large corporations. Michelle collects data from *Fortune 500*, which ranks the 500 largest industrial corporations by sales. Her random sample of 30 corporations covers the following potential predictor variables: sales, profits, assets, and stockholders' equity.

Corporation	Earnings per share, y	Sales (millions), x_2	Assets (millions), x_3	Stockholders' equity (millions), x_4	Profits as percentage of equity (%), x_5
IBM	8.72	54,217	63,688	38,263	13.7
Boeing	3.10	15,355	12,566	4,987	9.6
Unisys	3.15	9,713	9,958	4,545	12.7
Coca-Cola	2.43	7,658	8,356	3,224	28.4
Northrop	2.01	6,053	3,124	948	9.9
Pfizer	4.08	4,920	6,923	3,882	17.8
Time, Inc.	4.18	4,194	4,424	1,248	20.0
United Brands	3.86	3,268	1,116	419	14.2
Hercules	14.74	2,693	3,492	2,190	37.5
Paccar	6.26	2,424	1,300	801	14.0
Squibb	3.42	2,157	2,782	1,526	23.5
Maytag	1.91	1,909	855	415	36.8
Trinova	2.20	1,682	1,320	631	11.9
Amdahl	2.82	1,505	1,508	766	19.1
Holly Farms	4.31	1,407	685	343	20.9
Dow Jones	2.10	1,314	1,943	848	24.0
Timken	0.78	1,230	1,467	923	1.1
Clorox	1.96	1,126	933	616	17.0
Ball	2.80	1,054	795	397	16.7
Potlatch	3.13	992	1,307	638	13.7
Ferro	2.30	871	532	260	12.2
Telex	5.24	822	618	3,541	22.0
Sealed Power	2.12	774	562	288	9.1
Roper	2.12	714	250	81	24.5
Ametek	0.94	620	538	253	16.3
Coleman	2.72	599	404	184	10.4
Shaklee	1.77	572	414	252	9.3
Carlisle	2.25	543	309	186	10.1
Lukens	3.87	503	323	152	14.3
Russell	1.17	480	445	280	16.6

a. Discuss the potential of each predictor variable.

b. Is multicollinearity a problem with this set of predictor variables?

c. Write a report to Michelle discussing your findings concerning the prediction of earnings per share for large corporations.

59*a.* Only x_5 has a high t value, 2.71
b. Yes, when sales, assets, and equity are included in the model.
c. $\hat{y} = 1.082 + .139x_5$, but $R^2 = .175$

60. Spendwise supermarket chain manager Anna Sheehan wants to predict paperback book sales (books per week) based on the amount of shelf display space (in feet) provided. Anna gathers data for a sample of 11 weeks:

Week	Number of books sold, y	Feet of shelf space, x
1	275	6.8
2	142	3.3
3	168	4.1
4	197	4.2
5	215	4.8
6	188	3.9
7	241	4.9

Week	Number of books sold, y	Feet of shelf space, x
8	295	7.7
9	125	3.1
10	266	5.9
11	200	5.0

a. Plot the data on a scatter diagram.

b. Develop a linear model.

c. Develop a curvilinear model.

d. Test both models using the .05 significance level.

e. Use the best model to predict paperback book sales for a week in which five feet of shelf space is provided.

60*b.* $\hat{y} = 32.5 + 36.4x$
c. $\hat{y} = -115.3 + 95.9x - 5.56x^2$
d. Linear: $t = 3.875$
Curvilinear: $t = 3.875$ and -2.43
Both are significant
e. Curvilinear: 225.3

61. Tom Dukich, analyst for Burgan Furniture Company, decides that production scheduling can be improved if an accurate method for predicting quarterly sales can be developed. He investigates the relationship between housing construction permits and furniture sales in the store's market area. Tom feels that permits will lead sales by two quarters. In addition, he wonders if quarterly sales are seasonal. After examining 1988–92 data, Tom decides to create a dummy variable. He uses a 0 to represent first- or second-quarter sales and a 1 to represent third- or fourth-quarter sales. Sales data are recorded in thousands of dollars.

Year	Quarter	Sales	Permits
1988	3	—	20
	4	—	4
1989	1	119	33
	2	77	9
	3	409	13
	4	198	18
1990	1	77	29
	2	121	9
	3	281	11
	4	160	22
1991	1	115	69
	2	145	28
	3	654	21
	4	269	14
1992	1	196	76
	2	276	39
	3	789	19
	4	318	13

a. Develop a simple regression model using housing construction permits as the predictor variable.

b. Develop a multiple regression model by adding the dummy variable.

c. Which model should Tom use?

d. Estimate quarterly sales for 1993 for Burgan Furniture Company.

e. Does this model violate any of the assumptions of multiple regression?

61*a.* $\hat{y} = 20.0 + 9.4x_2$
b. $\hat{y} = 10.1 + 8.5x_2 + 65.5x_3$
c. Simple, since $t_3 = 1.69$
d. 197.823, 141.675

EXTENDED EXERCISES

62. MURPHY TRANSPORT

Charles Murphy is president of Murphy Transport, which hauls and stores household goods in the Midwest. He has been concerned lately about his fleet of trucks, specifically, about the annual cost of maintaining them. He decides to try to find variables that correlate well with this key variable. Mr. Murphy uses a random selection method to choose a sample of 39 trucks.

In addition to the dependent variable (annual truck maintenance cost), four potential predictor variables are selected:

x_2 = Age of truck, in years
x_3 = Weight of truck when empty
x_4 = Average number of trips taken per year
x_5 = Current odometer reading, in miles

He selects the random sample, makes five measurements, and analyzes the data on his personal computer using a statistical program that performs multiple regression. Table 15.21 presents the correlation matrix.

TABLE 15.21 Correlation Matrix for Extended Exercise 62

	1	2	3	4	5
1	1	.795	.338	.811	.949
2	.795	1	.490	.651	.754
3	.338	.490	1	.261	.238
4	.811	.651	.261	1	.780
5	.949	.754	.238	.780	1

After considering this correlation matrix, where the dependent variable is number 1, Mr. Murphy decides he would like to see the following regression runs:

Dependent variable: y
Predictor variables: x_5
x_4, x_5
x_2, x_5
x_2, x_4
x_2, x_3, x_4, x_5

The computer program performs these runs and generates the results. The program Mr. Murphy is using prepares a summary of the regression runs (Table 15.22). Mr. Murphy sits down in his office at the end of the day, closes the door, and begins to study these results.

a. Comment on the choices Mr. Murphy made for regressions he would like to see.

b. Based on the correlation matrix and the summary of the regression runs in Table 15.22, which variable(s) do you think should be used to predict annual maintenance cost?

c. Based on your answer to part *b*, how good a prediction equation will Mr. Murphy have?

TABLE 15.22 Regression Analysis Summary for Extended Exercise 62

Predictor variables	R^2	t values	F value
x_5	.90118	18.37	337.4
x_4, x_5	.91411	2.33	191.6
		10.35	
x_2, x_5	.91572	2.49	195.58
		11.00	
x_2, x_4	.78212	4.52	64.62
		4.97	
x_2, x_3, x_4, x_5	.92866	1.37	110.64
		1.32	
		2.03	
		8.34	

63. SILOS ELECTRONICS

Silos Electronics Company retails various electronic components for businesses, including telephones, paging systems, intercoms, and shortwave radios. Silos has collected a great deal of data over its five years in business, and its president wonders if there's any way to predict dollar amount per sale. This question has become more acute since the company began considering a substantial modification of its product line to include personal computers. "The Data Deluge," an article in the *Washington Post* business section (September 24, 1989), addressed this matter.

The president and his staff begin thinking about other variables from company records that might correlate with dollar amount per sale. The following candidates are finally selected, and a plan is finalized to randomly sample 100 sales over the company's history:

x_2 = Number of employees in purchasing company
x_3 = Distance, in miles, between Silos and purchasing company
x_4 = Size of purchasing company, in annual dollar sales
x_5 = Nature of purchasing company; retail (coded 1), wholesale (coded 2), or both (coded 3)
x_6 = Number of past orders placed by purchasing company

The dependent variable, dollar amount per sale, is designated y. The random sample of measurements for all six variables yields the correlation matrix in Table 15.23.

a. What do you think of the predictor variables selected by Silos?

b. Based on the correlation matrix, which predictor variable combinations would you run?

TABLE 15.23 Correlation Matrix for Extended Exercise 63

	1	2	3	4	5	6
1	1	.23	−.84	.79	−.37	.71
2	.23	1	−.17	.22	−.25	.31
3	−.84	−.17	1	−.81	.33	−.72
4	.79	.22	−.81	1	−.29	.22
5	−.37	−.25	.33	−.29	1	−.83
6	.71	.31	−.72	.22	−.83	1

c. Which combination indicated in part *b* would be best? How good a prediction equation would it produce?

64. Southern Hawaiian University

Ralph Ty is registrar for Southern Hawaiian University, which is experiencing excessive enrollment. The university administration has decided to restrict the number of entering freshmen using "some reasonable criteria." It is Ralph's job to find a way to do this.

Ralph decides that a person's college grade point average would be a good measure of success in college. He chooses this as the dependent variable and plans a multiple regression analysis in an attempt to find a good prediction equation. He thinks that if he can do this, he can make a good case to the Southern Hawaiian administration that a fair and impartial method has been found for admitting freshmen to the university.

Ralph thinks about other quantitative variables that might correlate well with college grade point average. He's not worried about having too many variables or too big a sample size, since he has access to work study students who can key the data into the university's computer. It would be easy for him to use the computer's statistical analysis package to perform the multiple regression.

Ralph has access to all university records in his attempts to find useful predictor variables. Also, he has the freedom to modify the university's application form if he determines that some variable not now being collected would be of use.

a. List as many variables as you can that you think would correlate well with Ralph's dependent variable.

b. Which of these variables do you think are recorded in the university's data system?

c. Which of the variables identified in part *a* would require special collecting? How might this be done?

65. Median Family Income

In this exercise, your objective is to build a model to forecast median family income. The variables are

y = Median family income
x_2 = Wages (in millions of dollars) for production workers in manufacturing industries
x_3 = Median gross rent
x_4 = Nonwhite population (percentage)
x_5 = Percentage of occupied households (with more than one person per room)

The population of 200 standard metropolitan statistical areas presented in the accompanying table was obtained from the *Statistical Abstract*, 1986. Choose a random sample of 40 areas and develop a good regression model to estimate median income.

Area	Median family income	Wages	Median rent	Nonwhite population (%)	Percentage of occupied households
001	19294	13400	233	20.30	05.2
002	18619	09688	251	18.23	05.7
003	19451	17261	263	17.70	06.0
004	20142	17402	221	04.84	01.9
005	20704	21331	216	11.00	01.9
006	18269	13107	251	35.56	07.6

Area	Median family income	Wages	Median rent	Nonwhite population (%)	Percentage of occupied households
007	23123	20983	246	01.96	01.8
008	18652	16909	239	12.16	06.1
009	20514	19605	231	06.43	02.1
010	23554	13303	315	66.89	15.5
011	20773	17780	260	02.87	02.0
012	21864	17607	222	08.98	02.2
013	21751	19805	228	14.43	02.9
014	22386	20275	252	05.67	02.1
015	18813	18388	193	04.46	03.8
016	19386	20807	232	34.61	06.9
017	21791	18774	244	27.10	03.0
018	20789	22500	223	11.26	02.2
019	24519	18339	252	04.95	02.0
020	18971	15743	232	01.11	04.0
021	18129	14146	224	41.78	07.3
022	15284	13505	165	02.33	02.8
023	21754	19186	226	18.17	04.0
024	17399	14770	203	02.60	02.5
025	20744	18259	231	04.16	02.2
026	21381	15289	231	04.14	01.4
027	21029	17326	301	15.58	05.0
028	18469	13306	256	16.43	03.0
029	19246	12027	215	20.98	04.3
030	17389	10797	191	08.65	03.8
031	21109	17000	232	02.15	02.4
032	18307	15125	216	04.64	01.9
033	21639	19848	212	11.91	03.6
034	22389	19851	238	16.60	02.1
035	20829	19086	227	12.20	02.3
036	20802	21010	222	13.54	02.1
037	21604	22035	238	12.83	02.1
038	19981	16944	238	14.43	03.3
039	20532	19131	237	14.26	03.0
040	19481	18908	253	03.86	02.6
041	17795	17848	253	03.29	03.6
042	21941	17711	270	06.67	02.3
043	19276	14081	244	05.40	02.9
044	21271	16419	232	03.04	01.5
045	20754	15750	233	07.42	01.7
046	20566	15215	229	04.16	02.2
047	21319	17245	251	20.95	02.8
048	21112	21565	223	08.21	02.2
049	20474	15544	219	03.42	01.9
050	19426	12643	219	05.29	02.6
051	17587	12753	181	17.57	04.7
052	17519	16043	237	32.66	05.3
053	19389	13573	240	30.11	04.1
054	20535	18517	220	01.94	01.7
055	17642	14381	216	14.56	04.0
056	18017	15400	201	40.71	06.4
057	19654	14466	237	16.95	03.6

Area	Median family income	Wages	Median rent	Nonwhite population (%)	Percentage of occupied households
058	14779	12277	222	24.12	04.4
059	17723	12975	228	13.70	04.9
060	20217	16819	223	10.52	04.1
061	20562	13006	262	20.29	05.4
062	21671	23232	236	23.82	04.9
063	12931	11500	186	23.04	23.4
064	18996	20351	231	18.12	11.1
065	21946	16110	261	20.45	04.9
066	22244	15179	262	22.24	05.2
067	21416	17757	253	15.82	04.3
068	15366	10485	194	41.44	13.0
069	24314	21193	278	27.20	06.7
070	24351	20687	279	28.17	06.7
071	14651	12222	220	25.96	06.0
072	17249	12405	214	18.87	09.1
073	19246	15912	236	24.33	04.7
074	16983	13602	204	20.99	04.8
075	20857	20917	250	18.92	08.0
076	17768	17535	213	05.37	09.1
077	21009	14946	244	03.11	04.5
078	20699	15633	259	01.39	02.4
079	19369	13163	279	16.11	03.3
080	16386	13272	166	30.32	04.7
081	18472	14321	207	21.02	03.3
082	19923	21654	246	05.44	02.6
083	21456	13600	246	07.62	02.6
084	21152	18864	259	05.58	02.7
085	24471	20803	301	07.85	04.3
086	23667	21202	273	10.61	02.5
087	24804	21371	284	10.10	02.3
088	20311	20169	239	12.29	03.0
089	19428	19267	224	04.57	02.1
090	17571	16453	214	17.08	06.9
091	20319	23468	221	05.80	03.0
092	19611	19015	190	02.59	02.7
093	21569	18478	219	01.55	02.2
094	18464	18738	219	00.91	02.6
095	21622	20431	223	02.31	02.5
096	21822	21425	230	04.34	02.0
097	19668	17362	227	00.99	02.0
098	23024	17178	246	03.81	01.7
099	23659	19701	251	12.73	02.5
100	23637	19936	252	13.02	02.5
101	23836	17772	243	11.35	02.7
102	25693	20000	327	03.43	03.0
103	16131	12215	185	18.74	04.4
104	18339	15697	208	27.64	04.3
105	15833	19093	180	43.32	06.9
106	15504	10875	197	22.48	05.0
107	17617	19157	194	12.94	03.6

Area	Median family income	Wages	Median rent	Nonwhite population (%)	Percentage of occupied households
108	16275	20759	169	13.83	03.5
109	19350	15913	223	21.58	03.9
110	17269	17929	202	29.54	05.7
111	17959	13569	195	35.35	05.9
112	17166	16426	197	27.78	05.0
113	30730	18111	374	14.78	04.0
114	20478	16615	288	13.36	05.2
115	19000	14736	246	16.66	05.8
116	18696	17163	224	11.05	04.3
117	18503	29447	201	15.08	03.9
118	15780	10932	213	03.25	03.8
119	15342	13336	188	08.86	04.8
120	18174	14794	218	20.26	04.1
121	18780	18276	240	23.25	07.9
122	16301	14441	228	06.83	03.5
123	18396	15125	236	26.30	08.3
124	21744	16582	288	26.50	09.4
125	25918	16742	358	13.63	05.6
126	21125	16491	277	32.15	11.2
127	23602	16437	317	19.56	07.5
128	17024	20281	240	04.34	04.3
129	20922	17400	247	16.49	03.5
130	20001	14932	289	31.13	10.2
131	20304	16953	281	18.68	05.5
132	24586	18581	297	24.34	04.9
133	24304	20593	273	27.62	04.1
134	25119	16853	309	28.83	05.7
135	26659	18556	334	21.41	05.3
136	20730	14048	303	12.45	06.0
137	21269	16260	289	07.24	03.3
138	21846	20268	254	20.74	04.1
139	21630	13865	300	17.07	06.0
140	19116	18578	223	23.98	06.3
141	16166	14683	226	26.72	09.9
142	16004	15231	206	16.79	05.9
143	18729	15407	225	12.67	02.6
144	23584	16655	264	13.15	02.4
145	17169	12280	260	04.88	02.0
146	23372	17349	252	10.30	02.5
147	21668	15013	258	11.49	02.7
148	20534	18290	249	05.96	02.4
149	16191	14949	261	10.27	03.3
150	15088	13107	241	12.15	03.1
151	16757	10926	278	09.65	03.8
152	16814	15060	259	17.29	05.1
153	16955	11636	224	11.67	03.0
154	16724	13367	244	21.25	04.6
155	17914	16389	240	23.15	04.3
156	16512	15414	219	17.03	05.0
157	19388	16672	259	10.06	02.9

Area	Median family income	Wages	Median rent	Nonwhite population (%)	Percentage of occupied households
158	19046	11788	282	18.52	08.0
159	19592	13771	312	12.39	03.9
160	18642	11055	272	22.36	12.1
161	19174	13167	264	13.16	05.9
162	13440	12000	216	17.27	04.9
163	18289	13491	255	15.02	04.2
164	15374	14700	212	14.27	04.1
165	16624	18487	223	19.21	04.1
166	17786	11625	285	06.20	02.1
167	16346	13177	240	10.63	03.1
168	19817	16132	279	15.49	04.5
169	17849	18893	205	41.62	08.8
170	16419	10855	202	19.14	04.1
171	21074	15204	252	25.64	03.7
172	17211	15836	202	32.54	05.2
173	15207	12477	182	37.36	05.3
174	18207	16597	186	34.36	05.6
175	17201	18550	204	37.80	05.1
176	23165	16818	240	05.26	01.7
177	21303	17735	241	11.85	02.5
178	24514	18558	252	25.85	05.0
179	25234	17023	275	09.04	03.9
180	24134	17380	251	29.34	05.3
181	24476	26376	239	23.43	04.9
182	25619	20748	260	12.05	03.3
183	23161	25158	236	04.28	02.9
184	28045	17150	285	10.31	03.3
185	21726	21485	238	11.17	02.5
186	20151	19151	239	15.72	03.9
187	23214	20746	262	07.04	02.4
188	22964	18341	238	09.51	02.6
189	22029	18789	241	06.98	02.2
190	20788	24483	208	07.48	02.7
191	18523	16062	215	05.38	03.0
192	19872	15016	223	05.36	02.4
193	21821	24590	225	05.09	02.2
194	20554	20219	227	03.93	03.0
195	20628	19848	223	10.57	02.1
196	18894	17281	227	11.83	03.5
197	18524	18434	197	05.64	03.2
198	23194	19575	248	03.64	01.8
199	23189	22903	253	06.59	02.5
200	22484	21838	224	00.78	03.0

The authors have selected a sample of 80 data points and analyzed these data using the MINITAB package. Please remember that your solution will be different from ours.

A random sample of 80 data points were selected and stored in a file called MEDIAN.DAT. An example of the data file is:

```
008 23194 19575 248 03.64 01.8
```

```
112 23189 22903 253 06.59 02.5
187 22484 21838 224 00.78 03.0
```

The MINITAB commands to read the file and run a regression analysis are:

```
MTB > READ 'MEDIAN.DAT' C1-C6
     80 ROWS READ

ROW    C1       C2       C3     C4       C5     C6

  1   117    18503    29447    201    15.08    3.9
  2   195    20628    19848    223    10.57    2.1
  3    72    17249    12405    214    18.87    9.1
  4    11    20773    17780    260     2.87    2.0
 . . .

MTB > NAME C2 'INCOME' C3 'WAGES' C4 'RENT' C5 'NONWHITE' C6 'HLDS'
MTB > CORR C2-C6

          INCOME     WAGES      RENT   NONWHITE
WAGES      0.562
RENT       0.677     0.131
NONWHITE  -0.230    -0.305    -0.141
HSLD      -0.319    -0.290    -0.115     0.524

MTB > STEP C2-C6;
SUBC> FENTER = 4.

STEPWISE REGRESSION OF INCOME ON 4 PREDICTORS, WITH N = 80

    STEP        1        2
CONSTANT     6432     1114

RENT         55.3     50.1
T RATIO      8.12     9.52

WAGES               0.393
T RATIO              7.47

S            2153     1650
R-SQ        45.80    68.58
 MORE? (YES, NO, SUBCOMMAND, OR HELP)
SUBC> NO

MTB > REGRESS C2 2 PREDICTORS C3 C4, STORE TRES IN C7

The regression equation is
INCOME = 1114 + 0.393 WAGES + 50.1 RENT

Predictor       Coef       Stdev    t ratio       p
Constant        1114        1445       0.77   0.443
WAGES        0.39310     0.05262       7.47   0.000
RENT          50.137       5.264       9.52   0.000

s = 1650     R-sq = 68.6%     R-sq (adj) = 67.8%

Analysis of Variance

SOURCE        DF          SS          MS        F        P
Regression     2   457258048   228629024    84.02    0.000
Error         77   209523920     2721090
Total         79   666781952

SOURCE       DF        SEQ SS
WAGES         1     210388880
RENT          1     246869184

Unusual Observations
Obs.       WAGES       INCOME          Fit       Stdev.Fit       Residual       St.Resid
   1       29447        18503        22767             749          -4264       -2.90RX
  42       17772        23836        20283             194           3553         2.17R
  63       14949        16191        20076             243          -3885        -2.38R
  74       18558        24514        21044             218           3470         2.12R

R denotes an obs. with a large st. resid.
X denotes an obs. whose X value gives it large influence.
```

```
MTB > HISTOGRAM C7

Histogram of C7 N = 80

MIDPOINT      COUNT
   -3.0           1   *
   -2.5           1   *
   -2.0           2   **
   -1.5           6   ******
   -1.0           7   *******
   -0.5          12   ************
    0.0          18   ******************
    0.5          15   ***************
    1.0          11   ***********
    1.5           5   *****
    2.0           2   **

MTB > NAME C7 'STDRES'
MTB > PLOT C7 VS C2

          -
          -
       2.0+                                           *   *
          -                      *     *       **
STDRES    -                   *    *     *   * * *  *        *
          -                          *          * *     *   *    *
          -               *     *  ** * **  2 *   * * * *     *
       0.0+                     3 * ****   **  *          *
          -               *       2 *2 *2  ** **
          -                  *   *    * *   **
          -       *          **    *  *  *
          -             2      *        *
      -2.0+          *         *
          -                  *
          -                          *
          -
          -
            ---+---------+---------+---------+---------+---------+----------+----INCOME
           12000     15000     18000     21000     24000      27000

MTB > STOP
```

Stepwise regression is used to identify the best variables to be used in the model: WAGES and RENT. These variables are then run so that the standardized residuals can be stored in C7. A histogram is run so that the normality assumption can be checked. A plot of standardized residuals is also run so that the rest of the regression assumptions can be checked.

Microcomputer Package

The micro package *Computerized Business Statistics* can be used to solve multiple regression problems.

In Exercise 40, Cindy Lawson bought a major league baseball team. Cindy asks you to write a report on how to develop a winning ball club. You decide to use stepwise multiple regression analysis to determine which statistics are important in creating a winning team.

Computer Solution:

From the main menu of *Computerized Business Statistics,* 10 is selected, indicating Multiple Regression Analysis. The multiple regression analysis menu is shown on the screen.

Since the problem involves entering data from the keyboard, a 1 is selected.

```
Multiple Regression Analysis-Define New Problem
Raw or Correlation Data: Enter R/C, Press ↵ R
Number of Variables: Enter 2–10, Press ↵ 7
```

Since the problem involves one dependent variable (WINS) and six predictor variables (ERA, SO, BA, RUNS, HR, and SB), a 7 is entered.

```
Number of Data Points: Enter 9–125, Press ↵ 26
```

Since there are 26 major league baseball teams, **26** is selected.

Next, the program asks for the variable names:

```
Multiple Variable Regression-Enter Variable Labels
        Variable 1 X1
        Variable 2 X2
        Variable 3 X3
        Variable 4 X4
        Variable 5 X5
        Variable 6 X6
        Variable Y
Press end when Finished
```

The variable names are ERA, SO, BA, RUNS, HR, SB, and WINS. **END** is pressed once the blanks have been completed.

```
Problem definition correct Y/N/Q, Press ↵ Y
```

After a **Y** response, the program is ready for the data to be entered. There are 26 observations for each of the seven variables. An **F** is entered once the blanks have been completed.

```
Select Dependent Variable: Enter 1–7, Press ↵ 7
```

Since variable 7, WINS, is the dependent variable, a **7** is entered. The screen then shows:

```
Regression Type: F = Full
                 S = Self Stepwise
                 A = Auto Stepwise
Select Type: Enter Letter and Press ↵ A
```

Since a stepwise regression is to be performed, **A** is entered.

Next, the computer asks:

```
Alpha Error 1 = 0.2, 2 = 0.1, 3 = 0.05, 4 = 0.025, 5 = 0.02, 6 = 0.01, 7 = Other
Select Alpha: Enter 1–7, Press ↵ 3
```

The screen shows:

```
Degrees of Freedom ................19
   Critical t ................. 2.093
dof (Numerator, Regression) = 6/ dof (Denominator, Error) = 19
   Critical F ................. 2.63
```

Next, you are asked:

```
Save Data? Enter Y/N, Press ↵ Y
```

A 7 is entered so that the problem can be run. The screen then shows the output menu. The choice in this case is **P**, for printer.

The program also provides the following alternatives for the user:

```
Multiple Regression Analysis-Optional Results
   R = Residual Analysis                    (No)
   C = Correlation Coefficients             (No)
   F = Forecasting                          (No)
Select Optional Results: Enter either (C, F, R) to toggle Option On/Off
Press P to Proceed . . . ?
```

MINITAB Computer Package

The MINITAB commands to solve Example 15.16 are:

```
MTB > READ 'CH15EX16.DAT' C1 C2
     14 ROWS READ

ROW     C1      C2

  1     1.1     3.9
  2     1.7     4.9
  3     2.6     7.6
  4     2.4     6.8

MTB > NAME C1 'SALES' C2 'EXP'
MTB > LOGE OF C2, PUT INTO C3
MTB > SQRT OF C2, PUT INTO C4
MTB > LET C5 = 1/C2
MTB > NAME C3 'LOGS' C4 'SQRT' C5 '1/EXP'
MTB > PRINT C1-C5
```

ROW	SALES	EXP	LOGS	SQRT	1/EXP
1	1.1	3.9	1.36098	1.97484	0.256410
2	1.7	4.9	1.58924	2.21359	0.204082
3	2.6	7.6	2.02815	2.75681	0.131579
4	2.4	6.8	1.91692	2.60768	0.147059
5	2.3	5.9	1.77495	2.42899	0.169492
6	2.9	9.1	2.20827	3.01662	0.109890
7	0.4	3.4	1.22378	1.84391	0.294118
8	3.2	11.6	2.45101	3.40588	0.086207
9	3.3	14.1	2.64617	3.75500	0.070922
10	3.1	14.9	2.70136	3.86005	0.067114
11	3.2	10.5	2.35138	3.24037	0.095238
12	3.0	9.9	2.29253	3.14643	0.101010
13	3.7	17.1	2.83908	4.13521	0.058480
14	3.3	12.4	2.51770	3.52136	0.080645

The LOGE command is used to calculate logarithms to base *e* (natural logarithms) for the data in C2 and store them in column C3. The SQRT command is used to calculate square roots for the data in C2 and store them in column C4. The LET command is used to compute the reciprocals for the data in C2 and store them in column C5. The PRINT command is used to show the data stored in columns C1 through C5 of the worksheet.

```
MTB > PLOT C1 VS C2
```

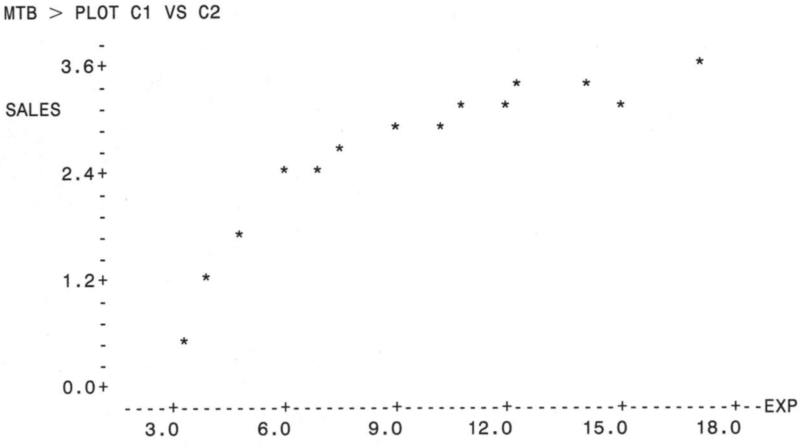

The original data are plotted with sales as the *y* variable and advertising expenditures as the *x* variable.

```
MTB > PLOT C1 VS C3
```

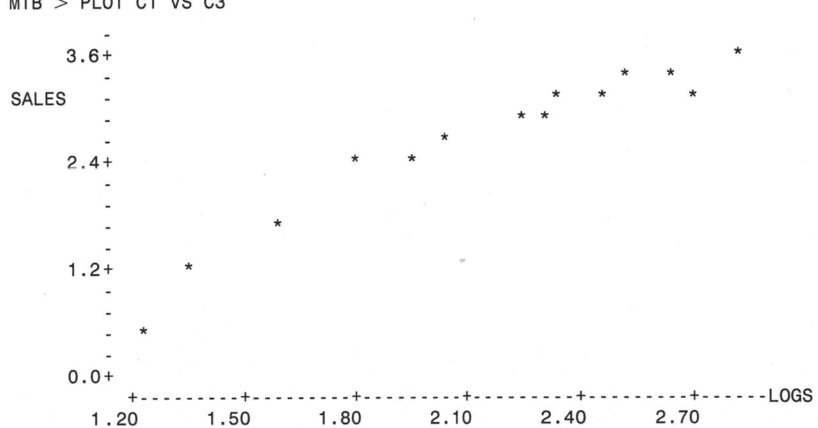

These data are plotted with sales as the y variable and the advertising expenditure variable transformed to natural logarithms as the x variable. Note that a straight line doesn't fit these data any better than the original data.

MTB > PLOT C1 VS C4

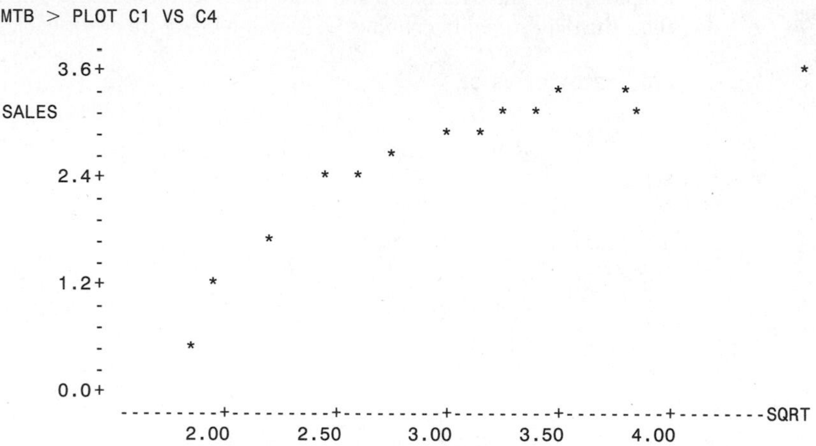

These data are plotted with sales as the y variable and the advertising expenditure variable transformed to square roots as the x variable. Note that a straight line should fit these data slightly better than the original data.

MTB > PLOT C1 VS C5

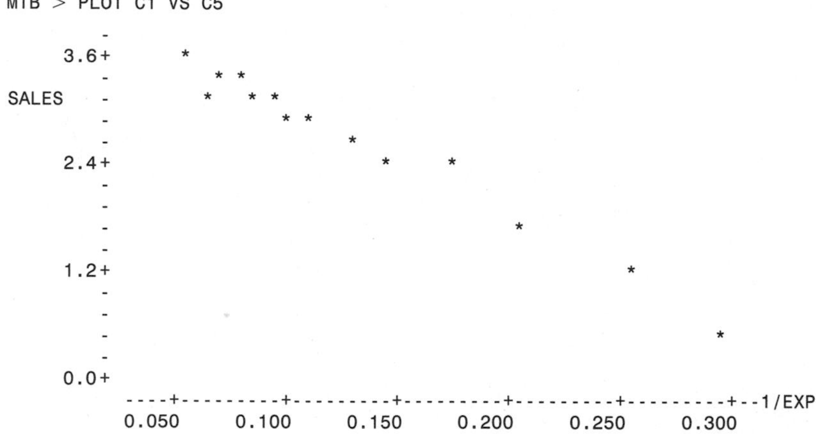

These data are plotted with sales as the y variable and the advertising expenditure variable transformed to reciprocals as the x variable. Note that a straight line should fit these data much better than the original data.

```
MTB > BRIEF 1
MTB > REGRESS C1 1 PREDICTOR C5

The regression equation is
SALES = 4.29 - 12.7 1/EXP

Predictor          Coef        Stdev      t ratio        p
Constant         4.28587     0.07695        55.69    0.000
1/EXP          -12.7132      0.5092       -24.97     0.000

s = 0.1342     R-sq = 98.1%     R-sq (adj) = 98.0%

Analysis of Variance

SOURCE        DF       SS         MS         F        P
Regression     1     11.221     11.221    623.44    0.000
Error         12      0.216      0.018
Total         13     11.437

MTB > STOP
```

The REGRESS command may be preceded by the BRIEF K command where K can equal 1, 2, or 3. Generally, $K = 1$ will produce enough statistics for most applications and will be assumed if the BRIEF command isn't used. When $K = 3$, a table of residuals is added to the basic output. The REGRESS command is used to run a simple regression with sales as the dependent variable and the advertising expenditure variable transformed to reciprocals as the x variable. This model explains 98.1% of the sales variable variance and seems to do a better job than the second-order model of Example 15.16.

SAS COMPUTER PACKAGE

The SAS computer package can be used to run stepwise regression analysis problems. The SAS commands to analyze Solved Exercise 1 are:

```
TITLE 'STEPWISE ANALYSIS FOR SOLVED EXERCISE 1';
DATA SALES;
INPUT SALES OUTLETS AUTOS INCOME;
CARDS;
52.3 2011 24.6 98.5
26.0 2850 22.1 31.1
20.2 650   7.9 34.8
16.0 480  12.5 32.7
30.0 1694  9.0 68.8
46.2 2302 11.5 94.7
35.0 2214 20.5 67.6
 3.5 125   4.1 19.7
33.1 1840  8.9 67.9
25.2 1233  6.1 61.4
38.2 1699  9.5 85.6
PROC STEPWISE;
 MODEL SALES = OUTLETS AUTOS INCOME/
       SLENTRY=.05;
```

The TITLE command names the SAS run. The DATA command gives the data a name. The INPUT command names and specifies the order for the four fields on the data lines. The 11 lines following the CARDS command represent the y variable and three x variables. The PROC STEPWISE command and MODEL subcommand indicate that the independent variables OUTLETS, AUTOS, and INCOME are to be entered in a regression equation to predict the dependent variable SALES. The SLENTRY = .05 statement specifies the significance level for entering a variable into the final regression model. Table 15.24 presents the output.

TABLE 15.24 SAS Output for Solved Exercise 1

```
                    STEPWISE ANALYSIS FOR SOLVED EXERCISE 1

                 Stepwise Procedure for Dependent Variable SALES

Step 1    Variable INCOME Entered     R-square = 0.87682179    C(p) = 25.76209947
                DF          Sum of Squares       Mean Square          F       Prob>F

Regression       1          1660.02452235     1660.02452235       64.06       0.0001
Error            9           233.20456856       25.91161873
Total           10          1893.22909091

                Parameter       Standard          Type II
Variable        Estimate         Error        Sum of Squares          F       Prob>F

INCEPTEP        1.03230539      3.88620209        1.82835352        0.07      0.7965
INCOME          0.47426771      0.05925344     1660.02452235       64.06      0.0001

Bounds on condition number:           1,        1
.................................................................................

Step 2    Variable AUTOS Entered     R-square = 0.96503519    C(p) = 4.29970153
                DF          Sum of Squares       Mean Square          F       Prob>F

Regression       2          1827.03269576      913.51634788      110.40       0.0001
Error            8            66.19639515        8.27454939
Total           10          1893.22909091

                Parameter       Standard          Type II
Variable        Estimate         Error        Sum of Squares          F       Prob>F

INTERCEP       -4.02689773      2.46798811       22.02923556        2.66      0.1414
AUTOS           0.62092180      0.13821024      167.00817341       20.18      0.0020
INCOME          0.43016878      0.03489322     1257.59286751      151.98      0.0001

Bounds on condition number:       1.085938,     4.343753
.................................................................................

All variables left in the model are significant at the 0.1500 level.
No other variable met the 0.0500 significance level for entry into the model.

           Summary of Stepwise Procedure for Dependent Variable SALES

      Variable            Number    Partial     Model
Step  Entered Removed       In       R**2       R**2        C(p)          F      Prob>F

  1   INCOME                 1      0.8768     0.8768     25.7621     65.0649    0.0001
  2   AUTOS                  2      0.0882     0.9650      4.2997     20.1834    0.0020
```

Chapter

16

Index Numbers and Time Series Analysis

The penguin flies backwards because he doesn't care to see where he's going, but wants to see where he's been.

Fred Allen

Objectives

When you have completed this chapter, you will be able to:

Explain how and why index numbers are used.

Compute price, quantity, and value indexes.

Develop a composite index.

Deflate a time series and change its base period.

Identify the component factors that influence a time series.

Explain what causes the trend in a time series and develop an equation to model it.

Compute the cyclical component in a time series and identify what causes this variation.

Identity the seasonal variation in a time series and compute seasonal indexes to describe it.

Isolate irregular or random variation in a time series.

Deseasonalize data.

Develop short-term and long-term series decomposition forecasting models.

The three-month T-bill rate was 3.64% on June 17, 1992, according to that day's *Wall Street Journal*, which also noted that the rate one year earlier was 5.62%.

Previous chapters' discussion of regression analysis and other techniques rests on the assumption that a random sample of items is selected for study, and measured. However, many variables are measured every week, month, quarter, or year. These variables, called *time series* variables, are usually important in business decisions. For this reason, observing and analyzing them carefully is vital in managing any organization.

Why Managers Need to Know about Index Numbers and Time Series Analysis

Thousands of index numbers are generated monthly by the federal government. These widely distributed indexes are designed to summarize one or several business time series values in a single, easy-to-understand number.

Companies typically follow many indexes closely, basing their decisions in part on the upward and downward movement of indexes they've decided are key *indicators*. Because of index numbers' widespread use, every manager must understand how they're computed and how they can be used.

This is the first of two chapters concerning analysis and forecasting of time series variables. This chapter presents the decomposition method of analyzing these variables. This approach identifies the component elements that influence each value in a series. Each component is identified so that the series can be projected into the future. The next chapter introduces other ways of accomplishing one of the manager's most important roles: forecasting.

Regarding three-month T-bill rate's sharp drop reported in *The Wall Street Journal*, many firms might want to track the T-bill rate over time. Some firms choose to watch this rate in its percentage form, while others prefer an index number based on a selected period in the past. Such index numbers are one of this chapter's subjects.

Purpose of Index Numbers

Time Series

Observations of data are frequently made over time. Any variable that consists of data collected, recorded, or observed over successive increments of time is called a **time series.**

> A **time series** consists of data that are collected, recorded, or observed over successive increments of time.

Index Numbers

Index numbers show the movement of values in a time series by converting the actual measured quantities to index, or *relative*, form. Index numbers are specified relative to a base period, usually designated as 100 or 100%. For example, if an index of factory wages has a base period of January 1993 and is currently at a level of 128, the analyst knows that wages are 28% higher now than in January 1993. If a unit production index for a jet airplane factory was based on the first quarter of 1993, an index of 95 in the current quarter would mean that production is 95% of what it was in the base quarter.

> **Index numbers** measure the movement of time series values relative to a base period; the index in the base period equals 100.

CONSTRUCTING AN INDEX

The first consideration in constructing an index is to choose an appropriate base period. The objective is to find a time period that's "normal" in the sense that it represents neither extremely good times nor extremely bad times.

The federal government has judged 1982 to be a "normal" year and has chosen it as the base year for many of its statistical indexes. Other indexes use different years as the base period. From time to time an index is updated by moving its base period forward to a more recent period. Conversion of an index to a new time period is covered later in this chapter.

EXAMPLE 16.1 The Worthrite Company has been keeping an index of its total monthly dollar sales for several years. When the index was started, January 1990 was chosen as the base period. For that month, the sales index was 100. In the latest month, Worthrite management computes the dollar sales index at 178. This means that sales for that month have increased 78% over what they were in the base period, January 1990.

EXAMPLE 16.2 The consumer price index (CPI), prepared by the federal government, consists of many items typically purchased by American consumers. The base period for this index is 1982–84. In March 1992, this index's value was 137. This value indicates that consumer prices in that month were 137% of what they were in the base period, 1982–84.

The usual reason for using index numbers is to summarize the values of a large number of items as a single value that can be monitored over time. For example, the CPI contains values of over 400 items. It would be difficult to assess the state of prices each month by studying all these items' prices, but it's easy to monitor a single value.

Even for a single variable, it's sometimes more convenient to follow an index than to track the variable in its original units. Company monthly sales, for example, might be monitored as an index number rather than in dollars. A company might use a unit production index or a defective item index rather than follow these important variables in their actual units of measurement.

A modification often considered by an analyst is the conversion of time series values measured in dollars to values in constant, or deflated, dollars. An appropriate index number is identified and used in this deflation process.

Index numbers are often of interest because they measure the changes in various economic conditions over time. They're commonly used to measure inflation's effects in various industries and to relate changes in quantities and values to a base period. The explanation and examples that follow show how different kinds of index numbers are computed and used.

Types of Indexes

Price Index

The basic type of index, and the one most commonly used, is the **price index.** This index measures changes in prices of selected goods and services over time.

> A **price index** measures changes in the prices of goods and services over time.

Equation 16.1 is used to calculate a price index. In this formula, PI represents the price index of the items being included. The idea is to calculate these items' current total price and compare it to the same calculation for the base period:

$$\text{PI} = \frac{\Sigma P_t}{\Sigma P_b}(100) \qquad (16.1)$$

where PI = Price index
P_t = Price in period t
P_b = Price in the base period

The numerator in Equation 16.1 sums the prices of all the items selected for the index in the current period. This total cost is divided by the sum of the prices of these same goods in the base period. The resulting value multiplied by 100 is the price index for that period. These steps are repeated for each period. If only one item is used for the index, the summation signs are ignored. The index in this case is the price of the item in the current period divided by the price of the item in the base period (times 100).

Example 16.3 Oil's price per gallon is monitored by a refinery in Anacortes, Washington. The refinery manager read a *New York Times* article (October 24, 1989) stating that oil companies' earnings had slipped—specifically, that Exxon and Phillips Petroleum reported lower third-quarter earnings in 1989. The manager then began a price index for oil so that prices could be more easily monitored.

The base period chosen for the price index was July 1985, when price per barrel was \$18. In January 1990, price per barrel was \$22. The price index for that month is calculated using Equation 16.1, with only a single item used in the index:

$$\text{PI} = \frac{P_t}{P_b}(100) = \frac{22}{18}(100) = 122$$

The refinery can conclude that oil's price per barrel is 22% higher in January 1990 than it was in the base period.

EXAMPLE 16.4 The Daly Manufacturing Company in Chico, California, makes electronic components that are shipped to assembly plants throughout the state. Ruth Kembel, personnel director, has been having trouble hiring qualified people and moving them to California. She has decided to keep track of the monthly cost of living for Chico. Ruth hopes to attract people on the basis of the town's low cost of living compared to other cities in California.

Ruth has defined a "market basket" of typical monthly purchases, including food, fuel, rent, clothing, and entertainment. Since 1982, the cost of this package of goods and services has been carefully measured (Table 16.1).

TABLE 16.1 Calculation of the Price Index for Example 16.4

Year	Monthly cost of market basket	Price index
1982	$435.78	100.00
1983	461.42	105.88
1984	478.83	109.88
1985	485.90	111.50
1986	491.82	112.86
1987	489.40	112.30
1988	495.71	113.75
1989	496.41	113.91
1990	501.14	115.00
1991	503.18	115.47
1992	505.27	115.95

Ruth thinks that the first year of the cost-of-living measurement, 1982, was a typical year, and she decides to use it as the base year in calculating the index. The cost of the package in 1982, $435.78, is divided into the cost of the same package for each year, using Equation 16.1. After moving the decimal point two places to the right to convert decimals to percentages, the cost-of-living indexes in the last column of Table 16.1 result. The index of 100.00 for 1982 indicates that it's the base year. Other years' indexes indicate the price of the market basket for those years relative to 1982. For example, the 1992 index is 505.27/435.78 = 1.1595, or 115.95%.

As these price indexes show, the cost of the defined packages of goods and services has grown steadily since 1982. In 1992, the package cost 115.95% of its price in 1982. In other words, there has been an inflationary effect of about 16% between 1982 and 1992. Ruth believes she can use this series of indexes in her recruiting efforts around the country to show that prices in Chico have risen less than in the rest of the country since 1982.

Quantity Index

Another important index, the **quantity index,** measures changes in quantities of selected goods over time.

> A **quantity index** measures changes in the quantities of goods over time.

Equation 16.2, used to calculate a quantity index, follows the same procedure as Equation 16.1 except that quantities of the selected items are used rather than prices. If only one item is tracked, the summation signs in Equation 16.2 are ignored and only the quantities for the single item are used:

$$QI = \frac{\Sigma Q_t}{\Sigma Q_b}(100) \tag{16.2}$$

where QI = Quantity index
Q_t = Quantity in period t
Q_b = Quantity in the base period

EXAMPLE 16.5 The Carmate Tire Company makes automobile tires and distributes them to wholesalers in a three-state area. Company analyst Calvin Shield has kept track of the number of tires shipped on a monthly basis for several years and has decided to convert these data to a quantity index. He begins the index in June 1991, but he chooses January 1992 as the index's base period (Table 16.2).

TABLE 16.2 Calculation of Quantity Index for Example 16.5

Month		Number of units shipped	Quantity index
1991	June	149	80.5
	July	135	73.0
	Aug.	163	88.1
	Sept.	160	86.5
	Oct.	175	94.6
	Nov.	142	76.8
	Dec.	163	88.1
1992	Jan.	185	100.0
	Feb.	179	96.8
	Mar.	190	102.7
	Apr.	188	101.6
	May	204	110.3
	June	162	87.6
	July	210	113.5
	Aug.	208	112.4
	Sept.	185	100.0
	Oct.	192	103.8
	Nov.	205	110.8
	Dec.	207	111.9

Each quantity in Table 16.2 is divided by 185 (the number of tires shipped in the base month, January 1992). Equation 16.2 is used for this computation, with the summation signs omitted since there's only one item. Multiplication by 100 produces the quantity indexes in the table's last column. For example, the index for June 1991 is 149/185 = .805, or 80.5%; the December 1992 index is 207/185 = 1.119, or 111.9%.

Calvin believes this quantity index will make managing the company easier since the number of tires shipped is now in index form relative to the base period.

Value Index

A third type of index, the **value index,** measures the dollar value of a group of goods or services.

A **value index** measures the total dollar value of a group of goods or services.

Equation 16.3 is used to calculate a value index. It calls for computing the value of each item in the selected mix. Each item's price is multiplied by its quantity, and these values are added for the current period. The same calculation is made for the base period, and the ratio is formed and multiplied by 100, resulting in the value index:

$$VI = \frac{\Sigma P_t Q_t}{\Sigma P_b Q_b}(100) \tag{16.3}$$

where
VI = Value index
P_t = Price in period t
P_b = Price in the base period
Q_t = Quantity in period t
Q_b = Quantity in the base period

To calculate a value index for only one item, ignore the summation signs in Equation 16.3.

EXAMPLE 16.6 The Boss Company wants to compare the value of the goods it produced last month with the value of its production in January 1991. Management considers January 1991 to be a "normal" month and wants to compare subsequent months with this period. Using Equation 16.3, the company analyst computes number of units produced for the current month, then multiplies this value by the total direct cost per unit. The result is the value of goods produced, excluding profit and overhead: $43,528. For January 1991, the same calculation produces a value of $29,743. Thus, the value index for Boss's most recent month is (43,528/29,743)100 = 146.35.

The Boss Company's management concludes that there has been a 46% increase in the value of its monthly production between January 1991 and the current month.

Aggregate Index

When an index is used to summarize several items, it's called an *aggregate index* because the prices, quantities, or values of several chosen goods or services are summed in its computation. The summation signs in Equations 16.1, 16.2, and 16.3 indicate the addition of the values for several items in each time period. If the price, quantity, or value history of only a single item is to be followed, the equations are simplified, using a single term in the numerator and denominator instead of the sum of several terms. Such indexes are called *simple indexes* (for example, the monthly price index of

Simple Index

wheat or the quantity index of trucks sold by a manufacturer). Example 16.3 illustrates a simple index.

Implicit in the concept of a "market basket" of goods is the *weighting* of the measured items in accordance with their frequency of use in the area being studied. The consumer price index, for example, doesn't include in its market basket one pound of butter, one car, one house, or one tube of toothpaste. Rather, items are weighted in the construction of the price index to reflect the fact that many tubes of toothpaste are purchased during a year, but a car is purchased only once every several years. This weighting of the items being studied is typically done when the index is constructed.

Consumer Price Index

The most commonly used aggregate index is the **consumer price index,** prepared monthly by the U.S. Dept. of Commerce. This index is widely followed by economists and business leaders as a measure of the prices U.S. consumers are paying for the products and services they commonly buy. Actually, beginning in 1978, the Bureau of Labor Statistics began publishing two consumer price indexes: one for wage earners and clerical workers (CPI-W) and another for all-urban consumers (CPI-U). Both of these important indexes price a market basket of goods and services believed to constitute an American worker's typical purchases. The CPI allows consumers to determine the degree to which price increases are eroding their purchasing power. The CPI has become a yardstick for revising pensions, wages, and other income payments that must keep pace with inflation.

Table 16.3 shows several recent values of the consumer price index (CPI-W). The base period chosen by the U.S. Dept. of Commerce is 1982–84. The index includes prices of about 400 items, such as milk, diapers, beer, bread, pop, gasoline, haircuts, interest rates, doctor fees, and taxes. As the table shows, the CPI-W's value was 136 in January 1992. This reflects an inflation rate of 36% between the base period and that month.

Table 16.3 Consumer Price Index and Purchasing Power of the Dollar

Month (1992)	Consumer price index (CPI-W)	Purchasing power (100/CPI-W)
January	136.0	.735
February	136.4	.733
March	137.0	.730

Source: *Survey of Current Business*, April 1992.

> The **consumer price index** measures the prices that U.S. consumers pay for the products and services they commonly buy.

In addition to measuring the change in prices of goods and services, the CPI is also used to deflate sales, to determine real disposable income, to find the purchasing power of the dollar, and to establish cost-of-living increases.

Table 16.3 also shows the purchasing power of the dollar for each period. The purchasing power varies inversely with the price index, since a rising price index means that a dollar purchases less. Equation 16.4 shows how purchasing power is computed:

$$\text{Current purchasing power of \$1} = \frac{100}{\text{Current consumer price index}} \tag{16.4}$$

Table 16.3 shows that in March 1992, the purchasing power was .73. This means that a dollar was worth only 73 cents in terms of its purchasing power relative to the base period.

EXERCISES

1. What is the purpose of calculating a price, quantity, or value index instead of using the original data values?
2. What is the advantage of using an index of the purchasing power of the dollar instead of a price index?
3. What is the advantage of a value index over either a price index or a quantity index?
4. The Data Company has recorded the average cost paid for one of its key computer components each month for several months. Compute a price index based on September using the following data:

Jan.	$123
Feb.	125
Mar.	132
Apr.	131
May	134
June	139
July	140
Aug.	138
Sept.	139
Oct.	142
Nov.	143
Dec.	143

4. Jan. 88.5
Feb. 89.9
Mar. 95.0
Apr. 94.2
May 96.4
June 100.0
July 100.7
Aug. 99.3
Sept. 100.0
Oct. 102.2
Nov. 102.9
Dec. 102.9

5. In the June 1993 base period, the price of a selected quantity of goods was $1,289.73. In the most recent month, the price index for these goods was 284.7. How much would the selected goods cost if purchased in the most recent month?

5. 3,671.86

6. A canning company buys aluminum in bulk for its operations. In addition to recording the number of pounds of aluminum it purchases each month, the company would like to form a quantity index. Construct such an index using the first month as the base period. The data are:

Pounds of aluminum
278
329

6. 100
118.3
65.8
90.6
103.2
154.3
112.2

Pounds of aluminum
183
252
287
429
312

7. 99.0
115.5
93.9
100.0

7. The Beyer Company wants to know the value of the sick leave benefits it gives its employees each operating quarter. The company records the number of sick days taken each quarter along with an estimate of such day's cost to the company. This value changes from quarter to quarter. Formulate a value index for Beyer based on the last quarter of data. The data are:

Quarter	Number of sick days	Cost per day ($)
1	198	125
2	258	112
3	178	132
4	205	122

8. 1.013
.962
.887
.906
.848
.772

8. Here are the price indexes for the purchase of an important commodity in the food business. Convert these values to represent purchasing power of the dollar for each period.

98.7
103.9
112.7
110.4
117.9
129.5

9. 1992
June 95.5
96.3
97.0
97.4
99.4
99.0
100.4
1993
Jan. 100.0
100.6
101.6
102.0
102.5
103.2
103.8

9. Here are figures for total U.S. personal income, in billions, for several months of 1992 and 1993. Convert these dollar values to an index based on January 1993.

1992	June	3,747.1
	July	3,778.6
	Aug.	3,803.7
	Sept.	3,820.8
	Oct.	3,897.2
	Nov.	3,884.1
	Dec.	3,939.0
1993	Jan.	3,921.8
	Feb.	3,946.7
	Mar.	3,985.9
	April	3,999.3
	May	4,020.6
	June	4,046.0
	July	4,071.2

10. 260, 299

10. According to the *Survey of Current Business*, the industrial production index for March 1988 was 134.1. This index has a base period of 1977. Suppose a company produces and ships 350,000 tons of aluminum during March. If this company is assumed to be in step

with the state of national production used to compute the industrial production index, what would its shipments have been during a typical month in 1977?

11. 100.0
69.1
90.7
99.5
96.0
91.9

11. The BeeWye Company wants a value index for the refrigerators it ships to customers. Here are the number of refrigerators it shipped along with average price charged, by month. Calculate a value index for the company using January 1993 as the base period.

	Month	Number of refrigerators shipped	Average price ($)
1993	Jan.	123	358
	Feb.	89	342
	Mar.	111	360
	Apr.	120	365
	May	114	371
	June	110	368

COMPOSITE INDEX

If a published index is available that accurately reflects the business or industry under study, the time and expense needed to calculate a new index can be avoided. The federal government publishes many indexes each month, each quarter, and each year, and these are widely used throughout business to study the overall economy or specific portions of it.

There may be no single published index that adequately matches the business for which an index is desired. Nevertheless, it may still be possible to avoid the large expense of forming a new index and updating it each time period. Two or more published indexes can be combined to form a new index that meets the analyst's specifications. A weighted average of the indexes being combined is calculated for each time period, and the analyst uses the resulting *composite index*.

Composite Index

EXAMPLE 16.7 Joe Fields wants to use a price index to study the annual dollar sales volume for his furniture business. Eighty percent of his business is retail; the other 20% is involved with wholesale trade. Joe can find separate government indexes for retail and for wholesale furniture prices and wants to combine these into a more accurate index. Table 16.4 shows the indexes Joe found along with the composite index he calculated by combining them.

Each composite index in Table 16.4 was calculated by multiplying the retail index by .80 and adding this value to the wholesale index multiplied by .20. In this way, Joe calculated a single index that reflects his store's sales split: 80% retail and 20% wholesale. For example, the index for 1992 was calculated as $(139.3)(.80) + (167.3)(.20) = 144.9$.

By using the composite index, Joe believes he has an accurate picture of the inflationary tendencies of the furniture business.

TABLE 16.4 Composite Index for Example 16.7

Period	Retail index	Wholesale index	Composite index
1982	123.7	156.9	130.3
1983	124.6	157.4	131.2
1984	127.8	160.2	134.3
1985	129.3	161.2	135.7
1986	130.7	162.5	137.1
1987	132.4	164.0	138.7
1988	133.1	164.7	139.4
1989	135.7	166.4	141.8
1990	136.8	165.1	142.5
1991	138.2	166.7	143.9
1992	139.3	167.3	144.9

DEFLATING A TIME SERIES

A primary reason for finding or calculating a good index number is to *deflate* a time series that's measured in dollars. The analyst often wants to remove the effects of price or value inflation before subjecting the series to further analysis. The first step in such price deflation is to find an appropriate price index, such as found in the federal government's *Survey of Current Business*. Alternatively, two or more published indexes can be combined to form a composite index, as in Example 16.7.

After the appropriate price index has been found or calculated, the decimal point in the index is moved two places to the left. The next step is to divide each dollar value in the time series by the price index for that period. Example 16.8 demonstrates this procedure.

EXAMPLE 16.8 Dollar sales volume for the Wing Company was \$35,758 in February; the price index is 243.9 for that month. Deflated dollar sales for the company are

$$\frac{\$35,758}{2.439} = \$14,661$$

Had there been no inflation since the price index's base period, the company's February sales volume would have been only \$14,661, not \$35,758. The difference between these two values reflects the amount of inflation since the price index base period.

The purpose of deflating a dollar time series is to enable the series to be examined with the effects of inflation removed. A dollar series that appears to be healthy because of its upward trend may actually show downward movement if inflationary effects are removed. A time series analysis (described later in this chapter) is often performed on a dollar time series after such an adjustment is made.

Deflating a Time Series

Steps for deflating a time series measured in dollars:

Step 1 Find an appropriate price index.
Step 2 Move the decimal point in the price index two places to the left.
Step 3 Divide each of the values in the time series by the price index for that period.

EXAMPLE 16.9 The Bentley Rug Company wants to examine its monthly dollar sales volume over the past three years. Because there has been some inflation over this period, chief accountant Sue Chen decides to deflate this time series before examining it. Sue decided to watch sales more closely after reading a *Wall Street Journal* article (October 23, 1989) showing that consumer installment debt is rising faster than GNP. Since Bentley finances almost all purchases, a drop in consumer willingness to incur debt would affect its sales.

Sue finds a price index published by the government that she thinks closely mirrors the rug business, and she records this index for the 12 months of her data. Table 16.5 shows this index, Bentley's actual dollar sales volume each month, and the deflated time series values. These deflated values were calculated by dividing each dollar value by the price index for the month, after moving the decimal point two places to the left. For example, the deflated dollar value for the last month was calculated as \$24,793/1.187 = \$20,887.

TABLE 16.5 Bentley Company Sales Deflation (Example 16.9)

Month number	Dollar sales	Price index	Deflated sales
1	15,428	110.7	13,937
2	13,538	111.2	12,174
3	16,479	111.0	14,846
4	19,421	112.5	17,263
5	21,937	113.2	19,379
6	18,233	113.9	16,008
7	22,751	115.7	19,664
8	21,840	114.2	19,124
9	25,841	115.0	22,470
10	22,556	116.7	19,328
11	20,779	118.0	17,609
12	24,793	118.7	20,887

Sue thinks that Table 16.5's final column (Bentley's deflated dollar sales volumes) contains figures that are much more meaningful than the unadjusted values. Since the effects of inflation have been removed, the company's performance independent of inflation can now be examined.

Changing the Base Period

Changing the Base Period

It is sometimes desirable to move the base period for an index forward in time. This adjustment is made when the original base period is many time periods in the past, and an index that better reflects a recent time period is needed. Care must be taken in choosing the new base period, just as for the original base period. A time period should be chosen that's as close as possible to "normal" in that neither extremely good nor extremely bad economic times were experienced in that period.

Example 16.10 Abby Smith, president and chief forecaster for the Abby Corporation, wants to update the base period for her company's price index. This index was formed five years ago, when a base period of January 1988 was chosen. She decides to update the base period to January 1992, which she considers to be an average operating month. Table 16.6 shows the old price indexes and the new price indexes for recent months.

Table 16.6 Change of Base Period for Example 16.10

	Month	Old price index	New price index
1991	Jan.	123.7	92.87
	Feb.	124.8	93.69
	Mar.	125.3	94.07
	Apr.	126.9	95.27
	May	127.4	95.65
	June	127.2	95.50
	July	128.0	96.10
	Aug.	128.2	96.25
	Sept.	129.7	97.37
	Oct.	130.5	97.97
	Nov.	131.5	98.72
	Dec.	132.9	99.77
1992	Jan.	133.2	100.00
	Feb.	133.8	100.45
	Mar.	134.4	100.90
	Apr.	134.9	101.28
	May	135.8	101.95
	June	135.6	101.80

For the new base period, January 1992, the old index value is 133.2. To compute the new price index for each month in Table 16.6, the old index is divided by 1.332 (the old index for January 1992 with the decimal moved two places left). The result is an index with a base period of January 1992. For example, the new index values for January 1991, January 1992, and June 1992 are

$$\text{January 1991: } 123.7/1.332 = 92.87$$
$$\text{January 1992: } 133.2/1.332 = 100.00$$
$$\text{June 1992: } 135.6/1.332 = 101.80$$

Abby has calculated a price index based on a recent time period, January 1992. She can now compare prices each month using the new price index.

EXERCISES

12. What is the advantage of a composite index over the indexes that might be found in a government publication?
13. What is the purpose of deflating a time series measured in dollars?
14. Which time series variable would yield the most information to the decision maker: raw dollars or deflated dollars?
15. What arithmetic operation is performed to deflate a dollar time series?
16. Why is it that only a time series measured in dollars is a candidate for deflating?
17. The Extra Company is involved equally with producing paper products and with printing newspapers. The company wants to find an index of production that closely matches its operations but is unable to do so. However, two relevant indexes are available: one for paper and related products, and one for printing and publishing. Assuming the company devotes 50% of its efforts to each endeavor, combine the two indexes to form a composite index.

17. 124.25
124.20
123.45
123.10

	Paper and products index (1982 = 100)	Printing and publishing index (1982 = 100)
1992 Jan.	133.3	115.2
Feb.	133.7	114.7
Mar.	134.4	112.5
Apr.	134.5	111.7

Source: *Survey of Current Business*, May 1992.

18. The Bluto Company wants to form a composite index for the cost of its workers, who are 80% blue-collar and 20% white-collar workers. Combine the following cost indexes to form such an index.

18. 77.2
81.8
86.2
90.7
94.0
97.7
103.9

	Blue-collar workers index	White-collar workers index
Dec. 1983	77.9	74.5
Dec. 1984	82.3	79.6
Dec. 1985	86.7	84.2
Dec. 1986	91.2	88.7
Dec. 1987	94.3	92.8
Dec. 1988	97.5	98.3
Dec. 1989	103.7	104.7

June 1989 = 100

Source: *Statistical Abstract of the United States*, 1991.

19. Deflate the following dollar sales volumes using the commodity price indexes shown. These indexes are for all commodities.

19. 281,631
233,139
280,624
295,097

		Sales volume (dollars)	Commodity price index (1982 = 100)
1992	Jan.	358,235	127.2
	Feb.	297,485	127.6
	Mar.	360,321	128.4
	Apr.	378,904	128.4

Source: *Survey of Current Business*, May 1992.

20. An analyst decides to deflate the variable of interest, total manufacturing and trade sales, in millions of dollars, using the consumer price index (CPI-W). Here are values for this time series, as found in the *Survey of Current Business*.

20*a*. 311,130
330,359
364,331

a. Calculate the deflated values for dollar sales.

b. Is it appropriate to use the CPI-W for deflating total sales dollars?

c. As shown, dollar sales are tending upward. How would you characterize deflated dollar sales?

		Sales	CPI-W (1982–84 = 100)
1992	Jan.	423,137	136.0
	Feb.	450,610	136.4
	Mar.	499,134	137.0

21. An analyst decides to study the dollar amounts of home mortgages insured or guaranteed by the Federal Housing Administration. A possible price index to use in deflating these dollar values is the consumer price index for all-urban consumers.

21*a*. 3231.44
2429.85
2119.36
1809.84
2545.15
2154.87

a. Deflate the dollar series using the CPI-U index.

b. How appropriate is the CPI-U for deflating this series?

c. How would you characterize the trend of FHA mortgages before and after deflation?

		FHA mortgages ($ millions)	CPI-U (1982–84 = 100)
1991	Nov.	4,452.92	137.8
	Dec.	3,350.77	137.9
1992	Jan.	2,926.84	138.1
	Feb.	2,508.44	138.6
	Mar.	3,545.40	139.3
	Apr.	3,006.04	139.5

Source: *Survey of Current Business*, May 1992.

Decomposition of a Time Series

Decomposition

Earlier in this chapter a time series was defined as data values that are collected, recorded, or observed over successive increments of time. When a time series variable is recorded and observed, it's often difficult or impossible to visualize its various components. The purpose of *decomposing* a time series variable is to observe each of its various elements in isolation. By doing so, we can gain insight into the causes of the series' variability. A second important reason for isolating time series components is to facilitate the forecasting process. If we understand the movements of the various components of a series, forecasting it into the future is much easier.

To understand the elements in a time series, we must consider the mathematical relationships among the various components. The most widely used model for time series decomposition is the *multiplicative model,* in which the series is analyzed as the product of its components:

$$Y = T \times C \times S \times I \tag{16.5}$$

where Y = Actual value of the variable of interest
T = Secular trend
C = Cyclical component
S = Seasonal component
I = Irregular component

In Equation 16.5, Y is the product of four elements acting in combination to produce the series. The multiplicative model is well suited to a wide variety of economic data in which percentage changes best represent the movement in the series. Additive models are also used occasionally and will be described in Chapter 17.

Trend

The **secular trend** of a time series is the long-term component that represents the series' growth or decline over an extended period of time. The basic forces responsible for a series' trend are population growth, price inflation, technological change, and productivity increases. Figure 16.1 shows that annual registration of new passenger cars in the United States from 1960 to 1991 has been increasing by a fairly constant amount, indicating a rising trend.

TM

FIGURE 16.1 New Passenger Car Registrations, 1960–1991

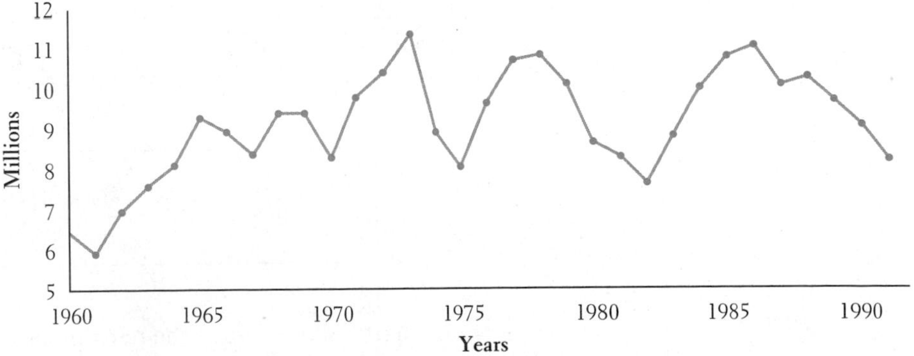

> The **secular trend** is the long-term component that represents the growth or decline in the time series over an extended period of time.

Cyclical Component

The **cyclical component** is the wavelike fluctuation around the trend. Any regular pattern of observations above or below the trend line is attributable to the cyclical component of the time series. Figure 16.2 shows a trend line fitted to the data for annual registration of new passenger cars in the United States for 1960 to 1991. The peaks and valleys above and below the trend line represent the cyclical component. Cyclical fluctuations are usually influenced by changing economic conditions.

FIGURE 16.2 Trend for New Passenger Car Registrations, 1960–1991

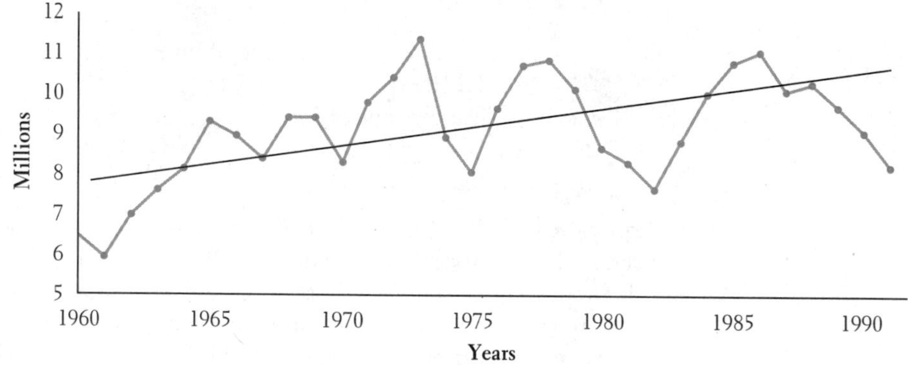

> The **cyclical component** is the wavelike fluctuation around the trend.

Seasonal Component

The **seasonal component** refers to a pattern of change that repeats itself year after year. For a monthly series, the seasonal component measures the variability of the series each January, each February, and so on. For a quarterly series, there are four seasonal measurements, one for each quarter. Seasonal variation may reflect weather conditions, holidays, or varying lengths of calendar months.

> The **seasonal component** is a pattern of change in quarterly or monthly data that repeats itself year to year.

Irregular Component

The **irregular component** is a measure of the remaining variability of the time series after the other components have been removed. It accounts for the random variability in a time series caused by unanticipated and nonrecurring factors. Most of the irregular component is made up of random variability. However, sometimes unpredictable events such as strikes, weather changes (droughts, floods, or earthquakes), election results, armed conflicts, or the passage of legislative bills cause irregularities in a variable.

> The **irregular component** measures the variability of the time series after the other components have been removed.

TREND

The multiplicative model Y = TC is used to analyze annual time series data.

The first component of interest in an annual time series is the secular trend. When an annual time series is observed over a very long time, say, 50 to 100 years, a curvilinear trend pattern is often seen. However, most annual time series are studied over a much shorter period, usually from 10 to 20 years. During such a period, either a typical series reveals a straight-line trend, or a straight line can be used as a close approximation to a slight curvilinear trend. Throughout this chapter, straight-line trends are usually used, although more advanced treatments of time series analyze curvilinear relationships as well. Two curvilinear models appear later in this chapter.

Trend Line

The least squares procedure is used to find the straight line that best fits the observed time series data. Equation 16.6 describes this linear trend function. This is the same procedure used to minimize $SSE = \Sigma(y - \hat{y})^2$ in regression analysis. For time series analysis, Y is the variable being analyzed, and X is a coded value used to represent the year, quarter, or month.

$$\hat{Y} = b_0 + b_1X \tag{16.6}$$

where $\hat{Y}$ = Forecast trend value of Y for selected coded time period X
b_0 = Constant or value of Y when X is coded as 0
b_1 = Slope of the trend line
X = Value of time selected

EXAMPLE 16.11 Annual registration of new passenger cars in the United States from 1960 to 1991 is shown in Table 16.7. Figure 16.1 plots these values as the Y variable; years are coded as the independent variable, X, with 1960 as 1, 1961 as 2, and so on. Equations 14.7 and 14.8 use the least squares procedure to compute the trend equation,

$$\hat{Y} = 7.902 + .076X$$

According to the MINITAB computer output, the trend equation explains 27.3% ($r^2 = .273$) of the variance for the new passenger car registration variable. The 1960 estimate for registrations based on the trend equation is 7.978 million (7.902 + .076). Each year, this trend estimate is expected to increase by an average of .076 million or 76,000 (rounded from 76,123) new passenger car registrations. This pattern of constant long-term growth might be attributed to the increase in the driving-age population for this time period. Figure 16.2 fits the trend equation to the actual data.

TABLE 16.7 Registration of New Passenger Cars in the United States, 1960–1991

Year	Registrations (millions) Y	X	$\hat{Y}$	Cyclical
1960	6.577	1	7.9780	82.439
1961	5.855	2	8.0542	72.695
1962	6.939	3	8.1303	85.348
1963	7.557	4	8.2064	92.087
1964	8.065	5	8.2825	97.374
1965	9.314	6	8.3586	111.430
1966	9.009	7	8.4348	106.808
1967	8.357	8	8.5109	98.192
1968	9.404	9	8.5870	109.514
1969	9.447	10	8.6631	109.048
1970	8.388	11	8.7393	95.981
1971	9.831	12	8.8154	111.521
1972	10.409	13	8.8915	117.067
1973	11.351	14	8.9676	126.577
1974	8.701	15	9.0438	96.210
1975	8.168	16	9.1199	89.563
1976	9.752	17	9.1960	106.046
1977	10.826	18	9.2721	116.759
1978	10.946	19	9.3482	117.091
1979	10.357	20	9.4244	109.896
1980	8.761	21	9.5005	92.216
1981	8.444	22	9.5766	88.173
1982	7.754	23	9.6527	80.330
1983	8.924	24	9.7289	91.727
1984	10.118	25	9.8050	103.192
1985	10.889	26	9.8811	110.200
1986	11.140	27	9.9572	111.879
1987	10.183	28	10.0333	101.492
1988	10.398	29	10.1095	102.854
1989	9.853	30	10.1856	96.735
1990	9.103	31	10.2617	88.708
1991	8.234	32	10.3378	79.649

Source: U.S. Dept. of Commerce, *Survey of Current Business*, various years.

The MINITAB computer package can be used to compute the trend equation. The MINITAB commands to solve Example 16.11 are:

```
MTB > SET C1
DATA> 6.577 5.855 6.939 7.557 8.065 9.314 9.009 8.357
DATA> 9.404 9.447 8.388 9.831 10.409 11.351 8.701
DATA> 8.168 9.752 10.826 10.946 10.357 8.761 8.444
DATA> 7.754 8.924 10.118 10.889 11.140 10.183 10.398 9.853 9.103 8.234
DATA> END
MTB > SET C2
DATA> 1:32
DATA> END
MTB > NAME C1 'REG' C2 'TIME'
MTB > REGRESS C1 1 PREDICTOR C2
```

```
The regression equation is
REG = 7.90 + 0.0761 TIME

Predictor        Coef       Stdev    t ratio       p
Constant      7.90190     0.42903      18.42   0.000
TIME         0.076123     0.02269       3.36   0.002

s = 1.185     R-sq = 27.3%     R-sq (adj) = 24.9%

Analysis of Variance

SOURCE        DF        SS        MS        F        P
Regression     1    15.808    15.808    11.26    0.002
Error         30    42.124     1.404
Total         31    57.932

Unusual Observations
Obs.    TIME       REG      Fit   Stdev.Fit   Residual   St.Resid
 14     14.0    11.351    8.968       0.217      2.383      2.05R

R denotes an obs. with a large st. resid.
```

Note that the DATA command 1:32 generates the time variable: integers 1 through 32.

Although the linear trend model is used more frequently than any other to describe long-term growth or decline of a time series, the use of curvilinear trends is sometimes necessary. Two of the more useful curvilinear trend models are described next.

Curvilinear and nonlinear trends are appropriate for describing growth patterns of new products, companies, or industries, especially over long periods of time. Figure 16.3 shows the life cycle of a typical new product, company, or industry. This growth pattern is divided into four stages: introduction, growth, maturity, and saturation. Time (represented on the horizontal axis) can vary from days to weeks to months to years, depending on the nature of the market. A linear model won't fit a typical life cycle pattern because the growth of most new products, companies, and industries increases at a *constant rate* (exponential model) instead of a *constant amount* (linear model).

TM

FIGURE 16.3 Life Cycle of a Typical New Product

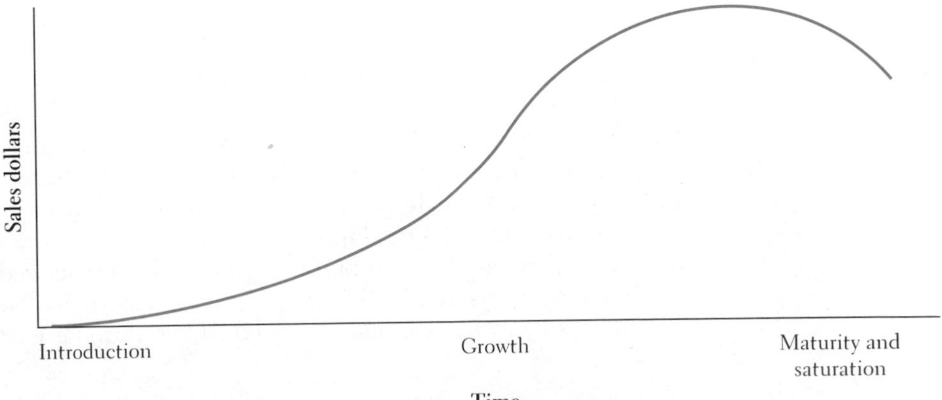

An exponential trend model should be fitted for a product that starts slowly (introduction stage, Figure 16.3) and then increases at a growing rate (growth stage, Figure 16.3) such that the percentage difference from observation to observation is constant. The number of handheld computers sold (Figure 16.4) reflects growth at a constant percentage rate instead of a constant amount. A linear trend might indicate an average growth of 800 computers per year. An exponential fit might indicate an average growth of 32% per year for the figure's data. If the exponential model estimated sales of 7,000 handheld computers for 1988, the increase estimated for 1989 would be 2,240 (7,000 × .32) instead of 800. Computations for various exponential models are complex, so use of appropriate computer programs is recommended.

TM

FIGURE 16.4 Exponential Trend for Handheld Computers

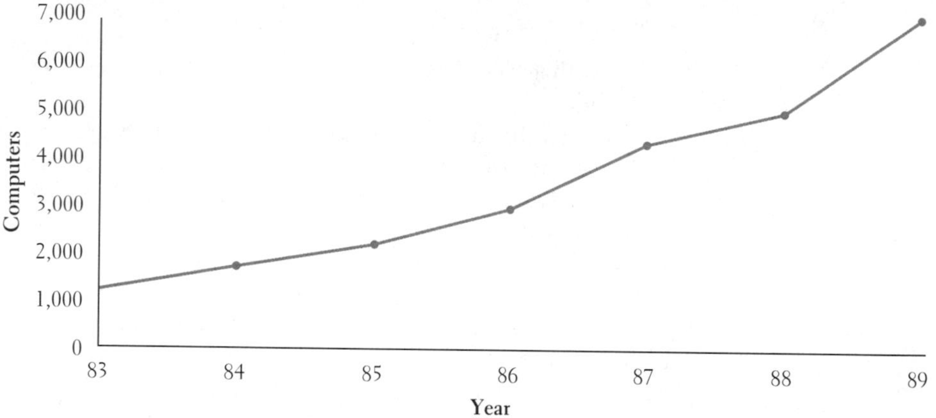

If the analyst isn't careful, the exponential trend model will provide an estimate that's higher than the actual growth of the variable. Note in Figure 16.4 that the exponential model would always forecast an increasing number of handheld computers sold. What happens when market maturity and saturation take place, and the growth rate slows down? The next section discusses growth curves that model this type of situation.

Growth curves of the Gompertz or logistic type represent the tendency of many industries and product lines to grow at a declining rate as they mature (the maturity and saturation stage of Figure 16.3). If product sales begin low, then catch on as sales "boom," and finally ease off as market saturation is reached, the Gompertz curve might be the appropriate trend model. Figure 16.5 shows the general shape of a Gompertz growth curve. Computations for various growth curve models are also complex; again, using appropriate computer programs is recommended.

When an analyst is deciding which trend model to use, the purpose for computing the trend should be carefully identified. If the purpose is to estimate demand for a

FIGURE 16.5 Gompertz Growth Curve

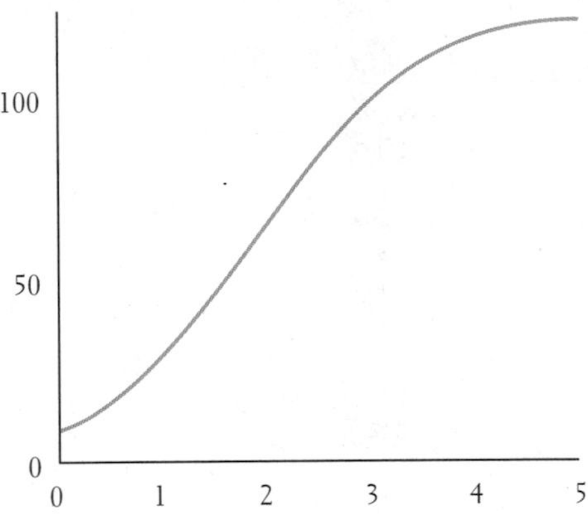

future quarter, you need to know the basic forces affecting long-term demand growth. Choice of the proper trend model is a matter of judgment so an analyst requires experience and common sense. The line or curve that best fits a set of data points might not make sense when projected as the future trend.

EXAMPLE 16.12 Decision Science Associates is doing a feasibility study for a proposed destination resort to be built within one half mile of the Grand Coulee Dam. Paul Nobisch, company president, feels that the large number of tourists who visit the dam each year might be a significant factor in determining whether the resort should be constructed. He assigns one of his employees, Mark Craze, to gather data and develop the appropriate trend model.

Visitors are counted by tour guides as they enter the visitors center. Table 16.8 shows that the number of visitors varied from a low of 161,524 in 1980 to a high of 617,737 in 1983.

Mark plotted the data (Figure 16.6) and decided that a linear trend would fit best. He computed the trend equation $\hat{Y} = 259{,}055 + 8{,}363X$. The correlation between the number of visitors and time is .358, so knowledge of time allows Mark to explain only 12.8% ($.358^2$) of the variance in the number of visitors. The regression equation indicates that the estimated number of visitors for 1969, based on the trend line, is 267,418 (259,055 + 8,363) and that the number has increased by an average of 8,363 persons per year.

The increasing trend for the *number of visitors* variable seems to be based mostly on population growth. The number of visitors increased an average of approximately 2–3% per year from 1969 to 1984. The population of the state of Washington also increased by approximately 2% per year from 1970 to 1984. Since time isn't highly related to the number of visitors, Mark decides that the cyclical component is extremely important.

TABLE 16.8 Number of Visitors Counted at the Grand Coulee Dam Visitors Center, 1969–1984 (Example 16.12)

Year	Visitors	Cyclical
1969	250,265	93.6
1970	250,929	91.0
1971	321,333	113.1
1972	342,269	117.0
1973	268,528	89.3
1974	468,136	151.4
1975	390,129	123.8
1976	300,140	92.1
1977	271,140	81.1
1978	282,752	83.5
1979	244,006	70.5
1980	161,524	44.9
1981	277,134	75.4
1982	382,343	101.7
1983	617,737	160.7
1984	453,881	115.5

Source: *Market Feasibility Study for a Proposed Development at Crescent Bay on Lake Roosevelt*, Spokane: Decision Science Associates, January–February 1985.

FIGURE 16.6 Grand Coulee Dam Visitors, 1969–1984 (Example 16.12)

EXERCISES

22. What is a time series?
23. Explain the concept of decomposing a time series.
24. In the decomposition of an annual time series, what components are analyzed?
25. Describe each of the four components in the decomposition of a seasonal time series.
26. Describe the secular trend component.

27. List the basic forces that affect the secular trend of most variables.

28. What kind of trend model should be used in each of the following cases?

28*a*. Exponential
b. Gompertz
c. Linear

a. The variable is increasing at a constant rate.

b. The variable increases at a constant rate until it reaches saturation and levels out.

c. The variable is increasing by a constant amount.

29. If

$$\hat{Y} = 1{,}600 + 85X$$
$$Y = \text{Annual sales, in units}$$
$$X = 1 \text{ unit/year } (X = 0 \text{ represents July 1, 1972})$$

29*a*. 1600
b. 85
c. 3,130

a. What were the expected sales based on the trend equation for 1972?

b. What is the average increase in sales per year?

c. Estimate the trend value for sales in 1993.

30. Triton Energy Corporation explores for and produces oil and gas. Company analyst Peter Feehan is studying the trend of the company's sales per share.

Year	Sales per share	Year	Sales per share
1972	0.39	1983	7.16
1973	0.81	1984	1.93
1974	0.93	1985	5.17
1975	1.35	1986	7.72
1976	1.48	1987	5.33
1977	2.36	1988	8.12
1978	2.45	1989	10.65
1979	2.52	1990	12.06
1980	2.81	1991	11.63
1981	3.82	1992	5.85*
1982	5.54	1993	6.40*

**Value Line* Estimates.
Source: *The Value Line Investment Survey* (New York: Value Line, 1988, 1989, 1991), p. 1844.

30*b*. Linear
c. $\hat{Y} = -1.29 + .571X$
d. $r^2 = 82.7\%$
e. .571
f. 1992: 10.71
1993: 11.28

a. Plot the data.

b. Determine the appropriate trend model. (Use 1972–91.)

c. If the appropriate model is linear, compute the straight-line trend model.

d. How well does the linear trend equation fit the data?

e. What has been the average increase in sales per share per year since 1972?

f. Estimate the trend value for sales in 1992 and 1993. Compare your trend estimates to *Value Line's*.

31. *Value Line's* estimates of sales and earnings growth for individual companies are derived by correlating sales, earnings, and dividends to appropriate components or subcomponents of the national income accounts, such as capital spending. *Value Line* employee Lynn Wallace examines the trend of capital spending from 1977 to 1993.

Year	($ billions)	Year	($ billions)
1977	214	1986	437
1978	259	1987	443
1979	303	1988	545
1980	323	1989	571
1981	369	1990	587
1982	367	1991	550
1983	357	1992	566*
1984	416	1993	623*
1985	443		

*Value Line estimates.
Source: *The Value Line Investment Survey* (New York: Value Line, 1988, 1989, 1991), p. 1750.

31*b*. Linear
c. $\hat{Y} = 212 + 25X$
d. 25
e. 612
637
f. 612 versus 566, 637 versus 623
g. Inflation, population growth

a. Plot the data.

b. Determine the appropriate trend model for the years 1977–91.

c. If the appropriate model is linear, compute the straight-line trend model for the years 1977–91.

d. What has the average increase in capital spending per year been since 1977?

e. Estimate the trend value for capital spending in 1992 and 1993.

f. Compare your trend estimate with *Value Line's*.

g. What factor(s) influence the trend of capital spending?

32. $\hat{Y} = -.3778 + .23X$
$r^2 = .8674$

32. The Graphic Scanning Corporation provides telecommunications services. Company analyst Roy Coumbs must determine the appropriate trend model for Graphic's sales per share.

Year	Sales per share	Year	Sales per share
1972	0.23	1981	2.09
1973	0.25	1982	2.32
1974	0.21	1983	2.85
1975	0.36	1984	3.89
1976	0.56	1985	3.29
1977	0.60	1986	3.03
1978	0.77	1987	3.20
1979	1.04	1988	3.51
1980	1.55	1989	2.78

Source: *The Value Line Investment Survey* (New York: Value Line, 1988, 1989), p. 781.

Write a memo describing the appropriate trend model for Graphic's sales per share.

CYCLICAL

Data collected annually obviously can't have a seasonal component. However, annual data can reveal certain cyclical effects. The cyclical component was defined as the wavelike fluctuation around the trend. In Example 16.11, the trend equation explained only 27.3% of the variance in new passenger car registrations. The peaks and valleys above and below the trend line in Figure 16.2 represents cyclical fluctuations in the number of annual registrations of new passenger cars in the United States from 1960 to 1991. These cyclical fluctuations are influenced by changing economic conditions such as interest rates, money supply, consumer demand, inventory levels, and market conditions. Equation 16.7 calculates the cyclical component for annual data:

Cyclical Index

$$C = \frac{Y}{\hat{Y}}(100) \tag{16.7}$$

where C = Cyclical component
Y = Actual value of the variable of interest
$\hat{Y}$ = Forecast trend value of Y for selected time period

EXAMPLE 16.13 Table 16.7 provides 1960–91 cyclical indexes for annual registrations of new passenger cars in the United States. Each cyclical relative is computed by dividing the actual number of registrations for each year (Y) by the expected number of registrations ($\hat{Y}$) based on the trend equation $\hat{Y} = 7.902 + .076X$. This ratio is then multiplied by 100 to put it in percentage or index number form.

For example, the first and last cyclical values in Table 16.7 are calculated as follows. (Disregard rounding errors.) The trend estimate for 1960 is

$$\hat{Y} = 7.902 + .076(1) = 7.978$$

The cyclical value in 1960 is

$$C = \frac{6.577}{7.978}(100) = 82.44$$

The trend estimate for 1991 is

$$\hat{Y} = 7.902 + .076123(32) = 10.338$$

The cyclical value for 1991 is

$$C = \frac{8.234}{10.338}(100) = 79.65$$

As Equation 16.7 shows, the cyclical indexes indicate the position of each Y value *relative* to the trend line. This position is indicated by a percentage. For example, in 1960, the Y value was 82.44% of the trend line. In 1965, Y was 111.43% of the trend line. Since the cyclical values are shown as percentages of the trend line, the trend is removed from the series, leaving only the cyclical component for evaluation. In 1960, new car passenger registrations were approximately 17–18% below what was expected based on the trend estimate. In 1965, new passenger car registrations were approximately 11–12% above what was expected based on the trend estimate.

The MINITAB computer package can also be used to compute cyclical relatives. The commands to enter the data and name the variables were given when Example 16.11 was solved. The MINITAB commands to solve Example 16.13 are:

```
MTB > REGRESS C1 1 PREDICTOR C2, TRESIDS IN C3, DHATS IN C4
MTB > LET C5 = (C1/C4)*100
MTB > PRINT C1-C5
```

ROW	REG	TIME	C3	C4	C5
1	6.577	1	−1.25990	7.9780	82.439
2	5.855	2	−1.96539	8.0542	72.695
3	6.939	3	−1.05857	8.1303	85.348
4	7.557	4	−0.57404	8.2064	92.087
5	8.065	5	−0.19136	8.2825	97.374
6	9.314	6	0.83677	8.3586	111.430
7	9.009	7	0.50098	8.4348	106.808
8	8.357	8	−0.13379	8.5109	98.192
9	9.404	9	0.70807	8.5870	109.514
10	9.447	10	0.67753	8.6631	109.048
11	8.388	11	−0.30292	8.7393	95.981
12	9.831	12	0.87416	8.8154	111.521
13	10.409	13	1.30415	8.8915	117.067
14	11.351	14	2.04596	8.9676	126.577
15	8.701	15	−0.29401	9.0438	96.210
16	8.168	16	−0.81619	9.1199	89.563
17	9.752	17	0.47675	9.1960	106.046
18	10.826	18	1.33289	9.2721	116.759
19	10.946	19	1.37156	9.3482	117.091
20	10.357	20	0.80151	9.4244	109.896
21	8.761	21	−0.63649	9.5005	92.216
22	8.444	22	−0.97672	9.5766	88.173
23	7.754	23	−1.64118	9.6527	80.330
24	8.924	24	−0.69756	9.7289	91.727
25	10.118	25	0.27213	9.8050	103.192
26	10.889	26	0.87933	9.8811	110.200
27	11.140	27	1.03597	9.9572	111.879
28	10.183	28	0.13165	10.0333	101.492
29	10.398	29	0.25504	10.1095	102.854
30	9.853	30	−0.29555	10.1856	96.735
31	9.103	31	−1.03555	10.2617	88.708
32	8.234	32	−1.89191	10.3378	79.649

```
MTB > STOP
```

The REGRESS command is producing standardized residuals (TRESIDS) and the predicted Y values (DHATS) and storing them in C3 and C4. The LET command is used so that the actual values, C1, can be divided by the predicted values, C4. The results are multiplied by 100 to create index numbers that are stored in C5.

Cyclical Chart

A cyclical chart, such as Figure 16.7, is developed to help analyze the cyclical component. The cyclical chart shows the trend equation as the base line, represented as 100%. Cyclical patterns are easier to see on a cyclical chart. This type of graph also allows the analyst to compare the variable of interest with the cyclical patterns for other variables and/or business indicators.

The following questions are answered by the cyclical indexes for any time series:

1. Is the series cyclical?
2. If so, how extreme is the cycle?
3. Does the series follow the general state of the economy (business cycle)?

Figure 16.7 Cyclical Chart for New Car Registrations, 1960–1991

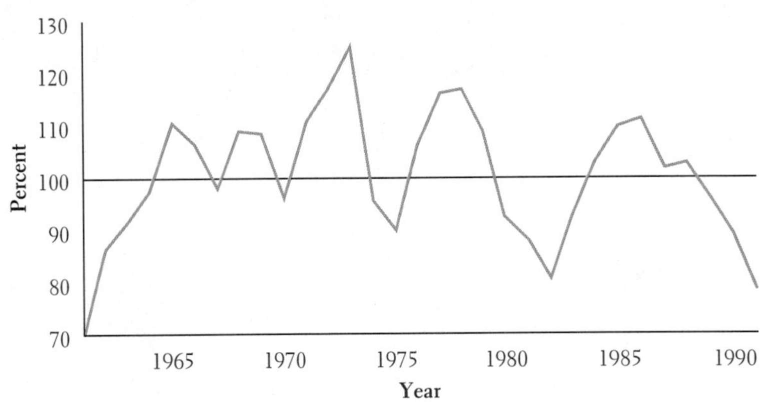

Example 16.14 Questions concerning the cyclical pattern for new passenger car registrations are answered in Figure 16.7. The series bottomed out in 1961 (72.7) and then gradually rose until it peaked in 1965 (111.4). Good times generally prevailed for the years 1966–79 (with the exception of 1974 and 1975), followed by a four-year slump in registrations in the early 1980s. In 1985 and 1986, the cyclical was above the trend line, indicating good times for registrations. The series has consistently decreased since 1988, reaching a low of 79.6 in 1991.

The cyclical pattern seems to indicate that new passenger car registrations are influenced to some extent by economic conditions. However, other factors also seem to be affecting the cyclical pattern of this variable.

A variable that might help explain the variability of the cyclical pattern for new passenger car registrations is the new-car price index. When prices are low, registrations should be higher than normal, and when prices are high, registrations should be down. The new-car price index must be adjusted for trend to eliminate effects of inflation. Figure 16.8 compares the cyclical index for new car prices with the cyclicals for registrations. These cyclical indexes are inversely related. Therefore, knowledge of proposed pricing policies should help an analyst forecast the cyclical pattern for new passenger car registrations.

Once a time series has been found to be cyclical and the locations of the peaks and valleys have been determined, the next concern is how much the cycle of the series matches other well-known cycle indicators. The federal government maintains a list of economic indicators (Table 16.9) that assist in this process.

The national economic indicators are divided into three groups. The *coincident indicators* define the economy's basic well-being. When these indicators are up and unemployment rate is down, the economy enjoys good times. When the reverse is true, the economy is depressed or in a recession.

The *leading indicators* in Table 16.9 tend to begin rising before a recession is over and to begin falling prior to the onset of a recession. *Lagging indicators* lag behind the ups and downs of the economy. By comparing the cycle of a company's time series to the behavior of the indicators, it may be possible to tie the series to one or more of

FIGURE 16.8 Cyclical Chart for New Car Registrations and Price Indexes, 1960–1991

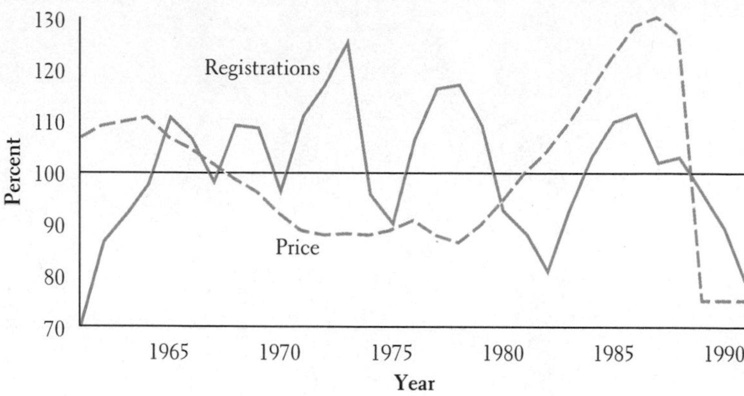

TABLE 16.9 Cyclical Indicators (NBER Short List)

Leading indicators	Roughly coincident indicators	Lagging indicators
Average hourly workweek, production workers, manufacturing	GNP in current dollars	Unemployment rate, persons unemployed 15 weeks or over
Average weekly initial claims, state unemployment insurance	GNP in 1972 dollars	Business expenditures, new plant and equipment
Index of net business formation	Index of industrial production	Book value, manufacturing and trade inventories
New orders, durable goods industries	Personal income	Index of labor cost per unit of output in manufacturing
Contracts and orders, plant and equipment	Manufacturing and trade sales	Commercial and industrial loans outstanding in large commercial banks
Index of new building permits, private-housing units	Sales of retail stores	Bank rates on short-term business loans
Change in book value, manufacturing and trade inventories	Employees on nonagricultural payrolls	
Index of industrial materials prices	Unemployment rate, total	
Index of stock prices, 500 common stocks		
Corporate profits after taxes (quarterly)		
Index: ratio, price to unit labor cost, manufacturing		
Change in consumer installment debt		

Source: U.S. Dept. of Commerce.

these national series. The cyclical component of the company series can then be estimated using predictions made by government officials and other experts. In addition, insights into the company series might be gained if it's demonstrated to be cycling in harmony with a national series.

Annual time series can be projected into the future using time series printouts such as those in Table 16.7 and Figure 16.7. The components used in such forecasts depend on the distance into the future for which the forecast is desired. For relatively short-term forecasts (say, one to two years), we can combine the trend and cyclical projections to calculate the forecast. For longer-term forecasts, only the trend estimate is used since it's not possible to anticipate the state of the economy with any precision more than one or two years into the future.

EXAMPLE 16.15 The multiplicative model is used to forecast new passenger car registrations for 1992. The trend estimate is computed using Equation 16.6. The appropriate value for X in 1992 is 33 (Table 16.7). This value is substituted into the equation, and the trend estimate for 1992 is

$$\begin{aligned}\hat{Y}\,(1992) &= b_0 + b_1X \\ &= 7.902 + .076(33) = 10.410\end{aligned}$$

Next, all the information that has been gathered concerning the cyclical pattern of new passenger car registrations is analyzed. Registrations have decreased consistently since 1988 (Figure 16.8). Will this pattern continue or will registrations level out or even turn upward again? How will the economy perform? What do the experts forecast for the business cycle? What are the proposed new-car pricing policies for 1992? Do election year politics affect new passenger car registrations? Once these questions are answered, we can choose an estimate for the cyclical relative for 1992. The most important aspect of the cyclical estimate process is to forecast the direction correctly. If the analyst successfully predicts whether a particular variable's cyclical pattern will continue to increase or decrease, level off, or turn upward or downward, the forecast will be fairly accurate. The actual value used for the estimate is not as important as the analyst's correct assessment of the direction.

Economic indicators point to the economy leveling off in 1992 since it's an election year. Therefore, we decided to forecast that the cyclical relative will also level off. The C for 1991 is 79.65 (Table 16.7). The cyclical for 1992 is estimated to be 78 and the forecast using Equation 16.6 is

$$Y(1992) = T \times C = 10.410(.78) = 8.120$$

Note that $\hat{Y}$ is used to estimate T (the trend) in this model.

The relative importance of the individual components of the multiplicative model dictates the accuracy of its forecasts. How well does the trend equation describe the long-term growth? If the trend equation does a good job of explaining a variable, a five-year projection into the future is reasonable. If the trend equation doesn't fit the data, the cyclical component is more important. Since it's extremely difficult to estimate the cyclical index for more than a year or two into the future, long-term forecasts are risky, at best.

EXAMPLE 16.16 In Example 16.12, Mark Craze developed a trend model for the number of visitors to Grand Coulee Dam. Now, he intends to analyze the cyclical so that he can forecast 1986.

Cyclical indexes are calculated in Table 16.8. Next Mark developed a cyclical chart (Figure 16.9) so that he could compare the cyclical indexes for the number of visitors

FIGURE 16.9 Visitors—Cyclical

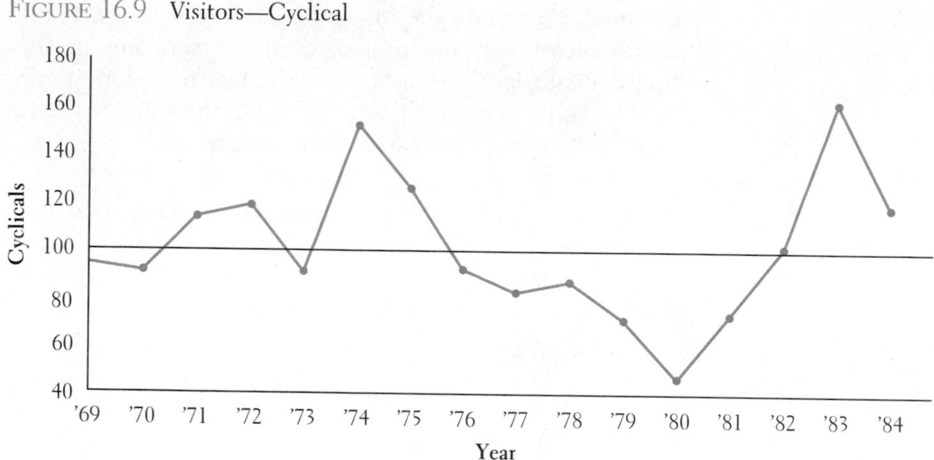

with other factors. He observed that the peak years for visits were 1974 and 1983, and that other above-average years were 1971, 1972, 1975, and 1984. The lowest year was 1980. Other below-average years were 1977, 1978, 1979, and 1981.

Mark compared the cyclical pattern in Figure 16.9 to economic indicators such as gross national product (GNP) and disposable personal income. He concluded that there was no relationship between the business cycle and the number of visitors. Next, he attempted to identify why peaks and troughs occurred for his variable. After a thorough investigation, Mark decided that the major reason 1983 was a good year was that it was the 50th anniversary of the Grand Coulee Dam. A well-advertised celebration during the summer months was extremely well attended. The primary reason 1974 was a good year was the World's Fair in Spokane, Washington, approximately 90 miles from Grand Coulee Dam. (A visit to the dam provided an excellent side trip for visitors to the fair.) Mark speculated that 1980 showed poor attendance because Mount St. Helens erupted in late May of that year.

Next, Mark decided to investigate the relationship between the price of gas and the number of visitors. Gas prices, as reported by the Independent Petroleum Association of America, are shown in Table 16.10. Mark computed the cyclical indexes (also shown in Table 16.10) and developed the cyclical chart in Figure 16.10 to compare them with the cyclical pattern for the number of visitors. This chart indicates an inverse relationship between the price of gas and the number of visitors. When gas prices are high, the number of visitors is generally low; when gas prices are down, the number of visitors is up.

Mark used the multiplicative model $Y = TC$ to estimate the number of people who would visit Grand Coulee Dam in 1986. The trend is estimated by substituting an X coded value of 18 into the regression equation:

$$\begin{aligned}\hat{Y} &= 259{,}055 + 8{,}363X \\ &= 259{,}055 + 8{,}363(18) = 409{,}589\end{aligned}$$

TABLE 16.10 Average National Gas Prices, 1969–1984 (Example 16.16)

Year	Average gas price	Cyclical
1969	34.8	179.3
1970	35.7	134.1
1971	36.5	107.9
1972	36.1	88.0
1973	38.8	80.4
1974	53.2	95.9
1975	56.7	90.5
1976	59.0	84.4
1977	62.2	80.7
1978	62.6	74.2
1979	85.7	93.6
1980	123.8	125.4
1981	131.7	124.3
1982	125.2	110.6
1983	117.0	97.2
1984	117.0	91.7

FIGURE 16.10 Gas Prices and Visitors—Cyclical Chart, 1969–84

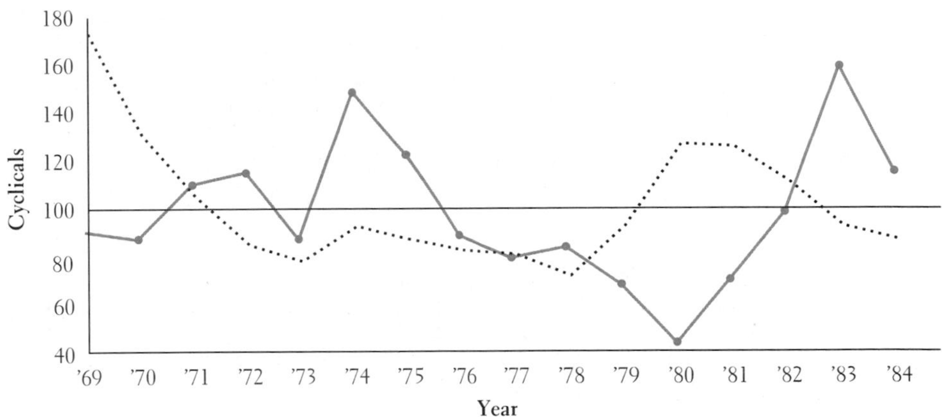

This equation seems appropriate because the population of Washington State is estimated to increase by an average of 2% annually through 1990.

Next, Mark estimated the cyclical index. The price of gasoline was forecast to be 4% less in 1985 and slightly lower in 1986. Vancouver, B.C., was to host Expo '86' in 1986, and 10 million visitors were expected to travel through Washington State. Since Grand Coulee Dam is approximately a day's drive southeast of Vancouver, many World's Fair visitors might include this attraction on their itinerary. Mark noted that large celebrations have had a very positive effect on the number of visitors in the past, so he chose a cyclical index of 193. The forecast for 1986 is

$$Y(1986) = TC = 409{,}589(1.93) = 790{,}507$$

EXERCISES

SM

33. Describe the cyclical component.
34. An analyst has decomposed an annual time series and is ready to forecast future values. Describe the process.
35. What is the basic force that affects the cyclical component of most variables?
36. Describe each of these time series established by the U.S. Dept. of Commerce: leading series, coincident series, lagging series.

SM

37. (This question refers to Exercise 30.) Analyze the cyclical component for Triton sales per share.

37*a*. No
b. Both are important
c. 12.28

   a. Does the economy affect the cyclical component?
   b. Which component is more important: trend or cyclical?
   c. Forecast Triton sales per share for 1992. Use the cyclical relative for 1991 as the estimate for 1992.
38. (This question refers to Exercise 31.) Analyze the cyclical component for the *capital spending* variable.

38*a*. No
b. Trend
c. Use trend

   a. Does the economy affect the cyclical component?
   b. Which component is more important: trend or cyclical?
   c. Forecast capital spending for 1992 and 1993.

39. Cyclicals
99.717
96.667
96.791
98.200
105.517
102.858
102.909
99.474
99.455
97.350

39. A large company's president read "Business Videos—Today's Hot Sales Weapon" in *Industry Week* (October 2, 1989, p. 38). As a result, the company is considering cutting back on TV advertising in favor of giving business videos to its customers. But before taking this action, the president wants to investigate the history of TV advertising in this country, especially the cyclical effect.

    Here are the total dollars spent on U.S. television advertising (in millions) from 1980 to 1989. Calculate cyclical indexes for this annual time series.

Year	Y	$\hat{Y}$
1980	11,424	11,456.4
1981	12,811	13,252.7
1982	14,566	15,049.0
1983	16,542	16,845.3
1984	19,670	18,641.6
1985	21,022	20,437.8
1986	22,881	22,234.1
1987	23,904	24,030.4
1988	25,686	25,826.7
1989	26,891	27,623.0

Source: *Statistical Abstract of the United States*, 1988, 1991.

    Analyze the peaks and bottoms of the cyclical component in U.S. TV advertising dollars. Forecast this variable for 1990.

40. The following annual data measure quantity of fish caught in millions of pounds from 1980 to 1989. The trend equation for this series appears also. Calculate the cyclical indicators for this annual series.

40. Cyclical
109.8
98.5
102.1
100.6
98.0
92.9
87.3
97.5
99.3
114.3

Year	Y	$\hat{Y}$
1980	6,482	5,902.25
1981	5,977	6,069.38
1982	6,367	6,236.50
1983	6,439	6,403.62
1984	6,438	6,570.74
1985	6,258	6,737.86
1986	6,031	6,904.98
1987	6,896	7,072.10
1988	7,192	7,239.22
1989	8,463	7,406.35

$\hat{Y} = 5735.1 + 167.12X$

Source: *Statistical Abstract of the United States*, 1988, 1991.

Based on the trend equation and the calculated cyclical indicators, summarize this time series with a brief statement about both the trend and cyclical components. Forecast the quantity of fish caught measured in millions of pounds for 1990.

SEASONAL DATA

Monthly or quarterly time series data are common because businesses generally use accounting techniques based on months or quarters. Projections of monthly and/or quarterly time series into the future are regular exercises for most organizations.

Decomposition of a monthly or quarterly time series can reveal the seasonal and irregular components, in addition to the trend and cyclical components. Examining each of these four components in isolation can reveal interesting and useful information and enables the analyst to combine these elements to produce a good forecast. Forecasts using monthly or quarterly time series are typically made for 1 to 12 months or 1 to 4 quarters into the future. The analyst should have from 4 to 7 years of monthly or quarterly data to perform the calculations necessary for a seasonal analysis.

The first component to be isolated in a monthly or quarterly time series is the seasonal component. An index for each of the 12 months or 4 quarters of the year is required; time series analysis computer programs are used to compute these indexes. Here's a description of the procedure typically used by such programs for monthly data.

The basic idea in calculating a monthly seasonal index is to compare the actual value of the variable (Y) with a 12-month average for the variable. In this way, we can determine whether the Y value is above or below the yearly average and by how much. If quarterly data are analyzed, a four-quarter average is computed for the comparison.

In computing a yearly average for the monthly comparison, an average should be used that is *centered* on the month being examined. Unfortunately, when 12 months are averaged, the center of the average isn't at the center of a month, but rather at the point where one month ends and another begins. For this reason, the following steps are used to center a 12-month average for Y on the month being examined. (These four steps assume that the data start in January.)

Step 1 Compute the 12-month moving total for January through December for the first year's data and place it opposite July 1. Compute the next 12-month moving total by removing January of the first year and adding January of the second year. This is the 12-month moving total from February of the first year through January of the second year; it's placed opposite August 1.

Step 2 Compute a two-year moving total by adding the 12-month moving totals opposite July 1 and August 1. The two-year total includes data for 24 months (January of the first year once, February through December twice, and January of the second year once). This total is centered opposite July 15.

Step 3 Divide the two-year moving total by 24 to obtain the 12-month average centered on July 15.

Seasonal Index

Step 4 The seasonal index for each month is calculated by dividing the actual value for each month by the 12-month centered average and multiplying by 100 so that the ratio is an index number. Equation 16.8 shows how this computation is performed:

$$S = \frac{TSCI}{TCI}(100) \tag{16.8}$$

where S = Seasonal index
$TSCI$ = Actual value of Y
TCI = 12-month centered average

Example 16.17 demonstrates the process of summarizing and computing the final adjusted seasonal indexes for each month.

EXAMPLE 16.17 Table 16.11 shows monthly 1985–86 data for new passenger car registrations. To illustrate the computation of monthly seasonal indexes, the four-step procedure is applied to these data. Each step is demonstrated in Table 16.11 and numbered to coincide with the following discussion:

Step 1 Registrations are summed for January through December 1985: 781 + 790 + 927 + 936 + 912 + 923 + 949 + 926 + 1105 + 973 + 828 + 849 = 10,899. This value is placed opposite July 1, 1985. The next 12-month moving total is computed by removing registrations for January 1985 and adding registrations for January 1986: 10,899 − 781 + 913 = 11,031.

Step 2 The two-year moving total is computed: 10,899 + 11,031 = 21,930.

Step 3 The 12-month centered moving average is computed: 21,930/24 = 913.75.

Step 4 The monthly seasonal index is computed using Equation 16.8:

$$S = \frac{\text{TSCI}}{\text{TCI}}(100) = \frac{949}{913.75}(100) = 103.86$$

The seasonal index of 103.86 for July 1985 indicates that registrations for this month were approximately 3 to 4% above normal.

The procedure just described is applied for each month, January 1985 to December 1991. Each of the monthly seasonal indexes is shown in Table 16.12. Note that the

TABLE 16.11 Registration of New Passenger Cars by Month, in Thousands, 1985–1986 (Example 16.17)

Period	Registrations	12-month moving total	2-year moving total	12-month centered moving average	Seasonal index
1985					
Jan.	781				
Feb.	790				
March	927				
April	936				
May	912				
June	923				
		10,899			
July	949	2	21,930 3	913.75	103.86 4
		11,031			
Aug.	926 1		22,094	920.58	100.59
		11,063			
Sept.	1,105		22,047	918.63	120.29
		10,984			
Oct.	973		21,938	914.08	106.45
		10,954			
Nov.	828		21,914	913.08	90.68
		10,960			
Dec.	849		22,009	917.04	92.58
		11,049			
1986					
Jan.	913		22,083	920.13	99.23
		11,034			
Feb.	822		22,036	918.17	89.53
		11,002			
March	848		22,048	918.67	92.31
		11,046			
April	906		22,067	919.46	98.54
		11,021			
May	918		21,933	913.88	100.45
		10,912			
June	1,012		21,877	911.54	111.02
		10,965			
July	934				
Aug.	894				
Sept.	1149				
Oct.	948				
Nov.	719				
Dec.	902				

TABLE 16.12 Summary of the Monthly Seasonal Indexes for Example 16.17

Month	1985	1986	1987	1988	1989	1990	1991	Modified monthly mean	Adjusted seasonal index mean (1.000324)
Jan.		99.23	91.29	89.33	86.85	80.06	83.67	87.79	87.8
Feb.		89.53	76.66	93.57	85.86	85.69	83.02	86.03	86.1
March		92.31	95.55	106.26	99.07	102.12	95.20	97.99	98.0
April		98.54	104.79	98.66	100.20	100.01	97.10	99.35	99.4
May		100.45	97.80	101.04	105.75	109.04	108.12	103.84	103.9
June		111.02	113.48	113.19	115.23	114.19	115.99	114.02	114.1
July	103.86	102.75	106.08	102.11	102.31	103.86		103.19	103.2
Aug.	100.59	99.55	105.96	104.84	109.48	104.09		103.87	103.9
Sept.	120.29	128.96	110.82	109.96	119.71	111.59		115.60	115.6
Oct.	106.45	106.55	94.82	95.14	100.98	107.54		102.28	102.3
Nov.	90.68	81.19	83.13	90.06	84.77	94.14		87.16	87.2
Dec.	92.58	102.51	104.00	105.73	89.08	94.91		98.50	98.5
								1,199.61	1,200.0

months of January–June 1985 don't have seasonal indexes. This is because July 1985 is the first month for which the previous six months of data are available. Likewise, the last six months of 1991 won't have seasonal indexes because when the analyst prepared the data, 1992 values weren't available.

Six seasonal indexes have been calculated for each month in Table 16.12. For January, these values are 99.23, 91.29, 89.33, 86.85, 80.06, and 83.67. We now want to combine these values into a single index for January. This might be done by adding them and dividing by 6 to create an average for the six values. But the usual procedure (and the one followed here) is to remove the highest and lowest of the calculated values and then average the rest. The lowest January index is 80.06 and the highest is 99.23. These are removed to eliminate any distortion that might result from extreme values, and the remaining four indexes are averaged:

$$(91.29 + 89.33 + 86.85 + 83.67)/4 = 87.79$$

This is the value in the "modified monthly mean" column in Table 16.12. The same procedure is followed for the other 11 months: the highest and lowest monthly indexes are removed and the other four are averaged to produce the modified monthly mean.

The modified monthly means just calculated add to 1,199.61 (Table 16.12). It would be convenient if they added to exactly 1,200 since their average would then be exactly 100, or 100%. This adjustment is easy to make since each modified mean can be increased slightly. If the adjusted seasonal indexes then add to exactly 1,200, the interpretation will be straightforward since each monthly index can be compared to their average of 100. The adjustment is made by dividing 1,200 by the sum of the modified monthly means and multiplying this ratio by each monthly index. For Table 16.12's January index, this ratio is

$$\frac{1{,}200}{1{,}199.61}(87.79) = 87.8$$

The "adjusted seasonal indexes" column is shown in Table 16.12. Following the adjustment, these values add to exactly 1,200 so their average is exactly 100.

The adjusted seasonal indexes in Table 16.12's last column are interpreted as the seasonal component of new passenger car registrations. Seasonal peaks occur in June and September; seasonal lows occur in January, February, and November. Weather is obviously important in explaining this variable's seasonal pattern. New passenger car registrations tend to be up in good-weather months and down in bad-weather months. September is generally a good month because of new models' introduction for the next year. Results of this analysis can be used to evaluate current sales, to schedule production and shipments, to plan personnel and financing, and to forecast monthly sales.

EXAMPLE 16.18 Julie Ruth is registrar of a midsized university in a Southern city. Among her responsibilities is planning for future enrollments. To do this, she needs some way to forecast the number of students for each quarter of the year.

Julie has quarterly records on the total student count over many years. She decides to use the past five years as an appropriate period to analyze in preparing forecasts for future quarters. Since the budget and facilities planning process is based to a considerable extent on these forecasts, she wants to use as accurate a process as possible in deriving predicted values. Julie knows that enrollments have been stable over the past five years. For this reason, she decides to base her forecasts strictly on the seasonal component.

Julie keys her enrollment data into the university's computer, using a program that will perform a time series decomposition. Part of the computer printout that results from this analysis is shown in Table 16.13.

The seasonal indexes indicate that fall is the most heavily enrolled quarter, followed by winter and then spring. The summer quarter has less than half the enrollment of the other quarters, with a seasonal index of 43.7. Julie can use these seasonal indexes to summarize quarterly enrollment loads and predict staffing and facility needs.

TABLE 16.13 Summary of the Quarterly Seasonal Indexes for Example 16.18

Quarter	1988	1989	1990	1991	1992	Modified qt. mean	Adjusted seasonal index
Fall		129.22	129.81	122.99	123.70	126.50	126.0
Winter		114.43	117.64	120.28	121.64	118.96	118.5
Spring	111.99	112.86	110.11	112.43		112.21	111.8
Summer	44.44	42.86	44.01	43.84		43.92	43.7
						401.59	400.0

Once the seasonal component has been identified, the next step is to compute a monthly or quarterly trend equation (seasonal trend equation). Recall that secular trend was defined as the *long-term* growth or decline in a time series. In conjunction with this definition, the trend of a monthly or quarterly series must be consistent with its long-term behavior. The trend for seasonal data can be computed using one of the following approaches:

1. If monthly or quarterly data are available for the entire annual series (all 10 to 20 years), the seasonal trend equation is computed using all of these values.
2. If the long-term trend equation has already been computed, it can be converted to be used with the seasonal data.
3. If the trend for the time period covered by the seasonal data appears to be similar to the pattern described by the long-term equation, the seasonal trend can be computed directly from the seasonal data.
4. If no long-term data are available, the seasonal trend must be computed directly from the seasonal data.

EXAMPLE 16.19 Figure 16.2 shows the long-term trend equation for the new passenger car registration series from 1960 to 1991. The simplest approach for developing a seasonal trend equation is to use the least squares procedure on the monthly data for 1985 through 1991. This is a reasonable solution if the resulting monthly trend equation accurately reflects the long-term growth pattern. According to Figure 16.2, the slope of a monthly trend equation developed from the monthly data for 1985 through 1991 would have a negative slope. Since the direction of the long-term trend has already been established as positive, the long-term trend equation will have to be converted for use with the seasonal data. This conversion process is demonstrated in Appendix B.

Monthly data for this series, measured in thousands, appear in the first column of Table 16.14 and are used as the Y variable. If the actual data were used to develop the trend equation, the months would represent the independent variable (X) with January 1985 as 1, February 1985 as 2, and so on. Equation 16.6 would then be used to compute the seasonal trend equation.

For this example, the long-term trend equation was converted to a seasonal equation (see Appendix B):

$$\hat{Y} = 819.990 + .5286X$$

Using the seasonal equation, the trend estimate for December 1984 (when $X = 0$) is 819,990. The resulting trend values using this equation are shown in column 2 of Table 16.14. Note that the trend estimate for January 1985 is 820,519 (819,990 + 529). Also note that the average increase each month is approximately 529 registrations.

Economic indicators are published in several sources, such as the *Survey of Current Business*. These indicators are frequently adjusted for seasonal influences to enable users to see patterns that are independent of seasonal variations. **Seasonally adjusted data** result when the monthly or quarterly values of a time series are divided by their corresponding seasonal indexes. Removal of the seasonal variation helps clarify basic strengths or weaknesses of the other components in the series. Equation 16.9 shows

Seasonally Adjusted Data

TABLE 16.14 Calculations for the Short-Term Components for Examples 16.19–16.23

PERIOD		DATA Y	REGRESSION T	SEAS. ADJ. TCI	CI	C	I
1985	JAN	781.00	820.52	889.39	108.39		
	FEB	790.00	821.05	918.04	111.81		
	MAR	927.00	821.58	945.75	115.11	111.32	103.41
	APR	936.00	822.10	941.81	114.56	109.31	104.81
	MAY	912.00	822.63	878.00	106.73	109.27	97.68
	JUN	923.00	823.16	809.23	98.31	107.87	91.14
	JUL	949.00	823.69	919.34	111.61	108.13	103.22
	AUG	926.00	824.22	891.21	108.13	109.83	98.45
	SEP	1105.00	824.75	955.56	115.86	113.17	102.38
	OCT	973.00	825.28	951.01	115.24	111.70	103.17
	NOV	828.00	825.80	949.67	115.00	115.22	99.81
	DEC	849.00	826.33	861.65	104.27	115.14	90.56
1986	JAN	913.00	826.86	1039.70	125.74	112.99	111.28
	FEB	822.00	827.39	955.22	115.45	112.00	103.08
	MAR	848.00	827.92	865.15	104.50	112.47	92.91
	APR	906.00	828.45	911.62	110.04	108.71	101.22
	MAY	918.00	828.98	883.77	106.61	107.42	99.24
	JUN	1012.00	829.50	887.26	106.96	107.24	99.74
	JUL	934.00	830.03	904.81	109.01	109.15	99.87
	AUG	894.00	830.56	860.42	103.59	110.11	94.08
	SEP	1149.00	831.09	993.60	119.55	108.54	110.15
	OCT	948.00	831.62	926.57	111.42	108.72	102.48
	NOV	719.00	832.15	824.65	99.10	109.87	90.20
	DEC	902.00	832.68	915.44	109.94	104.66	105.04
1987	JAN	800.00	833.21	911.02	109.34	102.66	106.51
	FEB	671.00	833.73	779.75	93.53	104.41	89.57
	MAR	829.00	834.26	845.77	101.38	101.56	99.83
	APR	895.00	834.79	900.56	107.88	99.89	108.00
	MAY	830.00	835.32	799.05	95.66	102.01	93.77
	JUN	963.00	835.85	844.30	101.01	102.50	98.54
	JUL	899.00	836.38	870.91	104.13	100.65	103.45
	AUG	903.00	836.91	869.08	103.84	100.63	103.20
	SEP	955.00	837.43	825.84	98.62	100.07	98.55
	OCT	819.00	837.96	800.49	95.53	101.04	94.55
	NOV	718.00	838.49	823.51	98.21	101.27	96.98
	DEC	901.00	839.02	914.42	108.99	103.95	104.84
1988	JAN	774.00	839.55	881.41	104.99	107.15	97.98
	FEB	810.00	840.08	941.28	112.05	107.90	103.85
	MAR	919.00	840.61	937.59	111.54	106.09	105.13
	APR	852.00	841.13	857.29	101.92	105.52	96.59
	MAY	874.00	841.66	841.41	99.97	103.41	96.67
	JUN	981.00	842.19	860.08	102.12	101.67	100.45
	JUL	883.00	842.72	855.41	101.51	100.49	101.01
	AUG	901.00	843.25	867.15	102.83	99.18	103.68
	SEP	937.00	843.78	810.28	96.03	99.50	96.51
	OCT	807.00	844.31	788.76	93.42	100.71	92.76
	NOV	764.00	844.84	876.27	103.72	99.88	103.84
	DEC	896.00	845.36	909.35	107.57	100.50	107.03
1989	JAN	733.00	845.89	834.72	98.68	101.89	96.85
	FEB	722.00	846.42	839.02	99.13	101.16	97.99
	MAR	833.00	846.95	849.85	100.34	99.74	100.60
	APR	843.00	847.48	848.23	100.09	99.64	100.45
	MAY	885.00	848.01	852.00	100.47	98.75	101.74
	JUN	950.00	848.54	832.90	98.16	98.62	99.53
	JUL	830.00	849.06	804.06	94.70	98.05	96.58
	AUG	880.00	849.59	846.94	99.69	96.34	103.47
	SEP	956.00	850.12	826.71	97.25	94.66	102.73
	OCT	800.00	850.65	781.92	91.92	92.26	99.63
	NOV	666.00	851.18	763.87	89.74	88.86	100.99
	DEC	694.00	851.71	704.34	82.70	87.32	94.71

TABLE 16.14 *concluded*

PERIOD		DATA Y	REGRESSION T	SEAS. ADJ. TCI	CI	C	I
1990	JAN	619.00	852.24	704.90	82.71	87.42	94.61
	FEB	657.00	852.76	763.48	89.53	87.17	102.70
	MAR	773.00	853.29	788.64	92.42	89.09	103.74
	APR	751.00	853.82	755.66	88.50	90.15	98.18
	MAY	819.00	854.35	788.46	92.29	89.89	102.67
	JUN	858.00	854.88	752.24	87.99	88.88	99.01
	JUL	779.00	855.41	754.66	88.22	87.83	100.44
	AUG	777.00	855.94	747.81	87.37	87.33	100.05
	SEP	825.00	856.47	713.42	83.30	88.00	94.66
	OCT	787.00	856.99	769.21	89.76	86.51	103.75
	NOV	683.00	857.52	783.36	91.35	84.93	107.56
	DEC	683.00	858.05	693.17	80.78	84.23	95.91
1991	JAN	599.00	858.58	682.13	79.45	82.16	96.70
	FEB	590.00	859.11	685.62	79.81	79.68	100.16
	MAR	669.00	859.64	682.53	79.40	80.17	99.04
	APR	675.00	860.17	679.19	78.96	80.40	98.21
	MAY	744.00	860.69	716.26	83.22	81.42	102.21
	JUN	792.00	861.22	694.38	80.63	80.60	100.03
	JUL	755.00	861.75	731.41	84.87	79.59	106.65
	AUG	675.00	862.28	649.64	75.34	78.61	95.84
	SEP	737.00	862.81	637.33	73.87	78.68	93.88
	OCT	692.00	863.34	676.36	78.34	76.45	102.47
	NOV	610.00	863.87	699.64	80.99		
	DEC	628.00	864.39	637.35	73.73		
1992	JAN		864.92				
	FEB		865.45				
	MAR		865.98				
	APR		866.51				
	MAY		867.04				
	JUN		867.57				
	JUL		868.09				
	AUG		868.62				
	SEP		869.15				
	OCT		869.68				
	NOV		870.21				
	DEC		870.74				

that seasonally adjusted values include the effects of trend, cyclical, and irregular components once the seasonal component has been eliminated:

$$TCI = \frac{TSCI}{S} \tag{16.9}$$

where TCI = Seasonally adjusted data value
$TSCI$ = Original Y value
S = Seasonal index

The unemployment rate, for example, is often seasonally adjusted so that the underlying pattern of this important index can be followed without the distorting effects of seasonal variations. Retail sales are often seasonally adjusted also, especially during the Christmas buying season.

Seasonally adjusted data result when the original monthly or quarterly values of a time series are divided by their corresponding seasonal indexes.

EXAMPLE 16.20 The third column of Table 16.14 (*TCI*) shows seasonally adjusted data for new passenger car registrations. These values were calculated by dividing the actual monthly values in column 1 by the seasonal indexes of Table 16.13 and multiplying the result by 100. The seasonally adjusted value for January 1985, for example, was computed using Equation 16.9:

$$TCI = \frac{TSCI}{S} = \frac{781}{.878} = 889.52$$

(Note: The computer carries more decimal places and produces slightly different values.)

Due to the seasonal component, January registrations typically are down by about 12.2% ($S = 87.8$). The seasonally adjusted value of 889.52 indicates what registrations would have been without the effect of the seasonal component.

Once the seasonal component has been removed for each month in the data, the *TCI* column shows that the number of new passenger car registrations for June (a high-registration month) of each year aren't higher than for January (a low-registration month). In fact, the seasonally adjusted data column shows that January was the best month of 1986. Seasonally adjusted data in Table 16.14 include only the effects of the trend, cyclical, and irregular components.

Next, the short-term cyclical component is computed. Since the data have already been seasonally adjusted, the cyclical and irregular components are isolated by dividing *TCI* by the trend *(T)*:

$$CI = \frac{TCI}{T}(100) \tag{16.10}$$

where CI = Cyclical-irregular index
TCI = Seasonally adjusted data
T = Trend value

The resulting values appear in the *CI* column. After the data have been adjusted for seasonal and trend influences, the cyclical and irregular components are separated. A moving average is developed to smooth out the irregularities of the *CI* column. This approach is similar to the analysis of the seasonal component, where a 12-month moving average is used to smooth out the trend, cyclical, and irregular influences. Recall that in the computation of the 12-month moving average, a centering problem occurred. Whenever an even number of time periods is used to compute a moving average, centering is a problem. For this reason, an odd number of time periods, such as 5,

7, 9, or 11, is usually used to smooth out irregularities. This approach is demonstrated in Example 16.21.

EXAMPLE 16.21 The CI column in Table 16.14 shows the cyclical-irregular indexes for new passenger car registrations. These values were calculated by dividing the seasonally adjusted data (*TCI*) by the trend estimates (*T*) and multiplying the result by 100. The cyclical-irregular index for January 1985, for example, is

$$CI = \frac{TCI}{T}(100) = \frac{889.39}{820.52}(100) = 108.39$$

The cyclical component is separated from the irregular component by using a five-month moving average. Table 16.15 shows the computations.

Compare the cyclical column (C) with the cyclical-irregular column (*CI*). Note that the five-month moving average has smoothed out the CI column's irregularities. The cyclical component rises and falls in a consistent manner, and the cycle is easier to identify. The cyclical index began at 111 in March 1985 and mostly stayed between 100 and 110 through 1988. From this point the cycle of new passenger car registrations dropped to a low of 76.45 in October 1991. This short-term cyclical index should parallel the long-term cyclical analyzed in Figure 16.7. If the short-term cyclical effect is radically different from the long-term cyclical, the monthly trend should be developed by either using all the monthly data or converting the long-term trend equation so that it can be used with the monthly data.

TABLE 16.15 Computational Procedure for Five-Month Moving Average for New Passenger Car Registration Data

Time period (1985)	*CI*	Five-month moving total	C
January	108.39		
February	111.81		
March	115.11	556.59	111.32
April	114.56	546.51	109.30
May	106.73	546.31	109.26
June	98.31		
July	111.61		

The final step in the decomposition of a seasonal time series is identification of the irregular component. We do this by dividing the *CI* column of Table 16.14 by the C column and multiplying the result by 100:

$$I = \frac{CI}{C}(100) \tag{16.11}$$

where I = Irregular index
CI = Cyclical-irregular index
C = Smoothed cyclical index

The irregular component measures the variability of the time series after the other components have been removed. Most of the irregular component is made up of random variability. However, sometimes unpredictable events cause irregularities in a variable.

EXAMPLE 16.22 The last column (I) in Table 16.14 shows the irregular indexes for new passenger car registrations. These values were calculated by dividing the cyclical-irregular indexes by the cyclical indexes and multiplying the result by 100. The irregular index for March 1985, for example, is

$$I = \frac{CI}{C}(100) = \frac{115.11}{111.32}(100) = 103.40$$

Sometimes the irregular variations in a time series can be explained. Examination of the irregular column in Table 16.14 shows that irregularities occurred in September (110.15) and November (90.20) of 1986. These irregularities were caused by wage and strike problems in the auto industry.

One of the key purposes of decomposing a time series is to examine the components of the series in isolation. Once the analyst can look at the trend, seasonal, cyclical, and irregular components of a monthly time series one at a time, valuable insights into the patterns hidden in the original data values may be gained and used to better manage the variable of interest. In addition, identifying the individual components will make it easier to forecast the series.

In forecasting a monthly time series, the decomposition process is reversed. Instead of separating the series into its individual components for examination, the components are recombined to form the forecasts. The trend, seasonal, cyclical, and irregular components are identified for each future period for which a forecast is desired, and the multiplicative model $Y = TSCI$ is used to develop the forecast.

Any monthly or quarterly time series can be used to project (forecast) future periods. This is often the sole objective in collecting time series data and subjecting them to the decomposition process. Since there are many time series values of vital importance to the future health of an organization, forecasting such variables is important in every manager's job, and the time series decomposition process is frequently used to produce accurate forecasts.

EXAMPLE 16.23 This example demonstrates the development of the short-term forecast for January 1992 for new passenger car registrations using Tables 16.12 and 16.14. The example illustrates how each individual component is computed.

1. *Trend.* The monthly trend equation is used to estimate the trend value for January 1992. Since January 1985 was represented by $X = 1$, January 1992 is represented by $X = 85$ in the trend equation. The trend estimate is 864.92:

$$\begin{aligned}\hat{Y} &= 819.990 + .5286X \\ &= 819.990 + .5286(85) \\ &= 864.92\end{aligned}$$

2. *Seasonal.* Table 16.12 gives the adjusted seasonal index for January, 87.8.
3. *Cyclical.* The cyclical index is estimated using all of the information gathered on the cyclical pattern. The analyst must answer the following questions: Was the cyclical pattern in Table 16.14 increasing or decreasing for the last few months of 1991? Have any leading indicators been identified? What is the economic forecast for 1992? To demonstrate the completion of this example, a cyclical index of 75 is estimated.
4. *Irregular.* Since most irregular fluctuations are random variations, an estimate of 100% or 1.0 is commonly used. Occasionally, an analyst can identify future irregularities. If an irregular event can be anticipated (such as a contract coming due along with a probable strike), the impact can be estimated by using a different irregular index. In this example, an irregular index of 100 is appropriate since no unusual events are foreseen. The forecast for January 1992 is

$$\begin{aligned} Y(\text{January 1992}) &= TSCI \\ &= (864.92)(.878)(.75)(1.00) \\ &= 569.55 \end{aligned}$$

EXERCISES

41. What components are analyzed in the decomposition of a seasonal (monthly or quarterly) time series?
42. For a seasonal time series, what method is used to isolate the trend component?
43. To compute a seasonal index for each month or quarter, the actual Y value is compared with an average. How many periods are averaged for monthly and quarterly data, and what is the center point for these averages?
44. How are the original data values deseasonalized? What arithmetic operation is used to generate the CI column in a monthly or quarterly time series printout?
45. How is the C column generated from the CI column in the printout? How is the I column computed for a monthly or quarterly time series analysis?

46. Yes

46. Do you agree with the statement, "A moving average is a smoothing technique"? Why or why not?

47. Averages 100 each quarter

47. What is the purpose of having the monthly seasonal indexes add to exactly 1,200 and the quarterly seasonal indexes add to exactly 400?

48. Multiplicative, $Y = TSCI$

48. What model is used to forecast a seasonal time series?

49. 84.15

49. Assume the following specific seasonal indexes for January, based on the ratio-to-moving-average method:

    88.2 85.9 64.3 92.4 80.1 82.4

    What is the seasonal index for January using the modified mean method?

50. 819

50. The expected trend value for September is \$900. Assuming a September seasonal index of 91, what would be the forecast for September?

51. 547.44

51. The following specific seasonal indexes are given for October:

    65.4 76.8 66.9 72.6 70.0

If the adjustment is 0.98, if the modified mean is used, and if the expected trend for October is $800, what is the forecast for October?

52. A large resort near Williamsburg, Virginia, has been tracking its quarterly sales for several years but has never analyzed these data. The resort manager has read an article in *Travel & Leisure* (July 1989, p. 100) on vacation opportunities in Williamsburg and wants to investigate his resort's sales history. She computes the seasonal indexes for quarterly sales. Which of the following statements about the index are correct?

52. *a*, *b*, *c*, and *e* are correct

a. The sum of the four quarterly index numbers should be 400.

b. An index of 75 for the first quarter indicates that sales were 25% lower than the average quarterly sales.

c. An index of 110 for the second quarter indicates that sales were 10% above the average quarterly sales.

d. The index for any quarter must be between 0 and 200.

e. The average index for each of the four quarters will be 100.

53. 97.3

53. In computing a seasonal index, the specific seasonals were tabulated and the extremes eliminated for each month. The averages for the 12 months were obtained and summed. If the mean for June was 96.9 and the sum for all 12 months is 1,195, what is the adjusted seasonal index for June?

54. No. The statistics should have been seasonally adjusted

54. Your report for Jim Rogers, Kona Department Store manager, includes the following statistics from last year's sales. Mr. Rogers says, "This report confirms what I've been telling you; business is getting better and better." Is this statement accurate? Why?

Month	Sales (thousands)	Adjusted seasonal index
Jan.	225	52
Feb.	213	49
Mar.	289	85
Apr.	301	92
May	306	93
June	341	98
July	330	95
Aug.	345	90
Sept.	371	100
Oct.	391	118
Nov.	420	129
Dec.	519	199

Source: Kona Department Store records.

SSM

55. John Managan, manager of Hallet Confections, is attempting to forecast sales for next year. He has the following adjusted seasonal indexes for sales based on the past four years. John has decided that no trend exists for his sales variable.

Month	Adjusted seasonal index	Month	Adjusted seasonal index
Jan.	60	July	72
Feb.	75	Aug.	78

Month	Adjusted seasonal index	Month	Adjusted seasonal index
Mar.	95	Sept.	105
Apr.	110	Oct.	116
May	107	Nov.	129
June	101	Dec.	152

Source: Hallet Confections records.

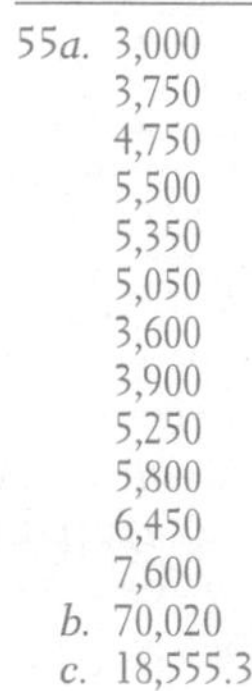

55*a.* 3,000
3,750
4,750
5,500
5,350
5,050
3,600
3,900
5,250
5,800
6,450
7,600
b. 70,020
c. 18,555.3

a. John forecasts that sales for the coming year will total \$60,000. On the basis of this forecast of total sales, make a forecast of sales for each month.

b. January sales were \$3,500. If this is the prevailing level of sales for the remaining 11 months and the adjusted seasonal indexes are accurate, what will be the total annual sales for this year?

c. On the basis of January sales and the adjusted seasonal indexes, forecast sales for the second quarter.

56. The adjusted seasonal indexes in the accompanying table reflect the changing volume of business of the Mt. Spokane Resort Hotel, which caters to the family tourist in summer and the skiing enthusiast during winter. No sharp cyclical variations are expected during 1993.

Month	Adjusted seasonal index	Month	Adjusted seasonal index
Jan.	120	July	153
Feb.	137	Aug.	151
Mar.	100	Sept.	95
Apr.	33	Oct.	60
May	47	Nov.	82
June	125	Dec.	97

Source: Mt. Spokane Resort Hotel records.

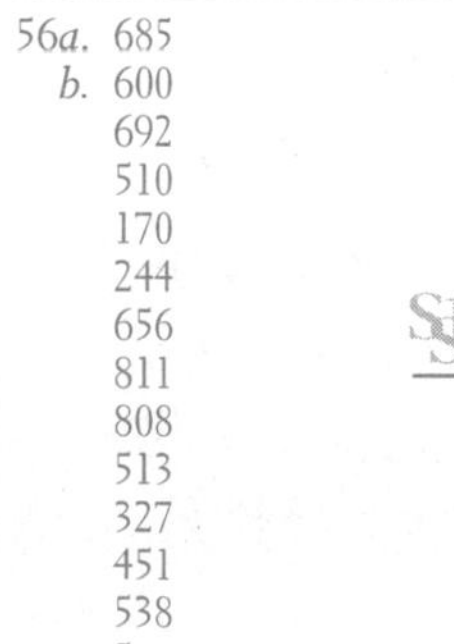

56*a.* 685
b. 600
692
510
170
244
656
811
808
513
327
451
538
c. 5

a. If 600 tourists visited the resort in January 1993, what is a reasonable estimate for February?

b. The monthly trend equation is $\hat{Y} = 135 + 5X$, where $X = 1$ represents January 15, 1987. What is the forecast for each month of 1993?

c. What is the average number of new tourists per month?

57. Goodyear Tire's quarterly sales appear below. Does there appear to be a significant seasonal effect in sales levels? Analyze this time series to get the four seasonal indexes and determine the extent of the seasonal component in Goodyear's sales.

Quarter:	1	2	3	4
1985	2292	2450	2363	2477
1986	2063	2358	2316	2366
1987	2268	2533	2479	2625
1988	2616	2793	2656	2746
1989	2643	2811	2679	2736

57. Q1 94.96
Q2 103.32
Q3 100.11
Q4 102.15

Quarter:	1	2	3	4
1990	2692	2871	2900	2810
1991	2497	2791	2838	2781

Source: *The Value Line Investment Survey* (New York: Value Line, 1988, 1989, 1991), p. 127.

58. The following data values represent monthly sales of all retail stores in the United States in billions of dollars. Analyze this series including comments on all four components of the series.

Year:	1985	1986	1987	1988	1989	1990	1991
Jan.	98.8	105.6	106.4	113.6	122.5	132.6	130.9
Feb.	95.6	99.7	105.8	115.0	118.9	127.3	128.6
March	110.2	114.2	120.4	131.6	139.7	148.3	149.3
April	113.1	115.7	125.4	130.9	137.9	145.0	148.5
May	120.3	125.4	129.1	136.0	148.2	154.1	159.8
June	115.0	120.4	129.0	137.5	147.1	153.5	153.9
July	115.5	120.7	129.3	134.1	142.6	148.9	154.6
Aug.	121.1	124.1	131.5	138.7	150.9	157.4	159.9
Sept.	113.8	124.4	124.5	131.9	142.1	145.6	146.7
Oct.	115.8	123.8	128.3	133.8	142.3	151.5	152.1
Nov.	118.1	121.4	126.9	140.2	148.8	156.1	155.6
Dec.	138.6	152.1	157.2	171.0	176.5	179.7	181.0

Source: *Survey of Current Business*, 1989, 1992.

SUMMARY

Price, quantity, and value indexes are widely used in business and government to monitor important economic and business conditions. It is frequently more useful to monitor these conditions using index numbers, which represent percentages of a base-period value, rather than use the original units of measurement. The basic calculations for the three major indexes have been demonstrated in this chapter, along with the calculations necessary to change a base period and to deflate a dollar time series.

Many businesses develop their own indexes to monitor important time series variables, such as sales levels, output quantities, and other monthly and quarterly variables. Almost all businesses take advantage of the hundreds of index numbers maintained by the federal government and by private organizations. The next section lists a few of these widely used indexes.

This chapter has presented a widely used technique for evaluating time series data. In the analysis of annual data, the trend and cyclical components are isolated, studied, and then employed in the forecasting process.

Next, the decomposition analysis for monthly data was presented. In addition to the trend and cyclical components, the seasonal and irregular components are examined in this analysis. The purpose is to study these components in isolation, and thus gain knowledge about the series, and to then recombine the components to forecast the future.

A final note is in order regarding the time horizon for forecasting. If a long-term forecast is needed, annual data are typically collected and analyzed. If the forecast is for one or two years ahead, we can anticipate the cyclical component and use it along with the projected trend to form the forecast. For forecasts three or more years into the future, the cyclical component isn't useful, and the forecast is based primarily on the trend projection.

Short-term forecasts are formed using monthly or quarterly data. Four to seven years of data are usually used to form these forecasts. After the decomposition process, forecasts of up to 12 months or four quarters are made. Forecasts for longer periods of time aren't usually made with monthly or quarterly data, since the data have been collected for too short a period, and since the trend and cyclical components may be considered suspect when used for forecasting far into the future.

Applications of Statistical Concepts in the Business World

The United States government and several private agencies maintain national and regional indexes used to monitor various aspects of the economy. Here are some of these indexes. They can be found in any issue of the *Survey of Current Business*, and some are found in the *Statistical Abstract of the United States*.

Consumer Price Index—Wage Earners and Clerical Workers (CPI-W)
Consumer Price Index—All-Urban Consumers (CPI-U)
Industrial Product Index
Producer Price Index (Wholesale Price Index)
Industrial Production—Nondurable Manufactures
Producer Prices—Farm Products
Producer Products—Textile Products and Apparel
Construction Cost Index
Employment Cost Index—Civilian Workers
Employment Cost Index—Blue-Collar Workers
Dow Jones Industrial Average
Standard & Poor's 500 Stock Index
NASDAQ Over-the-Counter Stock Price Index

Price indexes are frequently used to convert dollar time series to constant dollars, that is, to remove the effects of inflation. Here are some of the time series monitored by the federal government in both real dollars and constant dollars. The latter values are calculated by dividing each dollar value by an appropriate price index for the period.

Gross national product
Auto output
Government purchases of goods and services
Personal consumption expenditures by major type of product
National defense purchases of goods and services
Exports and imports of goods and services
Change in business inventories by industry
New plant and equipment expenditures by business

As mentioned earlier in this chapter, many variables are measured each year, quarter, or month that are vital to the successful operation of a business. Time series analysis is a valuable source of information on current operations and often provides the basis for successful forecasting.

Here are variables that might be analyzed by time series decomposition. These are only examples; many businesses have hundreds of time series variables that are carefully watched by managers in various departments and various management levels. Some variables are measured on an annual basis, although most are monitored each month or quarter.

Production:
Labor hours by product
Overtime hours
Product defects

Finance:
Return on investment
Dividends paid
Income per share

Personnel:
Number of employees
Sick days taken
Average hourly wage
Number of employees leaving company

Computer Department:
Number of CPU hours consumed
Number of network transactions

Marketing:
Share of market
Minutes of advertising on television

Accounting:
Cash balance
Accounts receivable
Accounts payable

Quality Control:
Defects per shift
Percentage defective by product line
Item deviation from specification

Glossary

Time series Data that are collected, recorded, or observed over successive increments of time.

Index number A value that measures the movement of time series values relative to a base period; the index in the base period equals 100.

Price index An index that measures changes in the prices of goods and services over time.

Quantity index An index that measures changes in the quantities of goods over time.

Value index An index that measures the total dollar value of a group of goods or services.

Consumer price index An index that measures the prices that U.S. consumers pay for the products and services they commonly buy.

Secular trend The long-term component that represents the growth or decline in a time series over an extended period of time.

Cyclical component The wavelike fluctuation around the trend.

Seasonal component A pattern of change in quarterly or monthly data that repeats itself from year to year.

Irregular component A measure of the variability of the time series after the other components have been removed.

Seasonally adjusted data The data that result when the original monthly or quarterly values of a time series are divided by their corresponding seasonal indexes.

Key Formulas

Price index

$$PI = \frac{\Sigma P_t}{\Sigma P_b}(100) \tag{16.1}$$

Quantity index

$$QI = \frac{\Sigma Q_t}{\Sigma Q_b}(100) \tag{16.2}$$

Value index

$$VI = \frac{\Sigma P_t Q_t}{\Sigma P_b Q_b}(100) \tag{16.3}$$

Purchasing power of the dollar

$$\text{Current purchasing power of \$1} = \frac{100}{\text{Current consumer price index}} \tag{16.4}$$

Time series decomposition model

$$Y = T \times C \times S \times I \tag{16.5}$$

Trend equation

$$\hat{Y} = b_0 + b_1 X \tag{16.6}$$

Cyclical component (annual data)

$$C = \frac{Y}{\hat{Y}}(100) \tag{16.7}$$

Seasonal component

$$S = \frac{TSCI}{TCI}(100) \tag{16.8}$$

Seasonally adjusted data

$$TCI = \frac{TSCI}{S} \tag{16.9}$$

Cyclical component (seasonal data)

$$CI = \frac{TCI}{T}(100) \tag{16.10}$$

Irregular component

$$I = \frac{CI}{C}(100) \tag{16.11}$$

SOLVED EXERCISES

1. FORMING A PRICE INDEX AND CHANGING THE BASE PERIOD

The Bayliner Corporation has decided to expand its manufacturing capacity. Company analyst Steve Donaldson is comparing the cost of housing in various sections of the country. The following data represent median purchase prices (in thousands of dollars) of existing one-family houses in the western region of the United States.

Year	Y
1980	89.3
1981	96.2
1982	98.9
1983	94.9
1984	95.8
1985	95.4
1986	100.9
1987	113.2
1988	124.9
1989	139.9

Source: National Association of Realtors.

a. Form a price index for Steve using 1980 as the base period.

b. Use the indexes from part *a* to change the base period to 1989.

Solution:

a. The price for each year is divided by the price in the base year, 1980, and multiplied by 100. The resulting values are the price indexes for the series with 1980 = 100.

1980: (89.3/89.3)100 = 100.0
1981: (96.2/89.3)100 = 107.7
1982: (98.9/89.3)100 = 110.8
1983: (94.9/89.3)100 = 106.3
1984: (95.8/89.3)100 = 107.3
1985: (95.4/89.3)100 = 106.8
1986: (100.9/89.3)100 = 113.0
1987: (113.2/89.3)100 = 126.8
1988: (124.9/89.3)100 = 139.9
1989: (139.9/89.3)100 = 156.7

b. The base period can be changed from 1980 to 1989 by using the indexes just calculated. Each index is divided by the index for the new base period, 156.7, and multiplied by 100. This changes the base period to 1989 where the new index is now 100.

1980: 100.0/156.7(100) = 63.8
1981: 107.7/156.7(100) = 68.7
1982: 110.8/156.7(100) = 70.7
1983: 106.3/156.7(100) = 67.8
1984: 107.3/156.7(100) = 68.5
1985: 106.8/156.7(100) = 68.2
1986: 113.0/156.7(100) = 72.1
1987: 126.8/156.7(100) = 80.9
1988: 139.9/156.7(100) = 89.3
1989: 156.7/156.7(100) = 100.0

2. Deflating a Time Series

Susan Meyer, sales manager for a cosmetics company, is concerned with the expense account totals turned in by her salespeople around the country. She computes the average amount her people spent on food and beverages per month over the past several years and sees that this amount has indeed gone up. However, she realizes that there has been inflation during the period of measurement and decides to deflate the actual dollar amounts. Here are the average monthly amounts for food and beverages during the measured years, along with the consumer price index for food and beverages found in the *Statistical Abstract of the United States.*

Year	Average monthly cost	CPI–Food and Beverages (1982–84 = 100)
1983	697	99.5
1984	721	103.2
1985	753	105.6
1986	761	109.1
1987	778	113.5
1988	784	118.2
1989	792	124.9
1990	811	132.1

a. Compute the dollar time series in deflated dollars using the food and beverage index.

b. What conclusion can be reached regarding the trend of salespeople's monthly food and beverage cost over the measured years?

Solution:

a. The dollar values are divided by the price index after moving the decimal on each index two places to the left. The result is the original time series in deflated dollars:

1983: 697/ .995 = 700.5
1984: 721/1.032 = 698.6
1985: 753/1.056 = 713.1
1986: 761/1.091 = 697.5
1987: 778/1.135 = 685.5
1988: 784/1.182 = 663.3
1989: 792/1.249 = 634.1
1990: 811/1.321 = 613.9

b. Susan is surprised to see that in terms of 1982–84 dollars, there has actually been a decrease in her salespeople's monthly food and beverage cost from 1983 to 1990. She decides that trying to reduce these expenditures isn't appropriate. In fact, she decides to compliment her sales staff at next month's sales meeting.

3. TREND

In Solved Exercise 1, the Bayliner Corporation has decided to expand its manufacturing capacity by building a new plant. Analyst Steve Donaldson needs to determine the long-term growth of the median purchase price of existing one-family houses in the western region of the United States, in thousands of dollars.

Year	Y
1980	89.3
1981	96.2
1982	98.9
1983	94.9
1984	95.8
1985	95.4
1986	100.9
1987	113.2
1988	124.9
1989	139.9

Source: National Association of Realtors.

a. Compute a linear trend equation.

b. Estimate the trend for 1990.

Solution:

a. Code time as the X variable with X = 1 representing 1980.

Year	Y	X	X^2	XY
1980	89.3	1	1	89.3
1981	96.2	2	4	192.4
1982	98.9	3	9	296.7
1983	94.9	4	16	379.6
1984	95.8	5	25	479.0
1985	95.4	6	36	572.4
1986	100.9	7	49	706.3
1987	113.2	8	64	905.6
1988	124.9	9	81	1124.1
1989	139.9	10	100	1399.0
Sums:	1,049.4	55	385	6,144.4

The slope, b_1, is computed using Equation 14.7:

$$b_1 = \frac{n\,\Sigma XY - (\Sigma X)(\Sigma Y)}{n\,\Sigma X^2 - (\Sigma X)^2} = \frac{10(6{,}144.4) - 55(1{,}049.4)}{10(385) - (55)^2}$$
$$= \frac{61{,}444 - 57{,}717}{3{,}850 - 3{,}025} = \frac{3{,}727}{825} = 4.5176$$

The constant b_0 (the value of the trend when X is 0) is computed using Equation 14.8:

$$b_0 = \frac{\Sigma Y}{n} - \frac{b_1\,\Sigma X}{n} = \frac{1{,}049.4}{10} - \frac{4.5176(55)}{10}$$
$$= 104.94 - 24.85 = 80.09$$

The trend equation is $\hat{Y} = 80.09 + 4.5176X$.

b. The trend estimate for 1990 is

$$\hat{Y} = 80.09 + 4.5176X$$
$$= 80.09 + 4.5176(11) = 129.784$$

4. Cyclical Component

This question refers to Solved Exercise 3.

a. Compute the cyclical component.

b. Forecast the median purchase price of existing one-family houses in the West for 1990. Use a cyclical estimate of 112.

Solution:

a. The cyclical for 1980 is

$$C = \frac{Y}{\hat{Y}}(100) = \frac{89.3}{84.6}(100) = 105.55$$

The cyclical components for each year are:

Year	Y	$\hat{Y}$	C
1980	89.3	84.611	105.54
1981	96.2	89.128	107.73

Year	Y	$\hat{Y}$	C
1982	98.9	93.646	105.61
1983	94.9	98.164	96.68
1984	95.8	102.681	93.30
1985	95.4	107.199	88.99
1986	100.9	111.716	90.32
1987	113.2	116.234	97.39
1988	124.9	120.752	103.44
1989	139.9	125.269	111.68

b. $$\begin{aligned} Y(1990) &= TC \\ &= 129.784(1.12) = 145{,}358 \end{aligned}$$

5. SEASONAL COMPONENT

The Consolidated Edison Company sells electricity and steam in New York City. Betty Springer, company analyst, must determine whether a seasonal pattern exists in the company's quarterly revenues. She collects the following data on quarterly revenues (in millions of dollars):

Year	Mar. 31	June 30	Sept. 30	Dec. 31
1985	1,441	1,209	1,526	1,321
1986	1,414	1,187	1,411	1,185
1987	1,284	1,125	1,493	1,192
1988	1,327	1,102	1,469	1,213

Source: *The Value Line Investment Survey* (New York: Value Line, 1988, 1989), p. 174.

a. Compute the quarterly seasonal indexes.

b. Compute the adjusted quarterly seasonal indexes.

c. Analyze the seasonal pattern for revenues.

Solution:

a. The seasonal variation analysis involves four steps, as Table 16.16 demonstrates.

Step 1 Revenues are summed for the four quarters of 1985:
1,411 + 1,209 + 1,526 + 1,321 = 5,497. This value is placed opposite July 1, 1985. The next four-quarter moving total is computed by removing first-quarter 1985 revenue and adding revenue for the first quarter of 1986:
5497 − 1,441 + 1,414 = 5,470.

Step 2 The two-year moving total is computed: 5,497 + 5,470 = 10,967.

Step 3 The four-quarter centered moving average is computed: 10,967/8 = 1,370.88.

Step 4 The quarterly seasonal index is computed using Equation 16.8:

$$S = \frac{TSCI}{TCI}(100) = \frac{1{,}526}{1{,}370.88}(100) = 111.32$$

The seasonal index of 111.32 for the third quarter of 1985 indicates that revenues for this quarter were approximately 11% to 12% above normal.

TABLE 16.16 Quarterly Revenues for the Consolidated Edison Corporation ($ millions), 1985–1988 (Solved Exercise 5)

Quarter	Revenue	Four-quarter moving total	Two-year moving total	Four-quarter centered moving average	Seasonal index
1985					
1st	1,441				
2d	1,209				
		5,497			
3d	1,526		10,967	1,370.88	111.32
		5,470			
4th	1,321		10,918	1,364.75	96.79
1986		5,448			
1st	1,414		10,781	1,347.63	104.93
		5,333			
2d	1,187		10,530	1,316.25	90.18
		5,197			
3d	1,411		10,264	1,283.00	109.98
		5,067			
4th	1,185		10,072	1,259.00	94.12
1987		5,005			
1st	1,284		10,092	1,261.50	101.78
		5,087			
2d	1,125		10,181	1,272.63	88.40
		5,094			
3d	1,493		10,231	1,278.88	116.74
		5,137			
4th	1,192		10,251	1,281.38	93.03
1988		5,114			
1st	1,327		10,204	1,275.50	104.04
		5,090			
2d	1,102		10,201	1,275.13	86.42
		5,111			
3d	1,469				
4th	1,213				

b. Table 16.17 shows each of the quarterly seasonal indexes. Three seasonal indexes have been calculated for each quarter. For the first quarter, these values are 104.93, 101.78, and 104.04. The lowest first-quarter index is 101.78 and the highest is 104.93. These are removed to eliminate any distortion that might result from extreme values, so the remaining index is 104.04 (the value shown in Table 16.17 in the "modified quarterly mean" column). The modified quarterly means add to 397.88; however, they should add up to 400, or an average of 100 for each of the four quarters. The adjustment is made by dividing 400 by the sum of the modified quarterly means and multiplying this ratio by each quarterly index. For the first-quarter index in the table, this ratio is

$$\frac{400}{397.88}(104.04) = 104.6$$

TABLE 16.17 Summary of the Quarterly Seasonal Indexes for Solved Exercise 5

Quarter	1985	1986	1987	1988	Modified quarterly mean	Adjusted seasonal index
1st		104.93	101.78	104.04	104.04	104.6
2d		90.18	88.40	86.42	88.40	88.9
3d	111.32	109.98	116.74		111.32	111.9
4th	96.79	94.12	93.03		94.12	94.6
					397.88	400.0

c. The adjusted seasonal indexes in the last column of Table 16.17 are interpreted as the seasonal component of the revenue variable. A seasonal peak occurs in the third quarter, and the seasonal low occurs in the second quarter.

EXERCISES

59. Describe the differences and similarities among price, quantity, and value indexes.
60. Describe three time series variables (recorded in dollars), one for each of the following:
    a. The series should be analyzed in original raw dollar form.
    b. The series should be deflated with an appropriate price index before analysis.
    c. The series should be analyzed both in raw dollars and in deflated dollars.
61. Describe the basic motivation for deflating a time series in dollars.
62. For which of the following time series variables would the analyst consider deflation, using an appropriate price index?
    a. Number of units produced per month.
    b. Number of overtime hours worked per week.
    c. Monthly dollar volume of spare parts received.
    d. Annual gross profit before taxes.
    e. Average weekly temperature of process.
    f. Dividends paid per quarter.
    g. Monthly cash balance.
    h. Miles driven per month by salespeople.

62. *c, d, f, g*

63. What are the criteria for choosing a base period in calculating any kind of index?
64. What are the advantages of updating the base period in an index? What are the disadvantages?
65. A market basket of goods is defined and priced in forming a price index. Over time, the market mix in the company or country will probably change. Discuss how to deal with this problem, recognizing both the advantages and disadvantages of changing the market basket at a later time.
66. Here is a composite price index developed by a company for use in deflating its annual net profit. The company now wishes to update the series to a more recent period, 1992. Calculate the new index values using this new base period.

66. 88.8
90.5
93.9
93.2
94.4
95.6
97.5
96.7
98.1
99.0
100.0

Year	Composite price index
1982	246.7
1983	251.4
1984	260.8
1985	259.0
1986	262.2
1987	265.7
1988	270.9
1989	268.6
1990	272.4
1991	275.1
1992	277.8

67. 106.4
104.9
102.7
100.5
100.0
102.5
101.9

67. Here are several values of the industrial production index. The series' base period is 1987. Calculate the new values of this series if the new base period is January 1992.

	Period	Industrial production index (1987 = 100)
1991	Sept.	111.4
	Oct.	109.8
	Nov.	107.5
	Dec.	105.2
1992	Jan.	104.7
	Feb.	107.3
	Mar.	106.7

Source: *Survey of Current Business.*

68. 1980–100.0
1985–101.5
100.4
100.5
99.9
100.6

68. Here are the number of marriages in the United States for selected years. Form an index for this time series using 1980 as the base year.

Year	Marriages (in thousands)
1980	2,390
1985	2,425
1986	2,400
1987	2,403
1988	2,389
1989	2,404

Source: *Statistical Abstract of the United States,* 1988, 1989, 1991.

69. 102.2
102.1
99.7
100.3
101.7
100.0

69. The number of divorces in the United States for selected years are shown. Form an index for this time series using 1989 as the base period.

Year	Divorces (in thousands)
1980	1,189
1985	1,187
1986	1,159
1987	1,166

Year	Divorces (in thousands)
1988	1,183
1989	1,163

Source: *Statistical Abstract of the United States,* 1988, 1991.

70. 324.6
348.3
370.3
397.8

70. Here are price indexes for prescription drugs and physicians' services. Form a composite index from these two indexes using weights of 20% for drugs and 80% for physicians' services.

Year	Prescription drugs	Physicians' services
1983	213.8	352.3
1984	234.3	376.8
1985	256.5	398.8
1986	278.6	427.7

Source: *Statistical Abstract of the United States,* 1988.

71. Here are consumer price indexes for all urban consumers by the four major regions in the United States for all items. Write a paragraph summarizing the price comparisons for these regions.

Region	CPI-U (Dec. 1977 = 100)			
	1983	1984	1985	1986
Northeast	157.1	164.5	170.7	175.0
Midwest	162.6	168.6	173.7	175.8
South	161.7	168.4	173.8	176.6
West	160.0	167.4	174.5	178.6

Source: *Statistical Abstract of the United States,* 1988.

72. Seasonal indexes of the sales for the CAM Corporation are:

Jan.	120	April	108	July	105	Oct.	100
Feb.	90	May	102	Aug.	90	Nov.	110
Mar.	100	June	110	Sept.	85	Dec.	80

72*a.* 15,500
b. 7,500
c. 5,000

a. Total 1994 sales for the CAM corporation are forecasted to be $60,000. Based on the seasonal indexes, what should sales in the first three months of 1994 total?

b. December 1993 CAM Corporation sales totaled $5,000. Give a reasonable estimate of sales for January 1994 based on the seasonal indexes.

c. CAM Corporation sales amounted to $5,500 in November 1993. Calculate November 1993 sales after adjustment for seasonal variation with the indexes just given.

73. Top, middle

73. What level of management would tend to be interested in a long-range forecast of annual data? Which level would be most interested in a monthly forecast for the next three months?

74. When would the cyclical component of a time series not be used in making a forecast?
75. What is wrong with this statement? "As president of the company, I want to plan our future plant capacity and so would like to see a monthly forecast of sales dollars including all four components. Prepare a forecast for the next two years."
76. What is wrong with this statement? "As a supervisor of the landing gear assembly line for 737s, I would like to see a forecast of demand for this aircraft. Prepare an annual forecast for 737s for the next 15 years."
77. Here are dollar values (in millions) spent on magazine advertising for beer, wine, and liquor in the United States.

Year	Y	$\hat{Y}$
1980	239	247.5
1981	252	245.1
1982	258	242.6
1983	243	240.2
1984	230	237.7
1985	240	235.3
1986	225	232.8
1987	208	230.4
1988	213	227.9
1989	257	225.5

Source: *Statistical Abstract of the United States,* 1988, 1991.

77*b.* $\hat{Y} = 250 - 2.455X$
c. 2.455
d. Inflation, population growth
f. A lot of fluctuation
h. Cyclical
i. 232

a. Calculate the cyclical indicators for this series.
b. What is the trend equation for this series?
c. Calculate the average decrease per year in magazine advertising since 1980.
d. What factor(s) affect the trend of this variable?
e. Develop a cyclical chart.
f. What can be said about the cyclical component in this series?
g. Does the economy affect this cyclical component?
h. Which component is more important: trend or cyclical?
i. Forecast the amount to be spent on magazine advertising for beer, wine, and liquor in the United States for 1990. Use the cyclical for 1989.

78. *Trend,*
$\hat{Y} = 113.1 + .61325X$
Cyclical:
Low 64 in March 1982
High 122 in Sept. 1983
Seasonal:
Jan. 74.8
Feb. 73.1
March 100.5
April 117.6
May 121.4
June 120.9
July 112.7
Aug. 106.9

78. Many firms watch the number of new housing starts in the United States as an indicator of the general level of economic prosperity in the country. The following data values are the monthly number of new housing starts in this country, in thousands.

	1982	1983	1984	1985	1986	1987
Jan.	47.6	92.9	109.2	105.4	115.7	105.1
Feb.	52.0	96.7	130.4	95.8	107.2	102.8
Mar.	78.7	135.8	138.1	145.2	151.0	141.3
Apr.	85.1	136.4	170.9	176.0	188.2	159.6
May	99.2	175.5	182.2	170.5	186.7	158.3
June	91.9	173.8	184.3	163.4	183.6	163.2
July	107.2	162.0	163.1	161.0	172.2	152.8
Aug.	97.2	177.7	147.8	161.1	163.8	143.8

Sept.	104.3
Oct.	106.7
Nov.	87.0
Dec.	74.1

	1982	1983	1984	1985	1986	1987
Sept.	108.4	156.8	149.6	148.6	153.2	152.3
Oct.	111.5	159.9	152.7	173.2	154.9	139.1
Nov.	110.0	136.4	126.5	124.1	115.7	118.9
Dec.	83.4	108.5	99.0	120.5	113.1	85.4

Source: *Survey of Current Business*, 1988.

a. Analyze this series, describing the trend, cyclical, seasonal, and irregular factors.

b. Forecast this series for the next four months by recombining the factors identified in the decomposition process.

79. $\hat{Y} = 908.84 - 4.33X$

1980	100.0
	110.9
	121.3
	86.4
	93.3
1985	94.7
	91.0
	78.7
	89.9
	111.3
1990	122.9

79. Here are dollar sales per share for selected bituminous coal firms. Calculate the trend equation for these data and the cyclical indicators. Briefly describe the series using these two components.

Year	Y
1980	904.13
1981	998.00
1982	1,086.22
1983	769.85
1984	827.31
1985	836.07
1986	799.43
1987	687.57
1988	781.77
1989	962.93
1990	1,058.02

Source: *Standard & Poor's Industry Surveys*, October 1988, 1991.

80. $\hat{Y} = .733 - .005X$

Q_1 58.2
Q_2 80.2
Q_3 62.3
Q_4 199.4

80. Here are quarterly earnings per share for the Kmart Corporation. Analyze this quarterly time series to determine the effects of the trend, cyclical, seasonal, and irregular components.

Quarter:	1	2	3	4
1985	.31	.41	.43	1.27
1986	.47	.59	.44	1.34
1987	.57	.71	.54	1.58
1988	.60	.81	.63	1.96
1989	.24	.37	.27	.98
1990	.25	.37	.27	1.00
1991	.27	.41	.25	1.06

Source: *The Value Line Investment Survey* (New York: Value Line, 1988, 1989, 1991), p. 1638.

81. A company that makes potato chips and other salty snack foods is interested in the time series of monthly liquor store retail sales. It finds the following sales levels (in millions of dollars) in the local library.

Year:	1985	1986	1987	1988	1989	1990	1991
Jan.	1636	1503	1592	1589	1623	1663	1826
Feb.	1575	1489	1628	1578	1614	1701	1819
March	1601	1520	1600	1586	1619	1716	1833
April	1625	1493	1620	1616	1633	1706	1783
May	1596	1497	1638	1634	1648	1678	1769
June	1592	1519	1593	1626	1641	1715	1760
July	1607	1499	1597	1606	1655	1731	1794
Aug.	1598	1464	1591	1585	1649	1761	1822
Sept.	1598	1443	1593	1561	1656	1755	1774
Oct.	1465	1635	1588	1555	1673	1772	1788
Nov.	1482	1600	1550	1571	1663	1778	1781
Dec.	1495	1585	1561	1590	1630	1785	1642

Source: *Survey of Current Business*, 1988, 1992.

81*a*. $\hat{Y} = 1499 + 3.177X$
No seasonality; some cyclical

a. Analyze this series, commenting on all four components.

b. How useful do you think your analysis would be to the snack food company?

82. $\hat{Y} = 9.942 - .213X$
1977 54.47
1978 75.66
1979 108.56
1980 125.40
1981 157.70
1982 122.33
1983 101.75
1984 115.31
1985 93.45
1986 76.79
1987 65.79
1988 90.79

82. The following values represent the average annual three-month Treasury bill rate, in percentages for the years 1977 through 1988, found in *The Value Line Investment Survey* (New York: Value Line, 1988). Analyze this time series, indicating the trend of the series and the extent of the cyclical effect. Also, estimate the rate for 1989 and compare your estimate with *Value Line*'s estimate of 8.1.

5.3, 7.2, 10.1, 11.4, 14.0, 10.6, 8.6, 9.5, 7.5, 6.0, 5.8, 6.7

83. After reading a *Financial World* article (November 14, 1989, p. 38) on how to increase technological development efforts to compete with Japan, a consulting company collects the following data to help it decide on a marketing strategy for its services. Data values represent monthly exports to China in millions of dollars.

Year:	1988	1989	1990	1991
Jan.	350.7	385.9	359.4	411.0
Feb.	375.2	499.2	516.7	486.3
March	401.6	581.8	356.4	472.9
April	348.9	355.2	499.8	505.8
May	401.0	471.0	381.4	630.9
June	348.9	355.2	499.8	505.8
July	399.7	644.7	385.7	538.5
Aug.	409.1	703.7	422.7	560.1
Sept.	406.5	456.2	354.8	470.8
Oct.	412.9	542.4	452.7	570.9
Nov.	449.3	305.0	329.9	621.5
Dec.	533.9	424.4	372.8	580.6

Source: *Survey of Current Business*, 1992.

83*a*. $\hat{Y} = 395 + 2.229X$
Jan. 89.0
109.6
103.4
108.3
99.0
100.4
102.2
105.6
99.2
110.8
78.7
Dec. 93.8
b. Seasonal, cyclical
c. Yes

a. Analyze this monthly series including comments on all four components of the series.

b. What do you think are the most significant factors in your analysis as far as the consulting firm is concerned?

c. Do you think your analysis would help the consulting firm in its marketing efforts?

d. Forecast this series for the next two months.

84. Describe the conditions under which the original units of measurement of a time series would be of more interest to the analyst than an index computed from these values.
85. Suppose you were president of a medium-sized company. If you could have any three indexes computed for you from company data and presented in a monthly report, which three would you choose?
86. If you were president of a company, which three dollar values would you like to see each month? Would you prefer that these values be in original dollars or deflated dollars?
87. Suppose your company is considering moving its operations to Kansas City. Before making a decision, what indexes would you like to see that summarize conditions in that city?
88. Locate *Value Line* in your library. Find a stock of interest to you and record the quarterly sales volume of this corporation. Analyze this time series to determine the trend, cyclical, seasonal, and irregular components. Summarize your findings in a brief memo, including the extent of your interest in investing your own money in this stock.
89. Locate the *Survey of Current Business* in your library. Find a monthly time series in this publication and record its values for five to seven years. Analyze this time series and report on the four components of the series.
90. Locate a copy of the *Statistical Abstract of the United States* in your library. Record the values of both an annual and a monthly time series from this publication and analyze each. Report your findings with reference to the major components of each series.

EXTENDED EXERCISES

91. GARRY PRODUCTS, INC.

Garry Products produces heat shields used on rocket motors and is under contract with NASA to provide shields for the next five years. The company's chief accountant, Barry Mano, has been trying to find a way to monitor the company's cost of producing these shields. The company is under constant pressure from NASA to justify the price of its shields, since its contract with NASA is of the "cost-plus" type. Barry would like to find a way to quickly and easily show how the cost of parts used in the manufacture of the shields increases.

In a current issue of the *Survey of Current Business*, Barry finds the producer price index prepared by the federal government. He decides that this measure of wholesale price inflation would be useful in showing how most or all of the price increases result from material and labor price increases rather than higher company profit margins.

Barry measures the costs of materials and hourly labor for shields produced during the past nine months (Table 16.18). He also records the producer price index for these same months. He hopes that after the shield costs are deflated using this index, a more favorable cost picture will emerge, and NASA's pressure on the company will decline.

a. Use Table 16.18's information to prepare a deflated shield cost for June 1991 through March 1992.

b. Do you think the Garry Company will be successful in reducing NASA's concerns regarding the cost of heat shields?

92. MOOREHOUSE DRY GOODS COMPANY

Sally Moorehouse is president of a company founded by her parents. It currently makes and imports various garments for the wholesale trade on the East Coast and has enjoyed increasing

TABLE 16.18 Garry Company Costs and Producer Price Index (Extended Exercise 91)

Time period	Average shield cost (in $)	Producer price index (1987 = 100)
1991		
June	105,328	116.4
July	104,935	116.1
Aug.	106,833	116.2
Sept.	106,462	116.1
Oct.	107,631	116.4
Nov.	108,003	116.4
Dec.	108,414	115.9
1992		
Jan.	108,286	115.6
Feb.	109,141	116.1
March	109,354	116.1

Source: *Survey of Current Business*, April 1992.

sales levels for the past several years. Sally's main job is to monitor its overall performance and plan for the future.

Sally has just read "Faking It—When You Want the Style But Not the Price" in *Glamour* (October 1989). This article has given her some ideas about the company's clothing line, and she's considering some changes. First, she would like an accurate picture of past sales levels.

During the past 10 years, annual sales, measured in dollars, have increased dramatically. However, profits haven't shown the same increase, which puzzles Sally. She suspects that inflation during these years has caused at least some of the increase in annual dollar sales, and she would like to see the sales picture with inflation removed. She suspects that the picture won't look so rosy if this is done, which might affect her view of the company's past history and her plans for the future.

a. Locate the most current issue of the *Survey of Current Business* in your library.

b. Find the best price index for deflating the Moorehouse Company's annual sales, and record its value for the past 10 years.

c. Based on the index values you found, do you think Sally's concern about inflation during the past 10 years is justified? Explain.

93. CONE LUMBER COMPANY

Mildred Cone, an elderly widow, owns Cone Lumber Company. Her grandson, Robert Thomas, has just graduated from a local business school and, at his grandmother's urging, has decided to manage the business.

One of the first problems Robert faces as he learns his new job is trying to predict monthly company sales volume. Robert decides he should first investigate the company's monthly sales so he knows where he stands.

Monthly sales seem to have a seasonal pattern, with winter being slowest and spring and summer being best. Robert would like to find a way of forecasting the next 12 months' sales volumes at the beginning of each year so rational methods of ordering materials and scheduling the work can be used.

Here are the monthly sales levels, in thousands of dollars, for the past several months. Robert found these data values in the company's records.

	1989	1990	1991	1992
Jan.	29.7	28.4	30.7	31.2
Feb.	21.3	25.7	25.9	29.2
Mar.	30.1	29.9	32.5	30.5
Apr.	35.8	34.6	38.7	37.0
May	42.9	40.2	44.5	45.5
June	44.6	48.9	50.1	51.3
July	50.6	51.4	52.7	54.4
Aug.	48.5	52.9	50.1	50.7
Sept.	51.0	48.8	46.3	44.8
Oct.	44.5	47.2	42.3	43.8
Nov.	40.0	39.2	41.6	40.9
Dec.	32.5	35.4	29.7	30.1

a. Using a time series decomposition computer program, perform the decomposition analysis and summarize what you find about the four components in the series.

b. Forecast the first three months of 1993.

MICROCOMPUTER PACKAGE

The micro package *Computerized Business Statistics* can be used to solve time series analysis problems.

In Solved Exercise 1, Steve Donaldson needs to determine the long-term growth of median purchase prices of existing one-family houses in the West.

Computer Solution:

From the main menu of *Computerized Business Statistics* an **11** is selected, indicating Time Series and Forecasting. The time series and forecasting menu is shown on the screen. Since the problem involves entering data from the keyboard, a **1** is selected.

```
Time Series and Forecasting-Define New Problem
OPTIONS:  1 = Least Squares
          2 = Moving Averages
          3 = Simple Exponential Smoothing
          4 = Smoothing with Trend Factoring
          5 = Trend and Seasonal Smoothing
          6 = Seasonal Indices
Select Model: Enter 1–6, press ↵ 1
```

Since the least squares trend line is desired, a **1** is selected.

```
Linear or Logarithmic Trend: L/O, Press ↵ L
```

Since a linear model is desired, an L is selected.

```
Number of Data Points: Enter 4–125, Press ↵ 10
```

The history period involves 10 years of data.

```
Enter Variable Name (0–5 Char.), Press ↵ Price
```

The variable is entered as **Price.**

```
Problem Definition Correct: Y/N/Q, Press ↵ Y
```

After a **Y** response, the program is ready for the data to be entered.

After the data have been entered the screen shows:

```
      Price
 1 =   89.3
 2 =   96.2
 3 =   98.9
 4 =   94.9
 5 =   95.8
 6 =   95.4
 7 =  100.9
 8 =  113.2
 9 =  124.9
10 =  139.9
Press F when Finished
```

There are 10 data points. An **F** is entered once the blanks have been filled in.

```
Save data? Enter Y/N, press ↵ N
```

The time series analysis menu reappears. A **7** is entered so that the problem can be run. The screen then displays the output menu. The choice in this case is **P** for printer.

In Solved Exercise 5, the Consolidated Edison Company sells electricity and steam in New York City. Betty Springer is trying to determine if a seasonal pattern exists in the company's quarter revenues.

Computer Solution

The steps are the same as for the previous example until the Time Series and Forecasting Options Menu reappears. This time the Seasonal Indexes option is chosen.

```
Select Model: Enter 1–6, & Press ↵ 6
Number of Years: Enter 2–10 & Press ↵ 4
```

The history period involves four years of data.

```
Enter Variable Name (0–5 Char.) & Press ↵ Rev
```

The variable is entered as **Rev.**

```
Problem Definition Correct: Y/N/Q, Press ↵ Y
```

After a **Y** response, the program is ready for the data to be entered. There are 16 data points. An **F** is entered once the blanks have been filled in.

After the data have been entered, the screen shows:

```
     Rev
 1 = 1441
 2 = 1209
 3 = 1526
 4 = 1321
 5 = 1414
 6 = 1187
 7 = 1411
 8 = 1185
 9 = 1284
```

```
10 = 1125
11 = 1493
12 = 1192
13 = 1327
14 = 1102
15 = 1469
16 = 1213
Press F when Finished
```

There are 16 data points. An **F** is entered once the blanks have been filled in.

```
Save data? Enter Y/N, press ↵ N
```

The time series analysis menu then reappears. A **7** is entered so that the problem can be run. Next, the screen shows the output menu. The choice in this case is **P** for printer.

MINITAB COMPUTER PACKAGE

MINITAB can be used to analyze seasonal time series data. The MINITAB commands to analyze Solved Exercise 5 are:

```
MTB > SET C1
DATA> 1441 1209 1526 1321 1414 1187 1411 1185
DATA> 1284 1125 1493 1192 1327 1102 1469 1213
DATA> END
MTB > LET C2 = C1
MTB > LET C3 = C1
MTB > LET C4 = C1
MTB > DELETE 1 C2
MTB > DELETE 1:2 C3
MTB > DELETE 1:3 C4
MTB > LET C5 = C1+C2+C3+C4
MTB > PRINT C1–C5
 ROW     C1     C2     C3     C4     C5
   1   1441   1209   1526   1321   5497
   2   1209   1526   1321   1414   5470
   3   1526   1321   1414   1187   5448
   4   1321   1414   1187   1411   5333
   5   1414   1187   1411   1185   5197
   6   1187   1411   1185   1284   5067
   7   1411   1185   1284   1125   5005
   8   1185   1284   1125   1493   5087
   9   1284   1125   1493   1192   5094
  10   1125   1493   1192   1327   5137
  11   1493   1192   1327   1102   5114
  12   1192   1327   1102   1469   5090
  13   1327   1102   1469   1213   5111
  14   1102   1469   1213
  15   1469   1213
  16   1213
```

The first step is to compute a four-quarter moving total. The data are copied into columns 2, 3, and 4. Next, the DELETE command is used to delete the first observation in column 2, the first two observations in column 3, and the first three observations in column 4. The LET command is then used to add columns 1 through 4 and store the resulting four-quarter moving total in C5. Next, the same type of process is used to compute a two-year moving total and eventually the quarterly seasonal indexes.

```
MTB > LET C6 = C5
MTB > DELETE 1 C6
MTB > LET C7 = C5+C6
MTB > PRINT C1-C7

 ROW     C1     C2     C3     C4     C5     C6      C7
   1   1441   1209   1526   1321   5497   5470   10967
   2   1209   1526   1321   1414   5470   5448   10918
   3   1526   1321   1414   1187   5448   5333   10781
   4   1321   1414   1187   1411   5333   5197   10530
   5   1414   1187   1411   1185   5197   5067   10264
   6   1187   1411   1185   1284   5067   5005   10072
   7   1411   1185   1284   1125   5005   5087   10092
   8   1185   1284   1125   1493   5087   5094   10181
   9   1284   1125   1493   1192   5094   5137   10231
  10   1125   1493   1192   1327   5137   5114   10251
  11   1493   1192   1327   1102   5114   5090   10204
  12   1192   1327   1102   1469   5090   5111   10201
  13   1327   1102   1469   1213   5111
  14   1102   1469   1213
  15   1469   1213
  16   1213

MTB > LET C8 = C7/8
MTB > LET C9 = (C3/C8)*100
MTB > PRINT C9

C9
  111.316    96.794    104.925    90.180    109.977    94.122
  101.784    88.400    116.743    93.025    104.038    86.423
```

The four-quarter centered moving average (C8) is computed by dividing the two-year moving total (C7) stored in column 7 by 8. Each quarterly seasonal index is computed by dividing the actual value for each quarter (C3) by the four-quarter centered average for that quarter and multiplying by 100 so the result is an index number. The next commands are used to compute the medians for each quarter.

```
MTB > SET C10
DATA> 3 4 1 2 3 4 1 2 3 4 1 2
DATA> END
MTB > DESCRIBE C9;
SUBC> BY C10.

            C10       N    MEDIAN
C9            1       3    104.04
              2       3     88.40
              3       3    111.32
              4       3     94.12

MTB > STOP
```

The SET command is used to identify each quarter. The DESCRIBE command and the BY subcommand are used to compute several statistics of C9 for each value of C10. Only the relevant portion of the output is shown here. The last step, not shown here, is to adjust these values so that they sum to 400.

Chapter 17

Business Forecasting

I never think of the future. It comes soon enough.
Albert Einstein

Objectives

When you have completed this chapter, you will be able to:

Choose the appropriate forecasting technique for a particular real-world situation.

Measure the errors generated by a forecasting procedure.

Use naive, moving average, and exponential smoothing techniques to create a forecast.

Compute an autocorrelation coefficient.

Construct a correlogram.

Identify whether data are random, nonstationary, or seasonal.

Detect serial correlation in a time series.

Discuss potential solutions to the problem of serial correlation.

Use autoregressive and regression models to forecast.

The chart on the front page of *The Wall Street Journal*, June 15, 1992, showed consumer price index values for the past several quarters. A downward trend was evident.

This chapter could be titled "More Business Forecasting" because the past three chapters have discussed aspects of this subject. In Chapter 14, regression analysis used knowledge of *one* predictor variable to forecast a dependent variable. In Chapter 15, multiple regression analysis used knowledge of *two or more* predictor variables to forecast a dependent variable. In Chapter 16, decomposition of a time series was used to study the components of a series in isolation, and this knowledge was used to make forecasts.

Why Managers Need to Know about Business Forecasting

This chapter describes additional techniques to generate forecasts of future values of a time series. The objective is to examine the pattern of the variable in past time periods and to use this pattern to extend values of the variable into the uncertain future. Methods of measuring forecast errors will be introduced, and the various forecasting methods discussed in this text will be summarized. As mentioned before, forecasting is one of a manager's most important tasks. This chapter concludes coverage of this critical topic.

Regarding *The Wall Street Journal* chart, many businesses closely watch the consumer price index as a measure of inflation. Forecasting this important indicator is of great interest to them. Many techniques in this chapter are commonly used to forecast such a series.

Choosing the Appropriate Forecasting Technique

Choosing a Forecasting Model

Forecasting involves extending past experiences into the future. The assumption is that the conditions that generated the historical data are indistinguishable from future conditions, except for those variables explicitly recognized by the forecasting model. To the extent that this assumption is not met, a forecast will be inaccurate unless modified by the judgment of the forecaster.

Recognition that forecasting techniques operate on data generated by historical events leads to identifying the following steps in the forecasting process:

1. Data collection and reduction.
2. Model building.
3. Model evaluation.
4. The forecast.

Often, the most challenging part of the forecasting process is obtaining the proper data and making sure they are correct. If the data are inappropriate or incorrect, the forecast will be inaccurate.

Model building means finding the appropriate model to use with the collected data. The simpler the model, the better the chances that the forecasting process will gain acceptance by managers who must make decisions. Often a balance must be struck between a sophisticated forecasting approach that offers slightly more accuracy and a simple approach that is easily understood by company decision makers.

A typical strategy for evaluating various forecasting methods involves the following steps:

TM

Step 1 A forecasting method is chosen based on the analyst's examination of the pattern of past data.

Step 2 The data set is divided into two sections: an initialization part and a test part.

Step 3 The chosen forecasting method is used to develop fitted values from the initialization part of the data.

Step 4 The model is used to forecast the test part of the data, and the forecasting errors are computed and evaluated. (Measurement error will be discussed in the next section.)

Step 5 A decision about the model is made. The decision might be to use the model in its present form, to modify the model, to develop a forecast using another model and compare the results, or to discard the model and try something else.

The final step is using the selected model to forecast future values of the variable of interest. The actual forecast should be both quantitative and qualitative. The forecasting model provides the quantitative value, and the analyst's judgment provides any qualitative adjustments.

Forecast Error Measurement

Several methods have been devised to measure the errors generated by a particular forecasting procedure. These methods basically consist of generating forecasts for past periods and comparing these forecasts to the actual values of the forecast variable. The difference between the forecast or estimated value and the observed value is similar to the residual in regression analysis. Equation 17.1 is used to compute the error for each forecast period:

$$e_t = Y_t - F_t \tag{17.1}$$

where e_t = Forecast error in time period t
Y_t = Actual value in time period t
F_t = Forecast value for time period t

One method for evaluating a forecasting technique uses the summation of the absolute errors. The *mean absolute deviation* (MAD) is the average of the absolute values of the errors:

$$\text{MAD} = \frac{\Sigma|e_t|}{n} \tag{17.2}$$

The *mean squared error* (MSE) method can also be used to evaluate a forecasting technique. Each error is squared and summed and then divided by the number of observations. This approach involves a penalty for large forecasting errors because each error is squared:

$$\text{MSE} = \frac{\Sigma e_t^2}{n} \tag{17.3}$$

Sometimes it's useful to compute the forecasting errors in terms of percentages rather than amounts. The *mean absolute percentage error* (MAPE) is computed by finding the absolute error in each period, dividing this by the value actually observed for that period, and then averaging these absolute percentage errors. This approach is useful when the magnitude of the forecast variable is important in evaluating the accuracy of the forecast:

$$\text{MAPE} = \frac{\sum \frac{|e_t|}{Y_t}}{n} \tag{17.4}$$

Finally, it is sometimes necessary to determine whether a forecasting method is biased (consistently forecasting high or low). The *mean percentage error* (MPE) is computed by finding the error in each period, dividing this by the observed value for that period, and then averaging these percentage errors. If the forecasting approach is unbiased, Equation 17.5 will produce a percentage close to 0. If the result is a large positive percentage, the forecasting method is consistently underestimating. If the result is a large negative percentage, the forecasting method is consistently overestimating.

$$\text{MPE} = \frac{\sum \frac{e_t}{Y_t}}{n} \tag{17.5}$$

Example 17.1 illustrates how each of these error measurements is computed.

EXAMPLE 17.1 Table 17.1 shows Cosmos Perfume Company's demand (in cases), Y_t, and a forecast of these data, F_t. The forecasting technique used the previous period's demand to derive the forecast for the current period. This simple model will be discussed in the next section. Table 17.1 shows the computations for evaluating this model using MAD, MSE, MAPE, and MPE.

$$\text{MAD} = \frac{\Sigma|e_t|}{n} = \frac{39}{9} = 4.3$$

$$\text{MSE} = \frac{\Sigma e_t^2}{n} = \frac{213}{9} = 23.7$$

$$\text{MAPE} = \frac{\sum \frac{|e_t|}{Y_t}}{n} = \frac{64.2\%}{9} = 7.1\%$$

$$\text{MPE} = \frac{\sum \frac{e_t}{Y_t}}{n} = \frac{24.8\%}{9} = 2.8\%$$

TM

TABLE 17.1 Computations for Forecast Evaluation Methods (Example 17.1)

Time, t	Demand (number of cases), Y_t	Forecast, F_t	Error, e_t	$\lvert e_t \rvert$	e_t^2	$\frac{\lvert e_t \rvert}{Y_t}$ (%)	$\frac{e_t}{Y_t}$ (%)
1	53	—	—	—	—	—	—
2	58	53	5	5	25	8.6	8.6
3	54	58	−4	4	16	7.4	−7.4
4	60	54	6	6	36	10.0	10.0
5	55	60	−5	5	25	9.1	−9.1
6	62	55	7	7	49	11.3	11.3
7	62	62	0	0	0	0.0	0.0
8	65	62	3	3	9	4.6	4.6
9	63	65	−2	2	4	3.2	−3.2
10	70	63	7	7	49	10.0	10.0
		Sums:	17	39	213	64.2	24.8

MAD indicates that each forecast deviated from the actual data by an average of 4.3 cases. The MSE of 23.7 and the MAPE of 7.1% can be compared to the MSE and MAPE for any other method used to forecast these data. Finally, the small MPE of 2.8% indicates that the model is not biased: since this value is close to 0, the model doesn't consistently over- or underestimate demand.

SIMPLE FORECASTING METHODS

Naive Forecasting Method

The easiest methods for forecasting a time series variable, **naive methods,** are intuitively appealing and are widely used by managers, either consciously or subconsciously. The simplest naive method uses the value for the current period as the forecast for the next period:

$$F_{t+1} = Y_t \tag{17.6}$$

where F_{t+1} = Forecast for time period $t + 1$

Y_t = Y value for time period t

Naive methods are very simple approaches to forecasting, such as using the value from the current period as the estimate for the next period.

This method is demonstrated in Example 17.2.

EXAMPLE 17.2 The Cosmos Perfume Company used the naive approach to forecast demand for cases in Table 17.1. The forecast for period 2 using Equation 17.6 is

$$F_{t+1} = Y_t$$
$$F_{1+1} = Y_1$$
$$F = 53$$

The forecast for period 11 is

$$F_{10+1} = Y_{10}$$
$$F_{11} = 70$$

The problem with this simple model is that it does not take trend or seasonality of the data into consideration. However, if the data have a trend, a naive model can be developed that takes into consideration the increase or decrease from one period to another. Also, if the data are seasonal, a model can be developed that forecasts, for example, this year's sales for June as the June sales from last year.

If a firm has been in business less than three years, the large amounts of data required for advanced forecasting models might not be available. Naive models are frequently used in situations where a new business hasn't had time to develop a useful historical data base.

Moving Averages

The **moving average** model uses the average of several past time periods as the forecast for the next period. In practice, the analyst must decide how many past periods to average. A trial-and-error process is often used to find the number of periods that would be best in minimizing the error; this process amounts to comparing the model's predictions against the known values of recent periods. The term *moving average* implies that as each new observation becomes available, a new mean is computed by dropping the oldest value used in the average and adding the newest one. This new mean is the forecast for the next period. Equation 17.7 is used to compute moving average forecasts:

Moving Average Method

$$F_{t+1} = \frac{Y_t + Y_{t-1} + Y_{t-2} + \cdots + Y_{t-m+1}}{m} \tag{17.7}$$

where F_{t+1} = Forecast for time period $t + 1$

Y_t = Y value for time period t

m = Number of terms in the moving average

> The **moving average** model uses the average of several past time periods as the forecast for the next period.

Example 17.3 The moving average method can be used with the data of Table 17.2 to produce a forecast for March (period 15). Suppose the analyst decides to use five periods in the averaging process. The forecast for June (period 6) is the average value of the variable for the five previous time periods, 132.4:

$$F_{t+1} = \frac{Y_t + Y_{t-1} + Y_{t-2} + \cdots + Y_{t-m+1}}{m}$$

TABLE 17.2 Moving Average Forecast for Example 17.3

t	Month	Cost of goods sold ($000s)	Five-month moving total	Five-month moving average	e_t
	1992				
1	Jan	125.7			
2	Feb	129.4			
3	Mar	131.7			
4	Apr	135.0			
5	May	140.2			
6	Jun	141.7	662.0	132.4	9.3
7	Jul	138.4	678.0	135.6	2.8
8	Aug	135.3	687.0	137.4	−2.1
9	Sep	130.9	690.6	138.1	−7.2
10	Oct	130.2	686.5	137.3	−7.1
11	Nov	131.8	676.5	135.3	−3.5
12	Dec	128.2	666.6	133.3	−5.1
	1993				
13	Jan	127.3	656.4	131.3	−4.0
14	Feb	129.3	646.8	129.4	−0.4

```
MEAN SQUARED ERROR (MSE)          =    28.41
MEAN ABSOLUTE PC ERROR (MAPE)     =     3.46%
MEAN PC ERROR (MPE) OR BIAS       =    -1.56%

PERIOD              FORECAST
  15                  129.36
```

$$F_{5+1} = \frac{Y_5 + Y_{5-1} + Y_{5-2} + \cdots + Y_{5-5+1}}{5}$$

$$F_6 = \frac{140.2 + 135.0 + 131.7 + 129.4 + 125.7}{5} = 132.4$$

This average is called " moving" because when the actual value for June becomes known, the averaging process will "move" down one month, dropping January's value and picking up the new June value. This process is repeated each month as a new data value becomes known. Finally, the forecast for period 15 (March) is 129.4:

$$F_{14+1} = \frac{Y_{14} + Y_{14-1} + Y_{14-2} + \cdots + Y_{14-5+1}}{m}$$

$$F_{15} = \frac{129.3 + 127.3 + 128.2 + 131.8 + 130.2}{5} = 129.4$$

EXPONENTIAL SMOOTHING

The disadvantage of the moving average process is that, regardless of how many time periods are used, every value is assumed to contribute equally to the forecast. In most actual situations, this isn't a realistic assumption. Rather, the forecast should usually

Exponential Smoothing

rely most heavily on the most recent value, less on the value before that, even less on the value before that, and so on. The **exponential smoothing** technique uses a weighted average of past time series values to arrive at a smoothed forecast.

Exponential smoothing is so named because the weights attached to past time periods in forming the forecast decline exponentially. That is, the weights decrease rapidly at first and then less and less so as the time period becomes older. The weight attached to a particular value approaches, but never quite reaches, 0. This method generates accurate forecasts for many time series variables, recognizing the decreasing impact of past time periods as they fade further into the past. The weights used are α for the most recent observation, $\alpha(1 - \alpha)$ for the next most recent, $\alpha(1 - \alpha)^2$ for the next, and so forth. α (alpha) is a constant between 0 and 1. An exponential smoothing forecast is formulated using Equation 17.8:

$$F_{t+1} = \alpha Y_t + (1 - \alpha)F_t \tag{17.8}$$

where F_{t+1} = Forecast for time period $t + 1$
Y_t = Y value for time period t
α = Smoothing constant, a value between 0 and 1
F_t = Average experience of the series smoothed to period t, or forecast value for period t

Equation 17.8 calls for combining two values in preparing the forecast: the most recent value for the time series (Y_t) and the average experience of the series smoothed to period t (F_t). The forecast is a weighted average of these two values. The smoothing constant, α, is the weight attached to the most recent observation in the series. When α is close to 1, the new forecast will be greatly affected by the most recent observation. When α is close to 0, the new forecast will be very similar to the old one.

> The **exponential smoothing** technique uses a weighted average of past time series values to arrive at smoothed forecasts.

The smoothing constant, α, is the key to the use of exponential smoothing. If forecasts need to be stable and random variations smoothed, a small α is required. If a rapid response to a real change in the pattern of observations is desired, a larger value of α is appropriate. Most exponential smoothing computer packages find the optimal smoothing constant by minimizing the sum of squares error: SSE $= \Sigma e_t^2$.

EXAMPLE 17.4 Jill Tilson owns a small art shop and is attempting to forecast her monthly sales based on past history. She specializes in abstract art and got some new ideas after reading "Exhibiting Abstract Painting in the Era of Its Belatedness" in *Arts Magazine* (March 1992, p. 60). She thinks it's essential to have a good forecast of future sales before initiating any changes suggested by the article.

In December, her forecast for January sales is \$12,703. At the end of January, actual sales turn out to be \$13,037. Exponential smoothing is being used to generate forecasts, and past experience has shown that a smoothing constant of .25 produces the most accurate forecast. Using Equation 17.8, the forecast prepared at the end of January for the month of February is

$$\begin{aligned} F_{t+1} &= \alpha Y_t + (1 - \alpha)F_t \\ &= (.25)(13{,}037) + (.75)(12{,}703) = 12{,}787 \end{aligned}$$

The forecast for February, \$12,787, is a weighted average of past time series values (the previous forecast, \$12,703) and the actual value of the time series in January (\$13,037). The reasoning behind this process is that the same basic forecast is made each month, with some modification based on the actual time series value for that month. In this example, the weighting constant of .25 recognizes a significant, but not overpowering, contribution of the current time series value to the forecast for the next month.

Example 17.4 used a smoothing or weighting constant of .25. In practice, small smoothing constants are generally used because more accurate forecasts are generated if each forecast is modified only slightly by the current value of the variable. The previous forecast, using the exponential smoothing formula, is based on many past values of the variable and should usually be modified only slightly by the current value.

EXAMPLE 17.5 The time series data of Table 17.2 can be forecast using exponential smoothing. A good place to start is January 1992. For this month, the actual value of the time series variable is 125.7. Suppose a smoothing constant of .20 is chosen. Equation 17.8 calls for these two values, along with the value of the previous forecast. Since this is the first data value, an arbitrary value for the previous forecast is chosen. This value should be in the same range as the actual values of the time series, and the actual value of the first period is usually used. In fact, the value chosen for the previous forecast is not critical, because after several forecasts are prepared for future time periods, the influence of this value will have died away exponentially and will not substantially affect the forecast. Using Equation 17.8, the forecast for February (time period 2) is

$$\begin{aligned} F_{t+1} &= \alpha Y_t + (1 - \alpha)F_t \\ F_{1+1} &= \alpha Y_1 + (1 - \alpha)F_1 \\ F_2 &= (.20)(125.7) + (.80)(125.7) = 125.7 \end{aligned}$$

Table 17.3 shows the forecast values. The next three forecasts are computed below. Note that for each forecast, the previous forecast is used as the second term in the averaging process.

$$\begin{aligned} F_3 &= (.20)(129.4) + (.80)(125.7) = 126.44 \\ F_4 &= (.20)(131.7) + (.80)(126.44) = 127.49 \\ F_5 &= (.20)(135.0) + (.80)(127.49) = 128.99 \end{aligned}$$

TABLE 17.3 Exponential Smoothing Forecast for Example 17.5

t		Y_t	F_t	e_t
	1992			
1	Jan	125.7	----	----
2	Feb	129.4	125.70	3.70
3	Mar	131.7	126.44	5.26
4	Apr	135.0	127.49	7.51
5	May	140.2	128.99	11.21
6	Jun	141.7	131.23	10.47
7	Jul	138.4	133.33	5.07
8	Aug	135.3	134.34	0.96
9	Sep	130.9	134.53	−3.63
10	Oct	130.2	133.81	−3.61
11	Nov	131.8	133.09	−1.29
12	Dec	128.2	132.83	−4.63
	1993			
13	Jan	127.3	131.90	−4.60
14	Feb	129.3	130.98	−1.68

```
MEAN SQUARED ERROR (MSE)          =     33.29
MEAN ABSOLUTE PC ERROR (MAPE)     =      3.63%
MEAN PC ERROR (MPE) OR BIAS       =      1.32%

PERIOD          FORECAST
  15            130.65
```

This process is continued until the forecast for March 1993 (period 15) is prepared:

$$F_{15} = (.20)(129.3) + (.80)(130.98) = 130.64$$

Note that the MSE for the smoothing constant of .2 is 33.29, the MAPE is 3.63%, and the MPE is 1.32%. If a smoothing constant of .6 is used, the MSE is reduced to 15.35, the MAPE is reduced to 2.6%, and the MPE is 0.26%. Knowledge of the cost of goods sold this month is evidently very important in forecasting for next month.

Actually, the optimal smoothing constant for these data is close to 1. This means that the naive forecasting model using Equation 17.6 would be appropriate.

The most basic exponential smoothing technique has just been presented. This forecasting method is often used in inventory control systems, where numerous items are to be forecast and low cost is a primary concern. Many statistical computer packages contain exponential smoothing procedures.

In addition to the basic method just described, extensions and modifications to this procedure are widely used. Details of these procedures can be found in more advanced texts on forecasting,[1] but the essential features of these methods are outlined here. Some of the more popular extensions of basic exponential smoothing include:

1. **Trend modifications.** When the time series experiences a trend over time, basic exponential smoothing will consistently underestimate a rising series and overestimate a falling one. This problem can be solved by adding or subtracting an

[1]Recommended is John E. Hanke and Arthur G. Reitsch, *Business Forecasting*, 4th ed. (Boston: Allyn & Bacon, 1992).

amount to each forecast reflecting the trend. The degree of adjustment is constantly upgraded based on the most recent trend indication. A procedure known as *Holt's two-parameter linear exponential smoothing* allows the analyst to estimate separately the smoothed value for the time series and the average trend change at each point in time. The resulting smoothed values will track time series values more accurately for a series containing a trend.

2. **Trend and seasonal modifications.** In addition to a trend adjustment, some time series forecasts benefit from recognition of a seasonal factor. In a monthly or quarterly time series, certain adjustments for the month or quarter being forecast may produce a more accurate prediction. In a monthly series, a seasonal adjustment factor is established for January, one for February, and so on. In a quarterly series, modifications for the first, second, third, and fourth quarters are developed and modified as new data become available. A procedure known as *Winter's linear and seasonal exponential smoothing* allows the analyst to estimate separately the smoothed value of the time series, the average trend gain at each point in time, and a seasonality factor for each time period.
3. **Adaptive filtering.** The adaptive filtering procedure is aimed at finding the best set of weights to use in combining past periods to develop the forecast. A program is used that tests various sets of weights leading to lower and lower measurements of error in forecasting past periods until the optimal weights have been determined. These weights are then used in the forecasting equation for future periods.

EXERCISES

1. Identify the basic steps used in the forecasting process.
2. Describe the typical strategy for evaluating various forecasting methods.
3. Explain the difference between the MAD and the MSE methods for evaluating a forecasting technique.
4. Which method for evaluating a forecasting technique should be used in each of the following situations?
   a. The analyst needs to penalize large forecasting errors.
   b. The analyst feels that the magnitude of the forecast variable is important in evaluating the forecast's accuracy.
   c. The analyst needs to determine whether a forecasting method is biased.

4*a.* MSE
b. MAPE
c. MPE

5. Which of the following statements are true concerning the methods used to evaluate forecasts?
   a. The MSE penalizes large errors.
   b. The MAPE takes into consideration the magnitude of the values being forecast.
   c. The advantage of the MAD method is that it relates the size of error to the actual observation.
   d. The MPE is used to determine whether a model is systematically predicting too high or too low.

5. *a, b, d*

6. Which forecasting model assumes that the pattern exhibited by the historical observations can best be represented by an arithmetic mean of those observations?

6. Moving average

7. Exponential smoothing

7. Which forecasting model continually revises an estimate in light of more recent experiences?

8. Decomposition

8. Which forecasting model identifies the component factors that influence each of the values in a series?

9. Naive

9. Which forecasting method uses the value for the current period as the forecast for the next period?

10. Given the following series:

Time period	Y_t	F_t	e_t
1	100	100	—
2	110		
3	115		
4	116		
5	119		
6	120		
7	125		

10*a*. 116
b. 106.6
c. 9.4

a. Using a five-month moving average, what is the forecast for period 7?

b. If a smoothing constant of .3 is used, what is the exponentially smoothed forecast for period 4?

c. Continuing part *b*, what is the forecast error for time period 4?

11. Columbia Mutual Fund invests primarily in technology stocks. The net asset value of the fund at the end of each month of 1992 is as follows:

Month	Mutual fund price
Jan.	9.39
Feb.	8.96
Mar.	8.20
Apr.	7.89
May	8.43
June	9.98
July	9.51
Aug.	10.63
Sept.	9.78
Oct.	11.25
Nov.	11.18
Dec.	12.14

11*a*. Feb. 9.39
Mar. 8.96
Apr. 8.20
May 7.89
June 8.43
July 9.98
Aug. 9.51
Sept. 10.63
Oct. 9.78
Nov. 11.25
Dec. 11.18
b. .78
c. .80
d. 7.78
e. 1.93
f. 12.14

a. Find the forecast value of the mutual fund for each month, starting with February, by using the naive model.

b. Evaluate this forecasting method using MAD.

c. Evaluate this forecasting method using MSE.

d. Evaluate this forecasting method using MAPE.

e. Evaluate this forecasting method using MPE.

f. Forecast the mutual fund price for January 1993.

g. Write a memo summarizing your findings.

12. MSE = 1.78, MAPE = 11.61%, no

12. (This question refers to Exercise 11.) Use a five-month moving average to forecast the mutual fund price for January 1993. Is this forecast better than the forecast made using the naive model? Explain.

13. The yield on a general obligation bond for a small city fluctuates with the market. Monthly quotations for 1992 are:

Month	Yield
Jan.	9.27
Feb.	9.96
Mar.	10.06
Apr.	10.28
May	10.63
June	11.08
July	11.51
Aug.	10.99
Sept.	10.78
Oct.	10.55
Nov.	10.82
Dec.	9.96

13*a*. June 10.04
b. April 9.76
c. 5-month .69
3-month .56
d. 5-month .51
3-month .32
e. 5-month 5.45%
3-month 4.66%
f. 5-month .71%
3-month .81%
g. 3-month 10.44

a. Find the forecast value of the yield for the obligation bonds for each month, starting with June, by using a five-month moving average.

b. Find the forecast value of the yield for the obligation bonds for each month, starting with April, by using a three-month moving average.

c. Evaluate these forecasting methods using MAD.

d. Evaluate these forecasting methods using MSE.

e. Evaluate these forecasting methods using MAPE.

f. Evaluate these forecasting methods using MPE.

g. Forecast the yield for January 1993 using the best model.

h. Write a memo summarizing your findings.

14. 10.51, MSE = .4332, no

14. (This question refers to Exercise 13.) Use exponential smoothing, with a smoothing constant of .3 and an initial value of 9.27, to forecast the yield for January 1993. Is this forecast better than the forecast made using the moving average model? Explain.

15. 292, MSE = 3,855.7

15. The Hughes Supply Company uses an inventory management method to determine monthly demands for various products. Demand values for the past 12 months for each product have been recorded and are available for future forecasting. Demand values for the past 12 months of 1992 for one electrical fixture are:

Month	Demand
Jan.	205
Feb.	251
Mar.	304
Apr.	284
May	352
June	300

Month	Demand
July	241
Aug.	284
Sept.	312
Oct.	289
Nov.	385
Dec.	256

Source: Hughes Supply Company records.

Use exponential smoothing with a smoothing constant of .2 and an initial value of 205 to forecast demand for January 1993.

16. Hugh Miller, analyst for Southdown Inc. (the nation's second largest cement producer) is attempting to forecast the company's quarterly revenues. The data in millions of dollars are:

Quarter:	1	2	3	4
1986	77.4	88.8	92.1	79.8
1987	77.5	89.1	92.4	80.1
1988	74.7	185.2	162.4	178.1
1989	129.1	158.4	160.6	138.7
1990	127.2	149.8	151.7	132.9
1991	103.0	136.8	141.3	123.5

Source: *Southdown Incorporated Annual Report,* various years.

16*a*. 127.2, MSE = 1,297.3, MAD = 24
b. 128.6, MSE = 751.6, MAD = 18.2
c. .1 gave a closer forecast
d. .6

a. Use exponential smoothing with a smoothing constant of .1 and an initial value of 77.4 to forecast earnings per share for first quarter 1992.

b. Use a smoothing constant of .6 and an initial value of 77.4 to forecast earnings per share for the first quarter of 1992.

c. Evaluate the two smoothing constants if actual quarterly revenue for first quarter 1992 is 107.6.

d. Estimate the smoothing constant that will provide the best forecast.

17. General American Investors Co., a closed-end regulated investment management company, invests primarily in medium- and high-quality stocks. Heather Campbell is studying the asset value per share for this company and would like to forecast this variable for first quarter 1992. The data are:

17. Exponential smoothing using $\alpha = .75$ was best. MSE = 7.26, MAPE = 9.95% forecast 29.97

Quarter:	1	2	3	4
1985	16.98	18.47	17.63	20.63
1986	21.95	23.85	20.44	19.29
1987	22.75	23.94	24.84	16.70
1988	18.04	19.19	18.97	17.03
1989	18.23	19.80	22.89	21.41
1990	21.50	25.05	20.33	20.60
1991	25.33	26.06	28.89	30.60

Source: *General American Investors Company Annual Report,* various years.

Evaluate the asset value per share variable using the following forecasting methods: naive, moving average, and exponential smoothing. Note that actual asset value per share for first quarter 1992 was 27.45. Write a report for Heather indicating which method she should use and why.

FORECASTING USING REGRESSION

In Chapters 14 and 15, regression analysis used knowledge of one or more predictor variables to forecast the variable of interest. In Chapter 16, a special case of regression analysis used time as the predictor variable to forecast the trend of the variable of interest. The use of a predictor variable allows the analyst to forecast the value of a dependent variable when there's a significant linear relationship between the dependent and predictor variables. When the dependent variable is in a time series, the regression analysis is known as an *econometric model*.

Econometric Model

In Chapter 16, new passenger car registrations were analyzed using the time series decomposition technique. In that example, the cyclical component seemed to be affected by economic conditions. If this is true, an econometric model might be used to predict new passenger car registrations. If the analyst knows that demand for automobiles (and hence new passenger car registrations) closely follows the pattern of overall economic activity as measured by GNP, then it's possible to derive a prediction equation for new passenger car registrations as a function of the GNP.

For the prediction equation to be useful in forecasting a future value of new passenger car registrations, the analyst must obtain an estimate of the value of the predictor variable, GNP, for the same period in the future. If the value for GNP is unknown and can't be estimated for next year, it cannot be used to forecast new passenger car registrations. This general principle holds true for the predictor variable in any linear regression model used to forecast some future value of the dependent variable.

The essence of econometric model building using regression analysis is the identification and specification of causative factors to be used in a prediction equation. However, recall from Chapter 14 that use of statistical analysis does not allow the analyst to claim cause and effect. In econometric model building, the analyst develops a model based on the theory that the predictor variables influence the behavior of the dependent variable in ways that can be explained on a commonsense basis.

Large-scale econometric models are being used today to model specific firms within an industry, selected industries within the economy, and the total economy. Econometric models include any number of simultaneous multiple linear regression equations. Thus, econometric models are systems of simultaneous equations involving several predictor variables. Further examination of econometric model building is beyond the scope of this text, but many source books are available.

EXAMPLE 17.6 Fred Robnett, economist for Divico Appliance Corporation, must develop a prediction equation to be used during June for forecasting quarterly sales of air conditioners. Fred decides to use as predictor variables disposable personal income, the typical price of an air conditioner unit, and the number of housing starts, lagged one quarter. His rationale for including the last variable is that air conditioners are one of the last items added to the house, so there is a two-quarter lag between a housing start and an air conditioner purchase. The model he develops is

$$\hat{Y} = b_0 + b_1X_1 + b_2X_2 + b_3X_3$$

where $\hat{Y}$ = Forecast of air conditioner sales for next quarter
X_1 = Estimate of disposable personal income for next quarter
X_2 = Housing starts last quarter
X_3 = Price of a typical air conditioner unit this quarter

To forecast air conditioner sales for the third quarter, Fred must obtain the following information: an estimate of disposable personal income for the third quarter, usually supplied by government agencies; the number of housing starts in the first quarter; and the price charged during the present (second) quarter. Fred has the potential for developing a good model. He has to estimate only one of the predictor variables, disposable personal income. Fred will have actual data on both the second-quarter price of a typical air conditioner and the number of housing starts during the first quarter.

In Chapter 16, a *multiplicative* time series model was described, in which the seasonal fluctuation is proportional to the trend level for each observation. This section introduces an *additive* time series model, in which a constant amount is added to the time series trend estimate corresponding to the expected increase in the value of the dependent variable due to seasonal factors. In the multiplicative model, the trend estimate is multiplied by a fixed percentage. In the additive model, a constant amount is *added* to the trend estimate. Equation 17.9 is used to regress quarterly data using this method:

$$\hat{Y}_t = b_0 + b_1S_1 + b_2S_2 + b_3S_3 \quad (17.9)$$

where $\hat{Y}$ = The forecast Y value
S_1 = 1 if first quarter of the year; 0 otherwise
S_2 = 1 if second quarter of the year; 0 otherwise
S_3 = 1 if third quarter of the year; 0 otherwise
b_0 = Constant
b_1, b_2, b_3 = Regression coefficients

The variables S_1, S_2, and S_3 are dummy variables representing the first, second, and third quarter, respectively. Note that the four levels of the qualitative variable have been described with only three dummy variables. This is because the fourth quarter's mean will be accounted for by the intercept b_0. If S_1, S_2, and S_3 are all 0, the fourth quarter is represented by b_0.

EXAMPLE 17.7 Washington Water Power Company forecaster Dana Byrnes is trying to forecast electrical usage for residential customers for the third and fourth quarters of 1992. She knows that the data are seasonal and decides to use Equation 17.9 to develop a seasonal regression model. She gathers quarterly data from 1980 through the first two quarters of 1992. Table 17.4 shows electrical usage measured in millions of kilowatt-hours.

TABLE 17.4 Electrical Usage for Washington Water Power Company, 1980–1992 (Example 17.7)

Year	Quarter	Kilowatts (millions)	Year	Quarter	Kilowatts (millions)
1980	1	1,071	1987	1	933
	2	648		2	582
	3	480		3	490
	4	746		4	708
1981	1	965	1988	1	953
	2	661		2	604
	3	501		3	508
	4	768		4	758
1982	1	1,065	1989	1	1,054
	2	667		2	635
	3	486		3	538
	4	780		4	752
1983	1	926	1990	1	969
	2	618		2	655
	3	483		3	568
	4	757		4	752
1984	1	1,047	1991	1	1,085
	2	667		2	692
	3	495		3	568
	4	794		4	783
1985	1	1,068	1992	1	928
	2	625		2	655
	3	499		3	
	4	850		4	
1986	1	975			
	2	623			
	3	496			
	4	728			

Source: *Washington Water Power Annual Report*, various years.

Dana creates dummy variables S_1, S_2, and S_3, representing the first, second, and third quarters, respectively. She stores the data in a file called USAGE.DAT. The data for the four quarters of 1980 are:

Y_t	S_1	S_2	S_3
1071	1	0	0
648	0	1	0
480	0	0	1
746	0	0	0

Dana uses the following MINITAB commands to develop her regression equation and forecast the third and fourth quarters of 1992:

```
MTB > READ 'USAGE.DAT' C1-C4
  ROW      C1      C2     C3     C4

    1    1071       1      0      0
    2     648       0      1      0
    3     480       0      0      1
    4     746       0      0      0
  .  .  .

MTB > NAME C1 'USAGE' C2 'S1' C3 'S2' C4 'S3'
MTB > REGRESS C1 3 PREDICTORS C2-C4
SUBC> PREDICT 0 0 1;
SUBC> PREDICT 0 0 0.
      THE OUTPUT IS SHOWN IN TABLE 17.5
MTB > STOP
```

TABLE 17.5 MINITAB Output for Seasonal Regression Model for WWP (Example 17.7)

```
The regression equation is
USAGE = 765 + 238 S1 - 124 S2 - 255 S3

Predictor        Coef      Stdev     t ratio       P
Constant       764.67      12.18       62.79   0.000
S1             238.33      16.89       14.11   0.000
S2            -123.74      16.89       -7.33   0.000
S3            -255.33      17.22      -14.82   0.000

s = 42.19     R-sq = 95.3%     R-sq(adj) = 95.0%

Analysis of Variance

SOURCE        DF         SS         MS          F        P
Regression     3    1670269     556756     312.81    0.000
Error         46      81872       1780
Total         49    1752141

SOURCE        DF     SEQ SS
S1             1    1278969
S2             1        130
S3             1     391171

Unusual Observations
Obs.      S1      USAGE          Fit    Stdev.Fit    Residual    St.Resid
 24     0.00     850.00       764.67        12.18       85.33       2.11R
 45     1.00    1085.00      1003.00        11.70       82.00       2.02R

R denotes an obs. with a large st. resid.

Fit       Stdev.Fit          95% C.I.             95% P.I.
509.33        12.18    (484.81, 533.85)     (420.93, 597.74)

764.67        12.18    (740.15, 789.19)     (676.26, 853.07)
```

The seasonal regression model is

$$\hat{Y} = b_0 + b_1 S_1 + b_1 S_2 + b_3 S_3$$

```
USAGE = 764.67 + 238.33 S1 - 123.74 S2 - 255.33 S3
```

Dana notes that this model explains 95.3% of the dependent variable. The third- and fourth-quarter predictions are

```
USAGE = 764.67 + 238.33(0) - 123.74(0) - 255.33(1) (Third quarter)  = 509.34
USAGE = 764.67 + 238.33(0) - 123.74(0) - 255.33(0) (Fourth quarter) = 764.67
```

Note that the constant, 764.67, is the forecast for the fourth quarter. This value is also the average or mean of fourth-quarter electrical usage.

EXERCISES

18. Describe how econometric models are developed and give an example.
19. Explain the difference between a multiplicative model and an additive model.
20. Explain how dummy variables are used in a regression model to represent seasonality.
21. The following multiple regression equation was used to forecast quarterly sales data measured in thousands of units:

$$\hat{Y}_t = 1.2 + 2.1t + 4S_1 - 2S_2 + 0.8S_3$$

where $\hat{Y}_t$ = Forecast Y value for time period t
t = Time or trend effect
S_1 = 1 if first quarter of the year; 0 otherwise
S_2 = 1 if second quarter of the year; 0 otherwise
S_3 = 1 if third quarter of the year; 0 otherwise

21*a*. 2.1 *b*. 1.2 *c*. 4 *d*. 41.2 *e*. 47.4

a. What is the average growth in sales each quarter if seasonal effects are held constant?

b. What is the forecast for the fourth quarter if the value for the trend is 0?

c. How much are first-quarter sales ahead of fourth-quarter sales on average if the trend effect is held constant?

d. Forecast sales for period 20 (a second quarter).

e. Forecast sales for period 22 (a fourth quarter).

22. Dibrell Brothers, Inc., one of the top three U.S. tobacco dealers, purchases and processes leaf tobacco worldwide for sale to cigarette manufacturers. Hershel Roberts has the task of predicting 1993 sales. Quarterly 1985–92 data in millions of dollars are:

Quarter:	1	2	3	4
1985	59.2	182.0	70.6	69.9
1986	58.7	131.4	85.3	66.8
1987	56.7	125.4	75.7	50.3
1988	93.2	192.1	163.8	105.9
1989	103.2	234.1	184.7	163.0
1990	132.0	220.4	242.4	170.6
1991	161.7	301.6	313.6	226.1
1992	219.3	299.9	264.4	

Source: *Dibrell Brothers Incorporated Annual Report*, various years.

22*a*. $\hat{Y} = 43 + 7.04t$, $r^2 = 63.5\%$, 268.26
b. $\hat{Y} = 122 - 11.3 S_1 + 89.1 S_2 + 53.3S_3$. $R^2 = 26.7\%$, 121.8
c. $\hat{Y} = 11.8 + 6.88t - 4.4 S_1 + 89.1 S_2 + 46.4 S_3$. $R^2 = 86.9\%$, 231.82.
d. Q1 234.3 Q2 334.6 Q3 298.8 Q4 259.3

a. Develop a regression model that uses time or the trend to predict sales. Evaluate the model's accuracy. Forecast fourth-quarter sales.

b. Develop a multiple regression model that uses dummy variables to model the seasonal effect. Evaluate the model's accuracy. Forecast fourth-quarter sales.

c. Develop a multiple regression model that uses both trend and seasonality. Evaluate the model's accuracy. Forecast fourth-quarter sales.

d. Forecast sales for each quarter of 1993 using the best model.

23. $\hat{Y} = 49.2 - 29.5\ S_1 - 30.2\ S_2 - 17.8\ S_3$. $R^2 = 70.3\%$. Q2 = 19.03 Q3 = 31.43 Q4 = 49.23

23. National Presto manufactures small electrical appliances and housewares. It appears that there's a strong seasonal effect in its business. Develop a multiple regression model using dummy variables to forecast sales for the second, third, and fourth quarters of 1992. Write a report summarizing your results. Quarterly sales (in millions of dollars) are:

Quarter	1	2	3	4
1985	16.3	17.7	28.1	34.3
1986	17.3	16.7	32.2	42.3
1987	17.4	16.9	30.9	36.5
1988	17.5	16.5	28.6	45.5
1989	24.3	24.2	33.8	45.2
1990	20.6	18.7	28.1	59.6
1991	19.5	22.5	38.3	81.2
1992	24.9			

Source: *The Value Line Investment Survey* (New York: Value Line, 1988, 1989, 1992), p. 133.

AUTOCORRELATION

Autocorrelation Coefficient

Recall that one underlying assumption of a regression model is that error terms are independent. With time series data, as discussed in Chapter 16, this assumption is questionable. When a variable is measured over time, it is frequently correlated with *itself,* when "lagged" one or more periods. This correlation between time series residuals is measured using the **autocorrelation** coefficient. Correlation between successive residuals is called *first-order autocorrelation.*

> **Autocorrelation** is the correlation between a variable, lagged one or more periods, and itself.

Autocorrelation is illustrated by Table 17.6. Note that variables Y_{t-1} and Y_{t-2} are actually the Y values lagged by one and two periods, respectively. Y_t values for March (shown on the row for time period 3) are: March sales, $Y_t = 67$; February sales, $Y_{t-1} = 62$; and January sales, $Y_{t-2} = 54$.

Equation 17.10 is commonly used to compute the first-order autocorrelation coefficient, r_1 (the correlation between Y_t and Y_{t-1}):

$$r_1 = \frac{\sum_{t=1}^{n-1} (Y_t - \bar{Y})(Y_{t-1} - \bar{Y})}{\sum_{t=1}^{n} (Y_t - \bar{Y})^2} \qquad (17.10)$$

TABLE 17.6 Wagner Florist Shop Monthly Sales (Example 17.8)

Time, t	Month	Original data, Y_t	Y lagged one period, Y_{t-1}	Y lagged two periods, Y_{t-2}
1	January	54	—	—
2	February	62	54	—
3	March	67	62	54
4	April	69	67	62
5	May	73	69	67
6	June	73	73	69
7	July	78	73	73
8	August	81	78	73
9	September	84	81	78
10	October	87	84	81
11	November	91	87	84
12	December	93	91	87

where r_1 = First-order autocorrelation coefficient
$\bar{Y}$ = Mean of the values of the series
Y_t = Observation at time period t
Y_{t-1} = Observation one time period earlier, or at time period $t - 1$

Equation 17.11 is the formula for computing the order k autocorrelation coefficient, r_k, between observations that are k periods apart: Y_t and Y_{t-k}:

$$r_k = \frac{\sum_{t=1}^{n-k} (Y_t - \bar{Y})(Y_{t-k} - \bar{Y})}{\sum_{t=1}^{n} (Y_t - \bar{Y})^2} \tag{17.11}$$

where r_k = Autocorrelation coefficient for a lag of k periods
$\bar{Y}$ = Mean of the values of the series
Y_t = Observation at time period t
Y_{t-k} = Observation k time periods earlier, or at time period $t - k$

EXAMPLE 17.8 Clara Wagner has collected monthly sales data for the last year for Wagner's Florist Shop (Table 17.6). Table 17.7 shows the computations that lead to the use of Equation 17.10.

The first-order autocorrelation coefficient, r_1 (the correlation between Y_t and Y_{t-1}) is computed using the summations from Table 17.7:

$$r_1 = \frac{\sum_{t=1}^{n-1} (Y_t - \bar{Y})(Y_{t-1} - \bar{Y})}{\sum_{t=1}^{n} (Y_t - \bar{Y})^2}$$

$$= \frac{1{,}079}{1{,}556} = .69$$

TABLE 17.7 Computations for the First-Order Autocorrelation (Example 17.8)

t	Y_t	Y_{t-1}	$(Y_t - \bar{Y})$	$(Y_{t-1} - \bar{Y})$	$(Y_t - \bar{Y})^2$	$(Y_t - \bar{Y})(Y_{t-1} - \bar{Y})$
1	54	—	−22	—	484	—
2	62	54	−14	−22	196	308
3	67	62	−9	−14	81	126
4	69	67	−7	−9	49	63
5	73	69	−3	−7	9	21
6	73	73	−3	−3	9	9
7	78	73	2	−3	4	−6
8	81	78	5	2	25	10
9	84	81	8	5	64	40
10	87	84	11	8	121	88
11	91	87	15	11	225	165
12	93	91	17	15	289	255
Sums:	912		0		1,556	1,079

$$\bar{Y} = \frac{912}{12} = 76$$

It appears that some autocorrelation exists in this time series lagged one time period. The correlation between Y_t and Y_{t-1} (the autocorrelation for lag 1) is .69. This means that the successive residuals for the monthly sales variable are somewhat correlated with each other. This information may give Clara valuable insights about her time series, may suggest use of an advanced forecasting method, and can warn her about using regression analysis with her data. The last situation will be discussed later in the chapter.

The second-order autocorrelation coefficient, r_2, or the correlation between Y_t and Y_{t-2}, is computed using Equation 17.11. The computations are shown in Table 17.8.

TABLE 17.8 Computations for the Second-Order Autocorrelation (Example 17.8)

t	Y_t	Y_{t-2}	$(Y_t - \bar{Y})$	$(Y_{t-2} - \bar{Y})$	$(Y_t - \bar{Y})^2$	$(Y_t - \bar{Y})(Y_{t-2} - \bar{Y})$
1	54	—	−22	—	484	—
2	62	—	−14	—	196	—
3	67	54	−9	−22	81	198
4	69	62	−7	−14	49	98
5	73	67	−3	−9	9	27
6	73	69	−3	−7	9	21
7	78	73	2	−3	4	−6
8	81	73	5	−3	25	−15
9	84	78	8	2	64	16
10	87	81	11	5	121	55
11	91	84	15	8	225	120
12	93	87	17	11	289	187
Sums:	912		0		1,556	701

$$r_2 = \frac{\sum_{t=1}^{n-2} (Y_t - \bar{Y})(Y_{t-2} - \bar{Y})}{\sum_{t=1}^{n} (Y_t - \bar{Y})^2}$$

$$= \frac{701}{1{,}556} = .45$$

It appears that moderate autocorrelation exists in this time series lagged two time periods. The correlation between Y_t and Y_{t-2} (the autocorrelation for lag 2) is .45. Note that the autocorrelation coefficient at lag 2 (.45) is less than the autocorrelation coefficient at lag 1 (.69). The denominator is the same for both computations; however, one fewer term is included in the numerator when the autocorrelation for lag 2 is computed. Generally, as the number of time lags, k, increases, the autocorrelation coefficient decreases.

Correlogram

Figure 17.1 shows a correlogram for the Wagner data in Example 17.8. The **correlogram** is a useful graphical tool for displaying autocorrelations for various lags of a time series. The vertical scale on the left shows the number of lagged time periods. The vertical scale on the right shows the autocorrelation coefficients (the correlations between Y_t and Y_{t-k}) corresponding to the number of lagged periods on the left. The horizontal scale at the bottom shows the possible range for an autocorrelation coefficient, -1 to $+1$. The autocorrelation coefficient for a particular time lag is shown relative to this horizontal scale. A vertical line is placed above 0 in the middle of the correlogram. Patterns in a correlogram are used to analyze patterns in the data. This concept is demonstrated in the next section.

TM

FIGURE 17.1 Autocorrelations for Example 17.8

```
TIME LAG                                                         AUTOCORRELATION
   6              .     *    I          .                            -0.23
   5              .         *I          .                            -0.07
   4              .          I*         .                             0.07
   3              .          I    *     .                             0.26
   2              .          I        * .                             0.45
   1              .          I          . *                           0.69
          I.I.I.I.I.I.I.I.I.I.I.I.I.I.I.I.I.I.I.I.I
         -1                  0                   +1
```

The **correlogram** is a graphical tool for displaying the autocorrelations for various lags of a time series.

The MINITAB computer package can be used to compute autocorrelations and draw correlograms. The MINITAB commands to solve Example 17.8 are:

```
MTB > SET C1
DATA> 54 62 67 69 73 73 78 81 84 87 91 93
DATA> END
MTB > ACF C1

          -1.0  -0.8  -0.6  -0.4  -0.2  0.0  0.2  0.4  0.6  0.8  1.0
          +----+----+----+----+----+----+----+----+----+----+
 1   0.693                              XXXXXXXXXXXXXXXXXX
 2   0.451                              XXXXXXXXXXXX
 3   0.259                              XXXXXXX
 4   0.073                              XXX
 5  -0.069                            XXX
 6  -0.231                        XXXXXXX
 7  -0.307                      XXXXXXXXX
 8  -0.375                     XXXXXXXXXX
 9  -0.389                    XXXXXXXXXXX
10  -0.365                     XXXXXXXXXX
11  -0.240                        XXXXXXX

MTB> STOP
```

Note that the MINITAB correlogram differs from Figure 17.1. The autocorrelation scale is shown on the top of the graph instead of at the bottom. The number of lags and their autocorrelation coefficients appear on the left.

Chapter 16 showed how to decompose a time series into its components, including trend, cyclical, seasonal, and irregular. Now data patterns, including some of these components, will be studied using the autocorrelation analysis approach. Autocorrelation coefficients for different time lags of a variable will be used to answer the following questions about a time series data collection:

1. Are the data random?
2. Do the data have a trend (i.e., are they nonstationary)?
3. Are the data seasonal?

If a series is random, the correlation between Y_t and Y_{t-1} is close to 0, indicating that the successive values of a time series are not related to each other.

If a series has a trend, Y_t and Y_{t-1} will be highly correlated; the autocorrelation coefficients will typically differ significantly from 0 for the first several time lags and then gradually drop toward 0 as the number of time lags increases. The autocorrelation coefficient for time lag 1 will be quite large (close to 1). The autocorrelation coefficient for time lag 2 will also be large. However, it won't be as large as for time lag 1 because one fewer term is used to calculate its numerator.

If a series has a seasonal pattern, a significant autocorrelation coefficient will occur at the appropriate time lag, which is 4 for quarterly data and 12 for monthly data.

Table 17.9 shows a time series of 40 three-digit random numbers selected from a random number table. The autocorrelations computed from these data should theoretically equal 0. Of course, the 40 values in Table 17.9 constitute only one of a large number of possible samples of size 40, each of which will produce a different autocorrelation coefficient. Most of these samples will produce autocorrelation coefficients

TABLE 17.9 Time Series with 40 Selected Random Numbers (Example 17.9)

t	Y_t	t	Y_t
1	269	21	465
2	219	22	675
3	058	23	950
4	030	24	013
5	554	25	617
6	221	26	536
7	264	27	767
8	903	28	591
9	082	29	357
10	172	30	961
11	333	31	860
12	602	32	155
13	466	33	491
14	875	34	268
15	119	35	556
16	869	36	183
17	446	37	018
18	505	38	865
19	484	39	191
20	632	40	713

close to 0. But a sample could produce an autocorrelation coefficient significantly different from 0 just by chance.

How does an analyst determine whether an autocorrelation coefficient for the data of Table 17.9 is significantly different from 0? A sampling distribution of autocorrelation coefficients could theoretically be developed by taking an infinite number of samples of 40 random numbers.

Quenouille[2] and others have demonstrated that the autocorrelation coefficients of random data have a sampling distribution that can be approximated by a normal curve with a mean of 0 and standard deviation of $1/\sqrt{n}$. Knowing this, the analyst can compare the sample autocorrelation coefficients with this theoretical sampling distribution and determine if they come from a population whose mean is 0 at particular time lags.

Autocorrelation Hypothesis Test

Actually, the autocorrelation coefficients for all time lags can be tested simultaneously. If the series is truly random, most of the sample autocorrelation coefficients should lie within the range specified by 0 plus or minus a certain number of standard errors. At a specified confidence level, a series can be considered random if the calculated autocorrelation coefficients are all within the interval produced by Equation 17.12:

$$0 \pm z(1/\sqrt{n}) \tag{17.12}$$

[2]M. H. Quenouille, "The Joint Distribution of Serial Correlation Coefficients," *Annuals of Mathematical Statistics* 20 (1949), pp. 561–71.

where z = Standard normal value for a given confidence level
n = Number of observations in the data series

This procedure is illustrated in Example 17.9.

EXAMPLE 17.9 A hypothesis test is developed to determine whether the series presented in Table 17.9 is random. The null and alternative hypotheses to test if the autocorrelation coefficient for a particular time lag is significantly different from 0 are

$$H_0: \rho_k = 0$$
$$H_1: \rho_k \neq 0$$

Since $n = 40$, the standard error (standard deviation of the sampling distribution of autocorrelation coefficients) is $1/\sqrt{40} = .158$. If the null hypothesis is tested at the .05 significance level, the correct standard normal z value is 1.96, and the critical value is $1.96(.158) = .310$. The decision rule is

If an autocorrelation coefficient is less than $-.310$ or greater than .310, reject the null hypothesis (reject H_0 if $r_k < -.310$ or $r_k > .310$).

The autocorrelation coefficients for the data of Table 17.9 are plotted on a correlogram (Figure 17.2). The two dotted lines parallel to the vertical axis are the 95% confidence limits ($-.310$ and .310). Twenty time lags are checked, and all autocorrelation coefficients lie within these limits. The analyst concludes that this series is random.

If a series has a trend, a significant relationship exists between successive time series values. The autocorrelation coefficients typically differ significantly from 0 for the first several time lags and then gradually drop toward 0 as the number of periods increases.

FIGURE 17.2 Autocorrelations for Random Data (Example 17.9)

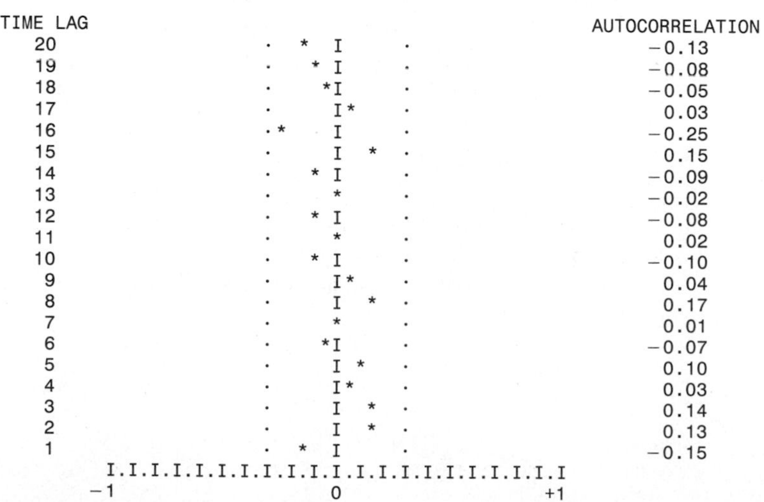

Stationary Series

Some advanced forecasting models, such as the Box-Jenkins models, are designed for use with stationary time series. A **stationary series** is one whose basic statistical properties, such as the mean and the variance, remain constant over time. A series that contains no growth or decline is said to be stationary. A series that contains a trend is said to be nonstationary. The autocorrelation coefficients of stationary data drop to 0 after the second or third time lag, whereas for a nonstationary series they differ significantly from 0 for several time periods. In a nonstationary series, the trend must be removed before any further analysis is undertaken, such as analyzing the series with the Box-Jenkins procedures.

> A **stationary series** is one whose mean and variance do not change over time.

Differencing

A method called *differencing* is used to remove the trend from a nonstationary series. Y_{t-1} is subtracted from Y_t, Y_{t-2} is subtracted from Y_{t-1}, and so forth, thus creating a new series. This process is illustrated in Table 17.10. The differenced series in Table 17.10 has transformed the original series to a new form. In this new form, the mean and variance remain constant over time; in other words, the series is stationary.

TABLE 17.10 Time Series Illustrating Differenced Data

t	Y_t	Y_{t-1}	$Y'_t = Y_t - Y_{t-1}$
1	21		—
2	24	21	3
3	29	24	5
4	38	29	9
5	40	38	2
6	39	40	−1
7	45	39	6
8	50	45	5
9	60	50	10
10	63	60	3
11	70	63	7
12	71	70	1

The MINITAB computer package can be used to difference data. The MINITAB commands to difference the data in Table 17.10 are:

```
MTB > SET C1
DATA> 21 24 29 38 40 39 45 50 60 63 70 71
MTB > END
MTB > DIFFERENCES 1 FOR C1, STORE IN C2
MTB > PRINT C1-C2
```

ROW	C1	C2
1	21	
2	24	3
3	29	5
4	38	9
5	40	2
6	39	−1
7	45	6
8	50	5
9	60	10
10	63	3
11	70	7
12	71	1

```
MTB > STOP
```

The data in column C1 are differenced and stored in column C2. The PRINT command shows the result, which is the same as for Table 17.10.

EXAMPLE 17.10 Jenny Jefferies, a Wall Street analyst, is forecasting the transportation index. She gathers data for a 24-day period from the *Survey of Current Business*. First, Jenny computes a 95% confidence interval for the autocorrelation coefficients:

$$0 \pm 1.96(1/\sqrt{24}) = 0 \pm .40$$

Next, she uses a computer program to compute the autocorrelation coefficients presented in the correlogram in Figure 17.3.

FIGURE 17.3 Autocorrelations for Trend Data (Example 17.10)

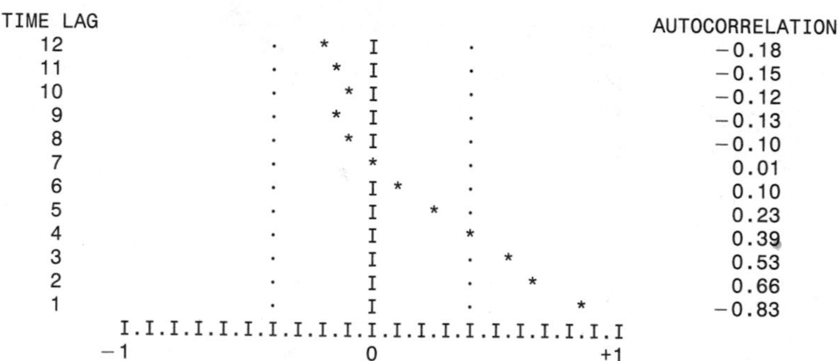

Examining the correlogram, she notices that the autocorrelations for the first three time lags differ significantly from 0: .83, .66, and .53. The values then drop gradually toward 0 rather than dropping exponentially. She decides that a trend exists in the data.

Jenny discovers that the advanced forecasting model she wants to experiment with requires that the series be stationary. She differences the data and uses a computer program to compute the autocorrelation coefficients for the differenced data. The correlogram shown in Figure 17.4 presents the results.

TM

FIGURE 17.4 Autocorrelations for Trend Data Differenced (Example 17.10)

```
TIME LAG                                                  AUTOCORRELATION
  11               .     * I       .                        -0.10
  10               .       I  *    .                         0.14
   9               .    *  I       .                        -0.15
   8               . *     I       .                        -0.23
   7               .       I    *  .                         0.25
   6               .      *I       .                        -0.04
   5               .      *I       .                        -0.06
   4               .       I*      .                         0.07
   3               .       I *     .                         0.12
   2               .       *       .                        -0.02
   1               .       I       .     *                  -0.76
         I.I.I.I.I.I.I.I.I.I.I.I.I.I.I.I.I.I.I.I.I
        -1                 0                    +1
```

Jenny is pleased because the autocorrelations for the differenced data are stationary and show that some pattern exists. (The first correlation coefficient equals .76; the autocorrelations then drop off to 0.) She can now use an appropriate advanced forecasting procedure.

If a series is seasonal, a pattern in the data repeats itself regularly during a particular interval of time (usually a year), and a significant autocorrelation coefficient will occur at the appropriate time lag. If quarterly data are analyzed, a significant autocorrelation coefficient will appear at time lag 4. If monthly data are analyzed, a significant autocorrelation coefficient will appear at time lag 12. That is, Januarys will correlate with other Januarys, Februarys with other Februarys, and so on. Example 17.11 illustrates a series that is seasonal.

EXAMPLE 17.11 Cordella Roberts (analyst for the Outboard Marine Corporation) long felt that sales were seasonal, but her company's absorption of six boat builders between 1986 and 1988 (*The Value Line Investment Survey*, 1988) makes her question this assumption. Cordella gathers 1984–92 quarterly sales data on Outboard Marine Corporation (Table 17.11) and computes a 95% confidence interval for the autocorrelation coefficients:

$$0 \pm 1.96\ 1/\sqrt{34}$$
$$0 \pm .336$$

Next, she uses a computer program to compute the autocorrelation coefficients presented in the correlogram shown in Figure 17.5.

Cordella notes that the autocorrelation coefficient at time lag 4 is significantly different from 0 (.73 > .336). She concludes that Outboard Marine sales are seasonal on a quarterly basis.

If the autocorrelation coefficients of stationary data drop to 0 after the second or third time lag, the series may have a pattern that can be modeled by advanced forecasting techniques, such as the Box-Jenkins models. Example 17.12 illustrates a series with a pattern that might be forecast using such techniques.

TABLE 17.11 Quarterly Sales for Outboard Marine, 1984–1992 (Example 17.11)

Fiscal year ends	Dec. 31	Mar. 31	June 30	Sept. 30
1984	147.6	251.8	273.1	249.1
1985	139.3	221.2	260.2	259.5
1986	140.5	245.5	298.8	287.0
1987	168.8	322.6	393.5	404.3
1988	259.7	401.1	464.6	479.7
1989	264.4	402.6	411.3	385.9
1990	232.7	309.2	310.7	293.0
1991	205.1	234.4	285.4	258.7
1992	193.2	263.7		

Source: *The Value Line Investment Survey* (New York: Value Line, 1988, 1992), p. 1768.

FIGURE 17.5 Autocorrelations for Seasonal Data (Example 17.11)

```
TIME LAG                                                            AUTOCORRELATION
   9                       .  *  I      .                                 -0.21
   8                       .     I     *.                                  0.28
   7                       .    *I      .                                 -0.06
   6                       .   * I      .                                 -0.12
   5                       .     I  *   .                                  0.17
   4                       .     I      .           *                      0.73
   3                       .     I      *                                  0.34
   2                       .     I     *.                                  0.22
   1                       .     I      .*                                 0.45
          I.I.I.I.I.I.I.I.I.I.I.I.I.I.I.I.I.I.I.I.I
         -1                      0                   +1
```

EXAMPLE 17.12 Evelyn Dunning of Central Chemical Corporation is responsible for anticipating the readings of a particular chemical process. Evelyn has gathered the past 75 readings for the process (Table 17.12) and wonders if there's some pattern to the data. First, she computes a 95% confidence interval for the autocorrelation coefficients:

$$0 \pm 1.96(1/\sqrt{75}) = 0 \pm .226$$

TABLE 17.12 Readings for the Cenex Chemical Process (in Sequence by Columns) (Example 17.12)

60	99	75	79	62	89	72	90
81	26	78	65	81	51	66	78
72	93	66	99	76	85	74	87
78	75	97	72	84	59	66	99
62	57	60	78	57	90	73	72
78	88	98	63	84	60	104	
57	77	61	66	74	78	60	
84	82	96	84	78	66	81	
82	72	80	66	49	97	87	
67	77	72	87	78	65	73	

Next, Evelyn uses a computer program to compute the autocorrelation coefficients (the correlogram in Figure 17.6).

FIGURE 17.6 Autocorrelations for Data with a Pattern (Example 17.12)

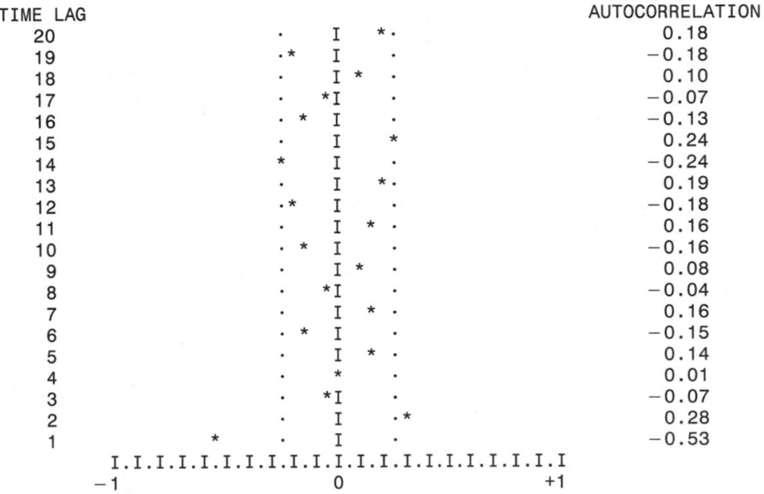

Evelyn notes that the first two autocorrelation coefficients, −.53 for time lag 1 and .28 for time lag 2, are significantly different from 0, and the autocorrelations then drop close to 0. She concludes that the data do have a pattern that might be modeled by an advanced forecasting technique.

EXAMPLE 17.13 Stu Miller (forecaster for Sears, Roebuck) is attempting to forecast 1992 operating revenue. He collects the data shown in Table 17.13 for the years 1955 through 1991. Stu considers regression analysis, but isn't sure that he can find the proper variables to explain the variability in Sears' sales. Instead, Stu decides to use autocorrelation analysis to study the patterns of his variable. Stu runs these data on a computer program that performs autocorrelation analysis (Figure 17.7).

Stu notes that a 95% confidence interval has been computed and is shown in Figure 17.7 by the dotted lines. Computations for the dotted lines are

$$0 \pm 1.96(1/\sqrt{37})$$
$$0 \pm .322$$

Stu examines the correlogram, noticing that the autocorrelations for the first seven time lags are significantly different from 0 (.92, .83, .73, .64, .55, .46, and .37) and the values then gradually drop to 0. He decides that the data have a trend.

Stu first differences the data and uses his computer program to calculate the autocorrelation coefficients in Figure 17.8. He notes that the autocorrelation coefficient at time lag 3, .65, is significantly different from 0 and that the first two autocorrelation

TABLE 17.13 Operating Revenue for Sears, Roebuck and Disposable Personal Income, 1955–1991 (Example 17.13)

Year	Sears sales Y_t	Disposable personal income X_t	Sears sales lagged one period Y_{t-1}
1955	3,307	273.4	—
1956	3,556	291.3	3,307
1957	3,601	306.9	3,556
1958	3,721	317.1	3,601
1959	4,036	336.1	3,721
1960	4,134	349.4	4,036
1961	4,268	362.9	4,134
1962	4,578	383.9	4,268
1963	5,093	402.8	4,578
1964	5,716	437.0	5,093
1965	6,357	472.2	5,716
1966	6,769	510.4	6,357
1967	7,296	544.5	6,769
1968	8,178	588.1	7,296
1969	8,844	630.4	8,178
1970	9,251	685.9	8,844
1971	10,006	776.8	9,251
1972	10,991	839.6	10,006
1973	12,306	949.8	10,991
1974	13,101	1,038.4	12,306
1975	13,639	1,142.8	13,101
1976	14,950	1,252.6	13,639
1977	17,224	1,379.3	14,950
1978	17,946	1,551.2	17,224
1979	17,514	1,729.3	17,946
1980	25,195	1,918.0	17,514
1981	27,357	2,127.6	25,195
1982	30,020	2,261.4	27,357
1983	35,883	2,428.1	30,020
1984	38,828	2,670.6	35,883
1985	40,715	2,841.1	38,828
1986	44,282	3,022.1	40.715
1987	48,440	3,205.9	44,282
1988	50,251	3,477.8	48.440
1989	53,794	3,725.5	50,251
1990	55,972	4,058.8	53,794
1991	57,242	4,218.4	55,972

Sources: Sears Operating Revenue: *Industry Surveys.* Disposable personal income: *Survey of Current Business,* various years.

coefficients and the fourth are close to being significant. After time lag 3, the pattern appears to drop to 0. Stu wonders whether there is some pattern in these data that can be modeled by one of the more advanced forecasting techniques.

EXERCISES

24. Explain the concept of autocorrelation.

TM

FIGURE 17.7 Autocorrelations for Sears, Roebuck Sales (Example 17.13)

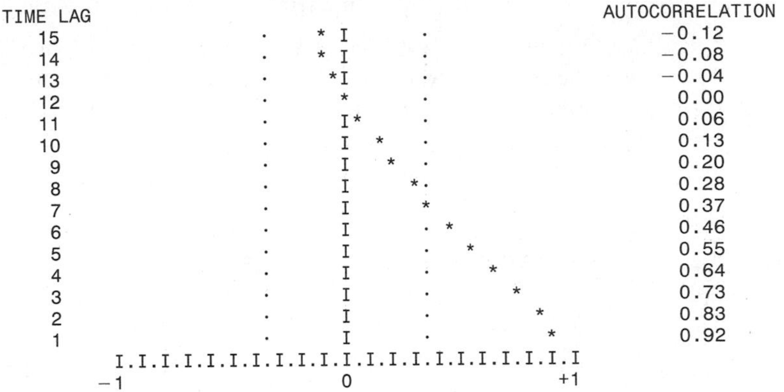

TM

FIGURE 17.8 Autocorrelations for Sears, Roebuck Sales First Differenced (Example 17.13)

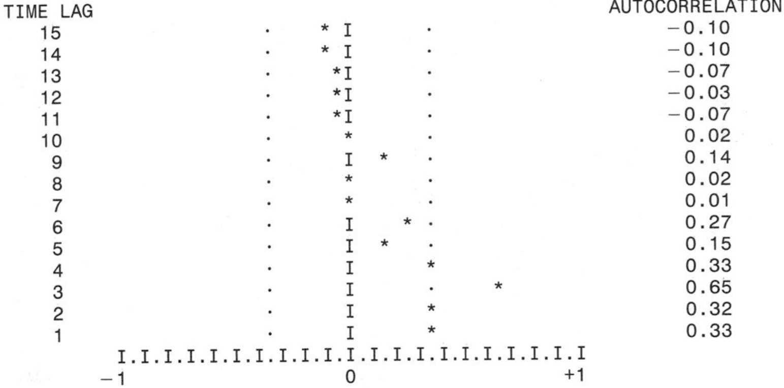

25. What does an autocorrelation coefficient measure?

26. Correlogram

SM

26. Name and describe the graphical tool analysts use to display the autocorrelations for various lags of a time series.

27. *a* and *b* are stationary

27. Each of the following statements describes either a stationary or nonstationary series. Indicate which.
    a. A series whose mean and variance remain constant over time.
    b. A series that contains no growth or decline.
    c. A series that has a trend.
    d. A series whose average value is changing over time.

28. How does an analyst determine whether an autocorrelation coefficient is significantly different from 0?

29. Each of the following statements describes a series that either is random, has a trend, or is seasonal. Identify which.

29*a*. Trend
b. Random
c. Seasonal
d. Trend

a. A high relationship exists between each successive value.

b. Successive values of a time series are not related to each other.

c. A significant autocorrelation coefficient appears at time lag 12.

d. The autocorrelation coefficients are typically significantly different from 0 for the first several time lags, and then gradually drop to 0 as the number of periods increases.

30. 1979 4
−2
−13
−20
−18
−15
1
248
53
549
82
34
35

30. The number of stores owned by Sears has been recorded from 1978 to 1991. Compute the first differences for these data.

Year	Sears stores
1978	862
1979	866
1980	864
1981	851
1982	831
1983	813
1984	798
1985	799
1986	1,047
1987	1,100
1988	1,649
1989	1,731
1990	1,765
1991	1,800

Source: *Statistical Abstract of the United States*, 1988, 1992.

31. Dominion Bank's chief loan officer wants to analyze the bank's loan portfolio from 1984 to 1991. The quarterly data (in millions of dollars) are:

Year	Mar. 31	June 30	Sept. 30	Dec. 31
1984	2313	2495	2609	2792
1985	2860	3099	3202	3161
1986	3399	3471	3545	3851
1987	4458	4850	5093	5318
1988	5756	6013	6158	6289
1989	6369	6568	6646	6861
1990	6836	6918	6782	6680
1991	6424	6283	6130	5939

Source: *The Value Line Investment Survey* (New York: Value Line, 1988, 1992), p. 2017.

31*a*. $r_1 = .942$, $r_2 = .873$
b. $r_1 = .633$

a. Compute the autocorrelations for time lags 1 and 2. Test to determine whether these autocorrelation coefficients are significantly different from 0 at the .05 significance level.

b. First difference the bank's quarterly loan data. Now compute the autocorrelation for time lag 1 using the first differenced data.

32. Trend, random, seasonal

32. Analyze the autocorrelation coefficients for the series in Figures 17.9, 17.10, and 17.11. Briefly describe each series.

FIGURE 17.9 Autocorrelations for Exercise 32

```
TIME LAG                                                    AUTOCORRELATION
  12                  .  *  I     .                             -0.18
  11                  .   * I     .                             -0.15
  10                  .    *I     .                             -0.12
   9                  .   * I     .                             -0.13
   8                  .    *I     .                             -0.10
   7                  .     *     .                              0.01
   6                  .     I*    .                              0.10
   5                  .     I    *.                              0.25
   4                  .     I     .*                             0.45
   3                  .     I     .   *                          0.60
   2                  .     I     .    *                         0.70
   1                  .     I     .        *                     0.85
         I.I.I.I.I.I.I.I.I.I.I.I.I.I.I.I.I.I.I.I.I
        -1                  0                   +1
```

FIGURE 17.10 Autocorrelations for Exercise 32

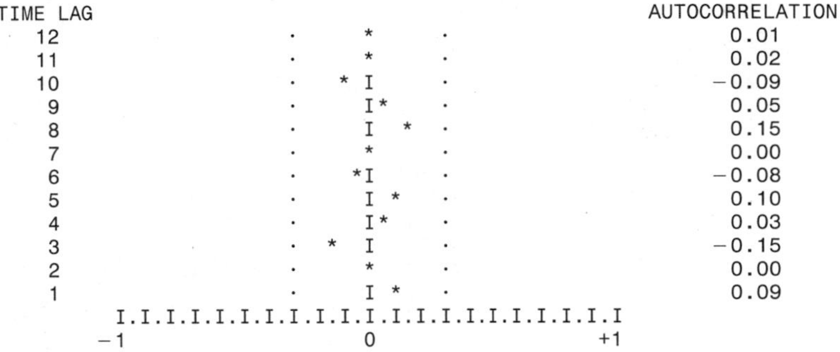

FIGURE 17.11 Autocorrelations for Exercise 32

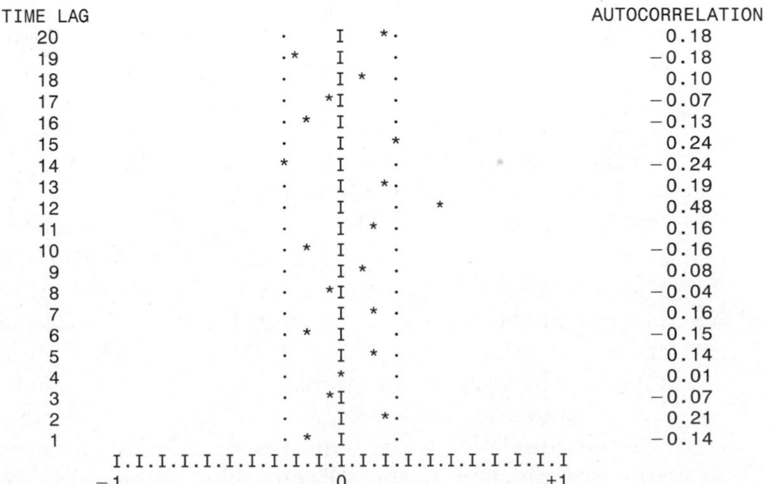

33. 0 ± .196

33. Compute the 95% confidence interval for the autocorrelation coefficients for a series of 100 items.

34. 0 ± .288

34. Compute the 99% confidence interval for the autocorrelation coefficients for a series of 80 items.

35. The Springtime Catering Corporation wants to expand to cater weddings. James Sloan, company analyst, is to analyze the pattern for the number of marriages for the past 20 years. He has 1965–89 data for the number of marriages (in thousands):

Year	Marriages	Year	Marriages
1965	1,800	1978	2,282
1966	1,857	1979	2,342
1967	1,927	1980	2,390
1968	2,069	1981	2,422
1969	2,145	1982	2,456
1970	2,159	1983	2,446
1971	2,190	1984	2,477
1972	2,282	1985	2,413
1973	2,284	1986	2,407
1974	2,230	1987	2,403
1975	2,153	1988	2,389
1976	2,155	1989	2,404
1977	2,178		

Source: U.S. Dept. of Health and Human Services, National Center for Health Statistics, and *Statistical Abstract of the United States.*

a. Compute the autocorrelations through lag 12 and construct a correlogram.

b. Are the data stationary? If not, compute the first differences for these data.

c. Are the first differences random or is there a pattern?

35*a.* 1 .822
2 .623
3 .431
4 .309
5 .220
6 .130
7 .067
8 .069
9 .082
10 .060
11 −.027
12 −.133
b. No
c. 1 .496
2 .168
3 −.096
4 −.074
5 −.217
6 −.238
7 −.399
8 −.172
9 −.002
10 .278
11 .263
12 .250
Pattern

The Problem of Autocorrelation in Regressing Time Series Data

In Chapters 14 and 15, regression analysis procedures used knowledge of linear relationships to predict the dependent variable of interest. In Chapter 16, a special case of regression analysis used time as a predictor variable to forecast the trend of the variable of interest. One of the underlying assumptions of the regression technique is that the error terms are independent of each other, which implies that a random sample has been selected from the population.

When time series variables are analyzed, this assumption of independence is frequently violated because time series are not randomly chosen samples. In most time series, there's some relationship between the value of the dependent variable in one time period and its value in the next. High sales in one month, for example, usually lead to high sales in the next month. A low unemployment rate in one quarter usually is followed by a low rate in the next quarter. For this reason, correlated error terms are likely whenever regression analysis is used to predict a time series variable.

Serial Correlation

Serial correlation is the term used to describe the situation in which each error term is a function of the previous time period's error term. The autocorrelation coefficient is used to measure serial correlation. Recall Equation 14.5: $y_t = \beta_0 + \beta_1 x_t + \varepsilon_t$. This equation indicates that the error term (ε_t) is the difference between an actual population y value and its value as predicted by the population regression line. As mentioned, one of the underlying assumptions of regression analysis is that the error terms are independent. This assumption can be evaluated using Equation 17.13:

$$\varepsilon_t = \rho_1 \varepsilon_{t-1} + v_t \tag{17.13}$$

where ε_t = Error term at time period t
ε_{t-1} = Error term at time period $t - 1$
ρ_1 = First-order autocorrelation coefficient measuring the correlation between successive error terms
v_t = Normally distributed independent disturbance term

For serial correlation to exist, all that's needed is for the level of the error term ε_{t-1} to directly affect the level of the next error term, ε_t. The magnitude of the first-order autocorrelation coefficient, ρ_1, indicates the strength of the serial correlation between successive error terms. If $\rho_1 = 0$, the error terms are independent ($\varepsilon_t = v_t$), and there's no serial correlation.

Serial correlation exists when successive observations over time are related to each other.

It should be reemphasized that the residual is the observed vertical deviation of y from the sample regression line and so is known. This residual is different from the model error term, ε_t. The error term is the vertical deviation of y from the unknown population regression line; hence it is unknown.

A major cause of autocorrelated residuals is a specification error, such as an omitted variable or an incorrect functional form. When the time-sequenced effects of a missing variable are positively related, the residuals tend to be positively autocorrelated because the effects of the missing variable are explained by time.

EXAMPLE 17.14 Chapter 16 forecast the number of new passenger car registrations using the decomposition approach. A linear trend line was fitted to the data, and the two variables (new passenger car registrations and time) were shown to be linearly related. In a technical sense, the number of new passenger cars registered can be thought of as unrelated to time. Instead, time is used as a substitute for variables that the registrations variable is actually related to, but that are ignored, unknown, difficult to measure, or too costly to measure.

The model using a linear trend might appear to be a good one, explaining a large portion of the variance in new passenger car registrations. Unfortunately, serial correlation is a potential problem. The model specification might have left out an important variable, such as the driving-age population, that might have a direct impact on auto registrations. If so, the time variable is explaining variance in new passenger car registrations that should be explained by driving-age population. If there's a shift in the direction of the driving-age population variable, the model using time may provide inaccurate forecasts.

Serial correlation in a time series, since it violates one of the key assumptions in regression analysis (a random sample), creates serious problems. Basically, the entire regression analysis must be considered suspect when autocorrelated residuals are present. More specifically, the following problems can result from regressing an autocorrelated series:

1. The regression coefficients in the regression equation are unreliable; that is, they tend to vary widely from one sample to the next. Interpretations based on the regression coefficients may therefore be misleading.
2. The standard error of estimate may be seriously understated, making R^2 spuriously high. The result is that the regression equation may appear to have much greater predictive power in the population than it really does.
3. Confidence intervals and tests employing the t and F distributions can be misleading. These tests rest on the assumption that a random sample has been taken. When this isn't the case, they may lead to erroneous conclusions about the population.

Because of these potential problems, it is always important to check for autocorrelated residuals when a time series variable is subjected to regression analysis. The following examples examine the possibility of serial correlation.

EXAMPLE 17.15 A study called "Using Segmentation to Improve Sales Forecasts Based on Purchase Intent: Which Intenders Actually Buy" (*Journal of Marketing Research*, November 1992) used segments (a stratification sampling as discussed in Chapter 2) to generate improved forecasts.[3] A sample of 12,116 persons indicated the intensity of their intention to buy cars and personal computers along with demographic characteristics such as income. The purpose of the study was improving the ability of forecasters to determine whether a person who intends to buy a product actually does so. Since the data were collected randomly during a short time period, serial correlation is not a problem.

EXAMPLE 17.16 Y. H. Kim and Fay D. Cobb (1992) investigated the accuracy of different models for forecasting corporate earnings.[4] They collected data on quarterly earnings per share from the first quarter 1981 through the fourth quarter 1991 from the *Industrial Compustat Data File* for 40 firms. Suppose a regression model for quarterly earnings per share for Abbott Laboratories and net profit after taxes pro-

[3] V. Morwitz and D. Schmittlein, "Using Segmentation to Improve Sales Forecasts Based on Purchase Intent: Which Intenders Actually Buy," *Journal of Marketing Research*, (November 1992), p. 291.

[4] Y. H. Kim and F. D. Cobb, "Forecasting Quarterly Earnings Per Share with Time-Series Methods" 1992 Proceedings Decision Sciences Institute, San Francisco, Vol. 3, p. 1145.

duced an r^2 of 97 percent. This value must be regarded as suspect because the dependent variable is a time series and so serial correlation is possible.

DETECTION OF SERIAL CORRELATION

Serial correlation is the condition in which successive values of the dependent variable in a time series are correlated. Another way of stating this condition is that the residuals, $Y - \hat{Y}$, are correlated from one time period to the next. In such a situation, the assumption of a random sample underlying the regression analysis procedure is violated.

Examination of the table of residuals may reveal the correlation, especially if it's strong. When autocorrelated residuals are present, the differences between the Y values and the regression line estimates, $\hat{Y}$, tend to be similar from one time period to the next, and strings of residuals with the same sign appear.

EXAMPLE 17.17 Birch Corporation analyst Arthur MacKelvie wants to predict yearly dollar sales of the company using regression analysis. The company is considering borrowing money to enter the water-selling market, and this projection is part of preparations for a meeting with Birch's banker. This market is of great interest to Birch management after an article on profits from selling water appeared in the *Los Angeles Times* business section, September 10, 1989.

Arthur is using disposable personal income as the predictor variable. Table 17.14 shows the results of this regression run. Arthur is happy with these results. R^2 equals .995, and the computed t value is 56.9. The model looks good until Arthur examines the table of residuals. Correlation exists between successive values of the dependent variable: the residuals are not randomly distributed but follow a definite pattern. The first five residuals are negative, followed by a string of seven positive residuals. The model starts out consistently overestimating Y, and then, beginning with period 6, it consistently underestimates Y.

Durbin-Watson Test

The serial correlation in Table 17.14 is easily detected because it is an extreme example. Many cases aren't so obvious, so a statistical test has been developed. The **Durbin-Watson test** is used to determine whether residuals are autocorrelated. The differences between successive residuals are used to calculate the test statistic. The Durbin-Watson statistic is an important feature of most regression analysis programs.

> The **Durbin-Watson test** detects the presence of autocorrelated residuals (serial correlation) in the regression of a time series.

$$\text{DW} = \frac{\sum_{t=2}^{n} (e_t - e_{t-1})^2}{\sum_{t=1}^{n} e_t^2} \tag{17.14}$$

TABLE 17.14 Table of Residuals for Birch Corporation (Example 17.17)

VARIABLE NO.	MEAN	STANDARD DEVIATION	CORRELATION X VS Y	REGRESSION COEFFICIENT	STD. ERROR OF REG COEF.	COMPUTED T VALUE
2	600.65	232.36	0.998	0.029	0.00051	56.9
DEPENDENT						
1	16.03	6.80				
INTERCEPT			−1.505	R SQUARED		0.9954
STD. ERROR OF ESTIMATE			0.47665	DURBIN-WATSON STATISTIC		0.7218

TABLE OF RESIDUALS

OBSERVATION	OBSERVED VALUE	PREDICTED VALUE	RESIDUAL
1	8.0	8.30671	−0.30671
2	8.2	8.69495	−0.49495
3	8.5	9.08904	−0.58904
4	9.2	9.08904	−0.50206
5	10.2	10.25378	−0.05378
6	11.4	11.25214	0.14786
7	12.8	12.27968	0.52032
8	13.6	13.39480	0.20520
9	14.6	14.39023	0.20977
10	16.4	15.66298	0.73701
11	17.8	16.89778	0.90222
12	18.6	18.51791	0.08209
13	20.0	20.17892	−0.17892
14	21.9	21.88663	0.01337
15	24.9	24.85834	0.04166
16	27.3	27.20825	0.09175
17	29.1	29.92599	−0.82599

where DW = Durbin-Watson statistic
e_t = Residual in current time period
e_{t-1} = Residual in preceding time period

Examining Equation 17.14, we see that if the residuals are autocorrelated, they'll be close to each other from one time period to the next. In this case, a small Durbin-Watson statistic will result since the numerator measures the error differences between adjacent time periods. On the other hand, if the residuals are not autocorrelated, a large Durbin-Watson statistic will result. This is because the error terms tend to vary widely from one time period to the next, resulting in a large numerator.

Appendix E.10 contains the Durbin-Watson table and is consulted once the Durbin-Watson statistic has been computed to see whether autocorrelated residuals are present. Note that there are two tables in Appendix E.10: one for the .05 significance level and one for the .01 level. Additional table listings would be necessary for other significance levels.

The column labeled k in the Durbin-Watson table indicates the number of predictor variables used in the regression. Note that there are two columns of Durbin-Watson values under each k. These values represent the lower limit (d_L) and upper limit (d_U) for the test. Sample size dictates which row to use. The Durbin-Watson statistic is interpreted as follows:

1. If the Durbin-Watson statistic computed from the data is below the lower limit, the residuals are positively autocorrelated.

2. If the test statistic is above the upper limit, the residuals are randomly distributed (no autocorrelation).
3. If the test statistic is between the lower and upper limits, the test is inconclusive. A larger sample is needed to determine whether the residuals are autocorrelated.

EXAMPLE 17.18 Continuing Example 17.17, Birch Corporation analyst Arthur MacKelvie is fairly sure that his residuals were autocorrelated. However, he decides to perform the appropriate hypothesis test.

The null and alternative hypotheses are

$$H_0: \quad \rho_1 \leq 0$$
$$H_1: \quad \rho_1 > 0$$

Arthur decides to use the .05 significance level and consults the Durbin-Watson table in Appendix E.10. Since he uses one predictor variable with a sample size of 17, the critical values are $d_L = 1.13$ and $d_U = 1.38$. The decision rule for the .05 significance level is

> Reject the null hypothesis if the calculated Durbin-Watson statistic is less than 1.13. Fail to reject the null hypothesis if the calculated Durbin-Watson statistic is greater than 1.38. If the calculated Durbin-Watson statistic lies between 1.13 and 1.38, the test is inconclusive.

Since the test statistic computed from the sample data (see Table 17.14) is below the critical value from the table ($0.72 < 1.13$), the null hypothesis is rejected. Arthur concludes that the residuals for Birch Corporation's yearly dollar sales volume are positively autocorrelated. He needs to take steps to correct this problem before a regression equation can be used for forecasting.

EXAMPLE 17.19 Parkins Company analyst Linda Lancaster wants to predict monthly cost of goods sold using regression analysis. She has identified four other variables measured each month as possible predictor variables. A combination of two predictor variables appears to produce an accurate prediction equation, with significant t, F, and R^2 values. The Durbin-Watson test statistic is computed to be 1.08 for the sample of 24 months.

Linda decides to use the .01 significance level and consults the Durbin-Watson table in Appendix E.10. For two predictor variables with a sample size of 24, the critical values are $d_L = 0.96$ and $d_U = 1.30$. The decision rule for the .01 significance level is

> Reject the null hypothesis if the calculated Durbin-Watson statistic is less than 0.96. Fail to reject the null hypothesis if the calculated Durbin-Watson statistic is greater than 1.30. If the calculated Durbin-Watson statistic lies between 0.96 and 1.30, the test is inconclusive.

Since the test statistic computed from the sample data is between the critical values from the table, $0.96 < 1.08 < 1.30$, the test is inconclusive. Linda must now consider the risks associated with having serial correlation in her regression equation. She decides that she can't trust the equation to produce accurate predictions using the present data.

Linda knows that if she can obtain data for three years instead of just two, the Durbin-Watson test might be more conclusive. However, only 24 months of data are available. Linda must find some other solution to her problem of serial correlation.

Solutions to the Problem of Serial Correlation

Analysts usually check for positively autocorrelated residuals when a regression analysis is performed on time series data. If positively autocorrelated residuals are revealed by the Durbin-Watson test, this situation must be corrected before evaluating the regression equation's effectiveness. The appropriate method for removing autocorrelated residuals depends on what caused them in the first place. Serial correlation can be caused by a specification error (such as an omitted variable), or the independent residuals may be correlated in a correctly specified equation.

The solution to the problem of serial correlation begins with an evaluation of the model specification. Is the model's functional form correct? Were any key variables omitted? Are there specification errors with some pattern over time that might have introduced correlation into the residuals? Since a major cause of positively autocorrelated residuals in business is the omission of a key variable, the best approach is to identify this missing variable. Unfortunately, it's not always possible to improve the model specification. The missing variable, even if known, may not be quantifiable.

Example 17.20 Nancy Anderson, analyst for the New England Financial Corporation, has found autocorrelated residuals in several of her regression models. She suspects that business investment in future periods is related to the attitudes of potential investors. However, Nancy has found it extremely difficult to quantify these attitudes. She knows that, whenever possible, her models should be specified in accordance with theoretically sound insight. She also knows that the problem of serial correlation won't be solved by applying any corrective technique to a theoretically unsound model. Nancy must look for another approach to eliminating autocorrelated residuals.

Only after the specification of a time series regression equation has been carefully reviewed should the possibility of some statistical adjustment be considered. Some possible techniques for eliminating serial correlation are:

1. **Autoregressive model.** The creation of an autoregressive model generates a new predictor variable by using the Y variable lagged one or more periods. The knowledge that successive time periods are correlated is incorporated into the model. The autoregressive model is discussed in depth in the next section.
2. **Differences.** Differencing generates new variables that use the actual differences in Y (increase or decrease) from period to period. This approach assumes that the relationship between the error terms as measured by the autocorrelation coefficient equals 1 ($\rho_1 = 1$ in Equation 17.13).
3. **Iterative approach.** The iterative approach also generates new variables that use the actual differences (increase or decrease) from period to period. Where the differencing approach assumes that the relationship between the error terms equals

1, the iterative approach actually estimates the value of the autocorrelation coefficient, ρ_1, in Equation 17.13. This approach has become very popular with the advent of the computer.

AUTOREGRESSIVE MODELS

Autoregressive Model

The creation of an **autoregressive model** generates a new predictor variable by using the Y variable lagged one or more periods. The knowledge that successive time periods are correlated is thus introduced into the model. Equation 17.15 expresses a kth-order autoregressive forecasting model.

> An **autoregressive model** generates a new predictor variable by using the Y variable lagged one or more periods.

$$Y_t = \beta_0 + \beta_1 Y_{t-1} + \cdots + \beta_k Y_{t-k} + \varepsilon_t \qquad (17.15)$$

where Y_t = Forecast Y value for time period t
Y_{t-1} = Y value for time period t lagged one period
Y_{t-k} = Y value for time period t lagged k periods
β_0 = Constant
β_1, β_k = Regression coefficients
ε_t = Random component at time t

A first-order autoregressive time series forecast is made using Equation 17.16:

$$\hat{Y}_t = b_0 + b_1 Y_{t-1} \qquad (17.16)$$

where $\hat{Y}_t$ = Forecast Y for time period t
Y_{t-1} = Y for time period t lagged one period
b_0, b_1 = Point estimates of β_0 and β_1

EXAMPLE 17.21 In Example 17.11, Outboard Marine Corporation analyst Cordella Roberts determined that sales were seasonal. Back in 1989, Cordella had decided to try a fourth-order autoregressive model to predict Outboard's quarterly sales. Cordella noted that a trend was present and included the variable time in her model. Her autoregressive equation was

$$\hat{Y}_t = b_0 + b_1 t + b_2 Y_{t-4}$$

where $\hat{Y}_t$ = Forecast Y for time period t
t = Time as measured by period number
Y_{t-4} = Y lagged four periods
b_0, b_1, b_2 = Point estimates of β_0, β_1, and β_2

When Cordella examined the SAS output in Table 17.15 she found that R^2 for the model was 92.7%. She tested the t values for both variables—both were significantly different from 0. However, the Durbin-Watson statistic of 1.13 was inconclusive at the .01 significance level ($.74 < 1.13 < 1.25$). She knew that a larger sample size was needed. Despite the potential serial correlation problem, Cordella decided to try the fourth-order autoregressive model. Her forecast for the first quarter of 1989 was

$$\begin{aligned} \hat{Y}_t &= b_0 + b_1 t + b_2 Y_{t-4} \\ Y_{21} &= -26.89 + 8.323 t_{21} + .848 Y_{21-4} \\ &= -26.89 + 8.323(21) + .848(2590.7) \\ &= 368.1 \end{aligned}$$

TABLE 17.15 SAS Computer Output for Autoregressive Forecast of Quarterly Sales for Outboard Marine, 1989 (Example 17.21)

```
                    SEASONAL AUTOREGRESSIVE MODEL

Model: MODEL 1
Dependent Variable: YT      SALES
                         Analysis of Variance

                             Sum of            Mean
Source          DF          Squares          Square    F Value     Prob>F

Model            2     140536.84715     70268.42358     82.946     0.0001
Error           13      11013.10285       847.16176
C Total         15     151549.95000

   Root MSE               29.10604        R-square      0.9273
   Dep Mean              292.57500        Adj R-sq      0.9162
   C.V.                    9.94823

                          Parameter Estimates
                     Parameter        Standard    T for H0:
Variable    DF        Estimate           Error    Parameter=0    Prob > |T|

INTERCEP     1      -26.892104     25.88135856         -1.039        0.3177
YT4          1        0.848400      0.11656553          7.278        0.0001
XT           1        8.322962      1.95951922          4.247        0.0010

DURBIN-WATSON D                1.128
(For Number of Obs.)              16
1st Order Autocorrelation      0.286
```

Outboard Marine sales were actually 264.4 for first quarter 1989, showing a forecasting error of 103.7. Cordella was disappointed and decided to use another model.

In 1992, Cordella has a large enough sample (Table 17.16) to give the model another try. She runs the data on SAS. (The instructions appear at the end of this chapter.)

Cordella examines the SAS output, shown in Table 17.17, noting that the model's R^2 is only 64.2%. She tests the t values and finds that the t value (-1.699) for the time variable coefficient isn't significantly different from 0. She also notes that serial correlation is still a problem since the Durbin-Watson statistic, 0.41, is significant at the .01 significance level ($0.41 < 1.07$). Cordella concludes that this fourth-order autoregressive model won't work for her data.

TABLE 17.16 Quarterly Sales for Outboard Marine, 1984–1992 (Example 17.21)

Year	Quarter	Time	Sales	Sales lagged 4 periods
1984	1	1	147.6	—
	2	2	251.8	—
	3	3	273.1	—
	4	4	249.1	—
1985	1	5	139.3	147.6
	2	6	221.2	251.8
	3	7	260.2	273.1
	4	8	259.5	249.1
1986	1	9	140.5	139.3
	2	10	245.5	221.2
	3	11	298.8	260.2
	4	12	287.0	259.5
1987	1	13	168.8	140.5
	2	14	322.6	245.5
	3	15	393.5	298.8
	4	16	404.3	287.0
1988	1	17	259.7	168.8
	2	18	401.1	322.6
	3	19	464.6	393.5
	4	20	479.7	404.3
1989	1	21	264.4	259.7
	2	22	402.6	401.1
	3	23	411.3	464.6
	4	24	385.9	479.7
1990	1	25	232.7	264.4
	2	26	309.2	402.6
	3	27	310.7	411.3
	4	28	293.0	385.9
1991	1	29	205.1	232.7
	2	30	234.4	309.2
	3	31	285.4	310.7
	4	32	258.7	293.0
1992	1	33	193.2	205.1
	2	34	263.7	234.4
	3			
	4			

Source: *The Value Line Investment Survey* (New York: Value Line, 1988, 1992), p. 1768.

EXAMPLE 17.22 Sears forecaster Stu Miller is still attempting to forecast yearly sales for 1992. He tried several sophisticated forecasting techniques, but couldn't find one that produced accurate forecasts. Stu has decided that regression analysis might be his best approach. He has chosen disposable personal income (Table 17.13) as his predictor variable and uses MINITAB to develop a regression analysis using disposable personal income to predict operation revenue:

TABLE 17.17 SAS Computer Output for Autoregressive Forecast of Outboard Marine's Quarterly Sales, 1992 (Example 17.21)

```
                        SEASONAL AUTOREGRESSIVE MODEL
Model: MODEL1
Dependent Variable: YT       SALES
                             Analysis of Variance
                                Sum of            Mean
Source              DF         Squares          Square    F Value    Prob>F
Model                2    151160.00562     75580.00281     24.246    0.0001
Error               27     84165.78238      3117.25120
C Total             29    235325.78800
   Root MSE                   55.83235       R-square      0.6423
   Dep Mean                  293.22000       Adj R-sq      0.6159
   C.V.                       19.04111
                                   Parameter Estimates
                      Parameter        Standard      T for HO:
Variable      DF       Estimate           Error    Parameter=0      Prob > |T|
INTERCEP       1      91.832977     35.81219998          2.564          0.0162
YT4            1       0.839530      0.12219363          6.870          0.0001
XT             1      -2.182468      1.28425647         -1.699          0.1007
Durbin-Watson D              0.410
(For Number of Obs.)            30
1st Order Autocorrelation    0.755
```

```
MTB > READ 'SEARS.DAT' C1-C2
     37 ROWS READ
 ROW       C1       C2
   1     3307    273.4
   2     3556    291.3
   3     3601    306.9
   4     3721    317.1
 . . .
MTB > NAME C1 'REVENUE' C2 'INCOME'
MTB > REGRESS C1 1 PREDICTOR C2;
SUBC> RESIDS C3;
SUBC> DW.
The regression equation is
REVENUE = -1201 + 14.4 INCOME
Predictor         Coef       Stdev     t ratio         P
Constant       -1201.0       444.8       -2.70     0.011
INCOME         14.3681      0.2366       60.72     0.000
s = 1729    R-sq = 99.1%    R-sq(adj) = 99.0%
Analysis of Variance
SOURCE         DF            SS             MS          F         P
Regression      1   11018152960    11018152960    3687.22     0.000
Error          35     104587136        2988204
Total          36   11122740224
```

```
Unusual Observations

Obs.      INCOME    REVENUE       Fit    Stdev.Fit   Residual    St.Resid
 25         1729      17514     23646          292      -6132      -3.60R
 33         3206      48440     44862          504       3578       2.16R
 37         4218      57242     59409          715      -2167      -1.38 X

R denotes an obs. with a large st. resid.
X denotes an obs. whose X-value gives it large influence.

Durbin-Watson statistic = 0.65

MTB > NAME C3 'RESIDUAL'
MTB > PRINT C1-C3

ROW   REVENUE    INCOME    RESIDUAL
  1      3307     273.4      579.77
  2      3556     291.3      571.58
  3      3601     306.9      392.44
  4      3721     317.1      365.89
  5      4036     336.1      407.89
  6      4134     349.4      314.80
  7      4268     362.9      254.83
  8      4578     383.9      263.10
  9      5093     402.8      506.54
 10      5716     437.0      638.16
 11      6357     472.2      773.40
 12      6769     510.4      636.54
 13      7296     544.5      673.59
 14      8178     588.1      929.14
 15      8844     630.4      987.37
 16      9251     685.9      596.94
 17     10006     776.8       45.89
 18     10991     839.6      128.57
 19     12306     949.8     -139.79
 20     13101    1038.4     -617.80
 21     13639    1142.8    -1579.83
 22     14950    1252.6    -1846.44
 23     17224    1379.3    -1392.88
 24     17946    1551.2    -3140.75
 25     17514    1729.3    -6131.70
 26     25195    1918.0    -1161.96
 27     27357    2127.6    -2011.51
 28     30020    2261.4    -1270.95
 29     35883    2428.1     2196.89
 30     38828    2670.6     1657.63
 31     40715    2841.1     1094.88
 32     44282    3022.1     2061.25
 33     48440    3205.9     3578.41
 34     50251    3477.8     1482.73
 35     53794    3725.5     1466.75
 36     55972    4058.8    -1144.13
 37     57242    4218.4    -2167.27
```

The data to run this analysis were stored in a data file called SEARS.DAT. The READ command is used to enter the data into the worksheet. The RESIDS subcommand is used to store the residuals in C3. The DW subcommand is used to compute the Durbin-Watson statistic.

Stu is pleased when he examines the results. R^2 is high (99.1 percent) and the t and F values are both significant. However, Stu notices that the first 18 residuals in the printout of residuals are positive, followed by a string of 10 negative residuals. He decides to test for serial correlation.

The null and alternative hypotheses are

$$H_0: \rho_1 \leq 0$$
$$H_1: \rho_1 > 0$$

Stu decides to use the .01 significance level and consults the Durbin-Watson table in Appendix E.10. For one predictor variable with a sample size of 37, the critical values are $d_L = 1.22$ and $d_U = 1.32$. The decision rule is

> Reject the null hypothesis if the calculated Durbin-Watson statistic is less than 1.22. Fail to reject the null hypothesis if the calculated Durbin-Watson statistic is greater than 1.32. If the calculated Durbin-Watson statistic lies between 1.22 and 1.32, the test is inconclusive.

Stu examines the computer output and finds that the Durbin-Watson statistic computed from the sample data is below the critical value from the table, $.65 < 1.22$. He rejects the null hypothesis and concludes that the residuals for Sears' operating revenue predicted by disposable personal income are positively autocorrelated.

Stu decides to develop an autoregressive model using disposable personal income and Sears sales lagged one period (Table 17.13). The MINITAB commands to lag the operating revenue variable and run the regression analysis are:

```
MTB > LAG 1 DATA IN C1, PUT IN C4
MTB > NAME C4 'REVLAG'
MTB > REGRESS C1 2 PREDICTORS C2 C4;
SUBC> RESIDS C3;
SUBC> DW.

The regression equation is
REVENUE = -256 + 5.58 INCOME + 0.650 REVLAG

36 cases used 1 cases contain missing values

Predictor        Coef      Stdev    t ratio        P
Constant       -256.2      378.4      -0.68    0.503
INCOME          5.579      1.576       3.54    0.001
REVLAG         0.6495     0.1155       5.62    0.000

s = 1270       R-sq = 99.5%  R-sq(adj) = 99.5%

Analysis of Variance

SOURCE        DF            SS            MS          F        P
Regression     2   10797421568    5398710784    3346.19    0.000
Error         33      53241960       1613393
Total         35   10850663424

SOURCE        DF        SEQ SS
INCOME         1   10746431488
REVLAG         1      50990308

Unusual Observations
Obs.    INCOME    REVENUE      Fit    Stdev.Fit    Residual    St.Resid
25        1729      17514    21047          508       -3533     -3.04R
26        1918      25195    21819          836        3376      3.53RX
29        2428      35883    32788          313        3095      2.51R
37        4218      57242    59631          528       -2389     -2.07R

R denotes an obs. with a large st. resid.
X denotes an obs. whose X-value gives it large influence.

Durbin-Watson statistic = 1.93
```

```
MTB > PRINT C1 C2 C4 C3
```

ROW	REVENUE	INCOME	REVLAG	RESIDUAL
1	3307	273.4	*	*
2	3556	291.3	3307	39.22
3	3601	306.9	3556	-164.54
4	3721	317.1	3601	-130.67
5	4036	336.1	3721	0.39
6	4134	349.4	4036	-180.40
7	4268	362.9	4134	-185.36
8	4578	383.9	4268	-79.55
9	5093	402.8	4578	128.66
10	5716	437.0	5093	226.37
11	6357	472.2	5716	266.35
12	6769	510.4	6357	48.91
13	7296	544.5	6769	118.08
14	8178	588.1	7296	414.55
15	8844	630.4	8178	271.70
16	9251	685.9	8844	-63.49
17	10006	776.8	9251	-79.94
18	10991	839.6	10006	64.34
19	12306	949.8	10991	124.80
20	13101	1038.4	12306	-428.58
21	13639	1142.8	13101	-989.35
22	14950	1252.6	13639	-640.32
23	17224	1379.3	14950	75.36
24	17946	1551.2	17224	-1638.61
25	17514	1729.3	17946	-3533.10
26	25195	1918.0	17514	3375.83
27	27357	2127.6	25195	-620.44
28	30020	2261.4	27357	-108.12
29	35883	2428.1	30020	3095.25
30	38828	2670.6	35883	879.29
31	40715	2841.1	38828	-97.70
32	44282	3022.1	40715	1233.93
33	48440	3205.9	44282	2049.74
34	50251	3477.8	48440	-356.79
35	53794	3725.5	50251	628.12
36	55972	4058.8	53794	-1354.47
37	57242	4218.4	55972	-2389.46

```
MTB > STOP
```

The LAG command is used to lag the data in C1 one time period and store it in C4. The PRINT command shows the new variable in C4.

Results of the computer run show that the R^2 is high (99.5 percent) and the t and F values are all significant. Stu examines the table of residuals and doesn't find a correlated pattern. Next, he tests the Durbin-Watson statistic. The critical values taken from the table for two predictor variables and a sample size of 36 are $d_L = 1.15$ and $d_U = 1.38$ ($\alpha = .01$). Since the calculated Durbin-Watson is 1.93, the null hypothesis is not rejected, and Stu concludes that the residuals are not autocorrelated.

ARIMA MODELS

Box-Jenkins Methods

An approach widely known as the **Box-Jenkins methodology** uses both the autoregressive and moving average techniques for forecasting. This methodology doesn't assume the presence of a particular pattern in the historical data of the series to be forecast. Instead, the Box-Jenkins technique, credited to George Box and Gwilym Jenkins, uses an iterative approach of identifying a potentially useful model from a general class of models. The selected model is then checked against the historical data to see if it accurately predicts the series. The model fits well if the residuals between the forecast values and the historical data points are small, randomly distributed, and independent. If the specified model is not satisfactory, the process is repeated using another model designed to improve on the original one. This process is repeated until a satisfactory model is found. Figure 17.12 shows the steps for the Box-Jenkins methodology.

> The **Box-Jenkins methodology** uses both the autoregressive and the moving average techniques for forecasting.

FIGURE 17.12 Flow Diagram of Box-Jenkins Method

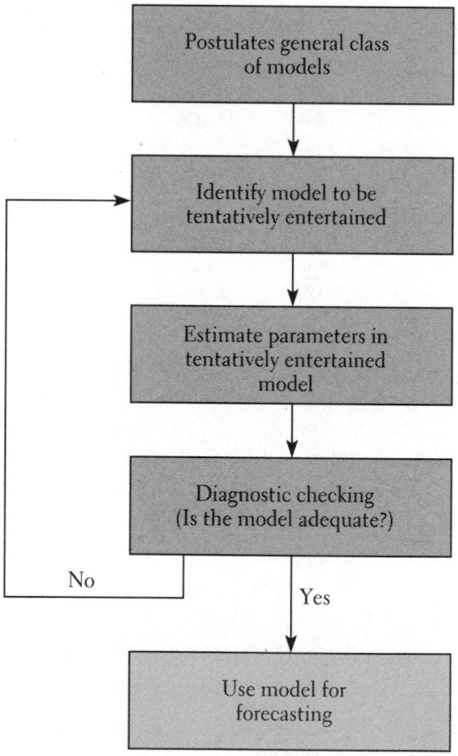

Postulates general class of models

Identify model to be tentatively entertained

Estimate parameters in tentatively entertained model

Diagnostic checking (Is the model adequate?)

No

Yes

Use model for forecasting

Source: G. P. Box and G. M. Jenkins, *Time Series Analysis Forecasting and Control* (San Francisco: Holden-Day, 1970), p. 19. Reprinted with permission.

To use the Box-Jenkins methodology, the time series of interest must be stationary. Earlier you learned that a stationary series is one whose basic statistical properties, the mean and variance, remain constant over time. You also learned that differencing a nonstationary series frequently produces a stationary series. Once a stationary series has been produced, the Box-Jenkins methodology can be applied. The degree of differencing is denoted by d in the Box-Jenkins model, which is more generally denoted by the expression ARIMA(p,d,q).

Several possible ARIMA models are:

ARIMA(1,0,0): First-order autoregressive model—original data
ARIMA (2,0,0): Second-order autoregressive model—original data
ARIMA(0,0,1): First-order moving average model—original data
ARIMA(0,0,2): Second-order moving average model—original data
ARIMA(1,1,0): First-order autoregressive model—differenced data
ARIMA(2,1,0): Second-order autoregressive model—differenced data
ARIMA(0,1,1): First-order moving average model—differenced data
ARIMA(0,1,2): Second-order moving average model—differenced data
ARIMA(1,0,1): First-order autoregressive moving average model—original data
ARIMA(1,1,1): First-order autoregressive moving average model—differenced data

Once a series has been identified as being stationary, the appropriate form of the ARIMA model is identified by examining a correlogram containing the sample autocorrelation coefficients. Sample partial autocorrelation coefficients are also used to identify the appropriate ARIMA model. Once the model has been selected, a computer program uses a nonlinear least squares procedure to estimate the model coefficients. A discussion of this process is beyond the scope of this introductory textbook.

As a final step in the model selection process, diagnostic checking of the residuals takes place to determine whether the model is appropriate. This is accomplished through examining a correlogram containing the sample autocorrelations of the residuals. If none of the autocorrelations is significantly different from 0, it is assumed that the sample residuals are independent with mean 0, and the model is deemed adequate.

The Box-Jenkins methodology is a powerful tool for providing accurate short-range forecasts. However, it's quite complex, requiring extensive computer analyses to perform the numerous computations required for identifying the model, estimating the parameters, and verifying that the model is adequate. To build a satisfactory model requires a great investment in terms of the analyst's time and computer resources. Also, the analyst should always remember that the more complicated the forecasting model, the less likely its results are to be understood and accepted by management and used in the decision-making process.

EXERCISES

36. Why are autocorrelated residuals a problem in the analysis of time series data?
37. What is the major cause of autocorrelated residuals?
38. When time series variables are analyzed, which underlying assumption is frequently violated?
39. How are autocorrelated residuals detected?

39. Durbin-Watson

40. All but *e* and *f* are true

40. If the residuals in a regression equation are positively autocorrelated, which of the following statements are true when the least squares procedure is used?
    a. The standard error of the regression coefficient underestimates the variability.
    b. Confidence intervals are no longer strictly applicable.
    c. The t and F distributions are no longer strictly applicable.
    d. The regression coefficient or coefficients are unreliable.
    e. The standard error of estimate seriously overestimates the variability of the error terms.
    f. R^2 is spuriously low.

41. Positive autocorrelation

41. You test a series of 26 observations with two independent variables at the .05 significance level, and the calculated Durbin-Watson statistic is 1.2. What is your conclusion?

42. You test a series of 57 observations with one independent variable at the .01 significance level, and the calculated Durbin-Watson statistic is 1.4. What is your conclusion?
43. How is the problem of autocorrelated residuals eliminated?
44. Explain the concept of an autoregressive model.

42. Test is inconclusive

45. How do the differencing and iterative techniques for solving autocorrelated residuals differ?
46. Examine the computer output presented in the accompanying table. Write a memo to your boss evaluating this model.

VARIABLE NO.	MEAN	STANDARD DEVIATION	CORRELATION X VS Y	REGRESSION COEFFICIENT	STD. ERROR OF REG COEF.	COMPUTED T-VALUE
2	542.85	241.16	0.975	4.22517	0.31627	13.45
DEPENDENT 1	1517.90	1078.70				

INTERCEPT −792
STD. ERROR OF ESTIMATE 341.1
R SQUARED 0.951
DURBIN-WATSON STATISTIC ____

TABLE OF RESIDUALS

OBSERVATION	OBSERVED VALUE	PREDICTED VALUE	RESIDUAL
1	295	371.36	−76.36
2	400	447.53	−47.53
3	390	513.91	−123.91
4	425	557.32	−132.32
5	547	638.16	−91.16
6	555	694.76	−139.76
7	620	752.20	−132.20
8	720	841.56	−121.56
9	880	921.98	−41.98
10	1050	1067.51	−17.51
11	1290	1217.29	72.71
12	1528	1379.84	148.16
13	1586	1524.94	61.06
14	1960	1710.47	249.53
15	2118	1890.46	227.54
16	2116	2126.62	−10.62
17	2477	2368.74	108.26
18	2199	2617.67	581.33
19	3702	3050.84	651.16
20	3316	3393.38	−77.38
21	2702	3789.54	−1087.54

47. Positive autocorrelation

47. (This question refers to Exercise 46.) The Durbin-Watson statistic, which was left out of the computer output, is 0.87. Test at the .01 significance level to determine if the residuals are autocorrelated.

48. A study attempts to relate personal savings and personal income (in billions of dollars) for the years 1935–54.

Year	Personal savings	Personal income
1935	2	60
1936	4	69
1937	4	74
1938	1	68
1939	3	73
1940	4	78
1941	11	96
1942	28	123
1943	33	151
1944	37	165
1945	30	171
1946	15	179
1947	7	191
1948	13	210
1949	9	207
1950	13	279
1951	18	257
1952	19	273
1953	20	288
1954	19	290

48*a*. (1). Reject H_0 if $t >$ 2.898; $t = 2.06$, fail to reject
(2) Reject H_0 if $F >$ 4.23; $F = 4.75$, fail to reject
(3) Reject H_0 if D.W. < 1.20; D.W. $=$ .41, reject

a. Evaluate the simple regression model in which personal income is used to predict personal savings. Specifically: (1) Test the regression coefficient for significance ($\alpha =$ .01). (2) Test the contribution of personal income to the prediction of personal savings, using the t or F test ($\alpha = .01$). (3) Test for serial correlation. How can the model be improved?

48*b*. (1) $t = 8.49$, reject
(2) D.W. $= 2.01$, fail to reject

b. Develop a dummy variable X_3, representing war years. Let $X_3 = 0$ for peacetime and $X_3 = 1$ for wartime. Consider the war years to be 1941–45. Evaluate this multiple regression model. Specifically: (1) Test to determine if knowledge of the war years variable contributes to the prediction of personal savings ($\alpha = .01$). (2) Test for serial correlation. Is the multiple regression model better than the simple regression model?

SUMMARY

This chapter has presented several ways of forecasting a time series variable. Along with the methods discussed in Chapter 16, these methods are valuable techniques for one of the most important jobs of every manager: predicting future values of variables of importance to the firm.

In terms of collecting data, performing the calculations, and explaining the results to others, simple methods are always preferable to elaborate ones. In addition, they sometimes produce the most accurate forecasts. Only when a more complicated and elaborate method substantially increases forecasting accuracy should such a method be considered. The danger is that the data needed for such techniques may be difficult to acquire or inaccurate, or that others in the organization won't understand and accept such techniques.

Here is a summary of the forecasting methods presented in recent chapters. All these techniques are widely used by forecasters in businesses of all kinds, utilizing the organization's past history to predict future values of important variables. Causal forecasting models include regression and multiple regression analysis. Time series forecasting models include the decomposition method, naive methods, moving averages, exponential smoothing, autoregression, and Box-Jenkins methods.

Regression analysis Regression analysis uses one or more related variables to form a prediction equation for *y*. Multicollinearity, a high correlation between predictor variables, is sometimes a problem. The necessity of obtaining accurate measurements for the predictor variables must be considered in deciding which variables to use. In developing a linear regression model for forecasting, the analyst should be aware that to predict some future value of the dependent variable, the future value of the predictor variable(s) must be known.

Decomposition method The decomposition method uses only past values of the time series variable to form forecasts. The series is decomposed into its components, which are then analyzed and recombined to form the forecast. Annual time series are decomposed into the secular trend and the cyclical component. Series measured by month or quarter use these two components along with the seasonal and irregular components. Forecasts are generated using the computed trend and seasonal values, along with the analyst's judgment of the values of the cyclical and irregular components.

Naive methods Very simple forecasting methods are often used by beginning forecasters, by businesses that are just starting, or by firms that are introducing a new product. Using the most recent value of *Y* as the forecast value for the next period is the simplest example of a naive method.

Moving averages The moving average method uses an average of recent periods to form the forecast for the next period. The analyst must decide how many past periods to use, a decision that is often made by trying different numbers of periods and finding the number that produces the most accurate forecasts for recent values of *Y*.

Exponential smoothing Exponential smoothing uses past periods to form the forecast for *Y* but assigns ever-decreasing weights to historical periods as they become older. This technique assumes that recent periods are more relevant to the forecast than are older ones. The basic exponential smoothing technique can be expanded to incorporate an adjustment for a trend in the series and/or a seasonal pattern in *Y*.

Autoregressive models The autoregressive technique takes advantage of the fact that *Y* values are often correlated with each other from one time period to the next.

"Predictor" variables are formed that are actually historical Y values lagged in time by one or more periods.

Box-Jenkins technique This sophisticated method doesn't assume that there's any particular pattern in the historical data of the series to be forecast. Instead, the technique uses both past values of Y and past error terms in the forecasting process to produce the model. The terms to be used and the weights assigned to past values are found through an iterative process.

Forecasting is widespread in every organization. It has always been performed on an informal, intuitive basis, and the use of more formal methods is constantly growing. The methods you've studied in these chapters, along with the availability of a computer and appropriate software, prepare you to utilize a wide range of formal forecasting methods in your career.

APPLICATIONS OF STATISTICAL CONCEPTS IN THE BUSINESS WORLD

Applications of the forecasting techniques discussed in this chapter are common in organizations of all sizes and types. These methods are widely used in business today, and their use is increasing as more and more business school graduates enter the work force with knowledge of these techniques.

The time series variables listed in the "Applications" section of Chapter 16 are candidates for the forecasting techniques that have just been summarized. It is worthwhile to review these applications and, armed with knowledge of many forecasting techniques, to consider how to approach forecasting each of these variables. Keep in mind that the analyst must seek a balance between a costly, time-consuming, and very accurate technique and a method that's fast, inexpensive, and easily understood by the firm's decision makers. Because of this dilemma, effective forecasting is as much an art as a science.

A summary of applications for the data analysis techniques discussed in these chapters follows.

Regression analysis Regression analysis is used for short- and medium-range forecasting of existing products and services, marketing strategies, production, personnel hiring, and facility planning.

Decomposition method Time series decomposition is used to make long-range forecasts for new plant and equipment planning, financing, new product development, and new methods of assembly. This technique is also used for short-range forecasting for personnel, advertising, inventory, financing, and production planning. It can be used in quality-control efforts to track and study such variables as defective rates over time.

Naive methods Naive methods are used to create short-range forecasts for sales and operations such as inventory, scheduling, and control measurements. This technique is especially useful for a new product or service.

Moving averages Moving average methods are used to make short-range forecasts for operations such as inventory, scheduling, control, pricing, and timing special promotions.

Exponential smoothing Exponential smoothing methods are used to create short-range forecasts of all types for operations such as inventory levels, scheduling of production, pricing decisions, and accounting balances. This technique is often used when a large number of forecasts are required and computer capabilities are available.

Autoregressive models Autoregressive methods are used for short- and medium-range forecasting for economic data ordered in a time series, such as prices, inventory, production, stock prices, and sales.

Box-Jenkins technique Box-Jenkins methods are used for short-range forecasting for such variables as earnings per share, stock prices, day-to-day demand, and inventory control.

Glossary

Naive methods Very simple approaches to forecasting, such as using the value from the current period as the estimate for the next period.

Moving average A model that uses the average of several past time periods as the forecast for the next period.

Exponential smoothing A technique that uses a weighted average of past time series values to arrive at smoothed forecasts.

Autocorrelation The correlation between a variable, lagged one or more periods, and itself.

Correlogram A graphical tool for displaying the autocorrelations for various lags of a time series.

Stationary series A series whose mean and variance do not change over time.

Serial correlation A condition that exists when successive observations over time are related to each other.

Durbin-Watson test A test that detects the presence of autocorrelated residuals (serial correlation) in the regression of a time series.

Autoregressive model A model that generates a new predictor variable by using the Y variable lagged one or more periods.

Box-Jenkins method A methodology that uses both the autoregressive and the moving average techniques for forecasting.

Key Formulas

Forecast error

$$e_t = Y_t - F_t \tag{17.1}$$

Mean absolute deviation

$$\text{MAD} = \frac{\Sigma|e_t|}{n} \tag{17.2}$$

Mean squared error

$$\text{MSE} = \frac{\Sigma e_t^2}{n} \tag{17.3}$$

Mean absolute percentage error

$$\text{MAPE} = \frac{\sum \frac{|e_t|}{Y_t}}{n} \tag{17.4}$$

Mean percentage error (BIAS)

$$\text{MPE} = \frac{\sum \frac{e_t}{Y_t}}{n} \tag{17.5}$$

Naive model

$$F_{t+1} = Y_t \tag{17.6}$$

Moving average model

$$F_{t+1} = \frac{Y_t + Y_{t-1} + Y_{t-2} + \cdots + Y_{t-m+1}}{m} \tag{17.7}$$

Exponential smoothing model

$$F_{t+1} = \alpha Y_t + (1 - \alpha)F_t \tag{17.8}$$

Seasonal regression model for quarterly data

$$\hat{Y}_t = b_0 + b_1 S_1 + b_2 S_2 + b_3 S_3 \tag{17.9}$$

First order autocorrelation coefficient

$$r_1 = \frac{\sum_{t=1}^{n-1} (Y_t - \bar{Y})(Y_{t-1} - \bar{Y})}{\sum_{t=1}^{n} (Y_t - \bar{Y})^2} \tag{17.10}$$

***k*th order autocorrelation coefficient**

$$r_k = \frac{\sum_{t=1}^{n-k} (Y_t - \bar{Y})(Y_{t-k} - \bar{Y})}{\sum_{t=1}^{n} (Y_t - \bar{Y})^2} \tag{17.11}$$

Autocorrelation coefficient confidence interval

$$0 \pm z\, 1/\sqrt{n} \tag{17.12}$$

First-order serial correlation

$$\varepsilon_t = \rho_1 \varepsilon_{t-1} + v_t \tag{17.13}$$

Durbin-Watson statistic

$$DW = \frac{\sum_{t=2}^{n} (e_t - e_{t-1})^2}{\sum_{t=1}^{n} e_t^2} \tag{17.14}$$

***k*th-order autoregressive model**

$$Y_t = \beta_0 + \beta_1 Y_{t-1} + \cdots + \beta_k Y_{t-k} + \varepsilon_t \tag{17.15}$$

First-order autoregressive model

$$\hat{Y}_t = b_0 + b_1 Y_{t-1} \tag{17.16}$$

Solved Exercises

1. Moving Average

Brunswick Corporation is the largest U.S. manufacturer of leisure and recreational products. Sid Foster has been assigned the job of forecasting sales for 1987. He has gathered the data (in millions of dollars) from 1978 to 1986: 1,126, 1,257, 1,200, 1,085, 1,068, 1,216, 1,468, 1,539, 1,717. (Source: *Brunswick Corporation Annual Report*, various years.)

a. Find the forecast value of sales for each year, starting with 1981, by using a three-year moving average.

b. Evaluate this forecasting method using MAD.

c. Evaluate this forecasting method using MSE.

d. Evaluate this forecasting method using MAPE.

e. Evaluate this forecasting method using MPE.

f. Summarize your evaluations of the forecasting errors.

g. Forecast sales for 1987.

Solution:

a. The moving average computations are shown in Table 17.18.

b. The error computations are shown in Table 17.19.

$$\text{MAD} = \frac{\Sigma|e_t|}{n} = \frac{1{,}262}{6} = 210.3$$

c.

$$\text{MSE} = \frac{\Sigma e_t^2}{n} = \frac{331{,}704}{6} = 55{,}284$$

d.

$$\text{MAPE} = \frac{\Sigma \frac{|e_t|}{Y_t}}{n} = \frac{88.9\%}{6} = 14.8\%$$

TABLE 17.18 Moving Average Forecast for Brunswick Sales (Solved Exercise 1)

t	Year	Sales ($ millions)	Three-year moving total	Three-year moving average	e_t
1	1978	1,126			
2	1979	1,257			
3	1980	1,200			
4	1981	1,085	3,583	1,194	−109
5	1982	1,068	3,542	1,181	−113
6	1983	1,216	3,353	1,118	98
7	1984	1,468	3,369	1,123	345
8	1985	1,539	3,752	1,251	288
9	1986	1,717	4,223	1,408	309

TABLE 17.19 Computations for Forecast Evaluation Methods (Solved Exercise 1)

Time, t	Sales, Y_t	Forecast, F_t	Error, e_t	$\lvert e_t \rvert$	e_t	$\frac{\lvert e_t \rvert}{Y_t}$ (%)	$\frac{e_t}{Y_t}$ (%)
1	1,126						
2	1,257						
3	1,200						
4	1,085	1,194	−109	109	11,881	10.0	−10.0
5	1,068	1,181	−113	113	12,769	10.6	−10.6
6	1,216	1,118	98	98	9,604	8.1	8.1
7	1,468	1,123	345	345	119,025	23.5	23.5
8	1,539	1,251	288	288	82,944	18.7	18.7
9	1,717	1,408	309	309	95,481	18.0	18.0
Sums:				1,262	331,704	88.9	47.7

e.

$$\text{MPE} = \frac{\sum \frac{e_t}{Y_t}}{n} = \frac{47.7\%}{6} = 8.0\%$$

f. The forecasting error averages about 210 for each forecast. The MPE or bias is fairly large, 8%. This means that the model is typically predicting on the low side, or underestimating. This might be caused by a trend in the data.

g. The forecast for 1987 is

$$F_{9+1} = \frac{Y_9 + Y_{9-1} + Y_{9-2}}{3}$$

$$F_{10} = \frac{1{,}717 + 1{,}539 + 1{,}468}{3} = \frac{4{,}724}{3} = 1{,}574.7 \text{ or } 1{,}575$$

2. EXPONENTIAL SMOOTHING

Forecast Brunswick Corporation sales using exponential smoothing.

a. Find the forecast value of sales for each year using a smoothing constant of .3 and an initial value of 1,126.

b. Evaluate this forecasting method using MAD.

c. Evaluate this forecasting method using MSE.

d. Evaluate this forecasting method using MAPE.

e. Evaluate this forecasting method using MPE.

f. Compare the smoothing model with the moving average model used in Solved Exercise 1.

g. Forecast sales for 1987.

Solution:

a. The exponential smoothing computations are shown in Table 17.20.

TABLE 17.20 Exponential Smoothing Forecast Computations for Brunswick Sales (Solved Exercise 2)

t	Year	Sales ($ millions)	F_t	e_t
1	1978	1,126	—	—
2	1979	1,257	1,126.0	131.0
3	1980	1,200	1,165.3	34.7
4	1981	1,085	1,175.7	−90.7
5	1982	1,068	1,148.5	−80.5
6	1983	1,216	1,124.4	91.6
7	1984	1,468	1,151.9	316.1
8	1985	1,539	1,246.7	292.3
9	1986	1,717	1,334.4	382.6

b. The error computations are shown in Table 17.21.

$$\text{MAD} = \frac{\Sigma|e_t|}{n} = \frac{1{,}421}{8} = 177.6$$

c.

$$\text{MSE} = \frac{\Sigma e_t^2}{n} = \frac{373{,}501}{8} = 46{,}687.6$$

d.

$$\text{MAPE} = \frac{\Sigma \frac{|e_t|}{Y_t}}{n} = \frac{99.7\%}{8} = 12.5\%$$

e.

$$\text{MPE} = \frac{\Sigma \frac{e_t}{Y_t}}{n} = \frac{67.7\%}{8} = 8.5\%$$

f. MAD, MSE, and MAPE are lower for the exponential smoothing model. If avoiding large forecasting errors is important, the MSE should be used for comparison purposes. The MPE is still too large.

TABLE 17.21 Computations for Forecast Evaluation Methods (Solved Exercise 2)

Time, t	Sales, Y_t	Forecast, F_t	Error, e_t	$\lvert e_t \rvert$	e_t^2	$\frac{\lvert e_t \rvert}{Y_t}$ (%)	$\frac{e_t}{Y_t}$ (%)
1	1,126						
2	1,257	1,126	131	131	17,161	10.4	10.4
3	1,200	1,165	35	35	1,225	2.9	2.9
4	1,085	1,176	−91	91	8,281	8.4	−8.4
5	1,068	1,149	−81	81	6,561	7.6	−7.6
6	1,216	1,124	92	92	8,464	7.6	7.6
7	1,468	1,152	316	316	99,856	21.5	21.5
8	1,539	1,247	292	292	85,264	19.0	19.0
9	1,717	1,334	383	383	146,689	22.3	22.3
Sums:				1,421	373,501	99.7	67.7

g. The forecast for 1987 is

$$F_{t+1} = \alpha Y_t + (1 - \alpha)F_t$$
$$F_{10} = \alpha Y_9 + (1 - \alpha)F_9$$
$$= (.3)(1{,}717) + (.7)(1{,}334.4) = 1{,}449.2 \text{ or } 1{,}449$$

3. AUTOCORRELATION COEFFICIENT COMPUTATION

Gail Robinson, analyst for Etta Life, is studying the amount of life premiums offered from 1982 through 1992 (Table 17.22). She decides to compute the autocorrelations to determine the data's pattern. Compute the autocorrelation coefficient for time lag 1.

TABLE 17.22 Etta Life Yearly Life Premiums (Solved Exercise 3)

Time, t	Year	Original data ($ millions), Y_t	Y lagged one period ($ millions), Y_{t-1}
1	1982	4,509	—
2	1983	5,439	4,509
3	1984	6,286	5,439
4	1985	6,669	6,286
5	1986	6,404	6,669
6	1987	6,169	6,404
7	1988	6,557	6,169
8	1989	8,029	6,557
9	1990	8,214	8,029
10	1991	9,161	8,214
11	1992	10,825	9,161

Source: Etta Company records.

Solution:

The summations to be used in the autocorrelation formula are presented in Table 17.23.

TABLE 17.23 Computations for Life Premiums (Solved Exercise 3)

t	Y_t	Y_{t-1}	$(Y_t - \bar{Y})$	$(Y_{t-1} - \bar{Y})$	$(Y_t - \bar{Y})^2$	$(Y_t - \bar{Y})(Y_{t-1} - \bar{Y})$
1	4,509	—	−2,606	—	6,791,236	—
2	5,439	4,509	−1,676	−2,606	2,808,976	4,367,656
3	6,286	5,439	−829	−1,676	687,241	1,389,404
4	6,669	6,286	−446	−829	198,916	369,734
5	6,404	6,669	−711	−446	505,521	317,106
6	6,169	6,404	−946	−711	894,916	672,606
7	6,557	6,169	−558	−946	311,364	527,868
8	8,029	6,557	914	−558	835,396	−510,012
9	8,214	8,029	1,099	914	1,207,801	1,004,486
10	9,161	8,214	2,046	1,099	4,186,116	2,248,554
11	10,825	9,161	3,710	2,046	13,764,100	7,590,660
Sums:	78,262		0		32,191,583	17,978,062

$$\bar{Y} = \frac{78{,}262}{11} = 7{,}115$$

$$r_1 = \frac{\sum_{t=1}^{n-1} (Y_t - \bar{Y})(Y_{t-1} - \bar{Y})}{\sum_{t=1}^{n} (Y_t - \bar{Y})^2}$$

$$= \frac{17{,}978{,}062}{32{,}191{,}583} = .56$$

It appears that moderate autocorrelation exists in this time series lagged one period. The correlation between Y_t and Y_{t-1}, or the autocorrelation for lag 1, is .56. However, a very small sample was used, so this autocorrelation coefficient should be tested to determine if it is significantly different from 0.

4. AUTOCORRELATION COEFFICIENT TEST OF SIGNIFICANCE

Gail Robinson, analyst for Etta Life, needs to determine whether the autocorrelation coefficient she computed is significantly different from 0.

Solution:

The null and alternative hypotheses to test whether the autocorrelation coefficient for time lag 1 is significantly different from 0 are

$$H_0: \rho_1 = 0$$
$$H_1: \rho_1 \neq 0$$

Since $n = 11$, the standard error (standard deviation of the sampling distribution of autocorrelation coefficients) is $1/\sqrt{11} = .302$. If the null hypothesis is tested at the .05 significance level, the critical value is $1.96(.302) = .592$, and the decision rule is

If the autocorrelation coefficient is less than $-.592$ or greater than .592, reject the null hypothesis (reject H_0 if $r_1 < -.592$ or $r_1 > .592$).

Gail concludes, based on her sample, that the data are not autocorrelated at time lag 1 (.56 < .592). However, she realizes that 11 time periods don't constitute a very large sample to test.

5. AUTOCORRELATION ANALYSIS

Eastman Kodak statistician Ron Wilson must estimate the company's operating revenue for 1991. He decides to analyze 1969–90 data (Table 17.24).

TABLE 17.24 Yearly Operating Revenue for Eastman Kodak and Disposable Personal Income, 1969–1990 (Solved Exercise 5)

Year	Operating revenue Y_t	Disposable income X_t	Operating revenue lagged one period Y_{t-1}
1969	2,747	630.4	—
1970	2,785	685.9	2,747
1971	2,976	776.8	2,785
1972	3,478	839.6	2,976
1973	4,036	949.8	3,478
1974	4,584	1,038.4	4,036
1975	4,959	1,142.8	4,584
1976	5,438	1,252.6	4,959
1977	5,967	1,379.3	5,438
1978	7,013	1,551.2	5,967
1979	8,028	1,729.3	7,013
1980	9,734	1,918.0	8,028
1981	10,337	2,127.6	9,734
1982	10,815	2,261.4	10,337
1983	10,170	2,428.1	10,815
1984	10,600	2,670.6	10,170
1985	10,631	2,841.1	10,600
1986	11,550	3,022.1	10,631
1987	13,305	3,205.9	11,550
1988	17,034	3,477.8	13,305
1989	18,398	3,725.5	17,034
1990	18,908	4,058.8	18,398

Sources: Eastman Kodak Operating Revenue: *Industry Surveys*. Disposable Personal Income: *Survey of Current Business*, various years.

Solution:

Ron runs an autocorrelation analysis of these data using the MINITAB computer program. The instructions are shown at the end of the chapter. Figure 17.13 shows the results.

The 95% confidence interval is

$$0 \pm 1.96\,(1/\sqrt{22})$$
$$0 \pm .418$$

FIGURE 17.13 Autocorrelations for Solved Exercise 5

```
ACF of REV
          -1.0 -0.8 -0.6 -0.4 -0.2  0.0  0.2  0.4  0.6  0.8  1.0
            +----+----+----+----+----+----+----+----+----+----+
  1   0.840                         XXXXXXXXXXXXXXXXXXXXXX
  2   0.652                         XXXXXXXXXXXXXXXXX
  3   0.468                         XXXXXXXXXXXXX
  4   0.352                         XXXXXXXXXX
  5   0.267                         XXXXXXXX
  6   0.203                         XXXXXX
  7   0.131                         XXXX
  8   0.057                         XX
  9  -0.047                        XX
 10  -0.147                     XXXXX
 11  -0.239                   XXXXXXX
 12  -0.288                   XXXXXXXX
 13  -0.318                  XXXXXXXXX
 14  -0.330                  XXXXXXXXX
```

Ron examines this correlogram and notices that the autocorrelations for the first three time lags (.84, .65, and .46) are significantly different from 0. The pattern then drops to 0 gradually rather than suddenly. He decides that the data have a trend.

Ron differences the data and uses MINITAB to compute the autocorrelation coefficients in Figure 17.14. Only the first autocorrelation coefficient (.44) is significantly different from 0 so Ron concludes that the first differenced data have some pattern that can be forecast.

FIGURE 17.14 Autocorrelations for Differenced Data for Solved Exercise 5

```
ACF of REVDIFF
          -1.0 -0.8 -0.6 -0.4 -0.2  0.0  0.2  0.4  0.6  0.8  1.0
            +----+----+----+----+----+----+----+----+----+----+
  1   0.443                         XXXXXXXXXXXX
  2   0.084                         XXX
  3  -0.260                   XXXXXXX
  4  -0.223                   XXXXXXX
  5  -0.361                XXXXXXXXXX
  6  -0.092                       XXX
  7   0.056                         XX
  8   0.220                         XXXXXXX
  9   0.105                         XXXX
 10   0.039                         XX
 11  -0.003                         X
 12  -0.014                         X
 13  -0.006                         X
 14  -0.025                        XX
```

6. SERIAL CORRELATION

Next, Ron develops a regression analysis using disposable personal income to predict yearly operating revenue. Ron employs MINITAB to do his regression analysis using the data in Table 17.24. The MINITAB commands are shown at the end of the chapter.

Ron is pleased when he examines the output (Table 17.25). R^2 is high, 96.2 percent, and the t and F values are both significant. But Ron knows that a test is needed to determine whether serial correlation is a problem.

TABLE 17.25 MINITAB Output for Solved Exercise 6, Disposable Income Used as the Predictor Variable

```
The regression equation is
REV = -313 + 4.58 INCOME

Predictor        Coef      Stdev     t ratio        P

Constant       -313.3      459.6       -0.68    0.503
INCOME         4.5841     0.2050       22.36    0.000

s = 999.0   R-sq = 96.2%   R-sq(adj) = 96.0%

Analysis of Variance

SOURCE        DF          SS           MS          F         P
Regression     1   499156352    499156352     500.14     0.000
Error         20    19960700       998035
Total         21   519117056

Unusual Observations
Obs.     INCOME      REV       Fit     Stdev.Fit     Residual     St.Resid
17         2841    10631     12711           276        -2080       -2.17R
18         3022    11550     13540           301        -1990       -2.09R

R denotes an obs. with a large st. resid.

Durbin-Watson statistic = 0.61
```

Solution:

The null and alternative hypotheses are

$$H_0: \quad \rho_1 \leq 0$$
$$H_1: \quad \rho_1 > 0$$

Ron decides to use the .01 significance level and consults the Durbin-Watson table in Appendix E.10. Since he used one predictor variable with a sample size of 22, the critical values are d_L = 1.00 and d_U = 1.17. The decision rule is

> Reject the null hypothesis if the calculated Durbin-Watson statistic is less than 1.00. Fail to reject the null hypothesis if the calculated Durbin-Watson statistic is greater than 1.17. If the calculated Durbin-Watson statistic lies between 1.00 and 1.17, the test is inconclusive.

Ron examines Table 17.25 and finds that the Durbin-Watson statistic computed from the sample data is below the critical value from the table, $.61 < 1.00$. He rejects the null hypothesis and concludes that the residuals for Eastman Kodak operating revenue predicted by disposable personal income are positively autocorrelated.

Ron decides to develop an autoregressive model using disposable personal income and Eastman Kodak operating revenue lagged one period. The MINITAB commands are shown at the end of the chapter. Table 17.26 shows the output for the autoregressive model.

Ron notices that the R^2 is high, 97.7 percent. However, the t value (1.95) for the disposable personal income variable is not significant at the .01 level. Ron checks the correlation matrix at the bottom of Table 17.26 and determines that multicollinearity is the reason why the disposable personal income variable is not significant. Next, Ron tests the Durbin-Watson statistic. The critical values taken from the table for two predictor variables and a sample size of 21 are d_L = 0.89 and d_U = 1.27 (α = .01). Since the calculated Durbin-Watson is 1.14, the test is inconclusive.

Ron decides to eliminate disposable personal income and runs Eastman Kodak operating revenue lagged one period as the only predictor variable (Table 17.27).

TABLE 17.26 MINITAB Output for Solved Exercise 6, Disposable Income and Revenue Lagged One Period Used as the Predictor Variables

```
The regression equation is
REV = -56 + 1.59 INCOME + 0.706 REVLAG

21 cases used 1 cases contain missing values

Predictor       Coef      Stdev    t ratio       P
Constant       -56.0      394.4      -0.14   0.889
INCOME        1.5938     0.8189       1.95   0.067
REVLAG        0.7060     0.1885       3.75   0.001

s = 788.8     R-sq = 97.7%    R-sq (adj) = 97.4%

Analysis of Variance

Source         DF         SS          MS          F        P
Regression      2  469596448   234798224     377.40    0.000
Error          18   11198757      622153
Total          20  480795200

SOURCE         DF     SEQ SS
INCOME          1  460867648
REVLAG          1    8728800

Unusual Observations
Obs.    INCOME      REV       Fit    Stdev.Fit    Residual    St.Resid
20        3478    17034     14880          358        2154       3.07R

R denotes an obs. with a large st. resid.

Durbin-Watson statistic = 1.14

             REV    INCOME
INCOME     0.981
REVLAG     0.986     0.979
```

TABLE 17.27 MINITAB Output for Solved Exercise 6, Revenue Lagged One Period Used as the Predictor Variable

```
The regression equation is
REV = 230 + 1.06 REVLAG

Predictor        Coef      Stdev    t ratio       P
Constant        229.5      392.0       0.59   0.565
REVLAG        1.06496    0.04161      25.59   0.000

s = 844.7     R-sq = 97.2%    R-sq(adj.) = 97.0%

Analysis of Variance

SOURCE         DF         SS          MS          F        P
Regression      1  467239840   467239840     654.91    0.000
Error          19   13555361      713440
Total          20  480795200

Unusual Observations
Obs.    REVLAG      REV       Fit    Stdev.Fit    Residual    St.Resid
20       13305    17034     14399          278        2635       3.30R
22       18398    18908     19823          458        -915      -1.29 X

R denotes an obs. with a large st. resid.
X denotes an obs. whose X-value gives it large influence.

Durbin-Watson statistic = 1.30
```

Again, the r^2 is high (97.2 percent) and this model has a significant t value (25.6). Ron tests the Durbin-Watson statistic. The critical values taken from the table for one predictor variable and a sample size of 21 are $d_L = 0.97$ and $d_U = 1.16$ ($\alpha = .01$). Since the calculated Durbin-Watson is 1.30, the null hypothesis is not rejected and Ron concludes that the residuals are not autocorrelated. He thinks he has found a good prediction equation for Eastman's operating revenue.

EXERCISES

49. What are the advantages and disadvantages of the naive forecasting model?
50. What are the advantages and disadvantages of the moving average forecasting model?
51. What are the advantages and disadvantages of the exponential smoothing forecasting model?
52. If large forecasting errors are considered disastrous, which evaluation method should be used to compare forecasting models?

53. Overestimating

53. If the MPE is a large negative value, what should the analyst conclude about the forecasting model?

54. Autoregressive Model

54. Which forecasting model generates a new predictor variable by using the dependent variable lagged one or more periods?

55. Box-Jenkins

55. Which forecasting model uses both the autoregressive and moving average techniques for forecasting?

56. Box-Jenkins

56. Which forecasting model does not assume the presence of any particular pattern in the historical data of the series to be forecast?
57. What are the disadvantages of using Box-Jenkins techniques to forecast?
58. What is a correlogram? How is it used?
59. How should the correlogram look for each of the following situations?
    a. A random series.
    b. A stationary series.
    c. A seasonal series.
60. What is serial correlation?
61. What problems arise when serial correlation is present in a regression equation?

62. $0 \pm .19$

62. Compute the 90% confidence interval for the autocorrelation coefficients for a series that contains 75 items.

63. Positive autocorrelation

63. A series of 43 observations with two independent variables is tested at the .05 significance level, and the calculated Durbin-Watson statistic is 1.0. What is your conclusion?
64. The AVX Corporation manufactures multilayer ceramic capacitors. Pam Williams has been assigned the job of forecasting book value per share for 1990. She has gathered the data from 1975 to 1989: 2.27, 2.59, 2.71, 3.17, 3.73, 5.90, 7.04, 9.64, 9.01, 9.38, 11.05, 12.24, 11.72, 11.81, 14.26. (Source: AVX *Corporation Annual Report*, various years.)
    a. Forecast book value per share for each year, starting with 1980, using a five-year moving average.

64*a*. 1990—12.22
b. 2.84
c. 9.19
d. 30.57%
e. 30.57%
g. 12.22

b. Evaluate this forecasting method using MAD.

c. Evaluate this forecasting method using MSE.

d. Evaluate this forecasting method using MAPE.

e. Evaluate this forecasting method using MPE.

f. Summarize your evaluation of the forecasting errors.

g. Forecast book value per share for 1990.

65. (This question refers to Exercise 64.) Forecast the AVX Corporation's book value per share using exponential smoothing.

a. Forecast book value per share for each year using a smoothing constant of .6 and an initial value of 2.27.

65*b*. 1.307
c. 2.78
d. 17.08%
e. 17.08%
g. 13.25

b. Evaluate this forecasting method using MAD.

c. Evaluate this forecasting method using MSE.

d. Evaluate this forecasting method using MAPE.

e. Evaluate this forecasting method using MPE.

f. Compare the smoothing model with the moving average model used in Exercise 64.

g. Forecast book value per share for 1990.

66. (This question refers to Exercise 64.) Forecast the AVX Corporation's book value per share using an autoregressive model.

66*a*. 1.01
b. $Y = .883 + .996Y_{t-1}$
c. 15.086

a. Evaluate this forecasting method using MSE.

b. Compare the autoregressive model with the models used in Exercises 64 and 65.

c. Forecast book value per share for 1990.

67*a*. Trend
b. Seasonal
c. Pattern in the data

67. Analyze the autocorrelation coefficients for each of the series shown in Figures 17.15, 17.16, and 17.17. Briefly describe each series.

FIGURE 17.15 Autocorrelations for Exercise 67

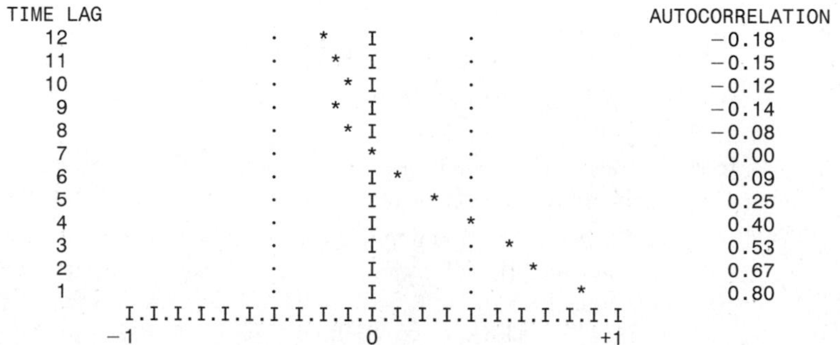

FIGURE 17.16 Autocorrelations for Exercise 67

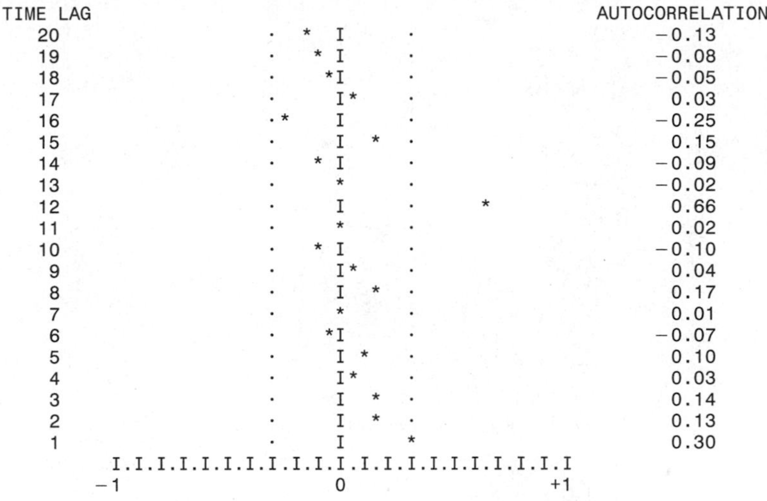

FIGURE 17.17 Autocorrelations for Exercise 67

```
TIME LAG                                              AUTOCORRELATION
   20               .  *  I     .                         −0.13
   19               .   * I     .                         −0.08
   18               .    *I     .                         −0.05
   17               .     I*    .                          0.03
   16               .*    I     .                         −0.25
   15               .     I  *  .                          0.15
   14               .   * I     .                         −0.09
   13               .     *     .                         −0.02
   12               .   * I     .                         −0.08
   11               .     *     .                          0.02
   10               .   * I     .                         −0.10
    9               .     I*    .                          0.04
    8               .     I  *  .                          0.17
    7               .     *     .                          0.01
    6               .    *I     .                         −0.07
    5               .     I *   .                          0.10
    4               .     I*    .                          0.03
    3               .     I*    .                          0.03
    2               .    *I     .                         −0.03
    1               .     I     .      *                   0.70
     I.I.I.I.I.I.I.I.I.I.I.I.I.I.I.I.I.I.I.I.I
    −1                    0                   +1
```

68. Sid Wynd, analyst for the Rockwell Clinic, must develop a model to predict the number of patients who will receive blood tests during a week. Sid has collected the following data on the number of patients receiving blood tests for the past 25 weeks.

Week	Number of patients	Week	Number of patients
1	249	14	300
2	255	15	298
3	248	16	306
4	258	17	308
5	254	18	308
6	268	19	313
7	260	20	320
8	270	21	323
9	265	22	323
10	287	23	337
11	298	24	340
12	291	25	342
13	291		

Source: Rockwell Clinic records.

68*a*. Trend
$r_1 = .86$
$r_2 = .75$
$r_3 = .61$
$r_4 = .52$
$r_5 = .39$
b. $\hat{Y} = 9.57 + .98039Y_{t-1}$.
c. 344.86
d. 341.76
e. Autoregressive is better

a. Construct a correlogram for these data.

b. Based on the results of the correlogram, develop an autoregressive model.

c. Use the model you developed to forecast period 26.

d. Use an exponential smoothing model.

e. Compare your results.

69*a*. 264.4, MAPE = 36.4%
b. 5 MO, 264.7 MAPE = 24.6%
c. 261.2, MAPE = 33.9%

69. (This question refers to Exercise 22.) Dibrell Brothers, Inc., purchases and processes leaf tobacco worldwide, for sale to cigarette manufacturers. Hershel Roberts has the task of predicting sales for 1993. Exercise 22 presents 1985–92 quarterly data.

a. Forecast sales using a naive model. Evaluate the accuracy of this model.

b. Forecast sales using a moving average model. Evaluate the accuracy of this model.

c. Forecast sales using an exponential smoothing model. Evaluate the accuracy of this model.

d. Write a report for Hershel that summarizes your findings and includes a forecast for 1993.

70. Burgan Furniture Company analyst Tom Dukich has decided that production scheduling can be improved by developing an accurate method for predicting quarterly sales. He investigated the relationship between housing construction permits and furniture sales in the store's market area in Exercise 61 in Chapter 15. In addition, he developed a model that used a 0 to represent first- or second-quarter sales and a 1 to represent third- or fourth-quarter sales. The sales data, recorded in thousands of dollars, are:

Year	Quarter	Sales	Year	Quarter	Sales
1989	1	119	1991	1	115
	2	77		2	145
	3	409		3	654
	4	198		4	269
1990	1	77	1992	1	196
	2	121		2	276
	3	281		3	789
	4	160		4	318

Source: Burgan Furniture Company records.

70*a*. .077
−.202
.051
.522
−.093
−.255
−.087
.185
−.204
−.280
b. $\hat{Y}_t = 45.986 + 1.085Y_{t-4}$
c. 258.65
d. $\hat{Y} = 56.75 + 17.95t - 55.6S_1 - 45.6S_2 + 314.95S_3$

a. Construct a correlogram for these data.

b. Based on the results of the correlogram, develop an autoregressive model.

c. Use the model you developed to forecast sales for the first quarter of 1993.

d. Develop a multiple regression model that uses dummy variables to model the seasonal effect.

e. Write a report indicating which model Tom should use.

71. Harvey Magnuson owns several large construction firms and is considering an investment project in the aerospace/defense industry. He hires you as a consultant to analyze capital expenditures for that industry. In the library you find the following data measured in billions of dollars:

Year	Expenditures
1979	32.65
1980	29.96
1981	26.81
1982	29.50
1983	27.20
1984	31.34
1985	38.99
1986	39.98
1987	39.57
1988	41.56
1989	41.87
1990	42.96

Source: Standard & Poor's *Industry Surveys*, 1988, 1992.

Analyze this series using any of the techniques covered in this text. Write a report for Mr. Magnuson including a 1991 forecast, an explanation of why you used the forecasting method, and an evaluation of that method's accuracy.

72. Harvey Magnuson liked the report that you wrote for him in Exercise 71 and hires you to analyze and forecast U.S. cement consumption for 1992. Again you go to the library and find the following data measured in thousands of short tons:

Year	Consumption
1972	84,559
1973	90,271
1974	82,415
1975	69,985
1976	74,282
1977	80,819
1978	87,284
1979	86,953
1980	77,258
1981	72,717
1982	65,496
1983	72,394
1984	83,784
1985	86,746

Year	Consumption
1986	91,191
1987	92,729
1988	92,379
1989	91,636
1990	88,863
1991	91,756

Source: Standard & Poor's, *Industry Surveys*, 1988, 1992.

Analyze this series using any of the techniques covered in this text. Write a report for Mr. Magnuson including a forecast for 1992, an explanation of why you used the forecasting method, and an evaluation of the forecasting method's accuracy.

73. Gilbert Sheely, analyst for the FCC, must predict the number of TV stations that will change hands in 1991. The data are:

Year	Number	Year	Number
1954	27	1973	25
1955	29	1974	24
1956	21	1975	22
1957	38	1976	32
1958	23	1977	25
1959	21	1978	51
1960	21	1979	47
1961	24	1980	35
1962	16	1981	24
1963	16	1982	30
1964	36	1983	61
1965	32	1984	82
1966	31	1985	99
1967	30	1986	128
1968	20	1987	59
1969	32	1988	70
1970	19	1989	84
1971	27	1990	75
1972	37		

Source: *Broadcasting Magazine*, 1991.

Analyze this series using any of the techniques covered in this text. Write a report for Mr. Sheely including a 1991 forecast, an explanation of why you used the forecasting method, and an evaluation of that method's accuracy.

74. $\alpha = .05$. Reject H_0 if D.W. < .98; D.W. = 2.37, fail to reject

74. Tracy Wilder, an economist working for the government, is trying to determine the demand function for passenger car motor fuel in the United States. Tracy developed a model using the variables actual price of a gallon of regular gasoline and U.S. population to predict motor fuel consumed per year. Her model explained 83.5% of the variance. Run the data on a regression program and determine whether serial correlation is a problem.

Year	Motor fuel consumed (billions of gallons) Y	Gas price x_2	U.S. population (millions) x_3
1973	78.8	.39	211.9
1974	75.1	.53	213.9
1975	76.4	.57	216.0
1976	79.7	.59	218.0
1977	80.4	.62	220.2
1978	81.7	.63	222.6
1979	77.1	.85	225.1
1980	71.9	1.19	227.7
1981	71.0	1.33	230.1
1982	70.1	1.26	232.5
1983	69.9	1.22	234.8
1984	68.7	1.21	236.3
1985	69.3	1.16	238.5
1986	71.4	.92	240.7
1987	70.6	.95	242.8
1988	71.7	.95	245.1

Source: *Statistical Abstract of the United States* and *Industry Surveys*, various years.

75. Best model uses use and change
$\alpha = .05$. Reject H_0 if D.W. < 1.19. If D.W. = .85, reject

75. (This question refers to Exercise 57 in Chapter 15.) Judy Johnson decided to investigate three potential predictor variables: residential use per kilowatt-hour (kwh), residential charge per kwh (cents/kwh), and number of residential electric customers. You were asked to write a report so that Judy could testify before the Rate Commission. The commission asked her if serial correlation was a problem. She has asked you to write a response to the commission's question.

76. You did an excellent job for Judy Johnson with the Rate Commission testimony in Exercise 75 so she recommended you to work on a problem for the company's president, Paul Chapman. Paul is worried about the possibility of a takeover attempt and the fact that the number of common shareholders has been decreasing since 1983. He instructs you to study the number of common shareholders since 1968 and forecast for 1992. You decide to investigate three potential predictor variables: earnings per share (common), dividends per share (common), and payout ratio. You collect the following data from 1968 to 1991

Year	Common shareholders Y	Earnings per share X_2	Dividends per share X_3	Payout ratio X_4
1968	26,472	1.68	1.21	72
1969	28,770	1.70	1.28	73
1970	29,681	1.80	1.32	73
1971	30,481	1.86	1.36	72
1972	30,111	1.96	1.39	71
1973	31,052	2.02	1.44	71
1974	30,845	2.11	1.49	71
1975	32,012	2.42	1.53	63
1976	32,846	2.79	1.65	55

Year	Common shareholders Y	Earnings per share X_2	Dividends per share X_3	Payout ratio X_4
1977	32,909	2.38	1.76	74
1978	34,593	2.95	1.94	61
1979	34,359	2.78	2.08	75
1980	36,161	2.33	2.16	93
1981	39,474	3.29	2.28	69
1982	46,278	3.17	2.40	76
1983	47,672	3.02	2.48	82
1984	45,462	2.46	2.48	101
1985	43,313	3.03	2.48	82
1986	41,368	2.06	2.48	120
1987	38,686	2.31	2.48	107
1988	37,072	2.54	2.48	98
1989	36,968	2.70	2.48	92
1990	34,348	2.87	2.48	86
1991	34,058	2.61	2.48	95

Source: "Financial and Operating Supplement," *Washington Water Power Annual Report*, 1978, 1986, 1991.

76*a*. $\hat{Y} = 16{,}504 + 9{,}639X_3$
$r^2 = 68.1\%$
D.W. = .31
b. Serial correlation is a problem

a. Run these data on the computer and find the best prediction model.

b. Is serial correlation a problem in this model?

c. If serial correlation is a problem, write a memo to Paul that discusses various solutions to the autocorrelation problem and includes your final recommendation.

EXTENDED EXERCISES

77. BUSINESS ACTIVITY INDEX

Dr. Shik Chun Young, professor of economics at Eastern Washington University, is attempting to develop a business activity index for Spokane County.[5] At the county level, personal income is judged as the best available indicator of local business conditions. Personal income is defined as the total income received by households before personal taxes are paid. Unfortunately, personal income data at the county level are estimated by the U.S. Dept. of Commerce on an annual basis and are released 16 months too late.

From Young's knowledge of the Spokane economy, he selects the following 10 series to try as predictor variables:

X_2 = Total employment
X_3 = Manufacturing employment
X_4 = Construction employment

[5]John E. Hanke and Arthur G. Reitsch, *Business Forecasting*, 4th ed. (Boston: Allyn & Bacon, 1992).

X_5 = Wholesale and retail trade employment
X_6 = Service employment
X_7 = Bank debits
X_8 = Bank demand deposits
X_9 = Building permits issued
X_{10} = Real estate mortgages
X_{11} = Commercial and industrial electricity consumption

Shik runs a regression model that includes all 10 predictor variables, and the variables are found to explain 96% of the variance. However, other regression statistics indicate several problems. First, of these 10 predictor variables, only 3 have computed t values which are significant at the .05 level. Second, the correlation matrix shows a high degree of interdependence among several of the independent variables—the problem of multicollinearity. For example, the variables for total employment and bank debits have a correlation coefficient of .88; total electricity consumption and bank demand deposits, .76; and building permits issued and real estate mortgages, .68. Finally, the Durbin-Watson statistic, 0.91, indicates a serial correlation problem.

a. Which problem should Dr. Young solve first: multicollinearity or serial correlation? Why?

b. How should Dr. Young attempt to eliminate the problem of serial correlation?

78. PROJECT

As mentioned throughout this chapter, many variables vital to a firm's health are measured every year, quarter, or month. For each of these, there may be several other variables that are highly correlated and that might provide valuable insights and forecasting power.

For this exercise, you are to simulate the identification of an important time series variable for a company of your choice and then analyze the patterns in the data using autocorrelation analysis. In addition, you can use a regression analysis computer program to see if a good prediction equation can be found.

a. Identify a company or organization that interests you. The company can be local, or it can be a national company that has published records including the measurement of time series variables.

b. Identify a key variable for your chosen company and record its values for several years, quarters, or months.

c. Either by hand or with a computer, calculate several autocorrelation coefficients and plot them on a correlogram.

d. Based on the correlogram pattern, describe the patterns in your time series.

e. Compute first differences for your data. Then compute the autocorrelation coefficients, plot them on a correlogram, and describe the resulting patterns.

f. Identify several potential predictor variables that you think might be correlated with the dependent variable. You can use company records along with other data sources in this process.

g. Run the data on a regression analysis computer program and obtain a correlation matrix. Assemble several predictor variable combinations that you think might be successful and run a regression analysis for each. See if you can find a good prediction equation for your dependent variable.

h. Check your model to make sure that serial correlation is not a problem.

79. Hyrum Brewery

Ralph Hyrum and his brother Claude have decided to open a brewery in a small New England town. They chose a town outside Manchester-Nashua, New Hampshire, after reading that this area is the fastest growing business area in the country (*Inc.* Magazine, March 1992).

To obtain financing for their brewery, the Hyrum brothers are told by their banker that they must have a method of forecasting demand, and hence production. After discussing this matter with the banker, and after the banker tastes some Hyrum beer that evening, they decide a general forecast of beer sales for the region will suffice. The banker is convinced that the Hyrum brothers have a good product and agrees that their sales can be projected as a percentage of overall demand for beer in the region.

This leaves the Hyrum brothers with the task of forecasting overall beer consumption for their part of the region. They hire you as a consultant to provide such a forecast. You begin by assembling the following figures for total beer sales in the region, in hundreds of kegs, which are to be used to develop a forecast for the next two years.

	1989	1990	1991	1992
Jan.	123	132	133	137
Feb.	124	129	131	135
Mar.	138	142	140	147
Apr.	135	151	155	159
May	145	153	158	162
June	179	183	192	188
July	180	193	204	211
Aug.	211	208	225	223
Sept.	187	200	192	199
Oct.	175	177	184	173
Nov.	139	144	148	151
Dec.	127	129	132	135

Forecast using the following methods:

1. Naive method
2. Moving average
3. Simple exponential smoothing
4. Regression analysis
5. Autoregressive model

   a. Are the data stationary? If not, do the data have a trend? Are the data seasonal?

   b. Discuss the pros and cons of each method. Keep in mind the need for collecting more data, the necessity of a computer program, and the need to choose parameters for some of the methods. Also remember that the method chosen must be as accurate as possible and must be understandable to the banker and the Hyrum brothers so they can use it to generate the forecasts they need.

c. Write a report for the Hyrum brothers. Compare each forecasting method using mean absolute percentage error (MAPE). Include a forecast for each month of 1993.

MICROCOMPUTER PACKAGE

The micro package *Computerized Business Statistics* can be used to solve moving average and exponential smoothing problems.

Sid Foster has been assigned the job of forecasting sales for the Brunswick Corporation for 1987 (Solved Exercise 1). He has gathered 1978–86 sales data (in millions of dollars). Sid would like to use the computer program to develop a moving average forecast.

Computer Solution

From the main menu of *Computerized Business Statistics* an 11 is selected, indicating Time Series and Forecasting. Since the problem involves entering data from the keyboard, a 1 is selected.

```
Time Series and Forecasting—Define New Problem
OPTIONS:  1 = Least Squares
          2 = Moving Averages
          3 = Simple Exponential Smoothing
          4 = Smoothing with Trend Factoring
          5 = Trend and Seasonal Smoothing
          6 = Seasonal Indices
Select Model: enter 1–6, press ↵ 2
```

Since a moving average is desired, a 2 is selected.

```
Simple or Weighted Averages: enter S/W, press ↵ S
Number of Data Points: enter 4–125, press ↵ 9
Number of Periods in Average: enter 2–9, press ↵ 3
Variable Name: enter 0–5 char., press ↵ Sales
```

The answers to this series of questions are: a simple average, **S**, is desired, for **9** data points, using a **3**-month moving average, and the variable is entered as **Sales**.

```
Problem definition correct Y/N, press ↵ Y
```

After a **Y** response, the program is ready for the data to be entered. There are nine data points. An **F** is entered once the blanks have been completed.

After the data have been entered the screen shows:

```
   Sales
1 = 1126
2 = 1257
3 = 1200
4 = 1085
5 = 1068
6 = 1216
7 = 1468
8 = 1539
9 = 1717
Save data? Y/N, press ↵ N
```

MINITAB COMPUTER PACKAGE

The MINITAB commands to analyze Solved Exercises 5 and 6 are:

```
MTB > READ 'KODAK.DAT' C1-C2
      22 ROWS READ
ROW     C1      C2
  1   2747   630.4
  2   2785   685.9
  3   2976   776.8
  4   3478   839.6
  . . .

MTB > NAME C1 'REV' C2 'INCOME'
MTB > ACF C1
MTB > DIFFERENCES 1 FOR C1, PUT IN C3
MTB > ACF C3
```

The READ command is used to import the KODAK.DAT file into columns 1 and 2. The ACF command is used to compute autocorrelations for the data in C1. The DIFFERENCES command is used to compute the differences for the data in C1 and store these differences in C3.

```
MTB > REGRESS C1 1 PREDICTOR C2;
SUBC> RESIDS C4;
SUBC> DW.
MTB > NAME C4 'RESIDUAL'
MTB > PRINT C1 C2 C4
ROW      REV    INCOME     RESIDUAL
  1     2747     630.4       170.49
  2     2785     685.9       -45.93
  3     2976     776.8      -271.62
  4     3478     839.6       -57.51
  5     4036     949.8        -4.68
  6     4584    1038.4       137.17
  7     4959    1142.8        33.58
  8     5438    1252.6         9.25
  9     5967    1379.3       -42.57
 10     7013    1551.2       215.42
 11     8028    1729.3       413.99
 12     9734    1918.0      1254.96
 13    10337    2127.6       897.12
 14    10815    2261.4       761.77
 15    10170    2428.1      -647.41
 16    10600    2670.6     -1329.06
 17    10631    2841.1     -2079.66
 18    11550    3022.1     -1990.38
 19    13305    3205.9     -1077.95
 20    17034    3477.8      1404.63
 21    18398    3725.5      1633.13
 22    18908    4058.8       615.24
```

The REGRESS command is used to run a regression analysis using disposable income to predict operating revenue. The RESIDS subcommand is used to store the residuals in C4. The DW subcommand is used to compute the Durbin-Watson statistic.

```
MTB > LAG 1 DATA IN C1, PUT IN C5
MTB > NAME C5 'REVLAG'
MTB > REGRESS C1 2 PREDICTORS C2 C5;
SUBC> RESIDS C4;
SUBC> DW.
MTB > CORR C1 C2 C5
```

The LAG command is used to lag the data in C1 one period and store the lagged data in C5. The REGRESS command is used to run a regression analysis using disposable income and operating revenue lagged one period to predict operating revenue. The CORR command is used to compute a correlation matrix for the variables operating revenue, disposable income, and operating revenue lagged one period.

```
MTB > REGRESS C1 1 PREDICTOR C5;
SUBC> RESIDS C4;
SUBC> DW.
```

SAS COMPUTER PACKAGE

The SAS computer package can be used to develop autoregressive models. The SAS commands to analyze Example 17.21 are:

```
TITLE "SEASONAL AUTOREGRESSIVE MODEL";
DATA OUTBOARD;
 INPUT YT XT;
 LABEL YT=SALES
       YT4=LAGSALES
        XT=TIME;
 YT4=LAG4(YT);
CARDS;
147.6 1
251.8 2
273.1 3
249.1 4
139.3 5
221.2 6
260.2 7
259.5 8
140.5 9
245.5 10
298.8 11
287.0 12
168.8 13
322.6 14
393.5 15
404.3 16
260.7 17
401.1 18
464.6 19
479.7 20
264.4 21
402.6 22
411.3 23
385.9 24
232.7 25
309.2 26
310.7 27
293.0 28
205.1 29
234.4 30
285.4 31
258.7 32
193.2 33
263.7 34
PROC REG;
 MODEL YT=YT4 XT/ DW;
ENDSAS;
```

The TITLE command names the SAS run. The DATA command gives the data a name. The INPUT command names and gives the correct order for the two data fields. The YT4= LAG4(YT) command provides YT4 with the value of YT lagged four periods. For example, the value of YT in case 1 is 147.6. Therefore, the value of YT4 in case 5 is also 147.6. The next 20 lines are card images that represent the YT variable (sales) and the XT variable (time). The PROC REG command and MODEL subcommand indicate that YT is the dependent variable and the predictor variables are XT and YT4. The DW subcommand computes the Durbin-Watson statistic.

The SAS computer package can also be used to determine significant autocorrelation coefficients. The SAS commands to analyze Solved Exercises 3 and 4 are:

```
TITLE "SAS ARIMA EXAMPLE";
DATA PREMIUMS;
INPUT Y;
CARDS;
4509
5439
6286
6669
6404
6169
6557
8029
8214
9161
10825
PROC ARIMA;
 IDENTIFY VAR=Y;
```

The TITLE command names the SAS run. The DATA command gives the data a name. The 11 lines of numbers are card images that represent the amount of life premiums offered from 1982 through 1992. The PROC ARIMA command determines the significant autocorrelations among the given lag periods. Table 17.28 shows the computer output for this SAS run.

TABLE 17.28 SAS Output for Solved Exercises 3 and 4

```
                              "SAS ARIMA EXAMPLE"
                               ARIMA PROCEDURE

                    NAME OF VARIABLE        =          Y

                    MEAN OF WORKING SERIES=     7114.73
                    STANDARD DEVIATION    =      1710.7
                    NUMBER OF OBSERVATIONS=          11

                               AUTOCORRELATIONS

LAG COVARIANCE CORRELATION -1 9 8 7 6 5 4 3 2 1 0 1 2 3 4 5 6 7 8 9 1        STD
 0    2926507    1.00000  |                    |********************|          0
 1    1634342    0.55846  |          •         |***********•        |   0.301511
 2     798635    0.27290  |  •                 |*****          •    |   0.384206
 3     358755    0.12259  |  •                 |**               •  |   0.401441
 4    -117672   -0.04021  |  •                *|                 •  |    0.40483
 5    -255636   -0.08735  |  •               **|                 •  |   0.405193
```

TABLE 17.28 SAS Output for Solved Exercises 3 and 4

```
 6    -412623    -0.14100  |  .          ***|          .  |  0.406901
 7    -688545    -0.23528  |  .        *****|          .  |  0.411319
 8    -851655    -0.29101  | .        ******|           . |  0.423377
 9   -1049949    -0.35877  | .       *******|            .|  0.441187
10    -878905    -0.30033  |.         ******|            .|  0.466957
                           |.. MARKS TWO STANDARD ERRORS

                      INVERSE AUTOCORRELATIONS

       LAG CORRELATION -1 9 8 7 6 5 4 3 2 1 0 1 2 3 4 5 6 7 8 9 1
        1   -0.46311   |        .  *********|          .          |
        2    0.07776   |        .           |**        .          |
        3   -0.10922   |        .         **|          .          |
        4    0.09891   |        .           |**        .          |
        5   -0.00004   |        .           |          .          |

                      PARTIAL AUTOCORRELATIONS

       LAG CORRELATION -1 9 8 7 6 5 4 3 2 1 0 1 2 3 4 5 6 7 8 9 1
        1    0.55846   |        .           |***********.         |
        2   -0.05665   |        .          *|          .          |
        3   -0.00993   |        .           |          .          |
        4   -0.13571   |        .        ***|          .          |
        5    0.00005   |        .           |          .          |
        6   -0.09434   |        .         **|          .          |
        7   -0.15075   |        .        ***|          .          |
        8   -0.13016   |        .        ***|          .          |
        9   -0.18591   |        .       ****|          .          |
       10   -0.02254   |        .           |          .          |

                AUTOCORRELATION CHECK FOR WHITE NOISE

    TO    CHI                      AUTOCORRELATIONS
   LAG  SQUARE DF   PROB
     6    6.70  6  0.350   0.558  0.273  0.123 -0.040 -0.087 -0.141
```

Chapter

18 Decision Making under Uncertainty

Yong Chu, weeping at the crossroads, said, "Isn't it here that you take a half step wrong and wake up a thousand miles astray?"
the Confucian Hsun-tzu

Objectives

When you have completed this chapter, you will be able to:

Use different criteria to make a decision by means of a payoff table.

Determine the value of perfect information in a complex decision.

Develop a tree diagram.

Make a decision by revising prior probabilities based on additional experimental or sample information.

Explain the concept of utility theory.

On September 21, 1989, *The Wall Street Journal* reported on the activities of The Procter & Gamble Co. The article indicated that this large company's decision-making process is complex and time-consuming, with every package redesign decision traveling through half a dozen management layers.

The title of this chapter is a good working definition of the management process. The concepts of this text are all designed to prepare the manager to make effective and timely decisions. This chapter examines the uncertainty that attends every business decision.

WHY MANAGERS NEED TO KNOW ABOUT DECISION MAKING

Managers are paid to make decisions for their organizations without all the information they might like. Those who become skilled in the decision-making process move up in the organization and are called on to make even more important decisions.

Since decision making under uncertainty is a daily part of a manager's job, it's only natural that a branch of study in business concentrates exclusively on this aspect of management. This chapter discusses techniques and approaches developed to assist the decision maker. Many of these techniques are commonly used in the automatic thought processes of every manager. Others are not so obvious, and a knowledge of them can help the manager make better decisions.

Procter & Gamble, as reported in *The Wall Street Journal,* saw its earnings rise by 18% in 1989. This achievement suggests an effective decision-making apparatus in spite of its complexity. Perhaps this successful company uses some of the formal decision-making techniques discussed in this chapter.

DECISION CRITERIA AND THE PAYOFF TABLE

All decision makers are faced with alternatives and states of nature. An *alternative* is a course of action or a strategy that may be chosen by a decision maker (for example, not wearing a coat tomorrow). A *state of nature* (or the world) is a situation over which the decision maker has little or no control (for example, tomorrow's weather). To present the decision alternatives, the analyst can develop either *payoff tables* or *tree diagrams.*

Payoff Table

In this section, different decision criteria are represented using the **payoff table.** This method of structuring a complex decision displays the financial consequences of every possible decision against every state of nature that could subsequently develop. In this table, the possible actions to be taken are listed in the columns, and the various states of the world are shown in the rows. By studying the payoff table, the decision maker can assess the financial consequences of different decisions as they relate to the state of the world.

The **payoff table** shows the payoff for every combination of decision and state of the world.

EXAMPLE 18.1 Jenny Hebert, manager of the Ward Department Store, must determine the number of units of a particular product to stock each day. From past experience she knows that the number of units that will be demanded on a given day is between one and six, so these are the stock units that will be considered. Depending on the number of units stocked and the number demanded, a different profit will result. These various profits are summarized in the payoff table in Table 18.1.

As the payoff table shows, there are 36 possible profits each day. Jenny must decide how many units to stock, or which column of the table to choose. The row, representing the true state of the world for the day, is unknown at the time the stocking decision is made and will be determined by the market. As indicated, profits can range anywhere from \$25 to \$150 each day.

Table 18.1 implies that each unit sold produces a profit of \$25. If one unit is stocked and one is demanded, the payoff, as indicated by the upper left value in the table, is \$25; this represents the profit generated by selling that unit. Beneath this value are other daily profits of \$25, indicating that the only possible profit for the day is the \$25 from selling the one unit in stock, regardless of how many additional units are demanded. Other matching values below the diagonal similarly indicate that profits won't rise after the total number of units in stock have been sold.

To the right of each profit along the diagonal, a \$10 reduction in daily profit is indicated for each additional unsold unit. For example, the profit of \$15 in the first row and second column indicates that if two units are stocked and only one is sold, net profit is \$25 for the unit sold, minus \$10 lost on the unsold unit. Thus, Table 18.1 indicates a \$10 reduction in profit for each additional unsold unit.

TABLE 18.1 Payoff Table for Example 18.1 (Profits in Dollars)

Number demanded	Decision: number of units to stock					
	1	2	3	4	5	6
1	25	15	5	−5	−15	−25
2	25	50	40	30	20	10
3	25	50	75	65	55	45
4	25	50	75	100	90	80
5	25	50	75	100	125	115
6	25	50	75	100	125	150

The payoff table enables the decision maker to view each possible combination of decision and subsequent development. In real situations, the payoff table may be quite large, incorporating many possible decisions and states of the world.

To complete the evaluation of a complex situation, the probabilities of the various events or states of the world identified in the payoff table must be estimated. The picture is then complete: the possible decisions have been identified, the states of the world that might develop have been specified, and the likelihood of each of these developments has been assessed. A rational decision that meets the decision maker's criteria can then be made.

Once the probabilities of the various events have been estimated, the expected monetary value (EMV) of each action or decision can be computed. Recall the concept of expected value discussed in Chapter 5. When the values of a discrete random variable have been identified along with their probabilities of occurring, the average value of this variable over many trials can be computed; this is known as the *expected value of the variable*. Equation 5.1 summarizes this computation of expected value.

Expected Monetary Value

The **expected monetary value** is the average profit that would result if a decision were repeated many times and the decision maker chose the same alternative each time. It is the expected profit for a decision, even though the decision is to be made only once. The EMV of each decision is found by multiplying each event's payoff by the probability of its occurrence and adding these products. This computation is illustrated in Example 18.2.

> The **expected monetary value** is the average profit that would result if a decision were repeated many times and each time the decision maker chose the same alternative.

EXAMPLE 18.2 In Example 18.1, Jenny Hebert needed to decide the number of units of a product to stock each day. From past experience she knows the probabilities of various numbers of units being demanded each day. (See Table 18.2, which indicates that the probability of three units being demanded is .40, for example.) The EMV is computed by multiplying each event's payoff by the probability of its occurrence. Thus, the expected monetary value for the decision to stock four units is

$$\text{EMV} = -5(.05) + 30(.15) + 65(.40) + 100(.25) + 100(.10) + 100(.05) = 70.25$$

TABLE 18.2 Payoff Table for Example 18.2: Expected Monetary Value

		Decision: number of units to stock					
Probability	Demand	1	2	3	4	5	6
.05	1	25	15	5	−5	−15	−25
.15	2	25	50	40	30	20	10
.40	3	25	50	75	65	55	45
.25	4	25	50	75	100	90	80
.10	5	25	50	75	100	125	115
.05	6	25	50	75	100	125	150
	EMV:	25	48.25	66.25	70.25	65.50	57.25

The EMV for each decision is shown in the last row of Table 18.2. Jenny can see from examining this row that the decision to stock four units will provide the highest expected profit (highest EMV).

Note that the payoff tables in this chapter use discrete decision levels and demand levels. For example, only certain demands such as 1, 2, 3, 4, 5, or 6 are considered. A more general treatment of the subject would permit any value for demand within some specified range. Such continuous distributions for demand are an extension of the basic ideas presented in this chapter and are covered in texts that discuss decision making under uncertainty in more detail.

EXAMPLE 18.3 King Hardware Store manager Joyce Cary must decide how many lawnmowers to order for summer. It is difficult to order additional units after the season has started, but then there is a cost associated with having more units on hand than can be sold. A lawnmower costs an average of $150 and sells for $200, resulting in a $50 profit. Units that are unsold at the end of the season are sold to a cut-rate mail order house for $25, resulting in a $125 loss per unit. Joyce needs a probability distribution for the season's demand so she can decide how many units to order. The situation is simplified because Joyce can place an order only in hundreds; thus, she knows that she must order either 300, 400, 500, 600, or 700 units.

After going over records from past years and projecting demand for the coming season, she formulates demand probabilities for each stock level. She then calculates the profits for each possible combination of stock level and demand. The result is a payoff table (Table 18.3).

TABLE 18.3 Payoff Table for Example 18.3 (Profits in Thousands of Dollars)

		Stock level: number of lawnmowers				
Probability	Demand	300	400	500	600	700
.10	300	15	2.5	−10	−22.5	−35
.20	400	15	20	7.5	−5	−17.5
.30	500	15	20	25	12.5	0
.25	600	15	20	25	30	17.5
.15	700	15	20	25	30	35
1.00						

The table shows a $15,000 profit for stocking and selling 300 lawnmowers, regardless of how many are demanded. For each additional 100 units stocked and sold, there's an additional $5,000 profit. These values appear along the diagonal of the payoff table and represent profits when the number of units stocked exactly equals the number demanded.

Beneath each profit along the primary diagonal is the same profit, since units demanded in excess of units stocked don't generate additional profits. To the right of each profit along the diagonal is a reduction of $12,500, representing the loss of 100 unsold units.

Joyce can now consider her decision criteria as she contemplates Table 18.3's payoffs. She must decide how many units to stock for the coming season; that is, she must decide which column of the table to use. To make this decision, she must first decide on her financial objective.

One objective is to aim for the highest possible profit. This very aggressive strategy would be implemented by stocking 700 units, since the 700 column contains the largest profit in the table: $35,000. This stock level would also be chosen if Joyce's objective were to meet all customer demand, regardless of profits.

Another objective might be to assume the worst will happen and stock accordingly. If the lowest profit in each column is identified, the maximum of these values is $15,000, found in the first column. Therefore, a very conservative decision maker might choose to stock 300 units: even under the worst conditions (only 300 units demanded), a profit of $15,000 is guaranteed. Another objective that would be met by stocking 300 units is to ensure that no inventory is left over at the end of the season.

Another approach is to stock the number of units that would generate the highest profits, while avoiding any possibility of a loss. This is a popular philosophy in business, sometimes known as the "cover your number" decision criterion. The best choice for this objective is to stock 400 units since the likely profit (90% chance) is $20,000, and no loss is possible.

Another possible objective is to choose that course of action that maximizes the expected profit for the season. To determine the stock level for this objective, calculate the expected monetary value (EMV) for each of the five stock levels, choosing the stock level with the highest EMV.

Here are the expected values for each column of the table. For each stock level, each payoff is multiplied by the probability of that row, and these products are added:

Stock 300: $(1.00)(15) = 15$
Stock 400: $(.10)(2.5) + (.90)(20) = 18.25$
Stock 500: $(.10)(-10) + (.20)(7.5) + (.70)(25) = 18.00$
Stock 600: $(.10)(-22.5) + (.20)(-5) + (.30)(12.5) + (.40)(30) = 12.50$
Stock 700: $(.10)(-35) + (.20)(-17.5) + (.30)(0) + (.25)(17.5) + (.15)(35) = 2.63$

The highest possible expected payoff results from stocking 400 units. The $18,250 payoff results from a combination of the probabilities of various demand levels, from the amount of profit for a unit sold, and from the loss suffered if a stocked unit is unsold. Joyce summarizes the situation as follows:

Decision	Rationale
Stock 300.	Find the highest profit if the worst situation develops.
	Do not have stock on hand at the end of the season.
Stock 400.	Maximize profits but avoid the possibility of a loss.
	Maximize expected profits.
Stock 700.	Try for the highest possible profit.
	Satisfy all possible demand.

Based on this summary, Joyce decides to stock 400 units.

EXPECTED VALUE OF PERFECT INFORMATION

It is often of value to consider what perfect information in a complex decision situation is worth. Although perfect information is seldom available to the decision maker, its value can be used as a benchmark to evaluate the benefit of acquiring additional information. If reliable information costs \$1,000 to acquire, but the value of perfect information in the situation is only \$500, the additional information is obviously not worth paying for. On the other hand, if the value of perfect information is \$10,000 for the same situation, the decision maker might be willing to pay \$1,000 to get additional information that would lead to a better decision.

Expected Value of Perfect Information

The **expected value of perfect information** (EVPI) is the difference between the expected payoff with perfect information and the expected payoff under uncertainty. If perfect information produces a profit of \$50,000, for example, and the best the decision maker could do under uncertainty is \$35,000, then the value of perfect information—should it exist—is the difference, \$15,000.

> The **expected value of perfect information** is the difference between the payoff that would result with perfect information and the payoff that would result under uncertainty.

EXAMPLE 18.4 Joyce Cary has decided to stock 400 lawnmowers for the season, reasoning that this stock level will maximize the expected payoff at \$18,250. She then begins thinking about an offer she received from a forecasting agency to provide her with a forecast of seasonal demand for lawnmowers in her area. She could use this forecast to predict her own sales level. The cost of this forecast is \$9,000, and Joyce wonders if such an expenditure is justified.

Joyce decides to calculate the value (to her) of perfect information regarding sales for the upcoming season. She can then compare this value with the cost of the good, but imperfect, information she's being offered.

If Joyce could foresee the season's demand with total accuracy, she'd realize one of the profits along the primary diagonal in Table 18.3. There's a 10% chance that she would correctly foresee a demand of 300 units, stock that number of lawnmowers, and make \$15,000. Likewise, there's a 20% chance that she would correctly predict sales of 400 units and make \$20,000, and so on. Under these conditions, she would experience the following expected profits for the season. This value is called *the expected profit under certainty*:

$$(.10)(15) + (.20)(20) + (.30)(25) + (.25)(30) + (.15)(35) = 25.75$$

Joyce can now calculate the expected value of perfect information. If she had perfect information, her expected seasonal profit would be \$25,750. As things stand, without knowledge of demand, she has calculated expected profit of \$18,250. This is the highest expected value she can choose and results from stocking 400 units. The difference between these two values is the expected value of perfect information.

Expected value of perfect information = Expected payoff with perfect information − Payoff resulting under uncertainty

EVPI = $25,750 − $18,250 = $7,500

Since *perfect* information about the season's demand is worth only $7,500, Joyce is not willing to pay $9,000 for a forecast of demand, even if it is very accurate. She turns down the offer.

EXERCISES

1. Why does an analyst construct a payoff table?

2. Why is it desirable to choose the action in a payoff table that results in the highest expected monetary value (EMV)?
3. Explain the concept of expected profit under certainty.
4. What is meant by the term *expected value of perfect information*? Why is it important to know the EVPI?
5. A year's supply of shoes of a certain popular type must be ordered in advance by a large department store. Each pair costs $30, sells for $60, and can be sold to a discounter for $15 if unsold at the end of the year. Stock levels being considered are 20, 30, 40, and 50 pairs. Construct a payoff table for the following demand levels: 20, 25, 30, 35, 40, 45, 50.
6. (This question refers to Exercise 5.) How many pairs of shoes should be ordered if expected profits are to be maximized? The demand levels, along with their associated probabilities, are:

Dozen	Probability
20	.20
25	.25
30	.20
35	.15
40	.10
45	.05
50	.05

7. Consider the following payoff table (where payoffs are in thousands of dollars):

		Stock level				
Probability	Sales	100	200	300	400	500
.25	100	5	3	1	−1	−3
.35	200	5	10	8	6	4
.25	300	5	10	15	13	11
.10	400	5	10	15	20	18
.05	500	5	10	15	20	25

a. What is the profit on a unit sold?

b. What is the loss on a unit unsold?

c. What is the expected monetary value if 300 units are stocked?

d. What is the optimal stocking level if expected profits are to be maximized?

e. What is the expected value of perfect information?

8. Barnes Tractor and Implement, a farm implement dealer, needs to decide how many large combines to order for the coming year. The matter is complicated by John Deere's new Maximizer combine, a machine featured in *Successful Farming* (February 1989, p. 26). It is the first new combine design by Deere in 20 years, and Barnes is uncertain how its appearance on the market will affect sales of conventional units.

   The choice of how many to order has been narrowed to 10, 20, 30, 40, or 50. The company believes the probabilities associated with selling these numbers of tractors are .15, .15, .20, .25, and .25, respectively. The profit to the dealer of selling a unit is $5,000; the loss associated with failing to sell a stocked unit is $1,000.

   a. Develop the payoff table.

   b. What is the expected monetary value if 50 units are ordered?

   c. What is the optimal stocking level, using the criterion of maximizing expected profit?

   d. What is the expected value of perfect information in this situation?

   e. What criteria would lead to stocking decisions other than the one identified in part *b*?

9. The Evergreen Corporation is trying to decide what size of can opener plant to build in the Cleveland area. Three alternatives are being considered: plants with capacities of 25,000, 40,000, and 55,000 can openers per year. Demand for Evergreen's can openers is uncertain, but management has assigned the following probabilities to five levels of demand. The payoff table also shows the profit, in millions of dollars, for each alternative and each possible level of demand. What size plant should Evergreen build?

		Action: Build plant with capacity of:		
Probability	Demand	25,000	40,000	55,000
.20	20,000	−3	−5	−7
.35	30,000	0	−2	−4
.25	40,000	1	4	5
.10	50,000	2	5	8
.10	60,000	2	6	10

TREE DIAGRAM ANALYSIS

Tree Diagrams

Decision makers frequently use **tree diagrams** to summarize complex situations so that their essential elements can be identified and used to make rational decisions. A valuable visual aid, the tree diagram, allows a complex situation to be easily understood by any manager. Two symbols are generally used in constructing a tree diagram:

1. A box is used to represent a *decision node* from which one of several alternatives may be selected.
2. A circle is used to represent a *state-of-nature node* out of which a particular state of nature will develop.

Example 18.5 and Figure 18.1 illustrate the use of these symbols.

FIGURE 18.1 Decision Tree Diagram for Example 18.5

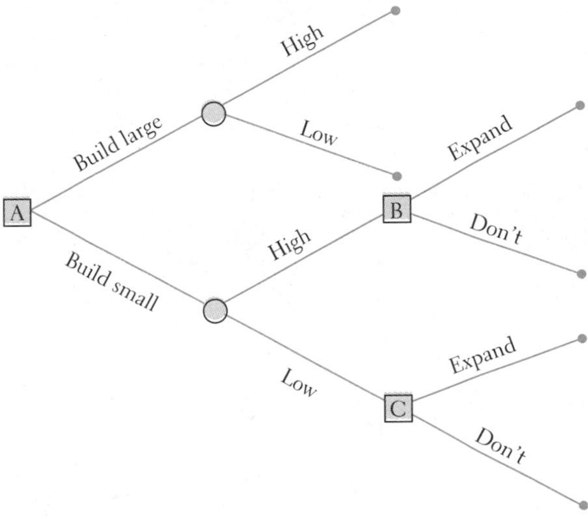

Tree diagrams are charts used by decision makers to summarize complex situations so that their essential elements can be identified.

EXAMPLE 18.5 The King Manufacturing Company must decide whether to build a small plant or a large plant to produce panels for a new product to be introduced next year. After the plant is built and the product produced, market demand will become known (market demand will be either high or low). If a small plant is built, it can be expanded once high market demand has occurred.

Gwynn Luvello, vice president of planning, constructs the tree diagram in Figure 18.1 to help make this decision. The box labeled A on the left side is a decision node. King must decide whether to build a small plant or a large plant. Since there are two alternatives, the tree diagram has two branches labeled *build small* and *build large*. Each branch leads to a circle. The circles are state-of-nature nodes, from which one of two states of nature will result: market demand will be either high or low.

After market demand has been determined, a small plant may or may not be expanded. Boxes B and C represent these decision nodes. The decision is to either expand the small plant or not to expand. Figure 18.1 summarizes the King Company's decision-making situation.

The tree diagram is useful for visualizing the King Company's problem, but by itself it isn't a complete decision-making tool. The next step is to assign cash flows to each tree segment to arrive at a cash value for each branch. These final cash values represent the payoffs.

Organizational decisions such as the ones in these examples are significant because they involve the possibility of more or less profit for the company. At the conclusion of each set of possible outcomes, or branches in a tree diagram, there is some payoff. There are also costs involved with certain branches that must be identified too. Along with the probability and decision branches in the tree diagram, the identification of the costs and payoffs for various possibilities enables the decision maker to assess the situation.

The next step in the process is to assign probabilities to the states of nature. This is usually done subjectively. (Subjective probabilities were discussed in Chapter 5.) Example 18.6 and Figure 18.2 illustrate the idea of assigning payoffs and subjective probabilities to a tree diagram.

FIGURE 18.2 Decision Tree Diagram for Example 18.6

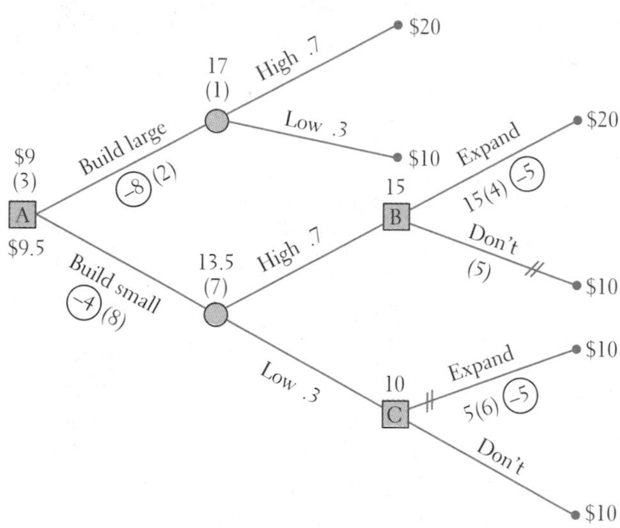

EXAMPLE 18.6 Gwynn Luvello decides to determine the cash flow for the tree diagram in Figure 18.1. Her analyst provides the following cost and payoff estimates:

Costs

Cost of building a large plant: $8 million
Cost of building a small plant: $4 million
Cost of expansion: $5 million

Payoffs

Revenue from high demand for a large or expanded plant: \$20 million

Revenue from high demand for a small plant: \$10 million

Revenue from low demand: \$10 million

Next, Gwynn has the marketing department provide her with estimates for high and low market demand for the new product. The marketing department feels that there is a .7 probability of high demand for the new product and a .3 probability of low demand. Armed with knowledge of the payoffs and probabilities, Gwynn develops Figure 18.2.

With the payoffs and probabilities indicated on the tree diagram, the final step is to find the best decision branch. The best decision usually amounts to the alternative with the highest expected monetary value (EMV). Identifying this alternative requires that the analyst work backward along the tree diagram, starting at the right-hand side of the tree and moving to the left until the first decision node is reached. There are two rules for working backward on a tree diagram:

1. For each state-of-nature node, find the EMV.
2. For each decision node, pick the alternative with the largest EMV.

Example 18.7 illustrates the implementation of these rules.

EXAMPLE 18.7 Gwynn is now ready to make a decision. She begins by computing the EMV for the *build large* decision branch. The analysis is done from right to left. The payoff for high market demand is \$20 million, and the probability of it occurring is .7. The payoff for low market demand is \$10 million, and the probability of it occurring is .3. Therefore, the EMV is \$17 million, as shown:

$$\text{EMV} = .7(20) + .3(10) = 17.0$$

Since the cost of building the large plant is \$8 million, as indicated by -8 in the circle coded (2) in Figure 18.2, the expected monetary value for this branch is actually \$9 million (\$17 − \$8), as indicated at the point of the figure coded (3).

Next, Gwynn analyzes the *build small* decision branch. Again, the analysis is done from right to left. Payoff for the *high demand–expand* branch is \$20 million. However, the cost of expansion is \$5 million, as indicated by -5 in the circle, so the EMV is \$15 million, the value coded (4), for this branch. This value is larger than the EMV for the *high demand–don't expand* branch (\$10 million), so she eliminates the *don't expand* branch by drawing two hashmarks, coded (5), through it.

The payoff for the *low demand–expand* branch is \$10 million. Since the cost of expansion is \$5 million, the EMV for this branch coded (6), is \$5 million. This value is smaller than that for the *low demand–don't expand* branch (\$10 million), so Gwynn eliminates the *low demand–expand* branch by drawing two hashmarks through it.

Now Gwynn knows that if a small plant is built and demand is high, she should expand, for an EMV of \$15 million. She also knows that if a small plant is built and demand is low, she should not expand, in which case the EMV is estimated to be $10 million.

Next, Gwynn computes an EMV of $13.5 million, coded (7), for the *high/low demand* state-of-nature node:

$$\text{EMV} = .7(15) + .3(10) = 13.5$$

Since the cost of building the small plant is $4 million, shown as −4 in the circle coded (8), the expected monetary value for this branch is actually $9.5 million ($13.5 − $4).

Based on the EMV criterion, Gwynn recommends that a small plant be built, and if market demand is high, the plant should be expanded.

BAYES' THEOREM

Bayes' Theorem

Bayes' theorem is designed to modify probability assessments on the basis of additional information. Such modification is a process that takes place in the minds of decision makers every day.

> **Bayes' theorem** involves the process of revising prior probabilities based on additional experimental or sample information.

In the 1700s, the Reverend Thomas Bayes, an English Presbyterian minister and mathematician, developed a formal procedure for using additional information to revise probabilities. This theorem is quite useful in the decision-making process since additional information is often obtained prior to an important decision. Recall the discussion of the expected value of perfect information earlier in this chapter. Although the information gathered from a sample or test market is not perfect, Bayes' theorem provides a way of modifying the decision maker's view of an uncertain world.

In utilizing Bayes' theorem, the tree diagram method will be used. In addition, the two basic rules of probability discussed in Chapter 5 need to be reviewed. Examples 18.8 and 18.9 demonstrate these rules.

EXAMPLE 18.8 The multiplication law of probability states that to determine the probability of a sequence of independent events occurring, the individual probabilities of the events are multiplied together. The multiplication law can also be used for dependent events as long as the sequence is known. The key concept is that if a sequence of events is specified along with their individual probabilities, the multiplication rule can be used to find the probability of that sequence.

Suppose there's a 45% chance that our competitor will reduce the price of a key product. If that happens, there will be an 80% chance that our own sales will be negatively affected. The probability that our sales will drop can be found using the multiplication rule, even though the two events are not independent:

$$P(\text{sales drop}) = (.45)(.80) = .36$$

We have a 36% chance that our sales will drop.

EXAMPLE 18.9 The addition rule states that to find the probability of an event that has more than one way of occurring, the probability of each possible way must be computed, and all these probabilities are then added together. Suppose a television set production line produces a perfect set only 50% of the time, and that the appearance of such a set is random. What is the probability of getting exactly two perfect sets in a random testing of four sets? There are several ways in which this can happen; therefore, each way must be identified, the probability computed, and the resulting probabilities added. Here are the different ways to get two perfect TV sets in a testing of four sets, where G represents good and N represents not good. The probability of each way is computed using the multiplication rule, and the sum of these probabilities is the correct answer:

$$\begin{aligned}
\text{P(GGNN)} &= .5 \times .5 \times .5 \times .5 = .0625 \\
\text{P(GNNG)} &= .5 \times .5 \times .5 \times .5 = .0625 \\
\text{P(NNGG)} &= .5 \times .5 \times .5 \times .5 = .0625 \\
\text{P(GNGN)} &= .5 \times .5 \times .5 \times .5 = .0625 \\
\text{P(NGNG)} &= .5 \times .5 \times .5 \times .5 = .0625 \\
\text{P(NGGN)} &= .5 \times .5 \times .5 \times .5 = \underline{.0625} \\
& \qquad\qquad\qquad\qquad\quad .3750
\end{aligned}$$

There's a 37.5% chance that we could select four TV sets at random and find that exactly two of them are good.

Bayes' theorem appears as Equation 18.1. This equation is actually a shortened version of the full mathematical expression for Bayes' theorem,[1] but the theorem will be used here in this form:

$$P(A|B) = \frac{P(\text{A and } B)}{P(B)} \tag{18.1}$$

where $P(A|B)$ = Probability of event A occurring given that event B has occurred
$P(\text{A and } B)$ = Joint probability of events A and B happening in succession, under conditions of statistical dependence
$P(B)$ = Probability that event B has occurred

EXAMPLE 18.10 Don Karger, production manager of the MacDonald Manufacturing Corporation, is trying to improve the efficiency of one of his assembly lines. Each Monday morning a machine that produces a key part is set up for the week. Setting up this particular machine is difficult and time-consuming. Don has studied past

[1]The general statement of Bayes' theorem for n events $A_1, A_2, \ldots, A_n$ is

$$P(A_1|B) = \frac{P(A_1)P(B|A_1)}{P(A_1)P(B|A_1) + P(A_2)P(B|A_2) + \cdots + P(A_n)P(B|A_n)}$$

records and discovered that the machine is set up correctly only 70% of the time. He also determined that if the machine is set up correctly, it will produce good parts 95% of the time, but if set up incorrectly, will produce good parts only 40% of the time.

Don decides to start the machine and produce one part before he begins the production run. The first part produced is tested and found to be good. What is the revised probability of proper machine setup given this sample evidence?

The application of Bayes' theorem is demonstrated using the tree diagram in Figure 18.3. The first branch shows the two mutually exclusive possibilities for the state of the machine once it's set up Monday morning: the machine is set up either correctly or incorrectly. Past experience indicates that the machine is set up correctly 70% of the time [$P(C) = .7$]. Since the probabilities of a mutually exclusive event must add to 1.0, the probability that the machine is set up incorrectly is .30 ($1.0 - .7 = .3$).

The secondary branches are based on whether the machine is set up correctly. Past experience indicates that if the machine is set up correctly, the probability that it will produce a good part is .95; incorrect setup reduces this probability to .40.

The numerator of the equation for Bayes' theorem for this example is found by using the multiplication rule in conjunction with Figure 18.3. The probability of a good setup followed by the production of a good part, the numerator is

$$(.70)(.95) = .665$$

FIGURE 18.3 Bayes' Theorem Tree Diagram for Example 18.10

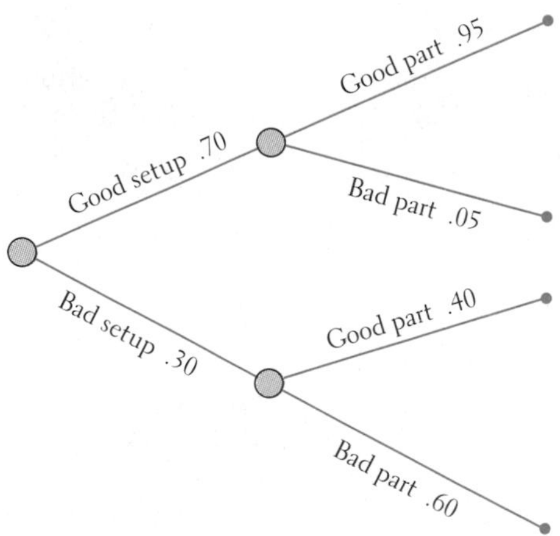

The denominator for Bayes' theorem represents the probability of the given event occurring; in this case, the appearance of a good part. One way to get a good part is following a correct setup, as just shown. The other way is to produce a good part following a bad setup. The denominator of Bayes' theorem is the sum of these two probabilities:

$$(.70)(.95) + (.30)(.40) = .665 + .12 = .785$$

The revised probability that the machine is set up correctly, given that it has produced a good part, is now computed using Equation 18.1.

$$P(A|B) = \frac{P(A \text{ and } B)}{P(B)}$$

$$P(C|GP) \frac{P(C \text{ and } GP)}{P(GP)} = \frac{.665}{.785} = .85$$

When the machine was set up Monday morning, the probability that it was set up correctly was .70. Now that the machine has produced a good part, Don knows that the revised probability of a correct setup is .85. If he wants more assurance, Don can test additional parts.

EXAMPLE 18.11 Loretta Lister, market researcher for the St. Ives Corporation, is using a test market to estimate the national market for her firm's new software product. An article in *The Futurist* (July–August 1992, p. 10) claims that advances in computer technology and information services may soon lead to a global web of networks capable of managing international problems.

She estimates demand for her new software product as either high (40% chance), medium (30% chance), or low (30% chance). St. Ives decides to test-market the product in a midwestern city it has used in the past to estimate national success. Loretta knows that the test market isn't infallible, however, and that it may mislead the company regarding public acceptance of a new product. Specifically, she calculates the following probabilities based on past experience with this test market:

1. For a product that later experiences high national sales, there is a 90% chance that the test market will indicate a successful product.
2. For a product that later experiences a medium national market, there is a 50% chance that the test market will indicate a successful product.
3. For a product that later experiences a low national market, there is a 20% chance that the test market will indicate a successful product.

St. Ives introduces the software product into the test market for a three-month trial period. At the end of this time, the product proves successful in this market. Loretta now wonders what the probability of national success is for this new product.

The initial probabilities of product success are shown in Figure 18.4, along with the probabilities based on the reaction of the test market.

The test market conclusion is that a good product has been developed. Given this result, what is the probability that the product will have high sales nationally? Bayes' theorem is used to compute this revised probability:

$$P(\text{high}|\text{good}) = \frac{P(\text{high and good})}{P(\text{good})}$$

$$= \frac{(.40)(.90)}{(.40)(.90) + (.30)(.50) + (.30)(.20)}$$

$$= \frac{.36}{.36 + .15 + .06} = .63$$

FIGURE 18.4 Test Market Tree Diagram for Example 18.11

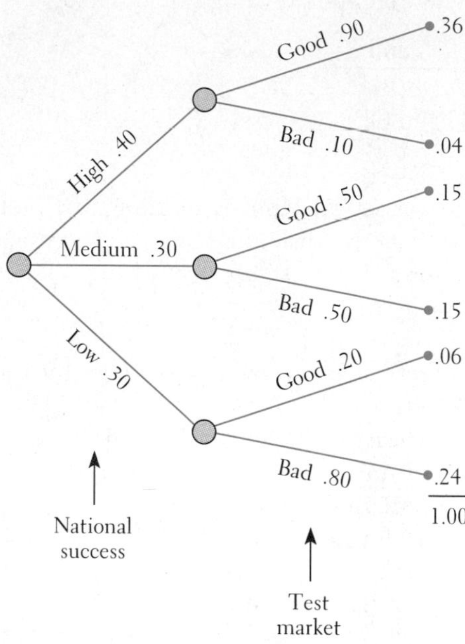

There's a 63% chance that the new product will be successful nationally, given that it has shown a good response in the test market. This is higher than the original probability of a national success (40%) and enables the company to make a more rational decision about committing the millions of dollars necessary to launch the product nationally.

UTILITY CONSIDERATIONS

The use of the EMV decision criterion is oversimplified in that it assumes indifference among various dollar amounts on the part of the decision maker. In fact, due to their varying asset bases, different companies have different utility functions. Furthermore, individual company managers may have different views of the impact of various sums of money on their organizations. A formal recognition of this matter is sometimes referred to as **utility theory**, because it reflects the usefulness (utility) of various payoffs to the firm.

Utility Theory

> **Utility theory** reflects the usefulness (utility) of various payoffs to the firm.

Suppose you were given the choice between taking \$500 or risking the money on a double-or-nothing investment (a .5 chance of a payoff of \$1,000 and a .5 chance of no payoff). The expected value of the gamble is also \$500 (.50 × \$1,000 + .50 × 0). Since the expected value of the gamble exactly equals the expected value of the certain payoff, the EMV criterion would result in indifference between these two choices.

Now suppose you are guaranteed \$5 million after taxes, and you may choose to risk the money on a double-or-nothing investment (a .5 chance of a payoff of \$10 million and a .5 chance of no payoff). The expected value approach again leads to indifference between these two choices, since the expected payoff is \$5 million. A very large corporation might actually be indifferent between these two choices, given identical expected values. As individuals, however, we would all choose the sure \$5 million rather than take a chance on getting nothing. The reason, based on utility theory, is that the first \$5 million has considerable utility (usefulness) in our lives, but the addition of a second \$5 million does not. That is, an additional \$5 million wouldn't appreciably alter our lives.

EXAMPLE 18.12 A company faces a choice between two propositions, or ventures. For each, the future is uncertain; however, probabilities of the possible outcomes can be estimated, and the payoffs for various alternatives are known. These two ventures are summarized in Figure 18.5.

FIGURE 18.5 Tree Diagrams for Example 18.12 (Millions of Dollars)

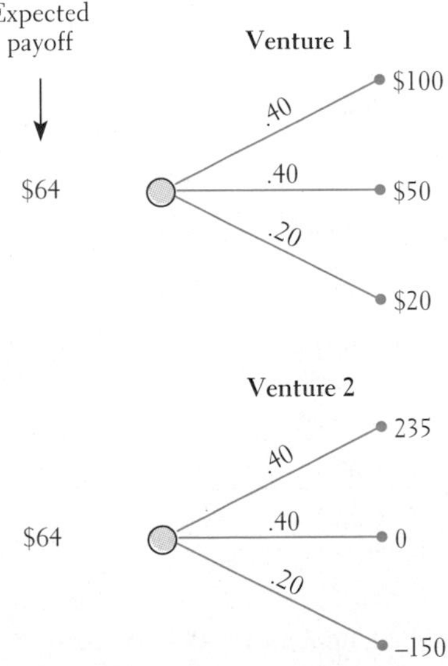

For each venture the expected payoff is \$64 million. These values were calculated by multiplying each payoff by its probability of occurring and adding these products. Using EMV reasoning, the two ventures are exactly the same, and the choice between them would result in indifference.

However, when payoffs are examined more closely, there appears to be a big difference between the two ventures. Venture 1 would appeal to a more conservative decision maker since there's no probability of a loss, a profit is guaranteed, and the largest payoff ($100 million) can be regarded as large enough. A more bold or aggressive decision maker might prefer Venture 2. The possibility of a $235 million payoff might be very attractive to the bold manager, and the possibility of no profits or a loss of $150 million might not be viewed as a strong negative factor.

The key point here is that different amounts of money are viewed differently from firm to firm and from one decision maker to another. Utility theory explicitly recognizes these viewpoints and incorporates them into the decision process. More advanced texts on decision making contain discussions about how utility theory is formally incorporated into complex decision-making situations.

EXERCISES

10. How are tree diagrams used by decision makers?
11. Explain how each of the following terms is used in reference to a tree diagram:
    a. State of nature
    b. Decision node
    c. Payoff
12. Bayes' theorem is designed to revise probabilities. What is the basis for such revision?
13. What is the disadvantage of collecting information to use in revising probabilities based on Bayes' theorem?
14. Explain how utility considerations might affect your decision regarding buying car insurance.
15. Explain how utility considerations might affect the Boeing Company's deliberations about designing and building a new commercial aircraft.

16. The national market for a new type of fishing reel is believed to be either strong, medium, or weak, with probabilities .45, .35, and .20, respectively. Probabilities for test market results (based on past experience with the chosen test market) are:

Test market results	National market: Strong	Medium	Weak
Good	.85	.50	.25
Bad	.15	.50	.75

    a. Draw the tree diagram that summarizes this situation.
    b. Compute the probabilities of a good test market result and a bad test market result.
    c. Suppose a test market study results in a good test. Compute the revised probabilities of strong, medium, and weak national markets.
17. About 70% of the finished goods produced by a factory are sent to chain store customers, and the remainder go to independent stores. There's a 10% chance that a chain store invoice will remain unpaid at the end of the billing period. For independent stores, this

probability is 50%. What is the probability that an unpaid account is for an independent store?

18. You think there's an 80% chance that you'll be offered a promotion during the next month. This probability is based on your own performance and on rumors of poor appraisals given some of your peers. "Poor Performance Appraisals," a September 1989 *Personnel Journal* article, leads you to believe your company's appraisal system is fair, since there are legal problems associated with a faulty system.

    From watching previous prepromotion activity, you know 90% of people about to be promoted receive an invitation to the executive dining room during the month preceding promotion. A person not about to be promoted has only a 25% chance of receiving such an invitation. If you receive an invitation to the executive dining room, what is the revised probability that you are about to be promoted?

19. Here is a summary of the situation faced by a large construction company regarding the possibility of building a new, large office building, building a smaller office building, or expanding the present building. The key factor is whether business during the next five years will be much greater, somewhat greater, the same, or smaller; the agreed-upon probabilities for these events are .35, .25, .20, and .20, respectively. Gross revenues to the company for each of these events are, in millions, $53, $35, $20, and $15, respectively.

    Cost of building a large building is $10 million. A smaller building could be built for $8 million, but if business turns out to be much larger, it would have to be enlarged at a cost of $4 million. Expanding the present building would cost $4 million and would be adequate to accommodate either the same or a smaller level of business. If business is somewhat greater, a $5 million expansion would be needed; and if business is much greater, a new site would have to be found and built on at a cost of $7 million.

    a. Draw a tree diagram that summarizes this situation.

    b. Compute the expected monetary values for each of three construction possibilities.

    c. Based on expected monetary values only, what is the rational decision sequence for the company?

    d. What utility considerations would enter into the construction decision?

Summary

This chapter has outlined some considerations that attend most decisions in modern organizations, where all the information necessary is usually not available at the time the decision must be made. Rather, estimates, probabilities, and expected values must be used to reach the best decision under conditions of uncertainty.

The payoff table is a way to show the payoffs that result from each combination of decision choice and state of the world. The expected value of perfect information constitutes the maximum amount the decision maker would pay for information that would improve the decision.

Tree diagrams are a way of focusing attention on the key elements in a decision. Tree diagrams incorporate uncertainty branches, decision choices, and final payoffs. Expected monetary value (EMV) calculations are used to evaluate each decision point and identify the best decision.

Finally, utility considerations are a means of recognizing the differences with which assorted firms and decision makers regard various payoffs. The purpose of utility theory is to formally incorporate these different viewpoints into the decision process.

Applications of Statistical Concepts in the Business World

Since decision making in the face of uncertainty is a common element of every manager's role, the concepts discussed in this chapter are used daily by every management decision maker. Unfortunately, these concepts are practiced only at the intuitive level by many managers. The decision process would be improved in many organizations if such concepts and tools as tree diagrams, expected monetary value, payoff tables, and utility theory were more formally incorporated into the process of evaluating complex situations.

Here are a number of hypothetical situations where formal use of the concepts in this chapter might prove helpful. In each situation, the decision is complex and involves many factors, including decision points, probabilities regarding the unknown future, costs of alternatives, final payoffs, and utility theory.

A company must decide whether to introduce a new laundry product or to modify a current product and introduce it as "new and improved."

A major car company is considering several design changes in its lineup. Top managers have spent a lot of time considering the future demands of American consumers as well as the costs and potential profits of various alternatives.

A quality-control manager is involved in the decision about which of five machines to install in a tire factory. The prices are all different, as are the production rates, maintenance costs, and quality of output. The labor needed to run and maintain the machines also varies.

An airplane manufacturer considers developing and introducing a new aircraft type. Because of the enormous cost of such an activity, only one of several contemplated designs can be chosen.

A company that makes computer chips is being wooed by several cities around the country. Management of the company must decide where to locate a new plant; staying in its present location is an alternative also.

Because of a drop in demand, a company that makes and distributes training films must change its way of doing business. Several alternative business activities have been considered along with simply maintaining the present business at a reduced level.

Leaders of a large city are trying to decide some policy matters regarding the city's future direction. Among the alternatives are attempting to expand "smokestack" industries, persuading modern-technology companies to relocate there, and planning a reduction in economic activity with an increase in the "quality of life."

A company is facing increased demand for its products and must decide how to expand operations. It is considering expanding on its present location, expanding to other U.S. locations, and locating some of its operations in other countries. The last consideration entails choosing from amongst several countries.

GLOSSARY

Payoff table A table showing the payoff for every combination of decision and state of the world.

Expected monetary value The average profit that would result if a decision were repeated many times and each time the decision maker chose the same alternative.

Expected value of perfect information The difference between the payoff that would result with perfect information and the payoff that would result under uncertainty.

Tree diagrams Charts used by decision makers to summarize complex situations so that their essential elements can be identified.

Bayes' theorem A theorem that involves the process of revising prior probabilities based on additional experimental or sample information.

Utility theory A concept that reflects the usefulness (utility) of various payoffs to the firm.

KEY FORMULA

Bayes' theorem

$$P(A|B) = \frac{P(A \text{ and } B)}{P(B)} \tag{18.1}$$

SOLVED EXERCISES

1. PAYOFF TABLE

Pat's Pies, a small shop, specializes in baking fancy pies. Pies are baked each morning, and any not sold the same day must be given away. Owner Pat Otten knows from past experience that she can always sell between 8 and 12 apple pies. However, Pat doesn't know how many to bake each day to maximize profits. Records from the past 100 business days show the following demand pattern:

Number of pies sold	Days
8	15
9	25
10	30
11	20
12	10

Each apple pie is sold for $7. The cost to bake an apple pie is $3. Develop a payoff table.

Solution:

Pat can choose one of five alternative decisions: baking 8, 9, 10, 11, or 12 pies, as shown across the top of Table 18.4. Actual demand for any particular day will also be for 8, 9, 10, 11, or 12 pies, as shown in the table's first column.

Note the last column of the first row, where the profit is $20. Twelve pies are baked, but only eight are sold. Profit for each pie sold is $4 ($7 − $3), so the profit for selling eight pies is $32

TABLE 18.4 Payoff Table for Solved Exercises 1 and 2 (Profits in Dollars)

Number demanded	Decision: number of pies to bake				
	8	9	10	11	12
8	32	29	26	23	20
9	32	36	33	30	27
10	32	36	40	37	34
11	32	36	40	44	41
12	32	36	40	44	48
EMV:	32	34.95	36.15	35.25	32.95

($4 × 8). However, four pies were baked and not sold, so the cost for the number of pies baked that exceeded demand is $12 ($3 × 4). Therefore, the payoff for baking 12 pies when demand is for only 8 is $20 ($32 − $12). For the last column of the last row, profit is $48. Twelve pies are baked, and all 12 are sold. Profit for selling 12 pies is $48 ($4 × 12).

Other entries in the payoff table are computed in a similar fashion.

2. EXPECTED MONETARY VALUE

For the situation in Solved Exercise 1, compute the expected monetary value if Pat decides to bake 11 pies. How many pies should Pat bake each day?

Solution:

The probability distribution for demand can be computed from the records in Solved Exercise 1. On 15 out of the 100 days observed, there was demand for eight pies. Therefore, on any given day the probability is .15 (15/100) that demand will be eight pies. Other entries in the following table were computed in the same fashion.

Demand	Days	Probability, $P(x)$
8	15	.15
9	25	.25
10	30	.30
11	20	.20
12	10	.10

The payoff for baking 11 pies when demand is for 8 pies is $23. Since Pat expects this to occur 15% of the time, the expected profit is $3.45 ($23 × .15) Expected profit for each possible demand is computed below in the last column. The expected monetary value for baking 11 pies is $35.25, the summation of the last column.

Demand, x	Probability, $P(x)$	Profit, z	EMV $z \times P(x)$
8	.15	$23	3.45
9	.25	30	7.50
10	.30	37	11.10
11	.20	44	8.80
12	.10	44	4.40
		EMV of baking 11 pies =	35.25

The bottom row of Table 18.4 shows the EMV for each possible action. Pat should bake 10 pies each day to maximize profits. The EMV for this course of action is $36.15.

3. EXPECTED VALUE OF PERFECT INFORMATION

Compute the expected value of perfect information for Solved Exercise 2.

Solution:

If Pat knows that demand is going to be for eight pies, that's the number she'll bake, and her payoff will be $32. With perfect information, the payoff for 9 pies is $36, for 10 pies $40, for 11 pies $44, and for 12 pies $48. The maximum payoff is:

Demand, x	Probability, $P(x)$	Profit, z	EMV $z \times P(x)$
8	.15	$32	4.80
9	.25	36	9.00
10	.30	40	12.00
11	.20	44	8.80
12	.10	48	4.80
			39.40

The EVPI is $3.25. This is the difference between the maximum payoff ($39.40) and expected monetary value of the best decision ($36.15).

4. TREE DIAGRAM ANALYSIS

Metropolitan Mortgage has just repossessed property on which a marina stands. The marina failed because there was no breakwater to prevent large waves from damaging the boat slips. Paul Sandifer, president of Metropolitan, feels that the company has three options:

1. The property can be sold in its present condition for $400,000.
2. The docks can be renovated, a breakwater built at a cost of $200,000, and the property sold. If the breakwater works, the property should sell for $800,000. If the breakwater doesn't work, the property can be sold for only $300,000. The probability that the breakwater will work is estimated at .9.
3. The docks can be renovated and a breakwater built at a cost of $200,000. Again, the breakwater might not work, in which case the property would have to be sold for $300,000. If the breakwater works, the marina will be operated for five years at a cost of $300,000.

Demand for boat slips will be either high, medium, or low. If demand is high (probability estimated at .1), the property can be sold for $1,300,000. If demand is medium (probability estimated at .5), the property can be sold for $1,100,000. If demand is low (probability estimated at .4), the property can be sold for $900,000. Develop a tree diagram.[2]

Solution:

Figure 18.6 is a tree diagram for this situation. The numbers at the end of each branch are the payoffs. (These payoffs don't include subtraction of the costs involved.) The numbers in rectangles are the EMVs for the decision branches. The tree is analyzed from right to left. The

[2]This exercise was adapted from a study by J. E. Hanke, M. Craze, and A. B. Cameron, "A Financial Institution's Dilemma Repossessed Property," *Management Accounting* (May 1991), pp. 44–49.

FIGURE 18.6 Tree Diagram for Solved Exercise 4

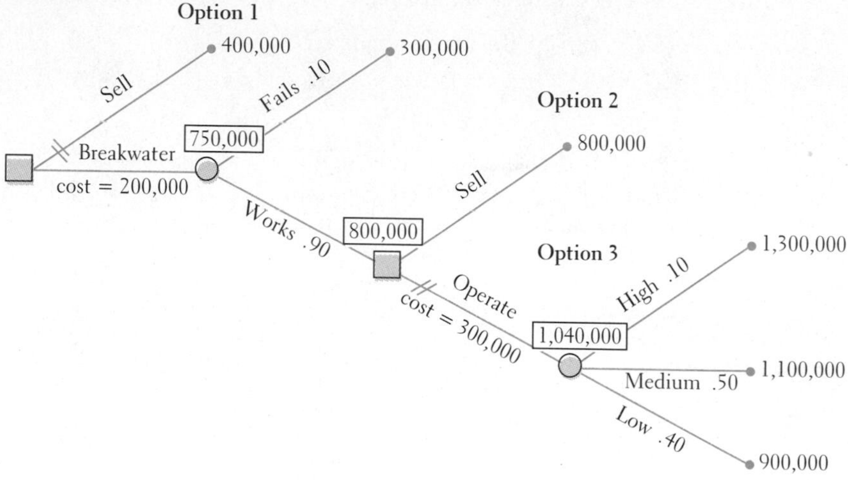

expected monetary value for option 3, the decision branch that involves operating the marina for five years, is about $1 million:

$$\begin{aligned} \text{EMV} &= .1(1{,}300{,}000) + .5(1{,}100{,}000) + .4(900{,}000) \\ &= 1{,}040{,}000 \end{aligned}$$

Since the cost of this decision is $300,000, the expected value for operating the marina for five years is $740,000 ($1,040,000 − $300,000). Therefore, this branch is eliminated because option 2, *build breakwater and sell*, has a higher value, $800,000. Next, the expected monetary value for option 2 is computed to be $750,000:

$$\text{EMV} = .1(300{,}000) + .9(800{,}000) = 750{,}000$$

Option 2 is now compared to option 1. Since the cost of renovating the docks and building the breakwater is $200,000, the expected payoff for option 2 is $550,000 ($750,000 − $200,000). Since this is a better expected payoff than simply selling the property for $400,000, option 2 is the best decision.

5. Bayes' Theorem

First Federal Savings Bank records show that 70% of its car loans are completely repaid. Analysis of the unpaid loans shows that 80% were made to applicants who had been employed at their present jobs for less than two years. Of the repaid loans, 30% were made to applicants who had been employed at their present jobs for less than two years.

a. What is the probability that a particular loan applicant will have been employed at his or her present job for less than two years?

b. Given that a particular loan applicant has spent only one year on the present job, what is the revised probability that this person will repay the loan?

c. Given that a particular loan applicant has spent five years on the present job, what is the revised probability that this person will repay the loan?

Solution:

a. Let R represent repaid loans, U represent unpaid loans, L represent less than two years on the job, and M represent more than two years on the job. The tree diagram for this problem (Figure 18.7) shows the probability that a particular loan applicant will have been employed at the present job for less than two years and repay a loan is .21:

$$P(\text{R and L}) = P(\text{R}) \times P(\text{L}|\text{R}) = .7 \times .3 = .21$$
$$P(\text{U and L}) = P(\text{U}) \times P(\text{L}|\text{U}) = .3 \times .8 = \underline{.24}$$
$$P(\text{L}) = .45$$

The probability that a particular loan applicant will have been employed on the present job for less than two years is .45.

b. $P(\text{R}|\text{L}) = \dfrac{P(\text{R and L})}{P(\text{L})} = \dfrac{.21}{.45} = .47$

c. $P(\text{R}|\text{M}) = \dfrac{P(\text{R and M})}{P(\text{M})} = \dfrac{.49}{.55} = .89$

FIGURE 18.7 Tree Diagram for Solved Exercise 5

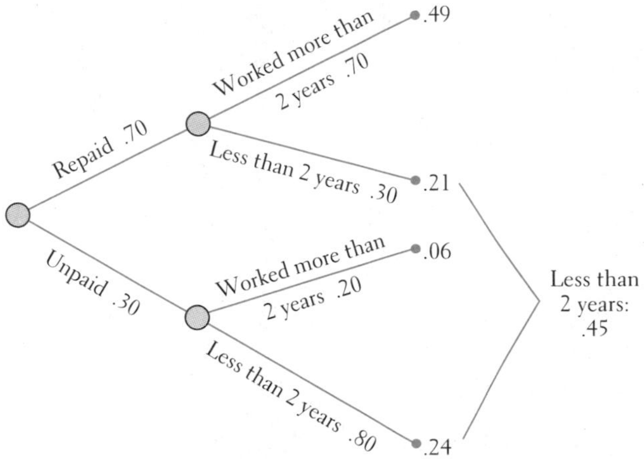

EXERCISES

20. Why is it sometimes useful to revise probabilities?
21. The Skil Corporation is trying to decide whether to introduce a new type of saw. The marketing department has supplied the following estimates:

Demand level	Probability	Expected payoff
Low	.1	−$400,000
Medium	.5	200,000
High	.4	800,000

a. The Skil Corporation must decide the best course of action (*introduce* or *don't introduce*). Develop a payoff table.

b. Compute the expected monetary value for the *introduce* option.

c. Write a memo summarizing the results and recommending a course of action.

22. Your company is developing a new product for the coming year and is concerned about the possibility of its major competitor developing a similar product. Since new products are common in your business, you've experienced similar situations in the past. The competitor is 50% likely to be developing a similar new product, based on the consensus of several of your company's executives.

    The annual new product convention can provide a clue as to whether you'll face competition. If the competitor is developing a competing product, there's an 80% chance it will send Sue Smith to the convention. If not the probability of Sue being there is only 40%. Suppose you attend the new product convention and see Sue Smith at a display booth. Find the revised probability that your major competitor is also developing a new competing product.

23. The Programming Institute is in the business of training computer programmers. It guarantees finding each new graduate a job within one week or else will refund the entire cost of training. For every graduate successfully placed, it makes a profit of $1,000. If the cost of training must be refunded, it loses $2,000. From past experience and by watching the want ads, the institute managers have determined demand for programmers during a typical one-week period to be:

Demand level	Probability
10	.10
11	.10
12	.20
13	.25
14	.30
15	.05

a. Develop a payoff table.

b. How large a class should the institute graduate at any one time?

c. Compute the EVPI.

24. Each steering assembly in a car manufacturer's inventory comes from either supplier A, supplier B, or supplier C, with probabilities .25, .45, and .30, respectively. The percentages defective, according to quality-control records, are:

    Supplier A: 5%
    Supplier B: 4%
    Supplier C: 2%

a. What is the probability that the next steering assembly randomly selected from inventory will be defective?

b. If the next assembly is found to be defective, what is the probability that it came from supplier B?

c. If the next assembly is found to operate properly, what is the probability that it came from supplier A?

25. A small community theater applies for many grants to supplement annual revenue. Over time, it has been awarded 40% of the grants it has applied for. By keeping careful records, the theater has noted that for grants that are subsequently awarded, there's a 75% chance that a person from the granting agency will call for clarification; for unsuccessful applications, this probability drops to 30%.

   a. The theater has just received a call from an agency requesting additional information about a grant request. What is the revised probability that the grant will be funded?

   b. Summarize the probability revision process and its results in a brief paragraph.

26. A retailer of airplanes makes $2,000 on a sale of its most popular model and loses $500 if the plane remains unsold at the end of the season. This loss is due to a lower selling price the next year, along with financing and storage costs. An article in *Flying*, "An Invitation to Fly" (June 1989, p. 56), leads the retailer to believe that business will increase during the coming year. This makes the inventory decision more difficult.

   Here are the probabilities of selling the various order units that the retailer is considering for the next year:

Amount	Probability
50	.20
75	.25
100	.30
125	.15
150	.10

   a. Construct a payoff table for this situation.

   b. What is the optimal stocking level if the objective is to maximize expected profits?

   c. What is the EVPI?

   d. State a rational reason for choosing a stocking level other than that identified in part *b.*

   e. What utility considerations might enter into the stocking decision?

27. A snowblower manufacturer must decide how many gasoline engines to order well before its plant begins production. Each engine produces a $250 profit for the company, and each unused engine results in a $50 loss due to financing and storage costs. The company must choose one of the following order levels; the corresponding probabilities for sales are also shown.

Number of engines	Probability of sales
500	.15
750	.25
1,000	.25
1,250	.20
1,500	.10
1,750	.05

   a. Construct a payoff table for this situation.

   b. What is the optimal stocking level for engines if the objective is to maximize expected profits?

c. What is the expected value of perfect information?

d. How would the optimal stocking level in part *b* change if the loss per engine unsold were $200?

e. How would the optimal stocking level in part *b* change if the profit per engine sold were $350?

28. Describe a marketing situation where a company would be willing to pay to get additional information for the purpose of revising a probability using Bayes' theorem.

29. Describe a situation where a manufacturing company would be willing to pay for additional information about its assembly line in order to revise a key probability using Bayes' theorem.

30. Describe the rationale behind the calculation of the expected value of perfect information.

31. Suppose a tree diagram has been devised that reflects a company's decision nodes, the probability branches of the situation, the costs associated with each branch, and the payoffs at the end of each branch. Describe the rationale used in computing the expected monetary value of the first decision the company must make.

32. Describe the philosophies of two companies that would be at opposite extremes in terms of utility considerations.

33. A company is considering entering one of two ventures described in the following table. Only one of these ventures can be undertaken due to limited company resources.

Venture A		Venture B	
Payoff	Probability	Payoff	Probability
$5,000	.20	−$10,000	.30
7,000	.25	−5,000	.30
10,000	.30	0	.20
15,000	.25	70,000	.20

a. Compute the EMV for each venture. Which venture would be preferred on the basis of maximizing expected profit?

b. Describe the kind of company that would strongly prefer venture A. Describe the kind of company that would strongly prefer venture B.

c. If you could borrow the money to enter one of these two ventures upon graduation, which would you prefer? Why?

34. As manager of a Las Vegas casino, you are confronted with an unusual game designed by one of your employees. The gambler pays a sum of money to play the game, which goes like this:

A fair coin is flipped.
- If heads appear, a pair of dice is thrown.
  - If the gambler throws two pairs in a row, the payoff is $1,000.
  - Otherwise, the coin is flipped again; heads pays $10, and tails pays nothing.
- If tails appears on the first flip, the gambler throws a pair of dice.
  - If a pair is thrown, the gambler wins $50.
  - If not, the coin is again thrown; heads pays $20, and tails pays $2.

a. What is the EMV of the game?

b. If the casino wants a 5% average payoff on this game, how much should each gambler be required to pay in order to play?

35. A company must choose either venture A, venture B, or venture C. Venture A has a 50% chance of returning $1 million, a 30% chance of returning $2 million, and a 20% chance of requiring a decision. If a certain branch of this decision point is taken, the payoff is $5 million. The other branch will return $10 million with a 30% chance, $8 million with a 40% chance, or nothing with a 30% chance.

    Venture B immediately requires a decision. Branch 1 returns $10 million. Branch 2 has a 40% chance of returning $25 million and a 60% chance of returning $8 million. Branch 3 will return $50 million with a 5% chance, $5 million with a 75% chance, and −$5 million with a 20% chance.

    Venture C either returns $50 million with a 10% chance or requires a decision. Branch 1 of this decision point produces either $10 million or $6 million with equal probability. Branch 2 requires another decision. The first brach returns either $5 million (60% chance) or $9 million (40% chance). The other branch results in either nothing (35% chance), −$10 million (35% chance), or $35 million (30% chance).

    a. Construct a tree diagram for this situation.

    b. What are the optimal decisions at each decision point?

    c. What is the EMV, using the decisions identified in part *b*?

    d. What utility considerations might modify the preceding analysis?

36. Based on several years of experience, a contractor knows there's a 40% chance that he will land any job he bids on. A consultant is willing to survey the market, including the contractor's competitors, to improve the contractor's ability to know in advance if the contract bid will be successful. Upon calling the consultant's references, the contractor finds that when the consultant evaluated bids that subsequently proved successful, she correctly identified a bid as successful 80% of the time. For bids that turned out to be unsuccessful, she incorrectly identified a bid as successful only 15% of the time.

    a. The consultant is hired and, after doing her research, reports that the upcoming bid will be successful. What is the revised probability of a successful bid?

    b. What is the probability of an unsuccessful bid if the consultant predicts the bid to be unsuccessful?

37. You have just won $1,000 in a game of chance at a casino. The casino offers to flip you for double or nothing using a fair coin and an impartial coin flipper.

    a. Would you flip for double or nothing?

    b. In utility terms, justify the answer you gave in part *a*.

38. Your company president makes the following statement to you:

    > We are evaluating a consultant's offer to conduct a market survey for us regarding our new breakfast cereal. We developed a payoff table for the various outcomes and have attached probabilities to each possible outcome. The people in the analysis section tell me that the expected value of perfect information is $48,000 and that this should help us reach a rational decision about the consultant's services. How do I use the $48,000 figure in reaching my decision? What does it mean, anyway?

    Write a memo to the president, answering her questions.

39. The utility considerations of the local water or electrical power company are probably quite different from a small firm that has just been organized to manufacture and sell computer software.
    a. Describe a venture that would be considered quite risky and describe how each company would probably react to it.
    b. Describe a venture that would be considered quite conservative and describe how each company would probably react to it.
    c. Which company would you prefer to work for in your first job? Does your choice reflect your own attitudes toward monetary utility?

EXTENDED EXERCISES

40. MARSHALL DRY GOODS COMPANY

The Marshall Dry Goods Company has been in the department store business for over 100 years and faces a major decision involving expansion of its operations in its major location, Atlanta, Georgia. Betty Bend is on Marshall's board of directors and is heading a committee of board members considering the matter.

A key element in the expansion decision is whether Marshall's major competitor will respond with an expansion of its own. The company believes there's a 60% chance that such competition will develop.

If the expansion is not followed by increased competition, Marshall believes profits will increase by $50 million per year. If the major competitor expands also, Betty and her committee believe this could take one of three forms: strong expansion, medium expansion, or weak expansion. The committee estimates the probabilities of these three outcomes at .30, .60, and .10, respectively.

For each of these alternatives, Marshall could respond by either increasing its advertising budget or not. Under certain conditions, the competitor might increase its advertising also, and Marshall would then be faced with another advertising budget decision. The situation as developed by Betty and her committee appears in Figure 18.8.

Each probability branch of the tree diagram shows the probabilities estimated by Betty's committee. For each decision branch, Marshall must decide which choice to make. The costs of taking certain branches are shown on the diagram. Finally, the estimated increases in annual profit are shown for each possible final outcome.

a. What is the optimal decision at each decision node, using the criterion of maximizing expected value?

b. If Marshall expands in Atlanta, what is the expected annual increase in profits, using the best decision at each decision node?

c. What utility factors should Betty Bend and her committee consider?

41. MURPHY BROTHERS

Jim Murphy, president of Murphy Brothers, is trying to decide whether to enter a fax machine market with a major company commitment, enter the market with a smaller commitment, or wait and see how the market develops before making a commitment. Jim has read an article about the fax market, "Challenge Is on for Fax Vendors" in *The Office* (September 1989). He understands that this will become an exciting market and thinks his company can be part of it.

FIGURE 18.8 Marshall Company Tree Diagram for Extended Exercise 40

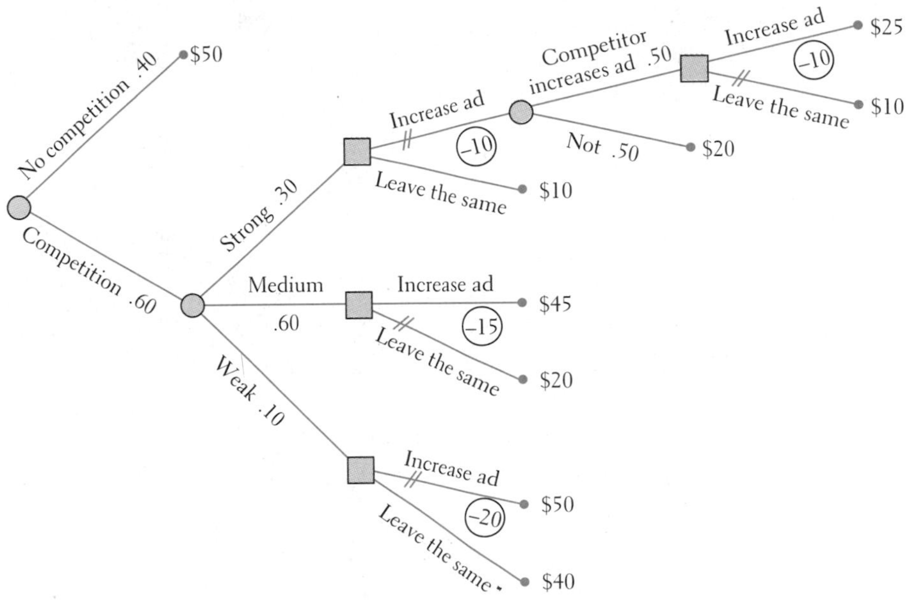

The following factors must be considered in his decision:

1. Entering the market in a major way would cost $60 million.
2. Entering the market on a smaller scale would cost $25 million. If a major market developed, it would cost money to expand the plant and sales staff to accommodate this market.
3. Waiting would cost the company $15 million in lost sales but would enable it to assess the market before making a commitment.

Jim wants to develop a rational way of weighing all the factors that bear on this important decision. He considers using a tree diagram to summarize the situation and to enable the company to find the best course of action. The decision is complicated by the fact that the market's size is unknown at the time the choice must be made. Figure 18.9 reveals the situation's complexity.

The first junction in the tree diagram is a decision node; hence, there are no probabilities attached to the three branches. Murphy Brothers may choose the *major entry* branch, the *small entry* branch, or the *wait* branch. If Jim chooses the *major entry* branch, a negative $60 million will be incurred—the cost of major entry into the market. The payoffs depend on the size of the market that develops. As shown, this market is either high, medium, or low with payoffs of $100, $70, and $30 million, respectively. The expected monetary value in this upper probability fan is $68.5 million, coded (1) in Figure 18.9. The calculation for this EMV is

$$\text{EMV} = (.35)(100) + (.35)(70) + (.30)(30) = 68.5$$

When the $60 million cost of major entry is subtracted from this EMV, the result is $8.5 million, coded (2); this is the EMV for choosing the *major entry* option. Jim Murphy will compare this

FIGURE 18.9 Decision Tree Diagram for Extended Exercise 41

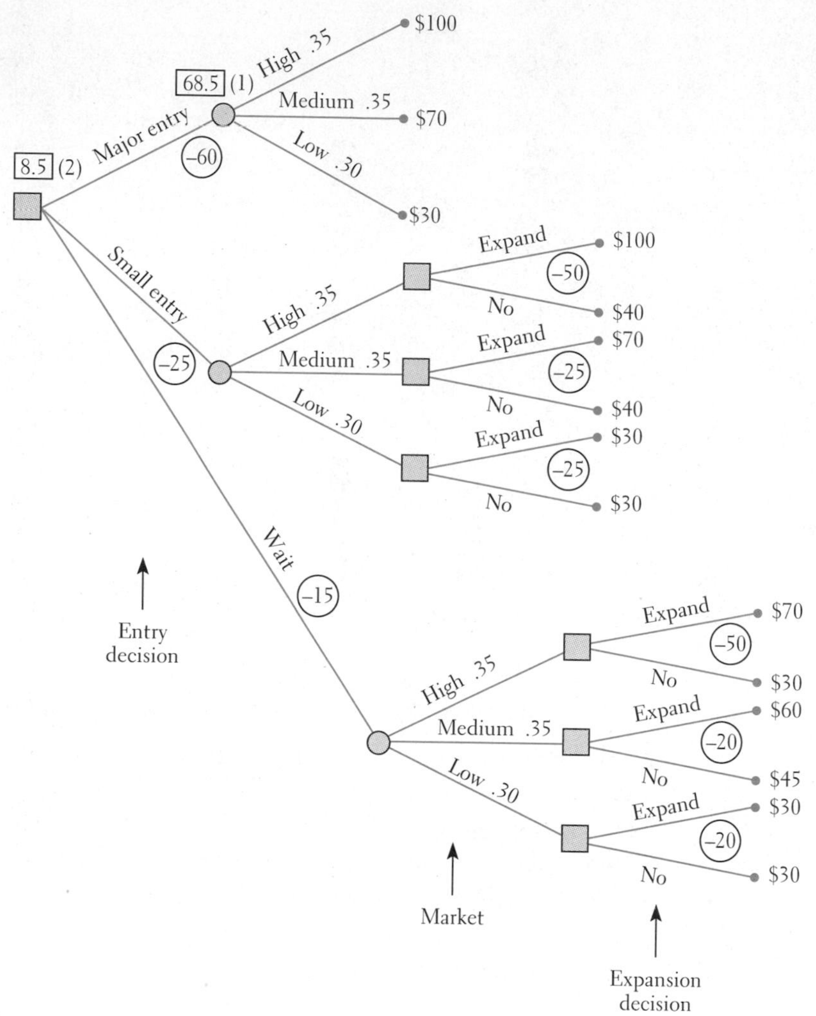

EMV with the expected monetary values of the other two options so that he can make the right decision regarding market entry.

a. Compute the EMV for the *small entry* branch of the tree diagram.

b. Compute the EMV for the *wait* branch of the figure's tree diagram.

c. What should Jim Murphy do?

MICROCOMPUTER PACKAGE

The micro package *Computerized Business Statistics* can be used to compute posterior and marginal probabilities using prior probabilities and a conditional probability table.

In Solved Exercise 5, the First Federal Savings Bank records show that 70% of its auto loans are completely repaid. An analysis of the unpaid loans shows that 80% were made to applicants who had been at their present jobs for less than two years. Of the repaid loans, 30% were made to applicants who had been employed at their present jobs for less than two years. First Federal wants to answer the following questions:

1. Given that a particular loan applicant has been employed for only one year at the present job, what is the revised probability that this person will repay the loan?
2. Given that a particular loan applicant has been employed for five years at the present job, what is the revised probability that this person will repay the loan?

Computer Solution

On the main menu of *Computerized Business Statistics* a **4** is selected, which indicates Probability Theory.

```
Probability Theory—Program Options Menu

0. CBS Configuration
1. Counting Rules
2. Probability Laws
3. Bayesian Analysis
4. Quick Reviews
5. Exit to Main Menu
6. Exit to Operating System
Press ↵ to select option under hi-lite bar. Press number or up/down arrow keys to
move hi-light bar.
```

A **3** is selected for Bayesian Analysis.

Since the problem involves entering data from the keyboard, a **1** is selected.

```
Number of States of Nature: Enter 2–10, Press ↵ 2
```

Since a loan is either unpaid or paid, two states exist.

```
Number of Indicators: Enter 2–10, Press ↵ 2
```

Since probabilities are given for loans being paid off by applicants employed at their present jobs for more than two years and for less than two years, two indicators are needed.

Next, the indicators are named:

```
Bayesian Analysis - Enter Indicator Labels
     Indicator 1     P1
     Indicator 2     P2
```

Indicator 1 is labeled **P1** and indicator 2 **P2**.

```
Problem definition correct? Enter Y/N/Q, Press ↵ Y
```

After a **Y** response, the program is ready for the data to be entered:

```
Table Commands Enter State Probabilities
     S1     0
     S2     0
Press F when Finished
```

An **F** is entered once the table has been completed.

After the table is completed, the screen shows:

```
     S1     .7
     S2     .3
Table Commands Enter Conditional Probabilities
            P1      P2
     S1      0       0
     S2      0       0
Press F when Finished
```

An **F** is entered once the table has been completed.

After the table has been completed, the screen shows:

```
            P1      P2
     S1     .7      .3
     S2     .2      .8
```

Note that each row must add to 1.0. Row 1 or (S1) gives the probabilities that the loan will be repaid. Row 2 or (S2) gives the probabilities that the loan will not be repaid. Column 1 or (P1) gives the probabilities that an applicant who has been employed on the present job for more than two years will repay the loan. Column 2 or (P2) gives the probabilities that an applicant who has been employed on the present job for less than two years will repay the loan.

The Bayesian Statistics menu reappears. A **7** is entered so that the problem can run. The screen shows the output menu. The choice in this case was **P** for printer.

Table 18.5 presents the results. The revised probability that a person who has been employed for only one year on the present job will repay the loan is .47. The revised probability that a person who has been employed for five years on the present job will repay the loan is .89.

TABLE 18.5 Bayesian Analysis Computer Output for Solved Exercise 5

```
                      Information Entered
  Number of States of Nature:     2
  Number of Indicators:           2
  State
1 = 0.7
2 = 0.3
  Conditional Probabilities
    p1       p2
1 = 0.7      0.3
2 = 0.2      0.8
                      Results
  Revised Conditional Table
    p1       p2
1 = 0.891    0.467
2 = 0.109    0.533
  Marginal Probabilities
    p1       p2
1 = 0.55     0.45
```

Chapter 19

Nonparametric Statistics

To par or to nonpar, that is the question. Whether t'is nobler in the mind to suffer the slings and arrows of outraged reviewers, or to breach the chasm of unfounded assumptions and light upon the ethereal shores of nonparameters.

Peter Vern Raven, "To Nonparametrics: a Poem"

Objectives

When you have completed this chapter, you will be able to:

Determine whether to use a nonparametric or a parametric test in a decision-making setting.

Apply the following nonparametric tests in decision-making situations: one-sample sign test, one-sample runs tests, Mann-Whitney *U* test, and Spearman rank correlation test.

The *New York Times* (July 31, 1992, p. C3) reported on *Field and Stream*'s and *Outdoor Life*'s efforts to improve their image with potential advertisers.

Most statistical techniques in this book make assumptions about the underlying form of the population data. Common assumptions are that the population is normally distributed, that several populations have equal variance, and that the data are measured on an interval or ratio scale. This chapter will discuss a group of techniques called *nonparametric tests* that are useful when these assumptions cannot be made.

WHY MANAGERS NEED TO KNOW ABOUT NONPARAMETRIC STATISTICS

The chi-square tests discussed in Chapter 11 are nonparametric tests. Both the contingency table test and the goodness-of-fit test analyze either nominal or ordinal data, that is, data collected in categories. These tests, especially the contingency table test, are widely used in business applications, which demonstrates the importance of the ability to deal with categorical or ranked data as well as quantitative data (interval or ratio scaled data).

There are many other statistical tests designed for situations where critical assumptions can't be met or where qualitative or categorical data are involved. Analysts who deal with such data should become familiar with books that focus on such tests, generally known as *nonparametric statistical tests*. A few of the more popular nonparametric tests are presented here.

Regarding the efforts of *Field and Stream* and *Outdoor Life*, these magazines might consider surveying their subscribers to determine their interests, life-styles, and income levels among other things. Such a survey would generate a lot of mostly nominal- or ordinal-scaled data. The statistical procedures in this chapter are designed to analyze such data.

NONPARAMETRIC VERSUS PARAMETRIC TESTS

Nonparametric Tests

Nonparametric tests do not require assumptions about the underlying form of the population data. Nonparametric tests are commonly used:

1. When the assumptions required of other popular techniques, usually called *parametric tests*, are not met.
2. When it is necessary to use a small sample size and it is not possible to verify that certain key assumptions are met.
3. When it is necessary to convert qualitative data (nominal or ordinal data) into useful decision-making information.

There are many cases, especially in business situations, where data measured on either a nominal or ordinal scale are collected. Many business applications involve opinions or feelings, and such data are usually in qualitative form.

Nonparametric tests have several advantages over parametric tests. Nonparametric tests:

1. Are generally easy to use and understand.
2. Eliminate the need for the restrictive assumptions of parametric tests.
3. Can be used with small samples.
4. Can be used with qualitative data (nominal or ordinal data).

Unfortunately, nonparametric tests also have disadvantages. Nonparametric tests:

1. Sometimes ignore, waste, or lose information.
2. Are not as efficient as parametric tests.
3. Lead to a greater probability of not rejecting a false null hypothesis (committing a type II error).

> **Nonparametric tests** are statistical tests that do not make assumptions about the underlying form of the population data.

Parametric tests are generally more powerful than nonparametric tests and should be used whenever possible. Also, it's important to note that although nonparametric tests don't make assumptions about the underlying distribution of the population being sampled, they often rely on sampling distributions such as the normal or the chi-square.

ONE-SAMPLE SIGN TEST

The one-sample mean test was discussed in Chapter 9. This test required that the population being sampled follow a normal distribution for a sample size less than 30. The flowchart in Figure 9.7 showed that when the assumption of a normal population is not met for such a small sample, a nonparametric test should be used. The one-sample sign test can be used with small samples where the normality assumption can't be made. However, it's not as discriminating as the one-sample mean test it replaces. The one-sample sign test requires that the population be symmetrical; that is, roughly half of the sample observations are expected to fall on either side of the true mean. If the population is not symmetrical, the null hypothesis should use the median rather than the mean.

The null hypothesis specifies an assumed mean. The test involves assigning each sample observation a plus or minus sign. If a sample value is greater than the assumed mean, a plus is assigned. If the value is less than the assumed mean, a minus is assigned. Values exactly equal to the assumed mean are ignored.

Sign Test

The sign test is virtually identical to a one-sample test for proportions. The cumulative binomial table is used for samples of 20 or less. The normal or Poisson approximation to the binomial is used for sample sizes 21 to 30. The z test for means (Figure

9.7) is used for samples of 30 or more. Example 19.1 illustrates the sign test for a sample of 20 or less.

EXAMPLE 19.1 Beverly Lundquist has just been hired to manage the Sandwich Garden Restaurant in the downtown shopping district of a large southern city. The restaurant gets a lot of lunch business during the noon hour, and people are usually asked to wait for a table. Beverly has been told that the mean time a customer waits between entering the restaurant and being served is 30 minutes. She's afraid that the mean time patrons must wait is more than 30 minutes, so she decides to time a random sample of 18 customers during the next week. Beverly tests at the .05 significance level. The results, measured in minutes, are

32	30	25	34	36	29	31	27	32
33	37	32	28	42	40	31	31	32

The null and alternative hypotheses are

$$H_0: \mu \leq 30$$
$$H_1: \mu > 30$$

Since Beverly doesn't think population waiting times follow a normal distribution, and since she has a small sample size, she chooses the sign test instead of the t test of Chapter 9. The first step is to determine whether each sample observation is less than, equal to, or greater than the claimed mean of 30 minutes. A plus sign is assigned to each sample value greater than 30 and a minus sign is assigned to each value less than 30. The next step is to count the plus signs and the minus signs: there are 13 plus signs and 4 minus signs. (Note that one value has been ignored because it equals the claimed mean of 30.)

The decision rule for this hypothesis test is

> If the chance of obtaining four or fewer minus signs is less than .05, reject the null hypothesis.

If the null hypothesis is true, the probability of a customer waiting less than 30 minutes is .5. The cumulative binomial table (Appendix E.3) is consulted using $n = 17$ and $p = .5$. The probability of obtaining four or fewer minus signs is .0245. Since this probability is less than .05, the null hypothesis is rejected. Beverly concludes that it takes more than 30 minutes, on average, for customers to receive service.

For samples between 21 and 30, Equation 19.1, for the normal approximation to the binomial, is used, as long as the probability of success is neither quite large nor quite small. (If it is, the Poisson approximation to the binomial is used.)

$$z = \frac{x - (n/2)}{(1/2)\sqrt{n}} \tag{19.1}$$

where x = Number of plus signs or minus signs of interest
n = Total number of plus signs and minus signs

Example 19.2 illustrates the sign test for a sample size of 21 to 30.

EXAMPLE 19.2 After completing the experiment in Example 19.1, Beverly realized that one of her cooks and two of her waitresses were new. She was afraid that this may have caused the average waiting time to be more than 30 minutes. So Beverly repeats the study using a new sample after the new people are properly experienced. She decides to sample 27 customers and test at the .05 significance level. The sample results, measured in minutes, are

22	33	25	34	36	29	30	27	31
23	30	32	28	32	40	29	31	35
26	34	33	26	27	37	38	32	34

The null and alternative hypotheses are

$$H_0: \mu \leq 30$$
$$H_1: \mu > 30$$

Again, the number of plus signs and minus signs is determined: there are 15 plus signs and 10 minus signs. (Note that two values have been ignored because they equal the claimed mean of 30.)

The decision rule for this hypothesis test is

If the computed z value is larger than 1.645, reject the null hypothesis.

The z value is computed using Equation 19.1:

$$z = \frac{x - (n/2)}{(1/2)\sqrt{n}} = \frac{15 - (25/2)}{(1/2)\sqrt{25}} = \frac{2.5}{2.5} = 1.0$$

Since the calculated z (1.0) is smaller than the critical z (1.645), the null hypothesis is not rejected. Beverly concludes that there's not enough evidence to reject the claimed average waiting time of 30 minutes.

EXERCISES

1. What is the essential difference between parametric statistical methods and nonparametric methods?
2. What is the disadvantage of converting numerical data, such as data measured on a ratio scale, to categorical data, such as those measured on an ordinal scale, in order to analyze the data using a nonparametric method?
3. List several reasons why a nonparametric method would be chosen to analyze sample data.
4. What are the advantages of using nonparametric tests instead of parametric tests? What are the disadvantages?

5. Parametric

5. Which tests, parametric or nonparametric, are more powerful?

6. When is the one-sample sign test used?
7. What parametric test is similar to the one-sample sign test?

8. L = 13 and S = 13 so $z = 0$, no bias

8. Here are indications of whether a sample of bridge girders are too long or too short, relative to specifications. Do these data suggest a bias toward either long or short girders at the .05 significance level? Girders too long are designated with an L, and those too short with an S.

L, L, S, S, L, S, S, L, S, S, L, L, S
S, S, S, L, L, S, L, L, S, L, L, L, S

9. A bicycle racing team coach randomly determines tire pressures for his team's bikes before each race. If the pressure is not correct, she records it either as too low (L) or too high (H). The data follow. Use the correct statistical test to determine, at the .10 significance level, if the tires tend to be either too high or too low, or whether the occurrence of highs and lows can be considered equal.

9. H = 6, L = 10 so $z = 1$. Don't reject H_0

H, H, L, L, L, H, H, L, L, L, L, H, H, L, L, L

ONE-SAMPLE RUNS TEST

The one-sample runs test is designed to see if a string of occurrences of two possible types is generated by a random process. A series of heads and tails resulting from coin flips could be tested for randomness, for example, as could a sequence of successes versus failures of some type. If there are only two possible outcomes for each trial and the objective is to determine if the sequence is randomly generated, the runs test can be used.

Special tables for the runs test using small samples can be found in texts devoted to nonparametric methods. If the number of occurrences of either type in the sequence is greater than 20, a normal curve approximation can be used. This is the procedure presented here.

Runs Test

The procedure for the runs test is to examine the sequence of observed events and count the number of runs. A *run* is an uninterrupted series of one of the outcomes. If a coin is flipped six times, for example, where H represents heads and T represents tails, the following sequences result in the number of runs indicated:

1. HHTTHH: There are three runs (two heads, followed by two tails, followed by two heads).
2. HHHTTT: There are two runs (three heads followed by three tails).
3. HTHTHT: There are six runs.

Once the number of runs in the sequence is known, the total number of outcomes of one type is determined (n_1), as is the number of outcomes of the other type (n_2). The test consists of finding if the number of runs can be considered to come from a normal curve with mean (Equation 19.2) and standard deviation (Equation 19.3), provided either n_1 or n_2 is greater than 20.

$$\mu_r = \frac{2n_1n_2}{n_1 + n_2} + 1 \tag{19.2}$$

$$\sigma_r = \sqrt{\frac{2n_1n_2(2n_1n_2 - n_1 - n_2)}{(n_1 + n_2)^2(n_1 + n_2 - 1)}} \tag{19.3}$$

where μ_r = Mean

σ_r = Standard deviation

n_1 = Number of occurrences of one kind

n_2 = Number of occurrences of the other kind

If it's unlikely that the observed number of runs could have come from the normal distribution, the null hypothesis of a random process is rejected. If the observed number of runs seems likely, the null hypothesis of a random process is not rejected.

The z value is calculated using Equation 19.4:

$$z = \frac{r - \mu_r}{\sigma_r} \tag{19.4}$$

where μ_r = Mean
σ_r = Standard deviation
r = Number of runs

EXAMPLE 19.3 Joe Short flew to Las Vegas and lost $150 playing roulette. He thought he had a foolproof system for playing red versus black, a system he developed at home using a small roulette wheel. After losing his money, he became suspicious about the fairness of the wheel and decided to record the occurrences of red and black for several minutes before hitchhiking back home.

Here is the string of reds and blacks he recorded, where R represents red and B represents black. (Zeros and double zeros were ignored.) The runs are underlined.

B B B R R B R B R R R B B R B R B R R B B B B R R R
B B B R B B B R R R R R R B R B R R R B B B B R R R

As shown, the number of runs Joe observed was 24. The number of reds was 27 (n_1 = 27), and the number of blacks was 25 (n_2 = 25). The normal distribution is used to test the null hypothesis that the process that generated this sequence is random. The mean and standard deviation of the normal distribution for this test are given by Equations 19.2 and 19.3:

$$\mu_r = \frac{2n_1n_2}{n_1 + n_2} + 1$$

$$= \frac{2(27)(25)}{27 + 25} + 1 = 26.96$$

$$\sigma_r = \sqrt{\frac{2n_1n_2(2n_1n_2 - n_1 - n_2)}{(n_1 + n_2)^2\,(n_1 + n_2 - 1)}}$$

$$= \sqrt{\frac{2(27)(25)[2(27)(25) - 27 - 25]}{(27 + 25)^2\,(27 + 25 - 1)}} = 3.56$$

Joe can now complete the randomness test by seeing if the number of runs he observed (24) can be considered unlikely to have come from a normal distribution with the mean and standard deviation shown. He decides to test for randomness at the .05 significance level.

The decision rule for this hypothesis test is

If the computed z value is less than -1.96 or larger than 1.96, reject the null hypothesis.

The z value is

$$z = \frac{r - \mu_r}{\sigma_r} = \frac{24 - 26.96}{3.56} = -0.83$$

Since the calculated z (-0.83) isn't less than the critical z (-1.96), the null hypothesis is not rejected. Joe concludes that the roulette wheel was generating reds and blacks in a random fashion, and that his gambling system was the cause of his losing money.

Figure 19.1 summarizes the test. As shown, an r value of 24 is only 0.83 standard deviations below the mean of 26.96. The standard normal table indicates that approximately 20.33% of the curve lies below a z value of -0.83. Since a two-tailed test was used, the p-value equals .4066 (2 × .2033).

TM

FIGURE 19.1 Runs Test Sampling Distribution for Example 19.3

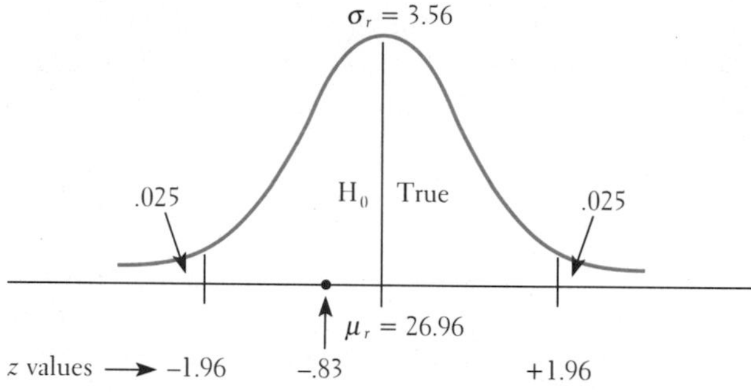

MINITAB can be used to perform a one-sample runs test. The MINITAB commands and output for Example 19.3 are:

```
MTB > SET C1
DATA> +1 +1 +1 −1 −1 +1 −1 +1 −1 −1 −1 +1 +1 −1 +1 −1 +1
DATA> −1 −1 +1 +1 +1 +1 −1 −1 −1 +1 +1 +1 −1 +1 +1 +1 −1
DATA> −1 −1 −1 −1 −1 +1 −1 +1 −1 −1 −1 +1 +1 +1 +1 −1 −1 −1
DATA> END
MTB > RUNS 0, USING C1

    C1

    K =     0.0000

    THE OBSERVED NO. OF RUNS = 24
    THE EXPECTED NO. OF RUNS = 26.9615
    25 OBSERVATIONS ABOVE K 27 BELOW
              THE TEST IS SIGNIFICANT AT 0.4063
              CANNOT REJECT AT ALPHA = 0.05

MTB > STOP
```

The black/red sequence is specified using +1 for black and −1 for red. Note that the solution contains the number of runs (24), the mean of the runs statistic if H_0 is true (26.96), and the p-value (.4063). The p-value is the probability of making a type I error if H_0 is rejected.

The runs test can also be used to examine the residuals from a regression analysis. In Chapter 14, you learned that one of the underlying assumptions of regression analysis is that the residuals are independent. This means that the analyst should observe a random pattern in the sample residuals. However, as discussed in Chapter 17, when observations are recorded across time (say, over consecutive months), the residuals are frequently correlated (autocorrelation). When this occurs, the Durbin-Watson statistic is computed to measure autocorrelation.

Use of the Durbin-Watson statistic assumes that the residuals follow a normal distribution. The nonparametric runs test can be used to examine the residuals when the normality assumption is questionable. This is done by recording the sign (+ or −) of each residual and counting the number of runs. This test is valid regardless of the distribution of the residuals and can be used for any model that assumes that residuals are independent.

EXAMPLE 19.4 In Example 17.22, Stu Miller developed a regression model that used disposable personal income to predict yearly sales for Sears Roebuck. Stu could have used MINITAB to perform the runs test for this situation. The MINITAB commands and results are:

```
MTB > READ 'SEARS.DAT' INTO C1-C2
MTB > REGRESS C1 1 PREDICTOR C2;
SUBC> RESIDS C3.
    COMPUTER OUTPUT WOULD BE SHOWN HERE
MTB > PRINT C3

C3
  378.60     379.25     207.81     186.29   237.68     151.15      97.84
  116.48     369.25     517.75     670.37   552.37     606.25     883.33
  962.44     599.41      93.23     206.92    -7.04    -441.32   -1351.80
-1564.21   -1048.10   -2711.11   -5614.14  -551.24   -1297.32   - 490.71
 3059.43    2639.88    2161.30

MTB> RUNS ABOVE AND BELOW 0, USING C3

     C3

     K =      0.0000

     THE OBSERVED NO. OF RUNS =   3
     THE EXPECTED NO. OF RUNS = 14.5484
     21 OBSERVATIONS ABOVE K    10 BELOW
               THE TEST IS SIGNIFICANT AT 0.0000

MTB> STOP
```

Note that the solution shows the number of runs, as well as the mean of the runs statistic if the null hypothesis is true. The p-value for this test is .0000. Because this value is smaller than both the .05 and .01 significance levels, H_0 is rejected. Stu concludes that the residuals are autocorrelated.

EXERCISES

SM

10. When is the one-sample runs test used?
11. What parametric test is similar to the one-sample runs test?

12. $r = 19$, $\mu = 17$, $\sigma = 2.78$, $z = .72$. Don't reject H_0

12. A production line is believed to generate good and bad assemblies in a random fashion. Data are recorded indicating whether the assembly produced is good (G) or defective in some way (D). The following string of devices was observed at a randomly chosen time. Does this string suggest a random process? Test at the .02 significance level.

G, G, D, D, G, D, D, D, G, G, D, G, G, D, G, D,
G, D, D, G, D, D, G, G, G, G, D, D, G, D, D, G

13. $r = 15$, $\mu = 16$, $\sigma = 2.60$, $z = -.38$. Don't reject H_0

13. A random number generator written for a company's computer is supposed to generate positive and negative numbers randomly. After checking the first series of numbers, the computer analyst thinks the series looks random but decides a statistical test should be undertaken before the program is widely used throughout the company. Here is the observed series of numbers, where P represents a positive number and N represents a negative number. Does the program appear to be random? Test at the .05 significance level.

P, P, N, N, P, P, P, P, N, N, P, P, P, N, N, P,
N, P, P, N, P, P, N, P, P, N, N, N, P, P, P, P

MANN-WHITNEY *U* TEST

Mann-Whitney U Test

The Mann-Whitney U test is designed to determine if two sample groups have been drawn from the same population. This test is used as an alternative to the small-sample t test for means described in Chapter 10. The Mann-Whitney U test is used to find whether two independent samples have come from symmetrical populations that have equal means or medians. The test is used when the assumption of two normal populations with equal variances cannot be verified. The data must be measured on at least an ordinal scale, making this test quite useful for ordinal, or ranked, data.

The procedure is to rank the data as if the values in both samples all belong to a single group. The lowest value is assigned a rank of 1, the next lowest a rank of 2, and so on, without regard to which sample the item came from. If the means of the two populations are equal, low and high ranks should be fairly evenly distributed between the two samples. If the means are not equal, one sample will tend to have more high or more low ranks than the other sample. The analysis focuses on the sum of ranks of one of the samples by comparing it with the sum of ranks that would be expected if the population means are equal.

For a combined sample size of 20 or less, special tables for testing the null hypothesis for the two groups are used; such tables are found in books dealing exclusively with nonparametric methods. If the combined sample size is greater than 20, the normal curve has been shown to be a good approximation of the sampling distribution. This normal curve has the parameters shown in Equations 19.6 and 19.7. The Mann-Whitney U statistic is computed using Equation 19.5:

$$U = n_1 n_2 + \frac{n_1(n_1 + 1)}{2} - R_1 \qquad (19.5)$$

where U = Mann-Whitney statistic
n_1 = Number of items in sample 1

n_2 = Number of items in sample 2
R_1 = Sum of the ranks in sample 1 (if ties in the rankings occur, average the rankings involved)

If the two samples are of unequal size, let sample 1 represent the sample with the lower number of observations to save computational time.

Standard normal curve procedures are employed to determine if the statistic U could reasonably have been drawn from a normal distribution with the specified parameters. If so, the null hypothesis that the samples came from symmetrical populations with equal means is not rejected. If it's quite unlikely that U could have come from this distribution, the null hypothesis is rejected.

If the null hypothesis is true, then the U statistic has a sampling distribution with the following mean and standard deviation (assuming sufficient sample sizes):

$$\mu_U = \frac{n_1 n_2}{2} \tag{19.6}$$

$$\sigma_U = \sqrt{\frac{n_1 n_2 (n_1 + n_2 + 1)}{12}} \tag{19.7}$$

where n_1 = Number of items in sample 1
n_2 = Number of items in sample 2

The z value is

$$z = \frac{U - \mu_U}{\sigma_U} \tag{19.8}$$

EXAMPLE 19.5 Two clerks, A and B, are employed in a children's clothing and toy store. The store manager is considering expansion to other locations after reading an article in *Marketing News* (October 1989) on the growing popularity of kid's stores. Comparing the two clerks' sales seems like a good way to determine if one of them could manage a new store. The null and alternative hypotheses are

H_0: $\mu_1 - \mu_2 = 0$
H_1: $\mu_1 - \mu_2 \neq 0$

If the .05 significance level is used, the decision rule for this hypothesis test is

If the computed z value is less than -1.96 or larger than 1.96, reject the null hypothesis.

The manager records weekly sales amounts for the two clerks for a sample of weeks and wants to know if they can be considered equal. The Mann-Whitney U test will be used to test the hypothesis that the two clerks are the same in this regard, since the sample size is small and since there is evidence that the population of sales amounts is not normal. Table 19.1 lists sales amounts for each clerk along with their rankings.

The U statistic is calculated using Equation 19.5. In this equation, n_1 equals 16 (the number of weeks clerk A was observed), $n_2 = 25$ (the number of weeks clerk B was

TABLE 19.1 Ranked Sales for Mann-Whitney U Test (Example 19.5)

Clerk A		Clerk B	
Sales	Rank	Sales	Rank
197	1	190	3
194	2	180	7
188	4	175	8
185	5	172	10
182	6	167	13
173	9	166	14
169	11	160	17
169	12	157	18
164	15	155	19
161	16	150	21
154	20	146	23
149	22	145	24
142	26	143	25
139	28	140	27
137	29	135	30
130	35	135	31
		134	32
		133	33
		131	34
		122	36
		120	37
		118	38
		109	39
		98	40
		95	41

observed), and $R_1 = 241$. This last value was calculated by summing all the ranks for clerk A. The calculation for U is

$$\begin{aligned} U &= n_1 n_2 + \frac{n_1(n_1 + 1)}{2} - R_1 \\ &= (16)(25) + \frac{16(16 + 1)}{2} - 241 \\ &= 295 \end{aligned}$$

The parameters of the normal sampling distribution must now be determined to see if a U value of 295 can be considered unusual. Using Equations 19.6 and 19.7, the mean and standard deviation of the normal sampling distribution are calculated:

$$\mu_U = \frac{n_1 n_2}{2} = \frac{(16)(25)}{2} = 200$$

$$\begin{aligned} \sigma_U &= \sqrt{\frac{n_1 n_2(n_1 + n_2 + 1)}{12}} \\ &= \sqrt{\frac{(16)(25)(16 + 25 + 1)}{12}} = 37.4 \end{aligned}$$

The z value for the sample statistic is computed using Equation 19.8:

$$z = \frac{U - \mu_U}{\sigma_U} = \frac{295 - 200}{37.4} = 2.54$$

The sample statistic (295) is 2.54 standard deviations above the curve mean of 200 if the null hypothesis of equal populations is true. This is an unlikely value for this curve, since this z value covers .4945 of the area under the curve, leaving only .0055 on the upper end. The store manager is justified in rejecting the hypothesis that the two clerks are equal in their ability to generate sales. The risk of a type I error in this rejection is only .011 (2 × .0055).

The MINITAB program can be used to conduct the Mann-Whitney U test. MINITAB commands to solve Example 19.5 and the test results are:

```
MTB> SET C1
DATA> 1 2 4 5 6 9 11 12 15 16 20 22 26 28 29 35
DATA> END
MTB> SET C2
DATA> 3 7 8 10 13 14 17 18 19 21 23 24 25 27 30 31 32
DATA> 33 34 36 37 38 39 40 41
DATA> END
MTB> MANN-WHITNEY USING C1 AND C2

Mann-Whitney Confidence Interval and Test

C1          N = 16    Median =         13.50
C2          N = 25    Median =         25.00
Point estimate for ETA1-ETA2 is      -10.00
95.1 pct c.i. for ETA1-ETA2 is (-18.00, -3.00)
W = 241.0
Test of ETA1 = ETA2 vs. ETA1 n.e. ETA2 is significant at 0.011

MTB> STOP
```

Note that W on the computer output is the same as R_1 for Example 19.5, 241. The statement "ETA1 n.e. ETA2 is significant at 0.011" indicates that for a two-tailed test the p-value is .011. If the original data had been used instead of the rankings, the value of W would be different; however, the p-value would still equal .011.

EXERCISES

SSM 14. When is the Mann-Whitney U test used?

15. What parametric test is similar to the Mann-Whitney U test?

SSM 16. The amounts of money won or lost by a husband (H) and wife (W) at Las Vegas are recorded for several trips and ranked from high to low. Here are the data:

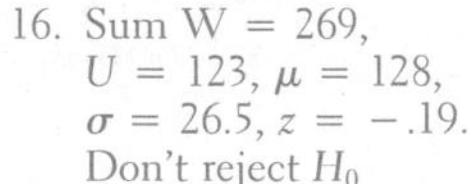

16. Sum W = 269, $U = 123$, $\mu = 128$, $\sigma = 26.5$, $z = -.19$. Don't reject H_0

W, W, H, H, H, W, W, H, W, H, W, H, H, H, W, W,
W, H, H, H, H, H, W, W, W, W, H, W, W, W, H, H

Can we conclude that the two gamblers have equal ability? Test using the .10 significance level.

17. The numbers of video games sold per week for several weeks are arranged in sequence from low to high and designated A or B, representing the two key company salespeople. The video wholesaler is interested in comparing their efforts, especially after reading an

17. Sum A = 192, $U = 183$, $\mu = 127.5$, $\sigma = 26.5$, $z = 2.09$. $z_{crit} = \pm 1.96$ so reject H_0

article in *Marketing and Media Decisions* (November 1989, p. 35) describing two high-power contenders entering the video game market to take on Nintendo, the industry leader. Since the wholesaler features Nintendo games, the owner is nervous about sales volume.

Can the two sellers be considered equally effective? Test using the .05 significance level. The data are

A, A, B, A, A, B, B, A, A, A, A, B, B, A, A, B,
A, B, A, B, B, B, A, B, A, B, B, B, A, B, B, B

Spearman Rank Correlation

The Pearson product-moment correlation coefficient, discussed in Chapter 14, is designed to measure the strength of the association between two quantitative variables. That is, the two variables being compared must be measured on either an interval or a ratio scale.

Rank Correlation

There is also a nonparametric counterpart to this measurement known as the *Spearman rank correlation coefficient.* This coefficient measures the extent of association between two variables each measured on an ordinal scale. As such, it's a valuable addition to the analyst's arsenal since many measurements in the business world are made on an ordinal scale.

The data for the Spearman rank correlation coefficient consist of two sets of rankings on the same subjects. The strength of the association between these two rankings is measured by the coefficient. This statistic ranges from -1 (perfect negative correlation) to $+1$ (perfect positive correlation), just as the Pearson coefficient does.

The procedure for calculating the Spearman correlation coefficient is to compare the rankings for the objects under study. The difference between each pair of ranks is denoted *d*. These differences are squared and added and then used to calculate the correlation coefficient:

$$r_s = 1 - \frac{6\Sigma d^2}{n^3 - n} \tag{19.9}$$

where r_s = Spearman rank correlation coefficient
d^2 = Squared differences between the two ranks
n = Number of objects being compared

The significance of the Spearman rank correlation coefficient is tested in the same way as for the Pearson correlation coefficient. Equation 14.3 is used to compute the test statistic, which has a t distribution based on $(n - 2)$ degrees of freedom. Example 19.6 illustrates this procedure.

Example 19.6 Jack Richer wants to see how good a leading sports magazine is at predicting the Big Nine football teams' final standings before the season. For each of the nine teams ranked prior to the season start, Jack records the magazine ranking and checks it against the actual ranking at the end of the season (Table 19.2).

TABLE 19.2 Ranking Data for Spearman Correlation Coefficient (Example 19.6)

Team	Preseason rank	Postseason rank	d	d^2
A	1	4	−3	9
B	2	2	0	0
C	3	5	−2	4
D	4	1	3	9
E	5	7	−2	4
F	6	3	3	9
G	7	9	−2	4
H	8	8	0	0
I	9	6	3	9
				48

Table 19.2 shows the difference between each preseason and postseason ranking, along with the squared differences. The sum of these squared differences for the nine teams is 48. Equation 19.9 is used to calculate the Spearman correlation coefficient:

$$r_s = 1 - \frac{6\Sigma d^2}{n^3 - n} = 1 - \frac{6(48)}{9^3 - 9} = 1 - .4 = .60$$

For the test of significance, the null and alternative hypotheses are

$$H_0\colon \rho_s \leq 0$$
$$H_1\colon \rho_s > 0$$

At the .01 significance level for 7 degrees of freedom (df $= n - 2 = 9 - 2 = 7$), the decision rule is

If the sample t statistic is greater than 2.998, reject the null hypothesis.

The standard error of r is computed using Equation 14.2:

$$s_r = \sqrt{\frac{1 - r^2}{n - 2}} = \sqrt{\frac{1 - (.60)^2}{7}} = .3$$

The t statistic is computed using Equation 14.3:

$$t = \frac{r_s - \rho_s}{s_r} = \frac{.60 - 0}{.3} = 2.0$$

Since the calculated t statistic (2.0) is less than the critical t value (2.998), the null hypothesis is not rejected. The correlation between the sports magazine's preseason rankings and the actual postseason rankings is not significant. Jack considered .60 to be a weak correlation for the "experts" on the magazine's staff and finds that, indeed, such a correlation cannot be generalized to the population of all the magazine's rankings. He immediately writes a letter to the magazine editor explaining his findings and hopes to see his letter published in an upcoming issue.

The MINITAB program can be used to compute the Spearman rank correlation coefficient. The MINITAB commands to solve Example 19.6 are:

```
MTB> SET C1
DATA> 1  2  3  4  5  6  7  8  9
DATA> END
MTB> SET C2
DATA> 4  2  5  1  7  3  9  8  6
DATA> END
MTB> CORRELATION BETWEEN C1 AND C2

Correlation of C1 and C2 = 0.600

MTB> STOP
```

If the original data were unranked, the following commands would be used to develop rankings:

```
MTB> RANK C1, PUT INTO C3
MTB> RANK C2, PUT INTO C4
```

Exercises

18. When is the Spearman rank test used?
19. What parametric test is similar to the Spearman rank test?

SM

20. Sum $d^2 = 110$, $r = .33$, $t = 1.00$. Don't reject H_0

20. The personnel department of a small company ranks its employees in terms of the number of sick days taken during the year, from highest to lowest. Near the end of this year a series of meetings is held with those who took the most sick days to correct the absentee problem. At the end of the next year, the ranking is again determined to see if the "pep talk" did any good. Here are the two rankings. Was there a significant change during the year if the rankings are tested at the .05 significance level?

Employee	First ranking	Second ranking
A	1	3
B	2	5
C	3	7
D	4	2
E	5	10
F	6	1
G	7	4
H	8	9
I	9	8
J	10	6

21. Sum $d^2 = 76$, $r = .095$, $t = .23$. Don't reject H_0

21. How similar are the following two rankings? Compute the Spearman rank correlation coefficient to answer this question. Test at the .01 significance level.

Rank 1	Rank 2
1	5
2	3
3	4
4	7
5	1

Rank 1	Rank 2
6	8
7	2
8	6

SUMMARY

This chapter has presented four statistical methods typically used to extract useful information from nominal or ordinal data. These methods are also employed when the underlying assumptions of more powerful parametric methods can't be met. The nonparametric methods are covered more fully in books devoted exclusively to this subject. Such books contain many statistical techniques designed for qualitative data.

The one-sample sign test was presented first as a nonparametric way of testing a claimed population mean. The runs test was presented as a method for determining if a sequence of *A*/*B* events is randomly generated. Next, the Mann-Whitney *U* test was discussed. This technique is designed to detect if two measurements made on an ordinal scale are drawn from the same population. Finally, the Spearman rank correlation coefficient was shown as a method for determining the strength of the relationship between two rankings on the same objects.

APPLICATIONS OF STATISTICAL CONCEPTS IN THE BUSINESS WORLD

Nonparametric methods are not as widely used as they perhaps should be for business applications. It is true that much business data—perhaps most—are quantitative in nature and are therefore properly analyzed using the methods that constitute most of this book. But in many cases, data are collected in categories. Marketing studies are especially involved with such data since these studies commonly measure attitudes.

Here are several questions that might arise in a business setting. For each, the collected data would likely fall in categories.

How do shoppers rank the three major department stores in the downtown area?

As a preliminary step to painting the office areas, what are our employees' favorite colors? Does color choice depend on age, sex, or department?

How do our customers rate the following characteristics of our store?

a. Prices.
b. Service.
c. Convenience.
d. Quality.

The amount by which the length of a manufactured part misses specification is measured for each part. Is there any difference between shifts 1 and 2 regarding these amounts?

Have the sales rankings of our salespeople changed during the past year?

What is the similarity between the rankings of our employees provided by the union's personnel committee and those of shop supervisors?

What is the relationship between the male/female variable and the ratings given the following factors in a recent employee survey?

a. Quality of company management.
b. Fairness of pay level.
c. Opportunity for advancement.

Last year the quality-control department ranked the company's 28 suppliers from best to worst. Rankings have again been made this year. How well do the two rankings correlate?

Glossary

Nonparametric tests Statistical tests that do not make assumptions about the underlying form of the population data.

Key Formulas

Normal approximation to the binomial

$$z = \frac{x - (n/2)}{(1/2)\sqrt{n}} \tag{19.1}$$

Mean for one-sample runs test

$$\mu_r = \frac{2n_1n_2}{n_1 + n_2} + 1 \tag{19.2}$$

Standard deviation for one-sample runs test

$$\sigma_r = \sqrt{\frac{2n_1n_2(2n_1n_2 - n_1 - n_2)}{(n_1 + n_2)^2(n_1 + n_2 - 1)}} \tag{19.3}$$

z value for one-sample runs test

$$z = \frac{r - \mu_r}{\sigma_r} \tag{19.4}$$

Mann-Whitney U statistic

$$U = n_1n_2 + \frac{n_1(n_1 + 1)}{2} - R_1 \tag{19.5}$$

Mean for Mann-Whitney U test

$$\mu_U = \frac{n_1n_2}{2} \tag{19.6}$$

Standard deviation for Mann-Whitney *U* test

$$\sigma_U = \sqrt{\frac{n_1 n_2 (n_1 + n_2 + 1)}{12}} \tag{19.7}$$

***z* value for Mann-Whitney *U* test**

$$z = \frac{U - \mu_U}{\sigma_U} \tag{19.8}$$

Spearman rank correlation coefficient

$$r_s = 1 - \frac{6\Sigma d^2}{n^3 - n} \tag{19.9}$$

SOLVED EXERCISES

1. ONE-SAMPLE SIGN TEST

A taste test is conducted to determine whether people prefer cherry diet cola or grape. A panel of 40 tasters is asked to rank each drink on a five-point scale. Table 19.3 shows the results. Use the .10 significance level to determine if the tasters indicate a significant difference between the two types of soft drink.

TABLE 19.3 Ranked Scores Assigned to Two Kinds of Diet Soft Drinks (Solved Exercise 1)

	Score				Score		
Taster	Cherry	Grape	Sign of difference	Taster	Cherry	Grape	Sign of difference
1	4	2	+	21	3	5	−
2	1	3	−	22	4	4	0
3	2	2	0	23	1	5	−
4	5	3	+	24	1	3	−
5	3	1	+	25	4	3	+
6	3	2	+	26	5	2	+
7	4	4	0	27	3	5	−
8	1	5	−	28	3	1	+
9	5	4	+	29	2	2	0
10	4	2	+	30	2	5	−
11	3	2	+	31	5	4	+
12	4	1	+	32	5	4	+
13	2	3	−	33	4	3	+
14	1	4	−	34	3	3	0
15	5	4	+	35	1	5	−
16	4	3	+	36	2	5	−
17	5	3	+	37	3	2	+
18	2	4	−	38	4	4	0
19	4	2	+	39	4	2	+
20	5	5	0	40	5	3	+

A 5 denotes the best score; a 1 denotes the worst score. + indicates that cherry was preferred; − indicates that grape was preferred.

Solution:

The null and alternative hypotheses are

$$H_0: p = .50$$
$$H_1: p \neq .50$$

The first step is to determine the number of plus signs and minus signs. A plus sign is assigned to each taster who ranked cherry diet cola higher than grape. A minus sign is assigned to each taster who ranked grape higher than cherry. The next step is to count the plus signs and minus signs. There are 21 plus signs and 12 minus signs. (Note that seven values have been ignored because the tasters gave the two beverages the same score.)

The normal-curve approximation to the binomial distribution is used. In terms of proportions, the mean and the standard deviation of the sampling distribution are

$$\mu_p = p = .50$$

$$\sigma_p = \sqrt{\frac{p(1 - p)}{n}} = \sqrt{\frac{.50(.50)}{33}} = \sqrt{.0076} = .087$$

The decision rule for this hypothesis test is

If the computed z value is less than -1.645 or larger than 1.645, reject the null hypothesis.

The observed proportion of plus signs is

$$\bar{p} = \frac{x}{n} = \frac{21}{33} = .\,,36$$

The z value is

$$z = \frac{\bar{p} - p}{\sigma_p} = \frac{.636 - .50}{.087} = 1.56$$

Since the calculated z (1.56) is less than the critical z (1.645), the null hypothesis is not rejected. There is *not* a significant difference in the number of tasters who preferred one beverage over the other.

2. One-Sample Runs Test

Chris Belmont has written a computer program to generate random numbers. He decides to test sequences of numbers to look for runs of numbers above and below the median value of 4.5. Consider the following string of 50 digits taken from the random number generator. Perform a one-sample runs test on this series at the .05 significance level.

07904675507234869595534089270867110682607982091123

Solution:

The first step is to identify the number of runs (r), the number of digits less than 4.5 (n_1), and the number of digits larger than 4.5 (n_2).

0 79 04 6755 0 7 234 8695955 340 89 2 7 0 867 110
68 2 6 0 798 20 9 1123

$$r = 23, \quad n_1 = 23, \quad n_2 = 27$$

$$\mu_r = \frac{2n_1n_2}{n_1 + n_2} + 1$$
$$= \frac{2(23)(27)}{23 + 27} + 1 = 25.84$$
$$\sigma_r = \sqrt{\frac{2n_1n_2(2n_1n_2 - n_1 - n_2)}{(n_1 + n_2)^2(n_1 + n_2 - 1)}}$$
$$= \sqrt{\frac{2(23)(27)[2(23)(27) - 23 - 27]}{(23 + 27)^2\,(23 + 27 - 1)}} = 3.48$$

The decision rule for this hypothesis test is

If the computed z value is less than -1.96 or larger than 1.96, reject the null hypothesis.

The z value is

$$z = \frac{r - \mu_r}{\sigma_r} = \frac{23 - 25.84}{3.48} = -0.82$$

Since the calculated z (-0.82) is not less than the critical z (-1.96), the null hypothesis is not rejected. The number of runs in the row of numbers is random.

3. MANN-WHITNEY *U* TEST

Dr. Tom Whitfield of Deaconess Hospital is testing the effectiveness of a new drug in treating paranoia. He records the lengths of hospital stays for paranoid patients treated with an old drug and those for similar patients treated with the new drug. A rank of 1 is assigned to the shortest hospital stay. Dr. Whitfield obtains the following ranks for the lengths of hospital stays for 25 patients:

Old drug	New drug
5	1
9	2
12	3
14	4
15	6
16	7
17	8
20	10
21	11
22	13
23	18
24	19
25	

Is the new drug more effective? Test at the .01 significance level.

Solution:

The null and alternative hypotheses are

$$H_0\colon \mu_1 - \mu_2 \le 0$$
$$H_1\colon \mu_1 - \mu_2 > 0$$

The U statistic is calculated using Equation 19.5. In this equation, $n_1 = 12$ (the number of patients using the new drug), $n_2 = 13$ (the number of patients using the old drug), and $R_1 = 102$. The last value was calculated by summing all the ranks for the new drug. The calculation for U is

$$\begin{aligned} U &= n_1 n_2 + \frac{n_1(n_1 + 1)}{2} - R_1 \\ &= (12)(13) + \frac{12(12 + 1)}{2} - 102 \\ &= 132 \end{aligned}$$

The U statistic computed from the sample data is 132.

Using Equations 19.6 and 19.7, the mean and standard deviation of the normal sampling distribution are

$$\begin{aligned} \mu_U &= \frac{n_1 n_2}{2} = \frac{(12)(13)}{2} = 78 \\ \sigma_U &= \sqrt{\frac{n_1 n_2(n_1 + n_2 + 1)}{12}} \\ &= \sqrt{\frac{(12)(13)(12 + 13 + 1)}{12}} = 18.4 \end{aligned}$$

The decision rule for this hypothesis test is

If the computed z value is larger than 2.33, reject the null hypothesis.

The z value for the sample statistic is

$$z = \frac{U - \mu_U}{\sigma_U} = \frac{132 - 78}{18.4} = 2.93$$

The calculated z (2.93) is greater than the critical z (2.33); therefore, the null hypothesis is rejected. Dr. Whitfield concludes that patients who used the new drug had a shorter hospital stay than patients who used the old drug.

4. Spearman Rank Correlation

Lester Roenfeldt, president of the Crescent Department Store chain, wants to measure the effect of a new incentive system on consumer preferences for various branches of the chain. On the basis of a marketing survey taken last year, 11 stores were ranked according to consumer preferences. This year, the same research was undertaken, with somewhat different rankings (Table 19.4). Lester wants to determine whether there's a significant change in preference rankings during the past year. Test at the .05 significance level.

Solution:

Table 19.4 shows the differences between rankings for each store, along with the squared differences. The sum of these squared differences is 67, and the total number of stores being ranked is 11. These values are used in Equation 19.9 to calculate the Spearman correlation coefficient:

$$r_s = 1 - \frac{6\Sigma d^2}{n^3 - n} = 1 - \frac{6(67)}{11^3 - 11} = 1 - .305 = .695$$

TABLE 19.4 Ranking Data for Solved Exercise 4

Branch	Last year's rank	This year's rank	d	d^2
A	1	5	−4	16
B	2	4	−2	4
C	3	1	2	4
D	4	2	2	4
E	5	9	−4	16
F	6	7	−1	1
G	7	3	4	16
H	8	8	0	0
I	9	11	−2	4
J	10	9	1	1
K	11	10	1	1
				67

For the test of significance, the null and alternative hypotheses are

$$H_0: \rho_s = 0$$
$$H_1: \rho_s \neq 0$$

At the .05 significance level, the decision rule is

If the sample t statistic is less than -2.262 or greater than 2.262, reject the null hypothesis.

The standard error of r is computed using Equation 14.2:

$$s_r = \sqrt{\frac{1 - r^2}{n - 2}} = \sqrt{\frac{1 - (.695)^2}{9}} = .24$$

The t statistic is computed using Equation 14.3:

$$t = \frac{r_s - \rho_s}{s_r} = \frac{.695 - 0}{.24} = 2.90$$

Since the calculated t statistic (2.90) is greater than the critical t value (2.262), the null hypothesis is rejected. Lester concludes that there's a significant similarity between the rankings last year and this year. Apparently the new incentive system has not been particularly effective.

EXERCISES

22. What is the disadvantage of converting quantitative data, such as those measured on a ratio scale, to categorical data, such as those measured on an ordinal scale, in order to analyze the data using a nonparametric method?

23. Here are sample observations for the weights of a new breakfast cereal fed into boxes by a filling machine. Since the sample size is small, and since there's evidence to suggest that the population of weights is not normal, a nonparametric test is in order. Can we conclude that the occurrences of overfills (O) and underfills (U) in the population are equal?

U, U, O, O, O, U, O, O, O, U, U, O, O,
U, O, O, U, U, O, O, O, O, U, U, O, O

23. Sign test: $n = 26$, $z = -1.18$. Don't reject H_0

24. U test: sum A = 177, $U = 152$, $\mu = 112$, $\sigma = 24.1$, $z = 1.66$, $z_{crit} = \pm 1.96$. Don't reject H_0

24. The number of bad parts found in a PC company's subassemblies is recorded for each order. Also recorded is whether the shipment of parts came from supplier A or supplier B. The plant manager is interested in the quality of units shipped, especially after reading "Five Hot 286 Bargains" in *PC Computing* (February 1989, p. 86). This article described five competitors' products and brought the subassemblies' quality level into sharp focus.

The shipments are arranged in ascending order, with the lowest number of bad parts appearing first, the next lowest second, and so on to the highest number of bad parts. Here is the ascending list denoted by supplier: A or B. Can the plant manager conclude at the .05 significance level that the two suppliers are supplying part batches of equal quality?

A, A, A, B, B, A, B, A, A, B, B, A, A, B, A,
A, B, B, B, A, B, A, A, B, B, B, A, B, B, B

25. Sum $d^2 = 150$, $r = .476$, moderate correlation

25. Determine the Spearman rank correlation coefficient for the following data. Describe the extent of similarity between the two ranks.

Rank 1	Rank 2
1	6
2	2
3	7
4	1
5	9
6	3
7	10
8	4
9	12
10	5
11	11
12	8

26. Runs test: runs = 16, $\mu = 15.9$, $\sigma = 2.68$, $z = .04$. Don't reject H_0

26. Howard Hindman, quality-control engineer for Spartan Manufacturing Company, needs to see if the production process for a particular part is in control. He examines a sample of 30 consecutive parts emerging from the production line and classifies each as either defective or nondefective. Howard wants to test at the .05 significance level if the process generates defective and nondefective parts randomly. Howard classifies the sequence as A = defective and B = nondefective:

A, A, A, B, B, A, B, A, A, B, B, A, A, B, A,
A, B, B, B, A, B, A, A, B, B, B, A, B, B, B

27. U test: sum reg. = 101, $U = 121$, $\mu = 72$, $\sigma = 17.3$, $z = 2.83$, $z_{crit} = 1.645$. Reject H_0

27. Evergreen Soft Drink Company President Julie Zappone has asked statistician Ben Showalter to analyze the effectiveness of free samples. Ben conducts an experiment by comparing sales of Evergreen soft drinks on regular days with sales on days when free samples are provided. The results, in sales units, are:

Regular days:	40	50	44	58	39	27	41	46	53	35	31	33
Free-sample days:	42	51	68	71	45	55	60	64	39	68	58	49

Test at the .05 significance level if free samples increase sales.

28. Sum $d^2 = 357.5$, $r = -.25$, $t = -.816$. Don't reject H_0

28. Art Lysone, foreman of the Amoca Plant, wants to know if the number of overtime hours worked is related to age. He records data for overtime hours and age for 12 employees:

Age:	58	47	35	24	60	29	38	42	22	54	28	39
Hours:	5	5	10	13	9	23	0	3	6	18	11	21

Test at the .02 significance level whether the number of hours worked overtime is related to age, using a nonparametric test.

29. Runs test: runs = 16, $\mu = 20.3$, $\sigma = 2.93$, $z = -1.47$, $z_{crit} = \pm 1.96$. Don't reject H_0

29. Eunice Stern, Dodge Corporation personnel director, analyzes the problem of employee absenteeism. Eunice carefully checks the records of employees with an unusually large number of absences. She wants to determine whether absences are random or occur for some reason. Here's the 42-day attendance record of Larry Wiley, one of these employees. A represents *absent* and P represents *present*.

PPPPPAAAPPAPPPPPAPPAAAPPPPPPAPPAPPAPPPAAAA

Test at the .05 significance level to determine whether Larry's absences have occurred randomly.

30. Runs test: runs = 30, $\mu = 30.7$, $\sigma = 3.80$, $z = -.18$. Don't reject H_0

30. Marian Campbell, a stockbroker for Weber-Payne, observes the behavior of the Dow Jones Industrial Average on the New York Stock Exchange for 60 market days. She wonders if day-to-day changes are random. Marian classifies market behavior each day, using I for *increase* and D for *decrease:*

DIDIIIIDIDDDIIDIIIIDDDDIDIIIDDDIIDIIIDDDIIIIDIDIIDDDDIIIDIDI

Test at the .01 significance level to determine if stock market ups and downs can be considered random.

31. Runs test: plus = 13, $z = 1.89$, $z_{crit} = 1.28$ so reject H_0

31. Sunkiss Vineyards tests its new grape juice, Purple-Power, against the leading seller, Grape-Wonderful. In a study of consumer preferences, 18 people were given unmarked samples of each brand and asked which they liked better. The brand each person tasted first was randomly selected. The results are:

Person	Brand preference	Sign
1	Purple-Power	+
2	Grape-Wonderful	−
3	Purple-Power	+
4	Purple-Power	+
5	Purple-Power	+
6	Grape-Wonderful	−
7	Purple-Power	+
8	Grape-Wonderful	−
9	Purple-Power	+
10	Purple-Power	+
11	Grape-Wonderful	−
12	Purple-Power	+
13	Purple-Power	+
14	Purple-Power	+
15	Purple-Power	+
16	Purple-Power	+
17	Grape-Wonderful	−
18	Purple-Power	+

Test at the .10 significance level whether people prefer Purple-Power.

32. Sum $d^2 = 168$, $r = -1$

32. Consider the following set of rankings:

Rank 1	Rank 2
1	8
2	7
3	6
4	5
5	4
6	3
7	2
8	1

a. What value would you expect for the Spearman rank correlation coefficient?

b. Compute the Spearman rank correlation coefficient.

33. Sum $d^2 = 78$, $r = .07$, $t = .17$, $t_{crit} = \pm 1.943$. Don't reject H_0

33. The Corker-White Advertising Agency decided to test eight different commercials on a group of men and women to determine if there's a relationship between the two groups' rankings. This study was requested by the agency president, who read an article on women in the workplace in *Training and Development Journal* (November 1989, p. 21). She believes men and women could react differently to the commercials.

Commercial	Ranked by women	Ranked by men
A	3	1
B	4	3
C	1	6
D	8	5
E	7	8
F	5	2
G	2	7
H	6	4

Test at the .10 significance level to determine if there is a significant difference between the way men and women rank the commercials.

34. Sign test: plus = 13, $z = 2.84$, $z_{crit} = 1.645$. Reject H_0

34. The Mayor of Deer Park, Tom Truelove, has just read a report stating that median income for his city is $13,329. This figure seems too low to Tom. He decides to take a random sample of 15 families and determine their median income. The results are

$14,100	$15,100	$12,789	$13,500	$14,010
$14,321	$13,560	$13,789	$20,900	$34,010
$12,150	$13,780	$14,189	$21,784	$68,543

Test at the .05 significance level to determine if the population median is higher than $13,329. Use a nonparametric test.

35. *U* test: $U = 256$, $\mu = 200$, $\sigma = 37.0$, $z = 1.51$, $z_{crit} = \pm 1.645$. Don't reject H_0

35. A consumer-testing group wishes to compare tires with five-year guarantees offered by two large mail order department stores. The group selects a random sample of 20 tires from store A and 20 tires from store B and tests them under similar conditions. The tire lives are ranked (the tire that lasted the longest is ranked number 1), and the summation of

the ranks for department store A is 354. Test at the .10 significance level to determine whether there's a significant difference in the lifetimes of the two stores' tires.

36. Runs test: runs = 22, $\mu = 20.5$, $\sigma = 3.08$, $z = .49$, $z_{crit} = \pm 2.578$. Don't reject H_0

36. From 1950 through 1989, National League baseball teams won the World Series 19 times, and American League teams won 21 times. The year-to-year results (with N representing the National League and A representing the American League) are

AAAANNANANNAANNNANANANAAANNAANNNNAAANAN

Test at the .01 significance level to determine if World Series victories have occurred randomly between the two leagues.

37. Sign test: remove unchanged value, $\mu = 8$, plus = 6, $z = 1.41$, $z_{crit} = 1.28$. Reject H_0

37. Frank Kasson, president of Zable Corporation, wants to know if an "Investment in Excellence" program will have a positive impact on potential for advancement within the company. Nine employees are rated as to their promotion potential on a 10-point scale, both before experiencing the program and after. The results are:

Employee	Before	After
A	7	9
B	4	3
C	4	6
D	8	10
E	7	7
F	5	2
G	2	8
H	3	9
I	6	8

Test at the .10 significance level to determine if the program has an impact on advancement potential.

38. U test: sum one = 42, $U = 21$, $\mu = 21$, $z = 0$. Don't reject H_0

38. The ROTC unit on campus has decided to test two methods of training cadets to break down and reassemble an automatic weapon. The results for the two groups are:

Time	Group	Rank
4.5	1	6
4.3	2	5
5.6	2	12
3.9	2	2
4.0	1	3.5
4.5	1	13
4.6	1	7
4.8	2	8
3.8	2	1
4.0	1	3.5
5.0	1	9
5.2	2	10.5
5.2	2	10.5

Test at the .05 significance level to determine if there is a significant difference between the two methods of training. Use a nonparametric method.

39. Sum $d^2 = 192$, $r = -.17, t = -.49$, $t_{crit} = \pm 2.306$. Don't reject H_0

39. Donald Barfield wants to test the relationship between his sales manager's ratings of salespeople and their years of experience.

Salesperson	Years of service	Rating
A	8	4
B	4	3
C	5	6
D	8	10
E	5	7
F	1	2
G	2	8
H	3	9
I	12	1
J	10	5

Test at the .05 significance level to determine if there is a significant relationship between the sales manager's ratings of salespeople and their years of experience. Use a nonparametric method.

40. Flip a coin 100 times and record the sequence of heads and tails. Is the sequence random if tested at the .10 significance level?

EXTENDED EXERCISES

41. THE FAIR COIN

An unpleasant fight with the company union is taking up a great deal of management time at the Bartlett Company. Irene Bartlett, company president, finally reaches an agreement with the union about the final point of contention in the new contract. They decide that the question of whether full disability pay will continue for six or nine months after injury will be resolved by a coin flip.

A local church minister has agreed to flip the coin at a meeting of the company's board of directors and the union leadership. Irene is stunned to learn that the union has now raised the question of which coin will be used and wants some assurance that the coin will be fair.

Irene realizes the union is trying to tax her patience but decides to let the minister select a coin and flip it many times. The outcomes will be recorded and given to a statistics professor, who will then use "some statistical test" to determine if the sequence of heads and tails can be regarded as randomly generated. Here are the test results, where H represents a head and T represents a tail:

H T H T T H H T H H T T T T H H T H T H H T T H T H
T T H H H T T H T H T T H T H H H T T H T T H H T T

Irene counts the number of runs in this sequence as 32, with 25 heads and 27 tails. The statistics professor leaves her a memo before he leaves on spring break: "The mean of the normal sampling distribution for the runs test is 27.0 with a standard deviation of 3.6."

a. Does the sequence of heads and tails appear to be randomly generated?

b. Use the runs test to determine if the claim of a random sequence can be statistically justified using the values Irene's analyst gave her.

c. What should Irene tell the union about the fairness of the coin?

42. THE SALES MOTIVATION PROGRAM

Charlie Fields became sales manager for a national life insurance company a year ago. At that time, he instituted a sales motivation program that he had used successfully in another company. Now, a year later, he wants to assess the impact on his key salespeople's performance. His interest increases after he reads "Productivity Improvement Begins Today" in *Management Solutions* (June 1988).

When he took the job, Charlie obtained a ranking of the 10 key salespeople in the company. A current ranking has just been issued by top management. These company rankings combine total dollar sales volume and other factors, such as number of new accounts, size of largest account, and total number of accounts.

Here are the key salespeople for the company along with their ratings, both one year ago and currently. After studying these rankings, Charlie isn't sure he has enough evidence to show top management that his first year on the job has paid big dividends to the company. He's especially concerned because company bonus time is only two weeks away.

Salesperson	Rating last year	Rating this year
Campion	1	3
Chapman	2	1
Lopez	3	5
Shapiro	4	2
Zurenko	5	6
Cameron	6	4
Bump	7	9
Kuo	8	8
Hartman	9	10
Faulkner	10	7

a. What is your opinion of Charlie's motivation program after looking at the two rankings?

b. Use the Spearman rank correlation procedure to determine the correlation between last year's rankings and this year's.

c. Based on the correlation coefficient, how effective has the program been?

43. BURNSIDE MANUFACTURING

Burnside Manufacturing Company produces small engines used in rototillers and garden tractors. The company has a contract with two companies that supply it with the pistons used in these engines. A continuing problem is out-of-tolerance pistons, which must be returned to the supplier. Recent meetings at Burnside have raised the question of whether the two suppliers are contributing equally to this problem.

To investigate this matter, records are kept for several days on the amount by which pistons are out of tolerance. These error amounts are then ranked from low to high, and the supplier is indicated for each. Burnside thinks it can determine if one supplier is worse than the other by examining these rankings. Obviously, if one supplier has most of the low rankings and the other has most of the high rankings, the higher-ranked supplier is creating most of the problem.

Here are the ranks for out-of-tolerance piston amounts, from low to high; R represents one supplier and S represents the other.

R R S R R R S S R R S R S R R S R R S S R S S S S S S R
S S S R S R R S S S S S R S S R S S S S R R S S S S S S

a. Do the sample results provide any clues about the quality comparison of the two suppliers?

b. Use the Mann-Whitney U test to determine if a quality difference can be supported statistically.

c. Assume the role of statistical analyst and write a paragraph summarizing your findings.

Microcomputer Package

The micro package *Computerized Business Statistics* can be used to solve nonparametric problems.

In Exercise 27, Ben Showalter analyzed the effectiveness of the policy of free samples. Ben conducted an experiment comparing sales of Evergreen soft drinks on regular days with sales on days when free samples are provided. The results, in sales units, are:

Regular days:	40	50	44	58	39	27	41	46	53	35	31	33
Free-sample days:	42	51	68	71	45	55	60	64	39	68	58	49

Test at the .05 significance level to determine if free samples increase sales.

Computer Solution

From the main menu of *Computerized Business Statistics* a **14** is selected, indicating Nonparametric Methods. The nonparametric methods menu is shown on the screen.

Since the problem involves entering data from the keyboard, a **1** is selected.

```
Nonparametric Methods - Define New Problem
Options:        1 = Wilcoxon Rank-Sum Test
                2 = Mann-Whitney Test
                3 = Wilcoxon Signed-Rank Test
                4 = Spearman Rank Correlation
                5 = Kruskal-Wallis Test
Select Method: Enter 1–5, press ↵ 2
```

Since the Mann-Whitney test is needed to solve Exercise 27, a **2** is selected.

```
Alpha Error: Enter 0–1, press ↵ .05
```

The significance level for this exercise is **.05**.

```
Nonparametric Methods - Enter Number of Data Points
      Population 1        __ 12 __
      Population 2        __ 12 __
Press F when Finished
```

Since each population had 12 observations, a **12** is entered in each blank space.

```
Nonparametric Methods - Enter Population Labels
       Population 1        ___ free
       Population 2        ___ reg ___
Press end when Finished
```

Population 1 is entered as **free,** and population 2 is entered as **reg.**

```
Problem definition correct Y/N/Q, Press ↵ Y
```

After a **Y** response, the program is ready for the data to be entered. There are 12 data points. An **F** is entered once the blanks have been completed.

After the data have been entered the screen shows:

```
          free    reg
 1 =       42      40
 2 =       51      50
 3 =       68      44
 4 =       71      58
 5 =       45      39
 6 =       55      27
 7 =       60      41
 8 =       64      46
 9 =       39      53
10 =       68      35
11 =       58      31
12 =       49      33
```

Next, the program asks:

```
Save data? Y/N, Press ↵ N
```

The nonparametric statistics menu reappears. A **7** is entered so that the problem can be run.

```
One or Two Tailed Test? Enter a '1' or a '2' and press ↵ 1
Lower or Upper Limit? Enter a 'L' or a 'U' and press ↵ U
```

Since the test involves determining whether the free samples increase sales, a one-tailed test at the upper limit is used. The screen shows the output menu. The choice in this case was **P** for printer.

MINITAB COMPUTER PACKAGE

MINITAB can be used to solve several nonparametric procedures. The MINITAB commands to solve the one-sample sign test for Example 19.1 are:

```
MTB > SET C1
DATA> 32 30 25 34 36 29 31 27 32 33 37 32 28 42 40 31 31 32
DATA> END
MTB > STEST 30 C1;
SUBC> ALTERNATIVE = +1.

SIGN TEST OF MEDIAN = 30.00 VERSUS G.T. 30.00

          N   BELOW   EQUAL   ABOVE   P-VALUE    MEDIAN
C1       18       4       1      13    0.0245     32.00
```

The data are entered into C1 using the SET command. The STEST command is used to compute a sign test for a hypothesized median of 30. The alternative subcommand is used for a one-sided test where the alternative hypothesis is greater than. Note that the p-value, .0245, is exactly the same as the probability of obtaining four or fewer successes from the cumulative binomial table.

Other nonparametric commands demonstrated in this chapter include RUNS (to test data to determine if the order is random), MANN-WHITNEY (to determine the difference between two population medians), and RANK and CORR (to compute the Spearman rank correlation for ordinal data).

Nonparametric commands not demonstrated in this chapter include WTEST (which performs a one-sample Wilcoxon signed-rank test), KRUSKAL WALLIS (which offers a nonparametric alternative to one-way analysis of variance), and FRIEDMAN (which performs a nonparametric analysis of a randomized block experiment).

SAS Computer Package

The SAS computer package can be used to solve nonparametric models. The SAS commands to analyze Exercise 39 are:

```
TITLE "SPEARMAN RANK FOR EXERCISE 39";
DATA SALESPEOPLE;
 INPUT YEARS RATING;
 LABEL YEARS ='YEARS OF EXPERIENCE'
       RATING ='RATING OF SALESPERSON';
CARDS;
8  4
4  3
5  6
8  10
5  7
1  2
2  8
3  9
12  1
10  5
PROC CORR NOSIMPLE SPEARMAN;
 VAR YEARS RATING;
```

The TITLE command names the SAS run. The DATA command gives the data a name. The INPUT command names and gives the correct order for the two data fields. The next 10 lines are card images that represent the years and rating variables. The PROC CORR NOSIMPLE SPEARMAN command calculates the Spearman rank correlation coefficient between the variables "years of experience" and "rating" indicated on the VAR subcommand. Figure 19.2 shows the results.

Other nonparametric techniques that can be analyzed in SAS using the PROC NPAR1WAY command are the Wilcoxon rank sum test, the Wilcoxon signed rank test, and the Kruskal-Wallis test.

FIGURE 19.2 SAS Output for Exercise 39

```
                        SPEARMAN RANK FOR EXERCISE 39

                            Correlation Analysis

                      2 'VAR' Variables:  YEARS   RATING
Spearman Correlation Coefficients/ Prob > |R| under H0: Rho=0 / N = 10

                             YEARS        RATING
YEARS                      1.00000      -0.17073
YEARS OF EXPERIENCE         0.0           0.6372

RATING                    -0.17073       1.00000
RATING OF SALESPERSON      0.6372         0.0
```

Appendixes

Appendix A
Effective Communications
924

Appendix B
Derivations
928

Appendix C
Company Data Base
931

Appendix D
Answers to Selected Odd-Numbered Exercises
936

Appendix E
Statistical Tables
967

APPENDIX A EFFECTIVE COMMUNICATIONS

Many of the exercises throughout this text have asked you to "prepare a memo for management explaining the results of your analysis." These assignments reflect our view that good communication is essential if research results are to be used in a firm's decision making. This is especially true when the analysis involves manipulating data and/or using a computer, the subjects of this text. We've seen many cases where a good analysis is ignored because of poor communications.

There are three essential steps to effectively communicating the results of a quantitative study. First, you must really *understand* these results. One purpose of studying statistics, and studying this text, is to develop your understanding of what happens when a computer performs an analysis on data.

Second, you need to *organize* the results before you begin any writing or verbal presentation. The importance of such organization seems obvious, but, again, it's easy to find instances where a presentation is sloppy and difficult to follow.

Third, in the actual written or verbal report, good presenters *practice* their techniques. Many good verbal models are available for you to study, such as TV newscasts and some political speeches. Good writing skills can be developed with practice as well. We can't overestimate the importance of good writing ability in a business career. The rest of this appendix is devoted to preparing written reports. Practice often!

Here are some guidelines to help you develop an effective communication style:

Think about your readers. What is their background? Why would they be interested? How much detail do they want? Do they just want the analysis, or do they want conclusions and recommendations as well? What is their connection to the firm's decision-making process, and what is the best way to get them to use your results?

Be as concise yet complete as you can. Once you've carefully considered your audience, how can you present the pertinent aspects of your research with just the right amount of detail?

Be prepared to present conclusions about your research as well as the results. What effect should your results have on the firm? How can the firm do its business better as a result of your efforts? What change in direction is suggested by your results?

Here is a sample memo written for a fictitious situation similar to those in this text's examples and exercises. The writer has decided that the length and amount of detail are appropriate for the intended audience. For other audiences, a much shorter memo might be appropriate, such as: "Bob/Judy: Average is up to $40.25. Recommend we buy." Another audience (for example, the company's board of directors or bank loan officer) might require a much longer written document.

MEMO

To: Bob and Judy, VPs

From: Art Hank, Analyst

Date: January 18, 1993

Subj.: Pamco Company Sales

Following your request of January 9, I conducted a study of the average dollar sales of the Pamco Company in conjunction with our proposed acquisition of Pamco during the next six months. Recall that in our last set of figures from Pamco, the average sales amount per customer visit was $37.59.

During the past three months, Pamco has initiated an intense advertising campaign designed to increase customers' average purchase amount. Pamco management has permitted me to take random samples of purchases during the past three weeks, and I've collected a total of 750 transactions during that time. I've used three trained interviewers for this purpose and have sampled during every day of the week at many different times of the day. As a result, I have a very representative view of Pamco's current performance.

The average purchase amount is $40.25, an increase of $2.66 over the previous reported average. With a sample standard deviation of $5.90, this results in a test z value of 12.3 and p-value of .0000. This means that we can make a virtually error-free statement that the average purchase amount at Pamco has increased.

In the face of this significant increase over a short period of time, I believe our faith in Pamco's potential has been justified. Subject to the financial considerations in this matter, I recommend that we move forward to purchase Pamco.

In determining the proper length of your report, remember that this memo is only an example. It would be good practice for you to take one of the exercises in this text that requires a written memo and write three different memos: a short one of two or three sentences, another of about the length of the one just presented, and a longer one of three or four pages.

The organization of a memo or report may vary just as the length, depending on the audience. The following sample outline is for reference in preparing any written report.[1] The topics are only suggestions since a given report might contain many more, or fewer, headings.

I. Title page
II. Table of contents

[1]From W. Dillon, T. Madden, and N. Firtle, *Marketing Research in a Marketing Environment* (St. Louis: Times Mirror/Mosby College Publishing, 1987), p. 718.

- III. Introduction
  - A. Background and objectives
  - B. Methodology
    1. Sample
    2. Procedure
    3. Questionnaire
- IV. Management summary
  - A. Key findings
  - B. Conclusions
  - C. Marketing implications and recommendations
- V. Detailed findings
  - A. Evaluation measures
  - B. Diagnostic measures
  - C. Profile composites
- VI. Appendixes
  - A. Questionnaire
  - B. Field materials
  - C. Statistical output

Two additional sample memos are shown next for your reference. Each is a solution to a text exercise. These will help you when your professor assigns a "memo" exercise.

Exercise 53, Chapter 4:

MEMO

To: Al

From: Bob

Date: January 24, 1993

Subj.: Income as a Percentage of Sales

Following your instructions, I've sampled 70 firms from the 500 largest industrial corporations in the United States and have recorded net income as a percentage of sales for each. In analyzing these data values, I find that the mean is 7.7%, the median is 8%, and the mode is also 8%. We can thus conclude that the mean return on sales is 7.7%, with half the returns being more than 8% and the other half less.

The standard deviation of returns is 2.0098, which tells us the typical amount by which the 70 returns differ from the mean of 7.7%.

Our own figure, according to last year's annual report, is 9%. This places us above the average for the nation, as indicated by my sample figures. I hope this analysis helps you with your upcoming presentation to the board.

Exercise 51, Chapter 12:

MEMO

To: Cindy Bane

From: Cathy Gant

Date: March 11, 1993

Subj.: ANOVA on Flavor and Price

I have completed the analysis of variance on flavor and price for our new ice cream flavors. This analysis is based on sampling sales volumes from 12 stores in the region. Here is a summary of the *F* test values I obtained, along with the critical values of *F* from the table using a .01 significance level:

Effect	Calculated *F*	Table *F*(.01)
Price	24.12*	4.68
Flavor	22.31*	5.57
Interaction	2.69	3.63

*Significant

The above results show that price has a definite effect on volume sold, as the null hypothesis of equal volume is rejected. Examination of the data indicates that lower prices result in higher volumes sold, as expected.

The null hypothesis of equal volume by flavor is also rejected. The data indicate that brandy and peach are about equal in terms of volume sold, but apricot lags behind.

The null hypothesis of no interaction has not been rejected. This means that unusual sales do not result when certain prices are attached to certain flavors.

On the basis of my analysis, I recommend that we seek to establish as low a price as possible in order to maximize sales, and that we drop the apricot flavor from our new line.

Appendix B Derivations

Correlation Derivation

$$
\begin{aligned}
r = \frac{\Sigma z_x z_y}{N} &= \sum \frac{[(x - \mu_x)/\sigma_x][(y - \mu_y)/\sigma_y]}{N} \\
&= \frac{\Sigma(x - \mu_x)(y - \mu_y)}{\sqrt{(\Sigma x^2/N) - (\Sigma x/N)^2}\sqrt{[(\Sigma y^2/N) - (\Sigma y/N)^2]/N}} \\
&= \frac{\Sigma(x - \mu_x)(y - \mu_y)}{\sqrt{[N\Sigma x^2 - (\Sigma x)^2]/N^2}\sqrt{[N\Sigma y^2 - (\Sigma y)^2]/(N^2/N)}} \\
&= \frac{N\Sigma(x - \mu_x)(y - \mu_y)}{\sqrt{N\Sigma x^2 - (\Sigma x)^2}\sqrt{N\Sigma y^2 - (\Sigma y)^2}} \\
&= \frac{N\Sigma(xy - y\mu_x - x\mu_y + \mu_x\mu_y)}{\sqrt{N\Sigma x^2 - (\Sigma x)^2}\sqrt{N\Sigma y^2 - (\Sigma y)^2}} \\
&= \frac{N[\Sigma xy - (\Sigma x\Sigma y/N) - (\Sigma x\Sigma y/N) + N(\Sigma x/N)(\Sigma y/N)]}{\sqrt{N\Sigma x^2 - (\Sigma x)^2}\sqrt{N\Sigma y^2 - (\Sigma y)^2}} \\
&= \frac{N[\Sigma xy - (\Sigma x\Sigma y/N) - (\Sigma x\Sigma y/N) + (\Sigma x\Sigma y/N)]}{\sqrt{N\Sigma x^2 - (\Sigma x)^2}\sqrt{N\Sigma y^2 - (\Sigma y)^2}} \\
&= \frac{N[\Sigma xy - (\Sigma x\Sigma y)/N]}{\sqrt{N\Sigma x^2 - (\Sigma x)^2}\sqrt{N\Sigma y^2 - (\Sigma y)^2}} \\
&= \frac{N\Sigma xy - \Sigma x\Sigma y}{\sqrt{N\Sigma x^2 - (\Sigma x)^2}\sqrt{N\Sigma y^2 - (\Sigma y)^2}}
\end{aligned}
$$

Least Squares Derivation

$$
\begin{aligned}
d &= y - \hat{y} \\
&= y - (b_0 + b_1 x) \\
d^2 &= [y - (b_0 + b_1 x)]^2 \\
\Sigma d^2 &= \Sigma[y - (b_0 + b_1 x)]^2 \\
&= \Sigma(y - b_0 \;\; b_1 x)^2
\end{aligned}
$$

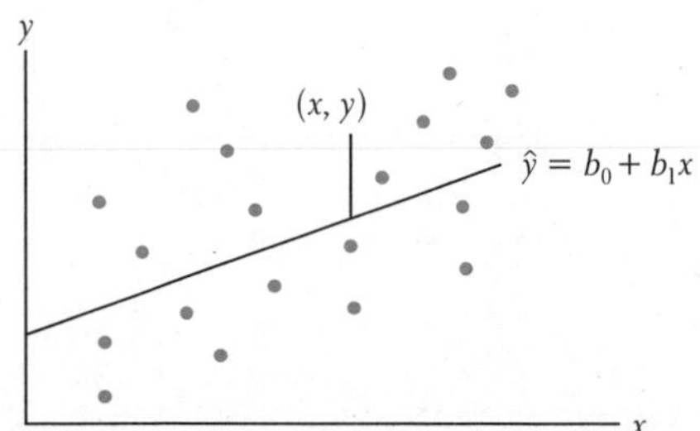

PARTIAL DERIVATIVES

$$\frac{\delta\Sigma}{\delta b_1} = 2\Sigma(y - b_1x - b_0)(-x) \qquad \frac{\delta\Sigma}{\delta b_0} = 2\Sigma(y - b_1x - b_0)(-1)$$

$$= 2\Sigma(-xy + b_1x^2 + b_0x) \qquad = 2\Sigma(-y + b_1x + b_0)$$

TO OBTAIN MINIMUMS, SET PARTIALS = 0

$$\frac{\delta\Sigma}{\delta b_1} = 0\text{: } 2\Sigma(-xy + b_1x^2 + b_0x) = 0 \qquad \frac{\delta\Sigma}{\delta b_0} = 0\text{: } 2\Sigma(-y + b_1x + b_0) = 0$$

$$\Sigma(-xy + b_1x^2 + b_0x) = 0 \qquad \Sigma(-y + b_1x + b_0) = 0$$

$$-\Sigma xy + b_0\Sigma x + b_1x^2 = 0 \qquad -\Sigma y + Nb_0 + b_1\Sigma x = 0$$

FIND A b_0 AND b_1 SUCH THAT $\Sigma\, d^2$ IS A MINIMUM

$$b_0\Sigma x + b_1\Sigma x^2 = \Sigma xy \qquad \times N$$

$$Nb_0 + b_1\Sigma x = \Sigma y \qquad \times \Sigma x$$

$$Nb_0\Sigma x + Nb_1\Sigma x^2 = N\Sigma xy$$

$$Nb_0\Sigma x + b_1(\Sigma x)^2 = \Sigma x\Sigma y \qquad \text{subtract}$$

$$Nb\Sigma x^2 - b_1(\Sigma x)^2 = N\Sigma xy - \Sigma x\Sigma y$$

$$b_1[N\Sigma x^2 - (\Sigma x)^2] = N\Sigma xy - \Sigma x\Sigma y$$

$$b_1 = \frac{N\Sigma xy - \Sigma x\Sigma y}{N\Sigma x^2 - (\Sigma x)^2} \qquad \text{slope formula}$$

$$Nb_0 + b_1\Sigma x = \Sigma y$$

$$Nb_0 = \Sigma y - b_1\Sigma x$$

$$b_0 = \frac{\Sigma y}{N} - \frac{b_1\Sigma x}{N} = \bar{\bar{y}} - b\bar{x} \qquad y\text{-intercept formula}$$

CONVERTING YEARLY TREND VALUES TO MONTHLY

Steps for converting the trend equation from annual to monthly:

1. The slope and constant must be converted from annual values to monthly values. To do so, divide b_0 and b_1 by 12. When the data are cumulative or when the annual figures are averages, this step is omitted. In other words, the monthly data must add to the annual totals in order for this step to apply. The annual equation for the new-car registration data is

   $$\hat{Y} = 7.901912 + .076123X$$

   where 1 unit of x represents 1 year and $x = 0$ represents July 1, 1959.

   $$\hat{Y} = 7.901912/12 + .076123/12(X)$$
   $$\hat{Y} = .658493 + .0063436X$$

2. The annual and monthly data must be recorded in the same type of units. If they are, skip this step. If they are not, convert the annual to monthly by moving the decimal point accordingly. Since the annual data are recorded in millions of

registrations and the monthly data in thousands, move the decimal point to the right three places.

$$\hat{Y} = 658.493 + 6.3436X$$

3. The x value must be converted from annual to monthly by dividing by 12. The x in the equation refers to units in terms of years. Convert x so that it represents months by dividing it by 12.

$$\hat{Y} = 658.493 + 6.3436/12(X)$$
$$\hat{Y} = 658.493 + 528.633X$$

4. The origin must be shifted to the middle of the first month of data, usually January 15. To move forward from July 1, 1959 to January 15, 1985, one must add 305.5 months to the x-coded value. The final monthly equation is

$$\hat{Y} = 658.493 + 528.633\ (X + 305.5)$$
$$\hat{Y} = 658.493 + 528.633X + 161{,}497$$
$$\hat{Y} = 819.990 + 528.633X$$

where $\hat{Y}$ = expected monthly trend values

X = monthly values with 0 located at January 15, 1985

APPENDIX C COMPANY DATA BASE

The following data base contains nine variables measured on N = 200 fictitious company employees. Each row represents the values of the nine variables for a single employee. The number in the first column (1–200) is the employee number. Each subsequent column represents the values of one variable for all 200 employees.

The nine variables are defined as follows:

x_1 = Number of years with the company
x_2 = Number of overtime hours worked during the past six months
x_3 = Gender: 1 = Female, 2 = Male
x_4 = Number of continuing education courses completed
x_5 = Number of sick days taken during the past six months
x_6 = Score on company aptitude test
x_7 = Amount of education: 0 = High school diploma, 1 = Some college, 2 = College degree, 3 = Postgraduate education
x_8 = Annual base salary
x_9 = Employee age

n	x_1	x_2	x_3	x_4	x_5	x_6	x_7	x_8	x_9
1	11	125	1	4	9	121.89	2	23065	44
2	24	225	2	2	2	114.20	1	27180	50
3	17	115	2	3	5	134.11	1	34875	48
4	9	117	1	1	1	113.95	1	23685	53
5	15	26	1	2	0	151.41	2	33550	62
6	6	43	1	4	3	96.65	1	22635	45
7	4	124	2	2	4	98.43	2	19575	26
8	2	71	2	1	1	110.06	1	20430	28
9	17	166	2	2	5	101.98	1	18955	33
10	17	158	1	3	2	101.01	1	25595	40
11	15	182	2	4	4	103.42	2	34975	63
12	21	81	2	3	6	106.88	2	26800	55
13	4	58	1	2	5	99.36	2	22400	50
14	12	203	1	2	3	105.66	2	31200	33
15	23	144	1	2	4	100.91	1	24750	41
16	20	179	1	3	5	73.76	2	30495	53
17	19	96	2	1	5	83.39	0	33965	58
18	12	96	2	4	7	88.41	1	30440	51
19	5	157	2	4	8	98.19	1	25545	39
20	11	27	2	2	4	101.72	1	23960	30
21	11	88	1	0	6	92.63	1	30630	45
22	8	177	2	4	6	92.59	1	38790	61
23	20	211	1	3	1	110.34	2	41705	68
24	1	125	1	0	9	102.91	2	19775	30
25	6	58	2	0	7	110.39	2	37600	57

(continued)

n	x_1	x_2	x_3	x_4	x_5	x_6	x_7	x_8	x_9
26	18	178	1	4	3	124.50	1	34250	49
27	21	166	1	3	5	116.35	1	36195	48
28	7	155	1	3	4	118.64	2	28090	31
29	21	45	2	2	6	115.64	2	35600	60
30	27	157	2	2	5	113.16	2	39975	67
31	20	99	2	0	4	96.92	2	37100	57
32	11	140	1	5	7	94.82	0	27500	32
33	11	101	1	3	9	102.62	1	24450	27
34	3	22	1	4	4	78.89	1	23150	37
35	16	93	1	3	5	83.88	1	35000	37
36	2	3	2	2	5	78.42	0	22025	25
37	12	142	1	4	9	98.67	1	26500	32
38	16	11	2	3	0	86.52	1	36475	53
39	9	124	2	1	5	87.65	2	27200	27
40	15	55	2	3	5	81.40	1	33975	37
41	3	6	2	9	3	107.87	2	19000	23
42	17	12	1	1	6	106.60	1	28650	35
43	17	112	1	3	0	117.57	1	38500	41
44	23	71	2	3	7	96.15	2	40400	63
45	6	28	2	1	3	107.97	1	38900	54
46	1	20	2	5	4	104.72	2	27050	31
47	7	43	1	3	3	85.54	0	26275	33
48	4	113	1	2	4	123.67	1	30000	40
49	22	77	2	5	4	80.55	0	40900	63
50	18	152	2	3	5	91.02	1	37000	54
51	22	0	1	1	4	105.08	1	42250	62
52	25	112	2	3	7	116.61	1	47300	63
53	15	103	1	2	1	120.90	1	30500	39
54	24	215	1	0	7	95.35	0	26180	41
55	15	50	1	3	6	95.94	0	27940	39
56	2	169	2	1	9	118.40	1	15625	26
57	17	92	2	1	3	82.45	0	23650	42
58	7	132	2	1	7	99.18	1	41910	41
59	8	48	1	1	7	107.17	1	38950	56
60	11	200	2	4	9	97.10	0	43650	70
61	10	149	2	4	4	92.41	0	31450	39
62	10	79	1	0	5	101.16	1	24650	40
63	8	48	1	1	8	93.92	0	26250	37
64	15	202	1	1	8	103.45	1	37225	57
65	8	74	1	1	3	103.89	1	23100	29
66	23	74	2	5	4	110.25	1	40370	65
67	24	138	2	5	4	103.60	1	42450	63
68	22	66	1	3	3	109.10	2	38300	65
69	6	68	1	2	5	87.58	1	39500	57
70	3	184	1	1	7	96.21	0	31400	29
71	16	123	2	1	4	101.75	1	32670	39
72	4	105	2	3	7	110.08	2	33110	47

n	x_1	x_2	x_3	x_4	x_5	x_6	x_7	x_8	x_9
73	12	0	2	6	8	104.85	1	35850	61
74	23	52	1	3	4	93.91	0	47100	61
75	13	121	2	4	8	103.45	1	41600	46
76	11	90	2	5	2	101.69	2	40700	42
77	4	31	2	0	3	110.25	1	28750	29
78	3	52	2	3	1	103.51	1	35200	35
79	9	79	2	3	4	109.97	1	38500	45
80	12	136	2	5	4	113.17	2	41800	42
81	3	169	2	2	3	118.46	1	23600	28
82	16	70	2	2	8	126.34	1	42000	46
83	23	26	2	2	7	108.45	1	43175	54
84	2	187	2	3	4	121.46	2	25150	29
85	18	198	2	2	5	106.49	1	37300	42
86	3	171	2	2	9	102.15	2	25100	27
87	7	132	2	5	7	126.34	1	28215	31
88	25	211	2	2	9	106.38	1	47025	65
89	2	112	1	2	1	102.35	2	40500	44
90	17	118	2	1	3	98.12	0	40425	45
91	22	204	2	3	2	96.82	0	42850	51
92	6	24	2	0	3	100.03	1	27500	20
93	27	11	1	3	2	112.69	1	45100	65
94	14	193	1	3	4	121.96	1	42450	57
95	12	100	1	3	8	93.77	0	41900	49
96	24	74	2	0	6	99.70	1	45375	68
97	14	61	1	1	3	93.21	0	34550	39
98	14	96	2	2	1	117.27	1	36100	38
99	11	138	2	3	7	103.46	1	27950	34
100	4	15	2	2	1	106.38	1	24525	28
101	3	13	2	0	7	102.35	1	27175	26
102	12	149	2	2	3	98.12	0	32775	38
103	12	158	2	2	5	122.27	1	35875	46
104	19	209	1	3	5	123.64	1	41800	52
105	12	180	2	0	4	134.53	1	41575	55
106	4	200	1	2	3	100.87	2	32350	31
107	5	182	2	1	7	124.09	1	34900	35
108	23	59	2	4	5	109.13	1	47950	66
109	9	28	1	3	8	102.32	1	23600	31
110	24	112	2	1	4	119.55	1	34875	47
111	21	169	1	1	4	113.04	1	32000	49
112	19	121	2	2	0	103.75	2	35000	46
113	14	28	1	2	8	103.89	1	33000	41
114	3	111	1	3	7	110.25	1	30600	38
115	3	132	2	4	1	93.18	1	27600	25
116	8	24	2	0	9	109.11	2	29900	36
117	15	160	1	4	7	87.58	2	37200	41
118	18	44	1	5	5	96.20	1	36200	51

(continued)

n	x_1	x_2	x_3	x_4	x_5	x_6	x_7	x_8	x_9
119	7	79	2	2	8	89.71	1	32000	34
120	11	187	2	4	0	108.64	1	35200	49
121	5	107	1	0	9	113.15	2	24650	28
122	18	182	1	5	8	104.37	1	36100	46
123	12	48	1	4	3	111.36	1	28150	35
124	2	217	1	2	0	123.07	1	34550	31
125	26	167	1	2	9	99.70	2	45375	67
126	26	33	1	3	2	93.21	0	41600	63
127	11	22	2	1	6	106.27	2	39500	47
128	11	44	2	3	4	102.83	1	37600	44
129	0	81	2	3	7	104.18	1	33900	31
130	7	123	1	0	2	107.48	2	34325	31
131	19	13	1	5	3	119.13	2	38300	40
132	5	189	2	4	0	92.42	0	39500	44
133	26	59	2	0	6	101.15	1	26500	58
134	1	147	2	2	5	93.91	0	26500	28
135	8	50	2	3	8	78.26	0	29000	35
136	3	70	2	1	2	97.98	0	27500	28
137	3	198	1	1	9	100.03	1	25100	25
138	14	193	1	1	3	120.54	1	32000	38
139	11	77	1	0	3	120.93	1	37750	45
140	22	125	2	4	5	125.95	2	44000	56
141	12	160	1	1	5	100.73	1	37750	44
142	17	28	2	0	3	105.08	2	37675	42
143	20	39	2	5	2	123.37	1	43945	62
144	11	154	1	0	1	119.53	3	43800	44
145	14	129	1	1	9	116.61	1	38170	40
146	22	204	2	2	7	119.69	1	40500	49
147	2	90	1	5	6	103.46	1	23325	25
148	14	37	2	4	3	106.38	2	31625	32
149	5	173	2	2	4	110.17	1	34325	35
150	19	6	1	2	4	105.01	1	40500	50
151	22	83	2	1	9	100.02	2	39275	52
152	26	125	1	1	9	135.22	1	43850	58
153	8	169	1	5	4	87.79	2	31625	34
154	16	55	2	4	3	103.14	1	39375	41
155	25	217	2	2	7	112.55	2	47200	66
156	7	19	1	1	1	109.11	1	28150	33
157	23	173	2	0	3	87.58	0	46900	63
158	7	173	2	4	4	92.91	0	29100	28
159	16	105	1	2	5	89.73	1	39400	41
160	2	11	1	1	8	108.57	1	23100	25
161	22	52	2	1	9	113.15	2	41650	46
162	13	103	2	0	5	104.36	1	35850	40
163	19	143	2	1	4	111.00	1	37350	41
164	7	123	2	4	2	111.00	1	31575	34
165	4	114	1	1	9	87.71	0	27350	28

n	x_1	x_2	x_3	x_4	x_5	x_6	x_7	x_8	x_9
166	24	37	1	5	4	99.12	1	47125	64
167	11	100	2	2	7	128.72	1	43675	55
168	8	100	2	2	6	107.85	2	40000	41
169	9	198	2	5	3	107.85	1	31570	44
170	22	198	1	1	9	122.66	0	41750	40
171	25	136	2	0	4	93.35	0	43780	52
172	14	0	2	4	2	115.46	1	43650	38
173	18	17	2	3	8	125.59	1	39750	44
174	8	103	2	0	9	92.37	0	29500	30
175	22	15	1	1	3	99.17	1	41150	44
176	8	107	2	0	3	102.84	1	33000	35
177	13	129	1	5	4	104.18	1	38300	38
178	27	167	2	0	8	107.75	1	46100	69
179	27	118	2	0	8	119.13	2	44000	66
180	3	209	2	5	3	92.42	0	23600	22
181	2	125	2	4	4	101.16	1	24850	29
182	23	22	1	2	5	91.35	1	45000	62
183	9	151	1	1	5	96.82	0	43850	52
184	15	11	2	4	2	96.82	0	40050	47
185	17	39	2	4	1	89.03	1	43800	58
186	5	193	2	0	5	112.67	2	35300	35
187	26	217	2	2	5	121.96	1	46550	68
188	27	189	1	3	7	104.50	2	45800	69
189	12	209	2	2	3	117.48	1	31450	34
190	1	70	2	5	4	96.38	0	20000	20
191	3	52	2	1	6	107.32	1	27300	29
192	0	138	2	0	4	121.36	1	20000	21
193	16	35	2	3	4	94.02	0	34850	47
194	3	9	1	1	3	129.13	1	41800	41
195	5	173	2	2	8	122.14	2	29000	29
196	1	11	2	1	4	93.86	3	30200	30
197	7	129	2	3	6	104.59	1	34450	35
198	2	162	1	3	3	107.85	1	23550	25
199	2	5	2	1	1	101.68	1	22000	26
200	5	74	2	3	6	111.00	1	33000	34

APPENDIX D ANSWERS TO SELECTED ODD-NUMBERED EXERCISES

We've selected several odd-numbered exercises in each chapter and present the final answers here so you can check your work. Your exact answer depends on the rounding used by you, your hand calculator, or your computer. If your answer is close, you probably did the exercise correctly.

CHAPTER 1

3*a*. $\Sigma x = 25$, $\Sigma y = 17$, $\Sigma xy = 255$, $\Sigma(x - y + 2z) = 74$ *b*. $\Sigma y^2 = 533$, $\Sigma(y)^2 = 289$

CHAPTER 2

3. *a*, *c*, *d*, *e*, and *g* are quantitative; *b* and *f* are qualitative.
13. Mail survey
29. Focus group and mail survey
31. *a*, *c*, *d*, and *e* are quantitative; *b*, *f*, and *g* are qualitative.

35*a*. Large: (.20)(1,200) = 240
Medium: (.35)(1,200) = 420
Small: (.20)(1,200) = 240
Compact: (.25)(1,200) = 300

CHAPTER 3

5. Ten
9. Using six classes,

Class	Freq.	Rel. freq.
40–49	18	.1500
50–59	18	.1500
60–69	22	.1833
70–79	22	.1833
80–89	20	.1667
90–99	20	.1667
	120	1.0000

13. All (100%)
15. With 486 observations, 9 classes would be better.

Class	Freq.	Rel. freq.	Cum. rel. freq.
5 or fewer	47	.0967	.0967
6–10	150	.3086	.4053
11–15	128	.2634	.6687
16–20	67	.1379	.8066
20 or more	94	.1934	1.0000
	486	1.000	

17.

Class	Freq.	Rel. freq.	Cum. freq. less	Dist. more
100–199	9	.1250	.1250	1.0000
200–299	22	.3056	.4306	.8751
300–399	24	.3333	.7639	.5695
400–499	13	.1806	.9445	.2362
500 and up	4	.0556	1.0000	.0556
	72	1.0000		

31. The pie chart and bar chart instructions are designed to give you practice in graphing. The relative frequency distribution is

Class	Relative frequency
Emp.	.5031
Spouse	.3067
Both	.1902
	1.0000

33*a*. The frequency distributions that can be used to construct the charts follow.

Class	Rel. FD	Cum less	Cum. more
20 < 25	.0467	.0467	1.0000
25 < 30	.0933	.1400	.9533
30 < 35	.1867	.3267	.8600
35 < 40	.3000	.6267	.6733
40 < 45	.2000	.8267	.3733
45 < 50	.1000	.9267	.1733
50 < 55	.0733	1.0000	.0733
	1.0000		

b. 37.33%
c. 67.33%

35*a*. Bar chart

37. The frequency distribution to be used in constructing the graphs is

Class	f
35 < 40	2
40 < 45	5
45 < 50	14
50 < 55	19
55 < 60	11
60 < 65	10
65 < 70	5
70 < 75	1
75 < 80	3
	70

Chapter 4

1. Mean
3. Weighted mean
5. Mean
7. Mean
9. Median
11. Mean
13. Median

17*a*. Right *b*. Symmetrical *c*. Left *d*. Right *e*. Symmetrical
19. Right
21. Left
23*a*. 8 *b*. 9 *c*. 11.6 *d*. The median (9)
25*a*. Median sales \$3,100 million, median units 5,361, mean sales \$5,252.4 million, mean units 5,601. *b*. \$937,761
27. Weighted mean = 2.11
29. Weighted mean = \$37.86
39*a*. $\sigma = 5$ *b*. Reduce it *c*. Increase it *d*. Increase it
41. Assuming a sample:
  a. Range = 33 *b*. $s = 10.38$ *c*. $s^2 = 107.74$ *d*. CV = 28.3%
43. Mean = \$64.52, s = \$62.18
45*a*. s^2 = \$178.76 *b*. s = \$13.37 *c*. CV = 62.7%
  d. Mean is 21.32, median is 17.5, mode is more than one, so distribution appears to be skewed right.
  e. Increase *f*. Decrease
47. Mean.
49*a*. Mean = 27. Median = 28 *b*. $\sigma = 5.54$ *c*. Decreases
  d. Both decrease *e*. Increases
51*a*. Mean = 14,774, s = 16,692 *b*. Mean = 156.2, s = 193.3
  c. Mean = 123, s = 155.9 *d*. Median = 7,168 *e*. Median = 79
  f. Median = 66.5 *g*. No *h*. Median
53*a*. Mean = 7.7 *b*. Median = 8 *c*. Mode = 8 *d*. $s = 2.01$
57*a*. 1985: Mean = 8.05%, s = 3.52%
  1988: Mean = 9.21%, s = 4.2%

Chapter 5

5*a*. Five outcomes are possible. *b*. 0: .20; 1: .30; 2: .24; 3: .16; 4+: .10
  c. .20 *d*. .26 *e*. (.10)(.10) = .01
7*a*. (.90)(.90) = .81 *b*. (.90)(.10) + (.90)(.10) = .18
  c. (.90)(.10) = .09 *d*. (.10)(.10) = .01
9*a*. (.45)(.45)(.45) = .091 *b*. (.55)(.55)(.55) = .166
  c. 3(.45)(.55)(.55) = .408
11. .66
19*a*. A frequency distribution

b.

Number	Probability
0	.5068
1	.2795
2	.1507
3	.0329
4+	.0301

23. $E(X) = \$85{,}500$
25. $E(X) = 48$
31. 21
33*a*. .189 *b*. .343 *c*. .657
35*a*. .005 *b*. .995 *c*. .000 *d*. .962
37. .8369
39. .6983
41. .0001
43. Yes
45. Mean = 10, SD = 2.24
47*a*. .9 to the 10th power = .349 *b*. Mean = 9 *c*. .95
49. Mean = 20, SD = 3.46
55. .308
61. .2681
63. .2231
65. .7745
67*b*. .0526
69*a*. .2138 *b*. .5438 *c*. .2424 *d*. .1404
73*a*. .3033 *b*. .0000
75*a*. .1353 *b*. .0361 *c*. .0166
77*a*. Discrete *b*. Continuous
c. Discrete *d*. Continuous
79. .9380
81. .9810
83. .8647
85. .9400
87. 6
89. \$480,000
91*a*. .0081 *b*. .3430 *c*. .2646
93. .9918
95. .4422

CHAPTER 6

5. x_1, x_2, x_6, x_8, x_9
7*a*. Mean = 112.5 *b*. SD = 21.7 *c*. 25/75 = 33%
9*a*. SD = 2.3 *b*. 6/8 = 75% *c*. 2/8 = 25%

13*a*. No *b*. No *c*. Yes *d*. Yes
e. No *f*. Yes *g*. Yes
15. Mean
19. Using the normal table and the z values calculated in Exercise 18:
a. .2734 *b*. .4599 *c*. .4931
d. .3593 *e*. .1587 *f*. .0013
21. 100,000 − (1.645)(25,000) = $58,875 and below.
23*a*. 692 *b*. 159 *c*. 736 *d*. 242
e. .2266 *f*. 10.96 *g*. 9.44
25. $x + 40{,}000 + 1.28(10{,}000) = 250{,}000$, $x = 197{,}200$
31*a*. .5557 *b*. .0968 *c*. .8438 *d*. .9032
33*a*. .7673 *b*. .9115
35. .2843
39*a*. $z = 0$ *b*. $z = -.52$
c. $z = \pm 1.645$ *d*. $z = \pm 1.96$
41. 3.92%
43*a*. $s = .58$ *b*. 35% *c*. 10%
45*a*. 24 *b*. .1711 *c*. .0853
47*a*. Mean = 35.5 *b*. 3/7 = 42.9%
49. .0548
51*a*. .9319, .6664, .2611, .0446 *b*. 70.8 years
53. .9936

Chapter 7

9*a*. Normal *b*. Not normal *c*. Normal
13. 2/6 = .33
15*a*. .1587 *b*. About 0 *c*. .6826 *d*. .0668
17. 96.8 to 103.2
19*a*. .9992 *b*. About 0 *c*. Variability would decrease
23. Decreases
25. Mean = .70, $s = .145$
27*a*. .20 *b*. .1894 *c*. .6368 *d*. .4038
29. .0336
31*a*. 1/6 = .17
b. With replacement, there will be $6^2 = 36$ different samples, with either an OK or a defective unit on the first draw, and likewise on the second.
c. Twenty-five pairs will be OK, OK ($p = 1.00$). Ten pairs will be one OK and one defective ($p = .50$). One pair will be both defective ($p = .00$)
d. .17; yes, the same
e. .266
f. .266, yes, the same
g. Sampling distribution
35*a*. .40 *b*. .248 *c*. .186
37*a*. .0764 *b*. .1112 *c*. .2668

39*a*. Mean = 5.75, s = 1.92 *c*. Mean = 5.75, yes, the same
d. 1.111 *e*. 1.111; yes, the same
41*a*. .3085 *b*. .2684 *c*. .2148
d. .0062 *e*. About 0
43*a*. 1.58 *b*. .63 *c*. .39
45*a*. .0778 *b*. .9544
47. .9641
49. .9836
51. .2776
53*a*. .7620 *b*. .0091 *c*. About 0
55*a*. For population: mean = 3, σ = 1.58
b. 5,4 5,2 5,1 4,5 4,2 4,1 2,5 2,4 2,1 1,5 1,4 1,2
c. 4.5 3.5 3 4.5 3 2.5 3.5 3 1.5 3 2.5 1.5
d. Mean = 3, yes
e. SD = .9129
f. Using the correction factor, σ = .9129; yes

CHAPTER 8

7. $\bar{x}$ = 16
9. 11.17 to 12.83
11*a*. 10.91 to 13.09 *b*. 11.3 to 12.7
c. Higher confidence yields a wider interval.
13. 1,891.75 to 2,008.25. It's 98% likely that the interval includes the population mean.
15. 7.54 to 8.66
19. 0 to .106
21*a*. 0 to .113 *b*. .01 to .09
c. A lower confidence level yields a smaller interval.
23. .10 to .22
25. .0077 to .0723
27. .508 to .617
33*a*. t *b*. Normal *c*. t *d*. Normal
35. 2.75 to 3.16
37. 2,443 to 2,531
39. 8.4% to 10.5%
43*a*. n = 34 *b*. n = 87 *c*. E = .047
45. n = 1,068
47. n = 189
49. n = 19
51*a*. 13.32 to 14.68 *b*. 122.74 to 133.26
c. .508 to .732 *d*. 1.795 to 1.805
53. 15.0 to 18.6 minutes
55. 89.85 to 100.15
57. $29,070 to $34,490

59. $n = 62, n = 151$
61. .2595 to .3905

CHAPTER 9

9*a*. H_0: $p \leq .02$ H_1: $p > .02$
b. H_0: $\mu = 7$ H_1: $\mu \neq 7$
c. H_0: $\mu \geq 600$ H_1: $\mu < 600$
d. H_0: $\mu = 21$ H_1: $\mu \neq 21$
e. H_0: $\mu \leq 5$ H_1: $\mu > 5$
f. H_0: $p = .10$ H_1: $p \neq .10$
15. Type II
19. No
23. No
27. If the z value is more than 2.33, reject the null hypothesis that $\mu = 30$ (one-tailed test). Since $z = 10$, reject the null hypothesis. The p-value is approximately .0000.
29. Reject the null hypothesis that $\mu = 3.2$ if z is outside the range, -2.575 to $+2.575$ (two-tailed test). Since $z = 7.5$, reject the hypothesis that $\mu = 2.1$. The p-value is approximately .0000.
31*a*. H_0: $\mu \geq 45{,}000$; H_1: $\mu < 45{,}000$
b. Reject the H_0 if $t < -2.518$
c. Reject
d. Type I
e. .007
33. H_0: $\mu \geq 19$; H_1: $\mu < 19$. Reject the H_0 if $t < -1.3836$. $s = .9$. $t = -.74$ Fail to reject.
37. H_0: $p \leq .12$ H_1: $p > .12$
39. Reject the null hypothesis that $p = .089$ if z is less than -2.33 (one-tailed test). Since $z = -3.44$, reject the null hypothesis.
41. When one fails to reject the H_0
51. $z = 1.2$; fail to reject; $\beta = .0301$
55. $z = .51$; fail to reject; $\beta = .6950$
57. Yes
61. $n = 54$
63. $n = 569$
69. .0228
71*a*. Normal *b*. t *c*. t
d. Binomial *e*. Binomial
75. Reject H_0 if $z < -2.05$ Since $z = -7.89$, reject.
77. Reject H_0 if $z > 2.33$ Since $z = .883$, fail to reject.
79. Reject H_0 if $z > 1.28$ Since $z = 1.52$, reject.
81. Since $z = -1.6$, fail to reject.
83. Since $z = -.6$, fail to reject.

85. Since $z = -1.35$, fail to reject.
87. Since $z = 1.41$, fail to reject.
89. Since $z = 2.12$, reject.
91*a*. $\beta = .48$, power $= .52$ *b*. $\beta = .61$, power $= .39$
93*a*. $\beta = .6293$ *b*. $\beta = .7486$

CHAPTER 10

7. Normal
9*a*. Yes *b*. Yes *c*. No *d*. Yes *e*. 6.5
f. Reject H_0 if $z < -1.96$ or $z > 1.96$ *g*. -4.62 *h*. Reject
11. Reject H_0 if $z < -1.28$. Calculated $z = -4.76$. Reject; females are earning significantly less than males.
13. Reject H_0 if $z < -2.575$ or $z > 2.575$. Calculated $z = .99$. Fail to reject; the average mileages using the two types of gas are not significantly different.
15. t
17*a*. Yes *b*. Yes *c*. Yes *d*. t
e. For the sample:

	A	B
$\bar{x}$	37.1	40.8
s	2.41	2.48

so s(pooled) $= 2.43$
f. $df = 11$ *g*. 1.35 *h*. Reject H_0 if $t < -2.201$ or $t > 2.201$
i. $t = -2.82$, reject; the populations have different means.
19*a*. H_0: $\mu_1 - \mu_2 = 0$ H_1: $\mu_1 - \mu_2 \neq 0$
b. t distribution
c. Reject H_0 if $t < -2.02$ or $t > 2.02$
d. Since $t = -5.59$, reject; sedans get better mileage than station wagons.
21*a*. H_0: $\mu_1 - \mu_2 = 0$, H_1: $\mu_1 - \mu_2 \neq 0$
b. Reject H_0 if $t < -2.048$ or $t > 2.048$ Since $t = 3.24$, reject; battery 1 lasts longer than battery 2
23*a*. H_0: $\mu_1 - \mu_2 \geq 0$, H_1: $\mu_1 - \mu_2 < 0$ *b*. t distribution with $n - 1 = 7$ df
c. Reject H_0 if $t < -1.895$ *d*. Since $t = -.98$, fail to reject
e. There hasn't been a significant change during the new ad campaign.
25*a*. H_0: $\mu_1 - \mu_2 = 0$, H_1: $\mu_1 - \mu_2 \neq 0$ *b*. t distribution with df $= 11$
c. Reject H_0 if $t < -1.796$ or $t > 1.796$ *d*. Since $t = -.48$, fail to reject
e. The two commercials are the same.
31. 0.
33*a*. H_0: $p_1 - p_2 = 0$, H_1: $p_1 - p_2 \neq 0$ *b*. Normal *c*. .0257
d. Reject H_0 if $z < -2.575$ or $z > 2.575$ *e*. Since $z = -2.335$, reject
f. Idaho and Oregon are the same with regard to preference for the wine.
35. Since the calculated $z = 1.2$, fail to reject. The data don't support the conclusion that small cars have more rollovers than large cars.

39. H_0: $\mu_1 - \mu_2 = 0$, H_1: $\mu_1 - \mu_2 \neq 0$. Normal.
Reject H_0 if $z < -1.645$ or $z > 1.645$. Since $z = -2.89$, reject.
Conclude different average heights

41*a*. H_0: $\mu_1 - \mu_2 \leq 0$, H_1: $\mu_1 - \mu_2 > 0$ *b.* t distribution for 10 *df*
c. Reject H_0 if $t < -1.812$ or $t > 1.812$ *d.* Since $t = 5.78$, reject
e. Sample supports the notion that the L cars have a lower impact force.

43*a*. H_0: $\mu_1 - \mu_2 = 0$, H_1: $\mu_1 - \mu_2 \neq 0$ *b.* Normal
c. Reject H_0 if $z < -1.96$ or $z > 1.96$ *d.* Since $z = -5.7$, reject
e. Conclude that one store is selling more per customer.

45*a*. t table $= \pm 2.228$ and $t = -5.04$ so reject H_0.
b. t table $= \pm 2.01$ (interpolated) and $t = 9.7$ so reject H_0.
c. t table $= \pm 2.045$ and $t = 3.33$ so reject H_0.

47*a*. H_0: $p_1 - p_2 = 0$, H_1: $p_1 - p_2 \neq 0$ *b.* Normal
c. Reject H_0 if $z < -1.645$ or $z > 1.645$ *d.* Since $z = -.5$, fail to reject
e. The death rates are the same.

49*a*. H_0: $p_1 - p_2 = 0$, H_1: $p_1 - p_2 \neq 0$ *b.* Normal
c. Reject H_0 if $z < -1.645$ or $z > 1.645$ *d.* Since $z = .69$, fail to reject
e. The percentage of towns with negative balance sheets hasn't changed significantly since 1991.

51*a*. H_0: $\mu_1 - \mu_2 \leq 0$, H_1: $\mu_1 - \mu_2 > 0$ *b.* Normal
c. Reject H_0 if $z > 2.064$ *d.* Since $t = 2.55$, reject
e. Claim seems correct

Chapter 11

1. Qualitative

7*a*. Proximity and payment status are independent. Proximity and payment status are dependent.
b. df $= (r - 1)(c - 1) = (2 - 1)(2 - 1) = 1$
c. Reject H_0 if $\chi^2 > 5.412$

	Expected		
	Paid	Over	Total
1 =	67.5	102.5	170
2 =	67.5	102.5	170
Total	135	205	340

Critical chi square value: 5.0200.
Computed chi square value: 2.7642.
Fail to reject the null; proximity and payment status are independent.

9*a*. Part quality and production shift are independent. Part quality and production shift are dependent.
b. df $= (r - 1)(c - 1) = (3 - 1)(2 - 1) = 2$
c. Reject H_0 if $\chi^2 > 5.99$

	Expected		
	Def	Good	Total
1 =	69.958	723.042	793
2 =	53.637	554.363	608
3 =	37.405	386.595	424
Total	161	1664	1825

Critical chi square value: 5.9900.
Computed chi square value: 25.1696.
Reject the null; part quality and production shift are dependent.

11*a*. Age and sports preference are independent. Age and sports preference are dependent.

b. df = $(r - 1)(c - 1) = (4 - 1)(4 - 1) = 9$

c. Reject H_0 if $\chi^2 > 14.68$
Critical chi square value: 14.68
Computed chi square value: 173.80
Reject the null; age and sports preference are dependent.

17. df = $k - 1 - c = 4 - 1 - 0 = 3$

21*a*. H_0: The population from which the accounts-having-errors data came is Poisson distributed. H_1: The population from which the accounts-having-errors data came isn't Poisson distributed.

b. df = $k - 1 - c = 5 - 1 - 1 = 3$

c. Reject H_0 if $\chi^2 > 7.18$

Frequency	Poisson prob. for $\mu = 1.4$	f_e (Prob. x 400)	f_o	$\frac{(f_o - f_e)^2}{f_e}$
0	.2466	98.6	102	.12
1	.3452	138.1	140	.03
2	.2417	96.7	75	4.87
3	.1128	45.1	52	1.06
4+	.0537	21.5	31	4.20
		Sum:	400	10.28

Reject the null; the population from which the accounts-having-errors data came isn't Poisson distributed.

23*a*. H_0: The population from which the data on number of service calls received came is Poisson distributed.
H_1: The population from which the data on number of service calls received came isn't Poisson distributed.

b. df = $k - 1 - c = 5 - 1 - 1 = 3$

c. Reject H_0 if $\chi^2 > 7.81$

Frequency	Poisson prob. for $\mu = 1.4$	f_e (Prob. x 400)	f_o	$\frac{(f_o - f_e)^2}{f_e}$
0	.3012	60.2	45	3.84
1	.3614	72.3	99	9.86
2	.2169	43.4	32	2.99
3	.0867	17.3	19	.17
4+	.0338	6.8	5	.48
		Sum:	400	17.34

Reject the null; the population from which the data on number of service calls received came isn't Poisson distributed.

27*a*. Income level and whether a person will vote yes for the aquifer protection area are independent. Income level and whether a person will vote yes for the aquifer protection area are dependent.

b. df $= (r - 1)(c - 1) = (3 - 1)(4 - 1) = 6$

c. Reject H_0 if $\chi^2 > 12.59$

	Expected			
	Yes	No	Un	Total
1 =	181.474	43.736	19.790	245
2 =	406.650	98.004	44.346	549
3 =	251.842	60.695	27.464	340
4 =	77.034	18.565	8.401	104
Total	917	221	100	1238

Critical chi square value: 12.5900
Computed chi square value: 33.6369
Reject the null; income level and whether a person will vote yes for the aquifer protection area are dependent.

29*a*. Type of advertising and sales are independent. Type of advertising and sales are dependent.

b. df $= (r - 1)(c - 1) = (3 - 1)(2 - 1) = 2$

c. Reject H_0 if $\chi^2 > 4.61$

	Expected		
	Inc	Sta	Total
1 =	15.423	18.577	34
2 =	14.062	16.938	31
3 =	14.515	17.485	32
Total	44	53	97

Critical chi square value: 4.6100
Computed chi square value: 1.3751
Fail to reject the null; type of advertising and sales are independent.

33*a*. Type of postage and response rate are independent. Type of postage and response rate are dependent.

b. df $= (r - 1)(c - 1) = (2 - 1)(2 - 1) = 1$

c. Reject H_0 if $\chi^2 > 6.63$

	Expected		
	Meter	Stamp	Total
1 =	762.5	762.5	1,525
2 =	1,237.5	1,237.5	2,475
Total	2,000	2,000	4,000

Critical chi square value: 6.6300
Computed chi square value: 0.6624
Fail to reject the null; type of postage and response rate are independent.

35*a*. H_0: The population from which the service-to-users data came is Poisson distributed. H_1: The population from which the service-to-users data came isn't Poisson distributed.

b. df $= k - 1 - c = 6 - 1 - 1 = 4$

c. At the .05 significance level, reject H_0 if $\chi^2 > 9.49$

$$\bar{x} = \frac{466}{365} = 1.276$$

Frequency	Poisson prob. for $\mu = 1.3$	f_e (Prob. x 365)	f_o	$\frac{(f_o - f_e)^2}{f_e}$
0	.2725	99.5	117	3.08
1	.3543	129.3	128	.01
2	.2303	84.1	63	5.29
3	.0998	36.4	30	1.13
4+	.0431	15.7	27	8.13
		Sum:	365	17.64

Reject the null; the population from which the service-to-users data came isn't Poisson distributed.

37*a*. Rider status and proximity to bus stop are independent. Rider status and proximity to bus stop are dependent.

b. df $= (r - 1)(c - 1) = (5 - 1)(2 - 1) = 5$.

c. Tested at the .05 level, reject H_0 if $\chi^2 > 11.07$.

	Expected		
	Riders	Nonriders	Total
1 =	176.708	257.292	434
2 =	159.200	231.800	391
3 =	67.996	99.004	167
4 =	68.810	100.190	169
5 =	16.286	23.714	40
Total	489.000	712	1,201

Critical chi square value: 9.4900
Computed chi square value: 19.4346
Reject the null; rider status and proximity to bus stop are dependent. The memo should indicate the surprising finding that nonriders are more likely to live closer to a bus stop than riders.

39*a*. H_0: The population of jelly doughnuts is normally distributed.
H_1: The population of jelly doughnuts isn't normally distributed. df $= k - 1 - c = 5 - 1 - 2 = 2$ Reject H_0 if $\chi^2 > 5.99$ $\bar{x} = 39.94$, $s = 3.97$

Jelly doughnuts	x	z	Area	f_e
30–32	32	−2.00	.0228	2
33–35	35	−1.25	.0828	8
36–38	38	−0.50	.2029	20
39–41	41	0.25	.2902	29
42–44	44	1.00	.2426	24

Jelly doughnuts	x	z	Area	f_e
45–47	47	1.75	.1186	12
48–50	50	2.50	.0401	4
			1.0000	99

Jelly doughnuts	f_o	f_e	$\frac{(f_o - f_e)^2}{f_e}$
30–35	12	10	.40
36–38	26	20	1.80
39–41	27	29	.14
42–44	19	24	1.04
45–50	16	16	.00
	100	99	3.38

Fail to reject the null; the population of jelly doughnuts is normally distributed.

41. Use x^2 goodness-of-fit test, reject H_0 because $27.82 > 12.59$.

CHAPTER 12

3*a*. H_0: $\sigma^2 \leq 16{,}000{,}000$ H_1: $\sigma^2 > 16{,}000{,}000$ *b*. $\text{df} = n - 1 = 12 - 1 = 11$

c. Reject the H_0 if $\chi^2 > 22.618$

d. $\chi^2 = \frac{(n-1)s^2}{\sigma^2} = \frac{(12-1)4{,}112^2}{4{,}000^2} = 11.62$

Fail to reject the null: $\sigma^2 = 16{,}000{,}000$

7. H_0: $\sigma_1^2 - \sigma_2^2 \leq 0$
H_1: $\sigma_1^2 - \sigma_2^2 > 0$

9*a*. H_0: $\sigma_1^2 - \sigma_2^2 \leq 0$ H_1: $\sigma_1^2 - \sigma_2^2 > 0$

b. $\text{df}_n = n - 1 = 20 - 1 = 19$
$\text{df}_d = n - 1 = 20 - 1 = 19$

c. Reject the H_0 if $F > 2.21$

d. $F = \frac{s_1^2}{s_2^2} = \frac{.002^2}{.0015^2} = 1.78$

Fail to reject the null; the variability of diameters of ball bearings is the same for the two machines.

25. $\bar{x}_a = 4$, $\bar{x}_b = 4$, $\bar{x}_c = 6$, $\bar{x}_d = 4.5$, $\bar{\bar{x}} = 4.625$

Source of variance	SS	df	Estimate σ^2	F ratio
Between:	10.750	3	3.583	.683
Within:	63	12	5.250	
Totals:	73.750	15		

27*a*. H_0: $\mu_1 = \mu_2 = \mu_3$ H_1: not equal *b*. $\text{df}_b = 2$ $\text{df}_w = 12$

c. Reject H_0 if $F > 6.93$

d.

Source of variance	SS	df	Estimate σ^2	*F* ratio
Between:	496.54	2	248.27	8.94
Within:	333.20	12	27.77	
Totals:	829.74	14		

e. Reject the null; the number of defectives differs for the three contractors.
f. No. He needs to compare the group means.

33*a.*

Source of variance	SS	df	Estimate σ^2	*F* ratio
Rows	5.1	3	1.7	1.63
Columns	18.1	2	9.1	8.72
Interaction	17.4	6	2.9	2.78
Within:	37.6	36	1.044	
Totals:	78.2	47		

b. 4 *c.* 3 *d.* 4
e. There's no interaction. There's no difference between row means. There's a difference between column means.

35*a.* H_0: no interaction present
H_1: interaction present
H_0: machine means are equal
H_1: machine means aren't equal
H_0: operator means are equal
H_1: operator means aren't equal

b. $\bar{x}_a = 11.17$, $\bar{x}_b = 21$, $\bar{x}_c = 12$
$\bar{x}_1 = 15.17$, $\bar{x}_2 = 15$, $\bar{x}_3 = 14$, $\bar{\bar{x}} = 14.72$

Source of variance	SS	df	Estimate σ^2	*F* ratio
Rows	4.778	2	2.39	.368
Columns	356.778	2	178.39	27.444
Interaction	19.556	4	4.89	.752
Within:	58.500	9	6.50	
Totals:	439.611	17		

c. There's no interaction. There's no difference between machines. There's a difference between operators.
d. The memo should emphasize the determination of which operators are different.

39. Fail to reject the H_0 because 8.4 isn't greater than 9.49.

41*a.*

Source of variance	SS	df	Estimate σ^2	*F* ratio
Between:	14,398	3	4,799.3	18.3
Within:	5,256	20	262.8	
Totals:	19,654	23		

b. Four groups *c.* Tabled $F = 3.10$
d. Calculated $F = 18.3$ *e.* Reject the null

43*a*. $H_0: \sigma_1^2 - \sigma_2^2 \leq 0$; $H_1: \sigma_1^2 - \sigma_2^2 > 0$.
b. $df_n = n - 1 = 30 - 1 = 29$
$df_d = n - 1 = 30 - 1 = 29$
c. Reject the H_0 if $F > 1.90$
d. $F = \frac{s_1^2}{s_2^2} = \frac{.93^2}{.68^2} = 1.87$
Fail to reject the null; the variability of the stocks is the same.

45*a*.

Source of variance	SS	df	Estimate σ^2	F ratio
Between:	695.8	2	347.9	64.4
Within:	129.6	24	5.4	
Totals:	825.4	26		

b. Three groups *c*. Tabled $F = 5.61$
d. Calculated $F = 64.4$ *e*. Reject the null

47*a*. $\bar{x}_1 = 87.44$, $\bar{x}_2 = 55.89$, $\bar{x}_3 = 129.89$, $\bar{\bar{x}} = 91.07$

Source of variance	SS	df	Estimate σ^2	F ratio
Between:	5,494.9	2	2,747.4	2.12
Within:	31,165.1	24	1,298.5	
Totals:	36,660	26		

Critical $F = 3.4$, so fail to reject null hypothesis. There's no difference in the mean amounts charged on the three credit cards.

49. $\bar{x}_1 = 13.33$, $\bar{x}_2 = 16.5$, $\bar{x}_3 = 24.5$, $\bar{\bar{x}} = 18.11$

Source of variance	SS	df	Estimate σ^2	F ratio
Between:	397.4	2	198.7	13.06
Within:	228.3	15	15.2	
Totals:	625.8	17		

Critical $F = 6.36$, so reject null hypothesis. The three shifts produce different mean rates of defective units.

51. $\bar{x}_b = 12.75$, $\bar{x}_p = 13.42$, $\bar{x}_a = 9.25$, $\bar{\bar{x}} = 11.81$
$\bar{x}_1 = 14.56$, $\bar{x}_2 = 13.11$, $\bar{x}_3 = 11.22$, $\bar{x}_4 = 8.33$

Source of variance	SS	df	Estimate σ^2	F ratio
Rows:	194.97	3	64.99	24.12
Columns:	120.22	2	60.11	22.319
Interaction:	31.78	6	5.30	1.976
Within:	64.67	24	2.69	
Totals:	411.64	35		

Critical F value (Int.): 2.51; fail to reject null hypothesis

Critical F value (Row): 3.01; reject null hypothesis
Critical F value (Col.): 3.4; reject null hypothesis

53. $\bar{x}_a = 77$, $\bar{x}_b = 76.25$, $\bar{x}_c = 76.75$
$\bar{x}_n = 76.5$, $\bar{x}_e = 76.83$, $\bar{\bar{x}} = 76.67$

Source of variance	Sum of squares	Degrees of freedom	Mean squared	Computed F value
Rows:	0.333	1	0.333	0.018
Columns:	1.167	2	0.583	0.031
Inter:	20.167	2	10.083	0.535
Error:	113.000	6	18.833	
Totals:	134.667	11		

Critical F value (Row): 5.99; fail to reject null hypothesis.
Critical F value (Int.): 5.14; fail to reject null hypothesis.
Critical F value (Col.): 5.14; fail to reject null hypothesis.

CHAPTER 13

7. SPC
13. .0026
15*a*. LCL = 26.4 UCL = 33.6 Process in control *b*. Process potentially out of control
21. Process in control
23. Process potentially out of control
25*a*. $\bar{x}$ chart *b*. $\bar{x} = 22.88$ LCL = 21.57, UCL = 24.20. Process in control.
31. Process in control
33. Process potentially out of control
35*a*. R chart
$\bar{R} = 2.722$
LCL = 0 UCL = 5.456
b. Process in control
41*a*. LCL = 0 UCL = .102 *b*. LCL = 0 UCL = .072
c. LCL = .001 UCL = .059
43*a*. CL = .07 LCL = .026 UCL = .114
b. Zone C: .055 to .085
Zone B: .041 to .055 and .085 to .099
Zone A: .026 to .041 and .099 to .114
c. Process potentially out of control
45*a*. p chart *b*. c chart *c*. p chart
d. c chart *e*. c chart
47*a*. CL = 55.33 LCL = 33.02 UCL = 77.65
b. Zone C: 47.89 to 62.77
Zone B: 40.46 to 47.89 and 62.77 to 70.21
Zone A: 33.02 to 40.46 and 70.21 to 77.65
c. Process potentially out of control

65*a*. Process in control *b*. Process potentially out of control
67*a*. H_0: $\mu \geq 20$; H_1: $\mu < 20$ *b*. Reject H_0 if $z < -1.645$
c. Example:

μ	β	$1 - \beta$
19.7	.7939	.2061
19.4	.5000	.5000
19.0	.1357	.8643

e. $\bar{x} = .19$ $z = -2.74$ Reject H_0
71*a*. $n = 31$ (one-tailed test)
b. Example:

μ	β	$1 - \beta$
5.30	.8238	.1762
5.55	.5000	.5000
5.80	.1762	.8238

73*a*. *p* chart
CL = .03467 LCL = 21.57 UCL = 24.20
b. Process potentially out of control
75*a*. *c* chart
CL = 1.55 LCL = 0 UCL = 5.285
b. Process potentially out of control

Chapter 14

9. H_0: $\rho = 0$; H_1: $\rho \neq 0$
Reject H_0 if $t < -1.98$ or $t > 1.98$ (using df = 120)

$$s_r = \sqrt{\frac{1 - r^2}{n - 2}} = \sqrt{\frac{1 - (.38)^2}{400 - 2}} = \sqrt{\frac{.86}{398}} = \sqrt{.00216} = .0465$$

$$t = \frac{r}{s_r} = \frac{.38}{.0465} = 8.17$$

Reject the null; the two variables are linearly related.
11*b*. Positive *c*. $r = .483$
e. H_0: $\rho = 0$; H_1: $\rho \neq 0$
Reject H_0 if $t < -2.365$ or $t > 2.365$

$$s_r = \sqrt{\frac{1 - r^2}{n - 2}} = \sqrt{\frac{1 - (.483)^2}{9 - 2}} = \sqrt{\frac{.767}{7}} = \sqrt{.11} = .332$$

$$t = \frac{r}{s_r} = \frac{.483}{.332} = 1.455$$

Fail to reject the null; minutes spent and account size aren't linearly related.
17. Yes. $\hat{y} = 12.1656 + 3.3758x$

19*a*. For every unit increase in GNP, AT&T earnings per share increase by an average amount of .05

b. When the GNP is 0, AT&T earnings per share equal .058

21*b*. Positive *c*. $r = .95$

d. $H_0: \rho = 0$; $H_1: \rho \neq 0$

Reject H_0 if $t < -1.833$ or $t > 1.833$

$t = 9.151$

Reject the null; feet of shelf space and number of books sold are linearly related.

e. Yes *f*. $\hat{y} = 32.4576 + 36.4053x$

g. $\hat{y} = 32.4576 + 36.4053(4) = 178.0779$

29. $\hat{y} = 208.20 + 70.918(10) = 917.4$

Prediction interval: 627.6 to 1,207.2

Confidence interval: 797.8 to 1,036.9

31*b*. $\hat{y} = .1774 + .0833x$

c. $\hat{y} = .1774 + .0833(19) = 1.7598$

$e = y - \hat{y} = 1.3 - 1.76 = -.46$

d. Standard error estimate: .9338

e. Each time the checkout time is estimated using amount of purchases, the prediction is typically off by .93 minutes.

f. $\hat{y} = .1774 + .0833(75) = 6.423$

g. 5.607 to 7.240 *h*. 4.596 to 8.250

35*a*. $r^2 = 1 - \dfrac{s_{y \cdot x}^{\ 2}}{s_y^{\ 2}} = 1 - \dfrac{6^2}{20^2} = 1 - .09 = .91$

When the price of unleaded gas increases by one unit, sales decrease by an average of 5,000 gallons.

b. $\hat{y} = 100 - 5(.95) = 95{,}230$

37*b*. $r = .9846$

c. Reject H_0 if $t < -2.306$ or $t > 2.306$

$t = 15.9352$

Reject the null; catalogs distributed and mail orders received are linearly related.

d. $\hat{y} = 11.95 + 1.77x$ *e*. 1,770 *f*. $r^2 = .9695$

g. Using knowledge of the linear relationship between catalogs distributed and mail orders received (.9846), we can explain 96.95% of the mail orders received variable variance.

41*b*. $\hat{y} = 75.4856 + .0449x$

c. The residual analysis is

Number	*y*-actual	*y*-pred	Residual
1	98	126	16.8600
2	94	141	12.1869
3	93	108	12.6678
4	84	121	3.0844
5	84	68	5.4628
6	78	111	−2.4668
7	77	159	−5.6209
8	77	117	−3.7361

Number	y-actual	y-pred	Residual
9	75	141	−6.8131
10	74	164	−8.8453
11	71	95	−8.7488
12	65	79	−14.0308

d. Sum of squares error: 1,082.31
e. Sum of squares total: 1,101.67
f. $r^2 = .0176$
g. $H_0\colon \rho^2 = 0;\quad H_1\colon \rho^2 > 0$
Reject H_0 if $F > 4.96$

$$F = \frac{\text{SSR}/(k-1)}{\text{SSE}/(n-k)} = \frac{19.4/(2-1)}{1{,}082.31/(12-2)} = \frac{19.4}{108.231} = .179$$

Fail to reject the null; the regression equation isn't explaining a significant percentage of the wins variable variance.

49. $r = 1.0.$
51*b.* $\hat{y} = 1.4539 + 2.0526x$
c. $\hat{y} = 1.4539 + 2.0526(10) = 21.9799$
53. $H_0\colon \beta \geq 0;\quad H_1\colon \beta < 0$
$df = n - 2 = 26 - 2 = 24$
Reject H_0 if $t < -1.711$

$$t = \frac{b}{s_b} = \frac{-.6}{2.3} = -.261$$

Fail to reject the null; the two variables aren't linearly related.

55*b.* $r = .9562$
c. The null and alternative hypotheses are
$H_0\colon \rho = 0;\quad H_1\colon \rho \neq 0$
$\text{df} = n - 2 = 13 - 2 = 11$
The decision rule is: If the sample t statistic is less than -2.2 or greater than 2.2, reject the null hypothesis. (Reject H_0 if $t < -2.2$ or $t > 2.2$.)
The standard error of r is

$$s_r = \sqrt{\frac{1-r^2}{n-2}} = \sqrt{\frac{1-(.9562)^2}{13-2}} = \sqrt{.0078} = .088$$

The t statistic is

$$t = \frac{r-\rho}{s_r} = \frac{.9562-0}{.088} = 10.87$$

The calculated t statistic (10.87) is greater than the tabled t value (2.2) so the null hypothesis is rejected. It's concluded that there's a linear relationship between miles and minutes.

d. $\hat{y} = 3.9095 + 2.2736x$ *e.* 2.27 minutes *f.* $r^2 = .9143$
g. Using knowledge of the linear relationship between miles and minutes (.9562), we can explain 91.43% of the amount of time variable variance.

h.

Number	y-actual	y-pred	Residual
1	28	28.9186	−0.9186
2	27	26.6451	0.3549
3	35	38.0129	−3.0129
4	15	19.8244	−4.8244
5	8	8.4566	−0.4566
6	14	15.2773	−1.2773
7	20	22.0980	−2.0980
8	29	24.3715	4.6285
9	13	13.0037	−0.0037
10	16	10.7302	5.2698
11	40	35.7393	4.2607
12	9	10.7302	−1.7302
13	31	31.1922	−0.1922

i. Sum of squares error: 109.9414 *j.* Sum of squares total: 1,282.9231

k. H_0: $\rho^2 = 0$; H_1: $\rho^2 > 0$

Reject H_0 if $F > 4.84$

$$F = \frac{\text{SSR}/(k-1)}{\text{SSE}/(n-k)} = \frac{1{,}172.98/(2-1)}{109.94/(13-2)} = \frac{1{,}172.98}{9.99} = 117.42$$

Reject the null; the regression equation is explaining a significant percentage of the time to make a delivery variable variance.

l. $\hat{y} = 3.9095 + 2.2736(10) = 26.2$ minutes *m.* 20.285 to 32.115

57. $\hat{y} = 3.24 + .39x$

$r^2 = .61898$

Computed $t = 4.03$

59*a.* $r = .92$ *b.* Yes, $t = 5.276$ *d.* $\hat{y} = 2.753 + .0042x$

CHAPTER 15

5*a.* Variables 2 and 3 are. *b.* No

c. Variables 2 and 3.

7*a.* Because the correlations for the bottom half would be exactly the same as those for the top half.

b. Variables 5 and 6. Variables 2 and 4 are possibilities.

c. Negative

d. Variable 5 $(r_{15} = .81)^2 = .66$ or 66%

e. Variables 5 and 6.

f. Variables 2, 4, and 5. Variables 2, 4, and 6.

13. $\hat{y} = 4.72 + 13(40) - 4.2(20) = 440.72$

15*a.* $\hat{y} = -622.313 + .067x_2 + .127x_3$ *b.* .127 minutes

c.

	y-actual	y-pred	Residual
1	576	588.1050	−12.1050
2	497	503.0244	−6.0244
3	789	741.4278	47.5722

c.

	y-actual	y-pred	Residual
4	862	863.2562	−1.2562
5	361	346.6572	14.3428
6	688	721.2757	−33.2757
7	532	541.2541	−9.2541

d. Standard error estimate: 31.0086

e. Each time a prediction is made using the multiple regression equation in part *a*, the estimate is typically off by about $31.

f. $\hat{y} = -622.313 + 2.398(150) + 9.914(100) = 728.8$

g. 633.25 to 824.356 *h.* 687.33 to 770.27

i. The correlation matrix shows potential for multicollinearity. The $R^2 = .98$ is good but Mario should obtain a larger sample.

19*a.* $R^2 = 1 - \frac{\text{SSE}}{\text{SST}} = 1 - \frac{424.81}{2{,}873.46} = 1 - .148 = .852$

b. $\text{df} = n - k = 22 - 4 = 18$

c. Yes, if no multicollinearity exists between the variables.

21*a.* Both variables are good potential predictor variables and multicollinearity shouldn't be a problem.

b. Reject the H_0 if $t > 1.703$

$$t = \frac{b_2}{s_{b2}} = \frac{.13589}{.04855} = 2.8 \qquad \text{Reject the null}$$

$$t = \frac{b_3}{s_{b3}} = \frac{.81245}{.19568} = 4.15 \qquad \text{Reject the null}$$

Both variables are making a contribution.

c. When the high temperature increases by one degree, holding traffic count constant, pop sales increase by an average of .81 quart bottles.

d. $\hat{y} = -31.85 + .13589(900) + .81245(70) = 147.3$ bottles.

e. $s_{y \cdot x} = \sqrt{\frac{3{,}125.61}{30 - 3}} = \sqrt{115.76} = 10.76$

f. $r^2 = 1 - \frac{\text{SSE}}{\text{SST}} = 1 - \frac{3{,}125.61}{15{,}271.15} = 1 - .205 = .795$

g. Reject the H_0 if $F > 5.57$

$$F = \frac{\text{SSR}/(k-1)}{\text{SSE}/(n-k)} = \frac{12{,}145.54/(3-1)}{3{,}125.61/(30-3)} = \frac{6{,}072.77}{115.76} = 52.46$$

h. No

i. This is a good equation that could only be made better by adding a new predictor variable.

23.

	y	x_2	x_3
y	1	−.864	.891
x_2		1	−.655
x_3			1

a. Both variables are good potential predictor variables and multicollinearity shouldn't be a problem.
b. Reject the H_0 if $t < -2.365$ or $t > 2.365$

Variable	β-coeff	Beta	t value
X3	0.006	0.571	4.377
X2	−0.008	−0.490	−3.756

Reject the null for both variables.
c. $\hat{y} = 16.406 - .0082x_2 + .0059x_3$
d. When the selling price increases by \$1, holding advertising expenditures constant, sales decrease by an average of .0082 units. When advertising expenditures increase by \$1, holding the selling price constant, sales increase by an average of .0059 units.
e. $R^2 = .932$ *f.* No
g. $\hat{y} = 16.406 - .0082(1500) + .0059(1000) = 10.006$
27*a.* The curvilinear model is a good model. *b.* 43.97
33. $\hat{y} = 6.95 - 1.1x_2 - .467x_3 + 1.3x_4$
$R^2 = .7106$

Source of variance	SS	df	Estimate σ^2	F ratio
Between:	18.61	3	6.203	16.37
Within:	7.57	20	.379	
Totals:	26.18	23		

35*a.* $\hat{y} = 9.667 + .833x_2 - 1.667x_3$ *b.* $\hat{y} = 9.667 + .833(1) - 1.667(0) = 10.5$
c. $\hat{y} = 9.667 + .833(0) - 1.667(1) = 8$ *d.* $\hat{y} = 9.667 + .833(0) - 1.667(0) =$ 9.667

e.

Source of variance	SS	df	Estimate σ^2	F ratio
Between:	19.44	2	9.72	4.19
Within:	34.83	15	2.32	
Totals:	54.28	17		

Reject H_0 if $F > 3.68$
Reject the null; there are significant differences in the hourly wages of bus drivers.
37*a.* Variable 2. $r_{12} = -.87$ *b.* Variable 3. $r_{13} = .78$ and $r_{23} = -.43$
c. Variables 2 and 3
39*a.* View: $r_{12} = .86$ *b.* Area: $r_{15} = .57$ $r_{25} = .38$
c. View and area
49. $\hat{y} = 7.81 + 1.5(2) - 8.46(1.4) + 10.68(3.5) = 36.35$
51. H_0: $\rho^2 = 0$; H_1: $\rho^2 > 0$
Reject H_0 if $F > 3.71$ $F = 189.04 \div 3.79 = 49.88$ Reject the null; the

regression equation explains a significant percentage of the miles per gallon variable variance.

53*b*. $\hat{y} = 7.319 - .0457x$.

c. $H_0: \beta = 0$; $H_1: \beta \neq 0$.
Reject H_0 if $t < -2.3$ or $t > 2.3$.
Since the computed t value is $-.47$, fail to reject the null hypothesis. The linear equation isn't a good model.

d. $\hat{y} = -18.633 + 1.347x - .017x^2$.

e. $H_0: \beta_2 = 0$; $H_1: \beta_2 \neq 0$
Reject H_0 if $t < -2.365$ or $t > 2.365$
Since the computed t value is 1.861, fail to reject the null hypothesis. The linear effect isn't significant.
$H_0: \beta_3 = 0$; $H_1: \beta_3 \neq 0$
Reject H_0 if $t < -2.365$ or $t > 2.365$
Since the computed t value is -1.938, fail to reject the null hypothesis. The curvilinear effect isn't significant.

Variable	*b* coefficient	Beta	*t*
AGE	1.347	4.817	1.861
AGE2	−0.017	−5.014	−1.938

f. The model isn't valid.

55. Answer to Exercise 47 in Chapter 12:

Source of variance	SS	df	Estimated σ^2	*F* ratio
Between	5,494.9	2	2,747.4	2.12
Within	31,165.1	24	1,298.5	
Total	36,660	26		

Critical *F* value = 3.4; fail to reject the null hypothesis. There's no difference in the mean amounts charged on the three credit cards.

57*a*. $\hat{y} = -69.1 + 0.0044(\text{Use}) + 31.7(\text{Charge})$ *b*. $\hat{y} = -69.1 + 0.0044(14{,}000) + 31.7(4.50) = 135.15$

c. The model is very accurate, explaining 98.4% of the revenue variance.

59*a*. $H_0: \beta_2 = 0; \beta_3 = 0; \beta_4 = 0; \beta_5 = 0$
$H_1: \beta_2 \neq 0; \beta_3 \neq 0; \beta_4 \neq 0; \beta_5 \neq 0$
Tested at the .05 significance level:
$df = n - k = 30 - 5 = 25$
Reject H_0 if $t < -2.06$ or $t > 2.06$.
Computed t values:
Sales: $t = .350$
Assets: $t = -.667$
Equity: $t = 1.142$
Profits: $t = 2.710$

Reject the null hypothesis for the profits as a percentage of equity variable. None of the rest of the variables explain much variance.

b. Yes. There's a multicollinearity problem when sales, assets, and equity are used as predictor variables.

c. $\hat{y} = 1.082 + .139(\text{Profits})$ is the only valid regression equation. It only explains 17.5% of the earnings per share variance.

61*a.* $\hat{y} = 20.021 + 9.358(\text{Permits})$ *b.* $\hat{y} = 10.131 + 8.496(\text{Permits}) + 65.531(\text{Season})$

c. The simple regression equation

Variable	*b* coefficient	Beta	*t*
PERM	8.496	.858	8.865
SEAS	64.531	.164	1.694

d. Quarter 1: $\hat{y} = 20.021 + 9.358(19) = 197.823$
Quarter 2: $\hat{y} = 20.021 + 9.358(13) = 141.675$

e. Yes. The observations don't constitute a random sample.

CHAPTER 16

5. $1{,}289.73(2.847) = 3{,}671.86$
7. Multiply the number of sick days by the cost per day for each quarter to get the new value series. Divide each of these values by the value in the last quarter base period (25,010), then multiply by 100 to get the value indexes:

   99.0 115.5 93.9 100.0
9. Divide each data value by the value for the base period, January 1993 (3,921.8), then multiply by 100:

1992	June	95.5	1993	Jan.	100.0
	July	96.3		Feb.	100.6
	Aug.	97.0		March	101.6
	Sept.	97.4		April	102.0
	Oct.	99.4		May	102.5
	Nov.	99.0		June	103.2
	Dec.	100.4		July	103.8

11.

Jan	100.0
Feb	69.1
March	90.7
April	99.5
May	96.0
June	91.9

17.

Jan	124.25
Feb	124.20
March	123.45
April	123.10

19.

Jan	281,631
Feb	233,139
March	280,624
April	295,097

21*a*.

Nov	3,231.44
Dec	2,429.85
Jan	2,119.36
Feb	1,809.84
March	2,545.15
April	2,154.87

29*a*. 1,600 *b*. 85 *c*. 3,130

31*b*. The linear model is best. *c*. $\hat{Y} = 212 + 25X$ *d*. 25

e. 612; 637 *f*. Compare 621 and 637 to 566 and 623

g. Inflation and population growth

37*a*. No *b*. Both are important

c. Trend estimate for 1992:

$\hat{Y} = -1.29 + .571(21) = 10.701$

Cyclical for 1991:

$\hat{Y} = -.7395 + .4904(20) = 10.13$

$C = Y/\hat{Y}(100) = 11.63/10.13 = 114.88$

$Y(1992) = TC = 10.701(1.148) = 12.285$

39.

Year	Cyclical
1980	99.717
1981	96.667
1982	96.791
1983	98.200
1984	105.517
1985	102.858
1986	102.909
1987	99.474
1988	99.455
1989	97.350

47. Average 100

49. 64.3 Eliminate the lowest (64.3) and the highest (92.4).
80.1 Average the remaining indexes.
82.4
85.9 $(80.1 + 82.4 + 85.9 + 88.2)/4 = 336.6/4 = 84.15$
88.2
92.4

51. 65.4 Eliminate the lowest (65.4) and the highest (76.8).
66.9 Average the remaining indexes.
70.0
72.6 $(66.9 + 70.0 + 72.6)/3 = 209.5/3 = 69.83$

76.8
69.83(.98) = 68.43
Y = TS = 800(.6843) = 547.44

53. (1,200/1,195)(96.9) = 97.3

55*a*.

Jan	3,000	Jul	3,600
Feb	3,750	Aug	3,900
Mar	4,750	Sep	5,250
Apr	5,500	Oct	5,800
May	5,350	Nov	6,450
Jun	5,050	Dec	7,600

b. 3,500/3,000 = 1.167
60,000(1.167) = 70,020

c. 70,020/12 = 5,835

5,835(1.10) = 6,418.50
5,835(1.07) = 6,243.45
5,835(1.01) = 5,893.35
18,555.30

57.

Quarter	
1	94.96
2	103.32
3	100.11
4	102.15

67.

Sep	106.4
Oct	104.9
Nov	102.7
Dec	100.5
Jan	100.0
Feb	102.5
Mar	101.9

69.

1980	102.2
1985	102.1
1986	99.7
1987	100.3
1988	101.7
1989	100.0

73. Top and middle management

77*a*. $\hat{Y} = 250 - 2.455X$ *b*. 2.455 *c*. Inflation and population growth
e. Lot of fluctuation *g*. Cyclical *h*. 195.67

79. $\hat{Y} = 908.84 - 4.33X$

1980	100.0
1981	110.9
1982	121.3

1983	86.4
1984	93.3
1985	94.7
1986	91.0
1987	78.7
1988	89.9
1989	111.3
1990	122.9

81*a*. $\hat{Y} = 1499 + 3.177X$
No seasonality and some cyclical variation.

83*a*. $\hat{Y} = 395 + 2.229X$

Jan.	89.0	July	102.2
Feb.	109.6	Aug.	105.6
March	103.4	Sept.	99.2
April	108.3	Oct.	110.8
May	99.0	Nov.	78.7
June	100.4	Dec.	93.8

b. Seasonal and cyclical *c*. Yes

Chapter 17

5. a, b, and d
7. Exponential smoothing
9. Naive

11*a*. $\Sigma e_t = 2.75$; $\Sigma|e_t| = 8.53$; $\Sigma e_t^2 = 8.83$; $\Sigma|e_t|/Y_t = 85.6$; $\Sigma e_t/Y_t = 21.2$
b. MAD = 8.53/11 = .78 *c*. MSE = 8.83/11 = .80 *d*. MAPE = 85.6/11 = 7.78 *e*. MPE = 21.2/11 = 1.93 *f*. Jan. 1993 = 12.14

13*a*.

Period	Actual	Predicted	Error	% error
6	11.08	10.04	1.04	9.39%
7	11.51	10.40	1.11	9.63%
8	10.99	10.71	0.28	2.53%
9	10.78	10.90	−0.12	1.09%
10	10.55	11.00	−0.45	4.25%
11	10.82	10.98	−0.16	1.50%
12	9.96	10.93	−0.97	9.74%

Mean squared error (MSE) = 0.51
Mean absolute percentage error (MAPE) = 5.45%
Mean percentage error (MPE) or bias = 0.71%

b.

Period	Actual	Predicted	Error	% error
4	10.28	9.76	0.52	5.03%
5	10.63	10.10	0.53	4.99%
6	11.08	10.32	0.76	6.83%

Period	Actual	Predicted	Error	% error
7	11.51	10.66	0.85	7.36%
8	10.99	11.07	−0.08	0.76%
9	10.78	11.19	−0.41	3.83%
10	10.55	11.09	−0.54	5.15%
11	10.82	10.77	0.05	0.43%
12	9.96	10.72	−0.76	7.60%

Mean squared error (MSE) = 0.32
Mean absolute percentage error (MAPE) = 4.66%
Mean percentage error (MPE) or bias = 0.81%

c. 5 month—MAD = .69 3 month—MAD = .56
d. 5 month—MSE = .51 3 month—MSE = .32
e. 5 month—MAPE = 5.45% 3 month—MAPE = 4.66%
f. 5 month—MPE = .71% 3 month—MPE = .81%
g. Three-month moving average forecast = 10.44

15.

Period	Y-actual	Y-pred
1	205	205.0
2	251	205.0
3	304	214.2
4	284	232.2
5	352	242.5
6	300	264.4
7	241	271.5
8	284	265.4
9	312	269.1
10	289	277.7
11	385	280.0
12	256	301.0

Demand for January 1993 = 292.0
Mean square error: 3,855.7

17. Exponential smoothing using $\alpha = .75$ was best.
MSE = 7.26, MAPE = 9.95%
Forecast for first quarter 1992 = 29.97

21*a.* 2.1 *b.* 1.2 *c.* 4.0
d. $Y_{20} = 1.2 + 2.1(20) + 4(0) - 2(1) + .8(0) = 41.2$
e. $Y_{22} = 1.2 + 2.1(22) + 4(0) - 2(0) + .8(0) = 47.2$

23. $\hat{Y} = 49.2 - 29.5S_1 - 30.2S_2 - 17.8S_3$.
$R^2 = 70.3\%$.
Second quarter 1992 = 19.03
Third quarter 1992 = 31.43
Fourth quarter 1992 = 49.23

27. a and b are stationary

29*a.* Trend *b.* Random *c.* Seasonal *d.* Trend

31*a.* $r_1 = .942$; $r_2 = .873$ *b.* $r_1 = .633$

33. $0 \pm .196$
35*a*. $r_1 = .822$, $r_2 = .623$, $r_3 = .431$, $r_4 = .309$,
$r_5 = .220$, $r_6 = .130$, $r_7 = .067$, $r_8 = .069$,
$r_9 = .082$, $r_{10} = .060$, $r_{11} = -.027$, $r_{12} = -.133$
b. No
c. $r_1 = .496$, $r_2 = .168$, $r_3 = -.096$, $r_4 = -.074$,
$r_5 = -.217$, $r_6 = -.238$, $r_7 = -.399$, $r_8 = -.172$,
$r_9 = -.002$, $r_{10} = .278$, $r_{11} = .263$, $r_{12} = .250$
d. Pattern
39. Durbin-Watson
41. Positive autocorrelation
47. Positive autocorrelation
53. Overestimating
55. Box-Jenkins
65*b*. 1.307 *c*. 2.78 *d*. 17.08%
e. 17.08% *g*. 13.25
67*a*. Trend *b*. Seasonal *c*. Pattern in data
69*a*. 264.4; MAPE = 36.4% *b*. 5-month: 264.7; MAPE = 24.6%
c. 261.2; MAPE = 33.9%
75. $\alpha = .05$; reject H_0 if D.W. < 1.19. Best model: $\hat{y} = -69.1 + .0044$ (use) + 31.7 (charge)
D.W. = .85; reject the null and conclude that serial correlation is a problem.

CHAPTER 18

5.

Prob.	Dem.	Stock (payoffs in hundreds) 20	30	40	50
.20	20	6	4.50	3.00	1.50
.25	25	6	6.75	5.25	3.75
.20	30	6	9.00	7.50	6.00
.15	35	6	9.00	9.75	8.25
.10	40	6	9.00	12.00	10.50
.05	45	6	9.00	12.00	12.75
.05	50	6	9.00	12.00	15.00

7*a*. \$5 per hundred (\$.05) *b*. \$2 per hundred (\$.02) *c*. \$9.05
d. Stock 300 since the expected payoffs, in order, are 5, 8.25, 9.05, 8.10, 6.45
e. EVPI = 11.75 − 9.05 = 2.70
9. The expected profits, in millions, are
Build 25,000: .05
Build 40,000: .40
Build 55,000: .25
So if the objective is to maximize expected profits, a 40,000-capacity plant should be built.
17. .682

19*b.* Large: 24.3; medium: 24.9; expand: 26.6.
c. Expand the present plant; expand again if much larger or somewhat larger demand results.
d. A conservative approach suggests expanding the present plant since less money would be needed.

21*a.* EMV = $380,000

23*a.*

		Class size (payoffs: in hundreds)					
P	Dem.	10	11	12	13	14	15
.10	10	10	8	6	4	2	0
.10	11	10	11	9	7	5	3
.20	12	10	11	12	10	8	6
.25	13	10	11	12.	13	11	9
.30	14	10	11	12	13	14	12
.05	15	10	11	12	13	14	15

b. The EMVs are, in order, 10, 10.7, 11.1, 10.9, 9.95, and 8.1 so the optimum class size is 12.
c. 12.7 − 11.1 = 1.6

25*a.* .625.

27*a.*

		Stock (payoffs: in hundreds)					
P	Dem.	500	750	1,000	1,250	1,500	1,750
.15	500	125	112.5	100	87.5	75	62.5
.25	750	125	187.5	175	162.5	150	137.5
.25	1000	125	187.5	250	237.5	225	212.5
.20	1250	125	187.5	250	312.5	300	287.5
.10	1500	125	187.5	250	312.5	375	362.5
.05	1750	125	187.5	250	312.5	375	437.5

b. The EMVs, in order, are 125, 176.3, 208.8, 222.5, 221.4, and 212.6 so 1,250 units should be stocked.
c. EVPI = 250.1 − 222.5 − 27.6
d. A higher marginal loss would result in fewer than 1,250 units stocked to maximize expected profits.
e. A higher marginal profit would increase the optimum stocking level above 1,250.

33*a.* The EMV for both projects is $9,500 so the choice would lead to indifference.
b. Venture A would be preferred by a conservative company while Venture B would be favored by an aggressive, risk-seeking company.

35*b.* EMVs: A: 2.34; B: 14.8; C: 12.2.
So the first choice is B. Then choose branch 2 of B since its payoff (14.8) is higher than the other two choices (10 and 5.25).
c. EMV = 14.8
d. The attractiveness of large payoffs and the negative aspect of negative amounts might affect the final decision.

Chapter 19

5. Parametric tests are more powerful.
7. The one-sample mean test of Chapter 9.
9. $H = 6$ and $L = 10$, so $z = 1$; fail to reject the null hypothesis. Neither high nor low pressures are favored.
11. The normal approximation to the binomial is similar.
13. $r = 15$, $\mu = 16$, $\sigma = 2.60$, and $z = -.38$. Fail to reject the null hypothesis of a random string.
15. The small sample t test is similar.
17. Sum of ranks for A is 192, $U = 183$, $\mu = 127.5$, $\sigma = 26.5$, so $z = 2.09$. At $\alpha = .05$, critical z values are ± 1.96, so the null hypothesis is rejected. B is a better seller than A.
19. The Spearman test is similar to the Pearson test used for quantitative data.
21. Sum of $d^2 = 76$, so $r = .095$ and $t = .23$. Fail to reject the null hypothesis of zero population correlation.
23. One-sample sign test: $n = 26$ and $X(U) = 10$; $z = -1.18$. Fail to reject the null hypothesis of equal overfills and underfills.
25. Sum of squared rank differences $= 150$ so $r = .476$, a moderate correlation.
27. U test: Sum of ranks for Regular $= 101$, $U = 121$, $\mu = 72$, and $\sigma = 17.3$. So $z = 2.83$ and table z for one-tailed test at $.05 = 1.645$ so the null hypothesis is rejected. Free days increase sales.
29. Runs test: runs $= 16$, $\mu = 20.3$, $\sigma = 2.93$, and $z = -1.47$. Since table $z = \pm 1.96$ (.05), fail to reject the null hypothesis of randomness.
31. One sample runs test: plus signs $= 13$ and $z = 1.89$. Since table z (one-tailed, $\alpha = .10) = 1.28$, the null hypothesis of equal preference is rejected. Purple-power is preferred.
33. Sum of squared ranks $= 78$ so $r = .07$. $t = .17$ and since table t (df $= 6$, two-tailed, $\alpha = .10$) is ± 1.943, fail to reject the null hypothesis of no population correlation. Men and women react differently to the commercials.
35. U test: $U = 256$, $\mu = 200$, $\sigma = 37.0$, and $z = 1.51$. Since table z (two-tailed, .10) $= \pm 1.645$, fail to reject the null hypothesis of equal tire lifetimes.
37. One-sample sign test: remove unchanged value and $n = 8$. Plus $= 6$ so $z = 1.41$. Table z (one-tailed, .10) $= 1.28$ and null hypothesis is rejected. There has been a significant increase in ratings after the program.
39. Sum of squared differences in ranks $= 192$ and $r = -.17$. $t = -.49$ and table t (two-tailed, df $= 8$, $\alpha = .05$) $= \pm 2.306$ so fail to reject the null hypothesis. There's no correlation between service and rating in the population.

APPENDIX E STATISTICAL TABLES

TABLE E.1 Table of Random Numbers

75421	11182	31304	08036	86922	77941	38944	30226	60766	90951
06692	19591	14171	04356	06744	46546	99184	97684	43285	86345
66065	12379	70386	09035	90126	74677	39885	84335	09442	21772
01098	06343	88773	94702	07203	60936	54445	12423	64560	99694
93526	56837	42025	45578	95193	97695	53146	51370	79913	83145
85129	31088	36253	40011	62078	72245	58783	47555	55681	45450
74312	81501	94303	30800	60660	69979	57625	00050	69795	15120
67348	11345	13361	40573	75687	78415	42407	97830	98069	98605
29241	77892	67728	60876	53046	75840	18933	18108	73509	76958
04366	94984	95131	22993	17240	63185	54786	31607	50705	61581
54205	61584	99698	74013	88263	96563	18003	77390	05762	40975
52801	44366	19745	74219	20982	91400	50685	56541	68392	96624
02573	59494	26362	40769	39340	19677	16923	04761	65952	03630
15896	32426	64984	99029	58073	28814	44849	39871	00825	29966
26032	33340	54573	55786	75383	14546	37499	43894	86358	19706
41349	18921	50835	65861	79521	38319	33999	74851	97319	17221
31246	35797	89051	36319	38137	11101	02808	36771	63163	00816
55704	87671	81967	18984	94617	89097	91625	49172	07106	06218
09107	53117	75664	25300	98186	29702	73632	77044	08238	08097
53779	05917	99367	58743	33981	66547	45685	11168	81086	29458
05252	99475	70537	29636	46984	49231	73571	64092	26162	26361
92966	81458	79792	39399	39278	20247	45367	76937	64563	73930
68109	88529	70116	11782	24198	68334	83184	26202	49315	38471
53118	70359	68973	95173	29213	29969	00445	24846	50957	80443
60924	44136	71034	80642	62977	93957	21006	66422	96753	69814
11151	59784	77446	64703	22038	40357	57749	62349	88018	20160
32731	14203	36222	13436	16935	26412	09878	27931	54679	35275
04037	48341	95595	26036	57521	16245	71204	44232	09527	49083
75807	89169	30622	23911	73689	50718	33796	30145	97763	75437
93509	65893	82351	54938	26829	04823	71697	46159	43465	99159
93528	38008	53069	29029	36617	09019	95758	52955	75018	83253
10603	93078	11673	36373	71957	89710	15378	52022	57934	86236
99155	30214	58351	16606	08569	19665	22531	58753	22759	90501
97268	87653	40124	51615	27365	26827	70255	23368	78952	05515
93564	66965	91850	25093	53517	39997	17521	57074	76743	11610
06959	27612	66188	10351	17367	84340	00247	49881	01997	33756
13172	61241	53558	59919	15082	75692	43138	22677	55844	70034
03690	57173	38889	03032	69496	42566	23096	43416	78732	12420
38005	70085	74744	32644	88440	12489	39538	64712	92792	51310
28758	45596	59049	79799	68763	49827	57854	76334	99237	11388
84260	58136	31250	88953	04929	06903	21175	42463	15227	15205
77800	77252	68397	37935	53941	59771	92875	37004	57044	18210
99505	24764	22807	54083	90303	43362	71223	96233	88058	03268
53803	68932	38510	87838	68543	73671	57403	50077	63351	55781
68379	47885	33501	10666	74222	81999	16699	51745	84672	11640
30033	45809	69655	31679	56931	40579	53867	22586	00794	67305
73888	69685	91050	60898	06171	01165	04192	03700	27979	76516
50935	51867	76172	52543	38383	43396	67725	68868	15571	78654
04689	09839	31801	18560	21328	87664	08203	82426	23946	82792
65860	84568	88383	49927	52267	63736	01964	86914	14949	55467

Source: Robert D. Mason and Douglas A. Lind, *Statistical Techniques in Business and Economics*, 7th ed. (Homewood, Ill.: Richard D. Irwin, 1990), p. 855.

TABLE E.2 Binomial Probability Distribution

$n = 1$
PROBABILITY

x	0.05	0.10	0.20	0.30	0.40	0.50	0.60	0.70	0.80	0.90	0.95
0	0.950	0.900	0.800	0.700	0.600	0.500	0.400	0.300	0.200	0.100	0.050
1	0.050	0.100	0.200	0.300	0.400	0.500	0.600	0.700	0.800	0.900	0.950

$n = 2$
PROBABILITY

x	0.05	0.10	0.20	0.30	0.40	0.50	0.60	0.70	0.80	0.90	0.95
0	0.903	0.810	0.640	0.490	0.360	0.250	0.160	0.090	0.040	0.010	0.003
1	0.095	0.180	0.320	0.420	0.480	0.500	0.480	0.420	0.320	0.180	0.095
2	0.003	0.010	0.040	0.090	0.160	0.250	0.360	0.490	0.640	0.810	0.903

$n = 3$
PROBABILITY

x	0.05	0.10	0.20	0.30	0.40	0.50	0.60	0.70	0.80	0.90	0.95
0	0.857	0.729	0.512	0.343	0.216	0.125	0.064	0.027	0.008	0.001	0.000
1	0.135	0.243	0.384	0.441	0.432	0.375	0.288	0.189	0.096	0.027	0.007
2	0.007	0.027	0.096	0.189	0.288	0.375	0.432	0.441	0.384	0.243	0.135
3	0.000	0.001	0.008	0.027	0.064	0.125	0.216	0.343	0.512	0.729	0.857

$n = 4$
PROBABILITY

x	0.05	0.10	0.20	0.30	0.40	0.50	0.60	0.70	0.80	0.90	0.95
0	0.815	0.656	0.410	0.240	0.130	0.063	0.026	0.008	0.002	0.000	0.000
1	0.171	0.292	0.410	0.412	0.346	0.250	0.154	0.076	0.026	0.004	0.000
2	0.014	0.049	0.154	0.265	0.346	0.375	0.346	0.265	0.154	0.049	0.014
3	0.000	0.004	0.026	0.076	0.154	0.250	0.346	0.412	0.410	0.292	0.171
4	0.000	0.000	0.002	0.008	0.026	0.063	0.130	0.240	0.410	0.656	0.815

$n = 5$
PROBABILITY

x	0.05	0.10	0.20	0.30	0.40	0.50	0.60	0.70	0.80	0.90	0.95
0	0.774	0.590	0.328	0.168	0.078	0.031	0.010	0.002	0.000	0.000	0.000
1	0.204	0.328	0.410	0.360	0.259	0.156	0.077	0.028	0.006	0.000	0.000
2	0.021	0.073	0.205	0.309	0.346	0.313	0.230	0.132	0.051	0.008	0.001
3	0.001	0.008	0.051	0.132	0.230	0.313	0.346	0.309	0.205	0.073	0.021
4	0.000	0.000	0.006	0.028	0.077	0.156	0.259	0.360	0.410	0.328	0.204
5	0.000	0.000	0.000	0.002	0.010	0.031	0.078	0.168	0.328	0.590	0.774

TABLE E.2 (continued)

$n = 6$
PROBABILITY

x	0.05	0.10	0.20	0.30	0.40	0.50	0.60	0.70	0.80	0.90	0.95
0	0.735	0.531	0.262	0.118	0.047	0.016	0.004	0.001	0.000	0.000	0.000
1	0.232	0.354	0.393	0.303	0.187	0.094	0.037	0.010	0.002	0.000	0.000
2	0.031	0.098	0.246	0.324	0.311	0.234	0.138	0.060	0.015	0.001	0.000
3	0.002	0.015	0.082	0.185	0.276	0.313	0.276	0.185	0.082	0.015	0.002
4	0.000	0.001	0.015	0.060	0.138	0.234	0.311	0.324	0.246	0.098	0.031
5	0.000	0.000	0.002	0.010	0.037	0.094	0.187	0.303	0.393	0.354	0.232
6	0.000	0.000	0.000	0.001	0.004	0.016	0.047	0.118	0.262	0.531	0.735

$n = 7$
PROBABILITY

x	0.05	0.10	0.20	0.30	0.40	0.50	0.60	0.70	0.80	0.90	0.95
0	0.698	0.478	0.210	0.082	0.028	0.008	0.002	0.000	0.000	0.000	0.000
1	0.257	0.372	0.367	0.247	0.131	0.055	0.017	0.004	0.000	0.000	0.000
2	0.041	0.124	0.275	0.318	0.261	0.164	0.077	0.025	0.004	0.000	0.000
3	0.004	0.023	0.115	0.227	0.290	0.273	0.194	0.097	0.029	0.003	0.000
4	0.000	0.003	0.029	0.097	0.194	0.273	0.290	0.227	0.115	0.023	0.004
5	0.000	0.000	0.004	0.025	0.077	0.164	0.261	0.318	0.275	0.124	0.041
6	0.000	0.000	0.000	0.004	0.017	0.055	0.131	0.247	0.367	0.372	0.257
7	0.000	0.000	0.000	0.000	0.002	0.008	0.028	0.082	0.210	0.478	0.698

$n = 8$
PROBABILITY

x	0.05	0.10	0.20	0.30	0.40	0.50	0.60	0.70	0.80	0.90	0.95
0	0.663	0.430	0.168	0.058	0.017	0.004	0.001	0.000	0.000	0.000	0.000
1	0.279	0.383	0.336	0.198	0.090	0.031	0.008	0.001	0.000	0.000	0.000
2	0.051	0.149	0.294	0.296	0.209	0.109	0.041	0.010	0.001	0.000	0.000
3	0.005	0.033	0.147	0.254	0.279	0.219	0.124	0.047	0.009	0.000	0.000
4	0.000	0.005	0.046	0.136	0.232	0.273	0.232	0.136	0.046	0.005	0.000
5	0.000	0.000	0.009	0.047	0.124	0.219	0.279	0.254	0.147	0.033	0.005
6	0.000	0.000	0.001	0.010	0.041	0.109	0.209	0.296	0.294	0.149	0.051
7	0.000	0.000	0.000	0.001	0.008	0.031	0.090	0.198	0.336	0.383	0.279
8	0.000	0.000	0.000	0.000	0.001	0.004	0.017	0.058	0.168	0.430	0.663

$n = 9$
PROBABILITY

x	0.05	0.10	0.20	0.30	0.40	0.50	0.60	0.70	0.80	0.90	0.95
0	0.630	0.387	0.134	0.040	0.010	0.002	0.000	0.000	0.000	0.000	0.000
1	0.299	0.387	0.302	0.156	0.060	0.018	0.004	0.000	0.000	0.000	0.000
2	0.063	0.172	0.302	0.267	0.161	0.070	0.021	0.004	0.000	0.000	0.000
3	0.008	0.045	0.176	0.267	0.251	0.164	0.074	0.021	0.003	0.000	0.000
4	0.001	0.007	0.066	0.172	0.251	0.246	0.167	0.074	0.017	0.001	0.000
5	0.000	0.001	0.017	0.074	0.167	0.246	0.251	0.172	0.066	0.007	0.001
6	0.000	0.000	0.003	0.021	0.074	0.164	0.251	0.267	0.176	0.045	0.008
7	0.000	0.000	0.000	0.004	0.021	0.070	0.161	0.267	0.302	0.172	0.063
8	0.000	0.000	0.000	0.000	0.004	0.018	0.060	0.156	0.302	0.387	0.299
9	0.000	0.000	0.000	0.000	0.000	0.002	0.010	0.040	0.134	0.387	0.630

TABLE E.2 (continued)

$n = 10$
PROBABILITY

x	0.05	0.10	0.20	0.30	0.40	0.50	0.60	0.70	0.80	0.90	0.95
0	0.599	0.349	0.107	0.028	0.006	0.001	0.000	0.000	0.000	0.000	0.000
1	0.315	0.387	0.268	0.121	0.040	0.010	0.002	0.000	0.000	0.000	0.000
2	0.075	0.194	0.302	0.233	0.121	0.044	0.011	0.001	0.000	0.000	0.000
3	0.010	0.057	0.201	0.267	0.215	0.117	0.042	0.009	0.001	0.000	0.000
4	0.001	0.011	0.088	0.200	0.251	0.205	0.111	0.037	0.006	0.000	0.000
5	0.000	0.001	0.026	0.103	0.201	0.246	0.201	0.103	0.026	0.001	0.000
6	0.000	0.000	0.006	0.037	0.111	0.205	0.251	0.200	0.088	0.011	0.001
7	0.000	0.000	0.001	0.009	0.042	0.117	0.215	0.267	0.201	0.057	0.010
8	0.000	0.000	0.000	0.001	0.011	0.044	0.121	0.233	0.302	0.194	0.075
9	0.000	0.000	0.000	0.000	0.002	0.010	0.040	0.121	0.268	0.387	0.315
10	0.000	0.000	0.000	0.000	0.000	0.001	0.006	0.028	0.107	0.349	0.599

$n = 11$
PROBABILITY

x	0.05	0.10	0.20	0.30	0.40	0.50	0.60	0.70	0.80	0.90	0.95
0	0.569	0.314	0.086	0.020	0.004	0.000	0.000	0.000	0.000	0.000	0.000
1	0.329	0.384	0.236	0.093	0.027	0.005	0.001	0.000	0.000	0.000	0.000
2	0.087	0.213	0.295	0.200	0.089	0.027	0.005	0.001	0.000	0.000	0.000
3	0.014	0.071	0.221	0.257	0.177	0.081	0.023	0.004	0.000	0.000	0.000
4	0.001	0.016	0.111	0.220	0.236	0.161	0.070	0.017	0.002	0.000	0.000
5	0.000	0.002	0.039	0.132	0.221	0.226	0.147	0.057	0.010	0.000	0.000
6	0.000	0.000	0.010	0.057	0.147	0.226	0.221	0.132	0.039	0.002	0.000
7	0.000	0.000	0.002	0.017	0.070	0.161	0.236	0.220	0.111	0.016	0.001
8	0.000	0.000	0.000	0.004	0.023	0.081	0.177	0.257	0.221	0.071	0.014
9	0.000	0.000	0.000	0.001	0.005	0.027	0.089	0.200	0.295	0.213	0.087
10	0.000	0.000	0.000	0.000	0.001	0.005	0.027	0.093	0.236	0.384	0.329
11	0.000	0.000	0.000	0.000	0.000	0.000	0.004	0.020	0.086	0.314	0.569

$n = 12$
PROBABILITY

x	0.05	0.10	0.20	0.30	0.40	0.50	0.60	0.70	0.80	0.90	0.95
0	0.540	0.282	0.069	0.014	0.002	0.000	0.000	0.000	0.000	0.000	0.000
1	0.341	0.377	0.206	0.071	0.017	0.003	0.000	0.000	0.000	0.000	0.000
2	0.099	0.230	0.283	0.168	0.064	0.016	0.002	0.000	0.000	0.000	0.000
3	0.017	0.085	0.236	0.240	0.142	0.054	0.012	0.001	0.000	0.000	0.000
4	0.002	0.021	0.133	0.231	0.213	0.121	0.042	0.008	0.001	0.000	0.000
5	0.000	0.004	0.053	0.158	0.227	0.193	0.101	0.029	0.003	0.000	0.000
6	0.000	0.000	0.016	0.079	0.177	0.226	0.177	0.079	0.016	0.000	0.000
7	0.000	0.000	0.003	0.029	0.101	0.193	0.227	0.158	0.053	0.004	0.000
8	0.000	0.000	0.001	0.008	0.042	0.121	0.213	0.231	0.133	0.021	0.002
9	0.000	0.000	0.000	0.001	0.012	0.054	0.142	0.240	0.236	0.085	0.017
10	0.000	0.000	0.000	0.000	0.002	0.016	0.064	0.168	0.283	0.230	0.099
11	0.000	0.000	0.000	0.000	0.000	0.003	0.017	0.071	0.206	0.377	0.341
12	0.000	0.000	0.000	0.000	0.000	0.000	0.002	0.014	0.069	0.282	0.540

TABLE E.2 (continued)

$n = 13$

PROBABILITY

x	0.05	0.10	0.20	0.30	0.40	0.50	0.60	0.70	0.80	0.90	0.95
0	0.513	0.254	0.055	0.010	0.001	0.000	0.000	0.000	0.000	0.000	0.000
1	0.351	0.367	0.179	0.054	0.011	0.002	0.000	0.000	0.000	0.000	0.000
2	0.111	0.245	0.268	0.139	0.045	0.010	0.001	0.000	0.000	0.000	0.000
3	0.021	0.100	0.246	0.218	0.111	0.035	0.006	0.001	0.000	0.000	0.000
4	0.003	0.028	0.154	0.234	0.184	0.087	0.024	0.003	0.000	0.000	0.000
5	0.000	0.006	0.069	0.180	0.221	0.157	0.066	0.014	0.001	0.000	0.000
6	0.000	0.001	0.023	0.103	0.197	0.209	0.131	0.044	0.006	0.000	0.000
7	0.000	0.000	0.006	0.044	0.131	0.209	0.197	0.103	0.023	0.001	0.000
8	0.000	0.000	0.001	0.014	0.066	0.157	0.221	0.180	0.069	0.006	0.000
9	0.000	0.000	0.000	0.003	0.024	0.087	0.184	0.234	0.154	0.028	0.003
10	0.000	0.000	0.000	0.001	0.006	0.035	0.111	0.218	0.246	0.100	0.021
11	0.000	0.000	0.000	0.000	0.001	0.010	0.045	0.139	0.268	0.245	0.111
12	0.000	0.000	0.000	0.000	0.000	0.002	0.011	0.054	0.179	0.367	0.351
13	0.000	0.000	0.000	0.000	0.000	0.000	0.001	0.010	0.055	0.254	0.513

$n = 14$

PROBABILITY

x	0.05	0.10	0.20	0.30	0.40	0.50	0.60	0.70	0.80	0.90	0.95
0	0.488	0.229	0.044	0.007	0.001	0.000	0.000	0.000	0.000	0.000	0.000
1	0.359	0.356	0.154	0.041	0.007	0.001	0.000	0.000	0.000	0.000	0.000
2	0.123	0.257	0.250	0.113	0.032	0.006	0.001	0.000	0.000	0.000	0.000
3	0.026	0.114	0.250	0.194	0.085	0.022	0.003	0.000	0.000	0.000	0.000
4	0.004	0.035	0.172	0.229	0.155	0.061	0.014	0.001	0.000	0.000	0.000
5	0.000	0.008	0.086	0.196	0.207	0.122	0.041	0.007	0.000	0.000	0.000
6	0.000	0.001	0.032	0.126	0.207	0.183	0.092	0.023	0.002	0.000	0.000
7	0.000	0.000	0.009	0.062	0.157	0.209	0.157	0.062	0.009	0.000	0.000
8	0.000	0.000	0.002	0.023	0.092	0.183	0.207	0.126	0.032	0.001	0.000
9	0.000	0.000	0.000	0.007	0.041	0.122	0.207	0.196	0.086	0.008	0.000
10	0.000	0.000	0.000	0.001	0.014	0.061	0.155	0.229	0.172	0.035	0.004
11	0.000	0.000	0.000	0.000	0.003	0.022	0.085	0.194	0.250	0.114	0.026
12	0.000	0.000	0.000	0.000	0.001	0.006	0.032	0.113	0.250	0.257	0.123
13	0.000	0.000	0.000	0.000	0.000	0.001	0.007	0.041	0.154	0.356	0.359
14	0.000	0.000	0.000	0.000	0.000	0.000	0.001	0.007	0.044	0.229	0.488

TABLE E.2 (continued)

$n = 15$
PROBABILITY

x	0.05	0.10	0.20	0.30	0.40	0.50	0.60	0.70	0.80	0.90	0.95
0	0.463	0.206	0.035	0.005	0.000	0.000	0.000	0.000	0.000	0.000	0.000
1	0.366	0.343	0.132	0.031	0.005	0.000	0.000	0.000	0.000	0.000	0.000
2	0.135	0.267	0.231	0.092	0.022	0.003	0.000	0.000	0.000	0.000	0.000
3	0.031	0.129	0.250	0.170	0.063	0.014	0.002	0.000	0.000	0.000	0.000
4	0.005	0.043	0.188	0.219	0.127	0.042	0.007	0.001	0.000	0.000	0.000
5	0.001	0.010	0.103	0.206	0.186	0.092	0.024	0.003	0.000	0.000	0.000
6	0.000	0.002	0.043	0.147	0.207	0.153	0.061	0.012	0.001	0.000	0.000
7	0.000	0.000	0.014	0.081	0.177	0.196	0.118	0.035	0.003	0.000	0.000
8	0.000	0.000	0.003	0.035	0.118	0.196	0.177	0.081	0.014	0.000	0.000
9	0.000	0.000	0.001	0.012	0.061	0.153	0.207	0.147	0.043	0.002	0.000
10	0.000	0.000	0.000	0.003	0.024	0.092	0.186	0.206	0.103	0.010	0.001
11	0.000	0.000	0.000	0.001	0.007	0.042	0.127	0.219	0.188	0.043	0.005
12	0.000	0.000	0.000	0.000	0.002	0.014	0.063	0.170	0.250	0.129	0.031
13	0.000	0.000	0.000	0.000	0.000	0.003	0.022	0.092	0.231	0.267	0.135
14	0.000	0.000	0.000	0.000	0.000	0.000	0.005	0.031	0.132	0.343	0.366
15	0.000	0.000	0.000	0.000	0.000	0.000	0.000	0.005	0.035	0.206	0.463

$n = 16$
PROBABILITY

x	0.05	0.10	0.20	0.30	0.40	0.50	0.60	0.70	0.80	0.90	0.95
0	0.440	0.185	0.028	0.003	0.000	0.000	0.000	0.000	0.000	0.000	0.000
1	0.371	0.329	0.113	0.023	0.003	0.000	0.000	0.000	0.000	0.000	0.000
2	0.146	0.275	0.211	0.073	0.015	0.002	0.000	0.000	0.000	0.000	0.000
3	0.036	0.142	0.246	0.146	0.047	0.009	0.001	0.000	0.000	0.000	0.000
4	0.006	0.051	0.200	0.204	0.101	0.028	0.004	0.000	0.000	0.000	0.000
5	0.001	0.014	0.120	0.210	0.162	0.067	0.014	0.001	0.000	0.000	0.000
6	0.000	0.003	0.055	0.165	0.198	0.122	0.039	0.006	0.000	0.000	0.000
7	0.000	0.000	0.020	0.101	0.189	0.175	0.084	0.019	0.001	0.000	0.000
8	0.000	0.000	0.006	0.049	0.142	0.196	0.142	0.049	0.006	0.000	0.000
9	0.000	0.000	0.001	0.019	0.084	0.175	0.189	0.101	0.020	0.000	0.000
10	0.000	0.000	0.000	0.006	0.039	0.122	0.198	0.165	0.055	0.003	0.000
11	0.000	0.000	0.000	0.001	0.014	0.067	0.162	0.210	0.120	0.014	0.001
12	0.000	0.000	0.000	0.000	0.004	0.028	0.101	0.204	0.200	0.051	0.006
13	0.000	0.000	0.000	0.000	0.001	0.009	0.047	0.146	0.246	0.142	0.036
14	0.000	0.000	0.000	0.000	0.000	0.002	0.015	0.073	0.211	0.275	0.146
15	0.000	0.000	0.000	0.000	0.000	0.000	0.003	0.023	0.113	0.329	0.371
16	0.000	0.000	0.000	0.000	0.000	0.000	0.000	0.003	0.028	0.185	0.440

TABLE E.2 (continued)

n = 17

PROBABILITY

x	0.05	0.10	0.20	0.30	0.40	0.50	0.60	0.70	0.80	0.90	0.95
0	0.418	0.167	0.023	0.002	0.000	0.000	0.000	0.000	0.000	0.000	0.000
1	0.374	0.315	0.096	0.017	0.002	0.000	0.000	0.000	0.000	0.000	0.000
2	0.158	0.280	0.191	0.058	0.010	0.001	0.000	0.000	0.000	0.000	0.000
3	0.041	0.156	0.239	0.125	0.034	0.005	0.000	0.000	0.000	0.000	0.000
4	0.008	0.060	0.209	0.187	0.080	0.018	0.002	0.000	0.000	0.000	0.000
5	0.001	0.017	0.136	0.208	0.138	0.047	0.008	0.001	0.000	0.000	0.000
6	0.000	0.004	0.068	0.178	0.184	0.094	0.024	0.003	0.000	0.000	0.000
7	0.000	0.001	0.027	0.120	0.193	0.148	0.057	0.009	0.000	0.000	0.000
8	0.000	0.000	0.008	0.064	0.161	0.185	0.107	0.028	0.002	0.000	0.000
9	0.000	0.000	0.002	0.028	0.107	0.185	0.161	0.064	0.008	0.000	0.000
10	0.000	0.000	0.000	0.009	0.057	0.148	0.193	0.120	0.027	0.001	0.000
11	0.000	0.000	0.000	0.003	0.024	0.094	0.184	0.178	0.068	0.004	0.000
12	0.000	0.000	0.000	0.001	0.008	0.047	0.138	0.208	0.136	0.017	0.001
13	0.000	0.000	0.000	0.000	0.002	0.018	0.080	0.187	0.209	0.060	0.008
14	0.000	0.000	0.000	0.000	0.000	0.005	0.034	0.125	0.239	0.156	0.041
15	0.000	0.000	0.000	0.000	0.000	0.001	0.010	0.058	0.191	0.280	0.158
16	0.000	0.000	0.000	0.000	0.000	0.000	0.002	0.017	0.096	0.315	0.374
17	0.000	0.000	0.000	0.000	0.000	0.000	0.000	0.002	0.023	0.167	0.418

n = 18

PROBABILITY

x	0.05	0.10	0.20	0.30	0.40	0.50	0.60	0.70	0.80	0.90	0.95
0	0.397	0.150	0.018	0.002	0.000	0.000	0.000	0.000	0.000	0.000	0.000
1	0.376	0.300	0.081	0.013	0.001	0.000	0.000	0.000	0.000	0.000	0.000
2	0.168	0.284	0.172	0.046	0.007	0.001	0.000	0.000	0.000	0.000	0.000
3	0.047	0.168	0.230	0.105	0.025	0.003	0.000	0.000	0.000	0.000	0.000
4	0.009	0.070	0.215	0.168	0.061	0.012	0.001	0.000	0.000	0.000	0.000
5	0.001	0.022	0.151	0.202	0.115	0.033	0.004	0.000	0.000	0.000	0.000
6	0.000	0.005	0.082	0.187	0.166	0.071	0.015	0.001	0.000	0.000	0.000
7	0.000	0.001	0.035	0.138	0.189	0.121	0.037	0.005	0.000	0.000	0.000
8	0.000	0.000	0.012	0.081	0.173	0.167	0.077	0.015	0.001	0.000	0.000
9	0.000	0.000	0.003	0.039	0.128	0.185	0.128	0.039	0.003	0.000	0.000
10	0.000	0.000	0.001	0.015	0.077	0.167	0.173	0.081	0.012	0.000	0.000
11	0.000	0.000	0.000	0.005	0.037	0.121	0.189	0.138	0.035	0.001	0.000
12	0.000	0.000	0.000	0.001	0.015	0.071	0.166	0.187	0.082	0.005	0.000
13	0.000	0.000	0.000	0.000	0.004	0.033	0.115	0.202	0.151	0.022	0.001
14	0.000	0.000	0.000	0.000	0.001	0.012	0.061	0.168	0.215	0.070	0.009
15	0.000	0.000	0.000	0.000	0.000	0.003	0.025	0.105	0.230	0.168	0.047
16	0.000	0.000	0.000	0.000	0.000	0.001	0.007	0.046	0.172	0.284	0.168
17	0.000	0.000	0.000	0.000	0.000	0.000	0.001	0.013	0.081	0.300	0.376
18	0.000	0.000	0.000	0.000	0.000	0.000	0.000	0.002	0.018	0.150	0.397

TABLE E.2 (concluded)

$n = 19$

PROBABILITY

x	0.05	0.10	0.20	0.30	0.40	0.50	0.60	0.70	0.80	0.90	0.95
0	0.377	0.135	0.014	0.001	0.000	0.000	0.000	0.000	0.000	0.000	0.000
1	0.377	0.285	0.068	0.009	0.001	0.000	0.000	0.000	0.000	0.000	0.000
2	0.179	0.285	0.154	0.036	0.005	0.000	0.000	0.000	0.000	0.000	0.000
3	0.053	0.180	0.218	0.087	0.017	0.002	0.000	0.000	0.000	0.000	0.000
4	0.011	0.080	0.218	0.149	0.047	0.007	0.001	0.000	0.000	0.000	0.000
5	0.002	0.027	0.164	0.192	0.093	0.022	0.002	0.000	0.000	0.000	0.000
6	0.000	0.007	0.095	0.192	0.145	0.052	0.008	0.001	0.000	0.000	0.000
7	0.000	0.001	0.044	0.153	0.180	0.096	0.024	0.002	0.000	0.000	0.000
8	0.000	0.000	0.017	0.098	0.180	0.144	0.053	0.008	0.000	0.000	0.000
9	0.000	0.000	0.005	0.051	0.146	0.176	0.098	0.022	0.001	0.000	0.000
10	0.000	0.000	0.001	0.022	0.098	0.176	0.146	0.051	0.005	0.000	0.000
11	0.000	0.000	0.000	0.008	0.053	0.144	0.180	0.098	0.017	0.000	0.000
12	0.000	0.000	0.000	0.002	0.024	0.096	0.180	0.153	0.044	0.001	0.000
13	0.000	0.000	0.000	0.001	0.008	0.052	0.145	0.192	0.095	0.007	0.000
14	0.000	0.000	0.000	0.000	0.002	0.022	0.093	0.192	0.164	0.027	0.002
15	0.000	0.000	0.000	0.000	0.001	0.007	0.047	0.149	0.218	0.080	0.011
16	0.000	0.000	0.000	0.000	0.000	0.002	0.017	0.087	0.218	0.180	0.053
17	0.000	0.000	0.000	0.000	0.000	0.000	0.005	0.036	0.154	0.285	0.179
18	0.000	0.000	0.000	0.000	0.000	0.000	0.001	0.009	0.068	0.285	0.377
19	0.000	0.000	0.000	0.000	0.000	0.000	0.000	0.001	0.014	0.135	0.377

$n = 20$

PROBABILITY

x	0.05	0.10	0.20	0.30	0.40	0.50	0.60	0.70	0.80	0.90	0.95
0	0.358	0.122	0.012	0.001	0.000	0.000	0.000	0.000	0.000	0.000	0.000
1	0.377	0.270	0.058	0.007	0.000	0.000	0.000	0.000	0.000	0.000	0.000
2	0.189	0.285	0.137	0.028	0.003	0.000	0.000	0.000	0.000	0.000	0.000
3	0.060	0.190	0.205	0.072	0.012	0.001	0.000	0.000	0.000	0.000	0.000
4	0.013	0.090	0.218	0.130	0.035	0.005	0.000	0.000	0.000	0.000	0.000
5	0.002	0.032	0.175	0.179	0.075	0.015	0.001	0.000	0.000	0.000	0.000
6	0.000	0.009	0.109	0.192	0.124	0.037	0.005	0.000	0.000	0.000	0.000
7	0.000	0.002	0.055	0.164	0.166	0.074	0.015	0.001	0.000	0.000	0.000
8	0.000	0.000	0.022	0.114	0.180	0.120	0.035	0.004	0.000	0.000	0.000
9	0.000	0.000	0.007	0.065	0.160	0.160	0.071	0.012	0.000	0.000	0.000
10	0.000	0.000	0.002	0.031	0.117	0.176	0.117	0.031	0.002	0.000	0.000
11	0.000	0.000	0.000	0.012	0.071	0.160	0.160	0.065	0.007	0.000	0.000
12	0.000	0.000	0.000	0.004	0.035	0.120	0.180	0.114	0.022	0.000	0.000
13	0.000	0.000	0.000	0.001	0.015	0.074	0.166	0.164	0.055	0.002	0.000
14	0.000	0.000	0.000	0.000	0.005	0.037	0.124	0.192	0.109	0.009	0.000
15	0.000	0.000	0.000	0.000	0.001	0.015	0.075	0.179	0.175	0.032	0.002
16	0.000	0.000	0.000	0.000	0.000	0.005	0.035	0.130	0.218	0.090	0.013
17	0.000	0.000	0.000	0.000	0.000	0.001	0.012	0.072	0.205	0.190	0.060
18	0.000	0.000	0.000	0.000	0.000	0.000	0.003	0.028	0.137	0.285	0.189
19	0.000	0.000	0.000	0.000	0.000	0.000	0.000	0.007	0.058	0.270	0.377
20	0.000	0.000	0.000	0.000	0.000	0.000	0.000	0.001	0.012	0.122	0.358

Source: Goldstein Software, Inc. for the program Goldspread Statistical, which was used to generate this table.

TABLE E.3 Cumulative Binomial Probability Distribution

$n = 1$

PROBABILITY

x	0.1	0.2	0.3	0.4	0.5	0.6	0.7	0.8	0.9
0	0.900	0.800	0.700	0.600	0.500	0.400	0.300	0.200	0.100
1	1.000	1.000	1.000	1.000	1.000	1.000	1.000	1.000	1.000

$n = 2$

PROBABILITY

x	0.1	0.2	0.3	0.4	0.5	0.6	0.7	0.8	0.9
0	0.810	0.640	0.490	0.360	0.250	0.160	0.090	0.040	0.010
1	0.990	0.960	0.910	0.840	0.750	0.640	0.510	0.360	0.190
2	1.000	1.000	1.000	1.000	1.000	1.000	1.000	1.000	1.000

$n = 3$

PROBABILITY

x	0.1	0.2	0.3	0.4	0.5	0.6	0.7	0.8	0.9
0	0.729	0.512	0.343	0.216	0.125	0.064	0.027	0.008	0.001
1	0.972	0.896	0.784	0.648	0.500	0.352	0.216	0.104	0.028
2	0.999	0.992	0.973	0.936	0.875	0.784	0.657	0.488	0.271
3	1.000	1.000	1.000	1.000	1.000	1.000	1.000	1.000	1.000

$n = 4$

PROBABILITY

x	0.1	0.2	0.3	0.4	0.5	0.6	0.7	0.8	0.9
0	0.656	0.410	0.240	0.130	0.063	0.026	0.008	0.002	0.000
1	0.948	0.819	0.652	0.475	0.313	0.179	0.084	0.027	0.004
2	0.996	0.973	0.916	0.821	0.688	0.525	0.348	0.181	0.052
3	1.000	0.998	0.992	0.974	0.938	0.870	0.760	0.590	0.344
4	1.000	1.000	1.000	1.000	1.000	1.000	1.000	1.000	1.000

$n = 5$

PROBABILITY

x	0.1	0.2	0.3	0.4	0.5	0.6	0.7	0.8	0.9
0	0.590	0.328	0.168	0.078	0.031	0.010	0.002	0.000	0.000
1	0.919	0.737	0.528	0.337	0.188	0.087	0.031	0.007	0.000
2	0.991	0.942	0.837	0.683	0.500	0.317	0.163	0.058	0.009
3	1.000	0.993	0.969	0.913	0.813	0.663	0.472	0.263	0.081
4	1.000	1.000	0.998	0.990	0.969	0.922	0.832	0.672	0.410
5	1.000	1.000	1.000	1.000	1.000	1.000	1.000	1.000	1.000

TABLE E.3 (continued)

n = 6

PROBABILITY

x	0.1	0.2	0.3	0.4	0.5	0.6	0.7	0.8	0.9
0	0.531	0.262	0.118	0.047	0.016	0.004	0.001	0.000	0.000
1	0.886	0.655	0.420	0.233	0.109	0.041	0.011	0.002	0.000
2	0.984	0.901	0.744	0.544	0.344	0.179	0.070	0.017	0.001
3	0.999	0.983	0.930	0.821	0.656	0.456	0.256	0.099	0.016
4	1.000	0.998	0.989	0.959	0.891	0.767	0.580	0.345	0.114
5	1.000	1.000	0.999	0.996	0.984	0.953	0.882	0.738	0.469
6	1.000	1.000	1.000	1.000	1.000	1.000	1.000	1.000	1.000

n = 7

PROBABILITY

x	0.1	0.2	0.3	0.4	0.5	0.6	0.7	0.8	0.9
0	0.478	0.210	0.082	0.028	0.008	0.002	0.000	0.000	0.000
1	0.850	0.577	0.329	0.159	0.063	0.019	0.004	0.000	0.000
2	0.974	0.852	0.647	0.420	0.227	0.096	0.029	0.005	0.000
3	0.997	0.967	0.874	0.710	0.500	0.290	0.126	0.033	0.003
4	1.000	0.995	0.971	0.904	0.773	0.580	0.353	0.148	0.026
5	1.000	1.000	0.996	0.981	0.938	0.841	0.671	0.423	0.150
6	1.000	1.000	1.000	0.998	0.992	0.972	0.918	0.790	0.522
7	1.000	1.000	1.000	1.000	1.000	1.000	1.000	1.000	1.000

n = 8

PROBABILITY

x	0.1	0.2	0.3	0.4	0.5	0.6	0.7	0.8	0.9
0	0.430	0.168	0.058	0.017	0.004	0.001	0.000	0.000	0.000
1	0.813	0.503	0.255	0.106	0.035	0.009	0.001	0.000	0.000
2	0.962	0.797	0.552	0.315	0.145	0.050	0.011	0.001	0.000
3	0.995	0.944	0.806	0.594	0.363	0.174	0.058	0.010	0.000
4	1.000	0.990	0.942	0.826	0.637	0.406	0.194	0.056	0.005
5	1.000	0.999	0.989	0.950	0.855	0.685	0.448	0.203	0.038
6	1.000	1.000	0.999	0.991	0.965	0.894	0.745	0.497	0.187
7	1.000	1.000	1.000	0.999	0.996	0.983	0.942	0.832	0.570
8	1.000	1.000	1.000	1.000	1.000	1.000	1.000	1.000	1.000

n = 9

PROBABILITY

x	0.1	0.2	0.3	0.4	0.5	0.6	0.7	0.8	0.9
0	0.387	0.134	0.040	0.010	0.002	0.000	0.000	0.000	0.000
1	0.775	0.436	0.196	0.071	0.020	0.004	0.000	0.000	0.000
2	0.947	0.738	0.463	0.232	0.090	0.025	0.004	0.000	0.000
3	0.992	0.914	0.730	0.483	0.254	0.099	0.025	0.003	0.000
4	0.999	0.980	0.901	0.733	0.500	0.267	0.099	0.020	0.001
5	1.000	0.997	0.975	0.901	0.746	0.517	0.270	0.086	0.008
6	1.000	1.000	0.996	0.975	0.910	0.768	0.537	0.262	0.053
7	1.000	1.000	1.000	0.996	0.980	0.929	0.804	0.564	0.225
8	1.000	1.000	1.000	1.000	0.998	0.990	0.960	0.866	0.613
9	1.000	1.000	1.000	1.000	1.000	1.000	1.000	1.000	1.000

TABLE E.3 (continued)

$n = 10$
PROBABILITY

x	0.1	0.2	0.3	0.4	0.5	0.6	0.7	0.8	0.9
0	0.349	0.107	0.028	0.006	0.001	0.000	0.000	0.000	0.000
1	0.736	0.376	0.149	0.046	0.011	0.002	0.000	0.000	0.000
2	0.930	0.678	0.383	0.167	0.055	0.012	0.002	0.000	0.000
3	0.987	0.879	0.650	0.382	0.172	0.055	0.011	0.001	0.000
4	0.998	0.967	0.850	0.633	0.377	0.166	0.047	0.006	0.000
5	1.000	0.994	0.953	0.834	0.623	0.367	0.150	0.033	0.002
6	1.000	0.999	0.989	0.945	0.828	0.618	0.350	0.121	0.013
7	1.000	1.000	0.998	0.988	0.945	0.833	0.617	0.322	0.070
8	1.000	1.000	1.000	0.998	0.989	0.954	0.851	0.624	0.264
9	1.000	1.000	1.000	1.000	0.999	0.994	0.972	0.893	0.651
10	1.000	1.000	1.000	1.000	1.000	1.000	1.000	1.000	1.000

$n = 11$
PROBABILITY

x	0.1	0.2	0.3	0.4	0.5	0.6	0.7	0.8	0.9
0	0.314	0.086	0.020	0.004	0.000	0.000	0.000	0.000	0.000
1	0.697	0.322	0.113	0.030	0.006	0.001	0.000	0.000	0.000
2	0.910	0.617	0.313	0.119	0.033	0.006	0.001	0.000	0.000
3	0.981	0.839	0.570	0.296	0.113	0.029	0.004	0.000	0.000
4	0.997	0.950	0.790	0.533	0.274	0.099	0.022	0.002	0.000
5	1.000	0.988	0.922	0.753	0.500	0.247	0.078	0.012	0.000
6	1.000	0.998	0.978	0.901	0.726	0.467	0.210	0.050	0.003
7	1.000	1.000	0.996	0.971	0.887	0.704	0.430	0.161	0.019
8	1.000	1.000	0.999	0.994	0.967	0.881	0.687	0.383	0.090
9	1.000	1.000	1.000	0.999	0.994	0.970	0.887	0.678	0.303
10	1.000	1.000	1.000	1.000	1.000	0.996	0.980	0.914	0.686
11	1.000	1.000	1.000	1.000	1.000	1.000	1.000	1.000	1.000

$n = 12$
PROBABILITY

x	0.1	0.2	0.3	0.4	0.5	0.6	0.7	0.8	0.9
0	0.282	0.069	0.014	0.002	0.000	0.000	0.000	0.000	0.000
1	0.659	0.275	0.085	0.020	0.003	0.000	0.000	0.000	0.000
2	0.889	0.558	0.253	0.083	0.019	0.003	0.000	0.000	0.000
3	0.974	0.795	0.493	0.225	0.073	0.015	0.002	0.000	0.000
4	0.996	0.927	0.724	0.438	0.194	0.057	0.009	0.001	0.000
5	0.999	0.981	0.882	0.665	0.387	0.158	0.039	0.004	0.000
6	1.000	0.996	0.961	0.842	0.613	0.335	0.118	0.019	0.001
7	1.000	0.999	0.991	0.943	0.806	0.562	0.276	0.073	0.004
8	1.000	1.000	0.998	0.985	0.927	0.775	0.507	0.205	0.026
9	1.000	1.000	1.000	0.997	0.981	0.917	0.747	0.442	0.111
10	1.000	1.000	1.000	1.000	0.997	0.980	0.915	0.725	0.341
11	1.000	1.000	1.000	1.000	1.000	0.998	0.986	0.931	0.718
12	1.000	1.000	1.000	1.000	1.000	1.000	1.000	1.000	1.000

TABLE E.3 (continued)

$n = 13$
PROBABILITY

x	0.1	0.2	0.3	0.4	0.5	0.6	0.7	0.8	0.9
0	0.254	0.055	0.010	0.001	0.000	0.000	0.000	0.000	0.000
1	0.621	0.234	0.064	0.013	0.002	0.000	0.000	0.000	0.000
2	0.866	0.502	0.202	0.058	0.011	0.001	0.000	0.000	0.000
3	0.966	0.747	0.421	0.169	0.046	0.008	0.001	0.000	0.000
4	0.994	0.901	0.654	0.353	0.133	0.032	0.004	0.000	0.000
5	0.999	0.970	0.835	0.574	0.291	0.098	0.018	0.001	0.000
6	1.000	0.993	0.938	0.771	0.500	0.229	0.062	0.007	0.000
7	1.000	0.999	0.982	0.902	0.709	0.426	0.165	0.030	0.001
8	1.000	1.000	0.996	0.968	0.867	0.647	0.346	0.099	0.006
9	1.000	1.000	0.999	0.992	0.954	0.831	0.579	0.253	0.034
10	1.000	1.000	1.000	0.999	0.989	0.942	0.798	0.498	0.134
11	1.000	1.000	1.000	1.000	0.998	0.987	0.936	0.766	0.379
12	1.000	1.000	1.000	1.000	1.000	0.999	0.990	0.945	0.746
13	1.000	1.000	1.000	1.000	1.000	1.000	1.000	1.000	1.000

$n = 14$
PROBABILITY

x	0.1	0.2	0.3	0.4	0.5	0.6	0.7	0.8	0.9
0	0.229	0.044	0.007	0.001	0.000	0.000	0.000	0.000	0.000
1	0.585	0.198	0.047	0.008	0.001	0.000	0.000	0.000	0.000
2	0.842	0.448	0.161	0.040	0.006	0.001	0.000	0.000	0.000
3	0.956	0.698	0.355	0.124	0.029	0.004	0.000	0.000	0.000
4	0.991	0.870	0.584	0.279	0.090	0.018	0.002	0.000	0.000
5	0.999	0.956	0.781	0.486	0.212	0.058	0.008	0.000	0.000
6	1.000	0.988	0.907	0.692	0.395	0.150	0.031	0.002	0.000
7	1.000	0.998	0.969	0.850	0.605	0.308	0.093	0.012	0.000
8	1.000	1.000	0.992	0.942	0.788	0.514	0.219	0.044	0.001
9	1.000	1.000	0.998	0.982	0.910	0.721	0.416	0.130	0.009
10	1.000	1.000	1.000	0.996	0.971	0.876	0.645	0.302	0.044
11	1.000	1.000	1.000	0.999	0.994	0.960	0.839	0.552	0.158
12	1.000	1.000	1.000	1.000	0.999	0.992	0.953	0.802	0.415
13	1.000	1.000	1.000	1.000	1.000	0.999	0.993	0.956	0.771
14	1.000	1.000	1.000	1.000	1.000	1.000	1.000	1.000	1.000

TABLE E.3 (continued)

$n = 15$
PROBABILITY

x	0.1	0.2	0.3	0.4	0.5	0.6	0.7	0.8	0.9
0	0.206	0.035	0.005	0.000	0.000	0.000	0.000	0.000	0.000
1	0.549	0.167	0.035	0.005	0.000	0.000	0.000	0.000	0.000
2	0.816	0.398	0.127	0.027	0.004	0.000	0.000	0.000	0.000
3	0.944	0.648	0.297	0.091	0.018	0.002	0.000	0.000	0.000
4	0.987	0.836	0.515	0.217	0.059	0.009	0.001	0.000	0.000
5	0.998	0.939	0.722	0.403	0.151	0.034	0.004	0.000	0.000
6	1.000	0.982	0.869	0.610	0.304	0.095	0.015	0.001	0.000
7	1.000	0.996	0.950	0.787	0.500	0.213	0.050	0.004	0.000
8	1.000	0.999	0.985	0.905	0.696	0.390	0.131	0.018	0.000
9	1.000	1.000	0.996	0.966	0.849	0.597	0.278	0.061	0.002
10	1.000	1.000	0.999	0.991	0.941	0.783	0.485	0.164	0.013
11	1.000	1.000	1.000	0.998	0.982	0.909	0.703	0.352	0.056
12	1.000	1.000	1.000	1.000	0.996	0.973	0.873	0.602	0.184
13	1.000	1.000	1.000	1.000	1.000	0.995	0.965	0.833	0.451
14	1.000	1.000	1.000	1.000	1.000	1.000	0.995	0.965	0.794
15	1.000	1.000	1.000	1.000	1.000	1.000	1.000	1.000	1.000

$n = 16$
PROBABILITY

x	0.1	0.2	0.3	0.4	0.5	0.6	0.7	0.8	0.9
0	0.185	0.028	0.003	0.000	0.000	0.000	0.000	0.000	0.000
1	0.515	0.141	0.026	0.003	0.000	0.000	0.000	0.000	0.000
2	0.789	0.352	0.099	0.018	0.002	0.000	0.000	0.000	0.000
3	0.932	0.598	0.246	0.065	0.011	0.001	0.000	0.000	0.000
4	0.983	0.798	0.450	0.167	0.038	0.005	0.000	0.000	0.000
5	0.997	0.918	0.660	0.329	0.105	0.019	0.002	0.000	0.000
6	0.999	0.973	0.825	0.527	0.227	0.058	0.007	0.000	0.000
7	1.000	0.993	0.926	0.716	0.402	0.142	0.026	0.001	0.000
8	1.000	0.999	0.974	0.858	0.598	0.284	0.074	0.007	0.000
9	1.000	1.000	0.993	0.942	0.773	0.473	0.175	0.027	0.001
10	1.000	1.000	0.998	0.981	0.895	0.671	0.340	0.082	0.003
11	1.000	1.000	1.000	0.995	0.962	0.833	0.550	0.202	0.017
12	1.000	1.000	1.000	0.999	0.989	0.935	0.754	0.402	0.068
13	1.000	1.000	1.000	1.000	0.998	0.982	0.901	0.648	0.211
14	1.000	1.000	1.000	1.000	1.000	0.997	0.974	0.859	0.485
15	1.000	1.000	1.000	1.000	1.000	1.000	0.997	0.972	0.815
16	1.000	1.000	1.000	1.000	1.000	1.000	1.000	1.000	1.000

TABLE E.3 (concluded)

n = 17
PROBABILITY

x	0.1	0.2	0.3	0.4	0.5	0.6	0.7	0.8	0.9
0	0.167	0.023	0.002	0.000	0.000	0.000	0.000	0.000	0.000
1	0.482	0.118	0.019	0.002	0.000	0.000	0.000	0.000	0.000
2	0.762	0.310	0.077	0.012	0.001	0.000	0.000	0.000	0.000
3	0.917	0.549	0.202	0.046	0.006	0.000	0.000	0.000	0.000
4	0.978	0.758	0.389	0.126	0.025	0.003	0.000	0.000	0.000
5	0.995	0.894	0.597	0.264	0.072	0.011	0.001	0.000	0.000
6	0.999	0.962	0.775	0.448	0.166	0.035	0.003	0.000	0.000
7	1.000	0.989	0.895	0.641	0.315	0.092	0.013	0.000	0.000
8	1.000	0.997	0.960	0.801	0.500	0.199	0.040	0.003	0.000
9	1.000	1.000	0.987	0.908	0.685	0.359	0.105	0.011	0.000
10	1.000	1.000	0.997	0.965	0.834	0.552	0.225	0.038	0.001
11	1.000	1.000	0.999	0.989	0.928	0.736	0.403	0.106	0.005
12	1.000	1.000	1.000	0.997	0.975	0.874	0.611	0.242	0.022
13	1.000	1.000	1.000	1.000	0.994	0.954	0.798	0.451	0.083
14	1.000	1.000	1.000	1.000	0.999	0.988	0.923	0.690	0.238
15	1.000	1.000	1.000	1.000	1.000	0.998	0.981	0.882	0.518
16	1.000	1.000	1.000	1.000	1.000	1.000	0.998	0.977	0.833
17	1.000	1.000	1.000	1.000	1.000	1.000	1.000	1.000	1.000

n = 18
PROBABILITY

x	0.1	0.2	0.3	0.4	0.5	0.6	0.7	0.8	0.9
0	0.150	0.018	0.002	0.000	0.000	0.000	0.000	0.000	0.000
1	0.450	0.099	0.014	0.001	0.000	0.000	0.000	0.000	0.000
2	0.734	0.271	0.060	0.008	0.001	0.000	0.000	0.000	0.000
3	0.902	0.501	0.165	0.033	0.004	0.000	0.000	0.000	0.000
4	0.972	0.716	0.333	0.094	0.015	0.001	0.000	0.000	0.000
5	0.994	0.867	0.534	0.209	0.048	0.006	0.000	0.000	0.000
6	0.999	0.949	0.722	0.374	0.119	0.020	0.001	0.000	0.000
7	1.000	0.984	0.859	0.563	0.240	0.058	0.006	0.000	0.000
8	1.000	0.996	0.940	0.737	0.407	0.135	0.021	0.001	0.000
9	1.000	0.999	0.979	0.865	0.593	0.263	0.060	0.004	0.000
10	1.000	1.000	0.994	0.942	0.760	0.437	0.141	0.016	0.000
11	1.000	1.000	0.999	0.980	0.881	0.626	0.278	0.051	0.001
12	1.000	1.000	1.000	0.994	0.952	0.791	0.466	0.133	0.006
13	1.000	1.000	1.000	0.999	0.985	0.906	0.667	0.284	0.028
14	1.000	1.000	1.000	1.000	0.996	0.967	0.835	0.499	0.098
15	1.000	1.000	1.000	1.000	0.999	0.992	0.940	0.729	0.266
16	1.000	1.000	1.000	1.000	1.000	0.999	0.986	0.901	0.550
17	1.000	1.000	1.000	1.000	1.000	1.000	0.998	0.982	0.850
18	1.000	1.000	1.000	1.000	1.000	1.000	1.000	1.000	1.000

Source: Goldstein Software, Inc. for the program Goldspread Statistical, which was used to generate this table.

Table E.4 Poisson Probabilities

	μ									
x	*0.1*	*0.2*	*0.3*	*0.4*	*0.5*	*0.6*	*0.7*	*0.8*	*0.9*	*1.0*
0	.9048	.8187	.7408	.6703	.6065	.5488	.4966	.4493	.4066	.3679
1	.0905	.1637	.2222	.2681	.3033	.3293	.3476	.3595	.3659	.3679
2	.0045	.0164	.0333	.0536	.0758	.0988	.1217	.1438	.1647	.1839
3	.0002	.0011	.0033	.0072	.0126	.0198	.0284	.3083	.0494	.0613
4	.0000	.0001	.0002	.0007	.0016	.0030	.0050	.0077	.0111	.0153
5	.0000	.0000	.0000	.0001	.0002	.0004	.0007	.0012	.0020	.0031
6	.0000	.0000	.0000	.0000	.0000	.0000	.0001	.0002	.0003	.0005
7	.0000	.0000	.0000	.0000	.0000	.0000	.0000	.0000	.0000	.0001

	μ									
x	*1.1*	*1.2*	*1.3*	*1.4*	*1.5*	*1.6*	*1.7*	*1.8*	*1.9*	*2.0*
0	.3329	.3012	.2725	.2466	.2231	.2019	.1827	.1653	.1496	.1353
1	.3662	.3614	.3543	.3452	.3347	.3230	.3106	.2975	.2842	.2707
2	.2014	.2169	.2303	.2417	.2510	.2584	.2640	.2678	.2700	.2707
3	.0738	.0867	.0998	.1128	.1255	.1378	.1496	.1607	.1710	.1804
4	.0203	.0260	.0324	.0395	.0471	.0551	.0636	.0723	.0812	.0902
5	.0045	.0062	.0084	.0111	.0141	.0176	.0216	.0260	.0309	.0361
6	.0008	.0012	.0018	.0026	.0035	.0047	.0061	.0078	.0098	.0120
7	.0001	.0002	.0003	.0005	.0008	.0011	.0015	.0020	.0027	.0034
8	.0000	.0000	.0001	.0001	.0001	.0002	.0003	.0005	.0006	.0009
9	.0000	.0000	.0000	.0000	.0000	.0000	.0001	.0001	.0001	.0002

	μ									
x	*2.1*	*2.2*	*2.3*	*2.4*	*2.5*	*2.6*	*2.7*	*2.8*	*2.9*	*3.0*
0	.1225	.1108	.1003	.0907	.0821	.0743	.0672	.0608	.0550	.0498
1	.2572	.2438	.2306	.2177	.2052	.1931	.1815	.1703	.1596	.1494
2	.2700	.2681	.2652	.2613	.2565	.2510	.2450	.2384	.2314	.2240
3	.1890	.1966	.2033	.2090	.2138	.2176	.2205	.2225	.2237	.2240
4	.0992	.1082	.1169	.1254	.1336	.1414	.1488	.1557	.1622	.1680
5	.0417	.0476	.0538	.0602	.0668	.0735	.0804	.0872	.0940	.1008
6	.0146	.0174	.0206	.0241	.0278	.0319	.0362	.0407	.0455	.0504
7	.0044	.0055	.0068	.0083	.0099	.0118	.0139	.0163	.0188	.0216
8	.0011	.0015	.0019	.0025	.0031	.0038	.0047	.0057	.0068	.0081
9	.0003	.0004	.0005	.0007	.0009	.0011	.0014	.0018	.0022	.0027
10	.0001	.0001	.0001	.0002	.0002	.0003	.0004	.0005	.0006	.0008
11	.0000	.0000	.0000	.0000	.0000	.0001	.0001	.0001	.0002	.0002
12	.0000	.0000	.0000	.0000	.0000	.0000	.0000	.0000	.0000	.0001

	μ									
x	*3.1*	*3.2*	*3.3*	*3.4*	*3.5*	*3.6*	*3.7*	*3.8*	*3.9*	*4.0*
0	.0450	.0408	.0369	.0334	.0302	.0273	.0247	.0224	.0202	.0183
1	.1397	.1304	.1217	.1135	.1057	.0984	.0915	.0850	.0789	.0733
2	.2165	.2087	.2008	.1929	.1850	.1771	.1692	.1615	.1539	.1465
3	.2237	.2226	.2209	.2186	.2158	.2125	.2087	.2046	.2001	.1954
4	.1734	.1781	.1823	.1858	.1888	.1912	.1931	.1944	.1951	.1954
5	.1075	.1140	.1203	.1264	.1322	.1377	.1429	.1477	.1522	.1563
6	.0555	.0608	.0662	.0716	.0771	.0826	.0881	.0936	.0989	.1042
7	.0246	.0278	.0312	.0348	.0385	.0425	.0466	.0508	.0551	.0595
8	.0095	.0111	.0129	.0148	.0169	.0191	.0215	.0241	.0269	.0298
9	.0033	.0040	.0047	.0056	.0066	.0076	.0089	.0102	.0116	.0132
10	.0010	.0013	.0016	.0019	.0023	.0028	.0033	.0039	.0045	.0053
11	.0003	.0004	.0005	.0006	.0007	.0009	.0011	.0013	.0016	.0019
12	.0001	.0001	.0001	.0002	.0002	.0003	.0003	.0004	.0005	.0006
13	.0000	.0000	.0000	.0000	.0001	.0001	.0001	.0001	.0002	.0002
14	.0000	.0000	.0000	.0000	.0000	.0000	.0000	.0000	.0000	.0001

TABLE E.4 (continued)

x	μ 4.1	4.2	4.3	4.4	4.5	4.6	4.7	4.8	4.9	5.0
0	.0166	.0150	.0136	.0123	.0111	.0101	.0091	.0082	.0074	.0067
1	.0679	.0630	.0583	.0540	.0500	.0462	.0427	.0395	.0365	.0337
2	.1393	.1323	.1254	.1188	.1125	.1063	.1005	.0948	.0894	.0842
3	.1904	.1852	.1798	.1743	.1687	.1631	.1574	.1517	.1460	.1404
4	.1951	.1944	.1933	.1917	.1898	.1875	.1849	.1820	.1789	.1755
5	.1600	.1633	.1662	.1687	.1708	.1725	.1738	.1747	.1753	.1755
6	.1093	.1143	.1191	.1237	.1281	.1323	.1362	.1398	.1432	.1462
7	.0640	.0686	.0732	.0778	.0824	.0869	.0914	.0959	.1002	.1044
8	.0328	.0360	.0393	.0428	.0463	.0500	.0537	.0575	.0614	.0653
9	.0150	.0168	.0188	.0209	.0232	.0255	.0280	.0307	.0334	.0363
10	.0061	.0071	.0081	.0092	.0104	.0118	.0132	.0147	.0164	.0181
11	.0023	.0027	.0032	.0037	.0043	.0049	.0056	.0064	.0073	.0082
12	.0008	.0009	.0011	.0014	.0016	.0019	.0022	.0026	.0030	.0034
13	.0002	.0003	.0004	.0005	.0006	.0007	.0008	.0009	.0011	.0013
14	.0001	.0001	.0001	.0001	.0002	.0002	.0003	.0003	.0004	.0005
15	.0000	.0000	.0000	.0000	.0001	.0001	.0001	.0001	.0001	.0002

x	μ 5.1	5.2	5.3	5.4	5.5	5.6	5.7	5.8	5.9	6.0
0	.0061	.0055	.0050	.0045	.0041	.0037	.0033	.0030	.0027	.0025
1	.0311	.0287	.0265	.0244	.0225	.0207	.0191	.0176	.0162	.0149
2	.0793	.0746	.0701	.0659	.0618	.0580	.0544	.0509	.0477	.0446
3	.1348	.1293	.1239	.1185	.1133	.1082	.1033	.0985	.0938	.0892
4	.1719	.1681	.1641	.1600	.1558	.1515	.1472	.1428	.1383	.1339
5	.1753	.1748	.1740	.1728	.1714	.1697	.1678	.1656	.1632	.1606
6	.1490	.1515	.1537	.1555	.1571	.1584	.1594	.1601	.1605	.1606
7	.1086	.1125	.1163	.1200	.1234	.1267	.1298	.1326	.1353	.1377
8	.0692	.0731	.0771	.0810	.0849	.0887	.0925	.0962	.0998	.1033
9	.0392	.0423	.0454	.0486	.0519	.0552	.0586	.0620	.0654	.0688
10	.0200	.0220	.0241	.0262	.0285	.0309	.0334	.0359	.0386	.0413
11	.0093	.0104	.0116	.0129	.0143	.0157	.0173	.0190	.0207	.0225
12	.0039	.0045	.0051	.0058	.0065	.0073	.0082	.0092	.0102	.0113
13	.0015	.0018	.0021	.0024	.0028	.0032	.0036	.0041	.0046	.0052
14	.0006	.0007	.0008	.0009	.0011	.0013	.0015	.0017	.0019	.0022
15	.0002	.0002	.0003	.0003	.0004	.0005	.0006	.0007	.0008	.0009
16	.0001	.0001	.0001	.0001	.0001	.0002	.0002	.0002	.0003	.0003
17	.0000	.0000	.0000	.0000	.0000	.0001	.0001	.0001	.0001	.0001

Table E.4 (continued)

x	μ 6.1	6.2	6.3	6.4	6.5	6.6	6.7	6.8	6.9	7.0
0	.0022	.0020	.0018	.0017	.0015	.0014	.0012	.0011	.0010	.0009
1	.0137	.0126	.0116	.0106	.0098	.0090	.0082	.0076	.0070	.0064
2	.0417	.0390	.0364	.0340	.0318	.0296	.0276	.0258	.0240	.0223
3	.0848	.0806	.0765	.0726	.0688	.0652	.0617	.0584	.0552	.0521
4	.1294	.1249	.1205	.1162	.1118	.1076	.1034	.0992	.0952	.0912
5	.1579	.1549	.1519	.1487	.1454	.1420	.1385	.1349	.1314	.1277
6	.1605	.1601	.1595	.1586	.1575	.1562	.1546	.1529	.1511	.1490
7	.1399	.1418	.1435	.1450	.1462	.1472	.1480	.1486	.1489	.1490
8	.1066	.1099	.1130	.1160	.1188	.1215	.1240	.1263	.1284	.1304
9	.0723	.0757	.0791	.0825	.0858	.0891	.0923	.0954	.0985	.1014
10	.0441	.0469	.0498	.0528	.0558	.0588	.0618	.0649	.0679	.0710
11	.0245	.0265	.0285	.0307	.0330	.0353	.0377	.0401	.0426	.0452
12	.0124	.0137	.0150	.0164	.0179	.0194	.0210	.0227	.0245	.0264
13	.0058	.0065	.0073	.0081	.0089	.0098	.0108	.0119	.0130	.0142
14	.0025	.0029	.0033	.0037	.0041	.0046	.0052	.0058	.0064	.0071
15	.0010	.0012	.0014	.0016	.0018	.0020	.0023	.0026	.0029	.0033
16	.0004	.0005	.0005	.0006	.0007	.0008	.0010	.0011	.0013	.0014
17	.0001	.0002	.0002	.0002	.0003	.0003	.0004	.0004	.0005	.0006
18	.0000	.0001	.0001	.0001	.0001	.0001	.0001	.0002	.0002	.0002
19	.0000	.0000	.0000	.0000	.0000	.0000	.0000	.0001	.0001	.0001

x	μ 7.1	7.2	7.3	7.4	7.5	7.6	7.7	7.8	7.9	8.0
0	.0008	.0007	.0007	.0006	.0006	.0005	.0005	.0004	.0004	.0003
1	.0059	.0054	.0049	.0045	.0041	.0038	.0035	.0032	.0029	.0027
2	.0208	.0194	.0180	.0167	.0156	.0145	.0134	.0125	.0116	.0107
3	.0492	.0464	.0438	.0413	.0389	.0366	.0345	.0324	.0305	.0286
4	.0874	.0836	.0799	.0764	.0729	.0696	.0663	.0632	.0602	.0573
5	.1241	.1204	.1167	.1130	.1094	.1057	.1021	.0986	.0951	.0916
6	.1468	.1445	.1420	.1394	.1367	.1339	.1311	.1282	.1252	.1221
7	.1489	.1486	.1481	.1474	.1465	.1454	.1442	.1428	.1413	.1396
8	.1321	.1337	.1351	.1363	.1373	.1382	.1388	.1392	.1395	.1396
9	.1042	.1070	.1096	.1121	.1144	.1167	.1187	.1207	.1224	.1241
10	.0740	.0770	.0800	.0829	.0858	.0887	.0914	.0941	.0967	.0993
11	.0478	.0504	.0531	.0558	.0585	.0613	.0640	.0667	.0695	.0722
12	.0283	.0303	.0323	.0344	.0366	.0388	.0411	.0434	.0457	.0481
13	.0154	.0168	.0181	.0196	.0211	.0227	.0243	.0260	.0278	.0296
14	.0078	.0086	.0095	.0104	.0113	.0123	.0134	.0145	.0157	.0169
15	.0037	.0041	.0046	.0051	.0057	.0062	.0069	.0075	.0083	.0090
16	.0016	.0019	.0021	.0024	.0026	.0030	.0033	.0037	.0041	.0045
17	.0007	.0008	.0009	.0010	.0012	.0013	.0015	.0017	.0019	.0021
18	.0003	.0003	.0004	.0004	.0005	.0006	.0006	.0007	.0008	.0009
19	.0001	.0001	.0001	.0002	.0002	.0002	.0003	.0003	.0003	.0004
20	.0000	.0000	.0001	.0001	.0001	.0001	.0001	.0001	.0001	.0002
21	.0000	.0000	.0000	.0000	.0000	.0000	.0000	.0000	.0001	.0001

TABLE E.4 (concluded)

x	μ 8.1	8.2	8.3	8.4	8.5	8.6	8.7	8.8	8.9	9.0
0	.0003	.0003	.0002	.0002	.0002	.0002	.0002	.0002	.0001	.0001
1	.0025	.0023	.0021	.0019	.0017	.0016	.0014	.0013	.0012	.0011
2	.0100	.0092	.0086	.0079	.0074	.0068	.0063	.0058	.0054	.0050
3	.0269	.0252	.0237	.0222	.0208	.0195	.0183	.0171	.0160	.0150
4	.0544	.0517	.0491	.0466	.0443	.0420	.0398	.0377	.0357	.0337
5	.0882	.0849	.0816	.0784	.0752	.0722	.0692	.0663	.0635	.0607
6	.1191	.1160	.1128	.1097	.1066	.1034	.1003	.0972	.0941	.0911
7	.1378	.1358	.1338	.1317	.1294	.1271	.1247	.1222	.1197	.1171
8	.1395	.1392	.1388	.1382	.1375	.1366	.1356	.1344	.1332	.1318
9	.1256	.1269	.1280	.1290	.1299	.1306	.1311	.1315	.1317	.1318
10	.1017	.1040	.1063	.1084	.1104	.1123	.1140	.1157	.1172	.1186
11	.0749	.0776	.0802	.0828	.0853	.0878	.0902	.0925	.0948	.0970
12	.0505	.0530	.0555	.0579	.0604	.0629	.0654	.0679	.0703	.0728
13	.0315	.0334	.0354	.0374	.0395	.0416	.0438	.0459	.0481	.0504
14	.0182	.0196	.0210	.0225	.0240	.0256	.0272	.0289	.0306	.0324
15	.0098	.0107	.0116	.0126	.0136	.0147	.0158	.0169	.0182	.0194
16	.0050	.0055	.0060	.0066	.0072	.0079	.0086	.0093	.0101	.0109
17	.0024	.0026	.0029	.0033	.0036	.0040	.0044	.0048	.0053	.0058
18	.0011	.0012	.0014	.0015	.0017	.0019	.0021	.0024	.0026	.0029
19	.0005	.0005	.0006	.0007	.0008	.0009	.0010	.0011	.0012	.0014
20	.0002	.0002	.0002	.0003	.0003	.0004	.0004	.0005	.0005	.0006
21	.0001	.0001	.0001	.0001	.0001	.0002	.0002	.0002	.0002	.0003
22	.0000	.0000	.0000	.0000	.0001	.0001	.0001	.0001	.0001	.0001

x	μ 9.1	9.2	9.3	9.4	9.5	9.6	9.7	9.8	9.9	10
0	.0001	.0001	.0001	.0001	.0001	.0001	.0001	.0001	.0001	.0000
1	.0010	.0009	.0009	.0008	.0007	.0007	.0006	.0005	.0005	.0005
2	.0046	.0043	.0040	.0037	.0034	.0031	.0029	.0027	.0025	.0023
3	.0140	.0131	.0123	.0115	.0107	.0100	.0093	.0087	.0081	.0076
4	.0319	.0302	.0285	.0269	.0254	.0240	.0226	.0213	.0201	.0189
5	.0581	.0555	.0530	.0506	.0483	.0460	.0439	.0418	.0398	.0378
6	.0881	.0851	.0822	.0793	.0764	.0736	.0709	.0682	.0656	.0631
7	.1145	.1118	.1091	.1064	.1037	.1010	.0982	.0955	.0928	.0901
8	.1302	.1286	.1269	.1251	.1232	.1212	.1191	.1170	.1148	.1126
9	.1317	.1315	.1311	.1306	.1300	.1293	.1284	.1274	.1263	.1251
10	.1198	.1210	.1219	.1228	.1235	.1241	.1245	.1249	.1250	.1251
11	.0991	.1012	.1031	.1049	.1067	.1083	.1098	.1112	.1125	.1137
12	.0752	.0776	.0799	.0822	.0844	.0866	.0888	.0908	.0928	.0948
13	.0526	.0549	.0572	.0594	.0617	.0640	.0662	.0685	.0707	.0729
14	.0342	.0361	.0380	.0399	.0419	.0439	.0459	.0479	.0500	.0521
15	.0208	.0221	.0235	.0250	.0265	.0281	.0297	.0313	.0330	.0347
16	.0118	.0127	.0137	.0147	.0157	.0168	.0180	.0192	.0204	.0217
17	.0063	.0069	.0075	.0081	.0088	.0095	.0103	.0111	.0119	.0128
18	.0032	.0035	.0039	.0042	.0046	.0051	.0055	.0060	.0065	.0071
19	.0015	.0017	.0019	.0021	.0023	.0026	.0028	.0031	.0034	.0037
20	.0007	.0008	.0009	.0010	.0011	.0012	.0014	.0015	.0017	.0019
21	.0003	.0003	.0004	.0004	.0005	.0006	.0006	.0007	.0008	.0009
22	.0001	.0001	.0002	.0002	.0002	.0002	.0003	.0003	.0004	.0004
23	.0000	.0001	.0001	.0001	.0001	.0001	.0001	.0001	.0002	.0002
24	.0000	.0000	.0000	.0000	.0000	.0000	.0000	.0001	.0001	.0001

Source: Adapted from Howard Gitlow, Shelly Gitlow, Alan Oppenheim, and Rosa Oppenheim, *Tools and Methods for the Improvement of Quality* (Homewood, Ill.: Richard D. Irwin, 1989), pp. 584–87.

TABLE E.5 Cumulative Poisson Table

x	μ .10	.20	.30	.40	.50	.60	.70	.80	.90
0	.9048	.8187	.7408	.6703	.6065	.5488	.4966	.4493	.4066
1	.9953	.9825	.9631	.9384	.9098	.8781	.8442	.8088	.7725
2	.9998	.9989	.9964	.9921	.9856	.9769	.9659	.9526	.9371
3	1.0000	.9999	.9997	.9992	.9982	.9966	.9942	.9909	.9865
4		1.0000	1.0000	.9999	.9998	.9996	.9992	.9986	.9977
5					1.0000	1.0000	.9999	.9998	.9997
6					1.0000	1.0000	1.0000	1.0000	1.0000

x	μ 1.0	1.1	1.2	1.3	1.4	1.5	1.6	1.7	1.8	1.9
0	.3679	.3329	.3012	.2725	.2466	.2231	.2019	.1827	.1653	.1496
1	.7358	.6990	.6626	.6268	.5918	.5578	.5249	.4932	.4628	.4337
2	.9197	.9004	.8795	.8571	.8335	.8088	.7834	.7572	.7306	.7037
3	.9810	.9743	.9662	.9569	.9463	.9344	.9212	.9068	.8913	.8747
4	.9963	.9946	.9923	.9893	.9857	.9814	.9763	.9704	.9636	.9559
5	.9994	.9990	.9985	.9978	.9968	.9955	.9940	.9920	.9896	.9868
6	.9999	.9999	.9997	.9996	.9994	.9991	.9987	.9981	.9974	.9966
7	1.0000	1.0000	1.0000	.9999	.9999	.9998	.9997	.9996	.9994	.9992
8	1.0000	1.0000	1.0000	1.0000	1.0000	1.0000	1.0000	.9999	.9999	.9998
9	1.0000	1.0000	1.0000	1.0000	1.0000	1.0000	1.0000	1.0000	1.0000	1.0000

x	μ 2.0	2.1	2.2	2.3	2.4	2.5	2.6	2.7	2.8	2.9
0	.1353	.1225	.1108	.1003	.0907	.0821	.0743	.0672	.0608	.0550
1	.4060	.3796	.3546	.3309	.3084	.2873	.2674	.2487	.2311	.2146
2	.6767	.6496	.6227	.5960	.5697	.5438	.5184	.4936	.4695	.4460
3	.8571	.8386	.8194	.7993	.7787	.7576	.7360	.7141	.6919	.6696
4	.9473	.9379	.9275	.9162	.9041	.8912	.8774	.8629	.8477	.8318
5	.9834	.9796	.9751	.9700	.9643	.9580	.9510	.9433	.9349	.9258
6	.9955	.9941	.9925	.9906	.9884	.9858	.9828	.9794	.9756	.9713
7	.9989	.9985	.9980	.9974	.9967	.9958	.9947	.9934	.9919	.9901
8	.9998	.9997	.9995	.9994	.9991	.9989	.9985	.9981	.9976	.9969
9	1.0000	.9999	.9999	.9999	.9998	.9997	.9996	.9995	.9993	.9991
10	1.0000	1.0000	1.0000	1.0000	1.0000	.9999	.9999	.9999	.9998	.9998
11	1.0000	1.0000	1.0000	1.0000	1.0000	1.0000	1.0000	1.0000	1.0000	.9999
12	1.0000	1.0000	1.0000	1.0000	1.0000	1.0000	1.0000	1.0000	1.0000	1.0000

TABLE E.5 (continued)

x	3.0	3.1	3.2	3.3	3.4	3.5	3.6	3.7	3.8	3.9
0	.0498	.0450	.0408	.0369	.0334	.0302	.0273	.0247	.0224	.0202
1	.1991	.1847	.1712	.1586	.1468	.1359	.1257	.1162	.1074	.0992
2	.4232	.4012	.3799	.3594	.3397	.3208	.3027	.2854	.2689	.2531
3	.6472	.6248	.6025	.5803	.5584	.5366	.5152	.4942	.4735	.4532
4	.8153	.7982	.7806	.7626	.7442	.7254	.7064	.6872	.6678	.6484
5	.9161	.9057	.8946	.8829	.8705	.8576	.8441	.8301	.8156	.8006
6	.9665	.9612	.9554	.9490	.9421	.9347	.9267	.9182	.9091	.8995
7	.9881	.9858	.9832	.9802	.9769	.9733	.9692	.9648	.9599	.9546
8	.9962	.9953	.9943	.9931	.9917	.9901	.9883	.9863	.9840	.9815
9	.9989	.9986	.9982	.9978	.9973	.9967	.9960	.9952	.9942	.9931
10	.9997	.9996	.9995	.9994	.9992	.9990	.9987	.9984	.9981	.9977
11	.9999	.9999	.9999	.9998	.9998	.9997	.9996	.9995	.9994	.9993
12	1.0000	1.0000	1.0000	1.0000	.9999	.9999	.9999	.9999	.9998	.9998
13	1.0000	1.0000	1.0000	1.0000	1.0000	1.0000	1.0000	1.0000	1.0000	.9999
14	1.0000	1.0000	1.0000	1.0000	1.0000	1.0000	1.0000	1.0000	1.0000	1.0000

					μ					
x	4.0	4.2	4.4	4.6	4.8	5.0	5.2	5.4	5.6	5.8
0	.0183	.0150	.0123	.0101	.0082	.0067	.0055	.0045	.0037	.0030
1	.0916	.0780	.0663	.0563	.0477	.0404	.0342	.0289	.0244	.0206
2	.2381	.2102	.1851	.1626	.1425	.1247	.1088	.0948	.0824	.0715
3	.4335	.3954	.3594	.3257	.2942	.2650	.2381	.2133	.1906	.1700
4	.6288	.5898	.5512	.5132	.4763	.4405	.4061	.3733	.3421	.3127
5	.7851	.7531	.7199	.6858	.6510	.6160	.5809	.5461	.5119	.4783
6	.8893	.8675	.8436	.8180	.7908	.7622	.7324	.7017	.6703	.6384
7	.9489	.9361	.9214	.9049	.8867	.8666	.8449	.8217	.7970	.7710
8	.9786	.9721	.9642	.9549	.9442	.9319	.9181	.9026	.8857	.8672
9	.9919	.9889	.9851	.9805	.9749	.9682	.9603	.9512	.9409	.9292
10	.9972	.9959	.9943	.9922	.9896	.9863	.9823	.9775	.9718	.9651
11	.9991	.9986	.9980	.9971	.9960	.9945	.9927	.9904	.9875	.9840
12	.9997	.9996	.9993	.9990	.9986	.9980	.9972	.9962	.9949	.9932
13	.9999	.9999	.9998	.9997	.9995	.9993	.9990	.9986	.9980	.9973
14	1.0000	1.0000	.9999	.9999	.9999	.9998	.9997	.9995	.9993	.9990
15	1.0000	1.0000	1.0000	1.0000	1.0000	.9999	.9999	.9998	.9998	.9996
16	1.0000	1.0000	1.0000	1.0000	1.0000	1.0000	1.0000	.9999	.9999	.9999
17	1.0000	1.0000	1.0000	1.0000	1.0000	1.0000	1.0000	1.0000	1.0000	1.0000

Table E.5 (continued)

	μ									
x	6.0	6.2	6.4	6.6	6.8	7.0	7.2	7.4	7.6	7.8
0	.0025	.0020	.0017	.0014	.0011	.0009	.0007	.0006	.0005	.0004
1	.0174	.0146	.0123	.0103	.0087	.0073	.0061	.0051	.0043	.0036
2	.0620	.0536	.0463	.0400	.0344	.0296	.0255	.0219	.0188	.0161
3	.1512	.1342	.1189	.1052	.0928	.0818	.0719	.0632	.0554	.0485
4	.2851	.2592	.2351	.2127	.1920	.1730	.1555	.1395	.1249	.1117
5	.4457	.4141	.3837	.3547	.3270	.3007	.2759	.2526	.2307	.2103
6	.6063	.5742	.5423	.5108	.4799	.4497	.4204	.3920	.3646	.3384
7	.7440	.7160	.6873	.6581	.6285	.5987	.5689	.5393	.5100	.4812
8	.8472	.8259	.8033	.7796	.7548	.7291	.7027	.6757	.6482	.6204
9	.9161	.9016	.8858	.8686	.8502	.8305	.8096	.7877	.7649	.7411
10	.9574	.9486	.9386	.9274	.9151	.9015	.8867	.8707	.8535	.8352
11	.9799	.9750	.9693	.9627	.9552	.9466	.9371	.9265	.9148	.9020
12	.9912	.9887	.9857	.9821	.9779	.9730	.9673	.9609	.9536	.9454
13	.9964	.9952	.9937	.9920	.9898	.9872	.9841	.9805	.9762	.9714
14	.9986	.9981	.9974	.9966	.9956	.9943	.9927	.9908	.9886	.9859
15	.9995	.9993	.9990	.9986	.9982	.9976	.9969	.9959	.9948	.9934
16	.9998	.9997	.9996	.9995	.9993	.9990	.9987	.9983	.9978	.9971
17	.9999	.9999	.9999	.9998	.9997	.9996	.9995	.9993	.9991	.9988
18	1.0000	1.0000	1.0000	.9999	.9999	.9999	.9998	.9997	.9996	.9995
19	1.0000	1.0000	1.0000	1.0000	1.0000	1.0000	.9999	.9999	.9999	.9998
20	1.0000	1.0000	1.0000	1.0000	1.0000	1.0000	1.0000	1.0000	1.0000	.9999
21	1.0000	1.0000	1.0000	1.0000	1.0000	1.0000	1.0000	1.0000	1.0000	1.0000

TABLE E.5 (concluded)

x	μ 8.0	8.5	9.0	9.5	10.0
0	.0003	.0002	.0001	.0001	.0000
1	.0030	.0019	.0012	.0008	.0005
2	.0138	.0093	.0062	.0042	.0028
3	.0424	.0301	.0212	.0149	.0103
4	.0996	.0744	.0550	.0403	.0293
5	.1912	.1496	.1157	.0885	.0671
6	.3134	.2562	.2068	.1649	.1301
7	.4530	.3856	.3239	.2687	.2202
8	.5925	.5231	.4557	.3918	.3328
9	.7166	.6530	.5874	.5218	.4579
10	.8159	.7634	.7060	.6453	.5830
11	.8881	.8487	.8030	.7520	.6968
12	.9362	.9091	.8758	.8364	.7916
13	.9658	.9486	.9261	.8981	.8645
14	.9827	.9726	.9585	.9400	.9165
15	.9918	.9862	.9780	.9665	.9513
16	.9963	.9934	.9889	.9823	.9730
17	.9984	.9970	.9947	.9911	.9857
18	.9993	.9987	.9976	.9957	.9928
19	.9997	.9995	.9989	.9980	.9965
20	.9999	.9998	.9996	.9991	.9984
21	1.0000	.9999	.9998	.9996	.9993
22	1.0000	1.0000	.9999	.9999	.9997
23	1.0000	1.0000	1.0000	.9999	.9999
24	1.0000	1.0000	1.0000	1.0000	1.0000
25	1.0000	1.0000	1.0000	1.0000	1.0000
26	1.0000	1.0000	1.0000	1.0000	1.0000
27	1.0000	1.0000	1.0000	1.0000	1.0000

TABLE E.6 Areas of the Standard Normal Distribution

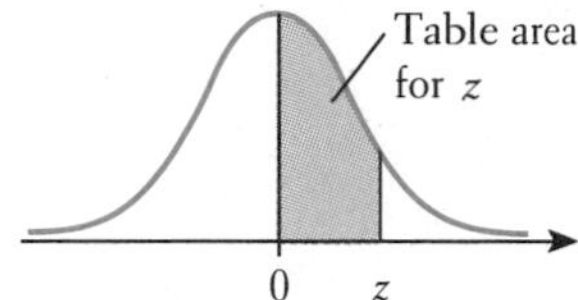

The table areas are probabilities that the standard normal random variable is between 0 and z.

	Second Decimal Place in z									
z	**0.00**	**0.01**	**0.02**	**0.03**	**0.04**	**0.05**	**0.06**	**0.07**	**0.08**	**0.09**
0.0	0.0000	0.0040	0.0080	0.0120	0.0160	0.0199	0.0239	0.0279	0.0319	0.0359
0.1	0.0398	0.0438	0.0478	0.0517	0.0557	0.0596	0.0636	0.0675	0.0714	0.0753
0.2	0.0793	0.0832	0.0871	0.0910	0.0948	0.0987	0.1026	0.1064	0.1103	0.1141
0.3	0.1179	0.1217	0.1255	0.1293	0.1331	0.1368	0.1406	0.1443	0.1480	0.1517
0.4	0.1554	0.1591	0.1628	0.1664	0.1700	0.1736	0.1772	0.1808	0.1844	0.1879
0.5	0.1915	0.1950	0.1985	0.2019	0.2054	0.2088	0.2123	0.2157	0.2190	0.2224
0.6	0.2257	0.2291	0.2324	0.2357	0.2389	0.2422	0.2454	0.2486	0.2517	0.2549
0.7	0.2580	0.2611	0.2642	0.2673	0.2704	0.2734	0.2764	0.2794	0.2823	0.2852
0.8	0.2881	0.2910	0.2939	0.2967	0.2995	0.3023	0.3051	0.3078	0.3106	0.3133
0.9	0.3159	0.3186	0.3212	0.3238	0.3264	0.3289	0.3315	0.3340	0.3365	0.3389
1.0	0.3413	0.3438	0.3461	0.3485	0.3508	0.3531	0.3554	0.3577	0.3599	0.3621
1.1	0.3643	0.3665	0.3686	0.3708	0.3729	0.3749	0.3770	0.3790	0.3810	0.3830
1.2	0.3849	0.3869	0.3888	0.3907	0.3925	0.3944	0.3962	0.3980	0.3997	0.4015
1.3	0.4032	0.4049	0.4066	0.4082	0.4099	0.4115	0.4131	0.4147	0.4162	0.4177
1.4	0.4192	0.4207	0.4222	0.4236	0.4251	0.4265	0.4279	0.4292	0.4306	0.4319
1.5	0.4332	0.4345	0.4357	0.4370	0.4382	0.4394	0.4406	0.4418	0.4429	0.4441
1.6	0.4452	0.4463	0.4474	0.4484	0.4495	0.4505	0.4515	0.4525	0.4535	0.4545
1.7	0.4554	0.4564	0.4573	0.4582	0.4591	0.4599	0.4608	0.4616	0.4625	0.4633
1.8	0.4641	0.4649	0.4656	0.4664	0.4671	0.4678	0.4686	0.4693	0.4699	0.4706
1.9	0.4713	0.4719	0.4726	0.4732	0.4738	0.4744	0.4750	0.4756	0.4761	0.4767
2.0	0.4772	0.4778	0.4783	0.4788	0.4793	0.4798	0.4803	0.4808	0.4812	0.4817
2.1	0.4821	0.4826	0.4830	0.4834	0.4838	0.4842	0.4846	0.4850	0.4854	0.4857
2.2	0.4861	0.4864	0.4868	0.4871	0.4875	0.4878	0.4881	0.4884	0.4887	0.4890
2.3	0.4893	0.4896	0.4898	0.4901	0.4904	0.4906	0.4909	0.4911	0.4913	0.4916
2.4	0.4918	0.4920	0.4922	0.4925	0.4927	0.4929	0.4931	0.4932	0.4934	0.4936
2.5	0.4938	0.4940	0.4941	0.4943	0.4945	0.4946	0.4948	0.4949	0.4951	0.4952
2.6	0.4953	0.4955	0.4956	0.4957	0.4959	0.4960	0.4961	0.4962	0.4963	0.4964
2.7	0.4965	0.4966	0.4967	0.4968	0.4969	0.4970	0.4971	0.4972	0.4973	0.4974
2.8	0.4974	0.4975	0.4976	0.4977	0.4977	0.4978	0.4979	0.4979	0.4980	0.4981
2.9	0.4981	0.4982	0.4982	0.4983	0.4984	0.4984	0.4985	0.4985	0.4986	0.4986
3.0	0.4987	0.4987	0.4987	0.4988	0.4988	0.4989	0.4989	0.4989	0.4990	0.4990
3.1	0.4990	0.4991	0.4991	0.4991	0.4992	0.4992	0.4992	0.4992	0.4993	0.4993
3.2	0.4993	0.4993	0.4994	0.4994	0.4994	0.4994	0.4994	0.4995	0.4995	0.4995
3.3	0.4995	0.4995	0.4995	0.4996	0.4996	0.4996	0.4996	0.4996	0.4996	0.4997
3.4	0.4997	0.4997	0.4997	0.4997	0.4997	0.4997	0.4997	0.4997	0.4997	0.4998
3.5	0.4998									
4.0	0.49997									
4.5	0.499997									
5.0	0.4999997									
6.0	0.499999999									

Source: Amir D. Aczel, *Complete Business Statistics* (Homewood, Ill.: Richard D. Irwin, 1989), p. 1018.

TABLE E.7 Student t-Distribution

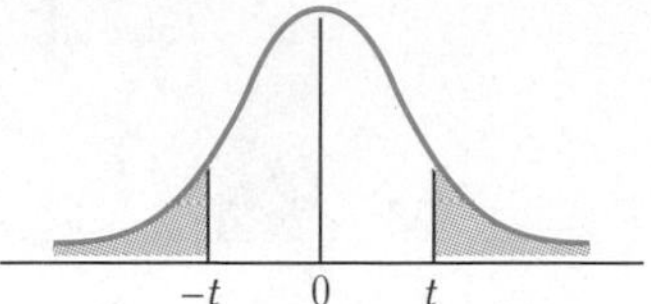

Two-tailed Area

df	.20	.10	.05	.02	.01	.001
1	3.078	6.314	12.706	31.821	63.657	636.619
2	1.886	2.920	4.303	6.965	9.925	31.598
3	1.638	2.353	3.182	4.541	5.841	12.941
4	1.533	2.132	2.776	3.747	4.604	8.610
5	1.476	2.015	2.571	3.365	4.032	6.859
6	1.440	1.943	2.447	3.143	3.707	5.959
7	1.415	1.895	2.365	2.998	3.499	5.405
8	1.397	1.860	2.306	2.896	3.355	5.041
9	1.383	1.833	2.262	2.821	3.250	4.781
10	1.372	1.812	2.228	2.764	3.169	4.587
11	1.363	1.796	2.201	2.718	3.106	4.437
12	1.356	1.782	2.179	2.681	3.055	4.318
13	1.350	1.771	2.160	2.650	3.012	4.221
14	1.345	1.761	2.145	2.624	2.977	4.140
15	1.341	1.753	2.131	2.602	2.947	4.073
16	1.337	1.746	2.120	2.583	2.921	4.015
17	1.333	1.740	2.110	2.567	2.898	3.965
18	1.330	1.734	2.101	2.552	2.878	3.922
19	1.328	1.729	2.093	2.539	2.681	3.883
20	1.325	1.725	2.086	2.528	2.845	3.850
21	1.323	1.721	2.080	2.518	2.831	3.819
22	1.321	1.717	2.074	2.508	2.819	3.792
23	1.319	1.714	2.069	2.500	2.807	3.767
24	1.318	1.711	2.064	2.492	2.797	3.745
25	1.316	1.708	2.060	2.485	2.787	3.725
26	1.315	1.706	2.056	2.479	2.779	3.707
27	1.314	1.703	2.052	2.473	2.771	3.690
28	1.313	1.701	2.048	2.467	2.763	3.674
29	1.311	1.699	2.045	2.462	2.756	3.659
30	1.310	1.697	2.042	2.457	2.750	3.646
40	1.303	1.684	2.021	2.423	2.704	3.551
60	1.296	1.671	2.000	2.390	2.660	3.460
120	1.289	1.658	1.980	2.358	2.617	3.373
∞	1.282	1.645	1.960	2.326	2.576	3.291
	.10	.05	.025	.01	.005	.0005

One-tailed Area

Source: Goldstein Software, Inc. for the program Goldspread Statistical, which was used to generate this table.

TABLE E.8 Critical Values of Chi-Square

This table contains the values of χ^2 that correspond to a specific right-tail area and specific numbers of degrees of freedom df.

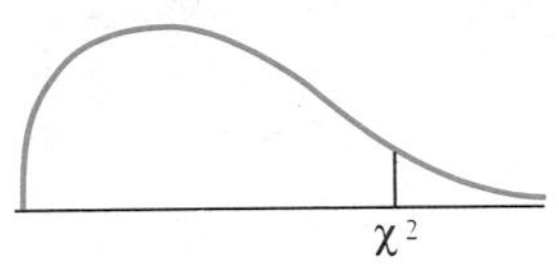

DEGREES OF FREEDOM df	RIGHT-TAIL AREA 0.10	0.05	0.02	0.01
1	2.706	3.841	5.412	6.635
2	4.605	5.991	7.824	9.210
3	6.251	7.815	9.837	11.345
4	7.779	9.488	11.668	13.277
5	9.236	11.070	13.388	15.086
6	10.645	12.592	15.033	16.812
7	12.017	14.067	16.622	18.475
8	13.362	15.507	18.168	20.090
9	14.684	16.919	19.679	21.666
10	15.987	18.307	21.161	23.209
11	17.275	19.675	22.618	24.725
12	18.549	21.026	24.054	26.217
13	19.812	22.362	25.472	27.688
14	21.064	23.685	26.873	29.141
15	22.307	24.996	28.259	30.578
16	23.542	26.296	29.633	32.000
17	24.769	27.587	30.995	33.409
18	25.989	28.869	32.346	34.805
19	27.204	30.144	33.687	36.191
20	28.412	31.410	35.020	37.566
21	29.615	32.671	36.343	38.932
22	30.813	33.924	37.659	40.289
23	32.007	35.172	38.968	41.638
24	33.196	36.415	40.270	42.980
25	34.382	37.652	41.566	44.314
26	35.563	38.885	42.856	45.642
27	36.741	40.113	44.140	46.963
28	37.916	41.337	45.419	48.278
29	39.087	42.557	46.693	49.588
30	40.256	43.773	47.962	50.892

Source: Robert D. Mason and Douglas A. Lind, *Statistical Techniques in Business and Economics*, 7th ed. (Homewood, Ill.: Richard D. Irwin, 1990), p. 860.

TABLE E.9 The F Distribution for $\alpha = 0.05$ and $\alpha = 0.01$ (**Bold**) for Many Possible Degrees of Freedom

Denominator Degrees of Freedom (k_2)	Numerator Degrees of Freedon (k_1)																							
	1	2	3	4	5	6	7	8	9	10	11	12	14	16	20	24	30	40	50	75	100	200	500	∞
1	161	200	216	225	230	234	237	239	241	242	243	244	245	246	248	249	250	251	252	253	253	254	254	254
	4,052	**5,000**	**5,403**	**5,625**	**5,764**	**5,859**	**5,928**	**5,981**	**6,022**	**6,056**	**6,083**	**6,106**	**6,143**	**6,170**	**6,209**	**6,235**	**6,261**	**6,287**	**6,303**	**6,324**	**6,334**	**6,350**	**6,360**	**6,366**
2	18.51	19.00	19.16	19.25	19.30	19.33	19.35	19.37	19.38	19.40	19.40	19.41	19.42	19.43	19.45	19.45	19.46	19.47	19.48	19.48	19.49	19.49	19.49	19.50
	98.50	**99.00**	**99.17**	**99.25**	**99.30**	**99.33**	**99.36**	**99.37**	**99.39**	**99.40**	**99.41**	**99.42**	**99.43**	**99.44**	**99.45**	**99.46**	**99.47**	**99.47**	**99.48**	**99.49**	**99.49**	**99.49**	**99.50**	**99.50**
3	10.13	9.55	9.28	9.12	9.01	8.94	8.89	8.85	8.81	8.79	8.76	8.74	8.71	8.69	8.66	8.64	8.62	8.59	8.58	8.56	8.55	8.54	8.53	8.53
	34.12	**30.82**	**29.46**	**28.71**	**28.24**	**27.91**	**27.67**	**27.49**	**27.35**	**27.23**	**27.13**	**27.05**	**26.92**	**26.83**	**26.69**	**26.60**	**26.50**	**26.41**	**26.35**	**26.28**	**26.24**	**26.18**	**26.15**	**26.13**
4	7.71	6.94	6.59	6.39	6.26	6.16	6.09	6.04	6.00	5.96	5.94	5.91	5.87	5.84	5.80	5.77	5.75	5.72	5.70	5.68	5.66	5.65	5.64	5.63
	21.20	**18.00**	**16.69**	**15.98**	**15.52**	**15.21**	**14.98**	**14.80**	**14.66**	**14.55**	**14.45**	**14.37**	**14.25**	**14.15**	**14.02**	**13.93**	**13.84**	**13.75**	**13.69**	**13.61**	**13.58**	**13.52**	**13.49**	**13.46**
5	6.61	5.79	5.41	5.19	5.05	4.95	4.88	4.82	4.77	4.74	4.70	4.68	4.64	4.60	4.56	4.53	4.50	4.46	4.44	4.42	4.41	4.39	4.37	4.37
	16.26	**13.27**	**12.06**	**11.39**	**10.97**	**10.67**	**10.46**	**10.29**	**10.16**	**10.05**	**9.96**	**9.89**	**9.77**	**9.68**	**9.55**	**9.47**	**9.38**	**9.29**	**9.24**	**9.17**	**9.13**	**9.08**	**9.04**	**9.02**
6	5.99	5.14	4.76	4.53	4.39	4.28	4.21	4.15	4.10	4.06	4.03	4.00	3.96	3.92	3.87	3.84	3.81	3.77	3.75	3.73	3.71	3.69	3.68	3.67
	13.75	**10.92**	**9.78**	**9.15**	**8.75**	**8.47**	**8.26**	**8.10**	**7.98**	**7.87**	**7.79**	**7.72**	**7.60**	**7.52**	**7.40**	**7.31**	**7.23**	**7.14**	**7.09**	**7.02**	**6.99**	**6.93**	**6.90**	**6.88**
7	5.59	4.74	4.35	4.12	3.97	3.87	3.79	3.73	3.68	3.64	3.60	3.57	3.53	3.49	3.44	3.41	3.38	3.34	3.32	3.29	3.27	3.25	3.24	3.23
	12.25	**9.55**	**8.45**	**7.85**	**7.46**	**7.19**	**6.99**	**6.84**	**6.72**	**6.62**	**6.54**	**6.47**	**6.36**	**6.28**	**6.16**	**6.07**	**5.99**	**5.91**	**5.86**	**5.79**	**5.75**	**5.70**	**5.67**	**5.65**
8	5.32	4.46	4.07	3.84	3.69	3.58	3.50	3.44	3.39	3.35	3.31	3.28	3.24	3.20	3.15	3.12	3.08	3.04	3.02	2.99	2.97	2.95	2.94	2.93
	11.26	**8.65**	**7.59**	**7.01**	**6.63**	**6.37**	**6.18**	**6.03**	**5.91**	**5.81**	**5.73**	**5.67**	**5.56**	**5.48**	**5.36**	**5.28**	**5.20**	**5.12**	**5.07**	**5.00**	**4.96**	**4.91**	**4.88**	**4.86**
9	5.12	4.26	3.86	3.63	3.48	3.37	3.29	3.23	3.18	3.14	3.10	3.07	3.03	2.99	2.94	2.90	2.86	2.83	2.80	2.77	2.76	2.73	2.72	2.71
	10.56	**8.02**	**6.99**	**6.42**	**6.06**	**5.80**	**5.61**	**5.47**	**5.35**	**5.26**	**5.18**	**5.11**	**5.01**	**4.92**	**4.81**	**4.73**	**4.65**	**4.57**	**4.52**	**4.45**	**4.41**	**4.36**	**4.33**	**4.31**
10	4.96	4.10	3.71	3.48	3.33	3.22	3.14	3.07	3.02	2.98	2.94	2.91	2.86	2.83	2.77	2.74	2.70	2.66	2.64	2.60	2.59	2.56	2.55	2.54
	10.04	**7.56**	**6.55**	**5.99**	**5.64**	**5.39**	**5.20**	**5.06**	**4.94**	**4.85**	**4.77**	**4.71**	**4.60**	**4.52**	**4.41**	**4.33**	**4.25**	**4.17**	**4.12**	**4.05**	**4.01**	**3.96**	**3.93**	**3.91**
11	4.84	3.98	3.59	3.36	3.20	3.09	3.01	2.95	2.90	2.85	2.82	2.79	2.74	2.70	2.65	2.61	2.57	2.53	2.51	2.47	2.46	2.43	2.42	2.40
	9.65	**7.21**	**6.22**	**5.67**	**5.32**	**5.07**	**4.89**	**4.74**	**4.63**	**4.54**	**4.46**	**4.40**	**4.29**	**4.21**	**4.10**	**4.02**	**3.94**	**3.86**	**3.81**	**3.74**	**3.71**	**3.66**	**3.62**	**3.60**
12	4.75	3.89	3.49	3.26	3.11	3.00	2.91	2.85	2.80	2.75	2.72	2.69	2.64	2.60	2.54	2.51	2.47	2.43	2.40	2.37	2.35	2.32	2.31	2.30
	9.33	**6.93**	**5.95**	**5.41**	**5.06**	**4.82**	**4.64**	**4.50**	**4.39**	**4.30**	**4.22**	**4.16**	**4.05**	**3.97**	**3.86**	**3.78**	**3.70**	**3.62**	**3.57**	**3.50**	**3.47**	**3.41**	**3.38**	**3.36**
13	4.67	3.81	3.41	3.18	3.03	2.92	2.83	2.77	2.71	2.67	2.63	2.60	2.55	2.51	2.46	2.42	2.38	2.34	2.31	2.28	2.26	2.23	2.22	2.21
	9.07	**6.70**	**5.74**	**5.21**	**4.86**	**4.62**	**4.44**	**4.30**	**4.19**	**4.10**	**4.02**	**3.96**	**3.86**	**3.78**	**3.66**	**3.59**	**3.51**	**3.43**	**3.38**	**3.31**	**3.27**	**3.22**	**3.19**	**3.17**

Denominator Degrees of Freedom (k_2)	Numerator Degrees of Freedon (k_1) 1	2	3	4	5	6	7	8	9	10	11	12	14	16	20	24	30	40	50	75	100	200	500	∞
14	4.60	3.74	3.34	3.11	2.96	2.85	2.76	2.70	2.65	2.60	2.57	2.53	2.48	2.44	2.39	2.35	2.31	2.27	2.24	2.21	2.19	2.16	2.14	2.13
	8.86	**6.51**	**5.56**	**5.04**	**4.69**	**4.46**	**4.28**	**4.14**	**4.03**	**3.94**	**3.86**	**3.80**	**3.70**	**3.62**	**3.51**	**3.43**	**3.35**	**3.27**	**3.22**	**3.15**	**3.11**	**3.06**	**3.03**	**3.00**
15	4.54	3.68	3.29	3.06	2.90	2.79	2.71	2.64	2.59	2.54	2.51	2.48	2.42	2.38	2.33	2.29	2.25	2.20	2.18	2.14	2.12	2.10	2.08	2.07
	8.68	**6.36**	**5.42**	**4.89**	**4.56**	**4.32**	**4.14**	**4.00**	**3.89**	**3.80**	**3.73**	**3.67**	**3.56**	**3.49**	**3.37**	**3.29**	**3.21**	**3.13**	**3.08**	**3.01**	**2.98**	**2.92**	**2.89**	**2.87**
16	4.49	3.63	3.24	3.01	2.85	2.74	2.66	2.59	2.54	2.49	2.46	2.42	2.37	2.33	2.28	2.24	2.19	2.15	2.12	2.09	2.07	2.04	2.02	2.01
	8.53	**6.23**	**5.29**	**4.77**	**4.44**	**4.20**	**4.03**	**3.89**	**3.78**	**3.69**	**3.62**	**3.55**	**3.45**	**3.37**	**3.26**	**3.18**	**3.10**	**3.02**	**2.97**	**2.90**	**2.86**	**2.81**	**2.78**	**2.75**
17	4.45	3.59	3.20	2.96	2.81	2.70	2.61	2.55	2.49	2.45	2.41	2.38	2.33	2.29	2.23	2.19	2.15	2.10	2.08	2.04	2.02	1.99	1.97	1.96
	8.40	**6.11**	**5.18**	**4.67**	**4.34**	**4.10**	**3.93**	**3.79**	**3.68**	**3.59**	**3.52**	**3.46**	**3.35**	**3.27**	**3.16**	**3.08**	**3.00**	**2.92**	**2.87**	**2.80**	**2.76**	**2.71**	**2.68**	**2.65**
18	4.41	3.55	3.16	2.93	2.77	2.66	2.58	2.51	2.46	2.41	2.37	2.34	2.29	2.25	2.19	2.15	2.11	2.06	2.04	2.00	1.98	1.95	1.93	1.92
	8.29	**6.01**	**5.09**	**4.58**	**4.25**	**4.01**	**3.84**	**3.71**	**3.60**	**3.51**	**3.43**	**3.37**	**3.27**	**3.19**	**3.08**	**3.00**	**2.92**	**2.84**	**2.78**	**2.71**	**2.68**	**2.62**	**2.59**	**2.57**
19	4.38	3.52	3.13	2.90	2.74	2.63	2.54	2.48	2.42	2.38	2.34	2.31	2.26	2.21	2.16	2.11	2.07	2.03	2.00	1.96	1.94	1.91	1.89	1.88
	8.18	**5.93**	**5.01**	**4.50**	**4.17**	**3.94**	**3.77**	**3.63**	**3.52**	**3.43**	**3.36**	**3.30**	**3.19**	**3.12**	**3.00**	**2.92**	**2.84**	**2.76**	**2.71**	**2.64**	**2.60**	**2.55**	**2.51**	**2.49**
20	4.35	3.49	3.10	2.87	2.71	2.60	2.51	2.45	2.39	2.35	2.31	2.28	2.22	2.18	2.12	2.08	2.04	1.99	1.97	1.93	1.91	1.88	1.86	1.84
	8.10	**5.85**	**4.94**	**4.43**	**4.10**	**3.87**	**3.70**	**3.56**	**3.46**	**3.37**	**3.29**	**3.23**	**3.13**	**3.05**	**2.94**	**2.86**	**2.78**	**2.69**	**2.64**	**2.57**	**2.54**	**2.48**	**2.44**	**2.42**
21	4.32	3.47	3.07	2.84	2.68	2.57	2.49	2.42	2.37	2.32	2.28	2.25	2.20	2.16	2.10	2.05	2.01	1.96	1.94	1.90	1.88	1.84	1.83	1.81
	8.02	**5.78**	**4.87**	**4.37**	**4.04**	**3.81**	**3.64**	**3.51**	**3.40**	**3.31**	**3.24**	**3.17**	**3.07**	**2.99**	**2.88**	**2.80**	**2.72**	**2.64**	**2.58**	**2.51**	**2.48**	**2.42**	**2.38**	**2.36**
22	4.30	3.44	3.05	2.82	2.66	2.55	2.46	2.40	2.34	2.30	2.26	2.23	2.17	2.13	2.07	2.03	1.98	1.94	1.91	1.87	1.85	1.82	1.80	1.78
	7.95	**5.72**	**4.82**	**4.31**	**3.99**	**3.76**	**3.59**	**3.45**	**3.35**	**3.26**	**3.18**	**3.12**	**3.02**	**2.94**	**2.83**	**2.75**	**2.67**	**2.58**	**2.53**	**2.46**	**2.42**	**2.36**	**2.33**	**2.31**
23	4.28	3.42	3.03	2.80	2.64	2.53	2.44	2.37	2.32	2.27	2.24	2.20	2.15	2.11	2.05	2.01	1.96	1.91	1.88	1.84	1.82	1.79	1.77	1.76
	7.88	**5.66**	**4.76**	**4.26**	**3.94**	**3.71**	**3.54**	**3.41**	**3.30**	**3.21**	**3.14**	**3.07**	**2.97**	**2.89**	**2.78**	**2.70**	**2.62**	**2.54**	**2.48**	**2.41**	**2.37**	**2.32**	**2.28**	**2.26**
24	4.26	3.40	3.01	2.78	2.62	2.51	2.42	2.36	2.30	2.25	2.22	2.18	2.13	2.09	2.03	1.98	1.94	1.89	1.86	1.82	1.80	1.77	1.75	1.73
	7.82	**5.61**	**4.72**	**4.22**	**3.90**	**3.67**	**3.50**	**3.36**	**3.26**	**3.17**	**3.09**	**3.03**	**2.93**	**2.85**	**2.74**	**2.66**	**2.58**	**2.49**	**2.44**	**2.37**	**2.33**	**2.27**	**2.24**	**2.21**
25	4.24	3.39	2.99	2.76	2.60	2.49	2.40	2.34	2.28	2.24	2.20	2.16	2.11	2.07	2.01	1.96	1.92	1.87	1.84	1.80	1.78	1.75	1.73	1.71
	7.77	**5.57**	**4.68**	**4.18**	**3.85**	**3.63**	**3.46**	**3.32**	**3.22**	**3.13**	**3.06**	**2.99**	**2.89**	**2.81**	**2.70**	**2.62**	**2.54**	**2.45**	**2.40**	**2.33**	**2.29**	**2.23**	**2.19**	**2.17**
26	4.23	3.37	2.98	2.74	2.59	2.47	2.39	2.32	2.27	2.22	2.18	2.15	2.09	2.05	1.99	1.95	1.90	1.85	1.82	1.78	1.76	1.73	1.71	1.69
	7.72	**5.53**	**4.64**	**4.14**	**3.82**	**3.59**	**3.42**	**3.29**	**3.18**	**3.09**	**3.02**	**2.96**	**2.86**	**2.78**	**2.66**	**2.58**	**2.50**	**2.42**	**2.36**	**2.29**	**2.25**	**2.19**	**2.16**	**2.13**

Denominator Degrees of Freedom (k_2)	Numerator Degrees of Freedon (k_1)																							
	1	2	3	4	5	6	7	8	9	10	11	12	14	16	20	24	30	40	50	75	100	200	500	∞
27	4.21	3.35	2.96	2.73	2.57	2.46	2.37	2.31	2.25	2.20	2.17	2.13	2.08	2.04	1.97	1.93	1.88	1.84	1.81	1.76	1.74	1.71	1.69	1.67
	7.68	**5.49**	**4.60**	**4.11**	**3.78**	**3.56**	**3.39**	**3.26**	**3.15**	**3.06**	**2.99**	**2.93**	**2.82**	**2.75**	**2.63**	**2.55**	**2.47**	**2.38**	**2.33**	**2.26**	**2.22**	**2.16**	**2.12**	**2.10**
28	4.20	3.34	2.95	2.71	2.56	2.45	2.36	2.29	2.24	2.19	2.15	2.12	2.06	2.02	1.96	1.91	1.87	1.82	1.79	1.75	1.73	1.69	1.67	1.65
	7.64	**5.45**	**4.57**	**4.07**	**3.75**	**3.53**	**3.36**	**3.23**	**3.12**	**3.03**	**2.96**	**2.90**	**2.79**	**2.72**	**2.60**	**2.52**	**2.44**	**2.35**	**2.30**	**2.23**	**2.19**	**2.13**	**2.09**	**2.06**
29	4.18	3.33	2.93	2.70	2.55	2.43	2.35	2.28	2.22	2.18	2.14	2.10	2.05	2.01	1.94	1.90	1.85	1.81	1.77	1.73	1.71	1.67	1.65	1.64
	7.60	**5.42**	**4.54**	**4.04**	**3.73**	**3.50**	**3.33**	**3.20**	**3.09**	**3.00**	**2.93**	**2.87**	**2.77**	**2.69**	**2.57**	**2.49**	**2.41**	**2.33**	**2.27**	**2.20**	**2.16**	**2.10**	**2.06**	**2.03**
30	4.17	3.32	2.92	2.69	2.53	2.42	2.33	2.27	2.21	2.16	2.13	2.09	2.04	1.99	1.93	1.89	1.84	1.79	1.76	1.72	1.70	1.66	1.64	1.62
	7.56	**5.39**	**4.51**	**4.02**	**3.70**	**3.47**	**3.30**	**3.17**	**3.07**	**2.98**	**2.91**	**2.84**	**2.74**	**2.66**	**2.55**	**2.47**	**2.39**	**2.30**	**2.25**	**2.17**	**2.13**	**2.07**	**2.03**	**2.01**
32	4.15	3.29	2.90	2.67	2.51	2.40	2.31	2.24	2.19	2.14	2.10	2.07	2.01	1.97	1.91	1.86	1.82	1.77	1.74	1.69	1.67	1.63	1.61	1.59
	7.50	**5.34**	**4.46**	**3.97**	**3.65**	**3.43**	**3.26**	**3.13**	**3.02**	**2.93**	**2.86**	**2.80**	**2.70**	**2.62**	**2.50**	**2.42**	**2.34**	**2.25**	**2.20**	**2.12**	**2.08**	**2.02**	**1.98**	**1.96**
34	4.13	3.28	2.88	2.65	2.49	2.38	2.29	2.23	2.17	2.12	2.08	2.05	1.99	1.95	1.89	1.84	1.80	1.75	1.71	1.67	1.65	1.61	1.59	1.57
	7.44	**5.29**	**4.42**	**3.93**	**3.61**	**3.39**	**3.22**	**3.09**	**2.98**	**2.89**	**2.82**	**2.76**	**2.66**	**2.58**	**2.46**	**2.38**	**2.30**	**2.21**	**2.16**	**2.08**	**2.04**	**1.98**	**1.94**	**1.91**
36	4.11	3.26	2.87	2.63	2.48	2.36	2.28	2.21	2.15	2.11	2.07	2.03	1.98	1.93	1.87	1.82	1.78	1.73	1.69	1.65	1.62	1.59	1.56	1.55
	7.40	**5.25**	**4.38**	**3.89**	**3.57**	**3.35**	**3.18**	**3.05**	**2.95**	**2.86**	**2.79**	**2.72**	**2.62**	**2.54**	**2.43**	**2.35**	**2.26**	**2.18**	**2.12**	**2.04**	**2.00**	**1.94**	**1.90**	**1.87**
38	4.10	3.24	2.85	2.62	2.46	2.35	2.26	2.19	2.14	2.09	2.05	2.02	1.96	1.92	1.85	1.81	1.76	1.71	1.68	1.63	1.61	1.57	1.54	1.53
	7.35	**5.21**	**4.34**	**3.86**	**3.54**	**3.32**	**3.15**	**3.02**	**2.92**	**2.83**	**2.75**	**2.69**	**2.59**	**2.51**	**2.40**	**2.32**	**2.23**	**2.14**	**2.09**	**2.01**	**1.97**	**1.90**	**1.86**	**1.84**
40	4.08	3.23	2.84	2.61	2.45	2.34	2.25	2.18	2.12	2.08	2.04	2.00	1.95	1.90	1.84	1.79	1.74	1.69	1.66	1.61	1.59	1.55	1.53	1.51
	7.31	**5.18**	**4.31**	**3.83**	**3.51**	**3.29**	**3.12**	**2.99**	**2.89**	**2.80**	**2.73**	**2.66**	**2.56**	**2.48**	**2.37**	**2.29**	**2.20**	**2.11**	**2.06**	**1.98**	**1.94**	**1.87**	**1.83**	**1.81**
42	4.07	3.22	2.83	2.59	2.44	2.32	2.24	2.17	2.11	2.06	2.03	1.99	1.94	1.89	1.83	1.78	1.73	1.68	1.65	1.60	1.57	1.53	1.51	1.49
	7.28	**5.15**	**4.29**	**3.80**	**3.49**	**3.27**	**3.10**	**2.97**	**2.86**	**2.78**	**2.70**	**2.64**	**2.54**	**2.46**	**2.34**	**2.26**	**2.18**	**2.09**	**2.03**	**1.95**	**1.91**	**1.85**	**1.80**	**1.78**
44	4.06	3.21	2.82	2.58	2.43	2.31	2.23	2.16	2.10	2.05	2.01	1.98	1.92	1.88	1.81	1.77	1.72	1.67	1.63	1.59	1.56	1.52	1.49	1.48
	7.25	**5.12**	**4.26**	**3.78**	**3.47**	**3.24**	**3.08**	**2.95**	**2.84**	**2.75**	**2.68**	**2.62**	**2.52**	**2.44**	**2.32**	**2.24**	**2.15**	**2.07**	**2.01**	**1.93**	**1.89**	**1.82**	**1.78**	**1.75**
46	4.05	3.20	2.81	2.57	2.42	2.30	2.22	2.15	2.09	2.04	2.00	1.97	1.91	1.87	1.80	1.76	1.71	1.65	1.62	1.57	1.55	1.51	1.48	1.46
	7.22	**5.10**	**4.24**	**3.76**	**3.44**	**3.22**	**3.06**	**2.93**	**2.82**	**2.73**	**2.66**	**2.60**	**2.50**	**2.42**	**2.30**	**2.22**	**2.13**	**2.04**	**1.99**	**1.91**	**1.86**	**1.80**	**1.76**	**1.73**
48	4.04	3.19	2.80	2.57	2.41	2.29	2.21	2.14	2.08	2.03	1.99	1.96	1.90	1.86	1.79	1.75	1.70	1.64	1.61	1.56	1.54	1.49	1.47	1.45
	7.19	**5.08**	**4.22**	**3.74**	**3.43**	**3.20**	**3.04**	**2.91**	**2.80**	**2.71**	**2.64**	**2.58**	**2.48**	**2.40**	**2.28**	**2.20**	**2.12**	**2.02**	**1.97**	**1.89**	**1.84**	**1.78**	**1.73**	**1.70**

Denominator Degrees of Freedom (k_2)	Numerator Degrees of Freedon (k_1)																							
	1	2	3	4	5	6	7	8	9	10	11	12	14	16	20	24	30	40	50	75	100	200	500	∞
50	4.03	3.18	2.79	2.56	2.40	2.29	2.20	2.13	2.07	2.03	1.99	1.95	1.89	1.85	1.78	1.74	1.69	1.63	1.60	1.55	1.52	1.48	1.46	1.44
	7.17	**5.06**	**4.20**	**3.72**	**3.41**	**3.19**	**3.02**	**2.89**	**2.78**	**2.70**	**2.63**	**2.56**	**2.46**	**2.38**	**2.27**	**2.18**	**2.10**	**2.01**	**1.95**	**1.87**	**1.82**	**1.76**	**1.71**	**1.68**
55	4.02	3.16	2.77	2.54	2.38	2.27	2.18	2.11	2.06	2.01	1.97	1.93	1.88	1.83	1.76	1.72	1.67	1.61	1.58	1.53	1.50	1.46	1.43	1.41
	7.12	**5.01**	**4.16**	**3.68**	**3.37**	**3.15**	**2.98**	**2.85**	**2.75**	**2.66**	**2.59**	**2.53**	**2.42**	**2.34**	**2.23**	**2.15**	**2.06**	**1.97**	**1.91**	**1.83**	**1.78**	**1.71**	**1.67**	**1.64**
60	4.00	3.15	2.76	2.53	2.37	2.25	2.17	2.10	2.04	1.99	1.95	1.92	1.86	1.82	1.75	1.70	1.65	1.59	1.56	1.51	1.48	1.44	1.41	1.39
	7.08	**4.98**	**4.13**	**3.65**	**3.34**	**3.12**	**2.95**	**2.82**	**2.72**	**2.63**	**2.56**	**2.50**	**2.39**	**2.31**	**2.20**	**2.12**	**2.03**	**1.94**	**1.88**	**1.79**	**1.75**	**1.68**	**1.63**	**1.60**
65	3.99	3.14	2.75	2.51	2.36	2.24	2.15	2.08	2.03	1.98	1.94	1.90	1.85	1.80	1.73	1.69	1.63	1.58	1.54	1.49	1.46	1.42	1.39	1.37
	7.04	**4.95**	**4.10**	**3.62**	**3.31**	**3.09**	**2.93**	**2.80**	**2.69**	**2.61**	**2.53**	**2.47**	**2.37**	**2.29**	**2.17**	**2.09**	**2.00**	**1.91**	**1.85**	**1.77**	**1.72**	**1.65**	**1.60**	**1.57**
70	3.98	3.13	2.74	2.50	2.35	2.23	2.14	2.07	2.02	1.97	1.93	1.89	1.84	1.79	1.72	1.67	1.62	1.57	1.53	1.48	1.45	1.40	1.37	1.35
	7.01	**4.92**	**4.07**	**3.60**	**3.29**	**3.07**	**2.91**	**2.78**	**2.67**	**2.59**	**2.51**	**2.45**	**2.35**	**2.27**	**2.15**	**2.07**	**1.98**	**1.89**	**1.83**	**1.74**	**1.70**	**1.62**	**1.57**	**1.54**
80	3.96	3.11	2.72	2.49	2.33	2.21	2.13	2.06	2.00	1.95	1.91	1.88	1.82	1.77	1.70	1.65	1.60	1.54	1.51	1.45	1.43	1.38	1.35	1.33
	6.96	**4.88**	**4.04**	**3.56**	**3.26**	**3.04**	**2.87**	**2.74**	**2.64**	**2.55**	**2.48**	**2.42**	**2.31**	**2.23**	**2.12**	**2.03**	**1.94**	**1.85**	**1.79**	**1.70**	**1.65**	**1.58**	**1.53**	**1.50**
100	3.94	3.09	2.70	2.46	2.31	2.19	2.10	2.03	1.97	1.93	1.89	1.85	1.79	1.75	1.68	1.63	1.57	1.52	1.48	1.42	1.39	1.34	1.31	1.28
	6.90	**4.82**	**3.98**	**3.51**	**3.21**	**2.99**	**2.82**	**2.69**	**2.59**	**2.50**	**2.43**	**2.37**	**2.27**	**2.19**	**2.07**	**1.98**	**1.89**	**1.80**	**1.74**	**1.65**	**1.60**	**1.52**	**1.47**	**1.43**
125	3.92	3.07	2.68	2.44	2.29	2.17	2.08	2.01	1.96	1.91	1.87	1.83	1.77	1.73	1.66	1.60	1.55	1.49	1.45	1.40	1.36	1.31	1.27	1.25
	6.84	**4.78**	**3.94**	**3.47**	**3.17**	**2.95**	**2.79**	**2.66**	**2.55**	**2.47**	**2.39**	**2.33**	**2.23**	**2.15**	**2.03**	**1.94**	**1.85**	**1.76**	**1.69**	**1.60**	**1.55**	**1.47**	**1.41**	**1.37**
150	3.90	3.06	2.66	2.43	2.27	2.16	2.07	2.00	1.94	1.89	1.85	1.82	1.76	1.71	1.64	1.59	1.54	1.48	1.44	1.38	1.34	1.29	1.25	1.22
	6.81	**4.75**	**3.91**	**3.45**	**3.14**	**2.92**	**2.76**	**2.63**	**2.53**	**2.44**	**2.37**	**2.31**	**2.20**	**2.12**	**2.00**	**1.92**	**1.83**	**1.73**	**1.66**	**1.57**	**1.52**	**1.43**	**1.38**	**1.33**
200	3.89	3.04	2.65	2.42	2.26	2.14	2.06	1.98	1.93	1.88	1.84	1.80	1.74	1.69	1.62	1.57	1.52	1.46	1.41	1.35	1.32	1.26	1.22	1.19
	6.76	**4.71**	**3.88**	**3.41**	**3.11**	**2.89**	**2.73**	**2.60**	**2.50**	**2.41**	**2.34**	**2.27**	**2.17**	**2.09**	**1.97**	**1.89**	**1.79**	**1.69**	**1.63**	**1.53**	**1.48**	**1.39**	**1.33**	**1.28**
400	3.86	3.02	2.63	2.39	2.24	2.12	2.03	1.96	1.90	1.85	1.81	1.78	1.72	1.67	1.60	1.54	1.49	1.42	1.38	1.32	1.28	1.22	1.17	1.13
	6.70	**4.66**	**3.83**	**3.37**	**3.06**	**2.85**	**2.68**	**2.56**	**2.45**	**2.37**	**2.29**	**2.23**	**2.13**	**2.05**	**1.92**	**1.84**	**1.75**	**1.64**	**1.58**	**1.48**	**1.42**	**1.32**	**1.25**	**1.19**
1000	3.85	3.00	2.61	2.38	2.22	2.11	2.02	1.95	1.89	1.84	1.80	1.76	1.70	1.65	1.58	1.53	1.47	1.41	1.36	1.30	1.26	1.19	1.13	1.08
	6.66	**4.63**	**3.80**	**3.34**	**3.04**	**2.82**	**2.66**	**2.53**	**2.43**	**2.34**	**2.27**	**2.20**	**2.10**	**2.02**	**1.90**	**1.81**	**1.72**	**1.61**	**1.54**	**1.44**	**1.38**	**1.28**	**1.19**	**1.12**
∞	3.84	3.00	2.60	2.37	2.21	2.10	2.01	1.94	1.88	1.83	1.79	1.75	1.69	1.64	1.57	1.52	1.46	1.39	1.35	1.28	1.24	1.17	1.11	1.00
	6.63	**4.61**	**3.78**	**3.32**	**3.02**	**2.80**	**2.64**	**2.51**	**2.41**	**2.32**	**2.25**	**2.18**	**2.08**	**2.00**	**1.88**	**1.79**	**1.70**	**1.59**	**1.52**	**1.42**	**1.36**	**1.25**	**1.18**	**1.00**

TABLE E.10 Critical Values of the Durbin-Watson Test Statistic for $\alpha = 0.05$

	$k = 1$		$k = 2$		$k = 3$		$k = 4$		$k = 5$	
n	d_L	d_U	d_L	d_U	d_L	d_U	d_L	d_U	d_L	d_U
15	0.81	1.07	0.70	1.25	0.59	1.46	0.49	1.70	0.39	1.96
16	0.84	1.09	0.74	1.25	0.63	1.44	0.53	1.66	0.44	1.90
17	0.87	1.10	0.77	1.25	0.67	1.43	0.57	1.63	0.48	1.85
18	0.90	1.12	0.80	1.26	0.71	1.42	0.61	1.60	0.52	1.80
19	0.93	1.13	0.83	1.26	0.74	1.41	0.65	1.58	0.56	1.77
20	0.95	1.15	0.86	1.27	0.77	1.41	0.68	1.57	0.60	1.74
21	0.97	1.16	0.89	1.27	0.80	1.41	0.72	1.55	0.63	1.71
22	1.00	1.17	0.91	1.28	0.83	1.40	0.75	1.54	0.66	1.69
23	1.02	1.19	0.94	1.29	0.86	1.40	0.77	1.53	0.70	1.67
24	1.05	1.20	0.96	1.30	0.88	1.41	0.80	1.53	0.72	1.66
25	1.05	1.21	0.98	1.30	0.90	1.41	0.83	1.52	0.75	1.65
26	1.07	1.22	1.00	1.31	0.93	1.41	0.85	1.52	0.78	1.64
27	1.09	1.23	1.02	1.32	0.95	1.41	0.88	1.51	0.81	1.63
28	1.10	1.24	1.04	1.32	0.97	1.41	0.90	1.51	0.83	1.62
29	1.12	1.25	1.05	1.33	0.99	1.42	0.92	1.51	0.85	1.61
30	1.13	1.26	1.07	1.34	1.01	1.42	0.94	1.51	0.88	1.61
31	1.15	1.27	1.08	1.34	1.02	1.42	0.96	1.51	0.90	1.60
32	1.16	1.28	1.10	1.35	1.04	1.43	0.98	1.51	0.92	1.60
33	1.17	1.29	1.11	1.36	1.05	1.43	1.00	1.51	0.94	1.59
34	1.18	1.30	1.13	1.36	1.07	1.43	1.01	1.51	0.95	1.59
35	1.19	1.31	1.14	1.37	1.08	1.44	1.03	1.51	0.97	1.59
36	1.21	1.32	1.15	1.38	1.10	1.44	1.04	1.51	0.99	1.59
37	1.22	1.32	1.16	1.38	1.11	1.45	1.06	1.51	1.00	1.59
38	1.23	1.33	1.18	1.39	1.12	1.45	1.07	1.52	1.02	1.58
39	1.24	1.34	1.19	1.39	1.14	1.45	1.09	1.52	1.03	1.58
40	1.25	1.34	1.20	1.40	1.15	1.46	1.10	1.52	1.05	1.58
45	1.29	1.38	1.24	1.42	1.20	1.48	1.16	1.53	1.11	1.58
50	1.32	1.40	1.28	1.45	1.24	1.49	1.20	1.54	1.16	1.59
55	1.36	1.43	1.32	1.47	1.28	1.51	1.25	1.55	1.21	1.59
60	1.38	1.45	1.35	1.48	1.32	1.52	1.28	1.56	1.25	1.60
65	1.41	1.47	1.38	1.50	1.35	1.53	1.31	1.57	1.28	1.61
70	1.43	1.49	1.40	1.52	1.37	1.55	1.34	1.58	1.31	1.61
75	1.45	1.50	1.42	1.53	1.39	1.56	1.37	1.59	1.34	1.62
80	1.47	1.52	1.44	1.54	1.42	1.57	1.39	1.60	1.36	1.62
85	1.48	1.53	1.46	1.55	1.43	1.58	1.41	1.60	1.39	1.63
90	1.50	1.54	1.47	1.56	1.45	1.59	1.43	1.61	1.41	1.64
95	1.51	1.55	1.49	1.57	1.47	1.60	1.45	1.62	1.42	1.64
100	1.52	1.56	1.50	1.58	1.48	1.60	1.46	1.63	1.44	1.65

TABLE E.10 Critical Values of the Durbin-Watson Test Statistic for $\alpha = 0.01$

	$k = 1$		$k = 2$		$k = 3$		$k = 4$		$k = 5$	
n	d_L	d_U	d_L	d_U	d_L	d_U	d_L	d_U	d_L	d_U
15	1.08	1.36	0.95	1.54	0.82	1.75	0.69	1.97	0.56	2.21
16	1.10	1.37	0.98	1.54	0.86	1.73	0.74	1.93	0.62	2.15
17	1.13	1.38	1.02	1.54	0.90	1.71	0.78	1.90	0.67	2.10
18	1.16	1.39	1.05	1.53	0.93	1.69	0.82	1.87	0.71	2.06
19	1.18	1.40	1.08	1.53	0.97	1.68	0.86	1.85	0.75	2.02
20	1.20	1.41	1.10	1.54	1.00	1.68	0.90	1.83	0.79	1.99
21	1.22	1.42	1.13	1.54	1.03	1.67	0.93	1.81	0.83	1.96
22	1.24	1.43	1.15	1.54	1.05	1.66	0.96	1.80	0.86	1.94
23	1.26	1.44	1.17	1.54	1.08	1.66	0.99	1.79	0.90	1.92
24	1.27	1.45	1.19	1.55	1.10	1.66	1.01	1.78	0.93	1.90
25	1.29	1.45	1.21	1.55	1.12	1.66	1.04	1.77	0.95	1.89
26	1.30	1.46	1.22	1.55	1.14	1.65	1.06	1.76	0.98	1.88
27	1.32	1.47	1.24	1.56	1.16	1.65	1.08	1.76	1.01	1.86
28	1.33	1.48	1.26	1.56	1.18	1.65	1.10	1.75	1.03	1.85
29	1.34	1.48	1.27	1.56	1.20	1.65	1.12	1.74	1.05	1.84
30	1.35	1.49	1.28	1.57	1.21	1.65	1.14	1.74	1.07	1.83
31	1.36	1.50	1.30	1.57	1.23	1.65	1.16	1.74	1.09	1.83
32	1.37	1.50	1.31	1.57	1.24	1.65	1.18	1.73	1.11	1.82
33	1.38	1.51	1.32	1.58	1.26	1.65	1.19	1.73	1.13	1.81
34	1.39	1.51	1.33	1.58	1.27	1.65	1.21	1.73	1.15	1.81
35	1.40	1.52	1.34	1.58	1.28	1.65	1.22	1.73	1.16	1.80
36	1.41	1.52	1.35	1.59	1.29	1.65	1.24	1.73	1.18	1.80
37	1.42	1.53	1.36	1.59	1.31	1.66	1.25	1.72	1.19	1.80
38	1.43	1.54	1.37	1.59	1.32	1.66	1.26	1.72	1.21	1.79
39	1.43	1.54	1.38	1.60	1.33	1.66	1.27	1.72	1.22	1.79
40	1.44	1.54	1.39	1.60	1.34	1.66	1.29	1.72	1.23	1.79
45	1.48	1.57	1.43	1.62	1.38	1.67	1.34	1.72	1.29	1.78
50	1.50	1.59	1.46	1.63	1.42	1.67	1.38	1.72	1.34	1.77
55	1.53	1.60	1.49	1.64	1.45	1.68	1.41	1.72	1.38	1.77
60	1.55	1.62	1.51	1.65	1.48	1.69	1.44	1.73	1.41	1.77
65	1.57	1.63	1.54	1.66	1.50	1.70	1.47	1.73	1.44	1.77
70	1.58	1.64	1.55	1.67	1.52	1.70	1.49	1.74	1.46	1.77
75	1.60	1.65	1.57	1.68	1.54	1.71	1.51	1.74	1.49	1.77
80	1.61	1.66	1.59	1.69	1.56	1.72	1.53	1.74	1.51	1.77
85	1.62	1.67	1.60	1.70	1.57	1.72	1.55	1.75	1.52	1.77
90	1.63	1.68	1.61	1.70	1.59	1.73	1.57	1.75	1.54	1.78
95	1.64	1.69	1.62	1.71	1.60	1.73	1.58	1.75	1.56	1.78
100	1.65	1.69	1.63	1.72	1.61	1.74	1.59	1.76	1.57	1.78

Source: Reproduced by permission from J. Durbin and G. S. Watson, "Testing for Serial Correlation in Least Squares Regression, II," *Biometrika* 38 (1951), pp. 159–78, as found in Amir D. Aczel, *Complete Business Statistics* (Homewood, Ill.: Richard D. Irwin, 1989), pp. 1036–37.

INDEX

Academy of Management Review, 558
A. C. Nielsen, 23
Accountancy, 93
Accounting Review, 256
Adaptive filtering, 783
Addition rule, 133–36, 172
Additive model, 788–91
Aggregate index, 709
Allen, Fred, 702
Alternative, 855
Alternative hypothesis, 292, 295–96, 521
American Demographics, 2, 135, 384
American Statistician, 162
American Statistics Index, 23
Annals of Surgery, 274
Analysis of variance, 421–66
  application to the business world, 450
  between method, 427, 430–32, 434, 435, 436, 443, 451
    degrees of freedom for, 432
  using the chi square statistic in, 422–23, 451
  and computers, 449–50
  dependent variable role in, 427, 449, 429
  experimental designs, 449
  F ratio, 433, 443, 444, 451
  F statistic, 424, 595
  importance to managers, 421
  interaction, 441–42, 452
  key assumption, 427
  and mean square error, 429
  one way, 421–38
  and quality control applications, 523
  randomized block designs, 449
  single-population variance test, 421–23
  sum of squares between, 431
  sum of squares within, 428
  table, 433–34, 451
    regression, 588
  two population variance test, 424–25
  two-way analysis of variance, 439–446
  within method, 427, 428–30, 433, 435, 436, 443, 444, 445, 450, 451
    degrees of freedom for, 429
ARIMA models, 821–23
Aristotle, 14
Arithmetic mean, 90–93, 114, 115
  advantages and disadvantages of using, 93, 96
  characteristics of, 92
  population formula, 91, 116, 224
  sample formula, 91, 116
Arts Magazine, 780
Assignable causes, 473, 530
The Atlantic Monthly, 269
Autocorrelation, 792–95, 796, 801, 803–4, 808–14, 828
  coefficient, 802
  correlogram, 795, 800, 828
  hypothesis test, 798
  stationary series, 799

The Banker, 293
Bar chart, 61–63, 76
Barron's Magazine, 61
Bayes theorem, 866–70
  revised, 866
Between method, 427, 430–32, 434, 435, 436, 443, 451
Binomial distribution, 146–57, 171, 172, 233; *see also* Poisson distribution, approximation to the binomial
  application to business, 171
  essential characteristics of, 147
  formula, 173
  mean of, 156, 173
  standard deviation of, 156, 173
  testing, 314
Binomial table, 152–54, 171
Blake, W, 220
Box, George, 821
Box-Jenkins, 799, 821–23, 827, 828
Business Conditions Digest, 23
Business forecasting, 773–828
  Box-Jenkins Models, 799, 821–23, 827, 828
    autoregressive/moving average models (ARIMA), 821–23
      application to the business world, 828
    differencing, 799
    stationary versus non-stationary series, 799
Business forecasting—*Cont.*
  choosing a model, 774–75
  forecast error measurement, 775, 828
  importance to managers, 774
  mean absolute deviation (MAD), 775, 777, 828
  mean absolute percentage error (MAPE), 776, 777, 829
  mean squared error (MSE), 775–76, 777, 829
Business forecasting methods, 777–828
  autoregressive/moving average models (ARIMA), 821–23
    application to the business world, 828
  Box-Jenkins Models, 799, 821–23, 827, 828
    autoregressive/moving average models (ARIMA), 821–23
      application to the business world, 828
    differencing, 799
    stationary versus non-stationary series, 799
  decomposition method, 747–48, 752
    application to the business world, 827
  exponential smoothing, 779–83, 828, 829
    adaptive filtering, 783
    application to the business world, 828
    trend modifications, 782–83
    trend and seasonal modifications, 783
  moving average, 778–79, 826, 828, 829
    application to the business world, 828
  naive methods, 777–78, 826, 828, 829
    application to the business world, 827
  regression analysis, 787–, 823 , 826
    additive model, 788–91
    application to the business world, 827
    autocorrelation, 792–95, 801, 803–4, 808–14, 828
      correlogram for, 795, 800,828
      hypothesis test for, 798
      serial correlation, 808–28
        detection of, 811–14
        differences, 814
        Durbin-Watson Test for, 811–14, 828, 830

Business forecasting methods—*Cont.*
regression analysis—*Cont.*
autocorrelation—*Cont.*
serial correlation—*Cont.*
problems with, 810
solutions for, 814
autoregressive model, 814, 815–26, 828
iterative approach, 814–15
application to the business world, 828
econometric model, 787–88
multiplicative model, 719, 733
Business Month, 221,
Business Monthly, 639
Business Periodicals Index, 23
Business Week, 468
Byron, John, 420

Calculated average; *see* Mean
Carroll, Lewis, 48
Categorical data, 17, 349, 405
C chart, 514–18, 524, 530, 531
steps in constructing, 515
Census, 26–27, 41
Central limit theorem, 226–27, 244, 171, 199, 430
Central tendency, 90–103, 114
Cervantes, 550
Chance causes, 473, 530
Changing base period, 716–17, 751
Charts and graphs, 60–69
bar chart, 61–63, 76
control charts, 481–83, 485–518, 524, 530
frequency polygon, 66, 76
histogram, 64–65, 76
ogive, 66, 76
less-than-ogive, 66
more-than-ogive, 67
Pareto chart, 63–64, 76
pie chart, 60–61, 76
scatter diagrams, 551–54, 563, 596
stem-and-leaf plot, 65–66, 76
time series graph, 68–69, 76
Chebyshev's theorem, 111, 203
Chi square tests, 383–406, 890
contingency table test, 384–86, 403, 405, 406, 890
application to the business world, 405–6, 523
degrees of freedom
contingency table test, 391–92, 407
goodness-of-fit test, 395, 407
difference between the contingency table and goodness-of-fit test, 394
expected frequencies, 386–91, 403, 406
goodness-of-fit test, 394–400, 403, 405, 406, 890
Chi square tests—*Cont.*
goodness-of-fit test—*Cont.*
application to the business world, 406, 524
importance to managers, 384
rule of five, 398–400
Chi square statistic, 387–92, 406
CIS/Index to Publications of the U.S. Government, 23
Classical probability, 131
Coefficient of simple determination, 579–84
Coefficient of variation, 109–10, 114, 116
Collectively exhaustive, 132, 172
Combination, 148–49, 172
formula for, 148, 173
Complement, 132, 172
Composite index, 713
Compuserve, 22
Computerized Business Statistics (CBS), 5, 6
computer output examples, 5, 6, 10, 46, 85, 126–27, 182–83, 218, 252, 287, 341–42, 380–81, 416–17, 462–63, 609–11, 696–98, 769–70, 849, 887–88, 918
Computers and statistics, 3
Constant data, 15, 41
Consumer price index, 710–11, 754
Contemporary Advertising, 93
Contingency table test, 384–86, 403, 405, 406, 890
application to the business world, 405–6, 523
Continuity correction factor, 206
Continuous probability distributions, 186–210; *see also* Normal distribution
importance to managers, 186
Continuous random variables, 139, 186, 210
Correlation analysis, 551–59, 595
versus causation, 559
dependent variable, 562
hypothesis testing, 556–59
independent variable; *see* Independent variable
predictor variable, 562
t test statistic for, 558
Correlation and regression analysis, 550–97
application to the business world, 551, 596
correlation coefficient, 554–56, 596, 614
correlation coefficient estimation, 557–59
F test, 589–92
importance to managers, 551
linear equations, 562–63
linear relationships, 556–59
Pearson product-moment correlation coefficient, 555
scatter diagrams, 551–54, 563, 596
Correlation coefficient, 554–56, 596, 614
Correlation matrix, 615, 674
Correlogram, 795, 800,828
Counting average; *see* Median
County and City Data Book, 23
Cross-classification table, 384; *see also* Chi square tests, contingency table test
Crosstabs; *see* Cross-classification table
Cumulative frequency distributions, 57–58, 76
defined, 57, 76
Cyclical indicators, 731–32
Cyclical trends; *see* Time series analysis, cyclical component

Data, 2, 15–21
categorical, 17, 394, 405
constant, 15
grouped, 112
hierarchy, 16
interval, 16, 18–19, 49
nominal, 16, 18–19, 20, 49, 60, 384, 890
ordinal, 16, 17–18, 20, 23, 49, 60, 384, 890
primary, 22, 40–41
qualitative, 15, 16–18, 20, 23, 49, 90, 405
quantitative, 15, 17–22, 49
ratio, 16, 19–22, 49
ratio scaled, 16
raw, 111–12
secondary, 22–23, 41
advantages and disadvantages of, 23
defined, 22
sources of, 22, 23
types, 15–22
variable, 15
Data file construction, 37–38
Data gathering techniques, 24–26
application to the business world, 39–41
door-to-door, 25
experiments, 25–26
focus groups, 24
importance to managers
interviews, 25
mail questionnaires, 24–25
observation, 25
registrations, 25
telephone, 24
Data presentation, 49–76
application to the business world, 74–76
importance to managers, 49
possible techniques, 75–76
Deciles, 111
Decision making, 855–75
alternative, 855
application to the business world, 874–75
Bayes theorem, 866–70, 875

Decision making—*Cont.*
  criteria, 855
  expected monetary value, 857–59, 873, 875
  expected value of perfect information, 861, 875
  importance to managers, 855
  payoff table, 855–56, 873, 875
  state of nature, 855
  tree diagrams, 855–57, 862–66, 873, 875
  utility theory, 870–72, 874, 875
Decision rules and hypothesis testing, 300–301, 303, 331
Decomposition; *see* Time series analysis, decomposition of
Degrees of freedom, 106–7, 116
  contingency table test, 391–92, 407
  F distribution, 424
  goodness-of-fit test, 395, 407
  for regression, 588, 590
  sum of squares error, 382
Deming, W. Edwards, 469
Dependent variable
  ANOVA, 427, 449, 429
  correlation analysis, 562
Descriptive statistics, 89–128
  application to the business world, 114–15
  importance to managers, 90
Deterministic model; *see* Functional model
Differencing, 799
Discrete probability distributions, 130–57
  importance to managers, 130
Discrete random variable, 138–39, 172
  expected value formula for, 173
  variance formula for, 173
Disraeli, B., 1
Distribution, 50, 76
Dollars and Sense, 424
Dow Jones News Retrieval Service, 22
Dryden, J., 254
Dummy variable, 653–56

Econometric model, 787–88
Economic Report of the President, 23
Educational and Psychological Measurement, 202, 202n
Einstein, Albert, 773
Empirical rule, 111, 198
Estimated standard error of the difference, 346–370
Estimation, 254–79
  application to the business world, 278
  confidence coefficient, 256
  difference between estimation and hypothesis testing, 290–91
  importance to managers, 255
Estimation—*Cont.*
  interval estimate, 256–88
    of population mean, 257
    of population proportion, 263–66
  point estimate, 255–56
  sample size and estimation error, 271–77
    and sample means, 271–74
    and proportions, 274–75
  small samples, 266–71
    estimation for means, 266
    and estimation for population proportions, 266
Events, 131, 138
  defined, 131, 172
  dependent, 134, 135
  independent, 134, 135
Expected monetary value, 857–59
Expected value, 143–44, 172, 857
  application to the business world, 171
  of a discrete random variable, formula for, 173
Expected value of perfect information, 861, 875
Experiment, 131, 138, 172, 449; *see also* Analysis of variance, experimental designs; Data gathering techniques, experiments
Exponential smoothing, 779–83, 828, 829
  adaptive filtering, 783
  application to the business world, 828
  trend modifications, 782–83
  trend and seasonal modifications, 783
Extended exercises
  Ace Custom Racing Tires, 180–81
  Amsbury Glass Showers, 83
  Babbet Electronics, 413–14
  Best Buy Stores, 46–61
  Brice Company, 378–79
  Business Activity Index, 846–48
  CEA Pension Fund, 285
  Cherry Lane Apple Orchard, 339
  Clinton Lawn Mowers, 546–48
  Cone Lumber Company, 768–69
  Consumers Automobile Insurance, 461–62
  Curtis Myers Company, 461
  Deer Park Credit Union, 44
  Eureka Dairy, 217–18
  The Fair Coin, 916–17
  Gady Electronics, 25–52
  Garry Products Incorporated, 767–68
  GMAT Scores for City University, 217
  Hyrum Brewery, 848–49
  Infrastructure Problems, 181–82
  IRS Refunds, 215–16
  Kane's Chemicals, 83
  Marshall Dry Goods Company, 884
  Median Family Income, 690–96
  Metropolitan Holding Company, 45
Extended exercises—*Cont.*
  Milgard Aluminum, 339–40
  Moorehouse Dry Goods
  Murford Electronics, 607
  Murphy Brothers, 884–86
  Murphy Transport, 688–89
  Olympic Manufacturing, 379–80
  Our Lady of Lourdes Hospital, 125, 252, 286–87, 340–41
  Park and Fly Car Rental, 286
  Pierone's Clothing Company, 124
  Platen Printing, 608–9
  Ranch Life Insurance Company of Florida, 216
  Rich Health Products, 338–39
  Sales Motivation Program, 917–18
  Second Avenue Car Stereos, 124–25
  Shelty Oil Company, 414
  Shives Investment Seminar, 608
  Silos Electronics, 689–90
  Southern Hawaiian University, 690
  Specific Electric, 216–17
  Spokane Indian Tribe Feasibility Study, 45
  Tenth Key Mail Orders, 284–85
  Valley Electronics, 544–45
  Valley Electronics II, 545
  Valley Hospital, 414–15
  Whitfield University Basketball, 285–86, 340
  Wickland Corporation, 249–50
  Wilco Vacuum Center, 84
  Wordan Wine Bottling, 123–24

Factorial; *see* Combination
F distribution, 424, 433
Federal Reserve Bulletin, 23
Feigenbaum, A. V., 469
Field and Stream, 890
Financial Executive, 90
Financial World, 551
Finite population multiplier, 239–43, 244, 245, 258
Focus groups; *see* Data gathering techniques, focus groups
Forecast error measurement, 775, 828
Fortune, 35, 164
Fortune Service, 35
Fourth Generation Management, 472
F ratio, 433, 443, 444, 451
Free China Review, 316
Frequency distributions, 19, 49–60, 74, 76
  cumulative frequency distribution, 57–58
  relative frequencies, 53–54
  steps in constructing, 51–52
Frequency polygon, 66, 76
F statistic, 424, 595
F test, 589–92

Functional model, 563–64, 596
Functional relationship, 563, 564
The Futurist, 869

Galton, Francis, 559
Gaussian curve; *see* Normal distribution
Giles, W. H., F. DeStefano, 291n
Gitlow, Gitlow, Oppenheim, 470
Glaub, V. E., and R. W. Kamphaus, 202n
Gompertz curve (logistic growth curve), 650, 675, 724
Goodness-of-fit test, 394–400, 403, 405, 406, 890
  application to the business world, 406, 524
Grosvenor, C. H., 89

Handbook of Labor Statistics, 23
Histogram, 64–65, 76
  check on normality, 669
Holt's two parameter linear exponential smoothing, 783
How to Lie with Statistics, 69, 69n
HR Focus, 515
Hsun-Tzu, 854
Huff, Darrell, 69n
Hypergeometric distribution, 158–60, 171, 172, 173, 239–40
Hypothesis testing, 290–331, 343–70
  alternative hypothesis, 292, 295–96, 330, 344, 385, 521
  application to the business world, 369–70,
  defined, 290, 330
  decision rule for, 300–1, 303, 331
  difference between estimation and hypothesis testing, 290–91
  errors in, 297–99
  importance to managers, 290
  level of significance, 299, 300, 328–29, 331
    normal distribution, 192–209, 210
  null hypothesis, 292, 294, 330, 344, 385, 421, 427, 521, 557
  one-tailed test, 295–96, 330
  pooled estimate of the variance, 354, 370
  about a population mean, 302, 305, 310–13
    for large samples, 302–310, 344–51
    for small samples, 310–14, 353–56
  about population proportion, 314–19
  possible outcomes, 298
  p values, 305–8, 331, 351, 437
  regression, 586–92
  sample size computation, 326–27
  steps and procedures, 292, 302, 368

Hypothesis testing—*Cont.*
  of two populations, 343–67
    application to the business world
    for dependent samples, 358–60
      matched pairs, 358–60, 370, 371
    importance to managers, 344
    for large samples, 343–51
    pooled estimate for population proportions, 366–67, 371
    for proportions, 363–67
    for small samples, 353–56
      t test statistic for, 354, 371
    standard error of the difference between population means, 346–47, 370, 371
      estimated, 346, 370
    Z test statistic for, 347, 370
  two-tailed test, 295–96, 330
  type I error, 297–99, 305, 320, 326, 328, 331, 520, 523
  type II error, 297–98, 320–24, 326, 328, 329, 331, 520, 523
    operating characteristic curve, 323–24, 331, 523
    power curve, 323–24, 331, 523

Independence, 134, 172
Independence of classification test; *see* Contingency table test
Independent variable, 562, 614, 774, 787
  selection of, 614–20
Indices
  aggregate index, 709
  application to the business world, 751
  changing base period, 716–17, 751
  composite index, 713
  Consumer Price Index, 710–11, 754
  price index, 706–7, 751, 754
  quantity index, 707–9, 754
  simple index, 709–10
  value index, 709, 754
Index numbers, 704–5, 754
  constructing an index, 705–6
  importance to managers, 704, 705, 706
  and time series, 714
Industrial Computstat Data File, 810
Industry Surveys, 94
Interaction, 441–42, 452
Interval estimate, 256–88
  of the population mean, 257–63, 279
    small samples, population standard deviation unknown, 267
  of the population proportions, 263–66, 279
  for sample mean, 279
    population standard deviation known, 258, 279

Interval estimate—*Cont.*
  for sample mean—*Cont.*
    population standard deviation unknown, 267–68, 279
    for small sample means, 267, 179
Interval scale, 18–19, 41
Interval scaled data, 16, 18–19, 49
  and ANOVA, 427
  chart presentation of, 64–65
  correlation and regression, 551
Interviews; *see* Data gathering techniques, interviews

Jenkins, Gwilym, 821
Joint Distribution of Serial Correlation Coefficients, 797n
Jones, D. H., 291n
Journal of the American Medical Association, 291
Journal of Marketing Research, 303, 442, 448, 810
Juran, Joseph, 469, 470

Less-than-ogive, 66
Level of significance, 299, 300, 328–29, 331
Linear relationship
  correlation and regression, 556–59
  functional model, 563–64, 596
Logistic Growth Curve (Gompertz Curve), 650, 675, 724

Malcolm Baldrige National Quality Award, 471–72
Management Accounting, 398, 488, 573
Management by process, 469, 470–71
Mann-Whitney U Test, 898–901, 905, 906
  Z value for, 901–7
Market Facts, Incorporated, 23
Market Research Corporation of America, 23
Matched pairs, 358–60; *see also* Hypothesis testing
Maximum tolerable error, 271–74, 279
  mean, 271–74
  proportion, 274–75
Mean, 19, 90–93, 114, 115
  characteristics of, 94
  defined, 94
  disadvantages of using, 93, 96, 100
  of a population, 91
  of a sample, 91
Mean absolute deviation (MAD), 775, 777, 828
Mean absolute percentage error (MAPE), 776, 777, 829

Mean squared error (MSE), 775–76, 777, 829
Measures of position, 110–12
Measures of variability, 104–10
Median, 93–95, 114, 115, 116
  characteristics of, 94
  defined, 94
  disadvantages of using, 100
  formula for median item number, 94, 116
Method of least squares, 566–67, 597, 622, 721
Minitab, 5, 6, 10–11, 30
  computer output examples, 11, 30, 31, 47, 69, 86–87, 108, 127–28, 153, 154, 164, 165, 169, 183–84, 190, 203, 218–19, 252–53, 260, 269, 288, 307, 313, 342, 381–82, 389–90, 417–18, 436–37, 463–64, 490, 491, 492–95, 496, 503, 511, 516, 517, 518, 549, 552–53, 556, 568–69, 611, 625, 634, 640, 646, 648, 649, 661, 662, 666, 667, 669, 694–96, 698–701, 722–23, 730, 771–72, 790, 796, 799–80, 818, 818–19, 820–21, 850–51, 904, 919–20
Mode, 95–96, 114, 115
  characteristics of, 96
  defined, 95
  disadvantages of using, 96, 100
Model building and regression analysis, 644–56
More-than-ogive, 67
Multicollinearity, 616, 620–21, 640, 672, 674
Multiple regression
  application to the business world, 673
  assumptions, 649
  asymptotic regression curve, 651, 675
  coefficient of multiple determination, 631
  correlation coefficient, 614
  curvilinear models, 644–50
  dummy variable, 653–56
  equation, 622
  estimated regression coefficient, 623–24, 674
  exponential model, 650, 675
  and hypothesis testing, 630–40
  model building, 644, 674
  multicollinearity, 616, 620–21, 640
  nonlinear models, 650–51
  qualitative variables in, 652–56
  point estimate, 624, 627
  polynomial regression model, 644, 674
    outlier, 671, 672
  prediction and confidence intervals, 627, 674
  quadratic model, 649, 675
  regression test, 633, 634
Multiple regression—*Cont.*
  residual analysis, 665
  residual plot, 666–68
  second order model, 645, 674
  selecting predictor (independent) variables, 614–630
  versus simple regression, 562
  standard error of the estimate, 626–27, 674
  stepwise regression, 659–64, 674
    problems with, 664
  third order model, 645, 675
  t values in, 632
Multiplication rule, 134–36, 172
Multiplicative model, 719, 733, 788
Mutually exclusive, 16, 17, 41, 132, 172

Naive method of business forecasting, 777–78, 826, 828, 829
  application to the business world, 827
NBER short list, 732
Newsweek, 530
New York Times, 130, 890
Nominal data, 16, 18–19, 20, 49, 60, 384, 890
Nominal scale, 16, 17, 41
  chart presentation, 60–62
Nonparametric tests, 20, 310, 889–906
  advantages over parametric, 891
  application to business world, 905–6
  importance to managers, 890
  Mann-Whitney U Test, 898–901, 905, 906
    Z value for, 901–7
  one-sample runs test, 894–97
    Z value for, 906
  one-sample sign test, 891–93, 905, 906
  Spearman rank correlation, 902–4, 905, 907
  when used, 890
Nonprobability samples; *see* Sampling techniques, nonrandom
Normal approximation to the binomial, 205–8
Normal curve; *see* Normal distribution
Normal distribution, 192–209, 210
  application to the business world, 209–10
  characteristics of, 192, 194
  importance to managers, 186
  importance to business statistics, 192
  and interval estimates, 259
  probability density function for, 193, 211
  and standard normal distribution, 195–203, 210
Null hypothesis, 292, 294, 330, 344, 385, 421, 427, 521, 557
Number of defects per unit, 484
Number of nonconforming units, 484
Observed average; *see* Mode
Ogive, 66–67, 76
  less-than-ogive, 66
  more-than-ogive, 67
One-sample runs test, 894–97
  Z value for, 906
One-sample sign test, 891–93, 905, 906
One-tailed test, 295–96, 330
Operating characteristic curve, 323–24, 331, 523
Ordinal scale, 17–18, 41
Ordinal scaled data, chart presentation, 60–62
Organic Gardening, 567
Outdoor Life, 890
Outlier, 671, 672, 674

Parameter of a population, 91, 115
Pareto Chart, 63–64, 76
P chart, 508–12, 524, 530, 531
  and sample size, 509
  steps in constructing, 510
Pauley, L. L., 349n
PC Magazine, 614
PC World, 235
Pearson product-moment correlation coefficient, 555
Percentile, 95, 111, 116
Personnel Journal, 421
Personnel Management, 226, 302, 344
Peterson, Donald, 524
Pie chart, 60–61, 76
Poe, E. A., 613
Point estimate, 255–56, 259, 279, 624, 627
  defined, 255
  of population proportions, 263
  problems with, 256
  of a sample, 255–56
Poisson distribution, 161–70, 171, 172, 398–99, 514
  application to the business world, 172
  approximation to the binomial, 168–70
  distribution table, 164–66
Pooled estimate of the proportion, 314–19
Pooled estimate of the variance, 354, 370
Population, 26, 41
  defined, 26
  stratification of (for sampling), 34
Power curve, 323–24, 331, 523
Prediction and confidence intervals, 574–77, 597, 598, 627, 674
  difference in, 576
  types of variation, 588
Predictor variable (independent variable), 562, 614, 774, 787
  selection of, 614–20
Price Index, 706–7, 751, 754
Primary data, 22, 40–41

Probablistic model; *see* Statistical model
Probability, 130–38
  defined, 130, 172
  distribution, 140–41, 172
  samples; *see* Sampling techniques, random
Process control, 481–519, 520, 525
Process mean, 484
Proportion defective, 484, 531
P value, 305–8, 331, 351, 437

Qualitative data, 15, 16–18, 20, 23, 49
Quality control, 63–64,
  and analysis of variance, 523
  application to the business world, 115, 525–30
  assignable causes, 473, 530
  average range, 501, 531
  chance causes, 473, 530
  c chart, 514–18, 524, 530, 531
    steps in constructing, 515
  control charts, 481–83, 485–518, 524, 530
  Deming, W. Edwards, 469
  Feigenbaum, A. V., 469
  fourteen points, 470–71
  fourth generation management, 472
  Gitlow, Gitlow, Oppenheim, 470
  importance to managers, 468
  Japanese influence on, 468-–69, 470
  Juran, Joseph, 469, 470
  lot acceptance, 520–22, 525
    acceptance sampling, 520
    consumers' risk, 520–21, 530
    producers' risk, 521, 530
  Malcolm Baldrige National Quality Award, 471–72
  management by process, 469, 470–71
  and measures of variability, 104
  and the normal distribution, 210
  number of defects per unit, 484
  number of nonconforming units, 484
  p chart, 508–12, 524, 530, 531
    and sample size, 509
    steps in constructing, 510
  Peterson, Donald, 524
  process control, 481–519, 520, 525
  process mean, 484
  proportion defective, 484, 531
  quality, defined, 469, 530
  r chart (range chart), 501–504, 524, 530, 531
    steps in constructing, 502
    range of measured values, 484
    Shewhart, Walter A., 468
    and standard deviation, 484
    standard error of average ranges, 502, 531
Quality control—*Cont.*
  r chart (range chart)—*Cont.*
    statistical process control (SPC), 473–78, 530
    total quality management (TQM), 472, 530
    x chart, 485–96, 501, 504, 502, 504, 524, 530
    defined, 486
    steps in constructing, 488d
Quantitative data, 15, 16–18, 20, 23, 49
Quantity index, 707–9, 754
Quartile, 95, 111
Quenouille, M. H., 797, 797n

r; *see* Pearson product-moment correlation coefficient
Range, 104, 114, 116
Raw data, 111–12
R chart (range chart), 501–504, 524, 530, 531
  steps in constructing, 502
Random number table, 29, 41
Random sample; *see* Sampling techniques, random
Random variable, 138, 172
Ratio scale, 19–20, 41
Ratio scaled data, 16
  charts for, 66–67
Range of measured values, 484
Reciprocal model, 649, 675
Regression analysis, 550–97, 613–74
  application to the business world, 596, 673
  assumptions, 564, 597, 598, 669, 673
  coefficient of simple determination, 579–84
  degrees of freedom, 588, 590
  deterministic; *see* Functional model
  functional model, 563–64, 596
    versus statistical relationships, 563
  hypothesis testing, 586–92
  method of least squares, 566–67, 597, 622
  model building, 644
  nonlinear models, 650–51
  prediction and confidence intervals, 574–77, 597, 598, 627, 674
    difference in, 576
    types of variation, 588
  probablistic model; *see* Statistical model
  reciprocal model, 649, 675
  regression coefficient, 567
  regression equation, use, 592–94
  residuals, 571–72, 597, 598
  sample regression line, 565–66, 590
  simple regression, 565–66, 590
    versus multiple regression, 562
Regression analysis—*Cont.*
  standard error of the prediction, 574, 598
  standard error of the regression coefficient, 586, 599
  statistical model, 564, 596
  t statistic for, 586, 599
Regression equation, use, 592–94
Relative frequencies, 53–54, 67, 76, 131, 172
  chart presentation, 67
Residual analysis, model building, 665–69
Residual plot, characteristics of, 666–68
Residuals, 571–72, 597, 598,

St. John, 383
Sample, 27–28, 41
  defined, 27
  representative, 27
Sample size
  balancing accuracy and cost, 37
  determination, 275, 279
  and estimation error, 271–77
  mean, 274–75, 279, 272
  proportion, 275–76, 279
Sample space, 131, 172
Sample statistic, 106, 271, 299, 300–301
Sampling distribution of proportions, 236–39, 244, 508
Sampling distribution of sample proportions, 233–35, 243
Sampling distributions, 222–30, 243
  application to the business world, 243–44
  importance to managers, 221
  mean of, 224–25, 244
  selection for test of population means, 268
  standard deviation of, 225
Sampling error, 37, 221, 224
Sampling techniques, 28–42
  balancing of, 37
  nonrandom, 28, 36
    convenience sampling, 36
    judgment sampling, 36
  objectives of, 39
  random, 28, 292
    advantages of, 29, 32
    cluster sampling, 35, 42
    difficulty in, 32
    simple, 28–29
    stratified, 34, 42
    systematic, 32, 41
Scatter diagrams, 551–54, 563, 596
Secondary data, 22–23, 41
  advantages and disadvantages of, 23
  defined, 22
  sources of, 22, 23
Secular trend, 719, 721–26, 754

Serial correlation, 808–28
detection of, 811–14
differences, 814
Durbin-Watson Test for, 811–14, 828, 830
problems with, 810
solutions for, 814
Shakespeare, 129, 185, 467
Shewhart, Walter A., 468
Shopping Journal, 396
Simple index, 709–10
Simple regression, 562–97
Single-population variance test, 421–23
Situations posed
Central Motors (5.1), 138
Central Motors (5.2), 143
Central Motors (5.3), 146
Central Motors (5.4), 151
Central Motors (5.5), 157
Central Motors (5.6), 160
Central Motors (5.7), 167
Sue and Bill Johnson (9.1), 291–92
Sue and Bill Johnson (9.2), 315
Situations resolved
Central Motors (5.1), 141
Central Motors (5.2), 145
Central Motors (5.3), 150
Central Motors (5.4), 156
Central Motors (5.5), 159
Central Motors (5.6), 162
Central Motors (5.7), 169
Sue and Bill Johnson (9.1), 295–96, 308–9
Sue and Bill Johnson (9.2), 318–19
Siwolf, S., 162n
Skewed distributions, 96, 97, 109, 116
Small sample estimation, 266
The Source, 22
Spearman rank correlation, 902–4, 905, 907
Spokane Chronicle, 263
Spokesman Review, 236, 263
Standard and Poor's Computstat, 22
Standard deviation, 105–9, 116
application to the business world, 114–15
Standard error of the difference, 346–47, 370, 371
Standard error of the estimate, 626–27, 674
Standard error of the mean, 244, 259
Standard error of the prediction, 574, 598
Standard error of the proportion, 235–36, 244, 245
Standardized test statistic, 301, 331
for a population mean (large sample), 303, 331
for a population mean (small sample), 310, 331
for a population proportion, 315, 331
Standardized value; *see* Z value
Standard normal distribution; *see* Normal distribution

State of nature, 855
Stationary series, 799
Statistic, 92, 115, 299
Statistical Decision Models for Management, 635
Statistical Package for the Social Sciences (SPSS-PC), computer output, 591
Statistics of Income Bulletin, 23
Statistical model, 564, 596
Statistical process control (SPC), 473–78, 530
Stem-and-leaf plot, 65–66, 76
Stepwise regression, 659–64, 674
problems with, 664
Student base questionnaire, 4
Subjective probability, 131, 172
Summation notation, 6–8, 9
Sum of squares error, 580–82
between method, 431
within method, 428
Sum of squares regression, 582
Sum of squares total, 580–82
Survey of Current Business, 23, 714, 800
Symmetrical distributions, 96, 97, 109, 116

Tchebysheff's theorem; *see* Chebyshev's theorem
Tests of dependence, independence; *see* Chi square tests, contingency table test
t distribution, 229, 266–71, 279, 311–13
and correlation, 558, 568, 597
and estimation of a population mean, 258
for matched pairs, 358–60
and small sample estimation, 266–71
similarity to normal distribution, 267
two population means, small samples, 353–56
Thoreau, H., 343
Time series analysis, 703–53, 754
application to the business world, 751, 752–53, 827
decomposition of, 718 -54
cyclical component, 720, 728–33, 754, 755
coincident indicators, 731
cyclical chart, 730
cyclical indicators, 731–32
lagging indicators, 731
leading indicators, 731
irregular component, 720–21, 746–47, 754, 755
and least squares method, 721
purpose of, 718–19
multiplicative model, 719, 733, 788
seasonal component, 720, 737–41, 754, 755
seasonal index, 738–41
secular trend, 719, 721–26, 754

Time series analysis—*Cont.*
deflating, 714–15
and forecasting, 747–48, 752
graph, 68–69, 75, 76
importance to managers, 704
Time series graph, 68–69, 75, 76
Total quality management (TQM), 472, 530
Training, 293
Trend, 719, 721–26, 754
Two population variance test, 424–25
Type I error, 297–99, 305, 320, 326, 328, 331, 520, 523
Type II error, 297–98, 320–24, 326, 328, 329, 331, 520, 523
operating characteristic curve, 323–24, 331, 523
power curve, 323–24, 331, 523

Uniform distribution, 187–92, 210
mean of, 189, 210
standard deviation of, 189, 211
Uniform probabilities, 188, 210
Utility theory, 870–72

Value index, 709, 754
Value Line, 22, 801
Variable, 15, 41
categorical, 17, 394, 405,551
continuous, 139, 186, 210
defined, 15
qualitative, 15, 16, 41, 90, 427, 508
quantitative, 15, 16, 41, 427, 508
Variability, measures of, 90, 104–110, 114
Variance, 105, 114
defined, 105
for population, 104, 116

Wall Street Journal, 7, 15, 27, 34, 37, 40, 49, 139, 186, 196, 216, 255, 274, 290, 347, 398, 704, 774, 855
Weighted mean, 98–99, 100, 114, 116

x chart, 485–96, 501, 502, 504, 524, 530
defined, 486
steps in constructing, 488

Z value, 195–203, 210, 211, 263–66, 301, 303, 305, 308, 557
estimation of population means, 257–58
formula for, 196
for Mann-Whitney, 901
two-sample for mean, 347, 370

Areas of the Standard Normal Distribution

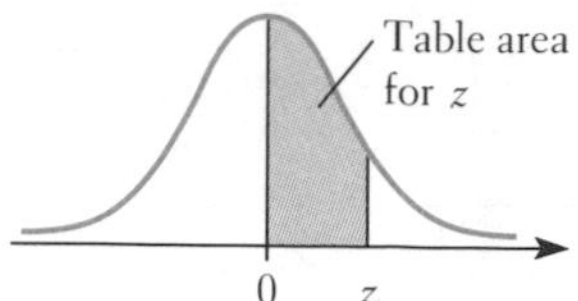

The table areas are probabilities that the standard normal random variable is between 0 and z.

Second Decimal Place in z

z	**0.00**	**0.01**	**0.02**	**0.03**	**0.04**	**0.05**	**0.06**	**0.07**	**0.08**	**0.09**
0.0	0.0000	0.0040	0.0080	0.0120	0.0160	0.0199	0.0239	0.0279	0.0319	0.0359
0.1	0.0398	0.0438	0.0478	0.0517	0.0557	0.0596	0.0636	0.0675	0.0714	0.0753
0.2	0.0793	0.0832	0.0871	0.0910	0.0948	0.0987	0.1026	0.1064	0.1103	0.1141
0.3	0.1179	0.1217	0.1255	0.1293	0.1331	0.1368	0.1406	0.1443	0.1480	0.1517
0.4	0.1554	0.1591	0.1628	0.1664	0.1700	0.1736	0.1772	0.1808	0.1844	0.1879
0.5	0.1915	0.1950	0.1985	0.2019	0.2054	0.2088	0.2123	0.2157	0.2190	0.2224
0.6	0.2257	0.2291	0.2324	0.2357	0.2389	0.2422	0.2454	0.2486	0.2517	0.2549
0.7	0.2580	0.2611	0.2642	0.2673	0.2704	0.2734	0.2764	0.2794	0.2823	0.2852
0.8	0.2881	0.2910	0.2939	0.2967	0.2995	0.3023	0.3051	0.3078	0.3106	0.3133
0.9	0.3159	0.3186	0.3212	0.3238	0.3264	0.3289	0.3315	0.3340	0.3365	0.3389
1.0	0.3413	0.3438	0.3461	0.3485	0.3508	0.3531	0.3554	0.3577	0.3599	0.3621
1.1	0.3643	0.3665	0.3686	0.3708	0.3729	0.3749	0.3770	0.3790	0.3810	0.3830
1.2	0.3849	0.3869	0.3888	0.3907	0.3925	0.3944	0.3962	0.3980	0.3997	0.4015
1.3	0.4032	0.4049	0.4066	0.4082	0.4099	0.4115	0.4131	0.4147	0.4162	0.4177
1.4	0.4192	0.4207	0.4222	0.4236	0.4251	0.4265	0.4279	0.4292	0.4306	0.4319
1.5	0.4332	0.4345	0.4357	0.4370	0.4382	0.4394	0.4406	0.4418	0.4429	0.4441
1.6	0.4452	0.4463	0.4474	0.4484	0.4495	0.4505	0.4515	0.4525	0.4535	0.4545
1.7	0.4554	0.4564	0.4573	0.4582	0.4591	0.4599	0.4608	0.4616	0.4625	0.4633
1.8	0.4641	0.4649	0.4656	0.4664	0.4671	0.4678	0.4686	0.4693	0.4699	0.4706
1.9	0.4713	0.4719	0.4726	0.4732	0.4738	0.4744	0.4750	0.4756	0.4761	0.4767
2.0	0.4772	0.4778	0.4783	0.4788	0.4793	0.4798	0.4803	0.4808	0.4812	0.4817
2.1	0.4821	0.4826	0.4830	0.4834	0.4838	0.4842	0.4846	0.4850	0.4854	0.4857
2.2	0.4861	0.4864	0.4868	0.4871	0.4875	0.4878	0.4881	0.4884	0.4887	0.4890
2.3	0.4893	0.4896	0.4898	0.4901	0.4904	0.4906	0.4909	0.4911	0.4913	0.4916
2.4	0.4918	0.4920	0.4922	0.4925	0.4927	0.4929	0.4931	0.4932	0.4934	0.4936
2.5	0.4938	0.4940	0.4941	0.4943	0.4945	0.4946	0.4948	0.4949	0.4951	0.4952
2.6	0.4953	0.4955	0.4956	0.4957	0.4959	0.4960	0.4961	0.4962	0.4963	0.4964
2.7	0.4965	0.4966	0.4967	0.4968	0.4969	0.4970	0.4971	0.4972	0.4973	0.4974
2.8	0.4974	0.4975	0.4976	0.4977	0.4977	0.4978	0.4979	0.4979	0.4980	0.4981
2.9	0.4981	0.4982	0.4982	0.4983	0.4984	0.4984	0.4985	0.4985	0.4986	0.4986
3.0	0.4987	0.4987	0.4987	0.4988	0.4988	0.4989	0.4989	0.4989	0.4990	0.4990
3.1	0.4990	0.4991	0.4991	0.4991	0.4992	0.4992	0.4992	0.4992	0.4993	0.4993
3.2	0.4993	0.4993	0.4994	0.4994	0.4994	0.4994	0.4994	0.4995	0.4995	0.4995
3.3	0.4995	0.4995	0.4995	0.4996	0.4996	0.4996	0.4996	0.4996	0.4996	0.4997
3.4	0.4997	0.4997	0.4997	0.4997	0.4997	0.4997	0.4997	0.4997	0.4997	0.4998
3.5	0.4998									
4.0	0.49997									
4.5	0.499997									
5.0	0.4999997									
6.0	0.499999999									